Texts in Computer Science

Editors
David Gries
Fred B. Schneider

For further volumes:
www.springer.com/series/3191

Richard Szeliski

Computer Vision

Algorithms and Applications

 Springer

Dr. Richard Szeliski
Microsoft Research
One Microsoft Way
98052-6399 Redmond
Washington
USA
szeliski@microsoft.com

Series Editors
David Gries
Department of Computer Science
Upson Hall
Cornell University
Ithaca, NY 14853-7501, USA

Fred B. Schneider
Department of Computer Science
Upson Hall
Cornell University
Ithaca, NY 14853-7501, USA

ISSN 1868-0941   e-ISSN 1868-095X
ISBN 978-1-84882-934-3   e-ISBN 978-1-84882-935-0
DOI 10.1007/978-1-84882-935-0
Springer London Dordrecht Heidelberg New York

British Library Cataloguing in Publication Data
A catalogue record for this book is available from the British Library

Library of Congress Control Number: 2010936817

Printed on acid-free paper

Springer is part of Springer Science+Business Media (www.springer.com)

This book is dedicated to my parents,

Zdzisław and Jadwiga,

and my family,

Lyn, Anne, and Stephen.

Preface

The seeds for this book were first planted in 2001 when Steve Seitz at the University of Washington invited me to co-teach a course called "Computer Vision for Computer Graphics". At that time, computer vision techniques were increasingly being used in computer graphics to create image-based models of real-world objects, to create visual effects, and to merge real-world imagery using computational photography techniques. Our decision to focus on the applications of computer vision to fun problems such as image stitching and photo-based 3D modeling from personal photos seemed to resonate well with our students.

Since that time, a similar syllabus and project-oriented course structure has been used to teach general computer vision courses both at the University of Washington and at Stanford. (The latter was a course I co-taught with David Fleet in 2003.) Similar curricula have been adopted at a number of other universities and also incorporated into more specialized courses on computational photography. (For ideas on how to use this book in your own course, please see Table 1.1 in Section 1.4.)

This book also reflects my 20 years' experience doing computer vision research in corporate research labs, mostly at Digital Equipment Corporation's Cambridge Research Lab and at Microsoft Research. In pursuing my work, I have mostly focused on problems and solution techniques (algorithms) that have practical real-world applications and that work well in practice. Thus, this book has more emphasis on basic techniques that work under real-world conditions and less on more esoteric mathematics that has intrinsic elegance but less practical applicability.

This book is suitable for teaching a senior-level undergraduate course in computer vision to students in both computer science and electrical engineering. I prefer students to have either an image processing or a computer graphics course as a prerequisite so that they can spend less time learning general background mathematics and more time studying computer vision techniques. The book is also suitable for teaching graduate-level courses in computer vision (by delving into the more demanding application and algorithmic areas) and as a general reference to fundamental techniques and the recent research literature. To this end, I have attempted wherever possible to at least cite the newest research in each sub-field, even if the technical details are too complex to cover in the book itself.

In teaching our courses, we have found it useful for the students to attempt a number of small implementation projects, which often build on one another, in order to get them used to working with real-world images and the challenges that these present. The students are then asked to choose an individual topic for each of their small-group, final projects. (Sometimes these projects even turn into conference papers!) The exercises at the end of each chapter contain numerous suggestions for smaller mid-term projects, as well as more open-ended problems whose solutions are still active research topics. Wherever possible, I encourage students to try their algorithms on their own personal photographs, since this better motivates them, often leads to creative variants on the problems, and better acquaints them with the variety and complexity of real-world imagery.

In formulating and solving computer vision problems, I have often found it useful to draw inspiration from three high-level approaches:

- **Scientific:** build detailed models of the image formation process and develop mathematical techniques to invert these in order to recover the quantities of interest (where necessary, making simplifying assumption to make the mathematics more tractable).

- **Statistical:** use probabilistic models to quantify the prior likelihood of your unknowns and the noisy measurement processes that produce the input images, then infer the best possible estimates of your desired quantities and analyze their resulting uncertainties. The inference algorithms used are often closely related to the optimization techniques used to invert the (scientific) image formation processes.

- **Engineering:** develop techniques that are simple to describe and implement but that are also known to work well in practice. Test these techniques to understand their limitation and failure modes, as well as their expected computational costs (run-time performance).

These three approaches build on each other and are used throughout the book.

My personal research and development philosophy (and hence the exercises in the book) have a strong emphasis on *testing* algorithms. It's too easy in computer vision to develop an algorithm that does something *plausible* on a few images rather than something *correct*. The best way to validate your algorithms is to use a three-part strategy.

First, test your algorithm on clean synthetic data, for which the exact results are known. Second, add noise to the data and evaluate how the performance degrades as a function of noise level. Finally, test the algorithm on real-world data, preferably drawn from a wide variety of sources, such as photos found on the Web. Only then can you truly know if your algorithm can deal with real-world complexity, i.e., images that do not fit some simplified model or assumptions.

In order to help students in this process, this books comes with a large amount of supplementary material, which can be found on the book's Web site http://szeliski.org/Book. This material, which is described in Appendix C, includes:

- pointers to commonly used data sets for the problems, which can be found on the Web

- pointers to software libraries, which can help students get started with basic tasks such as reading/writing images or creating and manipulating images

- slide sets corresponding to the material covered in this book

- a BibTeX bibliography of the papers cited in this book.

The latter two resources may be of more interest to instructors and researchers publishing new papers in this field, but they will probably come in handy even with regular students. Some of the software libraries contain implementations of a wide variety of computer vision algorithms, which can enable you to tackle more ambitious projects (with your instructor's consent).

Acknowledgements

I would like to gratefully acknowledge all of the people whose passion for research and inquiry as well as encouragement have helped me write this book.

Steve Zucker at McGill University first introduced me to computer vision, taught all of his students to question and debate research results and techniques, and encouraged me to pursue a graduate career in this area.

Takeo Kanade and Geoff Hinton, my Ph. D. thesis advisors at Carnegie Mellon University, taught me the fundamentals of good research, writing, and presentation. They fired up my interest in visual processing, 3D modeling, and statistical methods, while Larry Matthies introduced me to Kalman filtering and stereo matching.

Demetri Terzopoulos was my mentor at my first industrial research job and taught me the ropes of successful publishing. Yvan Leclerc and Pascal Fua, colleagues from my brief interlude at SRI International, gave me new perspectives on alternative approaches to computer vision.

During my six years of research at Digital Equipment Corporation's Cambridge Research Lab, I was fortunate to work with a great set of colleagues, including Ingrid Carlbom, Gudrun Klinker, Keith Waters, Richard Weiss, Stéphane Lavallée, and Sing Bing Kang, as well as to supervise the first of a long string of outstanding summer interns, including David Tonnesen, Sing Bing Kang, James Coughlan, and Harry Shum. This is also where I began my long-term collaboration with Daniel Scharstein, now at Middlebury College.

At Microsoft Research, I've had the outstanding fortune to work with some of the world's best researchers in computer vision and computer graphics, including Michael Cohen, Hugues Hoppe, Stephen Gortler, Steve Shafer, Matthew Turk, Harry Shum, Anandan, Phil Torr, Antonio Criminisi, Georg Petschnigg, Kentaro Toyama, Ramin Zabih, Shai Avidan, Sing Bing Kang, Matt Uyttendaele, Patrice Simard, Larry Zitnick, Richard Hartley, Simon Winder, Drew Steedly, Chris Pal, Nebojsa Jojic, Patrick Baudisch, Dani Lischinski, Matthew Brown, Simon Baker, Michael Goesele, Eric Stollnitz, David Nistér, Blaise Aguera y Arcas, Sudipta Sinha, Johannes Kopf, Neel Joshi, and Krishnan Ramnath. I was also lucky to have as interns such great students as Polina Golland, Simon Baker, Mei Han, Arno Schödl, Ron Dror, Ashley Eden, Jinxiang Chai, Rahul Swaminathan, Yanghai Tsin, Sam Hasinoff, Anat Levin, Matthew Brown, Eric Bennett, Vaibhav Vaish, Jan-Michael Frahm, James Diebel, Ce Liu, Josef Sivic, Grant Schindler, Colin Zheng, Neel Joshi, Sudipta Sinha, Zeev Farbman, Rahul Garg, Tim Cho, Yekeun Jeong, Richard Roberts, Varsha Hedau, and Dilip Krishnan.

While working at Microsoft, I've also had the opportunity to collaborate with wonderful colleagues at the University of Washington, where I hold an Affiliate Professor appointment. I'm indebted to Tony DeRose and David Salesin, who first encouraged me to get involved with the research going on at UW, my long-time collaborators Brian Curless, Steve Seitz, Maneesh Agrawala, Sameer Agarwal, and Yasu Furukawa, as well as the students I have had the privilege to supervise and interact with, including Fréderic Pighin, Yung-Yu Chuang, Doug Zongker, Colin Zheng, Aseem Agarwala, Dan Goldman, Noah Snavely, Rahul Garg, and Ryan Kaminsky. As I mentioned at the beginning of this preface, this book owes its inception to the vision course that Steve Seitz invited me to co-teach, as well as to Steve's encouragement, course notes, and editorial input.

I'm also grateful to the many other computer vision researchers who have given me so many constructive suggestions about the book, including Sing Bing Kang, who was my informal book editor, Vladimir Kolmogorov, who contributed Appendix B.5.5 on linear programming techniques for MRF inference, Daniel Scharstein, Richard Hartley, Simon Baker, Noah Snavely, Bill Freeman, Svetlana Lazebnik, Matthew Turk, Jitendra Malik, Alyosha Efros, Michael Black, Brian Curless, Sameer Agarwal, Li Zhang, Deva Ramanan, Olga Veksler, Yuri Boykov, Carsten Rother, Phil Torr, Bill Triggs, Bruce Maxwell, Jana Košecká, Eero Simoncelli, Aaron Hertzmann, Antonio Torralba, Tomaso Poggio, Theo Pavlidis, Baba Vemuri, Nando de Freitas, Chuck Dyer, Song Yi, Falk Schubert, Roman Pflugfelder, Marshall Tappen, James Coughlan, Sammy Rogmans, Klaus Strobel, Shanmuganathan, Andreas Siebert, Yongjun Wu, Fred Pighin, Juan Cockburn, Ronald Mallet, Tim Soper, Georgios Evangelidis, Dwight Fowler, Itzik Bayaz, Daniel O'Connor, and Srikrishna Bhat. Shena Deuchers did a fantastic job copy-editing the book and suggesting many useful improvements and Wayne Wheeler and Simon Rees at Springer were most helpful throughout the whole book publishing process. Keith Price's Annotated Computer Vision Bibliography was invaluable in tracking down references and finding related work.

If you have any suggestions for improving the book, please send me an e-mail, as I would like to keep the book as accurate, informative, and timely as possible.

Lastly, this book would not have been possible or worthwhile without the incredible support and encouragement of my family. I dedicate this book to my parents, Zdzisław and Jadwiga, whose love, generosity, and accomplishments have always inspired me; to my sister Basia for her lifelong friendship; and especially to Lyn, Anne, and Stephen, whose daily encouragement in all matters (including this book project) makes it all worthwhile.

Lake Wenatchee
August, 2010

Contents

Chapter 1

Introduction

Figure 1.1 The human visual system has no problem interpreting the subtle variations in translucency and shading in this photograph and correctly segmenting the object from its background.

R. Szeliski, *Computer Vision: Algorithms and Applications*, Texts in Computer Science,
DOI 10.1007/978-1-84882-935-0_1, © Springer-Verlag London Limited 2011

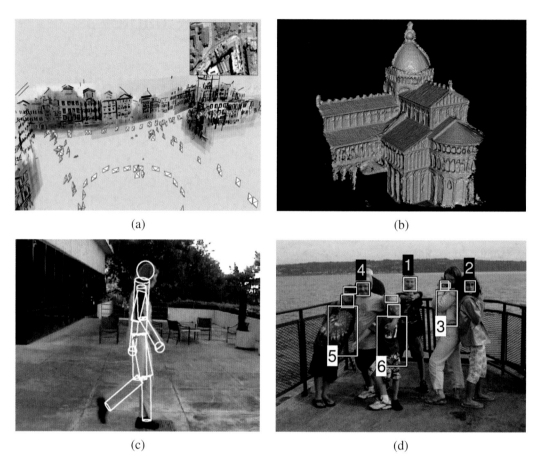

(a)

(b)

(c)

(d)

Figure 1.2 Some examples of computer vision algorithms and applications. (a) *Structure from motion* algorithms can reconstruct a sparse 3D point model of a large complex scene from hundreds of partially overlapping photographs (Snavely, Seitz, and Szeliski 2006) ⓒ 2006 ACM. (b) *Stereo matching* algorithms can build a detailed 3D model of a building façade from hundreds of differently exposed photographs taken from the Internet (Goesele, Snavely, Curless *et al.* 2007) ⓒ 2007 IEEE. (c) *Person tracking* algorithms can track a person walking in front of a cluttered background (Sidenbladh, Black, and Fleet 2000) ⓒ 2000 Springer. (d) *Face detection* algorithms, coupled with color-based clothing and hair detection algorithms, can locate and recognize the individuals in this image (Sivic, Zitnick, and Szeliski 2006) ⓒ 2006 Springer.

1.1 What is computer vision?

As humans, we perceive the three-dimensional structure of the world around us with apparent ease. Think of how vivid the three-dimensional percept is when you look at a vase of flowers sitting on the table next to you. You can tell the shape and translucency of each petal through the subtle patterns of light and shading that play across its surface and effortlessly segment each flower from the background of the scene (Figure 1.1). Looking at a framed group portrait, you can easily count (and name) all of the people in the picture and even guess at their emotions from their facial appearance. Perceptual psychologists have spent decades trying to understand how the visual system works and, even though they can devise optical illusions[1] to tease apart some of its principles (Figure 1.3), a complete solution to this puzzle remains elusive (Marr 1982; Palmer 1999; Livingstone 2008).

Researchers in computer vision have been developing, in parallel, mathematical techniques for recovering the three-dimensional shape and appearance of objects in imagery. We now have reliable techniques for accurately computing a partial 3D model of an environment from thousands of partially overlapping photographs (Figure 1.2a). Given a large enough set of views of a particular object or façade, we can create accurate dense 3D surface models using stereo matching (Figure 1.2b). We can track a person moving against a complex background (Figure 1.2c). We can even, with moderate success, attempt to find and name all of the people in a photograph using a combination of face, clothing, and hair detection and recognition (Figure 1.2d). However, despite all of these advances, the dream of having a computer interpret an image at the same level as a two-year old (for example, counting all of the animals in a picture) remains elusive.   Why is vision so difficult? In part, it is because vision is an *inverse problem*, in which we seek to recover some unknowns given insufficient information to fully specify the solution. We must therefore resort to physics-based and probabilistic *models* to disambiguate between potential solutions. However, modeling the visual world in all of its rich complexity is far more difficult than, say, modeling the vocal tract that produces spoken sounds.

The *forward* models that we use in computer vision are usually developed in physics (radiometry, optics, and sensor design) and in computer graphics. Both of these fields model how objects move and animate, how light reflects off their surfaces, is scattered by the atmosphere, refracted through camera lenses (or human eyes), and finally projected onto a flat (or curved) image plane. While computer graphics are not yet perfect (no fully computer-animated movie with human characters has yet succeeded at crossing the *uncanny valley*[2] that separates real humans from android robots and computer-animated humans), in limited domains, such as rendering a still scene composed of everyday objects or animating extinct creatures such as dinosaurs, the illusion of reality *is* perfect.

In computer vision, we are trying to do the inverse, i.e., to describe the world that we see in one or more images and to reconstruct its properties, such as shape, illumination, and color distributions. It is amazing that humans and animals do this so effortlessly, while computer vision algorithms are so error prone. People who have not worked in the field often underestimate the difficulty of the problem. (Colleagues at work often ask me for software to find and name all the people in photos, so they can get on with the more "interesting" work.) This

---

[1] http://www.michaelbach.de/ot/sze_muelue

[2] The term *uncanny valley* was originally coined by roboticist Masahiro Mori as applied to robotics (Mori 1970). It is also commonly applied to computer-animated films such as *Final Fantasy* and *Polar Express* (Geller 2008).

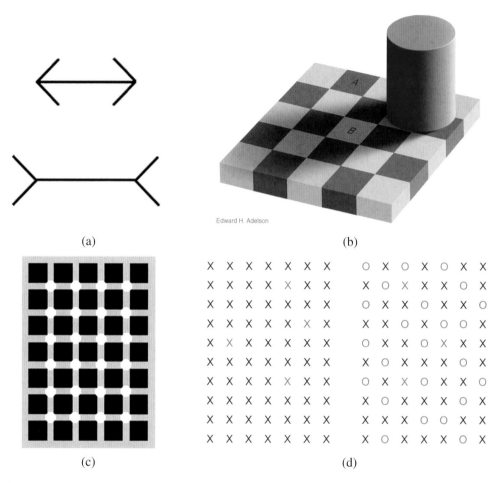

Edward H. Adelson

(a)   (b)

(c)   (d)

Figure 1.3 Some common optical illusions and what they might tell us about the visual system: (a) The classic Müller-Lyer illusion, where the length of the two horizontal lines appear different, probably due to the imagined perspective effects. (b) The "white" square B in the shadow and the "black" square A in the light actually have the same absolute intensity value. The percept is due to *brightness constancy*, the visual system's attempt to discount illumination when interpreting colors. Image courtesy of Ted Adelson, http://web.mit.edu/persci/people/adelson/checkershadow_illusion.html. (c) A variation of the Hermann grid illusion, courtesy of Hany Farid, http://www.cs.dartmouth.edu/~farid/illusions/hermann.html. As you move your eyes over the figure, gray spots appear at the intersections. (d) Count the red *X*s in the left half of the figure. Now count them in the right half. Is it significantly harder? The explanation has to do with a *pop-out* effect (Treisman 1985), which tells us about the operations of parallel perception and integration pathways in the brain.

misperception that vision should be easy dates back to the early days of artificial intelligence (see Section 1.2), when it was initially believed that the *cognitive* (logic proving and planning) parts of intelligence were intrinsically more difficult than the *perceptual* components (Boden 2006).

The good news is that computer vision *is* being used today in a wide variety of real-world applications, which include:

- **Optical character recognition (OCR):** reading handwritten postal codes on letters (Figure 1.4a) and automatic number plate recognition (ANPR);

- **Machine inspection:** rapid parts inspection for quality assurance using stereo vision with specialized illumination to measure tolerances on aircraft wings or auto body parts (Figure 1.4b) or looking for defects in steel castings using X-ray vision;

- **Retail:** object recognition for automated checkout lanes (Figure 1.4c);

- **3D model building (photogrammetry):** fully automated construction of 3D models from aerial photographs used in systems such as Bing Maps;

- **Medical imaging:** registering pre-operative and intra-operative imagery (Figure 1.4d) or performing long-term studies of people's brain morphology as they age;

- **Automotive safety:** detecting unexpected obstacles such as pedestrians on the street, under conditions where active vision techniques such as radar or lidar do not work well (Figure 1.4e; see also Miller, Campbell, Huttenlocher *et al.* (2008); Montemerlo, Becker, Bhat *et al.* (2008); Urmson, Anhalt, Bagnell *et al.* (2008) for examples of fully automated driving);

- **Match move:** merging computer-generated imagery (CGI) with live action footage by tracking feature points in the source video to estimate the 3D camera motion and shape of the environment. Such techniques are widely used in Hollywood (e.g., in movies such as Jurassic Park) (Roble 1999; Roble and Zafar 2009); they also require the use of precise *matting* to insert new elements between foreground and background elements (Chuang, Agarwala, Curless *et al.* 2002).

- **Motion capture (mocap):** using retro-reflective markers viewed from multiple cameras or other vision-based techniques to capture actors for computer animation;

- **Surveillance:** monitoring for intruders, analyzing highway traffic (Figure 1.4f), and monitoring pools for drowning victims;

- **Fingerprint recognition and biometrics:** for automatic access authentication as well as forensic applications.

David Lowe's Web site of industrial vision applications (http://www.cs.ubc.ca/spider/lowe/vision.html) lists many other interesting industrial applications of computer vision. While the above applications are all extremely important, they mostly pertain to fairly specialized kinds of imagery and narrow domains.

In this book, we focus more on broader *consumer-level* applications, such as fun things you can do with your own personal photographs and video. These include:

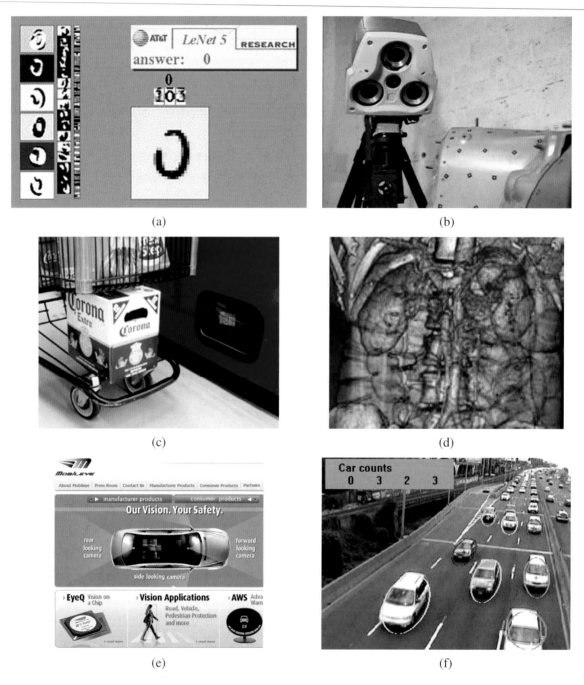

Figure 1.4 Some industrial applications of computer vision: (a) optical character recognition (OCR) http://yann. lecun.com/exdb/lenet/; (b) mechanical inspection http://www.cognitens.com/; (c) retail http://www.evoretail. com/; (d) medical imaging http://www.clarontech.com/; (e) automotive safety http://www.mobileye.com/; (f) surveillance and traffic monitoring http://www.honeywellvideo.com/, courtesy of Honeywell International Inc.

- **Stitching:** turning overlapping photos into a single seamlessly stitched panorama (Figure 1.5a), as described in Chapter 9;

- **Exposure bracketing:** merging multiple exposures taken under challenging lighting conditions (strong sunlight and shadows) into a single perfectly exposed image (Figure 1.5b), as described in Section 10.2;

- **Morphing:** turning a picture of one of your friends into another, using a seamless *morph* transition (Figure 1.5c);

- **3D modeling:** converting one or more snapshots into a 3D model of the object or person you are photographing (Figure 1.5d), as described in Section 12.6

- **Video match move and stabilization:** inserting 2D pictures or 3D models into your videos by automatically tracking nearby reference points (see Section 7.4.2)[3] or using motion estimates to remove shake from your videos (see Section 8.2.1);

- **Photo-based walkthroughs:** navigating a large collection of photographs, such as the interior of your house, by flying between different photos in 3D (see Sections 13.1.2 and 13.5.5)

- **Face detection:** for improved camera focusing as well as more relevant image searching (see Section 14.1.1);

- **Visual authentication:** automatically logging family members onto your home computer as they sit down in front of the webcam (see Section 14.2).

The great thing about these applications is that they are already familiar to most students; they are, at least, technologies that students can immediately appreciate and use with their own personal media. Since computer vision is a challenging topic, given the wide range of mathematics being covered[4] and the intrinsically difficult nature of the problems being solved, having fun and relevant problems to work on can be highly motivating and inspiring.

The other major reason why this book has a strong focus on applications is that they can be used to *formulate* and *constrain* the potentially open-ended problems endemic in vision. For example, if someone comes to me and asks for a good edge detector, my first question is usually to ask *why?* What kind of problem are they trying to solve and why do they believe that edge detection is an important component? If they are trying to locate faces, I usually point out that most successful face detectors use a combination of skin color detection (Exercise 2.8) and simple blob features Section 14.1.1; they do not rely on edge detection. If they are trying to match door and window edges in a building for the purpose of 3D reconstruction, I tell them that edges are a fine idea but it is better to tune the edge detector for long edges (see Sections 3.2.3 and 4.2) and link them together into straight lines with common vanishing points before matching (see Section 4.3).

Thus, it is better to think back from the problem at hand to suitable techniques, rather than to grab the first technique that you may have heard of. This kind of working back from

---

[3] For a fun student project on this topic, see the "PhotoBook" project at http://www.cc.gatech.edu/dvfx/videos/dvfx2005.html.

[4] These techniques include physics, Euclidean and projective geometry, statistics, and optimization. They make computer vision a fascinating field to study and a great way to learn techniques widely applicable in other fields.

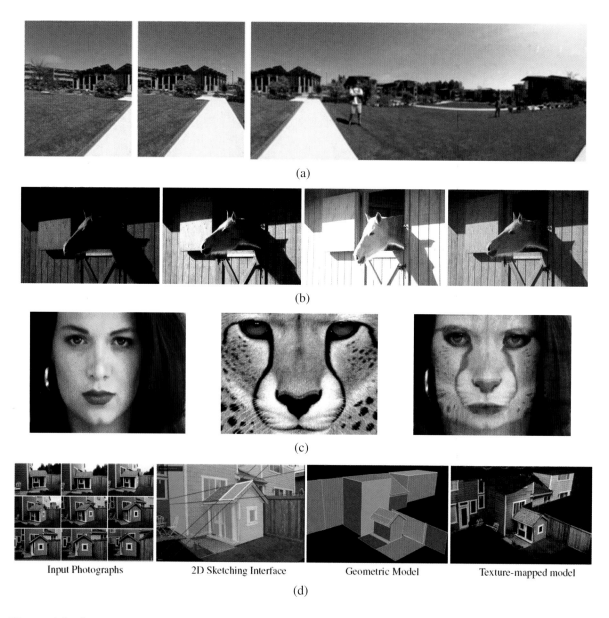

(a)

(b)

(c)

| Input Photographs | 2D Sketching Interface | Geometric Model | Texture-mapped model |

(d)

Figure 1.5 Some consumer applications of computer vision: (a) image stitching: merging different views (Szeliski and Shum 1997) © 1997 ACM; (b) exposure bracketing: merging different exposures; (c) morphing: blending between two photographs (Gomes, Darsa, Costa *et al.* 1999) © 1999 Morgan Kaufmann; (d) turning a collection of photographs into a 3D model (Sinha, Steedly, Szeliski *et al.* 2008) © 2008 ACM.

problems to solutions is typical of an **engineering** approach to the study of vision and reflects my own background in the field. First, I come up with a detailed problem definition and decide on the constraints and specifications for the problem. Then, I try to find out which techniques are known to work, implement a few of these, evaluate their performance, and finally make a selection. In order for this process to work, it is important to have realistic **test data**, both synthetic, which can be used to verify correctness and analyze noise sensitivity, and real-world data typical of the way the system will finally be used.

However, this book is not just an engineering text (a source of recipes). It also takes a **scientific** approach to basic vision problems. Here, I try to come up with the best possible models of the physics of the system at hand: how the scene is created, how light interacts with the scene and atmospheric effects, and how the sensors work, including sources of noise and uncertainty. The task is then to try to invert the acquisition process to come up with the best possible description of the scene.

The book often uses a **statistical** approach to formulating and solving computer vision problems. Where appropriate, probability distributions are used to model the scene and the noisy image acquisition process. The association of prior distributions with unknowns is often called *Bayesian modeling* (Appendix B). It is possible to associate a risk or loss function with mis-estimating the answer (Section B.2) and to set up your inference algorithm to minimize the expected risk. (Consider a robot trying to estimate the distance to an obstacle: it is usually safer to underestimate than to overestimate.) With statistical techniques, it often helps to gather lots of training data from which to learn probabilistic models. Finally, statistical approaches enable you to use proven inference techniques to estimate the best answer (or distribution of answers) and to quantify the uncertainty in the resulting estimates.

Because so much of computer vision involves the solution of inverse problems or the estimation of unknown quantities, my book also has a heavy emphasis on **algorithms**, especially those that are known to work well in practice. For many vision problems, it is all too easy to come up with a mathematical description of the problem that either does not match realistic real-world conditions or does not lend itself to the stable estimation of the unknowns. What we need are algorithms that are both **robust** to noise and deviation from our models and reasonably **efficient** in terms of run-time resources and space. In this book, I go into these issues in detail, using Bayesian techniques, where applicable, to ensure robustness, and efficient search, minimization, and linear system solving algorithms to ensure efficiency. Most of the algorithms described in this book are at a high level, being mostly a list of steps that have to be filled in by students or by reading more detailed descriptions elsewhere. In fact, many of the algorithms are sketched out in the exercises.

Now that I've described the goals of this book and the frameworks that I use, I devote the rest of this chapter to two additional topics. Section 1.2 is a brief synopsis of the history of computer vision. It can easily be skipped by those who want to get to "the meat" of the new material in this book and do not care as much about who invented what when.

The second is an overview of the book's contents, Section 1.3, which is useful reading for everyone who intends to make a study of this topic (or to jump in partway, since it describes chapter inter-dependencies). This outline is also useful for instructors looking to structure one or more courses around this topic, as it provides sample curricula based on the book's contents.

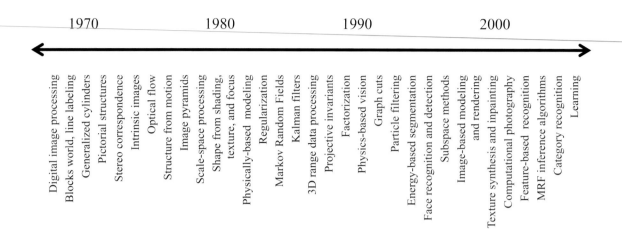

Figure 1.6 A rough timeline of some of the most active topics of research in computer vision.

1.2 A brief history

In this section, I provide a brief personal synopsis of the main developments in computer vision over the last 30 years (Figure 1.6); at least, those that I find personally interesting and which appear to have stood the test of time. Readers not interested in the provenance of various ideas and the evolution of this field should skip ahead to the book overview in Section 1.3.

1970s. When computer vision first started out in the early 1970s, it was viewed as the visual perception component of an ambitious agenda to mimic human intelligence and to endow robots with intelligent behavior. At the time, it was believed by some of the early pioneers of artificial intelligence and robotics (at places such as MIT, Stanford, and CMU) that solving the "visual input" problem would be an easy step along the path to solving more difficult problems such as higher-level reasoning and planning. According to one well-known story, in 1966, Marvin Minsky at MIT asked his undergraduate student Gerald Jay Sussman to "spend the summer linking a camera to a computer and getting the computer to describe what it saw" (Boden 2006, p. 781).[5] We now know that the problem is slightly more difficult than that.[6]

What distinguished computer vision from the already existing field of digital image processing (Rosenfeld and Pfaltz 1966; Rosenfeld and Kak 1976) was a desire to recover the three-dimensional structure of the world from images and to use this as a stepping stone towards full scene understanding. Winston (1975) and Hanson and Riseman (1978) provide two nice collections of classic papers from this early period.

Early attempts at scene understanding involved extracting edges and then inferring the 3D structure of an object or a "blocks world" from the topological structure of the 2D lines

---

[5] Boden (2006) cites (Crevier 1993) as the original source. The actual Vision Memo was authored by Seymour Papert (1966) and involved a whole cohort of students.

[6] To see how far robotic vision has come in the last four decades, have a look at the towel-folding robot at http://rll.eecs.berkeley.edu/pr/icra10/ (Maitin-Shepard, Cusumano-Towner, Lei *et al.* 2010).

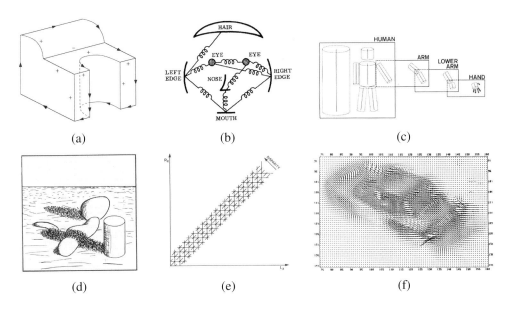

Figure 1.7 Some early (1970s) examples of computer vision algorithms: (a) line labeling (Nalwa 1993) © 1993 Addison-Wesley, (b) pictorial structures (Fischler and Elschlager 1973) © 1973 IEEE, (c) articulated body model (Marr 1982) © 1982 David Marr, (d) intrinsic images (Barrow and Tenenbaum 1981) © 1973 IEEE, (e) stereo correspondence (Marr 1982) © 1982 David Marr, (f) optical flow (Nagel and Enkelmann 1986) © 1986 IEEE.

(Roberts 1965). Several *line labeling* algorithms (Figure 1.7a) were developed at that time (Huffman 1971; Clowes 1971; Waltz 1975; Rosenfeld, Hummel, and Zucker 1976; Kanade 1980). Nalwa (1993) gives a nice review of this area. The topic of edge detection was also an active area of research; a nice survey of contemporaneous work can be found in (Davis 1975).

Three-dimensional modeling of non-polyhedral objects was also being studied (Baumgart 1974; Baker 1977). One popular approach used *generalized cylinders*, i.e., solids of revolution and swept closed curves (Agin and Binford 1976; Nevatia and Binford 1977), often arranged into parts relationships[7] (Hinton 1977; Marr 1982) (Figure 1.7c). Fischler and Elschlager (1973) called such *elastic* arrangements of parts *pictorial structures* (Figure 1.7b). This is currently one of the favored approaches being used in object recognition (see Section 14.4 and Felzenszwalb and Huttenlocher 2005).

A qualitative approach to understanding intensities and shading variations and explaining them by the effects of image formation phenomena, such as surface orientation and shadows, was championed by Barrow and Tenenbaum (1981) in their paper on *intrinsic images* (Figure 1.7d), along with the related *2½-D sketch* ideas of Marr (1982). This approach is again seeing a bit of a revival in the work of Tappen, Freeman, and Adelson (2005).

More quantitative approaches to computer vision were also developed at the time, including the first of many feature-based stereo correspondence algorithms (Figure 1.7e) (Dev 1974; Marr and Poggio 1976; Moravec 1977; Marr and Poggio 1979; Mayhew and Frisby 1981; Baker 1982; Barnard and Fischler 1982; Ohta and Kanade 1985; Grimson 1985; Pollard, Mayhew, and Frisby 1985; Prazdny 1985) and intensity-based optical flow algorithms

---

[7] In robotics and computer animation, these linked-part graphs are often called *kinematic chains*.

(Figure 1.7f) (Horn and Schunck 1981; Huang 1981; Lucas and Kanade 1981; Nagel 1986). The early work in simultaneously recovering 3D structure and camera motion (see Chapter 7) also began around this time (Ullman 1979; Longuet-Higgins 1981).

A lot of the philosophy of how vision was believed to work at the time is summarized in David Marr's (1982) book.[8] In particular, Marr introduced his notion of the three levels of description of a (visual) information processing system. These three levels, very loosely paraphrased according to my own interpretation, are:

- **Computational theory:** What is the goal of the computation (task) and what are the constraints that are known or can be brought to bear on the problem?

- **Representations and algorithms:** How are the input, output, and intermediate information represented and which algorithms are used to calculate the desired result?

- **Hardware implementation:** How are the representations and algorithms mapped onto actual hardware, e.g., a biological vision system or a specialized piece of silicon? Conversely, how can hardware constraints be used to guide the choice of representation and algorithm? With the increasing use of graphics chips (GPUs) and many-core architectures for computer vision (see Section C.2), this question is again becoming quite relevant.

As I mentioned earlier in this introduction, it is my conviction that a careful analysis of the problem specification and known constraints from image formation and priors (the scientific and statistical approaches) must be married with efficient and robust algorithms (the engineering approach) to design successful vision algorithms. Thus, it seems that Marr's philosophy is as good a guide to framing and solving problems in our field today as it was 25 years ago.

1980s.   In the 1980s, a lot of attention was focused on more sophisticated mathematical techniques for performing quantitative image and scene analysis.

Image pyramids (see Section 3.5) started being widely used to perform tasks such as image blending (Figure 1.8a) and coarse-to-fine correspondence search (Rosenfeld 1980; Burt and Adelson 1983a,b; Rosenfeld 1984; Quam 1984; Anandan 1989). Continuous versions of pyramids using the concept of *scale-space* processing were also developed (Witkin 1983; Witkin, Terzopoulos, and Kass 1986; Lindeberg 1990). In the late 1980s, wavelets (see Section 3.5.4) started displacing or augmenting regular image pyramids in some applications (Adelson, Simoncelli, and Hingorani 1987; Mallat 1989; Simoncelli and Adelson 1990a,b; Simoncelli, Freeman, Adelson *et al.* 1992).

The use of stereo as a quantitative shape cue was extended by a wide variety of *shape-from-X* techniques, including shape from shading (Figure 1.8b) (see Section 12.1.1 and Horn 1975; Pentland 1984; Blake, Zimmerman, and Knowles 1985; Horn and Brooks 1986, 1989), photometric stereo (see Section 12.1.1 and Woodham 1981), shape from texture (see Section 12.1.2 and Witkin 1981; Pentland 1984; Malik and Rosenholtz 1997), and shape from focus (see Section 12.1.3 and Nayar, Watanabe, and Noguchi 1995). Horn (1986) has a nice discussion of most of these techniques.

---

[8] More recent developments in visual perception theory are covered in (Palmer 1999; Livingstone 2008).

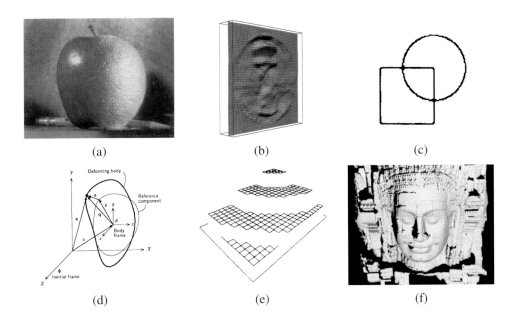

Figure 1.8 Examples of computer vision algorithms from the 1980s: (a) pyramid blending (Burt and Adelson 1983b) ⓒ 1983 ACM, (b) shape from shading (Freeman and Adelson 1991) ⓒ 1991 IEEE, (c) edge detection (Freeman and Adelson 1991) ⓒ 1991 IEEE, (d) physically based models (Terzopoulos and Witkin 1988) ⓒ 1988 IEEE, (e) regularization-based surface reconstruction (Terzopoulos 1988) ⓒ 1988 IEEE, (f) range data acquisition and merging (Banno, Masuda, Oishi *et al.* 2008) ⓒ 2008 Springer.

Research into better edge and contour detection (Figure 1.8c) (see Section 4.2) was also active during this period (Canny 1986; Nalwa and Binford 1986), including the introduction of dynamically evolving contour trackers (Section 5.1.1) such as *snakes* (Kass, Witkin, and Terzopoulos 1988), as well as three-dimensional *physically based models* (Figure 1.8d) (Terzopoulos, Witkin, and Kass 1987; Kass, Witkin, and Terzopoulos 1988; Terzopoulos and Fleischer 1988; Terzopoulos, Witkin, and Kass 1988).

Researchers noticed that a lot of the stereo, flow, shape-from-X, and edge detection algorithms could be unified, or at least described, using the same mathematical framework if they were posed as variational optimization problems (see Section 3.7) and made more robust (well-posed) using regularization (Figure 1.8e) (see Section 3.7.1 and Terzopoulos 1983; Poggio, Torre, and Koch 1985; Terzopoulos 1986b; Blake and Zisserman 1987; Bertero, Poggio, and Torre 1988; Terzopoulos 1988). Around the same time, Geman and Geman (1984) pointed out that such problems could equally well be formulated using discrete *Markov Random Field* (MRF) models (see Section 3.7.2), which enabled the use of better (global) search and optimization algorithms, such as simulated annealing.

Online variants of MRF algorithms that modeled and updated uncertainties using the Kalman filter were introduced a little later (Dickmanns and Graefe 1988; Matthies, Kanade, and Szeliski 1989; Szeliski 1989). Attempts were also made to map both regularized and MRF algorithms onto parallel hardware (Poggio and Koch 1985; Poggio, Little, Gamble *et al.* 1988; Fischler, Firschein, Barnard *et al.* 1989). The book by Fischler and Firschein (1987) contains a nice collection of articles focusing on all of these topics (stereo, flow,

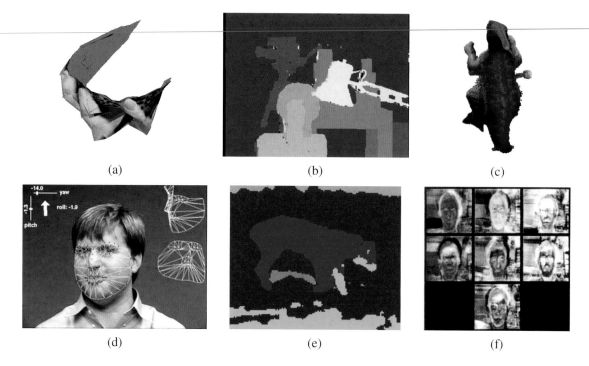

Figure 1.9   Examples of computer vision algorithms from the 1990s: (a) factorization-based structure from motion (Tomasi and Kanade 1992) © 1992 Springer, (b) dense stereo matching (Boykov, Veksler, and Zabih 2001), (c) multi-view reconstruction (Seitz and Dyer 1999) © 1999 Springer, (d) face tracking (Matthews, Xiao, and Baker 2007), (e) image segmentation (Belongie, Fowlkes, Chung *et al.* 2002) © 2002 Springer, (f) face recognition (Turk and Pentland 1991a).

regularization, MRFs, and even higher-level vision).

Three-dimensional range data processing (acquisition, merging, modeling, and recognition; see Figure 1.8f) continued being actively explored during this decade (Agin and Binford 1976; Besl and Jain 1985; Faugeras and Hebert 1987; Curless and Levoy 1996). The compilation by Kanade (1987) contains a lot of the interesting papers in this area.

1990s.   While a lot of the previously mentioned topics continued to be explored, a few of them became significantly more active.

A burst of activity in using projective invariants for recognition (Mundy and Zisserman 1992) evolved into a concerted effort to solve the structure from motion problem (see Chapter 7). A lot of the initial activity was directed at *projective reconstructions*, which did not require knowledge of camera calibration (Faugeras 1992; Hartley, Gupta, and Chang 1992; Hartley 1994a; Faugeras and Luong 2001; Hartley and Zisserman 2004). Simultaneously, *factorization* techniques (Section 7.3) were developed to solve efficiently problems for which orthographic camera approximations were applicable (Figure 1.9a) (Tomasi and Kanade 1992; Poelman and Kanade 1997; Anandan and Irani 2002) and then later extended to the perspective case (Christy and Horaud 1996; Triggs 1996). Eventually, the field started using full global optimization (see Section 7.4 and Taylor, Kriegman, and Anandan 1991; Szeliski and

Kang 1994; Azarbayejani and Pentland 1995), which was later recognized as being the same as the *bundle adjustment* techniques traditionally used in photogrammetry (Triggs, McLauchlan, Hartley *et al.* 1999). Fully automated (sparse) 3D modeling systems were built using such techniques (Beardsley, Torr, and Zisserman 1996; Schaffalitzky and Zisserman 2002; Brown and Lowe 2003; Snavely, Seitz, and Szeliski 2006).

Work begun in the 1980s on using detailed measurements of color and intensity combined with accurate physical models of radiance transport and color image formation created its own subfield known as *physics-based vision*. A good survey of the field can be found in the three-volume collection on this topic (Wolff, Shafer, and Healey 1992a; Healey and Shafer 1992; Shafer, Healey, and Wolff 1992).

Optical flow methods (see Chapter 8) continued to be improved (Nagel and Enkelmann 1986; Bolles, Baker, and Marimont 1987; Horn and Weldon Jr. 1988; Anandan 1989; Bergen, Anandan, Hanna *et al.* 1992; Black and Anandan 1996; Bruhn, Weickert, and Schnörr 2005; Papenberg, Bruhn, Brox *et al.* 2006), with (Nagel 1986; Barron, Fleet, and Beauchemin 1994; Baker, Black, Lewis *et al.* 2007) being good surveys. Similarly, a lot of progress was made on dense stereo correspondence algorithms (see Chapter 11, Okutomi and Kanade (1993, 1994); Boykov, Veksler, and Zabih (1998); Birchfield and Tomasi (1999); Boykov, Veksler, and Zabih (2001), and the survey and comparison in Scharstein and Szeliski (2002)), with the biggest breakthrough being perhaps global optimization using *graph cut* techniques (Figure 1.9b) (Boykov, Veksler, and Zabih 2001).

Multi-view stereo algorithms (Figure 1.9c) that produce complete 3D surfaces (see Section 11.6) were also an active topic of research (Seitz and Dyer 1999; Kutulakos and Seitz 2000) that continues to be active today (Seitz, Curless, Diebel *et al.* 2006). Techniques for producing 3D volumetric descriptions from binary silhouettes (see Section 11.6.2) continued to be developed (Potmesil 1987; Srivasan, Liang, and Hackwood 1990; Szeliski 1993; Laurentini 1994), along with techniques based on tracking and reconstructing smooth occluding contours (see Section 11.2.1 and Cipolla and Blake 1992; Vaillant and Faugeras 1992; Zheng 1994; Boyer and Berger 1997; Szeliski and Weiss 1998; Cipolla and Giblin 2000).

Tracking algorithms also improved a lot, including contour tracking using *active contours* (see Section 5.1), such as *snakes* (Kass, Witkin, and Terzopoulos 1988), *particle filters* (Blake and Isard 1998), and *level sets* (Malladi, Sethian, and Vemuri 1995), as well as intensity-based (*direct*) techniques (Lucas and Kanade 1981; Shi and Tomasi 1994; Rehg and Kanade 1994), often applied to tracking faces (Figure 1.9d) (Lanitis, Taylor, and Cootes 1997; Matthews and Baker 2004; Matthews, Xiao, and Baker 2007) and whole bodies (Sidenbladh, Black, and Fleet 2000; Hilton, Fua, and Ronfard 2006; Moeslund, Hilton, and Krüger 2006).

Image segmentation (see Chapter 5) (Figure 1.9e), a topic which has been active since the earliest days of computer vision (Brice and Fennema 1970; Horowitz and Pavlidis 1976; Riseman and Arbib 1977; Rosenfeld and Davis 1979; Haralick and Shapiro 1985; Pavlidis and Liow 1990), was also an active topic of research, producing techniques based on minimum energy (Mumford and Shah 1989) and minimum description length (Leclerc 1989), *normalized cuts* (Shi and Malik 2000), and *mean shift* (Comaniciu and Meer 2002).

Statistical learning techniques started appearing, first in the application of principal component *eigenface* analysis to face recognition (Figure 1.9f) (see Section 14.2.1 and Turk and Pentland 1991a) and linear dynamical systems for curve tracking (see Section 5.1.1 and Blake and Isard 1998).

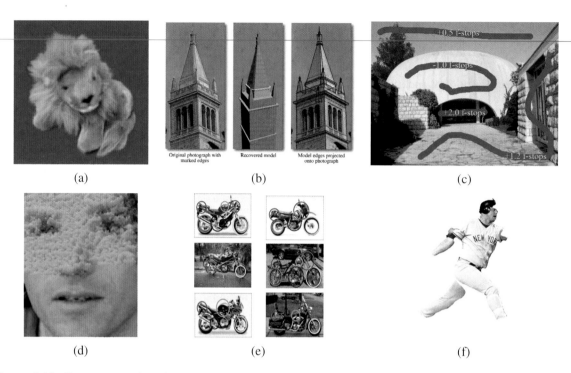

Figure 1.10 Recent examples of computer vision algorithms: (a) image-based rendering (Gortler, Grzeszczuk, Szeliski *et al.* 1996), (b) image-based modeling (Debevec, Taylor, and Malik 1996) © 1996 ACM, (c) interactive tone mapping (Lischinski, Farbman, Uyttendaele *et al.* 2006a) (d) texture synthesis (Efros and Freeman 2001), (e) feature-based recognition (Fergus, Perona, and Zisserman 2007), (f) region-based recognition (Mori, Ren, Efros *et al.* 2004) © 2004 IEEE.

Perhaps the most notable development in computer vision during this decade was the increased interaction with computer graphics (Seitz and Szeliski 1999), especially in the cross-disciplinary area of *image-based modeling and rendering* (see Chapter 13). The idea of manipulating real-world imagery directly to create new animations first came to prominence with *image morphing* techniques (Figure1.5c) (see Section 3.6.3 and Beier and Neely 1992) and was later applied to *view interpolation* (Chen and Williams 1993; Seitz and Dyer 1996), panoramic image stitching (Figure1.5a) (see Chapter 9 and Mann and Picard 1994; Chen 1995; Szeliski 1996; Szeliski and Shum 1997; Szeliski 2006a), and full light-field rendering (Figure 1.10a) (see Section 13.3 and Gortler, Grzeszczuk, Szeliski *et al.* 1996; Levoy and Hanrahan 1996; Shade, Gortler, He *et al.* 1998). At the same time, image-based modeling techniques (Figure 1.10b) for automatically creating realistic 3D models from collections of images were also being introduced (Beardsley, Torr, and Zisserman 1996; Debevec, Taylor, and Malik 1996; Taylor, Debevec, and Malik 1996).

2000s. This past decade has continued to see a deepening interplay between the vision and graphics fields. In particular, many of the topics introduced under the rubric of image-based rendering, such as image stitching (see Chapter 9), light-field capture and rendering (see Section 13.3), and *high dynamic range* (HDR) image capture through exposure bracketing (Figure1.5b) (see Section 10.2 and Mann and Picard 1995; Debevec and Malik 1997), were re-christened as *computational photography* (see Chapter 10) to acknowledge the increased use of such techniques in everyday digital photography. For example, the rapid adoption of exposure bracketing to create high dynamic range images necessitated the development of *tone mapping* algorithms (Figure 1.10c) (see Section 10.2.1) to convert such images back to displayable results (Fattal, Lischinski, and Werman 2002; Durand and Dorsey 2002; Reinhard, Stark, Shirley *et al.* 2002; Lischinski, Farbman, Uyttendaele *et al.* 2006a). In addition to merging multiple exposures, techniques were developed to merge flash images with non-flash counterparts (Eisemann and Durand 2004; Petschnigg, Agrawala, Hoppe *et al.* 2004) and to interactively or automatically select different regions from overlapping images (Agarwala, Dontcheva, Agrawala *et al.* 2004).

Texture synthesis (Figure 1.10d) (see Section 10.5), quilting (Efros and Leung 1999; Efros and Freeman 2001; Kwatra, Schödl, Essa *et al.* 2003) and inpainting (Bertalmio, Sapiro, Caselles *et al.* 2000; Bertalmio, Vese, Sapiro *et al.* 2003; Criminisi, Pérez, and Toyama 2004) are additional topics that can be classified as computational photography techniques, since they re-combine input image samples to produce new photographs.

A second notable trend during this past decade has been the emergence of feature-based techniques (combined with learning) for object recognition (see Section 14.3 and Ponce, Hebert, Schmid *et al.* 2006). Some of the notable papers in this area include the *constellation model* of Fergus, Perona, and Zisserman (2007) (Figure 1.10e) and the *pictorial structures* of Felzenszwalb and Huttenlocher (2005). Feature-based techniques also dominate other recognition tasks, such as scene recognition (Zhang, Marszalek, Lazebnik *et al.* 2007) and panorama and location recognition (Brown and Lowe 2007; Schindler, Brown, and Szeliski 2007). And while *interest point* (patch-based) features tend to dominate current research, some groups are pursuing recognition based on contours (Belongie, Malik, and Puzicha 2002) and region segmentation (Figure 1.10f) (Mori, Ren, Efros *et al.* 2004).

Another significant trend from this past decade has been the development of more efficient algorithms for complex global optimization problems (see Sections 3.7 and B.5 and Szeliski, Zabih, Scharstein *et al.* 2008; Blake, Kohli, and Rother 2010). While this trend began with work on graph cuts (Boykov, Veksler, and Zabih 2001; Kohli and Torr 2007), a lot of progress has also been made in message passing algorithms, such as *loopy belief propagation* (LBP) (Yedidia, Freeman, and Weiss 2001; Kumar and Torr 2006).

The final trend, which now dominates a lot of the visual recognition research in our community, is the application of sophisticated machine learning techniques to computer vision problems (see Section 14.5.1 and Freeman, Perona, and Schölkopf 2008). This trend coincides with the increased availability of immense quantities of partially labelled data on the Internet, which makes it more feasible to learn object categories without the use of careful human supervision.

1.3 Book overview

In the final part of this introduction, I give a brief tour of the material in this book, as well as a few notes on notation and some additional general references. Since computer vision is such a broad field, it is possible to study certain aspects of it, e.g., geometric image formation and 3D structure recovery, without engaging other parts, e.g., the modeling of reflectance and shading. Some of the chapters in this book are only loosely coupled with others, and it is not strictly necessary to read all of the material in sequence.

Figure 1.11 shows a rough layout of the contents of this book. Since computer vision involves going from images to a structural description of the scene (and computer graphics the converse), I have positioned the chapters horizontally in terms of which major component they address, in addition to vertically according to their dependence.

Going from left to right, we see the major column headings as Images (which are 2D in nature), Geometry (which encompasses 3D descriptions), and Photometry (which encompasses object appearance). (An alternative labeling for these latter two could also be *shape* and *appearance*—see, e.g., Chapter 13 and Kang, Szeliski, and Anandan (2000).) Going from top to bottom, we see increasing levels of modeling and abstraction, as well as techniques that build on previously developed algorithms. Of course, this taxonomy should be taken with a large grain of salt, as the processing and dependencies in this diagram are not strictly sequential and subtle additional dependencies and relationships also exist (e.g., some recognition techniques make use of 3D information). The placement of topics along the horizontal axis should also be taken lightly, as most vision algorithms involve mapping between at least two different representations.[9]

Interspersed throughout the book are sample **applications**, which relate the algorithms and mathematical material being presented in various chapters to useful, real-world applications. Many of these applications are also presented in the exercises sections, so that students can write their own.

At the end of each section, I provide a set of **exercises** that the students can use to implement, test, and refine the algorithms and techniques presented in each section. Some of the exercises are suitable as written homework assignments, others as shorter one-week projects, and still others as open-ended research problems that make for challenging final projects. Motivated students who implement a reasonable subset of these exercises will, by the end of the book, have a computer vision software library that can be used for a variety of interesting tasks and projects.

As a reference book, I try wherever possible to discuss which techniques and algorithms work well in practice, as well as providing up-to-date pointers to the latest research results in the areas that I cover. The exercises can be used to build up your own personal library of self-tested and validated vision algorithms, which is more worthwhile in the long term (assuming you have the time) than simply pulling algorithms out of a library whose performance you do not really understand.

The book begins in Chapter 2 with a review of the image formation processes that create the images that we see and capture. Understanding this process is fundamental if you want to take a scientific (model-based) approach to computer vision. Students who are eager to just start implementing algorithms (or courses that have limited time) can skip ahead to the next chapter and dip into this material later. In Chapter 2, we break down image formation into three major components. Geometric image formation (Section 2.1) deals with points, lines, and planes, and how these are mapped onto images using *projective geometry* and other models (including radial lens distortion). Photometric image formation (Section 2.2) covers *radiometry*, which describes how light interacts with surfaces in the world, and *optics*, which projects light onto the sensor plane. Finally, Section 2.3 covers how sensors work, including

---

[9] For an interesting comparison with what is known about the human visual system, e.g., the largely parallel *what* and *where* pathways, see some textbooks on human perception (Palmer 1999; Livingstone 2008).

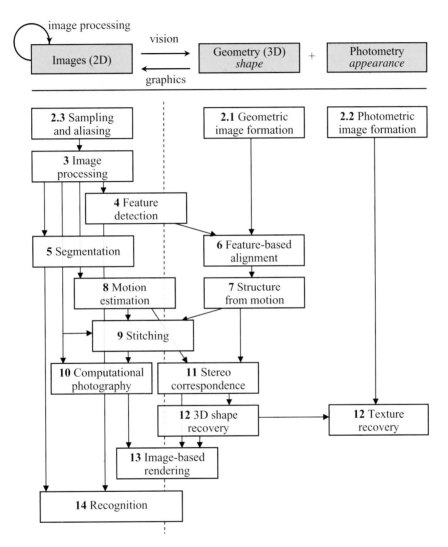

Figure 1.11 Relationship between images, geometry, and photometry, as well as a taxonomy of the topics covered in this book. Topics are roughly positioned along the left–right axis depending on whether they are more closely related to image-based (left), geometry-based (middle) or appearance-based (right) representations, and on the vertical axis by increasing level of abstraction. The whole figure should be taken with a large grain of salt, as there are many additional subtle connections between topics not illustrated here.

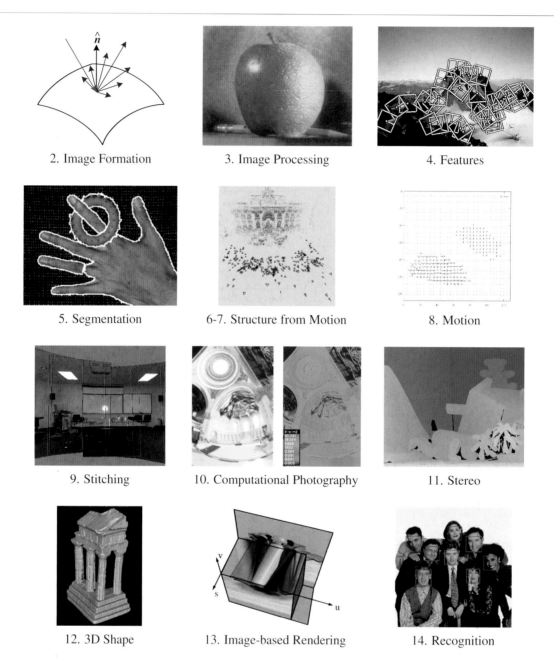

Figure 1.12 A pictorial summary of the chapter contents. Sources: Brown, Szeliski, and Winder (2005); Comaniciu and Meer (2002); Snavely, Seitz, and Szeliski (2006); Nagel and Enkelmann (1986); Szeliski and Shum (1997); Debevec and Malik (1997); Gortler, Grzeszczuk, Szeliski *et al.* (1996); Viola and Jones (2004)—see the figures in the respective chapters for copyright information.

topics such as sampling and aliasing, color sensing, and in-camera compression.

Chapter 3 covers image processing, which is needed in almost all computer vision applications. This includes topics such as linear and non-linear filtering (Section 3.3), the Fourier transform (Section 3.4), image pyramids and wavelets (Section 3.5), geometric transformations such as image warping (Section 3.6), and global optimization techniques such as *regularization* and *Markov Random Fields* (MRFs) (Section 3.7). While most of this material is covered in courses and textbooks on image processing, the use of optimization techniques is more typically associated with computer vision (although MRFs are now being widely used in image processing as well). The section on MRFs is also the first introduction to the use of Bayesian inference techniques, which are covered at a more abstract level in Appendix B. Chapter 3 also presents applications such as seamless image blending and image restoration.

In Chapter 4, we cover feature detection and matching. A lot of current 3D reconstruction and recognition techniques are built on extracting and matching *feature points* (Section 4.1), so this is a fundamental technique required by many subsequent chapters (Chapters 6, 7, 9 and 14). We also cover edge and straight line detection in Sections 4.2 and 4.3.

Chapter 5 covers region segmentation techniques, including active contour detection and tracking (Section 5.1). Segmentation techniques include top-down (split) and bottom-up (merge) techniques, mean shift techniques that find modes of clusters, and various graph-based segmentation approaches. All of these techniques are essential building blocks that are widely used in a variety of applications, including performance-driven animation, interactive image editing, and recognition.

In Chapter 6, we cover geometric alignment and camera calibration. We introduce the basic techniques of feature-based alignment in Section 6.1 and show how this problem can be solved using either linear or non-linear least squares, depending on the motion involved. We also introduce additional concepts, such as uncertainty weighting and robust regression, which are essential to making real-world systems work. Feature-based alignment is then used as a building block for 3D pose estimation (*extrinsic calibration*) in Section 6.2 and camera (*intrinsic*) calibration in Section 6.3. Chapter 6 also describes applications of these techniques to photo alignment for flip-book animations, 3D pose estimation from a hand-held camera, and single-view reconstruction of building models.

Chapter 7 covers the topic of *structure from motion*, which involves the simultaneous recovery of 3D camera motion and 3D scene structure from a collection of tracked 2D features. This chapter begins with the easier problem of 3D point *triangulation* (Section 7.1), which is the 3D reconstruction of points from matched features when the camera positions are known. It then describes two-frame structure from motion (Section 7.2), for which algebraic techniques exist, as well as robust sampling techniques such as RANSAC that can discount erroneous feature matches. The second half of Chapter 7 describes techniques for multi-frame structure from motion, including factorization (Section 7.3), bundle adjustment (Section 7.4), and constrained motion and structure models (Section 7.5). It also presents applications in view morphing, sparse 3D model construction, and match move.

In Chapter 8, we go back to a topic that deals directly with image intensities (as opposed to feature tracks), namely dense intensity-based motion estimation (*optical flow*). We start with the simplest possible motion models, translational motion (Section 8.1), and cover topics such as hierarchical (coarse-to-fine) motion estimation, Fourier-based techniques, and iterative refinement. We then present parametric motion models, which can be used to compensate for camera rotation and zooming, as well as affine or planar perspective motion (Section 8.2). This is then generalized to spline-based motion models (Section 8.3) and finally to general per-pixel optical flow (Section 8.4), including layered and learned motion models (Section 8.5). Applications of these techniques include automated morphing, frame interpolation (slow motion), and motion-based user interfaces.

Chapter 9 is devoted to *image stitching*, i.e., the construction of large panoramas and composites. While stitching is just one example of *computation photography* (see Chapter 10), there is enough depth here to warrant a separate chapter. We start by discussing various possible motion models (Section 9.1), including planar motion and pure camera rotation. We then discuss global alignment (Section 9.2), which is a special (simplified) case of general bundle adjustment, and then present *panorama recognition*, i.e., techniques for automatically discovering which images actually form overlapping panoramas. Finally, we cover the topics of *image compositing* and *blending* (Section 9.3), which involve both selecting which pixels from which images to use and blending them together so as to disguise exposure differences.

Image stitching is a wonderful application that ties together most of the material covered in earlier parts of this book. It also makes for a good mid-term course project that can build on previously developed techniques such as image warping and feature detection and matching. Chapter 9 also presents more specialized variants of stitching such as whiteboard and document scanning, video summarization, *panography*, full 360° spherical panoramas, and interactive photomontage for blending repeated action shots together.

Chapter 10 presents additional examples of *computational photography*, which is the process of creating new images from one or more input photographs, often based on the careful modeling and calibration of the image formation process (Section 10.1). Computational photography techniques include merging multiple exposures to create *high dynamic range* images (Section 10.2), increasing image resolution through blur removal and *super-resolution* (Section 10.3), and image editing and compositing operations (Section 10.4). We also cover the topics of texture analysis, synthesis and *inpainting* (hole filling) in Section 10.5, as well as non-photorealistic rendering (Section 10.5.2).

In Chapter 11, we turn to the issue of stereo correspondence, which can be thought of as a special case of motion estimation where the camera positions are already known (Section 11.1). This additional knowledge enables stereo algorithms to search over a much smaller space of correspondences and, in many cases, to produce dense depth estimates that can be converted into visible surface models (Section 11.3). We also cover multi-view stereo algorithms that build a true 3D surface representation instead of just a single depth map (Section 11.6). Applications of stereo matching include head and gaze tracking, as well as depth-based background replacement (*Z-keying*).

Chapter 12 covers additional 3D shape and appearance modeling techniques. These include classic *shape-from-X* techniques such as shape from shading, shape from texture, and shape from focus (Section 12.1), as well as shape from smooth occluding contours (Section 11.2.1) and silhouettes (Section 12.5). An alternative to all of these *passive* computer vision techniques is to use *active rangefinding* (Section 12.2), i.e., to project patterned light onto scenes and recover the 3D geometry through triangulation. Processing all of these 3D representations often involves interpolating or simplifying the geometry (Section 12.3), or using alternative representations such as surface point sets (Section 12.4).

The collection of techniques for going from one or more images to partial or full 3D models is often called *image-based modeling* or *3D photography*. Section 12.6 examines three more specialized application areas (architecture, faces, and human bodies), which can use *model-based reconstruction* to fit parameterized models to the sensed data. Section 12.7 examines the topic of *appearance modeling*, i.e., techniques for estimating the texture maps, albedos, or even sometimes complete *bi-directional reflectance distribution functions* (BRDFs) that describe the appearance of 3D surfaces.

In Chapter 13, we discuss the large number of image-based rendering techniques that have been developed in the last two decades, including simpler techniques such as view interpolation (Section 13.1), layered depth images (Section 13.2), and sprites and layers (Section 13.2.1), as well as the more general framework of light fields and Lumigraphs (Section 13.3) and higher-order fields such as environment mattes (Section 13.4). Applications of these techniques include navigating 3D collections of photographs using *photo tourism* and viewing 3D models as *object movies*.

In Chapter 13, we also discuss video-based rendering, which is the temporal extension of image-based rendering. The topics we cover include video-based animation (Section 13.5.1), periodic video turned into *video textures* (Section 13.5.2), and 3D video constructed from multiple video streams (Section 13.5.4). Applications of these techniques include video denoising, morphing, and tours based on $360°$ video.

Chapter 14 describes different approaches to recognition. It begins with techniques for detecting and recognizing faces (Sections 14.1 and 14.2), then looks at techniques for finding and recognizing particular objects (*instance recognition*) in Section 14.3. Next, we cover the most difficult variant of recognition, namely the recognition of broad *categories*, such as cars, motorcycles, horses and other animals (Section 14.4), and the role that scene context plays in recognition (Section 14.5).

To support the book's use as a textbook, the appendices and associated Web site contain more detailed mathematical topics and additional material. Appendix A covers linear algebra and numerical techniques, including matrix algebra, least squares, and iterative techniques. Appendix B covers Bayesian estimation theory, including maximum likelihood estimation, robust statistics, Markov random fields, and uncertainty modeling. Appendix C describes the supplementary material available to complement this book, including images and data sets, pointers to software, course slides, and an on-line bibliography.

1.4 Sample syllabus

Teaching all of the material covered in this book in a single quarter or semester course is a Herculean task and likely one not worth attempting. It is better to simply pick and choose topics related to the lecturer's preferred emphasis and tailored to the set of mini-projects envisioned for the students.

Steve Seitz and I have successfully used a 10-week syllabus similar to the one shown in Table 1.1 (omitting the parenthesized weeks) as both an undergraduate and a graduate-level course in computer vision. The undergraduate course[10] tends to go lighter on the mathematics and takes more time reviewing basics, while the graduate-level course[11] dives more deeply into techniques and assumes the students already have a decent grounding in either vision

---

[10] http://www.cs.washington.edu/education/courses/455/
[11] http://www.cs.washington.edu/education/courses/576/

Week	Material	Project
(1.)	Chapter 2 Image formation	
2.	Chapter 3 Image processing	
3.	Chapter 4 Feature detection and matching	P1
4.	Chapter 6 Feature-based alignment	
5.	Chapter 9 Image stitching	P2
6.	Chapter 8 Dense motion estimation	
7.	Chapter 7 Structure from motion	PP
8.	Chapter 14 Recognition	
(9.)	Chapter 10 Computational photography	
10.	Chapter 11 Stereo correspondence	
(11.)	Chapter 12 3D reconstruction	
12.	Chapter 13 Image-based rendering	
13.	Final project presentations	FP

Table 1.1 Sample syllabi for 10-week and 13-week courses. The weeks in parentheses are not used in the shorter version. P1 and P2 are two early-term mini-projects, PP is when the (student-selected) final project proposals are due, and FP is the final project presentations.

or related mathematical techniques. (See also the *Introduction to Computer Vision* course at Stanford,[12] which uses a similar curriculum.) Related courses have also been taught on the topics of 3D photography[13] and computational photography.[14]

When Steve and I teach the course, we prefer to give the students several small programming projects early in the course rather than focusing on written homework or quizzes. With a suitable choice of topics, it is possible for these projects to build on each other. For example, introducing feature matching early on can be used in a second assignment to do image alignment and stitching. Alternatively, direct (optical flow) techniques can be used to do the alignment and more focus can be put on either graph cut seam selection or multi-resolution blending techniques.

We also ask the students to propose a final project (we provide a set of suggested topics for those who need ideas) by the middle of the course and reserve the last week of the class for student presentations. With any luck, some of these final projects can actually turn into conference submissions!

No matter how you decide to structure the course or how you choose to use this book, I encourage you to try at least a few small programming tasks to get a good feel for how vision techniques work, and when they do not. Better yet, pick topics that are fun and can be used on your own photographs, and try to push your creative boundaries to come up with surprising results.

---

[12]http://vision.stanford.edu/teaching/cs223b/
[13] http://www.cs.washington.edu/education/courses/558/06sp/
[14] http://graphics.cs.cmu.edu/courses/15-463/

1.5 A note on notation

For better or worse, the notation found in computer vision and multi-view geometry textbooks tends to vary all over the map (Faugeras 1993; Hartley and Zisserman 2004; Girod, Greiner, and Niemann 2000; Faugeras and Luong 2001; Forsyth and Ponce 2003). In this book, I use the convention I first learned in my high school physics class (and later multi-variate calculus and computer graphics courses), which is that vectors v are lower case bold, matrices M are upper case bold, and scalars (T, s) are mixed case italic. Unless otherwise noted, vectors operate as column vectors, i.e., they post-multiply matrices, Mv, although they are sometimes written as comma-separated parenthesized lists $x = (x, y)$ instead of bracketed column vectors $x = [x \ y]^T$. Some commonly used matrices are R for rotations, K for calibration matrices, and I for the identity matrix. Homogeneous coordinates (Section 2.1) are denoted with a tilde over the vector, e.g., $\tilde{x} = (\tilde{x}, \tilde{y}, \tilde{w}) = \tilde{w}(x, y, 1) = \tilde{w}\bar{x}$ in $\mathcal{P}^2$. The cross product operator in matrix form is denoted by $[\ ]_\times$.

1.6 Additional reading

This book attempts to be self-contained, so that students can implement the basic assignments and algorithms described here without the need for outside references. However, it does presuppose a general familiarity with basic concepts in linear algebra and numerical techniques, which are reviewed in Appendix A, and image processing, which is reviewed in Chapter 3.

Students who want to delve more deeply into these topics can look in (Golub and Van Loan 1996) for matrix algebra and (Strang 1988) for linear algebra. In image processing, there are a number of popular textbooks, including (Crane 1997; Gomes and Velho 1997; Jähne 1997; Pratt 2007; Russ 2007; Burger and Burge 2008; Gonzales and Woods 2008). For computer graphics, popular texts include (Foley, van Dam, Feiner *et al.* 1995; Watt 1995), with (Glassner 1995) providing a more in-depth look at image formation and rendering. For statistics and machine learning, Chris Bishop's (2006) book is a wonderful and comprehensive introduction with a wealth of exercises. Students may also want to look in other textbooks on computer vision for material that we do not cover here, as well as for additional project ideas (Ballard and Brown 1982; Faugeras 1993; Nalwa 1993; Trucco and Verri 1998; Forsyth and Ponce 2003).

There is, however, no substitute for reading the latest research literature, both for the latest ideas and techniques and for the most up-to-date references to related literature.[15] In this book, I have attempted to cite the most recent work in each field so that students can read them directly and use them as inspiration for their own work. Browsing the last few years' conference proceedings from the major vision and graphics conferences, such as CVPR, ECCV, ICCV, and SIGGRAPH, will provide a wealth of new ideas. The tutorials offered at these conferences, for which slides or notes are often available on-line, are also an invaluable resource.

---

[15] For a comprehensive bibliography and taxonomy of computer vision research, Keith Price's Annotated Computer Vision Bibliography http://www.visionbib.com/bibliography/contents.html is an invaluable resource.

Chapter 2

Image formation

R. Szeliski, *Computer Vision: Algorithms and Applications*, Texts in Computer Science,
DOI 10.1007/978-1-84882-935-0_2, © Springer-Verlag London Limited 2011

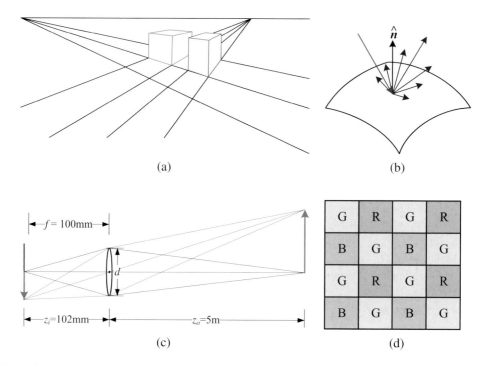

(a)   (b)

(c)   (d)

Figure 2.1   A few components of the image formation process: (a) perspective projection; (b) light scattering when hitting a surface; (c) lens optics; (d) Bayer color filter array.

Before we can intelligently analyze and manipulate images, we need to establish a vocabulary for describing the geometry of a scene. We also need to understand the image formation process that produced a particular image given a set of lighting conditions, scene geometry, surface properties, and camera optics. In this chapter, we present a simplified model of such an image formation process.

Section 2.1 introduces the basic geometric primitives used throughout the book (points, lines, and planes) and the *geometric* transformations that project these 3D quantities into 2D image features (Figure 2.1a). Section 2.2 describes how lighting, surface properties (Figure 2.1b), and camera *optics* (Figure 2.1c) interact in order to produce the color values that fall onto the image sensor. Section 2.3 describes how continuous color images are turned into discrete digital *samples* inside the image sensor (Figure 2.1d) and how to avoid (or at least characterize) sampling deficiencies, such as aliasing.

The material covered in this chapter is but a brief summary of a very rich and deep set of topics, traditionally covered in a number of separate fields. A more thorough introduction to the geometry of points, lines, planes, and projections can be found in textbooks on multi-view geometry (Hartley and Zisserman 2004; Faugeras and Luong 2001) and computer graphics (Foley, van Dam, Feiner *et al.* 1995). The image formation (synthesis) process is traditionally taught as part of a computer graphics curriculum (Foley, van Dam, Feiner *et al.* 1995; Glassner 1995; Watt 1995; Shirley 2005) but it is also studied in physics-based computer vision (Wolff, Shafer, and Healey 1992a). The behavior of camera lens systems is studied in optics (Möller 1988; Hecht 2001; Ray 2002). Two good books on color theory are (Wyszecki and Stiles 2000; Healey and Shafer 1992), with (Livingstone 2008) providing a more fun and informal introduction to the topic of color perception. Topics relating to sampling and aliasing are covered in textbooks on signal and image processing (Crane 1997; Jähne 1997; Oppenheim and Schafer 1996; Oppenheim, Schafer, and Buck 1999; Pratt 2007; Russ 2007; Burger and Burge 2008; Gonzales and Woods 2008).

A note to students: If you have already studied computer graphics, you may want to skim the material in Section 2.1, although the sections on projective depth and object-centered projection near the end of Section 2.1.5 may be new to you. Similarly, physics students (as well as computer graphics students) will mostly be familiar with Section 2.2. Finally, students with a good background in image processing will already be familiar with sampling issues (Section 2.3) as well as some of the material in Chapter 3.

2.1 Geometric primitives and transformations

In this section, we introduce the basic 2D and 3D primitives used in this textbook, namely points, lines, and planes. We also describe how 3D features are projected into 2D features. More detailed descriptions of these topics (along with a gentler and more intuitive introduction) can be found in textbooks on multiple-view geometry (Hartley and Zisserman 2004; Faugeras and Luong 2001).

2.1.1 Geometric primitives

Geometric primitives form the basic building blocks used to describe three-dimensional shapes. In this section, we introduce points, lines, and planes. Later sections of the book discuss

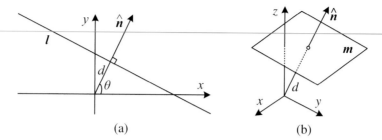

Figure 2.2 (a) 2D line equation and (b) 3D plane equation, expressed in terms of the normal $\hat{n}$ and distance to the origin d.

curves (Sections 5.1 and 11.2), surfaces (Section 12.3), and volumes (Section 12.5).

2D points. 2D points (pixel coordinates in an image) can be denoted using a pair of values, $\boldsymbol{x} = (x, y) \in \mathcal{R}^2$, or alternatively,

$$\boldsymbol{x} = \left[\begin{array}{c} x \\ y \end{array} \right]. \tag{2.1}$$

(As stated in the introduction, we use the $(x_1, x_2, \ldots)$ notation to denote column vectors.)

2D points can also be represented using *homogeneous coordinates*, $\tilde{\boldsymbol{x}} = (\tilde{x}, \tilde{y}, \tilde{w}) \in \mathcal{P}^2$, where vectors that differ only by scale are considered to be equivalent. $\mathcal{P}^2 = \mathcal{R}^3 - (0, 0, 0)$ is called the 2D *projective space*.

A homogeneous vector $\tilde{\boldsymbol{x}}$ can be converted back into an *inhomogeneous* vector $\boldsymbol{x}$ by dividing through by the last element $\tilde{w}$, i.e.,

$$\tilde{\boldsymbol{x}} = (\tilde{x}, \tilde{y}, \tilde{w}) = \tilde{w}(x, y, 1) = \tilde{w}\bar{\boldsymbol{x}}, \tag{2.2}$$

where $\bar{\boldsymbol{x}} = (x, y, 1)$ is the *augmented vector*. Homogeneous points whose last element is $\tilde{w} = 0$ are called *ideal points* or *points at infinity* and do not have an equivalent inhomogeneous representation.

2D lines. 2D lines can also be represented using homogeneous coordinates $\tilde{\boldsymbol{l}} = (a, b, c)$. The corresponding *line equation* is

$$\bar{\boldsymbol{x}} \cdot \tilde{\boldsymbol{l}} = ax + by + c = 0. \tag{2.3}$$

We can normalize the line equation vector so that $\boldsymbol{l} = (\hat{n}_x, \hat{n}_y, d) = (\hat{\boldsymbol{n}}, d)$ with $\|\hat{\boldsymbol{n}}\| = 1$. In this case, $\hat{\boldsymbol{n}}$ is the *normal vector* perpendicular to the line and d is its distance to the origin (Figure 2.2). (The one exception to this normalization is the *line at infinity* $\tilde{\boldsymbol{l}} = (0, 0, 1)$, which includes all (ideal) points at infinity.)

We can also express $\hat{\boldsymbol{n}}$ as a function of rotation angle θ, $\hat{\boldsymbol{n}} = (\hat{n}_x, \hat{n}_y) = (\cos\theta, \sin\theta)$ (Figure 2.2a). This representation is commonly used in the *Hough transform* line-finding algorithm, which is discussed in Section 4.3.2. The combination (θ, d) is also known as *polar coordinates*.

When using homogeneous coordinates, we can compute the intersection of two lines as

$$\tilde{\boldsymbol{x}} = \tilde{\boldsymbol{l}}_1 \times \tilde{\boldsymbol{l}}_2, \tag{2.4}$$

where $\times$ is the cross product operator. Similarly, the line joining two points can be written as

$$\tilde{l} = \tilde{\boldsymbol{x}}_1 \times \tilde{\boldsymbol{x}}_2. \tag{2.5}$$

When trying to fit an intersection point to multiple lines or, conversely, a line to multiple points, least squares techniques (Section 6.1.1 and Appendix A.2) can be used, as discussed in Exercise 2.1.

2D conics. There are other algebraic curves that can be expressed with simple polynomial homogeneous equations. For example, the *conic sections* (so called because they arise as the intersection of a plane and a 3D cone) can be written using a *quadric* equation

$$\tilde{\boldsymbol{x}}^T \boldsymbol{Q} \tilde{\boldsymbol{x}} = 0. \tag{2.6}$$

Quadric equations play useful roles in the study of multi-view geometry and camera calibration (Hartley and Zisserman 2004; Faugeras and Luong 2001) but are not used extensively in this book.

3D points. Point coordinates in three dimensions can be written using inhomogeneous coordinates $\boldsymbol{x} = (x, y, z) \in \mathcal{R}^3$ or homogeneous coordinates $\tilde{\boldsymbol{x}} = (\tilde{x}, \tilde{y}, \tilde{z}, \tilde{w}) \in \mathcal{P}^3$. As before, it is sometimes useful to denote a 3D point using the augmented vector $\bar{\boldsymbol{x}} = (x, y, z, 1)$ with $\tilde{\boldsymbol{x}} = \tilde{w}\bar{\boldsymbol{x}}$.

3D planes. 3D planes can also be represented as homogeneous coordinates $\tilde{\boldsymbol{m}} = (a, b, c, d)$ with a corresponding plane equation

$$\bar{\boldsymbol{x}} \cdot \tilde{\boldsymbol{m}} = ax + by + cz + d = 0. \tag{2.7}$$

We can also normalize the plane equation as $\boldsymbol{m} = (\hat{n}_x, \hat{n}_y, \hat{n}_z, d) = (\hat{\boldsymbol{n}}, d)$ with $\|\hat{\boldsymbol{n}}\| = 1$. In this case, $\hat{\boldsymbol{n}}$ is the *normal vector* perpendicular to the plane and d is its distance to the origin (Figure 2.2b). As with the case of 2D lines, the *plane at infinity* $\tilde{\boldsymbol{m}} = (0, 0, 0, 1)$, which contains all the points at infinity, cannot be normalized (i.e., it does not have a unique normal or a finite distance).

We can express $\hat{\boldsymbol{n}}$ as a function of two angles (θ, ϕ),

$$\hat{\boldsymbol{n}} = (\cos\theta\cos\phi, \sin\theta\cos\phi, \sin\phi), \tag{2.8}$$

i.e., using *spherical coordinates*, but these are less commonly used than polar coordinates since they do not uniformly sample the space of possible normal vectors.

3D lines. Lines in 3D are less elegant than either lines in 2D or planes in 3D. One possible representation is to use two points on the line, $(\boldsymbol{p}, \boldsymbol{q})$. Any other point on the line can be expressed as a linear combination of these two points

$$\boldsymbol{r} = (1 - \lambda)\boldsymbol{p} + \lambda\boldsymbol{q}, \tag{2.9}$$

as shown in Figure 2.3. If we restrict $0 \leq \lambda \leq 1$, we get the *line segment* joining $\boldsymbol{p}$ and $\boldsymbol{q}$.

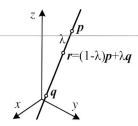

Figure 2.3 3D line equation, $r = (1 - \lambda)p + \lambda q$.

If we use homogeneous coordinates, we can write the line as

$$\tilde{r} = \mu\tilde{p} + \lambda\tilde{q}. \tag{2.10}$$

A special case of this is when the second point is at infinity, i.e., $\tilde{q} = (\hat{d}_x, \hat{d}_y, \hat{d}_z, 0) = (\hat{d}, 0)$. Here, we see that $\hat{d}$ is the *direction* of the line. We can then re-write the inhomogeneous 3D line equation as

$$r = p + \lambda\hat{d}. \tag{2.11}$$

A disadvantage of the endpoint representation for 3D lines is that it has too many degrees of freedom, i.e., six (three for each endpoint) instead of the four degrees that a 3D line truly has. However, if we fix the two points on the line to lie in specific planes, we obtain a representation with four degrees of freedom. For example, if we are representing nearly vertical lines, then $z = 0$ and $z = 1$ form two suitable planes, i.e., the (x, y) coordinates in both planes provide the four coordinates describing the line. This kind of two-plane parameterization is used in the *light field* and *Lumigraph* image-based rendering systems described in Chapter 13 to represent the collection of rays seen by a camera as it moves in front of an object. The two-endpoint representation is also useful for representing line segments, even when their exact endpoints cannot be seen (only guessed at).

If we wish to represent all possible lines without bias towards any particular orientation, we can use *Plücker coordinates* (Hartley and Zisserman 2004, Chapter 2; Faugeras and Luong 2001, Chapter 3). These coordinates are the six independent non-zero entries in the 4×4 skew symmetric matrix

$$L = \tilde{p}\tilde{q}^T - \tilde{q}\tilde{p}^T, \tag{2.12}$$

where $\tilde{p}$ and $\tilde{q}$ are *any* two (non-identical) points on the line. This representation has only four degrees of freedom, since L is homogeneous and also satisfies $det(L) = 0$, which results in a quadratic constraint on the Plücker coordinates.

In practice, the minimal representation is not essential for most applications. An adequate model of 3D lines can be obtained by estimating their direction (which may be known ahead of time, e.g., for architecture) and some point within the visible portion of the line (see Section 7.5.1) or by using the two endpoints, since lines are most often visible as finite line segments. However, if you are interested in more details about the topic of minimal line parameterizations, Förstner (2005) discusses various ways to infer and model 3D lines in projective geometry, as well as how to estimate the uncertainty in such fitted models.

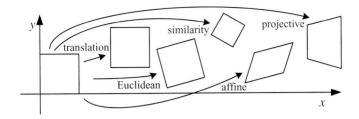

Figure 2.4 Basic set of 2D planar transformations.

3D quadrics. The 3D analog of a conic section is a quadric surface

$$\bar{x}^T Q \bar{x} = 0 \tag{2.13}$$

(Hartley and Zisserman 2004, Chapter 2). Again, while quadric surfaces are useful in the study of multi-view geometry and can also serve as useful modeling primitives (spheres, ellipsoids, cylinders), we do not study them in great detail in this book.

2.1.2 2D transformations

Having defined our basic primitives, we can now turn our attention to how they can be transformed. The simplest transformations occur in the 2D plane and are illustrated in Figure 2.4.

Translation. 2D translations can be written as $x' = x + t$ or

$$x' = \begin{bmatrix} I & t \end{bmatrix} \bar{x} \tag{2.14}$$

where I is the (2×2) identity matrix or

$$\bar{x}' = \begin{bmatrix} I & t \\ 0^T & 1 \end{bmatrix} \bar{x} \tag{2.15}$$

where 0 is the zero vector. Using a 2×3 matrix results in a more compact notation, whereas using a full-rank 3×3 matrix (which can be obtained from the 2×3 matrix by appending a $[0^T \ 1]$ row) makes it possible to chain transformations using matrix multiplication. Note that in any equation where an augmented vector such as $\bar{x}$ appears on both sides, it can always be replaced with a full homogeneous vector $\tilde{x}$.

Rotation + translation. This transformation is also known as *2D rigid body motion* or the *2D Euclidean transformation* (since Euclidean distances are preserved). It can be written as $x' = Rx + t$ or

$$x' = \begin{bmatrix} R & t \end{bmatrix} \bar{x} \tag{2.16}$$

where

$$R = \begin{bmatrix} \cos\theta & -\sin\theta \\ \sin\theta & \cos\theta \end{bmatrix} \tag{2.17}$$

is an orthonormal rotation matrix with $RR^T = I$ and $|R| = 1$.

Scaled rotation.   Also known as the *similarity transform*, this transformation can be expressed as $x' = sRx + t$ where s is an arbitrary scale factor. It can also be written as

$$x' = \begin{bmatrix} sR & t \end{bmatrix} \bar{x} = \begin{bmatrix} a & -b & t_x \\ b & a & t_y \end{bmatrix} \bar{x}, \qquad (2.18)$$

where we no longer require that $a^2 + b^2 = 1$. The similarity transform preserves angles between lines.

Affine.   The affine transformation is written as $x' = A\bar{x}$, where A is an arbitrary 2×3 matrix, i.e.,

$$x' = \begin{bmatrix} a_{00} & a_{01} & a_{02} \\ a_{10} & a_{11} & a_{12} \end{bmatrix} \bar{x}. \qquad (2.19)$$

Parallel lines remain parallel under affine transformations.

Projective.   This transformation, also known as a *perspective transform* or *homography*, operates on homogeneous coordinates,

$$\tilde{x}' = \tilde{H}\tilde{x}, \qquad (2.20)$$

where $\tilde{H}$ is an arbitrary 3×3 matrix. Note that $\tilde{H}$ is homogeneous, i.e., it is only defined up to a scale, and that two $\tilde{H}$ matrices that differ only by scale are equivalent. The resulting homogeneous coordinate $\tilde{x}'$ must be normalized in order to obtain an inhomogeneous result x, i.e.,

$$x' = \frac{h_{00}x + h_{01}y + h_{02}}{h_{20}x + h_{21}y + h_{22}} \text{ and } y' = \frac{h_{10}x + h_{11}y + h_{12}}{h_{20}x + h_{21}y + h_{22}}. \qquad (2.21)$$

Perspective transformations preserve straight lines (i.e., they remain straight after the transformation).

Hierarchy of 2D transformations.   The preceding set of transformations are illustrated in Figure 2.4 and summarized in Table 2.1. The easiest way to think of them is as a set of (potentially restricted) 3×3 matrices operating on 2D homogeneous coordinate vectors. Hartley and Zisserman (2004) contains a more detailed description of the hierarchy of 2D planar transformations.

The above transformations form a nested set of *groups*, i.e., they are closed under composition and have an inverse that is a member of the same group. (This will be important later when applying these transformations to images in Section 3.6.) Each (simpler) group is a subset of the more complex group below it.

Co-vectors.   While the above transformations can be used to transform points in a 2D plane, can they also be used directly to transform a line equation? Consider the homogeneous equation $\tilde{l} \cdot \tilde{x} = 0$. If we transform $x' = \tilde{H}x$, we obtain

$$\tilde{l}' \cdot \tilde{x}' = \tilde{l}'^T \tilde{H}\tilde{x} = (\tilde{H}^T \tilde{l}')^T \tilde{x} = \tilde{l} \cdot \tilde{x} = 0, \qquad (2.22)$$

i.e., $\tilde{l}' = \tilde{H}^{-T}\tilde{l}$. Thus, the action of a projective transformation on a *co-vector* such as a 2D line or 3D normal can be represented by the transposed inverse of the matrix, which is equivalent to the *adjoint* of $\tilde{H}$, since projective transformation matrices are homogeneous. Jim

Transformation	Matrix	# DoF	Preserves	Icon
translation	$\left[\ \boldsymbol{I}\ \mid\ \boldsymbol{t}\ \right]_{2\times3}$	2	orientation	
rigid (Euclidean)	$\left[\ \boldsymbol{R}\ \mid\ \boldsymbol{t}\ \right]_{2\times3}$	3	lengths	
similarity	$\left[\ s\boldsymbol{R}\ \mid\ \boldsymbol{t}\ \right]_{2\times3}$	4	angles	
affine	$\left[\ \boldsymbol{A}\ \right]_{2\times3}$	6	parallelism	
projective	$\left[\ \tilde{\boldsymbol{H}}\ \right]_{3\times3}$	8	straight lines	

Table 2.1 Hierarchy of 2D coordinate transformations. Each transformation also preserves the properties listed in the rows below it, i.e., similarity preserves not only angles but also parallelism and straight lines. The 2×3 matrices are extended with a third $[\mathbf{0}^T\ 1]$ row to form a full 3×3 matrix for homogeneous coordinate transformations.

Blinn (1998) describes (in Chapters 9 and 10) the ins and outs of notating and manipulating co-vectors.

While the above transformations are the ones we use most extensively, a number of additional transformations are sometimes used.

Stretch/squash.   This transformation changes the aspect ratio of an image,

$$
\begin{aligned}
x' &= s_x x + t_x \\
y' &= s_y y + t_y,
\end{aligned}
$$

and is a restricted form of an affine transformation. Unfortunately, it does not nest cleanly with the groups listed in Table 2.1.

Planar surface flow.   This eight-parameter transformation (Horn 1986; Bergen, Anandan, Hanna *et al.* 1992; Girod, Greiner, and Niemann 2000),

$$
\begin{aligned}
x' &= a_0 + a_1 x + a_2 y + a_6 x^2 + a_7 xy \\
y' &= a_3 + a_4 x + a_5 y + a_7 x^2 + a_6 xy,
\end{aligned}
$$

arises when a planar surface undergoes a small 3D motion. It can thus be thought of as a small motion approximation to a full homography. Its main attraction is that it is *linear* in the motion parameters, a_k, which are often the quantities being estimated.

Bilinear interpolant.   This eight-parameter transform (Wolberg 1990),

$$
\begin{aligned}
x' &= a_0 + a_1 x + a_2 y + a_6 xy \\
y' &= a_3 + a_4 x + a_5 y + a_7 xy,
\end{aligned}
$$

can be used to interpolate the deformation due to the motion of the four corner points of a square. (In fact, it can interpolate the motion of any four non-collinear points.) While

Transformation	Matrix	# DoF	Preserves	Icon
translation	$\left[\ I\ \mid\ t\ \right]_{3\times4}$	3	orientation	
rigid (Euclidean)	$\left[\ R\ \mid\ t\ \right]_{3\times4}$	6	lengths	
similarity	$\left[\ sR\ \mid\ t\ \right]_{3\times4}$	7	angles	
affine	$\left[\ A\ \right]_{3\times4}$	12	parallelism	
projective	$\left[\ \tilde{H}\ \right]_{4\times4}$	15	straight lines	

Table 2.2 Hierarchy of 3D coordinate transformations. Each transformation also preserves the properties listed in the rows below it, i.e., similarity preserves not only angles but also parallelism and straight lines. The 3×4 matrices are extended with a fourth $[0^T\ 1]$ row to form a full 4×4 matrix for homogeneous coordinate transformations. The mnemonic icons are drawn in 2D but are meant to suggest transformations occurring in a full 3D cube.

the deformation is linear in the motion parameters, it does not generally preserve straight lines (only lines parallel to the square axes). However, it is often quite useful, e.g., in the interpolation of sparse grids using splines (Section 8.3).

2.1.3 3D transformations

The set of three-dimensional coordinate transformations is very similar to that available for 2D transformations and is summarized in Table 2.2. As in 2D, these transformations form a nested set of groups. Hartley and Zisserman (2004, Section 2.4) give a more detailed description of this hierarchy.

Translation. 3D translations can be written as $x' = x + t$ or

$$x' = \left[\ I\ \ t\ \right] \bar{x} \tag{2.23}$$

where I is the (3×3) identity matrix and 0 is the zero vector.

Rotation + translation. Also known as 3D *rigid body motion* or the 3D *Euclidean transformation*, it can be written as $x' = Rx + t$ or

$$x' = \left[\ R\ \ t\ \right] \bar{x} \tag{2.24}$$

where R is a 3×3 orthonormal rotation matrix with $RR^T = I$ and $|R| = 1$. Note that sometimes it is more convenient to describe a rigid motion using

$$x' = R(x - c) = Rx - Rc, \tag{2.25}$$

where c is the center of rotation (often the camera center).

Compactly parameterizing a 3D rotation is a non-trivial task, which we describe in more detail below.

Scaled rotation. The 3D *similarity transform* can be expressed as $x' = sRx + t$ where s is an arbitrary scale factor. It can also be written as

$$x' = \begin{bmatrix} sR & t \end{bmatrix} \bar{x}. \tag{2.26}$$

This transformation preserves angles between lines and planes.

Affine. The affine transform is written as $x' = A\bar{x}$, where A is an arbitrary 3×4 matrix, i.e.,

$$x' = \begin{bmatrix} a_{00} & a_{01} & a_{02} & a_{03} \\ a_{10} & a_{11} & a_{12} & a_{13} \\ a_{20} & a_{21} & a_{22} & a_{23} \end{bmatrix} \bar{x}. \tag{2.27}$$

Parallel lines and planes remain parallel under affine transformations.

Projective. This transformation, variously known as a *3D perspective transform*, *homography*, or *collineation*, operates on homogeneous coordinates,

$$\tilde{x}' = \tilde{H}\tilde{x}, \tag{2.28}$$

where $\tilde{H}$ is an arbitrary 4×4 homogeneous matrix. As in 2D, the resulting homogeneous coordinate $\tilde{x}'$ must be normalized in order to obtain an inhomogeneous result x. Perspective transformations preserve straight lines (i.e., they remain straight after the transformation).

2.1.4 3D rotations

The biggest difference between 2D and 3D coordinate transformations is that the parameterization of the 3D rotation matrix R is not as straightforward but several possibilities exist.

Euler angles

A rotation matrix can be formed as the product of three rotations around three cardinal axes, e.g., x, y, and z, or x, y, and x. This is generally a bad idea, as the result depends on the order in which the transforms are applied. What is worse, it is not always possible to move smoothly in the parameter space, i.e., sometimes one or more of the Euler angles change dramatically in response to a small change in rotation.[1] For these reasons, we do not even give the formula for Euler angles in this book—interested readers can look in other textbooks or technical reports (Faugeras 1993; Diebel 2006). Note that, in some applications, if the rotations are known to be a set of uni-axial transforms, they can always be represented using an explicit set of rigid transformations.

Axis/angle (exponential twist)

A rotation can be represented by a rotation axis $\hat{n}$ and an angle θ, or equivalently by a 3D vector $\omega = \theta\hat{n}$. Figure 2.5 shows how we can compute the equivalent rotation. First, we project the vector v onto the axis $\hat{n}$ to obtain

$$v_{\parallel} = \hat{n}(\hat{n} \cdot v) = (\hat{n}\hat{n}^T)v, \tag{2.29}$$

---

[1] In robotics, this is sometimes referred to as *gimbal lock*.

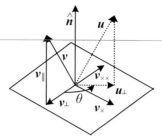

Figure 2.5 Rotation around an axis $\hat{n}$ by an angle θ.

which is the component of v that is not affected by the rotation. Next, we compute the perpendicular residual of v from $\hat{n}$,

$$v_\perp = v - v_\parallel = (I - \hat{n}\hat{n}^T)v. \tag{2.30}$$

We can rotate this vector by $90°$ using the cross product,

$$v_\times = \hat{n} \times v = [\hat{n}]_\times v, \tag{2.31}$$

where $[\hat{n}]_\times$ is the matrix form of the cross product operator with the vector $\hat{n} = (\hat{n}_x, \hat{n}_y, \hat{n}_z)$,

$$[\hat{n}]_\times = \left[\begin{array}{ccc} 0 & -\hat{n}_z & \hat{n}_y \\ \hat{n}_z & 0 & -\hat{n}_x \\ -\hat{n}_y & \hat{n}_x & 0 \end{array} \right]. \tag{2.32}$$

Note that rotating this vector by another $90°$ is equivalent to taking the cross product again,

$$v_{\times\times} = \hat{n} \times v_\times = [\hat{n}]_\times^2 v = -v_\perp,$$

and hence

$$v_\parallel = v - v_\perp = v + v_{\times\times} = (I + [\hat{n}]_\times^2)v.$$

We can now compute the in-plane component of the rotated vector u as

$$u_\perp = \cos\theta v_\perp + \sin\theta v_\times = (\sin\theta[\hat{n}]_\times - \cos\theta[\hat{n}]_\times^2)v.$$

Putting all these terms together, we obtain the final rotated vector as

$$u = u_\perp + v_\parallel = (I + \sin\theta[\hat{n}]_\times + (1 - \cos\theta)[\hat{n}]_\times^2)v. \tag{2.33}$$

We can therefore write the rotation matrix corresponding to a rotation by θ around an axis $\hat{n}$ as

$$R(\hat{n}, \theta) = I + \sin\theta[\hat{n}]_\times + (1 - \cos\theta)[\hat{n}]_\times^2, \tag{2.34}$$

which is known as *Rodriguez's formula* (Ayache 1989).

The product of the axis $\hat{n}$ and angle θ, $\omega = \theta\hat{n} = (\omega_x, \omega_y, \omega_z)$, is a minimal representation for a 3D rotation. Rotations through common angles such as multiples of $90°$ can be represented exactly (and converted to exact matrices) if θ is stored in degrees. Unfortunately, this representation is not unique, since we can always add a multiple of $360°$ (2π radians) to θ and get the same rotation matrix. As well, $(\hat{\boldsymbol{n}}, \theta)$ and $(-\hat{\boldsymbol{n}}, -\theta)$ represent the same rotation.

However, for small rotations (e.g., corrections to rotations), this is an excellent choice. In particular, for small (infinitesimal or instantaneous) rotations and θ expressed in radians, Rodriguez's formula simplifies to

$$\boldsymbol{R}(\boldsymbol{\omega}) \approx \boldsymbol{I} + \sin\theta[\hat{\boldsymbol{n}}]_\times \approx \boldsymbol{I} + [\theta\hat{\boldsymbol{n}}]_\times = \begin{bmatrix} 1 & -\omega_z & \omega_y \\ \omega_z & 1 & -\omega_x \\ -\omega_y & \omega_x & 1 \end{bmatrix}, \qquad (2.35)$$

which gives a nice linearized relationship between the rotation parameters $\boldsymbol{\omega}$ and $\boldsymbol{R}$. We can also write $\boldsymbol{R}(\boldsymbol{\omega})\boldsymbol{v} \approx \boldsymbol{v} + \boldsymbol{\omega} \times \boldsymbol{v}$, which is handy when we want to compute the derivative of $\boldsymbol{R}\boldsymbol{v}$ with respect to $\boldsymbol{\omega}$,

$$\frac{\partial \boldsymbol{R}\boldsymbol{v}}{\partial \boldsymbol{\omega}^T} = -[\boldsymbol{v}]_\times = \begin{bmatrix} 0 & z & -y \\ -z & 0 & x \\ y & -x & 0 \end{bmatrix}. \qquad (2.36)$$

Another way to derive a rotation through a finite angle is called the *exponential twist* (Murray, Li, and Sastry 1994). A rotation by an angle θ is equivalent to k rotations through θ/k. In the limit as $k \to \infty$, we obtain

$$\boldsymbol{R}(\hat{\boldsymbol{n}}, \theta) = \lim_{k \to \infty} (\boldsymbol{I} + \frac{1}{k}[\theta\hat{\boldsymbol{n}}]_\times)^k = \exp[\boldsymbol{\omega}]_\times. \qquad (2.37)$$

If we expand the matrix exponential as a Taylor series (using the identity $[\hat{\boldsymbol{n}}]_\times^{k+2} = -[\hat{\boldsymbol{n}}]_\times^k$, $k > 0$, and again assuming θ is in radians),

$$\begin{aligned} \exp[\boldsymbol{\omega}]_\times &= \boldsymbol{I} + \theta[\hat{\boldsymbol{n}}]_\times + \frac{\theta^2}{2}[\hat{\boldsymbol{n}}]_\times^2 + \frac{\theta^3}{3!}[\hat{\boldsymbol{n}}]_\times^3 + \cdots \\ &= \boldsymbol{I} + (\theta - \frac{\theta^3}{3!} + \cdots)[\hat{\boldsymbol{n}}]_\times + (\frac{\theta^2}{2} - \frac{\theta^3}{4!} + \cdots)[\hat{\boldsymbol{n}}]_\times^2 \\ &= \boldsymbol{I} + \sin\theta[\hat{\boldsymbol{n}}]_\times + (1 - \cos\theta)[\hat{\boldsymbol{n}}]_\times^2, \end{aligned} \qquad (2.38)$$

which yields the familiar Rodriguez's formula.

Unit quaternions

The unit quaternion representation is closely related to the angle/axis representation. A unit quaternion is a unit length 4-vector whose components can be written as $\boldsymbol{q} = (q_x, q_y, q_z, q_w)$ or $\boldsymbol{q} = (x, y, z, w)$ for short. Unit quaternions live on the unit sphere $\|\boldsymbol{q}\| = 1$ and *antipodal* (opposite sign) quaternions, $\boldsymbol{q}$ and $-\boldsymbol{q}$, represent the same rotation (Figure 2.6). Other than this ambiguity (dual covering), the unit quaternion representation of a rotation is unique. Furthermore, the representation is *continuous*, i.e., as rotation matrices vary continuously, one can find a continuous quaternion representation, although the path on the quaternion sphere may wrap all the way around before returning to the "origin" $\boldsymbol{q}_o = (0, 0, 0, 1)$. For these and other reasons given below, quaternions are a very popular representation for pose and for pose interpolation in computer graphics (Shoemake 1985).

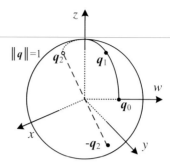

Figure 2.6 Unit quaternions live on the unit sphere $\|q\| = 1$. This figure shows a smooth trajectory through the three quaternions q_0, q_1, and q_2. The *antipodal* point to q_2, namely $-q_2$, represents the same rotation as q_2.

Quaternions can be derived from the axis/angle representation through the formula

$$q = (\boldsymbol{v}, w) = (\sin\frac{\theta}{2}\hat{\boldsymbol{n}}, \cos\frac{\theta}{2}), \tag{2.39}$$

where $\hat{\boldsymbol{n}}$ and θ are the rotation axis and angle. Using the trigonometric identities $\sin\theta = 2\sin\frac{\theta}{2}\cos\frac{\theta}{2}$ and $(1 - \cos\theta) = 2\sin^2\frac{\theta}{2}$, Rodriguez's formula can be converted to

$$\begin{aligned} \boldsymbol{R}(\hat{\boldsymbol{n}}, \theta) &= \boldsymbol{I} + \sin\theta[\hat{\boldsymbol{n}}]_\times + (1 - \cos\theta)[\hat{\boldsymbol{n}}]_\times^2 \\ &= \boldsymbol{I} + 2w[\boldsymbol{v}]_\times + 2[\boldsymbol{v}]_\times^2. \end{aligned} \tag{2.40}$$

This suggests a quick way to rotate a vector $\boldsymbol{v}$ by a quaternion using a series of cross products, scalings, and additions. To obtain a formula for $\boldsymbol{R}(\boldsymbol{q})$ as a function of (x, y, z, w), recall that

$$[\boldsymbol{v}]_\times = \begin{bmatrix} 0 & -z & y \\ z & 0 & -x \\ -y & x & 0 \end{bmatrix} \text{ and } [\boldsymbol{v}]_\times^2 = \begin{bmatrix} -y^2 - z^2 & xy & xz \\ xy & -x^2 - z^2 & yz \\ xz & yz & -x^2 - y^2 \end{bmatrix}.$$

We thus obtain

$$\boldsymbol{R}(\boldsymbol{q}) = \begin{bmatrix} 1 - 2(y^2 + z^2) & 2(xy - zw) & 2(xz + yw) \\ 2(xy + zw) & 1 - 2(x^2 + z^2) & 2(yz - xw) \\ 2(xz - yw) & 2(yz + xw) & 1 - 2(x^2 + y^2) \end{bmatrix}. \tag{2.41}$$

The diagonal terms can be made more symmetrical by replacing $1 - 2(y^2 + z^2)$ with $(x^2 + w^2 - y^2 - z^2)$, etc.

The nicest aspect of unit quaternions is that there is a simple algebra for composing rotations expressed as unit quaternions. Given two quaternions $\boldsymbol{q}_0 = (\boldsymbol{v}_0, w_0)$ and $\boldsymbol{q}_1 = (\boldsymbol{v}_1, w_1)$, the *quaternion multiply* operator is defined as

$$\boldsymbol{q}_2 = \boldsymbol{q}_0\boldsymbol{q}_1 = (\boldsymbol{v}_0 \times \boldsymbol{v}_1 + w_0\boldsymbol{v}_1 + w_1\boldsymbol{v}_0, \ w_0w_1 - \boldsymbol{v}_0 \cdot \boldsymbol{v}_1), \tag{2.42}$$

with the property that $\boldsymbol{R}(\boldsymbol{q}_2) = \boldsymbol{R}(\boldsymbol{q}_0)\boldsymbol{R}(\boldsymbol{q}_1)$. Note that quaternion multiplication is *not* commutative, just as 3D rotations and matrix multiplications are not.

procedure $slerp(\boldsymbol{q}_0, \boldsymbol{q}_1, \alpha)$:

1. $\boldsymbol{q}_r = \boldsymbol{q}_1/\boldsymbol{q}_0 = (\boldsymbol{v}_r, w_r)$

2. if $w_r < 0$ then $\boldsymbol{q}_r \leftarrow -\boldsymbol{q}_r$

3. $\theta_r = 2\tan^{-1}(\|\boldsymbol{v}_r\|/w_r)$

4. $\hat{\boldsymbol{n}}_r = \mathcal{N}(\boldsymbol{v}_r) = \boldsymbol{v}_r/\|\boldsymbol{v}_r\|$

5. $\theta_\alpha = \alpha\,\theta_r$

6. $\boldsymbol{q}_\alpha = (\sin\frac{\theta_\alpha}{2}\hat{\boldsymbol{n}}_r, \cos\frac{\theta_\alpha}{2})$

7. **return** $\boldsymbol{q}_2 = \boldsymbol{q}_\alpha \boldsymbol{q}_0$

Algorithm 2.1 Spherical linear interpolation (slerp). The axis and total angle are first computed from the quaternion ratio. (This computation can be lifted outside an inner loop that generates a set of interpolated position for animation.) An incremental quaternion is then computed and multiplied by the starting rotation quaternion.

Taking the inverse of a quaternion is easy: Just flip the sign of $\boldsymbol{v}$ or w (but not both!). (You can verify this has the desired effect of transposing the $\boldsymbol{R}$ matrix in (2.41).) Thus, we can also define *quaternion division* as

$$\boldsymbol{q}_2 = \boldsymbol{q}_0/\boldsymbol{q}_1 = \boldsymbol{q}_0\boldsymbol{q}_1^{-1} = (\boldsymbol{v}_0 \times \boldsymbol{v}_1 + w_0\boldsymbol{v}_1 - w_1\boldsymbol{v}_0, \; -w_0 w_1 - \boldsymbol{v}_0 \cdot \boldsymbol{v}_1). \qquad (2.43)$$

This is useful when the *incremental rotation* between two rotations is desired.

In particular, if we want to determine a rotation that is partway between two given rotations, we can compute the incremental rotation, take a fraction of the angle, and compute the new rotation. This procedure is called *spherical linear interpolation* or *slerp* for short (Shoemake 1985) and is given in Algorithm 2.1. Note that Shoemake presents two formulas other than the one given here. The first exponentiates $\boldsymbol{q}_r$ by alpha before multiplying the original quaternion,

$$\boldsymbol{q}_2 = \boldsymbol{q}_r^\alpha \boldsymbol{q}_0, \qquad (2.44)$$

while the second treats the quaternions as 4-vectors on a sphere and uses

$$\boldsymbol{q}_2 = \frac{\sin(1-\alpha)\theta}{\sin\theta}\boldsymbol{q}_0 + \frac{\sin\alpha\theta}{\sin\theta}\boldsymbol{q}_1, \qquad (2.45)$$

where $\theta = \cos^{-1}(\boldsymbol{q}_0 \cdot \boldsymbol{q}_1)$ and the dot product is directly between the quaternion 4-vectors. All of these formulas give comparable results, although care should be taken when $\boldsymbol{q}_0$ and $\boldsymbol{q}_1$ are close together, which is why I prefer to use an arctangent to establish the rotation angle.

Which rotation representation is better?

The choice of representation for 3D rotations depends partly on the application.

The axis/angle representation is minimal, and hence does not require any additional constraints on the parameters (no need to re-normalize after each update). If the angle is expressed in degrees, it is easier to understand the pose (say, $90°$ twist around x-axis), and also easier to express exact rotations. When the angle is in radians, the derivatives of R with respect to ω can easily be computed (2.36).

Quaternions, on the other hand, are better if you want to keep track of a smoothly moving camera, since there are no discontinuities in the representation. It is also easier to interpolate between rotations and to chain rigid transformations (Murray, Li, and Sastry 1994; Bregler and Malik 1998).

My usual preference is to use quaternions, but to update their estimates using an incremental rotation, as described in Section 6.2.2.

2.1.5 3D to 2D projections

Now that we know how to represent 2D and 3D geometric primitives and how to transform them spatially, we need to specify how 3D primitives are projected onto the image plane. We can do this using a linear 3D to 2D projection matrix. The simplest model is orthography, which requires no division to get the final (inhomogeneous) result. The more commonly used model is perspective, since this more accurately models the behavior of real cameras.

Orthography and para-perspective

An orthographic projection simply drops the z component of the three-dimensional coordinate p to obtain the 2D point x. (In this section, we use p to denote 3D points and x to denote 2D points.) This can be written as

$$x = [I_{2\times 2}|0]\, p. \tag{2.46}$$

If we are using homogeneous (projective) coordinates, we can write

$$\tilde{x} = \begin{bmatrix} 1 & 0 & 0 & 0 \\ 0 & 1 & 0 & 0 \\ 0 & 0 & 0 & 1 \end{bmatrix} \tilde{p}, \tag{2.47}$$

i.e., we drop the z component but keep the w component. Orthography is an approximate model for long focal length (telephoto) lenses and objects whose depth is *shallow* relative to their distance to the camera (Sawhney and Hanson 1991). It is exact only for *telecentric* lenses (Baker and Nayar 1999, 2001).

In practice, world coordinates (which may measure dimensions in meters) need to be scaled to fit onto an image sensor (physically measured in millimeters, but ultimately measured in pixels). For this reason, *scaled orthography* is actually more commonly used,

$$x = [sI_{2\times 2}|0]\, p. \tag{2.48}$$

This model is equivalent to first projecting the world points onto a local fronto-parallel image plane and then scaling this image using regular perspective projection. The scaling can be the same for all parts of the scene (Figure 2.7b) or it can be different for objects that are being modeled independently (Figure 2.7c). More importantly, the scaling can vary from frame to frame when estimating *structure from motion*, which can better model the scale change that occurs as an object approaches the camera.

Scaled orthography is a popular model for reconstructing the 3D shape of objects far away from the camera, since it greatly simplifies certain computations. For example, *pose* (camera

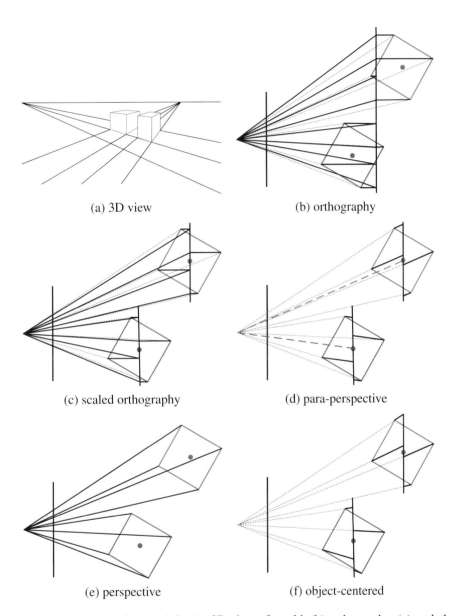

(a) 3D view   (b) orthography

(c) scaled orthography   (d) para-perspective

(e) perspective   (f) object-centered

Figure 2.7 Commonly used projection models: (a) 3D view of world, (b) orthography, (c) scaled orthography, (d) para-perspective, (e) perspective, (f) object-centered. Each diagram shows a top-down view of the projection. Note how parallel lines on the ground plane and box sides remain parallel in the non-perspective projections.

orientation) can be estimated using simple least squares (Section 6.2.1). Under orthography, structure and motion can simultaneously be estimated using *factorization* (singular value decomposition), as discussed in Section 7.3 (Tomasi and Kanade 1992).

A closely related projection model is *para-perspective* (Aloimonos 1990; Poelman and Kanade 1997). In this model, object points are again first projected onto a local reference parallel to the image plane. However, rather than being projected orthogonally to this plane, they are projected *parallel* to the line of sight to the object center (Figure 2.7d). This is followed by the usual projection onto the final image plane, which again amounts to a scaling. The combination of these two projections is therefore *affine* and can be written as

$$\tilde{x} = \begin{bmatrix} a_{00} & a_{01} & a_{02} & a_{03} \\ a_{10} & a_{11} & a_{12} & a_{13} \\ 0 & 0 & 0 & 1 \end{bmatrix} \tilde{p}. \tag{2.49}$$

Note how parallel lines in 3D remain parallel after projection in Figure 2.7b–d. Para-perspective provides a more accurate projection model than scaled orthography, without incurring the added complexity of per-pixel perspective division, which invalidates traditional factorization methods (Poelman and Kanade 1997).

Perspective

The most commonly used projection in computer graphics and computer vision is true 3D *perspective* (Figure 2.7e). Here, points are projected onto the image plane by dividing them by their z component. Using inhomogeneous coordinates, this can be written as

$$\bar{x} = \mathcal{P}_z(\boldsymbol{p}) = \begin{bmatrix} x/z \\ y/z \\ 1 \end{bmatrix}. \tag{2.50}$$

In homogeneous coordinates, the projection has a simple linear form,

$$\tilde{x} = \begin{bmatrix} 1 & 0 & 0 & 0 \\ 0 & 1 & 0 & 0 \\ 0 & 0 & 1 & 0 \end{bmatrix} \tilde{p}, \tag{2.51}$$

i.e., we drop the w component of $\boldsymbol{p}$. Thus, after projection, it is not possible to recover the *distance* of the 3D point from the image, which makes sense for a 2D imaging sensor.

A form often seen in computer graphics systems is a two-step projection that first projects 3D coordinates into *normalized device coordinates* in the range $(x, y, z) \in [-1, -1] \times [-1, 1] \times [0, 1]$, and then rescales these coordinates to integer pixel coordinates using a *viewport* transformation (Watt 1995; OpenGL-ARB 1997). The (initial) perspective projection is then represented using a 4×4 matrix

$$\tilde{x} = \begin{bmatrix} 1 & 0 & 0 & 0 \\ 0 & 1 & 0 & 0 \\ 0 & 0 & -z_{\text{far}}/z_{\text{range}} & z_{\text{near}}z_{\text{far}}/z_{\text{range}} \\ 0 & 0 & 1 & 0 \end{bmatrix} \tilde{p}, \tag{2.52}$$

where z_{near} and z_{far} are the near and far z *clipping planes* and $z_{\text{range}} = z_{\text{far}} - z_{\text{near}}$. Note that the first two rows are actually scaled by the focal length and the aspect ratio so that

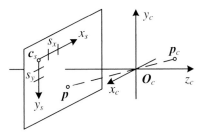

Figure 2.8 Projection of a 3D camera-centered point p_c onto the sensor planes at location p. O_c is the camera center (nodal point), c_s is the 3D origin of the sensor plane coordinate system, and s_x and s_y are the pixel spacings.

visible rays are mapped to $(x, y, z) \in [-1, -1]^2$. The reason for keeping the third row, rather than dropping it, is that visibility operations, such as *z-buffering*, require a depth for every graphical element that is being rendered.

If we set $z_{\text{near}} = 1$, $z_{\text{far}} \to \infty$, and switch the sign of the third row, the third element of the normalized screen vector becomes the inverse depth, i.e., the *disparity* (Okutomi and Kanade 1993). This can be quite convenient in many cases since, for cameras moving around outdoors, the inverse depth to the camera is often a more well-conditioned parameterization than direct 3D distance.

While a regular 2D image sensor has no way of measuring distance to a surface point, *range sensors* (Section 12.2) and stereo matching algorithms (Chapter 11) can compute such values. It is then convenient to be able to map from a sensor-based depth or disparity value d directly back to a 3D location using the inverse of a 4×4 matrix (Section 2.1.5). We can do this if we represent perspective projection using a full-rank 4×4 matrix, as in (2.64).

Camera intrinsics

Once we have projected a 3D point through an ideal pinhole using a projection matrix, we must still transform the resulting coordinates according to the pixel sensor spacing and the relative position of the sensor plane to the origin. Figure 2.8 shows an illustration of the geometry involved. In this section, we first present a mapping from 2D pixel coordinates to 3D rays using a sensor homography M_s, since this is easier to explain in terms of physically measurable quantities. We then relate these quantities to the more commonly used camera intrinsic matrix K, which is used to map 3D camera-centered points p_c to 2D pixel coordinates $\tilde{x}_s$.

Image sensors return pixel values indexed by integer *pixel coordinates* (x_s, y_s), often with the coordinates starting at the upper-left corner of the image and moving down and to the right. (This convention is not obeyed by all imaging libraries, but the adjustment for other coordinate systems is straightforward.) To map pixel centers to 3D coordinates, we first scale the (x_s, y_s) values by the pixel spacings (s_x, s_y) (sometimes expressed in microns for solid-state sensors) and then describe the orientation of the sensor array relative to the camera projection center O_c with an origin c_s and a 3D rotation R_s (Figure 2.8).

The combined 2D to 3D projection can then be written as

$$
p = \begin{bmatrix} R_s & | & c_s \end{bmatrix} \begin{bmatrix} s_x & 0 & 0 \\ 0 & s_y & 0 \\ 0 & 0 & 0 \\ 0 & 0 & 1 \end{bmatrix} \begin{bmatrix} x_s \\ y_s \\ 1 \end{bmatrix} = M_s \bar{x}_s. \tag{2.53}
$$

The first two columns of the 3×3 matrix M_s are the 3D vectors corresponding to unit steps in the image pixel array along the x_s and y_s directions, while the third column is the 3D image array origin c_s.

The matrix M_s is parameterized by eight unknowns: the three parameters describing the rotation R_s, the three parameters describing the translation c_s, and the two scale factors (s_x, s_y). Note that we ignore here the possibility of *skew* between the two axes on the image plane, since solid-state manufacturing techniques render this negligible. In practice, unless we have accurate external knowledge of the sensor spacing or sensor orientation, there are only seven degrees of freedom, since the distance of the sensor from the origin cannot be teased apart from the sensor spacing, based on external image measurement alone.

However, estimating a camera model M_s with the required seven degrees of freedom (i.e., where the first two columns are orthogonal after an appropriate re-scaling) is impractical, so most practitioners assume a general 3×3 homogeneous matrix form.

The relationship between the 3D pixel center p and the 3D camera-centered point p_c is given by an unknown scaling s, $p = sp_c$. We can therefore write the complete projection between p_c and a homogeneous version of the pixel address $\tilde{x}_s$ as

$$
\tilde{x}_s = \alpha M_s^{-1} p_c = K p_c. \tag{2.54}
$$

The 3×3 matrix K is called the *calibration matrix* and describes the camera *intrinsics* (as opposed to the camera's orientation in space, which are called the *extrinsics*).

From the above discussion, we see that K has seven degrees of freedom in theory and eight degrees of freedom (the full dimensionality of a 3×3 homogeneous matrix) in practice. Why, then, do most textbooks on 3D computer vision and multi-view geometry (Faugeras 1993; Hartley and Zisserman 2004; Faugeras and Luong 2001) treat K as an upper-triangular matrix with five degrees of freedom?

While this is usually not made explicit in these books, it is because we cannot recover the full K matrix based on external measurement alone. When calibrating a camera (Chapter 6) based on external 3D points or other measurements (Tsai 1987), we end up estimating the intrinsic (K) and extrinsic (R, t) camera parameters simultaneously using a series of measurements,

$$
\tilde{x}_s = K \begin{bmatrix} R & | & t \end{bmatrix} p_w = P p_w, \tag{2.55}
$$

where p_w are known 3D world coordinates and

$$
P = K[R|t] \tag{2.56}
$$

is known as the *camera matrix*. Inspecting this equation, we see that we can post-multiply K by R_1 and pre-multiply $[R|t]$ by R_1^T, and still end up with a valid calibration. Thus, it is impossible based on image measurements alone to know the true orientation of the sensor and the true camera intrinsics.

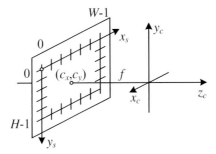

Figure 2.9 Simplified camera intrinsics showing the focal length f and the optical center (c_x, c_y). The image width and height are W and H.

The choice of an upper-triangular form for K seems to be conventional. Given a full 3×4 camera matrix $P = K[R|t]$, we can compute an upper-triangular K matrix using QR factorization (Golub and Van Loan 1996). (Note the unfortunate clash of terminologies: In matrix algebra textbooks, R represents an upper-triangular (right of the diagonal) matrix; in computer vision, R is an orthogonal rotation.)

There are several ways to write the upper-triangular form of K. One possibility is

$$K = \begin{bmatrix} f_x & s & c_x \\ 0 & f_y & c_y \\ 0 & 0 & 1 \end{bmatrix}, \tag{2.57}$$

which uses independent *focal lengths* f_x and f_y for the sensor x and y dimensions. The entry s encodes any possible *skew* between the sensor axes due to the sensor not being mounted perpendicular to the optical axis and (c_x, c_y) denotes the *optical center* expressed in pixel coordinates. Another possibility is

$$K = \begin{bmatrix} f & s & c_x \\ 0 & af & c_y \\ 0 & 0 & 1 \end{bmatrix}, \tag{2.58}$$

where the *aspect ratio* a has been made explicit and a common focal length f is used.

In practice, for many applications an even simpler form can be obtained by setting $a = 1$ and $s = 0$,

$$K = \begin{bmatrix} f & 0 & c_x \\ 0 & f & c_y \\ 0 & 0 & 1 \end{bmatrix}. \tag{2.59}$$

Often, setting the origin at roughly the center of the image, e.g., $(c_x, c_y) = (W/2, H/2)$, where W and H are the image height and width, can result in a perfectly usable camera model with a single unknown, i.e., the focal length f.

Figure 2.9 shows how these quantities can be visualized as part of a simplified imaging model. Note that now we have placed the image plane *in front* of the nodal point (projection center of the lens). The sense of the y axis has also been flipped to get a coordinate system compatible with the way that most imaging libraries treat the vertical (row) coordinate. Certain graphics libraries, such as Direct3D, use a left-handed coordinate system, which can lead to some confusion.

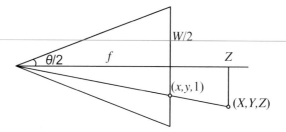

Figure 2.10 Central projection, showing the relationship between the 3D and 2D coordinates, p and x, as well as the relationship between the focal length f, image width W, and the field of view θ.

A note on focal lengths

The issue of how to express focal lengths is one that often causes confusion in implementing computer vision algorithms and discussing their results. This is because the focal length depends on the units used to measure pixels.

If we number pixel coordinates using integer values, say $[0, W) \times [0, H)$, the focal length f and camera center (c_x, c_y) in (2.59) can be expressed as pixel values. How do these quantities relate to the more familiar focal lengths used by photographers?

Figure 2.10 illustrates the relationship between the focal length f, the sensor width W, and the field of view θ, which obey the formula

$$\tan \frac{\theta}{2} = \frac{W}{2f} \quad \text{or} \quad f = \frac{W}{2}\left[\tan \frac{\theta}{2}\right]^{-1}. \tag{2.60}$$

For conventional film cameras, $W = 35\text{mm}$, and hence f is also expressed in millimeters. Since we work with digital images, it is more convenient to express W in pixels so that the focal length f can be used directly in the calibration matrix $\boldsymbol{K}$ as in (2.59).

Another possibility is to scale the pixel coordinates so that they go from $[-1, 1)$ along the longer image dimension and $[-a^{-1}, a^{-1})$ along the shorter axis, where $a \geq 1$ is the *image aspect ratio* (as opposed to the *sensor cell aspect ratio* introduced earlier). This can be accomplished using *modified normalized device coordinates*,

$$x'_s = (2x_s - W)/S \quad \text{and} \quad y'_s = (2y_s - H)/S, \quad \text{where} \quad S = \max(W, H). \tag{2.61}$$

This has the advantage that the focal length f and optical center (c_x, c_y) become independent of the image resolution, which can be useful when using multi-resolution, image-processing algorithms, such as image pyramids (Section 3.5).[2] The use of S instead of W also makes the focal length the same for landscape (horizontal) and portrait (vertical) pictures, as is the case in 35mm photography. (In some computer graphics textbooks and systems, normalized device coordinates go from $[-1, 1] \times [-1, 1]$, which requires the use of two different focal lengths to describe the camera intrinsics (Watt 1995; OpenGL-ARB 1997).) Setting $S = W = 2$ in (2.60), we obtain the simpler (unitless) relationship

$$f^{-1} = \tan \frac{\theta}{2}. \tag{2.62}$$

---

[2] To make the conversion truly accurate after a downsampling step in a pyramid, floating point values of W and H would have to be maintained since they can become non-integral if they are ever odd at a larger resolution in the pyramid.

The conversion between the various focal length representations is straightforward, e.g., to go from a unitless f to one expressed in pixels, multiply by $W/2$, while to convert from an f expressed in pixels to the equivalent 35mm focal length, multiply by $35/W$.

Camera matrix

Now that we have shown how to parameterize the calibration matrix K, we can put the camera intrinsics and extrinsics together to obtain a single 3×4 *camera matrix*

$$P = K \left[\ R\ |\ t\ \right]. \tag{2.63}$$

It is sometimes preferable to use an invertible 4×4 matrix, which can be obtained by not dropping the last row in the P matrix,

$$\tilde{P} = \begin{bmatrix} K & 0 \\ 0^T & 1 \end{bmatrix} \begin{bmatrix} R & t \\ 0^T & 1 \end{bmatrix} = \tilde{K} E, \tag{2.64}$$

where E is a 3D rigid-body (Euclidean) transformation and $\tilde{K}$ is the full-rank calibration matrix. The 4×4 camera matrix $\tilde{P}$ can be used to map directly from 3D world coordinates $\bar{p}_w = (x_w, y_w, z_w, 1)$ to screen coordinates (plus disparity), $x_s = (x_s, y_s, 1, d)$,

$$x_s \sim \tilde{P} \bar{p}_w, \tag{2.65}$$

where $\sim$ indicates equality up to scale. Note that after multiplication by $\tilde{P}$, the vector is divided by the *third* element of the vector to obtain the normalized form $x_s = (x_s, y_s, 1, d)$.

Plane plus parallax (projective depth)

In general, when using the 4×4 matrix $\tilde{P}$, we have the freedom to remap the last row to whatever suits our purpose (rather than just being the "standard" interpretation of disparity as inverse depth). Let us re-write the last row of $\tilde{P}$ as $p_3 = s_3[\hat{n}_0|c_0]$, where $\|\hat{n}_0\| = 1$. We then have the equation

$$d = \frac{s_3}{z}(\hat{n}_0 \cdot p_w + c_0), \tag{2.66}$$

where $z = p_2 \cdot \bar{p}_w = r_z \cdot (p_w - c)$ is the distance of p_w from the camera center C (2.25) along the optical axis Z (Figure 2.11). Thus, we can interpret d as the *projective disparity* or *projective depth* of a 3D scene point p_w from the *reference plane* $\hat{n}_0 \cdot p_w + c_0 = 0$ (Szeliski and Coughlan 1997; Szeliski and Golland 1999; Shade, Gortler, He *et al.* 1998; Baker, Szeliski, and Anandan 1998). (The projective depth is also sometimes called *parallax* in reconstruction algorithms that use the term *plane plus parallax* (Kumar, Anandan, and Hanna 1994; Sawhney 1994).) Setting $\hat{n}_0 = 0$ and $c_0 = 1$, i.e., putting the reference plane at infinity, results in the more standard $d = 1/z$ version of disparity (Okutomi and Kanade 1993).

Another way to see this is to invert the $\tilde{P}$ matrix so that we can map pixels plus disparity directly back to 3D points,

$$\tilde{p}_w = \tilde{P}^{-1} x_s. \tag{2.67}$$

In general, we can choose $\tilde{P}$ to have whatever form is convenient, i.e., to sample space using an arbitrary projection. This can come in particularly handy when setting up multi-view

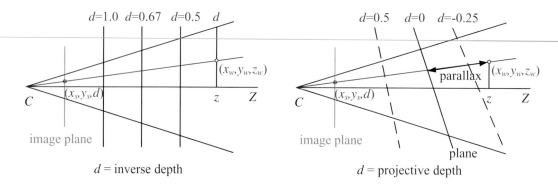

Figure 2.11 Regular disparity (inverse depth) and projective depth (parallax from a reference plane).

stereo reconstruction algorithms, since it allows us to sweep a series of planes (Section 11.1.2) through space with a variable (projective) sampling that best matches the sensed image motions (Collins 1996; Szeliski and Golland 1999; Saito and Kanade 1999).

Mapping from one camera to another

What happens when we take two images of a 3D scene from different camera positions or orientations (Figure 2.12a)? Using the full rank 4×4 camera matrix $\tilde{P} = \tilde{K}E$ from (2.64), we can write the projection from world to screen coordinates as

$$\tilde{x}_0 \sim \tilde{K}_0 E_0 p = \tilde{P}_0 p. \tag{2.68}$$

Assuming that we know the z-buffer or disparity value d_0 for a pixel in one image, we can compute the 3D point location p using

$$p \sim E_0^{-1} \tilde{K}_0^{-1} \tilde{x}_0 \tag{2.69}$$

and then project it into another image yielding

$$\tilde{x}_1 \sim \tilde{K}_1 E_1 p = \tilde{K}_1 E_1 E_0^{-1} \tilde{K}_0^{-1} \tilde{x}_0 = \tilde{P}_1 \tilde{P}_0^{-1} \tilde{x}_0 = M_{10} \tilde{x}_0. \tag{2.70}$$

Unfortunately, we do not usually have access to the depth coordinates of pixels in a regular photographic image. However, for a *planar scene*, as discussed above in (2.66), we can replace the last row of P_0 in (2.64) with a general *plane equation*, $\hat{n}_0 \cdot p + c_0$ that maps points on the plane to $d_0 = 0$ values (Figure 2.12b). Thus, if we set $d_0 = 0$, we can ignore the last column of M_{10} in (2.70) and also its last row, since we do not care about the final z-buffer depth. The mapping equation (2.70) thus reduces to

$$\tilde{x}_1 \sim \tilde{H}_{10} \tilde{x}_0, \tag{2.71}$$

where $\tilde{H}_{10}$ is a general 3×3 homography matrix and $\tilde{x}_1$ and $\tilde{x}_0$ are now 2D homogeneous coordinates (i.e., 3-vectors) (Szeliski 1996).This justifies the use of the 8-parameter homography as a general alignment model for mosaics of planar scenes (Mann and Picard 1994; Szeliski 1996).

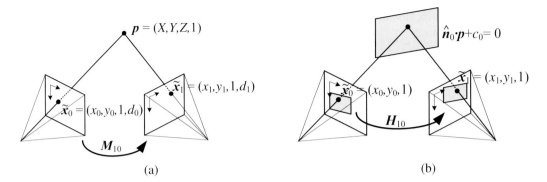

Figure 2.12 A point is projected into two images: (a) relationship between the 3D point coordinate $(X, Y, Z, 1)$ and the 2D projected point $(x, y, 1, d)$; (b) planar homography induced by points all lying on a common plane $\hat{n}_0 \cdot p + c_0 = 0$.

The other special case where we do not need to know depth to perform inter-camera mapping is when the camera is undergoing pure rotation (Section 9.1.3), i.e., when $t_0 = t_1$. In this case, we can write

$$\tilde{x}_1 \sim K_1 R_1 R_0^{-1} K_0^{-1} \tilde{x}_0 = K_1 R_{10} K_0^{-1} \tilde{x}_0, \qquad (2.72)$$

which again can be represented with a 3×3 homography. If we assume that the calibration matrices have known aspect ratios and centers of projection (2.59), this homography can be parameterized by the rotation amount and the two unknown focal lengths. This particular formulation is commonly used in image-stitching applications (Section 9.1.3).

Object-centered projection

When working with long focal length lenses, it often becomes difficult to reliably estimate the focal length from image measurements alone. This is because the focal length and the distance to the object are highly correlated and it becomes difficult to tease these two effects apart. For example, the change in scale of an object viewed through a zoom telephoto lens can either be due to a zoom change or a motion towards the user. (This effect was put to dramatic use in some of Alfred Hitchcock's film *Vertigo*, where the simultaneous change of zoom and camera motion produces a disquieting effect.)

This ambiguity becomes clearer if we write out the projection equation corresponding to the simple calibration matrix K (2.59),

$$x_s = f \frac{r_x \cdot p + t_x}{r_z \cdot p + t_z} + c_x \qquad (2.73)$$

$$y_s = f \frac{r_y \cdot p + t_y}{r_z \cdot p + t_z} + c_y, \qquad (2.74)$$

where r_x, r_y, and r_z are the three rows of R. If the distance to the object center $t_z \gg \|p\|$ (the size of the object), the denominator is approximately t_z and the overall scale of the projected object depends on the ratio of f to t_z. It therefore becomes difficult to disentangle these two quantities.

To see this more clearly, let $\eta_z = t_z^{-1}$ and $s = \eta_z f$. We can then re-write the above equations as

$$x_s = s\frac{\boldsymbol{r}_x \cdot \boldsymbol{p} + t_x}{1 + \eta_z \boldsymbol{r}_z \cdot \boldsymbol{p}} + c_x \qquad (2.75)$$

$$y_s = s\frac{\boldsymbol{r}_y \cdot \boldsymbol{p} + t_y}{1 + \eta_z \boldsymbol{r}_z \cdot \boldsymbol{p}} + c_y \qquad (2.76)$$

(Szeliski and Kang 1994; Pighin, Hecker, Lischinski *et al.* 1998). The scale of the projection s can be reliably estimated if we are looking at a known object (i.e., the 3D coordinates $\boldsymbol{p}$ are known). The inverse distance η_z is now mostly decoupled from the estimates of s and can be estimated from the amount of *foreshortening* as the object rotates. Furthermore, as the lens becomes longer, i.e., the projection model becomes orthographic, there is no need to replace a perspective imaging model with an orthographic one, since the same equation can be used, with $\eta_z \to 0$ (as opposed to f and t_z both going to infinity). This allows us to form a natural link between orthographic reconstruction techniques such as factorization and their projective/perspective counterparts (Section 7.3).

2.1.6 Lens distortions

The above imaging models all assume that cameras obey a *linear* projection model where straight lines in the world result in straight lines in the image. (This follows as a natural consequence of linear matrix operations being applied to homogeneous coordinates.) Unfortunately, many wide-angle lenses have noticeable *radial distortion*, which manifests itself as a visible curvature in the projection of straight lines. (See Section 2.2.3 for a more detailed discussion of lens optics, including chromatic aberration.) Unless this distortion is taken into account, it becomes impossible to create highly accurate photorealistic reconstructions. For example, image mosaics constructed without taking radial distortion into account will often exhibit blurring due to the mis-registration of corresponding features before pixel blending (Chapter 9).

Fortunately, compensating for radial distortion is not that difficult in practice. For most lenses, a simple quartic model of distortion can produce good results. Let (x_c, y_c) be the pixel coordinates obtained *after* perspective division but *before* scaling by focal length f and shifting by the optical center (c_x, c_y), i.e.,

$$x_c = \frac{\boldsymbol{r}_x \cdot \boldsymbol{p} + t_x}{\boldsymbol{r}_z \cdot \boldsymbol{p} + t_z}$$

$$y_c = \frac{\boldsymbol{r}_y \cdot \boldsymbol{p} + t_y}{\boldsymbol{r}_z \cdot \boldsymbol{p} + t_z}. \qquad (2.77)$$

The radial distortion model says that coordinates in the observed images are displaced away (*barrel* distortion) or towards (*pincushion* distortion) the image center by an amount proportional to their radial distance (Figure 2.13a–b).[3] The simplest radial distortion models use low-order polynomials, e.g.,

$$\hat{x}_c = x_c(1 + \kappa_1 r_c^2 + \kappa_2 r_c^4)$$

$$\hat{y}_c = y_c(1 + \kappa_1 r_c^2 + \kappa_2 r_c^4), \qquad (2.78)$$

---

[3] Anamorphic lenses, which are widely used in feature film production, do not follow this radial distortion model. Instead, they can be thought of, to a first approximation, as inducing different vertical and horizontal scalings, i.e., non-square pixels.

(a) (b) (c)

Figure 2.13 Radial lens distortions: (a) barrel, (b) pincushion, and (c) fisheye. The fisheye image spans almost 180° from side-to-side.

where $r_c^2 = x_c^2 + y_c^2$ and κ_1 and κ_2 are called the *radial distortion parameters*.[4] After the radial distortion step, the final pixel coordinates can be computed using

$$\begin{aligned} x_s &= f x_c' + c_x \\ y_s &= f y_c' + c_y. \end{aligned} \quad (2.79)$$

A variety of techniques can be used to estimate the radial distortion parameters for a given lens, as discussed in Section 6.3.5.

Sometimes the above simplified model does not model the true distortions produced by complex lenses accurately enough (especially at very wide angles). A more complete analytic model also includes *tangential distortions* and *decentering distortions* (Slama 1980), but these distortions are not covered in this book.

Fisheye lenses (Figure 2.13c) require a model that differs from traditional polynomial models of radial distortion. Fisheye lenses behave, to a first approximation, as *equi-distance* projectors of angles away from the optical axis (Xiong and Turkowski 1997), which is the same as the *polar projection* described by Equations (9.22–9.24). Xiong and Turkowski (1997) describe how this model can be extended with the addition of an extra quadratic correction in ϕ and how the unknown parameters (center of projection, scaling factor s, etc.) can be estimated from a set of overlapping fisheye images using a direct (intensity-based) non-linear minimization algorithm.

For even larger, less regular distortions, a parametric distortion model using splines may be necessary (Goshtasby 1989). If the lens does not have a single center of projection, it may become necessary to model the 3D *line* (as opposed to *direction*) corresponding to each pixel separately (Gremban, Thorpe, and Kanade 1988; Champleboux, Lavallée, Sautot *et al.* 1992; Grossberg and Nayar 2001; Sturm and Ramalingam 2004; Tardif, Sturm, Trudeau *et al.* 2009). Some of these techniques are described in more detail in Section 6.3.5, which discusses how to calibrate lens distortions.

---

[4] Sometimes the relationship between x_c and $\hat{x}_c$ is expressed the other way around, i.e., $x_c = \hat{x}_c(1 + \kappa_1 \hat{r}_c^2 + \kappa_2 \hat{r}_c^4)$. This is convenient if we map image pixels into (warped) rays by dividing through by f. We can then undistort the rays and have true 3D rays in space.

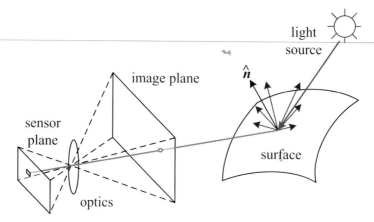

Figure 2.14 A simplified model of photometric image formation. Light is emitted by one or more light sources and is then reflected from an object's surface. A portion of this light is directed towards the camera. This simplified model ignores multiple reflections, which often occur in real-world scenes.

There is one subtle issue associated with the simple radial distortion model that is often glossed over. We have introduced a non-linearity between the perspective projection and final sensor array projection steps. Therefore, we cannot, in general, post-multiply an arbitrary 3×3 matrix K with a rotation to put it into upper-triangular form and absorb this into the global rotation. However, this situation is not as bad as it may at first appear. For many applications, keeping the simplified diagonal form of (2.59) is still an adequate model. Furthermore, if we correct radial and other distortions to an accuracy where straight lines are preserved, we have essentially converted the sensor back into a linear imager and the previous decomposition still applies.

2.2 Photometric image formation

In modeling the image formation process, we have described how 3D geometric features in the world are projected into 2D features in an image. However, images are not composed of 2D features. Instead, they are made up of discrete color or intensity values. Where do these values come from? How do they relate to the lighting in the environment, surface properties and geometry, camera optics, and sensor properties (Figure 2.14)? In this section, we develop a set of models to describe these interactions and formulate a generative process of image formation. A more detailed treatment of these topics can be found in other textbooks on computer graphics and image synthesis (Glassner 1995; Weyrich, Lawrence, Lensch *et al.* 2008; Foley, van Dam, Feiner *et al.* 1995; Watt 1995; Cohen and Wallace 1993; Sillion and Puech 1994).

2.2.1 Lighting

Images cannot exist without light. To produce an image, the scene must be illuminated with one or more light sources. (Certain modalities such as fluorescent microscopy and X-ray tomography do not fit this model, but we do not deal with them in this book.) Light sources can generally be divided into point and area light sources.

A point light source originates at a single location in space (e.g., a small light bulb), potentially at infinity (e.g., the sun). (Note that for some applications such as modeling soft shadows (*penumbras*), the sun may have to be treated as an area light source.) In addition to its location, a point light source has an intensity and a color spectrum, i.e., a distribution over wavelengths $L(\lambda)$. The intensity of a light source falls off with the square of the distance between the source and the object being lit, because the same light is being spread over a larger (spherical) area. A light source may also have a directional falloff (dependence), but we ignore this in our simplified model.

Area light sources are more complicated. A simple area light source such as a fluorescent ceiling light fixture with a diffuser can be modeled as a finite rectangular area emitting light equally in all directions (Cohen and Wallace 1993; Sillion and Puech 1994; Glassner 1995). When the distribution is strongly directional, a four-dimensional lightfield can be used instead (Ashdown 1993).

A more complex light distribution that approximates, say, the incident illumination on an object sitting in an outdoor courtyard, can often be represented using an *environment map* (Greene 1986) (originally called a *reflection map* (Blinn and Newell 1976)). This representation maps incident light directions $\hat{\boldsymbol{v}}$ to color values (or wavelengths, λ),

$$L(\hat{\boldsymbol{v}}; \lambda), \tag{2.80}$$

and is equivalent to assuming that all light sources are at infinity. Environment maps can be represented as a collection of cubical faces (Greene 1986), as a single longitude–latitude map (Blinn and Newell 1976), or as the image of a reflecting sphere (Watt 1995). A convenient way to get a rough model of a real-world environment map is to take an image of a reflective mirrored sphere and to unwrap this image onto the desired environment map (Debevec 1998). Watt (1995) gives a nice discussion of environment mapping, including the formulas needed to map directions to pixels for the three most commonly used representations.

2.2.2 Reflectance and shading

When light hits an object's surface, it is scattered and reflected (Figure 2.15a). Many different models have been developed to describe this interaction. In this section, we first describe the most general form, the bidirectional reflectance distribution function, and then look at some more specialized models, including the diffuse, specular, and Phong shading models. We also discuss how these models can be used to compute the *global illumination* corresponding to a scene.

The Bidirectional Reflectance Distribution Function (BRDF)

The most general model of light scattering is the *bidirectional reflectance distribution function* (BRDF).[5] Relative to some local coordinate frame on the surface, the BRDF is a four-dimensional function that describes how much of each wavelength arriving at an *incident*

---

[5] Actually, even more general models of light transport exist, including some that model spatial variation along the surface, sub-surface scattering, and atmospheric effects—see Section 12.7.1—(Dorsey, Rushmeier, and Sillion 2007; Weyrich, Lawrence, Lensch *et al.* 2008).

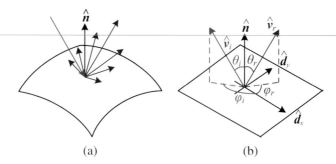

Figure 2.15   (a) Light scatters when it hits a surface. (b) The bidirectional reflectance distribution function (BRDF) $f(\theta_i, \phi_i, \theta_r, \phi_r)$ is parameterized by the angles that the incident, $\hat{\boldsymbol{v}}_i$, and reflected, $\hat{\boldsymbol{v}}_r$, light ray directions make with the local surface coordinate frame $(\hat{\boldsymbol{d}}_x, \hat{\boldsymbol{d}}_y, \hat{\boldsymbol{n}})$.

direction $\hat{\boldsymbol{v}}_i$ is emitted in a *reflected* direction $\hat{\boldsymbol{v}}_r$ (Figure 2.15b). The function can be written in terms of the angles of the incident and reflected directions relative to the surface frame as

$$f_r(\theta_i, \phi_i, \theta_r, \phi_r; \lambda). \tag{2.81}$$

The BRDF is *reciprocal*, i.e., because of the physics of light transport, you can interchange the roles of $\hat{\boldsymbol{v}}_i$ and $\hat{\boldsymbol{v}}_r$ and still get the same answer (this is sometimes called *Helmholtz reciprocity*).

Most surfaces are *isotropic*, i.e., there are no preferred directions on the surface as far as light transport is concerned. (The exceptions are *anisotropic* surfaces such as brushed (scratched) aluminum, where the reflectance depends on the light orientation relative to the direction of the scratches.) For an isotropic material, we can simplify the BRDF to

$$f_r(\theta_i, \theta_r, |\phi_r - \phi_i|; \lambda) \quad \text{or} \quad f_r(\hat{\boldsymbol{v}}_i, \hat{\boldsymbol{v}}_r, \hat{\boldsymbol{n}}; \lambda), \tag{2.82}$$

since the quantities θ_i, θ_r and $\phi_r - \phi_i$ can be computed from the directions $\hat{\boldsymbol{v}}_i$, $\hat{\boldsymbol{v}}_r$, and $\hat{\boldsymbol{n}}$.

To calculate the amount of light exiting a surface point $\boldsymbol{p}$ in a direction $\hat{\boldsymbol{v}}_r$ under a given lighting condition, we integrate the product of the incoming light $L_i(\hat{\boldsymbol{v}}_i; \lambda)$ with the BRDF (some authors call this step a *convolution*). Taking into account the *foreshortening* factor $\cos^+ \theta_i$, we obtain

$$L_r(\hat{\boldsymbol{v}}_r; \lambda) = \int L_i(\hat{\boldsymbol{v}}_i; \lambda) f_r(\hat{\boldsymbol{v}}_i, \hat{\boldsymbol{v}}_r, \hat{\boldsymbol{n}}; \lambda) \cos^+ \theta_i \, d\hat{\boldsymbol{v}}_i, \tag{2.83}$$

where

$$\cos^+ \theta_i = \max(0, \cos \theta_i). \tag{2.84}$$

If the light sources are discrete (a finite number of point light sources), we can replace the integral with a summation,

$$L_r(\hat{\boldsymbol{v}}_r; \lambda) = \sum_i L_i(\lambda) f_r(\hat{\boldsymbol{v}}_i, \hat{\boldsymbol{v}}_r, \hat{\boldsymbol{n}}; \lambda) \cos^+ \theta_i. \tag{2.85}$$

BRDFs for a given surface can be obtained through physical modeling (Torrance and Sparrow 1967; Cook and Torrance 1982; Glassner 1995), heuristic modeling (Phong 1975), or

Figure 2.16 This close-up of a statue shows both diffuse (smooth shading) and specular (shiny highlight) reflection, as well as darkening in the grooves and creases due to reduced light visibility and interreflections. (Photo courtesy of the Caltech Vision Lab, http://www.vision.caltech.edu/archive.html.)

through empirical observation (Ward 1992; Westin, Arvo, and Torrance 1992; Dana, van Ginneken, Nayar *et al.* 1999; Dorsey, Rushmeier, and Sillion 2007; Weyrich, Lawrence, Lensch *et al.* 2008).[6] Typical BRDFs can often be split into their *diffuse* and *specular* components, as described below.

Diffuse reflection

The diffuse component (also known as *Lambertian* or *matte* reflection) scatters light uniformly in all directions and is the phenomenon we most normally associate with *shading*, e.g., the smooth (non-shiny) variation of intensity with surface normal that is seen when observing a statue (Figure 2.16). Diffuse reflection also often imparts a strong *body color* to the light since it is caused by selective absorption and re-emission of light inside the object's material (Shafer 1985; Glassner 1995).

While light is scattered uniformly in all directions, i.e., the BRDF is constant,

$$f_d(\hat{\boldsymbol{v}}_i, \hat{\boldsymbol{v}}_r, \hat{\boldsymbol{n}}; \lambda) = f_d(\lambda), \tag{2.86}$$

the amount of light depends on the angle between the incident light direction and the surface normal θ_i. This is because the surface area exposed to a given amount of light becomes larger at oblique angles, becoming completely self-shadowed as the outgoing surface normal points away from the light (Figure 2.17a). (Think about how you orient yourself towards the sun or fireplace to get maximum warmth and how a flashlight projected obliquely against a wall is less bright than one pointing directly at it.) The *shading equation* for diffuse reflection can thus be written as

$$L_d(\hat{\boldsymbol{v}}_r; \lambda) = \sum_i L_i(\lambda) f_d(\lambda) \cos^+ \theta_i = \sum_i L_i(\lambda) f_d(\lambda) [\hat{\boldsymbol{v}}_i \cdot \hat{\boldsymbol{n}}]^+, \tag{2.87}$$

---

[6] See http://www1.cs.columbia.edu/CAVE/software/curet/ for a database of some empirically sampled BRDFs.

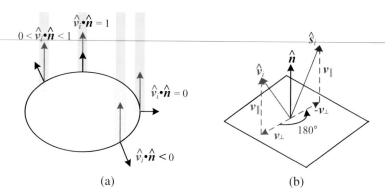

Figure 2.17 (a) The diminution of returned light caused by *foreshortening* depends on $\hat{\boldsymbol{v}}_i \cdot \hat{\boldsymbol{n}}$, the cosine of the angle between the incident light direction $\hat{\boldsymbol{v}}_i$ and the surface normal $\hat{\boldsymbol{n}}$. (b) Mirror (specular) reflection: The incident light ray direction $\hat{\boldsymbol{v}}_i$ is reflected onto the specular direction $\hat{\boldsymbol{s}}_i$ around the surface normal $\hat{\boldsymbol{n}}$.

where

$$[\hat{\boldsymbol{v}}_i \cdot \hat{\boldsymbol{n}}]^+ = \max(0, \hat{\boldsymbol{v}}_i \cdot \hat{\boldsymbol{n}}). \tag{2.88}$$

Specular reflection

The second major component of a typical BRDF is *specular* (gloss or highlight) reflection, which depends strongly on the direction of the outgoing light. Consider light reflecting off a mirrored surface (Figure 2.17b). Incident light rays are reflected in a direction that is rotated by $180°$ around the surface normal $\hat{\boldsymbol{n}}$. Using the same notation as in Equations (2.29–2.30), we can compute the *specular reflection* direction $\hat{\boldsymbol{s}}_i$ as

$$\hat{\boldsymbol{s}}_i = \boldsymbol{v}_\| - \boldsymbol{v}_\perp = (2\hat{\boldsymbol{n}}\hat{\boldsymbol{n}}^T - \boldsymbol{I})\boldsymbol{v}_i. \tag{2.89}$$

The amount of light reflected in a given direction $\hat{\boldsymbol{v}}_r$ thus depends on the angle $\theta_s = \cos^{-1}(\hat{\boldsymbol{v}}_r \cdot \hat{\boldsymbol{s}}_i)$ between the view direction $\hat{\boldsymbol{v}}_r$ and the specular direction $\hat{\boldsymbol{s}}_i$. For example, the Phong (1975) model uses a power of the cosine of the angle,

$$f_s(\theta_s; \lambda) = k_s(\lambda) \cos^{k_e} \theta_s, \tag{2.90}$$

while the Torrance and Sparrow (1967) micro-facet model uses a Gaussian,

$$f_s(\theta_s; \lambda) = k_s(\lambda) \exp(-c_s^2 \theta_s^2). \tag{2.91}$$

Larger exponents k_e (or inverse Gaussian widths c_s) correspond to more specular surfaces with distinct highlights, while smaller exponents better model materials with softer gloss.

Phong shading

Phong (1975) combined the diffuse and specular components of reflection with another term, which he called the *ambient illumination*. This term accounts for the fact that objects are generally illuminated not only by point light sources but also by a general diffuse illumination corresponding to inter-reflection (e.g., the walls in a room) or distant sources, such as the

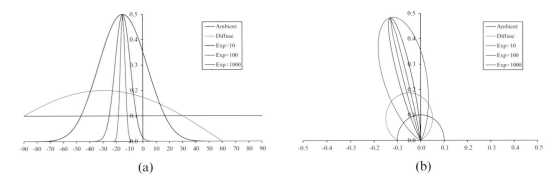

Figure 2.18 Cross-section through a Phong shading model BRDF for a fixed incident illumination direction: (a) component values as a function of angle away from surface normal; (b) polar plot. The value of the Phong exponent k_e is indicated by the "Exp" labels and the light source is at an angle of $30°$ away from the normal.

blue sky. In the Phong model, the ambient term does not depend on surface orientation, but depends on the color of both the ambient illumination $L_a(\lambda)$ and the object $k_a(\lambda)$,

$$f_a(\lambda) = k_a(\lambda)L_a(\lambda). \tag{2.92}$$

Putting all of these terms together, we arrive at the *Phong shading* model,

$$L_r(\hat{\boldsymbol{v}}_r; \lambda) = k_a(\lambda)L_a(\lambda) + k_d(\lambda) \sum_i L_i(\lambda)[\hat{\boldsymbol{v}}_i \cdot \hat{\boldsymbol{n}}]^+ + k_s(\lambda) \sum_i L_i(\lambda)(\hat{\boldsymbol{v}}_r \cdot \hat{\boldsymbol{s}}_i)^{k_e}. \tag{2.93}$$

Figure 2.18 shows a typical set of Phong shading model components as a function of the angle away from the surface normal (in a plane containing both the lighting direction and the viewer).

Typically, the ambient and diffuse reflection color distributions $k_a(\lambda)$ and $k_d(\lambda)$ are the same, since they are both due to sub-surface scattering (body reflection) inside the surface material (Shafer 1985). The specular reflection distribution $k_s(\lambda)$ is often uniform (white), since it is caused by interface reflections that do not change the light color. (The exception to this are *metallic* materials, such as copper, as opposed to the more common *dielectric* materials, such as plastics.)

The ambient illumination $L_a(\lambda)$ often has a different color cast from the direct light sources $L_i(\lambda)$, e.g., it may be blue for a sunny outdoor scene or yellow for an interior lit with candles or incandescent lights. (The presence of ambient sky illumination in shadowed areas is what often causes shadows to appear bluer than the corresponding lit portions of a scene). Note also that the diffuse component of the Phong model (or of any shading model) depends on the angle of the *incoming* light source $\hat{\boldsymbol{v}}_i$, while the specular component depends on the relative angle between the viewer $\boldsymbol{v}_r$ and the specular reflection direction $\hat{\boldsymbol{s}}_i$ (which itself depends on the incoming light direction $\hat{\boldsymbol{v}}_i$ and the surface normal $\hat{\boldsymbol{n}}$).

The Phong shading model has been superseded in terms of physical accuracy by a number of more recently developed models in computer graphics, including the model developed by Cook and Torrance (1982) based on the original micro-facet model of Torrance and Sparrow (1967). Until recently, most computer graphics hardware implemented the Phong model but the recent advent of programmable pixel shaders makes the use of more complex models feasible.

Di-chromatic reflection model

The Torrance and Sparrow (1967) model of reflection also forms the basis of Shafer's (1985) *di-chromatic reflection model*, which states that the apparent color of a uniform material lit from a single source depends on the sum of two terms,

$$L_r(\hat{\boldsymbol{v}}_r; \lambda) = L_i(\hat{\boldsymbol{v}}_r, \hat{\boldsymbol{v}}_i, \hat{\boldsymbol{n}}; \lambda) + L_b(\hat{\boldsymbol{v}}_r, \hat{\boldsymbol{v}}_i, \hat{\boldsymbol{n}}; \lambda) \tag{2.94}$$

$$= c_i(\lambda) m_i(\hat{\boldsymbol{v}}_r, \hat{\boldsymbol{v}}_i, \hat{\boldsymbol{n}}) + c_b(\lambda) m_b(\hat{\boldsymbol{v}}_r, \hat{\boldsymbol{v}}_i, \hat{\boldsymbol{n}}), \tag{2.95}$$

i.e., the radiance of the light reflected at the *interface*, L_i, and the radiance reflected at the *surface body*, L_b. Each of these, in turn, is a simple product between a relative power spectrum $c(\lambda)$, which depends only on wavelength, and a magnitude $m(\hat{\boldsymbol{v}}_r, \hat{\boldsymbol{v}}_i, \hat{\boldsymbol{n}})$, which depends only on geometry. (This model can easily be derived from a generalized version of Phong's model by assuming a single light source and no ambient illumination, and re-arranging terms.) The di-chromatic model has been successfully used in computer vision to segment specular colored objects with large variations in shading (Klinker 1993) and more recently has inspired local two-color models for applications such Bayer pattern demosaicing (Bennett, Uyttendaele, Zitnick *et al.* 2006).

Global illumination (ray tracing and radiosity)

The simple shading model presented thus far assumes that light rays leave the light sources, bounce off surfaces visible to the camera, thereby changing in intensity or color, and arrive at the camera. In reality, light sources can be shadowed by occluders and rays can bounce multiple times around a scene while making their trip from a light source to the camera.

Two methods have traditionally been used to model such effects. If the scene is mostly specular (the classic example being scenes made of glass objects and mirrored or highly polished balls), the preferred approach is *ray tracing* or *path tracing* (Glassner 1995; Akenine-Möller and Haines 2002; Shirley 2005), which follows individual rays from the camera across multiple bounces towards the light sources (or vice versa). If the scene is composed mostly of uniform albedo simple geometry illuminators and surfaces, *radiosity* (*global illumination*) techniques are preferred (Cohen and Wallace 1993; Sillion and Puech 1994; Glassner 1995). Combinations of the two techniques have also been developed (Wallace, Cohen, and Greenberg 1987), as well as more general *light transport* techniques for simulating effects such as the *caustics* cast by rippling water.

The basic ray tracing algorithm associates a light ray with each pixel in the camera image and finds its intersection with the nearest surface. A *primary* contribution can then be computed using the simple shading equations presented previously (e.g., Equation (2.93)) for all light sources that are visible for that surface element. (An alternative technique for computing which surfaces are illuminated by a light source is to compute a *shadow map*, or *shadow buffer*, i.e., a rendering of the scene from the light source's perspective, and then compare the depth of pixels being rendered with the map (Williams 1983; Akenine-Möller and Haines 2002).) Additional *secondary* rays can then be cast along the specular direction towards other objects in the scene, keeping track of any attenuation or color change that the specular reflection induces.

Radiosity works by associating lightness values with rectangular surface areas in the scene (including area light sources). The amount of light interchanged between any two (mutually

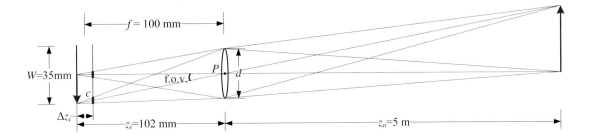

Figure 2.19 A thin lens of focal length f focuses the light from a plane a distance z_o in front of the lens at a distance z_i behind the lens, where $\frac{1}{z_o} + \frac{1}{z_i} = \frac{1}{f}$. If the focal plane (vertical gray line next to c) is moved forward, the images are no longer in focus and the *circle of confusion* c (small thick line segments) depends on the distance of the image plane motion Δz_i relative to the lens aperture diameter d. The field of view (f.o.v.) depends on the ratio between the sensor width W and the focal length f (or, more precisely, the focusing distance z_i, which is usually quite close to f).

visible) areas in the scene can be captured as a *form factor*, which depends on their relative orientation and surface reflectance properties, as well as the $1/r^2$ fall-off as light is distributed over a larger effective sphere the further away it is (Cohen and Wallace 1993; Sillion and Puech 1994; Glassner 1995). A large linear system can then be set up to solve for the final lightness of each area patch, using the light sources as the forcing function (right hand side). Once the system has been solved, the scene can be rendered from any desired point of view. Under certain circumstances, it is possible to recover the global illumination in a scene from photographs using computer vision techniques (Yu, Debevec, Malik *et al.* 1999).

The basic radiosity algorithm does not take into account certain *near field* effects, such as the darkening inside corners and scratches, or the limited ambient illumination caused by partial shadowing from other surfaces. Such effects have been exploited in a number of computer vision algorithms (Nayar, Ikeuchi, and Kanade 1991; Langer and Zucker 1994).

While all of these global illumination effects can have a strong effect on the appearance of a scene, and hence its 3D interpretation, they are not covered in more detail in this book. (But see Section 12.7.1 for a discussion of recovering BRDFs from real scenes and objects.)

2.2.3 Optics

Once the light from a scene reaches the camera, it must still pass through the lens before reaching the sensor (analog film or digital silicon). For many applications, it suffices to treat the lens as an ideal pinhole that simply projects all rays through a common center of projection (Figures 2.8 and 2.9).

However, if we want to deal with issues such as focus, exposure, vignetting, and aberration, we need to develop a more sophisticated model, which is where the study of *optics* comes in (Möller 1988; Hecht 2001; Ray 2002).

Figure 2.19 shows a diagram of the most basic lens model, i.e., the *thin lens* composed of a single piece of glass with very low, equal curvature on both sides. According to the *lens law* (which can be derived using simple geometric arguments on light ray refraction), the relationship between the distance to an object z_o and the distance behind the lens at which a

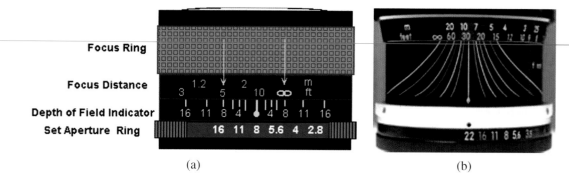

Focus Ring

Focus Distance

Depth of Field Indicator

Set Aperture Ring

(a)   (b)

Figure 2.20 Regular and zoom lens depth of field indicators.

focused image is formed z_i can be expressed as

$$\frac{1}{z_o} + \frac{1}{z_i} = \frac{1}{f},\qquad(2.96)$$

where f is called the *focal length* of the lens. If we let $z_o \rightarrow \infty$, i.e., we adjust the lens (move the image plane) so that objects at infinity are in focus, we get $z_i = f$, which is why we can think of a lens of focal length f as being equivalent (to a first approximation) to a pinhole a distance f from the focal plane (Figure 2.10), whose field of view is given by (2.60).

If the focal plane is moved away from its proper in-focus setting of z_i (e.g., by twisting the focus ring on the lens), objects at z_o are no longer in focus, as shown by the gray plane in Figure 2.19. The amount of mis-focus is measured by the *circle of confusion* c (shown as short thick blue line segments on the gray plane).[7] The equation for the circle of confusion can be derived using similar triangles; it depends on the distance of travel in the focal plane Δz_i relative to the original focus distance z_i and the diameter of the aperture d (see Exercise 2.4).

The allowable depth variation in the scene that limits the circle of confusion to an acceptable number is commonly called the *depth of field* and is a function of both the focus distance and the aperture, as shown diagrammatically by many lens markings (Figure 2.20). Since this depth of field depends on the aperture diameter d, we also have to know how this varies with the commonly displayed *f-number*, which is usually denoted as $f/\#$ or N and is defined as

$$f/\# = N = \frac{f}{d},\qquad(2.97)$$

where the focal length f and the aperture diameter d are measured in the same unit (say, millimeters).

The usual way to write the f-number is to replace the $\#$ in $f/\#$ with the actual number, i.e., $f/1.4, f/2, f/2.8, \ldots, f/22$. (Alternatively, we can say $N = 1.4$, etc.) An easy way to interpret these numbers is to notice that dividing the focal length by the f-number gives us the diameter d, so these are just formulas for the aperture diameter.[8]

---

[7] If the aperture is not completely circular, e.g., if it is caused by a hexagonal diaphragm, it is sometimes possible to see this effect in the actual blur function (Levin, Fergus, Durand *et al.* 2007; Joshi, Szeliski, and Kriegman 2008) or in the "glints" that are seen when shooting into the sun.

[8] This also explains why, with zoom lenses, the f-number varies with the current zoom (focal length) setting.

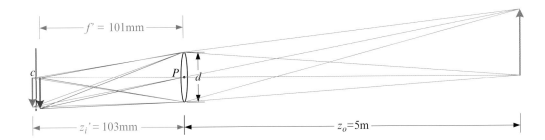

Figure 2.21 In a lens subject to *chromatic aberration*, light at different wavelengths (e.g., the red and blur arrows) is focused with a different focal length f' and hence a different depth z_i', resulting in both a geometric (in-plane) displacement and a loss of focus.

Notice that the usual progression for f-numbers is in *full stops*, which are multiples of $\sqrt{2}$, since this corresponds to doubling the area of the entrance pupil each time a smaller f-number is selected. (This doubling is also called changing the exposure by one *exposure value* or EV. It has the same effect on the amount of light reaching the sensor as doubling the exposure duration, e.g., from $1/125$ to $1/250$, see Exercise 2.5.)

Now that you know how to convert between f-numbers and aperture diameters, you can construct your own plots for the depth of field as a function of focal length f, circle of confusion c, and focus distance z_o, as explained in Exercise 2.4 and see how well these match what you observe on actual lenses, such as those shown in Figure 2.20.

Of course, real lenses are not infinitely thin and therefore suffer from geometric aberrations, unless compound elements are used to correct for them. The classic five *Seidel aberrations*, which arise when using *third-order optics*, include spherical aberration, coma, astigmatism, curvature of field, and distortion (Möller 1988; Hecht 2001; Ray 2002).

Chromatic aberration

Because the index of refraction for glass varies slightly as a function of wavelength, simple lenses suffer from *chromatic aberration*, which is the tendency for light of different colors to focus at slightly different distances (and hence also with slightly different magnification factors), as shown in Figure 2.21. The wavelength-dependent magnification factor, i.e., the *transverse chromatic aberration*, can be modeled as a per-color radial distortion (Section 2.1.6) and, hence, calibrated using the techniques described in Section 6.3.5. The wavelength-dependent blur caused by *longitudinal chromatic aberration* can be calibrated using techniques described in Section 10.1.4. Unfortunately, the blur induced by longitudinal aberration can be harder to undo, as higher frequencies can get strongly attenuated and hence hard to recover.

In order to reduce chromatic and other kinds of aberrations, most photographic lenses today are *compound lenses* made of different glass elements (with different coatings). Such lenses can no longer be modeled as having a single *nodal point* P through which all of the rays must pass (when approximating the lens with a pinhole model). Instead, these lenses have both a *front nodal point*, through which the rays enter the lens, and a *rear nodal point*, through which they leave on their way to the sensor. In practice, only the location of the front

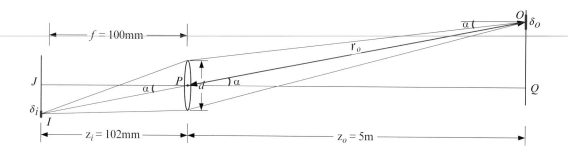

Figure 2.22   The amount of light hitting a pixel of surface area δi depends on the square of the ratio of the aperture diameter d to the focal length f, as well as the fourth power of the off-axis angle α cosine, $\cos^4 \alpha$.

nodal point is of interest when performing careful camera calibration, e.g., when determining the point around which to rotate to capture a parallax-free panorama (see Section 9.1.3).

Not all lenses, however, can be modeled as having a single nodal point. In particular, very wide-angle lenses such as fisheye lenses (Section 2.1.6) and certain *catadioptric* imaging systems consisting of lenses and curved mirrors (Baker and Nayar 1999) do not have a single point through which all of the acquired light rays pass. In such cases, it is preferable to explicitly construct a mapping function (look-up table) between pixel coordinates and 3D rays in space (Gremban, Thorpe, and Kanade 1988; Champleboux, Lavallée, Sautot *et al.* 1992; Grossberg and Nayar 2001; Sturm and Ramalingam 2004; Tardif, Sturm, Trudeau *et al.* 2009), as mentioned in Section 2.1.6.

Vignetting

Another property of real-world lenses is *vignetting*, which is the tendency for the brightness of the image to fall off towards the edge of the image.

Two kinds of phenomena usually contribute to this effect (Ray 2002). The first is called *natural vignetting* and is due to the foreshortening in the object surface, projected pixel, and lens aperture, as shown in Figure 2.22. Consider the light leaving the object surface patch of size δo located at an *off-axis angle* α. Because this patch is foreshortened with respect to the camera lens, the amount of light reaching the lens is reduced by a factor $\cos \alpha$. The amount of light reaching the lens is also subject to the usual $1/r^2$ fall-off; in this case, the distance $r_o = z_o / \cos \alpha$. The actual area of the aperture through which the light passes is foreshortened by an additional factor $\cos \alpha$, i.e., the aperture as seen from point O is an ellipse of dimensions $d \times d \cos \alpha$. Putting all of these factors together, we see that the amount of light leaving O and passing through the aperture on its way to the image pixel located at I is proportional to

$$\frac{\delta o \cos \alpha}{r_o^2} \pi \left(\frac{d}{2} \right)^2 \cos \alpha = \delta o \frac{\pi}{4} \frac{d^2}{z_o^2} \cos^4 \alpha. \tag{2.98}$$

Since triangles $\triangle OPQ$ and $\triangle IPJ$ are similar, the projected areas of of the object surface δo and image pixel δi are in the same (squared) ratio as $z_o : z_i$,

$$\frac{\delta o}{\delta i} = \frac{z_o^2}{z_i^2}. \tag{2.99}$$

Putting these together, we obtain the final relationship between the amount of light reaching pixel i and the aperture diameter d, the focusing distance $z_i \approx f$, and the off-axis angle α,

$$\delta o \frac{\pi}{4} \frac{d^2}{z_o^2} \cos^4 \alpha = \delta i \frac{\pi}{4} \frac{d^2}{z_i^2} \cos^4 \alpha \approx \delta i \frac{\pi}{4} \left(\frac{d}{f} \right)^2 \cos^4 \alpha, \qquad (2.100)$$

which is called the *fundamental radiometric relation* between the scene radiance L and the light (irradiance) E reaching the pixel sensor,

$$E = L \frac{\pi}{4} \left(\frac{d}{f} \right)^2 \cos^4 \alpha, \qquad (2.101)$$

(Horn 1986; Nalwa 1993; Hecht 2001; Ray 2002). Notice in this equation how the amount of light depends on the pixel surface area (which is why the smaller sensors in point-and-shoot cameras are so much noisier than digital single lens reflex (SLR) cameras), the inverse square of the f-stop $N = f/d$ (2.97), and the fourth power of the $\cos^4 \alpha$ off-axis fall-off, which is the natural vignetting term.

The other major kind of vignetting, called *mechanical vignetting*, is caused by the internal occlusion of rays near the periphery of lens elements in a compound lens, and cannot easily be described mathematically without performing a full ray-tracing of the actual lens design.[9] However, unlike natural vignetting, mechanical vignetting can be decreased by reducing the camera aperture (increasing the f-number). It can also be calibrated (along with natural vignetting) using special devices such as integrating spheres, uniformly illuminated targets, or camera rotation, as discussed in Section 10.1.3.

2.3 The digital camera

After starting from one or more light sources, reflecting off one or more surfaces in the world, and passing through the camera's optics (lenses), light finally reaches the imaging sensor. How are the photons arriving at this sensor converted into the digital (R, G, B) values that we observe when we look at a digital image? In this section, we develop a simple model that accounts for the most important effects such as exposure (gain and shutter speed), non-linear mappings, sampling and aliasing, and noise. Figure 2.23, which is based on camera models developed by Healey and Kondepudy (1994); Tsin, Ramesh, and Kanade (2001); Liu, Szeliski, Kang *et al.* (2008), shows a simple version of the processing stages that occur in modern digital cameras. Chakrabarti, Scharstein, and Zickler (2009) developed a sophisticated 24-parameter model that is an even better match to the processing performed in today's cameras.

Light falling on an imaging sensor is usually picked up by an *active sensing area*, integrated for the duration of the exposure (usually expressed as the shutter speed in a fraction of a second, e.g., $\frac{1}{125}$, $\frac{1}{60}$, $\frac{1}{30}$), and then passed to a set of *sense amplifiers* . The two main kinds of sensor used in digital still and video cameras today are charge-coupled device (CCD) and complementary metal oxide on silicon (CMOS).

In a CCD, photons are accumulated in each active *well* during the exposure time. Then, in a *transfer* phase, the charges are transferred from well to well in a kind of "bucket brigade"

---

[9] There are some empirical models that work well in practice (Kang and Weiss 2000; Zheng, Lin, and Kang 2006).

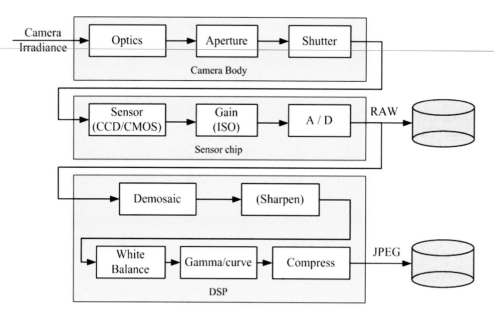

Figure 2.23 Image sensing pipeline, showing the various sources of noise as well as typical digital post-processing steps.

until they are deposited at the sense amplifiers, which amplify the signal and pass it to an analog-to-digital converter (ADC).[10] Older CCD sensors were prone to *blooming*, when charges from one over-exposed pixel spilled into adjacent ones, but most newer CCDs have anti-blooming technology ("troughs" into which the excess charge can spill).

In CMOS, the photons hitting the sensor directly affect the conductivity (or gain) of a photodetector, which can be selectively gated to control exposure duration, and locally amplified before being read out using a multiplexing scheme. Traditionally, CCD sensors outperformed CMOS in quality sensitive applications, such as digital SLRs, while CMOS was better for low-power applications, but today CMOS is used in most digital cameras.

The main factors affecting the performance of a digital image sensor are the shutter speed, sampling pitch, fill factor, chip size, analog gain, sensor noise, and the resolution (and quality) of the analog-to-digital converter. Many of the actual values for these parameters can be read from the EXIF tags embedded with digital images. while others can be obtained from the camera manufacturers' specification sheets or from camera review or calibration Web sites.[11]

Shutter speed. The shutter speed (exposure time) directly controls the amount of light reaching the sensor and, hence, determines if images are under- or over-exposed. (For bright scenes, where a large aperture or slow shutter speed are desired to get a shallow depth of field or motion blur, *neutral density filters* are sometimes used by photographers.) For dynamic scenes, the shutter speed also determines the amount of *motion blur* in the resulting picture.

---

[10] In digital still cameras, a complete frame is captured and then read out sequentially at once. However, if video is being captured, a *rolling shutter*, which exposes and transfers each line separately, is often used. In older video cameras, the even fields (lines) were scanned first, followed by the odd fields, in a process that is called *interlacing*.

[11] http://www.clarkvision.com/imagedetail/digital.sensor.performance.summary/ .

Usually, a higher shutter speed (less motion blur) makes subsequent analysis easier (see Section 10.3 for techniques to remove such blur). However, when video is being captured for display, some motion blur may be desirable to avoid stroboscopic effects.

Sampling pitch. The sampling pitch is the physical spacing between adjacent sensor cells on the imaging chip. A sensor with a smaller sampling pitch has a higher *sampling density* and hence provides a higher *resolution* (in terms of pixels) for a given active chip area. However, a smaller pitch also means that each sensor has a smaller area and cannot accumulate as many photons; this makes it not as *light sensitive* and more prone to noise.

Fill factor. The fill factor is the active sensing area size as a fraction of the theoretically available sensing area (the product of the horizontal and vertical sampling pitches). Higher fill factors are usually preferable, as they result in more light capture and less *aliasing* (see Section 2.3.1). However, this must be balanced with the need to place additional electronics between the active sense areas. The fill factor of a camera can be determined empirically using a photometric camera calibration process (see Section 10.1.4).

Chip size. Video and point-and-shoot cameras have traditionally used small chip areas ($\frac{1}{4}$-inch to $\frac{1}{2}$-inch sensors[12]), while digital SLR cameras try to come closer to the traditional size of a 35mm film frame.[13] When overall device size is not important, having a larger chip size is preferable, since each sensor cell can be more photo-sensitive. (For compact cameras, a smaller chip means that all of the optics can be shrunk down proportionately.) However, larger chips are more expensive to produce, not only because fewer chips can be packed into each wafer, but also because the probability of a chip defect goes up linearly with the chip area.

Analog gain. Before analog-to-digital conversion, the sensed signal is usually boosted by a *sense amplifier*. In video cameras, the gain on these amplifiers was traditionally controlled by *automatic gain control* (AGC) logic, which would adjust these values to obtain a good overall exposure. In newer digital still cameras, the user now has some additional control over this gain through the *ISO setting*, which is typically expressed in ISO standard units such as 100, 200, or 400. Since the automated exposure control in most cameras also adjusts the aperture and shutter speed, setting the ISO manually removes one degree of freedom from the camera's control, just as manually specifying aperture and shutter speed does. In theory, a higher gain allows the camera to perform better under low light conditions (less motion blur due to long exposure times when the aperture is already maxed out). In practice, however, higher ISO settings usually amplify the *sensor noise*.

---

[12] These numbers refer to the "tube diameter" of the old vidicon tubes used in video cameras (http://www.dpreview.com/learn/?/Glossary/Camera_System/sensor_sizes_01.htm). The 1/2.5" sensor on the Canon SD800 camera actually measures 5.76mm × 4.29mm, i.e., a sixth of the size (on side) of a 35mm full-frame (36mm × 24mm) DSLR sensor.

[13] When a DSLR chip does not fill the 35mm full frame, it results in a *multiplier effect* on the lens focal length. For example, a chip that is only 0.6 the dimension of a 35mm frame will make a 50mm lens image the same angular extent as a $50/0.6 = 50 \times 1.6 = 80$mm lens, as demonstrated in (2.60).

Sensor noise. Throughout the whole sensing process, noise is added from various sources, which may include *fixed pattern noise*, *dark current noise*, *shot noise*, *amplifier noise* and *quantization noise* (Healey and Kondepudy 1994; Tsin, Ramesh, and Kanade 2001). The final amount of noise present in a sampled image depends on all of these quantities, as well as the incoming light (controlled by the scene radiance and aperture), the exposure time, and the sensor gain. Also, for low light conditions where the noise is due to low photon counts, a Poisson model of noise may be more appropriate than a Gaussian model.

As discussed in more detail in Section 10.1.1, Liu, Szeliski, Kang *et al.* (2008) use this model, along with an empirical database of camera response functions (CRFs) obtained by Grossberg and Nayar (2004), to estimate the *noise level function* (NLF) for a given image, which predicts the overall noise variance at a given pixel as a function of its brightness (a separate NLF is estimated for each color channel). An alternative approach, when you have access to the camera before taking pictures, is to pre-calibrate the NLF by taking repeated shots of a scene containing a variety of colors and luminances, such as the Macbeth Color Chart shown in Figure 10.3b (McCamy, Marcus, and Davidson 1976). (When estimating the variance, be sure to throw away or downweight pixels with large gradients, as small shifts between exposures will affect the sensed values at such pixels.) Unfortunately, the pre-calibration process may have to be repeated for different exposure times and gain settings because of the complex interactions occurring within the sensing system.

In practice, most computer vision algorithms, such as image denoising, edge detection, and stereo matching, all benefit from at least a rudimentary estimate of the noise level. Barring the ability to pre-calibrate the camera or to take repeated shots of the same scene, the simplest approach is to look for regions of near-constant value and to estimate the noise variance in such regions (Liu, Szeliski, Kang *et al.* 2008).

ADC resolution. The final step in the analog processing chain occurring within an imaging sensor is the *analog to digital conversion* (ADC). While a variety of techniques can be used to implement this process, the two quantities of interest are the *resolution* of this process (how many bits it yields) and its noise level (how many of these bits are useful in practice). For most cameras, the number of bits quoted (eight bits for compressed JPEG images and a nominal 16 bits for the RAW formats provided by some DSLRs) exceeds the actual number of usable bits. The best way to tell is to simply calibrate the noise of a given sensor, e.g., by taking repeated shots of the same scene and plotting the estimated noise as a function of brightness (Exercise 2.6).

Digital post-processing. Once the irradiance values arriving at the sensor have been converted to digital bits, most cameras perform a variety of *digital signal processing* (DSP) operations to enhance the image before compressing and storing the pixel values. These include color filter array (CFA) demosaicing, white point setting, and mapping of the luminance values through a *gamma function* to increase the perceived dynamic range of the signal. We cover these topics in Section 2.3.2 but, before we do, we return to the topic of aliasing, which was mentioned in connection with sensor array fill factors.

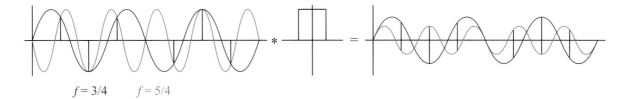

$f = 3/4$ $f = 5/4$

Figure 2.24 Aliasing of a one-dimensional signal: The blue sine wave at $f = 3/4$ and the red sine wave at $f = 5/4$ have the same digital samples, when sampled at $f = 2$. Even after convolution with a 100% fill factor box filter, the two signals, while no longer of the same magnitude, are still aliased in the sense that the sampled red signal looks like an inverted lower magnitude version of the blue signal. (The image on the right is scaled up for better visibility. The actual sine magnitudes are 30% and -18% of their original values.)

2.3.1 Sampling and aliasing

What happens when a field of light impinging on the image sensor falls onto the active sense areas in the imaging chip? The photons arriving at each active cell are integrated and then digitized. However, if the fill factor on the chip is small and the signal is not otherwise *band-limited*, visually unpleasing aliasing can occur.

To explore the phenomenon of aliasing, let us first look at a one-dimensional signal (Figure 2.24), in which we have two sine waves, one at a frequency of $f = {}^3\!/_4$ and the other at $f = {}^5\!/_4$. If we sample these two signals at a frequency of $f = 2$, we see that they produce the same samples (shown in black), and so we say that they are *aliased*.[14] Why is this a bad effect? In essence, we can no longer reconstruct the original signal, since we do not know which of the two original frequencies was present.

In fact, Shannon's Sampling Theorem shows that the minimum sampling (Oppenheim and Schafer 1996; Oppenheim, Schafer, and Buck 1999) rate required to reconstruct a signal from its instantaneous samples must be at least twice the highest frequency,[15]

$$f_{\rm s} \geq 2f_{\max}. \tag{2.102}$$

The maximum frequency in a signal is known as the *Nyquist frequency* and the inverse of the minimum sampling frequency $r_{\rm s} = 1/f_{\rm s}$ is known as the *Nyquist rate*.

However, you may ask, since an imaging chip actually *averages* the light field over a finite area, are the results on point sampling still applicable? Averaging over the sensor area does tend to attenuate some of the higher frequencies. However, even if the fill factor is 100%, as in the right image of Figure 2.24, frequencies above the Nyquist limit (half the sampling frequency) still produce an aliased signal, although with a smaller magnitude than the corresponding band-limited signals.

A more convincing argument as to why aliasing is bad can be seen by downsampling a signal using a poor quality filter such as a box (square) filter. Figure 2.25 shows a high-frequency *chirp* image (so called because the frequencies increase over time), along with the results of sampling it with a 25% fill-factor area sensor, a 100% fill-factor sensor, and a high-

---

[14] An alias is an alternate name for someone, so the sampled signal corresponds to two different *aliases*.

[15] The actual theorem states that $f_{\rm s}$ must be at least twice the signal *bandwidth* but, since we are not dealing with modulated signals such as radio waves during image capture, the maximum frequency suffices.

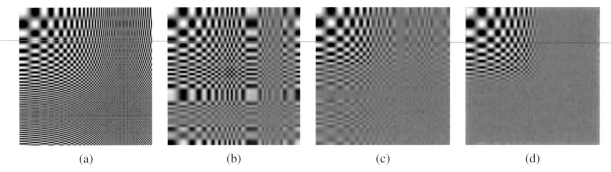

(a)   (b)   (c)   (d)

Figure 2.25   Aliasing of a two-dimensional signal: (a) original full-resolution image; (b) downsampled $4\times$ with a 25% fill factor box filter; (c) downsampled $4\times$ with a 100% fill factor box filter; (d) downsampled $4\times$ with a high-quality 9-tap filter. Notice how the higher frequencies are aliased into visible frequencies with the lower quality filters, while the 9-tap filter completely removes these higher frequencies.

quality 9-tap filter. Additional examples of downsampling (*decimation*) filters can be found in Section 3.5.2 and Figure 3.30.

The best way to predict the amount of aliasing that an imaging system (or even an image processing algorithm) will produce is to estimate the *point spread function* (PSF), which represents the response of a particular pixel sensor to an ideal point light source. The PSF is a combination (convolution) of the blur induced by the optical system (lens) and the finite integration area of a chip sensor.[16]

If we know the blur function of the lens and the fill factor (sensor area shape and spacing) for the imaging chip (plus, optionally, the response of the anti-aliasing filter), we can convolve these (as described in Section 3.2) to obtain the PSF. Figure 2.26a shows the one-dimensional cross-section of a PSF for a lens whose blur function is assumed to be a disc of a radius equal to the pixel spacing s plus a sensing chip whose horizontal fill factor is 80%. Taking the Fourier transform of this PSF (Section 3.4), we obtain the *modulation transfer function* (MTF), from which we can estimate the amount of aliasing as the area of the Fourier magnitude outside the $f \le f_s$ Nyquist frequency.[17] If we de-focus the lens so that the blur function has a radius of $2s$ (Figure 2.26c), we see that the amount of aliasing decreases significantly, but so does the amount of image detail (frequencies closer to $f = f_s$).

Under laboratory conditions, the PSF can be estimated (to pixel precision) by looking at a point light source such as a pin hole in a black piece of cardboard lit from behind. However, this PSF (the actual image of the pin hole) is only accurate to a pixel resolution and, while it can model larger blur (such as blur caused by defocus), it cannot model the sub-pixel shape of the PSF and predict the amount of aliasing. An alternative technique, described in Section 10.1.4, is to look at a calibration pattern (e.g., one consisting of slanted step edges (Reichenbach, Park, and Narayanswamy 1991; Williams and Burns 2001; Joshi, Szeliski, and Kriegman 2008)) whose ideal appearance can be re-synthesized to sub-pixel precision.

In addition to occurring during image acquisition, aliasing can also be introduced in var-

---

[16] Imaging chips usually interpose an optical *anti-aliasing filter* just before the imaging chip to reduce or control the amount of aliasing.

[17] The complex Fourier transform of the PSF is actually called the *optical transfer function* (OTF) (Williams 1999). Its magnitude is called the *modulation transfer function* (MTF) and its phase is called the *phase transfer function* (PTF).

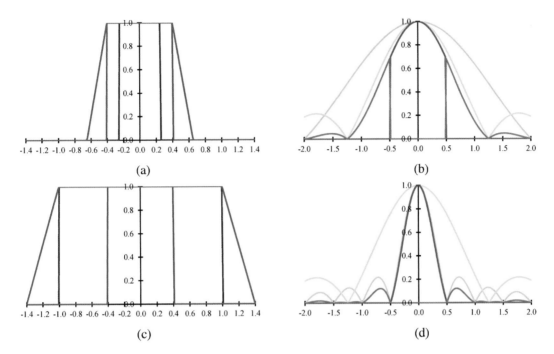

Figure 2.26 Sample point spread functions (PSF): The diameter of the blur disc (blue) in (a) is equal to half the pixel spacing, while the diameter in (c) is twice the pixel spacing. The horizontal fill factor of the sensing chip is 80% and is shown in brown. The convolution of these two kernels gives the point spread function, shown in green. The Fourier response of the PSF (the MTF) is plotted in (b) and (d). The area above the Nyquist frequency where aliasing occurs is shown in red.

ious image processing operations, such as resampling, upsampling, and downsampling. Sections 3.4 and 3.5.2 discuss these issues and show how careful selection of filters can reduce the amount of aliasing that operations inject.

2.3.2 Color

In Section 2.2, we saw how lighting and surface reflections are functions of wavelength. When the incoming light hits the imaging sensor, light from different parts of the spectrum is somehow integrated into the discrete red, green, and blue (RGB) color values that we see in a digital image. How does this process work and how can we analyze and manipulate color values?

You probably recall from your childhood days the magical process of mixing paint colors to obtain new ones. You may recall that blue+yellow makes green, red+blue makes purple, and red+green makes brown. If you revisited this topic at a later age, you may have learned that the proper *subtractive* primaries are actually cyan (a light blue-green), magenta (pink), and yellow (Figure 2.27b), although black is also often used in four-color printing (CMYK). (If you ever subsequently took any painting classes, you learned that colors can have even more fanciful names, such as alizarin crimson, cerulean blue, and chartreuse.) The subtractive colors are called subtractive because pigments in the paint absorb certain wavelengths in the color spectrum.

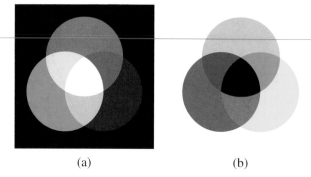

(a)   (b)

Figure 2.27 Primary and secondary colors: (a) additive colors red, green, and blue can be mixed to produce cyan, magenta, yellow, and white; (b) subtractive colors cyan, magenta, and yellow can be mixed to produce red, green, blue, and black.

Later on, you may have learned about the *additive* primary colors (red, green, and blue) and how they can be added (with a slide projector or on a computer monitor) to produce cyan, magenta, yellow, white, and all the other colors we typically see on our TV sets and monitors (Figure 2.27a).

Through what process is it possible for two different colors, such as red and green, to interact to produce a third color like yellow? Are the wavelengths somehow mixed up to produce a new wavelength?

You probably know that the correct answer has nothing to do with physically mixing wavelengths. Instead, the existence of three primaries is a result of the *tri-stimulus* (or *tri-chromatic*) nature of the human visual system, since we have three different kinds of cone, each of which responds selectively to a different portion of the color spectrum (Glassner 1995; Wyszecki and Stiles 2000; Fairchild 2005; Reinhard, Ward, Pattanaik *et al.* 2005; Livingstone 2008).[18] Note that for machine vision applications, such as remote sensing and terrain classification, it is preferable to use many more wavelengths. Similarly, surveillance applications can often benefit from sensing in the near-infrared (NIR) range.

CIE RGB and XYZ

To test and quantify the tri-chromatic theory of perception, we can attempt to reproduce all *monochromatic* (single wavelength) colors as a mixture of three suitably chosen primaries. (Pure wavelength light can be obtained using either a prism or specially manufactured color filters.) In the 1930s, the Commission Internationale d'Eclairage (CIE) standardized the RGB representation by performing such *color matching* experiments using the primary colors of red (700.0nm wavelength), green (546.1nm), and blue (435.8nm).

Figure 2.28 shows the results of performing these experiments with a *standard observer*, i.e., averaging perceptual results over a large number of subjects. You will notice that for certain pure spectra in the blue–green range, a *negative* amount of red light has to be added, i.e., a certain amount of red has to be added to the color being matched in order to get a color match. These results also provided a simple explanation for the existence of *metamers*, which are colors with different spectra that are perceptually indistinguishable. Note that two fabrics

---

[18] See also Mark Fairchild's Web page, http://www.cis.rit.edu/fairchild/WhyIsColor/books_links.html.

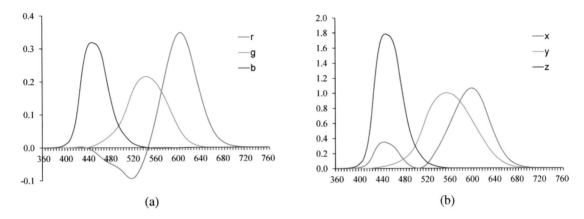

Figure 2.28 Standard CIE color matching functions: (a) $\bar{r}(\lambda)$, $\bar{g}(\lambda)$, $\bar{b}(\lambda)$ color spectra obtained from matching pure colors to the R=700.0nm, G=546.1nm, and B=435.8nm primaries; (b) $\bar{x}(\lambda)$, $\bar{y}(\lambda)$, $\bar{z}(\lambda)$ color matching functions, which are linear combinations of the $(\bar{r}(\lambda), \bar{g}(\lambda), \bar{b}(\lambda))$ spectra.

or paint colors that are metamers under one light may no longer be so under different lighting.

Because of the problem associated with mixing negative light, the CIE also developed a new color space called XYZ, which contains all of the pure spectral colors within its positive octant. (It also maps the Y axis to the *luminance*, i.e., perceived relative brightness, and maps pure white to a diagonal (equal-valued) vector.) The transformation from RGB to XYZ is given by

$$
\begin{bmatrix} X \\ Y \\ Z \end{bmatrix} = \frac{1}{0.17697} \begin{bmatrix} 0.49 & 0.31 & 0.20 \\ 0.17697 & 0.81240 & 0.01063 \\ 0.00 & 0.01 & 0.99 \end{bmatrix} \begin{bmatrix} R \\ G \\ B \end{bmatrix}. \tag{2.103}
$$

While the official definition of the CIE XYZ standard has the matrix normalized so that the Y value corresponding to pure red is 1, a more commonly used form is to omit the leading fraction, so that the second row adds up to one, i.e., the RGB triplet $(1, 1, 1)$ maps to a Y value of 1. Linearly blending the $(\bar{r}(\lambda), \bar{g}(\lambda), \bar{b}(\lambda))$ curves in Figure 2.28a according to (2.103), we obtain the resulting $(\bar{x}(\lambda), \bar{y}(\lambda), \bar{z}(\lambda))$ curves shown in Figure 2.28b. Notice how all three spectra (color matching functions) now have only positive values and how the $\bar{y}(\lambda)$ curve matches that of the luminance perceived by humans.

If we divide the XYZ values by the sum of X+Y+Z, we obtain the *chromaticity coordinates*

$$
x = \frac{X}{X + Y + Z}, \quad y = \frac{Y}{X + Y + Z}, \quad z = \frac{Z}{X + Y + Z}, \tag{2.104}
$$

which sum up to 1. The chromaticity coordinates discard the absolute intensity of a given color sample and just represent its pure color. If we sweep the monochromatic color λ parameter in Figure 2.28b from $\lambda = 380$nm to $\lambda = 800$nm, we obtain the familiar *chromaticity diagram* shown in Figure 2.29. This figure shows the (x, y) value for every color value perceivable by most humans. (Of course, the CMYK reproduction process in this book does not actually span the whole gamut of perceivable colors.) The outer curved rim represents where

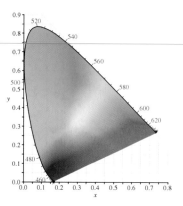

Figure 2.29 CIE chromaticity diagram, showing colors and their corresponding (x, y) values. Pure spectral colors are arranged around the outside of the curve.

all of the pure monochromatic color values map in (x, y) space, while the lower straight line, which connects the two endpoints, is known as the *purple line*.

A convenient representation for color values, when we want to tease apart luminance and chromaticity, is therefore Yxy (luminance plus the two most distinctive chrominance components).

L*a*b* color space

While the XYZ color space has many convenient properties, including the ability to separate luminance from chrominance, it does not actually predict how well humans perceive *differences* in color or luminance.

Because the response of the human visual system is roughly logarithmic (we can perceive *relative* luminance differences of about 1%), the CIE defined a non-linear re-mapping of the XYZ space called L*a*b* (also sometimes called CIELAB), where differences in luminance or chrominance are more perceptually uniform.[19]

The L* component of *lightness* is defined as

$$L^* = 116 f \left(\frac{Y}{Y_n} \right),$$ (2.105)

where Y_n is the luminance value for nominal white (Fairchild 2005) and

$$f(t) = \begin{cases} t^{1/3} & t > \delta^3 \\ t/(3\delta^2) + 2\delta/3 & \text{else,} \end{cases}$$ (2.106)

is a finite-slope approximation to the cube root with $\delta = 6/29$. The resulting $0 \ldots 100$ scale roughly measures equal amounts of lightness perceptibility.

In a similar fashion, the a* and b* components are defined as

$$a^* = 500 \left[f \left(\frac{X}{X_n} \right) - f \left(\frac{Y}{Y_n} \right) \right] \quad \text{and} \quad b^* = 200 \left[f \left(\frac{Y}{Y_n} \right) - f \left(\frac{Z}{Z_n} \right) \right],$$ (2.107)

[19] Another perceptually motivated color space called L*u*v* was developed and standardized simultaneously (Fairchild 2005).

where again, (X_n, Y_n, Z_n) is the measured white point. Figure 2.32i–k show the L*a*b* representation for a sample color image.

Color cameras

While the preceding discussion tells us how we can uniquely describe the perceived tri-stimulus description of any color (spectral distribution), it does not tell us how RGB still and video cameras actually work. Do they just measure the amount of light at the nominal wavelengths of red (700.0nm), green (546.1nm), and blue (435.8nm)? Do color monitors just emit exactly these wavelengths and, if so, how can they emit negative red light to reproduce colors in the cyan range?

In fact, the design of RGB video cameras has historically been based around the availability of colored phosphors that go into television sets. When standard-definition color television was invented (NTSC), a mapping was defined between the RGB values that would drive the three color guns in the cathode ray tube (CRT) and the XYZ values that unambiguously define perceived color (this standard was called ITU-R BT.601). With the advent of HDTV and newer monitors, a new standard called ITU-R BT.709 was created, which specifies the XYZ values of each of the color primaries,

$$\begin{bmatrix} X \\ Y \\ Z \end{bmatrix} = \begin{bmatrix} 0.412453 & 0.357580 & 0.180423 \\ 0.212671 & 0.715160 & 0.072169 \\ 0.019334 & 0.119193 & 0.950227 \end{bmatrix} \begin{bmatrix} R_{709} \\ G_{709} \\ B_{709} \end{bmatrix}. \tag{2.108}$$

In practice, each color camera integrates light according to the *spectral response function* of its red, green, and blue sensors,

$$\begin{aligned} R &= \int L(\lambda) S_R(\lambda) d\lambda, \\ G &= \int L(\lambda) S_G(\lambda) d\lambda, \\ B &= \int L(\lambda) S_B(\lambda) d\lambda, \end{aligned} \tag{2.109}$$

where $L(\lambda)$ is the incoming spectrum of light at a given pixel and $\{S_R(\lambda), S_G(\lambda), S_B(\lambda)\}$ are the red, green, and blue *spectral sensitivities* of the corresponding sensors.

Can we tell what spectral sensitivities the cameras actually have? Unless the camera manufacturer provides us with this data or we observe the response of the camera to a whole spectrum of monochromatic lights, these sensitivities are *not* specified by a standard such as BT.709. Instead, all that matters is that the tri-stimulus values for a given color produce the specified RGB values. The manufacturer is free to use sensors with sensitivities that do not match the standard XYZ definitions, so long as they can later be converted (through a linear transform) to the standard colors.

Similarly, while TV and computer monitors are supposed to produce RGB values as specified by Equation (2.108), there is no reason that they cannot use digital logic to transform the incoming RGB values into different signals to drive each of the color channels. Properly calibrated monitors make this information available to software applications that perform *color management*, so that colors in real life, on the screen, and on the printer all match as closely as possible.

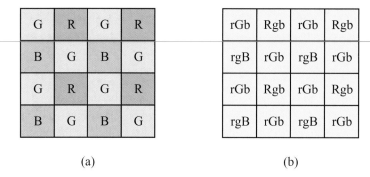

(a)   (b)

Figure 2.30 Bayer RGB pattern: (a) color filter array layout; (b) interpolated pixel values, with unknown (guessed) values shown as lower case.

Color filter arrays

While early color TV cameras used three *vidicons* (tubes) to perform their sensing and later cameras used three separate RGB sensing chips, most of today's digital still and video cameras cameras use a *color filter array* (CFA), where alternating sensors are covered by different colored filters.[20]

The most commonly used pattern in color cameras today is the *Bayer pattern* (Bayer 1976), which places green filters over half of the sensors (in a checkerboard pattern), and red and blue filters over the remaining ones (Figure 2.30). The reason that there are twice as many green filters as red and blue is because the luminance signal is mostly determined by green values and the visual system is much more sensitive to high frequency detail in luminance than in chrominance (a fact that is exploited in color image compression—see Section 2.3.3). The process of *interpolating* the missing color values so that we have valid RGB values for all the pixels is known as *demosaicing* and is covered in detail in Section 10.3.1.

Similarly, color LCD monitors typically use alternating stripes of red, green, and blue filters placed in front of each liquid crystal active area to simulate the experience of a full color display. As before, because the visual system has higher resolution (acuity) in luminance than chrominance, it is possible to digitally pre-filter RGB (and monochrome) images to enhance the perception of crispness (Betrisey, Blinn, Dresevic *et al.* 2000; Platt 2000).

Color balance

Before encoding the sensed RGB values, most cameras perform some kind of *color balancing* operation in an attempt to move the white point of a given image closer to pure white (equal RGB values). If the color system and the illumination are the same (the BT.709 system uses the daylight illuminant D_{65} as its reference white), the change may be minimal. However, if the illuminant is strongly colored, such as incandescent indoor lighting (which generally results in a yellow or orange hue), the compensation can be quite significant.

A simple way to perform color correction is to multiply each of the RGB values by a different factor (i.e., to apply a diagonal matrix transform to the RGB color space). More

---

[20] A newer chip design by Foveon (http://www.foveon.com) stacks the red, green, and blue sensors beneath each other, but it has not yet gained widespread adoption.

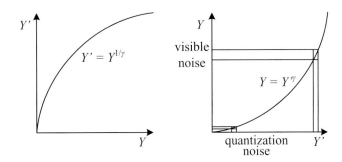

Figure 2.31 Gamma compression: (a) The relationship between the input signal luminance Y and the transmitted signal Y' is given by $Y' = Y^{1/\gamma}$. (b) At the receiver, the signal Y' is exponentiated by the factor γ, $\hat{Y} = Y'^{\gamma}$. Noise introduced during transmission is squashed in the dark regions, which corresponds to the more noise-sensitive region of the visual system.

complicated transforms, which are sometimes the result of mapping to XYZ space and back, actually perform a *color twist*, i.e., they use a general 3×3 color transform matrix.[21] Exercise 2.9 has you explore some of these issues.

Gamma

In the early days of black and white television, the phosphors in the CRT used to display the TV signal responded non-linearly to their input voltage. The relationship between the voltage and the resulting brightness was characterized by a number called *gamma* (γ), since the formula was roughly

$$B = V^{\gamma}, \tag{2.110}$$

with a γ of about 2.2. To compensate for this effect, the electronics in the TV camera would pre-map the sensed luminance Y through an inverse gamma,

$$Y' = Y^{\frac{1}{\gamma}}, \tag{2.111}$$

with a typical value of $\frac{1}{\gamma} = 0.45$.

The mapping of the signal through this non-linearity before transmission had a beneficial side effect: noise added during transmission (remember, these were analog days!) would be reduced (after applying the gamma at the receiver) in the darker regions of the signal where it was more visible (Figure 2.31).[22] (Remember that our visual system is roughly sensitive to relative differences in luminance.)

When color television was invented, it was decided to separately pass the red, green, and blue signals through the same gamma non-linearity before combining them for encoding. Today, even though we no longer have analog noise in our transmission systems, signals are still quantized during compression (see Section 2.3.3), so applying inverse gamma to sensed values is still useful.

---

[21] Those of you old enough to remember the early days of color television will naturally think of the *hue* adjustment knob on the television set, which could produce truly bizarre results.

[22] A related technique called *companding* was the basis of the Dolby noise reduction systems used with audio tapes.

Unfortunately, for both computer vision and computer graphics, the presence of gamma in images is often problematic. For example, the proper simulation of radiometric phenomena such as shading (see Section 2.2 and Equation (2.87)) occurs in a linear radiance space. Once all of the computations have been performed, the appropriate gamma should be applied before display. Unfortunately, many computer graphics systems (such as shading models) operate directly on RGB values and display these values directly. (Fortunately, newer color imaging standards such as the 16-bit scRGB use a linear space, which makes this less of a problem (Glassner 1995).)

In computer vision, the situation can be even more daunting. The accurate determination of surface normals, using a technique such as photometric stereo (Section 12.1.1) or even a simpler operation such as accurate image deblurring, require that the measurements be in a linear space of intensities. Therefore, it is imperative when performing detailed quantitative computations such as these to first undo the gamma and the per-image color re-balancing in the sensed color values. Chakrabarti, Scharstein, and Zickler (2009) develop a sophisticated 24-parameter model that is a good match to the processing performed by today's digital cameras; they also provide a database of color images you can use for your own testing.[23]

For other vision applications, however, such as feature detection or the matching of signals in stereo and motion estimation, this linearization step is often not necessary. In fact, determining whether it is necessary to undo gamma can take some careful thinking, e.g., in the case of compensating for exposure variations in image stitching (see Exercise 2.7).

If all of these processing steps sound confusing to model, they are. Exercise 2.10 has you try to tease apart some of these phenomena using empirical investigation, i.e., taking pictures of color charts and comparing the RAW and JPEG compressed color values.

Other color spaces

While RGB and XYZ are the primary color spaces used to describe the spectral content (and hence tri-stimulus response) of color signals, a variety of other representations have been developed both in video and still image coding and in computer graphics.

The earliest color representation developed for video transmission was the YIQ standard developed for NTSC video in North America and the closely related YUV standard developed for PAL in Europe. In both of these cases, it was desired to have a *luma* channel Y (so called since it only roughly mimics true luminance) that would be comparable to the regular black-and-white TV signal, along with two lower frequency *chroma* channels.

In both systems, the Y signal (or more appropriately, the Y' luma signal since it is gamma compressed) is obtained from

$$Y'_{601} = 0.299R' + 0.587G' + 0.114B', \tag{2.112}$$

where R'G'B' is the triplet of gamma-compressed color components. When using the newer color definitions for HDTV in BT.709, the formula is

$$Y'_{709} = 0.2125R' + 0.7154G' + 0.0721B'. \tag{2.113}$$

The UV components are derived from scaled versions of $(B' - Y')$ and $(R' - Y')$, namely,

$$U = 0.492111(B' - Y') \text{ and } V = 0.877283(R' - Y'), \tag{2.114}$$

---

[23] http://vision.middlebury.edu/color/.

whereas the IQ components are the UV components rotated through an angle of $33°$. In composite (NTSC and PAL) video, the chroma signals were then low-pass filtered horizontally before being modulated and superimposed on top of the Y' luma signal. Backward compatibility was achieved by having older black-and-white TV sets effectively ignore the high-frequency chroma signal (because of slow electronics) or, at worst, superimposing it as a high-frequency pattern on top of the main signal.

While these conversions were important in the early days of computer vision, when frame grabbers would directly digitize the composite TV signal, today all digital video and still image compression standards are based on the newer YCbCr conversion. YCbCr is closely related to YUV (the C_b and C_r signals carry the blue and red color difference signals and have more useful mnemonics than UV) but uses different scale factors to fit within the eight-bit range available with digital signals.

For video, the Y' signal is re-scaled to fit within the $[16 \ldots 235]$ range of values, while the Cb and Cr signals are scaled to fit within $[16 \ldots 240]$ (Gomes and Velho 1997; Fairchild 2005). For still images, the JPEG standard uses the full eight-bit range with no reserved values,

$$\begin{bmatrix} Y' \\ C_b \\ C_r \end{bmatrix} = \begin{bmatrix} 0.299 & 0.587 & 0.114 \\ -0.168736 & -0.331264 & 0.5 \\ 0.5 & -0.418688 & -0.081312 \end{bmatrix} \begin{bmatrix} R' \\ G' \\ B' \end{bmatrix} + \begin{bmatrix} 0 \\ 128 \\ 128 \end{bmatrix}, \quad (2.115)$$

where the R'G'B' values are the eight-bit gamma-compressed color components (i.e., the actual RGB values we obtain when we open up or display a JPEG image). For most applications, this formula is not that important, since your image reading software will directly provide you with the eight-bit gamma-compressed R'G'B' values. However, if you are trying to do careful image deblocking (Exercise 3.30), this information may be useful.

Another color space you may come across is *hue, saturation, value* (HSV), which is a projection of the RGB color cube onto a non-linear chroma angle, a radial saturation percentage, and a luminance-inspired value. In more detail, value is defined as either the mean or maximum color value, saturation is defined as scaled distance from the diagonal, and hue is defined as the direction around a color wheel (the exact formulas are described by Hall (1989); Foley, van Dam, Feiner *et al.* (1995)). Such a decomposition is quite natural in graphics applications such as color picking (it approximates the Munsell chart for color description). Figure 2.32l–n shows an HSV representation of a sample color image, where saturation is encoded using a gray scale (saturated = darker) and hue is depicted as a color.

If you want your computer vision algorithm to only affect the value (luminance) of an image and not its saturation or hue, a simpler solution is to use either the Yxy (luminance + chromaticity) coordinates defined in (2.104) or the even simpler *color ratios*,

$$r = \frac{R}{R+G+B}, \quad g = \frac{G}{R+G+B}, \quad b = \frac{B}{R+G+B} \quad (2.116)$$

(Figure 2.32e–h). After manipulating the luma (2.112), e.g., through the process of histogram equalization (Section 3.1.4), you can multiply each color ratio by the ratio of the new to old luma to obtain an adjusted RGB triplet.

While all of these color systems may sound confusing, in the end, it often may not matter that much which one you use. Poynton, in his *Color FAQ*, http://www.poynton.com/ColorFAQ.html, notes that the perceptually motivated L*a*b* system is qualitatively similar

Figure 2.32 Color space transformations: (a–d) RGB; (e–h) rgb. (i–k) L*a*b*; (l–n) HSV. Note that the rgb, L*a*b*, and HSV values are all re-scaled to fit the dynamic range of the printed page.

to the gamma-compressed R'G'B' system we mostly deal with, since both have a fractional power scaling (which approximates a logarithmic response) between the actual intensity values and the numbers being manipulated. As in all cases, think carefully about what you are trying to accomplish before deciding on a technique to use.[24]

2.3.3 Compression

The last stage in a camera's processing pipeline is usually some form of image compression (unless you are using a lossless compression scheme such as camera RAW or PNG).

All color video and image compression algorithms start by converting the signal into YCbCr (or some closely related variant), so that they can compress the luminance signal with

---

[24] If you are at a loss for questions at a conference, you can always ask why the speaker did not use a perceptual color space, such as L*a*b*. Conversely, if they did use L*a*b*, you can ask if they have any concrete evidence that this works better than regular colors.

Figure 2.33 Image compressed with JPEG at three quality settings. Note how the amount of block artifact and high-frequency aliasing ("mosquito noise") increases from left to right.

higher fidelity than the chrominance signal. (Recall that the human visual system has poorer frequency response to color than to luminance changes.) In video, it is common to subsample Cb and Cr by a factor of two horizontally; with still images (JPEG), the subsampling (averaging) occurs both horizontally and vertically.

Once the luminance and chrominance images have been appropriately subsampled and separated into individual images, they are then passed to a *block transform* stage. The most common technique used here is the *discrete cosine transform* (DCT), which is a real-valued variant of the discrete Fourier transform (DFT) (see Section 3.4.3). The DCT is a reasonable approximation to the Karhunen–Loève or eigenvalue decomposition of natural image patches, i.e., the decomposition that simultaneously packs the most energy into the first coefficients and diagonalizes the joint covariance matrix among the pixels (makes transform coefficients statistically independent). Both MPEG and JPEG use 8×8 DCT transforms (Wallace 1991; Le Gall 1991), although newer variants use smaller 4×4 blocks or alternative transformations, such as wavelets (Taubman and Marcellin 2002) and lapped transforms (Malvar 1990, 1998, 2000) are now used.

After transform coding, the coefficient values are quantized into a set of small integer values that can be coded using a variable bit length scheme such as a Huffman code or an arithmetic code (Wallace 1991). (The DC (lowest frequency) coefficients are also adaptively predicted from the previous block's DC values. The term "DC" comes from "direct current", i.e., the non-sinusoidal or non-alternating part of a signal.) The step size in the quantization is the main variable controlled by the *quality* setting on the JPEG file (Figure 2.33).

With video, it is also usual to perform block-based *motion compensation*, i.e., to encode the difference between each block and a *predicted* set of pixel values obtained from a shifted block in the previous frame. (The exception is the *motion-JPEG* scheme used in older DV camcorders, which is nothing more than a series of individually JPEG compressed image frames.) While basic MPEG uses 16×16 motion compensation blocks with integer motion values (Le Gall 1991), newer standards use adaptively sized block, sub-pixel motions, and the ability to reference blocks from older frames. In order to recover more gracefully from failures and to allow for random access to the video stream, predicted P frames are interleaved among independently coded I frames. (Bi-directional B frames are also sometimes used.)

The quality of a compression algorithm is usually reported using its *peak signal-to-noise ratio* (PSNR), which is derived from the average *mean square error*,

$$MSE = \frac{1}{n} \sum_{\boldsymbol{x}} \left[I(\boldsymbol{x}) - \hat{I}(\boldsymbol{x}) \right]^2 , \tag{2.117}$$

where $I(\boldsymbol{x})$ is the original uncompressed image and $\hat{I}(\boldsymbol{x})$ is its compressed counterpart, or equivalently, the *root mean square error* (RMS error), which is defined as

$$RMS = \sqrt{MSE}. \tag{2.118}$$

The PSNR is defined as

$$PSNR = 10 \log_{10} \frac{I_{\max}^2}{MSE} = 20 \log_{10} \frac{I_{\max}}{RMS}, \tag{2.119}$$

where $I_{\max}$ is the maximum signal extent, e.g., 255 for eight-bit images.

While this is just a high-level sketch of how image compression works, it is useful to understand so that the artifacts introduced by such techniques can be compensated for in various computer vision applications.

2.4 Additional reading

As we mentioned at the beginning of this chapter, it provides but a brief summary of a very rich and deep set of topics, traditionally covered in a number of separate fields.

A more thorough introduction to the geometry of points, lines, planes, and projections can be found in textbooks on multi-view geometry (Hartley and Zisserman 2004; Faugeras and Luong 2001) and computer graphics (Foley, van Dam, Feiner *et al.* 1995; Watt 1995; OpenGL-ARB 1997). Topics covered in more depth include higher-order primitives such as quadrics, conics, and cubics, as well as three-view and multi-view geometry.

The image formation (synthesis) process is traditionally taught as part of a computer graphics curriculum (Foley, van Dam, Feiner *et al.* 1995; Glassner 1995; Watt 1995; Shirley 2005) but it is also studied in physics-based computer vision (Wolff, Shafer, and Healey 1992a).

The behavior of camera lens systems is studied in optics (Möller 1988; Hecht 2001; Ray 2002).

Some good books on color theory have been written by Healey and Shafer (1992); Wyszecki and Stiles (2000); Fairchild (2005), with Livingstone (2008) providing a more fun and informal introduction to the topic of color perception. Mark Fairchild's page of color books and links[25] lists many other sources.

Topics relating to sampling and aliasing are covered in textbooks on signal and image processing (Crane 1997; Jähne 1997; Oppenheim and Schafer 1996; Oppenheim, Schafer, and Buck 1999; Pratt 2007; Russ 2007; Burger and Burge 2008; Gonzales and Woods 2008).

2.5 Exercises

A note to students: This chapter is relatively light on exercises since it contains mostly background material and not that many usable techniques. If you really want to understand

---

[25] http://www.cis.rit.edu/fairchild/WhyIsColor/books_links.html.

multi-view geometry in a thorough way, I encourage you to read and do the exercises provided by Hartley and Zisserman (2004). Similarly, if you want some exercises related to the image formation process, Glassner's (1995) book is full of challenging problems.

Ex 2.1: Least squares intersection point and line fitting—advanced Equation (2.4) shows how the intersection of two 2D lines can be expressed as their cross product, assuming the lines are expressed as homogeneous coordinates.

1. If you are given more than two lines and want to find a point $\tilde{x}$ that minimizes the sum of squared distances to each line,

$$D = \sum_i (\tilde{x} \cdot \tilde{l}_i)^2, \tag{2.120}$$

how can you compute this quantity? (Hint: Write the dot product as $\tilde{x}^T \tilde{l}_i$ and turn the squared quantity into a *quadratic form*, $\tilde{x}^T A \tilde{x}$.)

2. To fit a line to a bunch of points, you can compute the *centroid* (mean) of the points as well as the *covariance matrix* of the points around this mean. Show that the line passing through the centroid along the major axis of the covariance ellipsoid (largest eigenvector) minimizes the sum of squared distances to the points.

3. These two approaches are fundamentally different, even though projective duality tells us that points and lines are interchangeable. Why are these two algorithms so apparently different? Are they actually minimizing different objectives?

Ex 2.2: 2D transform editor Write a program that lets you interactively create a set of rectangles and then modify their "pose" (2D transform). You should implement the following steps:

1. Open an empty window ("canvas").

2. Shift drag (rubber-band) to create a new rectangle.

3. Select the deformation mode (motion model): translation, rigid, similarity, affine, or perspective.

4. Drag any corner of the outline to change its transformation.

This exercise should be built on a set of pixel coordinate and transformation classes, either implemented by yourself or from a software library. Persistence of the created representation (save and load) should also be supported (for each rectangle, save its transformation).

Ex 2.3: 3D viewer Write a simple viewer for 3D points, lines, and polygons. Import a set of point and line commands (primitives) as well as a viewing transform. Interactively modify the object or camera transform. This viewer can be an extension of the one you created in (Exercise 2.2). Simply replace the viewing transformations with their 3D equivalents.

(Optional) Add a z-buffer to do hidden surface removal for polygons.

(Optional) Use a 3D drawing package and just write the viewer control.

Ex 2.4: Focus distance and depth of field Figure out how the focus distance and depth of field indicators on a lens are determined.

1. Compute and plot the focus distance z_o as a function of the distance traveled from the focal length $\Delta z_i = f - z_i$ for a lens of focal length f (say, 100mm). Does this explain the hyperbolic progression of focus distances you see on a typical lens (Figure 2.20)?

2. Compute the depth of field (minimum and maximum focus distances) for a given focus setting z_o as a function of the circle of confusion diameter c (make it a fraction of the sensor width), the focal length f, and the f-stop number N (which relates to the aperture diameter d). Does this explain the usual depth of field markings on a lens that bracket the in-focus marker, as in Figure 2.20a?

3. Now consider a zoom lens with a varying focal length f. Assume that as you zoom, the lens stays in focus, i.e., the distance from the rear nodal point to the sensor plane z_i adjusts itself automatically for a fixed focus distance z_o. How do the depth of field indicators vary as a function of focal length? Can you reproduce a two-dimensional plot that mimics the curved depth of field lines seen on the lens in Figure 2.20b?

Ex 2.5: F-numbers and shutter speeds   List the common f-numbers and shutter speeds that your camera provides. On older model SLRs, they are visible on the lens and shutter speed dials. On newer cameras, you have to look at the electronic viewfinder (or LCD screen/indicator) as you manually adjust exposures.

1. Do these form geometric progressions; if so, what are the ratios? How do these relate to exposure values (EVs)?

2. If your camera has shutter speeds of $\frac{1}{60}$ and $\frac{1}{125}$, do you think that these two speeds are exactly a factor of two apart or a factor of $125/60 = 2.083$ apart?

3. How accurate do you think these numbers are? Can you devise some way to measure exactly how the aperture affects how much light reaches the sensor and what the exact exposure times actually are?

Ex 2.6: Noise level calibration   Estimate the amount of noise in your camera by taking repeated shots of a scene with the camera mounted on a tripod. (Purchasing a remote shutter release is a good investment if you own a DSLR.) Alternatively, take a scene with constant color regions (such as a color checker chart) and estimate the variance by fitting a smooth function to each color region and then taking differences from the predicted function.

1. Plot your estimated variance as a function of level for each of your color channels separately.

2. Change the ISO setting on your camera; if you cannot do that, reduce the overall light in your scene (turn off lights, draw the curtains, wait until dusk). Does the amount of noise vary a lot with ISO/gain?

3. Compare your camera to another one at a different price point or year of make. Is there evidence to suggest that "you get what you pay for"? Does the quality of digital cameras seem to be improving over time?

Ex 2.7: Gamma correction in image stitching   Here's a relatively simple puzzle. Assume you are given two images that are part of a panorama that you want to stitch (see Chapter 9). The two images were taken with different exposures, so you want to adjust the RGB values so that they match along the seam line. Is it necessary to undo the gamma in the color values in order to achieve this?

Ex 2.8: Skin color detection   Devise a simple skin color detector (Forsyth and Fleck 1999; Jones and Rehg 2001; Vezhnevets, Sazonov, and Andreeva 2003; Kakumanu, Makrogiannis, and Bourbakis 2007) based on chromaticity or other color properties.

1. Take a variety of photographs of people and calculate the *xy chromaticity values* for each pixel.

2. Crop the photos or otherwise indicate with a painting tool which pixels are likely to be skin (e.g. face and arms).

3. Calculate a color (chromaticity) distribution for these pixels. You can use something as simple as a mean and covariance measure or as complicated as a mean-shift segmentation algorithm (see Section 5.3.2). You can optionally use non-skin pixels to model the *background distribution*.

4. Use your computed distribution to find the skin regions in an image. One easy way to visualize this is to paint all non-skin pixels a given color, such as white or black.

5. How sensitive is your algorithm to color balance (scene lighting)?

6. Does a simpler chromaticity measurement, such as a color ratio (2.116), work just as well?

Ex 2.9: White point balancing—tricky   A common (in-camera or post-processing) technique for performing white point adjustment is to take a picture of a white piece of paper and to adjust the RGB values of an image to make this a neutral color.

1. Describe how you would adjust the RGB values in an image given a sample "white color" of (R_w, G_w, B_w) to make this color neutral (without changing the exposure too much).

2. Does your transformation involve a simple (per-channel) scaling of the RGB values or do you need a full 3×3 color twist matrix (or something else)?

3. Convert your RGB values to XYZ. Does the appropriate correction now only depend on the XY (or xy) values? If so, when you convert back to RGB space, do you need a full 3×3 color twist matrix to achieve the same effect?

4. If you used pure diagonal scaling in the direct RGB mode but end up with a twist if you work in XYZ space, how do you explain this apparent dichotomy? Which approach is correct? (Or is it possible that neither approach is actually correct?)

If you want to find out what your camera *actually* does, continue on to the next exercise.

Ex 2.10: In-camera color processing—challenging   If your camera supports a RAW pixel mode, take a pair of RAW and JPEG images, and see if you can infer what the camera is doing when it converts the RAW pixel values to the final color-corrected and gamma-compressed eight-bit JPEG pixel values.

1. Deduce the pattern in your color filter array from the correspondence between co-located RAW and color-mapped pixel values. Use a color checker chart at this stage if it makes your life easier. You may find it helpful to split the RAW image into four separate images (subsampling even and odd columns and rows) and to treat each of these new images as a "virtual" sensor.

2. Evaluate the quality of the demosaicing algorithm by taking pictures of challenging scenes which contain strong color edges (such as those shown in in Section 10.3.1).

3. If you can take the same exact picture after changing the color balance values in your camera, compare how these settings affect this processing.

4. Compare your results against those presented by Chakrabarti, Scharstein, and Zickler (2009) or use the data available in their database of color images.[26]

---

[26] http://vision.middlebury.edu/color/.

Chapter 3

Image processing

R. Szeliski, *Computer Vision: Algorithms and Applications*, Texts in Computer Science,
DOI 10.1007/978-1-84882-935-0_3, © Springer-Verlag London Limited 2011

Figure 3.1 Some common image processing operations: (a) original image; (b) increased contrast; (c) change in hue; (d) "posterized" (quantized colors); (e) blurred; (f) rotated.

Now that we have seen how images are formed through the interaction of 3D scene elements, lighting, and camera optics and sensors, let us look at the first stage in most computer vision applications, namely the use of image processing to preprocess the image and convert it into a form suitable for further analysis. Examples of such operations include exposure correction and color balancing, the reduction of image noise, increasing sharpness, or straightening the image by rotating it (Figure 3.1). While some may consider image processing to be outside the purview of computer vision, most computer vision applications, such as computational photography and even recognition, require care in designing the image processing stages in order to achieve acceptable results.

In this chapter, we review standard image processing operators that map pixel values from one image to another. Image processing is often taught in electrical engineering departments as a follow-on course to an introductory course in signal processing (Oppenheim and Schafer 1996; Oppenheim, Schafer, and Buck 1999). There are several popular textbooks for image processing (Crane 1997; Gomes and Velho 1997; Jähne 1997; Pratt 2007; Russ 2007; Burger and Burge 2008; Gonzales and Woods 2008).

We begin this chapter with the simplest kind of image transforms, namely those that manipulate each pixel independently of its neighbors (Section 3.1). Such transforms are often called *point operators* or *point processes*. Next, we examine *neighborhood* (area-based) operators, where each new pixel's value depends on a small number of neighboring input values (Sections 3.2 and 3.3). A convenient tool to analyze (and sometimes accelerate) such neighborhood operations is the *Fourier Transform*, which we cover in Section 3.4. Neighborhood operators can be cascaded to form *image pyramids* and *wavelets*, which are useful for analyzing images at a variety of resolutions (scales) and for accelerating certain operations (Section 3.5). Another important class of global operators are *geometric transformations*, such as rotations, shears, and perspective deformations (Section 3.6). Finally, we introduce *global optimization* approaches to image processing, which involve the minimization of an energy functional or, equivalently, optimal estimation using Bayesian *Markov random field* models (Section 3.7).

3.1 Point operators

The simplest kinds of image processing transforms are *point operators*, where each output pixel's value depends on only the corresponding input pixel value (plus, potentially, some globally collected information or parameters). Examples of such operators include brightness and contrast adjustments (Figure 3.2) as well as color correction and transformations. In the image processing literature, such operations are also known as *point processes* (Crane 1997).

We begin this section with a quick review of simple point operators such as brightness scaling and image addition. Next, we discuss how colors in images can be manipulated. We then present *image compositing* and *matting* operations, which play an important role in computational photography (Chapter 10) and computer graphics applications. Finally, we describe the more global process of *histogram equalization*. We close with an example application that manipulates *tonal values* (exposure and contrast) to improve image appearance.

Figure 3.2 Some local image processing operations: (a) original image along with its three color (per-channel) histograms; (b) brightness increased (additive offset, $b = 16$); (c) contrast increased (multiplicative gain, $a = 1.1$); (d) gamma (partially) linearized ($\gamma = 1.2$); (e) full histogram equalization; (f) partial histogram equalization.

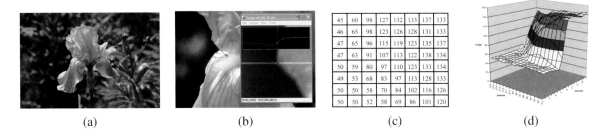

       (a)   (b)   (c)   (d)

Figure 3.3 Visualizing image data: (a) original image; (b) cropped portion and scanline plot using an image inspection tool; (c) grid of numbers; (d) surface plot. For figures (c)–(d), the image was first converted to grayscale.

3.1.1 Pixel transforms

A general image processing *operator* is a function that takes one or more input images and produces an output image. In the continuous domain, this can be denoted as

$$g(\boldsymbol{x}) = h(f(\boldsymbol{x})) \ \text{ or } \ g(\boldsymbol{x}) = h(f_0(\boldsymbol{x}),\ldots,f_n(\boldsymbol{x})), \tag{3.1}$$

where $\boldsymbol{x}$ is in the D-dimensional *domain* of the functions (usually $D = 2$ for images) and the functions f and g operate over some *range*, which can either be scalar or vector-valued, e.g., for color images or 2D motion. For discrete (sampled) images, the domain consists of a finite number of *pixel locations*, $\boldsymbol{x} = (i,j)$, and we can write

$$g(i,j) = h(f(i,j)). \tag{3.2}$$

Figure 3.3 shows how an image can be represented either by its color (appearance), as a grid of numbers, or as a two-dimensional function (surface plot).

Two commonly used point processes are multiplication and addition with a constant,

$$g(\boldsymbol{x}) = af(\boldsymbol{x}) + b. \tag{3.3}$$

The parameters $a > 0$ and b are often called the *gain* and *bias* parameters; sometimes these parameters are said to control *contrast* and *brightness*, respectively (Figures 3.2b–c).[1] The bias and gain parameters can also be spatially varying,

$$g(\boldsymbol{x}) = a(\boldsymbol{x})f(\boldsymbol{x}) + b(\boldsymbol{x}), \tag{3.4}$$

e.g., when simulating the *graded density filter* used by photographers to selectively darken the sky or when modeling vignetting in an optical system.

Multiplicative gain (both global and spatially varying) is a *linear* operation, since it obeys the *superposition principle*,

$$h(f_0 + f_1) = h(f_0) + h(f_1). \tag{3.5}$$

(We will have more to say about linear shift invariant operators in Section 3.2.) Operators such as image squaring (which is often used to get a local estimate of the *energy* in a bandpass filtered signal, see Section 3.5) are not linear.

---

[1] An image's luminance characteristics can also be summarized by its *key* (average luminanance) and *range* (Kopf, Uyttendaele, Deussen *et al.* 2007).

Another commonly used *dyadic* (two-input) operator is the *linear blend* operator,

$$g(\boldsymbol{x}) = (1 - \alpha)f_0(\boldsymbol{x}) + \alpha f_1(\boldsymbol{x}). \tag{3.6}$$

By varying α from $0 \rightarrow 1$, this operator can be used to perform a temporal *cross-dissolve* between two images or videos, as seen in slide shows and film production, or as a component of image *morphing* algorithms (Section 3.6.3).

One highly used non-linear transform that is often applied to images before further processing is *gamma correction*, which is used to remove the non-linear mapping between input radiance and quantized pixel values (Section 2.3.2). To invert the gamma mapping applied by the sensor, we can use

$$g(\boldsymbol{x}) = [f(\boldsymbol{x})]^{1/\gamma}, \tag{3.7}$$

where a gamma value of $\gamma \approx 2.2$ is a reasonable fit for most digital cameras.

3.1.2 Color transforms

While color images can be treated as arbitrary vector-valued functions or collections of independent bands, it usually makes sense to think about them as highly correlated signals with strong connections to the image formation process (Section 2.2), sensor design (Section 2.3), and human perception (Section 2.3.2). Consider, for example, brightening a picture by adding a constant value to all three channels, as shown in Figure 3.2b. Can you tell if this achieves the desired effect of making the image look brighter? Can you see any undesirable side-effects or artifacts?

In fact, adding the same value to each color channel not only increases the apparent *intensity* of each pixel, it can also affect the pixel's *hue* and *saturation*. How can we define and manipulate such quantities in order to achieve the desired perceptual effects?

As discussed in Section 2.3.2, chromaticity coordinates (2.104) or even simpler color ratios (2.116) can first be computed and then used after manipulating (e.g., brightening) the luminance Y to re-compute a valid RGB image with the same hue and saturation. Figure 2.32g–i shows some color ratio images multiplied by the middle gray value for better visualization.

Similarly, color balancing (e.g., to compensate for incandescent lighting) can be performed either by multiplying each channel with a different scale factor or by the more complex process of mapping to XYZ color space, changing the nominal white point, and mapping back to RGB, which can be written down using a linear 3×3 *color twist* transform matrix. Exercises 2.9 and 3.1 have you explore some of these issues.

Another fun project, best attempted after you have mastered the rest of the material in this chapter, is to take a picture with a rainbow in it and enhance the strength of the rainbow (Exercise 3.29).

3.1.3 Compositing and matting

In many photo editing and visual effects applications, it is often desirable to cut a *foreground* object out of one scene and put it on top of a different *background* (Figure 3.4). The process of extracting the object from the original image is often called *matting* (Smith and Blinn

Figure 3.4 Image matting and compositing (Chuang, Curless, Salesin *et al.* 2001) © 2001 IEEE: (a) source image; (b) extracted foreground object F; (c) alpha matte α shown in grayscale; (d) new composite C.

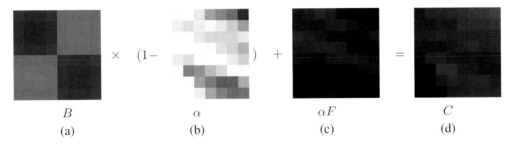

$$B \qquad \alpha \qquad \alpha F \qquad C$$
$$\text{(a)} \qquad \text{(b)} \qquad \text{(c)} \qquad \text{(d)}$$

Figure 3.5 Compositing equation $C = (1 - \alpha)B + \alpha F$. The images are taken from a close-up of the region of the hair in the upper right part of the lion in Figure 3.4.

1996), while the process of inserting it into another image (without visible artifacts) is called *compositing* (Porter and Duff 1984; Blinn 1994a).

The intermediate representation used for the foreground object between these two stages is called an *alpha-matted color image* (Figure 3.4b–c). In addition to the three color RGB channels, an alpha-matted image contains a fourth *alpha* channel α (or A) that describes the relative amount of *opacity* or *fractional coverage* at each pixel (Figures 3.4c and 3.5b). The opacity is the opposite of the *transparency*. Pixels within the object are fully opaque ($\alpha = 1$), while pixels fully outside the object are transparent ($\alpha = 0$). Pixels on the boundary of the object vary smoothly between these two extremes, which hides the perceptual visible *jaggies* that occur if only binary opacities are used.

To composite a new (or foreground) image on top of an old (background) image, the *over operator*, first proposed by Porter and Duff (1984) and then studied extensively by Blinn (1994a; 1994b), is used,

$$C = (1 - \alpha)B + \alpha F. \tag{3.8}$$

This operator *attenuates* the influence of the background image B by a factor $(1 - \alpha)$ and then adds in the color (and opacity) values corresponding to the foreground layer F, as shown in Figure 3.5.

In many situations, it is convenient to represent the foreground colors in *pre-multiplied* form, i.e., to store (and manipulate) the αF values directly. As Blinn (1994b) shows, the pre-multiplied RGBA representation is preferred for several reasons, including the ability to blur or resample (e.g., rotate) alpha-matted images without any additional complications (just treating each RGBA band independently). However, when matting using local color consistency (Ruzon and Tomasi 2000; Chuang, Curless, Salesin *et al.* 2001), the pure un-

Figure 3.6 An example of light reflecting off the transparent glass of a picture frame (Black and Anandan 1996) © 1996 Elsevier. You can clearly see the woman's portrait inside the picture frame superimposed with the reflection of a man's face off the glass.

multiplied foreground colors F are used, since these remain constant (or vary slowly) in the vicinity of the object edge.

The over operation is not the only kind of compositing operation that can be used. Porter and Duff (1984) describe a number of additional operations that can be useful in photo editing and visual effects applications. In this book, we concern ourselves with only one additional, commonly occurring case (but see Exercise 3.2).

When light reflects off clean transparent glass, the light passing through the glass and the light reflecting off the glass are simply added together (Figure 3.6). This model is useful in the analysis of *transparent motion* (Black and Anandan 1996; Szeliski, Avidan, and Anandan 2000), which occurs when such scenes are observed from a moving camera (see Section 8.5.2).

The actual process of *matting*, i.e., recovering the foreground, background, and alpha matte values from one or more images, has a rich history, which we study in Section 10.4. Smith and Blinn (1996) have a nice survey of traditional *blue-screen matting* techniques, while Toyama, Krumm, Brumitt *et al.* (1999) review *difference matting*. More recently, there has been a lot of activity in computational photography relating to *natural image matting* (Ruzon and Tomasi 2000; Chuang, Curless, Salesin *et al.* 2001; Wang and Cohen 2007a), which attempts to extract the mattes from a single natural image (Figure 3.4a) or from extended video sequences (Chuang, Agarwala, Curless *et al.* 2002). All of these techniques are described in more detail in Section 10.4.

3.1.4 Histogram equalization

While the brightness and gain controls described in Section 3.1.1 can improve the appearance of an image, how can we automatically determine their best values? One approach might be to look at the darkest and brightest pixel values in an image and map them to pure black and pure white. Another approach might be to find the *average* value in the image, push it towards middle gray, and expand the *range* so that it more closely fills the displayable values (Kopf, Uyttendaele, Deussen *et al.* 2007).

How can we visualize the set of lightness values in an image in order to test some of

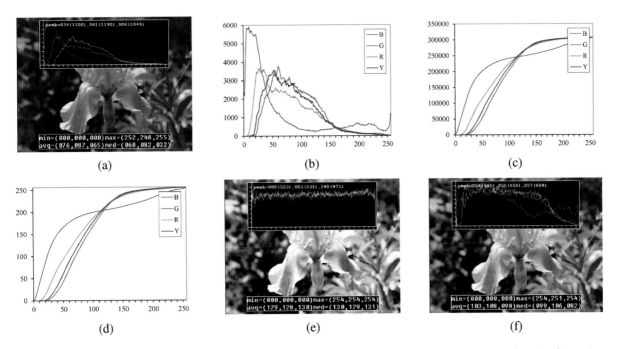

Figure 3.7 Histogram analysis and equalization: (a) original image (b) color channel and intensity (luminance) histograms; (c) cumulative distribution functions; (d) equalization (transfer) functions; (e) full histogram equalization; (f) partial histogram equalization.

these heuristics? The answer is to plot the *histogram* of the individual color channels and luminance values, as shown in Figure 3.7b.[2] From this distribution, we can compute relevant statistics such as the minimum, maximum, and average intensity values. Notice that the image in Figure 3.7a has both an excess of dark values and light values, but that the mid-range values are largely under-populated. Would it not be better if we could simultaneously brighten some dark values and darken some light values, while still using the full extent of the available dynamic range? Can you think of a mapping that might do this?

One popular answer to this question is to perform *histogram equalization*, i.e., to find an intensity mapping function $f(I)$ such that the resulting histogram is flat. The trick to finding such a mapping is the same one that people use to generate random samples from a *probability density function*, which is to first compute the *cumulative distribution function* shown in Figure 3.7c.

Think of the original histogram $h(I)$ as the distribution of grades in a class after some exam. How can we map a particular grade to its corresponding *percentile*, so that students at the 75% percentile range scored better than $3/4$ of their classmates? The answer is to integrate the distribution $h(I)$ to obtain the cumulative distribution $c(I)$,

$$c(I) = \frac{1}{N} \sum_{i=0}^{I} h(i) = c(I-1) + \frac{1}{N} h(I), \qquad (3.9)$$

---

[2] The histogram is simply the *count* of the number of pixels at each gray level value. For an eight-bit image, an accumulation table with 256 entries is needed. For higher bit depths, a table with the appropriate number of entries (probably fewer than the full number of gray levels) should be used.

(a)   (b)   (c)

Figure 3.8 Locally adaptive histogram equalization: (a) original image; (b) block histogram equalization; (c) full locally adaptive equalization.

where N is the number of pixels in the image or students in the class. For any given grade or intensity, we can look up its corresponding percentile $c(I)$ and determine the final value that pixel should take. When working with eight-bit pixel values, the I and c axes are rescaled from $[0, 255]$.

Figure 3.7d shows the result of applying $f(I) = c(I)$ to the original image. As we can see, the resulting histogram is flat; so is the resulting image (it is "flat" in the sense of a lack of contrast and being muddy looking). One way to compensate for this is to only *partially* compensate for the histogram unevenness, e.g., by using a mapping function $f(I) = \alpha c(I) + (1 - \alpha)I$, which is a linear blend between the cumulative distribution function and the identity transform (a straight line). As you can see in Figure 3.7e, the resulting image maintains more of its original grayscale distribution while having a more appealing balance.

Another potential problem with histogram equalization (or, in general, image brightening) is that noise in dark regions can be amplified and become more visible. Exercise 3.6 suggests some possible ways to mitigate this, as well as alternative techniques to maintain contrast and "punch" in the original images (Larson, Rushmeier, and Piatko 1997; Stark 2000).

Locally adaptive histogram equalization

While global histogram equalization can be useful, for some images it might be preferable to apply different kinds of equalization in different regions. Consider for example the image in Figure 3.8a, which has a wide range of luminance values. Instead of computing a single curve, what if we were to subdivide the image into $M \times M$ pixel blocks and perform separate histogram equalization in each sub-block? As you can see in Figure 3.8b, the resulting image exhibits a lot of blocking artifacts, i.e., intensity discontinuities at block boundaries.

One way to eliminate blocking artifacts is to use a *moving window*, i.e., to recompute the histogram for every $M \times M$ block centered at each pixel. This process can be quite slow (M^2 operations per pixel), although with clever programming only the histogram entries corresponding to the pixels entering and leaving the block (in a raster scan across the image) need to be updated (M operations per pixel). Note that this operation is an example of the *non-linear neighborhood operations* we study in more detail in Section 3.3.1.

A more efficient approach is to compute non-overlapped block-based equalization functions as before, but to then smoothly interpolate the transfer functions as we move between blocks. This technique is known as *adaptive histogram equalization* (AHE) and its contrast-

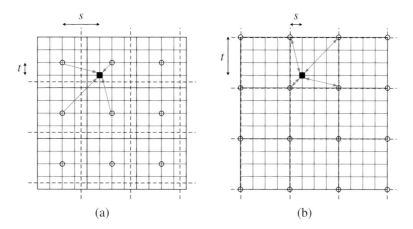

(a)   (b)

Figure 3.9 Local histogram interpolation using relative (s, t) coordinates: (a) block-based histograms, with block centers shown as circles; (b) corner-based "spline" histograms. Pixels are located on grid intersections. The black square pixel's transfer function is interpolated from the four adjacent lookup tables (gray arrows) using the computed (s, t) values. Block boundaries are shown as dashed lines.

limited (gain-limited) version is known as CLAHE (Pizer, Amburn, Austin *et al.* 1987).[3] The weighting function for a given pixel (i, j) can be computed as a function of its horizontal and vertical position (s, t) within a block, as shown in Figure 3.9a. To blend the four lookup functions $\{f_{00}, \ldots, f_{11}\}$, a *bilinear* blending function,

$$f_{s,t}(I) = (1 - s)(1 - t)f_{00}(I) + s(1 - t)f_{10}(I) + (1 - s)tf_{01}(I) + stf_{11}(I) \qquad (3.10)$$

can be used. (See Section 3.5.2 for higher-order generalizations of such *spline* functions.) Note that instead of blending the four lookup tables for each output pixel (which would be quite slow), we can instead blend the results of mapping a given pixel through the four neighboring lookups.

A variant on this algorithm is to place the lookup tables at the *corners* of each $M \times M$ block (see Figure 3.9b and Exercise 3.7). In addition to blending four lookups to compute the final value, we can also *distribute* each input pixel into four adjacent lookup tables during the histogram accumulation phase (notice that the gray arrows in Figure 3.9b point both ways), i.e.,

$$h_{k,l}(I(i, j)) \mathrel{+}= w(i, j, k, l), \qquad (3.11)$$

where $w(i, j, k, l)$ is the bilinear weighting function between pixel (i, j) and lookup table (k, l). This is an example of *soft histogramming*, which is used in a variety of other applications, including the construction of SIFT feature descriptors (Section 4.1.3) and vocabulary trees (Section 14.3.2).

3.1.5 *Application*: Tonal adjustment

One of the most widely used applications of point-wise image processing operators is the manipulation of contrast or *tone* in photographs, to make them look either more attractive or

---

[3]This algorithm is implemented in the MATLAB `adapthist` function.

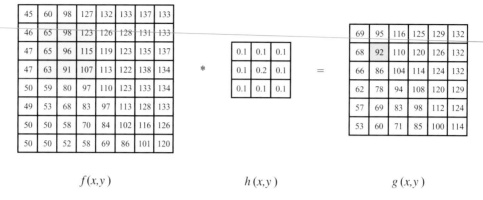

$$f(x,y) \qquad\qquad h(x,y) \qquad\qquad g(x,y)$$

Figure 3.10 Neighborhood filtering (convolution): The image on the left is convolved with the filter in the middle to yield the image on the right. The light blue pixels indicate the source neighborhood for the light green destination pixel.

more interpretable. You can get a good sense of the range of operations possible by opening up any photo manipulation tool and trying out a variety of contrast, brightness, and color manipulation options, as shown in Figures 3.2 and 3.7.

Exercises 3.1, 3.5, and 3.6 have you implement some of these operations, in order to become familiar with basic image processing operators. More sophisticated techniques for tonal adjustment (Reinhard, Ward, Pattanaik *et al.* 2005; Bae, Paris, and Durand 2006) are described in the section on high dynamic range tone mapping (Section 10.2.1).

3.2 Linear filtering

Locally adaptive histogram equalization is an example of a *neighborhood operator* or *local operator*, which uses a collection of pixel values in the vicinity of a given pixel to determine its final output value (Figure 3.10). In addition to performing local tone adjustment, neighborhood operators can be used to *filter* images in order to add soft blur, sharpen details, accentuate edges, or remove noise (Figure 3.11b–d). In this section, we look at *linear* filtering operators, which involve weighted combinations of pixels in small neighborhoods. In Section 3.3, we look at non-linear operators such as morphological filters and distance transforms.

The most commonly used type of neighborhood operator is a *linear filter*, in which an output pixel's value is determined as a weighted sum of input pixel values (Figure 3.10),

$$g(i,j) = \sum_{k,l} f(i+k, j+l)h(k,l). \tag{3.12}$$

The entries in the weight *kernel* or *mask* $h(k,l)$ are often called the *filter coefficients*. The above *correlation* operator can be more compactly notated as

$$g = f \otimes h. \tag{3.13}$$

Figure 3.11 Some neighborhood operations: (a) original image; (b) blurred; (c) sharpened; (d) smoothed with edge-preserving filter; (e) binary image; (f) dilated; (g) distance transform; (h) connected components. For the dilation and connected components, black (ink) pixels are assumed to be active, i.e., to have a value of 1 in Equations (3.41–3.45).

$$\boxed{72}\;\boxed{88}\;\boxed{62}\;\boxed{52}\;\boxed{37}\;*\;\boxed{1/4\;\;1/2\;\;1/4}\;\;\Leftrightarrow\;\;\frac{1}{4}\begin{bmatrix} 2 & 1 & . & . & . \\ 1 & 2 & 1 & . & . \\ . & 1 & 2 & 1 & . \\ . & . & 1 & 2 & 1 \\ . & . & . & 1 & 2 \end{bmatrix}\begin{bmatrix} 72 \\ 88 \\ 62 \\ 52 \\ 37 \end{bmatrix}$$

Figure 3.12 One-dimensional signal convolution as a sparse matrix-vector multiply, $g = Hf$.

A common variant on this formula is

$$g(i,j) = \sum_{k,l} f(i-k, j-l)h(k,l) = \sum_{k,l} f(k,l)h(i-k, j-l), \qquad (3.14)$$

where the sign of the offsets in f has been reversed. This is called the *convolution* operator,

$$g = f * h, \qquad (3.15)$$

and h is then called the *impulse response function*.[4] The reason for this name is that the kernel function, h, convolved with an impulse signal, $\delta(i,j)$ (an image that is 0 everywhere except at the origin) reproduces itself, $h * \delta = h$, whereas correlation produces the reflected signal. (Try this yourself to verify that it is so.)

In fact, Equation (3.14) can be interpreted as the superposition (addition) of shifted impulse response functions $h(i-k, j-l)$ multiplied by the input pixel values $f(k,l)$. Convolution has additional nice properties, e.g., it is both commutative and associative. As well, the Fourier transform of two convolved images is the product of their individual Fourier transforms (Section 3.4).

Both correlation and convolution are *linear shift-invariant* (LSI) operators, which obey both the superposition principle (3.5),

$$h \circ (f_0 + f_1) = h \circ f_0 + h \circ f_1, \qquad (3.16)$$

and the *shift invariance* principle,

$$g(i,j) = f(i+k, j+l) \;\;\Leftrightarrow\;\; (h \circ g)(i,j) = (h \circ f)(i+k, j+l), \qquad (3.17)$$

which means that shifting a signal commutes with applying the operator ($\circ$ stands for the LSI operator). Another way to think of shift invariance is that the operator "behaves the same everywhere".

Occasionally, a shift-variant version of correlation or convolution may be used, e.g.,

$$g(i,j) = \sum_{k,l} f(i-k, j-l)h(k,l; i,j), \qquad (3.18)$$

where $h(k,l; i,j)$ is the convolution kernel at pixel (i,j). For example, such a spatially varying kernel can be used to model blur in an image due to variable depth-dependent defocus.

Correlation and convolution can both be written as a matrix-vector multiply, if we first convert the two-dimensional images $f(i,j)$ and $g(i,j)$ into raster-ordered vectors f and g,

$$g = Hf, \qquad (3.19)$$

---

[4] The continuous version of convolution can be written as $g(x) = \int f(x - u)h(u)du$.

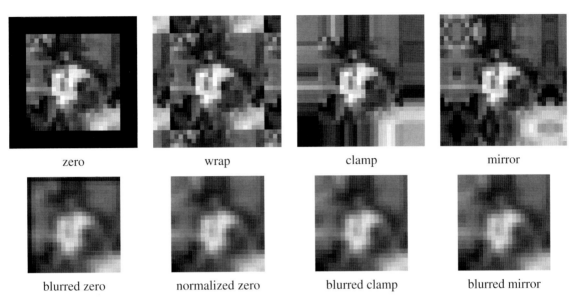

zero	wrap	clamp	mirror

blurred zero	normalized zero	blurred clamp	blurred mirror

Figure 3.13 Border padding (top row) and the results of blurring the padded image (bottom row). The normalized zero image is the result of dividing (normalizing) the blurred zero-padded RGBA image by its corresponding soft alpha value.

where the (sparse) H matrix contains the convolution kernels. Figure 3.12 shows how a one-dimensional convolution can be represented in matrix-vector form.

Padding (border effects)

The astute reader will notice that the matrix multiply shown in Figure 3.12 suffers from *boundary effects*, i.e., the results of filtering the image in this form will lead to a *darkening* of the corner pixels. This is because the original image is effectively being padded with 0 values wherever the convolution kernel extends beyond the original image boundaries.

To compensate for this, a number of alternative *padding* or extension modes have been developed (Figure 3.13):

- *zero*: set all pixels outside the source image to 0 (a good choice for alpha-matted cutout images);

- *constant (border color)*: set all pixels outside the source image to a specified *border* value;

- *clamp (replicate or clamp to edge)*: repeat edge pixels indefinitely;

- *(cyclic) wrap (repeat or tile)*: loop "around" the image in a "toroidal" configuration;

- *mirror*: reflect pixels across the image edge;

- *extend*: extend the signal by subtracting the mirrored version of the signal from the edge pixel value.

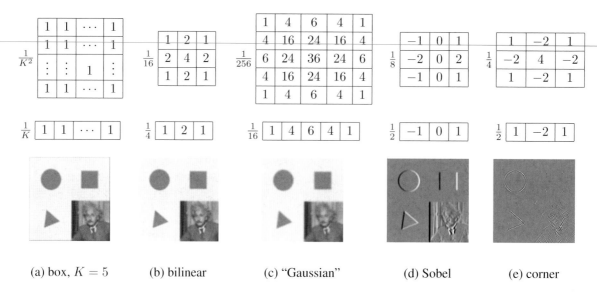

(a) box, $K = 5$ (b) bilinear   (c) "Gaussian"   (d) Sobel   (e) corner

Figure 3.14 Separable linear filters: For each image (a)–(e), we show the 2D filter kernel (top), the corresponding horizontal 1D kernel (middle), and the filtered image (bottom). The filtered Sobel and corner images are signed, scaled up by $2\times$ and $4\times$, respectively, and added to a gray offset before display.

In the computer graphics literature (Akenine-Möller and Haines 2002, p. 124), these mechanisms are known as the *wrapping mode* (OpenGL) or *texture addressing mode* (Direct3D). The formulas for each of these modes are left to the reader (Exercise 3.8).

Figure 3.13 shows the effects of padding an image with each of the above mechanisms and then blurring the resulting padded image. As you can see, zero padding darkens the edges, clamp (replication) padding propagates border values inward, mirror (reflection) padding preserves colors near the borders. Extension padding (not shown) keeps the border pixels fixed (during blur).

An alternative to padding is to blur the zero-padded RGBA image and to then divide the resulting image by its alpha value to remove the darkening effect. The results can be quite good, as seen in the normalized zero image in Figure 3.13.

3.2.1 Separable filtering

The process of performing a convolution requires K^2 (multiply-add) operations per pixel, where K is the size (width or height) of the convolution kernel, e.g., the box filter in Figure 3.14a. In many cases, this operation can be significantly sped up by first performing a one-dimensional horizontal convolution followed by a one-dimensional vertical convolution (which requires a total of $2K$ operations per pixel). A convolution kernel for which this is possible is said to be *separable*.

It is easy to show that the two-dimensional kernel $\boldsymbol{K}$ corresponding to successive convolution with a horizontal kernel $\boldsymbol{h}$ and a vertical kernel $\boldsymbol{v}$ is the *outer product* of the two kernels,

$$\boldsymbol{K} = \boldsymbol{v}\boldsymbol{h}^T \qquad (3.20)$$

(see Figure 3.14 for some examples). Because of the increased efficiency, the design of convolution kernels for computer vision applications is often influenced by their separability.

How can we tell if a given kernel K is indeed separable? This can often be done by inspection or by looking at the analytic form of the kernel (Freeman and Adelson 1991). A more direct method is to treat the 2D kernel as a 2D matrix K and to take its singular value decomposition (SVD),

$$K = \sum_i \sigma_i u_i v_i^T \qquad (3.21)$$

(see Appendix A.1.1 for the definition of the SVD). If only the first singular value σ_0 is non-zero, the kernel is separable and $\sqrt{\sigma_0} u_0$ and $\sqrt{\sigma_0} v_0^T$ provide the vertical and horizontal kernels (Perona 1995). For example, the Laplacian of Gaussian kernel (3.26 and 4.23) can be implemented as the sum of two separable filters (4.24) (Wiejak, Buxton, and Buxton 1985).

What if your kernel is not separable and yet you still want a faster way to implement it? Perona (1995), who first made the link between kernel separability and SVD, suggests using more terms in the (3.21) series, i.e., summing up a number of separable convolutions. Whether this is worth doing or not depends on the relative sizes of K and the number of significant singular values, as well as other considerations, such as cache coherency and memory locality.

3.2.2 Examples of linear filtering

Now that we have described the process for performing linear filtering, let us examine a number of frequently used filters.

The simplest filter to implement is the *moving average* or *box* filter, which simply averages the pixel values in a $K \times K$ window. This is equivalent to convolving the image with a kernel of all ones and then scaling (Figure 3.14a). For large kernels, a more efficient implementation is to slide a moving window across each scanline (in a separable filter) while adding the newest pixel and subtracting the oldest pixel from the running sum. This is related to the concept of *summed area tables*, which we describe shortly.

A smoother image can be obtained by separably convolving the image with a piecewise linear "tent" function (also known as a *Bartlett* filter). Figure 3.14b shows a 3×3 version of this filter, which is called the *bilinear* kernel, since it is the outer product of two linear (first-order) splines (see Section 3.5.2).

Convolving the linear tent function with itself yields the cubic approximating spline, which is called the "Gaussian" kernel (Figure 3.14c) in Burt and Adelson's (1983a) *Laplacian pyramid* representation (Section 3.5). Note that approximate Gaussian kernels can also be obtained by iterated convolution with box filters (Wells 1986). In applications where the filters really need to be rotationally symmetric, carefully tuned versions of sampled Gaussians should be used (Freeman and Adelson 1991) (Exercise 3.10).

The kernels we just discussed are all examples of blurring (smoothing) or *low-pass* kernels (since they pass through the lower frequencies while attenuating higher frequencies). How good are they at doing this? In Section 3.4, we use frequency-space Fourier analysis to examine the exact frequency response of these filters. We also introduce the *sinc* $((\sin x)/x)$ filter, which performs *ideal* low-pass filtering.

In practice, smoothing kernels are often used to reduce high-frequency noise. We have much more to say about using variants on smoothing to remove noise later (see Sections 3.3.1, 3.4, and 3.7).

Surprisingly, smoothing kernels can also be used to *sharpen* images using a process called
unsharp masking. Since blurring the image reduces high frequencies, adding some of the
difference between the original and the blurred image makes it sharper,

$$g_{\text{sharp}} = f + \gamma(f - h_{\text{blur}} * f). \tag{3.22}$$

In fact, before the advent of digital photography, this was the standard way to sharpen images
in the darkroom: create a blurred ("positive") negative from the original negative by mis-
focusing, then overlay the two negatives before printing the final image, which corresponds
to

$$g_{\text{unsharp}} = f(1 - \gamma h_{\text{blur}} * f). \tag{3.23}$$

This is no longer a linear filter but it still works well.

Linear filtering can also be used as a pre-processing stage to edge extraction (Section 4.2)
and interest point detection (Section 4.1) algorithms. Figure 3.14d shows a simple 3×3 edge
extractor called the Sobel operator, which is a separable combination of a horizontal *central
difference* (so called because the horizontal derivative is centered on the pixel) and a vertical
tent filter (to smooth the results). As you can see in the image below the kernel, this filter
effectively emphasizes horizontal edges.

The simple corner detector (Figure 3.14e) looks for simultaneous horizontal and vertical
second derivatives. As you can see however, it responds not only to the corners of the square,
but also along diagonal edges. Better corner detectors, or at least interest point detectors that
are more rotationally invariant, are described in Section 4.1.

3.2.3 Band-pass and steerable filters

The Sobel and corner operators are simple examples of band-pass and oriented filters. More
sophisticated kernels can be created by first smoothing the image with a (unit area) Gaussian
filter,

$$G(x, y; \sigma) = \frac{1}{2\pi\sigma^2} e^{-\frac{x^2 + y^2}{2\sigma^2}}, \tag{3.24}$$

and then taking the first or second derivatives (Marr 1982; Witkin 1983; Freeman and Adelson
1991). Such filters are known collectively as *band-pass filters*, since they filter out both low
and high frequencies.

The (undirected) second derivative of a two-dimensional image,

$$\nabla^2 f = \frac{\partial^2 f}{\partial x^2} + \frac{\partial^2 y}{\partial y^2}, \tag{3.25}$$

is known as the *Laplacian* operator. Blurring an image with a Gaussian and then taking its
Laplacian is equivalent to convolving directly with the *Laplacian of Gaussian* (LoG) filter,

$$\nabla^2 G(x, y; \sigma) = \left(\frac{x^2 + y^2}{\sigma^4} - \frac{2}{\sigma^2} \right) G(x, y; \sigma), \tag{3.26}$$

which has certain nice *scale-space properties* (Witkin 1983; Witkin, Terzopoulos, and Kass
1986). The five-point Laplacian is just a compact approximation to this more sophisticated
filter.

Likewise, the Sobel operator is a simple approximation to a *directional* or *oriented* filter,
which can obtained by smoothing with a Gaussian (or some other filter) and then taking a

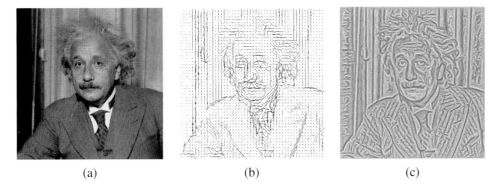

(a) (b) (c)

Figure 3.15 Second-order steerable filter (Freeman 1992) © 1992 IEEE: (a) original image of Einstein; (b) orientation map computed from the second-order oriented energy; (c) original image with oriented structures enhanced.

directional derivative $\nabla_{\hat{u}} = \frac{\partial}{\partial \hat{u}}$, which is obtained by taking the dot product between the gradient field ∇ and a unit direction $\hat{u} = (\cos\theta, \sin\theta)$,

$$\hat{u} \cdot \nabla(G * f) = \nabla_{\hat{u}}(G * f) = (\nabla_{\hat{u}} G) * f. \tag{3.27}$$

The smoothed directional derivative filter,

$$G_{\hat{u}} = uG_x + vG_y = u\frac{\partial G}{\partial x} + v\frac{\partial G}{\partial y}, \tag{3.28}$$

where $\hat{u} = (u, v)$, is an example of a *steerable* filter, since the value of an image convolved with $G_{\hat{u}}$ can be computed by first convolving with the pair of filters (G_x, G_y) and then *steering* the filter (potentially locally) by multiplying this gradient field with a unit vector $\hat{u}$ (Freeman and Adelson 1991). The advantage of this approach is that a whole *family* of filters can be evaluated with very little cost.

How about steering a directional second derivative filter $\nabla_{\hat{u}} \cdot \nabla_{\hat{u}} G_{\hat{u}}$, which is the result of taking a (smoothed) directional derivative and then taking the directional derivative again? For example, G_{xx} is the second directional derivative in the x direction.

At first glance, it would appear that the steering trick will not work, since for every direction $\hat{u}$, we need to compute a different first directional derivative. Somewhat surprisingly, Freeman and Adelson (1991) showed that, for directional Gaussian derivatives, it is possible to steer *any* order of derivative with a relatively small number of basis functions. For example, only three basis functions are required for the second-order directional derivative,

$$G_{\hat{u}\hat{u}} = u^2 G_{xx} + 2uv G_{xy} + v^2 G_{yy}. \tag{3.29}$$

Furthermore, each of the basis filters, while not itself necessarily separable, can be computed using a linear combination of a small number of separable filters (Freeman and Adelson 1991).

This remarkable result makes it possible to construct directional derivative filters of increasingly greater *directional selectivity*, i.e., filters that only respond to edges that have strong local consistency in orientation (Figure 3.15). Furthermore, higher order steerable

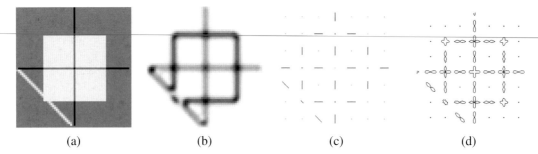

(a)   (b)   (c)   (d)

Figure 3.16 Fourth-order steerable filter (Freeman and Adelson 1991) © 1991 IEEE: (a) test image containing bars (lines) and step edges at different orientations; (b) average oriented energy; (c) dominant orientation; (d) oriented energy as a function of angle (polar plot).

filters can respond to potentially more than a single edge orientation at a given location, and they can respond to both *bar* edges (thin lines) and the classic step edges (Figure 3.16). In order to do this, however, full *Hilbert transform pairs* need to be used for second-order and higher filters, as described in (Freeman and Adelson 1991).

Steerable filters are often used to construct both feature descriptors (Section 4.1.3) and edge detectors (Section 4.2). While the filters developed by Freeman and Adelson (1991) are best suited for detecting linear (edge-like) structures, more recent work by Koethe (2003) shows how a combined 2×2 boundary tensor can be used to encode both edge and junction ("corner") features. Exercise 3.12 has you implement such steerable filters and apply them to finding both edge and corner features.

Summed area table (integral image)

If an image is going to be repeatedly convolved with different box filters (and especially filters of different sizes at different locations), you can precompute the *summed area table* (Crow 1984), which is just the running sum of all the pixel values from the origin,

$$s(i,j) = \sum_{k=0}^{i} \sum_{l=0}^{j} f(k,l). \tag{3.30}$$

This can be efficiently computed using a recursive (raster-scan) algorithm,

$$s(i,j) = s(i-1,j) + s(i,j-1) - s(i-1,j-1) + f(i,j). \tag{3.31}$$

The image $s(i,j)$ is also often called an *integral image* (see Figure 3.17) and can actually be computed using only two additions per pixel if separate row sums are used (Viola and Jones 2004). To find the summed area (integral) inside a rectangle $[i_0, i_1] \times [j_0, j_1]$, we simply combine four samples from the summed area table,

$$S(i_0 \ldots i_1, j_0 \ldots j_1) = \sum_{i=i_0}^{i_1} \sum_{j=j_0}^{j_1} s(i_1, j_1) - s(i_1, j_0 - 1) - s(i_0 - 1, j_1) + s(i_0 - 1, j_0 - 1). \tag{3.32}$$

A potential disadvantage of summed area tables is that they require $\log M + \log N$ extra bits in the accumulation image compared to the original image, where M and N are the image

3	2	7	2	3
1	5	1	3	4
5	1	3	5	1
4	3	2	1	6
2	4	1	4	8

3	5	12	14	17
4	*11*	**19**	24	31
9	**17**	**28**	38	46
13	24	37	48	62
15	30	44	59	81

3	5	12	*14*	17
4	11	19	24	31
9	17	28	38	46
13	24	37	**48**	62
15	30	44	59	81

(a) S = 24   (b) s = 28   (c) S = 24

Figure 3.17 Summed area tables: (a) original image; (b) summed area table; (c) computation of area sum. Each value in the summed area table $s(i, j)$ (red) is computed recursively from its three adjacent (blue) neighbors (3.31). Area sums S (green) are computed by combining the four values at the rectangle corners (purple) (3.32). Positive values are shown in **bold** and negative values in *italics*.

width and height. Extensions of summed area tables can also be used to approximate other convolution kernels (Wolberg (1990, Section 6.5.2) contains a review).

In computer vision, summed area tables have been used in face detection (Viola and Jones 2004) to compute simple multi-scale low-level features. Such features, which consist of adjacent rectangles of positive and negative values, are also known as *boxlets* (Simard, Bottou, Haffner *et al.* 1998). In principle, summed area tables could also be used to compute the sums in the sum of squared differences (SSD) stereo and motion algorithms (Section 11.4). In practice, separable moving average filters are usually preferred (Kanade, Yoshida, Oda *et al.* 1996), unless many different window shapes and sizes are being considered (Veksler 2003).

Recursive filtering

The incremental formula (3.31) for the summed area is an example of a *recursive filter*, i.e., one whose values depends on previous filter outputs. In the signal processing literature, such filters are known as *infinite impulse response* (IIR), since the output of the filter to an impulse (single non-zero value) goes on forever. For example, for a summed area table, an impulse generates an infinite rectangle of 1s below and to the right of the impulse. The filters we have previously studied in this chapter, which involve the image with a finite extent kernel, are known as *finite impulse response* (FIR).

Two-dimensional IIR filters and recursive formulas are sometimes used to compute quantities that involve large area interactions, such as two-dimensional distance functions (Section 3.3.3) and connected components (Section 3.3.4).

More commonly, however, IIR filters are used inside one-dimensional separable filtering stages to compute large-extent smoothing kernels, such as efficient approximations to Gaussians and edge filters (Deriche 1990; Nielsen, Florack, and Deriche 1997). Pyramid-based algorithms (Section 3.5) can also be used to perform such large-area smoothing computations.

$$(a) \qquad\qquad (b) \qquad\qquad (c) \qquad\qquad (d)$$

$$(e) \qquad\qquad (f) \qquad\qquad (g) \qquad\qquad (h)$$

Figure 3.18 Median and bilateral filtering: (a) original image with Gaussian noise; (b) Gaussian filtered; (c) median filtered; (d) bilaterally filtered; (e) original image with shot noise; (f) Gaussian filtered; (g) median filtered; (h) bilaterally filtered. Note that the bilateral filter fails to remove the shot noise because the noisy pixels are too different from their neighbors.

3.3 More neighborhood operators

As we have just seen, linear filters can perform a wide variety of image transformations. However non-linear filters, such as edge-preserving median or bilateral filters, can sometimes perform even better. Other examples of neighborhood operators include *morphological* operators that operate on binary images, as well as *semi-global* operators that compute *distance transforms* and find *connected components* in binary images (Figure 3.11f–h).

3.3.1 Non-linear filtering

The filters we have looked at so far have all been *linear*, i.e., their response to a sum of two signals is the same as the sum of the individual responses. This is equivalent to saying that each output pixel is a weighted summation of some number of input pixels (3.19). Linear filters are easier to compose and are amenable to frequency response analysis (Section 3.4).

In many cases, however, better performance can be obtained by using a *non-linear* combination of neighboring pixels. Consider for example the image in Figure 3.18e, where the noise, rather than being Gaussian, is *shot noise*, i.e., it occasionally has very large values. In this case, regular blurring with a Gaussian filter fails to remove the noisy pixels and instead turns them into softer (but still visible) spots (Figure 3.18f).

Median filtering

A better filter to use in this case is the *median* filter, which selects the median value from each pixel's neighborhood (Figure 3.19a). Median values can be computed in expected linear time using a randomized select algorithm (Cormen 2001) and incremental variants have also been

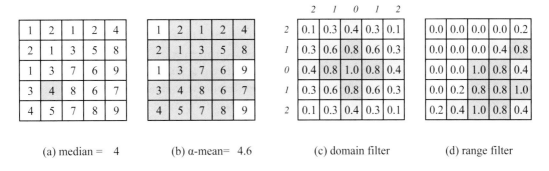

(a) median = 4 (b) α-mean= 4.6 (c) domain filter (d) range filter

Figure 3.19 Median and bilateral filtering: (a) median pixel (green); (b) selected α-trimmed mean pixels; (c) domain filter (numbers along edge are pixel distances); (d) range filter.

developed by Tomasi and Manduchi (1998) and Bovik (2000, Section 3.2). Since the shot noise value usually lies well outside the true values in the neighborhood, the median filter is able to filter away such bad pixels (Figure 3.18c).

One downside of the median filter, in addition to its moderate computational cost, is that since it selects only one input pixel value to replace each output pixel, it is not as *efficient* at averaging away regular Gaussian noise (Huber 1981; Hampel, Ronchetti, Rousseeuw *et al.* 1986; Stewart 1999). A better choice may be the α-trimmed mean (Lee and Redner 1990) (Crane 1997, p. 109), which averages together all of the pixels except for the α fraction that are the smallest and the largest (Figure 3.19b).

Another possibility is to compute a *weighted median*, in which each pixel is used a number of times depending on its distance from the center. This turns out to be equivalent to minimizing the weighted objective function

$$\sum_{k,l} w(k,l)|f(i+k,j+l) - g(i,j)|^p, \tag{3.33}$$

where $g(i,j)$ is the desired output value and $p = 1$ for the weighted median. The value $p = 2$ is the usual *weighted mean*, which is equivalent to correlation (3.12) after normalizing by the sum of the weights (Bovik 2000, Section 3.2) (Haralick and Shapiro 1992, Section 7.2.6). The weighted mean also has deep connections to other methods in robust statistics (see Appendix B.3), such as influence functions (Huber 1981; Hampel, Ronchetti, Rousseeuw *et al.* 1986).

Non-linear smoothing has another, perhaps even more important property, especially since shot noise is rare in today's cameras. Such filtering is more *edge preserving*, i.e., it has less tendency to soften edges while filtering away high-frequency noise.

Consider the noisy image in Figure 3.18a. In order to remove most of the noise, the Gaussian filter is forced to smooth away high-frequency detail, which is most noticeable near strong edges. Median filtering does better but, as mentioned before, does not do as good a job at smoothing away from discontinuities. See (Tomasi and Manduchi 1998) for some additional references to edge-preserving smoothing techniques.

While we could try to use the α-trimmed mean or weighted median, these techniques still have a tendency to round sharp corners, since the majority of pixels in the smoothing area come from the background distribution.

Bilateral filtering

What if we were to combine the idea of a weighted filter kernel with a better version of outlier rejection? What if instead of rejecting a fixed percentage α, we simply reject (in a soft way) pixels whose *values* differ too much from the central pixel value? This is the essential idea in *bilateral filtering*, which was first popularized in the computer vision community by Tomasi and Manduchi (1998). Chen, Paris, and Durand (2007) and Paris, Kornprobst, Tumblin *et al.* (2008) cite similar earlier work (Aurich and Weule 1995; Smith and Brady 1997) as well as the wealth of subsequent applications in computer vision and computational photography.

In the bilateral filter, the output pixel value depends on a weighted combination of neighboring pixel values

$$g(i,j) = \frac{\sum_{k,l} f(k,l)w(i,j,k,l)}{\sum_{k,l} w(i,j,k,l)}. \tag{3.34}$$

The weighting coefficient $w(i,j,k,l)$ depends on the product of a *domain kernel* (Figure 3.19c),

$$d(i,j,k,l) = \exp\left(-\frac{(i-k)^2 + (j-l)^2}{2\sigma_d^2}\right), \tag{3.35}$$

and a data-dependent *range kernel* (Figure 3.19d),

$$r(i,j,k,l) = \exp\left(-\frac{\|f(i,j) - f(k,l)\|^2}{2\sigma_r^2}\right). \tag{3.36}$$

When multiplied together, these yield the data-dependent *bilateral weight function*

$$w(i,j,k,l) = \exp\left(-\frac{(i-k)^2 + (j-l)^2}{2\sigma_d^2} - \frac{\|f(i,j) - f(k,l)\|^2}{2\sigma_r^2}\right). \tag{3.37}$$

Figure 3.20 shows an example of the bilateral filtering of a noisy step edge. Note how the domain kernel is the usual Gaussian, the range kernel measures appearance (intensity) similarity to the center pixel, and the bilateral filter kernel is a product of these two.

Notice that the range filter (3.36) uses the *vector distance* between the center and the neighboring pixel. This is important in color images, since an edge in any *one* of the color bands signals a change in material and hence the need to downweight a pixel's influence.[5]

Since bilateral filtering is quite slow compared to regular separable filtering, a number of acceleration techniques have been developed (Durand and Dorsey 2002; Paris and Durand 2006; Chen, Paris, and Durand 2007; Paris, Kornprobst, Tumblin *et al.* 2008). Unfortunately, these techniques tend to use more memory than regular filtering and are hence not directly applicable to filtering full-color images.

Iterated adaptive smoothing and anisotropic diffusion

Bilateral (and other) filters can also be applied in an iterative fashion, especially if an appearance more like a "cartoon" is desired (Tomasi and Manduchi 1998). When iterated filtering is applied, a much smaller neighborhood can often be used.

[5] Tomasi and Manduchi (1998) show that using the vector distance (as opposed to filtering each color band separately) reduces color fringing effects. They also recommend taking the color difference in the more perceptually uniform CIELAB color space (see Section 2.3.2).

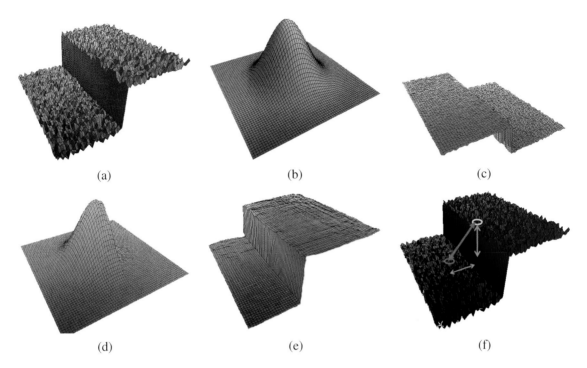

(a) (b) (c)

(d) (e) (f)

Figure 3.20 Bilateral filtering (Durand and Dorsey 2002) © 2002 ACM: (a) noisy step edge input; (b) domain filter (Gaussian); (c) range filter (similarity to center pixel value); (d) bilateral filter; (e) filtered step edge output; (f) 3D distance between pixels.

Consider, for example, using only the four nearest neighbors, i.e., restricting $|k - i| + |l - j| \leq 1$ in (3.34). Observe that

$$d(i, j, k, l) = \exp\left(-\frac{(i - k)^2 + (j - l)^2}{2\sigma_d^2}\right) \tag{3.38}$$

$$= \begin{cases} 1, & |k - i| + |l - j| = 0, \\ \lambda = e^{-1/2\sigma_d^2}, & |k - i| + |l - j| = 1. \end{cases} \tag{3.39}$$

We can thus re-write (3.34) as

$$f^{(t+1)}(i, j) = \frac{f^{(t)}(i, j) + \eta \sum_{k,l} f^{(t)}(k, l) r(i, j, k, l)}{1 + \eta \sum_{k,l} r(i, j, k, l)} \tag{3.40}$$

$$= f^{(t)}(i, j) + \frac{\eta}{1 + \eta R} \sum_{k,l} r(i, j, k, l)[f^{(t)}(k, l) - f^{(t)}(i, j)],$$

where $R = \sum_{(k,l)} r(i, j, k, l)$, (k, l) are the $\mathcal{N}_4$ neighbors of (i, j), and we have made the iterative nature of the filtering explicit.

As Barash (2002) notes, (3.40) is the same as the discrete *anisotropic diffusion* equation first proposed by Perona and Malik (1990b).[6] Since its original introduction, anisotropic diffusion has been extended and applied to a wide range of problems (Nielsen, Florack, and Deriche 1997; Black, Sapiro, Marimont *et al.* 1998; Weickert, ter Haar Romeny, and Viergever

---

[6] The $1/(1 + \eta R)$ factor is not present in anisotropic diffusion but becomes negligible as $\eta \to 0$.

1998; Weickert 1998). It has also been shown to be closely related to other *adaptive smoothing* techniques (Saint-Marc, Chen, and Medioni 1991; Barash 2002; Barash and Comaniciu 2004) as well as Bayesian regularization with a non-linear smoothness term that can be derived from image statistics (Scharr, Black, and Haussecker 2003).

In its general form, the range kernel $r(i, j, k, l) = r(\|f(i, j) - f(k, l)\|)$, which is usually called the *gain* or *edge-stopping* function, or diffusion coefficient, can be any monotonically increasing function with $r'(x) \to 0$ as $x \to \infty$. Black, Sapiro, Marimont *et al.* (1998) show how anisotropic diffusion is equivalent to minimizing a robust penalty function on the image gradients, which we discuss in Sections 3.7.1 and 3.7.2). Scharr, Black, and Haussecker (2003) show how the edge-stopping function can be derived in a principled manner from local image statistics. They also extend the diffusion neighborhood from $\mathcal{N}_4$ to $\mathcal{N}_8$, which allows them to create a diffusion operator that is both rotationally invariant and incorporates information about the eigenvalues of the local structure tensor.

Note that, without a bias term towards the original image, anisotropic diffusion and iterative adaptive smoothing converge to a constant image. Unless a small number of iterations is used (e.g., for speed), it is usually preferable to formulate the smoothing problem as a joint minimization of a smoothness term and a data fidelity term, as discussed in Sections 3.7.1 and 3.7.2 and by Scharr, Black, and Haussecker (2003), which introduce such a bias in a principled manner.

3.3.2 Morphology

While non-linear filters are often used to enhance grayscale and color images, they are also used extensively to process binary images. Such images often occur after a *thresholding* operation,

$$\theta(f, t) = \begin{cases} 1 & \text{if } f \geq t, \\ 0 & \text{else,} \end{cases} \tag{3.41}$$

e.g., converting a scanned grayscale document into a binary image for further processing such as *optical character recognition*.

The most common binary image operations are called *morphological operations*, since they change the *shape* of the underlying binary objects (Ritter and Wilson 2000, Chapter 7). To perform such an operation, we first convolve the binary image with a binary *structuring element* and then select a binary output value depending on the thresholded result of the convolution. (This is not the usual way in which these operations are described, but I find it a nice simple way to unify the processes.) The structuring element can be any shape, from a simple 3×3 box filter, to more complicated disc structures. It can even correspond to a particular shape that is being sought for in the image.

Figure 3.21 shows a close-up of the convolution of a binary image f with a 3×3 structuring element s and the resulting images for the operations described below. Let

$$c = f \otimes s \tag{3.42}$$

be the integer-valued *count* of the number of 1s inside each structuring element as it is scanned over the image and S be the size of the structuring element (number of pixels). The standard operations used in binary morphology include:

- **dilation**: $\text{dilate}(f, s) = \theta(c, 1)$;

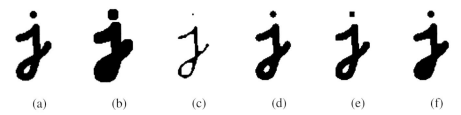

(a)   (b)   (c)   (d)   (e)   (f)

Figure 3.21 Binary image morphology: (a) original image; (b) dilation; (c) erosion; (d) majority; (e) opening; (f) closing. The structuring element for all examples is a 5×5 square. The effects of majority are a subtle rounding of sharp corners. Opening fails to eliminate the dot, since it is not wide enough.

- **erosion**: $\mathrm{erode}(f, s) = \theta(c, S)$;

- **majority**: $\mathrm{maj}(f, s) = \theta(c, S/2)$;

- **opening**: $\mathrm{open}(f, s) = \mathrm{dilate}(\mathrm{erode}(f, s), s)$;

- **closing**: $\mathrm{close}(f, s) = \mathrm{erode}(\mathrm{dilate}(f, s), s)$.

As we can see from Figure 3.21, dilation grows (thickens) objects consisting of 1s, while erosion shrinks (thins) them. The opening and closing operations tend to leave large regions and smooth boundaries unaffected, while removing small objects or holes and smoothing boundaries.

While we will not use mathematical morphology much in the rest of this book, it is a handy tool to have around whenever you need to clean up some thresholded images. You can find additional details on morphology in other textbooks on computer vision and image processing (Haralick and Shapiro 1992, Section 5.2) (Bovik 2000, Section 2.2) (Ritter and Wilson 2000, Section 7) as well as articles and books specifically on this topic (Serra 1982; Serra and Vincent 1992; Yuille, Vincent, and Geiger 1992; Soille 2006).

3.3.3 Distance transforms

The distance transform is useful in quickly precomputing the distance to a curve or set of points using a two-pass raster algorithm (Rosenfeld and Pfaltz 1966; Danielsson 1980; Borgefors 1986; Paglieroni 1992; Breu, Gil, Kirkpatrick *et al.* 1995; Felzenszwalb and Huttenlocher 2004a; Fabbri, Costa, Torelli *et al.* 2008). It has many applications, including level sets (Section 5.1.4), fast *chamfer matching* (binary image alignment) (Huttenlocher, Klanderman, and Rucklidge 1993), feathering in image stitching and blending (Section 9.3.2), and nearest point alignment (Section 12.2.1).

The distance transform $D(i, j)$ of a binary image $b(i, j)$ is defined as follows. Let $d(k, l)$ be some *distance metric* between pixel offsets. Two commonly used metrics include the *city block* or *Manhattan* distance

$$d_1(k, l) = |k| + |l| \tag{3.43}$$

and the *Euclidean* distance

$$d_2(k, l) = \sqrt{k^2 + l^2}. \tag{3.44}$$

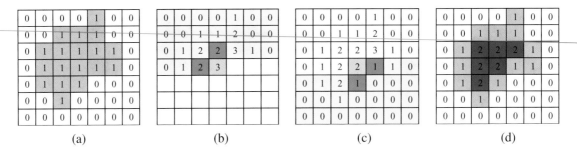

Figure 3.22 City block distance transform: (a) original binary image; (b) top to bottom (forward) raster sweep: green values are used to compute the orange value; (c) bottom to top (backward) raster sweep: green values are merged with old orange value; (d) final distance transform.

The distance transform is then defined as

$$D(i, j) = \min_{k,l:b(k,l)=0} d(i - k, j - l), \tag{3.45}$$

i.e., it is the distance to the *nearest* background pixel whose value is 0.

The D_1 city block distance transform can be efficiently computed using a forward and backward pass of a simple raster-scan algorithm, as shown in Figure 3.22. During the forward pass, each non-zero pixel in b is replaced by the minimum of 1 + the distance of its north or west neighbor. During the backward pass, the same occurs, except that the minimum is both over the current value D and 1 + the distance of the south and east neighbors (Figure 3.22).

Efficiently computing the Euclidean distance transform is more complicated. Here, just keeping the minimum scalar distance to the boundary during the two passes is not sufficient. Instead, a *vector-valued* distance consisting of both the x and y coordinates of the distance to the boundary must be kept and compared using the squared distance (hypotenuse) rule. As well, larger search regions need to be used to obtain reasonable results. Rather than explaining the algorithm (Danielsson 1980; Borgefors 1986) in more detail, we leave it as an exercise for the motivated reader (Exercise 3.13).

Figure 3.11g shows a distance transform computed from a binary image. Notice how the values grow away from the black (ink) regions and form ridges in the white area of the original image. Because of this linear growth from the starting boundary pixels, the distance transform is also sometimes known as the *grassfire transform*, since it describes the time at which a fire starting inside the black region would consume any given pixel, or a *chamfer*, because it resembles similar shapes used in woodworking and industrial design. The ridges in the distance transform become the *skeleton* (or *medial axis transform (MAT)*) of the region where the transform is computed, and consist of pixels that are of equal distance to two (or more) boundaries (Tek and Kimia 2003; Sebastian and Kimia 2005).

A useful extension of the basic distance transform is the *signed distance transform*, which computes distances to boundary pixels for *all* the pixels (Lavallée and Szeliski 1995). The simplest way to create this is to compute the distance transforms for both the original binary image and its complement and to negate one of them before combining. Because such distance fields tend to be smooth, it is possible to store them more compactly (with minimal loss in *relative* accuracy) using a spline defined over a quadtree or octree data structure

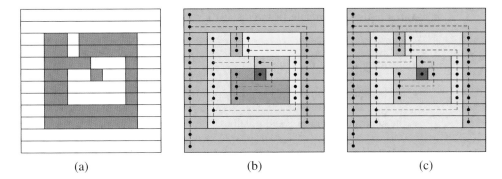

Figure 3.23 Connected component computation: (a) original grayscale image; (b) horizontal runs (nodes) connected by vertical (graph) edges (dashed blue)—runs are pseudocolored with unique colors inherited from parent nodes; (c) re-coloring after merging adjacent segments.

(Lavallée and Szeliski 1995; Szeliski and Lavallée 1996; Frisken, Perry, Rockwood *et al.* 2000). Such precomputed signed distance transforms can be extremely useful in efficiently aligning and merging 2D curves and 3D surfaces (Huttenlocher, Klanderman, and Rucklidge 1993; Szeliski and Lavallée 1996; Curless and Levoy 1996), especially if the *vectorial* version of the distance transform, i.e., a pointer from each pixel or voxel to the nearest boundary or surface element, is stored and interpolated. Signed distance fields are also an essential component of level set evolution (Section 5.1.4), where they are called *characteristic functions*.

3.3.4 Connected components

Another useful semi-global image operation is finding *connected components*, which are defined as regions of adjacent pixels that have the same input value (or label). (In the remainder of this section, consider pixels to be *adjacent* if they are immediate $\mathcal{N}_4$ neighbors and they have the same input value.) Connected components can be used in a variety of applications, such as finding individual letters in a scanned document or finding objects (say, cells) in a thresholded image and computing their area statistics.

Consider the grayscale image in Figure 3.23a. There are four connected components in this figure: the outermost set of white pixels, the large ring of gray pixels, the white enclosed region, and the single gray pixel. These are shown pseudocolored in Figure 3.23c as pink, green, blue, and brown.

To compute the connected components of an image, we first (conceptually) split the image into horizontal *runs* of adjacent pixels, and then color the runs with unique labels, re-using the labels of vertically adjacent runs whenever possible. In a second phase, adjacent runs of different colors are then merged.

While this description is a little sketchy, it should be enough to enable a motivated student to implement this algorithm (Exercise 3.14). Haralick and Shapiro (1992, Section 2.3) give a much longer description of various connected component algorithms, including ones that avoid the creation of a potentially large re-coloring (equivalence) table. Well-debugged connected component algorithms are also available in most image processing libraries.

Once a binary or multi-valued image has been segmented into its connected components, it is often useful to compute the area statistics for each individual region $\mathcal{R}$. Such statistics include:

- the area (number of pixels);

- the perimeter (number of boundary pixels);

- the centroid (average x and y values);

- the second moments,

$$M = \sum_{(x,y)\in\mathcal{R}} \left[\begin{array}{c} x - \overline{x} \\ y - \overline{y} \end{array} \right] \left[\begin{array}{cc} x - \overline{x} & y - \overline{y} \end{array} \right], \tag{3.46}$$

from which the major and minor axis orientation and lengths can be computed using eigenvalue analysis.[7]

These statistics can then be used for further processing, e.g., for sorting the regions by the area size (to consider the largest regions first) or for preliminary matching of regions in different images.

3.4 Fourier transforms

In Section 3.2, we mentioned that Fourier analysis could be used to analyze the frequency characteristics of various filters. In this section, we explain both how Fourier analysis lets us determine these characteristics (or equivalently, the frequency *content* of an image) and how using the Fast Fourier Transform (FFT) lets us perform large-kernel convolutions in time that is independent of the kernel's size. More comprehensive introductions to Fourier transforms are provided by Bracewell (1986); Glassner (1995); Oppenheim and Schafer (1996); Oppenheim, Schafer, and Buck (1999).

How can we analyze what a given filter does to high, medium, and low frequencies? The answer is to simply pass a sinusoid of known frequency through the filter and to observe by how much it is attenuated. Let

$$s(x) = \sin(2\pi f x + \phi_i) = \sin(\omega x + \phi_i) \tag{3.47}$$

be the input sinusoid whose *frequency* is f, *angular frequency* is $\omega = 2\pi f$, and *phase* is ϕ_i. Note that in this section, we use the variables x and y to denote the spatial coordinates of an image, rather than i and j as in the previous sections. This is both because the letters i and j are used for the *imaginary* number (the usage depends on whether you are reading complex variables or electrical engineering literature) and because it is clearer how to distinguish the horizontal (x) and vertical (y) components in frequency space. In this section, we use the letter j for the imaginary number, since that is the form more commonly found in the signal processing literature (Bracewell 1986; Oppenheim and Schafer 1996; Oppenheim, Schafer, and Buck 1999).

---

[7] Moments can also be computed using Green's theorem applied to the boundary pixels (Yang and Albregtsen 1996).

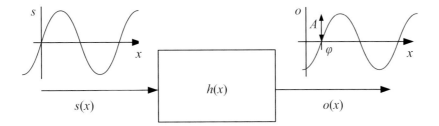

Figure 3.24 The Fourier Transform as the response of a filter $h(x)$ to an input sinusoid $s(x) = e^{j\omega x}$ yielding an output sinusoid $o(x) = h(x) * s(x) = Ae^{j\omega x + \phi}$.

If we convolve the sinusoidal signal $s(x)$ with a filter whose impulse response is $h(x)$, we get another sinusoid of the same frequency but different magnitude A and phase ϕ_o,

$$o(x) = h(x) * s(x) = A\sin(\omega x + \phi_o), \tag{3.48}$$

as shown in Figure 3.24. To see that this is the case, remember that a convolution can be expressed as a weighted summation of shifted input signals (3.14) and that the summation of a bunch of shifted sinusoids of the same frequency is just a single sinusoid at that frequency.[8] The new magnitude A is called the *gain* or *magnitude* of the filter, while the phase difference $\Delta\phi = \phi_o - \phi_i$ is called the *shift* or *phase*.

In fact, a more compact notation is to use the complex-valued sinusoid

$$s(x) = e^{j\omega x} = \cos \omega x + j \sin \omega x. \tag{3.49}$$

In that case, we can simply write,

$$o(x) = h(x) * s(x) = Ae^{j\omega x + \phi}. \tag{3.50}$$

The *Fourier transform* is simply a tabulation of the magnitude and phase response at each frequency,

$$H(\omega) = \mathcal{F}\{h(x)\} = Ae^{j\phi}, \tag{3.51}$$

i.e., it is the response to a complex sinusoid of frequency ω passed through the filter $h(x)$. The Fourier transform pair is also often written as

$$h(x) \overset{\mathcal{F}}{\leftrightarrow} H(\omega). \tag{3.52}$$

Unfortunately, (3.51) does not give an actual *formula* for computing the Fourier transform. Instead, it gives a *recipe*, i.e., convolve the filter with a sinusoid, observe the magnitude and phase shift, repeat. Fortunately, closed form equations for the Fourier transform exist both in the continuous domain,

$$H(\omega) = \int_{-\infty}^{\infty} h(x)e^{-j\omega x}dx, \tag{3.53}$$

---

[8] If h is a general (non-linear) transform, additional *harmonic* frequencies are introduced. This was traditionally the bane of audiophiles, who insisted on equipment with no *harmonic distortion*. Now that digital audio has introduced pure distortion-free sound, some audiophiles are buying retro tube amplifiers or digital signal processors that simulate such distortions because of their "warmer sound".

Property	Signal		Transform
superposition	$f_1(x) + f_2(x)$		$F_1(\omega) + F_2(\omega)$
shift	$f(x - x_0)$		$F(\omega)e^{-j\omega x_0}$
reversal	$f(-x)$		$F^*(\omega)$
convolution	$f(x) * h(x)$		$F(\omega)H(\omega)$
correlation	$f(x) \otimes h(x)$		$F(\omega)H^*(\omega)$
multiplication	$f(x)h(x)$		$F(\omega) * H(\omega)$
differentiation	$f'(x)$		$j\omega F(\omega)$
domain scaling	$f(ax)$		$1/aF(\omega/a)$
real images	$f(x) = f^*(x)$	$\Leftrightarrow$	$F(\omega) = F(-\omega)$
Parseval's Theorem	$\sum_x [f(x)]^2$	$=$	$\sum_\omega [F(\omega)]^2$

Table 3.1 Some useful properties of Fourier transforms. The original transform pair is $F(\omega) = \mathcal{F}\{f(x)\}$.

and in the discrete domain,

$$H(k) = \frac{1}{N} \sum_{x=0}^{N-1} h(x)e^{-j\frac{2\pi kx}{N}}, \tag{3.54}$$

where N is the length of the signal or region of analysis. These formulas apply both to filters, such as $h(x)$, and to signals or images, such as $s(x)$ or $g(x)$.

The discrete form of the Fourier transform (3.54) is known as the *Discrete Fourier Transform* (DFT). Note that while (3.54) can be evaluated for any value of k, it only makes sense for values in the range $k \in [-\frac{N}{2}, \frac{N}{2}]$. This is because larger values of k *alias* with lower frequencies and hence provide no additional information, as explained in the discussion on aliasing in Section 2.3.1.

At face value, the DFT takes $O(N^2)$ operations (multiply-adds) to evaluate. Fortunately, there exists a faster algorithm called the *Fast Fourier Transform* (FFT), which requires only $O(N \log_2 N)$ operations (Bracewell 1986; Oppenheim, Schafer, and Buck 1999). We do not explain the details of the algorithm here, except to say that it involves a series of $\log_2 N$ stages, where each stage performs small 2×2 transforms (matrix multiplications with known coefficients) followed by some semi-global permutations. (You will often see the term *butterfly* applied to these stages because of the pictorial shape of the signal processing graphs involved.) Implementations for the FFT can be found in most numerical and signal processing libraries.

Now that we have defined the Fourier transform, what are some of its properties and how can they be used? Table 3.1 lists a number of useful properties, which we describe in a little more detail below:

- **Superposition**: The Fourier transform of a sum of signals is the sum of their Fourier transforms. Thus, the Fourier transform is a linear operator.

- **Shift**: The Fourier transform of a shifted signal is the transform of the original signal multiplied by a *linear phase shift* (complex sinusoid).

- **Reversal**: The Fourier transform of a reversed signal is the complex conjugate of the signal's transform.

- **Convolution**: The Fourier transform of a pair of convolved signals is the product of their transforms.

- **Correlation**: The Fourier transform of a correlation is the product of the first transform times the complex conjugate of the second one.

- **Multiplication**: The Fourier transform of the product of two signals is the convolution of their transforms.

- **Differentiation**: The Fourier transform of the derivative of a signal is that signal's transform multiplied by the frequency. In other words, differentiation linearly emphasizes (magnifies) higher frequencies.

- **Domain scaling**: The Fourier transform of a stretched signal is the equivalently compressed (and scaled) version of the original transform and *vice versa*.

- **Real images**: The Fourier transform of a real-valued signal is symmetric around the origin. This fact can be used to save space and to double the speed of image FFTs by packing alternating scanlines into the real and imaginary parts of the signal being transformed.

- **Parseval's Theorem**: The energy (sum of squared values) of a signal is the same as the energy of its Fourier transform.

All of these properties are relatively straightforward to prove (see Exercise 3.15) and they will come in handy later in the book, e.g., when designing optimum Wiener filters (Section 3.4.3) or performing fast image correlations (Section 8.1.2).

3.4.1 Fourier transform pairs

Now that we have these properties in place, let us look at the Fourier transform pairs of some commonly occurring filters and signals, as listed in Table 3.2. In more detail, these pairs are as follows:

- **Impulse**: The impulse response has a constant (all frequency) transform.

- **Shifted impulse**: The shifted impulse has unit magnitude and linear phase.

- **Box filter**: The box (moving average) filter

$$\text{box}(x) = \begin{cases} 1 & \text{if } |x| \leq 1 \\ 0 & \text{else} \end{cases} \tag{3.55}$$

has a sinc Fourier transform,

$$\text{sinc}(\omega) = \frac{\sin \omega}{\omega}, \tag{3.56}$$

which has an infinite number of side lobes. Conversely, the sinc filter is an ideal low-pass filter. For a non-unit box, the width of the box a and the spacing of the zero crossings in the sinc $1/a$ are inversely proportional.

Name	Signal		Transform	
impulse		$\delta(x)$ $\Leftrightarrow$	1	
shifted impulse		$\delta(x-u)$ $\Leftrightarrow$	$e^{-j\omega u}$	
box filter		$\text{box}(x/a)$ $\Leftrightarrow$	$a\,\text{sinc}(a\omega)$	
tent		$\text{tent}(x/a)$ $\Leftrightarrow$	$a\,\text{sinc}^2(a\omega)$	
Gaussian		$G(x;\sigma)$ $\Leftrightarrow$	$\frac{\sqrt{2\pi}}{\sigma}G(\omega;\sigma^{-1})$	
Laplacian of Gaussian		$(\frac{x^2}{\sigma^4}-\frac{1}{\sigma^2})G(x;\sigma)$ $\Leftrightarrow$	$-\frac{\sqrt{2\pi}}{\sigma}\omega^2 G(\omega;\sigma^{-1})$	
Gabor		$\cos(\omega_0 x)G(x;\sigma)$ $\Leftrightarrow$	$\frac{\sqrt{2\pi}}{\sigma}G(\omega\pm\omega_0;\sigma^{-1})$	
unsharp mask		$(1+\gamma)\delta(x)$ $-\gamma G(x;\sigma)$ $\Leftrightarrow$	$(1+\gamma)-$ $\frac{\sqrt{2\pi}\gamma}{\sigma}G(\omega;\sigma^{-1})$	
windowed sinc		$\text{rcos}(x/(aW))$ $\text{sinc}(x/a)$ $\Leftrightarrow$	(see Figure 3.29)	

Table 3.2 Some useful (continuous) Fourier transform pairs: The dashed line in the Fourier transform of the shifted impulse indicates its (linear) phase. All other transforms have zero phase (they are real-valued). Note that the figures are not necessarily drawn to scale but are drawn to illustrate the general shape and characteristics of the filter or its response. In particular, the Laplacian of Gaussian is drawn inverted because it resembles more a "Mexican hat", as it is sometimes called.

- **Tent**: The piecewise linear tent function,

$$\text{tent}(x) = \max(0, 1 - |x|), \tag{3.57}$$

has a sinc^2 Fourier transform.

- **Gaussian**: The (unit area) Gaussian of width σ,

$$G(x; \sigma) = \frac{1}{\sqrt{2\pi}\sigma} e^{-\frac{x^2}{2\sigma^2}}, \tag{3.58}$$

has a (unit height) Gaussian of width σ^{-1} as its Fourier transform.

- **Laplacian of Gaussian**: The second derivative of a Gaussian of width σ,

$$LoG(x; \sigma) = (\frac{x^2}{\sigma^4} - \frac{1}{\sigma^2})G(x; \sigma) \tag{3.59}$$

has a band-pass response of

$$-\frac{\sqrt{2\pi}}{\sigma}\omega^2 G(\omega; \sigma^{-1}) \tag{3.60}$$

as its Fourier transform.

- **Gabor**: The even Gabor function, which is the product of a cosine of frequency ω_0 and a Gaussian of width σ, has as its transform the sum of the two Gaussians of width σ^{-1} centered at $\omega = \pm\omega_0$. The odd Gabor function, which uses a sine, is the difference of two such Gaussians. Gabor functions are often used for oriented and band-pass filtering, since they can be more frequency selective than Gaussian derivatives.

- **Unsharp mask**: The unsharp mask introduced in (3.22) has as its transform a unit response with a slight boost at higher frequencies.

- **Windowed sinc**: The windowed (masked) sinc function shown in Table 3.2 has a response function that approximates an ideal low-pass filter better and better as additional side lobes are added (W is increased). Figure 3.29 shows the shapes of these such filters along with their Fourier transforms. For these examples, we use a one-lobe raised cosine,

$$\text{rcos}(x) = \frac{1}{2}(1 + \cos \pi x)\text{box}(x), \tag{3.61}$$

also known as the *Hann window*, as the windowing function. Wolberg (1990) and Oppenheim, Schafer, and Buck (1999) discuss additional windowing functions, which include the *Lanczos* window, the positive first lobe of a sinc function.

We can also compute the Fourier transforms for the small discrete kernels shown in Figure 3.14 (see Table 3.3). Notice how the moving average filters do not uniformly dampen higher frequencies and hence can lead to ringing artifacts. The binomial filter (Gomes and Velho 1997) used as the "Gaussian" in Burt and Adelson's (1983a) Laplacian pyramid (see Section 3.5), does a decent job of separating the high and low frequencies, but still leaves a fair amount of high-frequency detail, which can lead to aliasing after downsampling. The Sobel edge detector at first linearly accentuates frequencies, but then decays at higher frequencies, and hence has trouble detecting fine-scale edges, e.g., adjacent black and white columns. We look at additional examples of small kernel Fourier transforms in Section 3.5.2, where we study better kernels for pre-filtering before decimation (size reduction).

Name	Kernel	Transform	Plot
box-3	$\frac{1}{3}$ [1 1 1]	$\frac{1}{3}(1 + 2\cos\omega)$	
box-5	$\frac{1}{5}$ [1 1 1 1 1]	$\frac{1}{5}(1 + 2\cos\omega + 2\cos 2\omega)$	
linear	$\frac{1}{4}$ [1 2 1]	$\frac{1}{2}(1 + \cos\omega)$	
binomial	$\frac{1}{16}$ [1 4 6 4 1]	$\frac{1}{4}(1 + \cos\omega)^2$	
Sobel	$\frac{1}{2}$ [−1 0 1]	$\sin\omega$	
corner	$\frac{1}{2}$ [−1 2 −1]	$\frac{1}{2}(1 - \cos\omega)$	

Table 3.3 Fourier transforms of the separable kernels shown in Figure 3.14.

3.4.2 Two-dimensional Fourier transforms

The formulas and insights we have developed for one-dimensional signals and their transforms translate directly to two-dimensional images. Here, instead of just specifying a horizontal or vertical frequency ω_x or ω_y, we can create an oriented sinusoid of frequency (ω_x, ω_y),

$$s(x, y) = \sin(\omega_x x + \omega_y y). \tag{3.62}$$

The corresponding two-dimensional Fourier transforms are then

$$H(\omega_x, \omega_y) = \int_{-\infty}^{\infty} \int_{-\infty}^{\infty} h(x, y) e^{-j(\omega_x x + \omega_y y)} dx \, dy, \tag{3.63}$$

and in the discrete domain,

$$H(k_x, k_y) = \frac{1}{MN} \sum_{x=0}^{M-1} \sum_{y=0}^{N-1} h(x, y) e^{-j2\pi \frac{k_x x + k_y y}{MN}}, \tag{3.64}$$

where M and N are the width and height of the image.

All of the Fourier transform properties from Table 3.1 carry over to two dimensions if we replace the scalar variables x, ω, x_0 and a with their 2D vector counterparts $\boldsymbol{x} = (x, y)$, $\boldsymbol{\omega} = (\omega_x, \omega_y)$, $\boldsymbol{x}_0 = (x_0, y_0)$, and $\boldsymbol{a} = (a_x, a_y)$, and use vector inner products instead of multiplications.

3.4.3 Wiener filtering

While the Fourier transform is a useful tool for analyzing the frequency characteristics of a filter kernel or image, it can also be used to analyze the frequency spectrum of a whole *class* of images.

A simple model for images is to assume that they are random noise fields whose expected magnitude at each frequency is given by this *power spectrum* $P_s(\omega_x, \omega_y)$, i.e.,

$$\left\langle [S(\omega_x, \omega_y)]^2 \right\rangle = P_s(\omega_x, \omega_y), \tag{3.65}$$

where the angle brackets $\langle \cdot \rangle$ denote the expected (mean) value of a random variable.[9] To generate such an image, we simply create a random Gaussian noise image $S(\omega_x, \omega_y)$ where each "pixel" is a zero-mean Gaussian[10] of variance $P_s(\omega_x, \omega_y)$ and then take its inverse FFT.

The observation that signal spectra capture a first-order description of spatial statistics is widely used in signal and image processing. In particular, assuming that an image is a sample from a correlated Gaussian random noise field combined with a statistical model of the measurement process yields an optimum restoration filter known as the *Wiener filter*.[11]

To derive the Wiener filter, we analyze each frequency component of a signal's Fourier transform independently. The noisy image formation process can be written as

$$o(x, y) = s(x, y) + n(x, y), \tag{3.66}$$

---

[9] The notation $E[\cdot]$ is also commonly used.

[10] We set the DC (i.e., constant) component at $S(0, 0)$ to the mean grey level. See Algorithm C.1 in Appendix C.2 for code to generate Gaussian noise.

[11] Wiener is pronounced "veener" since, in German, the "w" is pronounced "v". Remember that next time you order "Wiener schnitzel".

where $s(x, y)$ is the (unknown) image we are trying to recover, $n(x, y)$ is the additive noise signal, and $o(x, y)$ is the *observed* noisy image. Because of the linearity of the Fourier transform, we can write

$$O(\omega_x, \omega_y) = S(\omega_x, \omega_y) + N(\omega_x, \omega_y), \qquad (3.67)$$

where each quantity in the above equation is the Fourier transform of the corresponding image.

At each frequency (ω_x, ω_y), we know from our image spectrum that the unknown transform component $S(\omega_x, \omega_y)$ has a *prior* distribution which is a zero-mean Gaussian with variance $P_s(\omega_x, \omega_y)$. We also have noisy measurement $O(\omega_x, \omega_y)$ whose variance is $P_n(\omega_x, \omega_y)$, i.e., the power spectrum of the noise, which is usually assumed to be constant (white), $P_n(\omega_x, \omega_y) = \sigma_n^2$.

According to Bayes' Rule (Appendix B.4), the *posterior estimate* of S can be written as

$$p(S|O) = \frac{p(O|S)p(S)}{p(O)}, \qquad (3.68)$$

where $p(O) = \int_S p(O|S)p(S)$ is a normalizing constant used to make the $p(S|O)$ distribution *proper* (integrate to 1). The prior distribution $p(S)$ is given by

$$p(S) = e^{-\frac{(S-\mu)^2}{2P_s}}, \qquad (3.69)$$

where μ is the expected mean at that frequency (0 everywhere except at the origin) and the measurement distribution $P(O|S)$ is given by

$$p(S) = e^{-\frac{(S-O)^2}{2P_n}}. \qquad (3.70)$$

Taking the negative logarithm of both sides of (3.68) and setting $\mu = 0$ for simplicity, we get

$$
\begin{aligned}
-\log p(S|O) &= -\log p(O|S) - \log p(S) + C && (3.71) \\
&= \tfrac{1}{2}P_n^{-1}(S-O)^2 + \tfrac{1}{2}P_s^{-1}S^2 + C, && (3.72)
\end{aligned}
$$

which is the *negative posterior log likelihood*. The minimum of this quantity is easy to compute,

$$S_{\text{opt}} = \frac{P_n^{-1}}{P_n^{-1} + P_s^{-1}}O = \frac{P_s}{P_s + P_n}O = \frac{1}{1 + P_n/P_s}O. \qquad (3.73)$$

The quantity

$$W(\omega_x, \omega_y) = \frac{1}{1 + \sigma_n^2/P_s(\omega_x, \omega_y)} \qquad (3.74)$$

is the Fourier transform of the optimum *Wiener filter* needed to remove the noise from an image whose power spectrum is $P_s(\omega_x, \omega_y)$.

Notice that this filter has the right qualitative properties, i.e., for low frequencies where $P_s \gg \sigma_n^2$, it has unit gain, whereas for high frequencies, it attenuates the noise by a factor P_s/σ_n^2. Figure 3.25 shows the one-dimensional transform $W(f)$ and the corresponding filter kernel $w(x)$ for the commonly assumed case of $P(f) = f^{-2}$ (Field 1987). Exercise 3.16 has you compare the Wiener filter as a denoising algorithm to hand-tuned Gaussian smoothing.

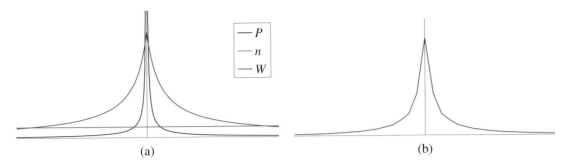

Figure 3.25 One-dimensional Wiener filter: (a) power spectrum of signal $P_s(f)$, noise level σ^2, and Wiener filter transform $W(f)$; (b) Wiener filter spatial kernel.

The methodology given above for deriving the Wiener filter can easily be extended to the case where the observed image is a noisy blurred version of the original image,

$$o(x, y) = b(x, y) * s(x, y) + n(x, y), \tag{3.75}$$

where $b(x, y)$ is the known blur kernel. Rather than deriving the corresponding Wiener filter, we leave it as an exercise (Exercise 3.17), which also encourages you to compare your de-blurring results with unsharp masking and naïve inverse filtering. More sophisticated algorithms for blur removal are discussed in Sections 3.7 and 10.3.

Discrete cosine transform

The *discrete cosine transform* (DCT) is a variant of the Fourier transform particularly well-suited to compressing images in a block-wise fashion. The one-dimensional DCT is computed by taking the dot product of each N-wide block of pixels with a set of cosines of different frequencies,

$$F(k) = \sum_{i=0}^{N-1} \cos\left(\frac{\pi}{N}(i + \frac{1}{2})k\right) f(i), \tag{3.76}$$

where k is the coefficient (frequency) index, and the $1/2$-pixel offset is used to make the basis coefficients symmetric (Wallace 1991). Some of the discrete cosine basis functions are shown in Figure 3.26. As you can see, the first basis function (the straight blue line) encodes the average DC value in the block of pixels, while the second encodes a slightly curvy version of the slope.

In turns out that the DCT is a good approximation to the optimal Karhunen–Loève decomposition of natural image statistics over small patches, which can be obtained by performing a principal component analysis (PCA) of images, as described in Section 14.2.1. The KL-transform de-correlates the signal optimally (assuming the signal is described by its spectrum) and thus, theoretically, leads to optimal compression.

The two-dimensional version of the DCT is defined similarly,

$$F(k, l) = \sum_{i=0}^{N-1} \sum_{j=0}^{N-1} \cos\left(\frac{\pi}{N}(i + \frac{1}{2})k\right) \cos\left(\frac{\pi}{N}(j + \frac{1}{2})l\right) f(i, j). \tag{3.77}$$

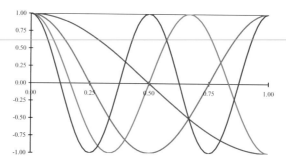

Figure 3.26 Discrete cosine transform (DCT) basis functions: The first DC (i.e., constant) basis is the horizontal blue line, the second is the brown half-cycle waveform, etc. These bases are widely used in image and video compression standards such as JPEG.

Like the 2D Fast Fourier Transform, the 2D DCT can be implemented separably, i.e., first computing the DCT of each line in the block and then computing the DCT of each resulting column. Like the FFT, each of the DCTs can also be computed in $O(N \log N)$ time.

As we mentioned in Section 2.3.3, the DCT is widely used in today's image and video compression algorithms, although it is slowly being supplanted by wavelet algorithms (Simoncelli and Adelson 1990b), as discussed in Section 3.5.4, and overlapped variants of the DCT (Malvar 1990, 1998, 2000), which are used in the new JPEG XR standard.[12] These newer algorithms suffer less from the *blocking artifacts* (visible edge-aligned discontinuities) that result from the pixels in each block (typically 8×8) being transformed and quantized independently. See Exercise 3.30 for ideas on how to remove blocking artifacts from compressed JPEG images.

3.4.4 *Application*: Sharpening, blur, and noise removal

Another common application of image processing is the enhancement of images through the use of sharpening and noise removal operations, which require some kind of neighborhood processing. Traditionally, these kinds of operation were performed using linear filtering (see Sections 3.2 and Section 3.4.3). Today, it is more common to use non-linear filters (Section 3.3.1), such as the weighted median or bilateral filter (3.34–3.37), anisotropic diffusion (3.39–3.40), or non-local means (Buades, Coll, and Morel 2008). Variational methods (Section 3.7.1), especially those using non-quadratic (robust) norms such as the L_1 norm (which is called *total variation*), are also often used. Figure 3.19 shows some examples of linear and non-linear filters being used to remove noise.

When measuring the effectiveness of image denoising algorithms, it is common to report the results as a *peak signal-to-noise ratio (PSNR)* measurement (2.119), where $I(x)$ is the original (noise-free) image and $\hat{I}(x)$ is the image after denoising; this is for the case where the noisy image has been synthetically generated, so that the clean image is known. A better way to measure the quality is to use a perceptually based similarity metric, such as the structural similarity (SSIM) index (Wang, Bovik, Sheikh *et al.* 2004; Wang, Bovik, and Simoncelli 2005).

---

[12] http://www.itu.int/rec/T-REC-T.832-200903-I/en.

Exercises 3.11, 3.16, 3.17, 3.21, and 3.28 have you implement some of these operations and compare their effectiveness. More sophisticated techniques for blur removal and the related task of super-resolution are discussed in Section 10.3.

3.5 Pyramids and wavelets

So far in this chapter, all of the image transformations we have studied produce output images of the same size as the inputs. Often, however, we may wish to change the resolution of an image before proceeding further. For example, we may need to interpolate a small image to make its resolution match that of the output printer or computer screen. Alternatively, we may want to reduce the size of an image to speed up the execution of an algorithm or to save on storage space or transmission time.

Sometimes, we do not even know what the appropriate resolution for the image should be. Consider, for example, the task of finding a face in an image (Section 14.1.1). Since we do not know the scale at which the face will appear, we need to generate a whole *pyramid* of differently sized images and scan each one for possible faces. (Biological visual systems also operate on a hierarchy of scales (Marr 1982).) Such a pyramid can also be very helpful in accelerating the search for an object by first finding a smaller instance of that object at a coarser level of the pyramid and then looking for the full resolution object only in the vicinity of coarse-level detections (Section 8.1.1). Finally, image pyramids are extremely useful for performing multi-scale editing operations such as blending images while maintaining details.

In this section, we first discuss good filters for changing image resolution, i.e., upsampling (*interpolation*, Section 3.5.1) and downsampling (*decimation*, Section 3.5.2). We then present the concept of multi-resolution pyramids, which can be used to create a complete hierarchy of differently sized images and to enable a variety of applications (Section 3.5.3). A closely related concept is that of *wavelets*, which are a special kind of pyramid with higher frequency selectivity and other useful properties (Section 3.5.4). Finally, we present a useful application of pyramids, namely the blending of different images in a way that hides the seams between the image boundaries (Section 3.5.5).

3.5.1 Interpolation

In order to *interpolate* (or *upsample*) an image to a higher resolution, we need to select some interpolation kernel with which to convolve the image,

$$g(i,j) = \sum_{k,l} f(k,l)h(i - rk, j - rl). \tag{3.78}$$

This formula is related to the discrete convolution formula (3.14), except that we replace k and l in $h()$ with rk and rl, where r is the upsampling rate. Figure 3.27a shows how to think of this process as the superposition of sample weighted interpolation kernels, one centered at each input sample k. An alternative mental model is shown in Figure 3.27b, where the kernel is centered at the output pixel value i (the two forms are equivalent). The latter form is sometimes called the *polyphase filter* form, since the kernel values $h(i)$ can be stored as r separate kernels, each of which is selected for convolution with the input samples depending on the *phase* of i relative to the upsampled grid.

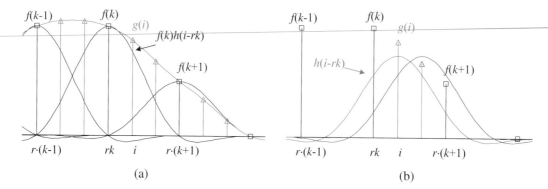

Figure 3.27 Signal interpolation, $g(i) = \sum_k f(k)h(i - rk)$: (a) weighted summation of input values; (b) polyphase filter interpretation.

What kinds of kernel make good interpolators? The answer depends on the application and the computation time involved. Any of the smoothing kernels shown in Tables 3.2 and 3.3 can be used after appropriate re-scaling.[13] The *linear* interpolator (corresponding to the tent kernel) produces interpolating piecewise linear curves, which result in unappealing *creases* when applied to images (Figure 3.28a). The cubic B-spline, whose discrete $1/2$-pixel sampling appears as the *binomial kernel* in Table 3.3, is an *approximating* kernel (the interpolated image does not pass through the input data points) that produces soft images with reduced high-frequency detail. The equation for the cubic B-spline is easiest to derive by convolving the tent function (linear B-spline) with itself.

While most graphics cards use the bilinear kernel (optionally combined with a MIP-map—see Section 3.5.3), most photo editing packages use *bicubic* interpolation. The cubic interpolant is a C^1 (derivative-continuous) piecewise-cubic *spline* (the term "spline" is synonymous with "piecewise-polynomial")[14] whose equation is

$$h(x) = \begin{cases} 1 - (a+3)x^2 + (a+2)|x|^3 & \text{if } |x| < 1 \\ a(|x| - 1)(|x| - 2)^2 & \text{if } 1 \le |x| < 2 \\ 0 & \text{otherwise,} \end{cases} \qquad (3.79)$$

where a specifies the derivative at $x = 1$ (Parker, Kenyon, and Troxel 1983). The value of a is often set to -1, since this best matches the frequency characteristics of a sinc function (Figure 3.29). It also introduces a small amount of sharpening, which can be visually appealing. Unfortunately, this choice does not linearly interpolate straight lines (intensity ramps), so some visible ringing may occur. A better choice for large amounts of interpolation is probably $a = -0.5$, which produces a *quadratic reproducing* spline; it interpolates linear and quadratic functions exactly (Wolberg 1990, Section 5.4.3). Figure 3.29 shows the $a = -1$ and $a = -0.5$ cubic interpolating kernel along with their Fourier transforms; Figure 3.28b and c shows them being applied to two-dimensional interpolation.

Splines have long been used for function and data value interpolation because of the abil-

---

[13] The smoothing kernels in Table 3.3 have a unit area. To turn them into interpolating kernels, we simply scale them up by the interpolation rate r.

[14] The term "spline" comes from the draughtsman's workshop, where it was the name of a flexible piece of wood or metal used to draw smooth curves.

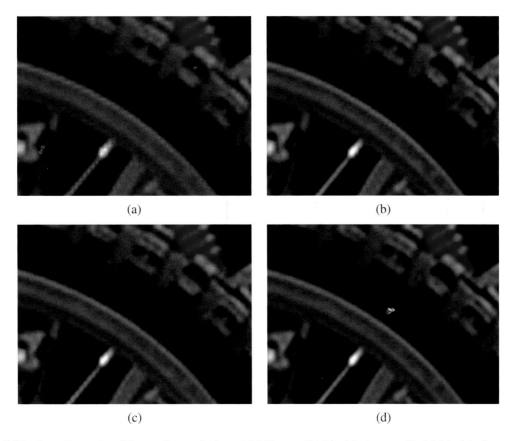

(a)   (b)

(c)   (d)

Figure 3.28 Two-dimensional image interpolation: (a) bilinear; (b) bicubic ($a = -1$); (c) bicubic ($a = -0.5$); (d) windowed sinc (nine taps).

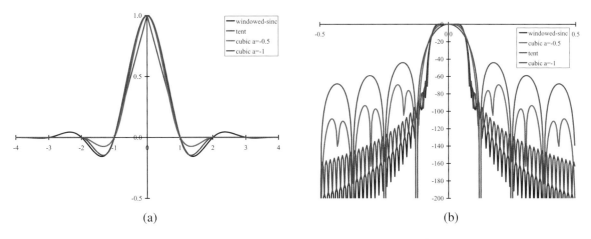

(a)   (b)

Figure 3.29 (a) Some windowed sinc functions and (b) their log Fourier transforms: raised-cosine windowed sinc in blue, cubic interpolators ($a = -1$ and $a = -0.5$) in green and purple, and tent function in brown. They are often used to perform high-accuracy low-pass filtering operations.

ity to precisely specify derivatives at control points and efficient *incremental* algorithms for their evaluation (Bartels, Beatty, and Barsky 1987; Farin 1992, 1996). Splines are widely used in geometric modeling and computer-aided design (CAD) applications, although they have started being displaced by subdivision surfaces (Zorin, Schröder, and Sweldens 1996; Peters and Reif 2008). In computer vision, splines are often used for elastic image deformations (Section 3.6.2), motion estimation (Section 8.3), and surface interpolation (Section 12.3). In fact, it is possible to carry out most image processing operations by representing images as splines and manipulating them in a multi-resolution framework (Unser 1999).

The highest quality interpolator is generally believed to be the windowed sinc function because it both preserves details in the lower resolution image and avoids aliasing. (It is also possible to construct a C^1 piecewise-cubic approximation to the windowed sinc by matching its derivatives at zero crossing (Szeliski and Ito 1986).) However, some people object to the excessive *ringing* that can be introduced by the windowed sinc and to the repetitive nature of the ringing frequencies (see Figure 3.28d). For this reason, some photographers prefer to repeatedly interpolate images by a small fractional amount (this tends to de-correlate the original pixel grid with the final image). Additional possibilities include using the bilateral filter as an interpolator (Kopf, Cohen, Lischinski *et al.* 2007), using global optimization (Section 3.6) or hallucinating details (Section 10.3).

3.5.2 Decimation

While interpolation can be used to increase the resolution of an image, decimation (downsampling) is required to reduce the resolution.[15] To perform decimation, we first (conceptually) convolve the image with a low-pass filter (to avoid aliasing) and then keep every rth sample. In practice, we usually only evaluate the convolution at every rth sample,

$$g(i, j) = \sum_{k,l} f(k, l) h(ri - k, rj - l), \tag{3.80}$$

as shown in Figure 3.30. Note that the smoothing kernel $h(k, l)$, in this case, is often a stretched and re-scaled version of an interpolation kernel. Alternatively, we can write

$$g(i, j) = \frac{1}{r} \sum_{k,l} f(k, l) h(i - k/r, j - l/r) \tag{3.81}$$

and keep the same kernel $h(k, l)$ for both interpolation and decimation.

One commonly used ($r = 2$) decimation filter is the *binomial* filter introduced by Burt and Adelson (1983a). As shown in Table 3.3, this kernel does a decent job of separating the high and low frequencies, but still leaves a fair amount of high-frequency detail, which can lead to aliasing after downsampling. However, for applications such as image blending (discussed later in this section), this aliasing is of little concern.

If, however, the downsampled images will be displayed directly to the user or, perhaps, blended with other resolutions (as in MIP-mapping, Section 3.5.3), a higher-quality filter is

---

[15] The term "decimation" has a gruesome etymology relating to the practice of killing every tenth soldier in a Roman unit guilty of cowardice. It is generally used in signal processing to mean any downsampling or rate reduction operation.

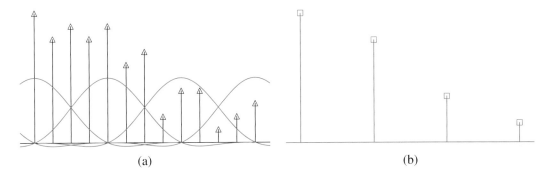

(a)   (b)

Figure 3.30 Signal decimation: (a) the original samples are (b) convolved with a low-pass filter before being downsampled.

desired. For high downsampling rates, the windowed sinc pre-filter is a good choice (Figure 3.29). However, for small downsampling rates, e.g., $r = 2$, more careful filter design is required.

Table 3.4 shows a number of commonly used $r = 2$ downsampling filters, while Figure 3.31 shows their corresponding frequency responses. These filters include:

- the linear $[1, 2, 1]$ filter gives a relatively poor response;

- the binomial $[1, 4, 6, 4, 1]$ filter cuts off a lot of frequencies but is useful for computer vision analysis pyramids;

- the cubic filters from (3.79); the $a = -1$ filter has a sharper fall-off than the $a = -0.5$ filter (Figure 3.31);

- a cosine-windowed sinc function (Table 3.2);

- the QMF-9 filter of Simoncelli and Adelson (1990b) is used for wavelet denoising and aliases a fair amount (note that the original filter coefficients are normalized to $\sqrt{2}$ gain so they can be "self-inverting");

- the 9/7 analysis filter from JPEG 2000 (Taubman and Marcellin 2002).

Please see the original papers for the full-precision values of some of these coefficients.

$|n|$	Linear	Binomial	Cubic $a = -1$	Cubic $a = -0.5$	Windowed sinc	QMF-9	JPEG 2000
0	0.50	0.3750	0.5000	0.50000	0.4939	0.5638	0.6029
1	0.25	0.2500	0.3125	0.28125	0.2684	0.2932	0.2669
2		0.0625	0.0000	0.00000	0.0000	-0.0519	-0.0782
3			-0.0625	-0.03125	-0.0153	-0.0431	-0.0169
4					0.0000	0.0198	0.0267

Table 3.4 Filter coefficients for $2\times$ decimation. These filters are of odd length, are symmetric, and are normalized to have unit DC gain (sum up to 1). See Figure 3.31 for their associated frequency responses.

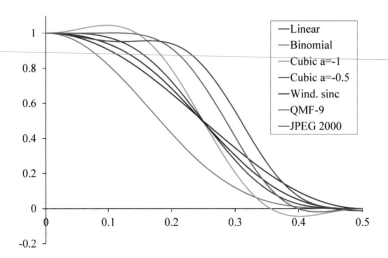

Figure 3.31 Frequency response for some 2× decimation filters. The cubic $a = -1$ filter has the sharpest fall-off but also a bit of ringing; the wavelet analysis filters (QMF-9 and JPEG 2000), while useful for compression, have more aliasing.

3.5.3 Multi-resolution representations

Now that we have described interpolation and decimation algorithms, we can build a complete image pyramid (Figure 3.32). As we mentioned before, pyramids can be used to accelerate coarse-to-fine search algorithms, to look for objects or patterns at different scales, and to perform multi-resolution blending operations. They are also widely used in computer graphics hardware and software to perform fractional-level decimation using the MIP-map, which we cover in Section 3.6.

The best known (and probably most widely used) pyramid in computer vision is Burt and Adelson's (1983a) Laplacian pyramid. To construct the pyramid, we first blur and subsample the original image by a factor of two and store this in the next level of the pyramid (Figure 3.33). Because adjacent levels in the pyramid are related by a sampling rate $r = 2$, this kind of pyramid is known as an *octave pyramid*. Burt and Adelson originally proposed a five-tap kernel of the form

$$\boxed{c} \boxed{b} \boxed{a} \boxed{b} \boxed{c} , \qquad\qquad (3.82)$$

with $b = 1/4$ and $c = 1/4 - a/2$. In practice, $a = 3/8$, which results in the familiar binomial kernel,

$$\frac{1}{16} \boxed{1} \boxed{4} \boxed{6} \boxed{4} \boxed{1} , \qquad\qquad (3.83)$$

which is particularly easy to implement using shifts and adds. (This was important in the days when multipliers were expensive.) The reason they call their resulting pyramid a *Gaussian* pyramid is that repeated convolutions of the binomial kernel converge to a Gaussian.[16]

To compute the *Laplacian* pyramid, Burt and Adelson first interpolate a lower resolution image to obtain a *reconstructed* low-pass version of the original image (Figure 3.34b). They then subtract this low-pass version from the original to yield the band-pass "Laplacian"

---

[16] Then again, this is true for any smoothing kernel (Wells 1986).

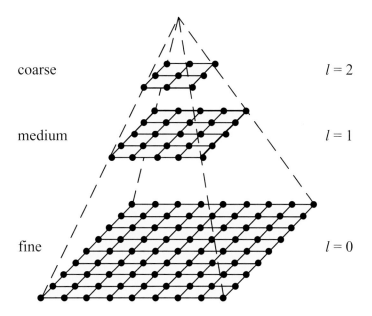

Figure 3.32 A traditional image pyramid: each level has half the resolution (width and height), and hence a quarter of the pixels, of its parent level.

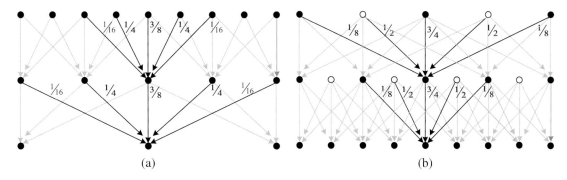

(a) (b)

Figure 3.33 The Gaussian pyramid shown as a signal processing diagram: The (a) analysis and (b) re-synthesis stages are shown as using similar computations. The white circles indicate zero values inserted by the $\uparrow 2$ upsampling operation. Notice how the reconstruction filter coefficients are twice the analysis coefficients. The computation is shown as flowing down the page, regardless of whether we are going from coarse to fine or *vice versa*.

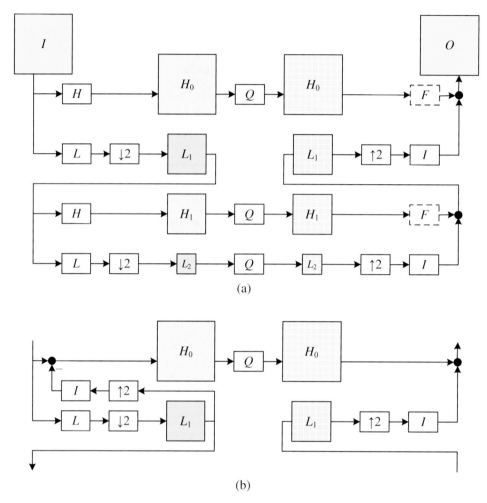

Figure 3.34 The Laplacian pyramid: (a) The conceptual flow of images through processing stages: images are high-pass and low-pass filtered, and the low-pass filtered images are processed in the next stage of the pyramid. During reconstruction, the interpolated image and the (optionally filtered) high-pass image are added back together. The Q box indicates quantization or some other pyramid processing, e.g., noise removal by *coring* (setting small wavelet values to 0). (b) The actual computation of the high-pass filter involves first interpolating the down-sampled low-pass image and then subtracting it. This results in perfect reconstruction when Q is the identity. The high-pass (or band-pass) images are typically called *Laplacian* images, while the low-pass images are called *Gaussian* images.

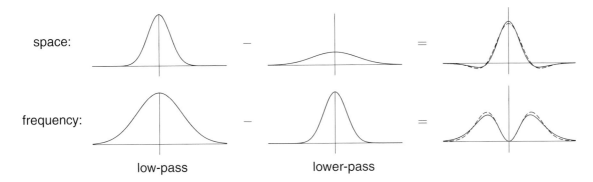

Figure 3.35 The difference of two low-pass filters results in a band-pass filter. The dashed blue lines show the close fit to a half-octave Laplacian of Gaussian.

image, which can be stored away for further processing. The resulting pyramid has *perfect reconstruction*, i.e., the Laplacian images plus the base-level Gaussian (L_2 in Figure 3.34b) are sufficient to exactly reconstruct the original image. Figure 3.33 shows the same computation in one dimension as a signal processing diagram, which completely captures the computations being performed during the analysis and re-synthesis stages.

Burt and Adelson also describe a variant on the Laplacian pyramid, where the low-pass image is taken from the original blurred image rather than the reconstructed pyramid (piping the output of the L box directly to the subtraction in Figure 3.34b). This variant has less aliasing, since it avoids one downsampling and upsampling round-trip, but it is not self-inverting, since the Laplacian images are no longer adequate to reproduce the original image.

As with the Gaussian pyramid, the term Laplacian is a bit of a misnomer, since their band-pass images are really differences of (approximate) Gaussians, or DoGs,

$$\text{DoG}\{I; \sigma_1, \sigma_2\} = G_{\sigma_1} * I - G_{\sigma_2} * I = (G_{\sigma_1} - G_{\sigma_2}) * I. \tag{3.84}$$

A Laplacian of Gaussian (which we saw in (3.26)) is actually its second derivative,

$$\text{LoG}\{I; \sigma\} = \nabla^2(G_\sigma * I) = (\nabla^2 G_\sigma) * I, \tag{3.85}$$

where

$$\nabla^2 = \frac{\partial^2}{\partial x^2} + \frac{\partial^2}{\partial y^2} \tag{3.86}$$

is the Laplacian (operator) of a function. Figure 3.35 shows how the Differences of Gaussian and Laplacians of Gaussian look in both space and frequency.

Laplacians of Gaussian have elegant mathematical properties, which have been widely studied in the *scale-space* community (Witkin 1983; Witkin, Terzopoulos, and Kass 1986; Lindeberg 1990; Nielsen, Florack, and Deriche 1997) and can be used for a variety of applications including edge detection (Marr and Hildreth 1980; Perona and Malik 1990b), stereo matching (Witkin, Terzopoulos, and Kass 1987), and image enhancement (Nielsen, Florack, and Deriche 1997).

A less widely used variant is *half-octave pyramids*, shown in Figure 3.36a. These were first introduced to the vision community by Crowley and Stern (1984), who call them *Difference of Low-Pass* (DOLP) transforms. Because of the small scale change between adja-

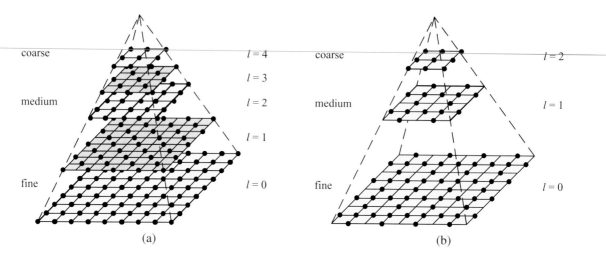

Figure 3.36 Multiresolution pyramids: (a) pyramid with half-octave (*quincunx*) sampling (odd levels are colored gray for clarity). (b) wavelet pyramid—each wavelet level stores $3/4$ of the original pixels (usually the horizontal, vertical, and mixed gradients), so that the total number of wavelet coefficients and original pixels is the same.

cent levels, the authors claim that coarse-to-fine algorithms perform better. In the image-processing community, half-octave pyramids combined with checkerboard sampling grids are known as *quincunx* sampling (Feilner, Van De Ville, and Unser 2005). In detecting multi-scale features (Section 4.1.1), it is often common to use half-octave or even quarter-octave pyramids (Lowe 2004; Triggs 2004). However, in this case, the subsampling only occurs at every octave level, i.e., the image is repeatedly blurred with wider Gaussians until a full octave of resolution change has been achieved (Figure 4.11).

3.5.4 Wavelets

While pyramids are used extensively in computer vision applications, some people use *wavelet* decompositions as an alternative. Wavelets are filters that localize a signal in both space and frequency (like the Gabor filter in Table 3.2) and are defined over a hierarchy of scales. Wavelets provide a smooth way to decompose a signal into frequency components without blocking and are closely related to pyramids.

Wavelets were originally developed in the applied math and signal processing communities and were introduced to the computer vision community by Mallat (1989). Strang (1989); Simoncelli and Adelson (1990b); Rioul and Vetterli (1991); Chui (1992); Meyer (1993) all provide nice introductions to the subject along with historical reviews, while Chui (1992) provides a more comprehensive review and survey of applications. Sweldens (1997) describes the more recent *lifting* approach to wavelets that we discuss shortly.

Wavelets are widely used in the computer graphics community to perform multi-resolution geometric processing (Stollnitz, DeRose, and Salesin 1996) and have also been used in computer vision for similar applications (Szeliski 1990b; Pentland 1994; Gortler and Cohen 1995; Yaou and Chang 1994; Lai and Vemuri 1997; Szeliski 2006b), as well as for multi-scale oriented filtering (Simoncelli, Freeman, Adelson *et al.* 1992) and denoising (Portilla, Strela, Wainwright *et al.* 2003).

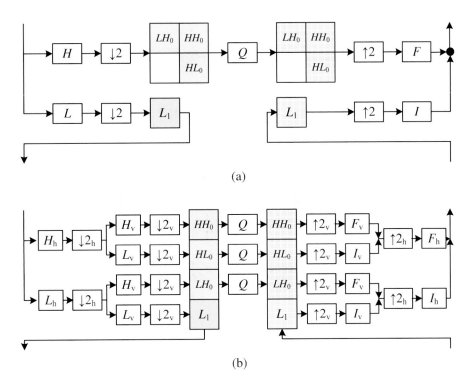

Figure 3.37 Two-dimensional wavelet decomposition: (a) high-level diagram showing the low-pass and high-pass transforms as single boxes; (b) separable implementation, which involves first performing the wavelet transform horizontally and then vertically. The I and F boxes are the interpolation and filtering boxes required to re-synthesize the image from its wavelet components.

Since both image pyramids and wavelets decompose an image into multi-resolution descriptions that are localized in both space and frequency, how do they differ? The usual answer is that traditional pyramids are *overcomplete*, i.e., they use more pixels than the original image to represent the decomposition, whereas wavelets provide a *tight frame*, i.e., they keep the size of the decomposition the same as the image (Figure 3.36b). However, some wavelet families *are*, in fact, overcomplete in order to provide better shiftability or steering in orientation (Simoncelli, Freeman, Adelson *et al.* 1992). A better distinction, therefore, might be that wavelets are more orientation selective than regular band-pass pyramids.

How are two-dimensional wavelets constructed? Figure 3.37a shows a high-level diagram of one stage of the (recursive) coarse-to-fine construction (analysis) pipeline alongside the complementary re-construction (synthesis) stage. In this diagram, the high-pass filter followed by decimation keeps $3/4$ of the original pixels, while $1/4$ of the low-frequency coefficients are passed on to the next stage for further analysis. In practice, the filtering is usually broken down into two separable sub-stages, as shown in Figure 3.37b. The resulting three wavelet images are sometimes called the high–high (HH), high–low (HL), and low–high (LH) images. The high–low and low–high images accentuate the horizontal and vertical edges and gradients, while the high–high image contains the less frequently occurring mixed derivatives.

How are the high-pass H and low-pass L filters shown in Figure 3.37b chosen and how

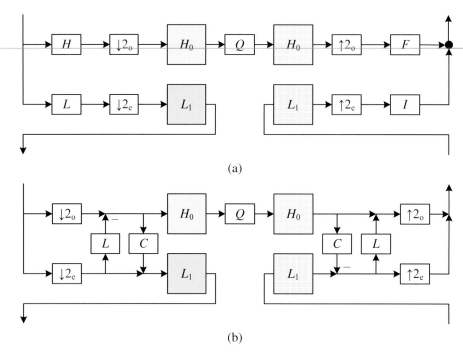

(a)

(b)

Figure 3.38 One-dimensional wavelet transform: (a) usual high-pass + low-pass filters followed by odd ($\downarrow 2_o$) and even ($\downarrow 2_e$) downsampling; (b) lifted version, which first selects the odd and even subsequences and then applies a low-pass prediction stage L and a high-pass correction stage C in an easily reversible manner.

can the corresponding reconstruction filters I and F be computed? Can filters be designed that all have finite impulse responses? This topic has been the main subject of study in the wavelet community for over two decades. The answer depends largely on the intended application, e.g., whether the wavelets are being used for compression, image analysis (feature finding), or denoising. Simoncelli and Adelson (1990b) show (in Table 4.1) some good odd-length quadrature mirror filter (QMF) coefficients that seem to work well in practice.

Since the design of wavelet filters is such a tricky art, is there perhaps a better way? Indeed, a simpler procedure is to split the signal into its even and odd components and then perform trivially reversible filtering operations on each sequence to produce what are called *lifted wavelets* (Figures 3.38 and 3.39). Sweldens (1996) gives a wonderfully understandable introduction to the *lifting scheme* for *second-generation wavelets*, followed by a comprehensive review (Sweldens 1997).

As Figure 3.38 demonstrates, rather than first filtering the whole input sequence (image) with high-pass and low-pass filters and then keeping the odd and even sub-sequences, the lifting scheme first splits the sequence into its even and odd sub-components. Filtering the even sequence with a low-pass filter L and subtracting the result from the even sequence is trivially reversible: simply perform the same filtering and then add the result back in. Furthermore, this operation can be performed in place, resulting in significant space savings. The same applies to filtering the even sequence with the correction filter C, which is used to ensure that the even sequence is low-pass. A series of such *lifting* steps can be used to create more complex filter responses with low computational cost and guaranteed reversibility.

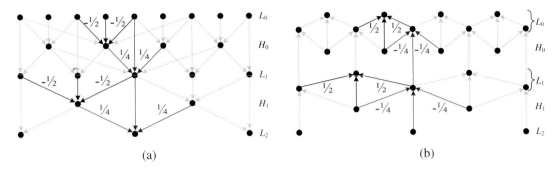

Figure 3.39 Lifted transform shown as a signal processing diagram: (a) The analysis stage first predicts the odd value from its even neighbors, stores the difference wavelet, and then compensates the coarser even value by adding in a fraction of the wavelet. (b) The synthesis stage simply reverses the flow of computation and the signs of some of the filters and operations. The light blue lines show what happens if we use four taps for the prediction and correction instead of just two.

This process can perhaps be more easily understood by considering the signal processing diagram in Figure 3.39. During analysis, the average of the even values is subtracted from the odd value to obtain a high-pass wavelet coefficient. However, the even samples still contain an aliased sample of the low-frequency signal. To compensate for this, a small amount of the high-pass wavelet is added back to the even sequence so that it is properly low-pass filtered. (It is easy to show that the effective low-pass filter is $[-\frac{1}{8}, \frac{1}{4}, \frac{3}{4}, \frac{1}{4}, -\frac{1}{8}]$, which is indeed a low-pass filter.) During synthesis, the same operations are reversed with a judicious change in sign.

Of course, we need not restrict ourselves to two-tap filters. Figure 3.39 shows as light blue arrows additional filter coefficients that could optionally be added to the lifting scheme without affecting its reversibility. In fact, the low-pass and high-pass filtering operations can be interchanged, e.g., we could use a five-tap cubic low-pass filter on the odd sequence (plus center value) first, followed by a four-tap cubic low-pass predictor to estimate the wavelet, although I have not seen this scheme written down.

Lifted wavelets are called *second-generation wavelets* because they can easily adapt to non-regular sampling topologies, e.g., those that arise in computer graphics applications such as multi-resolution surface manipulation (Schröder and Sweldens 1995). It also turns out that lifted *weighted wavelets*, i.e., wavelets whose coefficients adapt to the underlying problem being solved (Fattal 2009), can be extremely effective for low-level image manipulation tasks and also for preconditioning the kinds of sparse linear systems that arise in the optimization-based approaches to vision algorithms that we discuss in Section 3.7 (Szeliski 2006b).

An alternative to the widely used "separable" approach to wavelet construction, which decomposes each level into horizontal, vertical, and "cross" sub-bands, is to use a representation that is more rotationally symmetric and orientationally selective and also avoids the aliasing inherent in sampling signals below their Nyquist frequency.[17] Simoncelli, Freeman, Adelson *et al.* (1992) introduce such a representation, which they call a *pyramidal radial frequency implementation* of *shiftable multi-scale transforms* or, more succinctly, *steerable pyramids.*

---

[17] Such aliasing can often be seen as the signal content moving between bands as the original signal is slowly shifted.

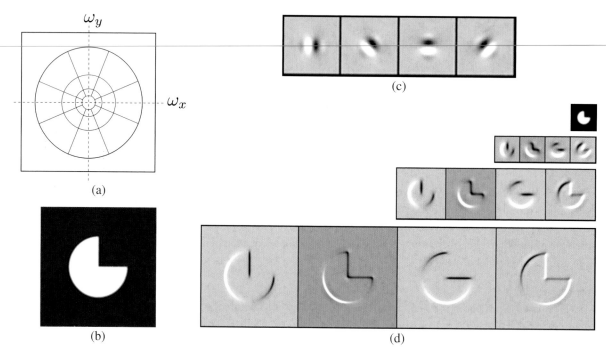

Figure 3.40 Steerable shiftable multiscale transforms (Simoncelli, Freeman, Adelson *et al.* 1992) © 1992 IEEE: (a) radial multi-scale frequency domain decomposition; (b) original image; (c) a set of four steerable filters; (d) the radial multi-scale wavelet decomposition.

Their representation is not only overcomplete (which eliminates the aliasing problem) but is also orientationally selective and has identical analysis and synthesis basis functions, i.e., it is *self-inverting*, just like "regular" wavelets. As a result, this makes steerable pyramids a much more useful basis for the structural analysis and matching tasks commonly used in computer vision.

Figure 3.40a shows how such a decomposition looks in frequency space. Instead of recursively dividing the frequency domain into 2×2 squares, which results in checkerboard high frequencies, radial arcs are used instead. Figure 3.40b illustrates the resulting pyramid sub-bands. Even through the representation is *overcomplete*, i.e., there are more wavelet coefficients than input pixels, the additional frequency and orientation selectivity makes this representation preferable for tasks such as texture analysis and synthesis (Portilla and Simoncelli 2000) and image denoising (Portilla, Strela, Wainwright *et al.* 2003; Lyu and Simoncelli 2009).

3.5.5 *Application*: Image blending

One of the most engaging and fun applications of the Laplacian pyramid presented in Section 3.5.3 is the creation of blended composite images, as shown in Figure 3.41 (Burt and Adelson 1983b). While splicing the apple and orange images together along the midline produces a noticeable cut, *splining* them together (as Burt and Adelson (1983b) called their procedure) creates a beautiful illusion of a truly hybrid fruit. The key to their approach is that the low-frequency color variations between the red apple and the orange are smoothly

(a)   (b)

(c)   (d)

Figure 3.41 Laplacian pyramid blending (Burt and Adelson 1983b) © 1983 ACM: (a) original image of apple, (b) original image of orange, (c) regular splice, (d) pyramid blend.

blended, while the higher-frequency textures on each fruit are blended more quickly to avoid "ghosting" effects when two textures are overlaid.

To create the blended image, each source image is first decomposed into its own Laplacian pyramid (Figure 3.42, left and middle columns). Each band is then multiplied by a smooth weighting function whose extent is proportional to the pyramid level. The simplest and most general way to create these weights is to take a binary mask image (Figure 3.43c) and to construct a *Gaussian* pyramid from this mask. Each Laplacian pyramid image is then multiplied by its corresponding Gaussian mask and the sum of these two weighted pyramids is then used to construct the final image (Figure 3.42, right column).

Figure 3.43 shows that this process can be applied to arbitrary mask images with surprising results. It is also straightforward to extend the pyramid blend to an arbitrary number of images whose pixel provenance is indicated by an integer-valued label image (see Exercise 3.20). This is particularly useful in image stitching and compositing applications, where the exposures may vary between different images, as described in Section 9.3.4.

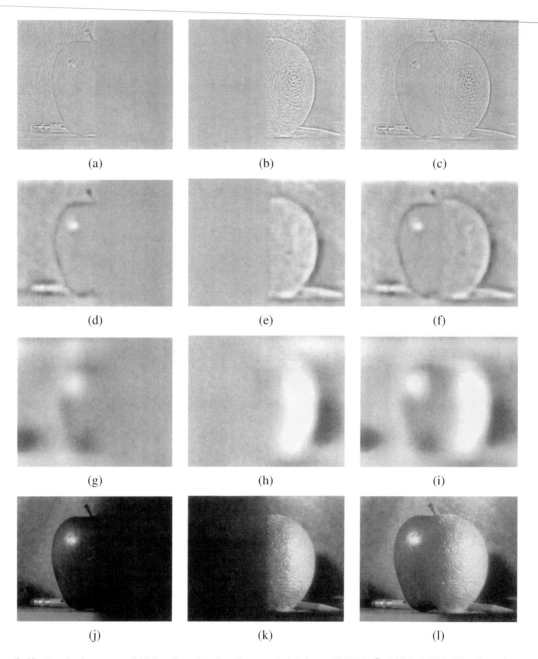

Figure 3.42 Laplacian pyramid blending details (Burt and Adelson 1983b) © 1983 ACM. The first three rows show the high, medium, and low frequency parts of the Laplacian pyramid (taken from levels 0, 2, and 4). The left and middle columns show the original apple and orange images weighted by the smooth interpolation functions, while the right column shows the averaged contributions.

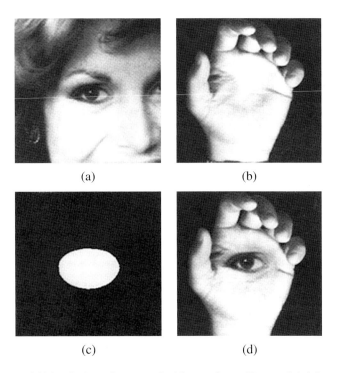

(a)   (b)

(c)   (d)

Figure 3.43 Laplacian pyramid blend of two images of arbitrary shape (Burt and Adelson 1983b) © 1983 ACM: (a) first input image; (b) second input image; (c) region mask; (d) blended image.

3.6 Geometric transformations

In the previous sections, we saw how interpolation and decimation could be used to change the *resolution* of an image. In this section, we look at how to perform more general transformations, such as image rotations or general warps. In contrast to the point processes we saw in Section 3.1, where the function applied to an image transforms the *range* of the image,

$$g(\boldsymbol{x}) = h(f(\boldsymbol{x})), \qquad (3.87)$$

here we look at functions that transform the *domain*,

$$g(\boldsymbol{x}) = f(\boldsymbol{h}(\boldsymbol{x})) \qquad (3.88)$$

(see Figure 3.44).

We begin by studying the global *parametric* 2D transformation first introduced in Section 2.1.2. (Such a transformation is called parametric because it is controlled by a small number of parameters.) We then turn our attention to more local general deformations such as those defined on meshes (Section 3.6.2). Finally, we show how image warps can be combined with cross-dissolves to create interesting *morphs* (in-between animations) in Section 3.6.3. For readers interested in more details on these topics, there is an excellent survey by Heckbert (1986) as well as very accessible textbooks by Wolberg (1990), Gomes, Darsa, Costa *et al.* (1999) and Akenine-Möller and Haines (2002). Note that Heckbert's survey is on *texture mapping*, which is how the computer graphics community refers to the topic of warping images onto surfaces.

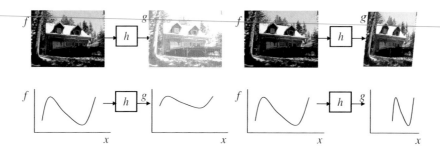

Figure 3.44 Image warping involves modifying the *domain* of an image function rather than its *range*.

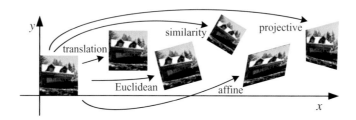

Figure 3.45 Basic set of 2D geometric image transformations.

Transformation	Matrix	# DoF	Preserves	Icon
translation	$\left[\; \boldsymbol{I} \mid \boldsymbol{t} \;\right]_{2\times 3}$	2	orientation	
rigid (Euclidean)	$\left[\; \boldsymbol{R} \mid \boldsymbol{t} \;\right]_{2\times 3}$	3	lengths	
similarity	$\left[\; s\boldsymbol{R} \mid \boldsymbol{t} \;\right]_{2\times 3}$	4	angles	
affine	$\left[\; \boldsymbol{A} \;\right]_{2\times 3}$	6	parallelism	
projective	$\left[\; \tilde{\boldsymbol{H}} \;\right]_{3\times 3}$	8	straight lines	

Table 3.5 Hierarchy of 2D coordinate transformations. Each transformation also preserves the properties listed in the rows below it, i.e., similarity preserves not only angles but also parallelism and straight lines. The 2×3 matrices are extended with a third $[\boldsymbol{0}^T\; 1]$ row to form a full 3×3 matrix for homogeneous coordinate transformations.

> **procedure** *forwardWarp*($f, h,$ **out** g):
>
> For every pixel x in $f(x)$
>
> 1. Compute the destination location $x' = h(x)$.
> 2. Copy the pixel $f(x)$ to $g(x')$.

Algorithm 3.1 Forward warping algorithm for transforming an image $f(x)$ into an image $g(x')$ through the parametric transform $x' = h(x)$.

(a)   (b)

Figure 3.46 Forward warping algorithm: (a) a pixel $f(x)$ is copied to its corresponding location $x' = h(x)$ in image $g(x')$; (b) detail of the source and destination pixel locations.

3.6.1 Parametric transformations

Parametric transformations apply a global deformation to an image, where the behavior of the transformation is controlled by a small number of parameters. Figure 3.45 shows a few examples of such transformations, which are based on the 2D geometric transformations shown in Figure 2.4. The formulas for these transformations were originally given in Table 2.1 and are reproduced here in Table 3.5 for ease of reference.

In general, given a transformation specified by a formula $x' = h(x)$ and a source image $f(x)$, how do we compute the values of the pixels in the new image $g(x)$, as given in (3.88)? Think about this for a minute before proceeding and see if you can figure it out.

If you are like most people, you will come up with an algorithm that looks something like Algorithm 3.1. This process is called *forward warping* or *forward mapping* and is shown in Figure 3.46a. Can you think of any problems with this approach?

In fact, this approach suffers from several limitations. The process of copying a pixel $f(x)$ to a location x' in g is not well defined when x' has a non-integer value. What do we do in such a case? What would you do?

You can round the value of x' to the nearest integer coordinate and copy the pixel there, but the resulting image has severe aliasing and pixels that jump around a lot when animating the transformation. You can also "distribute" the value among its four nearest neighbors in a weighted (bilinear) fashion, keeping track of the per-pixel weights and normalizing at the end. This technique is called *splatting* and is sometimes used for volume rendering in the graphics community (Levoy and Whitted 1985; Levoy 1988; Westover 1989; Rusinkiewicz and Levoy 2000). Unfortunately, it suffers from both moderate amounts of aliasing and a fair amount of blur (loss of high-resolution detail).

> **procedure** *inverseWarp*$(f, \mathbf{h}, \textbf{out } g)$:
>
>   For every pixel $\mathbf{x}'$ in $g(\mathbf{x}')$
>
>   1. Compute the source location $\mathbf{x} = \hat{\mathbf{h}}(\mathbf{x}')$
>
>   2. Resample $f(\mathbf{x})$ at location $\mathbf{x}$ and copy to $g(\mathbf{x}')$

Algorithm 3.2 Inverse warping algorithm for creating an image $g(\mathbf{x}')$ from an image $f(\mathbf{x})$ using the parametric transform $\mathbf{x}' = \mathbf{h}(\mathbf{x})$.

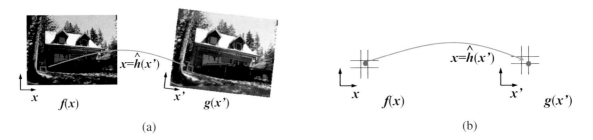

(a)   (b)

Figure 3.47 Inverse warping algorithm: (a) a pixel $g(\mathbf{x}')$ is sampled from its corresponding location $\mathbf{x} = \hat{\mathbf{h}}(\mathbf{x}')$ in image $f(\mathbf{x})$; (b) detail of the source and destination pixel locations.

The second major problem with forward warping is the appearance of cracks and holes, especially when magnifying an image. Filling such holes with their nearby neighbors can lead to further aliasing and blurring.

What can we do instead? A preferable solution is to use *inverse warping* (Algorithm 3.2), where each pixel in the destination image $g(\mathbf{x}')$ is sampled from the original image $f(\mathbf{x})$ (Figure 3.47).

How does this differ from the forward warping algorithm? For one thing, since $\hat{\mathbf{h}}(\mathbf{x}')$ is (presumably) defined for all pixels in $g(\mathbf{x}')$, we no longer have holes. More importantly, resampling an image at non-integer locations is a well-studied problem (general image interpolation, see Section 3.5.2) and high-quality filters that control aliasing can be used.

Where does the function $\hat{\mathbf{h}}(\mathbf{x}')$ come from? Quite often, it can simply be computed as the inverse of $\mathbf{h}(\mathbf{x})$. In fact, all of the parametric transforms listed in Table 3.5 have closed form solutions for the inverse transform: simply take the inverse of the 3×3 matrix specifying the transform.

In other cases, it is preferable to formulate the problem of image warping as that of re-sampling a source image $f(\mathbf{x})$ given a mapping $\mathbf{x} = \hat{\mathbf{h}}(\mathbf{x}')$ from destination pixels $\mathbf{x}'$ to source pixels $\mathbf{x}$. For example, in optical flow (Section 8.4), we estimate the flow field as the location of the *source* pixel which produced the current pixel whose flow is being estimated, as opposed to computing the *destination* pixel to which it is going. Similarly, when correcting for radial distortion (Section 2.1.6), we calibrate the lens by computing for each pixel in the final (undistorted) image the corresponding pixel location in the original (distorted) image.

What kinds of interpolation filter are suitable for the resampling process? Any of the filters we studied in Section 3.5.2 can be used, including nearest neighbor, bilinear, bicubic, and windowed sinc functions. While bilinear is often used for speed (e.g., inside the inner loop of a patch-tracking algorithm, see Section 8.1.3), bicubic, and windowed sinc are preferable where visual quality is important.

To compute the value of $f(\boldsymbol{x})$ at a non-integer location $\boldsymbol{x}$, we simply apply our usual FIR resampling filter,

$$g(x, y) = \sum_{k,l} f(k,l) h(x - k, y - l), \tag{3.89}$$

where (x, y) are the sub-pixel coordinate values and $h(x, y)$ is some interpolating or smoothing kernel. Recall from Section 3.5.2 that when decimation is being performed, the smoothing kernel is stretched and re-scaled according to the downsampling rate r.

Unfortunately, for a general (non-zoom) image transformation, the resampling rate r is not well defined. Consider a transformation that stretches the x dimensions while squashing the y dimensions. The resampling kernel should be performing regular interpolation along the x dimension and smoothing (to anti-alias the blurred image) in the y direction. This gets even more complicated for the case of general affine or perspective transforms.

What can we do? Fortunately, Fourier analysis can help. The two-dimensional generalization of the one-dimensional *domain scaling* law given in Table 3.1 is

$$g(\boldsymbol{A}\boldsymbol{x}) \Leftrightarrow |\boldsymbol{A}|^{-1} G(\boldsymbol{A}^{-T} \boldsymbol{f}). \tag{3.90}$$

For all of the transforms in Table 3.5 except perspective, the matrix $\boldsymbol{A}$ is already defined. For perspective transformations, the matrix $\boldsymbol{A}$ is the linearized *derivative* of the perspective transformation (Figure 3.48a), i.e., the local affine approximation to the stretching induced by the projection (Heckbert 1986; Wolberg 1990; Gomes, Darsa, Costa *et al.* 1999; Akenine-Möller and Haines 2002).

To prevent aliasing, we need to pre-filter the image $f(\boldsymbol{x})$ with a filter whose frequency response is the projection of the final desired spectrum through the $\boldsymbol{A}^{-T}$ transform (Szeliski, Winder, and Uyttendaele 2010). In general (for non-zoom transforms), this filter is non-separable and hence is very slow to compute. Therefore, a number of approximations to this filter are used in practice, include MIP-mapping, elliptically weighted Gaussian averaging, and anisotropic filtering (Akenine-Möller and Haines 2002).

MIP-mapping

MIP-mapping was first proposed by Williams (1983) as a means to rapidly pre-filter images being used for *texture mapping* in computer graphics. A MIP-map[18] is a standard image pyramid (Figure 3.32), where each level is pre-filtered with a high-quality filter rather than a poorer quality approximation, such as Burt and Adelson's (1983b) five-tap binomial. To resample an image from a MIP-map, a scalar estimate of the resampling rate r is first computed. For example, r can be the maximum of the absolute values in $\boldsymbol{A}$ (which suppresses aliasing) or it can be the minimum (which reduces blurring). Akenine-Möller and Haines (2002) discuss these issues in more detail.

Once a resampling rate has been specified, a *fractional* pyramid level is computed using the base 2 logarithm,

$$l = \log_2 r. \tag{3.91}$$

---

[18] The term 'MIP' stands for *multi in parvo*, meaning 'many in one'.

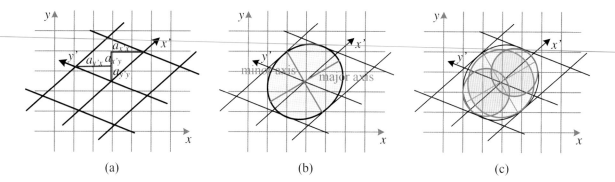

Figure 3.48 Anisotropic texture filtering: (a) Jacobian of transform A and the induced horizontal and vertical resampling rates $\{a_{x'x}, a_{x'y}, a_{y'x}, a_{y'y}\}$; (b) elliptical footprint of an EWA smoothing kernel; (c) anisotropic filtering using multiple samples along the major axis. Image pixels lie at line intersections.

One simple solution is to resample the texture from the next higher or lower pyramid level, depending on whether it is preferable to reduce aliasing or blur. A better solution is to resample *both* images and blend them linearly using the fractional component of l. Since most MIP-map implementations use bilinear resampling within each level, this approach is usually called *trilinear MIP-mapping*. Computer graphics rendering APIs, such as OpenGL and Direct3D, have parameters that can be used to select which variant of MIP-mapping (and of the sampling rate r computation) should be used, depending on the desired tradeoff between speed and quality. Exercise 3.22 has you examine some of these tradeoffs in more detail.

Elliptical Weighted Average

The Elliptical Weighted Average (EWA) filter invented by Greene and Heckbert (1986) is based on the observation that the affine mapping $x = Ax'$ defines a skewed two-dimensional coordinate system in the vicinity of each source pixel x (Figure 3.48a). For every destination pixel x', the ellipsoidal projection of a small pixel grid in x' onto x is computed (Figure 3.48b). This is then used to filter the source image $g(x)$ with a Gaussian whose inverse covariance matrix is this ellipsoid.

Despite its reputation as a high-quality filter (Akenine-Möller and Haines 2002), we have found in our work (Szeliski, Winder, and Uyttendaele 2010) that because a Gaussian kernel is used, the technique suffers simultaneously from both blurring and aliasing, compared to higher-quality filters. The EWA is also quite slow, although faster variants based on MIP-mapping have been proposed (Szeliski, Winder, and Uyttendaele (2010) provide some additional references).

Anisotropic filtering

An alternative approach to filtering oriented textures, which is sometimes implemented in graphics hardware (GPUs), is to use anisotropic filtering (Barkans 1997; Akenine-Möller and Haines 2002). In this approach, several samples at different resolutions (fractional levels in the MIP-map) are combined along the major axis of the EWA Gaussian (Figure 3.48c).

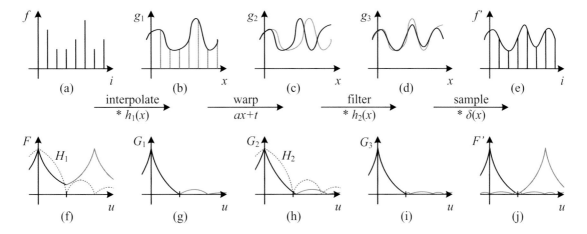

Figure 3.49 One-dimensional signal resampling (Szeliski, Winder, and Uyttendaele 2010): (a) original sampled signal $f(i)$; (b) interpolated signal $g_1(x)$; (c) warped signal $g_2(x)$; (d) filtered signal $g_3(x)$; (e) sampled signal $f'(i)$. The corresponding spectra are shown below the signals, with the aliased portions shown in red.

Multi-pass transforms

The optimal approach to warping images without excessive blurring or aliasing is to adaptively pre-filter the source image at each pixel using an ideal low-pass filter, i.e., an oriented skewed sinc or low-order (e.g., cubic) approximation (Figure 3.48a). Figure 3.49 shows how this works in one dimension. The signal is first (theoretically) interpolated to a continuous waveform, (ideally) low-pass filtered to below the new Nyquist rate, and then re-sampled to the final desired resolution. In practice, the interpolation and decimation steps are concatenated into a single *polyphase* digital filtering operation (Szeliski, Winder, and Uyttendaele 2010).

For parametric transforms, the oriented two-dimensional filtering and resampling operations can be approximated using a series of one-dimensional resampling and shearing transforms (Catmull and Smith 1980; Heckbert 1989; Wolberg 1990; Gomes, Darsa, Costa *et al.* 1999; Szeliski, Winder, and Uyttendaele 2010). The advantage of using a series of one-dimensional transforms is that they are much more efficient (in terms of basic arithmetic operations) than large, non-separable, two-dimensional filter kernels.

In order to prevent aliasing, however, it may be necessary to upsample in the opposite direction before applying a shearing transformation (Szeliski, Winder, and Uyttendaele 2010). Figure 3.50 shows this process for a rotation, where a vertical upsampling stage is added before the horizontal shearing (and upsampling) stage. The upper image shows the appearance of the letter being rotated, while the lower image shows its corresponding Fourier transform.

3.6.2 Mesh-based warping

While parametric transforms specified by a small number of global parameters have many uses, *local* deformations with more degrees of freedom are often required.

Consider, for example, changing the appearance of a face from a frown to a smile (Figure 3.51a). What is needed in this case is to curve the corners of the mouth upwards while

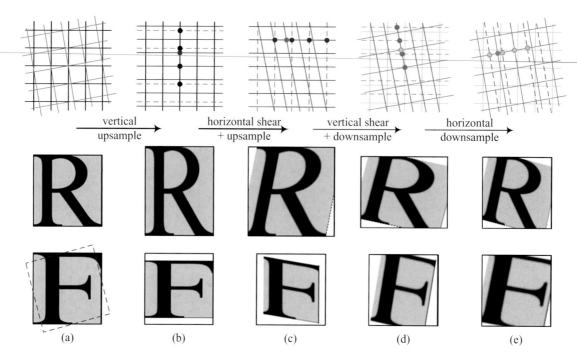

Figure 3.50 Four-pass rotation (Szeliski, Winder, and Uyttendaele 2010): (a) original pixel grid, image, and its Fourier transform; (b) vertical upsampling; (c) horizontal shear and upsampling; (d) vertical shear and downsampling; (e) horizontal downsampling. The general affine case looks similar except that the first two stages perform general resampling.

leaving the rest of the face intact.[19] To perform such a transformation, different amounts of motion are required in different parts of the image. Figure 3.51 shows some of the commonly used approaches.

The first approach, shown in Figure 3.51a–b, is to specify a *sparse* set of corresponding points. The displacement of these points can then be interpolated to a dense *displacement field* (Chapter 8) using a variety of techniques (Nielson 1993). One possibility is to *triangulate* the set of points in one image (de Berg, Cheong, van Kreveld *et al.* 2006; Litwinowicz and Williams 1994; Buck, Finkelstein, Jacobs *et al.* 2000) and to use an *affine* motion model (Table 3.5), specified by the three triangle vertices, inside each triangle. If the destination image is triangulated according to the new vertex locations, an inverse warping algorithm (Figure 3.47) can be used. If the source image is triangulated and used as a *texture map*, computer graphics rendering algorithms can be used to draw the new image (but care must be taken along triangle edges to avoid potential aliasing).

Alternative methods for interpolating a sparse set of displacements include moving nearby quadrilateral mesh vertices, as shown in Figure 3.51a, using *variational* (energy minimizing) interpolants such as regularization (Litwinowicz and Williams 1994), see Section 3.7.1, or using locally weighted (*radial basis function*) combinations of displacements (Nielson 1993). (See (Section 12.3.1) for additional *scattered data interpolation* techniques.) If quadrilateral

---

[19] Rowland and Perrett (1995); Pighin, Hecker, Lischinski *et al.* (1998); Blanz and Vetter (1999); Leyvand, Cohen-Or, Dror *et al.* (2008) show more sophisticated examples of changing facial expression and appearance.

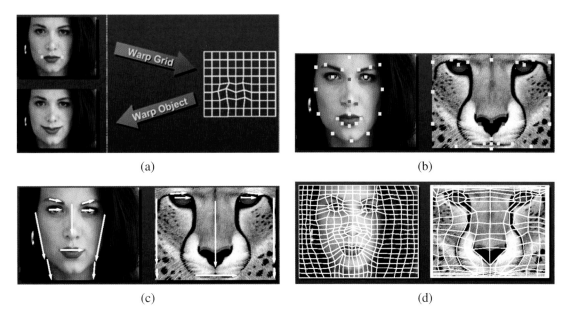

(a)   (b)

(c)   (d)

Figure 3.51 Image warping alternatives (Gomes, Darsa, Costa *et al.* 1999) © 1999 Morgan Kaufmann: (a) sparse control points ⟶ deformation grid; (b) denser set of control point correspondences; (c) oriented line correspondences; (d) uniform quadrilateral grid.

meshes are used, it may be desirable to interpolate displacements down to individual pixel values using a smooth interpolant such as a quadratic B-spline (Farin 1996; Lee, Wolberg, Chwa *et al.* 1996).[20]

In some cases, e.g., if a dense depth map has been estimated for an image (Shade, Gortler, He *et al.* 1998), we only know the forward displacement for each pixel. As mentioned before, drawing source pixels at their destination location, i.e., forward warping (Figure 3.46), suffers from several potential problems, including aliasing and the appearance of small cracks. An alternative technique in this case is to forward warp the *displacement field* (or depth map) to its new location, fill small holes in the resulting map, and then use inverse warping to perform the resampling (Shade, Gortler, He *et al.* 1998). The reason that this generally works better than forward warping is that displacement fields tend to be much smoother than images, so the aliasing introduced during the forward warping of the displacement field is much less noticeable.

A second approach to specifying displacements for local deformations is to use corresponding *oriented line segments* (Beier and Neely 1992), as shown in Figures 3.51c and 3.52. Pixels along each line segment are transferred from source to destination exactly as specified, and other pixels are warped using a smooth interpolation of these displacements. Each line segment correspondence specifies a translation, rotation, and scaling, i.e., a *similarity transform* (Table 3.5), for pixels in its vicinity, as shown in Figure 3.52a. Line segments influence the overall displacement of the image using a weighting function that depends on the minimum distance to the line segment (v in Figure 3.52a if $u \in [0, 1]$, else the shorter of the two

---

[20] Note that the *block-based* motion models used by many video compression standards (Le Gall 1991) can be thought of as a 0th-order (piecewise-constant) displacement field.

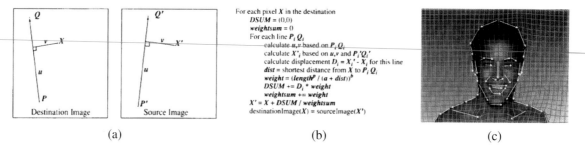

Figure 3.52 Line-based image warping (Beier and Neely 1992) © 1992 ACM: (a) distance computation and position transfer; (b) rendering algorithm; (c) two intermediate warps used for morphing.

distances to P and Q).

For each pixel X, the target location X' for each line correspondence is computed along with a weight that depends on the distance and the line segment length (Figure 3.52b). The weighted average of all target locations X'_i then becomes the final destination location. Note that while Beier and Neely describe this algorithm as a forward warp, an equivalent algorithm can be written by sequencing through the destination pixels. The resulting warps are not identical because line lengths or distances to lines may be different. Exercise 3.23 has you implement the Beier–Neely (line-based) warp and compare it to a number of other local deformation methods.

Yet another way of specifying correspondences in order to create image warps is to use snakes (Section 5.1.1) combined with B-splines (Lee, Wolberg, Chwa *et al.* 1996). This technique is used in Apple's Shake software and is popular in the medical imaging community.

One final possibility for specifying displacement fields is to use a mesh specifically *adapted* to the underlying image content, as shown in Figure 3.51d. Specifying such meshes by hand can involve a fair amount of work; Gomes, Darsa, Costa *et al.* (1999) describe an interactive system for doing this. Once the two meshes have been specified, intermediate warps can be generated using linear interpolation and the displacements at mesh nodes can be interpolated using splines.

3.6.3 *Application*: Feature-based morphing

While warps can be used to change the appearance of or to animate a *single* image, even more powerful effects can be obtained by warping and blending two or more images using a process now commonly known as *morphing* (Beier and Neely 1992; Lee, Wolberg, Chwa *et al.* 1996; Gomes, Darsa, Costa *et al.* 1999).

Figure 3.53 shows the essence of image morphing. Instead of simply cross-dissolving between two images, which leads to ghosting as shown in the top row, each image is warped toward the other image before blending, as shown in the bottom row. If the correspondences have been set up well (using any of the techniques shown in Figure 3.51), corresponding features are aligned and no ghosting results.

The above process is repeated for each intermediate frame being generated during a morph, using different blends (and amounts of deformation) at each interval. Let $t \in [0, 1]$ be

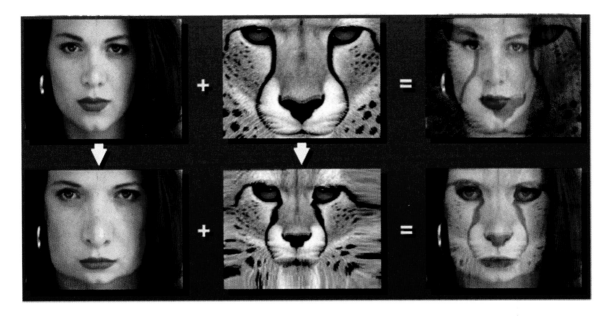

Figure 3.53 Image morphing (Gomes, Darsa, Costa *et al.* 1999) © 1999 Morgan Kaufmann. Top row: if the two images are just blended, visible ghosting results. Bottom row: both images are first warped to the same intermediate location (e.g., halfway towards the other image) and the resulting warped images are then blended resulting in a seamless morph.

the time parameter that describes the sequence of interpolated frames. The weighting functions for the two warped images in the blend go as $(1 - t)$ and t. Conversely, the amount of motion that image 0 undergoes at time t is t of the total amount of motion that is specified by the correspondences. However, some care must be taken in defining what it means to partially warp an image towards a destination, especially if the desired motion is far from linear (Sederberg, Gao, Wang *et al.* 1993). Exercise 3.25 has you implement a morphing algorithm and test it out under such challenging conditions.

3.7 Global optimization

So far in this chapter, we have covered a large number of image processing operators that take as input one or more images and produce some filtered or transformed version of these images. In many applications, it is more useful to first *formulate* the goals of the desired transformation using some optimization criterion and then find or infer the solution that best meets this criterion.

In this final section, we present two different (but closely related) variants on this idea. The first, which is often called *regularization* or *variational methods* (Section 3.7.1), constructs a continuous global energy function that describes the desired characteristics of the solution and then finds a minimum energy solution using sparse linear systems or related iterative techniques. The second formulates the problem using Bayesian statistics, modeling both the noisy measurement process that produced the input images as well as *prior assumptions* about the solution space, which are often encoded using a *Markov random field*

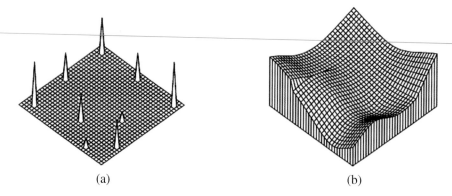

(a)   (b)

Figure 3.54 A simple surface interpolation problem: (a) nine data points of various height scattered on a grid; (b) second-order, controlled-continuity, thin-plate spline interpolator, with a tear along its left edge and a crease along its right (Szeliski 1989) © 1989 Springer.

(Section 3.7.2).

Examples of such problems include surface interpolation from scattered data (Figure 3.54), image denoising and the restoration of missing regions (Figure 3.57), and the segmentation of images into foreground and background regions (Figure 3.61).

3.7.1 Regularization

The theory of regularization was first developed by statisticians trying to fit models to data that severely underconstrained the solution space (Tikhonov and Arsenin 1977; Engl, Hanke, and Neubauer 1996). Consider, for example, finding a smooth surface that passes through (or near) a set of measured data points (Figure 3.54). Such a problem is described as *ill-posed* because many possible surfaces can fit this data. Since small changes in the input can sometimes lead to large changes in the fit (e.g., if we use polynomial interpolation), such problems are also often *ill-conditioned*. Since we are trying to recover the unknown function $f(x, y)$ from which the data point $d(x_i, y_i)$ were sampled, such problems are also often called *inverse problems*. Many computer vision tasks can be viewed as inverse problems, since we are trying to recover a full description of the 3D world from a limited set of images.

In order to quantify what it means to find a *smooth* solution, we can define a norm on the solution space. For one-dimensional functions $f(x)$, we can integrate the squared first derivative of the function,

$$\mathcal{E}_1 = \int f_x^2(x) \, dx \qquad (3.92)$$

or perhaps integrate the squared second derivative,

$$\mathcal{E}_2 = \int f_{xx}^2(x) \, dx. \qquad (3.93)$$

(Here, we use subscripts to denote differentiation.) Such energy measures are examples of *functionals*, which are operators that map functions to scalar values. They are also often called *variational methods*, because they measure the variation (non-smoothness) in a function.

In two dimensions (e.g., for images, flow fields, or surfaces), the corresponding smoothness functionals are

$$\mathcal{E}_1 = \int f_x^2(x,y) + f_y^2(x,y)\,dx\,dy = \int \|\nabla f(x,y)\|^2\,dx\,dy \qquad (3.94)$$

and

$$\mathcal{E}_2 = \int f_{xx}^2(x,y) + 2f_{xy}^2(x,y) + f_{yy}^2(x,y)\,dx\,dy, \qquad (3.95)$$

where the mixed $2f_{xy}^2$ term is needed to make the measure rotationally invariant (Grimson 1983).

The first derivative norm is often called the *membrane*, since interpolating a set of data points using this measure results in a tent-like structure. (In fact, this formula is a small-deflection approximation to the surface area, which is what soap bubbles minimize.) The second-order norm is called the *thin-plate spline*, since it approximates the behavior of thin plates (e.g., flexible steel) under small deformations. A blend of the two is called the *thin-plate spline under tension*; versions of these formulas where each derivative term is multiplied by a local weighting function are called *controlled-continuity splines* (Terzopoulos 1988). Figure 3.54 shows a simple example of a controlled-continuity interpolator fit to nine scattered data points. In practice, it is more common to find first-order smoothness terms used with images and flow fields (Section 8.4) and second-order smoothness associated with surfaces (Section 12.3.1).

In addition to the smoothness term, regularization also requires a data term (or *data penalty*). For scattered data interpolation (Nielson 1993), the data term measures the distance between the function $f(x,y)$ and a set of data points $d_i = d(x_i, y_i)$,

$$\mathcal{E}_d = \sum_i [f(x_i,y_i) - d_i]^2. \qquad (3.96)$$

For a problem like noise removal, a continuous version of this measure can be used,

$$\mathcal{E}_d = \int [f(x,y) - d(x,y)]^2\,dx\,dy. \qquad (3.97)$$

To obtain a global energy that can be minimized, the two energy terms are usually added together,

$$\mathcal{E} = \mathcal{E}_d + \lambda \mathcal{E}_s, \qquad (3.98)$$

where $\mathcal{E}_s$ is the *smoothness penalty* ($\mathcal{E}_1$, $\mathcal{E}_2$ or some weighted blend) and λ is the *regularization parameter*, which controls how smooth the solution should be.

In order to find the minimum of this continuous problem, the function $f(x,y)$ is usually first discretized on a regular grid.[21] The most principled way to perform this discretization is to use *finite element analysis*, i.e., to approximate the function with a piecewise continuous spline, and then perform the analytic integration (Bathe 2007).

Fortunately, for both the first-order and second-order smoothness functionals, the judicious selection of appropriate finite elements results in particularly simple discrete forms

---

[21] The alternative of using *kernel basis functions* centered on the data points (Boult and Kender 1986; Nielson 1993) is discussed in more detail in Section 12.3.1.

(Terzopoulos 1983). The corresponding *discrete* smoothness energy functions become

$$E_1 = \sum_{i,j} s_x(i,j)[f(i+1,j) - f(i,j) - g_x(i,j)]^2 \tag{3.99}$$
$$+ s_y(i,j)[f(i,j+1) - f(i,j) - g_y(i,j)]^2$$

and

$$E_2 = h^{-2} \sum_{i,j} c_x(i,j)[f(i+1,j) - 2f(i,j) + f(i-1,j)]^2 \tag{3.100}$$
$$+ 2c_m(i,j)[f(i+1,j+1) - f(i+1,j) - f(i,j+1) + f(i,j)]^2$$
$$+ c_y(i,j)[f(i,j+1) - 2f(i,j) + f(i,j-1)]^2,$$

where h is the size of the finite element grid. The h factor is only important if the energy is being discretized at a variety of resolutions, as in coarse-to-fine or multigrid techniques.

The optional smoothness weights $s_x(i,j)$ and $s_y(i,j)$ control the location of horizontal and vertical tears (or weaknesses) in the surface. For other problems, such as colorization (Levin, Lischinski, and Weiss 2004) and interactive tone mapping (Lischinski, Farbman, Uyttendaele *et al.* 2006a), they control the smoothness in the interpolated chroma or exposure field and are often set inversely proportional to the local luminance gradient strength. For second-order problems, the crease variables $c_x(i,j)$, $c_m(i,j)$, and $c_y(i,j)$ control the locations of creases in the surface (Terzopoulos 1988; Szeliski 1990a).

The data values $g_x(i,j)$ and $g_y(i,j)$ are gradient data terms (constraints) used by algorithms, such as photometric stereo (Section 12.1.1), HDR tone mapping (Section 10.2.1) (Fattal, Lischinski, and Werman 2002), Poisson blending (Section 9.3.4) (Pérez, Gangnet, and Blake 2003), and gradient-domain blending (Section 9.3.4) (Levin, Zomet, Peleg *et al.* 2004). They are set to zero when just discretizing the conventional first-order smoothness functional (3.94).

The two-dimensional discrete data energy is written as

$$E_d = \sum_{i,j} w(i,j)[f(i,j) - d(i,j)]^2, \tag{3.101}$$

where the local weights $w(i,j)$ control how strongly the data constraint is enforced. These values are set to zero where there is no data and can be set to the inverse variance of the data measurements when there is data (as discussed by Szeliski (1989) and in Section 3.7.2).

The total energy of the discretized problem can now be written as a *quadratic form*

$$E = E_d + \lambda E_s = \boldsymbol{x}^T \boldsymbol{A} \boldsymbol{x} - 2\boldsymbol{x}^T \boldsymbol{b} + c, \tag{3.102}$$

where $\boldsymbol{x} = [f(0,0) \dots f(m-1, n-1)]$ is called the *state vector*.[22]

The sparse symmetric positive-definite matrix $\boldsymbol{A}$ is called the *Hessian* since it encodes the second derivative of the energy function.[23] For the one-dimensional, first-order problem, $\boldsymbol{A}$

---

[22] We use $\boldsymbol{x}$ instead of $\boldsymbol{f}$ because this is the more common form in the numerical analysis literature (Golub and Van Loan 1996).

[23] In numerical analysis, $\boldsymbol{A}$ is called the *coefficient* matrix (Saad 2003); in finite element analysis (Bathe 2007), it is called the *stiffness* matrix.

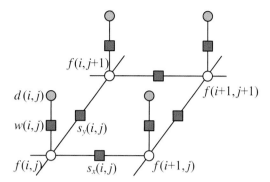

Figure 3.55   Graphical model interpretation of first-order regularization. The white circles are the unknowns $f(i,j)$ while the dark circles are the input data $d(i,j)$. In the resistive grid interpretation, the d and f values encode input and output voltages and the black squares denote resistors whose *conductance* is set to $s_x(i,j)$, $s_y(i,j)$, and $w(i,j)$. In the spring-mass system analogy, the circles denote elevations and the black squares denote springs. The same graphical model can be used to depict a first-order Markov random field (Figure 3.56).

is tridiagonal; for the two-dimensional, first-order problem, it is multi-banded with five non-zero entries per row. We call b the *weighted data vector*. Minimizing the above quadratic form is equivalent to solving the sparse linear system

$$Ax = b, \qquad\qquad (3.103)$$

which can be done using a variety of sparse matrix techniques, such as multigrid (Briggs, Henson, and McCormick 2000) and hierarchical preconditioners (Szeliski 2006b), as described in Appendix A.5.

While regularization was first introduced to the vision community by Poggio, Torre, and Koch (1985) and Terzopoulos (1986b) for problems such as surface interpolation, it was quickly adopted by other vision researchers for such varied problems as edge detection (Section 4.2), optical flow (Section 8.4), and shape from shading (Section 12.1) (Poggio, Torre, and Koch 1985; Horn and Brooks 1986; Terzopoulos 1986b; Bertero, Poggio, and Torre 1988; Brox, Bruhn, Papenberg *et al.* 2004). Poggio, Torre, and Koch (1985) also showed how the discrete energy defined by Equations (3.100–3.101) could be implemented in a resistive grid, as shown in Figure 3.55. In computational photography (Chapter 10), regularization and its variants are commonly used to solve problems such as high-dynamic range tone mapping (Fattal, Lischinski, and Werman 2002; Lischinski, Farbman, Uyttendaele *et al.* 2006a), Poisson and gradient-domain blending (Pérez, Gangnet, and Blake 2003; Levin, Zomet, Peleg *et al.* 2004; Agarwala, Dontcheva, Agrawala *et al.* 2004), colorization (Levin, Lischinski, and Weiss 2004), and natural image matting (Levin, Lischinski, and Weiss 2008).

Robust regularization

While regularization is most commonly formulated using quadratic (L_2) norms (compare with the squared derivatives in (3.92–3.95) and squared differences in (3.100–3.101)), it can also be formulated using non-quadratic *robust* penalty functions (Appendix B.3). For example, (3.100) can be generalized to

$$E_{1r} = \sum_{i,j} s_x(i,j)\rho(f(i+1,j) - f(i,j)) \tag{3.104}$$

$$+ s_y(i,j)\rho(f(i,j+1) - f(i,j)),$$

where $\rho(x)$ is some monotonically increasing penalty function. For example, the family of norms $\rho(x) = |x|^p$ is called p-norms. When $p < 2$, the resulting smoothness terms become more piecewise continuous than totally smooth, which can better model the discontinuous nature of images, flow fields, and 3D surfaces.

An early example of robust regularization is the *graduated non-convexity* (GNC) algorithm introduced by Blake and Zisserman (1987). Here, the norms on the data and derivatives are clamped to a maximum value

$$\rho(x) = \min(x^2, V). \tag{3.105}$$

Because the resulting problem is highly non-convex (it has many local minima), a *continuation* method is proposed, where a quadratic norm (which is convex) is gradually replaced by the non-convex robust norm (Allgower and Georg 2003). (Around the same time, Terzopoulos (1988) was also using continuation to infer the tear and crease variables in his surface interpolation problems.)

Today, it is more common to use the L_1 ($p = 1$) norm, which is often called *total variation* (Chan, Osher, and Shen 2001; Tschumperlé and Deriche 2005; Tschumperlé 2006; Kaftory, Schechner, and Zeevi 2007). Other norms, for which the *influence* (derivative) more quickly decays to zero, are presented by Black and Rangarajan (1996); Black, Sapiro, Marimont *et al.* (1998) and discussed in Appendix B.3.

Even more recently, *hyper-Laplacian* norms with $p < 1$ have gained popularity, based on the observation that the log-likelihood distribution of image derivatives follows a $p \approx 0.5 - 0.8$ slope and is therefore a hyper-Laplacian distribution (Simoncelli 1999; Levin and Weiss 2007; Weiss and Freeman 2007; Krishnan and Fergus 2009). Such norms have an even stronger tendency to prefer large discontinuities over small ones. See the related discussion in Section 3.7.2 (3.114).

While least squares regularized problems using L_2 norms can be solved using linear systems, other p-norms require different iterative techniques, such as iteratively reweighted least squares (IRLS), Levenberg–Marquardt, or alternation between local non-linear subproblems and global quadratic regularization (Krishnan and Fergus 2009). Such techniques are discussed in Section 6.1.3 and Appendices A.3 and B.3.

3.7.2 Markov random fields

As we have just seen, regularization, which involves the minimization of energy functionals defined over (piecewise) continuous functions, can be used to formulate and solve a variety of low-level computer vision problems. An alternative technique is to formulate a *Bayesian* model, which separately models the noisy image formation (*measurement*) process, as well as assuming a statistical *prior* model over the solution space. In this section, we look at priors based on Markov random fields, whose log-likelihood can be described using local neighborhood interaction (or penalty) terms (Kindermann and Snell 1980; Geman and Geman 1984; Marroquin, Mitter, and Poggio 1987; Li 1995; Szeliski, Zabih, Scharstein *et al.* 2008).

The use of Bayesian modeling has several potential advantages over regularization (see also Appendix B). The ability to model measurement processes statistically enables us to extract the maximum information possible from each measurement, rather than just guessing what weighting to give the data. Similarly, the parameters of the prior distribution can often be *learned* by observing samples from the class we are modeling (Roth and Black 2007a; Tappen 2007; Li and Huttenlocher 2008). Furthermore, because our model is probabilistic, it is possible to estimate (in principle) complete probability *distributions* over the unknowns being recovered and, in particular, to model the *uncertainty* in the solution, which can be useful in latter processing stages. Finally, Markov random field models can be defined over *discrete* variables, such as image labels (where the variables have no proper ordering), for which regularization does not apply.

Recall from (3.68) in Section 3.4.3 (or see Appendix B.4) that, according to Bayes' Rule, the *posterior* distribution for a given set of measurements $\boldsymbol{y}$, $p(\boldsymbol{y}|\boldsymbol{x})$, combined with a prior $p(\boldsymbol{x})$ over the unknowns $\boldsymbol{x}$, is given by

$$p(\boldsymbol{x}|\boldsymbol{y}) = \frac{p(\boldsymbol{y}|\boldsymbol{x})p(\boldsymbol{x})}{p(\boldsymbol{y})}, \tag{3.106}$$

where $p(\boldsymbol{y}) = \int_{\boldsymbol{x}} p(\boldsymbol{y}|\boldsymbol{x})p(\boldsymbol{x})$ is a normalizing constant used to make the $p(\boldsymbol{x}|\boldsymbol{y})$ distribution *proper* (integrate to 1). Taking the negative logarithm of both sides of (3.106), we get

$$-\log p(\boldsymbol{x}|\boldsymbol{y}) = -\log p(\boldsymbol{y}|\boldsymbol{x}) - \log p(\boldsymbol{x}) + C, \tag{3.107}$$

which is the *negative posterior log likelihood*.

To find the most likely (*maximum a posteriori* or MAP) solution $\boldsymbol{x}$ given some measurements $\boldsymbol{y}$, we simply minimize this negative log likelihood, which can also be thought of as an *energy*,

$$E(\boldsymbol{x}, \boldsymbol{y}) = E_d(\boldsymbol{x}, \boldsymbol{y}) + E_p(\boldsymbol{x}). \tag{3.108}$$

(We drop the constant C because its value does not matter during energy minimization.) The first term $E_d(\boldsymbol{x}, \boldsymbol{y})$ is the *data energy* or *data penalty*; it measures the negative log likelihood that the data were observed given the unknown state $\boldsymbol{x}$. The second term $E_p(\boldsymbol{x})$ is the *prior energy*; it plays a role analogous to the smoothness energy in regularization. Note that the MAP estimate may not always be desirable, since it selects the "peak" in the posterior distribution rather than some more stable statistic—see the discussion in Appendix B.2 and by Levin, Weiss, Durand *et al.* (2009).

For image processing applications, the unknowns $\boldsymbol{x}$ are the set of output pixels

$$\boldsymbol{x} = [f(0,0) \ldots f(m-1, n-1)],$$

and the data are (in the simplest case) the input pixels

$$\boldsymbol{y} = [d(0,0) \ldots d(m-1, n-1)]$$

as shown in Figure 3.56.

For a Markov random field, the probability $p(\boldsymbol{x})$ is a *Gibbs* or *Boltzmann distribution*, whose negative log likelihood (according to the Hammersley–Clifford theorem) can be written as a sum of pairwise interaction potentials,

$$E_p(\boldsymbol{x}) = \sum_{\{(i,j),(k,l)\}\in\mathcal{N}} V_{i,j,k,l}(f(i,j), f(k,l)), \tag{3.109}$$

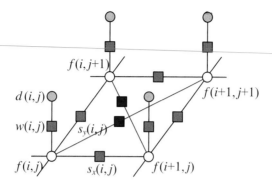

Figure 3.56   Graphical model for an $\mathcal{N}_4$ neighborhood Markov random field. (The blue edges are added for an $\mathcal{N}_8$ neighborhood.) The white circles are the unknowns $f(i,j)$, while the dark circles are the input data $d(i,j)$. The $s_x(i,j)$ and $s_y(i,j)$ black boxes denote arbitrary *interaction potentials* between adjacent nodes in the random field, and the $w(i,j)$ denote the *data penalty* functions. The same graphical model can be used to depict a discrete version of a first-order regularization problem (Figure 3.55).

where $\mathcal{N}(i,j)$ denotes the *neighbors* of pixel (i,j). In fact, the general version of the theorem says that the energy may have to be evaluated over a larger set of *cliques*, which depend on the *order* of the Markov random field (Kindermann and Snell 1980; Geman and Geman 1984; Bishop 2006; Kohli, Ladický, and Torr 2009; Kohli, Kumar, and Torr 2009).

The most commonly used neighborhood in Markov random field modeling is the $\mathcal{N}_4$ neighborhood, where each pixel in the field $f(i,j)$ interacts only with its immediate neighbors. The model in Figure 3.56, which we previously used in Figure 3.55 to illustrate the discrete version of first-order regularization, shows an $\mathcal{N}_4$ MRF. The $s_x(i,j)$ and $s_y(i,j)$ black boxes denote arbitrary *interaction potentials* between adjacent nodes in the random field and the $w(i,j)$ denote the data penalty functions. These square nodes can also be interpreted as *factors* in a *factor graph* version of the (undirected) graphical model (Bishop 2006), which is another name for interaction potentials. (Strictly speaking, the factors are (improper) probability functions whose product is the (un-normalized) posterior distribution.)

As we will see in (3.112–3.113), there is a close relationship between these interaction potentials and the discretized versions of regularized image restoration problems. Thus, to a first approximation, we can view energy minimization being performed when solving a regularized problem and the maximum a posteriori inference being performed in an MRF as equivalent.

While $\mathcal{N}_4$ neighborhoods are most commonly used, in some applications $\mathcal{N}_8$ (or even higher order) neighborhoods perform better at tasks such as image segmentation because they can better model discontinuities at different orientations (Boykov and Kolmogorov 2003; Rother, Kohli, Feng *et al.* 2009; Kohli, Ladický, and Torr 2009; Kohli, Kumar, and Torr 2009).

Binary MRFs

The simplest possible example of a Markov random field is a binary field. Examples of such fields include 1-bit (black and white) scanned document images as well as images segmented into foreground and background regions.

To denoise a scanned image, we set the data penalty to reflect the agreement between the scanned and final images,

$$E_d(i,j) = w\delta(f(i,j), d(i,j)) \tag{3.110}$$

and the smoothness penalty to reflect the agreement between neighboring pixels

$$E_p(i,j) = E_x(i,j) + E_y(i,j) = s\delta(f(i,j), f(i+1,j)) + s\delta(f(i,j), f(i,j+1)). \tag{3.111}$$

Once we have formulated the energy, how do we minimize it? The simplest approach is to perform gradient descent, flipping one state at a time if it produces a lower energy. This approach is known as *contextual classification* (Kittler and Föglein 1984), *iterated conditional modes* (ICM) (Besag 1986), or *highest confidence first* (HCF) (Chou and Brown 1990) if the pixel with the largest energy decrease is selected first.

Unfortunately, these downhill methods tend to get easily stuck in local minima. An alternative approach is to add some randomness to the process, which is known as *stochastic gradient descent* (Metropolis, Rosenbluth, Rosenbluth *et al.* 1953; Geman and Geman 1984). When the amount of noise is decreased over time, this technique is known as *simulated annealing* (Kirkpatrick, Gelatt, and Vecchi 1983; Carnevali, Coletti, and Patarnello 1985; Wolberg and Pavlidis 1985; Swendsen and Wang 1987) and was first popularized in computer vision by Geman and Geman (1984) and later applied to stereo matching by Barnard (1989), among others.

Even this technique, however, does not perform that well (Boykov, Veksler, and Zabih 2001). For binary images, a much better technique, introduced to the computer vision community by Boykov, Veksler, and Zabih (2001) is to re-formulate the energy minimization as a *max-flow/min-cut* graph optimization problem (Greig, Porteous, and Seheult 1989). This technique has informally come to be known as *graph cuts* in the computer vision community (Boykov and Kolmogorov 2010). For simple energy functions, e.g., those where the penalty for non-identical neighboring pixels is a constant, this algorithm is guaranteed to produce the *global minimum*. Kolmogorov and Zabih (2004) formally characterize the class of binary energy potentials (*regularity conditions*) for which these results hold, while newer work by Komodakis, Tziritas, and Paragios (2008) and Rother, Kolmogorov, Lempitsky *et al.* (2007) provide good algorithms for the cases when they do not.

In addition to the above mentioned techniques, a number of other optimization approaches have been developed for MRF energy minimization, such as (loopy) belief propagation and dynamic programming (for one-dimensional problems). These are discussed in more detail in Appendix B.5 as well as the comparative survey paper by Szeliski, Zabih, Scharstein *et al.* (2008).

Ordinal-valued MRFs

In addition to binary images, Markov random fields can be applied to ordinal-valued labels such as grayscale images or depth maps. The term "ordinal" indicates that the labels have an implied ordering, e.g., that higher values are lighter pixels. In the next section, we look at unordered labels, such as source image labels for image compositing.

In many cases, it is common to extend the binary data and smoothness prior terms as

$$E_d(i,j) = w(i,j)\rho_d(f(i,j) - d(i,j)) \tag{3.112}$$

(a)   (b)   (c)   (d)

Figure 3.57   Grayscale image denoising and inpainting: (a) original image; (b) image corrupted by noise and with missing data (black bar); (c) image restored using loopy belief propagation; (d) image restored using expansion move graph cuts. Images are from http://vision.middlebury.edu/MRF/results/ (Szeliski, Zabih, Scharstein *et al.* 2008).

and

$$E_p(i,j) = s_x(i,j)\rho_p(f(i,j) - f(i+1,j)) + s_y(i,j)\rho_p(f(i,j) - f(i,j+1)), \quad (3.113)$$

which are robust generalizations of the quadratic penalty terms (3.101) and (3.100), first introduced in (3.105). As before, the $w(i,j)$, $s_x(i,j)$ and $s_y(i,j)$ weights can be used to locally control the data weighting and the horizontal and vertical smoothness. Instead of using a quadratic penalty, however, a general monotonically increasing penalty function $\rho()$ is used. (Different functions can be used for the data and smoothness terms.) For example, ρ_p can be a hyper-Laplacian penalty

$$\rho_p(d) = |d|^p, \quad p < 1, \quad (3.114)$$

which better encodes the distribution of gradients (mainly edges) in an image than either a quadratic or linear (total variation) penalty.[24]   Levin and Weiss (2007) use such a penalty to separate a transmitted and reflected image (Figure 8.17) by encouraging gradients to lie in one or the other image, but not both. More recently, Levin, Fergus, Durand *et al.* (2007) use the hyper-Laplacian as a prior for image deconvolution (deblurring) and Krishnan and Fergus (2009) develop a faster algorithm for solving such problems. For the data penalty, ρ_d can be quadratic (to model Gaussian noise) or the log of a *contaminated Gaussian* (Appendix B.3).

When ρ_p is a quadratic function, the resulting Markov random field is called a Gaussian Markov random field (GMRF) and its minimum can be found by sparse linear system solving (3.103). When the weighting functions are uniform, the GMRF becomes a special case of Wiener filtering (Section 3.4.3). Allowing the weighting functions to depend on the input image (a special kind of conditional random field, which we describe below) enables quite sophisticated image processing algorithms to be performed, including colorization (Levin, Lischinski, and Weiss 2004), interactive tone mapping (Lischinski, Farbman, Uyttendaele *et*

---

[24] Note that, unlike a quadratic penalty, the sum of the horizontal and vertical derivative p-norms is not rotationally invariant. A better approach may be to locally estimate the gradient direction and to impose different norms on the perpendicular and parallel components, which Roth and Black (2007b) call a *steerable random field*.

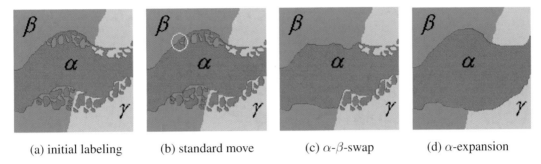

| (a) initial labeling | (b) standard move | (c) α-β-swap | (d) α-expansion |

Figure 3.58 Multi-level graph optimization from (Boykov, Veksler, and Zabih 2001) © 2001 IEEE: (a) initial problem configuration; (b) the standard move only changes one pixel; (c) the α-β-swap optimally exchanges all α and β-labeled pixels; (d) the α-expansion move optimally selects among current pixel values and the α label.

al. 2006a), natural image matting (Levin, Lischinski, and Weiss 2008), and image restoration (Tappen, Liu, Freeman *et al.* 2007).

When ρ_d or ρ_p are non-quadratic functions, gradient descent techniques such as non-linear least squares or iteratively re-weighted least squares can sometimes be used (Appendix A.3). However, if the search space has lots of local minima, as is the case for stereo matching (Barnard 1989; Boykov, Veksler, and Zabih 2001), more sophisticated techniques are required.

The extension of graph cut techniques to multi-valued problems was first proposed by Boykov, Veksler, and Zabih (2001). In their paper, they develop two different algorithms, called the *swap move* and the *expansion move*, which iterate among a series of binary labeling sub-problems to find a good solution (Figure 3.58). Note that a global solution is generally not achievable, as the problem is provably NP-hard for general energy functions. Because both these algorithms use a binary MRF optimization inside their inner loop, they are subject to the kind of constraints on the energy functions that occur in the binary labeling case (Kolmogorov and Zabih 2004). Appendix B.5.4 discusses these algorithms in more detail, along with some more recently developed approaches to this problem.

Another MRF inference technique is *belief propagation* (BP). While belief propagation was originally developed for inference over trees, where it is exact (Pearl 1988), it has more recently been applied to graphs with loops such as Markov random fields (Freeman, Pasztor, and Carmichael 2000; Yedidia, Freeman, and Weiss 2001). In fact, some of the better performing stereo-matching algorithms use loopy belief propagation (LBP) to perform their inference (Sun, Zheng, and Shum 2003). LBP is discussed in more detail in Appendix B.5.3 as well as the comparative survey paper on MRF optimization (Szeliski, Zabih, Scharstein *et al.* 2008).

Figure 3.57 shows an example of image denoising and inpainting (hole filling) using a non-quadratic energy function (non-Gaussian MRF). The original image has been corrupted by noise and a portion of the data has been removed (the black bar). In this case, the loopy belief propagation algorithm computes a slightly lower energy and also a smoother image than the alpha-expansion graph cut algorithm.

Of course, the above formula (3.113) for the smoothness term $E_p(i, j)$ just shows the simplest case. In more recent work, Roth and Black (2009) propose a *Field of Experts* (FoE) model, which sums up a large number of exponentiated local filter outputs to arrive at the

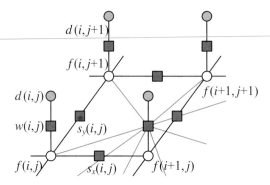

Figure 3.59 Graphical model for a Markov random field with a more complex measurement model. The additional colored edges show how combinations of unknown values (say, in a sharp image) produce the measured values (a noisy blurred image). The resulting graphical model is still a classic MRF and is just as easy to sample from, but some inference algorithms (e.g., those based on graph cuts) may not be applicable because of the increased network complexity, since state changes during the inference become more entangled and the posterior MRF has much larger cliques.

smoothness penalty. Weiss and Freeman (2007) analyze this approach and compare it to the simpler hyper-Laplacian model of natural image statistics. Lyu and Simoncelli (2009) use *Gaussian Scale Mixtures* (GSMs) to construct an inhomogeneous multi-scale MRF, with one (positive exponential) GMRF modulating the variance (amplitude) of another Gaussian MRF.

It is also possible to extend the *measurement* model to make the sampled (noise-corrupted) input pixels correspond to blends of unknown (latent) image pixels, as in Figure 3.59. This is the commonly occurring case when trying to de-blur an image. While this kind of a model is still a traditional generative Markov random field, finding an optimal solution can be difficult because the clique sizes get larger. In such situations, gradient descent techniques, such as iteratively reweighted least squares, can be used (Joshi, Zitnick, Szeliski *et al.* 2009). Exercise 3.31 has you explore some of these issues.

Unordered labels

Another case with multi-valued labels where Markov random fields are often applied are *unordered labels*, i.e., labels where there is no semantic meaning to the numerical difference between the values of two labels. For example, if we are classifying terrain from aerial imagery, it makes no sense to take the numeric difference between the labels assigned to forest, field, water, and pavement. In fact, the adjacencies of these various kinds of terrain each have different likelihoods, so it makes more sense to use a prior of the form

$$E_p(i,j) = s_x(i,j)V(l(i,j), l(i+1,j)) + s_y(i,j)V(l(i,j), l(i,j+1)), \qquad (3.115)$$

where $V(l_0, l_1)$ is a general *compatibility* or *potential* function. (Note that we have also replaced $f(i,j)$ with $l(i,j)$ to make it clearer that these are labels rather than discrete function samples.) An alternative way to write this prior energy (Boykov, Veksler, and Zabih 2001;

Figure 3.60 An unordered label MRF (Agarwala, Dontcheva, Agrawala *et al.* 2004) © 2004 ACM: Strokes in each of the source images on the left are used as constraints on an MRF optimization, which is solved using graph cuts. The resulting multi-valued label field is shown as a color overlay in the middle image, and the final composite is shown on the right.

Szeliski, Zabih, Scharstein *et al.* 2008) is

$$E_p = \sum_{(p,q)\in\mathcal{N}} V_{p,q}(l_p, l_q), \tag{3.116}$$

where the (p, q) are neighboring pixels and a spatially varying potential function $V_{p,q}$ is evaluated for each neighboring pair.

An important application of unordered MRF labeling is seam finding in image compositing (Davis 1998; Agarwala, Dontcheva, Agrawala *et al.* 2004) (see Figure 3.60, which is explained in more detail in Section 9.3.2). Here, the compatibility $V_{p,q}(l_p, l_q)$ measures the quality of the visual appearance that would result from placing a pixel p from image l_p next to a pixel q from image l_q. As with most MRFs, we assume that $V_{p,q}(l, l) = 0$, i.e., it is perfectly fine to choose contiguous pixels from the same image. For different labels, however, the compatibility $V_{p,q}(l_p, l_q)$ may depend on the values of the underlying pixels $I_{l_p}(p)$ and $I_{l_q}(q)$.

Consider, for example, where one image I_0 is all sky blue, i.e., $I_0(p) = I_0(q) = B$, while the other image I_1 has a transition from sky blue, $I_1(p) = B$, to forest green, $I_1(q) = G$.

$$I_0 : \boxed{\begin{array}{c|c} p & q \end{array}} \qquad \boxed{\begin{array}{c|c} p & q \end{array}} : I_1$$

In this case, $V_{p,q}(1, 0) = 0$ (the colors agree), while $V_{p,q}(0, 1) > 0$ (the colors disagree).

Conditional random fields

In a classic Bayesian model (3.106–3.108),

$$p(\boldsymbol{x}|\boldsymbol{y}) \propto p(\boldsymbol{y}|\boldsymbol{x})p(\boldsymbol{x}), \tag{3.117}$$

the prior distribution $p(\boldsymbol{x})$ is independent of the observations $\boldsymbol{y}$. Sometimes, however, it is useful to modify our prior assumptions, say about the smoothness of the field we are trying to estimate, in response to the sensed data. Whether this makes sense from a probability viewpoint is something we discuss once we have explained the new model.

Figure 3.61   Image segmentation (Boykov and Funka-Lea 2006) © 2006 Springer: The user draws a few red strokes in the foreground object and a few blue ones in the background. The system computes color distributions for the foreground and background and solves a binary MRF. The smoothness weights are modulated by the intensity gradients (edges), which makes this a conditional random field (CRF).

Consider the interactive image segmentation problem shown in Figure 3.61 (Boykov and Funka-Lea 2006). In this application, the user draws foreground (red) and background (blue) strokes, and the system then solves a binary MRF labeling problem to estimate the extent of the foreground object. In addition to minimizing a data term, which measures the pointwise similarity between pixel colors and the inferred region distributions (Section 5.5), the MRF is modified so that the smoothness terms $s_x(x, y)$ and $s_y(x, y)$ in Figure 3.56 and (3.113) depend on the magnitude of the gradient between adjacent pixels.[25]

Since the smoothness term now depends on the data, Bayes' Rule (3.117) no longer applies. Instead, we use a direct model for the posterior distribution $p(\boldsymbol{x}|\boldsymbol{y})$, whose negative log likelihood can be written as

$$
\begin{aligned}
E(\boldsymbol{x}|\boldsymbol{y}) &= E_d(\boldsymbol{x}, \boldsymbol{y}) + E_s(\boldsymbol{x}, \boldsymbol{y}) \\
&= \sum_p V_p(x_p, \boldsymbol{y}) + \sum_{(p,q)\in\mathcal{N}} V_{p,q}(x_p, x_q, \boldsymbol{y}),
\end{aligned}
\tag{3.118}
$$

using the notation introduced in (3.116). The resulting probability distribution is called a *conditional random field* (CRF) and was first introduced to the computer vision field by Kumar and Hebert (2003), based on earlier work in text modeling by Lafferty, McCallum, and Pereira (2001).

Figure 3.62 shows a graphical model where the smoothness terms depend on the data values. In this particular model, each smoothness term depends only on its adjacent pair of data values, i.e., terms are of the form $V_{p,q}(x_p, x_q, y_p, y_q)$ in (3.118).

The idea of modifying smoothness terms in response to input data is not new. For example, Boykov and Jolly (2001) used this idea for interactive segmentation, as shown in Figure 3.61, and it is now widely used in image segmentation (Section 5.5) (Blake, Rother, Brown *et al.* 2004; Rother, Kolmogorov, and Blake 2004), denoising (Tappen, Liu, Freeman *et al.* 2007), and object recognition (Section 14.4.3) (Winn and Shotton 2006; Shotton, Winn, Rother *et al.* 2009).

---

[25] An alternative formulation that also uses detected edges to modulate the smoothness of a depth or motion field and hence to integrate multiple lower level vision modules is presented by Poggio, Gamble, and Little (1988).

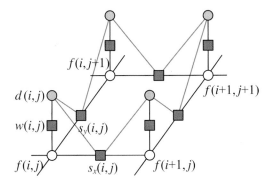

Figure 3.62 Graphical model for a conditional random field (CRF). The additional green edges show how combinations of sensed data influence the smoothness in the underlying MRF prior model, i.e., $s_x(i,j)$ and $s_y(i,j)$ in (3.113) depend on adjacent $d(i,j)$ values. These additional links (factors) enable the smoothness to depend on the input data. However, they make sampling from this MRF more complex.

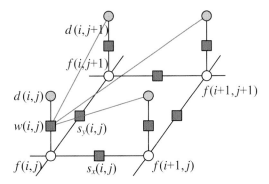

Figure 3.63 Graphical model for a discriminative random field (DRF). The additional green edges show how combinations of sensed data, e.g., $d(i,j+1)$, influence the data term for $f(i,j)$. The generative model is therefore more complex, i.e., we cannot just apply a simple function to the unknown variables and add noise.

In stereo matching, the idea of encouraging disparity discontinuities to coincide with intensity edges goes back even further to the early days of optimization and MRF-based algorithms (Poggio, Gamble, and Little 1988; Fua 1993; Bobick and Intille 1999; Boykov, Veksler, and Zabih 2001) and is discussed in more detail in (Section 11.5).

In addition to using smoothness terms that adapt to the input data, Kumar and Hebert (2003) also compute a neighborhood function over the input data for each $V_p(x_p, \boldsymbol{y})$ term, as illustrated in Figure 3.63, instead of using the classic unary MRF data term $V_p(x_p, y_p)$ shown in Figure 3.56.[26] Because such neighborhood functions can be thought of as *discriminant* functions (a term widely used in machine learning (Bishop 2006)), they call the resulting graphical model a *discriminative random field* (DRF). In their paper, Kumar and Hebert (2006) show that DRFs outperform similar CRFs on a number of applications, such as structure detection (Figure 3.64) and binary image denoising.

Here again, one could argue that previous stereo correspondence algorithms also look at

---

[26] Kumar and Hebert (2006) call the unary potentials $V_p(x_p, \boldsymbol{y})$ *association potentials* and the pairwise potentials $V_{p,q}(x_p, y_q, \boldsymbol{y})$ *interaction potentials*.

Figure 3.64   Structure detection results using an MRF (left) and a DRF (right) (Kumar and Hebert 2006) ©
2006 Springer.

a neighborhood of input data, either explicitly, because they compute correlation measures
(Criminisi, Cross, Blake *et al.* 2006) as data terms, or implicitly, because even pixel-wise
disparity costs look at several pixels in either the left or right image (Barnard 1989; Boykov,
Veksler, and Zabih 2001).

What, then are the advantages and disadvantages of using conditional or discriminative
random fields instead of MRFs?

Classic Bayesian inference (MRF) assumes that the prior distribution of the data is independent of the measurements. This makes a lot of sense: if you see a pair of sixes when
you first throw a pair of dice, it would be unwise to assume that they will always show up
thereafter. However, if after playing for a long time you detect a statistically significant bias,
you may want to adjust your prior. What CRFs do, in essence, is to select or modify the prior
model based on observed data. This can be viewed as making a partial inference over additional hidden variables or correlations between the unknowns (say, a label, depth, or clean
image) and the knowns (observed images).

In some cases, the CRF approach makes a lot of sense and is, in fact, the only plausible way to proceed. For example, in grayscale image colorization (Section 10.3.2) (Levin,
Lischinski, and Weiss 2004), the best way to transfer the continuity information from the
input grayscale image to the unknown color image is to modify local smoothness constraints.
Similarly, for simultaneous segmentation and recognition (Winn and Shotton 2006; Shotton,
Winn, Rother *et al.* 2009), it makes a lot of sense to permit strong color edges to influence
the semantic image label continuities.

In other cases, such as image denoising, the situation is more subtle. Using a non-
quadratic (robust) smoothness term as in (3.113) plays a qualitatively similar role to setting
the smoothness based on local gradient information in a Gaussian MRF (GMRF) (Tappen,
Liu, Freeman *et al.* 2007). (In more recent work, Tanaka and Okutomi (2008) use a larger
neighborhood and full covariance matrix on a related Gaussian MRF.) The advantage of Gaussian MRFs, when the smoothness can be correctly inferred, is that the resulting quadratic
energy can be minimized in a single step. However, for situations where the discontinuities
are not self-evident in the input data, such as for piecewise-smooth sparse data interpolation
(Blake and Zisserman 1987; Terzopoulos 1988), classic robust smoothness energy minimization may be preferable. Thus, as with most computer vision algorithms, a careful analysis of

the problem at hand and desired robustness and computation constraints may be required to choose the best technique.

Perhaps the biggest advantage of CRFs and DRFs, as argued by Kumar and Hebert (2006), Tappen, Liu, Freeman *et al.* (2007) and Blake, Rother, Brown *et al.* (2004), is that learning the model parameters is sometimes easier. While learning parameters in MRFs and their variants is not a topic that we cover in this book, interested readers can find more details in recently published articles (Kumar and Hebert 2006; Roth and Black 2007a; Tappen, Liu, Freeman *et al.* 2007; Tappen 2007; Li and Huttenlocher 2008).

3.7.3 *Application*: Image restoration

In Section 3.4.4, we saw how two-dimensional linear and non-linear filters can be used to remove noise or enhance sharpness in images. Sometimes, however, images are degraded by larger problems, such as scratches and blotches (Kokaram 2004). In this case, Bayesian methods such as MRFs, which can model spatially varying per-pixel measurement noise, can be used instead. An alternative is to use hole filling or inpainting techniques (Bertalmio, Sapiro, Caselles *et al.* 2000; Bertalmio, Vese, Sapiro *et al.* 2003; Criminisi, Pérez, and Toyama 2004), as discussed in Sections 5.1.4 and 10.5.1.

Figure 3.57 shows an example of image denoising and inpainting (hole filling) using a Markov random field. The original image has been corrupted by noise and a portion of the data has been removed. In this case, the loopy belief propagation algorithm computes a slightly lower energy and also a smoother image than the alpha-expansion graph cut algorithm.

3.8 Additional reading

If you are interested in exploring the topic of image processing in more depth, some popular textbooks have been written by Lim (1990); Crane (1997); Gomes and Velho (1997); Jähne (1997); Pratt (2007); Russ (2007); Burger and Burge (2008); Gonzales and Woods (2008). The pre-eminent conference and journal in this field are the IEEE Conference on Image Processsing and the IEEE Transactions on Image Processing.

For image compositing operators, the seminal reference is by Porter and Duff (1984) while Blinn (1994a,b) provides a more detailed tutorial. For image compositing, Smith and Blinn (1996) were the first to bring this topic to the attention of the graphics community, while Wang and Cohen (2007a) provide a recent in-depth survey.

In the realm of linear filtering, Freeman and Adelson (1991) provide a great introduction to separable and steerable oriented band-pass filters, while Perona (1995) shows how to approximate any filter as a sum of separable components.

The literature on non-linear filtering is quite wide and varied; it includes such topics as bilateral filtering (Tomasi and Manduchi 1998; Durand and Dorsey 2002; Paris and Durand 2006; Chen, Paris, and Durand 2007; Paris, Kornprobst, Tumblin *et al.* 2008), related iterative algorithms (Saint-Marc, Chen, and Medioni 1991; Nielsen, Florack, and Deriche 1997; Black, Sapiro, Marimont *et al.* 1998; Weickert, ter Haar Romeny, and Viergever 1998; Weickert 1998; Barash 2002; Scharr, Black, and Haussecker 2003; Barash and Comaniciu 2004), and variational approaches (Chan, Osher, and Shen 2001; Tschumperlé and Deriche 2005; Tschumperlé 2006; Kaftory, Schechner, and Zeevi 2007).

Good references to image morphology include (Haralick and Shapiro 1992, Section 5.2; Bovik 2000, Section 2.2; Ritter and Wilson 2000, Section 7; Serra 1982; Serra and Vincent 1992; Yuille, Vincent, and Geiger 1992; Soille 2006).

The classic papers for image pyramids and pyramid blending are by Burt and Adelson (1983a,b). Wavelets were first introduced to the computer vision community by Mallat (1989) and good tutorial and review papers and books are available (Strang 1989; Simoncelli and Adelson 1990b; Rioul and Vetterli 1991; Chui 1992; Meyer 1993; Sweldens 1997). Wavelets are widely used in the computer graphics community to perform multi-resolution geometric processing (Stollnitz, DeRose, and Salesin 1996) and have been used in computer vision for similar applications (Szeliski 1990b; Pentland 1994; Gortler and Cohen 1995; Yaou and Chang 1994; Lai and Vemuri 1997; Szeliski 2006b), as well as for multi-scale oriented filtering (Simoncelli, Freeman, Adelson *et al.* 1992) and denoising (Portilla, Strela, Wainwright *et al.* 2003).

While image pyramids (Section 3.5.3) are usually constructed using linear filtering operators, some recent work has started investigating non-linear filters, since these can better preserve details and other salient features. Some representative papers in the computer vision literature are by Gluckman (2006a,b); Lyu and Simoncelli (2008) and in computational photography by Bae, Paris, and Durand (2006); Farbman, Fattal, Lischinski *et al.* (2008); Fattal (2009).

High-quality algorithms for image warping and resampling are covered both in the image processing literature (Wolberg 1990; Dodgson 1992; Gomes, Darsa, Costa *et al.* 1999; Szeliski, Winder, and Uyttendaele 2010) and in computer graphics (Williams 1983; Heckbert 1986; Barkans 1997; Akenine-Möller and Haines 2002), where they go under the name of *texture mapping*. Combination of image warping and image blending techniques are used to enable *morphing* between images, which is covered in a series of seminal papers and books (Beier and Neely 1992; Gomes, Darsa, Costa *et al.* 1999).

The regularization approach to computer vision problems was first introduced to the vision community by Poggio, Torre, and Koch (1985) and Terzopoulos (1986a,b, 1988) and continues to be a popular framework for formulating and solving low-level vision problems (Ju, Black, and Jepson 1996; Nielsen, Florack, and Deriche 1997; Nordström 1990; Brox, Bruhn, Papenberg *et al.* 2004; Levin, Lischinski, and Weiss 2008). More detailed mathematical treatment and additional applications can be found in the applied mathematics and statistics literature (Tikhonov and Arsenin 1977; Engl, Hanke, and Neubauer 1996).

The literature on Markov random fields is truly immense, with publications in related fields such as optimization and control theory of which few vision practitioners are even aware. A good guide to the latest techniques is the book edited by Blake, Kohli, and Rother (2010). Other recent articles that contain nice literature reviews or experimental comparisons include (Boykov and Funka-Lea 2006; Szeliski, Zabih, Scharstein *et al.* 2008; Kumar, Veksler, and Torr 2010).

The seminal paper on Markov random fields is the work of Geman and Geman (1984), who introduced this formalism to computer vision researchers and also introduced the notion of *line processes*, additional binary variables that control whether smoothness penalties are enforced or not. Black and Rangarajan (1996) showed how independent line processes could be replaced with robust pairwise potentials; Boykov, Veksler, and Zabih (2001) developed iterative binary, graph cut algorithms for optimizing multi-label MRFs; Kolmogorov and Zabih (2004) characterized the class of binary energy potentials required for these techniques to work; and Freeman, Pasztor, and Carmichael (2000) popularized the use of loopy belief propagation for MRF inference. Many more additional references can be found in Sections 3.7.2 and 5.5, and Appendix B.5.

3.9 Exercises

Ex 3.1: Color balance   Write a simple application to change the color balance of an image by multiplying each color value by a different user-specified constant. If you want to get fancy, you can make this application interactive, with sliders.

1. Do you get different results if you take out the gamma transformation before or after doing the multiplication? Why or why not?

2. Take the same picture with your digital camera using different color balance settings (most cameras control the color balance from one of the menus). Can you recover what the color balance ratios are between the different settings? You may need to put your camera on a tripod and align the images manually or automatically to make this work. Alternatively, use a color checker chart (Figure 10.3b), as discussed in Sections 2.3 and 10.1.1.

3. If you have access to the RAW image for the camera, perform the demosaicing yourself (Section 10.3.1) or downsample the image resolution to get a "true" RGB image. Does your camera perform a simple linear mapping between RAW values and the color-balanced values in a JPEG? Some high-end cameras have a RAW+JPEG mode, which makes this comparison much easier.

4. Can you think of any reason why you might want to perform a color twist (Section 3.1.2) on the images? See also Exercise 2.9 for some related ideas.

Ex 3.2: Compositing and reflections   Section 3.1.3 describes the process of compositing an alpha-matted image on top of another. Answer the following questions and optionally validate them experimentally:

1. Most captured images have gamma correction applied to them. Does this invalidate the basic compositing equation (3.8); if so, how should it be fixed?

2. The additive (pure reflection) model may have limitations. What happens if the glass is tinted, especially to a non-gray hue? How about if the glass is dirty or smudged? How could you model wavy glass or other kinds of refractive objects?

Ex 3.3: Blue screen matting   Set up a blue or green background, e.g., by buying a large piece of colored posterboard. Take a picture of the empty background, and then of the background with a new object in front of it. *Pull the matte* using the difference between each colored pixel and its assumed corresponding background pixel, using one of the techniques described in Section 3.1.3) or by Smith and Blinn (1996).

Ex 3.4: Difference keying Implement a difference keying algorithm (see Section 3.1.3) (Toyama, Krumm, Brumitt *et al.* 1999), consisting of the following steps:

1. Compute the mean and variance (or median and robust variance) at each pixel in an "empty" video sequence.

2. For each new frame, classify each pixel as foreground or background (set the background pixels to RGBA=0).

3. (Optional) Compute the alpha channel and composite over a new background.

4. (Optional) Clean up the image using morphology (Section 3.3.1), label the connected components (Section 3.3.4), compute their centroids, and track them from frame to frame. Use this to build a "people counter".

Ex 3.5: Photo effects Write a variety of photo enhancement or effects filters: contrast, solarization (quantization), etc. Which ones are useful (perform sensible corrections) and which ones are more creative (create unusual images)?

Ex 3.6: Histogram equalization Compute the gray level (luminance) histogram for an image and equalize it so that the tones look better (and the image is less sensitive to exposure settings). You may want to use the following steps:

1. Convert the color image to luminance (Section 3.1.2).

2. Compute the histogram, the cumulative distribution, and the compensation transfer function (Section 3.1.4).

3. (Optional) Try to increase the "punch" in the image by ensuring that a certain fraction of pixels (say, 5%) are mapped to pure black and white.

4. (Optional) Limit the local *gain* $f'(I)$ in the transfer function. One way to do this is to limit $f(I) < \gamma I$ or $f'(I) < \gamma$ while performing the accumulation (3.9), keeping any unaccumulated values "in reserve". (I'll let you figure out the exact details.)

5. Compensate the luminance channel through the lookup table and re-generate the color image using color ratios (2.116).

6. (Optional) Color values that are *clipped* in the original image, i.e., have one or more saturated color channels, may appear unnatural when remapped to a non-clipped value. Extend your algorithm to handle this case in some useful way.

Ex 3.7: Local histogram equalization Compute the gray level (luminance) histograms for each patch, but add to vertices based on distance (a spline).

1. Build on Exercise 3.6 (luminance computation).

2. Distribute values (counts) to adjacent vertices (bilinear).

3. Convert to CDF (look-up functions).

4. (Optional) Use low-pass filtering of CDFs.

5. Interpolate adjacent CDFs for final lookup.

Ex 3.8: Padding for neighborhood operations   Write down the formulas for computing the padded pixel values $\tilde{f}(i, j)$ as a function of the original pixel values $f(k, l)$ and the image width and height (M, N) for *each* of the padding modes shown in Figure 3.13. For example, for replication (clamping),

$$\tilde{f}(i, j) = f(k, l), \quad \begin{aligned} k &= \max(0, \min(M - 1, i)), \\ l &= \max(0, \min(N - 1, j)), \end{aligned}$$

(Hint: you may want to use the min, max, mod, and absolute value operators in addition to the regular arithmetic operators.)

- Describe in more detail the advantages and disadvantages of these various modes.

- (Optional) Check what your graphics card does by drawing a texture-mapped rectangle where the texture coordinates lie beyond the $[0.0, 1.0]$ range and using different texture clamping modes.

Ex 3.9: Separable filters   Implement convolution with a separable kernel. The input should be a grayscale or color image along with the horizontal and vertical kernels. Make sure you support the padding mechanisms developed in the previous exercise. You will need this functionality for some of the later exercises. If you already have access to separable filtering in an image processing package you are using (such as IPL), skip this exercise.

- (Optional) Use Pietro Perona's (1995) technique to approximate convolution as a sum of a number of separable kernels. Let the user specify the number of kernels and report back some sensible metric of the approximation fidelity.

Ex 3.10: Discrete Gaussian filters   Discuss the following issues with implementing a discrete Gaussian filter:

- If you just sample the equation of a continuous Gaussian filter at discrete locations, will you get the desired properties, e.g., will the coefficients sum up to 0? Similarly, if you sample a derivative of a Gaussian, do the samples sum up to 0 or have vanishing higher-order moments?

- Would it be preferable to take the original signal, interpolate it with a sinc, blur with a continuous Gaussian, then pre-filter with a sinc before re-sampling? Is there a simpler way to do this in the frequency domain?

- Would it make more sense to produce a Gaussian frequency response in the Fourier domain and to then take an inverse FFT to obtain a discrete filter?

- How does truncation of the filter change its frequency response? Does it introduce any additional artifacts?

- Are the resulting two-dimensional filters as rotationally invariant as their continuous analogs? Is there some way to improve this? In fact, can any 2D discrete (separable or non-separable) filter be truly rotationally invariant?

Ex 3.11: Sharpening, blur, and noise removal   Implement some softening, sharpening, and non-linear diffusion (selective sharpening or noise removal) filters, such as Gaussian, median, and bilateral (Section 3.3.1), as discussed in Section 3.4.4.

Take blurry or noisy images (shooting in low light is a good way to get both) and try to improve their appearance and legibility.

Ex 3.12: Steerable filters   Implement Freeman and Adelson's (1991) steerable filter algorithm. The input should be a grayscale or color image and the output should be a multi-banded image consisting of $G_1^{0°}$ and $G_1^{90°}$. The coefficients for the filters can be found in the paper by Freeman and Adelson (1991).

Test the various order filters on a number of images of your choice and see if you can reliably find corner and intersection features. These filters will be quite useful later to detect elongated structures, such as lines (Section 4.3).

Ex 3.13: Distance transform   Implement some (raster-scan) algorithms for city block and Euclidean distance transforms. Can you do it without peeking at the literature (Danielsson 1980; Borgefors 1986)? If so, what problems did you come across and resolve?

Later on, you can use the distance functions you compute to perform *feathering* during image stitching (Section 9.3.2).

Ex 3.14: Connected components   Implement one of the connected component algorithms from Section 3.3.4 or Section 2.3 from Haralick and Shapiro's book (1992) and discuss its computational complexity.

- Threshold or quantize an image to obtain a variety of input labels and then compute the area statistics for the regions that you find.

- Use the connected components that you have found to track or match regions in different images or video frames.

Ex 3.15: Fourier transform   Prove the properties of the Fourier transform listed in Table 3.1 and derive the formulas for the Fourier transforms listed in Tables 3.2 and 3.3. These exercises are very useful if you want to become comfortable working with Fourier transforms, which is a very useful skill when analyzing and designing the behavior and efficiency of many computer vision algorithms.

Ex 3.16: Wiener filtering   Estimate the frequency spectrum of your personal photo collection and use it to perform Wiener filtering on a few images with varying degrees of noise.

1. Collect a few hundred of your images by re-scaling them to fit within a 512×512 window and cropping them.

2. Take their Fourier transforms, throw away the phase information, and average together all of the spectra.

3. Pick two of your favorite images and add varying amounts of Gaussian noise, $\sigma_n \in \{1, 2, 5, 10, 20\}$ gray levels.

4. For each combination of image and noise, determine by eye which width of a Gaussian blurring filter σ_s gives the best denoised result. You will have to make a subjective decision between sharpness and noise.

5. Compute the Wiener filtered version of all the noised images and compare them against your hand-tuned Gaussian-smoothed images.

6. (Optional) Do your image spectra have a lot of energy concentrated along the horizontal and vertical axes ($f_x = 0$ and $f_y = 0$)? Can you think of an explanation for this? Does rotating your image samples by $45°$ move this energy to the diagonals? If not, could it be due to edge effects in the Fourier transform? Can you suggest some techniques for reducing such effects?

Ex 3.17: Deblurring using Wiener filtering   Use Wiener filtering to deblur some images.

1. Modify the Wiener filter derivation (3.66–3.74) to incorporate blur (3.75).

2. Discuss the resulting Wiener filter in terms of its noise suppression and frequency boosting characteristics.

3. Assuming that the blur kernel is Gaussian and the image spectrum follows an inverse frequency law, compute the frequency response of the Wiener filter, and compare it to the unsharp mask.

4. Synthetically blur two of your sample images with Gaussian blur kernels of different radii, add noise, and then perform Wiener filtering.

5. Repeat the above experiment with a "pillbox" (disc) blurring kernel, which is characteristic of a finite aperture lens (Section 2.2.3). Compare these results to Gaussian blur kernels (be sure to inspect your frequency plots).

6. It has been suggested that regular apertures are anathema to de-blurring because they introduce zeros in the sensed frequency spectrum (Veeraraghavan, Raskar, Agrawal *et al.* 2007). Show that this is indeed an issue if no prior model is assumed for the signal, i.e., $P_s^{-1}\mathit{l}1$. If a reasonable power spectrum is assumed, is this still a problem (do we still get banding or ringing artifacts)?

Ex 3.18: High-quality image resampling   Implement several of the low-pass filters presented in Section 3.5.2 and also the discussion of the windowed sinc shown in Table 3.2 and Figure 3.29. Feel free to implement other filters (Wolberg 1990; Unser 1999).

Apply your filters to continuously resize an image, both magnifying (interpolating) and minifying (decimating) it; compare the resulting animations for several filters. Use both a synthetic chirp image (Figure 3.65a) and natural images with lots of high-frequency detail (Figure 3.65b-c).[27]

You may find it helpful to write a simple visualization program that continuously plays the animations for two or more filters at once and that let you "blink" between different results.

Discuss the merits and deficiencies of each filter, as well as its tradeoff between speed and quality.

Ex 3.19: Pyramids   Construct an image pyramid. The inputs should be a grayscale or color image, a separable filter kernel, and the number of desired levels. Implement at least the following kernels:

---

[27] These particular images are available on the book's Web site.

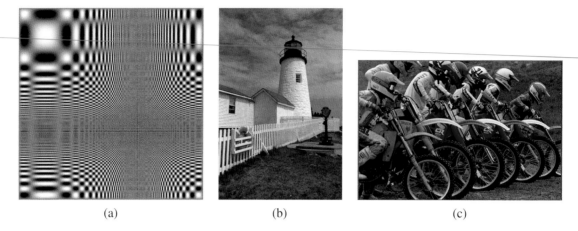

(a)   (b)   (c)

Figure 3.65 Sample images for testing the quality of resampling algorithms: (a) a synthetic chirp; (b) and (c) some high-frequency images from the image compression community.

- 2×2 block filtering;

- Burt and Adelson's binomial kernel $^1/_{16}(1, 4, 6, 4, 1)$ (Burt and Adelson 1983a);

- a high-quality seven- or nine-tap filter.

Compare the visual quality of the various decimation filters. Also, shift your input image by 1 to 4 pixels and compare the resulting decimated (quarter size) image sequence.

Ex 3.20: Pyramid blending   Write a program that takes as input two color images and a binary mask image and produces the Laplacian pyramid blend of the two images.

1. Construct the Laplacian pyramid for each image.

2. Construct the Gaussian pyramid for the two mask images (the input image and its complement).

3. Multiply each Laplacian image by its corresponding mask and sum the images (see Figure 3.43).

4. Reconstruct the final image from the blended Laplacian pyramid.

Generalize your algorithm to input n images and a label image with values $1 \ldots n$ (the value 0 can be reserved for "no input"). Discuss whether the weighted summation stage (step 3) needs to keep track of the total weight for renormalization, or whether the math just works out. Use your algorithm either to blend two differently exposed image (to avoid under- and over-exposed regions) or to make a creative blend of two different scenes.

Ex 3.21: Wavelet construction and applications   Implement one of the wavelet families described in Section 3.5.4 or by Simoncelli and Adelson (1990b), as well as the basic Laplacian pyramid (Exercise 3.19). Apply the resulting representations to one of the following two tasks:

- **Compression:** Compute the entropy in each band for the different wavelet implementations, assuming a given quantization level (say, $\frac{1}{4}$ gray level, to keep the rounding error acceptable). Quantize the wavelet coefficients and reconstruct the original images. Which technique performs better? (See (Simoncelli and Adelson 1990b) or any of the multitude of wavelet compression papers for some typical results.)

- **Denoising.** After computing the wavelets, suppress small values using *coring*, i.e., set small values to zero using a piecewise linear or other C^0 function. Compare the results of your denoising using different wavelet and pyramid representations.

Ex 3.22: Parametric image warping Write the code to do affine and perspective image warps (optionally bilinear as well). Try a variety of interpolants and report on their visual quality. In particular, discuss the following:

- In a MIP-map, selecting only the coarser level adjacent to the computed fractional level will produce a blurrier image, while selecting the finer level will lead to aliasing. Explain why this is so and discuss whether blending an aliased and a blurred image (tri-linear MIP-mapping) is a good idea.

- When the ratio of the horizontal and vertical resampling rates becomes very different (anisotropic), the MIP-map performs even worse. Suggest some approaches to reduce such problems.

Ex 3.23: Local image warping Open an image and deform its appearance in one of the following ways:

1. Click on a number of pixels and move (drag) them to new locations. Interpolate the resulting sparse displacement field to obtain a dense motion field (Sections 3.6.2 and 3.5.1).

2. Draw a number of lines in the image. Move the endpoints of the lines to specify their new positions and use the Beier–Neely interpolation algorithm (Beier and Neely 1992), discussed in Section 3.6.2, to get a dense motion field.

3. Overlay a spline control grid and move one grid point at a time (optionally select the level of the deformation).

4. Have a dense per-pixel flow field and use a soft "paintbrush" to design a horizontal and vertical velocity field.

5. (Optional): Prove whether the Beier–Neely warp does or does not reduce to a sparse point-based deformation as the line segments become shorter (reduce to points).

Ex 3.24: Forward warping Given a displacement field from the previous exercise, write a forward warping algorithm:

1. Write a forward warper using splatting, either nearest neighbor or soft accumulation (Section 3.6.1).

2. Write a two-pass algorithm, which forward warps the displacement field, fills in small holes, and then uses inverse warping (Shade, Gortler, He *et al.* 1998).

3. Compare the quality of these two algorithms.

Ex 3.25: Feature-based morphing   Extend the warping code you wrote in Exercise 3.23 to import two different images and specify correspondences (point, line, or mesh-based) between the two images.

1. Create a morph by partially warping the images towards each other and cross-dissolving (Section 3.6.3).

2. Try using your morphing algorithm to perform an image rotation and discuss whether it behaves the way you want it to.

Ex 3.26: 2D image editor   Extend the program you wrote in Exercise 2.2 to import images and let you create a "collage" of pictures. You should implement the following steps:

1. Open up a new image (in a separate window).

2. Shift drag (rubber-band) to crop a subregion (or select whole image).

3. Paste into the current canvas.

4. Select the deformation mode (motion model): translation, rigid, similarity, affine, or perspective.

5. Drag any corner of the outline to change its transformation.

6. (Optional) Change the relative ordering of the images and which image is currently being manipulated.

The user should see the composition of the various images' pieces on top of each other.

This exercise should be built on the image transformation classes supported in the software library. Persistence of the created representation (save and load) should also be supported (for each image, save its transformation).

Ex 3.27: 3D texture-mapped viewer   Extend the viewer you created in Exercise 2.3 to include texture-mapped polygon rendering. Augment each polygon with (u, v, w) coordinates into an image.

Ex 3.28: Image denoising   Implement at least two of the various image denoising techniques described in this chapter and compare them on both synthetically noised image sequences and real-world (low-light) sequences. Does the performance of the algorithm depend on the correct choice of noise level estimate? Can you draw any conclusions as to which techniques work better?

Ex 3.29: Rainbow enhancer—challenging   Take a picture containing a rainbow, such as Figure 3.66, and enhance the strength (saturation) of the rainbow.

1. Draw an arc in the image delineating the extent of the rainbow.

Figure 3.66 There is a faint image of a rainbow visible in the right hand side of this picture. Can you think of a way to enhance it (Exercise 3.29)?

2. Fit an *additive* rainbow function (explain why it is additive) to this arc (it is best to work with linearized pixel values), using the spectrum as the cross section, and estimating the width of the arc and the amount of color being added. This is the trickiest part of the problem, as you need to tease apart the (low-frequency) rainbow pattern and the natural image hiding behind it.

3. Amplify the rainbow signal and add it back into the image, re-applying the gamma function if necessary to produce the final image.

Ex 3.30: Image deblocking—challenging Now that you have some good techniques to distinguish signal from noise, develop a technique to remove the *blocking artifacts* that occur with JPEG at high compression settings (Section 2.3.3). Your technique can be as simple as looking for unexpected edges along block boundaries, to looking at the quantization step as a projection of a convex region of the transform coefficient space onto the corresponding quantized values.

1. Does the knowledge of the compression factor, which is available in the JPEG header information, help you perform better deblocking?

2. Because the quantization occurs in the DCT transformed YCbCr space (2.115), it may be preferable to perform the analysis in this space. On the other hand, image priors make more sense in an RGB space (or do they?). Decide how you will approach this dichotomy and discuss your choice.

3. While you are at it, since the YCbCr conversion is followed by a chrominance subsampling stage (before the DCT), see if you can restore some of the lost high-frequency chrominance signal using one of the better restoration techniques discussed in this chapter.

4. If your camera has a RAW + JPEG mode, how close can you come to the noise-free true pixel values? (This suggestion may not be that useful, since cameras generally use reasonably high quality settings for their RAW + JPEG models.)

Ex 3.31: Inference in de-blurring—challenging   Write down the graphical model corresponding to Figure 3.59 for a non-blind image deblurring problem, i.e., one where the blur kernel is known ahead of time.

What kind of efficient inference (optimization) algorithms can you think of for solving such problems?

Chapter 4

Feature detection and matching

R. Szeliski, *Computer Vision: Algorithms and Applications*, Texts in Computer Science,
DOI 10.1007/978-1-84882-935-0_4, © Springer-Verlag London Limited 2011

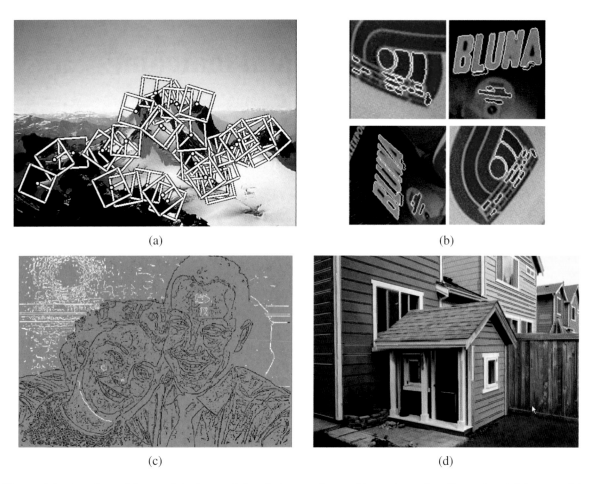

Figure 4.1   A variety of feature detectors and descriptors can be used to analyze, describe and match images: (a) point-like interest operators (Brown, Szeliski, and Winder 2005) © 2005 IEEE; (b) region-like interest operators (Matas, Chum, Urban *et al.* 2004) © 2004 Elsevier; (c) edges (Elder and Goldberg 2001) © 2001 IEEE; (d) straight lines (Sinha, Steedly, Szeliski *et al.* 2008) © 2008 ACM.

Feature detection and matching are an essential component of many computer vision applications. Consider the two pairs of images shown in Figure 4.2. For the first pair, we may wish to *align* the two images so that they can be seamlessly stitched into a composite mosaic (Chapter 9). For the second pair, we may wish to establish a dense set of *correspondences* so that a 3D model can be constructed or an in-between view can be generated (Chapter 11). In either case, what kinds of *features* should you detect and then match in order to establish such an alignment or set of correspondences? Think about this for a few moments before reading on.

The first kind of feature that you may notice are specific locations in the images, such as mountain peaks, building corners, doorways, or interestingly shaped patches of snow. These kinds of localized feature are often called *keypoint features* or *interest points* (or even *corners*) and are often described by the appearance of patches of pixels surrounding the point location (Section 4.1). Another class of important features are *edges*, e.g., the profile of mountains against the sky, (Section 4.2). These kinds of features can be matched based on their orientation and local appearance (edge profiles) and can also be good indicators of object boundaries and *occlusion* events in image sequences. Edges can be grouped into longer *curves* and *straight line segments*, which can be directly matched or analyzed to find *vanishing points* and hence internal and external camera parameters (Section 4.3).

In this chapter, we describe some practical approaches to detecting such features and also discuss how feature correspondences can be established across different images. Point features are now used in such a wide variety of applications that it is good practice to read and implement some of the algorithms from (Section 4.1). Edges and lines provide information that is complementary to both keypoint and region-based descriptors and are well-suited to describing object boundaries and man-made objects. These alternative descriptors, while extremely useful, can be skipped in a short introductory course.

4.1 Points and patches

Point features can be used to find a sparse set of corresponding locations in different images, often as a pre-cursor to computing camera pose (Chapter 7), which is a prerequisite for computing a denser set of correspondences using stereo matching (Chapter 11). Such correspondences can also be used to align different images, e.g., when stitching image mosaics or performing video stabilization (Chapter 9). They are also used extensively to perform object instance and category recognition (Sections 14.3 and 14.4). A key advantage of keypoints is that they permit matching even in the presence of clutter (occlusion) and large scale and orientation changes.

Feature-based correspondence techniques have been used since the early days of stereo matching (Hannah 1974; Moravec 1983; Hannah 1988) and have more recently gained popularity for image-stitching applications (Zoghlami, Faugeras, and Deriche 1997; Brown and Lowe 2007) as well as fully automated 3D modeling (Beardsley, Torr, and Zisserman 1996; Schaffalitzky and Zisserman 2002; Brown and Lowe 2003; Snavely, Seitz, and Szeliski 2006).

There are two main approaches to finding feature points and their correspondences. The first is to find features in one image that can be accurately *tracked* using a local search technique, such as correlation or least squares (Section 4.1.4). The second is to independently

Figure 4.2 Two pairs of images to be matched. What kinds of feature might one use to establish a set of *correspondences* between these images?

detect features in all the images under consideration and then *match* features based on their local appearance (Section 4.1.3). The former approach is more suitable when images are taken from nearby viewpoints or in rapid succession (e.g., video sequences), while the latter is more suitable when a large amount of motion or appearance change is expected, e.g., in stitching together panoramas (Brown and Lowe 2007), establishing correspondences in *wide baseline stereo* (Schaffalitzky and Zisserman 2002), or performing object recognition (Fergus, Perona, and Zisserman 2007).

In this section, we split the keypoint detection and matching pipeline into four separate stages. During the *feature detection* (extraction) stage (Section 4.1.1), each image is searched for locations that are likely to match well in other images. At the *feature description* stage (Section 4.1.2), each region around detected keypoint locations is converted into a more compact and stable (invariant) *descriptor* that can be matched against other descriptors. The *feature matching* stage (Section 4.1.3) efficiently searches for likely matching candidates in other images. The *feature tracking* stage (Section 4.1.4) is an alternative to the third stage that only searches a small neighborhood around each detected feature and is therefore more suitable for video processing.

A wonderful example of all of these stages can be found in David Lowe's (2004) paper, which describes the development and refinement of his *Scale Invariant Feature Transform* (SIFT). Comprehensive descriptions of alternative techniques can be found in a series of survey and evaluation papers covering both feature detection (Schmid, Mohr, and Bauckhage 2000; Mikolajczyk, Tuytelaars, Schmid *et al.* 2005; Tuytelaars and Mikolajczyk 2007) and feature descriptors (Mikolajczyk and Schmid 2005). Shi and Tomasi (1994) and Triggs (2004) also provide nice reviews of feature detection techniques.

Figure 4.3 Image pairs with extracted patches below. Notice how some patches can be localized or matched with higher accuracy than others.

4.1.1 Feature detectors

How can we find image locations where we can reliably find correspondences with other images, i.e., what are good features to track (Shi and Tomasi 1994; Triggs 2004)? Look again at the image pair shown in Figure 4.3 and at the three sample *patches* to see how well they might be matched or tracked. As you may notice, textureless patches are nearly impossible to localize. Patches with large contrast changes (gradients) are easier to localize, although straight line segments at a single orientation suffer from the *aperture problem* (Horn and Schunck 1981; Lucas and Kanade 1981; Anandan 1989), i.e., it is only possible to align the patches along the direction *normal* to the edge direction (Figure 4.4b). Patches with gradients in at least two (significantly) different orientations are the easiest to localize, as shown schematically in Figure 4.4a.

These intuitions can be formalized by looking at the simplest possible matching criterion for comparing two image patches, i.e., their (weighted) summed square difference,

$$E_{\text{WSSD}}(\boldsymbol{u}) = \sum_i w(\boldsymbol{x}_i)[I_1(\boldsymbol{x}_i + \boldsymbol{u}) - I_0(\boldsymbol{x}_i)]^2, \quad (4.1)$$

where I_0 and I_1 are the two images being compared, $\boldsymbol{u} = (u, v)$ is the *displacement* vector, $w(\boldsymbol{x})$ is a spatially varying weighting (or window) function, and the summation i is over all the pixels in the patch. Note that this is the same formulation we later use to estimate motion between complete images (Section 8.1).

When performing feature detection, we do not know which other image locations the feature will end up being matched against. Therefore, we can only compute how stable this metric is with respect to small variations in position $\Delta\boldsymbol{u}$ by comparing an image patch against

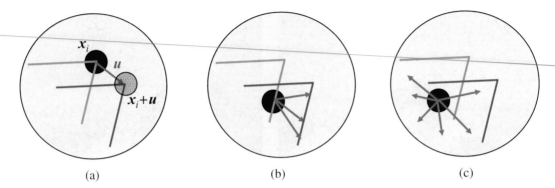

(a)   (b)   (c)

Figure 4.4 Aperture problems for different image patches: (a) stable ("corner-like") flow; (b) classic aperture problem (barber-pole illusion); (c) textureless region. The two images I_0 (yellow) and I_1 (red) are overlaid. The red vector $\boldsymbol{u}$ indicates the displacement between the patch centers and the $w(\boldsymbol{x}_i)$ weighting function (patch window) is shown as a dark circle.

itself, which is known as an *auto-correlation function* or *surface*

$$E_{\mathrm{AC}}(\Delta\boldsymbol{u}) = \sum_i w(\boldsymbol{x}_i)[I_0(\boldsymbol{x}_i + \Delta\boldsymbol{u}) - I_0(\boldsymbol{x}_i)]^2 \tag{4.2}$$

(Figure 4.5).[1] Note how the auto-correlation surface for the textured flower bed (Figure 4.5b and the red cross in the lower right quadrant of Figure 4.5a) exhibits a strong minimum, indicating that it can be well localized. The correlation surface corresponding to the roof edge (Figure 4.5c) has a strong ambiguity along one direction, while the correlation surface corresponding to the cloud region (Figure 4.5d) has no stable minimum.

Using a Taylor Series expansion of the image function $I_0(\boldsymbol{x}_i + \Delta\boldsymbol{u}) \approx I_0(\boldsymbol{x}_i) + \nabla I_0(\boldsymbol{x}_i) \cdot \Delta\boldsymbol{u}$ (Lucas and Kanade 1981; Shi and Tomasi 1994), we can approximate the auto-correlation surface as

$$
\begin{aligned}
E_{\mathrm{AC}}(\Delta\boldsymbol{u}) &= \sum_i w(\boldsymbol{x}_i)[I_0(\boldsymbol{x}_i + \Delta\boldsymbol{u}) - I_0(\boldsymbol{x}_i)]^2 & (4.3)\\
&\approx \sum_i w(\boldsymbol{x}_i)[I_0(\boldsymbol{x}_i) + \nabla I_0(\boldsymbol{x}_i) \cdot \Delta\boldsymbol{u} - I_0(\boldsymbol{x}_i)]^2 & (4.4)\\
&= \sum_i w(\boldsymbol{x}_i)[\nabla I_0(\boldsymbol{x}_i) \cdot \Delta\boldsymbol{u}]^2 & (4.5)\\
&= \Delta\boldsymbol{u}^T \boldsymbol{A} \Delta\boldsymbol{u}, & (4.6)
\end{aligned}
$$

where

$$\nabla I_0(\boldsymbol{x}_i) = (\frac{\partial I_0}{\partial x}, \frac{\partial I_0}{\partial y})(\boldsymbol{x}_i) \tag{4.7}$$

is the *image gradient* at $\boldsymbol{x}_i$. This gradient can be computed using a variety of techniques (Schmid, Mohr, and Bauckhage 2000). The classic "Harris" detector (Harris and Stephens 1988) uses a [-2 -1 0 1 2] filter, but more modern variants (Schmid, Mohr, and Bauckhage 2000; Triggs 2004) convolve the image with horizontal and vertical derivatives of a Gaussian (typically with $\sigma = 1$).

---

[1] Strictly speaking, a correlation is the *product* of two patches (3.12); I'm using the term here in a more qualitative sense. The weighted sum of squared differences is often called an *SSD surface* (Section 8.1).

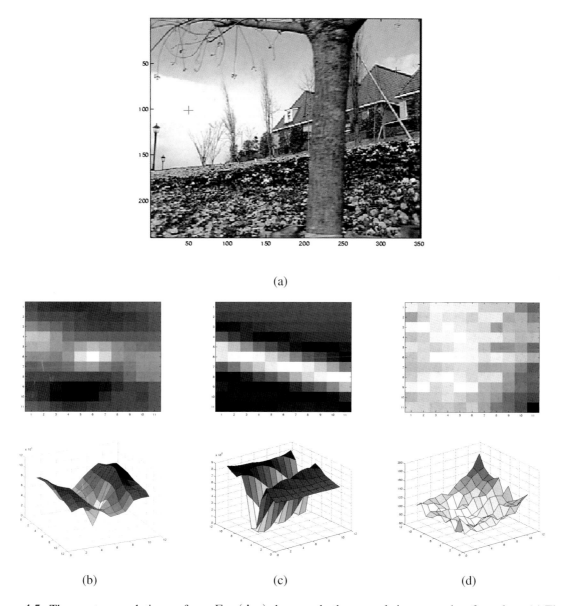

(a)

(b)   (c)   (d)

Figure 4.5 Three auto-correlation surfaces $E_{\mathrm{AC}}(\Delta u)$ shown as both grayscale images and surface plots: (a) The original image is marked with three red crosses to denote where the auto-correlation surfaces were computed; (b) this patch is from the flower bed (good unique minimum); (c) this patch is from the roof edge (one-dimensional aperture problem); and (d) this patch is from the cloud (no good peak). Each grid point in figures b–d is one value of Δu.

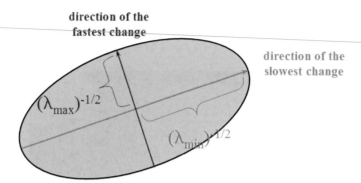

Figure 4.6 Uncertainty ellipse corresponding to an eigenvalue analysis of the auto-correlation matrix A.

The auto-correlation matrix A can be written as

$$A = w * \begin{bmatrix} I_x^2 & I_x I_y \\ I_x I_y & I_y^2 \end{bmatrix}, \tag{4.8}$$

where we have replaced the weighted summations with discrete convolutions with the weighting kernel w. This matrix can be interpreted as a tensor (multiband) image, where the outer products of the gradients ∇I are convolved with a weighting function w to provide a per-pixel estimate of the local (quadratic) shape of the auto-correlation function.

As first shown by Anandan (1984; 1989) and further discussed in Section 8.1.3 and (8.44), the inverse of the matrix A provides a lower bound on the uncertainty in the location of a matching patch. It is therefore a useful indicator of which patches can be reliably matched. The easiest way to visualize and reason about this uncertainty is to perform an eigenvalue analysis of the auto-correlation matrix A, which produces two eigenvalues (λ_0, λ_1) and two eigenvector directions (Figure 4.6). Since the larger uncertainty depends on the smaller eigenvalue, i.e., $\lambda_0^{-1/2}$, it makes sense to find maxima in the smaller eigenvalue to locate good features to track (Shi and Tomasi 1994).

Förstner–Harris. While Anandan and Lucas and Kanade (1981) were the first to analyze the uncertainty structure of the auto-correlation matrix, they did so in the context of associating certainties with optic flow measurements. Förstner (1986) and Harris and Stephens (1988) were the first to propose using local maxima in rotationally invariant scalar measures derived from the auto-correlation matrix to locate keypoints for the purpose of sparse feature matching. (Schmid, Mohr, and Bauckhage (2000); Triggs (2004) give more detailed historical reviews of feature detection algorithms.) Both of these techniques also proposed using a Gaussian weighting window instead of the previously used square patches, which makes the detector response insensitive to in-plane image rotations.

The minimum eigenvalue λ_0 (Shi and Tomasi 1994) is not the only quantity that can be used to find keypoints. A simpler quantity, proposed by Harris and Stephens (1988), is

$$\det(A) - \alpha \operatorname{trace}(A)^2 = \lambda_0 \lambda_1 - \alpha(\lambda_0 + \lambda_1)^2 \tag{4.9}$$

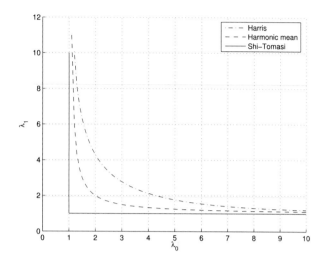

Figure 4.7 Isocontours of popular keypoint detection functions (Brown, Szeliski, and Winder 2004). Each detector looks for points where the eigenvalues λ_0, λ_1 of $\boldsymbol{A} = w * \nabla I \nabla I^T$ are both large.

with $\alpha = 0.06$. Unlike eigenvalue analysis, this quantity does not require the use of square roots and yet is still rotationally invariant and also downweights edge-like features where $\lambda_1 \gg \lambda_0$. Triggs (2004) suggests using the quantity

$$\lambda_0 - \alpha \lambda_1 \tag{4.10}$$

(say, with $\alpha = 0.05$), which also reduces the response at 1D edges, where aliasing errors sometimes inflate the smaller eigenvalue. He also shows how the basic 2×2 Hessian can be extended to parametric motions to detect points that are also accurately localizable in scale and rotation. Brown, Szeliski, and Winder (2005), on the other hand, use the harmonic mean,

$$\frac{\det \boldsymbol{A}}{\operatorname{tr} \boldsymbol{A}} = \frac{\lambda_0 \lambda_1}{\lambda_0 + \lambda_1}, \tag{4.11}$$

which is a smoother function in the region where $\lambda_0 \approx \lambda_1$. Figure 4.7 shows isocontours of the various interest point operators, from which we can see how the two eigenvalues are blended to determine the final interest value.

The steps in the basic auto-correlation-based keypoint detector are summarized in Algorithm 4.1. Figure 4.8 shows the resulting interest operator responses for the classic Harris detector as well as the difference of Gaussian (DoG) detector discussed below.

Adaptive non-maximal suppression (ANMS). While most feature detectors simply look for local maxima in the interest function, this can lead to an uneven distribution of feature points across the image, e.g., points will be denser in regions of higher contrast. To mitigate this problem, Brown, Szeliski, and Winder (2005) only detect features that are both local maxima and whose response value is significantly (10%) greater than that of all of its neighbors within a radius r (Figure 4.9c–d). They devise an efficient way to associate suppression radii with all local maxima by first sorting them by their response strength and then creating a second list sorted by decreasing suppression radius (Brown, Szeliski, and

1. Compute the horizontal and vertical derivatives of the image I_x and I_y by convolving the original image with derivatives of Gaussians (Section 3.2.3).

2. Compute the three images corresponding to the outer products of these gradients. (The matrix A is symmetric, so only three entries are needed.)

3. Convolve each of these images with a larger Gaussian.

4. Compute a scalar interest measure using one of the formulas discussed above.

5. Find local maxima above a certain threshold and report them as detected feature point locations.

Algorithm 4.1 Outline of a basic feature detection algorithm.

(a)   (b)   (c)

Figure 4.8 Interest operator responses: (a) Sample image, (b) Harris response, and (c) DoG response. The circle sizes and colors indicate the scale at which each interest point was detected. Notice how the two detectors tend to respond at complementary locations.

Winder 2005). Figure 4.9 shows a qualitative comparison of selecting the top n features and using ANMS.

Measuring repeatability. Given the large number of feature detectors that have been developed in computer vision, how can we decide which ones to use? Schmid, Mohr, and Bauckhage (2000) were the first to propose measuring the *repeatability* of feature detectors, which they define as the frequency with which keypoints detected in one image are found within ϵ (say, $\epsilon = 1.5$) pixels of the corresponding location in a transformed image. In their paper, they transform their planar images by applying rotations, scale changes, illumination changes, viewpoint changes, and adding noise. They also measure the *information content* available at each detected feature point, which they define as the entropy of a set of rotationally invariant local grayscale descriptors. Among the techniques they survey, they find that the improved (Gaussian derivative) version of the Harris operator with $\sigma_d = 1$ (scale of the derivative Gaussian) and $\sigma_i = 2$ (scale of the integration Gaussian) works best.

(a) Strongest 250   (b) Strongest 500

(c) ANMS 250, $r = 24$ (d) ANMS 500, $r = 16$

Figure 4.9 Adaptive non-maximal suppression (ANMS) (Brown, Szeliski, and Winder 2005) © 2005 IEEE: The upper two images show the strongest 250 and 500 interest points, while the lower two images show the interest points selected with adaptive non-maximal suppression, along with the corresponding suppression radius r. Note how the latter features have a much more uniform spatial distribution across the image.

Scale invariance

In many situations, detecting features at the finest stable scale possible may not be appropriate. For example, when matching images with little high frequency detail (e.g., clouds), fine-scale features may not exist.

One solution to the problem is to extract features at a variety of scales, e.g., by performing the same operations at multiple resolutions in a pyramid and then matching features at the same level. This kind of approach is suitable when the images being matched do not undergo large scale changes, e.g., when matching successive aerial images taken from an airplane or stitching panoramas taken with a fixed-focal-length camera. Figure 4.10 shows the output of one such approach, the multi-scale, oriented patch detector of Brown, Szeliski, and Winder (2005), for which responses at five different scales are shown.

However, for most object recognition applications, the scale of the object in the image is unknown. Instead of extracting features at many different scales and then matching all of them, it is more efficient to extract features that are stable in both location *and* scale (Lowe 2004; Mikolajczyk and Schmid 2004).

Early investigations into scale selection were performed by Lindeberg (1993; 1998b), who first proposed using extrema in the Laplacian of Gaussian (LoG) function as interest

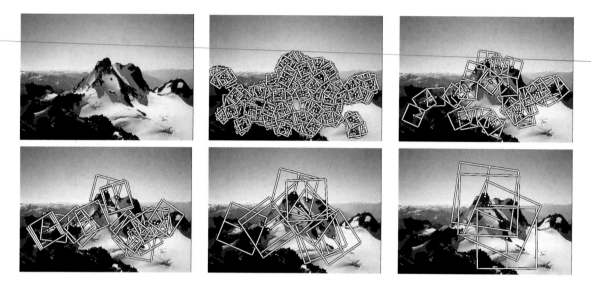

Figure 4.10   Multi-scale oriented patches (MOPS) extracted at five pyramid levels (Brown, Szeliski, and Winder 2005) © 2005 IEEE. The boxes show the feature orientation and the region from which the descriptor vectors are sampled.

point locations. Based on this work, Lowe (2004) proposed computing a set of sub-octave Difference of Gaussian filters (Figure 4.11a), looking for 3D (space+scale) maxima in the resulting structure (Figure 4.11b), and then computing a sub-pixel space+scale location using a quadratic fit (Brown and Lowe 2002). The number of sub-octave levels was determined, after careful empirical investigation, to be three, which corresponds to a quarter-octave pyramid, which is the same as used by Triggs (2004).

As with the Harris operator, pixels where there is strong asymmetry in the local curvature of the indicator function (in this case, the DoG) are rejected. This is implemented by first computing the local Hessian of the difference image D,

$$H = \left[\begin{array}{cc} D_{xx} & D_{xy} \\ D_{xy} & D_{yy} \end{array} \right],$$
(4.12)

and then rejecting keypoints for which

$$\frac{\mathrm{Tr}(H)^2}{\mathrm{Det}(H)} > 10.$$
(4.13)

While Lowe's Scale Invariant Feature Transform (SIFT) performs well in practice, it is not based on the same theoretical foundation of maximum spatial stability as the auto-correlation-based detectors. (In fact, its detection locations are often complementary to those produced by such techniques and can therefore be used in conjunction with these other approaches.) In order to add a scale selection mechanism to the Harris corner detector, Mikolajczyk and Schmid (2004) evaluate the Laplacian of Gaussian function at each detected Harris point (in a multi-scale pyramid) and keep only those points for which the Laplacian is extremal (larger or smaller than both its coarser and finer-level values). An optional iterative refinement for both scale and position is also proposed and evaluated. Additional examples of scale invariant

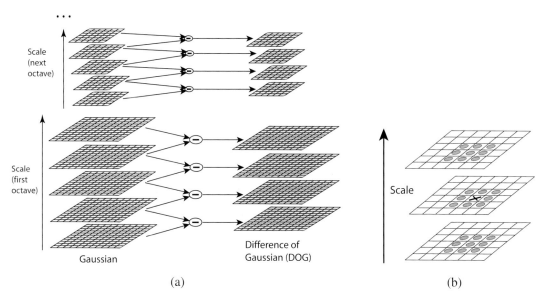

Figure 4.11 Scale-space feature detection using a sub-octave Difference of Gaussian pyramid (Lowe 2004) ©
2004 Springer: (a) Adjacent levels of a sub-octave Gaussian pyramid are subtracted to produce Difference of
Gaussian images; (b) extrema (maxima and minima) in the resulting 3D volume are detected by comparing a
pixel to its 26 neighbors.

region detectors are discussed by Mikolajczyk, Tuytelaars, Schmid *et al.* (2005); Tuytelaars
and Mikolajczyk (2007).

Rotational invariance and orientation estimation

In addition to dealing with scale changes, most image matching and object recognition algorithms need to deal with (at least) in-plane image rotation. One way to deal with this problem
is to design descriptors that are rotationally invariant (Schmid and Mohr 1997), but such
descriptors have poor discriminability, i.e. they map different looking patches to the same
descriptor.

A better method is to estimate a *dominant orientation* at each detected keypoint. Once
the local orientation and scale of a keypoint have been estimated, a scaled and oriented patch
around the detected point can be extracted and used to form a feature descriptor (Figures 4.10
and 4.17).

The simplest possible orientation estimate is the average gradient within a region around
the keypoint. If a Gaussian weighting function is used (Brown, Szeliski, and Winder 2005),
this average gradient is equivalent to a first-order steerable filter (Section 3.2.3), i.e., it can be
computed using an image convolution with the horizontal and vertical derivatives of Gaussian filter (Freeman and Adelson 1991). In order to make this estimate more reliable, it is
usually preferable to use a larger aggregation window (Gaussian kernel size) than detection
window (Brown, Szeliski, and Winder 2005). The orientations of the square boxes shown in
Figure 4.10 were computed using this technique.

Sometimes, however, the averaged (signed) gradient in a region can be small and therefore

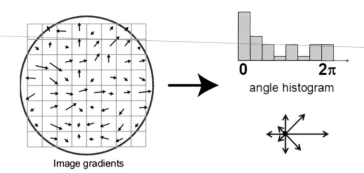

Image gradients   angle histogram

Figure 4.12 A dominant orientation estimate can be computed by creating a histogram of all the gradient orientations (weighted by their magnitudes or after thresholding out small gradients) and then finding the significant peaks in this distribution (Lowe 2004) © 2004 Springer.

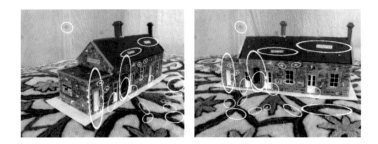

Figure 4.13 Affine region detectors used to match two images taken from dramatically different viewpoints (Mikolajczyk and Schmid 2004) © 2004 Springer.

an unreliable indicator of orientation. A more reliable technique is to look at the *histogram* of orientations computed around the keypoint. Lowe (2004) computes a 36-bin histogram of edge orientations weighted by both gradient magnitude and Gaussian distance to the center, finds all peaks within 80% of the global maximum, and then computes a more accurate orientation estimate using a three-bin parabolic fit (Figure 4.12).

Affine invariance

While scale and rotation invariance are highly desirable, for many applications such as *wide baseline stereo matching* (Pritchett and Zisserman 1998; Schaffalitzky and Zisserman 2002) or location recognition (Chum, Philbin, Sivic *et al.* 2007), full affine invariance is preferred. Affine-invariant detectors not only respond at consistent locations after scale and orientation changes, they also respond consistently across affine deformations such as (local) perspective foreshortening (Figure 4.13). In fact, for a small enough patch, any continuous image warping can be well approximated by an affine deformation.

To introduce affine invariance, several authors have proposed fitting an ellipse to the autocorrelation or Hessian matrix (using eigenvalue analysis) and then using the principal axes and ratios of this fit as the affine coordinate frame (Lindeberg and Garding 1997; Baumberg

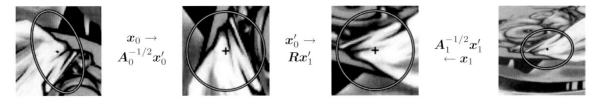

Figure 4.14 Affine normalization using the second moment matrices, as described by Mikolajczyk, Tuytelaars, Schmid *et al.* (2005) © 2005 Springer. After image coordinates are transformed using the matrices $A_0^{-1/2}$ and $A_1^{-1/2}$, they are related by a pure rotation R, which can be estimated using a dominant orientation technique.

Figure 4.15 Maximally stable extremal regions (MSERs) extracted and matched from a number of images (Matas, Chum, Urban *et al.* 2004) © 2004 Elsevier.

2000; Mikolajczyk and Schmid 2004; Mikolajczyk, Tuytelaars, Schmid *et al.* 2005; Tuytelaars and Mikolajczyk 2007). Figure 4.14 shows how the square root of the moment matrix can be used to transform local patches into a frame which is similar up to rotation.

Another important affine invariant region detector is the maximally stable extremal region (MSER) detector developed by Matas, Chum, Urban *et al.* (2004). To detect MSERs, binary regions are computed by thresholding the image at all possible gray levels (the technique therefore only works for grayscale images). This operation can be performed efficiently by first sorting all pixels by gray value and then incrementally adding pixels to each connected component as the threshold is changed (Nistér and Stewénius 2008). As the threshold is changed, the area of each component (region) is monitored; regions whose rate of change of area with respect to the threshold is minimal are defined as *maximally stable*. Such regions are therefore invariant to both affine geometric and photometric (linear bias-gain or smooth monotonic) transformations (Figure 4.15). If desired, an affine coordinate frame can be fit to each detected region using its moment matrix.

The area of feature point detectors continues to be very active, with papers appearing every year at major computer vision conferences (Xiao and Shah 2003; Koethe 2003; Carneiro and Jepson 2005; Kenney, Zuliani, and Manjunath 2005; Bay, Tuytelaars, and Van Gool 2006; Platel, Balmachnova, Florack *et al.* 2006; Rosten and Drummond 2006). Mikolajczyk, Tuytelaars, Schmid *et al.* (2005) survey a number of popular affine region detectors and provide experimental comparisons of their invariance to common image transformations such as scaling, rotations, noise, and blur. These experimental results, code, and pointers to the surveyed papers can be found on their Web site at http://www.robots.ox.ac.uk/~vgg/research/affine/.

Of course, keypoints are not the only features that can be used for registering images. Zoghlami, Faugeras, and Deriche (1997) use line segments as well as point-like features to estimate homographies between pairs of images, whereas Bartoli, Coquerelle, and Sturm (2004) use line segments with local correspondences along the edges to extract 3D structure

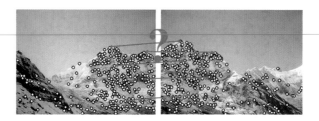

Figure 4.16 Feature matching: how can we extract local descriptors that are invariant to inter-image variations and yet still discriminative enough to establish correct correspondences?

and motion. Tuytelaars and Van Gool (2004) use affine invariant regions to detect correspondences for wide baseline stereo matching, whereas Kadir, Zisserman, and Brady (2004) detect salient regions where patch entropy and its rate of change with scale are locally maximal. Corso and Hager (2005) use a related technique to fit 2D oriented Gaussian kernels to homogeneous regions. More details on techniques for finding and matching curves, lines, and regions can be found later in this chapter.

4.1.2 Feature descriptors

After detecting features (keypoints), we must *match* them, i.e., we must determine which features come from corresponding locations in different images. In some situations, e.g., for video sequences (Shi and Tomasi 1994) or for stereo pairs that have been *rectified* (Zhang, Deriche, Faugeras *et al.* 1995; Loop and Zhang 1999; Scharstein and Szeliski 2002), the local motion around each feature point may be mostly translational. In this case, simple error metrics, such as the *sum of squared differences* or *normalized cross-correlation*, described in Section 8.1 can be used to directly compare the intensities in small patches around each feature point. (The comparative study by Mikolajczyk and Schmid (2005), discussed below, uses cross-correlation.) Because feature points may not be exactly located, a more accurate matching score can be computed by performing incremental motion refinement as described in Section 8.1.3 but this can be time consuming and can sometimes even decrease performance (Brown, Szeliski, and Winder 2005).

In most cases, however, the local appearance of features will change in orientation and scale, and sometimes even undergo affine deformations. Extracting a local scale, orientation, or affine frame estimate and then using this to resample the patch before forming the feature descriptor is thus usually preferable (Figure 4.17).

Even after compensating for these changes, the local appearance of image patches will usually still vary from image to image. How can we make image descriptors more invariant to such changes, while still preserving discriminability between different (non-corresponding) patches (Figure 4.16)? Mikolajczyk and Schmid (2005) review some recently developed view-invariant local image descriptors and experimentally compare their performance. Below, we describe a few of these descriptors in more detail.

Bias and gain normalization (MOPS). For tasks that do not exhibit large amounts of foreshortening, such as image stitching, simple normalized intensity patches perform reasonably well and are simple to implement (Brown, Szeliski, and Winder 2005) (Figure 4.17). In

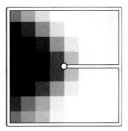

Figure 4.17 MOPS descriptors are formed using an 8×8 sampling of bias and gain normalized intensity values, with a sample spacing of five pixels relative to the detection scale (Brown, Szeliski, and Winder 2005) © 2005 IEEE. This low frequency sampling gives the features some robustness to interest point location error and is achieved by sampling at a higher pyramid level than the detection scale.

order to compensate for slight inaccuracies in the feature point detector (location, orientation, and scale), these multi-scale oriented patches (MOPS) are sampled at a spacing of five pixels relative to the detection scale, using a coarser level of the image pyramid to avoid aliasing. To compensate for affine photometric variations (linear exposure changes or bias and gain, (3.3)), patch intensities are re-scaled so that their mean is zero and their variance is one.

Scale invariant feature transform (SIFT). SIFT features are formed by computing the gradient at each pixel in a 16×16 window around the detected keypoint, using the appropriate level of the Gaussian pyramid at which the keypoint was detected. The gradient magnitudes are downweighted by a Gaussian fall-off function (shown as a blue circle in (Figure 4.18a) in order to reduce the influence of gradients far from the center, as these are more affected by small misregistrations.

In each 4×4 quadrant, a gradient orientation histogram is formed by (conceptually) adding the weighted gradient value to one of eight orientation histogram bins. To reduce the effects of location and dominant orientation misestimation, each of the original 256 weighted gradient magnitudes is softly added to $2 \times 2 \times 2$ histogram bins using trilinear interpolation. Softly distributing values to adjacent histogram bins is generally a good idea in any application where histograms are being computed, e.g., for Hough transforms (Section 4.3.2) or local histogram equalization (Section 3.1.4).

The resulting 128 non-negative values form a raw version of the SIFT descriptor vector. To reduce the effects of contrast or gain (additive variations are already removed by the gradient), the 128-D vector is normalized to unit length. To further make the descriptor robust to other photometric variations, values are clipped to 0.2 and the resulting vector is once again renormalized to unit length.

PCA-SIFT. Ke and Sukthankar (2004) propose a simpler way to compute descriptors inspired by SIFT; it computes the x and y (gradient) derivatives over a 39×39 patch and then reduces the resulting 3042-dimensional vector to 36 using principal component analysis (PCA) (Section 14.2.1 and Appendix A.1.2). Another popular variant of SIFT is SURF (Bay, Tuytelaars, and Van Gool 2006), which uses box filters to approximate the derivatives and

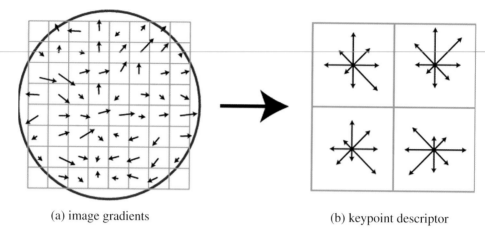

(a) image gradients   (b) keypoint descriptor

Figure 4.18 A schematic representation of Lowe's (2004) scale invariant feature transform (SIFT): (a) Gradient orientations and magnitudes are computed at each pixel and weighted by a Gaussian fall-off function (blue circle). (b) A weighted gradient orientation histogram is then computed in each subregion, using trilinear interpolation. While this figure shows an 8×8 pixel patch and a 2×2 descriptor array, Lowe's actual implementation uses 16×16 patches and a 4×4 array of eight-bin histograms.

integrals used in SIFT.

Gradient location-orientation histogram (GLOH).   This descriptor, developed by Mikolajczyk and Schmid (2005), is a variant on SIFT that uses a log-polar binning structure instead of the four quadrants used by Lowe (2004) (Figure 4.19). The spatial bins are of radius 6, 11, and 15, with eight angular bins (except for the central region), for a total of 17 spatial bins and 16 orientation bins. The 272-dimensional histogram is then projected onto a 128-dimensional descriptor using PCA trained on a large database. In their evaluation, Mikolajczyk and Schmid (2005) found that GLOH, which has the best performance overall, outperforms SIFT by a small margin.

Steerable filters.   Steerable filters (Section 3.2.3) are combinations of derivative of Gaussian filters that permit the rapid computation of even and odd (symmetric and anti-symmetric) edge-like and corner-like features at all possible orientations (Freeman and Adelson 1991). Because they use reasonably broad Gaussians, they too are somewhat insensitive to localization and orientation errors.

Performance of local descriptors.   Among the local descriptors that Mikolajczyk and Schmid (2005) compared, they found that GLOH performed best, followed closely by SIFT (see Figure 4.25). They also present results for many other descriptors not covered in this book.

The field of feature descriptors continues to evolve rapidly, with some of the newer techniques looking at local color information (van de Weijer and Schmid 2006; Abdel-Hakim and Farag 2006). Winder and Brown (2007) develop a multi-stage framework for feature descriptor computation that subsumes both SIFT and GLOH (Figure 4.20a) and also allows

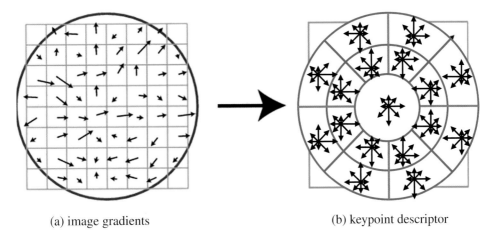

(a) image gradients   (b) keypoint descriptor

Figure 4.19 The gradient location-orientation histogram (GLOH) descriptor uses log-polar bins instead of square bins to compute orientation histograms (Mikolajczyk and Schmid 2005).

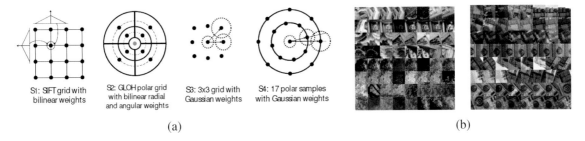

(a)   (b)

Figure 4.20 Spatial summation blocks for SIFT, GLOH, and some newly developed feature descriptors (Winder and Brown 2007) © 2007 IEEE: (a) The parameters for the new features, e.g., their Gaussian weights, are learned from a training database of (b) matched real-world image patches obtained from robust structure from motion applied to Internet photo collections (Hua, Brown, and Winder 2007).

them to learn optimal parameters for newer descriptors that outperform previous hand-tuned descriptors. Hua, Brown, and Winder (2007) extend this work by learning lower-dimensional projections of higher-dimensional descriptors that have the best discriminative power. Both of these papers use a database of real-world image patches (Figure 4.20b) obtained by sampling images at locations that were reliably matched using a robust structure-from-motion algorithm applied to Internet photo collections (Snavely, Seitz, and Szeliski 2006; Goesele, Snavely, Curless *et al.* 2007). In concurrent work, Tola, Lepetit, and Fua (2010) developed a similar DAISY descriptor for dense stereo matching and optimized its parameters based on ground truth stereo data.

While these techniques construct feature detectors that optimize for repeatability across *all* object classes, it is also possible to develop class- or instance-specific feature detectors that maximize *discriminability* from other classes (Ferencz, Learned-Miller, and Malik 2008).

Figure 4.21 Recognizing objects in a cluttered scene (Lowe 2004) © 2004 Springer. Two of the training images in the database are shown on the left. These are matched to the cluttered scene in the middle using SIFT features, shown as small squares in the right image. The affine warp of each recognized database image onto the scene is shown as a larger parallelogram in the right image.

4.1.3 Feature matching

Once we have extracted features and their descriptors from two or more images, the next step is to establish some preliminary feature matches between these images. In this section, we divide this problem into two separate components. The first is to select a *matching strategy*, which determines which correspondences are passed on to the next stage for further processing. The second is to devise efficient *data structures* and *algorithms* to perform this matching as quickly as possible. (See the discussion of related techniques in Section 14.3.2.)

Matching strategy and error rates

Determining which feature matches are reasonable to process further depends on the context in which the matching is being performed. Say we are given two images that overlap to a fair amount (e.g., for image stitching, as in Figure 4.16, or for tracking objects in a video). We know that most features in one image are likely to match the other image, although some may not match because they are occluded or their appearance has changed too much.

On the other hand, if we are trying to recognize how many known objects appear in a cluttered scene (Figure 4.21), most of the features may not match. Furthermore, a large number of potentially matching objects must be searched, which requires more efficient strategies, as described below.

To begin with, we assume that the feature descriptors have been designed so that Euclidean (vector magnitude) distances in feature space can be directly used for ranking potential matches. If it turns out that certain parameters (axes) in a descriptor are more reliable than others, it is usually preferable to re-scale these axes ahead of time, e.g., by determining how much they vary when compared against other known good matches (Hua, Brown, and Winder 2007). A more general process, which involves transforming feature vectors into a new scaled basis, is called *whitening* and is discussed in more detail in the context of eigenface-based face recognition (Section 14.2.1).

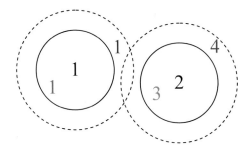

Figure 4.22 False positives and negatives: The black digits 1 and 2 are features being matched against a database of features in other images. At the current threshold setting (the solid circles), the green 1 is a *true positive* (good match), the blue 1 is a *false negative* (failure to match), and the red 3 is a *false positive* (incorrect match). If we set the threshold higher (the dashed circles), the blue 1 becomes a true positive but the brown 4 becomes an additional false positive.

	True matches	True non-matches		
Predicted matches	TP = 18	FP = 4	P' = 22	PPV = 0.82
Predicted non-matches	FN = 2	TN = 76	N' = 78	
	P = 20	N = 80	Total = 100	
	TPR = 0.90	FPR = 0.05		ACC = 0.94

Table 4.1 The number of matches correctly and incorrectly estimated by a feature matching algorithm, showing the number of true positives (TP), false positives (FP), false negatives (FN) and true negatives (TN). The columns sum up to the actual number of positives (P) and negatives (N), while the rows sum up to the predicted number of positives (P') and negatives (N'). The formulas for the true positive rate (TPR), the false positive rate (FPR), the positive predictive value (PPV), and the accuracy (ACC) are given in the text.

Given a Euclidean distance metric, the simplest matching strategy is to set a threshold (maximum distance) and to return all matches from other images within this threshold. Setting the threshold too high results in too many *false positives*, i.e., incorrect matches being returned. Setting the threshold too low results in too many *false negatives*, i.e., too many correct matches being missed (Figure 4.22).

We can quantify the performance of a matching algorithm at a particular threshold by first counting the number of true and false matches and match failures, using the following definitions (Fawcett 2006):

- TP: true positives, i.e., number of correct matches;

- FN: false negatives, matches that were not correctly detected;

- FP: false positives, proposed matches that are incorrect;

- TN: true negatives, non-matches that were correctly rejected.

Table 4.1 shows a sample *confusion matrix* (contingency table) containing such numbers.

We can convert these numbers into *unit rates* by defining the following quantities (Fawcett 2006):

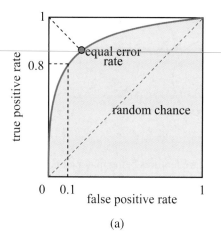
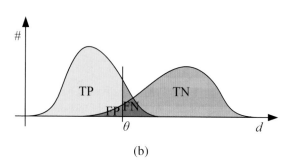

(a)   (b)

Figure 4.23 ROC curve and its related rates: (a) The ROC curve plots the true positive rate against the false positive rate for a particular combination of feature extraction and matching algorithms. Ideally, the true positive rate should be close to 1, while the false positive rate is close to 0. The area under the ROC curve (AUC) is often used as a single (scalar) measure of algorithm performance. Alternatively, the equal error rate is sometimes used. (b) The distribution of positives (matches) and negatives (non-matches) as a function of inter-feature distance d. As the threshold θ is increased, the number of true positives (TP) and false positives (FP) increases.

- true positive rate (TPR),

$$\text{TPR} = \frac{\text{TP}}{\text{TP+FN}} = \frac{\text{TP}}{\text{P}}; \tag{4.14}$$

- false positive rate (FPR),

$$\text{FPR} = \frac{\text{FP}}{\text{FP+TN}} = \frac{\text{FP}}{\text{N}}; \tag{4.15}$$

- positive predictive value (PPV),

$$\text{PPV} = \frac{\text{TP}}{\text{TP+FP}} = \frac{\text{TP}}{\text{P'}}; \tag{4.16}$$

- accuracy (ACC),

$$\text{ACC} = \frac{\text{TP+TN}}{\text{P+N}}. \tag{4.17}$$

In the *information retrieval* (or document retrieval) literature (Baeza-Yates and Ribeiro-Neto 1999; Manning, Raghavan, and Schütze 2008), the term *precision* (how many returned documents are relevant) is used instead of PPV and *recall* (what fraction of relevant documents was found) is used instead of TPR.

Any particular matching strategy (at a particular threshold or parameter setting) can be rated by the TPR and FPR numbers; ideally, the true positive rate will be close to 1 and the false positive rate close to 0. As we vary the matching threshold, we obtain a family of such points, which are collectively known as the *receiver operating characteristic (ROC curve)* (Fawcett 2006) (Figure 4.23a). The closer this curve lies to the upper left corner, i.e., the larger the area under the curve (AUC), the better its performance. Figure 4.23b shows how we can plot the number of matches and non-matches as a function of inter-feature distance d.

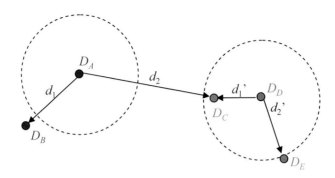

Figure 4.24 Fixed threshold, nearest neighbor, and nearest neighbor distance ratio matching. At a fixed distance threshold (dashed circles), descriptor D_A fails to match D_B and D_D incorrectly matches D_C and D_E. If we pick the nearest neighbor, D_A correctly matches D_B but D_D incorrectly matches D_C. Using nearest neighbor distance ratio (NNDR) matching, the small NNDR d_1/d_2 correctly matches D_A with D_B, and the large NNDR d_1'/d_2' correctly rejects matches for D_D.

These curves can then be used to plot an ROC curve (Exercise 4.3). The ROC curve can also be used to calculate the *mean average precision*, which is the average precision (PPV) as you vary the threshold to select the best results, then the two top results, etc.

The problem with using a fixed threshold is that it is difficult to set; the useful range of thresholds can vary a lot as we move to different parts of the feature space (Lowe 2004; Mikolajczyk and Schmid 2005). A better strategy in such cases is to simply match the *nearest neighbor* in feature space. Since some features may have no matches (e.g., they may be part of background clutter in object recognition or they may be occluded in the other image), a threshold is still used to reduce the number of false positives.

Ideally, this threshold itself will adapt to different regions of the feature space. If sufficient training data is available (Hua, Brown, and Winder 2007), it is sometimes possible to learn different thresholds for different features. Often, however, we are simply given a collection of images to match, e.g., when stitching images or constructing 3D models from unordered photo collections (Brown and Lowe 2007, 2003; Snavely, Seitz, and Szeliski 2006). In this case, a useful heuristic can be to compare the nearest neighbor distance to that of the second nearest neighbor, preferably taken from an image that is known not to match the target (e.g., a different object in the database) (Brown and Lowe 2002; Lowe 2004). We can define this *nearest neighbor distance ratio* (Mikolajczyk and Schmid 2005) as

$$\text{NNDR} = \frac{d_1}{d_2} = \frac{\|D_A - D_B\|}{\|D_A - D_C\|}, \tag{4.18}$$

where d_1 and d_2 are the nearest and second nearest neighbor distances, D_A is the target descriptor, and D_B and D_C are its closest two neighbors (Figure 4.24).

The effects of using these three different matching strategies for the feature descriptors evaluated by Mikolajczyk and Schmid (2005) are shown in Figure 4.25. As you can see, the nearest neighbor and NNDR strategies produce improved ROC curves.

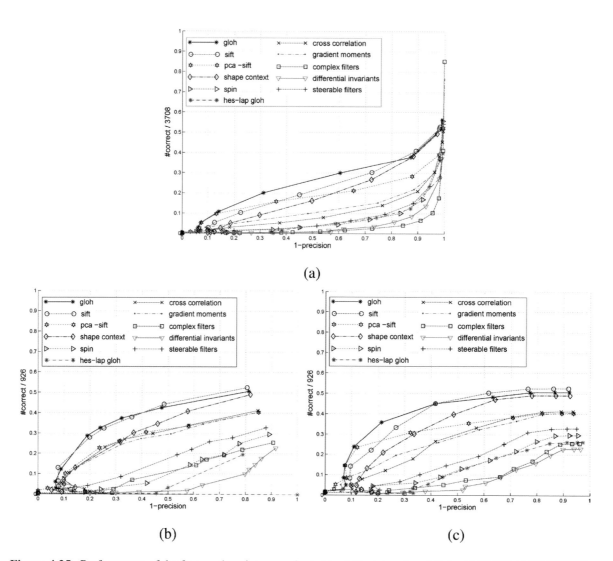

(a)

(b)   (c)

Figure 4.25 Performance of the feature descriptors evaluated by Mikolajczyk and Schmid (2005) © 2005 IEEE, shown for three matching strategies: (a) fixed threshold; (b) nearest neighbor; (c) nearest neighbor distance ratio (NNDR). Note how the ordering of the algorithms does not change that much, but the overall performance varies significantly between the different matching strategies.

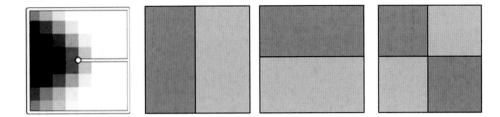

Figure 4.26 The three Haar wavelet coefficients used for hashing the MOPS descriptor devised by Brown, Szeliski, and Winder (2005) are computed by summing each 8×8 normalized patch over the light and dark gray regions and taking their difference.

Efficient matching

Once we have decided on a matching strategy, we still need to search efficiently for potential candidates. The simplest way to find all corresponding feature points is to compare all features against all other features in each pair of potentially matching images. Unfortunately, this is quadratic in the number of extracted features, which makes it impractical for most applications.

A better approach is to devise an *indexing structure*, such as a multi-dimensional search tree or a hash table, to rapidly search for features near a given feature. Such indexing structures can either be built for each image independently (which is useful if we want to only consider certain potential matches, e.g., searching for a particular object) or globally for all the images in a given database, which can potentially be faster, since it removes the need to iterate over each image. For extremely large databases (millions of images or more), even more efficient structures based on ideas from document retrieval (e.g., *vocabulary trees*, (Nistér and Stewénius 2006)) can be used (Section 14.3.2).

One of the simpler techniques to implement is multi-dimensional hashing, which maps descriptors into fixed size buckets based on some function applied to each descriptor vector. At matching time, each new feature is hashed into a bucket, and a search of nearby buckets is used to return potential candidates, which can then be sorted or graded to determine which are valid matches.

A simple example of hashing is the Haar wavelets used by Brown, Szeliski, and Winder (2005) in their MOPS paper. During the matching structure construction, each 8×8 scaled, oriented, and normalized MOPS patch is converted into a three-element index by performing sums over different quadrants of the patch (Figure 4.26). The resulting three values are normalized by their expected standard deviations and then mapped to the two (of $b = 10$) nearest 1D bins. The three-dimensional indices formed by concatenating the three quantized values are used to index the $2^3 = 8$ bins where the feature is stored (added). At query time, only the primary (closest) indices are used, so only a single three-dimensional bin needs to be examined. The coefficients in the bin can then be used to select k approximate nearest neighbors for further processing (such as computing the NNDR).

A more complex, but more widely applicable, version of hashing is called *locality sensitive hashing*, which uses unions of independently computed hashing functions to index the features (Gionis, Indyk, and Motwani 1999; Shakhnarovich, Darrell, and Indyk 2006). Shakhnarovich, Viola, and Darrell (2003) extend this technique to be more sensitive to the

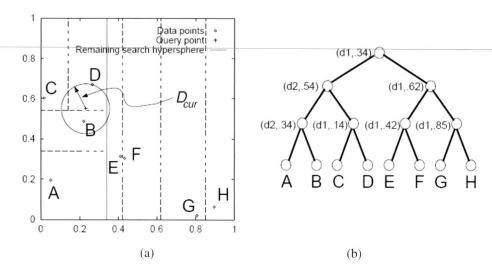

(a)   (b)

Figure 4.27 K-d tree and best bin first (BBF) search (Beis and Lowe 1999) © 1999 IEEE: (a) The spatial arrangement of the axis-aligned cutting planes is shown using dashed lines. Individual data points are shown as small diamonds. (b) The same subdivision can be represented as a tree, where each interior node represents an axis-aligned cutting plane (e.g., the top node cuts along dimension d1 at value .34) and each leaf node is a data point. During a BBF search, a query point (denoted by "+") first looks in its containing bin (D) and then in its nearest adjacent bin (B), rather than its closest neighbor in the tree (C).

distribution of points in parameter space, which they call *parameter-sensitive hashing*. Even more recent work converts high-dimensional descriptor vectors into binary codes that can be compared using Hamming distances (Torralba, Weiss, and Fergus 2008; Weiss, Torralba, and Fergus 2008) or that can accommodate arbitrary kernel functions (Kulis and Grauman 2009; Raginsky and Lazebnik 2009).

Another widely used class of indexing structures are multi-dimensional search trees. The best known of these are *k-d trees*, also often written as *k*d-trees, which divide the multi-dimensional feature space along alternating axis-aligned hyperplanes, choosing the threshold along each axis so as to maximize some criterion, such as the search tree balance (Samet 1989). Figure 4.27 shows an example of a two-dimensional k-d tree. Here, eight different data points A–H are shown as small diamonds arranged on a two-dimensional plane. The k-d tree recursively splits this plane along axis-aligned (horizontal or vertical) cutting planes. Each split can be denoted using the dimension number and split value (Figure 4.27b). The splits are arranged so as to try to balance the tree, i.e., to keep its maximum depth as small as possible. At query time, a classic k-d tree search first locates the query point (+) in its appropriate bin (D), and then searches nearby leaves in the tree (C, B, ...) until it can guarantee that the nearest neighbor has been found. The best bin first (BBF) search (Beis and Lowe 1999) searches bins in order of their spatial proximity to the query point and is therefore usually more efficient.

Many additional data structures have been developed over the years for solving nearest neighbor problems (Arya, Mount, Netanyahu *et al.* 1998; Liang, Liu, Xu *et al.* 2001; Hjaltason and Samet 2003). For example, Nene and Nayar (1997) developed a technique they call *slicing* that uses a series of 1D binary searches on the point list sorted along different dimensions to efficiently cull down a list of candidate points that lie within a hypercube of the query point. Grauman and Darrell (2005) reweight the matches at different levels of an indexing tree, which allows their technique to be less sensitive to discretization errors in the tree construction. Nistér and Stewénius (2006) use a *metric tree*, which compares feature descriptors to a small number of prototypes at each level in a hierarchy. The resulting quantized *visual words* can then be used with classical information retrieval (document relevance) techniques to quickly winnow down a set of potential candidates from a database of millions of images (Section 14.3.2). Muja and Lowe (2009) compare a number of these approaches, introduce a new one of their own (priority search on hierarchical k-means trees), and conclude that multiple randomized k-d trees often provide the best performance. Despite all of this promising work, the rapid computation of image feature correspondences remains a challenging open research problem.

Feature match verification and densification

Once we have some hypothetical (putative) matches, we can often use geometric alignment (Section 6.1) to verify which matches are *inliers* and which ones are *outliers*. For example, if we expect the whole image to be translated or rotated in the matching view, we can fit a global geometric transform and keep only those feature matches that are sufficiently close to this estimated transformation. The process of selecting a small set of seed matches and then verifying a larger set is often called *random sampling* or RANSAC (Section 6.1.4). Once an initial set of correspondences has been established, some systems look for additional matches, e.g., by looking for additional correspondences along epipolar lines (Section 11.1) or in the vicinity of estimated locations based on the global transform. These topics are discussed further in Sections 6.1, 11.2, and 14.3.1.

4.1.4 Feature tracking

An alternative to independently finding features in all candidate images and then matching them is to find a set of likely feature locations in a first image and to then *search* for their corresponding locations in subsequent images. This kind of *detect then track* approach is more widely used for video tracking applications, where the expected amount of motion and appearance deformation between adjacent frames is expected to be small.

The process of selecting good features to track is closely related to selecting good features for more general recognition applications. In practice, regions containing high gradients in both directions, i.e., which have high eigenvalues in the auto-correlation matrix (4.8), provide stable locations at which to find correspondences (Shi and Tomasi 1994).

In subsequent frames, searching for locations where the corresponding patch has low squared difference (4.1) often works well enough. However, if the images are undergoing brightness change, explicitly compensating for such variations (8.9) or using *normalized cross-correlation* (8.11) may be preferable. If the search range is large, it is also often more efficient to use a *hierarchical* search strategy, which uses matches in lower-resolution images to provide better initial guesses and hence speed up the search (Section 8.1.1). Alternatives to this strategy involve learning what the appearance of the patch being tracked should be and then searching for it in the vicinity of its predicted position (Avidan 2001; Jurie and Dhome

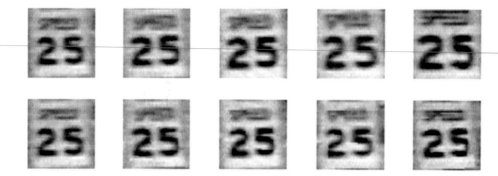

Figure 4.28 Feature tracking using an affine motion model (Shi and Tomasi 1994) © 1994 IEEE, Top row: image patch around the tracked feature location. Bottom row: image patch after warping back toward the first frame using an affine deformation. Even though the speed sign gets larger from frame to frame, the affine transformation maintains a good resemblance between the original and subsequent tracked frames.

2002; Williams, Blake, and Cipolla 2003). These topics are all covered in more detail in Section 8.1.3.

If features are being tracked over longer image sequences, their appearance can undergo larger changes. You then have to decide whether to continue matching against the originally detected patch (feature) or to re-sample each subsequent frame at the matching location. The former strategy is prone to failure as the original patch can undergo appearance changes such as foreshortening. The latter runs the risk of the feature drifting from its original location to some other location in the image (Shi and Tomasi 1994). (Mathematically, small misregistration errors compound to create a *Markov Random Walk*, which leads to larger drift over time.)

A preferable solution is to compare the original patch to later image locations using an *affine* motion model (Section 8.2). Shi and Tomasi (1994) first compare patches in neighboring frames using a translational model and then use the location estimates produced by this step to initialize an affine registration between the patch in the current frame and the base frame where a feature was first detected (Figure 4.28). In their system, features are only detected infrequently, i.e., only in regions where tracking has failed. In the usual case, an area around the current *predicted* location of the feature is searched with an incremental registration algorithm (Section 8.1.3). The resulting tracker is often called the Kanade–Lucas–Tomasi (KLT) tracker.

Since their original work on feature tracking, Shi and Tomasi's approach has generated a string of interesting follow-on papers and applications. Beardsley, Torr, and Zisserman (1996) use extended feature tracking combined with structure from motion (Chapter 7) to incrementally build up sparse 3D models from video sequences. Kang, Szeliski, and Shum (1997) tie together the corners of adjacent (regularly gridded) patches to provide some additional stability to the tracking, at the cost of poorer handling of occlusions. Tommasini, Fusiello, Trucco *et al.* (1998) provide a better spurious match rejection criterion for the basic Shi and Tomasi algorithm, Collins and Liu (2003) provide improved mechanisms for feature selection and dealing with larger appearance changes over time, and Shafique and Shah (2005) develop algorithms for feature matching (data association) for videos with large numbers of

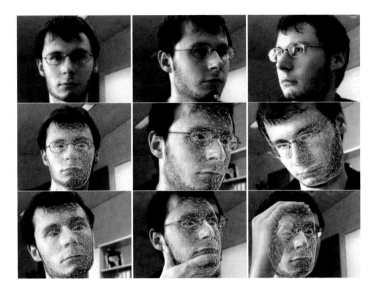

Figure 4.29 Real-time head tracking using the fast trained classifiers of Lepetit, Pilet, and Fua (2004) © 2004 IEEE.

moving objects or points. Yilmaz, Javed, and Shah (2006) and Lepetit and Fua (2005) survey the larger field of object tracking, which includes not only feature-based techniques but also alternative techniques based on contour and region (Section 5.1).

One of the newest developments in feature tracking is the use of learning algorithms to build special-purpose recognizers to rapidly search for matching features anywhere in an image (Lepetit, Pilet, and Fua 2006; Hinterstoisser, Benhimane, Navab *et al.* 2008; Rogez, Rihan, Ramalingam *et al.* 2008; Özuysal, Calonder, Lepetit *et al.* 2010).[2] By taking the time to train classifiers on sample patches and their affine deformations, extremely fast and reliable feature detectors can be constructed, which enables much faster motions to be supported (Figure 4.29). Coupling such features to deformable models (Pilet, Lepetit, and Fua 2008) or structure-from-motion algorithms (Klein and Murray 2008) can result in even higher stability.

4.1.5 *Application*: Performance-driven animation

One of the most compelling applications of fast feature tracking is *performance-driven animation*, i.e., the interactive deformation of a 3D graphics model based on tracking a user's motions (Williams 1990; Litwinowicz and Williams 1994; Lepetit, Pilet, and Fua 2004).

Buck, Finkelstein, Jacobs *et al.* (2000) present a system that tracks a user's facial expressions and head motions and then uses them to morph among a series of hand-drawn sketches. An animator first extracts the eye and mouth regions of each sketch and draws control lines over each image (Figure 4.30a). At run time, a face-tracking system (Toyama 1998) determines the current location of these features (Figure 4.30b). The animation system decides

---

[2] See also my previous comment on earlier work in learning-based tracking (Avidan 2001; Jurie and Dhome 2002; Williams, Blake, and Cipolla 2003).

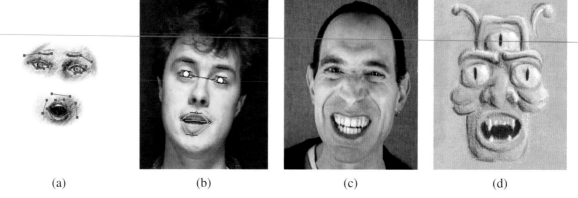

(a)   (b)   (c)   (d)

Figure 4.30 Performance-driven, hand-drawn animation (Buck, Finkelstein, Jacobs *et al.* 2000) © 2000 ACM: (a) eye and mouth portions of hand-drawn sketch with their overlaid control lines; (b) an input video frame with the tracked features overlaid; (c) a different input video frame along with its (d) corresponding hand-drawn animation.

which input images to morph based on nearest neighbor feature appearance matching and triangular barycentric interpolation. It also computes the global location and orientation of the head from the tracked features. The resulting morphed eye and mouth regions are then composited back into the overall head model to yield a frame of hand-drawn animation (Figure 4.30d).

In more recent work, Barnes, Jacobs, Sanders *et al.* (2008) watch users animate paper cutouts on a desk and then turn the resulting motions and drawings into seamless 2D animations.

4.2 Edges

While interest points are useful for finding image locations that can be accurately matched in 2D, edge points are far more plentiful and often carry important semantic associations. For example, the boundaries of objects, which also correspond to occlusion events in 3D, are usually delineated by visible contours. Other kinds of edges correspond to shadow boundaries or crease edges, where surface orientation changes rapidly. Isolated edge points can also be grouped into longer *curves* or *contours*, as well as *straight line segments* (Section 4.3). It is interesting that even young children have no difficulty in recognizing familiar objects or animals from such simple line drawings.

4.2.1 Edge detection

Given an image, how can we find the salient edges? Consider the color images in Figure 4.31. If someone asked you to point out the most "salient" or "strongest" edges or the object boundaries (Martin, Fowlkes, and Malik 2004; Arbeláez, Maire, Fowlkes *et al.* 2010), which ones would you trace? How closely do your perceptions match the edge images shown in Figure 4.31?

Figure 4.31 Human boundary detection (Martin, Fowlkes, and Malik 2004) © 2004 IEEE. The darkness of the edges corresponds to how many human subjects marked an object boundary at that location.

Qualitatively, edges occur at boundaries between regions of different color, intensity, or texture. Unfortunately, segmenting an image into coherent regions is a difficult task, which we address in Chapter 5. Often, it is preferable to detect edges using only purely local information.

Under such conditions, a reasonable approach is to define an edge as a location of *rapid intensity variation*.[3] Think of an image as a height field. On such a surface, edges occur at locations of *steep slopes*, or equivalently, in regions of closely packed contour lines (on a topographic map).

A mathematical way to define the slope and direction of a surface is through its gradient,

$$\boldsymbol{J}(\boldsymbol{x}) = \nabla I(\boldsymbol{x}) = (\frac{\partial I}{\partial x}, \frac{\partial I}{\partial y})(\boldsymbol{x}). \tag{4.19}$$

The local gradient vector $\boldsymbol{J}$ points in the direction of *steepest ascent* in the intensity function. Its magnitude is an indication of the slope or strength of the variation, while its orientation points in a direction *perpendicular* to the local contour.

Unfortunately, taking image derivatives accentuates high frequencies and hence amplifies noise, since the proportion of noise to signal is larger at high frequencies. It is therefore prudent to smooth the image with a low-pass filter prior to computing the gradient. Because we would like the response of our edge detector to be independent of orientation, a circularly symmetric smoothing filter is desirable. As we saw in Section 3.2, the Gaussian is the only separable circularly symmetric filter and so it is used in most edge detection algorithms. Canny (1986) discusses alternative filters and a number of researcher review alternative edge detection algorithms and compare their performance (Davis 1975; Nalwa and Binford 1986; Nalwa 1987; Deriche 1987; Freeman and Adelson 1991; Nalwa 1993; Heath, Sarkar, Sanocki *et al.* 1998; Crane 1997; Ritter and Wilson 2000; Bowyer, Kranenburg, and Dougherty 2001; Arbeláez, Maire, Fowlkes *et al.* 2010).

Because differentiation is a linear operation, it commutes with other linear filtering oper-

---

[3] We defer the topic of edge detection in color images.

ations. The gradient of the smoothed image can therefore be written as

$$\boldsymbol{J}_\sigma(\boldsymbol{x}) = \nabla[G_\sigma(\boldsymbol{x}) * I(\boldsymbol{x})] = [\nabla G_\sigma](\boldsymbol{x}) * I(\boldsymbol{x}), \tag{4.20}$$

i.e., we can convolve the image with the horizontal and vertical derivatives of the Gaussian kernel function,

$$\nabla G_\sigma(\boldsymbol{x}) = (\frac{\partial G_\sigma}{\partial x}, \frac{\partial G_\sigma}{\partial y})(\boldsymbol{x}) = [-x \ -y]\frac{1}{\sigma^3}\exp\left(-\frac{x^2+y^2}{2\sigma^2}\right) \tag{4.21}$$

(The parameter σ indicates the width of the Gaussian.) This is the same computation that is performed by Freeman and Adelson's (1991) first-order steerable filter, which we already covered in Section 3.2.3.

For many applications, however, we wish to thin such a continuous gradient image to only return isolated edges, i.e., as single pixels at discrete locations along the edge contours. This can be achieved by looking for *maxima* in the edge strength (gradient magnitude) in a direction *perpendicular* to the edge orientation, i.e., along the gradient direction.

Finding this maximum corresponds to taking a directional derivative of the strength field in the direction of the gradient and then looking for zero crossings. The desired directional derivative is equivalent to the dot product between a second gradient operator and the results of the first,

$$S_\sigma(\boldsymbol{x}) = \nabla \cdot \boldsymbol{J}_\sigma(\boldsymbol{x}) = [\nabla^2 G_\sigma](\boldsymbol{x}) * I(\boldsymbol{x})]. \tag{4.22}$$

The gradient operator dot product with the gradient is called the *Laplacian*. The convolution kernel

$$\nabla^2 G_\sigma(\boldsymbol{x}) = \frac{1}{\sigma^3}\left(2 - \frac{x^2+y^2}{2\sigma^2}\right)\exp\left(-\frac{x^2+y^2}{2\sigma^2}\right) \tag{4.23}$$

is therefore called the *Laplacian of Gaussian* (LoG) kernel (Marr and Hildreth 1980). This kernel can be split into two separable parts,

$$\nabla^2 G_\sigma(\boldsymbol{x}) = \frac{1}{\sigma^3}\left(1 - \frac{x^2}{2\sigma^2}\right)G_\sigma(x)G_\sigma(y) + \frac{1}{\sigma^3}\left(1 - \frac{y^2}{2\sigma^2}\right)G_\sigma(y)G_\sigma(x) \tag{4.24}$$

(Wiejak, Buxton, and Buxton 1985), which allows for a much more efficient implementation using separable filtering (Section 3.2.1).

In practice, it is quite common to replace the Laplacian of Gaussian convolution with a Difference of Gaussian (DoG) computation, since the kernel shapes are qualitatively similar (Figure 3.35). This is especially convenient if a "Laplacian pyramid" (Section 3.5) has already been computed.[4]

In fact, it is not strictly necessary to take differences between adjacent levels when computing the edge field. Think about what a zero crossing in a "generalized" difference of Gaussians image represents. The finer (smaller kernel) Gaussian is a noise-reduced version of the original image. The coarser (larger kernel) Gaussian is an estimate of the average intensity over a larger region. Thus, whenever the DoG image changes sign, this corresponds to the (slightly blurred) image going from relatively darker to relatively lighter, as compared to the average intensity in that neighborhood.

---

[4] Recall that Burt and Adelson's (1983a) "Laplacian pyramid" actually computed differences of Gaussian-filtered levels.

Once we have computed the sign function $S(\boldsymbol{x})$, we must find its *zero crossings* and convert these into edge elements (*edgels*). An easy way to detect and represent zero crossings is to look for adjacent pixel locations $\boldsymbol{x}_i$ and $\boldsymbol{x}_j$ where the sign changes value, i.e., $[S(\boldsymbol{x}_i) > 0] \neq [S(\boldsymbol{x}_j) > 0]$.

The sub-pixel location of this crossing can be obtained by computing the "x-intercept" of the "line" connecting $S(\boldsymbol{x}_i)$ and $S(\boldsymbol{x}_j)$,

$$\boldsymbol{x}_{\mathrm{z}} = \frac{\boldsymbol{x}_i S(\boldsymbol{x}_j) - \boldsymbol{x}_j S(\boldsymbol{x}_i)}{S(\boldsymbol{x}_j) - S(\boldsymbol{x}_i)}. \qquad (4.25)$$

The orientation and strength of such edgels can be obtained by linearly interpolating the gradient values computed on the original pixel grid.

An alternative edgel representation can be obtained by linking adjacent edgels on the dual grid to form edgels that live *inside* each square formed by four adjacent pixels in the original pixel grid.[5] The (potential) advantage of this representation is that the edgels now live on a grid offset by half a pixel from the original pixel grid and are thus easier to store and access.   As before, the orientations and strengths of the edges can be computed by interpolating the gradient field or estimating these values from the difference of Gaussian image (see Exercise 4.7).

In applications where the accuracy of the edge orientation is more important, higher-order steerable filters can be used (Freeman and Adelson 1991) (see Section 3.2.3). Such filters are more selective for more elongated edges and also have the possibility of better modeling curve intersections because they can represent multiple orientations at the same pixel (Figure 3.16). Their disadvantage is that they are more expensive to compute and the directional derivative of the edge strength does not have a simple closed form solution.[6]

Scale selection and blur estimation

As we mentioned before, the derivative, Laplacian, and Difference of Gaussian filters (4.20–4.23) all require the selection of a spatial scale parameter σ. If we are only interested in detecting sharp edges, the width of the filter can be determined from image noise characteristics (Canny 1986; Elder and Zucker 1998). However, if we want to detect edges that occur at different resolutions (Figures 4.32b–c), a *scale-space* approach that detects and then selects edges at different scales may be necessary (Witkin 1983; Lindeberg 1994, 1998a; Nielsen, Florack, and Deriche 1997).

Elder and Zucker (1998) present a principled approach to solving this problem. Given a known image noise level, their technique computes, for every pixel, the minimum scale at which an edge can be reliably detected (Figure 4.32d). Their approach first computes gradients densely over an image by selecting among gradient estimates computed at different scales, based on their gradient magnitudes. It then performs a similar estimate of minimum scale for directed second derivatives and uses zero crossings of this latter quantity to robustly select edges (Figures 4.32e–f). As an optional final step, the blur width of each edge can be computed from the distance between extrema in the second derivative response minus the width of the Gaussian filter.

---

[5] This algorithm is a 2D version of the 3D *marching cubes* isosurface extraction algorithm (Lorensen and Cline 1987).

[6] In fact, the edge orientation can have a $180°$ ambiguity for "bar edges", which makes the computation of zero crossings in the derivative more tricky.

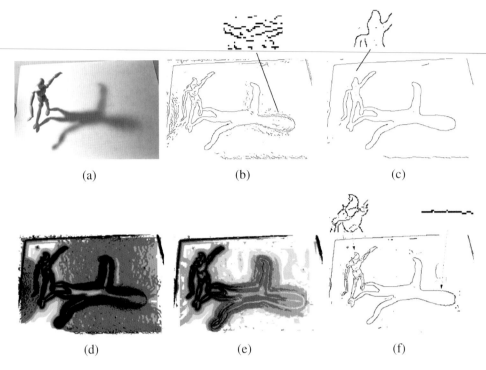

(a)   (b)   (c)

(d)   (e)   (f)

Figure 4.32 Scale selection for edge detection (Elder and Zucker 1998) © 1998 IEEE: (a) original image; (b–c) Canny/Deriche edge detector tuned to the finer (mannequin) and coarser (shadow) scales; (d) minimum reliable scale for gradient estimation; (e) minimum reliable scale for second derivative estimation; (f) final detected edges.

Color edge detection

While most edge detection techniques have been developed for grayscale images, color images can provide additional information. For example, noticeable edges between *iso-luminant* colors (colors that have the same luminance) are useful cues but fail to be detected by grayscale edge operators.

One simple approach is to combine the outputs of grayscale detectors run on each color band separately.[7] However, some care must be taken. For example, if we simply sum up the gradients in each of the color bands, the signed gradients may actually cancel each other! (Consider, for example a pure red-to-green edge.) We could also detect edges independently in each band and then take the union of these, but this might lead to thickened or doubled edges that are hard to link.

A better approach is to compute the *oriented energy* in each band (Morrone and Burr 1988; Perona and Malik 1990a), e.g., using a second-order steerable filter (Section 3.2.3) (Freeman and Adelson 1991), and then sum up the orientation-weighted energies and find their joint best orientation. Unfortunately, the directional derivative of this energy may not have a closed form solution (as in the case of signed first-order steerable filters), so a simple zero crossing-based strategy cannot be used. However, the technique described by Elder and

---

[7] Instead of using the raw RGB space, a more perceptually uniform color space such as L*a*b* (see Section 2.3.2) can be used instead. When trying to match human performance (Martin, Fowlkes, and Malik 2004), this makes sense. However, in terms of the physics of the underlying image formation and sensing, it may be a questionable strategy.

Zucker (1998) can be used to compute these zero crossings numerically instead.

An alternative approach is to estimate local color statistics in regions around each pixel (Ruzon and Tomasi 2001; Martin, Fowlkes, and Malik 2004). This has the advantage that more sophisticated techniques (e.g., 3D color histograms) can be used to compare regional statistics and that additional measures, such as texture, can also be considered. Figure 4.33 shows the output of such detectors.

Of course, many other approaches have been developed for detecting color edges, dating back to early work by Nevatia (1977). Ruzon and Tomasi (2001) and Gevers, van de Weijer, and Stokman (2006) provide good reviews of these approaches, which include ideas such as fusing outputs from multiple channels, using multidimensional gradients, and vector-based methods.

Combining edge feature cues

If the goal of edge detection is to match human *boundary detection* performance (Bowyer, Kranenburg, and Dougherty 2001; Martin, Fowlkes, and Malik 2004; Arbeláez, Maire, Fowlkes *et al.* 2010), as opposed to simply finding stable features for matching, even better detectors can be constructed by combining multiple low-level cues such as brightness, color, and texture.

Martin, Fowlkes, and Malik (2004) describe a system that combines brightness, color, and texture edges to produce state-of-the-art performance on a database of hand-segmented natural color images (Martin, Fowlkes, Tal *et al.* 2001). First, they construct and train[8] separate oriented half-disc detectors for measuring significant differences in brightness (luminance), color (a* and b* channels, summed responses), and texture (un-normalized filter bank responses from the work of Malik, Belongie, Leung *et al.* (2001)). Some of the responses are then sharpened using a soft non-maximal suppression technique. Finally, the outputs of the three detectors are combined using a variety of machine-learning techniques, from which logistic regression is found to have the best tradeoff between speed, space and accuracy . The resulting system (see Figure 4.33 for some examples) is shown to outperform previously developed techniques. Maire, Arbelaez, Fowlkes *et al.* (2008) improve on these results by combining the detector based on local appearance with a *spectral* (segmentation-based) detector (Belongie and Malik 1998). In more recent work, Arbeláez, Maire, Fowlkes *et al.* (2010) build a hierarchical segmentation on top of this edge detector using a variant of the watershed algorithm.

4.2.2 Edge linking

While isolated edges can be useful for a variety of applications, such as line detection (Section 4.3) and sparse stereo matching (Section 11.2), they become even more useful when linked into continuous contours.

If the edges have been detected using zero crossings of some function, linking them up is straightforward, since adjacent edgels share common endpoints. Linking the edgels into chains involves picking up an unlinked edgel and following its neighbors in both directions. Either a sorted list of edgels (sorted first by x coordinates and then by y coordinates, for example) or a 2D array can be used to accelerate the neighbor finding. If edges were not

---

[8] The training uses 200 labeled images and testing is performed on a different set of 100 images.

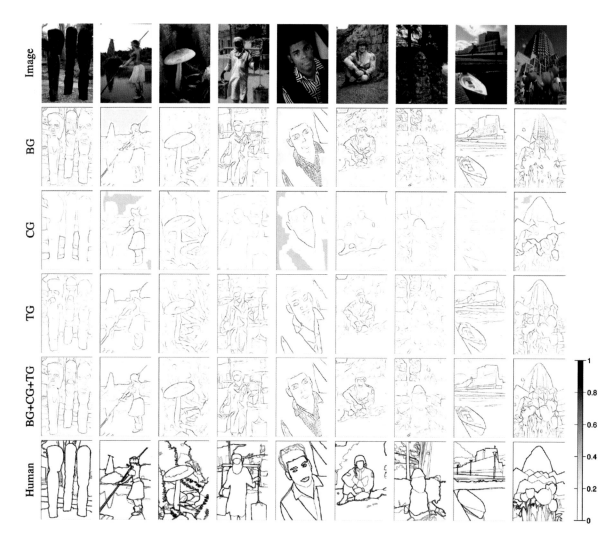

Figure 4.33 Combined brightness, color, texture boundary detector (Martin, Fowlkes, and Malik 2004) © 2004 IEEE. Successive rows show the outputs of the brightness gradient (BG), color gradient (CG), texture gradient (TG), and combined (BG+CG+TG) detectors. The final row shows human-labeled boundaries derived from a database of hand-segmented images (Martin, Fowlkes, Tal *et al.* 2001).

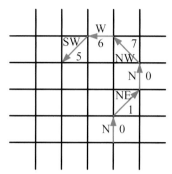

Figure 4.34 Chain code representation of a grid-aligned linked edge chain. The code is represented as a series of direction codes, e.g, 0 1 0 7 6 5, which can further be compressed using predictive and run-length coding.

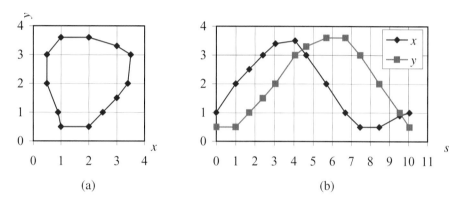

(a)   (b)

Figure 4.35 Arc-length parameterization of a contour: (a) discrete points along the contour are first transcribed as (b) (x, y) pairs along the arc length s. This curve can then be regularly re-sampled or converted into alternative (e.g., Fourier) representations.

detected using zero crossings, finding the continuation of an edgel can be tricky. In this case, comparing the orientation (and, optionally, phase) of adjacent edgels can be used for disambiguation. Ideas from connected component computation can also sometimes be used to make the edge linking process even faster (see Exercise 4.8).

Once the edgels have been linked into chains, we can apply an optional thresholding with hysteresis to remove low-strength contour segments (Canny 1986). The basic idea of hysteresis is to set two different thresholds and allow a curve being tracked above the higher threshold to dip in strength down to the lower threshold.

Linked edgel lists can be encoded more compactly using a variety of alternative representations. A *chain code* encodes a list of connected points lying on an $\mathcal{N}_8$ grid using a three-bit code corresponding to the eight cardinal directions (N, NE, E, SE, S, SW, W, NW) between a point and its successor (Figure 4.34). While this representation is more compact than the original edgel list (especially if predictive variable-length coding is used), it is not very suitable for further processing.

A more useful representation is the *arc length parameterization* of a contour, $\boldsymbol{x}(s)$, where s denotes the arc length along a curve. Consider the linked set of edgels shown in Fig-

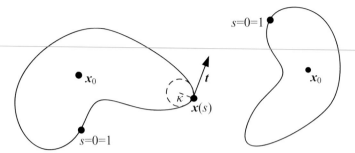

Figure 4.36 Matching two contours using their arc-length parameterization. If both curves are normalized to unit length, $s \in [0, 1]$ and centered around their centroid x_0, they will have the same descriptor up to an overall "temporal" shift (due to different starting points for $s = 0$) and a phase (x-y) shift (due to rotation).

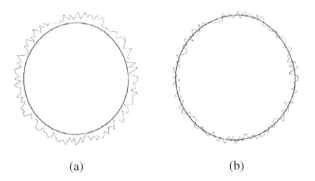

(a)   (b)

Figure 4.37 Curve smoothing with a Gaussian kernel (Lowe 1988) © 1998 IEEE: (a) without a shrinkage correction term; (b) with a shrinkage correction term.

ure 4.35a. We start at one point (the dot at $(1.0, 0.5)$ in Figure 4.35a) and plot it at coordinate $s = 0$ (Figure 4.35b). The next point at $(2.0, 0.5)$ gets plotted at $s = 1$, and the next point at $(2.5, 1.0)$ gets plotted at $s = 1.7071$, i.e., we increment s by the length of each edge segment. The resulting plot can be resampled on a regular (say, integral) s grid before further processing.

The advantage of the arc-length parameterization is that it makes matching and processing (e.g., smoothing) operations much easier. Consider the two curves describing similar shapes shown in Figure 4.36. To compare the curves, we first subtract the average values $x_0 = \int_s x(s)$ from each descriptor. Next, we rescale each descriptor so that s goes from 0 to 1 instead of 0 to S, i.e., we divide $x(s)$ by S. Finally, we take the Fourier transform of each normalized descriptor, treating each $x = (x, y)$ value as a complex number. If the original curves are the same (up to an unknown scale and rotation), the resulting Fourier transforms should differ only by a scale change in magnitude plus a constant complex phase shift, due to rotation, and a linear phase shift in the domain, due to different starting points for s (see Exercise 4.9).

Arc-length parameterization can also be used to smooth curves in order to remove digitization noise. However, if we just apply a regular smoothing filter, the curve tends to shrink

Figure 4.38 Changing the character of a curve without affecting its sweep (Finkelstein and Salesin 1994) ©
1994 ACM: higher frequency wavelets can be replaced with exemplars from a style library to effect different local
appearances.

on itself (Figure 4.37a). Lowe (1989) and Taubin (1995) describe techniques that compensate
for this shrinkage by adding an offset term based on second derivative estimates or a larger
smoothing kernel (Figure 4.37b). An alternative approach, based on selectively modifying
different frequencies in a wavelet decomposition, is presented by Finkelstein and Salesin
(1994). In addition to controlling shrinkage without affecting its "sweep", wavelets allow the
"character" of a curve to be interactively modified, as shown in Figure 4.38.

The evolution of curves as they are smoothed and simplified is related to "grassfire" (distance) transforms and region skeletons (Section 3.3.3) (Tek and Kimia 2003), and can be used
to recognize objects based on their contour shape (Sebastian and Kimia 2005). More local descriptors of curve shape such as *shape contexts* (Belongie, Malik, and Puzicha 2002) can also
be used for recognition and are potentially more robust to missing parts due to occlusions.

The field of contour detection and linking continues to evolve rapidly and now includes
techniques for global contour grouping, boundary completion, and junction detection (Maire,
Arbelaez, Fowlkes *et al.* 2008), as well as grouping contours into likely regions (Arbeláez,
Maire, Fowlkes *et al.* 2010) and wide-baseline correspondence (Meltzer and Soatto 2008).

4.2.3 *Application*: Edge editing and enhancement

While edges can serve as components for object recognition or features for matching, they
can also be used directly for image editing.

In fact, if the edge magnitude and blur estimate are kept along with each edge, a visually
similar image can be reconstructed from this information (Elder 1999). Based on this principle, Elder and Goldberg (2001) propose a system for "image editing in the contour domain".
Their system allows users to selectively remove edges corresponding to unwanted features
such as specularities, shadows, or distracting visual elements. After reconstructing the image
from the remaining edges, the undesirable visual features have been removed (Figure 4.39).

Another potential application is to enhance perceptually salient edges while simplifying
the underlying image to produce a cartoon-like or "pen-and-ink" stylized image (DeCarlo and
Santella 2002). This application is discussed in more detail in Section 10.5.2.

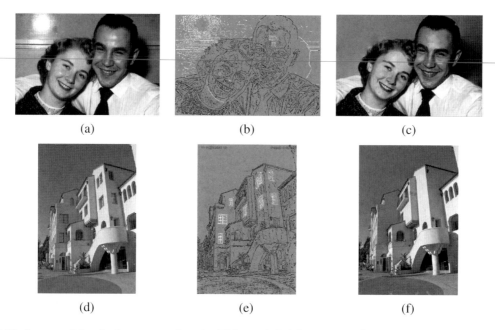

(a)   (b)   (c)

(d)   (e)   (f)

Figure 4.39 Image editing in the contour domain (Elder and Goldberg 2001) © 2001 IEEE: (a) and (d) original images; (b) and (e) extracted edges (edges to be deleted are marked in white); (c) and (f) reconstructed edited images.

4.3 Lines

While edges and general curves are suitable for describing the contours of natural objects, the man-made world is full of straight lines. Detecting and matching these lines can be useful in a variety of applications, including architectural modeling, pose estimation in urban environments, and the analysis of printed document layouts.

In this section, we present some techniques for extracting *piecewise linear* descriptions from the curves computed in the previous section. We begin with some algorithms for approximating a curve as a piecewise-linear polyline. We then describe the *Hough transform*, which can be used to group edgels into line segments even across gaps and occlusions. Finally, we describe how 3D lines with common *vanishing points* can be grouped together. These vanishing points can be used to calibrate a camera and to determine its orientation relative to a rectahedral scene, as described in Section 6.3.2.

4.3.1 Successive approximation

As we saw in Section 4.2.2, describing a curve as a series of 2D locations $x_i = x(s_i)$ provides a general representation suitable for matching and further processing. In many applications, however, it is preferable to approximate such a curve with a simpler representation, e.g., as a piecewise-linear polyline or as a B-spline curve (Farin 1996), as shown in Figure 4.40.

Many techniques have been developed over the years to perform this approximation, which is also known as *line simplification*. One of the oldest, and simplest, is the one proposed by Ramer (1972) and Douglas and Peucker (1973), who recursively subdivide the curve at

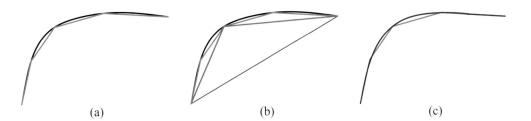

Figure 4.40 Approximating a curve (shown in black) as a polyline or B-spline: (a) original curve and a polyline approximation shown in red; (b) successive approximation by recursively finding points furthest away from the current approximation; (c) smooth interpolating spline, shown in dark blue, fit to the polyline vertices.

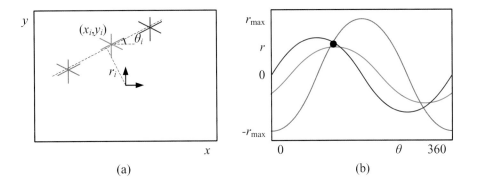

Figure 4.41 Original Hough transform: (a) each point votes for a complete family of potential lines $r_i(\theta) = x_i \cos\theta + y_i \sin\theta$; (b) each pencil of lines sweeps out a sinusoid in (r, θ); their intersection provides the desired line equation.

the point furthest away from the line joining the two endpoints (or the current coarse polyline approximation), as shown in Figure 4.40. Hershberger and Snoeyink (1992) provide a more efficient implementation and also cite some of the other related work in this area.

Once the line simplification has been computed, it can be used to approximate the original curve. If a smoother representation or visualization is desired, either approximating or interpolating splines or curves can be used (Sections 3.5.1 and 5.1.1) (Szeliski and Ito 1986; Bartels, Beatty, and Barsky 1987; Farin 1996), as shown in Figure 4.40c.

4.3.2 Hough transforms

While curve approximation with polylines can often lead to successful line extraction, lines in the real world are sometimes broken up into disconnected components or made up of many collinear line segments. In many cases, it is desirable to group such collinear segments into extended lines. At a further processing stage (described in Section 4.3.3), we can then group such lines into collections with common vanishing points.

The Hough transform, named after its original inventor (Hough 1962), is a well-known technique for having edges "vote" for plausible line locations (Duda and Hart 1972; Ballard 1981; Illingworth and Kittler 1988). In its original formulation (Figure 4.41), each edge point votes for *all* possible lines passing through it, and lines corresponding to high *accumulator* or

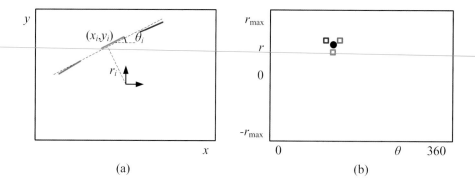

Figure 4.42 Oriented Hough transform: (a) an edgel re-parameterized in polar (r, θ) coordinates, with $\hat{n}_i = (\cos \theta_i, \sin \theta_i)$ and $r_i = \hat{n}_i \cdot x_i$; (b) (r, θ) accumulator array, showing the votes for the three edgels marked in red, green, and blue.

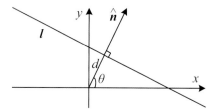

Figure 4.43 2D line equation expressed in terms of the normal $\hat{n}$ and distance to the origin d.

bin values are examined for potential line fits.[9] Unless the points on a line are truly punctate, a better approach (in my experience) is to use the local orientation information at each edgel to vote for a *single* accumulator cell (Figure 4.42), as described below. A hybrid strategy, where each edgel votes for a number of possible orientation or location pairs centered around the estimate orientation, may be desirable in some cases.

Before we can vote for line hypotheses, we must first choose a suitable representation. Figure 4.43 (copied from Figure 2.2a) shows the normal-distance $(\hat{n}, d)$ parameterization for a line. Since lines are made up of edge segments, we adopt the convention that the line normal $\hat{n}$ points in the same direction (i.e., has the same sign) as the image gradient $J(x) = \nabla I(x)$ (4.19). To obtain a minimal two-parameter representation for lines, we convert the normal vector into an angle

$$\theta = \tan^{-1} n_y/n_x, \tag{4.26}$$

as shown in Figure 4.43. The range of possible (θ, d) values is $[-180°, 180°] \times [-\sqrt{2}, \sqrt{2}]$, assuming that we are using normalized pixel coordinates (2.61) that lie in $[-1, 1]$. The number of bins to use along each axis depends on the accuracy of the position and orientation estimate available at each edgel and the expected line density, and is best set experimentally with some test runs on sample imagery.

Given the line parameterization, the Hough transform proceeds as shown in Algorithm 4.2.

---

[9] The Hough transform can also be *generalized* to look for other geometric features such as circles (Ballard 1981), but we do not cover such extensions in this book.

procedure $Hough(\{(x, y, \theta)\})$:

1. Clear the accumulator array.

2. For each detected edgel at location (x, y) and orientation $\theta = \tan^{-1} n_y/n_x$, compute the value of

$$d = x \, n_x + y \, n_y$$

and increment the accumulator corresponding to (θ, d).

3. Find the peaks in the accumulator corresponding to lines.

4. Optionally re-fit the lines to the constituent edgels.

Algorithm 4.2 Outline of a Hough transform algorithm based on oriented edge segments.

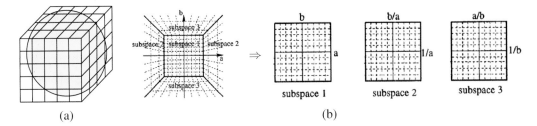

Figure 4.44 Cube map representation for line equations and vanishing points: (a) a cube map surrounding the unit sphere; (b) projecting the half-cube onto three subspaces (Tuytelaars, Van Gool, and Proesmans 1997) © 1997 IEEE.

Note that the original formulation of the Hough transform, which assumed no knowledge of the edgel orientation θ, has an additional loop inside Step 2 that iterates over all possible values of θ and increments a whole series of accumulators.

There are a lot of details in getting the Hough transform to work well, but these are best worked out by writing an implementation and testing it out on sample data. Exercise 4.12 describes some of these steps in more detail, including using edge segment lengths or strengths during the voting process, keeping a list of constituent edgels in the accumulator array for easier post-processing, and optionally combining edges of different "polarity" into the same line segments.

An alternative to the 2D polar (θ, d) representation for lines is to use the full 3D $\boldsymbol{m} = (\hat{\boldsymbol{n}}, d)$ line equation, projected onto the unit sphere. While the sphere can be parameterized using spherical coordinates (2.8),

$$\hat{\boldsymbol{m}} = (\cos\theta\cos\phi, \sin\theta\cos\phi, \sin\phi), \tag{4.27}$$

this does not uniformly sample the sphere and still requires the use of trigonometry.

An alternative representation can be obtained by using a *cube map*, i.e., projecting $\boldsymbol{m}$ onto the face of a unit cube (Figure 4.44a). To compute the cube map coordinate of a 3D vector $\boldsymbol{m}$, first find the largest (absolute value) component of $\boldsymbol{m}$, i.e., $m = \pm \max(|n_x|, |n_y|, |d|)$, and use this to select one of the six cube faces. Divide the remaining two coordinates by m and use these as indices into the cube face. While this avoids the use of trigonometry, it does require some decision logic.

One advantage of using the cube map, first pointed out by Tuytelaars, Van Gool, and Proesmans (1997), is that all of the lines passing through a point correspond to line segments on the cube faces, which is useful if the original (full voting) variant of the Hough transform is being used. In their work, they represent the line equation as $ax + b + y = 0$, which does not treat the x and y axes symmetrically. Note that if we restrict $d \geq 0$ by ignoring the polarity of the edge orientation (gradient sign), we can use a half-cube instead, which can be represented using only three cube faces, as shown in Figure 4.44b (Tuytelaars, Van Gool, and Proesmans 1997).

RANSAC-based line detection. Another alternative to the Hough transform is the RANdom SAmple Consensus (RANSAC) algorithm described in more detail in Section 6.1.4. In brief, RANSAC randomly chooses pairs of edgels to form a line hypothesis and then tests how many other edgels fall onto this line. (If the edge orientations are accurate enough, a single edgel can produce this hypothesis.) Lines with sufficiently large numbers of *inliers* (matching edgels) are then selected as the desired line segments.

An advantage of RANSAC is that no accumulator array is needed and so the algorithm can be more space efficient and potentially less prone to the choice of bin size. The disadvantage is that many more hypotheses may need to be generated and tested than those obtained by finding peaks in the accumulator array.

In general, there is no clear consensus on which line estimation technique performs best. It is therefore a good idea to think carefully about the problem at hand and to implement several approaches (successive approximation, Hough, and RANSAC) to determine the one that works best for your application.

4.3.3 Vanishing points

In many scenes, structurally important lines have the same vanishing point because they are parallel in 3D. Examples of such lines are horizontal and vertical building edges, zebra crossings, railway tracks, the edges of furniture such as tables and dressers, and of course, the ubiquitous calibration pattern (Figure 4.45). Finding the vanishing points common to such line sets can help refine their position in the image and, in certain cases, help determine the intrinsic and extrinsic orientation of the camera (Section 6.3.2).

Over the years, a large number of techniques have been developed for finding vanishing points, including (Quan and Mohr 1989; Collins and Weiss 1990; Brillaut-O'Mahoney 1991; McLean and Kotturi 1995; Becker and Bove 1995; Shufelt 1999; Tuytelaars, Van Gool, and Proesmans 1997; Schaffalitzky and Zisserman 2000; Antone and Teller 2002; Rother 2002; Košecká and Zhang 2005; Pflugfelder 2008; Tardif 2009)—see some of the more recent papers for additional references. In this section, we present a simple Hough technique based on having line pairs vote for potential vanishing point locations, followed by a robust least squares fitting stage. For alternative approaches, please see some of the more recent papers listed above.

The first stage in my vanishing point detection algorithm uses a Hough transform to accumulate votes for likely vanishing point candidates. As with line fitting, one possible approach

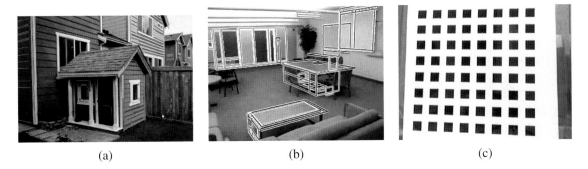

$$(a) \qquad\qquad\qquad (b) \qquad\qquad\qquad (c)$$

Figure 4.45 Real-world vanishing points: (a) architecture (Sinha, Steedly, Szeliski *et al.* 2008), (b) furniture (Mičušík, Wildenauer, and Košecká 2008) ⓒ 2008 IEEE, and (c) calibration patterns (Zhang 2000).

is to have each line vote for *all* possible vanishing point directions, either using a cube map (Tuytelaars, Van Gool, and Proesmans 1997; Antone and Teller 2002) or a Gaussian sphere (Collins and Weiss 1990), optionally using knowledge about the uncertainty in the vanishing point location to perform a weighted vote (Collins and Weiss 1990; Brillaut-O'Mahoney 1991; Shufelt 1999). My preferred approach is to use pairs of detected line segments to form candidate vanishing point locations. Let $\hat{m}_i$ and $\hat{m}_j$ be the (unit norm) line equations for a pair of line segments and l_i and l_j be their corresponding segment lengths. The location of the corresponding vanishing point hypothesis can be computed as

$$v_{ij} = \hat{m}_i \times \hat{m}_j \qquad\qquad (4.28)$$

and the corresponding weight set to

$$w_{ij} = \|v_{ij}\| l_i l_j. \qquad\qquad (4.29)$$

This has the desirable effect of downweighting (near-)collinear line segments and short line segments. The Hough space itself can either be represented using spherical coordinates (4.27) or as a cube map (Figure 4.44a).

Once the Hough accumulator space has been populated, peaks can be detected in a manner similar to that previously discussed for line detection. Given a set of candidate line segments that voted for a vanishing point, which can optionally be kept as a list at each Hough accumulator cell, I then use a robust least squares fit to estimate a more accurate location for each vanishing point.

Consider the relationship between the two line segment endpoints $\{p_{i0}, p_{i1}\}$ and the vanishing point v, as shown in Figure 4.46. The area A of the triangle given by these three points, which is the magnitude of their triple product

$$A_i = |(p_{i0} \times p_{i1}) \cdot v|, \qquad\qquad (4.30)$$

is proportional to the perpendicular distance d_1 between each endpoint and the line through v and the other endpoint, as well as the distance between p_{i0} and v. Assuming that the accuracy of a fitted line segment is proportional to its endpoint accuracy (Exercise 4.13), this therefore serves as an optimal metric for how well a vanishing point fits a set of extracted lines (Leibowitz (2001, Section 3.6.1) and Pflugfelder (2008, Section 2.1.1.3)). A robustified

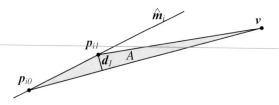

Figure 4.46 Triple product of the line segments endpoints $\boldsymbol{p}_{i0}$ and $\boldsymbol{p}_{i1}$ and the vanishing point $\boldsymbol{v}$. The area A is proportional to the perpendicular distance d_1 and the distance between the other endpoint $\boldsymbol{p}_{i0}$ and the vanishing point.

least squares estimate (Appendix B.3) for the vanishing point can therefore be written as

$$\mathcal{E} = \sum_i \rho(A_i) = \boldsymbol{v}^T \left(\sum_i w_i(A_i) \boldsymbol{m}_i \boldsymbol{m}_i^T \right) \boldsymbol{v} = \boldsymbol{v}^T \boldsymbol{M} \boldsymbol{v}, \qquad (4.31)$$

where $\boldsymbol{m}_i = \boldsymbol{p}_{i0} \times \boldsymbol{p}_{i1}$ is the segment line equation weighted by its length l_i, and $w_i = \rho'(A_i)/A_i$ is the *influence* of each robustified (reweighted) measurement on the final error (Appendix B.3). Notice how this metric is closely related to the original formula for the pairwise weighted Hough transform accumulation step. The final desired value for $\boldsymbol{v}$ is computed as the least eigenvector of $\boldsymbol{M}$.

While the technique described above proceeds in two discrete stages, better results may be obtained by alternating between assigning lines to vanishing points and refitting the vanishing point locations (Antone and Teller 2002; Košecká and Zhang 2005; Pflugfelder 2008). The results of detecting individual vanishing points can also be made more robust by simultaneously searching for pairs or triplets of mutually orthogonal vanishing points (Shufelt 1999; Antone and Teller 2002; Rother 2002; Sinha, Steedly, Szeliski *et al.* 2008). Some results of such vanishing point detection algorithms can be seen in Figure 4.45.

4.3.4 *Application*: Rectangle detection

Once sets of mutually orthogonal vanishing points have been detected, it now becomes possible to search for 3D rectangular structures in the image (Figure 4.47). Over the last decade, a variety of techniques have been developed to find such rectangles, primarily focused on architectural scenes (Košecká and Zhang 2005; Han and Zhu 2005; Shaw and Barnes 2006; Mičušìk, Wildenauer, and Košecká 2008; Schindler, Krishnamurthy, Lublinerman *et al.* 2008).

After detecting orthogonal vanishing directions, Košecká and Zhang (2005) refine the fitted line equations, search for corners near line intersections, and then verify rectangle hypotheses by rectifying the corresponding patches and looking for a preponderance of horizontal and vertical edges (Figures 4.47a–b). In follow-on work, Mičušìk, Wildenauer, and Košecká (2008) use a Markov random field (MRF) to disambiguate between potentially overlapping rectangle hypotheses. They also use a plane sweep algorithm to match rectangles between different views (Figures 4.47d–f).

A different approach is proposed by Han and Zhu (2005), who use a grammar of potential rectangle shapes and nesting structures (between rectangles and vanishing points) to infer the most likely assignment of line segments to rectangles (Figure 4.47c).

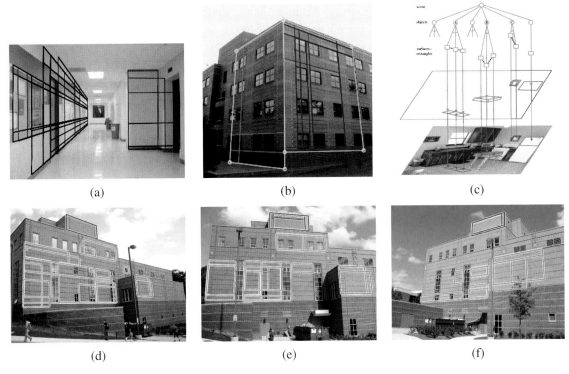

(a)

(b)

(c)

(d)

(e)

(f)

Figure 4.47 Rectangle detection: (a) indoor corridor and (b) building exterior with grouped facades (Košecká and Zhang 2005) ⓒ 2005 Elsevier; (c) grammar-based recognition (Han and Zhu 2005) ⓒ 2005 IEEE; (d–f) rectangle matching using a plane sweep algorithm (Mičušík, Wildenauer, and Košecká 2008) ⓒ 2008 IEEE.

4.4 Additional reading

One of the seminal papers on feature detection, description, and matching is by Lowe (2004). Comprehensive surveys and evaluations of such techniques have been made by Schmid, Mohr, and Bauckhage (2000); Mikolajczyk and Schmid (2005); Mikolajczyk, Tuytelaars, Schmid *et al.* (2005); Tuytelaars and Mikolajczyk (2007) while Shi and Tomasi (1994) and Triggs (2004) also provide nice reviews.

In the area of feature detectors (Mikolajczyk, Tuytelaars, Schmid *et al.* 2005), in addition to such classic approaches as Förstner–Harris (Förstner 1986; Harris and Stephens 1988) and difference of Gaussians (Lindeberg 1993, 1998b; Lowe 2004), maximally stable extremal regions (MSERs) are widely used for applications that require affine invariance (Matas, Chum, Urban *et al.* 2004; Nistér and Stewénius 2008). More recent interest point detectors are discussed by Xiao and Shah (2003); Koethe (2003); Carneiro and Jepson (2005); Kenney, Zuliani, and Manjunath (2005); Bay, Tuytelaars, and Van Gool (2006); Platel, Balmachnova, Florack *et al.* (2006); Rosten and Drummond (2006), as well as techniques based on line matching (Zoghlami, Faugeras, and Deriche 1997; Bartoli, Coquerelle, and Sturm 2004) and region detection (Kadir, Zisserman, and Brady 2004; Matas, Chum, Urban *et al.* 2004; Tuytelaars and Van Gool 2004; Corso and Hager 2005).

A variety of local feature descriptors (and matching heuristics) are surveyed and compared by Mikolajczyk and Schmid (2005). More recent publications in this area include those by van de Weijer and Schmid (2006); Abdel-Hakim and Farag (2006); Winder and Brown (2007); Hua, Brown, and Winder (2007). Techniques for efficiently matching features include k-d trees (Beis and Lowe 1999; Lowe 2004; Muja and Lowe 2009), pyramid matching kernels (Grauman and Darrell 2005), metric (vocabulary) trees (Nistér and Stewénius 2006), and a variety of multi-dimensional hashing techniques (Shakhnarovich, Viola, and Darrell 2003; Torralba, Weiss, and Fergus 2008; Weiss, Torralba, and Fergus 2008; Kulis and Grauman 2009; Raginsky and Lazebnik 2009).

The classic reference on feature detection and tracking is (Shi and Tomasi 1994). More recent work in this field has focused on learning better matching functions for specific features (Avidan 2001; Jurie and Dhome 2002; Williams, Blake, and Cipolla 2003; Lepetit and Fua 2005; Lepetit, Pilet, and Fua 2006; Hinterstoisser, Benhimane, Navab *et al.* 2008; Rogez, Rihan, Ramalingam *et al.* 2008; Özuysal, Calonder, Lepetit *et al.* 2010).

A highly cited and widely used edge detector is the one developed by Canny (1986). Alternative edge detectors as well as experimental comparisons can be found in publications by Nalwa and Binford (1986); Nalwa (1987); Deriche (1987); Freeman and Adelson (1991); Nalwa (1993); Heath, Sarkar, Sanocki *et al.* (1998); Crane (1997); Ritter and Wilson (2000); Bowyer, Kranenburg, and Dougherty (2001); Arbeláez, Maire, Fowlkes *et al.* (2010). The topic of scale selection in edge detection is nicely treated by Elder and Zucker (1998), while approaches to color and texture edge detection can be found in (Ruzon and Tomasi 2001; Martin, Fowlkes, and Malik 2004; Gevers, van de Weijer, and Stokman 2006). Edge detectors have also recently been combined with region segmentation techniques to further improve the detection of semantically salient boundaries (Maire, Arbelaez, Fowlkes *et al.* 2008; Arbeláez, Maire, Fowlkes *et al.* 2010). Edges linked into contours can be smoothed and manipulated for artistic effect (Lowe 1989; Finkelstein and Salesin 1994; Taubin 1995) and used for recognition (Belongie, Malik, and Puzicha 2002; Tek and Kimia 2003; Sebastian and Kimia 2005).

An early, well-regarded paper on straight line extraction in images was written by Burns, Hanson, and Riseman (1986). More recent techniques often combine line detection with vanishing point detection (Quan and Mohr 1989; Collins and Weiss 1990; Brillaut-O'Mahoney 1991; McLean and Kotturi 1995; Becker and Bove 1995; Shufelt 1999; Tuytelaars, Van Gool, and Proesmans 1997; Schaffalitzky and Zisserman 2000; Antone and Teller 2002; Rother 2002; Košecká and Zhang 2005; Pflugfelder 2008; Sinha, Steedly, Szeliski *et al.* 2008; Tardif 2009).

4.5 Exercises

Ex 4.1: Interest point detector   Implement one or more keypoint detectors and compare their performance (with your own or with a classmate's detector).

Possible detectors:

- Laplacian or Difference of Gaussian;

- Förstner–Harris Hessian (try different formula variants given in (4.9–4.11));

- oriented/steerable filter, looking for either second-order high second response or two edges in a window (Koethe 2003), as discussed in Section 4.1.1.

Other detectors are described by Mikolajczyk, Tuytelaars, Schmid *et al.* (2005); Tuytelaars and Mikolajczyk (2007). Additional optional steps could include:

1. Compute the detections on a sub-octave pyramid and find 3D maxima.

2. Find local orientation estimates using steerable filter responses or a gradient histogramming method.

3. Implement non-maximal suppression, such as the adaptive technique of Brown, Szeliski, and Winder (2005).

4. Vary the window shape and size (pre-filter and aggregation).

To test for repeatability, download the code from http://www.robots.ox.ac.uk/~vgg/research/affine/ (Mikolajczyk, Tuytelaars, Schmid *et al.* 2005; Tuytelaars and Mikolajczyk 2007) or simply rotate or shear your own test images. (Pick a domain you may want to use later, e.g., for outdoor stitching.)

Be sure to measure and report the stability of your scale and orientation estimates.

Ex 4.2: Interest point descriptor   Implement one or more descriptors (steered to local scale and orientation) and compare their performance (with your own or with a classmate's detector).

Some possible descriptors include

- contrast-normalized patches (Brown, Szeliski, and Winder 2005);

- SIFT (Lowe 2004);

- GLOH (Mikolajczyk and Schmid 2005);

- DAISY (Winder and Brown 2007; Tola, Lepetit, and Fua 2010).

Other detectors are described by Mikolajczyk and Schmid (2005).

Ex 4.3: ROC curve computation   Given a pair of curves (histograms) plotting the number of matching and non-matching features as a function of Euclidean distance d as shown in Figure 4.23b, derive an algorithm for plotting a ROC curve (Figure 4.23a). In particular, let $t(d)$ be the distribution of true matches and $f(d)$ be the distribution of (false) non-matches. Write down the equations for the ROC, i.e., TPR(FPR), and the AUC.

(Hint: Plot the cumulative distributions $T(d) = \int t(d)$ and $F(d) = \int f(d)$ and see if these help you derive the TPR and FPR at a given threshold θ.)

Ex 4.4: Feature matcher   After extracting features from a collection of overlapping or distorted images,[10] match them up by their descriptors either using nearest neighbor matching or a more efficient matching strategy such as a k-d tree.

See whether you can improve the accuracy of your matches using techniques such as the nearest neighbor distance ratio.

---

[10] http://www.robots.ox.ac.uk/~vgg/research/affine/.

Ex 4.5: Feature tracker Instead of finding feature points independently in multiple images and then matching them, find features in the first image of a video or image sequence and then re-locate the corresponding points in the next frames using either search and gradient descent (Shi and Tomasi 1994) or learned feature detectors (Lepetit, Pilet, and Fua 2006; Fossati, Dimitrijevic, Lepetit *et al.* 2007). When the number of tracked points drops below a threshold or new regions in the image become visible, find additional points to track.

(Optional) Winnow out incorrect matches by estimating a homography (6.19–6.23) or fundamental matrix (Section 7.2.1).

(Optional) Refine the accuracy of your matches using the iterative registration algorithm described in Section 8.2 and Exercise 8.2.

Ex 4.6: Facial feature tracker Apply your feature tracker to tracking points on a person's face, either manually initialized to interesting locations such as eye corners or automatically initialized at interest points.

(Optional) Match features between two people and use these features to perform image morphing (Exercise 3.25).

Ex 4.7: Edge detector Implement an edge detector of your choice. Compare its performance to that of your classmates' detectors or code downloaded from the Internet.

A simple but well-performing sub-pixel edge detector can be created as follows:

1. Blur the input image a little,

$$B_\sigma(\boldsymbol{x}) = G_\sigma(\boldsymbol{x}) * I(\boldsymbol{x}).$$

2. Construct a Gaussian pyramid (Exercise 3.19),

$$P = \mathrm{Pyramid}\{B_\sigma(\boldsymbol{x})\}$$

3. Subtract an interpolated coarser-level pyramid image from the original resolution blurred image,

$$S(\boldsymbol{x}) = B_\sigma(\boldsymbol{x}) - P.\mathrm{InterpolatedLevel}(L).$$

4. For each quad of pixels, $\{(i,j), (i+1,j), (i,j+1), (i+1,j+1)\}$, count the number of zero crossings along the four edges.

5. When there are exactly two zero crossings, compute their locations using (4.25) and store these edgel endpoints along with the midpoint in the edgel structure (Figure 4.48).

6. For each edgel, compute the local gradient by taking the horizontal and vertical differences between the values of S along the zero crossing edges.

7. Store the magnitude of this gradient as the edge strength and either its orientation or that of the segment joining the edgel endpoints as the edge orientation.

8. Add the edgel to a list of edgels or store it in a 2D array of edgels (addressed by pixel coordinates).

Figure 4.48 shows a possible representation for each computed edgel.

```
struct SEdgel {
    float e[2][2];      // edgel endpoints (zero crossing)
    float x, y;         // sub-pixel edge position (midpoint)
    float n_x, n_y;     // orientation, as normal vector
    float theta;        // orientation, as angle (degrees)
    float length;       // length of edgel
    float strength;     // strength of edgel (gradient magnitude)
};

struct SLine : public SEdgel {
    float line_length;  // length of line (est. from ellipsoid)
    float sigma;        // estimated std. dev. of edgel noise
    float r;            // line equation: x * n_y - y * n_x = r
};
```

Figure 4.48 A potential C++ structure for edgel and line elements.

Ex 4.8: Edge linking and thresholding   Link up the edges computed in the previous exercise into chains and optionally perform thresholding with hysteresis.

The steps may include:

1. Store the edgels either in a 2D array (say, an integer image with indices into the edgel list) or pre-sort the edgel list first by (integer) x coordinates and then y coordinates, for faster neighbor finding.

2. Pick up an edgel from the list of unlinked edgels and find its neighbors in both directions until no neighbor is found or a closed contour is obtained. Flag edgels as linked as you visit them and push them onto your list of linked edgels.

3. Alternatively, generalize a previously developed connected component algorithm (Exercise 3.14) to perform the linking in just two raster passes.

4. (Optional) Perform hysteresis-based thresholding (Canny 1986). Use two thresholds "hi" and "lo" for the edge strength. A candidate edgel is considered an edge if either its strength is above the "hi" threshold or its strength is above the "lo" threshold and it is (recursively) connected to a previously detected edge.

5. (Optional) Link together contours that have small gaps but whose endpoints have similar orientations.

6. (Optional) Find junctions between adjacent contours, e.g., using some of the ideas (or references) from Maire, Arbelaez, Fowlkes *et al.* (2008).

Ex 4.9: Contour matching   Convert a closed contour (linked edgel list) into its arc-length parameterization and use this to match object outlines.

The steps may include:

1. Walk along the contour and create a list of (x_i, y_i, s_i) triplets, using the arc-length formula

$$s_{i+1} = s_i + \|x_{i+1} - x_i\|. \tag{4.32}$$

2. Resample this list onto a regular set of (x_j, y_j, j) samples using linear interpolation of each segment.

3. Compute the average values of x and y, i.e., $\bar{x}$ and $\bar{y}$ and subtract them from your sampled curve points.

4. Resample the original (x_i, y_i, s_i) piecewise-linear function onto a length-independent set of samples, say $j \in [0, 1023]$. (Using a length which is a power of two makes subsequent Fourier transforms more convenient.)

5. Compute the Fourier transform of the curve, treating each (x, y) pair as a complex number.

6. To compare two curves, fit a linear equation to the phase difference between the two curves. (Careful: phase wraps around at $360°$. Also, you may wish to weight samples by their Fourier spectrum magnitude—see Section 8.1.2.)

7. (Optional) Prove that the constant phase component corresponds to the temporal shift in s, while the linear component corresponds to rotation.

Of course, feel free to try any other curve descriptor and matching technique from the computer vision literature (Tek and Kimia 2003; Sebastian and Kimia 2005).

Ex 4.10: Jigsaw puzzle solver—challenging   Write a program to automatically solve a jigsaw puzzle from a set of scanned puzzle pieces. Your software may include the following components:

1. Scan the pieces (either face up or face down) on a flatbed scanner with a distinctively colored background.

2. (Optional) Scan in the box top to use as a low-resolution reference image.

3. Use color-based thresholding to isolate the pieces.

4. Extract the contour of each piece using edge finding and linking.

5. (Optional) Re-represent each contour using an arc-length or some other re-parameterization. Break up the contours into meaningful matchable pieces. (Is this hard?)

6. (Optional) Associate color values with each contour to help in the matching.

7. (Optional) Match pieces to the reference image using some rotationally invariant feature descriptors.

8. Solve a global optimization or (backtracking) search problem to snap pieces together and place them in the correct location relative to the reference image.

9. Test your algorithm on a succession of more difficult puzzles and compare your results with those of others.

Ex 4.11: Successive approximation line detector Implement a line simplification algorithm (Section 4.3.1) (Ramer 1972; Douglas and Peucker 1973) to convert a hand-drawn curve (or linked edge image) into a small set of polylines.

(Optional) Re-render this curve using either an approximating or interpolating spline or Bezier curve (Szeliski and Ito 1986; Bartels, Beatty, and Barsky 1987; Farin 1996).

Ex 4.12: Hough transform line detector Implement a Hough transform for finding lines in images:

1. Create an accumulator array of the appropriate user-specified size and clear it. The user can specify the spacing in degrees between orientation bins and in pixels between distance bins. The array can be allocated as integer (for simple counts), floating point (for weighted counts), or as an array of vectors for keeping back pointers to the constituent edges.

2. For each detected edgel at location (x, y) and orientation $\theta = \tan^{-1} n_y/n_x$, compute the value of

$$d = xn_x + yn_y \qquad (4.33)$$

   and increment the accumulator corresponding to (θ, d).

   (Optional) Weight the vote of each edge by its length (see Exercise 4.7) or the strength of its gradient.

3. (Optional) Smooth the scalar accumulator array by adding in values from its immediate neighbors. This can help counteract the *discretization* effect of voting for only a single bin—see Exercise 3.7.

4. Find the largest peaks (local maxima) in the accumulator corresponding to lines.

5. (Optional) For each peak, re-fit the lines to the constituent edgels, using *total least squares* (Appendix A.2). Use the original edgel lengths or strength weights to weight the least squares fit, as well as the agreement between the hypothesized line orientation and the edgel orientation. Determine whether these heuristics help increase the accuracy of the fit.

6. After fitting each peak, zero-out or eliminate that peak and its adjacent bins in the array, and move on to the next largest peak.

Test out your Hough transform on a variety of images taken indoors and outdoors, as well as checkerboard calibration patterns.

For checkerboard patterns, you can modify your Hough transform by collapsing *antipodal* bins $(\theta \pm 180°, -d)$ with (θ, d) to find lines that do not care about polarity changes. Can you think of examples in real-world images where this might be desirable as well?

Ex 4.13: Line fitting uncertainty Estimate the uncertainty (covariance) in your line fit using uncertainty analysis.

1. After determining which edgels belong to the line segment (using either successive approximation or Hough transform), re-fit the line segment using total least squares (Van Huffel and Vandewalle 1991; Van Huffel and Lemmerling 2002), i.e., find the

mean or centroid of the edgels and then use eigenvalue analysis to find the dominant orientation.

2. Compute the perpendicular errors (deviations) to the line and robustly estimate the variance of the fitting noise using an estimator such as MAD (Appendix B.3).

3. (Optional) re-fit the line parameters by throwing away outliers or using a robust norm or influence function.

4. Estimate the error in the perpendicular location of the line segment and its orientation.

Ex 4.14: Vanishing points   Compute the vanishing points in an image using one of the techniques described in Section 4.3.3 and optionally refine the original line equations associated with each vanishing point. Your results can be used later to track a target (Exercise 6.5) or reconstruct architecture (Section 12.6.1).

Ex 4.15: Vanishing point uncertainty   Perform an uncertainty analysis on your estimated vanishing points. You will need to decide how to represent your vanishing point, e.g., homogeneous coordinates on a sphere, to handle vanishing points near infinity.

See the discussion of Bingham distributions by Collins and Weiss (1990) for some ideas.

Chapter 5

Segmentation

R. Szeliski, *Computer Vision: Algorithms and Applications*, Texts in Computer Science,
DOI 10.1007/978-1-84882-935-0_5, © Springer-Verlag London Limited 2011

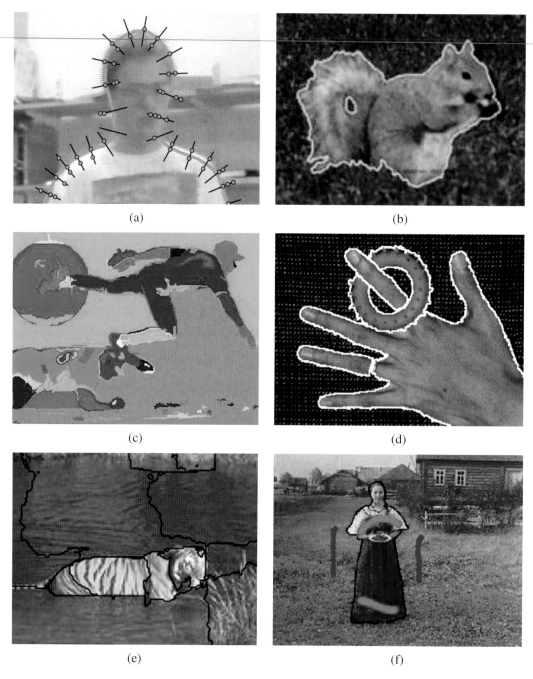

Figure 5.1 Some popular image segmentation techniques: (a) active contours (Isard and Blake 1998) © 1998 Springer; (b) level sets (Cremers, Rousson, and Deriche 2007) © 2007 Springer; (c) graph-based merging (Felzenszwalb and Huttenlocher 2004b) © 2004 Springer; (d) mean shift (Comaniciu and Meer 2002) © 2002 IEEE; (e) texture and intervening contour-based normalized cuts (Malik, Belongie, Leung *et al.* 2001) © 2001 Springer; (f) binary MRF solved using graph cuts (Boykov and Funka-Lea 2006) © 2006 Springer.

Image segmentation is the task of finding groups of pixels that "go together". In statistics, this problem is known as *cluster analysis* and is a widely studied area with hundreds of different algorithms (Jain and Dubes 1988; Kaufman and Rousseeuw 1990; Jain, Duin, and Mao 2000; Jain, Topchy, Law *et al.* 2004).

In computer vision, image segmentation is one of the oldest and most widely studied problems (Brice and Fennema 1970; Pavlidis 1977; Riseman and Arbib 1977; Ohlander, Price, and Reddy 1978; Rosenfeld and Davis 1979; Haralick and Shapiro 1985). Early techniques tend to use region splitting or merging (Brice and Fennema 1970; Horowitz and Pavlidis 1976; Ohlander, Price, and Reddy 1978; Pavlidis and Liow 1990), which correspond to *divisive* and *agglomerative* algorithms in the clustering literature (Jain, Topchy, Law *et al.* 2004). More recent algorithms often optimize some global criterion, such as intra-region consistency and inter-region boundary lengths or dissimilarity (Leclerc 1989; Mumford and Shah 1989; Shi and Malik 2000; Comaniciu and Meer 2002; Felzenszwalb and Huttenlocher 2004b; Cremers, Rousson, and Deriche 2007).

We have already seen examples of image segmentation in Sections 3.3.2 and 3.7.2. In this chapter, we review some additional techniques that have been developed for image segmentation. These include algorithms based on active contours (Section 5.1) and level sets (Section 5.1.4), region splitting and merging (Section 5.2), *mean shift* (mode finding) (Section 5.3), *normalized cuts* (splitting based on pixel similarity metrics) (Section 5.4), and binary Markov random fields solved using graph cuts (Section 5.5). Figure 5.1 shows some examples of these techniques applied to different images.

Since the literature on image segmentation is so vast, a good way to get a handle on some of the better performing algorithms is to look at experimental comparisons on human-labeled databases (Arbeláez, Maire, Fowlkes *et al.* 2010). The best known of these is the Berkeley Segmentation Dataset and Benchmark[1] (Martin, Fowlkes, Tal *et al.* 2001), which consists of 1000 images from a Corel image dataset that were hand-labeled by 30 human subjects. Many of the more recent image segmentation algorithms report comparative results on this database. For example, Unnikrishnan, Pantofaru, and Hebert (2007) propose new metrics for comparing such algorithms. Estrada and Jepson (2009) compare four well-known segmentation algorithms on the Berkeley data set and conclude that while their own SE-MinCut algorithm (Estrada, Jepson, and Chennubhotla 2004) algorithm outperforms the others by a small margin, there still exists a wide gap between automated and human segmentation performance.[2] A new database of foreground and background segmentations, used by Alpert, Galun, Basri *et al.* (2007), is also available.[3]

5.1 Active contours

While lines, vanishing points, and rectangles are commonplace in the man-made world, curves corresponding to object boundaries are even more common, especially in the natural environment. In this section, we describe three related approaches to locating such boundary curves in images.

---

[1] http://www.eecs.berkeley.edu/Research/Projects/CS/vision/grouping/segbench/

[2] An interesting observation about their ROC plots is that automated techniques cluster tightly along similar curves, but human performance is all over the map.

[3] http://www.wisdom.weizmann.ac.il/~vision/Seg_Evaluation_DB/index.html

The first, originally called *snakes* by its inventors (Kass, Witkin, and Terzopoulos 1988) (Section 5.1.1), is an energy-minimizing, two-dimensional spline curve that evolves (moves) towards image features such as strong edges. The second, *intelligent scissors* (Mortensen and Barrett 1995) (Section 5.1.3), allow the user to sketch in real time a curve that clings to object boundaries. Finally, *level set* techniques (Section 5.1.4) evolve the curve as the zero-set of a *characteristic function*, which allows them to easily change topology and incorporate region-based statistics.

All three of these are examples of *active contours* (Blake and Isard 1998; Mortensen 1999), since these boundary detectors iteratively move towards their final solution under the combination of image and optional user-guidance forces.

5.1.1 Snakes

Snakes are a two-dimensional generalization of the 1D energy-minimizing splines first introduced in Section 3.7.1,

$$\mathcal{E}_{\text{int}} = \int \alpha(s)\|\boldsymbol{f}_s(s)\|^2 + \beta(s)\|\boldsymbol{f}_{ss}(s)\|^2\, ds, \tag{5.1}$$

where s is the arc-length along the curve $\boldsymbol{f}(s) = (x(s), y(s))$ and $\alpha(s)$ and $\beta(s)$ are first- and second-order continuity weighting functions analogous to the $s(x, y)$ and $c(x, y)$ terms introduced in (3.100–3.101). We can discretize this energy by sampling the initial curve position evenly along its length (Figure 4.35) to obtain

$$
\begin{aligned}
E_{\text{int}} \;=\; & \sum_i \alpha(i)\|f(i+1) - f(i)\|^2/h^2 \\
& + \beta(i)\|f(i+1) - 2f(i) + f(i-1)\|^2/h^4,
\end{aligned} \tag{5.2}
$$

where h is the step size, which can be neglected if we resample the curve along its arc-length after each iteration.

In addition to this *internal* spline energy, a snake simultaneously minimizes external image-based and constraint-based potentials. The image-based potentials are the sum of several terms

$$\mathcal{E}_{\text{image}} = w_{\text{line}}\mathcal{E}_{\text{line}} + w_{\text{edge}}\mathcal{E}_{\text{edge}} + w_{\text{term}}\mathcal{E}_{\text{term}}, \tag{5.3}$$

where the *line* term attracts the snake to dark ridges, the *edge* term attracts it to strong gradients (edges), and the *term* term attracts it to line terminations. In practice, most systems only use the edge term, which can either be directly proportional to the image gradients,

$$E_{\text{edge}} = \sum_i -\|\nabla I(\boldsymbol{f}(i))\|^2, \tag{5.4}$$

or to a smoothed version of the image Laplacian,

$$E_{\text{edge}} = \sum_i -|(G_\sigma * \nabla^2 I)(\boldsymbol{f}(i))|^2. \tag{5.5}$$

People also sometimes extract edges and then use a distance map to the edges as an alternative to these two originally proposed potentials.

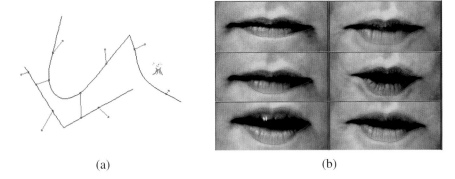

(a)   (b)

Figure 5.2 Snakes (Kass, Witkin, and Terzopoulos 1988) © 1988 Springer: (a) the "snake pit" for interactively controlling shape; (b) lip tracking.

In interactive applications, a variety of user-placed constraints can also be added, e.g., attractive (spring) forces towards anchor points $\boldsymbol{d}(i)$,

$$E_{\text{spring}} = k_i \|\boldsymbol{f}(i) - \boldsymbol{d}(i)\|^2, \tag{5.6}$$

as well as repulsive $1/r$ ("volcano") forces (Figure 5.2a). As the snakes evolve by minimizing their energy, they often "wiggle" and "slither", which accounts for their popular name. Figure 5.2b shows snakes being used to track a person's lips.

Because regular snakes have a tendency to shrink (Exercise 5.1), it is usually better to initialize them by drawing the snake outside the object of interest to be tracked. Alternatively, an expansion *ballooning* force can be added to the dynamics (Cohen and Cohen 1993), essentially moving each point outwards along its normal.

To efficiently solve the sparse linear system arising from snake energy minimization, a sparse direct solver (Appendix A.4) can be used, since the linear system is essentially penta-diagonal.[4] Snake evolution is usually implemented as an alternation between this linear system solution and the linearization of non-linear constraints such as edge energy. A more direct way to find a global energy minimum is to use dynamic programming (Amini, Weymouth, and Jain 1990; Williams and Shah 1992), but this is not often used in practice, since it has been superseded by even more efficient or interactive algorithms such as intelligent scissors (Section 5.1.3) and GrabCut (Section 5.5).

Elastic nets and slippery springs

An interesting variant on snakes, first proposed by Durbin and Willshaw (1987) and later re-formulated in an energy-minimizing framework by Durbin, Szeliski, and Yuille (1989), is the *elastic net* formulation of the Traveling Salesman Problem (TSP). Recall that in a TSP, the salesman must visit each city once while minimizing the total distance traversed. A snake that is constrained to pass through each city could solve this problem (without any optimality guarantees) but it is impossible to tell ahead of time which snake control point should be associated with each city.

---

[4] A closed snake has a Toeplitz matrix form, which can still be factored and solved in $O(N)$ time.

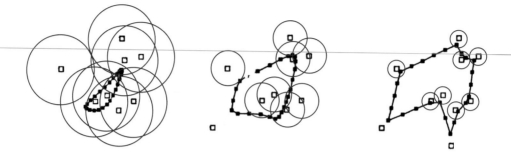

Figure 5.3 Elastic net: The open squares indicate the cities and the closed squares linked by straight line segments are the tour points. The blue circles indicate the approximate extent of the attraction force of each city, which is reduced over time. Under the Bayesian interpretation of the elastic net, the blue circles correspond to one standard deviation of the circular Gaussian that generates each city from some unknown tour point.

Instead of having a fixed constraint between snake nodes and cities, as in (5.6), a city is assumed to pass near *some* point along the tour (Figure 5.3). In a probabilistic interpretation, each city is generated as a *mixture* of Gaussians centered at each tour point,

$$p(\boldsymbol{d}(j)) = \sum_i p_{ij} \text{ with } p_{ij} = e^{-d_{ij}^2/(2\sigma^2)} \tag{5.7}$$

where σ is the standard deviation of the Gaussian and

$$d_{ij} = \|\boldsymbol{f}(i) - \boldsymbol{d}(j)\| \tag{5.8}$$

is the Euclidean distance between a tour point $\boldsymbol{f}(i)$ and a city location $\boldsymbol{d}(j)$. The corresponding data fitting energy (negative log likelihood) is

$$E_{\text{slippery}} = -\sum_j \log p(\boldsymbol{d}(j)) = -\sum_j \log \left[\sum e^{-\|\boldsymbol{f}(i)-\boldsymbol{d}(j)\|^2/2\sigma^2}\right]. \tag{5.9}$$

This energy derives its name from the fact that, unlike a regular spring, which couples a given snake point to a given constraint (5.6), this alternative energy defines a *slippery spring* that allows the association between constraints (cities) and curve (tour) points to evolve over time (Szeliski 1989). Note that this is a soft variant of the popular *iterated closest point* data constraint that is often used in fitting or aligning surfaces to data points or to each other (Section 12.2.1) (Besl and McKay 1992; Zhang 1994).

To compute a good solution to the TSP, the slippery spring data association energy is combined with a regular first-order internal smoothness energy (5.3) to define the cost of a tour. The tour $\boldsymbol{f}(s)$ is initialized as a small circle around the mean of the city points and σ is progressively lowered (Figure 5.3). For large σ values, the tour tries to stay near the centroid of the points but as σ decreases each city pulls more and more strongly on its closest tour points (Durbin, Szeliski, and Yuille 1989). In the limit as $\sigma \to 0$, each city is guaranteed to capture at least one tour point and the tours between subsequent cites become straight lines.

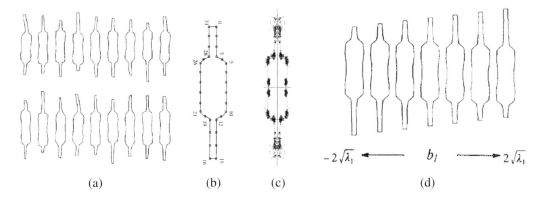

Figure 5.4 Point distribution model for a set of resistors (Cootes, Cooper, Taylor *et al.* 1995) © 1995 Elsevier: (a) set of input resistor shapes; (b) assignment of control points to the boundary; (c) distribution (scatter plot) of point locations; (d) first (largest) mode of variation in the ensemble shapes.

Splines and shape priors

While snakes can be very good at capturing the fine and irregular detail in many real-world contours, they sometimes exhibit too many degrees of freedom, making it more likely that they can get trapped in local minima during their evolution.

One solution to this problem is to control the snake with fewer degrees of freedom through the use of B-spline approximations (Menet, Saint-Marc, and Medioni 1990b,a; Cipolla and Blake 1990). The resulting *B-snake* can be written as

$$\boldsymbol{f}(s) = \sum_k B_k(s)\boldsymbol{x}_k \tag{5.10}$$

or in discrete form as

$$\boldsymbol{F} = \boldsymbol{B}\boldsymbol{X} \tag{5.11}$$

with

$$\boldsymbol{F} = \begin{bmatrix} \boldsymbol{f}^T(0) \\ \vdots \\ \boldsymbol{f}^T(N) \end{bmatrix}, \quad \boldsymbol{B} = \begin{bmatrix} B_0(s_0) & \dots & B_K(s_0) \\ \vdots & \ddots & \vdots \\ B_0(s_N) & \dots & B_K(s_N) \end{bmatrix}, \quad \text{and} \quad \boldsymbol{X} = \begin{bmatrix} \boldsymbol{x}^T(0) \\ \vdots \\ \boldsymbol{x}^T(K) \end{bmatrix}. \tag{5.12}$$

If the object being tracked or recognized has large variations in location, scale, or orientation, these can be modeled as an additional transformation on the control points, e.g., $\boldsymbol{x}'_k = s\boldsymbol{R}\boldsymbol{x}_k + \boldsymbol{t}$ (2.18), which can be estimated at the same time as the values of the control points. Alternatively, separate *detection* and *alignment* stages can be run to first localize and orient the objects of interest (Cootes, Cooper, Taylor *et al.* 1995).

In a B-snake, because the snake is controlled by fewer degrees of freedom, there is less need for the internal smoothness forces used with the original snakes, although these can still be derived and implemented using finite element analysis, i.e., taking derivatives and integrals of the B-spline basis functions (Terzopoulos 1983; Bathe 2007).

In practice, it is more common to estimate a set of *shape priors* on the typical distribution of the control points $\{\boldsymbol{x}_k\}$ (Cootes, Cooper, Taylor *et al.* 1995). Consider the set of resistor

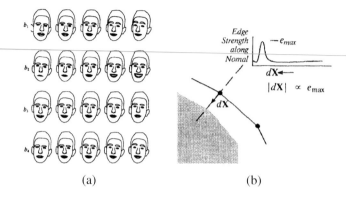

                                        (a)   (b)

Figure 5.5 Active Shape Model (ASM): (a) the effect of varying the first four shape parameters for a set of faces (Cootes, Taylor, Lanitis *et al.* 1993) © 1993 IEEE; (b) searching for the strongest gradient along the normal to each control point (Cootes, Cooper, Taylor *et al.* 1995) © 1995 Elsevier.

shapes shown in Figure 5.4a. If we describe each contour with the set of control points shown in Figure 5.4b, we can plot the distribution of each point in a scatter plot, as shown in Figure 5.4c.

One potential way of describing this distribution would be by the location $\bar{x}_k$ and 2D covariance C_k of each individual point x_k. These could then be turned into a quadratic penalty (prior energy) on the point location,

$$E_{\mathrm{loc}}(x_k) = \frac{1}{2}(x_k - \bar{x}_k)^T C_k^{-1}(x_k - \bar{x}_k). \qquad (5.13)$$

In practice, however, the variation in point locations is usually highly correlated.

A preferable approach is to estimate the joint covariance of all the points simultaneously. First, concatenate all of the point locations $\{x_k\}$ into a single vector x, e.g., by interleaving the x and y locations of each point. The distribution of these vectors across all training examples (Figure 5.4a) can be described with a mean $\bar{x}$ and a covariance

$$C = \frac{1}{P}\sum_p (x_p - \bar{x})(x_p - \bar{x})^T, \qquad (5.14)$$

where x_p are the P training examples. Using *eigenvalue analysis* (Appendix A.1.2), which is also known as *Principal Component Analysis* (PCA) (Appendix B.1.1), the covariance matrix can be written as,

$$C = \Phi \, \mathrm{diag}(\lambda_0 \ldots \lambda_{K-1}) \, \Phi^T. \qquad (5.15)$$

In most cases, the likely appearance of the points can be modeled using only a few eigenvectors with the largest eigenvalues. The resulting *point distribution model* (Cootes, Taylor, Lanitis *et al.* 1993; Cootes, Cooper, Taylor *et al.* 1995) can be written as

$$x = \bar{x} + \hat{\Phi}\, b, \qquad (5.16)$$

where b is an $M \ll K$ element *shape parameter* vector and $\hat{\Phi}$ are the first m columns of Φ. To constrain the shape parameters to reasonable values, we can use a quadratic penalty of the form

$$E_{\text{shape}} = \frac{1}{2} \boldsymbol{b}^T \operatorname{diag}(\lambda_0 \ldots \lambda_{M-1}) \, \boldsymbol{b} = \sum_m b_m^2 / 2\lambda_m. \qquad (5.17)$$

Alternatively, the range of allowable b_m values can be limited to some range, e.g., $|b_m| \leq 3\sqrt{\lambda_m}$ (Cootes, Cooper, Taylor *et al.* 1995). Alternative approaches for deriving a set of shape vectors are reviewed by Isard and Blake (1998).

Varying the individual shape parameters b_m over the range $-2\sqrt{\lambda_m} \leq 2\sqrt{\lambda_m}$ can give a good indication of the expected variation in appearance, as shown in Figure 5.4d. Another example, this time related to face contours, is shown in Figure 5.5a.

In order to align a point distribution model with an image, each control point searches in a direction normal to the contour to find the most likely corresponding image edge point (Figure 5.5b). These individual measurements can be combined with priors on the shape parameters (and, if desired, position, scale, and orientation parameters) to estimate a new set of parameters. The resulting *Active Shape Model* (ASM) can be iteratively minimized to fit images to non-rigidly deforming objects such as medical images or body parts such as hands (Cootes, Cooper, Taylor *et al.* 1995). The ASM can also be combined with a PCA analysis of the underlying gray-level distribution to create an *Active Appearance Model* (AAM) (Cootes, Edwards, and Taylor 2001), which we discuss in more detail in Section 14.2.2.

5.1.2 Dynamic snakes and CONDENSATION

In many applications of active contours, the object of interest is being tracked from frame to frame as it deforms and evolves. In this case, it makes sense to use estimates from the previous frame to predict and constrain the new estimates.

One way to do this is to use Kalman filtering, which results in a formulation called *Kalman snakes* (Terzopoulos and Szeliski 1992; Blake, Curwen, and Zisserman 1993). The Kalman filter is based on a linear dynamic model of shape parameter evolution,

$$\boldsymbol{x}_t = \boldsymbol{A}\boldsymbol{x}_{t-1} + \boldsymbol{w}_t, \qquad (5.18)$$

where $\boldsymbol{x}_t$ and $\boldsymbol{x}_{t-1}$ are the current and previous state variables, $\boldsymbol{A}$ is the linear *transition matrix*, and $\boldsymbol{w}$ is a noise (perturbation) vector, which is often modeled as a Gaussian (Gelb 1974). The matrices $\boldsymbol{A}$ and the noise covariance can be learned ahead of time by observing typical sequences of the object being tracked (Blake and Isard 1998).

The qualitative behavior of the Kalman filter can be seen in Figure 5.6a. The linear dynamic model causes a deterministic change (drift) in the previous estimate, while the process noise (perturbation) causes a stochastic diffusion that increases the system entropy (lack of certainty). New measurements from the current frame restore some of the certainty (peakedness) in the updated estimate.

In many situations, however, such as when tracking in clutter, a better estimate for the contour can be obtained if we remove the assumptions that the distribution are Gaussian, which is what the Kalman filter requires. In this case, a general multi-modal distribution is propagated, as shown in Figure 5.6b. In order to model such multi-modal distributions, Isard and Blake (1998) introduced the use of *particle filtering* to the computer vision community.[5]

---

[5] Alternatives to modeling multi-modal distributions include *mixtures of Gaussians* (Bishop 2006) and *multiple hypothesis tracking* (Bar-Shalom and Fortmann 1988; Cham and Rehg 1999).

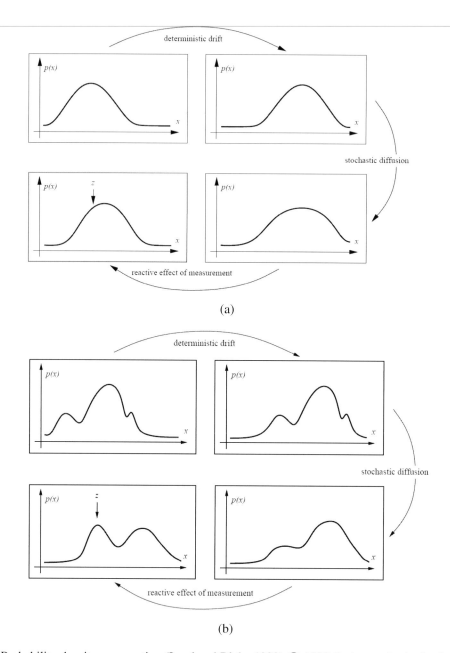

(a)

(b)

Figure 5.6 Probability density propagation (Isard and Blake 1998) © 1998 Springer. At the beginning of each estimation step, the probability density is updated according to the linear dynamic model (deterministic drift) and its certainty is reduced due to process noise (stochastic diffusion). New measurements introduce additional information that helps refine the current estimate. (a) The Kalman filter models the distributions as uni-modal, i.e., using a mean and covariance. (b) Some applications require more general multi-modal distributions.

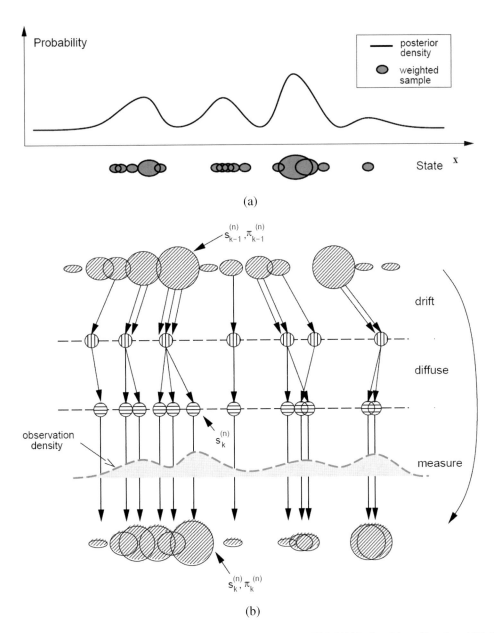

Figure 5.7 Factored sampling using particle filter in the CONDENSATION algorithm (Isard and Blake 1998) © 1998 Springer: (a) each density distribution is represented using a superposition of weighted *particles*; (b) the drift-diffusion-measurement cycle implemented using random sampling, perturbation, and re-weighting stages.

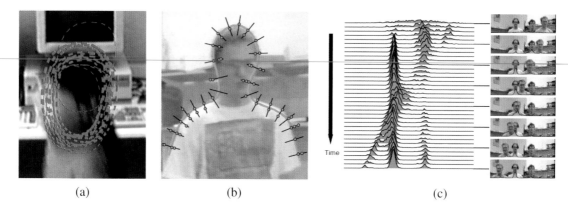

$$(a) \qquad\qquad\qquad (b) \qquad\qquad\qquad (c)$$

Figure 5.8 Head tracking using CONDENSATION (Isard and Blake 1998) © 1998 Springer: (a) sample set representation of head estimate distribution; (b) multiple measurements at each control vertex location; (c) multi-hypothesis tracking over time.

Particle filtering techniques represent a probability distribution using a collection of weighted point samples (Figure 5.7a) (Andrieu, de Freitas, Doucet *et al.* 2003; Bishop 2006; Koller and Friedman 2009). To update the locations of the samples according to the linear dynamics (deterministic drift), the centers of the samples are updated according to (5.18) and multiple samples are generated for each point (Figure 5.7b). These are then perturbed to account for the stochastic diffusion, i.e., their locations are moved by random vectors taken from the distribution of w.[6] Finally, the weights of these samples are multiplied by the measurement probability density, i.e., we take each sample and measure its likelihood given the current (new) measurements. Because the point samples represent and propagate conditional estimates of the multi-modal density, Isard and Blake (1998) dubbed their algorithm CONditional DENSity propagATION or CONDENSATION.

Figure 5.8a shows what a factored sample of a head tracker might look like, drawing a red B-spline contour for each of (a subset of) the particles being tracked. Figure 5.8b shows why the measurement density itself is often multi-modal: the locations of the edges perpendicular to the spline curve can have multiple local maxima due to background clutter. Finally, Figure 5.8c shows the temporal evolution of the conditional density (x coordinate of the head and shoulder tracker centroid) as it tracks several people over time.

5.1.3 Scissors

Active contours allow a user to roughly specify a boundary of interest and have the system evolve the contour towards a more accurate location as well as track it over time. The results of this curve evolution, however, may be unpredictable and may require additional user-based hints to achieve the desired result.

An alternative approach is to have the system optimize the contour in real time as the user is drawing (Mortensen 1999). The *intelligent scissors* system developed by Mortensen and Barrett (1995) does just that. As the user draws a rough outline (the white curve in Figure 5.9a), the system computes and draws a better curve that clings to high-contrast edges

---

[6] Note that because of the structure of these steps, non-linear dynamics and non-Gaussian noise can be used.

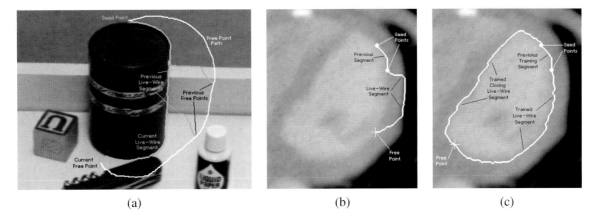

(a)   (b)   (c)

Figure 5.9 Intelligent scissors: (a) as the mouse traces the white path, the scissors follow the orange path along the object boundary (the green curves show intermediate positions) (Mortensen and Barrett 1995) © 1995 ACM; (b) regular scissors can sometimes jump to a stronger (incorrect) boundary; (c) after training to the previous segment, similar edge profiles are preferred (Mortensen and Barrett 1998) © 1995 Elsevier.

(the orange curve).

To compute the optimal curve path (*live-wire*), the image is first pre-processed to associate low costs with edges (links between neighboring horizontal, vertical, and diagonal, i.e., $\mathcal{N}_8$ neighbors) that are likely to be boundary elements. Their system uses a combination of zero-crossing, gradient magnitudes, and gradient orientations to compute these costs.

Next, as the user traces a rough curve, the system continuously recomputes the lowest-cost path between the starting *seed point* and the current mouse location using Dijkstra's algorithm, a breadth-first dynamic programming algorithm that terminates at the current target location.

In order to keep the system from jumping around unpredictably, the system will "freeze" the curve to date (reset the seed point) after a period of inactivity. To prevent the live wire from jumping onto adjacent higher-contrast contours, the system also "learns" the intensity profile under the current optimized curve, and uses this to preferentially keep the wire moving along the same (or a similar looking) boundary (Figure 5.9b–c).

Several extensions have been proposed to the basic algorithm, which works remarkably well even in its original form. Mortensen and Barrett (1999) use *tobogganing*, which is a simple form of watershed region segmentation, to pre-segment the image into regions whose boundaries become candidates for optimized curve paths. The resulting region boundaries are turned into a much smaller graph, where nodes are located wherever three or four regions meet. The Dijkstra algorithm is then run on this reduced graph, resulting in much faster (and often more stable) performance. Another extension to intelligent scissors is to use a probabilistic framework that takes into account the current trajectory of the boundary, resulting in a system called JetStream (Pérez, Blake, and Gangnet 2001).

Instead of re-computing an optimal curve at each time instant, a simpler system can be developed by simply "snapping" the current mouse position to the nearest likely boundary point (Gleicher 1995). Applications of these boundary extraction techniques to image cutting and pasting are presented in Section 10.4.

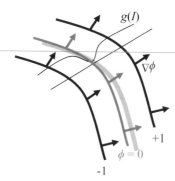

Figure 5.10 Level set evolution for a geodesic active contour. The embedding function ϕ is updated based on the curvature of the underlying surface modulated by the edge/speed function $g(I)$, as well as the gradient of $g(I)$, thereby attracting it to strong edges.

5.1.4 Level Sets

A limitation of active contours based on parametric curves of the form $f(s)$, e.g., snakes, B-snakes, and CONDENSATION, is that it is challenging to change the topology of the curve as it evolves. (McInerney and Terzopoulos (1999, 2000) describe one approach to doing this.) Furthermore, if the shape changes dramatically, curve reparameterization may also be required.

An alternative representation for such closed contours is to use a *level set*, where the *zero-crossing(s)* of a *characteristic* (or signed distance (Section 3.3.3)) function define the curve. Level sets evolve to fit and track objects of interest by modifying the underlying *embedding function* (another name for this 2D function) $\phi(x, y)$ instead of the curve $f(s)$ (Malladi, Sethian, and Vemuri 1995; Sethian 1999; Sapiro 2001; Osher and Paragios 2003). To reduce the amount of computation required, only a small strip (frontier) around the locations of the current zero-crossing needs to updated at each step, which results in what are called *fast marching methods* (Sethian 1999).

An example of an evolution equation is the *geodesic active contour* proposed by Caselles, Kimmel, and Sapiro (1997) and Yezzi, Kichenassamy, Kumar *et al.* (1997),

$$
\begin{aligned}
\frac{d\phi}{dt} &= |\nabla\phi|\,\text{div}\left(g(I)\frac{\nabla\phi}{|\nabla\phi|}\right) \\
&= g(I)|\nabla\phi|\,\text{div}\left(\frac{\nabla\phi}{|\nabla\phi|}\right) + \nabla g(I) \cdot \nabla\phi,
\end{aligned}
\tag{5.19}
$$

where $g(I)$ is a generalized version of the snake edge potential (5.5). To get an intuitive sense of the curve's behavior, assume that the embedding function ϕ is a signed distance function away from the curve (Figure 5.10), in which case $|\phi| = 1$. The first term in Equation (5.19) moves the curve in the direction of its curvature, i.e., it acts to straighten the curve, under the influence of the modulation function $g(I)$. The second term moves the curve down the gradient of $g(I)$, encouraging the curve to migrate towards minima of $g(I)$.

While this level-set formulation can readily change topology, it is still susceptible to local minima, since it is based on local measurements such as image gradients. An alternative

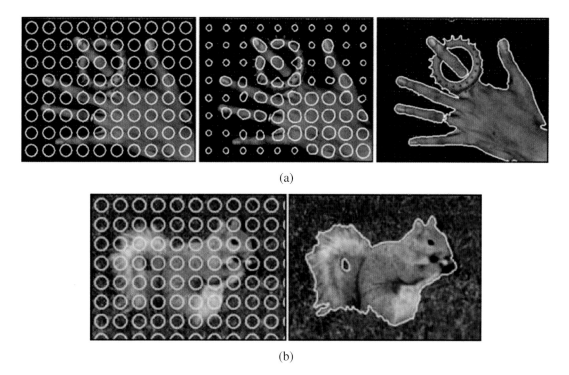

(a)

(b)

Figure 5.11 Level set segmentation (Cremers, Rousson, and Deriche 2007) © 2007 Springer: (a) grayscale image segmentation and (b) color image segmentation. Uni-variate and multi-variate Gaussians are used to model the foreground and background pixel distributions. The initial circles evolve towards an accurate segmentation of foreground and background, adapting their topology as they evolve.

approach is to re-cast the problem in a segmentation framework, where the energy measures the consistency of the image statistics (e.g., color, texture, motion) inside and outside the segmented regions (Cremers, Rousson, and Deriche 2007; Rousson and Paragios 2008; Houhou, Thiran, and Bresson 2008). These approaches build on earlier energy-based segmentation frameworks introduced by Leclerc (1989), Mumford and Shah (1989), and Chan and Vese (1992), which are discussed in more detail in Section 5.5. Examples of such level-set segmentations are shown in Figure 5.11, which shows the evolution of the level sets from a series of distributed circles towards the final binary segmentation.

For more information on level sets and their applications, please see the collection of papers edited by Osher and Paragios (2003) as well as the series of Workshops on Variational and Level Set Methods in Computer Vision (Paragios, Faugeras, Chan *et al.* 2005) and Special Issues on Scale Space and Variational Methods in Computer Vision (Paragios and Sgallari 2009).

5.1.5 *Application*: Contour tracking and rotoscoping

Active contours can be used in a wide variety of object-tracking applications (Blake and Isard 1998; Yilmaz, Javed, and Shah 2006). For example, they can be used to track facial features for performance-driven animation (Terzopoulos and Waters 1990; Lee, Terzopoulos, and Wa-

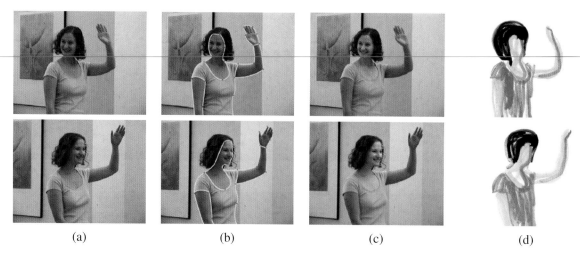

(a)   (b)   (c)   (d)

Figure 5.12   Keyframe-based rotoscoping (Agarwala, Hertzmann, Seitz *et al.* 2004) © 2004 ACM: (a) original frames; (b) rotoscoped contours; (c) re-colored blouse; (d) rotoscoped hand-drawn animation.

ters 1995; Parke and Waters 1996; Bregler, Covell, and Slaney 1997) (Figure 5.2b). They can also be used to track heads and people, as shown in Figure 5.8, as well as moving vehicles (Paragios and Deriche 2000). Additional applications include medical image segmentation, where contours can be tracked from slice to slice in computerized tomography (3D medical imagery) (Cootes and Taylor 2001) or over time, as in ultrasound scans.

An interesting application that is closer to computer animation and visual effects is *rotoscoping*, which uses the tracked contours to deform a set of hand-drawn animations (or to modify or replace the original video frames).[7] Agarwala, Hertzmann, Seitz *et al.* (2004) present a system based on tracking hand-drawn B-spline contours drawn at selected keyframes, using a combination of geometric and appearance-based criteria (Figure 5.12). They also provide an excellent review of previous rotoscoping and image-based, contour-tracking systems.

Additional applications of rotoscoping (object contour detection and segmentation), such as cutting and pasting objects from one photograph into another, are presented in Section 10.4.

5.2 Split and merge

As mentioned in the introduction to this chapter, the simplest possible technique for segmenting a grayscale image is to select a threshold and then compute connected components (Section 3.3.2). Unfortunately, a single threshold is rarely sufficient for the whole image because of lighting and intra-object statistical variations.

In this section, we describe a number of algorithms that proceed either by recursively splitting the whole image into pieces based on region statistics or, conversely, merging pixels and regions together in a hierarchical fashion. It is also possible to combine both splitting and merging by starting with a medium-grain segmentation (in a quadtree representation) and

---

[7] The term comes from a device (a rotoscope) that projected frames of a live-action film underneath an acetate so that artists could draw animations directly over the actors' shapes.

then allowing both merging and splitting operations (Horowitz and Pavlidis 1976; Pavlidis and Liow 1990).

5.2.1 Watershed

A technique related to thresholding, since it operates on a grayscale image, is *watershed* computation (Vincent and Soille 1991). This technique segments an image into several *catchment basins*, which are the regions of an image (interpreted as a height field or landscape) where rain would flow into the same lake. An efficient way to compute such regions is to start flooding the landscape at all of the local minima and to label ridges wherever differently evolving components meet. The whole algorithm can be implemented using a priority queue of pixels and breadth-first search (Vincent and Soille 1991).[8]

Since images rarely have dark regions separated by lighter ridges, watershed segmentation is usually applied to a smoothed version of the gradient magnitude image, which also makes it usable with color images. As an alternative, the maximum oriented energy in a steerable filter (3.28–3.29) (Freeman and Adelson 1991) can be used as the basis of the *oriented watershed transform* developed by Arbeláez, Maire, Fowlkes *et al.* (2010). Such techniques end up finding smooth regions separated by visible (higher gradient) boundaries. Since such boundaries are what active contours usually follow, active contour algorithms (Mortensen and Barrett 1999; Li, Sun, Tang *et al.* 2004) often precompute such a segmentation using either the watershed or the related *tobogganing* technique (Section 5.1.3).

Unfortunately, watershed segmentation associates a unique region with each local minimum, which can lead to over-segmentation. Watershed segmentation is therefore often used as part of an interactive system, where the user first marks seed locations (with a click or a short stroke) that correspond to the centers of different desired components. Figure 5.13 shows the results of running the watershed algorithm with some manually placed markers on a confocal microscopy image. It also shows the result for an improved version of watershed that uses local morphology to smooth out and optimize the boundaries separating the regions (Beare 2006).

5.2.2 Region splitting (divisive clustering)

Splitting the image into successively finer regions is one of the oldest techniques in computer vision. Ohlander, Price, and Reddy (1978) present such a technique, which first computes a histogram for the whole image and then finds a threshold that best separates the large peaks in the histogram. This process is repeated until regions are either fairly uniform or below a certain size.

More recent splitting algorithms often optimize some metric of intra-region similarity and inter-region dissimilarity. These are covered in Sections 5.4 and 5.5.

5.2.3 Region merging (agglomerative clustering)

Region merging techniques also date back to the beginnings of computer vision. Brice and Fennema (1970) use a dual grid for representing boundaries between pixels and merge re-

---

[8] A related algorithm can be used to compute maximally stable extremal regions (MSERs) efficiently (Section 4.1.1) (Nistér and Stewénius 2008).

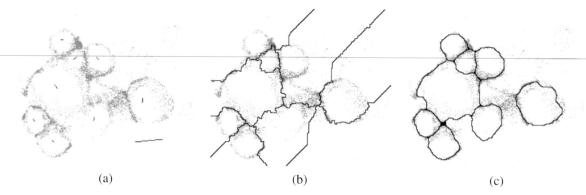

(a)   (b)   (c)

Figure 5.13 Locally constrained watershed segmentation (Beare 2006) © 2006 IEEE: (a) original confocal microscopy image with marked seeds (line segments); (b) standard watershed segmentation; (c) locally constrained watershed segmentation.

gions based on their relative boundary lengths and the strength of the visible edges at these boundaries.

In data clustering, algorithms can link clusters together based on the distance between their closest points (single-link clustering), their farthest points (complete-link clustering), or something in between (Jain, Topchy, Law *et al.* 2004). Kamvar, Klein, and Manning (2002) provide a probabilistic interpretation of these algorithms and show how additional models can be incorporated within this framework.

A very simple version of pixel-based merging combines adjacent regions whose average color difference is below a threshold or whose regions are too small. Segmenting the image into such *superpixels* (Mori, Ren, Efros *et al.* 2004), which are not semantically meaningful, can be a useful pre-processing stage to make higher-level algorithms such as stereo matching (Zitnick, Kang, Uyttendaele *et al.* 2004; Taguchi, Wilburn, and Zitnick 2008), optic flow (Zitnick, Jojic, and Kang 2005; Brox, Bregler, and Malik 2009), and recognition (Mori, Ren, Efros *et al.* 2004; Mori 2005; Gu, Lim, Arbelaez *et al.* 2009; Lim, Arbeláez, Gu *et al.* 2009) both faster and more robust.

5.2.4 Graph-based segmentation

While many merging algorithms simply apply a fixed rule that groups pixels and regions together, Felzenszwalb and Huttenlocher (2004b) present a merging algorithm that uses *relative dissimilarities* between regions to determine which ones should be merged; it produces an algorithm that provably optimizes a global grouping metric. They start with a pixel-to-pixel dissimilarity measure $w(e)$ that measures, for example, intensity differences between $\mathcal{N}_8$ neighbors. (Alternatively, they can use the *joint feature space* distances (5.42) introduced by Comaniciu and Meer (2002), which we discuss in Section 5.3.2.)

For any region R, its *internal difference* is defined as the largest edge weight in the region's minimum spanning tree,

$$Int(R) = \min_{e \in MST(R)} w(e). \tag{5.20}$$

For any two adjacent regions with at least one edge connecting their vertices, the difference

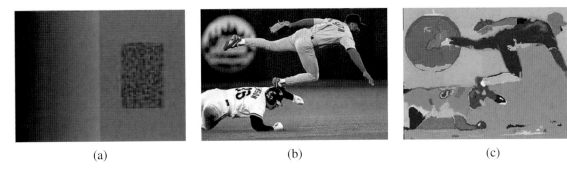

(a)   (b)   (c)

Figure 5.14 Graph-based merging segmentation (Felzenszwalb and Huttenlocher 2004b) © 2004 Springer: (a) input grayscale image that is successfully segmented into three regions even though the variation inside the smaller rectangle is larger than the variation across the middle edge; (b) input grayscale image; (c) resulting segmentation using an $\mathcal{N}_8$ pixel neighborhood.

between these regions is defined as the minimum weight edge connecting the two regions,

$$Dif(R_1, R_2) = \min_{e=(v_1,v_2)|v_1 \in R_1, v_2 \in R_2} w(e). \tag{5.21}$$

Their algorithm merges any two adjacent regions whose difference is smaller than the minimum internal difference of these two regions,

$$MInt(R_1, R_2) = \min(Int(R_1) + \tau(R_1), Int(R_2) + \tau(R_2)), \tag{5.22}$$

where $\tau(R)$ is a heuristic region penalty that Felzenszwalb and Huttenlocher (2004b) set to $k/|R|$, but which can be set to any application-specific measure of region goodness.

By merging regions in decreasing order of the edges separating them (which can be efficiently evaluated using a variant of Kruskal's minimum spanning tree algorithm), they provably produce segmentations that are neither too fine (there exist regions that could have been merged) nor too coarse (there are regions that could be split without being mergeable). For fixed-size pixel neighborhoods, the running time for this algorithm is $O(N \log N)$, where N is the number of image pixels, which makes it one of the fastest segmentation algorithms (Paris and Durand 2007). Figure 5.14 shows two examples of images segmented using their technique.

5.2.5 Probabilistic aggregation

Alpert, Galun, Basri *et al.* (2007) develop a probabilistic merging algorithm based on two cues, namely gray-level similarity and texture similarity. The gray-level similarity between regions R_i and R_j is based on the *minimal external difference* from other neighboring regions,

$$\sigma_{local}^+ = \min(\Delta_i^+, \Delta_j^+), \tag{5.23}$$

where $\Delta_i^+ = \min_k |\Delta_{ik}|$ and Δ_{ik} is the difference in average intensities between regions R_i and R_k. This is compared to the *average intensity difference*,

$$\sigma_{local}^- = \frac{\Delta_i^- + \Delta_j^-}{2}, \tag{5.24}$$

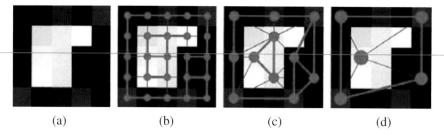

(a)   (b)   (c)   (d)

Figure 5.15 Coarse to fine node aggregation in segmentation by weighted aggregation (SWA) (Sharon, Galun, Sharon *et al.* 2006) © 2006 Macmillan Publishers Ltd [Nature]: (a) original gray-level pixel grid; (b) inter-pixel couplings, where thicker lines indicate stronger couplings; (c) after one level of coarsening, where each original pixel is strongly coupled to one of the coarse-level nodes; (d) after two levels of coarsening.

where $\Delta_i^- = \sum_k (\tau_{ik} \Delta_{ik}) / \sum_k (\tau_{ik})$ and τ_{ik} is the boundary length between regions R_i and R_k. The texture similarity is defined using relative differences between histogram bins of simple oriented Sobel filter responses. The pairwise statistics σ_{local}^+ and σ_{local}^- are used to compute the likelihoods p_{ij} that two regions should be merged. (See the paper by Alpert, Galun, Basri *et al.* (2007) for more details.)

Merging proceeds in a hierarchical fashion inspired by algebraic multigrid techniques (Brandt 1986; Briggs, Henson, and McCormick 2000) and previously used by Alpert, Galun, Basri *et al.* (2007) in their segmentation by weighted aggregation (SWA) algorithm (Sharon, Galun, Sharon *et al.* 2006), which we discuss in Section 5.4. A subset of the nodes $C \subset V$ that are (collectively) *strongly coupled* to all of the original nodes (regions) are used to define the problem at a coarser scale (Figure 5.15), where strong coupling is defined as

$$\frac{\sum_{j \in C} p_{ij}}{\sum_{j \in V} p_{ij}} > \phi, \tag{5.25}$$

with ϕ usually set to 0.2. The intensity and texture similarity statistics for the coarser nodes are recursively computed using weighted averaging, where the relative strengths (couplings) between coarse- and fine-level nodes are based on their merge probabilities p_{ij}. This allows the algorithm to run in essentially $O(N)$ time, using the same kind of hierarchical aggregation operations that are used in pyramid-based filtering or preconditioning algorithms. After a segmentation has been identified at a coarser level, the exact memberships of each pixel are computed by propagating coarse-level assignments to their finer-level "children" (Sharon, Galun, Sharon *et al.* 2006; Alpert, Galun, Basri *et al.* 2007). Figure 5.22 shows the segmentations produced by this algorithm compared to other popular segmentation algorithms.

5.3 Mean shift and mode finding

Mean-shift and mode finding techniques, such as k-means and mixtures of Gaussians, model the feature vectors associated with each pixel (e.g., color and position) as samples from an unknown probability density function and then try to find clusters (modes) in this distribution.

Consider the color image shown in Figure 5.16a. How would you segment this image based on color alone? Figure 5.16b shows the distribution of pixels in L*u*v* space, which is equivalent to what a vision algorithm that ignores spatial location would see. To make the

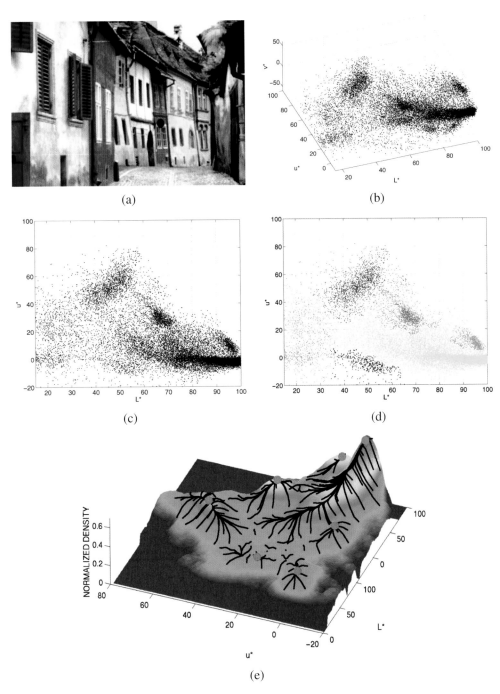

Figure 5.16 Mean-shift image segmentation (Comaniciu and Meer 2002) © 2002 IEEE: (a) input color image; (b) pixels plotted in L*u*v* space; (c) L*u* space distribution; (d) clustered results after 159 mean-shift procedures; (e) corresponding trajectories with peaks marked as red dots.

visualization simpler, let us only consider the L*u* coordinates, as shown in Figure 5.16c. How many obvious (elongated) clusters do you see? How would you go about finding these clusters?

The k-means and mixtures of Gaussians techniques use a *parametric* model of the density function to answer this question, i.e., they assume the density is the superposition of a small number of simpler distributions (e.g., Gaussians) whose locations (centers) and shape (covariance) can be estimated. Mean shift, on the other hand, smoothes the distribution and finds its peaks as well as the regions of feature space that correspond to each peak. Since a complete density is being modeled, this approach is called *non-parametric* (Bishop 2006). Let us look at these techniques in more detail.

5.3.1 K-means and mixtures of Gaussians

While k-means implicitly models the probability density as a superposition of spherically symmetric distributions, it does not require any probabilistic reasoning or modeling (Bishop 2006). Instead, the algorithm is given the number of clusters k it is supposed to find; it then iteratively updates the cluster center location based on the samples that are closest to each center. The algorithm can be initialized by randomly sampling k centers from the input feature vectors. Techniques have also been developed for splitting or merging cluster centers based on their statistics, and for accelerating the process of finding the nearest mean center (Bishop 2006).

In mixtures of Gaussians, each cluster center is augmented by a covariance matrix whose values are re-estimated from the corresponding samples. Instead of using nearest neighbors to associate input samples with cluster centers, a *Mahalanobis distance* (Appendix B.1.1) is used:

$$d(\boldsymbol{x}_i, \boldsymbol{\mu}_k; \boldsymbol{\Sigma}_k) = \|\boldsymbol{x}_i - \boldsymbol{\mu}_k\|_{\boldsymbol{\Sigma}_k^{-1}} = (\boldsymbol{x}_i - \boldsymbol{\mu}_k)^T \boldsymbol{\Sigma}_k^{-1} (\boldsymbol{x}_i - \boldsymbol{\mu}_k) \tag{5.26}$$

where $\boldsymbol{x}_i$ are the input samples, $\boldsymbol{\mu}_k$ are the cluster centers, and $\boldsymbol{\Sigma}_k$ are their covariance estimates. Samples can be associated with the nearest cluster center (a *hard assignment* of membership) or can be *softly assigned* to several nearby clusters.

This latter, more commonly used, approach corresponds to iteratively re-estimating the parameters for a mixture of Gaussians density function,

$$p(\boldsymbol{x}|\{\pi_k, \boldsymbol{\mu}_k, \boldsymbol{\Sigma}_k\}) = \sum_k \pi_k \mathcal{N}(\boldsymbol{x}|\boldsymbol{\mu}_k, \boldsymbol{\Sigma}_k), \tag{5.27}$$

where π_k are the *mixing coefficients*, $\boldsymbol{\mu}_k$ and $\boldsymbol{\Sigma}_k$ are the Gaussian means and covariances, and

$$\mathcal{N}(\boldsymbol{x}|\boldsymbol{\mu}_k, \boldsymbol{\Sigma}_k) = \frac{1}{|\boldsymbol{\Sigma}_k|} e^{-d(\boldsymbol{x}, \boldsymbol{\mu}_k; \boldsymbol{\Sigma}_k)} \tag{5.28}$$

is the *normal* (Gaussian) distribution (Bishop 2006).

To iteratively compute (a local) maximum likely estimate for the unknown mixture parameters $\{\pi_k, \boldsymbol{\mu}_k, \boldsymbol{\Sigma}_k\}$, the *expectation maximization* (EM) algorithm (Dempster, Laird, and Rubin 1977) proceeds in two alternating stages:

1. The *expectation* stage (E step) estimates the *responsibilities*

$$z_{ik} = \frac{1}{Z_i} \pi_k \mathcal{N}(\boldsymbol{x}|\boldsymbol{\mu}_k, \boldsymbol{\Sigma}_k) \quad \text{with} \quad \sum_k z_{ik} = 1, \tag{5.29}$$

which are the estimates of how likely a sample x_i was generated from the kth Gaussian cluster.

2. The *maximization* stage (M step) updates the parameter values

$$\boldsymbol{\mu}_k = \frac{1}{N_k} \sum_i z_{ik} \boldsymbol{x}_i, \tag{5.30}$$

$$\boldsymbol{\Sigma}_k = \frac{1}{N_k} \sum_i z_{ik} (\boldsymbol{x}_i - \boldsymbol{\mu}_k)(\boldsymbol{x}_i - \boldsymbol{\mu}_k)^T, \tag{5.31}$$

$$\pi_k = \frac{N_k}{N}, \tag{5.32}$$

where

$$N_k = \sum_i z_{ik}. \tag{5.33}$$

is an estimate of the number of sample points assigned to each cluster.

Bishop (2006) has a wonderful exposition of both mixture of Gaussians estimation and the more general topic of expectation maximization.

In the context of image segmentation, Ma, Derksen, Hong *et al.* (2007) present a nice review of segmentation using mixtures of Gaussians and develop their own extension based on Minimum Description Length (MDL) coding, which they show produces good results on the Berkeley segmentation database.

5.3.2 Mean shift

While k-means and mixtures of Gaussians use a parametric form to model the probability density function being segmented, mean shift implicitly models this distribution using a smooth continuous *non-parametric model*. The key to mean shift is a technique for efficiently finding peaks in this high-dimensional data distribution without ever computing the complete function explicitly (Fukunaga and Hostetler 1975; Cheng 1995; Comaniciu and Meer 2002).

Consider once again the data points shown in Figure 5.16c, which can be thought of as having been drawn from some probability density function. If we could compute this density function, as visualized in Figure 5.16e, we could find its major peaks (*modes*) and identify regions of the input space that climb to the same peak as being part of the same region. This is the inverse of the *watershed* algorithm described in Section 5.2.1, which climbs downhill to find *basins of attraction*.

The first question, then, is how to estimate the density function given a sparse set of samples. One of the simplest approaches is to just smooth the data, e.g., by convolving it with a fixed kernel of width h,

$$f(\boldsymbol{x}) = \sum_i K(\boldsymbol{x} - \boldsymbol{x}_i) = \sum_i k\left(\frac{\|\boldsymbol{x} - \boldsymbol{x}_i\|^2}{h^2}\right), \tag{5.34}$$

where x_i are the input samples and $k(r)$ is the kernel function (or *Parzen window*).[9] This approach is known as *kernel density estimation* or the *Parzen window technique* (Duda, Hart,

---

[9] In this simplified formula, a Euclidean metric is used. We discuss a little later (5.42) how to generalize this to non-uniform (scaled or oriented) metrics. Note also that this distribution may not be *proper*, i.e., integrate to 1. Since we are looking for maxima in the density, this does not matter.

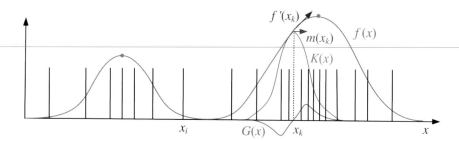

Figure 5.17 One-dimensional visualization of the kernel density estimate, its derivative, and a mean shift. The kernel density estimate $f(x)$ is obtained by convolving the sparse set of input samples x_i with the kernel function $K(x)$. The derivative of this function, $f'(x)$, can be obtained by convolving the inputs with the derivative kernel $G(x)$. Estimating the local displacement vectors around a current estimate x_k results in the mean-shift vector $m(x_k)$, which, in a multi-dimensional setting, point in the same direction as the function gradient $\nabla f(\boldsymbol{x}_k)$. The red dots indicate local maxima in $f(x)$ to which the mean shifts converge.

and Stork 2001, Section 4.3; Bishop 2006, Section 2.5.1). Once we have computed $f(\boldsymbol{x})$, as shown in Figures 5.16e and 5.17, we can find its local maxima using gradient ascent or some other optimization technique.

The problem with this "brute force" approach is that, for higher dimensions, it becomes computationally prohibitive to evaluate $f(\boldsymbol{x})$ over the complete search space.[10] Instead, mean shift uses a variant of what is known in the optimization literature as *multiple restart gradient descent*. Starting at some guess for a local maximum, $\boldsymbol{y}_k$, which can be a random input data point $\boldsymbol{x}_i$, mean shift computes the gradient of the density estimate $f(\boldsymbol{x})$ at $\boldsymbol{y}_k$ and takes an uphill step in that direction (Figure 5.17). The gradient of $f(\boldsymbol{x})$ is given by

$$\nabla f(\boldsymbol{x}) = \sum_i (\boldsymbol{x}_i - \boldsymbol{x}) G(\boldsymbol{x} - \boldsymbol{x}_i) = \sum_i (\boldsymbol{x}_i - \boldsymbol{x}) g\left(\frac{\|\boldsymbol{x} - \boldsymbol{x}_i\|^2}{h^2}\right), \tag{5.35}$$

where

$$g(r) = -k'(r), \tag{5.36}$$

and $k'(r)$ is the first derivative of $k(r)$. We can re-write the gradient of the density function as

$$\nabla f(\boldsymbol{x}) = \left[\sum_i G(\boldsymbol{x} - \boldsymbol{x}_i)\right] \boldsymbol{m}(\boldsymbol{x}), \tag{5.37}$$

where the vector

$$\boldsymbol{m}(\boldsymbol{x}) = \frac{\sum_i \boldsymbol{x}_i G(\boldsymbol{x} - \boldsymbol{x}_i)}{\sum_i G(\boldsymbol{x} - \boldsymbol{x}_i)} - \boldsymbol{x} \tag{5.38}$$

is called the *mean shift*, since it is the difference between the weighted mean of the neighbors $\boldsymbol{x}_i$ around $\boldsymbol{x}$ and the current value of $\boldsymbol{x}$.

In the mean-shift procedure, the current estimate of the mode $\boldsymbol{y}_k$ at iteration k is replaced by its locally weighted mean,

$$\boldsymbol{y}_{k+1} = \boldsymbol{y}_k + \boldsymbol{m}(\boldsymbol{y}_k) = \frac{\sum_i \boldsymbol{x}_i G(\boldsymbol{y}_k - \boldsymbol{x}_i)}{\sum_i G(\boldsymbol{y}_k - \boldsymbol{x}_i)}. \tag{5.39}$$

---

[10] Even for one dimension, if the space is extremely sparse, it may be inefficient.

Comaniciu and Meer (2002) prove that this algorithm converges to a local maximum of $f(\boldsymbol{x})$ under reasonably weak conditions on the kernel $k(r)$, i.e., that it is monotonically decreasing. This convergence is not guaranteed for regular gradient descent unless appropriate step size control is used.

The two kernels that Comaniciu and Meer (2002) studied are the Epanechnikov kernel,

$$k_E(r) = \max(0, 1 - r), \tag{5.40}$$

which is a radial generalization of a bilinear kernel, and the Gaussian (normal) kernel,

$$k_N(r) = \exp\left(-\frac{1}{2}r\right). \tag{5.41}$$

The corresponding derivative kernels $g(r)$ are a unit ball and another Gaussian, respectively. Using the Epanechnikov kernel converges in a finite number of steps, while the Gaussian kernel has a smoother trajectory (and produces better results), but converges very slowly near a mode (Exercise 5.5).

The simplest way to apply mean shift is to start a separate mean-shift mode estimate $\boldsymbol{y}$ at every input point $\boldsymbol{x}_i$ and to iterate for a fixed number of steps or until the mean-shift magnitude is below a threshold. A faster approach is to randomly subsample the input points $\boldsymbol{x}_i$ and to keep track of each point's temporal evolution. The remaining points can then be classified based on the nearest evolution path (Comaniciu and Meer 2002). Paris and Durand (2007) review a number of other more efficient implementations of mean shift, including their own approach, which is based on using an efficient low-resolution estimate of the complete multi-dimensional space of $f(\boldsymbol{x})$ along with its stationary points.

The color-based segmentation shown in Figure 5.16 only looks at pixel colors when determining the best clustering. It may therefore cluster together small isolated pixels that happen to have the same color, which may not correspond to a semantically meaningful segmentation of the image.

Better results can usually be obtained by clustering in the *joint domain* of color and location. In this approach, the spatial coordinates of the image $\boldsymbol{x}_s = (x, y)$, which are called the *spatial domain*, are concatenated with the color values $\boldsymbol{x}_r$, which are known as the *range domain*, and mean-shift clustering is applied in this five-dimensional space $\boldsymbol{x}_j$. Since location and color may have different scales, the kernels are adjusted accordingly, i.e., we use a kernel of the form

$$K(\boldsymbol{x}_j) = k\left(\frac{\|\boldsymbol{x}_r\|^2}{h_r^2}\right) k\left(\frac{\|\boldsymbol{x}_s\|^2}{h_s^2}\right), \tag{5.42}$$

where separate parameters h_s and h_r are used to control the spatial and range bandwidths of the filter kernels. Figure 5.18 shows an example of mean-shift clustering in the joint domain, with parameters $(h_s, h_r, M) = (16, 19, 40)$, where spatial regions containing less than M pixels are eliminated.

The form of the joint domain filter kernel (5.42) is reminiscent of the bilateral filter kernel (3.34–3.37) discussed in Section 3.3.1. The difference between mean shift and bilateral filtering, however, is that in mean shift the spatial coordinates of each pixel are adjusted along with its color values, so that the pixel migrates more quickly towards other pixels with similar colors, and can therefore later be used for clustering and segmentation.

Determining the best bandwidth parameters h to use with mean shift remains something of an art, although a number of approaches have been explored. These include optimizing

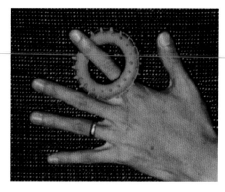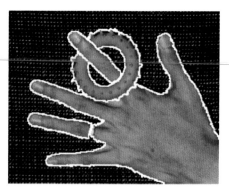

Figure 5.18 Mean-shift color image segmentation with parameters $(h_s, h_r, M) = (16, 19, 40)$ (Comaniciu and Meer 2002) © 2002 IEEE.

the bias–variance tradeoff, looking for parameter ranges where the number of clusters varies slowly, optimizing some external clustering criterion, or using top-down (application domain) knowledge (Comaniciu and Meer 2003). It is also possible to change the orientation of the kernel in joint parameter space for applications such as spatio-temporal (video) segmentations (Wang, Thiesson, Xu *et al.* 2004).

Mean shift has been applied to a number of different problems in computer vision, including face tracking, 2D shape extraction, and texture segmentation (Comaniciu and Meer 2002), and more recently in stereo matching (Chapter 11) (Wei and Quan 2004), non-photorealistic rendering (Section 10.5.2) (DeCarlo and Santella 2002), and video editing (Section 10.4.5) (Wang, Bhat, Colburn *et al.* 2005). Paris and Durand (2007) provide a nice review of such applications, as well as techniques for more efficiently solving the mean-shift equations and producing hierarchical segmentations.

5.4 Normalized cuts

While bottom-up merging techniques aggregate regions into coherent wholes and mean-shift techniques try to find clusters of similar pixels using mode finding, the normalized cuts technique introduced by Shi and Malik (2000) examines the *affinities* (similarities) between nearby pixels and tries to separate groups that are connected by weak affinities.

Consider the simple graph shown in Figure 5.19a. The pixels in group A are all strongly connected with high affinities, shown as thick red lines, as are the pixels in group B. The connections between these two groups, shown as thinner blue lines, are much weaker. A *normalized cut* between the two groups, shown as a dashed line, separates them into two clusters.

The cut between two groups A and B is defined as the sum of all the weights being cut,

$$cut(A, B) = \sum_{i \in A, j \in B} w_{ij}, \tag{5.43}$$

where the weights between two pixels (or regions) i and j measure their similarity. Using a minimum cut as a segmentation criterion, however, does not result in reasonable clusters, since the smallest cuts usually involve isolating a single pixel.

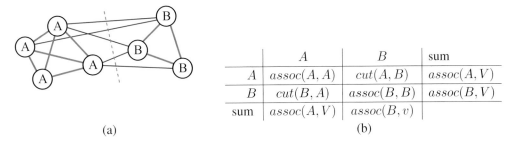

	A	B	sum
A	$assoc(A, A)$	$cut(A, B)$	$assoc(A, V)$
B	$cut(B, A)$	$assoc(B, B)$	$assoc(B, V)$
sum	$assoc(A, V)$	$assoc(B, v)$	

(a)   (b)

Figure 5.19 Sample weighted graph and its normalized cut: (a) a small sample graph and its smallest normalized cut; (b) tabular form of the associations and cuts for this graph. The $assoc$ and cut entries are computed as area sums of the associated weight matrix W (Figure 5.20). Normalizing the table entries by the row or column sums produces normalized associations and cuts $Nassoc$ and $Ncut$.

A better measure of segmentation is the normalized cut, which is defined as

$$Ncut(A, B) = \frac{cut(A, B)}{assoc(A, V)} + \frac{cut(A, B)}{assoc(B, V)}, \tag{5.44}$$

where $assoc(A, A) = \sum_{i \in A, j \in A} w_{ij}$ is the *association* (sum of all the weights) within a cluster and $assoc(A, V) = assoc(A, A) + cut(A, B)$ is the sum of *all* the weights associated with nodes in A. Figure 5.19b shows how the cuts and associations can be thought of as area sums in the weight matrix $W = [w_{ij}]$, where the entries of the matrix have been arranged so that the nodes in A come first and the nodes in B come second. Figure 5.20 shows an actual weight matrix for which these area sums can be computed. Dividing each of these areas by the corresponding row sum (the rightmost column of Figure 5.19b) results in the normalized cut and association values. These normalized values better reflect the fitness of a particular segmentation, since they look for collections of edges that are weak relative to all of the edges both inside and emanating from a particular region.

Unfortunately, computing the optimal normalized cut is NP-complete. Instead, Shi and Malik (2000) suggest computing a real-valued assignment of nodes to groups. Let x be the *indicator vector* where $x_i = +1$ iff $i \in A$ and $x_i = -1$ iff $i \in B$. Let $d = W1$ be the row sums of the symmetric matrix W and $D = \text{diag}(d)$ be the corresponding diagonal matrix. Shi and Malik (2000) show that minimizing the normalized cut over all possible indicator vectors x is equivalent to minimizing

$$\min_{y} \frac{y^T(D - W)y}{y^T Dy}, \tag{5.45}$$

where $y = ((1 + x) - b(1 - x))/2$ is a vector consisting of all 1s and $-b$s such that $y \cdot d = 0$. Minimizing this *Rayleigh quotient* is equivalent to solving the generalized eigenvalue system

$$(D - W)y = \lambda Dy, \tag{5.46}$$

which can be turned into a regular eigenvalue problem

$$(I - N)z = \lambda z, \tag{5.47}$$

where $N = D^{-1/2}WD^{-1/2}$ is the *normalized* affinity matrix (Weiss 1999) and $z = D^{1/2}y$. Because these eigenvectors can be interpreted as the large modes of vibration in

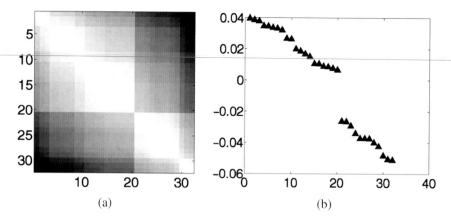

Figure 5.20 Sample weight table and its second smallest eigenvector (Shi and Malik 2000) © 2000 IEEE: (a) sample 32×32 weight matrix $\boldsymbol{W}$; (b) eigenvector corresponding to the second smallest eigenvalue of the generalized eigenvalue problem $(\boldsymbol{D} - \boldsymbol{W})\boldsymbol{y} = \lambda \boldsymbol{D}\boldsymbol{y}$.

a spring-mass system, normalized cuts is an example of a *spectral method* for image segmentation.

Extending an idea originally proposed by Scott and Longuet-Higgins (1990), Weiss (1999) suggests normalizing the affinity matrix and then using the top k eigenvectors to reconstitute a $\boldsymbol{Q}$ matrix. Other papers have extended the basic normalized cuts framework by modifying the affinity matrix in different ways, finding better discrete solutions to the minimization problem, or applying multi-scale techniques (Meilă and Shi 2000, 2001; Ng, Jordan, and Weiss 2001; Yu and Shi 2003; Cour, Bénézit, and Shi 2005; Tolliver and Miller 2006).

Figure 5.20b shows the second smallest (real-valued) eigenvector corresponding to the weight matrix shown in Figure 5.20a. (Here, the rows have been permuted to separate the two groups of variables that belong to the different components of this eigenvector.) After this real-valued vector is computed, the variables corresponding to positive and negative eigenvector values are associated with the two cut components. This process can be further repeated to hierarchically subdivide an image, as shown in Figure 5.21.

The original algorithm proposed by Shi and Malik (2000) used spatial position and image feature differences to compute the pixel-wise affinities,

$$ w_{ij} = \exp\left(-\frac{\|\boldsymbol{F}_i - \boldsymbol{F}_j\|^2}{\sigma_F^2} - \frac{\|\boldsymbol{x}_i - \boldsymbol{x}_j\|^2}{\sigma_s^2} \right), \tag{5.48} $$

for pixels within a radius $\|\boldsymbol{x}_i - \boldsymbol{x}_j\| < r$, where $\boldsymbol{F}$ is a feature vector that consists of intensities, colors, or oriented filter histograms. (Note how (5.48) is the negative exponential of the joint feature space distance (5.42).)

In subsequent work, Malik, Belongie, Leung *et al.* (2001) look for *intervening contours* between pixels i and j and define an intervening contour weight

$$ w_{ij}^{IC} = 1 - \max_{\boldsymbol{x} \in l_{ij}} p_{con}(\boldsymbol{x}), \tag{5.49} $$

where l_{ij} is the image line joining pixels i and j and $p_{con}(\boldsymbol{x})$ is the probability of an intervening contour perpendicular to this line, which is defined as the negative exponential of the

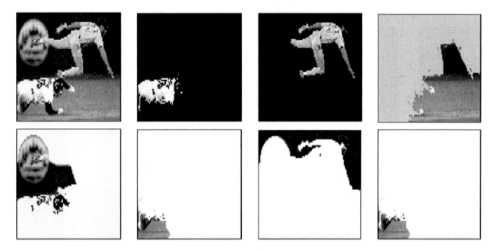

Figure 5.21 Normalized cuts segmentation (Shi and Malik 2000) © 2000 IEEE: The input image and the components returned by the normalized cuts algorithm.

oriented energy in the perpendicular direction. They multiply these weights with a texton-based texture similarity metric and use an initial over-segmentation based purely on local pixel-wise features to re-estimate intervening contours and texture statistics in a region-based manner. Figure 5.22 shows the results of running this improved algorithm on a number of test images.

Because it requires the solution of large sparse eigenvalue problems, normalized cuts can be quite slow. Sharon, Galun, Sharon *et al.* (2006) present a way to accelerate the computation of the normalized cuts using an approach inspired by algebraic multigrid (Brandt 1986; Briggs, Henson, and McCormick 2000). To coarsen the original problem, they select a smaller number of variables such that the remaining fine-level variables are *strongly coupled* to at least one coarse-level variable. Figure 5.15 shows this process schematically, while (5.25) gives the definition for strong coupling except that, in this case, the original weights w_{ij} in the normalized cut are used instead of merge probabilities p_{ij}.

Once a set of coarse variables has been selected, an inter-level interpolation matrix with elements similar to the left hand side of (5.25) is used to define a reduced version of the normalized cuts problem. In addition to computing the weight matrix using interpolation-based coarsening, additional region statistics are used to modulate the weights. After a normalized cut has been computed at the coarsest level of analysis, the membership values of finer-level nodes are computed by interpolating parent values and mapping values within $\epsilon = 0.1$ of 0 and 1 to pure Boolean values.

An example of the segmentation produced by weighted aggregation (SWA) is shown in Figure 5.22, along with the most recent probabilistic bottom-up merging algorithm by Alpert, Galun, Basri *et al.* (2007), which was described in Section 5.2. In even more recent work, Wang and Oliensis (2010) show how to estimate statistics over segmentations (e.g., mean region size) directly from the affinity graph. They use this to produce segmentations that are more *central* with respect to other possible segmentations.

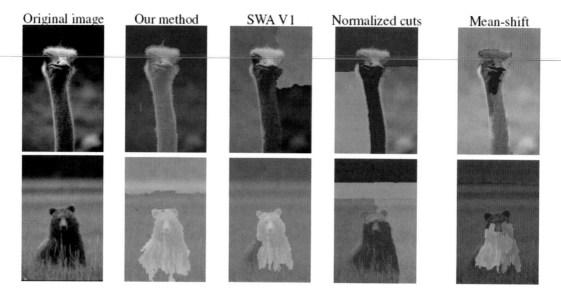

Figure 5.22 Comparative segmentation results (Alpert, Galun, Basri *et al.* 2007) © 2007 IEEE. "Our method" refers to the probabilistic bottom-up merging algorithm developed by Alpert *et al.*

5.5 Graph cuts and energy-based methods

A common theme in image segmentation algorithms is the desire to group pixels that have similar appearance (statistics) and to have the boundaries between pixels in different regions be of short length and across visible discontinuities. If we restrict the boundary measurements to be between immediate neighbors and compute region membership statistics by summing over pixels, we can formulate this as a classic pixel-based energy function using either a *variational formulation* (regularization, see Section 3.7.1) or as a binary Markov random field (Section 3.7.2).

Examples of the continuous approach include (Mumford and Shah 1989; Chan and Vese 1992; Zhu and Yuille 1996; Tabb and Ahuja 1997) along with the level set approaches discussed in Section 5.1.4. An early example of a discrete labeling problem that combines both region-based and boundary-based energy terms is the work of Leclerc (1989), who used minimum description length (MDL) coding to derive the energy function being minimized. Boykov and Funka-Lea (2006) present a wonderful survey of various energy-based techniques for binary object segmentation, some of which we discuss below.

As we saw in Section 3.7.2, the energy corresponding to a segmentation problem can be written (c.f. Equations (3.100) and (3.108–3.113)) as

$$E(f) = \sum_{i,j} E_r(i,j) + E_b(i,j), \qquad (5.50)$$

where the region term

$$E_r(i,j) = E_S(I(i,j); R(f(i,j))) \qquad (5.51)$$

is the negative log likelihood that pixel intensity (or color) $I(i,j)$ is consistent with the statis-

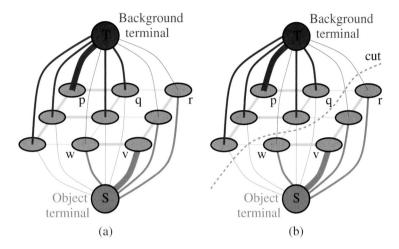

Figure 5.23 Graph cuts for region segmentation (Boykov and Jolly 2001) © 2001 IEEE: (a) the energy function is encoded as a maximum flow problem; (b) the minimum cut determines the region boundary.

tics of region $R(f(i,j))$ and the boundary term

$$E_b(i,j) = s_x(i,j)\delta(f(i,j) - f(i+1,j)) + s_y(i,j)\delta(f(i,j) - f(i,j+1)) \qquad (5.52)$$

measures the inconsistency between $\mathcal{N}_4$ neighbors modulated by local horizontal and vertical smoothness terms $s_x(i,j)$ and $s_y(i,j)$.

Region statistics can be something as simple as the mean gray level or color (Leclerc 1989), in which case

$$E_S(I;\mu_k) = \|I - \mu_k\|^2. \qquad (5.53)$$

Alternatively, they can be more complex, such as region intensity histograms (Boykov and Jolly 2001) or color Gaussian mixture models (Rother, Kolmogorov, and Blake 2004). For smoothness (boundary) terms, it is common to make the strength of the smoothness $s_x(i,j)$ inversely proportional to the local edge strength (Boykov, Veksler, and Zabih 2001).

Originally, energy-based segmentation problems were optimized using iterative gradient descent techniques, which were slow and prone to getting trapped in local minima. Boykov and Jolly (2001) were the first to apply the binary MRF optimization algorithm developed by Greig, Porteous, and Seheult (1989) to binary object segmentation.

In this approach, the user first delineates pixels in the background and foreground regions using a few strokes of an image brush (Figure 3.61). These pixels then become the *seeds* that tie nodes in the *S–T graph* to the source and sink labels S and T (Figure 5.23a). Seed pixels can also be used to estimate foreground and background region statistics (intensity or color histograms).

The capacities of the other edges in the graph are derived from the region and boundary energy terms, i.e., pixels that are more compatible with the foreground or background region get stronger connections to the respective source or sink; adjacent pixels with greater smoothness also get stronger links. Once the minimum-cut/maximum-flow problem has been solved using a polynomial time algorithm (Goldberg and Tarjan 1988; Boykov and Kolmogorov 2004), pixels on either side of the computed cut are labeled according to the source or sink to

(a)

(b)

(c)

Figure 5.24 GrabCut image segmentation (Rother, Kolmogorov, and Blake 2004) © 2004 ACM: (a) the user draws a bounding box in red; (b) the algorithm guesses color distributions for the object and background and performs a binary segmentation; (c) the process is repeated with better region statistics.

which they remain connected (Figure 5.23b). While graph cuts is just one of several known techniques for MRF energy minimization (Appendix B.5.4), it is still the one most commonly used for solving binary MRF problems.

The basic binary segmentation algorithm of Boykov and Jolly (2001) has been extended in a number of directions. The *GrabCut* system of Rother, Kolmogorov, and Blake (2004) iteratively re-estimates the region statistics, which are modeled as a mixtures of Gaussians in color space. This allows their system to operate given minimal user input, such as a single bounding box (Figure 5.24a)—the background color model is initialized from a strip of pixels around the box outline. (The foreground color model is initialized from the interior pixels, but quickly converges to a better estimate of the object.) The user can also place additional strokes to refine the segmentation as the solution progresses. In more recent work, Cui, Yang, Wen *et al.* (2008) use color and edge models derived from previous segmentations of similar objects to improve the local models used in GrabCut.

Another major extension to the original binary segmentation formulation is the addition of *directed edges*, which allows boundary regions to be oriented, e.g., to prefer light to dark transitions or *vice versa* (Kolmogorov and Boykov 2005). Figure 5.25 shows an example where the directed graph cut correctly segments the light gray liver from its dark gray surround. The same approach can be used to measure the *flux* exiting a region, i.e., the signed gradient projected normal to the region boundary. Combining oriented graphs with larger neighborhoods enables approximating continuous problems such as those traditionally solved using level sets in the globally optimal graph cut framework (Boykov and Kolmogorov 2003; Kolmogorov and Boykov 2005).

Even more recent developments in graph cut-based segmentation techniques include the addition of connectivity priors to force the foreground to be in a single piece (Vicente, Kolmogorov, and Rother 2008) and shape priors to use knowledge about an object's shape during the segmentation process (Lempitsky and Boykov 2007; Lempitsky, Blake, and Rother 2008).

While optimizing the binary MRF energy (5.50) requires the use of combinatorial optimization techniques, such as maximum flow, an approximate solution can be obtained by converting the binary energy terms into quadratic energy terms defined over a continuous $[0, 1]$ random field, which then becomes a classical membrane-based regularization problem (3.100–3.102). The resulting quadratic energy function can then be solved using standard linear system solvers (3.102–3.103), although if speed is an issue, you should use multigrid

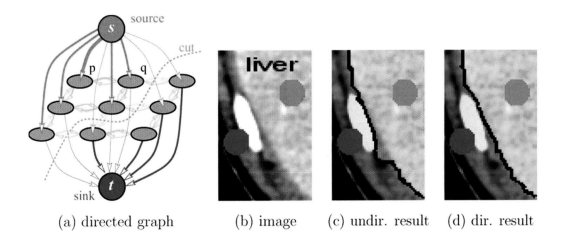

(a) directed graph (b) image (c) undir. result (d) dir. result

Figure 5.25 Segmentation with a directed graph cut (Boykov and Funka-Lea 2006) © 2006 Springer: (a) directed graph; (b) image with seed points; (c) the undirected graph incorrectly continues the boundary along the bright object; (d) the directed graph correctly segments the light gray region from its darker surround.

or one of its variants (Appendix A.5). Once the continuous solution has been computed, it can be thresholded at 0.5 to yield a binary segmentation.

The $[0, 1]$ continuous optimization problem can also be interpreted as computing the probability at each pixel that a *random walker* starting at that pixel ends up at one of the labeled seed pixels, which is also equivalent to computing the potential in a resistive grid where the resistors are equal to the edge weights (Grady 2006; Sinop and Grady 2007). K-way segmentations can also be computed by iterating through the seed labels, using a binary problem with one label set to 1 and all the others set to 0 to compute the relative membership probabilities for each pixel. In follow-on work, Grady and Ali (2008) use a precomputation of the eigenvectors of the linear system to make the solution with a novel set of seeds faster, which is related to the Laplacian matting problem presented in Section 10.4.3 (Levin, Acha, and Lischinski 2008). Couprie, Grady, Najman *et al.* (2009) relate the random walker to watersheds and other segmentation techniques. Singaraju, Grady, and Vidal (2008) add directed-edge constraints in order to support flux, which makes the energy piecewise quadratic and hence not solvable as a single linear system. The random walker algorithm can also be used to solve the Mumford–Shah segmentation problem (Grady and Alvino 2008) and to compute fast multigrid solutions (Grady 2008). A nice review of these techniques is given by Singaraju, Grady, Sinop *et al.* (2010).

An even faster way to compute a continuous $[0, 1]$ approximate segmentation is to compute *weighted geodesic distances* between the 0 and 1 seed regions (Bai and Sapiro 2009), which can also be used to estimate soft alpha mattes (Section 10.4.3). A related approach by Criminisi, Sharp, and Blake (2008) can be used to find fast approximate solutions to general binary Markov random field optimization problems.

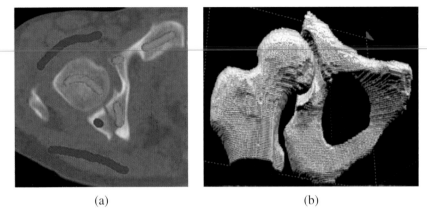

(a)   (b)

Figure 5.26   3D volumetric medical image segmentation using graph cuts (Boykov and Funka-Lea 2006) ©
2006 Springer: (a) computed tomography (CT) slice with some seeds; (b) recovered 3D volumetric bone model
(on a $256 \times 256 \times 119$ voxel grid).

5.5.1 *Application*: Medical image segmentation

One of the most promising applications of image segmentation is in the medical imaging
domain, where it can be used to segment anatomical tissues for later quantitative analysis.
Figure 5.25 shows a binary graph cut with directed edges being used to segment the liver tissue (light gray) from its surrounding bone (white) and muscle (dark gray) tissue. Figure 5.26
shows the segmentation of bones in a $256 \times 256 \times 119$ computed X-ray tomography (CT)
volume. Without the powerful optimization techniques available in today's image segmentation algorithms, such processing used to require much more laborious manual tracing of
individual X-ray slices.

The fields of medical image segmentation (McInerney and Terzopoulos 1996) and medical image registration (Kybic and Unser 2003) (Section 8.3.1) are rich research fields with
their own specialized conferences, such as *Medical Imaging Computing and Computer Assisted Intervention (MICCAI)*,[11] and journals, such as *Medical Image Analysis* and *IEEE
Transactions on Medical Imaging*. These can be great sources of references and ideas for
research in this area.

5.6 Additional reading

The topic of image segmentation is closely related to clustering techniques, which are treated
in a number of monographs and review articles (Jain and Dubes 1988; Kaufman and Rousseeuw
1990; Jain, Duin, and Mao 2000; Jain, Topchy, Law *et al.* 2004). Some early segmentation
techniques include those describerd by Brice and Fennema (1970); Pavlidis (1977); Riseman
and Arbib (1977); Ohlander, Price, and Reddy (1978); Rosenfeld and Davis (1979); Haralick
and Shapiro (1985), while examples of newer techniques are developed by Leclerc (1989);
Mumford and Shah (1989); Shi and Malik (2000); Felzenszwalb and Huttenlocher (2004b).

---

[11] http://www.miccai.org/.

Arbeláez, Maire, Fowlkes *et al.* (2010) provide a good review of automatic segmentation techniques and also compare their performance on the Berkeley Segmentation Dataset and Benchmark (Martin, Fowlkes, Tal *et al.* 2001).[12] Additional comparison papers and databases include those by Unnikrishnan, Pantofaru, and Hebert (2007); Alpert, Galun, Basri *et al.* (2007); Estrada and Jepson (2009).

The topic of active contours has a long history, beginning with the seminal work on snakes and other energy-minimizing variational methods (Kass, Witkin, and Terzopoulos 1988; Cootes, Cooper, Taylor *et al.* 1995; Blake and Isard 1998), continuing through techniques such as intelligent scissors (Mortensen and Barrett 1995, 1999; Pérez, Blake, and Gangnet 2001), and culminating in level sets (Malladi, Sethian, and Vemuri 1995; Caselles, Kimmel, and Sapiro 1997; Sethian 1999; Paragios and Deriche 2000; Sapiro 2001; Osher and Paragios 2003; Paragios, Faugeras, Chan *et al.* 2005; Cremers, Rousson, and Deriche 2007; Rousson and Paragios 2008; Paragios and Sgallari 2009), which are currently the most widely used active contour methods.

Techniques for segmenting images based on local pixel similarities combined with aggregation or splitting methods include watersheds (Vincent and Soille 1991; Beare 2006; Arbeláez, Maire, Fowlkes *et al.* 2010), region splitting (Ohlander, Price, and Reddy 1978), region merging (Brice and Fennema 1970; Pavlidis and Liow 1990; Jain, Topchy, Law *et al.* 2004), as well as graph-based and probabilistic multi-scale approaches (Felzenszwalb and Huttenlocher 2004b; Alpert, Galun, Basri *et al.* 2007).

Mean-shift algorithms, which find modes (peaks) in a density function representation of the pixels, are presented by Comaniciu and Meer (2002); Paris and Durand (2007). Parametric mixtures of Gaussians can also be used to represent and segment such pixel densities (Bishop 2006; Ma, Derksen, Hong *et al.* 2007).

The seminal work on spectral (eigenvalue) methods for image segmentation is the *normalized cut* algorithm of Shi and Malik (2000). Related work includes that by Weiss (1999); Meilă and Shi (2000, 2001); Malik, Belongie, Leung *et al.* (2001); Ng, Jordan, and Weiss (2001); Yu and Shi (2003); Cour, Bénézit, and Shi (2005); Sharon, Galun, Sharon *et al.* (2006); Tolliver and Miller (2006); Wang and Oliensis (2010).

Continuous-energy-based (variational) approaches to interactive segmentation include Leclerc (1989); Mumford and Shah (1989); Chan and Vese (1992); Zhu and Yuille (1996); Tabb and Ahuja (1997). Discrete variants of such problems are usually optimized using binary graph cuts or other combinatorial energy minimization methods (Boykov and Jolly 2001; Boykov and Kolmogorov 2003; Rother, Kolmogorov, and Blake 2004; Kolmogorov and Boykov 2005; Cui, Yang, Wen *et al.* 2008; Vicente, Kolmogorov, and Rother 2008; Lempitsky and Boykov 2007; Lempitsky, Blake, and Rother 2008), although continuous optimization techniques followed by thresholding can also be used (Grady 2006; Grady and Ali 2008; Singaraju, Grady, and Vidal 2008; Criminisi, Sharp, and Blake 2008; Grady 2008; Bai and Sapiro 2009; Couprie, Grady, Najman *et al.* 2009). Boykov and Funka-Lea (2006) present a good survey of various energy-based techniques for binary object segmentation.

---

[12] http://www.eecs.berkeley.edu/Research/Projects/CS/vision/grouping/segbench/.

5.7 Exercises

Ex 5.1: Snake evolution   Prove that, in the absence of external forces, a snake will always shrink to a small circle and eventually a single point, regardless of whether first- or second-order smoothness (or some combination) is used.

(Hint: If you can show that the evolution of the $x(s)$ and $y(s)$ components are independent, you can analyze the 1D case more easily.)

Ex 5.2: Snake tracker   Implement a snake-based contour tracker:

1. Decide whether to use a large number of contour points or a smaller number interpolated with a B-spline.

2. Define your internal smoothness energy function and decide what image-based attractive forces to use.

3. At each iteration, set up the banded linear system of equations (quadratic energy function) and solve it using banded Cholesky factorization (Appendix A.4).

Ex 5.3: Intelligent scissors   Implement the intelligent scissors (live-wire) interactive segmentation algorithm (Mortensen and Barrett 1995) and design a graphical user interface (GUI) to let you draw such curves over an image and use them for segmentation.

Ex 5.4: Region segmentation   Implement one of the region segmentation algorithms described in this chapter. Some popular segmentation algorithms include:

- k-means (Section 5.3.1);

- mixtures of Gaussians (Section 5.3.1);

- mean shift (Section 5.3.2) and Exercise 5.5;

- normalized cuts (Section 5.4);

- similarity graph-based segmentation (Section 5.2.4);

- binary Markov random fields solved using graph cuts (Section 5.5).

Apply your region segmentation to a video sequence and use it to track moving regions from frame to frame.

Alternatively, test out your segmentation algorithm on the Berkeley segmentation database (Martin, Fowlkes, Tal *et al.* 2001).

Ex 5.5: Mean shift   Develop a mean-shift segmentation algorithm for color images (Comaniciu and Meer 2002).

1. Convert your image to L*a*b* space, or keep the original RGB colors, and augment them with the pixel (x, y) locations.

2. For every pixel (L, a, b, x, y), compute the weighted mean of its neighbors using either a unit ball (Epanechnikov kernel) or finite-radius Gaussian, or some other kernel of your choosing. Weight the color and spatial scales differently, e.g., using values of $(h_s, h_r, M) = (16, 19, 40)$ as shown in Figure 5.18.

3. Replace the current value with this weighted mean and iterate until either the motion is below a threshold or a finite number of steps has been taken.

4. Cluster all final values (modes) that are within a threshold, i.e., find the connected components. Since each pixel is associated with a final mean-shift (mode) value, this results in an image segmentation, i.e., each pixel is labeled with its final component.

5. (Optional) Use a random subset of the pixels as starting points and find which component each unlabeled pixel belongs to, either by finding its nearest neighbor or by iterating the mean shift until it finds a neighboring track of mean-shift values. Describe the data structures you use to make this efficient.

6. (Optional) Mean shift divides the kernel density function estimate by the local weighting to obtain a step size that is guaranteed to converge but may be slow. Use an alternative step size estimation algorithm from the optimization literature to see if you can make the algorithm converge faster.

Chapter 6

Feature-based alignment

R. Szeliski, *Computer Vision: Algorithms and Applications*, Texts in Computer Science,
DOI 10.1007/978-1-84882-935-0_6, © Springer-Verlag London Limited 2011

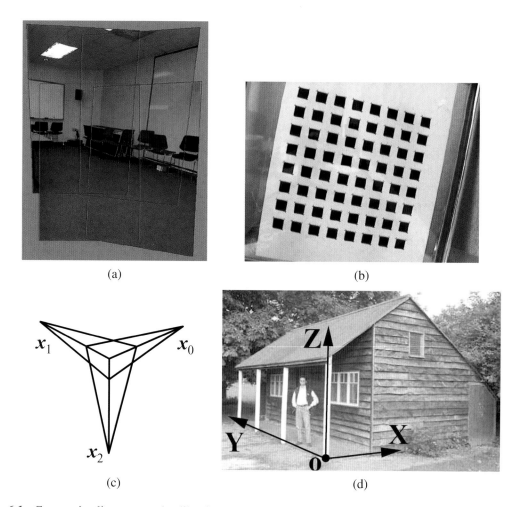

(a)

(b)

x_1 x_0

x_2

(c)

(d)

Figure 6.1 Geometric alignment and calibration: (a) geometric alignment of 2D images for stitching (Szeliski and Shum 1997) © 1997 ACM; (b) a two-dimensional calibration target (Zhang 2000) © 2000 IEEE; (c) calibration from vanishing points; (d) scene with easy-to-find lines and vanishing directions (Criminisi, Reid, and Zisserman 2000) © 2000 Springer.

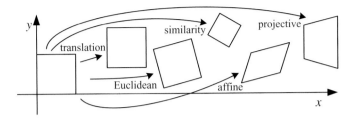

Figure 6.2 Basic set of 2D planar transformations

Once we have extracted features from images, the next stage in many vision algorithms is to match these features across different images (Section 4.1.3). An important component of this matching is to verify whether the set of matching features is geometrically consistent, e.g., whether the feature displacements can be described by a simple 2D or 3D geometric transformation. The computed motions can then be used in other applications such as image stitching (Chapter 9) or augmented reality (Section 6.2.3).

In this chapter, we look at the topic of geometric image registration, i.e., the computation of 2D and 3D transformations that map features in one image to another (Section 6.1). One special case of this problem is *pose estimation*, which is determining a camera's position relative to a known 3D object or scene (Section 6.2). Another case is the computation of a camera's *intrinsic calibration*, which consists of the internal parameters such as focal length and radial distortion (Section 6.3). In Chapter 7, we look at the related problems of how to estimate 3D point structure from 2D matches (*triangulation*) and how to simultaneously estimate 3D geometry and camera motion (*structure from motion*).

6.1 2D and 3D feature-based alignment

Feature-based alignment is the problem of estimating the motion between two or more sets of matched 2D or 3D points. In this section, we restrict ourselves to global *parametric* transformations, such as those described in Section 2.1.2 and shown in Table 2.1 and Figure 6.2, or higher order transformation for curved surfaces (Shashua and Toelg 1997; Can, Stewart, Roysam *et al.* 2002). Applications to non-rigid or elastic deformations (Bookstein 1989; Szeliski and Lavallée 1996; Torresani, Hertzmann, and Bregler 2008) are examined in Sections 8.3 and 12.6.4.

6.1.1 2D alignment using least squares

Given a set of matched feature points $\{(\boldsymbol{x}_i, \boldsymbol{x}'_i)\}$ and a planar parametric transformation[1] of the form

$$\boldsymbol{x}' = \boldsymbol{f}(\boldsymbol{x}; \boldsymbol{p}), \tag{6.1}$$

---

[1] For examples of non-planar parametric models, such as quadrics, see the work of Shashua and Toelg (1997); Shashua and Wexler (2001).

Transform	Matrix	Parameters p	Jacobian J
translation	$\begin{bmatrix} 1 & 0 & t_x \\ 0 & 1 & t_y \end{bmatrix}$	(t_x, t_y)	$\begin{bmatrix} 1 & 0 \\ 0 & 1 \end{bmatrix}$
Euclidean	$\begin{bmatrix} c_\theta & -s_\theta & t_x \\ s_\theta & c_\theta & t_y \end{bmatrix}$	(t_x, t_y, θ)	$\begin{bmatrix} 1 & 0 & -s_\theta x - c_\theta y \\ 0 & 1 & c_\theta x - s_\theta y \end{bmatrix}$
similarity	$\begin{bmatrix} 1+a & -b & t_x \\ b & 1+a & t_y \end{bmatrix}$	(t_x, t_y, a, b)	$\begin{bmatrix} 1 & 0 & x & -y \\ 0 & 1 & y & x \end{bmatrix}$
affine	$\begin{bmatrix} 1+a_{00} & a_{01} & t_x \\ a_{10} & 1+a_{11} & t_y \end{bmatrix}$	$(t_x, t_y, a_{00}, a_{01}, a_{10}, a_{11})$	$\begin{bmatrix} 1 & 0 & x & y & 0 & 0 \\ 0 & 1 & 0 & 0 & x & y \end{bmatrix}$
projective	$\begin{bmatrix} 1+h_{00} & h_{01} & h_{02} \\ h_{10} & 1+h_{11} & h_{12} \\ h_{20} & h_{21} & 1 \end{bmatrix}$	$(h_{00}, h_{01}, \ldots, h_{21})$	(see Section 6.1.3)

Table 6.1 Jacobians of the 2D coordinate transformations $x' = f(x; p)$ shown in Table 2.1, where we have re-parameterized the motions so that they are identity for $p = 0$.

how can we produce the best estimate of the motion parameters p? The usual way to do this is to use least squares, i.e., to minimize the sum of squared residuals

$$E_{\text{LS}} = \sum_i \|r_i\|^2 = \sum_i \|f(x_i; p) - x'_i\|^2, \tag{6.2}$$

where

$$r_i = f(x_i; p) - x'_i = \hat{x}'_i - \tilde{x}'_i \tag{6.3}$$

is the *residual* between the measured location $\hat{x}'_i$ and its corresponding current *predicted* location $\tilde{x}'_i = f(x_i; p)$. (See Appendix A.2 for more on least squares and Appendix B.2 for a statistical justification.)

Many of the motion models presented in Section 2.1.2 and Table 2.1, i.e., translation, similarity, and affine, have a *linear* relationship between the amount of motion $\Delta x = x' - x$ and the unknown parameters p,

$$\Delta x = x' - x = J(x)p, \tag{6.4}$$

where $J = \partial f/\partial p$ is the *Jacobian* of the transformation f with respect to the motion parameters p (see Table 6.1). In this case, a simple *linear* regression (linear least squares problem) can be formulated as

$$E_{\text{LLS}} = \sum_i \|J(x_i)p - \Delta x_i\|^2 \tag{6.5}$$

$$= p^T \left[\sum_i J^T(x_i) J(x_i) \right] p - 2p^T \left[\sum_i J^T(x_i) \Delta x_i \right] + \sum_i \|\Delta x_i\|^2 \tag{6.6}$$

$$= p^T A p - 2p^T b + c. \tag{6.7}$$

The minimum can be found by solving the symmetric positive definite (SPD) system of *normal equations*[2]

$$\boldsymbol{A}\boldsymbol{p} = \boldsymbol{b}, \tag{6.8}$$

where

$$\boldsymbol{A} = \sum_i \boldsymbol{J}^T(\boldsymbol{x}_i)\boldsymbol{J}(\boldsymbol{x}_i) \tag{6.9}$$

is called the *Hessian* and $\boldsymbol{b} = \sum_i \boldsymbol{J}^T(\boldsymbol{x}_i)\Delta\boldsymbol{x}_i$. For the case of pure translation, the resulting equations have a particularly simple form, i.e., the translation is the average translation between corresponding points or, equivalently, the translation of the point centroids.

Uncertainty weighting. The above least squares formulation assumes that all feature points are matched with the same accuracy. This is often not the case, since certain points may fall into more textured regions than others. If we associate a scalar variance estimate σ_i^2 with each correspondence, we can minimize the *weighted least squares* problem instead,[3]

$$E_{\text{WLS}} = \sum_i \sigma_i^{-2}\|\boldsymbol{r}_i\|^2. \tag{6.10}$$

As shown in Section 8.1.3, a covariance estimate for patch-based matching can be obtained by multiplying the inverse of the *patch Hessian* $\boldsymbol{A}_i$ (8.55) with the per-pixel noise covariance σ_n^2 (8.44). Weighting each squared residual by its inverse covariance $\Sigma_i^{-1} = \sigma_n^{-2}\boldsymbol{A}_i$ (which is called the *information matrix*), we obtain

$$E_{\text{CWLS}} = \sum_i \|\boldsymbol{r}_i\|^2_{\Sigma_i^{-1}} = \sum_i \boldsymbol{r}_i^T \Sigma_i^{-1} \boldsymbol{r}_i = \sum_i \sigma_n^{-2} \boldsymbol{r}_i^T \boldsymbol{A}_i \boldsymbol{r}_i. \tag{6.11}$$

6.1.2 *Application*: Panography

One of the simplest (and most fun) applications of image alignment is a special form of image stitching called *panography*. In a panograph, images are translated and optionally rotated and scaled before being blended with simple averaging (Figure 6.3). This process mimics the photographic collages created by artist David Hockney, although his compositions use an opaque overlay model, being created out of regular photographs.

In most of the examples seen on the Web, the images are aligned by hand for best artistic effect.[4] However, it is also possible to use feature matching and alignment techniques to perform the registration automatically (Nomura, Zhang, and Nayar 2007; Zelnik-Manor and Perona 2007).

Consider a simple translational model. We want all the corresponding features in different images to line up as best as possible. Let $\boldsymbol{t}_j$ be the location of the jth image coordinate frame in the global composite frame and $\boldsymbol{x}_{ij}$ be the location of the ith matched feature in the jth image. In order to align the images, we wish to minimize the least squares error

$$E_{\text{PLS}} = \sum_{ij} \|(\boldsymbol{t}_j + \boldsymbol{x}_{ij}) - \boldsymbol{x}_i\|^2, \tag{6.12}$$

---

[2] For poorly conditioned problems, it is better to use QR decomposition on the set of linear equations $\boldsymbol{J}(\boldsymbol{x}_i)\boldsymbol{p} = \Delta\boldsymbol{x}_i$ instead of the normal equations (Björck 1996; Golub and Van Loan 1996). However, such conditions rarely arise in image registration.

[3] Problems where each measurement can have a different variance or certainty are called *heteroscedastic models*.

[4] http://www.flickr.com/groups/panography/.

Figure 6.3 A simple panograph consisting of three images automatically aligned with a translational model and then averaged together.

where $\boldsymbol{x}_i$ is the consensus (average) position of feature i in the global coordinate frame. (An alternative approach is to register each pair of overlapping images separately and then compute a consensus location for each frame—see Exercise 6.2.)

The above least squares problem is indeterminate (you can add a constant offset to all the frame and point locations $\boldsymbol{t}_j$ and $\boldsymbol{x}_i$). To fix this, either pick one frame as being at the origin or add a constraint to make the average frame offsets be 0.

The formulas for adding rotation and scale transformations are straightforward and are left as an exercise (Exercise 6.2). See if you can create some collages that you would be happy to share with others on the Web.

6.1.3 Iterative algorithms

While linear least squares is the simplest method for estimating parameters, most problems in computer vision do not have a simple linear relationship between the measurements and the unknowns. In this case, the resulting problem is called *non-linear least squares* or *non-linear regression*.

Consider, for example, the problem of estimating a rigid Euclidean 2D transformation (translation plus rotation) between two sets of points. If we parameterize this transformation by the translation amount (t_x, t_y) and the rotation angle θ, as in Table 2.1, the Jacobian of this transformation, given in Table 6.1, depends on the current value of θ. Notice how in Table 6.1, we have re-parameterized the motion matrices so that they are always the identity at the origin $\boldsymbol{p} = 0$, which makes it easier to initialize the motion parameters.

To minimize the non-linear least squares problem, we iteratively find an update $\Delta\boldsymbol{p}$ to the current parameter estimate $\boldsymbol{p}$ by minimizing

$$E_{\mathrm{NLS}}(\Delta\boldsymbol{p}) \quad = \quad \sum_i \|\boldsymbol{f}(\boldsymbol{x}_i; \boldsymbol{p} + \Delta\boldsymbol{p}) - \boldsymbol{x}_i'\|^2 \tag{6.13}$$

$$\approx \quad \sum_i \|\boldsymbol{J}(\boldsymbol{x}_i; \boldsymbol{p})\Delta\boldsymbol{p} - \boldsymbol{r}_i\|^2 \tag{6.14}$$

$$= \Delta p^T \left[\sum_i J^T J \right] \Delta p - 2\Delta p^T \left[\sum_i J^T r_i \right] + \sum_i \|r_i\|^2 \quad (6.15)$$

$$= \Delta p^T A \Delta p - 2\Delta p^T b + c, \quad (6.16)$$

where the "Hessian"[5] A is the same as Equation (6.9) and the right hand side vector

$$b = \sum_i J^T(x_i) r_i \quad (6.17)$$

is now a Jacobian-weighted sum of residual vectors. This makes intuitive sense, as the parameters are pulled in the direction of the prediction error with a strength proportional to the Jacobian.

Once A and b have been computed, we solve for Δp using

$$(A + \lambda \text{diag}(A))\Delta p = b, \quad (6.18)$$

and update the parameter vector $p \leftarrow p + \Delta p$ accordingly. The parameter λ is an additional damping parameter used to ensure that the system takes a "downhill" step in energy (squared error) and is an essential component of the Levenberg–Marquardt algorithm (described in more detail in Appendix A.3). In many applications, it can be set to 0 if the system is successfully converging.

For the case of our 2D translation+rotation, we end up with a 3×3 set of normal equations in the unknowns $(\delta t_x, \delta t_y, \delta \theta)$. An initial guess for (t_x, t_y, θ) can be obtained by fitting a four-parameter similarity transform in (t_x, t_y, c, s) and then setting $\theta = \tan^{-1}(s/c)$. An alternative approach is to estimate the translation parameters using the centroids of the 2D points and to then estimate the rotation angle using polar coordinates (Exercise 6.3).

For the other 2D motion models, the derivatives in Table 6.1 are all fairly straightforward, except for the projective 2D motion (homography), which arises in image-stitching applications (Chapter 9). These equations can be re-written from (2.21) in their new parametric form as

$$x' = \frac{(1 + h_{00})x + h_{01}y + h_{02}}{h_{20}x + h_{21}y + 1} \quad \text{and} \quad y' = \frac{h_{10}x + (1 + h_{11})y + h_{12}}{h_{20}x + h_{21}y + 1}. \quad (6.19)$$

The Jacobian is therefore

$$J = \frac{\partial f}{\partial p} = \frac{1}{D} \begin{bmatrix} x & y & 1 & 0 & 0 & 0 & -x'x & -x'y \\ 0 & 0 & 0 & x & y & 1 & -y'x & -y'y \end{bmatrix}, \quad (6.20)$$

where $D = h_{20}x + h_{21}y + 1$ is the denominator in (6.19), which depends on the current parameter settings (as do x' and y').

An initial guess for the eight unknowns $\{h_{00}, h_{01}, \ldots, h_{21}\}$ can be obtained by multiplying both sides of the equations in (6.19) through by the denominator, which yields the linear set of equations,

$$\begin{bmatrix} \hat{x}' - x \\ \hat{y}' - y \end{bmatrix} = \begin{bmatrix} x & y & 1 & 0 & 0 & 0 & -\hat{x}'x & -\hat{x}'y \\ 0 & 0 & 0 & x & y & 1 & -\hat{y}'x & -\hat{y}'y \end{bmatrix} \begin{bmatrix} h_{00} \\ \vdots \\ h_{21} \end{bmatrix}. \quad (6.21)$$

---

[5] The "Hessian" A is not the true Hessian (second derivative) of the non-linear least squares problem (6.13). Instead, it is the approximate Hessian, which neglects second (and higher) order derivatives of $f(x_i; p + \Delta p)$.

However, this is not optimal from a statistical point of view, since the denominator D, which was used to multiply each equation, can vary quite a bit from point to point.[6]

One way to compensate for this is to *reweight* each equation by the inverse of the current estimate of the denominator, D,

$$\frac{1}{D} \begin{bmatrix} \hat{x}' - x \\ \hat{y}' - y \end{bmatrix} = \frac{1}{D} \begin{bmatrix} x & y & 1 & 0 & 0 & 0 & -\hat{x}'x & -\hat{x}'y \\ 0 & 0 & 0 & x & y & 1 & -\hat{y}'x & -\hat{y}'y \end{bmatrix} \begin{bmatrix} h_{00} \\ \vdots \\ h_{21} \end{bmatrix}. \qquad (6.22)$$

While this may at first seem to be the exact same set of equations as (6.21), because least squares is being used to solve the over-determined set of equations, the weightings *do* matter and produce a different set of normal equations that performs better in practice.

The most principled way to do the estimation, however, is to directly minimize the squared residual equations (6.13) using the Gauss–Newton approximation, i.e., performing a first-order Taylor series expansion in p, as shown in (6.14), which yields the set of equations

$$\begin{bmatrix} \hat{x}' - \tilde{x}' \\ \hat{y}' - \tilde{y}' \end{bmatrix} = \frac{1}{D} \begin{bmatrix} x & y & 1 & 0 & 0 & 0 & -\tilde{x}'x & -\tilde{x}'y \\ 0 & 0 & 0 & x & y & 1 & -\tilde{y}'x & -\tilde{y}'y \end{bmatrix} \begin{bmatrix} \Delta h_{00} \\ \vdots \\ \Delta h_{21} \end{bmatrix}. \qquad (6.23)$$

While these look similar to (6.22), they differ in two important respects. First, the left hand side consists of unweighted *prediction errors* rather than point displacements and the solution vector is a *perturbation* to the parameter vector p. Second, the quantities inside J involve *predicted* feature locations $(\tilde{x}', \tilde{y}')$ instead of *sensed* feature locations $(\hat{x}', \hat{y}')$. Both of these differences are subtle and yet they lead to an algorithm that, when combined with proper checking for downhill steps (as in the Levenberg–Marquardt algorithm), will converge to a local minimum. Note that iterating Equations (6.22) is not guaranteed to converge, since it is not minimizing a well-defined energy function.

Equation (6.23) is analogous to the *additive* algorithm for direct intensity-based registration (Section 8.2), since the change to the full transformation is being computed. If we prepend an incremental homography to the current homography instead, i.e., we use a *compositional* algorithm (described in Section 8.2), we get $D = 1$ (since $p = 0$) and the above formula simplifies to

$$\begin{bmatrix} \hat{x}' - x \\ \hat{y}' - y \end{bmatrix} = \begin{bmatrix} x & y & 1 & 0 & 0 & 0 & -x^2 & -xy \\ 0 & 0 & 0 & x & y & 1 & -xy & -y^2 \end{bmatrix} \begin{bmatrix} \Delta h_{00} \\ \vdots \\ \Delta h_{21} \end{bmatrix}, \qquad (6.24)$$

where we have replaced $(\tilde{x}', \tilde{y}')$ with (x, y) for conciseness. (Notice how this results in the same Jacobian as (8.63).)

---

[6] Hartley and Zisserman (2004) call this strategy of forming linear equations from rational equations the *direct linear transform*, but that term is more commonly associated with pose estimation (Section 6.2). Note also that our definition of the h_{ij} parameters differs from that used in their book, since we define h_{ii} to be the *difference* from unity and we do not leave h_{22} as a free parameter, which means that we cannot handle certain extreme homographies.

6.1.4 Robust least squares and RANSAC

While regular least squares is the method of choice for measurements where the noise follows a normal (Gaussian) distribution, more robust versions of least squares are required when there are outliers among the correspondences (as there almost always are). In this case, it is preferable to use an *M-estimator* (Huber 1981; Hampel, Ronchetti, Rousseeuw *et al.* 1986; Black and Rangarajan 1996; Stewart 1999), which involves applying a robust penalty function $\rho(r)$ to the residuals

$$E_{\text{RLS}}(\Delta \boldsymbol{p}) = \sum_i \rho(\|\boldsymbol{r}_i\|) \tag{6.25}$$

instead of squaring them.

We can take the derivative of this function with respect to $\boldsymbol{p}$ and set it to 0,

$$\sum_i \psi(\|\boldsymbol{r}_i\|) \frac{\partial \|\boldsymbol{r}_i\|}{\partial \boldsymbol{p}} = \sum_i \frac{\psi(\|\boldsymbol{r}_i\|)}{\|\boldsymbol{r}_i\|} \boldsymbol{r}_i^T \frac{\partial \boldsymbol{r}_i}{\partial \boldsymbol{p}} = 0, \tag{6.26}$$

where $\psi(r) = \rho'(r)$ is the derivative of ρ and is called the *influence function*. If we introduce a *weight function*, $w(r) = \Psi(r)/r$, we observe that finding the stationary point of (6.25) using (6.26) is equivalent to minimizing the *iteratively reweighted least squares* (IRLS) problem

$$E_{\text{IRLS}} = \sum_i w(\|\boldsymbol{r}_i\|)\|\boldsymbol{r}_i\|^2, \tag{6.27}$$

where the $w(\|\boldsymbol{r}_i\|)$ play the same local weighting role as σ_i^{-2} in (6.10). The IRLS algorithm alternates between computing the influence functions $w(\|\boldsymbol{r}_i\|)$ and solving the resulting weighted least squares problem (with fixed w values). Other incremental robust least squares algorithms can be found in the work of Sawhney and Ayer (1996); Black and Anandan (1996); Black and Rangarajan (1996); Baker, Gross, Ishikawa *et al.* (2003) and textbooks and tutorials on robust statistics (Huber 1981; Hampel, Ronchetti, Rousseeuw *et al.* 1986; Rousseeuw and Leroy 1987; Stewart 1999).

While M-estimators can definitely help reduce the influence of outliers, in some cases, starting with too many outliers will prevent IRLS (or other gradient descent algorithms) from converging to the global optimum. A better approach is often to find a starting set of *inlier* correspondences, i.e., points that are consistent with a dominant motion estimate.[7]

Two widely used approaches to this problem are called RANdom SAmple Consensus, or RANSAC for short (Fischler and Bolles 1981), and *least median of squares* (LMS) (Rousseeuw 1984). Both techniques start by selecting (at random) a subset of k correspondences, which is then used to compute an initial estimate for $\boldsymbol{p}$. The *residuals* of the full set of correspondences are then computed as

$$\boldsymbol{r}_i = \tilde{\boldsymbol{x}}_i'(\boldsymbol{x}_i; \boldsymbol{p}) - \hat{\boldsymbol{x}}_i', \tag{6.28}$$

where $\tilde{\boldsymbol{x}}_i'$ are the *estimated* (mapped) locations and $\hat{\boldsymbol{x}}_i'$ are the sensed (detected) feature point locations.

The RANSAC technique then counts the number of *inliers* that are within ϵ of their predicted location, i.e., whose $\|\boldsymbol{r}_i\| \leq \epsilon$. (The ϵ value is application dependent but is often around 1–3 pixels.) Least median of squares finds the median value of the $\|\boldsymbol{r}_i\|^2$ values. The

---

[7] For pixel-based alignment methods (Section 8.1.1), hierarchical (coarse-to-fine) techniques are often used to lock onto the *dominant motion* in a scene.

k	p	S
3	0.5	35
6	0.6	97
6	0.5	293

Table 6.2 Number of trials S to attain a 99% probability of success (Stewart 1999).

random selection process is repeated S times and the sample set with the largest number of inliers (or with the smallest median residual) is kept as the final solution. Either the initial parameter guess p or the full set of computed inliers is then passed on to the next data fitting stage.

When the number of measurements is quite large, it may be preferable to only score a subset of the measurements in an initial round that selects the most plausible hypotheses for additional scoring and selection. This modification of RANSAC, which can significantly speed up its performance, is called *Preemptive RANSAC* (Nistér 2003). In another variant on RANSAC called PROSAC (PROgressive SAmple Consensus), random samples are initially added from the most "confident" matches, thereby speeding up the process of finding a (statistically) likely good set of inliers (Chum and Matas 2005).

To ensure that the random sampling has a good chance of finding a true set of inliers, a sufficient number of trials S must be tried. Let p be the probability that any given correspondence is valid and P be the total probability of success after S trials. The likelihood in one trial that all k random samples are inliers is p^k. Therefore, the likelihood that S such trials will all fail is

$$1 - P = (1 - p^k)^S \tag{6.29}$$

and the required minimum number of trials is

$$S = \frac{\log(1 - P)}{\log(1 - p^k)}. \tag{6.30}$$

Stewart (1999) gives examples of the required number of trials S to attain a 99% probability of success. As you can see from Table 6.2, the number of trials grows quickly with the number of sample points used. This provides a strong incentive to use the *minimum* number of sample points k possible for any given trial, which is how RANSAC is normally used in practice.

Uncertainty modeling

In addition to robustly computing a good alignment, some applications require the computation of uncertainty (see Appendix B.6). For linear problems, this estimate can be obtained by inverting the Hessian matrix (6.9) and multiplying it by the feature position noise (if these have not already been used to weight the individual measurements, as in Equations (6.10) and 6.11)). In statistics, the Hessian, which is the inverse covariance, is sometimes called the (Fisher) *information matrix* (Appendix B.1.1).

When the problem involves non-linear least squares, the inverse of the Hessian matrix provides the *Cramer–Rao lower bound* on the covariance matrix, i.e., it provides the *minimum* amount of covariance in a given solution, which can actually have a wider spread ("longer tails") if the energy flattens out away from the local minimum where the optimal solution is found.

6.1.5 3D alignment

Instead of aligning 2D sets of image features, many computer vision applications require the alignment of 3D points. In the case where the 3D transformations are linear in the motion parameters, e.g., for translation, similarity, and affine, regular least squares (6.5) can be used.

The case of rigid (Euclidean) motion,

$$E_{\text{R3D}} = \sum_i \| \boldsymbol{x}_i' - \boldsymbol{R}\boldsymbol{x}_i - \boldsymbol{t} \|^2, \tag{6.31}$$

which arises more frequently and is often called the *absolute orientation* problem (Horn 1987), requires slightly different techniques. If only scalar weightings are being used (as opposed to full 3D per-point anisotropic covariance estimates), the weighted centroids of the two point clouds $\boldsymbol{c}$ and $\boldsymbol{c}'$ can be used to estimate the translation $\boldsymbol{t} = \boldsymbol{c}' - \boldsymbol{R}\boldsymbol{c}$.[8] We are then left with the problem of estimating the rotation between two sets of points $\{\hat{\boldsymbol{x}}_i = \boldsymbol{x}_i - \boldsymbol{c}\}$ and $\{\hat{\boldsymbol{x}}_i' = \boldsymbol{x}_i' - \boldsymbol{c}'\}$ that are both centered at the origin.

One commonly used technique is called the *orthogonal Procrustes algorithm* (Golub and Van Loan 1996, p. 601) and involves computing the singular value decomposition (SVD) of the 3×3 correlation matrix

$$\boldsymbol{C} = \sum_i \hat{\boldsymbol{x}}' \hat{\boldsymbol{x}}^T = \boldsymbol{U}\boldsymbol{\Sigma}\boldsymbol{V}^T. \tag{6.32}$$

The rotation matrix is then obtained as $\boldsymbol{R} = \boldsymbol{U}\boldsymbol{V}^T$. (Verify this for yourself when $\hat{\boldsymbol{x}}' = \boldsymbol{R}\hat{\boldsymbol{x}}$.)

Another technique is the absolute orientation algorithm (Horn 1987) for estimating the unit quaternion corresponding to the rotation matrix $\boldsymbol{R}$, which involves forming a 4×4 matrix from the entries in $\boldsymbol{C}$ and then finding the eigenvector associated with its largest positive eigenvalue.

Lorusso, Eggert, and Fisher (1995) experimentally compare these two techniques to two additional techniques proposed in the literature, but find that the difference in accuracy is negligible (well below the effects of measurement noise).

In situations where these closed-form algorithms are not applicable, e.g., when full 3D covariances are being used or when the 3D alignment is part of some larger optimization, the incremental rotation update introduced in Section 2.1.4 (2.35–2.36), which is parameterized by an instantaneous rotation vector $\boldsymbol{\omega}$, can be used (See Section 9.1.3 for an application to image stitching.)

In some situations, e.g., when merging range data maps, the correspondence between data points is not known *a priori*. In this case, iterative algorithms that start by matching nearby points and then update the most likely correspondence can be used (Besl and McKay 1992; Zhang 1994; Szeliski and Lavallée 1996; Gold, Rangarajan, Lu *et al.* 1998; David, DeMenthon, Duraiswami *et al.* 2004; Li and Hartley 2007; Enqvist, Josephson, and Kahl 2009). These techniques are discussed in more detail in Section 12.2.1.

---

[8] When full covariances are used, they are transformed by the rotation and so a closed-form solution for translation is not possible.

6.2 Pose estimation

A particular instance of feature-based alignment, which occurs very often, is estimating an object's 3D pose from a set of 2D point projections. This *pose estimation* problem is also known as *extrinsic* calibration, as opposed to the *intrinsic* calibration of internal camera parameters such as focal length, which we discuss in Section 6.3. The problem of recovering pose from three correspondences, which is the minimal amount of information necessary, is known as the *perspective-3-point-problem* (P3P), with extensions to larger numbers of points collectively known as PnP (Haralick, Lee, Ottenberg *et al.* 1994; Quan and Lan 1999; Moreno-Noguer, Lepetit, and Fua 2007).

In this section, we look at some of the techniques that have been developed to solve such problems, starting with the *direct linear transform* (DLT), which recovers a 3×4 camera matrix, followed by other "linear" algorithms, and then looking at statistically optimal iterative algorithms.

6.2.1 Linear algorithms

The simplest way to recover the pose of the camera is to form a set of linear equations analogous to those used for 2D motion estimation (6.19) from the camera matrix form of perspective projection (2.55–2.56),

$$x_i = \frac{p_{00}X_i + p_{01}Y_i + p_{02}Z_i + p_{03}}{p_{20}X_i + p_{21}Y_i + p_{22}Z_i + p_{23}} \tag{6.33}$$

$$y_i = \frac{p_{10}X_i + p_{11}Y_i + p_{12}Z_i + p_{13}}{p_{20}X_i + p_{21}Y_i + p_{22}Z_i + p_{23}}, \tag{6.34}$$

where (x_i, y_i) are the measured 2D feature locations and (X_i, Y_i, Z_i) are the known 3D feature locations (Figure 6.4). As with (6.21), this system of equations can be solved in a linear fashion for the unknowns in the camera matrix P by multiplying the denominator on both sides of the equation.[9] The resulting algorithm is called the *direct linear transform* (DLT) and is commonly attributed to Sutherland (1974). (For a more in-depth discussion, refer to the work of Hartley and Zisserman (2004).) In order to compute the 12 (or 11) unknowns in P, at least six correspondences between 3D and 2D locations must be known.

As with the case of estimating homographies (6.21–6.23), more accurate results for the entries in P can be obtained by directly minimizing the set of Equations (6.33–6.34) using non-linear least squares with a small number of iterations.

Once the entries in P have been recovered, it is possible to recover both the intrinsic calibration matrix K and the rigid transformation (R, t) by observing from Equation (2.56) that

$$P = K[R|t]. \tag{6.35}$$

Since K is by convention upper-triangular (see the discussion in Section 2.1.5), both K and R can be obtained from the front 3×3 sub-matrix of P using RQ factorization (Golub and Van Loan 1996).[10]

---

[9] Because P is unknown up to a scale, we can either fix one of the entries, e.g., $p_{23} = 1$, or find the smallest singular vector of the set of linear equations.

[10] Note the unfortunate clash of terminologies: In matrix algebra textbooks, R represents an upper-triangular matrix; in computer vision, R is an orthogonal rotation.

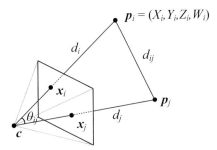

Figure 6.4 Pose estimation by the direct linear transform and by measuring visual angles and distances between pairs of points.

In most applications, however, we have some prior knowledge about the intrinsic calibration matrix K, e.g., that the pixels are square, the skew is very small, and the optical center is near the center of the image (2.57–2.59). Such constraints can be incorporated into a non-linear minimization of the parameters in K and (R, t), as described in Section 6.2.2.

In the case where the camera is already calibrated, i.e., the matrix K is known (Section 6.3), we can perform pose estimation using as few as three points (Fischler and Bolles 1981; Haralick, Lee, Ottenberg *et al.* 1994; Quan and Lan 1999). The basic observation that these *linear PnP* (*perspective n-point*) algorithms employ is that the visual angle between any pair of 2D points $\hat{x}_i$ and $\hat{x}_j$ must be the same as the angle between their corresponding 3D points p_i and p_j (Figure 6.4).

Given a set of corresponding 2D and 3D points $\{(\hat{x}_i, p_i)\}$, where the $\hat{x}_i$ are unit directions obtained by transforming 2D pixel measurements x_i to unit norm 3D directions $\hat{x}_i$ through the inverse calibration matrix K,

$$\hat{x}_i = \mathcal{N}(K^{-1}x_i) = K^{-1}x_i/\|K^{-1}x_i\|, \tag{6.36}$$

the unknowns are the distances d_i from the camera origin c to the 3D points p_i, where

$$p_i = d_i\hat{x}_i + c \tag{6.37}$$

(Figure 6.4). The cosine law for triangle $\Delta(c, p_i, p_j)$ gives us

$$f_{ij}(d_i, d_j) = d_i^2 + d_j^2 - 2d_id_jc_{ij} - d_{ij}^2 = 0, \tag{6.38}$$

where

$$c_{ij} = \cos\theta_{ij} = \hat{x}_i \cdot \hat{x}_j \tag{6.39}$$

and

$$d_{ij}^2 = \|p_i - p_j\|^2. \tag{6.40}$$

We can take any triplet of constraints (f_{ij}, f_{ik}, f_{jk}) and eliminate the d_j and d_k using Sylvester resultants (Cox, Little, and O'Shea 2007) to obtain a quartic equation in d_i^2,

$$g_{ijk}(d_i^2) = a_4d_i^8 + a_3d_i^6 + a_2d_i^4 + a_1d_i^2 + a_0 = 0. \tag{6.41}$$

Given five or more correspondences, we can generate $\frac{(n-1)(n-2)}{2}$ triplets to obtain a linear estimate (using SVD) for the values of $(d_i^8, d_i^6, d_i^4, d_i^2)$ (Quan and Lan 1999). Estimates for

d_i^2 can computed as ratios of successive d_i^{2n+2}/d_i^{2n} estimates and these can be averaged to obtain a final estimate of d_i^2 (and hence d_i).

Once the individual estimates of the d_i distances have been computed, we can generate a 3D structure consisting of the scaled point directions $d_i \hat{x}_i$, which can then be aligned with the 3D point cloud $\{p_i\}$ using absolute orientation (Section 6.1.5) to obtained the desired pose estimate. Quan and Lan (1999) give accuracy results for this and other techniques, which use fewer points but require more complicated algebraic manipulations. The paper by Moreno-Noguer, Lepetit, and Fua (2007) reviews more recent alternatives and also gives a lower complexity algorithm that typically produces more accurate results.

Unfortunately, because minimal PnP solutions can be quite noise sensitive and also suffer from *bas-relief ambiguities* (e.g., depth reversals) (Section 7.4.3), it is often preferable to use the linear six-point algorithm to guess an initial pose and then optimize this estimate using the iterative technique described in Section 6.2.2.

An alternative pose estimation algorithm involves starting with a scaled orthographic projection model and then iteratively refining this initial estimate using a more accurate perspective projection model (DeMenthon and Davis 1995). The attraction of this model, as stated in the paper's title, is that it can be implemented "in 25 lines of [Mathematica] code".

6.2.2 Iterative algorithms

The most accurate (and flexible) way to estimate pose is to directly minimize the squared (or robust) reprojection error for the 2D points as a function of the unknown pose parameters in (R, t) and optionally K using non-linear least squares (Tsai 1987; Bogart 1991; Gleicher and Witkin 1992). We can write the projection equations as

$$x_i = f(p_i; R, t, K) \tag{6.42}$$

and iteratively minimize the robustified linearized reprojection errors

$$E_{\text{NLP}} = \sum_i \rho \left(\frac{\partial f}{\partial R} \Delta R + \frac{\partial f}{\partial t} \Delta t + \frac{\partial f}{\partial K} \Delta K - r_i \right), \tag{6.43}$$

where $r_i = \tilde{x}_i - \hat{x}_i$ is the current residual vector (2D error in predicted position) and the partial derivatives are with respect to the unknown pose parameters (rotation, translation, and optionally calibration). Note that if full 2D covariance estimates are available for the 2D feature locations, the above squared norm can be weighted by the inverse point covariance matrix, as in Equation (6.11).

An easier to understand (and implement) version of the above non-linear regression problem can be constructed by re-writing the projection equations as a concatenation of simpler steps, each of which transforms a 4D homogeneous coordinate p_i by a simple transformation such as translation, rotation, or perspective division (Figure 6.5). The resulting projection equations can be written as

$$
\begin{align}
y^{(1)} &= f_{\text{T}}(p_i; c_j) = p_i - c_j, \tag{6.44} \\
y^{(2)} &= f_{\text{R}}(y^{(1)}; q_j) = R(q_j) y^{(1)}, \tag{6.45} \\
y^{(3)} &= f_{\text{P}}(y^{(2)}) = \frac{y^{(2)}}{z^{(2)}}, \tag{6.46} \\
x_i &= f_{\text{C}}(y^{(3)}; k) = K(k) y^{(3)}. \tag{6.47}
\end{align}
$$

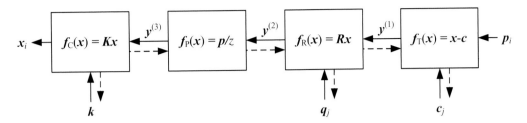

Figure 6.5 A set of chained transforms for projecting a 3D point p_i to a 2D measurement x_i through a series of transformations $f^{(k)}$, each of which is controlled by its own set of parameters. The dashed lines indicate the flow of information as partial derivatives are computed during a backward pass.

Note that in these equations, we have indexed the camera centers c_j and camera rotation quaternions q_j by an index j, in case more than one pose of the calibration object is being used (see also Section 7.4.) We are also using the camera center c_j instead of the world translation t_j, since this is a more natural parameter to estimate.

The advantage of this chained set of transformations is that each one has a simple partial derivative with respect both to its parameters and to its input. Thus, once the predicted value of $\tilde{x}_i$ has been computed based on the 3D point location p_i and the current values of the pose parameters (c_j, q_j, k), we can obtain all of the required partial derivatives using the chain rule

$$\frac{\partial r_i}{\partial p^{(k)}} = \frac{\partial r_i}{\partial y^{(k)}} \frac{\partial y^{(k)}}{\partial p^{(k)}}, \tag{6.48}$$

where $p^{(k)}$ indicates one of the parameter vectors that is being optimized. (This same "trick" is used in neural networks as part of the *backpropagation* algorithm (Bishop 2006).)

The one special case in this formulation that can be considerably simplified is the computation of the rotation update. Instead of directly computing the derivatives of the 3×3 rotation matrix $R(q)$ as a function of the unit quaternion entries, you can prepend the incremental rotation matrix $\Delta R(\omega)$ given in Equation (2.35) to the current rotation matrix and compute the partial derivative of the transform with respect to these parameters, which results in a simple cross product of the backward chaining partial derivative and the outgoing 3D vector (2.36).

6.2.3 *Application*: Augmented reality

A widely used application of pose estimation is *augmented reality*, where virtual 3D images or annotations are superimposed on top of a live video feed, either through the use of see-through glasses (a head-mounted display) or on a regular computer or mobile device screen (Azuma, Baillot, Behringer *et al.* 2001; Haller, Billinghurst, and Thomas 2007). In some applications, a special pattern printed on cards or in a book is tracked to perform the augmentation (Kato, Billinghurst, Poupyrev *et al.* 2000; Billinghurst, Kato, and Poupyrev 2001). For a desktop application, a grid of dots printed on a mouse pad can be tracked by a camera embedded in an augmented mouse to give the user control of a full six degrees of freedom over their position and orientation in a 3D space (Hinckley, Sinclair, Hanson *et al.* 1999), as shown in Figure 6.6.

Sometimes, the scene itself provides a convenient object to track, such as the rectangle defining a desktop used in *through-the-lens camera control* (Gleicher and Witkin 1992). In

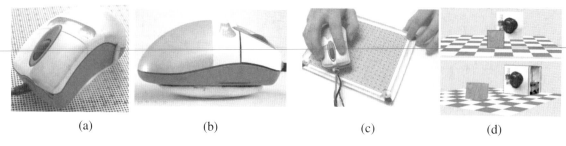

(a)   (b)   (c)   (d)

Figure 6.6 The VideoMouse can sense six degrees of freedom relative to a specially printed mouse pad using its embedded camera (Hinckley, Sinclair, Hanson *et al.* 1999) © 1999 ACM: (a) top view of the mouse; (b) view of the mouse showing the curved base for rocking; (c) moving the mouse pad with the other hand extends the interaction capabilities; (d) the resulting movement seen on the screen.

outdoor locations, such as film sets, it is more common to place special markers such as brightly colored balls in the scene to make it easier to find and track them (Bogart 1991). In older applications, surveying techniques were used to determine the locations of these balls before filming. Today, it is more common to apply structure-from-motion directly to the film footage itself (Section 7.4.2).

Rapid pose estimation is also central to tracking the position and orientation of the hand-held remote controls used in Nintendo's Wii game systems. A high-speed camera embedded in the remote control is used to track the locations of the infrared (IR) LEDs in the bar that is mounted on the TV monitor. Pose estimation is then used to infer the remote control's location and orientation at very high frame rates. The Wii system can be extended to a variety of other user interaction applications by mounting the bar on a hand-held device, as described by Johnny Lee.[11]

Exercises 6.4 and 6.5 have you implement two different tracking and pose estimation systems for augmented-reality applications. The first system tracks the outline of a rectangular object, such as a book cover or magazine page, and the second has you track the pose of a hand-held Rubik's cube.

6.3 Geometric intrinsic calibration

As described above in Equations (6.42–6.43), the computation of the internal (intrinsic) camera calibration parameters can occur simultaneously with the estimation of the (extrinsic) pose of the camera with respect to a known calibration target. This, indeed, is the "classic" approach to camera calibration used in both the photogrammetry (Slama 1980) and the computer vision (Tsai 1987) communities. In this section, we look at alternative formulations (which may not involve the full solution of a non-linear regression problem), the use of alternative calibration targets, and the estimation of the non-linear part of camera optics such as radial distortion.[12]

---

[11] http://johnnylee.net/projects/wii/.

[12] In some applications, you can use the EXIF tags associated with a JPEG image to obtain a rough estimate of a camera's focal length but this technique should be used with caution as the results are often inaccurate.

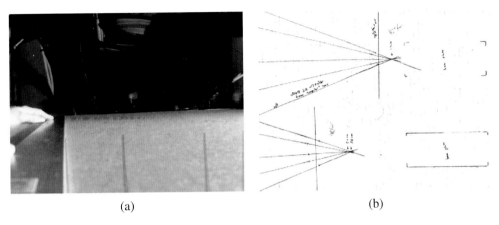

(a) (b)

Figure 6.7 Calibrating a lens by drawing straight lines on cardboard (Debevec, Wenger, Tchou *et al.* 2002) ©
2002 ACM: (a) an image taken by the video camera showing a hand holding a metal ruler whose right edge
appears vertical in the image; (b) the set of lines drawn on the cardboard converging on the front nodal point
(center of projection) of the lens and indicating the horizontal field of view.

6.3.1 Calibration patterns

The use of a calibration pattern or set of markers is one of the more reliable ways to estimate
a camera's intrinsic parameters. In photogrammetry, it is common to set up a camera in a
large field looking at distant calibration targets whose exact location has been precomputed
using surveying equipment (Slama 1980; Atkinson 1996; Kraus 1997). In this case, the translational component of the pose becomes irrelevant and only the camera rotation and intrinsic
parameters need to be recovered.

If a smaller calibration rig needs to be used, e.g., for indoor robotics applications or for
mobile robots that carry their own calibration target, it is best if the calibration object can span
as much of the workspace as possible (Figure 6.8a), as planar targets often fail to accurately
predict the components of the pose that lie far away from the plane. A good way to determine
if the calibration has been successfully performed is to estimate the covariance in the parameters (Section 6.1.4) and then project 3D points from various points in the workspace into the
image in order to estimate their 2D positional uncertainty.

An alternative method for estimating the focal length and center of projection of a lens
is to place the camera on a large flat piece of cardboard and use a long metal ruler to draw
lines on the cardboard that appear vertical in the image, as shown in Figure 6.7a (Debevec,
Wenger, Tchou *et al.* 2002). Such lines lie on planes that are parallel to the vertical axis of
the camera sensor and also pass through the lens' front nodal point. The location of the nodal
point (projected vertically onto the cardboard plane) and the horizontal field of view (determined from lines that graze the left and right edges of the visible image) can be recovered by
intersecting these lines and measuring their angular extent (Figure 6.7b).

If no calibration pattern is available, it is also possible to perform calibration simultaneously with structure and pose recovery (Sections 6.3.4 and 7.4), which is known as *self-
calibration* (Faugeras, Luong, and Maybank 1992; Hartley and Zisserman 2004; Moons, Van
Gool, and Vergauwen 2010). However, such an approach requires a large amount of imagery
to be accurate.

(a)   (b)

Figure 6.8 Calibration patterns: (a) a three-dimensional target (Quan and Lan 1999) © 1999 IEEE; (b) a two-dimensional target (Zhang 2000) © 2000 IEEE. Note that radial distortion needs to be removed from such images before the feature points can be used for calibration.

Planar calibration patterns

When a finite workspace is being used and accurate machining and motion control platforms are available, a good way to perform calibration is to move a planar calibration target in a controlled fashion through the workspace volume. This approach is sometimes called the *N-planes* calibration approach (Gremban, Thorpe, and Kanade 1988; Champleboux, Lavallée, Szeliski *et al.* 1992; Grossberg and Nayar 2001) and has the advantage that each camera pixel can be mapped to a unique 3D ray in space, which takes care of both linear effects modeled by the calibration matrix K and non-linear effects such as radial distortion (Section 6.3.5).

A less cumbersome but also less accurate calibration can be obtained by waving a planar calibration pattern in front of a camera (Figure 6.8b). In this case, the pattern's pose has (in principle) to be recovered in conjunction with the intrinsics. In this technique, each input image is used to compute a separate homography (6.19–6.23) $\tilde{H}$ mapping the plane's calibration points $(X_i, Y_i, 0)$ into image coordinates (x_i, y_i),

$$x_i = \begin{bmatrix} x_i \\ y_i \\ 1 \end{bmatrix} \sim K \begin{bmatrix} r_0 & r_1 & t \end{bmatrix} \begin{bmatrix} X_i \\ Y_i \\ 1 \end{bmatrix} \sim \tilde{H}p_i, \qquad (6.49)$$

where the r_i are the first two columns of R and $\sim$ indicates equality up to scale. From these, Zhang (2000) shows how to form linear constraints on the nine entries in the $B = K^{-T}K^{-1}$ matrix, from which the calibration matrix K can be recovered using a matrix square root and inversion. (The matrix B is known as the *image of the absolute conic* (IAC) in projective geometry and is commonly used for camera calibration (Hartley and Zisserman 2004, Section 7.5).) If only the focal length is being recovered, the even simpler approach of using vanishing points can be used instead.

6.3.2 Vanishing points

A common case for calibration that occurs often in practice is when the camera is looking at a man-made scene with strong extended rectahedral objects such as boxes or room walls. In this case, we can intersect the 2D lines corresponding to 3D parallel lines to compute their

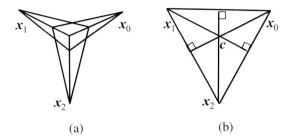

Figure 6.9 Calibration from vanishing points: (a) any pair of finite vanishing points $(\hat{x}_i, \hat{x}_j)$ can be used to estimate the focal length; (b) the orthocenter of the vanishing point triangle gives the optical center of the image c.

vanishing points, as described in Section 4.3.3, and use these to determine the intrinsic and extrinsic calibration parameters (Caprile and Torre 1990; Becker and Bove 1995; Liebowitz and Zisserman 1998; Cipolla, Drummond, and Robertson 1999; Antone and Teller 2002; Criminisi, Reid, and Zisserman 2000; Hartley and Zisserman 2004; Pflugfelder 2008).

Let us assume that we have detected two or more orthogonal vanishing points, all of which are *finite*, i.e., they are not obtained from lines that appear to be parallel in the image plane (Figure 6.9a). Let us also assume a simplified form for the calibration matrix K where only the focal length is unknown (2.59). (It is often safe for rough 3D modeling to assume that the optical center is at the center of the image, that the aspect ratio is 1, and that there is no skew.) In this case, the projection equation for the vanishing points can be written as

$$\hat{x}_i = \begin{bmatrix} x_i - c_x \\ y_i - c_y \\ f \end{bmatrix} \sim Rp_i = r_i, \tag{6.50}$$

where p_i corresponds to one of the cardinal directions $(1,0,0)$, $(0,1,0)$, or $(0,0,1)$, and r_i is the ith column of the rotation matrix R.

From the orthogonality between columns of the rotation matrix, we have

$$r_i \cdot r_j \sim (x_i - c_x)(x_j - c_y) + (y_i - c_y)(y_j - c_y) + f^2 = 0 \tag{6.51}$$

from which we can obtain an estimate for f^2. Note that the accuracy of this estimate increases as the vanishing points move closer to the center of the image. In other words, it is best to tilt the calibration pattern a decent amount around the $45°$ axis, as in Figure 6.9a. Once the focal length f has been determined, the individual columns of R can be estimated by normalizing the left hand side of (6.50) and taking cross products. Alternatively, an SVD of the initial R estimate, which is a variant on orthogonal Procrustes (6.32), can be used.

If all three vanishing points are visible and finite in the same image, it is also possible to estimate the optical center as the orthocenter of the triangle formed by the three vanishing points (Caprile and Torre 1990; Hartley and Zisserman 2004, Section 7.6) (Figure 6.9b). In practice, however, it is more accurate to re-estimate any unknown intrinsic calibration parameters using non-linear least squares (6.42).

(a)   (b)

Figure 6.10 Single view metrology (Criminisi, Reid, and Zisserman 2000) © 2000 Springer: (a) input image showing the three coordinate axes computed from the two horizontal vanishing points (which can be determined from the sidings on the shed); (b) a new view of the 3D reconstruction.

6.3.3 *Application*: Single view metrology

A fun application of vanishing point estimation and camera calibration is the *single view metrology* system developed by Criminisi, Reid, and Zisserman (2000). Their system allows people to interactively measure heights and other dimensions as well as to build piecewise-planar 3D models, as shown in Figure 6.10.

The first step in their system is to identify two orthogonal vanishing points on the ground plane and the vanishing point for the vertical direction, which can be done by drawing some parallel sets of lines in the image. (Alternatively, automated techniques such as those discussed in Section 4.3.3 or by Schaffalitzky and Zisserman (2000) could be used.) The user then marks a few dimensions in the image, such as the height of a reference object, and the system can automatically compute the height of another object. Walls and other planar impostors (geometry) can also be sketched and reconstructed.

In the formulation originally developed by Criminisi, Reid, and Zisserman (2000), the system produces an *affine* reconstruction, i.e., one that is only known up to a set of independent scaling factors along each axis. A potentially more useful system can be constructed by assuming that the camera is calibrated up to an unknown focal length, which can be recovered from orthogonal (finite) vanishing directions, as we just described in Section 6.3.2. Once this is done, the user can indicate an origin on the ground plane and another point a known distance away. From this, points on the ground plane can be directly projected into 3D and points above the ground plane, when paired with their ground plane projections, can also be recovered. A fully metric reconstruction of the scene then becomes possible.

Exercise 6.9 has you implement such a system and then use it to model some simple 3D scenes. Section 12.6.1 describes other, potentially multi-view, approaches to architectural reconstruction, including an interactive piecewise-planar modeling system that uses vanishing points to establish 3D line directions and plane normals (Sinha, Steedly, Szeliski *et al.* 2008).

Figure 6.11 Four images taken with a hand-held camera registered using a 3D rotation motion model, which can be used to estimate the focal length of the camera (Szeliski and Shum 1997) © 2000 ACM.

6.3.4 Rotational motion

When no calibration targets or known structures are available but you can rotate the camera around its front nodal point (or, equivalently, work in a large open environment where all objects are distant), the camera can be calibrated from a set of overlapping images by assuming that it is undergoing pure rotational motion, as shown in Figure 6.11 (Stein 1995; Hartley 1997b; Hartley, Hayman, de Agapito *et al.* 2000; de Agapito, Hayman, and Reid 2001; Kang and Weiss 1999; Shum and Szeliski 2000; Frahm and Koch 2003). When a full 360° motion is used to perform this calibration, a very accurate estimate of the focal length f can be obtained, as the accuracy in this estimate is proportional to the total number of pixels in the resulting cylindrical panorama (Section 9.1.6) (Stein 1995; Shum and Szeliski 2000).

To use this technique, we first compute the homographies $\tilde{H}_{ij}$ between all overlapping pairs of images, as explained in Equations (6.19–6.23). Then, we use the observation, first made in Equation (2.72) and explored in more detail in Section 9.1.3 (9.5), that each homography is related to the inter-camera rotation R_{ij} through the (unknown) calibration matrices K_i and K_j,

$$\tilde{H}_{ij} = K_i R_i R_j^{-1} K_j^{-1} = K_i R_{ij} K_j^{-1}. \tag{6.52}$$

The simplest way to obtain the calibration is to use the simplified form of the calibration matrix (2.59), where we assume that the pixels are square and the optical center lies at the center of the image, i.e., $K_k = \mathrm{diag}(f_k, f_k, 1)$. (We number the pixel coordinates accordingly, i.e., place pixel $(x, y) = (0, 0)$ at the center of the image.) We can then rewrite Equation (6.52) as

$$R_{10} \sim K_1^{-1} \tilde{H}_{10} K_0 \sim \begin{bmatrix} h_{00} & h_{01} & f_0^{-1} h_{02} \\ h_{10} & h_{11} & f_0^{-1} h_{12} \\ f_1 h_{20} & f_1 h_{21} & f_0^{-1} f_1 h_{22} \end{bmatrix}, \tag{6.53}$$

where h_{ij} are the elements of $\tilde{H}_{10}$.

Using the orthonormality properties of the rotation matrix $\boldsymbol{R}_{10}$ and the fact that the right hand side of (6.53) is known only up to a scale, we obtain

$$h_{00}^2 + h_{01}^2 + f_0^{-2}h_{02}^2 = h_{10}^2 + h_{11}^2 + f_0^{-2}h_{12}^2 \tag{6.54}$$

and

$$h_{00}h_{10} + h_{01}h_{11} + f_0^{-2}h_{02}h_{12} = 0. \tag{6.55}$$

From this, we can compute estimates for f_0 of

$$f_0^2 = \frac{h_{12}^2 - h_{02}^2}{h_{00}^2 + h_{01}^2 - h_{10}^2 - h_{11}^2} \quad \text{if } h_{00}^2 + h_{01}^2 \neq h_{10}^2 + h_{11}^2 \tag{6.56}$$

or

$$f_0^2 = -\frac{h_{02}h_{12}}{h_{00}h_{10} + h_{01}h_{11}} \quad \text{if } h_{00}h_{10} \neq -h_{01}h_{11}. \tag{6.57}$$

(Note that the equations originally given by Szeliski and Shum (1997) are erroneous; the correct equations are given by Shum and Szeliski (2000).) If neither of these conditions holds, we can also take the dot products between the first (or second) row and the third one. Similar results can be obtained for f_1 as well, by analyzing the columns of $\tilde{\boldsymbol{H}}_{10}$. If the focal length is the same for both images, we can take the geometric mean of f_0 and f_1 as the estimated focal length $f = \sqrt{f_1 f_0}$. When multiple estimates of f are available, e.g., from different homographies, the median value can be used as the final estimate.

A more general (upper-triangular) estimate of $\boldsymbol{K}$ can be obtained in the case of a fixed-parameter camera $\boldsymbol{K}_i = \boldsymbol{K}$ using the technique of Hartley (1997b). Observe from (6.52) that $\boldsymbol{R}_{ij} \sim \boldsymbol{K}^{-1}\tilde{\boldsymbol{H}}_{ij}\boldsymbol{K}$ and $\boldsymbol{R}_{ij}^{-T} \sim \boldsymbol{K}^T\tilde{\boldsymbol{H}}_{ij}^{-T}\boldsymbol{K}^{-T}$. Equating $\boldsymbol{R}_{ij} = \boldsymbol{R}_{ij}^{-T}$ we obtain $\boldsymbol{K}^{-1}\tilde{\boldsymbol{H}}_{ij}\boldsymbol{K} \sim \boldsymbol{K}^T\tilde{\boldsymbol{H}}_{ij}^{-T}\boldsymbol{K}^{-T}$, from which we get

$$\tilde{\boldsymbol{H}}_{ij}(\boldsymbol{K}\boldsymbol{K}^T) \sim (\boldsymbol{K}\boldsymbol{K}^T)\tilde{\boldsymbol{H}}_{ij}^{-T}. \tag{6.58}$$

This provides us with some homogeneous linear constraints on the entries in $\boldsymbol{A} = \boldsymbol{K}\boldsymbol{K}^T$, which is known as the *dual of the image of the absolute conic* (Hartley 1997b; Hartley and Zisserman 2004). (Recall that when we estimate a homography, we can only recover it up to an unknown scale.) Given a sufficient number of independent homography estimates $\tilde{\boldsymbol{H}}_{ij}$, we can recover $\boldsymbol{A}$ (up to a scale) using either SVD or eigenvalue analysis and then recover $\boldsymbol{K}$ through Cholesky decomposition (Appendix A.1.4). Extensions to the cases of temporally varying calibration parameters and non-stationary cameras are discussed by Hartley, Hayman, de Agapito *et al.* (2000) and de Agapito, Hayman, and Reid (2001).

The quality of the intrinsic camera parameters can be greatly increased by constructing a full $360°$ panorama, since mis-estimating the focal length will result in a gap (or excessive overlap) when the first image in the sequence is stitched to itself (Figure 9.5). The resulting mis-alignment can be used to improve the estimate of the focal length and to re-adjust the rotation estimates, as described in Section 9.1.4. Rotating the camera by $90°$ around its optic axis and re-shooting the panorama is a good way to check for aspect ratio and skew pixel problems, as is generating a full hemi-spherical panorama when there is sufficient texture.

Ultimately, however, the most accurate estimate of the calibration parameters (including radial distortion) can be obtained using a full simultaneous non-linear minimization of the intrinsic and extrinsic (rotation) parameters, as described in Section 9.2.

6.3.5 Radial distortion

When images are taken with wide-angle lenses, it is often necessary to model *lens distortions* such as *radial distortion*. As discussed in Section 2.1.6, the radial distortion model says that coordinates in the observed images are displaced away from (*barrel* distortion) or towards (*pincushion* distortion) the image center by an amount proportional to their radial distance (Figure 2.13a–b). The simplest radial distortion models use low-order polynomials (c.f. Equation (2.78)),

$$\hat{x} = x(1 + \kappa_1 r^2 + \kappa_2 r^4)$$
$$\hat{y} = y(1 + \kappa_1 r^2 + \kappa_2 r^4), \tag{6.59}$$

where $r^2 = x^2 + y^2$ and κ_1 and κ_2 are called the *radial distortion parameters* (Brown 1971; Slama 1980).[13]

A variety of techniques can be used to estimate the radial distortion parameters for a given lens.[14] One of the simplest and most useful is to take an image of a scene with a lot of straight lines, especially lines aligned with and near the edges of the image. The radial distortion parameters can then be adjusted until all of the lines in the image are straight, which is commonly called the *plumb-line method* (Brown 1971; Kang 2001; El-Melegy and Farag 2003). Exercise 6.10 gives some more details on how to implement such a technique.

Another approach is to use several overlapping images and to combine the estimation of the radial distortion parameters with the image alignment process, i.e., by extending the pipeline used for stitching in Section 9.2.1. Sawhney and Kumar (1999) use a hierarchy of motion models (translation, affine, projective) in a coarse-to-fine strategy coupled with a quadratic radial distortion correction term. They use direct (intensity-based) minimization to compute the alignment. Stein (1997) uses a feature-based approach combined with a general 3D motion model (and quadratic radial distortion), which requires more matches than a parallax-free rotational panorama but is potentially more general. More recent approaches sometimes simultaneously compute both the unknown intrinsic parameters and the radial distortion coefficients, which may include higher-order terms or more complex rational or non-parametric forms (Claus and Fitzgibbon 2005; Sturm 2005; Thirthala and Pollefeys 2005; Barreto and Daniilidis 2005; Hartley and Kang 2005; Steele and Jaynes 2006; Tardif, Sturm, Trudeau *et al.* 2009).

When a known calibration target is being used (Figure 6.8), the radial distortion estimation can be folded into the estimation of the other intrinsic and extrinsic parameters (Zhang 2000; Hartley and Kang 2007; Tardif, Sturm, Trudeau *et al.* 2009). This can be viewed as adding another stage to the general non-linear minimization pipeline shown in Figure 6.5 between the intrinsic parameter multiplication box f_C and the perspective division box f_P. (See Exercise 6.11 on more details for the case of a planar calibration target.)

Of course, as discussed in Section 2.1.6, more general models of lens distortion, such as fisheye and non-central projection, may sometimes be required. While the parameterization of such lenses may be more complicated (Section 2.1.6), the general approach of either using calibration rigs with known 3D positions or self-calibration through the use of multiple

---

[13] Sometimes the relationship between x and $\hat{x}$ is expressed the other way around, i.e., using primed (final) coordinates on the right-hand side, $x = \hat{x}(1 + \kappa_1 \hat{r}^2 + \kappa_2 \hat{r}^4)$. This is convenient if we map image pixels into (warped) rays and then undistort the rays to obtain 3D rays in space, i.e., if we are using inverse warping.

[14] Some of today's digital cameras are starting to remove radial distortion using software in the camera itself.

overlapping images of a scene can both be used (Hartley and Kang 2007; Tardif, Sturm, and Roy 2007). The same techniques used to calibrate for radial distortion can also be used to reduce the amount of chromatic aberration by separately calibrating each color channel and then warping the channels to put them back into alignment (Exercise 6.12).

6.4 Additional reading

Hartley and Zisserman (2004) provide a wonderful introduction to the topics of feature-based alignment and optimal motion estimation, as well as an in-depth discussion of camera calibration and pose estimation techniques.

Techniques for robust estimation are discussed in more detail in Appendix B.3 and in monographs and review articles on this topic (Huber 1981; Hampel, Ronchetti, Rousseeuw *et al.* 1986; Rousseeuw and Leroy 1987; Black and Rangarajan 1996; Stewart 1999). The most commonly used robust initialization technique in computer vision is RANdom SAmple Consensus (RANSAC) (Fischler and Bolles 1981), which has spawned a series of more efficient variants (Nistér 2003; Chum and Matas 2005).

The topic of registering 3D point data sets is called *absolute orientation* (Horn 1987) and *3D pose estimation* (Lorusso, Eggert, and Fisher 1995). A variety of techniques has been developed for simultaneously computing 3D point correspondences and their corresponding rigid transformations (Besl and McKay 1992; Zhang 1994; Szeliski and Lavallée 1996; Gold, Rangarajan, Lu *et al.* 1998; David, DeMenthon, Duraiswami *et al.* 2004; Li and Hartley 2007; Enqvist, Josephson, and Kahl 2009).

Camera calibration was first studied in photogrammetry (Brown 1971; Slama 1980; Atkinson 1996; Kraus 1997) but it has also been widely studied in computer vision (Tsai 1987; Gremban, Thorpe, and Kanade 1988; Champleboux, Lavallée, Szeliski *et al.* 1992; Zhang 2000; Grossberg and Nayar 2001). Vanishing points observed either from rectahedral calibration objects or man-made architecture are often used to perform rudimentary calibration (Caprile and Torre 1990; Becker and Bove 1995; Liebowitz and Zisserman 1998; Cipolla, Drummond, and Robertson 1999; Antone and Teller 2002; Criminisi, Reid, and Zisserman 2000; Hartley and Zisserman 2004; Pflugfelder 2008). Performing camera calibration without using known targets is known as *self-calibration* and is discussed in textbooks and surveys on structure from motion (Faugeras, Luong, and Maybank 1992; Hartley and Zisserman 2004; Moons, Van Gool, and Vergauwen 2010). One popular subset of such techniques uses pure rotational motion (Stein 1995; Hartley 1997b; Hartley, Hayman, de Agapito *et al.* 2000; de Agapito, Hayman, and Reid 2001; Kang and Weiss 1999; Shum and Szeliski 2000; Frahm and Koch 2003).

6.5 Exercises

Ex 6.1: Feature-based image alignment for flip-book animations   Take a set of photos of an action scene or portrait (preferably in motor-drive—continuous shooting—mode) and align them to make a composite or flip-book animation.

1. Extract features and feature descriptors using some of the techniques described in Sections 4.1.1–4.1.2.

2. Match your features using nearest neighbor matching with a nearest neighbor distance ratio test (4.18).

3. Compute an optimal 2D translation and rotation between the first image and all subsequent images, using least squares (Section 6.1.1) with optional RANSAC for robustness (Section 6.1.4).

4. Resample all of the images onto the first image's coordinate frame (Section 3.6.1) using either bilinear or bicubic resampling and optionally crop them to their common area.

5. Convert the resulting images into an animated GIF (using software available from the Web) or optionally implement cross-dissolves to turn them into a "slo-mo" video.

6. (Optional) Combine this technique with feature-based (Exercise 3.25) morphing.

Ex 6.2: Panography Create the kind of panograph discussed in Section 6.1.2 and commonly found on the Web.

1. Take a series of interesting overlapping photos.

2. Use the feature detector, descriptor, and matcher developed in Exercises 4.1–4.4 (or existing software) to match features among the images.

3. Turn each connected component of matching features into a *track*, i.e., assign a unique index i to each track, discarding any tracks that are inconsistent (contain two different features in the same image).

4. Compute a global translation for each image using Equation (6.12).

5. Since your matches probably contain errors, turn the above least square metric into a robust metric (6.25) and re-solve your system using iteratively reweighted least squares.

6. Compute the size of the resulting composite canvas and resample each image into its final position on the canvas. (Keeping track of bounding boxes will make this more efficient.)

7. Average all of the images, or choose some kind of ordering and implement translucent *over* compositing (3.8).

8. (Optional) Extend your parametric motion model to include rotations and scale, i.e., the similarity transform given in Table 6.1. Discuss how you could handle the case of translations and rotations only (no scale).

9. (Optional) Write a simple tool to let the user adjust the ordering and opacity, and add or remove images.

10. (Optional) Write down a different least squares problem that involves pairwise matching of images. Discuss why this might be better or worse than the global matching formula given in (6.12).

Ex 6.3: 2D rigid/Euclidean matching Several alternative approaches are given in Section 6.1.3 for estimating a 2D rigid (Euclidean) alignment.

1. Implement the various alternatives and compare their accuracy on synthetic data, i.e., random 2D point clouds with noisy feature positions.

2. One approach is to estimate the translations from the centroids and then estimate rotation in polar coordinates. Do you need to weight the angles obtained from a polar decomposition in some way to get the statistically correct estimate?

3. How can you modify your techniques to take into account either scalar (6.10) or full two-dimensional point covariance weightings (6.11)? Do all of the previously developed "shortcuts" still work or does full weighting require iterative optimization?

Ex 6.4: 2D match move/augmented reality   Replace a picture in a magazine or a book with a different image or video.

1. With a webcam, take a picture of a magazine or book page.

2. Outline a figure or picture on the page with a rectangle, i.e., draw over the four sides as they appear in the image.

3. Match features in this area with each new image frame.

4. Replace the original image with an "advertising" insert, warping the new image with the appropriate homography.

5. Try your approach on a clip from a sporting event (e.g., indoor or outdoor soccer) to implement a billboard replacement.

Ex 6.5: 3D joystick   Track a Rubik's cube to implement a 3D joystick/mouse control.

1. Get out an old Rubik's cube (or get one from your parents).

2. Write a program to detect the center of each colored square.

3. Group these centers into lines and then find the vanishing points for each face.

4. Estimate the rotation angle and focal length from the vanishing points.

5. Estimate the full 3D pose (including translation) by finding one or more 3×3 grids and recovering the plane's full equation from this known homography using the technique developed by Zhang (2000).

6. Alternatively, since you already know the rotation, simply estimate the unknown translation from the known 3D corner points on the cube and their measured 2D locations using either linear or non-linear least squares.

7. Use the 3D rotation and position to control a VRML or 3D game viewer.

Ex 6.6: Rotation-based calibration   Take an outdoor or indoor sequence from a rotating camera with very little parallax and use it to calibrate the focal length of your camera using the techniques described in Section 6.3.4 or Sections 9.1.3–9.2.1.

1. Take out any radial distortion in the images using one of the techniques from Exercises 6.10–6.11 or using parameters supplied for a given camera by your instructor.

2. Detect and match feature points across neighboring frames and chain them into feature tracks.

3. Compute homographies between overlapping frames and use Equations (6.56–6.57) to get an estimate of the focal length.

4. Compute a full $360°$ panorama and update your focal length estimate to close the gap (Section 9.1.4).

5. (Optional) Perform a complete bundle adjustment in the rotation matrices and focal length to obtain the highest quality estimate (Section 9.2.1).

Ex 6.7: Target-based calibration   Use a three-dimensional target to calibrate your camera.

1. Construct a three-dimensional calibration pattern with known 3D locations. It is not easy to get high accuracy unless you use a machine shop, but you can get close using heavy plywood and printed patterns.

2. Find the corners, e.g, using a line finder and intersecting the lines.

3. Implement one of the iterative calibration and pose estimation algorithms described in Tsai (1987); Bogart (1991); Gleicher and Witkin (1992) or the system described in Section 6.2.2.

4. Take many pictures at different distances and orientations relative to the calibration target and report on both your re-projection errors and accuracy. (To do the latter, you may need to use simulated data.)

Ex 6.8: Calibration accuracy   Compare the three calibration techniques (plane-based, rotation-based, and 3D-target-based).

One approach is to have a different student implement each one and to compare the results. Another approach is to use synthetic data, potentially re-using the software you developed for Exercise 2.3. The advantage of using synthetic data is that you know the ground truth for the calibration and pose parameters, you can easily run lots of experiments, and you can synthetically vary the noise in your measurements.

Here are some possible guidelines for constructing your test sets:

1. Assume a medium-wide focal length (say, $50°$ field of view).

2. For the plane-based technique, generate a 2D grid target and project it at different inclinations.

3. For a 3D target, create an inner cube corner and position it so that it fills most of field of view.

4. For the rotation technique, scatter points uniformly on a sphere until you get a similar number of points as for other techniques.

Before comparing your techniques, predict which one will be the most accurate (normalize your results by the square root of the number of points used).

Add varying amounts of noise to your measurements and describe the noise sensitivity of your various techniques.

Ex 6.9: Single view metrology   Implement a system to measure dimensions and reconstruct a 3D model from a single image of a man-made scene using visible vanishing directions (Section 6.3.3) (Criminisi, Reid, and Zisserman 2000).

1. Find the three orthogonal vanishing points from parallel lines and use them to establish the three coordinate axes (rotation matrix R of the camera relative to the scene). If two of the vanishing points are finite (not at infinity), use them to compute the focal length, assuming a known optical center. Otherwise, find some other way to calibrate your camera; you could use some of the techniques described by Schaffalitzky and Zisserman (2000).

2. Click on a ground plane point to establish your origin and click on a point a known distance away to establish the scene scale. This lets you compute the translation t between the camera and the scene. As an alternative, click on a pair of points, one on the ground plane and one above it, and use the known height to establish the scene scale.

3. Write a user interface that lets you click on ground plane points to recover their 3D locations. (Hint: you already know the camera matrix, so knowledge of a point's z value is sufficient to recover its 3D location.) Click on pairs of points (one on the ground plane, one above it) to measure vertical heights.

4. Extend your system to let you draw quadrilaterals in the scene that correspond to axis-aligned rectangles in the world, using some of the techniques described by Sinha, Steedly, Szeliski *et al.* (2008). Export your 3D rectangles to a VRML or PLY[15] file.

5. (Optional) Warp the pixels enclosed by the quadrilateral using the correct homography to produce a texture map for each planar polygon.

Ex 6.10: Radial distortion with plumb lines   Implement a plumb-line algorithm to determine the radial distortion parameters.

1. Take some images of scenes with lots of straight lines, e.g., hallways in your home or office, and try to get some of the lines as close to the edges of the image as possible.

2. Extract the edges and link them into curves, as described in Section 4.2.2 and Exercise 4.8.

3. Fit quadratic or elliptic curves to the linked edges using a generalization of the successive line approximation algorithm described in Section 4.3.1 and Exercise 4.11 and keep the curves that fit this form well.

4. For each curved segment, fit a straight line and minimize the perpendicular distance between the curve and the line while adjusting the radial distortion parameters.

5. Alternate between re-fitting the straight line and adjusting the radial distortion parameters until convergence.

---

[15] http://meshlab.sf.net.

Ex 6.11: Radial distortion with a calibration target   Use a grid calibration target to determine the radial distortion parameters.

1. Print out a planar calibration target, mount it on a stiff board, and get it to fill your field of view.

2. Detect the squares, lines, or dots in your calibration target.

3. Estimate the homography mapping the target to the camera from the central portion of the image that does not have any radial distortion.

4. Predict the positions of the remaining targets and use the differences between the observed and predicted positions to estimate the radial distortion.

5. (Optional) Fit a general spline model (for severe distortion) instead of the quartic distortion model.

6. (Optional) Extend your technique to calibrate a fisheye lens.

Ex 6.12: Chromatic aberration   Use the radial distortion estimates for each color channel computed in the previous exercise to clean up wide-angle lens images by warping all of the channels into alignment. (Optional) Straighten out the images at the same time.

Can you think of any reasons why this warping strategy may not always work?

Chapter 7

Structure from motion

R. Szeliski, *Computer Vision: Algorithms and Applications*, Texts in Computer Science,
DOI 10.1007/978-1-84882-935-0_7, © Springer-Verlag London Limited 2011

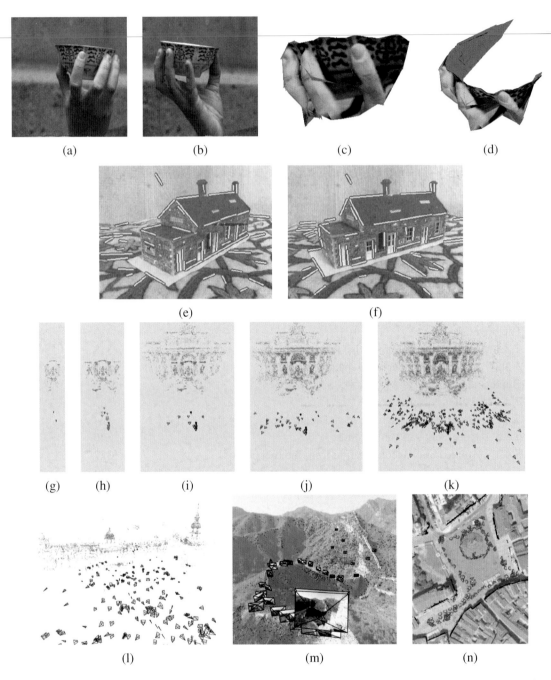

Figure 7.1 Structure from motion systems: (a–d) orthographic factorization (Tomasi and Kanade 1992) © 1992 Springer; (e–f) line matching (Schmid and Zisserman 1997) © 1997 IEEE; (g–k) incremental structure from motion (Snavely, Seitz, and Szeliski 2006); (l) 3D reconstruction of Trafalgar Square (Snavely, Seitz, and Szeliski 2006); (m) 3D reconstruction of the Great Wall of China (Snavely, Seitz, and Szeliski 2006); (n) 3D reconstruction of the Old Town Square, Prague (Snavely, Seitz, and Szeliski 2006) © 2006 ACM.

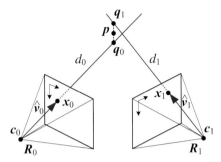

Figure 7.2   3D point triangulation by finding the point p that lies nearest to all of the optical rays $c_j + d_j\hat{v}_j$.

In the previous chapter, we saw how 2D and 3D point sets could be aligned and how such alignments could be used to estimate both a camera's pose and its internal calibration parameters. In this chapter, we look at the converse problem of estimating the locations of 3D points from multiple images given only a sparse set of correspondences between image features. While this process often involves simultaneously estimating both 3D geometry (structure) and camera pose (motion), it is commonly known as *structure from motion* (Ullman 1979).

The topics of projective geometry and structure from motion are extremely rich and some excellent textbooks and surveys have been written on them (Faugeras and Luong 2001; Hartley and Zisserman 2004; Moons, Van Gool, and Vergauwen 2010). This chapter skips over a lot of the richer material available in these books, such as the trifocal tensor and algebraic techniques for full self-calibration, and concentrates instead on the basics that we have found useful in large-scale, image-based reconstruction problems (Snavely, Seitz, and Szeliski 2006).

We begin with a brief discussion of *triangulation* (Section 7.1), which is the problem of estimating a point's 3D location when it is seen from multiple cameras. Next, we look at the two-frame structure from motion problem (Section 7.2), which involves the determination of the *epipolar geometry* between two cameras and which can also be used to recover certain information about the camera intrinsics using self-calibration (Section 7.2.2). Section 7.3 looks at *factorization* approaches to simultaneously estimating structure and motion from large numbers of point tracks using orthographic approximations to the projection model. We then develop a more general and useful approach to structure from motion, namely the simultaneous *bundle adjustment* of all the camera and 3D structure parameters (Section 7.4). We also look at special cases that arise when there are higher-level structures, such as lines and planes, in the scene (Section 7.5).

7.1 Triangulation

The problem of determining a point's 3D position from a set of corresponding image locations and known camera positions is known as *triangulation*. This problem is the converse of the pose estimation problem we studied in Section 6.2.

One of the simplest ways to solve this problem is to find the 3D point p that lies closest to all of the 3D rays corresponding to the 2D matching feature locations $\{x_j\}$ observed by cameras $\{P_j = K_j[R_j|t_j]\}$, where $t_j = -R_j c_j$ and c_j is the jth camera center (2.55–2.56). As you can see in Figure 7.2, these rays originate at c_j in a direction $\hat{v}_j = \mathcal{N}(R_j^{-1} K_j^{-1} x_j)$. The nearest point to p on this ray, which we denote as q_j, minimizes the distance

$$\|c_j + d_j \hat{v}_j - p\|^2, \tag{7.1}$$

which has a minimum at $d_j = \hat{v}_j \cdot (p - c_j)$. Hence,

$$q_j = c_j + (\hat{v}_j \hat{v}_j^T)(p - c_j) = c_j + (p - c_j)_\|, \tag{7.2}$$

in the notation of Equation (2.29), and the squared distance between p and q_j is

$$r_j^2 = \|(I - \hat{v}_j \hat{v}_j^T)(p - c_j)\|^2 = \|(p - c_j)_\perp\|^2. \tag{7.3}$$

The optimal value for p, which lies closest to all of the rays, can be computed as a regular least squares problem by summing over all the r_j^2 and finding the optimal value of p,

$$p = \left[\sum_j (I - \hat{v}_j \hat{v}_j^T) \right]^{-1} \left[\sum_j (I - \hat{v}_j \hat{v}_j^T) c_j \right]. \tag{7.4}$$

An alternative formulation, which is more statistically optimal and which can produce significantly better estimates if some of the cameras are closer to the 3D point than others, is to minimize the residual in the measurement equations

$$x_j = \frac{p_{00}^{(j)} X + p_{01}^{(j)} Y + p_{02}^{(j)} Z + p_{03}^{(j)} W}{p_{20}^{(j)} X + p_{21}^{(j)} Y + p_{22}^{(j)} Z + p_{23}^{(j)} W} \tag{7.5}$$

$$y_j = \frac{p_{10}^{(j)} X + p_{11}^{(j)} Y + p_{12}^{(j)} Z + p_{13}^{(j)} W}{p_{20}^{(j)} X + p_{21}^{(j)} Y + p_{22}^{(j)} Z + p_{23}^{(j)} W}, \tag{7.6}$$

where (x_j, y_j) are the measured 2D feature locations and $\{p_{00}^{(j)} \ldots p_{23}^{(j)}\}$ are the known entries in camera matrix P_j (Sutherland 1974).

As with Equations (6.21, 6.33, and 6.34), this set of non-linear equations can be converted into a linear least squares problem by multiplying both sides of the denominator. Note that if we use homogeneous coordinates $p = (X, Y, Z, W)$, the resulting set of equations is homogeneous and is best solved as a singular value decomposition (SVD) or eigenvalue problem (looking for the smallest singular vector or eigenvector). If we set $W = 1$, we can use regular linear least squares, but the resulting system may be singular or poorly conditioned, i.e., if all of the viewing rays are parallel, as occurs for points far away from the camera.

For this reason, it is generally preferable to parameterize 3D points using homogeneous coordinates, especially if we know that there are likely to be points at greatly varying distances from the cameras. Of course, minimizing the set of observations (7.5–7.6) using non-linear least squares, as described in (6.14 and 6.23), is preferable to using linear least squares, regardless of the representation chosen.

For the case of two observations, it turns out that the location of the point p that exactly minimizes the true reprojection error (7.5–7.6) can be computed using the solution of degree six equations (Hartley and Sturm 1997). Another problem to watch out for with triangulation is the issue of *chirality*, i.e., ensuring that the reconstructed points lie in front of all the

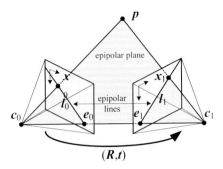

Figure 7.3 Epipolar geometry: The vectors $t = c_1 - c_0$, $p - c_0$ and $p - c_1$ are co-planar and define the basic epipolar constraint expressed in terms of the pixel measurements x_0 and x_1.

cameras (Hartley 1998). While this cannot always be guaranteed, a useful heuristic is to take the points that lie behind the cameras because their rays are diverging (imagine Figure 7.2 where the rays were pointing *away* from each other) and to place them on the plane at infinity by setting their W values to 0.

7.2 Two-frame structure from motion

So far in our study of 3D reconstruction, we have always assumed that either the 3D point positions or the 3D camera poses are known in advance. In this section, we take our first look at *structure from motion*, which is the simultaneous recovery of 3D structure and pose from image correspondences.

Consider Figure 7.3, which shows a 3D point p being viewed from two cameras whose relative position can be encoded by a rotation R and a translation t. Since we do not know anything about the camera positions, without loss of generality, we can set the first camera at the origin $c_0 = 0$ and at a canonical orientation $R_0 = I$.

Now notice that the observed location of point p in the first image, $p_0 = d_0 \hat{x}_0$ is mapped into the second image by the transformation

$$d_1 \hat{x}_1 = p_1 = R p_0 + t = R(d_0 \hat{x}_0) + t, \tag{7.7}$$

where $\hat{x}_j = K_j^{-1} x_j$ are the (local) ray direction vectors. Taking the cross product of both sides with t in order to annihilate it on the right hand side yields[1]

$$d_1 [t]_\times \hat{x}_1 = d_0 [t]_\times R \hat{x}_0. \tag{7.8}$$

Taking the dot product of both sides with $\hat{x}_1$ yields

$$d_0 \hat{x}_1^T ([t]_\times R) \hat{x}_0 = d_1 \hat{x}_1^T [t]_\times \hat{x}_1 = 0, \tag{7.9}$$

since the right hand side is a triple product with two identical entries. (Another way to say this is that the cross product matrix $[t]_\times$ is skew symmetric and returns 0 when pre- and post-multiplied by the same vector.)

---

[1] The cross-product operator $[\ ]_\times$ was introduced in (2.32).

We therefore arrive at the basic *epipolar constraint*

$$\hat{x}_1^T E \hat{x}_0 = 0, \tag{7.10}$$

where

$$E = [t]_\times R \tag{7.11}$$

is called the *essential matrix* (Longuet-Higgins 1981).

An alternative way to derive the epipolar constraint is to notice that in order for the cameras to be oriented so that the rays $\hat{x}_0$ and $\hat{x}_1$ intersect in 3D at point p, the vectors connecting the two camera centers $c_1 - c_0 = -R_1^{-1}t$ and the rays corresponding to pixels x_0 and x_1, namely $R_j^{-1}\hat{x}_j$, must be co-planar. This requires that the triple product

$$(\hat{x}_0, R^{-1}\hat{x}_1, -R^{-1}t) = (R\hat{x}_0, \hat{x}_1, -t) = \hat{x}_1 \cdot (t \times R\hat{x}_0) = \hat{x}_1^T([t]_\times R)\hat{x}_0 = 0. \tag{7.12}$$

Notice that the essential matrix E maps a point $\hat{x}_0$ in image 0 into a line $l_1 = E\hat{x}_0$ in image 1, since $\hat{x}_1^T l_1 = 0$ (Figure 7.3). All such lines must pass through the second *epipole* e_1, which is therefore defined as the left singular vector of E with a 0 singular value, or, equivalently, the projection of the vector t into image 1. The dual (transpose) of these relationships gives us the epipolar line in the first image as $l_0 = E^T\hat{x}_1$ and e_0 as the zero-value right singular vector of E.

Given this fundamental relationship (7.10), how can we use it to recover the camera motion encoded in the essential matrix E? If we have N corresponding measurements $\{(x_{i0}, x_{i1})\}$, we can form N homogeneous equations in the nine elements of $E = \{e_{00} \ldots e_{22}\}$,

$$\begin{aligned}
x_{i0}x_{i1}e_{00} &+& y_{i0}x_{i1}e_{01} &+& x_{i1}e_{02} &+ \\
x_{i0}y_{i1}e_{00} &+& y_{i0}y_{i1}e_{11} &+& y_{i1}e_{12} &+ \\
x_{i0}e_{20} &+& y_{i0}e_{21} &+& e_{22} &= 0
\end{aligned} \tag{7.13}$$

where $x_{ij} = (x_{ij}, y_{ij}, 1)$. This can be written more compactly as

$$[x_{i1} x_{i0}^T] \otimes E = Z_i \otimes E = z_i \cdot f = 0, \tag{7.14}$$

where $\otimes$ indicates an element-wise multiplication and summation of matrix elements, and z_i and f are the rasterized (vector) forms of the $Z_i = \hat{x}_{i1}\hat{x}_{i0}^T$ and E matrices.[2] Given $N \geq 8$ such equations, we can compute an estimate (up to scale) for the entries in E using an SVD.

In the presence of noisy measurements, how close is this estimate to being statistically optimal? If you look at the entries in (7.13), you can see that some entries are the products of image measurements such as $x_{i0}y_{i1}$ and others are direct image measurements (or even the identity). If the measurements have comparable noise, the terms that are products of measurements have their noise amplified by the other element in the product, which can lead to very poor scaling, e.g., an inordinately large influence of points with large coordinates (far away from the image center).

In order to counteract this trend, Hartley (1997a) suggests that the point coordinates should be translated and scaled so that their centroid lies at the origin and their variance is unity, i.e.,

$$\tilde{x}_i = s(x_i - \mu_x) \tag{7.15}$$

$$\tilde{y}_i = s(x_i - \mu_y) \tag{7.16}$$

---

[2] We use f instead of e to denote the rasterized form of E to avoid confusion with the epipoles e_j.

such that $\sum_i \tilde{x}_i = \sum_i \tilde{y}_i = 0$ and $\sum_i \tilde{x}_i^2 + \sum_i \tilde{y}_i^2 = 2n$, where n is the number of points.[3]

Once the essential matrix $\tilde{E}$ has been computed from the transformed coordinates $\{(\tilde{x}_{i0}, \tilde{x}_{i1})\}$, where $\tilde{x}_{ij} = T_j \hat{x}_{ij}$, the original essential matrix E can be recovered as

$$E = T_1 \tilde{E} T_0. \tag{7.17}$$

In his paper, Hartley (1997a) compares the improvement due to his re-normalization strategy to alternative distance measures proposed by others such as Zhang (1998a,b) and concludes that his simple re-normalization in most cases is as effective as (or better than) alternative techniques. Torr and Fitzgibbon (2004) recommend a variant on this algorithm where the norm of the upper 2×2 sub-matrix of E is set to 1 and show that it has even better stability with respect to 2D coordinate transformations.

Once an estimate for the essential matrix E has been recovered, the direction of the translation vector t can be estimated. Note that the absolute distance between the two cameras can never be recovered from pure image measurements alone, regardless of how many cameras or points are used. Knowledge about absolute camera and point positions or distances, often called *ground control points* in photogrammetry, is always required to establish the final scale, position, and orientation.

To estimate this direction $\hat{t}$, observe that under ideal noise-free conditions, the essential matrix E is singular, i.e., $\hat{t}^T E = 0$. This singularity shows up as a singular value of 0 when an SVD of E is performed,

$$E = [\hat{t}]_\times R = U \Sigma V^T = \begin{bmatrix} u_0 & u_1 & \hat{t} \end{bmatrix} \begin{bmatrix} 1 & & \\ & 1 & \\ & & 0 \end{bmatrix} \begin{bmatrix} v_0^T \\ v_1^T \\ v_2^T \end{bmatrix} \tag{7.18}$$

When E is computed from noisy measurements, the singular vector associated with the smallest singular value gives us $\hat{t}$. (The other two singular values should be similar but are not, in general, equal to 1 because E is only computed up to an unknown scale.)

Because E is rank-deficient, it turns out that we actually only need seven correspondences of the form of Equation (7.14) instead of eight to estimate this matrix (Hartley 1994a; Torr and Murray 1997; Hartley and Zisserman 2004). (The advantage of using fewer correspondences inside a RANSAC robust fitting stage is that fewer random samples need to be generated.) From this set of seven homogeneous equations (which we can stack into a 7×9 matrix for SVD analysis), we can find two independent vectors, say f_0 and f_1 such that $z_i \cdot f_j = 0$. These two vectors can be converted back into 3×3 matrices E_0 and E_1, which span the solution space for

$$E = \alpha E_0 + (1 - \alpha) E_1. \tag{7.19}$$

To find the correct value of α, we observe that E has a zero determinant, since it is rank deficient, and hence

$$\det |\alpha E_0 + (1 - \alpha) E_1| = 0. \tag{7.20}$$

This gives us a cubic equation in α, which has either one or three solutions (roots). Substituting these values into (7.19) to obtain E, we can test this essential matrix against other unused feature correspondences to select the correct one.

---

[3] More precisely, Hartley (1997a) suggests scaling the points "so that the average distance from the origin is equal to $\sqrt{2}$" but the heuristic of unit variance is faster to compute (does not require per-point square roots) and should yield comparable improvements.

Once $\hat{t}$ has been recovered, how can we estimate the corresponding rotation matrix R? Recall that the cross-product operator $[\hat{t}]_\times$ (2.32) projects a vector onto a set of orthogonal basis vectors that include $\hat{t}$, zeros out the $\hat{t}$ component, and rotates the other two by $90°$,

$$[\hat{t}]_\times = SZR_{90°}S^T = \begin{bmatrix} s_0 & s_1 & \hat{t} \end{bmatrix} \begin{bmatrix} 1 & & \\ & 1 & \\ & & 0 \end{bmatrix} \begin{bmatrix} 0 & -1 & \\ 1 & 0 & \\ & & 1 \end{bmatrix} \begin{bmatrix} s_0^T \\ s_1^T \\ \hat{t}^T \end{bmatrix}, \quad (7.21)$$

where $\hat{t} = s_0 \times s_1$. From Equations (7.18 and 7.21), we get

$$E = [\hat{t}]_\times R = SZR_{90°}S^T R = U\Sigma V^T, \quad (7.22)$$

from which we can conclude that $S = U$. Recall that for a noise-free essential matrix, $(\Sigma = Z)$, and hence

$$R_{90°}U^T R = V^T \quad (7.23)$$

and

$$R = UR_{90°}^T V^T. \quad (7.24)$$

Unfortunately, we only know both E and $\hat{t}$ up to a sign. Furthermore, the matrices U and V are not guaranteed to be rotations (you can flip both their signs and still get a valid SVD). For this reason, we have to generate all four possible rotation matrices

$$R = \pm UR_{\pm 90°}^T V^T \quad (7.25)$$

and keep the two whose determinant $|R| = 1$. To disambiguate between the remaining pair of potential rotations, which form a *twisted pair* (Hartley and Zisserman 2004, p. 240), we need to pair them with both possible signs of the translation direction $\pm\hat{t}$ and select the combination for which the largest number of points is seen in front of both cameras.[4]

The property that points must lie in front of the camera, i.e., at a positive distance along the viewing rays emanating from the camera, is known as *chirality* (Hartley 1998). In addition to determining the signs of the rotation and translation, as described above, the chirality (sign of the distances) of the points in a reconstruction can be used inside a RANSAC procedure (along with the reprojection errors) to distinguish between likely and unlikely configurations.[5] Chirality can also be used to transform projective reconstructions (Sections 7.2.1 and 7.2.2) into *quasi-affine* reconstructions (Hartley 1998).

The normalized "eight-point algorithm" (Hartley 1997a) described above is not the only way to estimate the camera motion from correspondences. Variants include using seven points while enforcing the rank two constraint in E (7.19–7.20) and a five-point algorithm that requires finding the roots of a 10th degree polynomial (Nistér 2004). Since such algorithms use fewer points to compute their estimates, they are less sensitive to outliers when used as part of a random sampling (RANSAC) strategy.

---

[4] In the noise-free case, a single point suffices. It is safer, however, to test all or a sufficient subset of points, downweighting the ones that lie close to the plane at infinity, for which it is easy to get depth reversals.

[5] Note that as points get further away from a camera, i.e., closer toward the plane at infinity, errors in chirality become more likely.

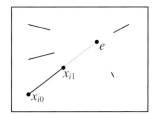

Figure 7.4 Pure translational camera motion results in visual motion where all the points move towards (or away from) a common *focus of expansion* (FOE) e. They therefore satisfy the triple product condition $(\boldsymbol{x}_0, \boldsymbol{x}_1, \boldsymbol{e}) = \boldsymbol{e} \cdot (\boldsymbol{x}_0 \times \boldsymbol{x}_1) = 0$.

Pure translation (known rotation)

In the case where we know the rotation, we can pre-rotate the points in the second image to match the viewing direction of the first. The resulting set of 3D points all move towards (or away from) the *focus of expansion* (FOE), as shown in Figure 7.4.[6] The resulting essential matrix $\boldsymbol{E}$ is (in the noise-free case) skew symmetric and so can be estimated more directly by setting $e_{ij} = -e_{ji}$ and $e_{ii} = 0$ in (7.13). Two points with non-zero parallax now suffice to estimate the FOE.

A more direct derivation of the FOE estimate can be obtained by minimizing the triple product

$$\sum_i (\boldsymbol{x}_{i0}, \boldsymbol{x}_{i1}, \boldsymbol{e})^2 = \sum_i ((\boldsymbol{x}_{i0} \times \boldsymbol{x}_{i1}) \cdot \boldsymbol{e})^2, \tag{7.26}$$

which is equivalent to finding the null space for the set of equations

$$(y_{i0} - y_{i1})e_0 + (x_{i1} - x_{i0})e_1 + (x_{i0}y_{i1} - y_{i0}x_{i1})e_2 = 0. \tag{7.27}$$

Note that, as in the eight-point algorithm, it is advisable to normalize the 2D points to have unit variance before computing this estimate.

In situations where a large number of points at infinity are available, e.g., when shooting outdoor scenes or when the camera motion is small compared to distant objects, this suggests an alternative RANSAC strategy for estimating the camera motion. First, pick a pair of points to estimate a rotation, hoping that both of the points lie at infinity (very far from the camera). Then, compute the FOE and check whether the residual error is small (indicating agreement with this rotation hypothesis) and whether the motions towards or away from the epipole (FOE) are all in the same direction (ignoring very small motions, which may be noise-contaminated).

Pure rotation

The case of pure rotation results in a degenerate estimate of the essential matrix $\boldsymbol{E}$ and of the translation direction $\hat{\boldsymbol{t}}$. Consider first the case of the rotation matrix being known. The estimates for the FOE will be degenerate, since $\boldsymbol{x}_{i0} \approx \boldsymbol{x}_{i1}$, and hence (7.27), is degenerate. A similar argument shows that the equations for the essential matrix (7.13) are also rank-deficient.

---

[6] Fans of *Star Trek* and *Star Wars* will recognize this as the "jump to hyperdrive" visual effect.

This suggests that it might be prudent before computing a full essential matrix to first compute a rotation estimate R using (6.32), potentially with just a small number of points, and then compute the residuals after rotating the points before proceeding with a full E computation.

7.2.1 Projective (uncalibrated) reconstruction

In many cases, such as when trying to build a 3D model from Internet or legacy photos taken by unknown cameras without any EXIF tags, we do not know ahead of time the intrinsic calibration parameters associated with the input images. In such situations, we can still estimate a two-frame reconstruction, although the true metric structure may not be available, e.g., orthogonal lines or planes in the world may not end up being reconstructed as orthogonal.

Consider the derivations we used to estimate the essential matrix E (7.10–7.12). In the uncalibrated case, we do not know the calibration matrices K_j, so we cannot use the normalized ray directions $\hat{x}_j = K_j^{-1} x_j$. Instead, we have access only to the image coordinates x_j, and so the essential matrix (7.10) becomes

$$\hat{x}_1^T E \hat{x}_1 = x_1^T K_1^{-T} E K_0^{-1} x_0 = x_1^T F x_0 = 0, \tag{7.28}$$

where

$$F = K_1^{-T} E K_0^{-1} = [e]_\times \tilde{H} \tag{7.29}$$

is called the *fundamental matrix* (Faugeras 1992; Hartley, Gupta, and Chang 1992; Hartley and Zisserman 2004).

Like the essential matrix, the fundamental matrix is (in principle) rank two,

$$F = [e]_\times \tilde{H} = U \Sigma V^T = \begin{bmatrix} u_0 & u_1 & e_1 \end{bmatrix} \begin{bmatrix} \sigma_0 & & \\ & \sigma_1 & \\ & & 0 \end{bmatrix} \begin{bmatrix} v_0^T \\ v_1^T \\ e_0^T \end{bmatrix}. \tag{7.30}$$

Its smallest left singular vector indicates the epipole e_1 in the image 1 and its smallest right singular vector is e_0 (Figure 7.3). The homography $\tilde{H}$ in (7.29), which in principle should equal

$$\tilde{H} = K_1^{-T} R K_0^{-1}, \tag{7.31}$$

cannot be uniquely recovered from F, since any homography of the form $\tilde{H}' = \tilde{H} + e v^T$ results in the same F matrix. (Note that $[e]_\times$ annihilates any multiple of e.)

Any one of these valid homographies $\tilde{H}$ maps some plane in the scene from one image to the other. It is not possible to tell in advance which one it is without either selecting four or more co-planar correspondences to compute $\tilde{H}$ as part of the F estimation process (in a manner analogous to guessing a rotation for E) or mapping all points in one image through $\tilde{H}$ and seeing which ones line up with their corresponding locations in the other.[7]

In order to create a *projective* reconstruction of the scene, we can pick any valid homography $\tilde{H}$ that satisfies Equation (7.29). For example, following a technique analogous to Equations (7.18–7.24), we get

$$F = [e]_\times \tilde{H} = S Z R_{90°} S^T \tilde{H} = U \Sigma V^T \tag{7.32}$$

---

[7] This process is sometimes referred to as *plane plus parallax* (Section 2.1.5) (Kumar, Anandan, and Hanna 1994; Sawhney 1994).

and hence

$$\tilde{\boldsymbol{H}} = \boldsymbol{U}\boldsymbol{R}_{90°}^T\hat{\boldsymbol{\Sigma}}\boldsymbol{V}^T, \tag{7.33}$$

where $\hat{\boldsymbol{\Sigma}}$ is the singular value matrix with the smallest value replaced by a reasonable alternative (say, the middle value).[8] We can then form a pair of camera matrices

$$\boldsymbol{P}_0 = [\boldsymbol{I}|\boldsymbol{0}] \quad \text{and} \quad \boldsymbol{P}_0 = [\tilde{\boldsymbol{H}}|\boldsymbol{e}], \tag{7.34}$$

from which a projective reconstruction of the scene can be computed using triangulation (Section 7.1).

While the projective reconstruction may not be useful in practice, it can often be *upgraded* to an affine or metric reconstruction, as detailed below. Even without this step, however, the fundamental matrix $\boldsymbol{F}$ can be very useful in finding additional correspondences, as they must all lie on corresponding epipolar lines, i.e., any feature $\boldsymbol{x}_0$ in image 0 must have its correspondence lying on the associated epipolar line $\boldsymbol{l}_1 = \boldsymbol{F}\boldsymbol{x}_0$ in image 1, assuming that the point motions are due to a rigid transformation.

7.2.2 Self-calibration

The results of structure from motion computation are much more useful (and intelligible) if a *metric* reconstruction is obtained, i.e., one in which parallel lines are parallel, orthogonal walls are at right angles, and the reconstructed model is a scaled version of reality. Over the years, a large number of *self-calibration* (or *auto-calibration*) techniques have been developed for converting a projective reconstruction into a metric one, which is equivalent to recovering the unknown calibration matrices $\boldsymbol{K}_j$ associated with each image (Hartley and Zisserman 2004; Moons, Van Gool, and Vergauwen 2010).

In situations where certain additional information is known about the scene, different methods may be employed. For example, if there are parallel lines in the scene (usually, having several lines converge on the same vanishing point is good evidence), three or more vanishing points, which are the images of points at infinity, can be used to establish the homography for the plane at infinity, from which focal lengths and rotations can be recovered. If two or more finite *orthogonal* vanishing points have been observed, the single-image calibration method based on vanishing points (Section 6.3.2) can be used instead.

In the absence of such external information, it is not possible to recover a fully parameterized independent calibration matrix $\boldsymbol{K}_j$ for each image from correspondences alone. To see this, consider the set of all camera matrices $\boldsymbol{P}_j = \boldsymbol{K}_j[\boldsymbol{R}_j|\boldsymbol{t}_j]$ projecting world coordinates $\boldsymbol{p}_i = (X_i, Y_i, Z_i, W_i)$ into screen coordinates $\boldsymbol{x}_{ij} \sim \boldsymbol{P}_j\boldsymbol{p}_i$. Now consider transforming the 3D scene $\{\boldsymbol{p}_i\}$ through an arbitrary 4×4 projective transformation $\tilde{\boldsymbol{H}}$, yielding a new model consisting of points $\boldsymbol{p}_i' = \tilde{\boldsymbol{H}}\boldsymbol{p}_i$. Post-multiplying each $\boldsymbol{P}_j$ matrix by $\tilde{\boldsymbol{H}}^{-1}$ still produces the same screen coordinates and a new set calibration matrices can be computed by applying RQ decomposition to the new camera matrix $\boldsymbol{P}_j' = \boldsymbol{P}_j\tilde{\boldsymbol{H}}^{-1}$.

For this reason, all self-calibration methods assume some restricted form of the calibration matrix, either by setting or equating some of their elements or by assuming that they do not vary over time. While most of the techniques discussed by Hartley and Zisserman (2004);

---

[8] Hartley and Zisserman (2004, p. 237) recommend using $\tilde{\boldsymbol{H}} = [\boldsymbol{e}]_\times \boldsymbol{F}$ (Luong and Viéville 1996), which places the camera on the plane at infinity.

Moons, Van Gool, and Vergauwen (2010) require three or more frames, in this section we present a simple technique that can recover the focal lengths (f_0, f_1) of both images from the fundamental matrix $\boldsymbol{F}$ in a two-frame reconstruction (Hartley and Zisserman 2004, p. 456).

To accomplish this, we assume that the camera has zero skew, a known aspect ratio (usually set to 1), and a known optical center, as in Equation (2.59). How reasonable is this assumption in practice? The answer, as with many questions, is "it depends".

If absolute metric accuracy is required, as in photogrammetry applications, it is imperative to pre-calibrate the cameras using one of the techniques from Section 6.3 and to use ground control points to pin down the reconstruction. If instead, we simply wish to reconstruct the world for visualization or image-based rendering applications, as in the Photo Tourism system of Snavely, Seitz, and Szeliski (2006), this assumption is quite reasonable in practice.

Most cameras today have square pixels and an optical center near the middle of the image, and are much more likely to deviate from a simple camera model due to radial distortion (Section 6.3.5), which should be compensated for whenever possible. The biggest problems occur when images have been cropped off-center, in which case the optical center will no longer be in the middle, or when perspective pictures have been taken of a different picture, in which case a general camera matrix becomes necessary.[9]

Given these caveats, the two-frame focal length estimation algorithm based on the Kruppa equations developed by Hartley and Zisserman (2004, p. 456) proceeds as follows. Take the left and right singular vectors $\{\boldsymbol{u}_0, \boldsymbol{u}_1, \boldsymbol{v}_0, \boldsymbol{v}_1\}$ of the fundamental matrix $\boldsymbol{F}$ (7.30) and their associated singular values $\{\sigma_0, \sigma_1\}$ and form the following set of equations:

$$\frac{\boldsymbol{u}_1^T \boldsymbol{D}_0 \boldsymbol{u}_1}{\sigma_0^2 \boldsymbol{v}_0^T \boldsymbol{D}_1 \boldsymbol{v}_0} = -\frac{\boldsymbol{u}_0^T \boldsymbol{D}_0 \boldsymbol{u}_1}{\sigma_0 \sigma_1 \boldsymbol{v}_0^T \boldsymbol{D}_1 \boldsymbol{v}_1} = \frac{\boldsymbol{u}_0^T \boldsymbol{D}_0 \boldsymbol{u}_0}{\sigma_1^2 \boldsymbol{v}_1^T \boldsymbol{D}_1 \boldsymbol{v}_1}, \tag{7.35}$$

where the two matrices

$$\boldsymbol{D}_j = \boldsymbol{K}_j \boldsymbol{K}_j^T = \mathrm{diag}(f_j^2, f_j^2, 1) = \begin{bmatrix} f_j^2 & & \\ & f_j^2 & \\ & & 1 \end{bmatrix} \tag{7.36}$$

encode the unknown focal lengths. For simplicity, let us rewrite each of the numerators and denominators in (7.35) as

$$e_{ij0}(f_0^2) = \boldsymbol{u}_i^T \boldsymbol{D}_0 \boldsymbol{u}_j = a_{ij} + b_{ij} f_0^2, \tag{7.37}$$
$$e_{ij1}(f_1^2) = \sigma_i \sigma_j \boldsymbol{v}_i^T \boldsymbol{D}_1 \boldsymbol{v}_j = c_{ij} + d_{ij} f_1^2. \tag{7.38}$$

Notice that each of these is affine (linear plus constant) in either f_0^2 or f_1^2. Hence, we can cross-multiply these equations to obtain quadratic equations in f_j^2, which can readily be solved. (See also the work by Bougnoux (1998) for some alternative formulations.)

An alternative solution technique is to observe that we have a set of three equations related by an unknown scalar λ, i.e.,

$$e_{ij0}(f_0^2) = \lambda e_{ij1}(f_1^2) \tag{7.39}$$

(Richard Hartley, personal communication, July 2009). These can readily be solved to yield $(f_0^2, \lambda f_1^2, \lambda)$ and hence (f_0, f_1).

---

[9] In Photo Tourism, our system registered photographs of an information sign outside Notre Dame with real pictures of the cathedral.

How well does this approach work in practice? There are certain degenerate configurations, such as when there is no rotation or when the optical axes intersect, when it does not work at all. (In such a situation, you can vary the focal lengths of the cameras and obtain a deeper or shallower reconstruction, which is an example of a *bas-relief ambiguity* (Section 7.4.3).) Hartley and Zisserman (2004) recommend using techniques based on three or more frames. However, if you find two images for which the estimates of $(f_0^2, \lambda f_1^2, \lambda)$ are well conditioned, they can be used to initialize a more complete bundle adjustment of all the parameters (Section 7.4). An alternative, which is often used in systems such as Photo Tourism, is to use camera EXIF tags or generic default values to initialize focal length estimates and refine them as part of bundle adjustment.

7.2.3 *Application*: View morphing

An interesting application of basic two-frame structure from motion is *view morphing* (also known as *view interpolation*, see Section 13.1), which can be used to generate a smooth 3D animation from one view of a 3D scene to another (Chen and Williams 1993; Seitz and Dyer 1996).

To create such a transition, you must first smoothly interpolate the camera matrices, i.e., the camera positions, orientations, and focal lengths. While simple linear interpolation can be used (representing rotations as quaternions (Section 2.1.4)), a more pleasing effect is obtained by *easing in* and *easing out* the camera parameters, e.g., using a raised cosine, as well as moving the camera along a more circular trajectory (Snavely, Seitz, and Szeliski 2006).

To generate in-between frames, either a full set of 3D correspondences needs to be established (Section 11.3) or 3D models (proxies) must be created for each reference view. Section 13.1 describes several widely used approaches to this problem. One of the simplest is to just triangulate the set of matched feature points in each image, e.g., using Delaunay triangulation. As the 3D points are re-projected into their intermediate views, pixels can be mapped from their original source images to their new views using affine or projective mapping (Szeliski and Shum 1997). The final image is then composited using a linear blend of the two reference images, as with usual morphing (Section 3.6.3).

7.3 Factorization

When processing video sequences, we often get extended *feature tracks* (Section 4.1.4) from which it is possible to recover the structure and motion using a process called *factorization*. Consider the tracks generated by a rotating ping pong ball, which has been marked with dots to make its shape and motion more discernable (Figure 7.5). We can readily see from the shape of the tracks that the moving object must be a sphere, but how can we infer this mathematically?

It turns out that, under orthography or related models we discuss below, the shape and motion can be recovered simultaneously using a singular value decomposition (Tomasi and Kanade 1992). Consider the orthographic and weak perspective projection models introduced in Equations (2.47–2.49). Since the last row is always $[0\,0\,0\,1]$, there is no perspective division and we can write

$$\boldsymbol{x}_{ji} = \tilde{\boldsymbol{P}}_j \bar{\boldsymbol{p}}_i, \tag{7.40}$$

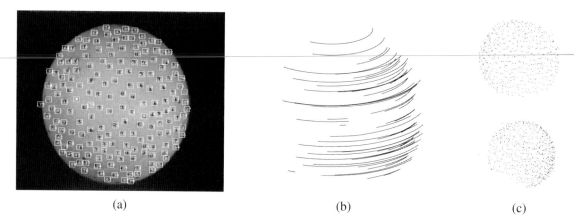

(a)   (b)   (c)

Figure 7.5 3D reconstruction of a rotating ping pong ball using factorization (Tomasi and Kanade 1992) © 1992 Springer: (a) sample image with tracked features overlaid; (b) subsampled feature motion stream; (c) two views of the reconstructed 3D model.

where $\boldsymbol{x}_{ji}$ is the location of the ith point in the jth frame, $\tilde{\boldsymbol{P}}_j$ is the upper 2×4 portion of the projection matrix $\boldsymbol{P}_j$, and $\bar{\boldsymbol{p}}_i = (X_i, Y_i, Z_i, 1)$ is the augmented 3D point position.[10]

Let us assume (for now) that every point i is visible in every frame j. We can take the *centroid* (average) of the projected point locations $\boldsymbol{x}_{ji}$ in frame j,

$$\bar{\boldsymbol{x}}_j = \frac{1}{N} \sum_i \boldsymbol{x}_{ji} = \tilde{\boldsymbol{P}}_j \frac{1}{N} \sum_i \bar{\boldsymbol{p}}_i = \tilde{\boldsymbol{P}}_j \bar{\boldsymbol{c}}, \tag{7.41}$$

where $\bar{\boldsymbol{c}} = (\bar{X}, \bar{Y}, \bar{Z}, 1)$ is the augmented 3D centroid of the point cloud.

Since world coordinate frames in structure from motion are always arbitrary, i.e., we cannot recover true 3D locations without ground control points (known measurements), we can place the origin of the world at the centroid of the points, i.e, $\bar{X} = \bar{Y} = \bar{Z} = 0$, so that $\bar{\boldsymbol{c}} = (0, 0, 0, 1)$. We see from this that the centroid of the 2D points in each frame $\bar{\boldsymbol{x}}_j$ directly gives us the last element of $\tilde{\boldsymbol{P}}_j$.

Let $\tilde{\boldsymbol{x}}_{ji} = \boldsymbol{x}_{ji} - \bar{\boldsymbol{x}}_j$ be the 2D point locations after their image centroid has been subtracted. We can now write

$$\tilde{\boldsymbol{x}}_{ji} = \boldsymbol{M}_j \boldsymbol{p}_i, \tag{7.42}$$

where $\boldsymbol{M}_j$ is the upper 2×3 portion of the projection matrix $\boldsymbol{P}_j$ and $\boldsymbol{p}_i = (X_i, Y_i, Z_i)$. We can concatenate all of these measurement equations into one large matrix

$$\hat{\boldsymbol{X}} = \begin{bmatrix} \tilde{\boldsymbol{x}}_{11} & \cdots & \tilde{\boldsymbol{x}}_{1i} & \cdots & \tilde{\boldsymbol{x}}_{1N} \\ \vdots & & \vdots & & \vdots \\ \tilde{\boldsymbol{x}}_{j1} & \cdots & \tilde{\boldsymbol{x}}_{ji} & \cdots & \tilde{\boldsymbol{x}}_{jN} \\ \vdots & & \vdots & & \vdots \\ \tilde{\boldsymbol{x}}_{M1} & \cdots & \tilde{\boldsymbol{x}}_{Mi} & \cdots & \tilde{\boldsymbol{x}}_{MN} \end{bmatrix} = \begin{bmatrix} \boldsymbol{M}_1 \\ \vdots \\ \boldsymbol{M}_j \\ \vdots \\ \boldsymbol{M}_M \end{bmatrix} \begin{bmatrix} \boldsymbol{p}_1 & \cdots & \boldsymbol{p}_i & \cdots & \boldsymbol{p}_N \end{bmatrix} = \hat{\boldsymbol{M}} \hat{\boldsymbol{S}}. \tag{7.43}$$

$\hat{\boldsymbol{X}}$ is called the *measurement* matrix and $\hat{\boldsymbol{M}}$ and ($\hat{\boldsymbol{S}}$ are the *motion*) and *structure* matrices, respectively (Tomasi and Kanade 1992).

---

[10] In this section, we index the 2D point positions as $\boldsymbol{x}_{ji}$ instead of $\boldsymbol{x}_{ij}$, since this is the convention adopted by factorization papers (Tomasi and Kanade 1992) and is consistent with the factorization given in (7.43).

Because the motion matrix $\hat{M}$ is $2M \times 3$ and the structure matrix $\hat{S}$ is $3 \times N$, an SVD applied to $\hat{X}$ has only three non-zero singular values. In the case where the measurements in $\hat{X}$ are noisy, SVD returns the rank-three factorization of $\hat{X}$ that is the closest to $\hat{X}$ in a least squares sense (Tomasi and Kanade 1992; Golub and Van Loan 1996; Hartley and Zisserman 2004).

It would be nice if the SVD of $\hat{X} = U\Sigma V^T$ directly returned the matrices $\hat{M}$ and $\hat{S}$, but it does not. Instead, we can write the relationship

$$\hat{X} = U\Sigma V^T = [UQ][Q^{-1}\Sigma V^T] \tag{7.44}$$

and set $\hat{M} = UQ$ and $\hat{S} = Q^{-1}\Sigma V^T$.[11]

How can we recover the values of the 3×3 matrix Q? This depends on the motion model being used. In the case of orthographic projection (2.47), the entries in M_j are the first two rows of rotation matrices R_j, so we have

$$\begin{aligned} m_{j0} \cdot m_{j0} = & \quad u_{2j}QQ^T u_{2j}^T & = 1, \\ m_{j0} \cdot m_{j1} = & \quad u_{2j}QQ^T u_{2j+1}^T & = 0, \\ m_{j1} \cdot m_{j1} = & \quad u_{2j+1}QQ^T u_{2j+1}^T & = 1, \end{aligned} \tag{7.45}$$

where u_k are the 3×1 *rows* of the matrix U. This gives us a large set of equations for the entries in the matrix QQ^T, from which the matrix Q can be recovered using a matrix square root (Appendix A.1.4). If we have scaled orthography (2.48), i.e., $M_j = s_j R_j$, the first and third equations are equal to s_j and can be set equal to each other.

Note that even once Q has been recovered, there still exists a bas-relief ambiguity, i.e., we can never be sure if the object is rotating left to right or if its depth reversed version is moving the other way. (This can be seen in the classic rotating Necker Cube visual illusion.) Additional cues, such as the appearance and disappearance of points, or perspective effects, both of which are discussed below, can be used to remove this ambiguity.

For motion models other than pure orthography, e.g., for scaled orthography or paraperspective, the approach above must be extended in the appropriate manner. Such techniques are relatively straightforward to derive from first principles; more details can be found in papers that extend the basic factorization approach to these more flexible models (Poelman and Kanade 1997). Additional extensions of the original factorization algorithm include multi-body rigid motion (Costeira and Kanade 1995), sequential updates to the factorization (Morita and Kanade 1997), the addition of lines and planes (Morris and Kanade 1998), and re-scaling the measurements to incorporate individual location uncertainties (Anandan and Irani 2002).

A disadvantage of factorization approaches is that they require a complete set of tracks, i.e., each point must be visible in each frame, in order for the factorization approach to work. Tomasi and Kanade (1992) deal with this problem by first applying factorization to smaller denser subsets and then using known camera (motion) or point (structure) estimates to *hallucinate* additional missing values, which allows them to incrementally incorporate more features and cameras. Huynh, Hartley, and Heyden (2003) extend this approach to view missing data as special cases of outliers. Buchanan and Fitzgibbon (2005) develop fast iterative algorithms for performing large matrix factorizations with missing data. The general topic of

---

[11] Tomasi and Kanade (1992) first take the square root of Σ and distribute this to U and V, but there is no particular reason to do this.

principal component analysis (PCA) with missing data also appears in other computer vision problems (Shum, Ikeuchi, and Reddy 1995; De la Torre and Black 2003; Gross, Matthews, and Baker 2006; Torresani, Hertzmann, and Bregler 2008; Vidal, Ma, and Sastry 2010).

7.3.1 Perspective and projective factorization

Another disadvantage of regular factorization is that it cannot deal with perspective cameras. One way to get around this problem is to perform an initial affine (e.g., orthographic) reconstruction and to then correct for the perspective effects in an iterative manner (Christy and Horaud 1996).

Observe that the object-centered projection model (2.76)

$$x_{ji} = s_j \frac{r_{xj} \cdot p_i + t_{xj}}{1 + \eta_j r_{zj} \cdot p_i} \tag{7.46}$$

$$y_{ji} = s_j \frac{r_{yj} \cdot p_i + t_{yj}}{1 + \eta_j r_{zj} \cdot p_i} \tag{7.47}$$

differs from the scaled orthographic projection model (7.40) by the inclusion of the denominator terms $(1 + \eta_j r_{zj} \cdot p_i)$.[12]

If we knew the correct values of $\eta_j = t_{zj}^{-1}$ and the structure and motion parameters R_j and p_i, we could cross-multiply the left hand side (visible point measurements x_{ji} and y_{ji}) by the denominator and get corrected values, for which the bilinear projection model (7.40) is exact. In practice, after an initial reconstruction, the values of η_j can be estimated independently for each frame by comparing reconstructed and sensed point positions. (The third row of the rotation matrix r_{zj} is always available as the cross-product of the first two rows.) Note that since the η_j are determined from the image measurements, the cameras do not have to be pre-calibrated, i.e., their focal lengths can be recovered from $f_j = s_j / \eta_j$.

Once the η_j have been estimated, the feature locations can then be corrected before applying another round of factorization. Note that because of the initial depth reversal ambiguity, both reconstructions have to be tried while calculating η_j. (The incorrect reconstruction will result in a negative η_j, which is not physically meaningful.) Christy and Horaud (1996) report that their algorithm usually converges in three to five iterations, with the majority of the time spent in the SVD computation.

An alternative approach, which does not assume partially calibrated cameras (known optical center, square pixels, and zero skew) is to perform a fully *projective* factorization (Sturm and Triggs 1996; Triggs 1996). In this case, the inclusion of the third row of the camera matrix in (7.40) is equivalent to multiplying each reconstructed measurement $x_{ji} = M_j p_i$ by its inverse (projective) depth $\eta_{ji} = d_{ji}^{-1} = 1/(P_{j2}p_i)$ or, equivalently, multiplying each measured position by its projective depth d_{ji},

$$\hat{X} = \begin{bmatrix} d_{11}\tilde{x}_{11} & \cdots & d_{1i}\tilde{x}_{1i} & \cdots & d_{1N}\tilde{x}_{1N} \\ \vdots & & \vdots & & \vdots \\ d_{j1}\tilde{x}_{j1} & \cdots & d_{ji}\tilde{x}_{ji} & \cdots & d_{jN}\tilde{x}_{jN} \\ \vdots & & \vdots & & \vdots \\ d_{M1}\tilde{x}_{M1} & \cdots & d_{Mi}\tilde{x}_{Mi} & \cdots & d_{MN}\tilde{x}_{MN} \end{bmatrix} = \hat{M}\hat{S}. \tag{7.48}$$

---

[12] Assuming that the optical center (c_x, c_y) lies at $(0, 0)$ and that pixels are square.

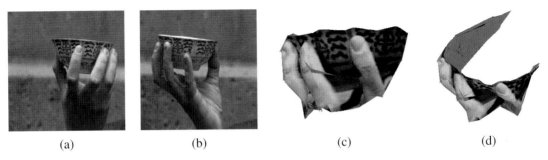

In the original paper by Sturm and Triggs (1996), the projective depths d_{ji} are obtained from two-frame reconstructions, while in later work (Triggs 1996; Oliensis and Hartley 2007), they are initialized to $d_{ji} = 1$ and updated after each iteration. Oliensis and Hartley (2007) present an update formula that is guaranteed to converge to a fixed point. None of these authors suggest actually estimating the third row of P_j as part of the projective depth computations. In any case, it is unclear when a fully projective reconstruction would be preferable to a partially calibrated one, especially if they are being used to initialize a full bundle adjustment of all the parameters.

One of the attractions of factorization methods is that they provide a "closed form" (sometimes called a "linear") method to initialize iterative techniques such as bundle adjustment. An alternative initialization technique is to estimate the homographies corresponding to some common plane seen by all the cameras (Rother and Carlsson 2002). In a calibrated camera setting, this can correspond to estimating consistent rotations for all of the cameras, for example, using matched vanishing points (Antone and Teller 2002). Once these have been recovered, the camera positions can then be obtained by solving a linear system (Antone and Teller 2002; Rother and Carlsson 2002; Rother 2003).

7.3.2 *Application*: Sparse 3D model extraction

Once a multi-view 3D reconstruction of the scene has been estimated, it then becomes possible to create a texture-mapped 3D model of the object and to look at it from new directions.

The first step is to create a denser 3D model than the sparse point cloud that structure from motion produces. One alternative is to run dense multi-view stereo (Sections 11.3–11.6). Alternatively, a simpler technique such as 3D triangulation can be used, as shown in Figure 7.6, in which 207 reconstructed 3D points are triangulated to produce a surface mesh.

In order to create a more realistic model, a *texture map* can be extracted for each triangle face. The equations to map points on the surface of a 3D triangle to a 2D image are straightforward: just pass the local 2D coordinates on the triangle through the 3×4 camera projection matrix to obtain a 3×3 homography (planar perspective projection). When multiple source images are available, as is usually the case in multi-view reconstruction, either the closest and most fronto-parallel image can be used or multiple images can be blended in to deal with view-dependent foreshortening (Wang, Kang, Szeliski *et al.* 2001) or to obtain super-resolved results (Goldluecke and Cremers 2009) Another alternative is to create a sep-

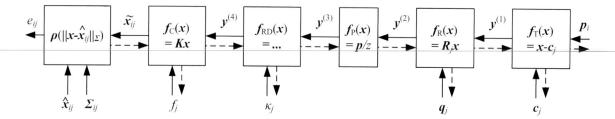

Figure 7.7   A set of chained transforms for projecting a 3D point p_i into a 2D measurement x_{ij} through a series of transformations $f^{(k)}$, each of which is controlled by its own set of parameters. The dashed lines indicate the flow of information as partial derivatives are computed during a backward pass. The formula for the radial distortion function is $f_{\mathrm{RD}}(x) = (1 + \kappa_1 r^2 + \kappa_2 r^4)x$.

arate texture map from each reference camera and to blend between them during rendering, which is known as *view-dependent texture mapping* (Section 13.1.1) (Debevec, Taylor, and Malik 1996; Debevec, Yu, and Borshukov 1998).

7.4 Bundle adjustment

As we have mentioned several times before, the most accurate way to recover structure and motion is to perform robust non-linear minimization of the measurement (re-projection) errors, which is commonly known in the photogrammetry (and now computer vision) communities as *bundle adjustment*.[13] Triggs, McLauchlan, Hartley *et al.* (1999) provide an excellent overview of this topic, including its historical development, pointers to the photogrammetry literature (Slama 1980; Atkinson 1996; Kraus 1997), and subtle issues with gauge ambiguities. The topic is also treated in depth in textbooks and surveys on multi-view geometry (Faugeras and Luong 2001; Hartley and Zisserman 2004; Moons, Van Gool, and Vergauwen 2010).

We have already introduced the elements of bundle adjustment in our discussion on iterative pose estimation (Section 6.2.2), i.e., Equations (6.42–6.48) and Figure 6.5. The biggest difference between these formulas and full bundle adjustment is that our feature location measurements x_{ij} now depend not only on the point (track index) i but also on the camera pose index j,

$$x_{ij} = f(p_i, R_j, c_j, K_j), \tag{7.49}$$

and that the 3D point positions p_i are also being simultaneously updated. In addition, it is common to add a stage for radial distortion parameter estimation (2.78),

$$f_{\mathrm{RD}}(x) = (1 + \kappa_1 r^2 + \kappa_2 r^4)x, \tag{7.50}$$

if the cameras being used have not been pre-calibrated, as shown in Figure 7.7.

While most of the boxes (transforms) in Figure 7.7 have previously been explained (6.47), the leftmost box has not. This box performs a robust comparison of the predicted and mea-

---

[13] The term "bundle" refers to the bundles of rays connecting camera centers to 3D points and the term "adjustment" refers to the iterative minimization of re-projection error. Alternative terms for this in the vision community include *optimal motion estimation* (Weng, Ahuja, and Huang 1993) and *non-linear least squares* (Appendix A.3) (Taylor, Kriegman, and Anandan 1991; Szeliski and Kang 1994).

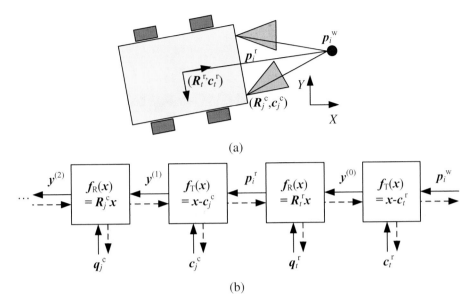

(a)

(b)

Figure 7.8 A camera rig and its associated transform chain. (a) As the mobile rig (robot) moves around in the world, its pose with respect to the world at time t is captured by $(\boldsymbol{R}_t^r, \boldsymbol{c}_t^r)$. Each camera's pose with respect to the rig is captured by $(\boldsymbol{R}_j^c, \boldsymbol{c}_j^c)$. (b) A 3D point with world coordinates $\boldsymbol{p}_i^w$ is first transformed into rig coordinates $\boldsymbol{p}_i^r$, and then through the rest of the camera-specific chain, as shown in Figure 7.7.

sured 2D locations $\hat{\boldsymbol{x}}_{ij}$ and $\tilde{\boldsymbol{x}}_{ij}$ after re-scaling by the measurement noise covariance Σ_{ij}. In more detail, this operation can be written as

$$\boldsymbol{r}_{ij} = \tilde{\boldsymbol{x}}_{ij} - \hat{\boldsymbol{x}}_{ij}, \tag{7.51}$$
$$s_{ij}^2 = \boldsymbol{r}_{ij}^T \Sigma_{ij}^{-1} \boldsymbol{r}_{ij}, \tag{7.52}$$
$$e_{ij} = \hat{\rho}(s_{ij}^2), \tag{7.53}$$

where $\hat{\rho}(r^2) = \rho(r)$. The corresponding Jacobians (partial derivatives) can be written as

$$\frac{\partial e_{ij}}{\partial s_{ij}^2} = \hat{\rho}'(s_{ij}^2), \tag{7.54}$$
$$\frac{\partial s_{ij}^2}{\partial \tilde{\boldsymbol{x}}_{ij}} = \Sigma_{ij}^{-1} \boldsymbol{r}_{ij}. \tag{7.55}$$

The advantage of the chained representation introduced above is that it not only makes the computations of the partial derivatives and Jacobians simpler but it can also be adapted to any camera configuration. Consider for example a pair of cameras mounted on a robot that is moving around in the world, as shown in Figure 7.8a. By replacing the rightmost two transformations in Figure 7.7 with the transformations shown in Figure 7.8b, we can simultaneously recover the position of the robot at each time and the calibration of each camera with respect to the rig, in addition to the 3D structure of the world.

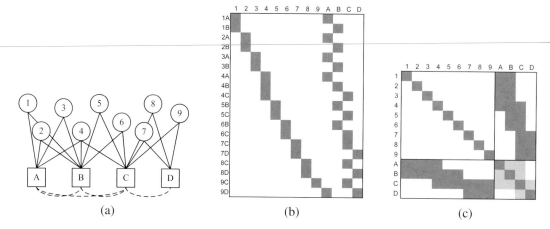

Figure 7.9 (a) Bipartite graph for a toy structure from motion problem and (b) its associated Jacobian J and (c) Hessian A. Numbers indicate 3D points and letters indicate cameras. The dashed arcs and light blue squares indicate the fill-in that occurs when the structure (point) variables are eliminated.

7.4.1 Exploiting sparsity

Large bundle adjustment problems, such as those involving reconstructing 3D scenes from thousands of Internet photographs (Snavely, Seitz, and Szeliski 2008b; Agarwal, Snavely, Simon *et al.* 2009; Agarwal, Furukawa, Snavely *et al.* 2010; Snavely, Simon, Goesele *et al.* 2010), can require solving non-linear least squares problems with millions of measurements (feature matches) and tens of thousands of unknown parameters (3D point positions and camera poses). Unless some care is taken, these kinds of problem can become intractable, since the (direct) solution of dense least squares problems is cubic in the number of unknowns.

Fortunately, structure from motion is a *bipartite* problem in structure and motion. Each feature point x_{ij} in a given image depends on one 3D point position p_i and one 3D camera pose (R_j, c_j). This is illustrated in Figure 7.9a, where each circle (1–9) indicates a 3D point, each square (A–D) indicates a camera, and lines (edges) indicate which points are visible in which cameras (2D features). If the values for all the points are known or fixed, the equations for all the cameras become independent, and vice versa.

If we order the structure variables before the motion variables in the Hessian matrix A (and hence also the right hand side vector b), we obtain a structure for the Hessian shown in Figure 7.9c.[14] When such a system is solved using sparse Cholesky factorization (see Appendix A.4) (Björck 1996; Golub and Van Loan 1996), the *fill-in* occurs in the smaller motion Hessian A_{cc} (Szeliski and Kang 1994; Triggs, McLauchlan, Hartley *et al.* 1999; Hartley and Zisserman 2004; Lourakis and Argyros 2009; Engels, Stewénius, and Nistér 2006). Some recent papers by (Byröd and øAström 2009), Jeong, Nistér, Steedly *et al.* (2010) and (Agarwal, Snavely, Seitz *et al.* 2010) explore the use of iterative (conjugate gradient) techniques for the solution of bundle adjustment problems.

---

[14] This ordering is preferable when there are fewer cameras than 3D points, which is the usual case. The exception is when we are tracking a small number of points through many video frames, in which case this ordering should be reversed.

In more detail, the *reduced* motion Hessian is computed using the *Schur complement*,

$$A'_{cc} = A_{cc} - A_{pc}^T A_{pp}^{-1} A_{pc}, \qquad (7.56)$$

where A_{pp} is the point (structure) Hessian (the top left block of Figure 7.9c), A_{pc} is the point-camera Hessian (the top right block), and A_{cc} and A'_{cc} are the motion Hessians before and after the point variable elimination (the bottom right block of Figure 7.9c). Notice that A'_{cc} has a non-zero entry between two cameras if they see any 3D point in common. This is indicated with dashed arcs in Figure 7.9a and light blue squares in Figure 7.9c.

Whenever there are global parameters present in the reconstruction algorithm, such as camera intrinsics that are common to all of the cameras, or camera rig calibration parameters such as those shown in Figure 7.8, they should be ordered last (placed along the right and bottom edges of A) in order to reduce fill-in.

Engels, Stewénius, and Nistér (2006) provide a nice recipe for sparse bundle adjustment, including all the steps needed to initialize the iterations, as well as typical computation times for a system that uses a fixed number of backward-looking frames in a real-time setting. They also recommend using homogeneous coordinates for the structure parameters p_i, which is a good idea, since it avoids numerical instabilities for points near infinity.

Bundle adjustment is now the standard method of choice for most structure-from-motion problems and is commonly applied to problems with hundreds of weakly calibrated images and tens of thousands of points, e.g., in systems such as Photosynth. (Much larger problems are commonly solved in photogrammetry and aerial imagery, but these are usually carefully calibrated and make use of surveyed ground control points.) However, as the problems become larger, it becomes impractical to re-solve full bundle adjustment problems at each iteration.

One approach to dealing with this problem is to use an incremental algorithm, where new cameras are added over time. (This makes particular sense if the data is being acquired from a video camera or moving vehicle (Nistér, Naroditsky, and Bergen 2006; Pollefeys, Nistér, Frahm *et al.* 2008).) A Kalman filter can be used to incrementally update estimates as new information is acquired. Unfortunately, such sequential updating is only statistically optimal for linear least squares problems.

For non-linear problems such as structure from motion, an extended Kalman filter, which linearizes measurement and update equations around the current estimate, needs to be used (Gelb 1974; Viéville and Faugeras 1990). To overcome this limitation, several passes can be made through the data (Azarbayejani and Pentland 1995). Because points disappear from view (and old cameras become irrelevant), a *variable state dimension filter* (VSDF) can be used to adjust the set of state variables over time, for example, by keeping only cameras and point tracks seen in the last k frames (McLauchlan 2000). A more flexible approach to using a fixed number of frames is to propagate corrections backwards through points and cameras until the changes on parameters are below a threshold (Steedly and Essa 2001). Variants of these techniques, including methods that use a fixed window for bundle adjustment (Engels, Stewénius, and Nistér 2006) or select keyframes for doing full bundle adjustment (Klein and Murray 2008) are now commonly used in real-time tracking and augmented-reality applications, as discussed in Section 7.4.2.

When maximum accuracy is required, it is still preferable to perform a full bundle adjustment over all the frames. In order to control the resulting computational complexity, one approach is to lock together subsets of frames into locally rigid configurations and to optimize the relative positions of these cluster (Steedly, Essa, and Dellaert 2003). A different approach is to select a smaller number of frames to form a *skeletal set* that still spans the whole dataset and produces reconstructions of comparable accuracy (Snavely, Seitz, and Szeliski 2008b). We describe this latter technique in more detail in Section 7.4.4, where we discuss applications of structure from motion to large image sets.

While bundle adjustment and other robust non-linear least squares techniques are the methods of choice for most structure-from-motion problems, they suffer from initialization problems, i.e., they can get stuck in local energy minima if not started sufficiently close to the global optimum. Many systems try to mitigate this by being conservative in what reconstruction they perform early on and which cameras and points they add to the solution (Section 7.4.4). An alternative, however, is to re-formulate the problem using a norm that supports the computation of global optima.

Kahl and Hartley (2008) describe techniques for using L_∞ norms in geometric reconstruction problems. The advantage of such norms is that globally optimal solutions can be efficiently computed using second-order cone programming (SOCP). The disadvantage is that L_∞ norms are particularly sensitive to outliers and so must be combined with good outlier rejection techniques before they can be used.

7.4.2 *Application*: Match move and augmented reality

One of the neatest applications of structure from motion is to estimate the 3D motion of a video or film camera, along with the geometry of a 3D scene, in order to superimpose 3D graphics or computer-generated images (CGI) on the scene. In the visual effects industry, this is known as the *match move* problem (Roble 1999), since the motion of the synthetic 3D camera used to render the graphics must be *matched* to that of the real-world camera. For very small motions, or motions involving pure camera rotations, one or two tracked points can suffice to compute the necessary visual motion. For planar surfaces moving in 3D, four points are needed to compute the homography, which can then be used to insert planar overlays, e.g., to replace the contents of advertising billboards during sporting events.

The general version of this problem requires the estimation of the full 3D camera pose along with the focal length (zoom) of the lens and potentially its radial distortion parameters (Roble 1999). When the 3D structure of the scene is known ahead of time, pose estimation techniques such as *view correlation* (Bogart 1991) or *through-the-lens camera control* (Gleicher and Witkin 1992) can be used, as described in Section 6.2.3.

For more complex scenes, it is usually preferable to recover the 3D structure simultaneously with the camera motion using structure-from-motion techniques. The trick with using such techniques is that in order to prevent any visible jitter between the synthetic graphics and the actual scene, features must be tracked to very high accuracy and ample feature tracks must be available in the vicinity of the insertion location. Some of today's best known match move software packages, such as the *boujou* package from 2d3,[15] which won an Emmy award in 2002, originated in structure-from-motion research in the computer vision community (Fitzgibbon and Zisserman 1998).

---

[15] http://www.2d3.com/.

(a)   (b)

Figure 7.10 3D augmented reality: (a) Darth Vader and a horde of Ewoks battle it out on a table-top recovered using real-time, keyframe-based structure from motion (Klein and Murray 2007) ©️ 2007 IEEE; (b) a virtual teapot is fixed to the top of a real-world coffee cup, whose pose is re-recognized at each time frame (Gordon and Lowe 2006) ©️ 2007 Springer.

Closely related to the match move problem is robotics navigation, where a robot must estimate its location relative to its environment, while simultaneously avoiding any dangerous obstacles. This problem is often known as *simultaneous localization and mapping* (SLAM) (Thrun, Burgard, and Fox 2005) or *visual odometry* (Levin and Szeliski 2004; Nistér, Naroditsky, and Bergen 2006; Maimone, Cheng, and Matthies 2007). Early versions of such algorithms used range-sensing techniques, such as ultrasound, laser range finders, or stereo matching, to estimate local 3D geometry, which could then be fused into a 3D model. Newer techniques can perform the same task based purely on visual feature tracking, sometimes not even requiring a stereo camera rig (Davison, Reid, Molton *et al.* 2007).

Another closely related application is *augmented reality*, where 3D objects are inserted into a video feed in real time, often to annotate or help users understand a scene (Azuma, Baillot, Behringer *et al.* 2001). While traditional systems require prior knowledge about the scene or object being visually tracked (Rosten and Drummond 2005), newer systems can simultaneously build up a model of the 3D environment and then track it, so that graphics can be superimposed.

Klein and Murray (2007) describe a *parallel tracking and mapping* (PTAM) system, which simultaneously applies full bundle adjustment to keyframes selected from a video stream, while performing robust real-time pose estimation on intermediate frames. Figure 7.10a shows an example of their system in use. Once an initial 3D scene has been reconstructed, a dominant plane is estimated (in this case, the table-top) and 3D animated characters are virtually inserted. Klein and Murray (2008) extend their previous system to handle even faster camera motion by adding edge features, which can still be detected even when interest points become too blurred. They also use a direct (intensity-based) rotation estimation algorithm for even faster motions.

Instead of modeling the whole scene as one rigid reference frame, Gordon and Lowe (2006) first build a 3D model of an individual object using feature matching and structure from motion. Once the system has been initialized, for every new frame, they find the object and its pose using a 3D instance recognition algorithm, and then superimpose a graphical object onto that model, as shown in Figure 7.10b.

While reliably tracking such objects and environments is now a well-solved problem, determining which pixels should be occluded by foreground scene elements still remains an open problem (Chuang, Agarwala, Curless *et al.* 2002; Wang and Cohen 2007a).

7.4.3 Uncertainty and ambiguities

Because structure from motion involves the estimation of so many highly coupled parameters, often with no known "ground truth" components, the estimates produced by structure from motion algorithms can often exhibit large amounts of uncertainty (Szeliski and Kang 1997). An example of this is the classic *bas-relief ambiguity*, which makes it hard to simultaneously estimate the 3D depth of a scene and the amount of camera motion (Oliensis 2005).[16]

As mentioned before, a unique coordinate frame and scale for a reconstructed scene cannot be recovered from monocular visual measurements alone. (When a stereo rig is used, the scale can be recovered if we know the distance (baseline) between the cameras.) This seven-degree-of-freedom *gauge ambiguity* makes it tricky to compute the covariance matrix associated with a 3D reconstruction (Triggs, McLauchlan, Hartley *et al.* 1999; Kanatani and Morris 2001). A simple way to compute a covariance matrix that ignores the gauge freedom (indeterminacy) is to throw away the seven smallest eigenvalues of the information matrix (inverse covariance), whose values are equivalent to the problem Hessian A up to noise scaling (see Section 6.1.4 and Appendix B.6). After we do this, the resulting matrix can be inverted to obtain an estimate of the parameter covariance.

Szeliski and Kang (1997) use this approach to visualize the largest directions of variation in typical structure from motion problems. Not surprisingly, they find that (ignoring the gauge freedoms), the greatest uncertainties for problems such as observing an object from a small number of nearby viewpoints are in the depths of the 3D structure relative to the extent of the camera motion.[17]

It is also possible to estimate *local* or *marginal* uncertainties for individual parameters, which corresponds simply to taking block sub-matrices from the full covariance matrix. Under certain conditions, such as when the camera poses are relatively certain compared to 3D point locations, such uncertainty estimates can be meaningful. However, in many cases, individual uncertainty measures can mask the extent to which reconstruction errors are correlated, which is why looking at the first few modes of greatest joint variation can be helpful.

The other way in which gauge ambiguities affect structure from motion and, in particular, bundle adjustment is that they make the system Hessian matrix A rank-deficient and hence impossible to invert. A number of techniques have been proposed to mitigate this problem (Triggs, McLauchlan, Hartley *et al.* 1999; Bartoli 2003). In practice, however, it appears that simply adding a small amount of the Hessian diagonal $\lambda\mathrm{diag}(A)$ to the Hessian A itself, as is done in the Levenberg–Marquardt non-linear least squares algorithm (Appendix A.3), usually works well.

---

[16] Bas-relief refers to a kind of sculpture in which objects, often on ornamental friezes, are sculpted with less depth than they actually occupy. When lit from above by sunlight, they appear to have true 3D depth because of the ambiguity between relative depth and the angle of the illuminant (Section 12.1.1).

[17] A good way to minimize the amount of such ambiguities is to use wide field of view cameras (Antone and Teller 2002; Levin and Szeliski 2006).

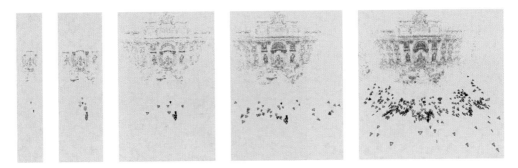

Figure 7.11 Incremental structure from motion (Snavely, Seitz, and Szeliski 2006) © 2006 ACM: Starting with an initial two-frame reconstruction of Trevi Fountain, batches of images are added using pose estimation, and their positions (along with the 3D model) are refined using bundle adjustment.

7.4.4 *Application*: Reconstruction from Internet photos

The most widely used application of structure from motion is in the reconstruction of 3D objects and scenes from video sequences and collections of images (Pollefeys and Van Gool 2002). The last decade has seen an explosion of techniques for performing this task automatically without the need for any manual correspondence or pre-surveyed ground control points. A lot of these techniques assume that the scene is taken with the same camera and hence the images all have the same intrinsics (Fitzgibbon and Zisserman 1998; Koch, Pollefeys, and Van Gool 2000; Schaffalitzky and Zisserman 2002; Tuytelaars and Van Gool 2004; Pollefeys, Nistér, Frahm *et al.* 2008; Moons, Van Gool, and Vergauwen 2010). Many of these techniques take the results of the sparse feature matching and structure from motion computation and then compute dense 3D surface models using multi-view stereo techniques (Section 11.6) (Koch, Pollefeys, and Van Gool 2000; Pollefeys and Van Gool 2002; Pollefeys, Nistér, Frahm *et al.* 2008; Moons, Van Gool, and Vergauwen 2010).

The latest innovation in this space has been the application of structure from motion and multi-view stereo techniques to thousands of images taken from the Internet, where very little is known about the cameras taking the photographs (Snavely, Seitz, and Szeliski 2008a). Before the structure from motion computation can begin, it is first necessary to establish sparse correspondences between different pairs of images and to then link such correspondences into *feature tracks*, which associate individual 2D image features with global 3D points. Because the $O(N^2)$ comparison of all pairs of images can be very slow, a number of techniques have been developed in the recognition community to make this process faster (Section 14.3.2) (Nistér and Stewénius 2006; Philbin, Chum, Sivic *et al.* 2008; Li, Wu, Zach *et al.* 2008; Chum, Philbin, and Zisserman 2008; Chum and Matas 2010).

To begin the reconstruction process, it is important to to select a good pair of images, where there are both a large number of consistent matches (to lower the likelihood of incorrect correspondences) and a significant amount of out-of-plane parallax,[18] to ensure that a stable reconstruction can be obtained (Snavely, Seitz, and Szeliski 2006). The EXIF tags associated with the photographs can be used to get good initial estimates for camera focal lengths, although this is not always strictly necessary, since these parameters are re-adjusted

---

[18] A simple way to compute this is to robustly fit a homography to the correspondences and measure reprojection errors.

(a)   (b)   (c)

Figure 7.12   3D reconstructions produced by the incremental structure from motion algorithm developed by Snavely, Seitz, and Szeliski (2006) © 2006 ACM: (a) cameras and point cloud from Trafalgar Square; (b) cameras and points overlaid on an image from the Great Wall of China; (c) overhead view of a reconstruction of the Old Town Square in Prague registered to an aerial photograph.

as part of the bundle adjustment process.

Once an initial pair has been reconstructed, the pose of cameras that see a sufficient number of the resulting 3D points can be estimated (Section 6.2) and the complete set of cameras and feature correspondences can be used to perform another round of bundle adjustment. Figure 7.11 shows the progression of the incremental bundle adjustment algorithm, where sets of cameras are added after each successive round of bundle adjustment, while Figure 7.12 shows some additional results. An alternative to this kind of *seed and grow* approach is to first reconstruct triplets of images and then hierarchically merge triplets into larger collections, as described by Fitzgibbon and Zisserman (1998).

Unfortunately, as the incremental structure from motion algorithm continues to add more cameras and points, it can become extremely slow. The direct solution of a dense system of $O(N)$ equations for the camera pose updates can take $O(N^3)$ time; while structure from motion problems are rarely dense, scenes such as city squares have a high percentage of cameras that see points in common. Re-running the bundle adjustment algorithm after every few camera additions results in a quartic scaling of the run time with the number of images in the dataset. One approach to solving this problem is to select a smaller number of images for the original scene reconstruction and to fold in the remaining images at the very end.

Snavely, Seitz, and Szeliski (2008b) develop an algorithm for computing such a *skeletal set* of images, which is guaranteed to produce a reconstruction whose error is within a bounded factor of the optimal reconstruction accuracy. Their algorithm first evaluates all pairwise uncertainties (position covariances) between overlapping images and then chains them together to estimate a lower bound for the relative uncertainty of any distant pair. The skeletal set is constructed so that the maximal uncertainty between any pair grows by no more than a constant factor. Figure 7.13 shows an example of the skeletal set computed for 784 images of the Pantheon in Rome. As you can see, even though the skeletal set contains just a fraction of the original images, the shapes of the skeletal set and full bundle adjusted reconstructions are virtually indistinguishable.

The ability to automatically reconstruct 3D models from large, unstructured image collections has opened a wide variety of additional applications, including the ability to automat-

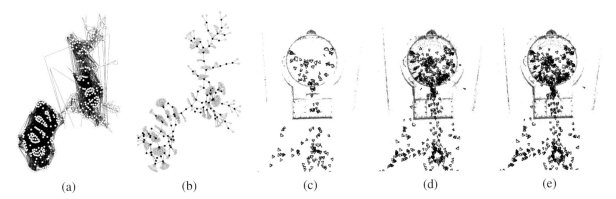

(a)   (b)   (c)   (d)   (e)

Figure 7.13 Large scale structure from motion using skeletal sets (Snavely, Seitz, and Szeliski 2008b) © 2008 IEEE: (a) original match graph for 784 images; (b) skeletal set containing 101 images; (c) top-down view of scene (Pantheon) reconstructed from the skeletal set; (d) reconstruction after adding in the remaining images using pose estimation; (e) final bundle adjusted reconstruction, which is almost identical.

ically find and label locations and regions of interest (Simon, Snavely, and Seitz 2007; Simon and Seitz 2008; Gammeter, Bossard, Quack *et al.* 2009) and to cluster large image collections so that they can be automatically labeled (Li, Wu, Zach *et al.* 2008; Quack, Leibe, and Van Gool 2008). Some of these application are discussed in more detail in Section 13.1.2.

7.5 Constrained structure and motion

The most general algorithms for structure from motion make no prior assumptions about the objects or scenes that they are reconstructing. In many cases, however, the scene contains higher-level geometric primitives, such as lines and planes. These can provide information complementary to interest points and also serve as useful building blocks for 3D modeling and visualization. Furthermore, these primitives are often arranged in particular relationships, i.e., many lines and planes are either parallel or orthogonal to each other. This is particularly true of architectural scenes and models, which we study in more detail in Section 12.6.1.

Sometimes, instead of exploiting regularity in the scene structure, it is possible to take advantage of a constrained motion model. For example, if the object of interest is rotating on a turntable (Szeliski 1991b), i.e., around a fixed but unknown axis, specialized techniques can be used to recover this motion (Fitzgibbon, Cross, and Zisserman 1998). In other situations, the camera itself may be moving in a fixed arc around some center of rotation (Shum and He 1999). Specialized capture setups, such as mobile stereo camera rigs or moving vehicles equipped with multiple fixed cameras, can also take advantage of the knowledge that individual cameras are (mostly) fixed with respect to the capture rig, as shown in Figure 7.8.[19]

---

[19] Because of mechanical compliance and jitter, it may be prudent to allow for a small amount of individual camera rotation around a nominal position.

Figure 7.14 Two images of a toy house along with their matched 3D line segments (Schmid and Zisserman 1997) © 1997 Springer.

7.5.1 Line-based techniques

It is well known that pairwise epipolar geometry cannot be recovered from line matches alone, even if the cameras are calibrated. To see this, think of projecting the set of lines in each image into a set of 3D planes in space. You can move the two cameras around into any configuration you like and still obtain a valid reconstruction for 3D lines.

When lines are visible in three or more views, the trifocal tensor can be used to transfer lines from one pair of images to another (Hartley and Zisserman 2004). The trifocal tensor can also be computed on the basis of line matches alone.

Schmid and Zisserman (1997) describe a widely used technique for matching 2D lines based on the average of 15×15 pixel correlation scores evaluated at all pixels along their common line segment intersection.[20] In their system, the epipolar geometry is assumed to be known, e.g., computed from point matches. For wide baselines, all possible homographies corresponding to planes passing through the 3D line are used to warp pixels and the maximum correlation score is used. For triplets of images, the trifocal tensor is used to verify that the lines are in geometric correspondence before evaluating the correlations between line segments. Figure 7.14 shows the results of using their system.

Bartoli and Sturm (2003) describe a complete system for extending three view relations (trifocal tensors) computed from manual line correspondences to a full bundle adjustment of all the line and camera parameters. The key to their approach is to use the Plücker coordinates (2.12) to parameterize lines and to directly minimize reprojection errors. It is also possible to represent 3D line segments by their endpoints and to measure either the reprojection error perpendicular to the detected 2D line segments in each image or the 2D errors using an elongated uncertainty ellipse aligned with the line segment direction (Szeliski and Kang 1994).

Instead of reconstructing 3D lines, Bay, Ferrari, and Van Gool (2005) use RANSAC to group lines into likely coplanar subsets. Four lines are chosen at random to compute a homography, which is then verified for these and other plausible line segment matches by evaluating color histogram-based correlation scores. The 2D intersection points of lines belonging to the same plane are then used as virtual measurements to estimate the epipolar geometry, which is more accurate than using the homographies directly.

---

[20] Because lines often occur at depth or orientation discontinuities, it may be preferable to compute correlation scores (or to match color histograms (Bay, Ferrari, and Van Gool 2005)) separately on each side of the line.

An alternative to grouping lines into coplanar subsets is to group lines by parallelism. Whenever three or more 2D lines share a common vanishing point, there is a good likelihood that they are parallel in 3D. By finding multiple vanishing points in an image (Section 4.3.3) and establishing correspondences between such vanishing points in different images, the relative rotations between the various images (and often the camera intrinsics) can be directly estimated (Section 6.3.2).

Shum, Han, and Szeliski (1998) describe a 3D modeling system which first constructs calibrated panoramas from multiple images (Section 7.4) and then has the user draw vertical and horizontal lines in the image to demarcate the boundaries of planar regions. The lines are initially used to establish an absolute rotation for each panorama and are later used (along with the inferred vertices and planes) to infer a 3D structure, which can be recovered up to scale from one or more images (Figure 12.15).

A fully automated approach to line-based structure from motion is presented vy Werner and Zisserman (2002). In their system, they first find lines and group them by common vanishing points in each image (Section 4.3.3). The vanishing points are then used to calibrate the camera, i.e., to performa a "metric upgrade" (Section 6.3.2). Lines corresponding to common vanishing points are then matched using both appearance (Schmid and Zisserman 1997) and trifocal tensors. The resulting set of 3D lines, color coded by common vanishing directions (3D orientations) is shown in Figure 12.16a. These lines are then used to infer planes and a block-structured model for the scene, as described in more detail in Section 12.6.1.

7.5.2 Plane-based techniques

In scenes that are rich in planar structures, e.g., in architecture and certain kinds of manufactured objects such as furniture, it is possible to directly estimate homographies between different planes, using either feature-based or intensity-based methods. In principle, this information can be used to simultaneously infer the camera poses and the plane equations, i.e., to compute plane-based structure from motion.

Luong and Faugeras (1996) show how a fundamental matrix can be directly computed from two or more homographies using algebraic manipulations and least squares. Unfortunately, this approach often performs poorly, since the algebraic errors do not correspond to meaningful reprojection errors (Szeliski and Torr 1998).

A better approach is to *hallucinate* virtual point correspondences within the areas from which each homography was computed and to feed them into a standard structure from motion algorithm (Szeliski and Torr 1998). An even better approach is to use full bundle adjustment with explicit plane equations, as well as additional constraints to force reconstructed co-planar features to lie exactly on their corresponding planes. (A principled way to do this is to establish a coordinate frame for each plane, e.g., at one of the feature points, and to use 2D in-plane parameterizations for the other points.) The system developed by Shum, Han, and Szeliski (1998) shows an example of such an approach, where the directions of lines and normals for planes in the scene are pre-specified by the user.

7.6 Additional reading

The topic of structure from motion is extensively covered in books and review articles on multi-view geometry (Faugeras and Luong 2001; Hartley and Zisserman 2004; Moons, Van Gool, and Vergauwen 2010). For two-frame reconstruction, Hartley (1997a) wrote a highly cited paper on the "eight-point algorithm" for computing an essential or fundamental matrix with reasonable point normalization. When the cameras are calibrated, the five-point algorithm of Nistér (2004) can be used in conjunction with RANSAC to obtain initial reconstructions from the minimum number of points. When the cameras are uncalibrated, various self-calibration techniques can be found in work by Hartley and Zisserman (2004); Moons, Van Gool, and Vergauwen (2010)—I only briefly mention one of the simplest techniques, the Kruppa equations (7.35).

In applications where points are being tracked from frame to frame, factorization techniques, based on either orthographic camera models (Tomasi and Kanade 1992; Poelman and Kanade 1997; Costeira and Kanade 1995; Morita and Kanade 1997; Morris and Kanade 1998; Anandan and Irani 2002) or projective extensions (Christy and Horaud 1996; Sturm and Triggs 1996; Triggs 1996; Oliensis and Hartley 2007), can be used.

Triggs, McLauchlan, Hartley *et al.* (1999) provide a good tutorial and survey on bundle adjustment, while Lourakis and Argyros (2009) and Engels, Stewénius, and Nistér (2006) provide tips on implementation and effective practices. Bundle adjustment is also covered in textbooks and surveys on multi-view geometry (Faugeras and Luong 2001; Hartley and Zisserman 2004; Moons, Van Gool, and Vergauwen 2010). Techniques for handling larger problems are described by Snavely, Seitz, and Szeliski (2008b); Agarwal, Snavely, Simon *et al.* (2009); Jeong, Nistér, Steedly *et al.* (2010); Agarwal, Snavely, Seitz *et al.* (2010). While bundle adjustment is often called as an inner loop inside incremental reconstruction algorithms (Snavely, Seitz, and Szeliski 2006), hierarchical (Fitzgibbon and Zisserman 1998; Farenzena, Fusiello, and Gherardi 2009) and global (Rother and Carlsson 2002; Martinec and Pajdla 2007) approaches for initialization are also possible and perhaps even preferable.

As structure from motion starts being applied to dynamic scenes, the topic of non-rigid structure from motion (Torresani, Hertzmann, and Bregler 2008), which we do not cover in this book, will become more important.

7.7 Exercises

Ex 7.1: Triangulation   Use the calibration pattern you built and tested in Exercise 6.7 to test your triangulation accuracy. As an alternative, generate synthetic 3D points and cameras and add noise to the 2D point measurements.

1. Assume that you know the camera pose, i.e., the camera matrices. Use the 3D distance to rays (7.4) or linearized versions of Equations (7.5–7.6) to compute an initial set of 3D locations. Compare these to your known ground truth locations.

2. Use iterative non-linear minimization to improve your initial estimates and report on the improvement in accuracy.

3. (Optional) Use the technique described by Hartley and Sturm (1997) to perform two-frame triangulation.

4. See if any of the failure modes reported by Hartley and Sturm (1997) or Hartley (1998) occur in practice.

Ex 7.2: Essential and fundamental matrix   Implement the two-frame E and F matrix estimation techniques presented in Section 7.2, with suitable re-scaling for better noise immunity.

1. Use the data from Exercise 7.1 to validate your algorithms and to report on their accuracy.

2. (Optional) Implement one of the improved F or E estimation algorithms, e.g., using renormalization (Zhang 1998b; Torr and Fitzgibbon 2004; Hartley and Zisserman 2004), RANSAC (Torr and Murray 1997), least media squares (LMS), or the five-point algorithm developed by Nistér (2004).

Ex 7.3: View morphing and interpolation   Implement automatic view morphing, i.e., compute two-frame structure from motion and then use these results to generate a smooth animation from one image to the next (Section 7.2.3).

1. Decide how to represent your 3D scene, e.g., compute a Delaunay triangulation of the matched point and decide what to do with the triangles near the border. (Hint: try fitting a plane to the scene, e.g., behind most of the points.)

2. Compute your in-between camera positions and orientations.

3. Warp each triangle to its new location, preferably using the correct perspective projection (Szeliski and Shum 1997).

4. (Optional) If you have a denser 3D model (e.g., from stereo), decide what to do at the "cracks".

5. (Optional) For a non-rigid scene, e.g., two pictures of a face with different expressions, not all of your matched points will obey the epipolar geometry. Decide how to handle them to achieve the best effect.

Ex 7.4: Factorization   Implement the factorization algorithm described in Section 7.3 using point tracks you computed in Exercise 4.5.

1. (Optional) Implement uncertainty rescaling (Anandan and Irani 2002) and comment on whether this improves your results.

2. (Optional) Implement one of the perspective improvements to factorization discussed in Section 7.3.1 (Christy and Horaud 1996; Sturm and Triggs 1996; Triggs 1996). Does this produce significantly lower reprojection errors? Can you upgrade this reconstruction to a metric one?

Ex 7.5: Bundle adjuster   Implement a full bundle adjuster. This may sound daunting, but it really is not.

1. Devise the internal data structures and external file representations to hold your camera parameters (position, orientation, and focal length), 3D point locations (Euclidean or homogeneous), and 2D point tracks (frame and point identifier as well as 2D locations).

2. Use some other technique, such as factorization, to initialize the 3D point and camera locations from your 2D tracks (e.g., a subset of points that appears in all frames).

3. Implement the code corresponding to the forward transformations in Figure 7.7, i.e., for each 2D point measurement, take the corresponding 3D point, map it through the camera transformations (including perspective projection and focal length scaling), and compare it to the 2D point measurement to get a residual error.

4. Take the residual error and compute its derivatives with respect to all the unknown motion and structure parameters, using backward chaining, as shown, e.g., in Figure 7.7 and Equation (6.47). This gives you the sparse Jacobian J used in Equations (6.13–6.17) and Equation (6.43).

5. Use a sparse least squares or linear system solver, e.g., MATLAB, SparseSuite, or SPARSKIT (see Appendix A.4 and A.5), to solve the corresponding linearized system, adding a small amount of diagonal preconditioning, as in Levenberg–Marquardt.

6. Update your parameters, make sure your rotation matrices are still orthonormal (e.g., by re-computing them from your quaternions), and continue iterating while monitoring your residual error.

7. (Optional) Use the "Schur complement trick" (7.56) to reduce the size of the system being solved (Triggs, McLauchlan, Hartley *et al.* 1999; Hartley and Zisserman 2004; Lourakis and Argyros 2009; Engels, Stewénius, and Nistér 2006).

8. (Optional) Implement your own iterative sparse solver, e.g., conjugate gradient, and compare its performance to a direct method.

9. (Optional) Make your bundle adjuster robust to outliers, or try adding some of the other improvements discussed in (Engels, Stewénius, and Nistér 2006). Can you think of any other ways to make your algorithm even faster or more robust?

Ex 7.6: Match move and augmented reality   Use the results of the previous exercise to superimpose a rendered 3D model on top of video. See Section 7.4.2 for more details and ideas. Check for how "locked down" the objects are.

Ex 7.7: Line-based reconstruction   Augment the previously developed bundle adjuster to include lines, possibly with known 3D orientations.

Optionally, use co-planar sets of points and lines to hypothesize planes and to enforce co-planarity (Schaffalitzky and Zisserman 2002; Robertson and Cipolla 2002)

Ex 7.8: Flexible bundle adjuster   Design a bundle adjuster that allows for arbitrary chains of transformations and prior knowledge about the unknowns, as suggested in Figures 7.7–7.8.

Ex 7.9: Unordered image matching   Compute the camera pose and 3D structure of a scene from an arbitrary collection of photographs (Brown and Lowe 2003; Snavely, Seitz, and Szeliski 2006).

Chapter 8

Dense motion estimation

R. Szeliski, *Computer Vision: Algorithms and Applications*, Texts in Computer Science,
DOI 10.1007/978-1-84882-935-0_8, © Springer-Verlag London Limited 2011

(a)   (b)

(c)   (d)

flow   initial layers   final layers

layers with pixel assignments and flow

(e)   (f)

Figure 8.1 Motion estimation: (a–b) regularization-based optical flow (Nagel and Enkelmann 1986) © 1986 IEEE; (c–d) layered motion estimation (Wang and Adelson 1994) © 1994 IEEE; (e–f) sample image and ground truth flow from evaluation database (Baker, Black, Lewis *et al.* 2007) © 2007 IEEE.

Algorithms for aligning images and estimating motion in video sequences are among the most widely used in computer vision. For example, frame-rate image alignment is widely used in camcorders and digital cameras to implement their image stabilization (IS) feature.

An early example of a widely used image registration algorithm is the patch-based translational alignment (optical flow) technique developed by Lucas and Kanade (1981). Variants of this algorithm are used in almost all motion-compensated video compression schemes such as MPEG and H.263 (Le Gall 1991). Similar parametric motion estimation algorithms have found a wide variety of applications, including video summarization (Teodosio and Bender 1993; Irani and Anandan 1998), video stabilization (Hansen, Anandan, Dana *et al.* 1994; Srinivasan, Chellappa, Veeraraghavan *et al.* 2005; Matsushita, Ofek, Ge *et al.* 2006), and video compression (Irani, Hsu, and Anandan 1995; Lee, ge Chen, lung Bruce Lin *et al.* 1997). More sophisticated image registration algorithms have also been developed for medical imaging and remote sensing. Image registration techniques are surveyed by Brown (1992), Zitov'aa and Flusser (2003), Goshtasby (2005), and Szeliski (2006a).

To estimate the motion between two or more images, a suitable *error metric* must first be chosen to compare the images (Section 8.1). Once this has been established, a suitable *search* technique must be devised. The simplest technique is to exhaustively try all possible alignments, i.e., to do a *full search*. In practice, this may be too slow, so *hierarchical* coarse-to-fine techniques (Section 8.1.1) based on image pyramids are normally used. Alternatively, Fourier transforms (Section 8.1.2) can be used to speed up the computation.

To get sub-pixel precision in the alignment, *incremental* methods (Section 8.1.3) based on a Taylor series expansion of the image function are often used. These can also be applied to *parametric motion models* (Section 8.2), which model global image transformations such as rotation or shearing. Motion estimation can be made more reliable by *learning* the typical dynamics or motion statistics of the scenes or objects being tracked, e.g., the natural gait of walking people (Section 8.2.2). For more complex motions, piecewise parametric *spline motion models* (Section 8.3) can be used. In the presence of multiple independent (and perhaps non-rigid) motions, general-purpose *optical flow* (or *optic flow*) techniques need to be used (Section 8.4). For even more complex motions that include a lot of occlusions, *layered motion models* (Section 8.5), which decompose the scene into coherently moving layers, can work well.

In this chapter, we describe each of these techniques in more detail. Additional details can be found in review and comparative evaluation papers on motion estimation (Barron, Fleet, and Beauchemin 1994; Mitiche and Bouthemy 1996; Stiller and Konrad 1999; Szeliski 2006a; Baker, Black, Lewis *et al.* 2007).

8.1 Translational alignment

The simplest way to establish an alignment between two images or image patches is to shift one image relative to the other. Given a *template* image $I_0(\boldsymbol{x})$ sampled at discrete pixel locations $\{\boldsymbol{x}_i = (x_i, y_i)\}$, we wish to find where it is located in image $I_1(\boldsymbol{x})$. A least squares solution to this problem is to find the minimum of the *sum of squared differences* (SSD) function

$$E_{\text{SSD}}(\boldsymbol{u}) = \sum_i [I_1(\boldsymbol{x}_i + \boldsymbol{u}) - I_0(\boldsymbol{x}_i)]^2 = \sum_i e_i^2, \qquad (8.1)$$

where $\boldsymbol{u} = (u, v)$ is the *displacement* and $e_i = I_1(\boldsymbol{x}_i + \boldsymbol{u}) - I_0(\boldsymbol{x}_i)$ is called the *residual error* (or the *displaced frame difference* in the video coding literature).[1] (We ignore for the moment the possibility that parts of I_0 may lie outside the boundaries of I_1 or be otherwise not visible.) The assumption that corresponding pixel values remain the same in the two images is often called the *brightness constancy constraint*.[2]

In general, the displacement $\boldsymbol{u}$ can be fractional, so a suitable interpolation function must be applied to image $I_1(\boldsymbol{x})$. In practice, a bilinear interpolant is often used but bicubic interpolation can yield slightly better results (Szeliski and Scharstein 2004). Color images can be processed by summing differences across all three color channels, although it is also possible to first transform the images into a different color space or to only use the luminance (which is often done in video encoders).

Robust error metrics. We can make the above error metric more robust to outliers by replacing the squared error terms with a robust function $\rho(e_i)$ (Huber 1981; Hampel, Ronchetti, Rousseeuw *et al.* 1986; Black and Anandan 1996; Stewart 1999) to obtain

$$E_{\mathrm{SRD}}(\boldsymbol{u}) = \sum_i \rho(I_1(\boldsymbol{x}_i + \boldsymbol{u}) - I_0(\boldsymbol{x}_i)) = \sum_i \rho(e_i). \tag{8.2}$$

The robust norm $\rho(e)$ is a function that grows less quickly than the quadratic penalty associated with least squares. One such function, sometimes used in motion estimation for video coding because of its speed, is the *sum of absolute differences* (SAD) metric[3] or L_1 norm, i.e.,

$$E_{\mathrm{SAD}}(\boldsymbol{u}) = \sum_i |I_1(\boldsymbol{x}_i + \boldsymbol{u}) - I_0(\boldsymbol{x}_i)| = \sum_i |e_i|. \tag{8.3}$$

However, since this function is not differentiable at the origin, it is not well suited to gradient-descent approaches such as the ones presented in Section 8.1.3.

Instead, a smoothly varying function that is quadratic for small values but grows more slowly away from the origin is often used. Black and Rangarajan (1996) discuss a variety of such functions, including the *Geman–McClure* function,

$$\rho_{\mathrm{GM}}(x) = \frac{x^2}{1 + x^2/a^2}, \tag{8.4}$$

where a is a constant that can be thought of as an *outlier threshold*. An appropriate value for the threshold can itself be derived using robust statistics (Huber 1981; Hampel, Ronchetti, Rousseeuw *et al.* 1986; Rousseeuw and Leroy 1987), e.g., by computing the *median absolute deviation*, $MAD = \mathrm{med}_i|e_i|$, and multiplying it by 1.4 to obtain a robust estimate of the standard deviation of the inlier noise process (Stewart 1999).

---

[1] The usual justification for using least squares is that it is the optimal estimate with respect to Gaussian noise. See the discussion below on robust error metrics as well as Appendix B.3.

[2] Brightness constancy (Horn 1974) is the tendency for objects to maintain their perceived brightness under varying illumination conditions.

[3] In video compression, e.g., the H.264 standard (http://www.itu.int/rec/T-REC-H.264), the sum of absolute transformed differences (SATD), which measures the differences in a frequency transform space, e.g., using a Hadamard transform, is often used since it more accurately predicts quality (Richardson 2003).

Spatially varying weights. The error metrics above ignore that fact that for a given alignment, some of the pixels being compared may lie outside the original image boundaries. Furthermore, we may want to partially or completely downweight the contributions of certain pixels. For example, we may want to selectively "erase" some parts of an image from consideration when stitching a mosaic where unwanted foreground objects have been cut out. For applications such as background stabilization, we may want to downweight the middle part of the image, which often contains independently moving objects being tracked by the camera.

All of these tasks can be accomplished by associating a spatially varying per-pixel weight value with each of the two images being matched. The error metric then becomes the weighted (or *windowed*) SSD function,

$$E_{\mathrm{WSSD}}(\boldsymbol{u}) = \sum_i w_0(\boldsymbol{x}_i) w_1(\boldsymbol{x}_i + \boldsymbol{u}) [I_1(\boldsymbol{x}_i + \boldsymbol{u}) - I_0(\boldsymbol{x}_i)]^2, \qquad (8.5)$$

where the weighting functions w_0 and w_1 are zero outside the image boundaries.

If a large range of potential motions is allowed, the above metric can have a bias towards smaller overlap solutions. To counteract this bias, the windowed SSD score can be divided by the overlap area

$$A = \sum_i w_0(\boldsymbol{x}_i) w_1(\boldsymbol{x}_i + \boldsymbol{u}) \qquad (8.6)$$

to compute a *per-pixel* (or mean) squared pixel error E_{WSSD}/A. The square root of this quantity is the *root mean square* intensity error

$$RMS = \sqrt{E_{\mathrm{WSSD}}/A} \qquad (8.7)$$

often reported in comparative studies.

Bias and gain (exposure differences). Often, the two images being aligned were not taken with the same exposure. A simple model of linear (affine) intensity variation between the two images is the *bias and gain* model,

$$I_1(\boldsymbol{x} + \boldsymbol{u}) = (1 + \alpha) I_0(\boldsymbol{x}) + \beta, \qquad (8.8)$$

where β is the *bias* and α is the *gain* (Lucas and Kanade 1981; Gennert 1988; Fuh and Maragos 1991; Baker, Gross, and Matthews 2003; Evangelidis and Psarakis 2008). The least squares formulation then becomes

$$E_{\mathrm{BG}}(\boldsymbol{u}) = \sum_i [I_1(\boldsymbol{x}_i + \boldsymbol{u}) - (1 + \alpha) I_0(\boldsymbol{x}_i) - \beta]^2 = \sum_i [\alpha I_0(\boldsymbol{x}_i) + \beta - e_i]^2. \qquad (8.9)$$

Rather than taking a simple squared difference between corresponding patches, it becomes necessary to perform a *linear regression* (Appendix A.2), which is somewhat more costly. Note that for color images, it may be necessary to estimate a different bias and gain for each color channel to compensate for the automatic *color correction* performed by some digital cameras (Section 2.3.2). Bias and gain compensation is also used in video codecs, where it is known as *weighted prediction* (Richardson 2003).

A more general (spatially varying, non-parametric) model of intensity variation, which is computed as part of the registration process, is used in (Negahdaripour 1998; Jia and Tang

2003; Seitz and Baker 2009). This can be useful for dealing with local variations such as the *vignetting* caused by wide-angle lenses, wide apertures, or lens housings. It is also possible to pre-process the images before comparing their values, e.g., using band-pass filtered images (Anandan 1989; Bergen, Anandan, Hanna *et al.* 1992), gradients (Scharstein 1994; Papenberg, Bruhn, Brox *et al.* 2006), or using other local transformations such as histograms or rank transforms (Cox, Roy, and Hingorani 1995; Zabih and Woodfill 1994), or to maximize *mutual information* (Viola and Wells III 1997; Kim, Kolmogorov, and Zabih 2003). Hirschmüller and Scharstein (2009) compare a number of these approaches and report on their relative performance in scenes with exposure differences.

Correlation. An alternative to taking intensity differences is to perform *correlation*, i.e., to maximize the *product* (or *cross-correlation*) of the two aligned images,

$$E_{\text{CC}}(\boldsymbol{u}) = \sum_i I_0(\boldsymbol{x}_i) I_1(\boldsymbol{x}_i + \boldsymbol{u}). \tag{8.10}$$

At first glance, this may appear to make bias and gain modeling unnecessary, since the images will prefer to line up regardless of their relative scales and offsets. However, this is actually not true. If a very bright patch exists in $I_1(\boldsymbol{x})$, the maximum product may actually lie in that area.

For this reason, *normalized cross-correlation* is more commonly used,

$$E_{\text{NCC}}(\boldsymbol{u}) = \frac{\sum_i [I_0(\boldsymbol{x}_i) - \overline{I_0}] \, [I_1(\boldsymbol{x}_i + \boldsymbol{u}) - \overline{I_1}]}{\sqrt{\sum_i [I_0(\boldsymbol{x}_i) - \overline{I_0}]^2} \sqrt{\sum_i [I_1(\boldsymbol{x}_i + \boldsymbol{u}) - \overline{I_1}]^2}}, \tag{8.11}$$

where

$$\overline{I_0} = \frac{1}{N} \sum_i I_0(\boldsymbol{x}_i) \quad \text{and} \tag{8.12}$$

$$\overline{I_1} = \frac{1}{N} \sum_i I_1(\boldsymbol{x}_i + \boldsymbol{u}) \tag{8.13}$$

are the *mean images* of the corresponding patches and N is the number of pixels in the patch. The normalized cross-correlation score is always guaranteed to be in the range $[-1, 1]$, which makes it easier to handle in some higher-level applications, such as deciding which patches truly match. Normalized correlation works well when matching images taken with different exposures, e.g., when creating high dynamic range images (Section 10.2). Note, however, that the NCC score is undefined if either of the two patches has zero variance (and, in fact, its performance degrades for noisy low-contrast regions).

A variant on NCC, which is related to the bias–gain regression implicit in the matching score (8.9), is the *normalized SSD* score

$$E_{\text{NSSD}}(\boldsymbol{u}) = \frac{1}{2} \frac{\sum_i \left[[I_0(\boldsymbol{x}_i) - \overline{I_0}] - [I_1(\boldsymbol{x}_i + \boldsymbol{u}) - \overline{I_1}] \right]^2}{\sqrt{\sum_i [I_0(\boldsymbol{x}_i) - \overline{I_0}]^2 + [I_1(\boldsymbol{x}_i + \boldsymbol{u}) - \overline{I_1}]^2}} \tag{8.14}$$

recently proposed by Criminisi, Shotton, Blake *et al.* (2007). In their experiments, they find that it produces comparable results to NCC, but is more efficient when applied to a large number of overlapping patches using a moving average technique (Section 3.2.2).

8.1.1 Hierarchical motion estimation

Now that we have a well-defined alignment cost function to optimize, how can we find its minimum? The simplest solution is to do a *full search* over some range of shifts, using either integer or sub-pixel steps. This is often the approach used for *block matching* in *motion compensated video compression*, where a range of possible motions (say, ±16 pixels) is explored.[4]

To accelerate this search process, *hierarchical motion estimation* is often used: an image pyramid (Section 3.5) is constructed and a search over a smaller number of discrete pixels (corresponding to the same range of motion) is first performed at coarser levels (Quam 1984; Anandan 1989; Bergen, Anandan, Hanna *et al.* 1992). The motion estimate from one level of the pyramid is then used to initialize a smaller *local* search at the next finer level. Alternatively, several seeds (good solutions) from the coarse level can be used to initialize the fine-level search. While this is not guaranteed to produce the same result as a full search, it usually works almost as well and is much faster.

More formally, let

$$I_k^{(l)}(\boldsymbol{x}_j) \leftarrow \tilde{I}_k^{(l-1)}(2\boldsymbol{x}_j) \tag{8.15}$$

be the *decimated* image at level l obtained by subsampling (*downsampling*) a smoothed version of the image at level $l-1$. See Section 3.5 for how to perform the required downsampling (pyramid construction) without introducing too much aliasing.

At the coarsest level, we search for the best displacement $\boldsymbol{u}^{(l)}$ that minimizes the difference between images $I_0^{(l)}$ and $I_1^{(l)}$. This is usually done using a full search over some range of displacements $\boldsymbol{u}^{(l)} \in 2^{-l}[-S, S]^2$, where S is the desired *search range* at the finest (original) resolution level, optionally followed by the incremental refinement step described in Section 8.1.3.

Once a suitable motion vector has been estimated, it is used to *predict* a likely displacement

$$\hat{\boldsymbol{u}}^{(l-1)} \leftarrow 2\boldsymbol{u}^{(l)} \tag{8.16}$$

for the next finer level.[5] The search over displacements is then repeated at the finer level over a much narrower range of displacements, say $\hat{\boldsymbol{u}}^{(l-1)} \pm 1$, again optionally combined with an incremental refinement step (Anandan 1989). Alternatively, one of the images can be *warped* (resampled) by the current motion estimate, in which case only small incremental motions need to be computed at the finer level. A nice description of the whole process, extended to parametric motion estimation (Section 8.2), is provided by Bergen, Anandan, Hanna *et al.* (1992).

8.1.2 Fourier-based alignment

When the search range corresponds to a significant fraction of the larger image (as is the case in image stitching, see Chapter 9), the hierarchical approach may not work that well, since

---

[4] In stereo matching (Section 11.1.2), an explicit search over all possible disparities (i.e., a *plane sweep*) is almost always performed, since the number of search hypotheses is much smaller due to the 1D nature of the potential displacements.

[5] This doubling of displacements is only necessary if displacements are defined in integer *pixel* coordinates, which is the usual case in the literature (Bergen, Anandan, Hanna *et al.* 1992). If *normalized device coordinates* (Section 2.1.5) are used instead, the displacements (and search ranges) need not change from level to level, although the step sizes will need to be adjusted, to keep search steps of roughly one pixel.

it is often not possible to coarsen the representation too much before significant features are blurred away. In this case, a Fourier-based approach may be preferable.

Fourier-based alignment relies on the fact that the Fourier transform of a shifted signal has the same magnitude as the original signal but a linearly varying phase (Section 3.4), i.e.,

$$\mathcal{F}\left\{I_1(\boldsymbol{x}+\boldsymbol{u})\right\} = \mathcal{F}\left\{I_1(\boldsymbol{x})\right\}e^{-ju\cdot\boldsymbol{\omega}} = \mathcal{I}_1(\boldsymbol{\omega})e^{-ju\cdot\boldsymbol{\omega}}, \tag{8.17}$$

where $\boldsymbol{\omega}$ is the vector-valued angular frequency of the Fourier transform and we use calligraphic notation $\mathcal{I}_1(\boldsymbol{\omega}) = \mathcal{F}\left\{I_1(\boldsymbol{x})\right\}$ to denote the Fourier transform of a signal (Section 3.4).

Another useful property of Fourier transforms is that convolution in the spatial domain corresponds to multiplication in the Fourier domain (Section 3.4).[6] Thus, the Fourier transform of the cross-correlation function E_{CC} can be written as

$$\mathcal{F}\left\{E_{\mathrm{CC}}(\boldsymbol{u})\right\} = \mathcal{F}\left\{\sum_i I_0(\boldsymbol{x}_i)I_1(\boldsymbol{x}_i+\boldsymbol{u})\right\} = \mathcal{F}\left\{I_0(\boldsymbol{u})\bar{*}I_1(\boldsymbol{u})\right\} = \mathcal{I}_0(\boldsymbol{\omega})\mathcal{I}_1^*(\boldsymbol{\omega}), \tag{8.18}$$

where

$$f(\boldsymbol{u})\bar{*}g(\boldsymbol{u}) = \sum_i f(\boldsymbol{x}_i)g(\boldsymbol{x}_i+\boldsymbol{u}) \tag{8.19}$$

is the *correlation* function, i.e., the convolution of one signal with the reverse of the other, and $\mathcal{I}_1^*(\boldsymbol{\omega})$ is the *complex conjugate* of $\mathcal{I}_1(\boldsymbol{\omega})$. This is because convolution is defined as the summation of one signal with the reverse of the other (Section 3.4).

Thus, to efficiently evaluate E_{CC} over the range of all possible values of $\boldsymbol{u}$, we take the Fourier transforms of both images $I_0(\boldsymbol{x})$ and $I_1(\boldsymbol{x})$, multiply both transforms together (after conjugating the second one), and take the inverse transform of the result. The Fast Fourier Transform algorithm can compute the transform of an $N \times M$ image in $\mathrm{O}(NM \log NM)$ operations (Bracewell 1986). This can be significantly faster than the $\mathrm{O}(N^2M^2)$ operations required to do a full search when the full range of image overlaps is considered.

While Fourier-based convolution is often used to accelerate the computation of image correlations, it can also be used to accelerate the sum of squared differences function (and its variants). Consider the SSD formula given in (8.1). Its Fourier transform can be written as

$$\begin{aligned}\mathcal{F}\left\{E_{\mathrm{SSD}}(\boldsymbol{u})\right\} &= \mathcal{F}\left\{\sum_i [I_1(\boldsymbol{x}_i+\boldsymbol{u}) - I_0(\boldsymbol{x}_i)]^2\right\} \\ &= \delta(\boldsymbol{\omega})\sum_i [I_0^2(\boldsymbol{x}_i) + I_1^2(\boldsymbol{x}_i)] - 2\mathcal{I}_0(\boldsymbol{\omega})\mathcal{I}_1^*(\boldsymbol{\omega}).\end{aligned} \tag{8.20}$$

Thus, the SSD function can be computed by taking twice the correlation function and subtracting it from the sum of the energies in the two images.

Windowed correlation. Unfortunately, the Fourier convolution theorem only applies when the summation over $\boldsymbol{x}_i$ is performed over *all* the pixels in both images, using a circular shift of the image when accessing pixels outside the original boundaries. While this is

---

[6] In fact, the Fourier shift property (8.17) derives from the convolution theorem by observing that shifting is equivalent to convolution with a displaced delta function $\delta(\boldsymbol{x}-\boldsymbol{u})$.

acceptable for small shifts and comparably sized images, it makes no sense when the images overlap by a small amount or one image is a small subset of the other.

In that case, the cross-correlation function should be replaced with a *windowed* (weighted) cross-correlation function,

$$E_{\mathrm{WCC}}(\boldsymbol{u}) = \sum_i w_0(\boldsymbol{x}_i)I_0(\boldsymbol{x}_i)\, w_1(\boldsymbol{x}_i + \boldsymbol{u})I_1(\boldsymbol{x}_i + \boldsymbol{u}), \qquad (8.21)$$

$$= [w_0(\boldsymbol{x})I_0(\boldsymbol{x})]\bar{*}[w_1(\boldsymbol{x})I_1(\boldsymbol{x})] \qquad (8.22)$$

where the weighting functions w_0 and w_1 are zero outside the valid ranges of the images and both images are padded so that circular shifts return 0 values outside the original image boundaries.

An even more interesting case is the computation of the *weighted* SSD function introduced in Equation (8.5),

$$E_{\mathrm{WSSD}}(\boldsymbol{u}) = \sum_i w_0(\boldsymbol{x}_i)w_1(\boldsymbol{x}_i + \boldsymbol{u})[I_1(\boldsymbol{x}_i + \boldsymbol{u}) - I_0(\boldsymbol{x}_i)]^2. \qquad (8.23)$$

Expanding this as a sum of correlations and deriving the appropriate set of Fourier transforms is left for Exercise 8.1.

The same kind of derivation can also be applied to the bias–gain corrected sum of squared difference function E_{BG} (8.9). Again, Fourier transforms can be used to efficiently compute all the correlations needed to perform the linear regression in the bias and gain parameters in order to estimate the exposure-compensated difference for each potential shift (Exercise 8.1).

Phase correlation. A variant of regular correlation (8.18) that is sometimes used for motion estimation is *phase correlation* (Kuglin and Hines 1975; Brown 1992). Here, the spectrum of the two signals being matched is *whitened* by dividing each per-frequency product in (8.18) by the magnitudes of the Fourier transforms,

$$\mathcal{F}\left\{E_{\mathrm{PC}}(\boldsymbol{u})\right\} = \frac{\mathcal{I}_0(\boldsymbol{\omega})\mathcal{I}_1^*(\boldsymbol{\omega})}{\|\mathcal{I}_0(\boldsymbol{\omega})\|\|\mathcal{I}_1(\boldsymbol{\omega})\|} \qquad (8.24)$$

before taking the final inverse Fourier transform. In the case of noiseless signals with perfect (cyclic) shift, we have $I_1(\boldsymbol{x} + \boldsymbol{u}) = I_0(\boldsymbol{x})$ and hence, from Equation (8.17), we obtain

$$\mathcal{F}\left\{I_1(\boldsymbol{x} + \boldsymbol{u})\right\} = \mathcal{I}_1(\boldsymbol{\omega})e^{-2\pi j u \cdot \boldsymbol{\omega}} = \mathcal{I}_0(\boldsymbol{\omega}) \;\; \text{and}$$

$$\mathcal{F}\left\{E_{\mathrm{PC}}(\boldsymbol{u})\right\} = e^{-2\pi j u \cdot \boldsymbol{\omega}}. \qquad (8.25)$$

The output of phase correlation (under ideal conditions) is therefore a single spike (impulse) located at the correct value of $\boldsymbol{u}$, which (in principle) makes it easier to find the correct estimate.

Phase correlation has a reputation in some quarters of outperforming regular correlation, but this behavior depends on the characteristics of the signals and noise. If the original images are contaminated by noise in a narrow frequency band (e.g., low-frequency noise or peaked frequency "hum"), the whitening process effectively de-emphasizes the noise in these regions. However, if the original signals have very low signal-to-noise ratio at some frequencies (say, two blurry or low-textured images with lots of high-frequency noise), the whitening process can actually decrease performance (see Exercise 8.1).

Recently, gradient cross-correlation has emerged as a promising alternative to phase correlation (Argyriou and Vlachos 2003), although further systematic studies are probably warranted. Phase correlation has also been studied by Fleet and Jepson (1990) as a method for estimating general optical flow and stereo disparity.

Rotations and scale. While Fourier-based alignment is mostly used to estimate translational shifts between images, it can, under certain limited conditions, also be used to estimate in-plane rotations and scales. Consider two images that are related *purely* by rotation, i.e.,

$$I_1(\hat{\boldsymbol{R}}\boldsymbol{x}) = I_0(\boldsymbol{x}). \tag{8.26}$$

If we re-sample the images into *polar coordinates*,

$$\tilde{I}_0(r,\theta) = I_0(r\cos\theta, r\sin\theta) \;\text{ and }\; \tilde{I}_1(r,\theta) = I_1(r\cos\theta, r\sin\theta), \tag{8.27}$$

we obtain

$$\tilde{I}_1(r,\theta + \hat{\theta}) = \tilde{I}_0(r,\theta). \tag{8.28}$$

The desired rotation can then be estimated using a Fast Fourier Transform (FFT) shift-based technique.

If the two images are also related by a scale,

$$I_1(e^{\hat{s}}\hat{\boldsymbol{R}}\boldsymbol{x}) = I_0(\boldsymbol{x}), \tag{8.29}$$

we can re-sample into *log-polar coordinates*,

$$\tilde{I}_0(s,\theta) = I_0(e^s\cos\theta, e^s\sin\theta) \;\text{ and }\; \tilde{I}_1(s,\theta) = I_1(e^s\cos\theta, e^s\sin\theta), \tag{8.30}$$

to obtain

$$\tilde{I}_1(s + \hat{s}, \theta + \hat{\theta}) = \tilde{I}_0(s,\theta). \tag{8.31}$$

In this case, care must be taken to choose a suitable range of s values that reasonably samples the original image.

For images that are also translated by a small amount,

$$I_1(e^{\hat{s}}\hat{\boldsymbol{R}}\boldsymbol{x} + \boldsymbol{t}) = I_0(\boldsymbol{x}), \tag{8.32}$$

De Castro and Morandi (1987) propose an ingenious solution that uses several steps to estimate the unknown parameters. First, both images are converted to the Fourier domain and only the magnitudes of the transformed images are retained. In principle, the Fourier magnitude images are insensitive to translations in the image plane (although the usual caveats about border effects apply). Next, the two magnitude images are aligned in rotation and scale using the polar or log-polar representations. Once rotation and scale are estimated, one of the images can be de-rotated and scaled and a regular translational algorithm can be applied to estimate the translational shift.

Unfortunately, this trick only applies when the images have large overlap (small translational motion). For more general motion of patches or images, the parametric motion estimator described in Section 8.2 or the feature-based approaches described in Section 6.1 need to be used.

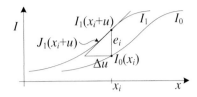

Figure 8.2 Taylor series approximation of a function and the incremental computation of the optical flow correction amount. $\boldsymbol{J}_1(\boldsymbol{x}_i + \boldsymbol{u})$ is the image gradient at $(\boldsymbol{x}_i + \boldsymbol{u})$ and e_i is the current intensity difference.

8.1.3 Incremental refinement

The techniques described up till now can estimate alignment to the nearest pixel (or potentially fractional pixel if smaller search steps are used). In general, image stabilization and stitching applications require much higher accuracies to obtain acceptable results.

To obtain better *sub-pixel* estimates, we can use one of several techniques described by Tian and Huhns (1986). One possibility is to evaluate several discrete (integer or fractional) values of (u, v) around the best value found so far and to *interpolate* the matching score to find an analytic minimum.

A more commonly used approach, first proposed by Lucas and Kanade (1981), is to perform *gradient descent* on the SSD energy function (8.1), using a Taylor series expansion of the image function (Figure 8.2),

$$E_{\text{LK–SSD}}(\boldsymbol{u} + \Delta\boldsymbol{u}) = \sum_i [I_1(\boldsymbol{x}_i + \boldsymbol{u} + \Delta\boldsymbol{u}) - I_0(\boldsymbol{x}_i)]^2 \tag{8.33}$$

$$\approx \sum_i [I_1(\boldsymbol{x}_i + \boldsymbol{u}) + \boldsymbol{J}_1(\boldsymbol{x}_i + \boldsymbol{u})\Delta\boldsymbol{u} - I_0(\boldsymbol{x}_i)]^2 \tag{8.34}$$

$$= \sum_i [\boldsymbol{J}_1(\boldsymbol{x}_i + \boldsymbol{u})\Delta\boldsymbol{u} + e_i]^2, \tag{8.35}$$

where

$$\boldsymbol{J}_1(\boldsymbol{x}_i + \boldsymbol{u}) = \nabla I_1(\boldsymbol{x}_i + \boldsymbol{u}) = (\frac{\partial I_1}{\partial x}, \frac{\partial I_1}{\partial y})(\boldsymbol{x}_i + \boldsymbol{u}) \tag{8.36}$$

is the *image gradient* or *Jacobian* at $(\boldsymbol{x}_i + \boldsymbol{u})$ and

$$e_i = I_1(\boldsymbol{x}_i + \boldsymbol{u}) - I_0(\boldsymbol{x}_i), \tag{8.37}$$

first introduced in (8.1), is the current intensity error.[7] The gradient at a particular sub-pixel location $(\boldsymbol{x}_i + \boldsymbol{u})$ can be computed using a variety of techniques, the simplest of which is to simply take the horizontal and vertical differences between pixels $\boldsymbol{x}$ and $\boldsymbol{x} + (1, 0)$ or $\boldsymbol{x} + (0, 1)$. More sophisticated derivatives can sometimes lead to noticeable performance improvements.

The linearized form of the incremental update to the SSD error (8.35) is often called the *optical flow constraint* or *brightness constancy constraint* equation

$$I_x u + I_y v + I_t = 0, \tag{8.38}$$

---

[7] We follow the convention, commonly used in robotics and by Baker and Matthews (2004), that derivatives with respect to (column) vectors result in row vectors, so that fewer transposes are needed in the formulas.

where the subscripts in I_x and I_y denote spatial derivatives, and I_t is called the *temporal derivative*, which makes sense if we are computing instantaneous velocity in a video sequence. When squared and summed or integrated over a region, it can be used to compute optic flow (Horn and Schunck 1981).

The above least squares problem (8.35) can be minimized by solving the associated *normal equations* (Appendix A.2),

$$A \Delta u = b \qquad (8.39)$$

where

$$A = \sum_i J_1^T (x_i + u) J_1 (x_i + u) \qquad (8.40)$$

and

$$b = - \sum_i e_i J_1^T (x_i + u) \qquad (8.41)$$

are called the (Gauss–Newton approximation of the) *Hessian* and *gradient-weighted residual vector*, respectively.[8] These matrices are also often written as

$$A = \begin{bmatrix} \sum I_x^2 & \sum I_x I_y \\ \sum I_x I_y & \sum I_y^2 \end{bmatrix} \quad \text{and} \quad b = - \begin{bmatrix} \sum I_x I_t \\ \sum I_y I_t \end{bmatrix}. \qquad (8.42)$$

The gradients required for $J_1(x_i + u)$ can be evaluated at the same time as the image warps required to estimate $I_1(x_i + u)$ (Section 3.6.1 (3.89)) and, in fact, are often computed as a side-product of image interpolation. If efficiency is a concern, these gradients can be replaced by the gradients in the *template* image,

$$J_1(x_i + u) \approx J_0(x_i), \qquad (8.43)$$

since near the correct alignment, the template and displaced target images should look similar. This has the advantage of allowing the pre-computation of the Hessian and Jacobian images, which can result in significant computational savings (Hager and Belhumeur 1998; Baker and Matthews 2004). A further reduction in computation can be obtained by writing the warped image $I_1(x_i + u)$ used to compute e_i in (8.37) as a convolution of a sub-pixel interpolation filter with the discrete samples in I_1 (Peleg and Rav-Acha 2006). Precomputing the inner product between the gradient field and shifted version of I_1 allows the iterative re-computation of e_i to be performed in constant time (independent of the number of pixels).

The effectiveness of the above incremental update rule relies on the quality of the Taylor series approximation. When far away from the true displacement (say, 1–2 pixels), several iterations may be needed. It is possible, however, to estimate a value for J_1 using a least squares fit to a series of larger displacements in order to increase the range of convergence (Jurie and Dhome 2002) or to "learn" a special-purpose recognizer for a given patch (Avidan 2001; Williams, Blake, and Cipolla 2003; Lepetit, Pilet, and Fua 2006; Hinterstoisser, Benhimane, Navab *et al.* 2008; Özuysal, Calonder, Lepetit *et al.* 2010) as discussed in Section 4.1.4.

A commonly used stopping criterion for incremental updating is to monitor the magnitude of the displacement correction $\|u\|$ and to stop when it drops below a certain threshold (say,

---

[8] The true Hessian is the full second derivative of the error function E, which may not be positive definite—see Section 6.1.3 and Appendix A.3.

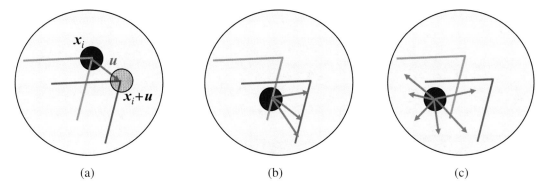

Figure 8.3 Aperture problems for different image regions, denoted by the orange and red L-shaped structures, overlaid in the same image to make it easier to diagram the flow. (a) A window $w(x_i)$ centered at x_i (black circle) can uniquely be matched to its corresponding structure at $x_i + u$ in the second (red) image. (b) A window centered on the edge exhibits the classic aperture problem, since it can be matched to a 1D family of possible locations. (c) In a completely textureless region, the matches become totally unconstrained.

$1/10$ of a pixel). For larger motions, it is usual to combine the incremental update rule with a hierarchical coarse-to-fine search strategy, as described in Section 8.1.1.

Conditioning and aperture problems. Sometimes, the inversion of the linear system (8.39) can be poorly conditioned because of lack of two-dimensional texture in the patch being aligned. A commonly occurring example of this is the *aperture problem*, first identified in some of the early papers on optical flow (Horn and Schunck 1981) and then studied more extensively by Anandan (1989). Consider an image patch that consists of a slanted edge moving to the right (Figure 8.3). Only the *normal* component of the velocity (displacement) can be reliably recovered in this case. This manifests itself in (8.39) as a *rank-deficient* matrix A, i.e., one whose smaller eigenvalue is very close to zero.[9]

When Equation (8.39) is solved, the component of the displacement along the edge is very poorly conditioned and can result in wild guesses under small noise perturbations. One way to mitigate this problem is to add a *prior* (soft constraint) on the expected range of motions (Simoncelli, Adelson, and Heeger 1991; Baker, Gross, and Matthews 2004; Govindu 2006). This can be accomplished by adding a small value to the diagonal of A, which essentially biases the solution towards smaller Δu values that still (mostly) minimize the squared error.

However, the pure Gaussian model assumed when using a simple (fixed) quadratic prior, as in (Simoncelli, Adelson, and Heeger 1991), does not always hold in practice, e.g., because of aliasing along strong edges (Triggs 2004). For this reason, it may be prudent to add some small fraction (say, 5%) of the larger eigenvalue to the smaller one before doing the matrix inversion.

Uncertainty modeling. The reliability of a particular patch-based motion estimate can be captured more formally with an *uncertainty model*. The simplest such model is a *covariance matrix*, which captures the expected variance in the motion estimate in all possible directions.

---

[9]The matrix A is by construction always guaranteed to be symmetric positive semi-definite, i.e., it has real non-negative eigenvalues.

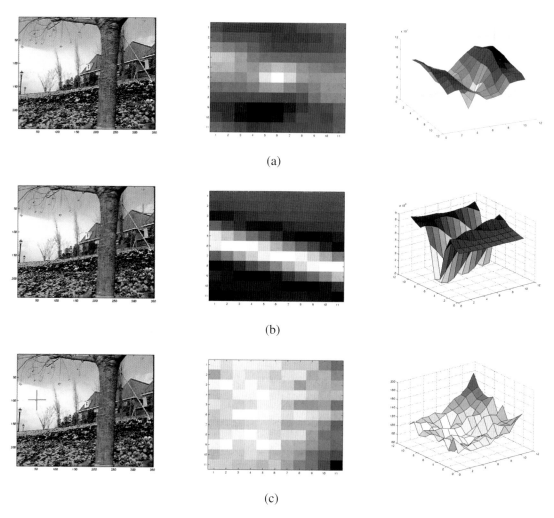

Figure 8.4 SSD surfaces corresponding to three locations (red crosses) in an image: (a) highly textured area, strong minimum, low uncertainty; (b) strong edge, aperture problem, high uncertainty in one direction; (c) weak texture, no clear minimum, large uncertainty.

As discussed in Section 6.1.4 and Appendix B.6, under small amounts of additive Gaussian noise, it can be shown that the covariance matrix $\Sigma_{\boldsymbol{u}}$ is proportional to the inverse of the Hessian $\boldsymbol{A}$,

$$\Sigma_{\boldsymbol{u}} = \sigma_n^2 \boldsymbol{A}^{-1}, \tag{8.44}$$

where σ_n^2 is the variance of the additive Gaussian noise (Anandan 1989; Matthies, Kanade, and Szeliski 1989; Szeliski 1989).

For larger amounts of noise, the linearization performed by the Lucas–Kanade algorithm in (8.35) is only approximate, so the above quantity becomes a *Cramer–Rao lower bound* on the true covariance. Thus, the minimum and maximum eigenvalues of the Hessian $\boldsymbol{A}$ can now be interpreted as the (scaled) inverse variances in the least-certain and most-certain directions of motion. (A more detailed analysis using a more realistic model of image noise is given by Steele and Jaynes (2005).) Figure 8.4 shows the local SSD surfaces for three different pixel locations in an image. As you can see, the surface has a clear minimum in the highly textured region and suffers from the aperture problem near the strong edge.

Bias and gain, weighting, and robust error metrics. The Lucas–Kanade update rule can also be applied to the bias–gain equation (8.9) to obtain

$$E_{\mathrm{LK-BG}}(\boldsymbol{u} + \Delta\boldsymbol{u}) = \sum_i [\boldsymbol{J}_1(\boldsymbol{x}_i + \boldsymbol{u})\Delta\boldsymbol{u} + e_i - \alpha I_0(\boldsymbol{x}_i) - \beta]^2 \tag{8.45}$$

(Lucas and Kanade 1981; Gennert 1988; Fuh and Maragos 1991; Baker, Gross, and Matthews 2003). The resulting 4×4 system of equations can be solved to simultaneously estimate the translational displacement update $\Delta\boldsymbol{u}$ and the bias and gain parameters β and α.

A similar formulation can be derived for images (templates) that have a *linear appearance variation*,

$$I_1(\boldsymbol{x} + \boldsymbol{u}) \approx I_0(\boldsymbol{x}) + \sum_j \lambda_j B_j(\boldsymbol{x}), \tag{8.46}$$

where the $B_j(\boldsymbol{x})$ are the *basis images* and the λ_j are the unknown coefficients (Hager and Belhumeur 1998; Baker, Gross, Ishikawa *et al.* 2003; Baker, Gross, and Matthews 2003). Potential linear appearance variations include illumination changes (Hager and Belhumeur 1998) and small non-rigid deformations (Black and Jepson 1998).

A weighted (windowed) version of the Lucas–Kanade algorithm is also possible:

$$E_{\mathrm{LK-WSSD}}(\boldsymbol{u} + \Delta\boldsymbol{u}) = \sum_i w_0(\boldsymbol{x}_i) w_1(\boldsymbol{x}_i + \boldsymbol{u})[\boldsymbol{J}_1(\boldsymbol{x}_i + \boldsymbol{u})\Delta\boldsymbol{u} + e_i]^2. \tag{8.47}$$

Note that here, in deriving the Lucas–Kanade update from the original weighted SSD function (8.5), we have neglected taking the derivative of the $w_1(\boldsymbol{x}_i + \boldsymbol{u})$ weighting function with respect to $\boldsymbol{u}$, which is usually acceptable in practice, especially if the weighting function is a binary mask with relatively few transitions.

Baker, Gross, Ishikawa *et al.* (2003) only use the $w_0(\boldsymbol{x})$ term, which is reasonable if the two images have the same extent and no (independent) cutouts in the overlap region. They also discuss the idea of making the weighting proportional to $\nabla I(\boldsymbol{x})$, which helps for very noisy images, where the gradient itself is noisy. Similar observations, formulated in terms of *total least squares* (Van Huffel and Vandewalle 1991; Van Huffel and Lemmerling 2002), have been made by other researchers studying optical flow (Weber and Malik 1995; Bab-Hadiashar and Suter 1998b; Mühlich and Mester 1998). Lastly, Baker, Gross, Ishikawa *et al.* (2003) show how evaluating Equation (8.47) at just the *most reliable* (highest gradient) pixels does not significantly reduce performance for large enough images, even if only 5–10% of the pixels are used. (This idea was originally proposed by Dellaert and Collins (1999), who used a more sophisticated selection criterion.)

The Lucas–Kanade incremental refinement step can also be applied to the robust error metric introduced in Section 8.1,

$$E_{\mathrm{LK-SRD}}(\boldsymbol{u} + \Delta \boldsymbol{u}) = \sum_i \rho(\boldsymbol{J}_1(\boldsymbol{x}_i + \boldsymbol{u})\Delta \boldsymbol{u} + e_i), \tag{8.48}$$

which can be solved using the *iteratively reweighted least squares* technique described in Section 6.1.4.

8.2 Parametric motion

Many image alignment tasks, for example image stitching with handheld cameras, require the use of more sophisticated motion models, as described in Section 2.1.2. Since these models, e.g., affine deformations, typically have more parameters than pure translation, a full search over the possible range of values is impractical. Instead, the incremental Lucas–Kanade algorithm can be generalized to parametric motion models and used in conjunction with a hierarchical search algorithm (Lucas and Kanade 1981; Rehg and Witkin 1991; Fuh and Maragos 1991; Bergen, Anandan, Hanna *et al.* 1992; Shashua and Toelg 1997; Shashua and Wexler 2001; Baker and Matthews 2004).

For parametric motion, instead of using a single constant translation vector $\boldsymbol{u}$, we use a spatially varying *motion field* or *correspondence map*, $\boldsymbol{x}'(\boldsymbol{x}; \boldsymbol{p})$, parameterized by a low-dimensional vector $\boldsymbol{p}$, where $\boldsymbol{x}'$ can be any of the motion models presented in Section 2.1.2. The parametric incremental motion update rule now becomes

$$E_{\mathrm{LK-PM}}(\boldsymbol{p} + \Delta \boldsymbol{p}) = \sum_i [I_1(\boldsymbol{x}'(\boldsymbol{x}_i; \boldsymbol{p} + \Delta \boldsymbol{p})) - I_0(\boldsymbol{x}_i)]^2 \tag{8.49}$$

$$\approx \sum_i [I_1(\boldsymbol{x}'_i) + \boldsymbol{J}_1(\boldsymbol{x}'_i)\Delta \boldsymbol{p} - I_0(\boldsymbol{x}_i)]^2 \tag{8.50}$$

$$= \sum_i [\boldsymbol{J}_1(\boldsymbol{x}'_i)\Delta \boldsymbol{p} + e_i]^2, \tag{8.51}$$

where the Jacobian is now

$$\boldsymbol{J}_1(\boldsymbol{x}'_i) = \frac{\partial I_1}{\partial \boldsymbol{p}} = \nabla I_1(\boldsymbol{x}'_i)\frac{\partial \boldsymbol{x}'}{\partial \boldsymbol{p}}(\boldsymbol{x}_i), \tag{8.52}$$

i.e., the product of the image gradient ∇I_1 with the Jacobian of the correspondence field, $\boldsymbol{J}_{x'} = \partial \boldsymbol{x}'/\partial \boldsymbol{p}$.

The motion Jacobians $\boldsymbol{J}_{x'}$ for the 2D planar transformations introduced in Section 2.1.2 and Table 2.1 are given in Table 6.1. Note how we have re-parameterized the motion matrices so that they are always the identity at the origin $\boldsymbol{p} = 0$. This becomes useful later, when we talk about the compositional and inverse compositional algorithms. (It also makes it easier to impose priors on the motions.)

For parametric motion, the (Gauss–Newton) *Hessian* and *gradient-weighted residual vector* become

$$A = \sum_i J_{x'}^T(x_i)[\nabla I_1^T(x_i')\nabla I_1(x_i')]J_{x'}(x_i) \tag{8.53}$$

and

$$b = -\sum_i J_{x'}^T(x_i)[e_i\nabla I_1^T(x_i')]. \tag{8.54}$$

Note how the expressions inside the square brackets are the same ones evaluated for the simpler translational motion case (8.40–8.41).

Patch-based approximation. The computation of the Hessian and residual vectors for parametric motion can be significantly more expensive than for the translational case. For parametric motion with n parameters and N pixels, the accumulation of A and b takes $O(n^2 N)$ operations (Baker and Matthews 2004). One way to reduce this by a significant amount is to divide the image up into smaller sub-blocks (patches) P_j and to only accumulate the simpler 2×2 quantities inside the square brackets at the pixel level (Shum and Szeliski 2000),

$$A_j = \sum_{i \in P_j} \nabla I_1^T(x_i')\nabla I_1(x_i') \tag{8.55}$$

$$b_j = \sum_{i \in P_j} e_i\nabla I_1^T(x_i'). \tag{8.56}$$

The full Hessian and residual can then be approximated as

$$A \approx \sum_j J_{x'}^T(\hat{x}_j)[\sum_{i \in P_j} \nabla I_1^T(x_i')\nabla I_1(x_i')]J_{x'}(\hat{x}_j) = \sum_j J_{x'}^T(\hat{x}_j)A_j J_{x'}(\hat{x}_j) \tag{8.57}$$

and

$$b \approx -\sum_j J_{x'}^T(\hat{x}_j)[\sum_{i \in P_j} e_i\nabla I_1^T(x_i')] = -\sum_j J_{x'}^T(\hat{x}_j)b_j, \tag{8.58}$$

where $\hat{x}_j$ is the *center* of each patch P_j (Shum and Szeliski 2000). This is equivalent to replacing the true motion Jacobian with a piecewise-constant approximation. In practice, this works quite well. The relationship of this approximation to feature-based registration is discussed in Section 9.2.4.

Compositional approach. For a complex parametric motion such as a homography, the computation of the motion Jacobian becomes complicated and may involve a per-pixel division. Szeliski and Shum (1997) observed that this can be simplified by first warping the target image I_1 according to the current motion estimate $x'(x; p)$,

$$\tilde{I}_1(x) = I_1(x'(x; p)), \tag{8.59}$$

and then comparing this *warped* image against the template $I_0(x)$,

$$E_{\text{LK-SS}}(\Delta p) = \sum_i [\tilde{I}_1(\tilde{x}(x_i; \Delta p)) - I_0(x_i)]^2 \tag{8.60}$$

$$\approx \sum_i [\tilde{J}_1(x_i)\Delta p + e_i]^2 \tag{8.61}$$

$$= \sum_i [\nabla \tilde{I}_1(x_i)J_{\tilde{x}}(x_i)\Delta p + e_i]^2. \tag{8.62}$$

Note that since the two images are assumed to be fairly similar, only an *incremental* parametric motion is required, i.e., the incremental motion can be evaluated around $\boldsymbol{p} = 0$, which can lead to considerable simplifications. For example, the Jacobian of the planar projective transform (6.19) now becomes

$$\boldsymbol{J}_{\tilde{\boldsymbol{x}}} = \left.\frac{\partial \tilde{\boldsymbol{x}}}{\partial \boldsymbol{p}}\right|_{\boldsymbol{p}=0} = \begin{bmatrix} x & y & 1 & 0 & 0 & 0 & -x^2 & -xy \\ 0 & 0 & 0 & x & y & 1 & -xy & -y^2 \end{bmatrix}. \tag{8.63}$$

Once the incremental motion $\tilde{\boldsymbol{x}}$ has been computed, it can be *prepended* to the previously estimated motion, which is easy to do for motions represented with transformation matrices, such as those given in Tables 2.1 and 6.1. Baker and Matthews (2004) call this the *forward compositional* algorithm, since the target image is being re-warped and the final motion estimates are being composed.

If the appearance of the warped and template images is similar enough, we can replace the gradient of $\tilde{I}_1(\boldsymbol{x})$ with the gradient of $I_0(\boldsymbol{x})$, as suggested previously (8.43). This has potentially a big advantage in that it allows the pre-computation (and inversion) of the Hessian matrix $\boldsymbol{A}$ given in Equation (8.53). The residual vector $\boldsymbol{b}$ (8.54) can also be partially precomputed, i.e., the *steepest descent images* $\nabla I_0(\boldsymbol{x})\boldsymbol{J}_{\tilde{\boldsymbol{x}}}(\boldsymbol{x})$ can precomputed and stored for later multiplication with the $e(\boldsymbol{x}) = \tilde{I}_1(\boldsymbol{x}) - I_0(\boldsymbol{x})$ error images (Baker and Matthews 2004). This idea was first suggested by Hager and Belhumeur (1998) in what Baker and Matthews (2004) call a *inverse additive* scheme.

Baker and Matthews (2004) introduce one more variant they call the *inverse compositional* algorithm. Rather than (conceptually) re-warping the warped target image $\tilde{I}_1(\boldsymbol{x})$, they instead warp the template image $I_0(\boldsymbol{x})$ and minimize

$$E_{\mathrm{LK-BM}}(\Delta\boldsymbol{p}) = \sum_i [\tilde{I}_1(\boldsymbol{x}_i) - I_0(\tilde{\boldsymbol{x}}(\boldsymbol{x}_i; \Delta\boldsymbol{p}))]^2 \tag{8.64}$$

$$\approx \sum_i [\nabla I_0(\boldsymbol{x}_i)\boldsymbol{J}_{\tilde{\boldsymbol{x}}}(\boldsymbol{x}_i)\Delta\boldsymbol{p} - e_i]^2. \tag{8.65}$$

This is identical to the forward warped algorithm (8.62) with the gradients $\nabla \tilde{I}_1(\boldsymbol{x})$ replaced by the gradients $\nabla I_0(\boldsymbol{x})$, except for the sign of e_i. The resulting update $\Delta\boldsymbol{p}$ is the *negative* of the one computed by the modified Equation (8.62) and hence the *inverse* of the incremental transformation must be prepended to the current transform. Because the inverse compositional algorithm has the potential of pre-computing the inverse Hessian and the steepest descent images, this makes it the preferred approach of those surveyed by Baker and Matthews (2004). Figure 8.5 (Baker, Gross, Ishikawa *et al.* 2003) beautifully shows all of the steps required to implement the inverse compositional algorithm.

Baker and Matthews (2004) also discuss the advantage of using Gauss–Newton iteration (i.e., the first-order expansion of the least squares, as above) compared to other approaches such as steepest descent and Levenberg–Marquardt. Subsequent parts of the series (Baker, Gross, Ishikawa *et al.* 2003; Baker, Gross, and Matthews 2003, 2004) discuss more advanced topics such as per-pixel weighting, pixel selection for efficiency, a more in-depth discussion of robust metrics and algorithms, linear appearance variations, and priors on parameters. They make for invaluable reading for anyone interested in implementing a highly tuned implementation of incremental image registration. Evangelidis and Psarakis (2008) provide some detailed experimental evaluations of these and other related approaches.

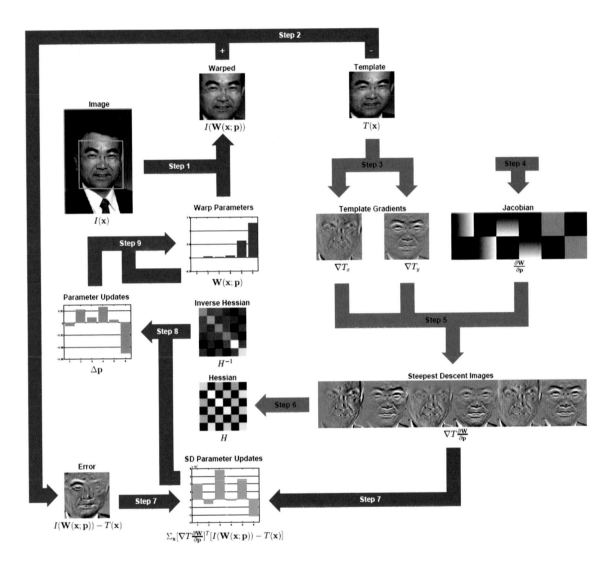

Figure 8.5 A schematic overview of the inverse compositional algorithm (copied, with permission, from (Baker, Gross, Ishikawa *et al.* 2003)). Steps 3–6 (light-colored arrows) are performed once as a pre-computation. The main algorithm simply consists of iterating: image warping (Step 1), image differencing (Step 2), image dot products (Step 7), multiplication with the inverse of the Hessian (Step 8), and the update to the warp (Step 9). All of these steps can be performed efficiently.

8.2.1 *Application*: Video stabilization

Video stabilization is one of the most widely used applications of parametric motion estimation (Hansen, Anandan, Dana *et al.* 1994; Irani, Rousso, and Peleg 1997; Morimoto and Chellappa 1997; Srinivasan, Chellappa, Veeraraghavan *et al.* 2005). Algorithms for stabilization run inside both hardware devices, such as camcorders and still cameras, and software packages for improving the visual quality of shaky videos.

In their paper on full-frame video stabilization, Matsushita, Ofek, Ge *et al.* (2006) give a nice overview of the three major stages of stabilization, namely motion estimation, motion smoothing, and image warping. Motion estimation algorithms often use a similarity transform to handle camera translations, rotations, and zooming. The tricky part is getting these algorithms to lock onto the background motion, which is a result of the camera movement, without getting distracted by independent moving foreground objects. Motion smoothing algorithms recover the low-frequency (slowly varying) part of the motion and then estimate the high-frequency shake component that needs to be removed. Finally, image warping algorithms apply the high-frequency correction to render the original frames as if the camera had undergone only the smooth motion.

The resulting stabilization algorithms can greatly improve the appearance of shaky videos but they often still contain visual artifacts. For example, image warping can result in missing borders around the image, which must be cropped, filled using information from other frames, or hallucinated using inpainting techniques (Section 10.5.1). Furthermore, video frames captured during fast motion are often blurry. Their appearance can be improved either using deblurring techniques (Section 10.3) or stealing sharper pixels from other frames with less motion or better focus (Matsushita, Ofek, Ge *et al.* 2006). Exercise 8.3 has you implement and test some of these ideas.

In situations where the camera is translating a lot in 3D, e.g., when the videographer is walking, an even better approach is to compute a full structure from motion reconstruction of the camera motion and 3D scene. A smooth 3D camera path can then be computed and the original video re-rendered using view interpolation with the interpolated 3D point cloud serving as the proxy geometry while preserving salient features (Liu, Gleicher, Jin *et al.* 2009). If you have access to a camera array instead of a single video camera, you can do even better using a light field rendering approach (Section 13.3) (Smith, Zhang, Jin *et al.* 2009).

8.2.2 Learned motion models

An alternative to parameterizing the motion field with a geometric deformation such as an affine transform is to learn a set of basis functions tailored to a particular application (Black, Yacoob, Jepson *et al.* 1997). First, a set of dense motion fields (Section 8.4) is computed from a set of training videos. Next, singular value decomposition (SVD) is applied to the stack of motion fields $u_t(x)$ to compute the first few singular vectors $v_k(x)$. Finally, for a new test sequence, a novel flow field is computed using a coarse-to-fine algorithm that estimates the unknown coefficient a_k in the parameterized flow field

$$u(x) = \sum_k a_k v_k(x). \tag{8.66}$$

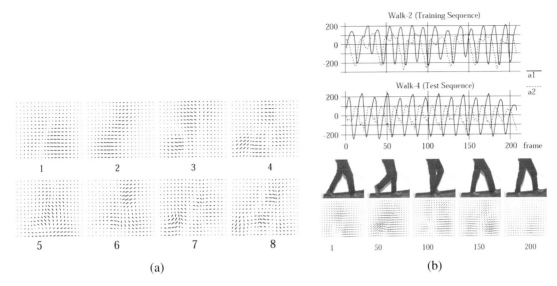

Figure 8.6 Learned parameterized motion fields for a walking sequence (Black, Yacoob, Jepson *et al.* 1997) ©
1997 IEEE: (a) learned basis flow fields; (b) plots of motion coefficients over time and corresponding estimated
motion fields.

Figure 8.6a shows a set of basis fields learned by observing videos of walking motions.
Figure 8.6b shows the temporal evolution of the basis coefficients as well as a few of the
recovered parametric motion fields. Note that similar ideas can also be applied to feature
tracks (Torresani, Hertzmann, and Bregler 2008), which is a topic we discuss in more detail
in Sections 4.1.4 and 12.6.4.

8.3 Spline-based motion

While parametric motion models are useful in a wide variety of applications (such as video
stabilization and mapping onto planar surfaces), most image motion is too complicated to be
captured by such low-dimensional models.

Traditionally, optical flow algorithms (Section 8.4) compute an independent motion estimate for each pixel, i.e., the number of flow vectors computed is equal to the number of input
pixels. The general optical flow analog to Equation (8.1) can thus be written as

$$E_{\mathrm{SSD-OF}}(\{\boldsymbol{u}_i\}) = \sum_i [I_1(\boldsymbol{x}_i + \boldsymbol{u}_i) - I_0(\boldsymbol{x}_i)]^2. \tag{8.67}$$

Notice how in the above equation, the number of variables $\{\boldsymbol{u}_i\}$ is twice the number of
measurements, so the problem is underconstrained.

The two classic approaches to this problem, which we study in Section 8.4, are to perform
the summation over overlapping regions (the *patch-based* or *window-based* approach) or to
add smoothness terms on the $\{\boldsymbol{u}_i\}$ field using *regularization* or *Markov random fields* (Section 3.7). In this section, we describe an alternative approach that lies somewhere between
general optical flow (independent flow at each pixel) and parametric flow (a small number of
global parameters). The approach is to represent the motion field as a two-dimensional *spline*

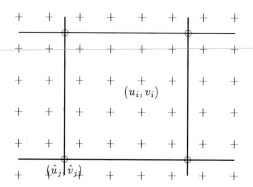

Figure 8.7 Spline motion field: the displacement vectors $\boldsymbol{u}_i = (u_i, v_i)$ are shown as pluses (+) and are controlled by the smaller number of control vertices $\hat{\boldsymbol{u}}_j = (\hat{u}_i, \hat{v}_j)$, which are shown as circles (○).

controlled by a smaller number of *control vertices* $\{\hat{\boldsymbol{u}}_j\}$ (Figure 8.7),

$$\boldsymbol{u}_i = \sum_j \hat{\boldsymbol{u}}_j B_j(\boldsymbol{x}_i) = \sum_j \hat{\boldsymbol{u}}_j w_{i,j}, \qquad (8.68)$$

where the $B_j(\boldsymbol{x}_i)$ are called the *basis functions* and are only non-zero over a small *finite sup-port* interval (Szeliski and Coughlan 1997). We call the $w_{ij} = B_j(\boldsymbol{x}_i)$ *weights* to emphasize that the $\{\boldsymbol{u}_i\}$ are known linear combinations of the $\{\hat{\boldsymbol{u}}_j\}$. Some commonly used spline basis functions are shown in Figure 8.8.

Substituting the formula for the individual per-pixel flow vectors $\boldsymbol{u}_i$ (8.68) into the SSD error metric (8.67) yields a parametric motion formula similar to Equation (8.50). The biggest difference is that the Jacobian $\boldsymbol{J}_1(\boldsymbol{x}_i')$ (8.52) now consists of the sparse entries in the weight matrix $\boldsymbol{W} = [w_{ij}]$.

In situations where we know something more about the motion field, e.g., when the motion is due to a camera moving in a static scene, we can use more specialized motion models. For example, the *plane plus parallax* model (Section 2.1.5) can be naturally combined with a spline-based motion representation, where the in-plane motion is represented by a homography (6.19) and the out-of-plane parallax d is represented by a scalar variable at each spline control point (Szeliski and Kang 1995; Szeliski and Coughlan 1997).

In many cases, the small number of spline vertices results in a motion estimation problem that is well conditioned. However, if large textureless regions (or elongated edges subject to the aperture problem) persist across several spline patches, it may be necessary to add a *regularization* term to make the problem well posed (Section 3.7.1). The simplest way to do this is to directly add squared difference penalties between adjacent vertices in the spline control mesh $\{\hat{\boldsymbol{u}}_j\}$, as in (3.100). If a multi-resolution (coarse-to-fine) strategy is being used, it is important to re-scale these smoothness terms while going from level to level.

The linear system corresponding to the spline-based motion estimator is sparse and regular. Because it is usually of moderate size, it can often be solved using direct techniques such as Cholesky decomposition (Appendix A.4). Alternatively, if the problem becomes too large and subject to excessive fill-in, iterative techniques such as hierarchically preconditioned conjugate gradient (Szeliski 1990b, 2006b) can be used instead (Appendix A.5).

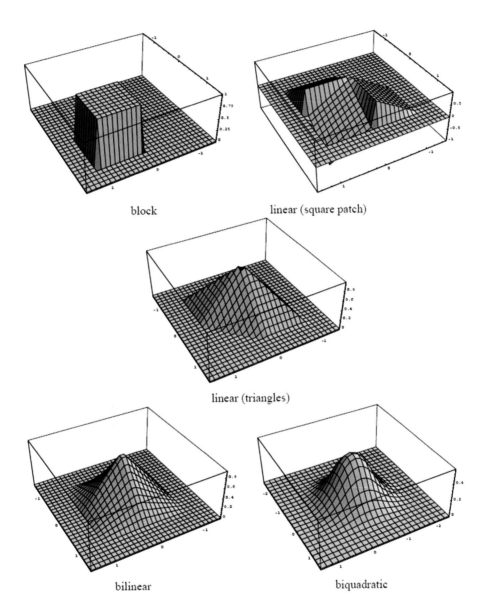

Figure 8.8 Sample spline basis functions (Szeliski and Coughlan 1997) © 1997 Springer. The block (constant) interpolator/basis corresponds to block-based motion estimation (Le Gall 1991). See Section 3.5.1 for more details on spline functions.

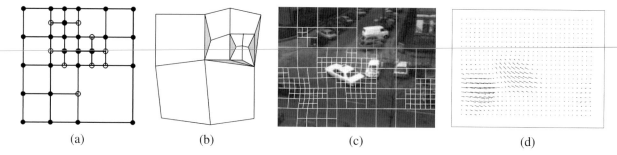

(a)   (b)   (c)   (d)

Figure 8.9 Quadtree spline-based motion estimation (Szeliski and Shum 1996) © 1996 IEEE: (a) quadtree spline representation, (b) which can lead to *cracks*, unless the white nodes are constrained to depend on their parents; (c) deformed quadtree spline mesh overlaid on grayscale image; (d) flow field visualized as a needle diagram.

Because of its robustness, spline-based motion estimation has been used for a number of applications, including visual effects (Roble 1999) and medical image registration (Section 8.3.1) (Szeliski and Lavallée 1996; Kybic and Unser 2003).

One disadvantage of the basic technique, however, is that the model does a poor job near motion discontinuities, unless an excessive number of nodes is used. To remedy this situation, Szeliski and Shum (1996) propose using a *quadtree* representation embedded in the spline control grid (Figure 8.9a). Large cells are used to present regions of smooth motion, while smaller cells are added in regions of motion discontinuities (Figure 8.9c).

To estimate the motion, a coarse-to-fine strategy is used. Starting with a regular spline imposed over a lower-resolution image, an initial motion estimate is obtained. Spline patches where the motion is inconsistent, i.e., the squared residual (8.67) is above a threshold, are subdivided into smaller patches. In order to avoid *cracks* in the resulting motion field (Figure 8.9b), the values of certain nodes in the refined mesh, i.e., those adjacent to larger cells, need to be *restricted* so that they depend on their parent values. This is most easily accomplished using a hierarchical basis representation for the quadtree spline (Szeliski 1990b) and selectively setting some of the hierarchical basis functions to 0, as described in (Szeliski and Shum 1996).

8.3.1 *Application*: Medical image registration

Because they excel at representing smooth *elastic* deformation fields, spline-based motion models have found widespread use in medical image registration (Bajcsy and Kovacic 1989; Szeliski and Lavallée 1996; Christensen, Joshi, and Miller 1997).[10] Registration techniques can be used both to track an individual patient's development or progress over time (a *longitudinal* study) or to match different patient images together to find commonalities and detect variations or pathologies (*cross-sectional* studies). When different imaging *modalities* are being registered, e.g., computed tomography (CT) scans and magnetic resonance images (MRI), *mutual information* measures of similarity are often necessary (Viola and Wells III 1997; Maes, Collignon, Vandermeulen *et al.* 1997).

---

[10] In computer graphics, such elastic volumetric deformation are known as *free-form deformations* (Sederberg and Parry 1986; Coquillart 1990; Celniker and Gossard 1991).

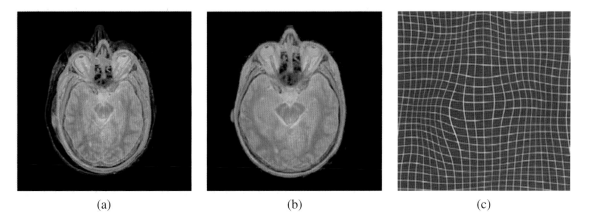

(a) (b) (c)

Figure 8.10 Elastic brain registration (Kybic and Unser 2003) © 2003 IEEE: (a) original brain atlas and patient MRI images overlaid in red–green; (b) after elastic registration with eight user-specified landmarks (not shown); (c) a cubic B-spline deformation field, shown as a deformed grid.

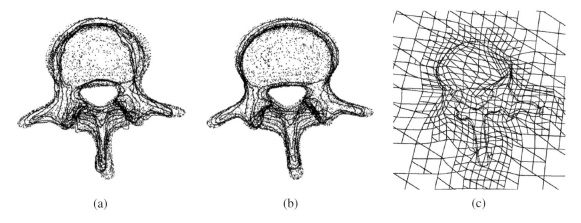

(a) (b) (c)

Figure 8.11 Octree spline-based image registration of two vertebral surface models (Szeliski and Lavallée 1996) © 1996 Springer: (a) after initial rigid alignment; (b) after elastic alignment; (c) a cross-section through the adapted octree spline deformation field.

Kybic and Unser (2003) provide a nice literature review and describe a complete working system based on representing both the images and the deformation fields as multi-resolution splines. Figure 8.10 shows an example of the Kybic and Unser system being used to register a patient's brain MRI with a labeled brain atlas image. The system can be run in a fully automatic mode but more accurate results can be obtained by locating a few key *landmarks*. More recent papers on deformable medical image registration, including performance evaluations, include (Klein, Staring, and Pluim 2007; Glocker, Komodakis, Tziritas *et al.* 2008).

As with other applications, regular volumetric splines can be enhanced using selective refinement. In the case of 3D volumetric image or surface registration, these are known as *octree splines* (Szeliski and Lavallée 1996) and have been used to register medical surface models such as vertebrae and faces from different patients (Figure 8.11).

8.4 Optical flow

The most general (and challenging) version of motion estimation is to compute an independent estimate of motion at *each* pixel, which is generally known as *optical* (or *optic*) *flow*. As we mentioned in the previous section, this generally involves minimizing the brightness or color difference between corresponding pixels summed over the image,

$$E_{\mathrm{SSD-OF}}(\{\boldsymbol{u}_i\}) = \sum_i [I_1(\boldsymbol{x}_i + \boldsymbol{u}_i) - I_0(\boldsymbol{x}_i)]^2. \tag{8.69}$$

Since the number of variables $\{\boldsymbol{u}_i\}$ is twice the number of measurements, the problem is underconstrained. The two classic approaches to this problem are to perform the summation *locally* over overlapping regions (the *patch-based* or *window-based* approach) or to add smoothness terms on the $\{\boldsymbol{u}_i\}$ field using regularization or Markov random fields (Section 3.7) and to search for a global minimum.

The patch-based approach usually involves using a Taylor series expansion of the displaced image function (8.35) in order to obtain sub-pixel estimates (Lucas and Kanade 1981). Anandan (1989) shows how a series of local discrete search steps can be interleaved with Lucas–Kanade incremental refinement steps in a coarse-to-fine pyramid scheme, which allows the estimation of large motions, as described in Section 8.1.1. He also analyzes how the *uncertainty* in local motion estimates is related to the eigenvalues of the local Hessian matrix A_i (8.44), as shown in Figures 8.3–8.4.

Bergen, Anandan, Hanna *et al.* (1992) develop a unified framework for describing both parametric (Section 8.2) and patch-based optic flow algorithms and provide a nice introduction to this topic. After each iteration of optic flow estimation in a coarse-to-fine pyramid, they re-warp one of the images so that only incremental flow estimates are computed (Section 8.1.1). When overlapping patches are used, an efficient implementation is to first compute the outer products of the gradients and intensity errors (8.40–8.41) at every pixel and then perform the overlapping window sums using a moving average filter.[11]

Instead of solving for each motion (or motion update) independently, Horn and Schunck (1981) develop a regularization-based framework where (8.69) is simultaneously minimized over all flow vectors $\{\boldsymbol{u}_i\}$. In order to constrain the problem, smoothness constraints, i.e., squared penalties on flow derivatives, are added to the basic per-pixel error metric. Because the technique was originally developed for small motions in a variational (continuous function) framework, the linearized *brightness constancy constraint* corresponding to (8.35), i.e., (8.38), is more commonly written as an analytic integral

$$E_{\mathrm{HS}} = \int (I_x u + I_y v + I_t)^2 \, dx \, dy, \tag{8.70}$$

where $(I_x, I_y) = \nabla I_1 = \boldsymbol{J}_1$ and $I_t = e_i$ is the *temporal derivative*, i.e., the brightness change between images. The Horn and Schunck model can also be viewed as the limiting case of spline-based motion estimation as the splines become 1x1 pixel patches.

It is also possible to combine ideas from local and global flow estimation into a single framework by using a locally aggregated (as opposed to single-pixel) Hessian as the brightness constancy term (Bruhn, Weickert, and Schnörr 2005). Consider the discrete analog

---

[11] Other smoothing or aggregation filters can also be used at this stage (Bruhn, Weickert, and Schnörr 2005).

(8.35) to the analytic global energy (8.70),

$$E_{\text{HSD}} = \sum_i \boldsymbol{u}_i^T [\boldsymbol{J}_i \boldsymbol{J}_i^T] \boldsymbol{u}_i + 2e_i \boldsymbol{J}_i^T \boldsymbol{u}_i + e_i^2. \qquad (8.71)$$

If we replace the per-pixel (rank 1) Hessians $\boldsymbol{A}_i = [\boldsymbol{J}_i \boldsymbol{J}_i^T]$ and residuals $\boldsymbol{b}_i = \boldsymbol{J}_i e_i$ with area-aggregated versions (8.40–8.41), we obtain a global minimization algorithm where region-based brightness constraints are used.

Another extension to the basic optic flow model is to use a combination of global (parametric) and local motion models. For example, if we know that the motion is due to a camera moving in a static scene (rigid motion), we can re-formulate the problem as the estimation of a per-pixel depth along with the parameters of the global camera motion (Adiv 1989; Hanna 1991; Bergen, Anandan, Hanna *et al.* 1992; Szeliski and Coughlan 1997; Nir, Bruckstein, and Kimmel 2008; Wedel, Cremers, Pock *et al.* 2009). Such techniques are closely related to stereo matching (Chapter 11). Alternatively, we can estimate either per-image or per-segment affine motion models combined with per-pixel *residual* corrections (Black and Jepson 1996; Ju, Black, and Jepson 1996; Chang, Tekalp, and Sezan 1997; Mémin and Pérez 2002). We revisit this topic in Section 8.5.

Of course, image brightness may not always be an appropriate metric for measuring appearance consistency, e.g., when the lighting in an image is varying. As discussed in Section 8.1, matching gradients, filtered images, or other metrics such as image Hessians (second derivative measures) may be more appropriate. It is also possible to locally compute the *phase* of steerable filters in the image, which is insensitive to both bias and gain transformations (Fleet and Jepson 1990). Papenberg, Bruhn, Brox *et al.* (2006) review and explore such constraints and also provide a detailed analysis and justification for iteratively re-warping images during incremental flow computation.

Because the brightness constancy constraint is evaluated at each pixel independently, rather than being summed over patches where the constant flow assumption may be violated, global optimization approaches tend to perform better near motion discontinuities. This is especially true if robust metrics are used in the smoothness constraint (Black and Anandan 1996; Bab-Hadiashar and Suter 1998a).[12] One popular choice for robust metrics in the L_1 norm, also known as *total variation* (TV), which results in a convex energy whose global minimum can be found (Bruhn, Weickert, and Schnörr 2005; Papenberg, Bruhn, Brox *et al.* 2006). Anisotropic smoothness priors, which apply a different smoothness in the directions parallel and perpendicular to the image gradient, are another popular choice (Nagel and Enkelmann 1986; Sun, Roth, Lewis *et al.* 2008; Werlberger, Trobin, Pock *et al.* 2009). It is also possible to learn a set of better smoothness constraints (derivative filters and robust functions) from a set of paired flow and intensity images (Sun, Roth, Lewis *et al.* 2008). Additional details on some of these techniques are given by Baker, Black, Lewis *et al.* (2007) and Baker, Scharstein, Lewis *et al.* (2009).

Because of the large, two-dimensional search space in estimating flow, most algorithms use variations of gradient descent and coarse-to-fine continuation methods to minimize the global energy function. This contrasts starkly with stereo matching (which is an "easier" one-dimensional disparity estimation problem), where combinatorial optimization techniques have been the method of choice for the last decade.

---

[12] Robust brightness metrics (Section 8.1, (8.2)) can also help improve the performance of window-based approaches (Black and Anandan 1996).

Optical flow evaluation results

Statistics: Average SD R0.5 R1.0 R2.0 A50 A75 A95
Error type: endpoint angle interpolation normalized interpolation

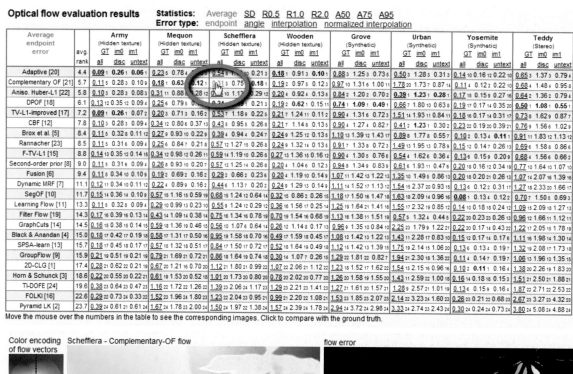

Average endpoint error	avg. rank	Army (Hidden texture) GT / im0 / im1 (all disc untext)	Mequon (Hidden texture)	Schefflera (Hidden texture)	Wooden (Hidden texture)	Grove (Synthetic)	Urban (Synthetic)	Yosemite (Synthetic)	Teddy (Stereo)
Adaptive [20]	4.4	0.09(1) 0.26(1) 0.06(1)	0.23(5) 0.78(4) —	0.54(8) — 0.21(3)	0.18(1) 0.91(3) 0.10(1)	0.88(3) 1.25(3) 0.73(5)	0.50(3) 1.28(3) 0.31(3)	0.14(10) 0.16(12) 0.22(10)	0.65(3) 1.37(3) 0.79(4)
Complementary OF [21]	5.7	0.11(5) 0.28(3) 0.10(9)	0.18(1) 0.63 0.12(1)	—(13) 0.75 0.18(1)	0.19(2) 0.97(5) 0.12(3)	0.97(10) 1.31(6) 1.00(11)	1.78(20) 1.73(7) 0.87(14)	0.11(4) 0.12(2) 0.22(10)	0.68(4) 1.48(4) 0.95(8)
Aniso. Huber-L1 [22]	5.8	0.10(3) 0.28(3) 0.08(3)	0.31(11) 0.88 0.28(12)	—(10) 1.13 0.29(12)	0.20(4) 0.92(4) 0.13(5)	0.84(2) 1.20(2) 0.70(2)	0.39(1) 1.23(1) 0.28(1)	0.17(15) 0.15(9) 0.27(16)	0.64(2) 1.36(2) 0.79(4)
DPOF [18]	6.1	0.13(12) 0.35(12) 0.09(4)	0.25(6) 0.79(5) —	— 0.21(3)	0.19(2) 0.62(1) 0.15(11)	0.74(1) 1.09(1) 0.49(1)	0.66(7) 1.80(10) 0.63(8)	0.19(17) 0.17(14) 0.35(20)	0.50(1) 1.08(1) 0.55(1)
TV-L1-improved [17]	7.2	0.09(1) 0.26(1) 0.07(2)	0.20(3) 0.71(3) 0.16(2)	0.53(7) 1.18(9) 0.22(5)	0.21(7) 1.24(11) 0.11(2)	0.90(4) 1.31(6) 0.72(3)	1.51(14) 1.93(11) 0.84(11)	0.18(16) 0.17(14) 0.31(17)	0.73(8) 1.62(9) 0.87(7)
CBF [12]	7.8	0.10(3) 0.28(3) 0.09(4)	0.34(12) 0.80(6) 0.37(13)	0.43(5) 0.95(5) 0.26(8)	0.21(7) 1.14(8) 0.13(5)	0.90(4) 1.27(4) 0.82(7)	0.41(2) 1.23(1) 0.30(2)	0.23(22) 0.19(20) 0.39(21)	0.76(9) 1.56(6) 1.02(9)
Brox et al. [5]	8.4	0.11(5) 0.32(8) 0.11(12)	0.27(9) 0.93(10) 0.22(9)	0.39(4) 0.94(4) 0.24(7)	0.24(9) 1.25(12) 0.13(5)	1.10(13) 1.39(12) 1.43(17)	0.89(8) 1.77(8) 0.55(7)	0.10(2) 0.13(4) 0.11(1)	0.91(11) 1.83(12) 1.13(12)
Rannacher [23]	8.5	0.11(5) 0.31(6) 0.09(4)	0.25(6) 0.84(7) 0.21(8)	0.57(12) 1.27(15) 0.26(8)	0.24(9) 1.32(14) 0.13(5)	0.91(7) 1.33(8) 0.72(3)	1.49(13) 1.95(13) 0.78(9)	0.15(12) 0.14(7) 0.26(13)	0.69(6) 1.58(8) 0.86(6)
F-TV-L1 [15]	8.8	0.14(13) 0.35(12) 0.14(16)	0.34(12) 0.98(12) 0.26(11)	0.59(14) 1.19(10) 0.26(8)	0.27(13) 1.36(15) 0.16(12)	0.90(4) 1.30(5) 0.76(6)	0.54(4) 1.62(6) 0.36(4)	0.13(6) 0.15(9) 0.20(9)	0.68(4) 1.56(6) 0.66(2)
Second-order prior [8]	9.0	0.11(5) 0.31(6) 0.09(4)	0.26(8) 0.93(10) 0.20(7)	0.57(12) 1.25(14) 0.26(8)	0.20(4) 1.04(6) 0.12(3)	0.94(8) 1.34(9) 0.83(9)	0.61(6) 1.93(11) 0.47(6)	0.20(18) 0.16(12) 0.34(19)	0.77(10) 1.64(10) 1.07(10)
Fusion [6]	9.4	0.11(5) 0.34(10) 0.10(9)	0.19(2) 0.69(2) 0.16(2)	0.29(2) 0.66(2) 0.23(6)	0.20(4) 1.19(10) 0.14(9)	1.07(11) 1.42(13) 1.22(13)	1.35(10) 1.49(5) 0.86(13)	0.20(18) 0.20(21) 0.26(13)	1.07(14) 2.07(16) 1.39(16)
Dynamic MRF [7]	11.1	0.12(11) 0.34(10) 0.11(12)	0.22(4) 0.89(8) 0.16(2)	0.44(6) 1.13(7) 0.20(2)	0.24(9) 1.29(13) 0.14(9)	1.11(14) 1.52(17) 1.13(12)	1.54(16) 2.37(20) 0.93(15)	0.13(6) 0.12(2) 0.31(17)	1.27(18) 2.33(20) 1.66(17)
SegOF [10]	11.7	0.15(14) 0.36(14) 0.10(9)	0.57(15) 1.16(15) 0.59(19)	0.68(15) 1.24(12) 0.64(14)	0.32(15) 0.86(2) 0.26(15)	1.18(17) 1.50(16) 1.47(18)	1.63(18) 2.09(14) 0.96(16)	0.08(1) 0.13(4) 0.12(2)	0.70(7) 1.50(5) 0.69(3)
Learning Flow [11]	13.3	0.11(5) 0.32(8) 0.09(4)	0.29(10) 0.99(13) 0.23(10)	0.55(9) 1.24(12) 0.29(12)	0.36(16) 1.56(17) 0.25(14)	1.25(19) 1.64(21) 1.41(16)	1.55(17) 2.32(19) 0.85(12)	0.14(10) 0.18(18) 0.24(12)	1.09(15) 2.09(18) 1.27(13)
Filter Flow [19]	14.3	0.17(16) 0.39(16) 0.13(14)	0.43(14) 1.09(14) 0.38(14)	0.75(16) 1.34(16) 0.78(19)	0.70(19) 1.54(16) 0.68(19)	1.13(16) 1.38(11) 1.51(19)	0.57(5) 1.32(4) 0.44(5)	0.22(20) 0.23(23) 0.26(13)	0.96(12) 1.66(11) 1.12(11)
GraphCuts [14]	14.5	0.16(15) 0.38(15) 0.14(15)	0.59(18) 1.36(19) 0.46(15)	0.56(10) 1.07(6) 0.64(14)	0.26(12) 1.14(6) 0.17(13)	0.96(9) 1.35(10) 0.84(10)	2.25(23) 1.79(9) 1.22(21)	0.22(20) 0.17(14) 0.43(22)	1.22(17) 2.05(15) 1.78(19)
Black & Anandan [4]	15.0	0.18(17) 0.42(17) 0.19(18)	0.58(17) 1.31(17) 0.50(16)	0.95(18) 1.58(18) 0.70(16)	0.49(17) 1.59(18) 0.45(17)	1.08(12) 1.42(13) 1.22(13)	1.43(11) 2.28(17) 0.83(10)	0.15(12) 0.17(14) 0.17(6)	1.11(16) 1.98(14) 1.30(14)
SPSA-learn [13]	15.7	0.18(17) 0.45(18) 0.17(17)	0.57(15) 1.32(18) 0.51(17)	0.84(17) 1.50(17) 0.72(17)	0.52(18) 1.64(19) 0.49(18)	1.12(15) 1.42(13) 1.39(15)	1.75(19) 2.14(15) 1.06(20)	0.13(6) 0.13(4) 0.19(7)	1.32(19) 2.08(17) 1.73(18)
GroupFlow [9]	15.9	0.21(19) 0.51(19) 0.21(19)	0.79(21) 1.69(21) 0.72(21)	0.86(18) 1.64(19) 0.74(18)	0.30(14) 1.07(7) 0.26(15)	1.29(22) 1.81(22) 0.82(7)	1.94(21) 2.30(18) 1.36(22)	0.11(4) 0.14(7) 0.19(7)	1.06(13) 1.96(13) 1.35(15)
2D-CLG [1]	17.4	0.28(21) 0.62(22) 0.21(19)	0.67(20) 1.21(16) 0.70(20)	1.12(21) 1.80(21) 0.99(22)	1.07(22) 2.06(21) 1.12(22)	1.23(18) 1.52(17) 1.62(22)	1.54(15) 2.15(16) 0.96(16)	0.10(2) 0.11(1) 0.16(4)	1.38(20) 2.26(19) 1.83(20)
Horn & Schunck [3]	18.6	0.22(20) 0.55(20) 0.22(21)	0.61(19) 1.53(20) 0.52(18)	1.01(20) 1.73(20) 0.80(20)	0.78(20) 2.02(20) 0.77(20)	1.26(20) 1.58(19) 1.55(20)	1.43(11) 2.59(22) 1.00(18)	0.16(14) 0.18(18) 0.15(3)	1.51(21) 2.50(21) 1.88(21)
TI-DOFE [24]	19.6	0.38(23) 0.64(23) 0.47(23)	1.16(22) 1.72(22) 1.26(22)	1.39(23) 2.06(24) 1.17(23)	1.29(23) 2.21(23) 1.41(23)	1.27(21) 1.61(20) 1.57(21)	1.28(9) 2.57(21) 1.01(19)	0.13(6) 0.15(9) 0.16(4)	1.87(22) 2.71(22) 2.53(22)
FOLKI [16]	22.6	0.29(22) 0.73(24) 0.33(22)	1.52(23) 1.96(24) 1.80(23)	1.23(22) 2.04(23) 0.95(21)	0.99(21) 2.20(22) 1.08(21)	1.53(23) 1.85(23) 2.07(23)	2.14(22) 3.23(24) 1.60(23)	0.26(23) 0.21(22) 0.68(23)	2.67(23) 3.27(23) 4.32(23)
Pyramid LK [2]	23.7	0.39(24) 0.61(21) 0.61(24)	1.67(24) 1.78(23) 2.00(24)	1.50(24) 1.97(22) 1.38(24)	1.57(24) 2.39(24) 1.78(24)	2.94(24) 3.72(24) 2.98(24)	3.33(24) 2.74(23) 2.43(24)	0.30(24) 0.24(24) 0.73(24)	3.80(24) 5.08(24) 4.88(24)

Move the mouse over the numbers in the table to see the corresponding images. Click to compare with the ground truth.

Color encoding of flow vectors   Schefflera – Complementary-OF flow   flow error

Figure 8.12 Evaluation of the results of 24 optical flow algorithms, October 2009, http://vision.middlebury.edu/flow/, (Baker, Scharstein, Lewis *et al.* 2009). By moving the mouse pointer over an underlined performance score, the user can interactively view the corresponding flow and error maps. Clicking on a score toggles between the computed and ground truth flows. Next to each score, the corresponding rank in the current column is indicated by a smaller blue number. The minimum (best) score in each column is shown in boldface. The table is sorted by the average rank (computed over all 24 columns, three region masks for each of the eight sequences). The average rank serves as an *approximate* measure of performance *under the selected metric/statistic*.

Fortunately, combinatorial optimization methods based on Markov random fields are beginning to appear and tend to be among the better-performing methods on the recently released optical flow database (Baker, Black, Lewis *et al.* 2007).[13]

Examples of such techniques include the one developed by Glocker, Paragios, Komodakis *et al.* (2008), who use a coarse-to-fine strategy with per-pixel 2D uncertainty estimates, which are then used to guide the refinement and search at the next finer level. Instead of using gradient descent to refine the flow estimates, a combinatorial search over discrete displacement labels (which is able to find better energy minima) is performed using their Fast-PD algorithm (Komodakis, Tziritas, and Paragios 2008).

Lempitsky, Roth, and Rother. (2008) use fusion moves (Lempitsky, Rother, and Blake 2007) over proposals generated from basic flow algorithms (Horn and Schunck 1981; Lucas and Kanade 1981) to find good solutions. The basic idea behind fusion moves is to replace portions of the current best estimate with hypotheses generated by more basic techniques (or their shifted versions) and to alternate them with local gradient descent for better energy minimization.

The field of accurate motion estimation continues to evolve at a rapid pace, with significant advances in performance occurring every year. The optical flow evaluation Web site (http://vision.middlebury.edu/flow/) is a good source of pointers to high-performing recently developed algorithms (Figure 8.12).

8.4.1 Multi-frame motion estimation

So far, we have looked at motion estimation as a two-frame problem, where the goal is to compute a motion field that aligns pixels from one image with those in another. In practice, motion estimation is usually applied to video, where a whole sequence of frames is available to perform this task.

One classic approach to multi-frame motion is to *filter* the spatio-temporal volume using oriented or steerable filters (Heeger 1988), in a manner analogous to oriented edge detection (Section 3.2.3). Figure 8.13 shows two frames from the commonly used *flower garden* sequence, as well as a horizontal slice through the spatio-temporal volume, i.e., the 3D volume created by stacking all of the video frames together. Because the pixel motion is mostly horizontal, the slopes of individual (textured) pixel tracks, which correspond to their horizontal velocities, can clearly be seen. Spatio-temporal filtering uses a 3D volume around each pixel to determine the best orientation in space–time, which corresponds directly to a pixel's velocity.

Unfortunately, in order to obtain reasonably accurate velocity estimates everywhere in an image, spatio-temporal filters have moderately large extents, which severely degrades the quality of their estimates near motion discontinuities. (This same problem is endemic in 2D window-based motion estimators.) An alternative to full spatio-temporal filtering is to estimate more local spatio-temporal derivatives and use them inside a global optimization framework to fill in textureless regions (Bruhn, Weickert, and Schnörr 2005; Govindu 2006).

Another alternative is to simultaneously estimate multiple motion estimates, while also optionally reasoning about occlusion relationships (Szeliski 1999). Figure 8.13c shows schematically one potential approach to this problem. The horizontal arrows show the locations of

---

[13] http://vision.middlebury.edu/flow/.

Figure 8.13 Slice through a spatio-temporal volume (Szeliski 1999) © 1999 IEEE: (a–b) two frames from the *flower garden* sequence; (c) a horizontal slice through the complete spatio-temporal volume, with the arrows indicating locations of potential key frames where flow is estimated. Note that the colors for the flower garden sequence are incorrect; the correct colors (yellow flowers) are shown in Figure 8.15.

keyframes s where motion is estimated, while other slices indicate video frames t whose colors are matched with those predicted by interpolating between the keyframes. Motion estimation can be cast as a global energy minimization problem that simultaneously minimizes brightness compatibility and flow compatibility terms between keyframes and other frames, in addition to using robust smoothness terms.

The multi-view framework is potentially even more appropriate for rigid scene motion (multi-view stereo) (Section 11.6), where the unknowns at each pixel are disparities and occlusion relationships can be determined directly from pixel depths (Szeliski 1999; Kolmogorov and Zabih 2002). However, it may also be applicable to general motion, with the addition of models for object accelerations and occlusion relationships.

8.4.2 *Application*: Video denoising

Video denoising is the process of removing noise and other artifacts such as scratches from film and video (Kokaram 2004). Unlike single image denoising, where the only information available is in the current picture, video denoisers can average or borrow information from adjacent frames. However, in order to do this without introducing blur or jitter (irregular motion), they need accurate per-pixel motion estimates.

Exercise 8.7 lists some of the steps required, which include the ability to determine if the current motion estimate is accurate enough to permit averaging with other frames. Gai and Kang (2009) describe their recently developed restoration process, which involves a series of additional steps to deal with the special characteristics of vintage film.

8.4.3 *Application*: De-interlacing

Another commonly used application of per-pixel motion estimation is video de-interlacing, which is the process of converting a video taken with alternating fields of even and odd lines to a non-interlaced signal that contains both fields in each frame (de Haan and Bellers 1998). Two simple de-interlacing techniques are *bob*, which copies the line above or below the missing line from the same field, and *weave*, which copies the corresponding line from the field before or after. The names come from the visual artifacts generated by these two simple techniques: bob introduces an up-and-down bobbing motion along strong horizontal

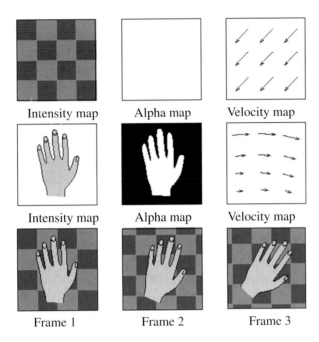

Figure 8.14 Layered motion estimation framework (Wang and Adelson 1994) © 1994 IEEE: The top two rows describe the two layers, each of which consists of an intensity (color) image, an alpha mask (black=transparent), and a parametric motion field. The layers are composited with different amounts of motion to recreate the video sequence.

lines; weave can lead to a "zippering" effect along horizontally translating edges. Replacing these copy operators with averages can help but does not completely remove these artifacts.

A wide variety of improved techniques have been developed for this process, which is often embedded in specialized DSP chips found inside video digitization boards in computers (since broadcast video is often interlaced, while computer monitors are not). A large class of these techniques estimates local per-pixel motions and interpolates the missing data from the information available in spatially and temporally adjacent fields. Dai, Baker, and Kang (2009) review this literature and propose their own algorithm, which selects among seven different interpolation functions at each pixel using an MRF framework.

8.5 Layered motion

In many situation, visual motion is caused by the movement of a small number of objects at different depths in the scene. In such situations, the pixel motions can be described more succinctly (and estimated more reliably) if pixels are grouped into appropriate objects or *layers* (Wang and Adelson 1994).

Figure 8.14 shows this approach schematically. The motion in this sequence is caused by the translational motion of the checkered background and the rotation of the foreground hand. The complete motion sequence can be reconstructed from the appearance of the foreground and background elements, which can be represented as alpha-matted images (*sprites* or *video objects*) and the parametric motion corresponding to each layer. Displacing and compositing

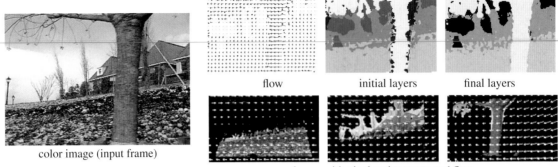

color image (input frame)   flow   initial layers   final layers

layers with pixel assignments and flow

Figure 8.15 Layered motion estimation results (Wang and Adelson 1994) © 1994 IEEE.

these layers in back to front order (Section 3.1.3) recreates the original video sequence.

Layered motion representations not only lead to compact representations (Wang and Adelson 1994; Lee, ge Chen, lung Bruce Lin *et al.* 1997), but they also exploit the information available in multiple video frames, as well as accurately modeling the appearance of pixels near motion discontinuities. This makes them particularly suited as a representation for image-based rendering (Section 13.2.1) (Shade, Gortler, He *et al.* 1998; Zitnick, Kang, Uyttendaele *et al.* 2004) as well as object-level video editing.

To compute a layered representation of a video sequence, Wang and Adelson (1994) first estimate affine motion models over a collection of non-overlapping patches and then cluster these estimates using k-means. They then alternate between assigning pixels to layers and recomputing motion estimates for each layer using the assigned pixels, using a technique first proposed by Darrell and Pentland (1991). Once the parametric motions and pixel-wise layer assignments have been computed for each frame independently, layers are constructed by warping and merging the various layer pieces from all of the frames together. Median filtering is used to produce sharp composite layers that are robust to small intensity variations, as well as to infer occlusion relationships between the layers. Figure 8.15 shows the results of this process on the *flower garden* sequence. You can see both the initial and final layer assignments for one of the frames, as well as the composite flow and the alpha-matted layers with their corresponding flow vectors overlaid.

In follow-on work, Weiss and Adelson (1996) use a formal probabilistic mixture model to infer both the optimal number of layers and the per-pixel layer assignments. Weiss (1997) further generalizes this approach by replacing the per-layer affine motion models with smooth regularized per-pixel motion estimates, which allows the system to better handle curved and undulating layers, such as those seen in most real-world sequences.

The above approaches, however, still make a distinction between estimating the motions and layer assignments and then later estimating the layer colors. In the system described by Baker, Szeliski, and Anandan (1998), the generative model illustrated in Figure 8.14 is generalized to account for real-world rigid motion scenes. The motion of each frame is described using a 3D camera model and the motion of each layer is described using a 3D plane equation plus per-pixel residual depth offsets (the *plane plus parallax* representation (Section 2.1.5)). The initial layer estimation proceeds in a manner similar to that of Wang and Adelson (1994),

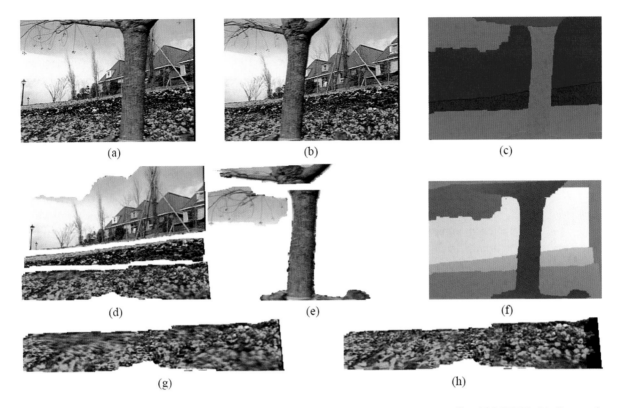

Figure 8.16 Layered stereo reconstruction (Baker, Szeliski, and Anandan 1998) © 1998 IEEE: (a) first and (b) last input images; (c) initial segmentation into six layers; (d) and (e) the six layer sprites; (f) depth map for planar sprites (darker denotes closer); front layer (g) before and (h) after residual depth estimation. Note that the colors for the flower garden sequence are incorrect; the correct colors (yellow flowers) are shown in Figure 8.15.

o

except that rigid planar motions (homographies) are used instead of affine motion models. The final model refinement, however, jointly re-optimizes the layer pixel color and opacity values L_l and the 3D depth, plane, and motion parameters z_l, n_l, and P_t by minimizing the discrepancy between the re-synthesized and observed motion sequences (Baker, Szeliski, and Anandan 1998).

Figure 8.16 shows the final results obtained with this algorithm. As you can see, the motion boundaries and layer assignments are much crisper than those in Figure 8.15. Because of the per-pixel depth offsets, the individual layer color values are also sharper than those obtained with affine or planar motion models. While the original system of Baker, Szeliski, and Anandan (1998) required a rough initial assignment of pixels to layers, Torr, Szeliski, and Anandan (2001) describe automated Bayesian techniques for initializing this system and determining the optimal number of layers.

Layered motion estimation continues to be an active area of research. Representative papers in this area include (Sawhney and Ayer 1996; Jojic and Frey 2001; Xiao and Shah 2005; Kumar, Torr, and Zisserman 2008; Thayananthan, Iwasaki, and Cipolla 2008; Schoenemann and Cremers 2008).

Of course, layers are not the only way to introduce segmentation into motion estimation.

A large number of algorithms have been developed that alternate between estimating optic flow vectors and segmenting them into coherent regions (Black and Jepson 1996; Ju, Black, and Jepson 1996; Chang, Tekalp, and Sezan 1997; Mémin and Pérez 2002; Cremers and Soatto 2005). Some of the more recent techniques rely on first segmenting the input color images and then estimating per-segment motions that produce a coherent motion field while also modeling occlusions (Zitnick, Kang, Uyttendaele *et al.* 2004; Zitnick, Jojic, and Kang 2005; Stein, Hoiem, and Hebert 2007; Thayananthan, Iwasaki, and Cipolla 2008).

8.5.1 *Application*: Frame interpolation

Frame interpolation is another widely used application of motion estimation, often implemented in the same circuitry as de-interlacing hardware required to match an incoming video to a monitor's actual refresh rate. As with de-interlacing, information from novel in-between frames needs to be interpolated from preceding and subsequent frames. The best results can be obtained if an accurate motion estimate can be computed at each unknown pixel's location. However, in addition to computing the motion, occlusion information is critical to prevent colors from being contaminated by moving foreground objects that might obscure a particular pixel in a preceding or subsequent frame.

In a little more detail, consider Figure 8.13c and assume that the arrows denote keyframes between which we wish to interpolate additional images. The orientations of the streaks in this figure encode the velocities of individual pixels. If the same motion estimate u_0 is obtained at location x_0 in image I_0 as is obtained at location $x_0 + u_0$ in image I_1, the flow vectors are said to be *consistent*. This motion estimate can be transferred to location $x_0 + tu_0$ in the image I_t being generated, where $t \in (0, 1)$ is the time of interpolation. The final color value at pixel $x_0 + tu_0$ can be computed as a linear blend,

$$I_t(x_0 + tu_0) = (1 - t)I_0(x_0) + tI_1(x_0 + u_0). \tag{8.72}$$

If, however, the motion vectors are different at corresponding locations, some method must be used to determine which is correct and which image contains colors that are occluded. The actual reasoning is even more subtle than this. One example of such an interpolation algorithm, based on earlier work in depth map interpolation (Shade, Gortler, He *et al.* 1998; Zitnick, Kang, Uyttendaele *et al.* 2004) which is the one used in the flow evaluation paper of Baker, Black, Lewis *et al.* (2007); Baker, Scharstein, Lewis *et al.* (2009). An even higher-quality frame interpolation algorithm, which uses gradient-based reconstruction, is presented by Mahajan, Huang, Matusik *et al.* (2009).

8.5.2 Transparent layers and reflections

A special case of layered motion that occurs quite often is transparent motion, which is usually caused by reflections seen in windows and picture frames (Figures 8.17 and 8.18).

Some of the early work in this area handles transparent motion by either just estimating the component motions (Shizawa and Mase 1991; Bergen, Burt, Hingorani *et al.* 1992; Darrell and Simoncelli 1993; Irani, Rousso, and Peleg 1994) or by assigning individual pixels to competing motion layers (Darrell and Pentland 1995; Black and Anandan 1996; Ju, Black, and Jepson 1996), which is appropriate for scenes partially seen through a fine occluder (e.g., foliage). However, to accurately separate truly transparent layers, a better model for

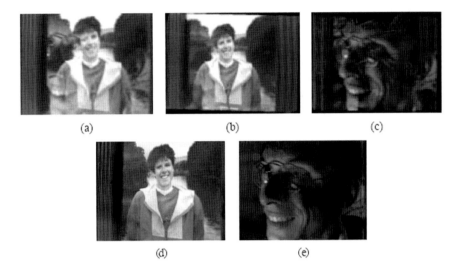

Figure 8.17 Light reflecting off the transparent glass of a picture frame: (a) first image from the input sequence; (b) dominant motion layer *min-composite*; (c) secondary motion residual layer *max-composite*; (d–e) final estimated picture and reflection layers The original images are from Black and Anandan (1996), while the separated layers are from Szeliski, Avidan, and Anandan (2000) © 2000 IEEE.

motion due to reflections is required. Because of the way that light is both reflected from and transmitted through a glass surface, the correct model for reflections is an *additive* one, where each moving layer contributes some intensity to the final image (Szeliski, Avidan, and Anandan 2000).

If the motions of the individual layers are known, the recovery of the individual layers is a simple constrained least squares problem, with the individual layer images are constrained to be positive. However, this problem can suffer from extended low-frequency ambiguities, especially if either of the layers lacks dark (black) pixels or the motion is uni-directional. In their paper, Szeliski, Avidan, and Anandan (2000) show that the simultaneous estimation of the motions and layer values can be obtained by alternating between robustly computing the motion layers and then making conservative (upper- or lower-bound) estimates of the layer intensities. The final motion and layer estimates can then be polished using gradient descent on a joint constrained least squares formulation similar to (Baker, Szeliski, and Anandan 1998), where the *over* compositing operator is replaced with addition.

Figures 8.17 and 8.18 show the results of applying these techniques to two different picture frames with reflections. Notice how, in the second sequence, the amount of reflected light is quite low compared to the transmitted light (the picture of the girl) and yet the algorithm is still able to recover both layers.

Unfortunately, the simple parametric motion models used in (Szeliski, Avidan, and Anandan 2000) are only valid for planar reflectors and scenes with shallow depth. The extension of these techniques to curved reflectors and scenes with significant depth has also been studied (Swaminathan, Kang, Szeliski *et al.* 2002; Criminisi, Kang, Swaminathan *et al.* 2005), as has the extension to scenes with more complex 3D depth (Tsin, Kang, and Szeliski 2006).

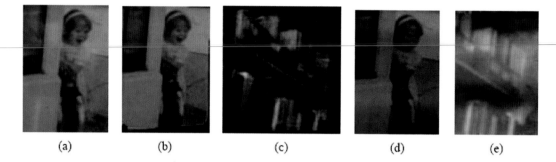

Figure 8.18 Transparent motion separation (Szeliski, Avidan, and Anandan 2000) © 2000 IEEE: (a) first image from input sequence; (b) dominant motion layer *min-composite*; (c) secondary motion residual layer *max-composite*; (d–e) final estimated picture and reflection layers. Note that the reflected layers in (c) and (e) are doubled in intensity to better show their structure.

8.6 Additional reading

Some of the earliest algorithms for motion estimation were developed for motion-compensated video coding (Netravali and Robbins 1979) and such techniques continue to be used in modern coding standards such as MPEG, H.263, and H.264 (Le Gall 1991; Richardson 2003).[14] In computer vision, this field was originally called *image sequence analysis* (Huang 1981). Some of the early seminal papers include the variational approaches developed by Horn and Schunck (1981) and Nagel and Enkelmann (1986), and the patch-based translational alignment technique developed by Lucas and Kanade (1981). Hierarchical (coarse-to-fine) versions of such algorithms were developed by Quam (1984), Anandan (1989), and Bergen, Anandan, Hanna *et al.* (1992), although they have also long been used in motion estimation for video coding.

Translational motion models were generalized to affine motion by Rehg and Witkin (1991), Fuh and Maragos (1991), and Bergen, Anandan, Hanna *et al.* (1992) and to quadric reference surfaces by Shashua and Toelg (1997) and Shashua and Wexler (2001)—see Baker and Matthews (2004) for a nice review. Such parametric motion estimation algorithms have found widespread application in video summarization (Teodosio and Bender 1993; Irani and Anandan 1998), video stabilization (Hansen, Anandan, Dana *et al.* 1994; Srinivasan, Chellappa, Veeraraghavan *et al.* 2005; Matsushita, Ofek, Ge *et al.* 2006), and video compression (Irani, Hsu, and Anandan 1995; Lee, ge Chen, lung Bruce Lin *et al.* 1997). Surveys of parametric image registration include those by Brown (1992), Zitov'aa and Flusser (2003), Goshtasby (2005), and Szeliski (2006a).

Good general surveys and comparisons of optic flow algorithms include those by Aggarwal and Nandhakumar (1988), Barron, Fleet, and Beauchemin (1994), Otte and Nagel (1994), Mitiche and Bouthemy (1996), Stiller and Konrad (1999), McCane, Novins, Crannitch *et al.* (2001), Szeliski (2006a), and Baker, Black, Lewis *et al.* (2007). The topic of matching primitives, i.e., pre-transforming images using filtering or other techniques before matching, is treated in a number of papers (Anandan 1989; Bergen, Anandan, Hanna *et al.* 1992; Scharstein 1994; Zabih and Woodfill 1994; Cox, Roy, and Hingorani 1995; Viola and

---

[14] http://www.itu.int/rec/T-REC-H.264.

Wells III 1997; Negahdaripour 1998; Kim, Kolmogorov, and Zabih 2003; Jia and Tang 2003; Papenberg, Bruhn, Brox *et al.* 2006; Seitz and Baker 2009). Hirschmüller and Scharstein (2009) compare a number of these approaches and report on their relative performance in scenes with exposure differences.

The publication of a new benchmark for evaluating optical flow algorithms (Baker, Black, Lewis *et al.* 2007) has led to rapid advances in the quality of estimation algorithms, to the point where new datasets may soon become necessary. According to their updated technical report (Baker, Scharstein, Lewis *et al.* 2009), most of the best performing algorithms use robust data and smoothness norms (often L_1 TV) and continuous variational optimization techniques, although some techniques use discrete optimization or segmentations (Papenberg, Bruhn, Brox *et al.* 2006; Trobin, Pock, Cremers *et al.* 2008; Xu, Chen, and Jia 2008; Lempitsky, Roth, and Rother. 2008; Werlberger, Trobin, Pock *et al.* 2009; Lei and Yang 2009; Wedel, Cremers, Pock *et al.* 2009).

8.7 Exercises

Ex 8.1: Correlation   Implement and compare the performance of the following correlation algorithms:

- sum of squared differences (8.1)

- sum of robust differences (8.2)

- sum of absolute differences (8.3)

- bias–gain compensated squared differences (8.9)

- normalized cross-correlation (8.11)

- windowed versions of the above (8.22–8.23)

- Fourier-based implementations of the above measures (8.18–8.20)

- phase correlation (8.24)

- gradient cross-correlation (Argyriou and Vlachos 2003).

Compare a few of your algorithms on different motion sequences with different amounts of noise, exposure variation, occlusion, and frequency variations (e.g., high-frequency textures, such as sand or cloth, and low-frequency images, such as clouds or motion-blurred video). Some datasets with illumination variation and ground truth correspondences (horizontal motion) can be found at http://vision.middlebury.edu/stereo/data/ (the 2005 and 2006 datasets).

Some additional ideas, variants, and questions:

1. When do you think that phase correlation will outperform regular correlation or SSD? Can you show this experimentally or justify it analytically?

2. For the Fourier-based masked or windowed correlation and sum of squared differences, the results should be the same as the direct implementations. Note that you will have to expand (8.5) into a sum of pairwise correlations, just as in (8.22). (This is part of the exercise.)

3. For the bias–gain corrected variant of squared differences (8.9), you will also have to expand the terms to end up with a 3×3 (least squares) system of equations. If implementing the Fast Fourier Transform version, you will need to figure out how all of these entries can be evaluated in the Fourier domain.

4. (Optional) Implement some of the additional techniques studied by Hirschmüller and Scharstein (2009) and see if your results agree with theirs.

Ex 8.2: Affine registration   Implement a coarse-to-fine direct method for affine and projective image alignment.

1. Does it help to use lower-order (simpler) models at coarser levels of the pyramid (Bergen, Anandan, Hanna *et al.* 1992)?

2. (Optional) Implement patch-based acceleration (Shum and Szeliski 2000; Baker and Matthews 2004).

3. See the Baker and Matthews (2004) survey for more comparisons and ideas.

Ex 8.3: Stabilization   Write a program to *stabilize* an input video sequence. You should implement the following steps, as described in Section 8.2.1:

1. Compute the translation (and, optionally, rotation) between successive frames with robust outlier rejection.

2. Perform temporal high-pass filtering on the motion parameters to remove the low-frequency component (smooth the motion).

3. Compensate for the high-frequency motion, zooming in slightly (a user-specified amount) to avoid missing edge pixels.

4. (Optional) Do not zoom in, but instead borrow pixels from previous or subsequent frames to fill in.

5. (Optional) Compensate for images that are blurry because of fast motion by "stealing" higher frequencies from adjacent frames.

Ex 8.4: Optical flow   Compute optical flow (spline-based or per-pixel) between two images, using one or more of the techniques described in this chapter.

1. Test your algorithms on the motion sequences available at http://vision.middlebury. edu/flow/ or http://people.csail.mit.edu/celiu/motionAnnotation/ and compare your results (visually) to those available on these Web sites. If you think your algorithm is competitive with the best, consider submitting it for formal evaluation.

2. Visualize the quality of your results by generating in-between images using frame interpolation (Exercise 8.5).

3. What can you say about the relative efficiency (speed) of your approach?

Ex 8.5: Automated morphing / frame interpolation   Write a program to automatically morph between pairs of images. Implement the following steps, as sketched out in Section 8.5.1 and by Baker, Scharstein, Lewis *et al.* (2009):

1. Compute the flow both ways (previous exercise). Consider using a multi-frame ($n > 2$) technique to better deal with occluded regions.

2. For each intermediate (morphed) image, compute a set of flow vectors and which images should be used in the final composition.

3. Blend (cross-dissolve) the images and view with a sequence viewer.

Try this out on images of your friends and colleagues and see what kinds of morphs you get. Alternatively, take a video sequence and do a high-quality slow-motion effect. Compare your algorithm with simple cross-fading.

Ex 8.6: Motion-based user interaction   Write a program to compute a low-resolution motion field in order to interactively control a simple application (Cutler and Turk 1998). For example:

1. Downsample each image using a pyramid and compute the optical flow (spline-based or pixel-based) from the previous frame.

2. Segment each training video sequence into different "actions" (e.g., hand moving inwards, moving up, no motion) and "learn" the velocity fields associated with each one. (You can simply find the mean and variance for each motion field or use something more sophisticated, such as a support vector machine (SVM).)

3. Write a recognizer that finds successive actions of approximately the right duration and hook it up to an interactive application (e.g., a sound generator or a computer game).

4. Ask your friends to test it out.

Ex 8.7: Video denoising   Implement the algorithm sketched in Application 8.4.2. Your algorithm should contain the following steps:

1. Compute accurate per-pixel flow.

2. Determine which pixels in the reference image have good matches with other frames.

3. Either average all of the matched pixels or choose the sharpest image, if trying to compensate for blur. Don't forget to use regular single-frame denoising techniques as part of your solution, (see Section 3.4.4, Section 3.7.3, and Exercise 3.11).

4. Devise a fall-back strategy for areas where you don't think the flow estimates are accurate enough.

Ex 8.8: Motion segmentation   Write a program to segment an image into separately moving regions or to reliably find motion boundaries.

Use the human-assisted motion segmentation database at http://people.csail.mit.edu/celiu/ motionAnnotation/ as some of your test data.

Ex 8.9: Layered motion estimation   Decompose into separate layers (Section 8.5) a video sequence of a scene taken with a moving camera:

1. Find the set of dominant (affine or planar perspective) motions, either by computing them in blocks or finding a robust estimate and then iteratively re-fitting outliers.

2. Determine which pixels go with each motion.

3. Construct the layers by blending pixels from different frames.

4. (Optional) Add per-pixel residual flows or depths.

5. (Optional) Refine your estimates using an iterative global optimization technique.

6. (Optional) Write an interactive renderer to generate in-between frames or view the scene from different viewpoints (Shade, Gortler, He *et al.* 1998).

7. (Optional) Construct an *unwrap mosaic* from a more complex scene and use this to do some video editing (Rav-Acha, Kohli, Fitzgibbon *et al.* 2008).

Ex 8.10: Transparent motion and reflection estimation   Take a video sequence looking through a window (or picture frame) and see if you can remove the reflection in order to better see what is inside.

The steps are described in Section 8.5.2 and by Szeliski, Avidan, and Anandan (2000). Alternative approaches can be found in work by Shizawa and Mase (1991), Bergen, Burt, Hingorani *et al.* (1992), Darrell and Simoncelli (1993), Darrell and Pentland (1995), Irani, Rousso, and Peleg (1994), Black and Anandan (1996), and Ju, Black, and Jepson (1996).

Chapter 9

Image stitching

R. Szeliski, *Computer Vision: Algorithms and Applications*, Texts in Computer Science,
DOI 10.1007/978-1-84882-935-0_9, © Springer-Verlag London Limited 2011

Figure 9.1 Image stitching: (a) portion of a cylindrical panorama and (b) a spherical panorama constructed from 54 photographs (Szeliski and Shum 1997) © 1997 ACM; (c) a multi-image panorama automatically assembled from an unordered photo collection; a multi-image stitch (d) without and (e) with moving object removal (Uyttendaele, Eden, and Szeliski 2001) © 2001 IEEE.

Algorithms for aligning images and stitching them into seamless photo-mosaics are among the oldest and most widely used in computer vision (Milgram 1975; Peleg 1981). image stitching algorithms create the high-resolution photo-mosaics used to produce today's digital maps and satellite photos. They also come bundled with most digital cameras and can be used to create beautiful ultra wide-angle panoramas.

image stitching originated in the photogrammetry community, where more manually intensive methods based on surveyed *ground control points* or manually registered *tie points* have long been used to register aerial photos into large-scale photo-mosaics (Slama 1980). One of the key advances in this community was the development of *bundle adjustment* algorithms (Section 7.4), which could simultaneously solve for the locations of all of the camera positions, thus yielding globally consistent solutions (Triggs, McLauchlan, Hartley *et al.* 1999). Another recurring problem in creating photo-mosaics is the elimination of visible seams, for which a variety of techniques have been developed over the years (Milgram 1975, 1977; Peleg 1981; Davis 1998; Agarwala, Dontcheva, Agrawala *et al.* 2004)

In film photography, special cameras were developed in the 1990s to take ultra-wide-angle panoramas, often by exposing the film through a vertical slit as the camera rotated on its axis (Meehan 1990). In the mid-1990s, image alignment techniques started being applied to the construction of wide-angle seamless panoramas from regular hand-held cameras (Mann and Picard 1994; Chen 1995; Szeliski 1996). More recent work in this area has addressed the need to compute globally consistent alignments (Szeliski and Shum 1997; Sawhney and Kumar 1999; Shum and Szeliski 2000), to remove "ghosts" due to parallax and object movement (Davis 1998; Shum and Szeliski 2000; Uyttendaele, Eden, and Szeliski 2001; Agarwala, Dontcheva, Agrawala *et al.* 2004), and to deal with varying exposures (Mann and Picard 1994; Uyttendaele, Eden, and Szeliski 2001; Levin, Zomet, Peleg *et al.* 2004; Agarwala, Dontcheva, Agrawala *et al.* 2004; Eden, Uyttendaele, and Szeliski 2006; Kopf, Uyttendaele, Deussen *et al.* 2007).[1] These techniques have spawned a large number of commercial stitching products (Chen 1995; Sawhney, Kumar, Gendel *et al.* 1998), of which reviews and comparisons can be found on the Web.[2]

While most of the earlier techniques worked by directly minimizing pixel-to-pixel dissimilarities, more recent algorithms usually extract a sparse set of features and match them to each other, as described in Chapter 4. Such feature-based approaches to image stitching have the advantage of being more robust against scene movement and are potentially faster, if implemented the right way. Their biggest advantage, however, is the ability to "recognize panoramas", i.e., to automatically discover the adjacency (overlap) relationships among an unordered set of images, which makes them ideally suited for fully automated stitching of panoramas taken by casual users (Brown and Lowe 2007).

What, then, are the essential problems in image stitching? As with image alignment, we must first determine the appropriate mathematical model relating pixel coordinates in one image to pixel coordinates in another; Section 9.1 reviews the basic models we have studied and presents some new motion models related specifically to panoramic image stitching. Next, we must somehow estimate the correct alignments relating various pairs (or collections) of images. Chapter 4 discussed how distinctive features can be found in each image and then

---

[1] A collection of some of these papers was compiled by Benosman and Kang (2001) and they are surveyed by Szeliski (2006a).

[2] The Photosynth Web site, http://photosynth.net, allows people to create and upload panoramas for free.

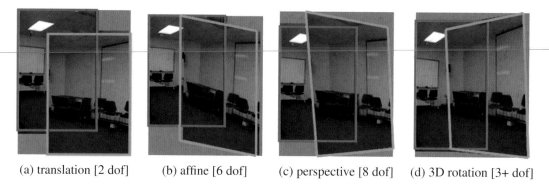

(a) translation [2 dof]   (b) affine [6 dof]   (c) perspective [8 dof]   (d) 3D rotation [3+ dof]

Figure 9.2 Two-dimensional motion models and how they can be used for image stitching.

efficiently matched to rapidly establish correspondences between pairs of images. Chapter 8 discussed how direct pixel-to-pixel comparisons combined with gradient descent (and other optimization techniques) can also be used to estimate these parameters. When multiple images exist in a panorama, bundle adjustment (Section 7.4) can be used to compute a globally consistent set of alignments and to efficiently discover which images overlap one another. In Section 9.2, we look at how each of these previously developed techniques can be modified to take advantage of the imaging setups commonly used to create panoramas.

Once we have aligned the images, we must choose a final compositing surface for warping the aligned images (Section 9.3.1). We also need algorithms to seamlessly cut and blend overlapping images, even in the presence of parallax, lens distortion, scene motion, and exposure differences (Section 9.3.2–9.3.4).

9.1 Motion models

Before we can register and align images, we need to establish the mathematical relationships that map pixel coordinates from one image to another. A variety of such *parametric motion models* are possible, from simple 2D transforms, to planar perspective models, 3D camera rotations, lens distortions, and mapping to non-planar (e.g., cylindrical) surfaces.

We already covered several of these models in Sections 2.1 and 6.1. In particular, we saw in Section 2.1.5 how the parametric motion describing the deformation of a planar surfaced as viewed from different positions can be described with an eight-parameter homography (2.71) (Mann and Picard 1994; Szeliski 1996). We also saw how a camera undergoing a pure rotation induces a different kind of homography (2.72).

In this section, we review both of these models and show how they can be applied to different stitching situations. We also introduce spherical and cylindrical compositing surfaces and show how, under favorable circumstances, they can be used to perform alignment using pure translations (Section 9.1.6). Deciding which alignment model is most appropriate for a given situation or set of data is a *model selection* problem (Hastie, Tibshirani, and Friedman 2001; Torr 2002; Bishop 2006; Robert 2007), an important topic we do not cover in this book.

9.1.1 Planar perspective motion

The simplest possible motion model to use when aligning images is to simply translate and rotate them in 2D (Figure 9.2a). This is exactly the same kind of motion that you would use if you had overlapping photographic prints. It is also the kind of technique favored by David Hockney to create the collages that he calls *joiners* (Zelnik-Manor and Perona 2007; Nomura, Zhang, and Nayar 2007). Creating such collages, which show visible seams and inconsistencies that add to the artistic effect, is popular on Web sites such as Flickr, where they more commonly go under the name *panography* (Section 6.1.2). Translation and rotation are also usually adequate motion models to compensate for small camera motions in applications such as photo and video stabilization and merging (Exercise 6.1 and Section 8.2.1).

In Section 6.1.3, we saw how the mapping between two cameras viewing a common plane can be described using a 3×3 homography (2.71). Consider the matrix M_{10} that arises when mapping a pixel in one image to a 3D point and then back onto a second image,

$$\tilde{x}_1 \sim \tilde{P}_1 \tilde{P}_0^{-1} \tilde{x}_0 = M_{10} \tilde{x}_0. \tag{9.1}$$

When the last row of the P_0 matrix is replaced with a plane equation $\hat{n}_0 \cdot p + c_0$ and points are assumed to lie on this plane, i.e., their disparity is $d_0 = 0$, we can ignore the last column of M_{10} and also its last row, since we do not care about the final z-buffer depth. The resulting homography matrix $\tilde{H}_{10}$ (the upper left 3×3 sub-matrix of M_{10}) describes the mapping between pixels in the two images,

$$\tilde{x}_1 \sim \tilde{H}_{10} \tilde{x}_0. \tag{9.2}$$

This observation formed the basis of some of the earliest automated image stitching algorithms (Mann and Picard 1994; Szeliski 1994, 1996). Because reliable feature matching techniques had not yet been developed, these algorithms used direct pixel value matching, i.e., direct parametric motion estimation, as described in Section 8.2 and Equations (6.19–6.20).

More recent stitching algorithms first extract features and then match them up, often using robust techniques such as RANSAC (Section 6.1.4) to compute a good set of inliers. The final computation of the homography (9.2), i.e., the solution of the least squares fitting problem given pairs of corresponding features,

$$x_1 = \frac{(1 + h_{00})x_0 + h_{01}y_0 + h_{02}}{h_{20}x_0 + h_{21}y_0 + 1} \quad \text{and} \quad y_1 = \frac{h_{10}x_0 + (1 + h_{11})y_0 + h_{12}}{h_{20}x_0 + h_{21}y_0 + 1}, \tag{9.3}$$

uses iterative least squares, as described in Section 6.1.3 and Equations (6.21–6.23).

9.1.2 *Application*: Whiteboard and document scanning

The simplest image-stitching application is to stitch together a number of image scans taken on a flatbed scanner. Say you have a large map, or a piece of child's artwork, that is too large to fit on your scanner. Simply take multiple scans of the document, making sure to overlap the scans by a large enough amount to ensure that there are enough common features. Next, take successive pairs of images that you know overlap, extract features, match them up, and estimate the 2D rigid transform (2.16),

$$x_{k+1} = R_k x_k + t_k, \tag{9.4}$$

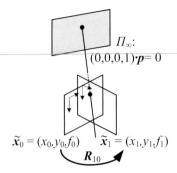

Π_∞:

$(0,0,0,1)\cdot p = 0$

$\tilde{x}_0 = (x_0, y_0, f_0)$ $\tilde{x}_1 = (x_1, y_1, f_1)$

R_{10}

Figure 9.3 Pure 3D camera rotation. The form of the homography (mapping) is particularly simple and depends only on the 3D rotation matrix and focal lengths.

that best matches the features, using two-point RANSAC, if necessary, to find a good set of inliers. Then, on a final compositing surface (aligned with the first scan, for example), resample your images (Section 3.6.1) and average them together. Can you see any potential problems with this scheme?

One complication is that a 2D rigid transformation is non-linear in the rotation angle θ, so you will have to either use non-linear least squares or constrain R to be orthonormal, as described in Section 6.1.3.

A bigger problem lies in the pairwise alignment process. As you align more and more pairs, the solution may drift so that it is no longer globally consistent. In this case, a global optimization procedure, as described in Section 9.2, may be required. Such global optimization often requires a large system of non-linear equations to be solved, although in some cases, such as linearized homographies (Section 9.1.3) or similarity transforms (Section 6.1.2), regular least squares may be an option.

A slightly more complex scenario is when you take multiple overlapping handheld pictures of a whiteboard or other large planar object (He and Zhang 2005; Zhang and He 2007). Here, the natural motion model to use is a homography, although a more complex model that estimates the 3D rigid motion relative to the plane (plus the focal length, if unknown), could in principle be used.

9.1.3 Rotational panoramas

The most typical case for panoramic image stitching is when the camera undergoes a pure rotation. Think of standing at the rim of the Grand Canyon. Relative to the distant geometry in the scene, as you snap away, the camera is undergoing a pure rotation, which is equivalent to assuming that all points are very far from the camera, i.e., on the *plane at infinity* (Figure 9.3). Setting $t_0 = t_1 = 0$, we get the simplified 3×3 homography

$$\tilde{H}_{10} = K_1 R_1 R_0^{-1} K_0^{-1} = K_1 R_{10} K_0^{-1}, \tag{9.5}$$

where $K_k = \text{diag}(f_k, f_k, 1)$ is the simplified camera intrinsic matrix (2.59), assuming that $c_x = c_y = 0$, i.e., we are indexing the pixels starting from the optical center (Szeliski 1996).

This can also be re-written as

$$
\begin{bmatrix} x_1 \\ y_1 \\ 1 \end{bmatrix} \sim \begin{bmatrix} f_1 & & \\ & f_1 & \\ & & 1 \end{bmatrix} \boldsymbol{R}_{10} \begin{bmatrix} f_0^{-1} & & \\ & f_0^{-1} & \\ & & 1 \end{bmatrix} \begin{bmatrix} x_0 \\ y_0 \\ 1 \end{bmatrix} \tag{9.6}
$$

or

$$
\begin{bmatrix} x_1 \\ y_1 \\ f_1 \end{bmatrix} \sim \boldsymbol{R}_{10} \begin{bmatrix} x_0 \\ y_0 \\ f_0 \end{bmatrix}, \tag{9.7}
$$

which reveals the simplicity of the mapping equations and makes all of the motion parameters explicit. Thus, instead of the general eight-parameter homography relating a pair of images, we get the three-, four-, or five-parameter *3D rotation* motion models corresponding to the cases where the focal length f is known, fixed, or variable (Szeliski and Shum 1997).[3] Estimating the 3D rotation matrix (and, optionally, focal length) associated with each image is intrinsically more stable than estimating a homography with a full eight degrees of freedom, which makes this the method of choice for large-scale image stitching algorithms (Szeliski and Shum 1997; Shum and Szeliski 2000; Brown and Lowe 2007).

Given this representation, how do we update the rotation matrices to best align two overlapping images? Given a current estimate for the homography $\tilde{\boldsymbol{H}}_{10}$ in (9.5), the best way to update $\boldsymbol{R}_{10}$ is to prepend an *incremental* rotation matrix $\boldsymbol{R}(\boldsymbol{\omega})$ to the current estimate $\boldsymbol{R}_{10}$ (Szeliski and Shum 1997; Shum and Szeliski 2000),

$$
\tilde{\boldsymbol{H}}(\boldsymbol{\omega}) = \boldsymbol{K}_1 \boldsymbol{R}(\boldsymbol{\omega}) \boldsymbol{R}_{10} \boldsymbol{K}_0^{-1} = [\boldsymbol{K}_1 \boldsymbol{R}(\boldsymbol{\omega}) \boldsymbol{K}_1^{-1}][\boldsymbol{K}_1 \boldsymbol{R}_{10} \boldsymbol{K}_0^{-1}] = \boldsymbol{D} \tilde{\boldsymbol{H}}_{10}. \tag{9.8}
$$

Note that here we have written the update rule in the *compositional* form, where the incremental update $\boldsymbol{D}$ is *prepended* to the current homography $\tilde{\boldsymbol{H}}_{10}$. Using the small-angle approximation to $\boldsymbol{R}(\boldsymbol{\omega})$ given in (2.35), we can write the incremental update matrix as

$$
\boldsymbol{D} = \boldsymbol{K}_1 \boldsymbol{R}(\boldsymbol{\omega}) \boldsymbol{K}_1^{-1} \approx \boldsymbol{K}_1 (\boldsymbol{I} + [\boldsymbol{\omega}]_\times) \boldsymbol{K}_1^{-1} = \begin{bmatrix} 1 & -\omega_z & f_1 \omega_y \\ \omega_z & 1 & -f_1 \omega_x \\ -\omega_y/f_1 & \omega_x/f_1 & 1 \end{bmatrix}. \tag{9.9}
$$

Notice how there is now a nice one-to-one correspondence between the entries in the $\boldsymbol{D}$ matrix and the $h_{00}, \ldots, h_{21}$ parameters used in Table 6.1 and Equation (6.19), i.e.,

$$
(h_{00}, h_{01}, h_{02}, h_{00}, h_{11}, h_{12}, h_{20}, h_{21}) = (0, -\omega_z, f_1 \omega_y, \omega_z, 0, -f_1 \omega_x, -\omega_y/f_1, \omega_x/f_1). \tag{9.10}
$$

We can therefore apply the chain rule to Equations (6.24 and 9.10) to obtain

$$
\begin{bmatrix} \hat{x}' - x \\ \hat{y}' - y \end{bmatrix} = \begin{bmatrix} -xy/f_1 & f_1 + x^2/f_1 & -y \\ -(f_1 + y^2/f_1) & xy/f_1 & x \end{bmatrix} \begin{bmatrix} \omega_x \\ \omega_y \\ \omega_z \end{bmatrix}, \tag{9.11}
$$

which give us the linearized update equations needed to estimate $\boldsymbol{\omega} = (\omega_x, \omega_y, \omega_z)$.[4] Notice that this update rule depends on the focal length f_1 of the *target* view and is independent

---

[3] An initial estimate of the focal lengths can be obtained using the intrinsic calibration techniques described in Section 6.3.4 or from EXIF tags.

[4] This is the same as the rotational component of instantaneous rigid flow (Bergen, Anandan, Hanna *et al.* 1992) and the update equations given by Szeliski and Shum (1997) and Shum and Szeliski (2000).

Figure 9.4 Four images taken with a hand-held camera registered using a 3D rotation motion model (Szeliski and Shum 1997) © 1997 ACM. Notice how the homographies, rather than being arbitrary, have a well-defined keystone shape whose width increases away from the origin.

of the focal length f_0 of the *template* view. This is because the compositional algorithm essentially makes small perturbations to the target. Once the incremental rotation vector $\boldsymbol{\omega}$ has been computed, the $\boldsymbol{R}_1$ rotation matrix can be updated using $\boldsymbol{R}_1 \leftarrow \boldsymbol{R}(\boldsymbol{\omega})\boldsymbol{R}_1$.

The formulas for updating the focal length estimates are a little more involved and are given in (Shum and Szeliski 2000). We will not repeat them here, since an alternative update rule, based on minimizing the difference between back-projected 3D rays, is given in Section 9.2.1. Figure 9.4 shows the alignment of four images under the 3D rotation motion model.

9.1.4 Gap closing

The techniques presented in this section can be used to estimate a series of rotation matrices and focal lengths, which can be chained together to create large panoramas. Unfortunately, because of accumulated errors, this approach will rarely produce a closed 360° panorama. Instead, there will invariably be either a gap or an overlap (Figure 9.5).

We can solve this problem by matching the first image in the sequence with the last one. The difference between the two rotation matrix estimates associated with the repeated first indicates the amount of misregistration. This error can be distributed evenly across the whole sequence by taking the quotient of the two quaternions associated with these rotations and dividing this "error quaternion" by the number of images in the sequence (assuming relatively constant inter-frame rotations). We can also update the estimated focal length based on the amount of misregistration. To do this, we first convert the error quaternion into a *gap angle*, θ_g and then update the focal length using the equation $f' = f(1 - \theta_g/360°)$.

Figure 9.5a shows the end of registered image sequence and the first image. There is a big gap between the last image and the first which are in fact the same image. The gap is 32° because the wrong estimate of focal length ($f = 510$) was used. Figure 9.5b shows the registration after closing the gap with the correct focal length ($f = 468$). Notice that both

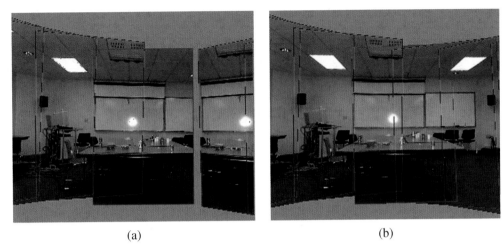

(a)   (b)

Figure 9.5 Gap closing (Szeliski and Shum 1997) © 1997 ACM: (a) A gap is visible when the focal length is wrong ($f = 510$). (b) No gap is visible for the correct focal length ($f = 468$).

mosaics show very little visual misregistration (except at the gap), yet Figure 9.5a has been computed using a focal length that has 9% error. Related approaches have been developed by Hartley (1994b), McMillan and Bishop (1995), Stein (1995), and Kang and Weiss (1997) to solve the focal length estimation problem using pure panning motion and cylindrical images.

Unfortunately, this particular gap-closing heuristic only works for the kind of "one-dimensional" panorama where the camera is continuously turning in the same direction. In Section 9.2, we describe a different approach to removing gaps and overlaps that works for arbitrary camera motions.

9.1.5 *Application*: Video summarization and compression

An interesting application of image stitching is the ability to summarize and compress videos taken with a panning camera. This application was first suggested by Teodosio and Bender (1993), who called their mosaic-based summaries *salient stills*. These ideas were then extended by Irani, Hsu, and Anandan (1995), Kumar, Anandan, Irani *et al.* (1995), and Irani and Anandan (1998) to additional applications, such as video compression and video indexing. While these early approaches used affine motion models and were therefore restricted to long focal lengths, the techniques were generalized by Lee, ge Chen, lung Bruce Lin *et al.* (1997) to full eight-parameter homographies and incorporated into the MPEG-4 video compression standard, where the stitched background layers were called *video sprites* (Figure 9.6).

While video stitching is in many ways a straightforward generalization of multiple-image stitching (Steedly, Pal, and Szeliski 2005; Baudisch, Tan, Steedly *et al.* 2006), the potential presence of large amounts of independent motion, camera zoom, and the desire to visualize dynamic events impose additional challenges. For example, moving foreground objects can often be removed using *median filtering*. Alternatively, foreground objects can be extracted into a separate layer (Sawhney and Ayer 1996) and later composited back into the stitched panoramas, sometimes as multiple instances to give the impressions of a "Chronophotograph" (Massey and Bender 1996) and sometimes as video overlays (Irani and Anandan 1998).

Figure 9.6 Video stitching the background scene to create a single *sprite* image that can be transmitted and used to re-create the background in each frame (Lee, ge Chen, lung Bruce Lin *et al.* 1997) © 1997 IEEE.

Videos can also be used to create animated *panoramic video textures* (Section 13.5.2), in which different portions of a panoramic scene are animated with independently moving video loops (Agarwala, Zheng, Pal *et al.* 2005; Rav-Acha, Pritch, Lischinski *et al.* 2005), or to shine "video flashlights" onto a composite mosaic of a scene (Sawhney, Arpa, Kumar *et al.* 2002).

Video can also provide an interesting source of content for creating panoramas taken from moving cameras. While this invalidates the usual assumption of a single point of view (optical center), interesting results can still be obtained. For example, the VideoBrush system of Sawhney, Kumar, Gendel *et al.* (1998) uses thin strips taken from the center of the image to create a panorama taken from a horizontally moving camera. This idea can be generalized to other camera motions and compositing surfaces using the concept of mosaics on adaptive manifold (Peleg, Rousso, Rav-Acha *et al.* 2000), and also used to generate panoramic stereograms (Peleg, Ben-Ezra, and Pritch 2001). Related ideas have been used to create panoramic matte paintings for multi-plane cel animation (Wood, Finkelstein, Hughes *et al.* 1997), for creating stitched images of scenes with parallax (Kumar, Anandan, Irani *et al.* 1995), and as 3D representations of more complex scenes using *multiple-center-of-projection images* (Rademacher and Bishop 1998) and *multi-perspective panoramas* (Román, Garg, and Levoy 2004; Román and Lensch 2006; Agarwala, Agrawala, Cohen *et al.* 2006).

Another interesting variant on video-based panoramas are *concentric mosaics* (Section 13.3.3) (Shum and He 1999). Here, rather than trying to produce a single panoramic image, the complete original video is kept and used to re-synthesize views (from different camera origins) using ray remapping (light field rendering), thus endowing the panorama with a sense of 3D depth. The same data set can also be used to explicitly reconstruct the depth using multibaseline stereo (Peleg, Ben-Ezra, and Pritch 2001; Li, Shum, Tang *et al.* 2004; Zheng, Kang, Cohen *et al.* 2007).

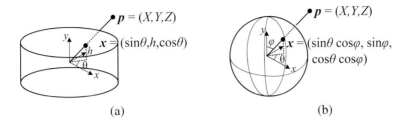

Figure 9.7 Projection from 3D to (a) cylindrical and (b) spherical coordinates.

9.1.6 Cylindrical and spherical coordinates

An alternative to using homographies or 3D motions to align images is to first warp the images into *cylindrical* coordinates and then use a pure translational model to align them (Chen 1995; Szeliski 1996). Unfortunately, this only works if the images are all taken with a level camera or with a known tilt angle.

Assume for now that the camera is in its canonical position, i.e., its rotation matrix is the identity, $R = I$, so that the optical axis is aligned with the z axis and the y axis is aligned vertically. The 3D ray corresponding to an (x, y) pixel is therefore (x, y, f).

We wish to project this image onto a *cylindrical surface* of unit radius (Szeliski 1996). Points on this surface are parameterized by an angle θ and a height h, with the 3D cylindrical coordinates corresponding to (θ, h) given by

$$(\sin \theta, h, \cos \theta) \propto (x, y, f),\tag{9.12}$$

as shown in Figure 9.7a. From this correspondence, we can compute the formula for the *warped* or *mapped* coordinates (Szeliski and Shum 1997),

$$x' = s\theta = s\tan^{-1}\frac{x}{f},\tag{9.13}$$

$$y' = sh = s\frac{y}{\sqrt{x^2 + f^2}},\tag{9.14}$$

where s is an arbitrary scaling factor (sometimes called the *radius* of the cylinder) that can be set to $s = f$ to minimize the distortion (scaling) near the center of the image.[5] The inverse of this mapping equation is given by

$$x = f\tan\theta = f\tan\frac{x'}{s},\tag{9.15}$$

$$y = h\sqrt{x^2 + f^2} = \frac{y'}{s}f\sqrt{1 + \tan^2 x'/s} = f\frac{y'}{s}\sec\frac{x'}{s}.\tag{9.16}$$

Images can also be projected onto a *spherical surface* (Szeliski and Shum 1997), which is useful if the final panorama includes a full sphere or hemisphere of views, instead of just a cylindrical strip. In this case, the sphere is parameterized by two angles (θ, ϕ), with 3D spherical coordinates given by

$$(\sin \theta \cos \phi, \sin \phi, \cos \theta \cos \phi) \propto (x, y, f),\tag{9.17}$$

---

[5] The scale can also be set to a larger or smaller value for the final compositing surface, depending on the desired output panorama resolution—see Section 9.3.

                        (a)   (b)

Figure 9.8 A cylindrical panorama (Szeliski and Shum 1997) © 1997 ACM: (a) two cylindrically warped images related by a horizontal translation; (b) part of a cylindrical panorama composited from a sequence of images.

as shown in Figure 9.7b.[6] The correspondence between coordinates is now given by (Szeliski and Shum 1997):

$$x' = s\theta = s\tan^{-1}\frac{x}{f}, \tag{9.18}$$

$$y' = s\phi = s\tan^{-1}\frac{y}{\sqrt{x^2+f^2}}, \tag{9.19}$$

while the inverse is given by

$$x = f\tan\theta = f\tan\frac{x'}{s}, \tag{9.20}$$

$$y = \sqrt{x^2+f^2}\tan\phi = \tan\frac{y'}{s}f\sqrt{1+\tan^2 x'/s} = f\tan\frac{y'}{s}\sec\frac{x'}{s}. \tag{9.21}$$

Note that it may be simpler to generate a scaled (x, y, z) direction from Equation (9.17) followed by a perspective division by z and a scaling by f.

Cylindrical image stitching algorithms are most commonly used when the camera is known to be level and only rotating around its vertical axis (Chen 1995). Under these conditions, images at different rotations are related by a pure horizontal translation.[7] This makes it attractive as an initial class project in an introductory computer vision course, since the full complexity of the perspective alignment algorithm (Sections 6.1, 8.2, and 9.1.3) can be avoided. Figure 9.8 shows how two cylindrically warped images from a leveled rotational panorama are related by a pure translation (Szeliski and Shum 1997).

Professional panoramic photographers often use pan-tilt heads that make it easy to control the tilt and to stop at specific *detents* in the rotation angle. Motorized rotation heads are also sometimes used for the acquisition of larger panoramas (Kopf, Uyttendaele, Deussen *et al.* 2007).[8] Not only do they ensure a uniform coverage of the visual field with a desired amount of image overlap but they also make it possible to stitch the images using cylindrical or spherical coordinates and pure translations. In this case, pixel coordinates (x, y, f) must first

---

[6] Note that these are not the usual spherical coordinates, first presented in Equation (2.8). Here, the y axis points at the north pole instead of the z axis, since we are used to viewing images taken horizontally, i.e., with the y axis pointing in the direction of the gravity vector.

[7] Small vertical tilts can sometimes be compensated for with vertical translations.

[8] See also http://gigapan.org.

Figure 9.9 A spherical panorama constructed from 54 photographs (Szeliski and Shum 1997) © 1997 ACM.

be rotated using the known tilt and panning angles before being projected into cylindrical or spherical coordinates (Chen 1995). Having a roughly known panning angle also makes it easier to compute the alignment, since the rough relative positioning of all the input images is known ahead of time, enabling a reduced search range for alignment. Figure 9.9 shows a full 3D rotational panorama unwrapped onto the surface of a sphere (Szeliski and Shum 1997).

One final coordinate mapping worth mentioning is the *polar* mapping, where the north pole lies along the optical axis rather than the vertical axis,

$$(\cos\theta\sin\phi, \sin\theta\sin\phi, \cos\phi) = s\,(x, y, z). \tag{9.22}$$

In this case, the mapping equations become

$$x' = s\phi\cos\theta = s\frac{x}{r}\tan^{-1}\frac{r}{z}, \tag{9.23}$$

$$y' = s\phi\sin\theta = s\frac{y}{r}\tan^{-1}\frac{r}{z}, \tag{9.24}$$

where $r = \sqrt{x^2 + y^2}$ is the *radial distance* in the (x, y) plane and $s\phi$ plays a similar role in the (x', y') plane. This mapping provides an attractive visualization surface for certain kinds of wide-angle panoramas and is also a good model for the distortion induced by *fisheye lenses*, as discussed in Section 2.1.6. Note how for small values of (x, y), the mapping equations reduce to $x' \approx sx/z$, which suggests that s plays a role similar to the focal length f.

9.2 Global alignment

So far, we have discussed how to register pairs of images using a variety of motion models. In most applications, we are given more than a single pair of images to register. The goal is then to find a globally consistent set of alignment parameters that minimize the mis-registration between all pairs of images (Szeliski and Shum 1997; Shum and Szeliski 2000; Sawhney and Kumar 1999; Coorg and Teller 2000).

In this section, we extend the pairwise matching criteria (6.2, 8.1, and 8.50) to a global energy function that involves all of the per-image pose parameters (Section 9.2.1). Once we have computed the global alignment, we often need to perform *local adjustments*, such as *parallax removal*, to reduce double images and blurring due to local mis-registrations (Section 9.2.2). Finally, if we are given an unordered set of images to register, we need to discover which images go together to form one or more panoramas. This process of *panorama recognition* is described in Section 9.2.3.

9.2.1 Bundle adjustment

One way to register a large number of images is to add new images to the panorama one at a time, aligning the most recent image with the previous ones already in the collection (Szeliski and Shum 1997) and discovering, if necessary, which images it overlaps (Sawhney and Kumar 1999). In the case of $360°$ panoramas, accumulated error may lead to the presence of a gap (or excessive overlap) between the two ends of the panorama, which can be fixed by stretching the alignment of all the images using a process called *gap closing* (Szeliski and Shum 1997). However, a better alternative is to simultaneously align all the images using a least-squares framework to correctly distribute any mis-registration errors.

The process of simultaneously adjusting pose parameters for a large collection of overlapping images is called *bundle adjustment* in the photogrammetry community (Triggs, McLauchlan, Hartley *et al.* 1999). In computer vision, it was first applied to the general structure from motion problem (Szeliski and Kang 1994) and then later specialized for panoramic image stitching (Shum and Szeliski 2000; Sawhney and Kumar 1999; Coorg and Teller 2000).

In this section, we formulate the problem of global alignment using a feature-based approach, since this results in a simpler system. An equivalent direct approach can be obtained either by dividing images into patches and creating a virtual feature correspondence for each one (as discussed in Section 9.2.4 and by Shum and Szeliski (2000)) or by replacing the per-feature error metrics with per-pixel metrics.

Consider the feature-based alignment problem given in Equation (6.2), i.e.,

$$E_{\text{pairwise}-\text{LS}} = \sum_i \|r_i\|^2 = \|\tilde{x}_i'(x_i; p) - \hat{x}_i'\|^2. \tag{9.25}$$

For multi-image alignment, instead of having a single collection of pairwise feature correspondences, $\{(x_i, \hat{x}_i')\}$, we have a collection of n features, with the location of the ith feature point in the jth image denoted by x_{ij} and its scalar confidence (i.e., inverse variance) denoted by c_{ij}.[9] Each image also has some associated pose parameters.

In this section, we assume that this pose consists of a rotation matrix R_j and a focal length f_j, although formulations in terms of homographies are also possible (Szeliski and Shum 1997; Sawhney and Kumar 1999). The equation mapping a 3D point x_i into a point x_{ij} in frame j can be re-written from Equations (2.68) and (9.5) as

$$\tilde{x}_{ij} \sim K_j R_j x_i \quad \text{and} \quad x_i \sim R_j^{-1} K_j^{-1} \tilde{x}_{ij}, \tag{9.26}$$

---

[9] Features that are not seen in image j have $c_{ij} = 0$. We can also use 2×2 inverse covariance matrices Σ_{ij}^{-1} in place of c_{ij}, as shown in Equation (6.11).

where $\boldsymbol{K}_j = \mathrm{diag}(f_j, f_j, 1)$ is the simplified form of the calibration matrix. The motion mapping a point $\boldsymbol{x}_{ij}$ from frame j into a point $\boldsymbol{x}_{ik}$ in frame k is similarly given by

$$\tilde{\boldsymbol{x}}_{ik} \sim \tilde{\boldsymbol{H}}_{kj}\tilde{\boldsymbol{x}}_{ij} = \boldsymbol{K}_k \boldsymbol{R}_k \boldsymbol{R}_j^{-1} \boldsymbol{K}_j^{-1} \tilde{\boldsymbol{x}}_{ij}. \tag{9.27}$$

Given an initial set of $\{(\boldsymbol{R}_j, f_j)\}$ estimates obtained from chaining pairwise alignments, how do we refine these estimates?

One approach is to directly extend the pairwise energy $E_{\mathrm{pairwise-LS}}$ (9.25) to a multiview formulation,

$$E_{\mathrm{all-pairs-2D}} = \sum_i \sum_{jk} c_{ij} c_{ik} \|\tilde{\boldsymbol{x}}_{ik}(\hat{\boldsymbol{x}}_{ij}; \boldsymbol{R}_j, f_j, \boldsymbol{R}_k, f_k) - \hat{\boldsymbol{x}}_{ik}\|^2, \tag{9.28}$$

where the $\tilde{\boldsymbol{x}}_{ik}$ function is the *predicted* location of feature i in frame k given by (9.27), $\hat{\boldsymbol{x}}_{ij}$ is the *observed* location, and the "2D" in the subscript indicates that an image-plane error is being minimized (Shum and Szeliski 2000). Note that since $\tilde{\boldsymbol{x}}_{ik}$ depends on the $\hat{\boldsymbol{x}}_{ij}$ observed value, we actually have an *errors-in-variable* problem, which in principle requires more sophisticated techniques than least squares to solve (Van Huffel and Lemmerling 2002; Matei and Meer 2006). However, in practice, if we have enough features, we can directly minimize the above quantity using regular non-linear least squares and obtain an accurate multi-frame alignment.

While this approach works well in practice, it suffers from two potential disadvantages. First, since a summation is taken over all pairs with corresponding features, features that are observed many times are overweighted in the final solution. (In effect, a feature observed m times gets counted $\binom{m}{2}$ times instead of m times.) Second, the derivatives of $\tilde{\boldsymbol{x}}_{ik}$ with respect to the $\{(\boldsymbol{R}_j, f_j)\}$ are a little cumbersome, although using the incremental correction to $\boldsymbol{R}_j$ introduced in Section 9.1.3 makes this more tractable.

An alternative way to formulate the optimization is to use true bundle adjustment, i.e., to solve not only for the pose parameters $\{(\boldsymbol{R}_j, f_j)\}$ but also for the 3D point positions $\{\boldsymbol{x}_i\}$,

$$E_{\mathrm{BA-2D}} = \sum_i \sum_j c_{ij} \|\tilde{\boldsymbol{x}}_{ij}(\boldsymbol{x}_i; \boldsymbol{R}_j, f_j) - \hat{\boldsymbol{x}}_{ij}\|^2, \tag{9.29}$$

where $\tilde{\boldsymbol{x}}_{ij}(\boldsymbol{x}_i; \boldsymbol{R}_j, f_j)$ is given by (9.26). The disadvantage of full bundle adjustment is that there are more variables to solve for, so each iteration and also the overall convergence may be slower. (Imagine how the 3D points need to "shift" each time some rotation matrices are updated.) However, the computational complexity of each linearized Gauss–Newton step can be reduced using sparse matrix techniques (Section 7.4.1) (Szeliski and Kang 1994; Triggs, McLauchlan, Hartley *et al.* 1999; Hartley and Zisserman 2004).

An alternative formulation is to minimize the error in 3D projected ray directions (Shum and Szeliski 2000), i.e.,

$$E_{\mathrm{BA-3D}} = \sum_i \sum_j c_{ij} \|\tilde{\boldsymbol{x}}_i(\hat{\boldsymbol{x}}_{ij}; \boldsymbol{R}_j, f_j) - \boldsymbol{x}_i\|^2, \tag{9.30}$$

where $\tilde{\boldsymbol{x}}_i(\boldsymbol{x}_{ij}; \boldsymbol{R}_j, f_j)$ is given by the second half of (9.26). This has no particular advantage over (9.29). In fact, since errors are being minimized in 3D ray space, there is a bias towards estimating longer focal lengths, since the angles between rays become smaller as f increases.

However, if we eliminate the 3D rays $\boldsymbol{x}_i$, we can derive a pairwise energy formulated in 3D ray space (Shum and Szeliski 2000),

$$E_{\text{all-pairs-3D}} = \sum_i \sum_{jk} c_{ij} c_{ik} \| \tilde{\boldsymbol{x}}_i(\hat{\boldsymbol{x}}_{ij}; \boldsymbol{R}_j, f_j) - \tilde{\boldsymbol{x}}_i(\hat{\boldsymbol{x}}_{ik}; \boldsymbol{R}_k, f_k) \|^2. \qquad (9.31)$$

This results in the simplest set of update equations (Shum and Szeliski 2000), since the f_k can be folded into the creation of the homogeneous coordinate vector as in Equation (9.7). Thus, even though this formula over-weights features that occur more frequently, it is the method used by Shum and Szeliski (2000) and Brown, Szeliski, and Winder (2005). In order to reduce the bias towards longer focal lengths, we multiply each residual (3D error) by $\sqrt{f_j f_k}$, which is similar to projecting the 3D rays into a "virtual camera" of intermediate focal length.

Up vector selection.   As mentioned above, there exists a global ambiguity in the pose of the 3D cameras computed by the above methods. While this may not appear to matter, people prefer that the final stitched image is "upright" rather than twisted or tilted. More concretely, people are used to seeing photographs displayed so that the vertical (gravity) axis points straight up in the image. Consider how you usually shoot photographs: while you may pan and tilt the camera any which way, you usually keep the horizontal edge of your camera (its x-axis) parallel to the ground plane (perpendicular to the world gravity direction).

Mathematically, this constraint on the rotation matrices can be expressed as follows. Recall from Equation (9.26) that the 3D to 2D projection is given by

$$\tilde{\boldsymbol{x}}_{ik} \sim \boldsymbol{K}_k \boldsymbol{R}_k \boldsymbol{x}_i. \qquad (9.32)$$

We wish to post-multiply each rotation matrix $\boldsymbol{R}_k$ by a global rotation $\boldsymbol{R}_{\text{g}}$ such that the projection of the global y-axis, $\hat{\boldsymbol{\jmath}} = (0, 1, 0)$ is perpendicular to the image x-axis, $\hat{\boldsymbol{\imath}} = (1, 0, 0)$.[10]

This constraint can be written as

$$\hat{\boldsymbol{\imath}}^T \boldsymbol{R}_k \boldsymbol{R}_{\text{g}} \hat{\boldsymbol{\jmath}} = 0 \qquad (9.33)$$

(note that the scaling by the calibration matrix is irrelevant here). This is equivalent to requiring that the first row of $\boldsymbol{R}_k$, $\boldsymbol{r}_{k0} = \hat{\boldsymbol{\imath}}^T \boldsymbol{R}_k$ be perpendicular to the second column of $\boldsymbol{R}_{\text{g}}$, $\boldsymbol{r}_{\text{g}1} = \boldsymbol{R}_{\text{g}} \hat{\boldsymbol{\jmath}}$. This set of constraints (one per input image) can be written as a least squares problem,

$$\boldsymbol{r}_{\text{g}1} = \arg\min_{\boldsymbol{r}} \sum_k (\boldsymbol{r}^T \boldsymbol{r}_{k0})^2 = \arg\min_{\boldsymbol{r}} \boldsymbol{r}^T \left[\sum_k \boldsymbol{r}_{k0} \boldsymbol{r}_{k0}^T \right] \boldsymbol{r}. \qquad (9.34)$$

Thus, $\boldsymbol{r}_{\text{g}1}$ is the smallest eigenvector of the *scatter* or *moment* matrix spanned by the individual camera rotation x-vectors, which should generally be of the form $(c, 0, s)$ when the cameras are upright.

To fully specify the $\boldsymbol{R}_{\text{g}}$ global rotation, we need to specify one additional constraint. This is related to the *view selection* problem discussed in Section 9.3.1. One simple heuristic is to prefer the average z-axis of the individual rotation matrices, $\bar{\boldsymbol{k}} = \sum_k \hat{\boldsymbol{k}}^T \boldsymbol{R}_k$ to be close to the world z-axis, $\boldsymbol{r}_{\text{g}2} = \boldsymbol{R}_{\text{g}} \hat{\boldsymbol{k}}$. We can therefore compute the full rotation matrix $\boldsymbol{R}_{\text{g}}$ in three steps:

---

[10] Note that here we use the convention common in computer graphics that the vertical world axis corresponds to y. This is a natural choice if we wish the rotation matrix associated with a "regular" image taken horizontally to be the identity, rather than a $90°$ rotation around the x-axis.

1. $\boldsymbol{r}_{g1} = \min \; \mathrm{eigenvector} \; (\sum_k \boldsymbol{r}_{k0} \boldsymbol{r}_{k0}^T)$;

2. $\boldsymbol{r}_{g0} = \mathcal{N}((\sum_k \boldsymbol{r}_{k2}) \times \boldsymbol{r}_{g1})$;

3. $\boldsymbol{r}_{g2} = \boldsymbol{r}_{g0} \times \boldsymbol{r}_{g1}$,

where $\mathcal{N}(\boldsymbol{v}) = \boldsymbol{v}/\|\boldsymbol{v}\|$ normalizes a vector $\boldsymbol{v}$.

9.2.2 Parallax removal

Once we have optimized the global orientations and focal lengths of our cameras, we may find that the images are still not perfectly aligned, i.e., the resulting stitched image looks blurry or ghosted in some places. This can be caused by a variety of factors, including unmodeled radial distortion, 3D parallax (failure to rotate the camera around its optical center), small scene motions such as waving tree branches, and large-scale scene motions such as people moving in and out of pictures.

Each of these problems can be treated with a different approach. Radial distortion can be estimated (potentially ahead of time) using one of the techniques discussed in Section 2.1.6. For example, the *plumb-line method* (Brown 1971; Kang 2001; El-Melegy and Farag 2003) adjusts radial distortion parameters until slightly curved lines become straight, while mosaic-based approaches adjust them until mis-registration is reduced in image overlap areas (Stein 1997; Sawhney and Kumar 1999).

3D parallax can be handled by doing a full 3D bundle adjustment, i.e., by replacing the projection equation (9.26) used in Equation (9.29) with Equation (2.68), which models camera translations. The 3D positions of the matched feature points and cameras can then be simultaneously recovered, although this can be significantly more expensive than parallax-free image registration. Once the 3D structure has been recovered, the scene could (in theory) be projected to a single (central) viewpoint that contains no parallax. However, in order to do this, dense *stereo* correspondence needs to be performed (Section 11.3) (Li, Shum, Tang *et al.* 2004; Zheng, Kang, Cohen *et al.* 2007), which may not be possible if the images contain only partial overlap. In that case, it may be necessary to correct for parallax only in the overlap areas, which can be accomplished using a *multi-perspective plane sweep* (MPPS) algorithm (Kang, Szeliski, and Uyttendaele 2004; Uyttendaele, Criminisi, Kang *et al.* 2004).

When the motion in the scene is very large, i.e., when objects appear and disappear completely, a sensible solution is to simply *select* pixels from only one image at a time as the source for the final composite (Milgram 1977; Davis 1998; Agarwala, Dontcheva, Agrawala *et al.* 2004), as discussed in Section 9.3.2. However, when the motion is reasonably small (on the order of a few pixels), general 2D motion estimation (optical flow) can be used to perform an appropriate correction before blending using a process called *local alignment* (Shum and Szeliski 2000; Kang, Uyttendaele, Winder *et al.* 2003). This same process can also be used to compensate for radial distortion and 3D parallax, although it uses a weaker motion model than explicitly modeling the source of error and may, therefore, fail more often or introduce unwanted distortions.

The local alignment technique introduced by Shum and Szeliski (2000) starts with the global bundle adjustment (9.31) used to optimize the camera poses. Once these have been estimated, the *desired* location of a 3D point $\boldsymbol{x}_i$ can be estimated as the *average* of the back-

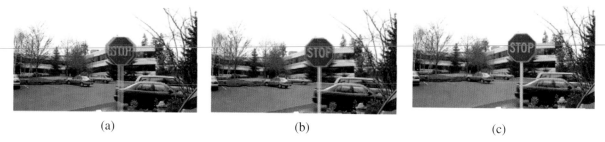

(a)   (b)   (c)

Figure 9.10 Deghosting a mosaic with motion parallax (Shum and Szeliski 2000) © 2000 IEEE: (a) composite with parallax; (b) after a single deghosting step (patch size 32); (c) after multiple steps (sizes 32, 16 and 8).

projected 3D locations,

$$\bar{x}_i \sim \sum_j c_{ij} \tilde{x}_i(\hat{x}_{ij}; R_j, f_j) \Big/ \sum_j c_{ij}, \qquad (9.35)$$

which can be projected into each image j to obtain a *target location* $\bar{x}_{ij}$. The difference between the target locations $\bar{x}_{ij}$ and the original features x_{ij} provide a set of local motion estimates

$$u_{ij} = \bar{x}_{ij} - x_{ij}, \qquad (9.36)$$

which can be interpolated to form a dense correction field $u_j(x_j)$. In their system, Shum and Szeliski (2000) use an *inverse warping* algorithm where the sparse $-u_{ij}$ values are placed at the new target locations $\bar{x}_{ij}$, interpolated using bilinear kernel functions (Nielson 1993) and then added to the original pixel coordinates when computing the warped (corrected) image. In order to get a reasonably dense set of features to interpolate, Shum and Szeliski (2000) place a feature point at the center of each patch (the patch size controls the smoothness in the local alignment stage), rather than relying of features extracted using an interest operator (Figure 9.10).

An alternative approach to motion-based de-ghosting was proposed by Kang, Uyttendaele, Winder *et al.* (2003), who estimate dense optical flow between each input image and a central *reference* image. The accuracy of the flow vector is checked using a photo-consistency measure before a given warped pixel is considered valid and is used to compute a high dynamic range radiance estimate, which is the goal of their overall algorithm. The requirement for a reference image makes their approach less applicable to general image mosaicing, although an extension to this case could certainly be envisaged.

9.2.3 Recognizing panoramas

The final piece needed to perform fully automated image stitching is a technique to recognize which images actually go together, which Brown and Lowe (2007) call *recognizing panoramas*. If the user takes images in sequence so that each image overlaps its predecessor and also specifies the first and last images to be stitched, bundle adjustment combined with the process of *topology inference* can be used to automatically assemble a panorama (Sawhney and Kumar 1999). However, users often jump around when taking panoramas, e.g., they may start a new row on top of a previous one, jump back to take a repeat shot, or create

$360°$ panoramas where end-to-end overlaps need to be discovered. Furthermore, the ability to discover multiple panoramas taken by a user over an extended period of time can be a big convenience.

To recognize panoramas, Brown and Lowe (2007) first find all pairwise image overlaps using a feature-based method and then find connected components in the overlap graph to "recognize" individual panoramas (Figure 9.11). The feature-based matching stage first extracts scale invariant feature transform (SIFT) feature locations and feature descriptors (Lowe 2004) from all the input images and places them in an indexing structure, as described in Section 4.1.3. For each image pair under consideration, the nearest matching neighbor is found for each feature in the first image, using the indexing structure to rapidly find candidates and then comparing feature descriptors to find the best match. RANSAC is used to find a set of *inlier* matches; pairs of matches are used to hypothesize similarity motion models that are then used to count the number of inliers. (A more recent RANSAC algorithm tailored specifically for rotational panoramas is described by Brown, Hartley, and Nistér (2007).)

In practice, the most difficult part of getting a fully automated stitching algorithm to work is deciding which pairs of images actually correspond to the same parts of the scene. Repeated structures such as windows (Figure 9.12) can lead to false matches when using a feature-based approach. One way to mitigate this problem is to perform a direct pixel-based comparison between the registered images to determine if they actually are different views of the same scene. Unfortunately, this heuristic may fail if there are moving objects in the scene (Figure 9.13). While there is no magic bullet for this problem, short of full scene understanding, further improvements can likely be made by applying domain-specific heuristics, such as priors on typical camera motions as well as machine learning techniques applied to the problem of match validation.

9.2.4 Direct vs. feature-based alignment

Given that there exist these two approaches to aligning images, which is preferable?

Early feature-based methods would get confused in regions that were either too textured or not textured enough. The features would often be distributed unevenly over the images, thereby failing to match image pairs that should have been aligned. Furthermore, establishing correspondences relied on simple cross-correlation between patches surrounding the feature points, which did not work well when the images were rotated or had foreshortening due to homographies.

Today, feature detection and matching schemes are remarkably robust and can even be used for known object recognition from widely separated views (Lowe 2004). Features not only respond to regions of high "cornerness" (Förstner 1986; Harris and Stephens 1988) but also to "blob-like" regions (Lowe 2004), and uniform areas (Matas, Chum, Urban *et al.* 2004; Tuytelaars and Van Gool 2004). Furthermore, because they operate in scale-space and use a dominant orientation (or orientation invariant descriptors), they can match images that differ in scale, orientation, and even foreshortening. Our own experience in working with feature-based approaches is that if the features are well distributed over the image and the descriptors reasonably designed for repeatability, enough correspondences to permit image stitching can usually be found (Brown, Szeliski, and Winder 2005).

The biggest disadvantage of direct pixel-based alignment techniques is that they have a limited range of convergence. Even though they can be used in a hierarchical (coarse-to-

(a)

(b)

(c)

Figure 9.11 Recognizing panoramas (Brown, Szeliski, and Winder 2005), figures courtesy of Matthew Brown: (a) input images with pairwise matches; (b) images grouped into connected components (panoramas); (c) individual panoramas registered and blended into stitched composites.

Figure 9.12 Matching errors (Brown, Szeliski, and Winder 2004): accidental matching of several features can lead to matches between pairs of images that do not actually overlap.

Figure 9.13 Validation of image matches by direct pixel error comparison can fail when the scene contains moving objects (Uyttendaele, Eden, and Szeliski 2001) © 2001 IEEE.

fine) estimation framework, in practice it is hard to use more than two or three levels of a pyramid before important details start to be blurred away.[11] For matching sequential frames in a video, direct approaches can usually be made to work. However, for matching partially overlapping images in photo-based panoramas or for image collections where the contrast or content varies too much, they fail too often to be useful and feature-based approaches are therefore preferred.

9.3 Compositing

Once we have registered all of the input images with respect to each other, we need to decide how to produce the final stitched mosaic image. This involves selecting a final compositing surface (flat, cylindrical, spherical, etc.) and view (reference image). It also involves selecting which pixels contribute to the final composite and how to optimally blend these pixels to minimize visible seams, blur, and ghosting.

In this section, we review techniques that address these problems, namely compositing surface parameterization, pixel and seam selection, blending, and exposure compensation. My emphasis is on fully automated approaches to the problem. Since the creation of high-quality panoramas and composites is as much an artistic endeavor as a computational one, various interactive tools have been developed to assist this process (Agarwala, Dontcheva, Agrawala et al. 2004; Li, Sun, Tang et al. 2004; Rother, Kolmogorov, and Blake 2004). Some of these are covered in more detail in Section 10.4.

9.3.1 Choosing a compositing surface

The first choice to be made is how to represent the final image. If only a few images are stitched together, a natural approach is to select one of the images as the *reference* and to then warp all of the other images into its reference coordinate system. The resulting composite is sometimes called a *flat* panorama, since the projection onto the final surface is still a perspective projection, and hence straight lines remain straight (which is often a desirable attribute).[12]

For larger fields of view, however, we cannot maintain a flat representation without excessively stretching pixels near the border of the image. (In practice, flat panoramas start to look severely distorted once the field of view exceeds 90° or so.) The usual choice for compositing larger panoramas is to use a cylindrical (Chen 1995; Szeliski 1996) or spherical (Szeliski and Shum 1997) projection, as described in Section 9.1.6. In fact, any surface used for *environment mapping* in computer graphics can be used, including a *cube map*, which represents the full viewing sphere with the six square faces of a cube (Greene 1986; Szeliski and Shum 1997). Cartographers have also developed a number of alternative methods for representing the globe (Bugayevskiy and Snyder 1995).

The choice of parameterization is somewhat application dependent and involves a trade-off between keeping the local appearance undistorted (e.g., keeping straight lines straight)

---

[11] Fourier-based correlation (Szeliski 1996; Szeliski and Shum 1997) can extend this range but requires cylindrical images or motion prediction to be useful.

[12] Recently, some techniques have been developed to straighten curved lines in cylindrical and spherical panoramas (Carroll, Agrawala, and Agarwala 2009; Kopf, Lischinski, Deussen et al. 2009).

and providing a reasonably uniform sampling of the environment. Automatically making this selection and smoothly transitioning between representations based on the extent of the panorama is an active area of current research (Kopf, Uyttendaele, Deussen *et al.* 2007).

An interesting recent development in panoramic photography has been the use of stereographic projections looking down at the ground (in an outdoor scene) to create "little planet" renderings.[13]

View selection. Once we have chosen the output parameterization, we still need to determine which part of the scene will be *centered* in the final view. As mentioned above, for a flat composite, we can choose one of the images as a reference. Often, a reasonable choice is the one that is geometrically most central. For example, for rotational panoramas represented as a collection of 3D rotation matrices, we can choose the image whose z-axis is closest to the average z-axis (assuming a reasonable field of view). Alternatively, we can use the average z-axis (or quaternion, but this is trickier) to define the reference rotation matrix.

For larger, e.g., cylindrical or spherical, panoramas, we can use the same heuristic if a subset of the viewing sphere has been imaged. In the case of full $360°$ panoramas, a better choice might be to choose the middle image from the sequence of inputs, or sometimes the first image, assuming this contains the object of greatest interest. In all of these cases, having the user control the final view is often highly desirable. If the "up vector" computation described in Section 9.2.1 is working correctly, this can be as simple as panning over the image or setting a vertical "center line" for the final panorama.

Coordinate transformations. After selecting the parameterization and reference view, we still need to compute the mappings between the input and output pixels coordinates.

If the final compositing surface is flat (e.g., a single plane or the face of a cube map) and the input images have no radial distortion, the coordinate transformation is the simple homography described by (9.5). This kind of warping can be performed in graphics hardware by appropriately setting texture mapping coordinates and rendering a single quadrilateral.

If the final composite surface has some other analytic form (e.g., cylindrical or spherical), we need to convert every pixel in the final panorama into a viewing ray (3D point) and then map it back into each image according to the projection (and optionally radial distortion) equations. This process can be made more efficient by precomputing some lookup tables, e.g., the partial trigonometric functions needed to map cylindrical or spherical coordinates to 3D coordinates or the radial distortion field at each pixel. It is also possible to accelerate this process by computing exact pixel mappings on a coarser grid and then interpolating these values.

When the final compositing surface is a texture-mapped polyhedron, a slightly more sophisticated algorithm must be used. Not only do the 3D and texture map coordinates have to be properly handled, but a small amount of *overdraw* outside the triangle footprints in the texture map is necessary, to ensure that the texture pixels being interpolated during 3D rendering have valid values (Szeliski and Shum 1997).

---

[13] These are inspired by *The Little Prince* by Antoine De Saint-Exupery. Go to http://www.flickr.com and search for "little planet projection".

Sampling issues. While the above computations can yield the correct (fractional) pixel addresses in each input image, we still need to pay attention to sampling issues. For example, if the final panorama has a lower resolution than the input images, pre-filtering the input images is necessary to avoid aliasing. These issues have been extensively studied in both the image processing and computer graphics communities. The basic problem is to compute the appropriate pre-filter, which depends on the distance (and arrangement) between neighboring samples in a source image. As discussed in Sections 3.5.2 and 3.6.1, various approximate solutions, such as MIP mapping (Williams 1983) or elliptically weighted Gaussian averaging (Greene and Heckbert 1986) have been developed in the graphics community. For highest visual quality, a higher order (e.g., cubic) interpolator combined with a spatially adaptive pre-filter may be necessary (Wang, Kang, Szeliski *et al.* 2001). Under certain conditions, it may also be possible to produce images with a higher resolution than the input images using the process of *super-resolution* (Section 10.3).

9.3.2 Pixel selection and weighting (de-ghosting)

Once the source pixels have been mapped onto the final composite surface, we must still decide how to blend them in order to create an attractive-looking panorama. If all of the images are in perfect registration and identically exposed, this is an easy problem, i.e., any pixel or combination will do. However, for real images, visible seams (due to exposure differences), blurring (due to mis-registration), or ghosting (due to moving objects) can occur.

Creating clean, pleasing-looking panoramas involves both deciding which pixels to use and how to weight or blend them. The distinction between these two stages is a little fluid, since per-pixel weighting can be thought of as a combination of selection and blending. In this section, we discuss spatially varying weighting, pixel selection (seam placement), and then more sophisticated blending.

Feathering and center-weighting. The simplest way to create a final composite is to simply take an *average* value at each pixel,

$$C(\boldsymbol{x}) = \sum_k w_k(\boldsymbol{x}) \tilde{I}_k(\boldsymbol{x}) \Big/ \sum_k w_k(\boldsymbol{x}) \,, \qquad (9.37)$$

where $\tilde{I}_k(\boldsymbol{x})$ are the *warped* (re-sampled) images and $w_k(\boldsymbol{x})$ is 1 at valid pixels and 0 elsewhere. On computer graphics hardware, this kind of summation can be performed in an *accumulation buffer* (using the A channel as the weight).

Simple averaging usually does not work very well, since exposure differences, mis-registrations, and scene movement are all very visible (Figure 9.14a). If rapidly moving objects are the only problem, taking a *median* filter (which is a kind of pixel selection operator) can often be used to remove them (Figure 9.14b) (Irani and Anandan 1998). Conversely, center-weighting (discussed below) and *minimum likelihood* selection (Agarwala, Dontcheva, Agrawala *et al.* 2004) can sometimes be used to retain multiple copies of a moving object (Figure 9.17).

A better approach to averaging is to weight pixels near the center of the image more heavily and to down-weight pixels near the edges. When an image has some cutout regions,

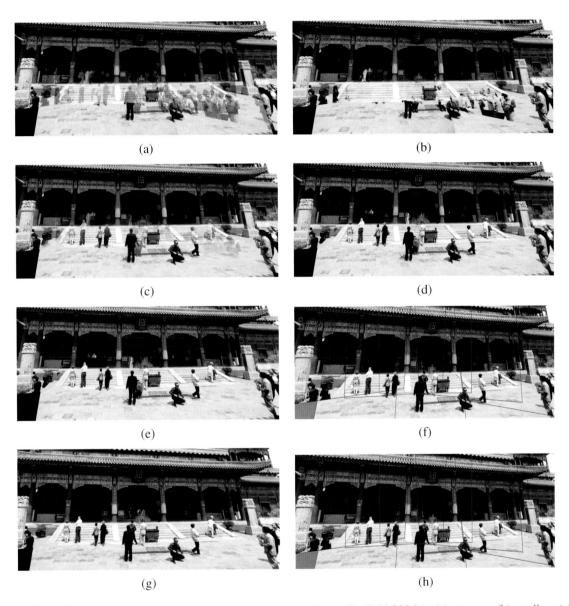

Figure 9.14 Final composites computed by a variety of algorithms (Szeliski 2006a): (a) average, (b) median, (c) feathered average, (d) *p-norm* $p = 10$, (e) Voronoi, (f) weighted ROD vertex cover with feathering, (g) graph cut seams with Poisson blending and (h) with pyramid blending.

down-weighting pixels near the edges of both cutouts and the image is preferable. This can be done by computing a *distance map* or *grassfire transform*,

$$w_k(\boldsymbol{x}) = \arg\min_{\boldsymbol{y}}\{\|\boldsymbol{y}\| \mid \tilde{I}_k(\boldsymbol{x} + \boldsymbol{y}) \text{ is invalid}\}, \tag{9.38}$$

where each valid pixel is tagged with its Euclidean distance to the nearest invalid pixel (Section 3.3.3). The Euclidean distance map can be efficiently computed using a two-pass raster algorithm (Danielsson 1980; Borgefors 1986).

Weighted averaging with a distance map is often called *feathering* (Szeliski and Shum 1997; Chen and Klette 1999; Uyttendaele, Eden, and Szeliski 2001) and does a reasonable job of blending over exposure differences. However, blurring and ghosting can still be problems (Figure 9.14c). Note that weighted averaging is *not* the same as compositing the individual images with the classic *over* operation (Porter and Duff 1984; Blinn 1994a), even when using the weight values (normalized to sum up to one) as *alpha* (translucency) channels. This is because the over operation attenuates the values from more distant surfaces and, hence, is not equivalent to a direct sum.

One way to improve feathering is to raise the distance map values to some large power, i.e., to use $w_k^p(\boldsymbol{x})$ in Equation (9.37). The weighted averages then become dominated by the larger values, i.e., they act somewhat like a *p-norm*. The resulting composite can often provide a reasonable tradeoff between visible exposure differences and blur (Figure 9.14d).

In the limit as $p \to \infty$, only the pixel with the maximum weight is selected,

$$C(\boldsymbol{x}) = \tilde{I}_{l(\boldsymbol{x})}(\boldsymbol{x}), \tag{9.39}$$

where

$$l = \arg\max_k w_k(\boldsymbol{x}) \tag{9.40}$$

is the *label assignment* or *pixel selection* function that selects which image to use at each pixel. This hard pixel selection process produces a visibility mask-sensitive variant of the familiar *Voronoi diagram*, which assigns each pixel to the nearest image center in the set (Wood, Finkelstein, Hughes *et al.* 1997; Peleg, Rousso, Rav-Acha *et al.* 2000). The resulting composite, while useful for artistic guidance and in high-overlap panoramas (*manifold mosaics*) tends to have very hard edges with noticeable seams when the exposures vary (Figure 9.14e).

Xiong and Turkowski (1998) use this Voronoi idea (local maximum of the grassfire transform) to select seams for Laplacian pyramid blending (which is discussed below). However, since the seam selection is performed sequentially as new images are added in, some artifacts can occur.

Optimal seam selection.   Computing the Voronoi diagram is one way to select the *seams* between regions where different images contribute to the final composite. However, Voronoi images totally ignore the local image structure underlying the seam.

A better approach is to place the seams in regions where the images agree, so that transitions from one source to another are not visible. In this way, the algorithm avoids "cutting through" moving objects where a seam would look unnatural (Davis 1998). For a pair of images, this process can be formulated as a simple dynamic program starting from one edge

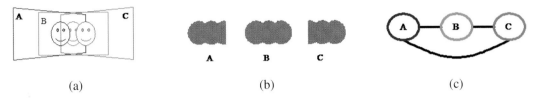

Figure 9.15   Computation of regions of difference (RODs) (Uyttendaele, Eden, and Szeliski 2001) © 2001 IEEE: (a) three overlapping images with a moving face; (b) corresponding RODs; (c) graph of coincident RODs.

of the overlap region and ending at the other (Milgram 1975, 1977; Davis 1998; Efros and Freeman 2001).

When multiple images are being composited, the dynamic program idea does not readily generalize. (For square texture tiles being composited sequentially, Efros and Freeman (2001) run a dynamic program along each of the four tile sides.)

To overcome this problem, Uyttendaele, Eden, and Szeliski (2001) observed that, for well-registered images, moving objects produce the most visible artifacts, namely translucent looking *ghosts*. Their system therefore decides which objects to keep and which ones to erase. First, the algorithm compares all overlapping input image pairs to determine *regions of difference* (RODs) where the images disagree. Next, a graph is constructed with the RODs as vertices and edges representing ROD pairs that overlap in the final composite (Figure 9.15). Since the presence of an edge indicates an area of disagreement, vertices (regions) must be removed from the final composite until no edge spans a pair of remaining vertices. The smallest such set can be computed using a *vertex cover* algorithm. Since several such covers may exist, a *weighted vertex cover* is used instead, where the vertex weights are computed by summing the feather weights in the ROD (Uyttendaele, Eden, and Szeliski 2001). The algorithm therefore prefers removing regions that are near the edge of the image, which reduces the likelihood that partially visible objects will appear in the final composite. (It is also possible to infer which object in a region of difference is the foreground object by the "edginess" (pixel differences) across the ROD boundary, which should be higher when an object is present (Herley 2005).) Once the desired excess regions of difference have been removed, the final composite can be created by feathering (Figure 9.14f).

A different approach to pixel selection and seam placement is described by Agarwala, Dontcheva, Agrawala *et al.* (2004). Their system computes the label assignment that optimizes the sum of two objective functions. The first is a per-pixel *image objective* that determines which pixels are likely to produce good composites,

$$\mathcal{C}_D = \sum_{\boldsymbol{x}} D(\boldsymbol{x}, l(\boldsymbol{x})), \qquad (9.41)$$

where $D(\boldsymbol{x}, l)$ is the *data penalty* associated with choosing image l at pixel $\boldsymbol{x}$. In their system, users can select which pixels to use by "painting" over an image with the desired object or appearance, which sets $D(\boldsymbol{x}, l)$ to a large value for all labels l other than the one selected by the user (Figure 9.16). Alternatively, automated selection criteria can be used, such as *maximum likelihood*, which prefers pixels that occur repeatedly in the background (for object removal), or *minimum likelihood* for objects that occur infrequently, i.e., for moving object retention. Using a more traditional center-weighted data term tends to favor objects that are

Figure 9.16 Photomontage (Agarwala, Dontcheva, Agrawala *et al.* 2004) ©️ 2004 ACM. From a set of five source images (of which four are shown on the left), Photomontage quickly creates a composite family portrait in which everyone is smiling and looking at the camera (right). Users simply flip through the stack and coarsely draw strokes using the designated source image objective over the people they wish to add to the composite. The user-applied strokes and computed regions (middle) are color-coded by the borders of the source images on the left.

centered in the input images (Figure 9.17).

The second term is a *seam objective* that penalizes differences in labelings between adjacent images,

$$C_S = \sum_{(\boldsymbol{x},\boldsymbol{y})\in\mathcal{N}} S(\boldsymbol{x},\boldsymbol{y},l(\boldsymbol{x}),l(\boldsymbol{y})), \qquad (9.42)$$

where $S(\boldsymbol{x},\boldsymbol{y},l_x,l_y)$ is the image-dependent *interaction penalty* or *seam cost* of placing a seam between pixels $\boldsymbol{x}$ and $\boldsymbol{y}$, and $\mathcal{N}$ is the set of $\mathcal{N}_4$ neighboring pixels. For example, the simple color-based seam penalty used in (Kwatra, Schödl, Essa *et al.* 2003; Agarwala, Dontcheva, Agrawala *et al.* 2004) can be written as

$$S(\boldsymbol{x},\boldsymbol{y},l_x,l_y) = \|\tilde{I}_{l_x}(\boldsymbol{x}) - \tilde{I}_{l_y}(\boldsymbol{x})\| + \|\tilde{I}_{l_x}(\boldsymbol{y}) - \tilde{I}_{l_y}(\boldsymbol{y})\|. \qquad (9.43)$$

More sophisticated seam penalties can also look at image gradients or the presence of image edges (Agarwala, Dontcheva, Agrawala *et al.* 2004). Seam penalties are widely used in other computer vision applications such as stereo matching (Boykov, Veksler, and Zabih 2001) to give the labeling function its *coherence* or *smoothness*. An alternative approach, which places seams along strong consistent edges in overlapping images using a watershed computation is described by Soille (2006).

The sum of these two objective functions gives rise to a *Markov random field* (MRF), for which good optimization algorithms are described in Sections 3.7.2 and 5.5 and Appendix B.5. For label computations of this kind, the α-*expansion* algorithm developed by Boykov, Veksler, and Zabih (2001) works particularly well (Szeliski, Zabih, Scharstein *et al.* 2008).

For the result shown in Figure 9.14g, Agarwala, Dontcheva, Agrawala *et al.* (2004) use a large data penalty for invalid pixels and 0 for valid pixels. Notice how the seam placement algorithm avoids regions of difference, including those that border the image and that might result in objects being cut off. Graph cuts (Agarwala, Dontcheva, Agrawala *et al.* 2004) and vertex cover (Uyttendaele, Eden, and Szeliski 2001) often produce similar looking results, although the former is significantly slower since it optimizes over all pixels, while the latter is more sensitive to the thresholds used to determine regions of difference.

Figure 9.17   Set of five photos tracking a snowboarder's jump stitched together into a seamless composite. Because the algorithm prefers pixels near the center of the image, multiple copies of the boarder are retained.

9.3.3 *Application*: Photomontage

While image stitching is normally used to composite partially overlapping photographs, it can also be used to composite repeated shots of a scene taken with the aim of obtaining the best possible composition and appearance of each element.

Figure 9.16 shows the *Photomontage* system developed by Agarwala, Dontcheva, Agrawala *et al.* (2004), where users draw strokes over a set of pre-aligned images to indicate which regions they wish to keep from each image. Once the system solves the resulting multi-label graph cut (9.41–9.42), the various pieces taken from each source photo are blended together using a variant of Poisson image blending (9.44–9.46). Their system can also be used to automatically composite an all-focus image from a series of bracketed focus images (Hasinoff, Kutulakos, Durand *et al.* 2009) or to remove wires and other unwanted elements from sets of photographs. Exercise 9.10 has you implement this system and try out some of its variants.

9.3.4 Blending

Once the seams between images have been determined and unwanted objects removed, we still need to blend the images to compensate for exposure differences and other mis-alignments. The spatially varying weighting (feathering) previously discussed can often be used to accomplish this. However, it is difficult in practice to achieve a pleasing balance between smoothing out low-frequency exposure variations and retaining sharp enough transitions to prevent blurring (although using a high exponent in feathering can help).

Laplacian pyramid blending.   An attractive solution to this problem is the Laplacian pyramid blending technique developed by Burt and Adelson (1983b), which we discussed in Section 3.5.5. Instead of using a single transition width, a frequency-adaptive width is used by creating a band-pass (Laplacian) pyramid and making the transition widths within each level

(a)   (b)   (c)

Figure 9.18   Poisson image editing (Pérez, Gangnet, and Blake 2003) © 2003 ACM: (a) The dog and the two children are chosen as source images to be pasted into the destination swimming pool. (b) Simple pasting fails to match the colors at the boundaries, whereas (c) Poisson image blending masks these differences.

a function of the level, i.e., the same width in pixels. In practice, a small number of levels, i.e., as few as two (Brown and Lowe 2007), may be adequate to compensate for differences in exposure. The result of applying this pyramid blending is shown in Figure 9.14h.

Gradient domain blending.   An alternative approach to multi-band image blending is to perform the operations in the *gradient domain*. Reconstructing images from their gradient fields has a long history in computer vision (Horn 1986), starting originally with work in brightness constancy (Horn 1974), shape from shading (Horn and Brooks 1989), and photometric stereo (Woodham 1981). More recently, related ideas have been used for reconstructing images from their edges (Elder and Goldberg 2001), removing shadows from images (Weiss 2001), separating reflections from a single image (Levin, Zomet, and Weiss 2004; Levin and Weiss 2007), and *tone mapping* high dynamic range images by reducing the magnitude of image edges (gradients) (Fattal, Lischinski, and Werman 2002).

Pérez, Gangnet, and Blake (2003) show how gradient domain reconstruction can be used to do seamless object insertion in image editing applications (Figure 9.18). Rather than copying pixels, the *gradients* of the new image fragment are copied instead. The actual pixel values for the copied area are then computed by solving a *Poisson equation* that locally matches the gradients while obeying the fixed *Dirichlet* (exact matching) conditions at the seam boundary. Pérez, Gangnet, and Blake (2003) show that this is equivalent to computing an additive *membrane* interpolant of the mismatch between the source and destination images along the boundary.[14] In earlier work, Peleg (1981) also proposed adding a smooth function to enforce consistency along the seam curve.

Agarwala, Dontcheva, Agrawala *et al.* (2004) extended this idea to a multi-source formulation, where it no longer makes sense to talk of a destination image whose exact pixel values must be matched at the seam. Instead, *each* source image contributes its own gradient field and the Poisson equation is solved using *Neumann* boundary conditions, i.e., dropping any

---

[14] The membrane interpolant is known to have nicer interpolation properties for arbitrary-shaped constraints than frequency-domain interpolants (Nielson 1993).

equations that involve pixels outside the boundary of the image.

Rather than solving the Poisson partial differential equations, Agarwala, Dontcheva, Agrawala *et al.* (2004) directly minimize a *variational problem*,

$$\min_{C(\boldsymbol{x})} \|\nabla C(\boldsymbol{x}) - \nabla \tilde{I}_{l(\boldsymbol{x})}(\boldsymbol{x})\|^2. \tag{9.44}$$

The discretized form of this equation is a set of gradient constraint equations

$$C(\boldsymbol{x} + \hat{\boldsymbol{\imath}}) - C(\boldsymbol{x}) = \tilde{I}_{l(\boldsymbol{x})}(\boldsymbol{x} + \hat{\boldsymbol{\imath}}) - \tilde{I}_{l(\boldsymbol{x})}(\boldsymbol{x}) \text{ and} \tag{9.45}$$

$$C(\boldsymbol{x} + \hat{\boldsymbol{\jmath}}) - C(\boldsymbol{x}) = \tilde{I}_{l(\boldsymbol{x})}(\boldsymbol{x} + \hat{\boldsymbol{\jmath}}) - \tilde{I}_{l(\boldsymbol{x})}(\boldsymbol{x}), \tag{9.46}$$

where $\hat{\boldsymbol{\imath}} = (1, 0)$ and $\hat{\boldsymbol{\jmath}} = (0, 1)$ are unit vectors in the x and y directions.[15] They then solve the associated sparse least squares problem. Since this system of equations is only defined up to an additive constraint, Agarwala, Dontcheva, Agrawala *et al.* (2004) ask the user to select the value of one pixel. In practice, a better choice might be to weakly bias the solution towards reproducing the original color values.

In order to accelerate the solution of this sparse linear system, Fattal, Lischinski, and Werman (2002) use multigrid, whereas Agarwala, Dontcheva, Agrawala *et al.* (2004) use hierarchical basis preconditioned conjugate gradient descent (Szeliski 1990b, 2006b) (Appendix A.5). In subsequent work, Agarwala (2007) shows how using a quadtree representation for the solution can further accelerate the computation with minimal loss in accuracy, while Szeliski, Uyttendaele, and Steedly (2008) show how representing the per-image offset fields using even coarser splines is even faster. This latter work also argues that blending in the log domain, i.e., using multiplicative rather than additive offsets, is preferable, as it more closely matches texture contrasts across seam boundaries. The resulting seam blending works very well in practice (Figure 9.14h), although care must be taken when copying large gradient values near seams so that a "double edge" is not introduced.

Copying gradients directly from the source images after seam placement is just one approach to gradient domain blending. The paper by Levin, Zomet, Peleg *et al.* (2004) examines several different variants of this approach, which they call *Gradient-domain Image STitching* (GIST). The techniques they examine include feathering (blending) the gradients from the source images, as well as using an L1 norm in performing the reconstruction of the image from the gradient field, rather than using an L2 norm as in Equation (9.44). Their preferred technique is the L1 optimization of a feathered (blended) cost function on the original image gradients (which they call GIST1-l_1). Since L1 optimization using linear programming can be slow, they develop a faster iterative median-based algorithm in a multigrid framework. Visual comparisons between their preferred approach and what they call *optimal seam on the gradients* (which is equivalent to the approach of Agarwala, Dontcheva, Agrawala *et al.* (2004)) show similar results, while significantly improving on pyramid blending and feathering algorithms.

Exposure compensation. Pyramid and gradient domain blending can do a good job of compensating for moderate amounts of exposure differences between images. However, when the exposure differences become large, alternative approaches may be necessary.

---

[15] At seam locations, the right hand side is replaced by the average of the gradients in the two source images.

Uyttendaele, Eden, and Szeliski (2001) iteratively estimate a local correction between each source image and a blended composite. First, a block-based quadratic transfer function is fit between each source image and an initial feathered composite. Next, transfer functions are averaged with their neighbors to get a smoother mapping and per-pixel transfer functions are computed by *splining* (interpolating) between neighboring block values. Once each source image has been smoothly adjusted, a new feathered composite is computed and the process is repeated (typically three times). The results shown by Uyttendaele, Eden, and Szeliski (2001) demonstrate that this does a better job of exposure compensation than simple feathering and can handle local variations in exposure due to effects such as lens vignetting.

Ultimately, however, the most principled way to deal with exposure differences is to stitch images in the radiance domain, i.e., to convert each image into a radiance image using its exposure value and then create a stitched, high dynamic range image, as discussed in Section 10.2 (Eden, Uyttendaele, and Szeliski 2006).

9.4 Additional reading

The literature on image stitching dates back to work in the photogrammetry community in the 1970s (Milgram 1975, 1977; Slama 1980). In computer vision, papers started appearing in the early 1980s (Peleg 1981), while the development of fully automated techniques came about a decade later (Mann and Picard 1994; Chen 1995; Szeliski 1996; Szeliski and Shum 1997; Sawhney and Kumar 1999; Shum and Szeliski 2000). Those techniques used direct pixel-based alignment but feature-based approaches are now the norm (Zoghlami, Faugeras, and Deriche 1997; Capel and Zisserman 1998; Cham and Cipolla 1998; Badra, Qumsieh, and Dudek 1998; McLauchlan and Jaenicke 2002; Brown and Lowe 2007). A collection of some of these papers can be found in the book by Benosman and Kang (2001). Szeliski (2006a) provides a comprehensive survey of image stitching, on which the material in this chapter is based.

High-quality techniques for optimal seam finding and blending are another important component of image stitching systems. Important developments in this field include work by Milgram (1977), Burt and Adelson (1983b), Davis (1998), Uyttendaele, Eden, and Szeliski (2001),Pérez, Gangnet, and Blake (2003), Levin, Zomet, Peleg *et al.* (2004), Agarwala, Dontcheva, Agrawala *et al.* (2004), Eden, Uyttendaele, and Szeliski (2006), and Kopf, Uyttendaele, Deussen *et al.* (2007).

In addition to the merging of multiple overlapping photographs taken for aerial or terrestrial panoramic image creation, stitching techniques can be used for automated whiteboard scanning (He and Zhang 2005; Zhang and He 2007), scanning with a mouse (Nakao, Kashitani, and Kaneyoshi 1998), and retinal image mosaics (Can, Stewart, Roysam *et al.* 2002). They can also be applied to video sequences (Teodosio and Bender 1993; Irani, Hsu, and Anandan 1995; Kumar, Anandan, Irani *et al.* 1995; Sawhney and Ayer 1996; Massey and Bender 1996; Irani and Anandan 1998; Sawhney, Arpa, Kumar *et al.* 2002; Agarwala, Zheng, Pal *et al.* 2005; Rav-Acha, Pritch, Lischinski *et al.* 2005; Steedly, Pal, and Szeliski 2005; Baudisch, Tan, Steedly *et al.* 2006) and can even be used for video compression (Lee, ge Chen, lung Bruce Lin *et al.* 1997).

9.5 Exercises

Ex 9.1: Direct pixel-based alignment   Take a pair of images, compute a coarse-to-fine affine alignment (Exercise 8.2) and then blend them using either averaging (Exercise 6.2) or a Laplacian pyramid (Exercise 3.20). Extend your motion model from affine to perspective (homography) to better deal with rotational mosaics and planar surfaces seen under arbitrary motion.

Ex 9.2: Featured-based stitching   Extend your feature-based alignment technique from Exercise 6.2 to use a full perspective model and then blend the resulting mosaic using either averaging or more sophisticated distance-based feathering (Exercise 9.9).

Ex 9.3: Cylindrical strip panoramas   To generate cylindrical or spherical panoramas from a horizontally panning (rotating) camera, it is best to use a tripod. Set your camera up to take a series of 50% overlapped photos and then use the following steps to create your panorama:

1. Estimate the amount of radial distortion by taking some pictures with lots of long straight lines near the edges of the image and then using the plumb-line method from Exercise 6.10.

2. Compute the focal length either by using a ruler and paper, as in Figure 6.7 (Debevec, Wenger, Tchou *et al.* 2002) or by rotating your camera on the tripod, overlapping the images by exactly 0% and counting the number of images it takes to make a $360°$ panorama.

3. Convert each of your images to cylindrical coordinates using (9.12–9.16).

4. Line up the images with a translational motion model using either a direct pixel-based technique, such as coarse-to-fine incremental or an FFT, or a feature-based technique.

5. (Optional) If doing a complete $360°$ panorama, align the first and last images. Compute the amount of accumulated vertical mis-registration and re-distribute this among the images.

6. Blend the resulting images using feathering or some other technique.

Ex 9.4: Coarse alignment   Use FFT or phase correlation (Section 8.1.2) to estimate the initial alignment between successive images. How well does this work? Over what range of overlaps? If it does not work, does aligning sub-sections (e.g., quarters) do better?

Ex 9.5: Automated mosaicing   Use feature-based alignment with four-point RANSAC for homographies (Section 6.1.3, Equations (6.19–6.23)) or three-point RANSAC for rotational motions (Brown, Hartley, and Nistér 2007) to match up all pairs of overlapping images.

Merge these pairwise estimates together by finding a spanning tree of pairwise relations. Visualize the resulting global alignment, e.g., by displaying a blend of each image with all other images that overlap it.

For greater robustness, try multiple spanning trees (perhaps randomly sampled based on the confidence in pairwise alignments) to see if you can recover from bad pairwise matches (Zach, Klopschitz, and Pollefeys 2010). As a measure of fitness, count how many pairwise estimates are consistent with the global alignment.

Ex 9.6: Global optimization Use the initialization from the previous algorithm to perform a full bundle adjustment over all of the camera rotations and focal lengths, as described in Section 7.4 and by Shum and Szeliski (2000). Optionally, estimate radial distortion parameters as well or support fisheye lenses (Section 2.1.6).

As in the previous exercise, visualize the quality of your registration by creating composites of each input image with its neighbors, optionally blinking between the original image and the composite to better see mis-alignment artifacts.

Ex 9.7: De-ghosting Use the results of the previous bundle adjustment to predict the location of each feature in a consensus geometry. Use the difference between the predicted and actual feature locations to correct for small mis-registrations, as described in Section 9.2.2 (Shum and Szeliski 2000).

Ex 9.8: Compositing surface Choose a compositing surface (Section 9.3.1), e.g., a single reference image extended to a larger plane, a sphere represented using cylindrical or spherical coordinates, a stereographic "little planet" projection, or a cube map.

Project all of your images onto this surface and blend them with equal weighting, for now (just to see where the original image seams are).

Ex 9.9: Feathering and blending Compute a feather (distance) map for each warped source image and use these maps to blend the warped images.

Alternatively, use Laplacian pyramid blending (Exercise 3.20) or gradient domain blending.

Ex 9.10: Photomontage and object removal Implement a "PhotoMontage" system in which users can indicate desired or unwanted regions in pre-registered images using strokes or other primitives (such as bounding boxes).

(Optional) Devise an automatic moving objects remover (or "keeper") by analyzing which inconsistent regions are more or less typical given some consensus (e.g., median filtering) of the aligned images. Figure 9.17 shows an example where the moving object was kept. Try to make this work for sequences with large amounts of overlaps and consider averaging the images to make the moving object look more ghosted.

Chapter 10

Computational photography

R. Szeliski, *Computer Vision: Algorithms and Applications*, Texts in Computer Science,
DOI 10.1007/978-1-84882-935-0_10, © Springer-Verlag London Limited 2011

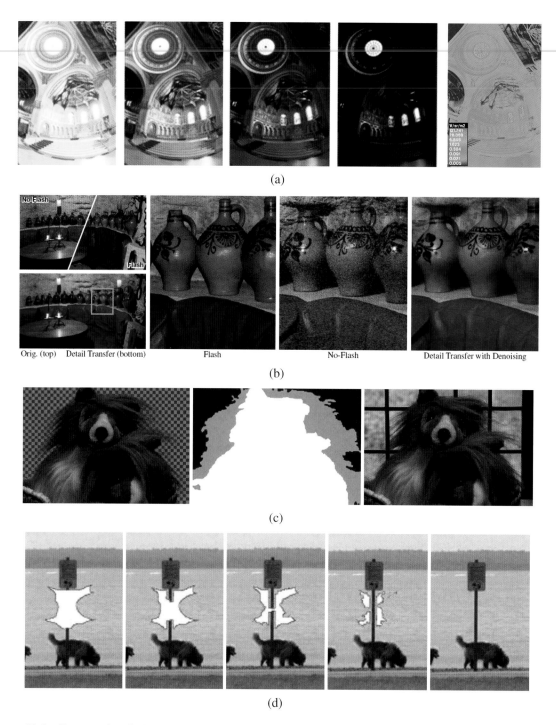

(a)

Orig. (top)   Detail Transfer (bottom)   Flash   No-Flash   Detail Transfer with Denoising

(b)

(c)

(d)

Figure 10.1 Computational photography: (a) merging multiple exposures to create high dynamic range images (Debevec and Malik 1997) © 1997 ACM; (b) merging flash and non-flash photographs; (Petschnigg, Agrawala, Hoppe *et al.* 2004) © 2004 ACM; (c) image matting and compositing; (Chuang, Curless, Salesin *et al.* 2001) © 2001 IEEE; (d) hole filling with inpainting (Criminisi, Pérez, and Toyama 2004) © 2004 IEEE.

Stitching multiple images into wide field of view panoramas, which we covered in Chapter 9, allows us create photographs that could not be captured with a regular camera. This is just one instance of *computational photography*, where image analysis and processing algorithms are applied to one or more photographs to create images that go beyond the capabilities of traditional imaging systems. Some of these techniques are now being incorporated directly into digital still cameras. For example, some of the newer digital still cameras have sweep panorama modes and take multiple shots in low-light conditions to reduce image noise.

In this chapter, we cover a number of additional computational photography algorithms. We begin with a review of photometric image calibration (Section 10.1), i.e., the measurement of camera and lens responses, which is a prerequisite for many of the algorithms we describe later. We then discuss *high dynamic range imaging* (Section 10.2), which captures the full range of brightness in a scene through the use of multiple exposures (Figure 10.1a). We also discuss *tone mapping operators*, which map rich images back into regular display devices, such as screens and printers, as well as algorithms that merge flash and regular images to obtain better exposures (Figure 10.1b).

Next, we discuss how the resolution of images can be improved either by merging multiple photographs together or using sophisticated image priors (Section 10.3). This includes algorithms for extracting full-color images from the patterned Bayer mosaics present in most cameras.

In Section 10.4, we discuss algorithms for cutting pieces of images from one photograph and pasting them into others (Figure 10.1c). In Section 10.5, we describe how to generate novel textures from real-world samples for applications such as filling holes in images (Figure 10.1d). We close with a brief overview of *non-photorealistic rendering* (Section 10.5.2), which can turn regular photographs into artistic renderings that resemble traditional drawings and paintings.

One topic that we do not cover extensively in this book is novel computational sensors, optics, and cameras. A nice survey can be found in an article by Nayar (2006), a recently published book by Raskar and Tumblin (2010), and more recent research papers (Levin, Fergus, Durand *et al.* 2007). Some related discussion can also be found in Sections 10.2 and 13.3.

A good general-audience introduction to computational photography can be found in the article by Hayes (2008) as well as survey papers by Nayar (2006), Cohen and Szeliski (2006), Levoy (2006), and Debevec (2006).[1] Raskar and Tumblin (2010) give extensive coverage of topics in this area, with particular emphasis on computational cameras and sensors. The sub-field of high dynamic range imaging has its own book discussing research in this area (Reinhard, Ward, Pattanaik *et al.* 2005), as well as a wonderful book aimed more at professional photographers (Freeman 2008).[2] A good survey of image matting is provided by Wang and Cohen (2007a).

There are also several courses on computational photography where the instructors have provided extensive on-line materials, e.g., Frédo Durand's Computation Photography course at MIT,[3] Alyosha Efros' class at Carnegie Mellon,[4] Marc Levoy's class at Stanford,[5] and a

---

[1] See also the two special issue journals edited by Bimber (2006) and Durand and Szeliski (2007).
[2] Gulbins and Gulbins (2009) discuss related photographic techniques.
[3] MIT 6.815/6.865, http://stellar.mit.edu/S/course/6/sp08/6.815/materials.html.
[4] CMU 15-463, http://graphics.cs.cmu.edu/courses/15-463/.
[5] Stanford CS 448A, http://graphics.stanford.edu/courses/cs448a-10/.

series of SIGGRAPH courses on Computational Photography.[6]

10.1 Photometric calibration

Before we can successfully merge multiple photographs, we need to characterize the functions that map incoming irradiance into pixel values and also the amounts of noise present in each image. In this section, we examine three components of the imaging pipeline (Figure 10.2) that affect this mapping.

The first is the *radiometric response function* (Mitsunaga and Nayar 1999), which maps photons arriving at the lens into digital values stored in the image file (Section 10.1.1). The second is *vignetting*, which darkens pixel values near the periphery of images, especially at large apertures (Section 10.1.3). The third is the *point spread function*, which characterizes the blur induced by the lens, anti-aliasing filters, and finite sensor areas (Section 10.1.4).[7] The material in this section builds on the image formation processes described in Sections 2.2.3 and 2.3.3, so if it has been a while since you looked at those sections, please go back and review them.

10.1.1 Radiometric response function

As we can see in Figure 10.2, a number of factors affect how the intensity of light arriving at the lens ends up being mapped into stored digital values. Let us ignore for now any non-uniform attenuation that may occur inside the lens, which we cover in Section 10.1.3.

The first factors to affect this mapping are the aperture and shutter speed (Section 2.3), which can be modeled as global multipliers on the incoming light, most conveniently measured in *exposure values* ($\log_2$ brightness ratios). Next, the analog to digital (A/D) converter on the sensing chip applies an electronic gain, usually controlled by the ISO setting on your camera. While in theory this gain is linear, as with any electronics non-linearities may be present (either unintentionally or by design). Ignoring, for now, photon noise, on-chip noise, amplifier noise, and quantization noise, which we discuss shortly, you can often assume that the mapping between incoming light and the values stored in a RAW camera file (if your camera supports this) is roughly linear.

If images are being stored in the more common JPEG format, the camera's digital signal processor (DSP) next performs Bayer pattern demosaicing (Sections 2.3.2 and 10.3.1), which is a mostly linear (but often non-stationary) process. Some sharpening is also often applied at this stage. Next, the color values are multiplied by different constants (or sometimes a 3×3 color twist matrix) to perform color balancing, i.e., to move the white point closer to pure white. Finally, a standard gamma is applied to the intensities in each color channel and the colors are converted into YCbCr format before being transformed by a DCT, quantized, and then compressed into the JPEG format (Section 2.3.3). Figure 10.2 shows all of these steps in pictorial form.

Given the complexity of all of this processing, it is difficult to model the camera response function (Figure 10.3a), i.e., the mapping between incoming irradiance and digital RGB val-

---

[6] http://web.media.mit.edu/~raskar/photo/.

[7] Additional photometric camera and lens effects include sensor glare, blooming, and chromatic aberration, which can also be thought of as a spectrally varying form of geometric aberration (Section 2.2.3).

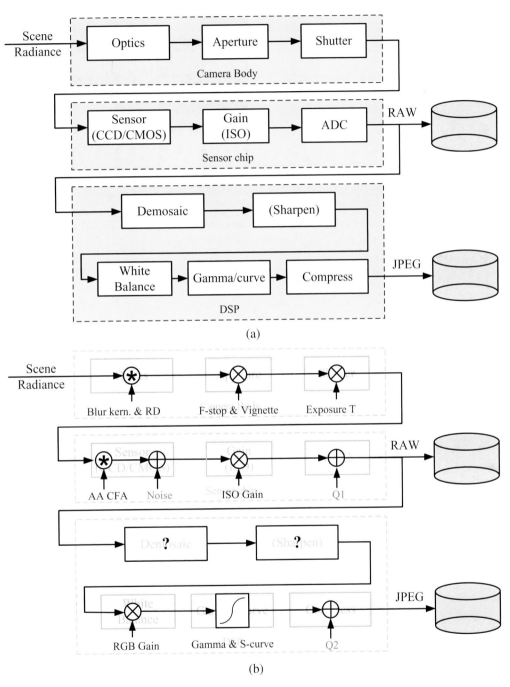

Figure 10.2 Image sensing pipeline: (a) block diagram showing the various sources of noise as well as the typical digital post-processing steps; (b) equivalent signal transforms, including convolution, gain, and noise injection. The abbreviations are: RD = radial distortion, AA = anti-aliasing filter, CFA = color filter array, Q1 and Q2 = quantization noise.

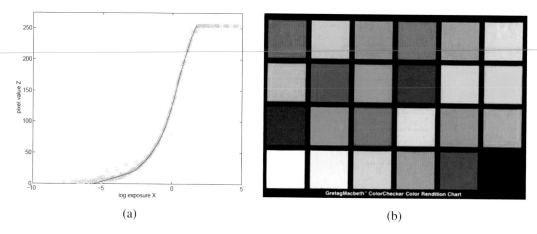

(a)   (b)

Figure 10.3 Radiometric response calibration: (a) typical camera response function, showing the mapping between incoming log irradiance (exposure) and output eight-bit pixel values, for one color channel (Debevec and Malik 1997) © 1997 ACM; (b) color checker chart.

ues, from first principles. A more practical approach is to calibrate the camera by measuring correspondences between incoming light and final values.

The most accurate, but most expensive, approach is to use an *integrating sphere*, which is a large (typically 1m diameter) sphere carefully painted on the inside with white matte paint. An accurately calibrated light at the top controls the amount of radiance inside the sphere (which is constant everywhere because of the sphere's radiometry) and a small opening at the side allows for a camera/lens combination to be mounted. By slowly varying the current going into the light, an accurate correspondence can be established between incoming radiance and measured pixel values. The vignetting and noise characteristics of the camera can also be simultaneously determined.

A more practical alternative is to use a calibration chart (Figure 10.3b) such as the Macbeth or Munsell ColorChecker Chart.[8] The biggest problem with this approach is to ensure uniform lighting. One approach is to use a large dark room with a high-quality light source far away from (and perpendicular to) the chart. Another is to place the chart outdoors away from any shadows. (The results will differ under these two conditions, because the color of the illuminant will be different).

The easiest approach is probably to take multiple exposures of the same scene while the camera is on a tripod and to recover the response function by simultaneously estimating the incoming irradiance at each pixel and the response curve (Mann and Picard 1995; Debevec and Malik 1997; Mitsunaga and Nayar 1999). This approach is discussed in more detail in Section 10.2 on high dynamic range imaging.

If all else fails, i.e., you just have one or more unrelated photos, you can use an International Color Consortium (ICC) profile for the camera (Fairchild 2005).[9] Even more simply, you can just assume that the response is linear if they are RAW files and that the images have a $\gamma = 2.2$ non-linearity (plus clipping) applied to each RGB channel if they are JPEG images.

---

[8] http://www.xrite.com.
[9] See also the ICC *Information on Profiles*, http://www.color.org/info_profiles2.xalter.

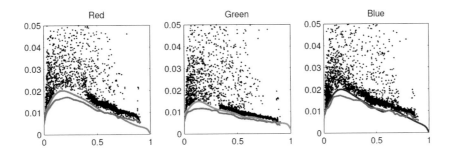

Figure 10.4 Noise level function estimates obtained from a single color photograph (Liu, Szeliski, Kang *et al.* 2008) © 2008 IEEE. The colored curves are the estimated NLF fit as the probabilistic lower envelope of the measured deviations between the noisy piecewise-smooth images. The ground truth NLFs obtained by averaging 29 images are shown in gray.

10.1.2 Noise level estimation

In addition to knowing the camera response function, it is also often important to know the amount of noise being injected under a particular camera setting (e.g., ISO/gain level). The simplest characterization of noise is a single standard deviation, usually measured in gray levels, independent of pixel value. A more accurate model can be obtained by estimating the noise level as a function of pixel value (Figure 10.4), which is known as the *noise level function* (Liu, Szeliski, Kang *et al.* 2008).

As with the camera response function, the simplest way to estimate these quantities is in the lab, using either an integrating sphere or a calibration chart. The noise can be estimated either at each pixel independently, by taking repeated exposures and computing the temporal variance in the measurements (Healey and Kondepudy 1994), or over regions, by assuming that pixel values should all be the same within some region (e.g., inside a color checker square) and computing a spatial variance.

This approach can be generalized to photos where there are regions of constant or slowly varying intensity (Liu, Szeliski, Kang *et al.* 2008). First, segment the image into such regions and fit a constant or linear function inside each region. Next, measure the (spatial) standard deviation of the differences between the noisy input pixels and the smooth fitted function away from large gradients and region boundaries. Plot these as a function of output level for each color channel, as shown in Figure 10.4. Finally, fit a lower envelope to this distribution in order to ignore pixels or deviations that are outliers. A fully Bayesian approach to this problem that models the statistical distribution of each quantity is presented by (Liu, Szeliski, Kang *et al.* 2008). A simpler approach, which should produce useful results in most cases, is to fit a low-dimensional function (e.g., positive valued B-spline) to the lower envelope (see Exercise 10.2).

In more recent work, Matsushita and Lin (2007) present a technique for simultaneously estimating a camera's response and noise level functions based on skew (asymmetries) in level-dependent noise distributions. Their paper also contains extensive references to previous work in these areas.

Figure 10.5 Single image vignetting correction (Zheng, Yu, Kang *et al.* 2008) © 2008 IEEE: (a) original image with strong visible vignetting; (b) vignetting compensation as described by Zheng, Zhou, Georgescu *et al.* (2006); (c–d) vignetting compensation as described by Zheng, Yu, Kang *et al.* (2008).

10.1.3 Vignetting

A common problem with using wide-angle and wide-aperture lenses is that the image tends to darken in the corners (Figure 10.5a). This problem is generally known as *vignetting* and comes in several different forms, including natural, optical, and mechanical vignetting (Section 2.2.3) (Ray 2002). As with radiometric response function calibration, the most accurate way to calibrate vignetting is to use an integrating sphere or a picture of a uniformly colored and illuminated blank wall.

An alternative approach is to stitch a panoramic scene and to assume that the true radiance at each pixel comes from the central portion of each input image. This is easier to do if the radiometric response function is already known (e.g., by shooting in RAW mode) and if the exposure is kept constant. If the response function, image exposures, and vignetting function are unknown, they can still be recovered by optimizing a large least squares fitting problem (Litvinov and Schechner 2005; Goldman 2011). Figure 10.6 shows an example of simultaneously estimating the vignetting, exposure, and radiometric response function from a set of overlapping photographs (Goldman 2011). Note that unless vignetting is modeled and compensated, regular gradient-domain image blending (Section 9.3.4) will not create an attractive image.

If only a single image is available, vignetting can be estimated by looking for slow consistent intensity variations in the radial direction. The original algorithm proposed by Zheng, Lin, and Kang (2006) first pre-segmented the image into smoothly varying regions and then performed an analysis inside each region. Instead of pre-segmenting the image, Zheng, Yu, Kang *et al.* (2008) compute the radial gradients at all the pixels and use the asymmetry in this distribution (since gradients away from the center are, on average, slightly negative) to estimate the vignetting. Figure 10.5 shows the results of applying each of these algorithms to an image with a large amount of vignetting. Exercise 10.3 has you implement some of the above techniques.

10.1.4 Optical blur (spatial response) estimation

One final characteristic of imaging systems that you should calibrate is the spatial response function, which encodes the optical blur that gets convolved with the incoming image to produce the point-sampled image. The shape of the convolution kernel, which is also known as *point spread function (PSF)* or *optical transfer function*, depends on several factors, including lens blur and radial distortion (Section 2.2.3), anti-aliasing filters in front of the sensor, and

(a)   (b)

(c)   (d)

Figure 10.6 Simultaneous estimation of vignetting, exposure, and radiometric response (Goldman 2011) ©
2011 IEEE: (a) original average of the input images; (b) after compensating for vignetting; (c) using gradient
domain blending only (note the remaining mottled look); (d) after both vignetting compensation and blending.

the shape and extent of each active pixel area (Section 2.3) (Figure 10.2). A good estimate of
this function is required for applications such as multi-image super-resolution and de-blurring
(Section 10.3).

In theory, one could estimate the PSF by simply observing an infinitely small point light
source everywhere in the image. Creating an array of samples by drilling through a dark plate
and backlighting with a very bright light source is difficult in practice.

A more practical approach is to observe an image composed of long straight lines or
bars, since these can be fitted to arbitrary precision. Because the location of a horizontal
or vertical edge can be *aliased* during acquisition, slightly slanted edges are preferred. The
profile and locations of such edges can be estimated to sub-pixel precision, which makes it
possible to estimate the PSF at sub-pixel resolutions (Reichenbach, Park, and Narayanswamy
1991; Burns and Williams 1999; Williams and Burns 2001; Goesele, Fuchs, and Seidel 2003).
The thesis by Murphy (2005) contains a nice survey of all aspects of camera calibration,
including the spatial frequency response (SFR), spatial uniformity, tone reproduction, color
reproduction, noise, dynamic range, color channel registration, and depth of field. It also
includes a description of a slant-edge calibration algorithm called `sfrmat2`.

The slant-edge technique can be used to recover a 1D projection of the 2D PSF, e.g.,
slightly vertical edges are used to recover the horizontal *line spread function* (LSF) (Williams
1999). The LSF is then often converted into the Fourier domain and its magnitude plotted as a
one-dimensional *modulation transfer function* (MTF), which indicates which image frequencies are lost (blurred) and aliased during the acquisition process (Section 2.3.1). For most
computational photography applications, it is preferable to directly estimate the full 2D PSF,
since it can be hard to recover from its projections (Williams 1999).

Figure 10.7 shows a pattern containing edges at all orientations, which can be used to
directly recover a two-dimensional PSF. First, corners in the pattern are located by extracting
edges in the sensed image, linking them, and finding the intersections of the circular arcs.
Next, the ideal pattern, whose analytic form is known, is warped (using a homography) to
fit the central portion of the input image and its intensities are adjusted to fit the ones in

Figure 10.7 Calibration pattern with edges equally distributed at all orientations that can be used for PSF and radial distortion estimation (Joshi, Szeliski, and Kriegman 2008) © 2008 IEEE. A portion of an actual sensed image is shown in the middle and a close-up of the ideal pattern is on the right.

the sensed image. If desired, the pattern can be rendered at a higher resolution than the input image, which enables the estimation of the PSF to sub-pixel resolution (Figure 10.8a). Finally a large linear least squares system is solved to recover the unknown PSF kernel K,

$$K = \arg\min_{K} \|B - D(I * K)\|^2, \tag{10.1}$$

where B is the sensed (blurred) image, I is the predicted (sharp) image, and D is an optional downsampling operator that matches the resolution of the ideal and sensed images (Joshi, Szeliski, and Kriegman 2008). In terms of the notation (3.75) introduced in Section 3.4.3, this could also be written as

$$b = \arg\min_{b} \|o - D(s * b)\|^2, \tag{10.2}$$

where o is the observed image, s is the sharp image, and b is the blur kernel.

If the process of estimating the PSF is done locally in overlapping patches of the image, it can also be used to estimate the radial distortion and chromatic aberration induced by the lens (Figure 10.8b). Because the homography mapping the ideal target to the sensed image is estimated in the central (undistorted) part of the image, any (per-channel) shifts induced by the optics manifest themselves as a displacement in the PSF centers.[10] Compensating for these shifts eliminates both the achromatic radial distortion and the inter-channel shifts that result in visible chromatic aberration. The color-dependent blurring caused by chromatic aberration (Figure 2.21) can also be removed using the de-blurring techniques discussed in Section 10.3. Figure 10.8b shows how the radial distortion and chromatic aberration manifest themselves as elongated and displaced PSFs, along with the result of removing these effects in a region of the calibration target.

The local 2D PSF estimation technique can also be used to estimate vignetting. Figure 10.8c shows how the mechanical vignetting manifests itself as clipping of the PSF in the corners of the image. In order for the overall dimming associated with vignetting to be properly captured, the modified intensities of the ideal pattern need to be extrapolated from the center, which is best done with a uniformly illuminated target.

---

[10] This process confounds the distinction between geometric and photometric calibration. In principle, any geometric distortion could be modeled by spatially varying displaced PSFs. In practice, it is easier to fold any large shifts into the geometric correction component.

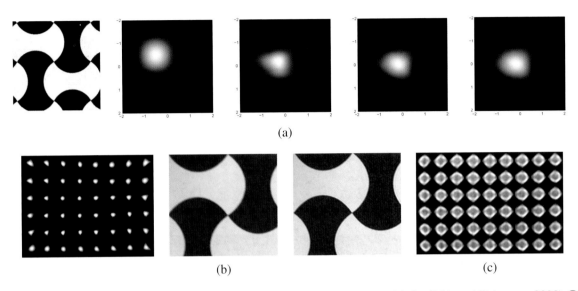

(a)

(b)   (c)

Figure 10.8 Point spread function estimation using a calibration target (Joshi, Szeliski, and Kriegman 2008) ©
2008 IEEE. (a) Sub-pixel PSFs at successively higher resolutions (note the interaction between the square sensing
area and the circular lens blur). (b) The radial distortion and chromatic aberration can also be estimated and
removed. (c) PSF for a mis-focused (blurred) lens showing some diffraction and vignetting effects in the corners.

When working with RAW Bayer-pattern images, the correct way to estimate the PSF is
to only evaluate the least squares terms in (10.1) at sensed pixel values, while interpolating
the ideal image to all values. For JPEG images, you should linearize your intensities first,
e.g., remove the gamma and any other non-linearities in your estimated radiometric response
function.

What if you have an image that was taken with an uncalibrated camera? Can you still
recover the PSF an use it to correct the image? In fact, with a slight modification, the previous
algorithms still work.

Instead of assuming a known calibration image, you can detect strong elongated edges
and fit ideal step edges in such regions (Figure 10.9b), resulting in the sharp image shown
in Figure 10.9d. For every pixel that is surrounded by a complete set of valid estimated
neighbors (green pixels in Figure 10.9c), apply the least squares formula (10.1) to estimate
the kernel K. The resulting locally estimated PSFs can be used to correct for chromatic
aberration (since the relative displacements between per-channel PSFs can be computed), as
shown by Joshi, Szeliski, and Kriegman (2008).

Exercise 10.4 provides some more detailed instructions for implementing and testing
edge-based PSF estimation algorithms. An alternative approach, which does not require the
explicit detection of edges but uses image statistics (gradient distributions) instead, is presented by Fergus, Singh, Hertzmann *et al.* (2006).

10.2 High dynamic range imaging

As we mentioned earlier in this chapter, registered images taken at different exposures can be
used to calibrate the radiometric response function of a camera. More importantly, they can

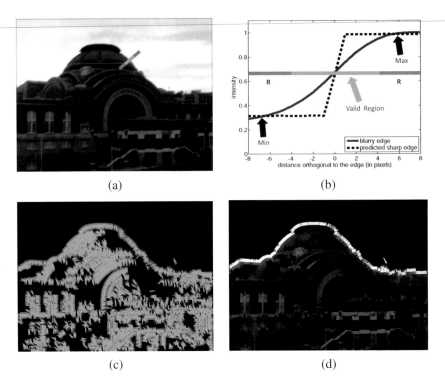

(a)   (b)

(c)   (d)

Figure 10.9 Estimating the PSF without using a calibration pattern (Joshi, Szeliski, and Kriegman 2008) © 2008 IEEE: (a) Input image with blue cross-section (profile) location, (b) Profile of sensed and predicted step edges, (c–d) Locations and values of the predicted colors near the edge locations.

Figure 10.10 Sample indoor image where the areas outside the window are overexposed and inside the room are too dark.

1   1,500   25,000   400,000   2,000,000

Figure 10.11 Relative brightness of different scenes, ranging from 1 inside a dark room lit by a monitor to 2,000,000 looking at the sun. Photos courtesy of Paul Debevec.

Figure 10.12 A bracketed set of shots (using the camera's automatic exposure bracketing (AEB) mode) and the resulting high dynamic range (HDR) composite.

help you create well-exposed photographs under challenging conditions, such as brightly lit scenes where any single exposure contains saturated (overexposed) and dark (underexposed) regions (Figure 10.10). This problem is quite common, because the natural world contains a range of radiance values that is far greater than can be captured with any photographic sensor or film (Figure 10.11). Taking a set of *bracketed exposures* (exposures taken by a camera in automatic exposure bracketing (AEB) mode to deliberately under- and over-expose the image) gives you the material from which to create a properly exposed photograph, as shown in Figure 10.12 (Reinhard, Ward, Pattanaik *et al.* 2005; Freeman 2008; Gulbins and Gulbins 2009; Hasinoff, Durand, and Freeman 2010).

While it is possible to combine pixels from different exposures directly into a final composite (Burt and Kolczynski 1993; Mertens, Kautz, and Reeth 2007), this approach runs the risk of creating contrast reversals and halos. Instead, the more common approach is to proceed in three stages:

1. Estimate the radiometric response function from the aligned images.

2. Estimate a *radiance map* by selecting or blending pixels from different exposures.

3. Tone map the resulting high dynamic range (HDR) image back into a displayable gamut.

The idea behind estimating the radiometric response function is relatively straightforward (Mann and Picard 1995; Debevec and Malik 1997; Mitsunaga and Nayar 1999; Reinhard, Ward, Pattanaik *et al.* 2005). Suppose you take three sets of images at different exposures (shutter speeds), say at ± 2 exposure values.[11] If we were able to determine the irradiance

---

[11] Changing the shutter speed is preferable to changing the aperture, as the latter can modify the vignetting and focus. Using ± 2 "f-stops" (technically, exposure values, or EVs, since f-stops refer to apertures) is usually the right compromise between capturing a good dynamic range and having properly exposed pixels everywhere.

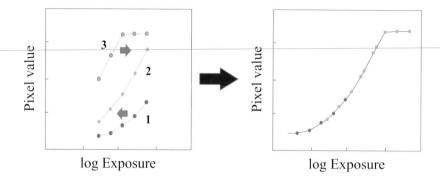

Figure 10.13 Radiometric calibration using multiple exposures (Debevec and Malik 1997). Corresponding pixel values are plotted as functions of log exposures (irradiance). The curves on the left are shifted to account for each pixel's unknown radiance until they all line up into a single smooth curve.

(exposure) E_i at each pixel (2.101), we could plot it against the measured pixel value z_{ij} for each exposure time t_j, as shown in Figure 10.13.

Unfortunately, we do not know the irradiance values E_i, so these have to be estimated at the same time as the radiometric response function f, which can be written (Debevec and Malik 1997) as

$$z_{ij} = f(E_i\, t_j), \tag{10.3}$$

where t_j is the exposure time for the jth image. The inverse response curve f^{-1} is given by

$$f^{-1}(z_{ij}) = E_i\, t_j. \tag{10.4}$$

Taking logarithms of both sides (base 2 is convenient, as we can now measure quantities in EVs), we obtain

$$g(z_{ij}) = \log f^{-1}(z_{ij}) = \log E_i + \log t_j, \tag{10.5}$$

where $g = \log f^{-1}$ (which maps pixel values z_{ij} into log irradiance) is the curve we are estimating (Figure 10.13 turned on its side).

Debevec and Malik (1997) assume that the exposure times t_j are known. (Recall that these can be obtained from a camera's EXIF tags, but that they actually follow a power of 2 progression ..., $1/128$, $1/64$, $1/32$, $1/16$, $1/8$, ... instead of the marked ..., $1/125$, $1/60$, $1/30$, $1/15$, $1/8$, ... values—see Exercise 2.5.) The unknowns are therefore the per-pixel exposures E_i and the response values $g_k = g(k)$, where g can be discretized according to the 256 pixel values commonly observed in eight-bit images. (The response curves are calibrated separately for each color channel.)

In order to make the response curve smooth, Debevec and Malik (1997) add a second-order smoothness constraint

$$\lambda \sum_k g''(k)^2 = \lambda \sum [g(k-1) - 2g(k) + g(k+1)]^2, \tag{10.6}$$

which is similar to the one used in snakes (5.3). Since pixel values are more reliable in the middle of their range (and the g function becomes singular near saturation values), they also

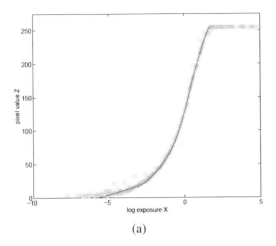
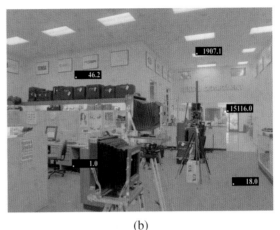

(a)   (b)

Figure 10.14 Recovered response function and radiance image for a real digital camera (DCS460) (Debevec and Malik 1997) © 1997 ACM.

add a weighting (hat) function $w(k)$ that decays to zero at both ends of the pixel value range,

$$w(z) = \begin{cases} z - z_{\min} & z \leq (z_{\min} + z_{\max})/2 \\ z_{\max} - z & z > (z_{\min} + z_{\max})/2. \end{cases} \qquad (10.7)$$

Putting all of these terms together, they obtain a least squares problem in the unknowns $\{g_k\}$ and $\{E_i\}$,

$$E = \sum_i \sum_j w(z_{i,j})[g(z_{i,j}) - \log E_i - \log t_j]^2 + \lambda \sum_k w(k)g''(k)^2. \qquad (10.8)$$

(In order to remove the overall shift ambiguity in the response curve and irradiance values, the middle of the response curve is set to 0.) Debevec and Malik (1997) show how this can be implemented in 21 lines of MATLAB code, which partially accounts for the popularity of their technique.

While Debevec and Malik (1997) assume that the exposure times t_j are known exactly, there is no reason why these additional variables cannot be thrown into the least squares problem, constraining their final estimated values to lie close to their nominal values $\hat{t}_j$ with an extra term $\eta \sum_j (t_j - \hat{t}_j)^2$.

Figure 10.14 shows the recovered radiometric response function for a digital camera along with select (relative) radiance values in the overall radiance map. Figure 10.15 shows the bracketed input images captured on color film and the corresponding radiance map.

While Debevec and Malik (1997) use a general second-order smooth curve g to parameterize their response curve, Mann and Picard (1995) use a three-parameter function

$$f(E) = \alpha + \beta E^\gamma, \qquad (10.9)$$

while Mitsunaga and Nayar (1999) use a low-order ($N \leq 10$) polynomial for the inverse response function g. Pal, Szeliski, Uyttendaele et al. (2004) derive a Bayesian model that estimates an independent smooth response function for each image, which can better model

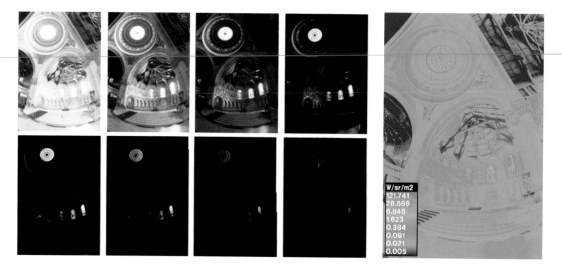

Figure 10.15 Bracketed set of exposures captured with a film camera and the resulting radiance image displayed in pseudocolor (Debevec and Malik 1997) © 1997 ACM.

the more sophisticated (and hence less predictable) automatic contrast and tone adjustment performed in today's digital cameras.

Once the response function has been estimated, the second step in creating high dynamic range photographs is to merge the input images into a composite *radiance map*. If the response function and images were known exactly, i.e., if they were noise free, you could use any non-saturated pixel value to estimate the corresponding radiance by mapping it through the inverse response curve $E = g(z)$.

Unfortunately, pixels are noisy, especially under low-light conditions when fewer photons arrive at the sensor. To compensate for this, Mann and Picard (1995) use the derivative of the response function as a weight in determining the final radiance estimate, since "flatter" regions of the curve tell us less about the incoming irradiance. Debevec and Malik (1997) use a hat function (10.7) which accentuates mid-tone pixels while avoiding saturated values. Mitsunaga and Nayar (1999) show that in order to maximize the signal-to-noise ratio (SNR), the weighting function must emphasize both higher pixel values and larger gradients in the transfer function, i.e.,

$$w(z) = g(z)/g'(z), \tag{10.10}$$

where the weights w are used to form the final irradiance estimate

$$\log E_i = \frac{\sum_j w(z_{ij})[g(z_{ij}) - \log t_j]}{\sum_j w(z_{ij})}. \tag{10.11}$$

Exercise 10.1 has you implement one of the radiometric response function calibration techniques and then use it to create radiance maps.

Under real-world conditions, casually acquired images may not be perfectly registered and may contain moving objects. Ward (2003) uses a global (parametric) transform to align the input images, while Kang, Uyttendaele, Winder *et al.* (2003) present an algorithm that combines global registration with local motion estimation (optical flow) to accurately align

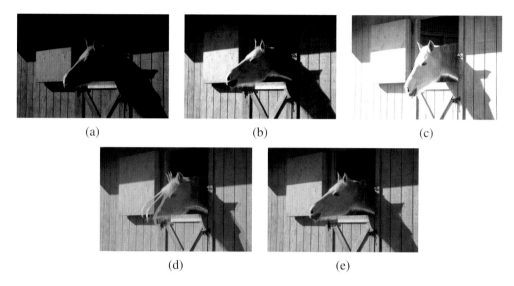

Figure 10.16 Merging multiple exposures to create a high dynamic range composite (Kang, Uyttendaele, Winder *et al.* 2003): (a–c) three different exposures; (d) merging the exposures using classic algorithms (note the ghosting due to the horse's head movement); (e) merging the exposures with motion compensation.

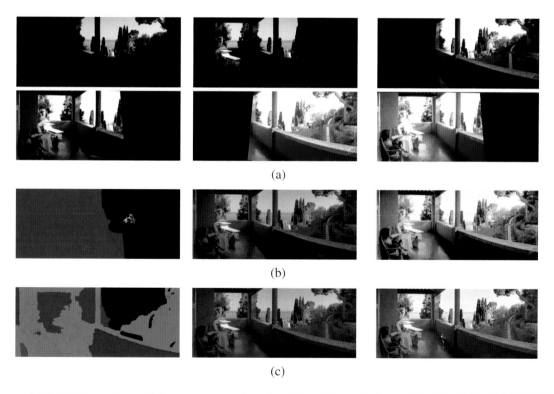

Figure 10.17 HDR merging with large amounts of motion (Eden, Uyttendaele, and Szeliski 2006) © 2006 IEEE: (a) registered bracketed input images; (b) results after the first pass of image selection: reference labels, image, and tone-mapped image; (c) results after the second pass of image selection: final labels, compressed HDR image, and tone-mapped image

Figure 10.18 Fuji SuperCCD high dynamic range image sensor. The paired large and small active areas provide two different effective exposures.

the images before blending their radiance estimates (Figure 10.16). Since the images may have widely different exposures, care must be taken when estimating the motions, which must themselves be checked for consistency to avoid the creation of ghosts and object fragments.

Even this approach, however, may not work when the camera is simultaneously undergoing large panning motions and exposure changes, which is a common occurrence in casually acquired panoramas. Under such conditions, different parts of the image may be seen at one or more exposures. Devising a method to blend all of these different sources while avoiding sharp transitions and dealing with scene motion is a challenging problem. One approach is to first find a consensus mosaic and to then selectively compute radiances in under- and over-exposed regions (Eden, Uyttendaele, and Szeliski 2006), as shown in Figure 10.17.

Recently, some cameras, such as the Sony α550 and Pentax K-7, have started integrating multiple exposure merging and tone mapping directly into the camera body. In the future, the need to compute high dynamic range images from multiple exposures may be eliminated by advances in camera sensor technology (Figure 10.18) (Yang, El Gamal, Fowler *et al.* 1999; Nayar and Mitsunaga 2000; Nayar and Branzoi 2003; Kang, Uyttendaele, Winder *et al.* 2003; Narasimhan and Nayar 2005; Tumblin, Agrawal, and Raskar 2005). However, the need to blend such images and to tone map them to lower-gamut displays is likely to remain.

HDR image formats.   Before we discuss techniques for mapping HDR images back to a displayable gamut, we should discuss the commonly used formats for storing HDR images.

If storage space is not an issue, storing each of the R, G, and B values as a 32-bit IEEE float is the best solution. The commonly used Portable PixMap (.ppm) format, which supports both uncompressed ASCII and raw binary encodings of values, can be extended to a Portable FloatMap (.pfm) format by modifying the header. TIFF also supports full floating point values.

A more compact representation is the Radiance format (.pic, .hdr) (Ward 1994), which uses a single common exponent and per-channel mantissas (10.19b). An intermediate encoding, OpenEXR from ILM,[12] uses 16-bit floats for each channel (10.19c), which is a format supported natively on most modern GPUs. Ward (2004) describes these and other data formats such as LogLuv (Larson 1998) in more detail, as do the books by Reinhard, Ward,

---

[12] http://www.openexr.net/.

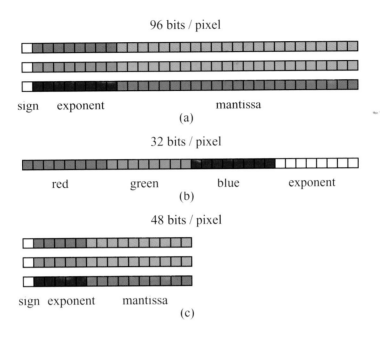

96 bits / pixel

sign   exponent   mantissa

(a)

32 bits / pixel

red   green   blue   exponent

(b)

48 bits / pixel

sign exponent   mantissa

(c)

Figure 10.19 HDR image encoding formats: (a) Portable PixMap (.ppm); (b) Radiance (.pic, .hdr); (c) OpenEXR (.exr).

Pattanaik *et al.* (2005) and Freeman (2008). An even more recent HDR image format is the JPEG XR standard.[13]

10.2.1 Tone mapping

Once a radiance map has been computed, it is usually necessary to display it on a lower gamut (i.e., eight-bit) screen or printer. A variety of *tone mapping* techniques has been developed for this purpose, which involve either computing spatially varying transfer functions or reducing image gradients to fit the available dynamic range (Reinhard, Ward, Pattanaik *et al.* 2005).

The simplest way to compress a high dynamic range radiance image into a low dynamic range gamut is to use a global transfer curve (Larson, Rushmeier, and Piatko 1997). Figure 10.20 shows one such example, where a gamma curve is used to map an HDR image back into a displayable gamut. If gamma is applied separately to each channel (Figure 10.20b), the colors become muted (less saturated), since higher-valued color channels contribute less (proportionately) to the final color. Splitting the image up into its luminance and chrominance (say, L*a*b*) components (Section 2.3.2), applying the global mapping to the luminance channel, and then reconstituting a color image works better (Figure 10.20c).

Unfortunately, when the image has a really wide range of exposures, this global approach still fails to preserve details in regions with widely varying exposures. What is needed, instead, is something akin to the dodging and burning performed by photographers in the darkroom. Mathematically, this is similar to dividing each pixel by the *average* brightness in a region around that pixel.

---

[13] http://www.itu.int/rec/T-REC-T.832-200903-I/en.

 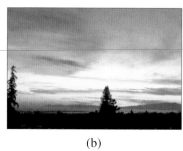 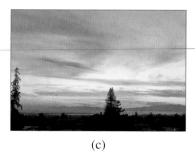

(a)   (b)   (c)

Figure 10.20 Global tone mapping: (a) input HDR image, linearly mapped; (b) gamma applied to each color channel independently; (c) gamma applied to intensity (colors are less washed out). Original HDR image courtesy of Paul Debevec, http://ict.debevec.org/~debevec/Research/HDR/. Processed images courtesy of Frédo Durand, MIT 6.815/6.865 course on Computational Photography.

Figure 10.21 shows how this process works. As before, the image is split into its luminance and chrominance channels. The log luminance image

$$H(x, y) = \log L(x, y) \tag{10.12}$$

is then low-pass filtered to produce a *base layer*

$$H_L(x, y) = B(x, y) * H(x, y), \tag{10.13}$$

and a high-pass *detail layer*

$$H_H(x, y) = H(x, y) - H_L(x, y). \tag{10.14}$$

The base layer is then contrast reduced by scaling to the desired log-luminance range,

$$H'_H(x, y) = s\, H_H(x, y) \tag{10.15}$$

and added to the detail layer to produce the new log-luminance image

$$I(x, y) = H'_H(x, y) + H_L(x, y), \tag{10.16}$$

which can then be exponentiated to produce the tone-mapped (compressed) luminance image. Note that this process is equivalent to dividing each luminance value by (a monotonic mapping of) the average log-luminance value in a region around that pixel.

Figure 10.21 shows the low-pass and high-pass log luminance image and the resulting tone-mapped color image. Note how the detail layer has visible *halos* around the high-contrast edges, which are visible in the final tone-mapped image. This is because linear filtering, which is not edge preserving, produces halos in the detail layer (Figure 10.23).

The solution to this problem is to use an edge-preserving filter to create the base layer. Durand and Dorsey (2002) study a number of such edge-preserving filters, including anisotropic and robust anisotropic diffusion, and select bilateral filtering (Section 3.3.1) as their edge-preserving filter. (A more recent paper by Farbman, Fattal, Lischinski *et al.* (2008) argues in favor of using a weighted least squares (WLF) filter as an alternative to the bilateral filter and Paris, Kornprobst, Tumblin *et al.* (2008) reviews bilateral filtering and its applications

(a) (b)

Figure 10.21 Local tone mapping using linear filters: (a) low-pass and high-pass filtered log luminance images and color (chrominance) image; (b) resulting tone-mapped image (after attenuating the low-pass log luminance image) shows visible halos around the trees. Processed images courtesy of Frédo Durand, MIT 6.815/6.865 course on Computational Photography.

(a) (b)

Figure 10.22 Local tone mapping using bilateral filter (Durand and Dorsey 2002): (a) low-pass and high-pass bilateral filtered log luminance images and color (chrominance) image; (b) resulting tone-mapped image (after attenuating the low-pass log luminance image) shows no halos. Processed images courtesy of Frédo Durand, MIT 6.815/6.865 course on Computational Photography.

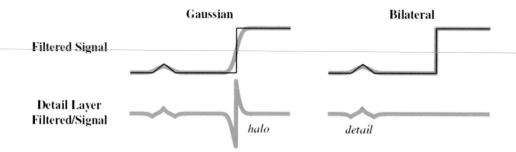

Figure 10.23 Gaussian vs. bilateral filtering (Petschnigg, Agrawala, Hoppe *et al.* 2004) © 2004 ACM: A Gaussian low-pass filter blurs across all edges and therefore creates strong peaks and valleys in the detail image that cause halos. The bilateral filter does not smooth across strong edges and thereby reduces halos while still capturing detail.

in computer vision and computational photography.) Figure 10.22 shows how replacing the linear low-pass filter with a bilateral filter produces tone-mapped images with no visible halos. Figure 10.24 summarizes the complete information flow in this process, starting with the decomposition into log luminance and chrominance images, bilateral filtering, contrast reduction, and re-composition into the final output image.

An alternative to compressing the base layer is to compress its *derivatives*, i.e., the gradient of the log-luminance image (Fattal, Lischinski, and Werman 2002). Figure 10.25 illustrates this process. The log-luminance image is differentiated to obtain a gradient image

$$H'(x,y) = \nabla H(x,y). \tag{10.17}$$

This gradient image is then attenuated by a spatially varying attenuation function $\Phi(x,y)$,

$$G(x,y) = H'(x,y)\,\Phi(x,y). \tag{10.18}$$

The attenuation function $I(x,y)$ is designed to attenuate large-scale brightness changes (Figure 10.26a) and is designed to take into account gradients at different spatial scales (Fattal, Lischinski, and Werman 2002).

After attenuation, the resulting gradient field is re-integrated by solving a first-order variational (least squares) problem,

$$\min \int \int \|\nabla I(x,y) - G(x,y)\|^2 dx\,dy \tag{10.19}$$

to obtain the compressed log-luminance image $I(x,y)$. This least squares problem is the same that was used for Poisson blending (Section 9.3.4) and was first introduced in our study of regularization (Section 3.7.1, 3.100). It can efficiently be solved using techniques such as multigrid and hierarchical basis preconditioning (Fattal, Lischinski, and Werman 2002; Szeliski 2006b; Farbman, Fattal, Lischinski *et al.* 2008). Once the new luminance image has been computed, it is combined with the original color image using

$$C_{\text{out}} = \left(\frac{C_{\text{in}}}{L_{\text{in}}}\right)^s L_{\text{out}}, \tag{10.20}$$

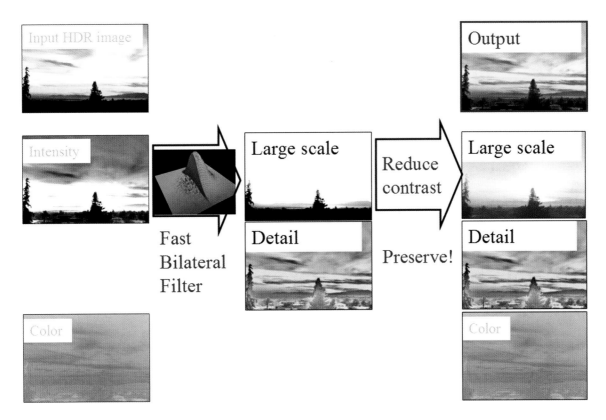

Figure 10.24 Local tone mapping using bilateral filter (Durand and Dorsey 2002): summary of algorithm workflow. Images courtesy of Frédo Durand, MIT 6.815/6.865 course on Computational Photography.

where $C = (R, G, B)$ and L_{in} and L_{out} are the original and compressed luminance images. The exponent s controls the saturation of the colors and is typically in the range $s \in [0.4, 0.6]$. Figure 10.26b shows the final tone-mapped color image, which shows no visible halos despite the extremely large variation in input radiance values.

Yet another alternative to these two approaches is to perform the local dodging and burning using a locally scale-selective operator (Reinhard, Stark, Shirley *et al.* 2002). Figure 10.27 shows how such a scale selection operator can determine a radius (scale) that only includes similar color values within the inner circle while avoiding much brighter values in the surrounding circle. In practice, a difference of Gaussians normalized by the inner Gaussian response is evaluated over a range of scales, and the largest scale whose metric is below a threshold is selected (Reinhard, Stark, Shirley *et al.* 2002).

What all of these techniques have in common is that they adaptively attenuate or brighten different regions of the image so that they can be displayed in a limited gamut without loss of contrast. Lischinski, Farbman, Uyttendaele *et al.* (2006b) introduce an *interactive* technique that performs this operation by interpolating a set of sparse user-drawn adjustments (strokes and associated exposure value corrections) to a piecewise-continuous exposure correction map (Figure 10.28). The interpolation is performed by minimizing a locally weighted least

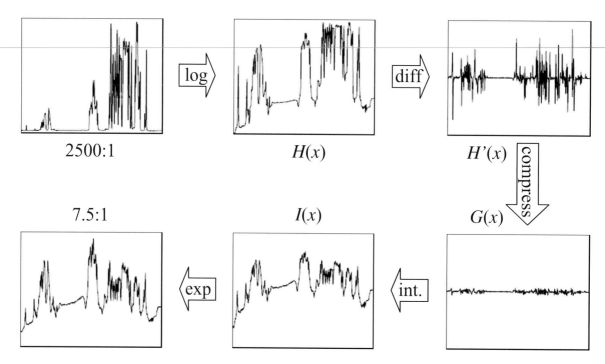

Figure 10.25 Gradient domain tone mapping (Fattal, Lischinski, and Werman 2002) © 2002 ACM. The original image with a dynamic range of 2415:1 is first converted into the log domain, $H(x)$, and its gradients are computed, $H'(x)$. These are attenuated (compressed) based on local contrast, $G(x)$, and integrated to produce the new logarithmic exposure image $I(x)$, which is exponentiated to produce the final intensity image, whose dynamic range is 7.5:1.

(a)   (b)

Figure 10.26 Gradient domain tone mapping (Fattal, Lischinski, and Werman 2002) © 2002 ACM: (a) attenuation map, with darker values corresponding to more attenuation; (b) final tone-mapped image.

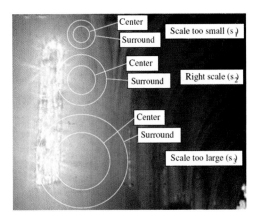

Figure 10.27 Scale selection for tone mapping (Reinhard, Stark, Shirley *et al.* 2002) © 2002 ACM.

square (WLS) variational problem,

$$\min \int\int w_d(x,y)\|f(x,y) - g(x,y)\|^2 dx\, dy + \lambda \int\int w_s(x,y)\|\nabla f(x,y)\|^2 dx\, dy,$$

$$(10.21)$$

where $g(x,y)$ and $f(x,y)$ are the input and output log exposure (attenuation) maps (Figure 10.28). The data weighting term $w_d(x,y)$ is 1 at stroke locations and 0 elsewhere. The smoothness weighting term $w_s(x,y)$ is inversely proportional to the log-luminance gradient,

$$w_s = \frac{1}{\|\nabla H\|^\alpha + \epsilon} \qquad (10.22)$$

and hence encourages the $f(x,y)$ map to be smoother in low-gradient areas than along high-gradient discontinuities.[14] The same approach can also be used for fully automated tone mapping by setting target exposure values at each pixel and allowing the weighted least squares to convert these into piecewise smooth adjustment maps.

The weighted least squares algorithm, which was originally developed for image colorization applications (Levin, Lischinski, and Weiss 2004), has recently been applied to general edge-preserving smoothing in applications such as contrast enhancement (Bae, Paris, and Durand 2006) and tone mapping (Farbman, Fattal, Lischinski *et al.* 2008) where the bilateral filtering was previously used. It can also be used to perform HDR merging and tone mapping simultaneously (Raman and Chaudhuri 2007, 2009).

Given the wide range of locally adaptive tone mapping algorithms that have been developed, which ones should be used in practice? Freeman (2008) provides a great discussion of commercially available algorithms, their artifacts, and the parameters that can be used to control them. He also has a wealth of tips for HDR photography and workflow. I highly recommend his book for anyone contemplating additional research (or personal photography) in this area.

---

[14] In practice, the x and y discrete derivatives are weighted separately (Lischinski, Farbman, Uyttendaele *et al.* 2006b). Their default parameter settings are $\lambda = 0.2$, $\alpha = 1$, and $\epsilon = 0.0001$.

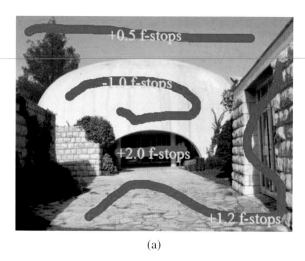
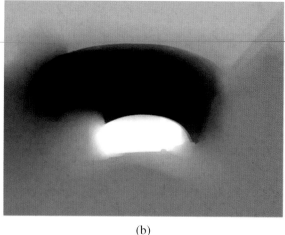

(a)   (b)

Figure 10.28 Interactive local tone mapping (Lischinski, Farbman, Uyttendaele *et al.* 2006b) © 2006 ACM: (a) user-drawn strokes with associated exposure values $g(x, y)$ (b) corresponding piecewise-smooth exposure adjustment map $f(x, y)$.

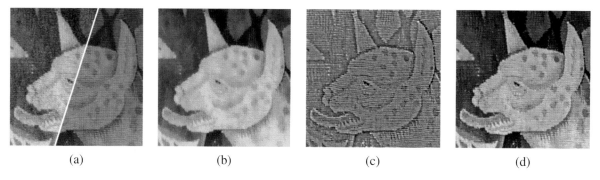

(a)   (b)   (c)   (d)

Figure 10.29 Detail transfer in flash/no-flash photography (Petschnigg, Agrawala, Hoppe *et al.* 2004) © 2004 ACM: (a) details of input ambient A and flash F images; (b) joint bilaterally filtered no-flash image A^{NR}; (c) detail layer F^{Detail} computed from the flash image F; (d) final merged image A^{Final}.

10.2.2 *Application*: Flash photography

While high dynamic range imaging combines images of a scene taken at different exposures, it is also possible to combine flash and non-flash images to achieve better exposure and color balance and to reduce noise (Eisemann and Durand 2004; Petschnigg, Agrawala, Hoppe *et al.* 2004).

The problem with flash images is that the color is often unnatural (it fails to capture the ambient illumination), there may be strong shadows or specularities, and there is a radial falloff in brightness away from the camera (Figures 10.1b and 10.29a). Non-flash photos taken under low light conditions often suffer from excessive noise (because of the high ISO gains and low photon counts) and blur (due to longer exposures). Is there some way to combine a non-flash photo taken just before the flash goes off with the flash photo to produce

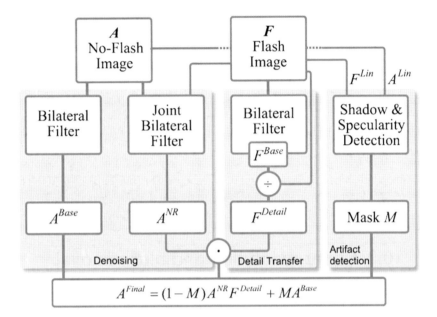

Figure 10.30 Flash/no-flash photography algorithm (Petschnigg, Agrawala, Hoppe *et al.* 2004) © 2004 ACM. The ambient (no-flash) image A is filtered with a regular bilateral filter to produce A^{Base}, which is used in shadow and specularity regions, and a joint bilaterally filtered noise reduced image A^{NR}. The flash image F is bilaterally filtered to produce a base image F^{Base} and a detail (ratio) image F^{Detail}, which is used to modulate the de-noised ambient image. The shadow/specularity mask M is computed by comparing linearized versions of the flash and no-flash images.

an image with good color values, sharpness, and low noise?[15]

Petschnigg, Agrawala, Hoppe *et al.* (2004) approach this problem by first filtering the no-flash (ambient) image A with a variant of the bilateral filter called the *joint bilateral filter*[16] in which the range kernel (3.36)

$$r(i, j, k, l) = \exp\left(-\frac{\|f(i, j) - f(k, l)\|^2}{2\sigma_r^2}\right) \qquad (10.23)$$

is evaluated on the flash image F instead of the ambient image A, since the flash image is less noisy and hence has more reliable edges (Figure 10.29b). Because the contents of the flash image can be unreliable inside and at the boundaries of shadows and specularities, these are detected and a regular bilaterally filtered image A^{Base} is used instead (Figure 10.30).

The second stage of their algorithm computes a flash detail image

$$F^{Detail} = \frac{F + \epsilon}{F^{Base} + \epsilon}, \qquad (10.24)$$

where F^{Base} is a bilaterally filtered version of the flash image F and $\epsilon = 0.02$. This detail image (Figure 10.29c) encodes details that may have been filtered away from the noise-reduced

---

[15] In fact, the discontinued FujiFilm FinePix F40fd camera takes a pair of flash and no flash images in quick succession; however, it only lets you decide to keep one of them.

[16] Eisemann and Durand (2004) call this the *cross bilateral filter*.

no-flash image A^{NR}, as well as additional details created by the flash camera, which often add crispness. The detail image is used to modulate the noise-reduced ambient image A^{NR} to produce the final results

$$A^{Final} = (1 - M)A^{NR}F^{Detail} + MA^{Base} \tag{10.25}$$

shown in Figures 10.1b and 10.29d.

Eisemann and Durand (2004) present an alternative algorithm that shares some of the same basic concepts. Both papers are well worth reading and contrasting (Exercise 10.6).

Flash images can also be used for a variety of additional applications such as extracting more reliable foreground mattes of objects (Raskar, Tan, Feris *et al.* 2004; Sun, Li, Kang *et al.* 2006). Flash photography is just one instance of the more general topic of *active illumination*, which is discussed in more detail by Raskar and Tumblin (2010).

10.3 Super-resolution and blur removal

While high dynamic range imaging enables us to obtain an image with a larger dynamic range than a single regular image, super-resolution enables us to create images with higher *spatial* resolution and less noise than regular camera images (Chaudhuri 2001; Park, Park, and Kang 2003; Capel and Zisserman 2003; Capel 2004; van Ouwerkerk 2006). Most commonly, super-resolution refers to the process of aligning and combining several input images to produce such high-resolution composites (Irani and Peleg 1991; Cheeseman, Kanefsky, Hanson *et al.* 1993; Pickup, Capel, Roberts *et al.* 2009). However, some newer techniques can super-resolve a single image (Freeman, Jones, and Pasztor 2002; Baker and Kanade 2002; Fattal 2007) and are hence closely related to techniques for removing blur (Sections 3.4.3 and 3.4.4).

The most principled way to formulate the super-resolution problem is to write down the stochastic image formation equations and image priors and to then use Bayesian inference to recover the super-resolved (original) sharp image. We can do this by generalizing the image formation equations (3.75) used for image deblurring (Section 3.4.3), which we also used in (10.2) for blur kernel (PSF) estimation (Section 10.1.4). In this case, we have several observed images $\{o_k(\boldsymbol{x})\}$, as well as an image warping function $\hat{\boldsymbol{h}}_k(\boldsymbol{x})$ for each observed image (Figure 3.47). Combining all of these elements, we get the (noisy) observation equations[17]

$$o_k(\boldsymbol{x}) = D\{b(\boldsymbol{x}) * s(\hat{\boldsymbol{h}}_k(\boldsymbol{x}))\} + n_k(\boldsymbol{x}), \tag{10.26}$$

where D is the downsampling operator, which operates *after* the super-resolved (sharp) warped image $s(\hat{\boldsymbol{h}}_k(\boldsymbol{x}))$ has been convolved with the blur kernel $b(\boldsymbol{x})$. The above image formation equations lead to the following least squares problem,

$$\sum_k \|o_k(\boldsymbol{x}) - D\{b_k(\boldsymbol{x}) * s(\hat{\boldsymbol{h}}_k(\boldsymbol{x}))\}\|^2. \tag{10.27}$$

In most super-resolution algorithms, the alignment (warping) $\hat{\boldsymbol{h}}_k$ is estimated using one of the input frames as the *reference frame*; either feature-based (Section 6.1.3) or direct (image-based) (Section 8.2) parametric alignment techniques can be used. (A few algorithms, such

---

[17] It is also possible to add an unknown bias–gain term to each observation (Capel 2004), as was done for motion estimation in (8.8).

as those described by Schultz and Stevenson (1996) or Capel (2004) use dense (per-pixel flow) estimates.) A better approach is to re-compute the alignment by directly minimizing (10.27) once an initial estimate of $s(\boldsymbol{x})$ has been computed (Hardie, Barnard, and Armstrong 1997) or to *marginalize* out the motion parameters altogether (Pickup, Capel, Roberts *et al.* 2007)—see also the work of Protter and Elad (2009) for some related video super-resolution work.

The point spread function (blur kernel) b_k is either inferred from knowledge of the image formation process (e.g., the amount of motion or defocus blur and the camera sensor optics) or calibrated from a test image or the observed images $\{o_k\}$ using one of the techniques described in Section 10.1.4. The problem of simultaneously inferring the blur kernel and the sharp image is known as *blind image deconvolution* (Kundur and Hatzinakos 1996; Levin 2006).[18]

Given an estimate of $\hat{\boldsymbol{h}}_k$ and $b_k(\boldsymbol{x})$, (10.27) can be re-written using matrix/vector notation as a large sparse least squares problem in the unknown values of the super-resolved pixels $\boldsymbol{s}$,

$$\sum_k \|\boldsymbol{o}_k - \boldsymbol{D}\boldsymbol{B}_k\boldsymbol{W}_k\boldsymbol{s}\|^2. \tag{10.28}$$

(Recall from (3.89) that once the warping function $\hat{\boldsymbol{h}}_k$ is known, values of $s(\hat{\boldsymbol{h}}_k(\boldsymbol{x}))$ depend linearly on those in $s(\boldsymbol{x})$.) An efficient way to solve this least squares problem is to use preconditioned conjugate gradient descent (Capel 2004), although some earlier algorithms, such as the one developed by Irani and Peleg (1991), used regular gradient descent (also known as iterative back projection (IBP), in the computed tomography literature).

The above formulation assumes that warping can be expressed as a simple (sinc or bicubic) interpolated resampling of the super-resolved sharp image, followed by a stationary (spatially invariant) blurring (PSF) and area integration process. However, if the surface is severely foreshortened, we have to take into account the spatially varying filtering that occurs during the image warping (Section 3.6.1), before we can then model the PSF induced by the optics and camera sensor (Wang, Kang, Szeliski *et al.* 2001; Capel 2004).

How well does this least squares (MLE) approach to super-resolution work? In practice, this depends a lot on the amount of blur and aliasing in the camera optics, as well as the accuracy in the motion and PSF estimates (Baker and Kanade 2002; Jiang, Wong, and Bao 2003; Capel 2004). Less blurring and more aliasing means that there is more (aliased) high frequency information available to be recovered. However, because the least squares (maximum likelihood) formulation uses no image prior, a lot of high-frequency noise can be introduced into the solution (Figure 10.31c).

For this reason, most super-resolution algorithms assume some form of image prior. The simplest of these is to place a penalty on the image derivatives similar to Equations (3.105 and 3.113), e.g.,

$$\sum_{(i,j)} \rho_p(s(i,j) - s(i+1,j)) + \rho_p(s(i,j) - s(i,j+1)). \tag{10.29}$$

---

[18] Notice that there is a chicken-and-egg problem if both the blur kernel and the super-resolved image are unknown. This can be "broken" either using structural assumptions about the sharp image, e.g., the presence of edges (Joshi, Szeliski, and Kriegman 2008) or prior models for the image, such as edge sparsity (Fergus, Singh, Hertzmann *et al.* 2006).

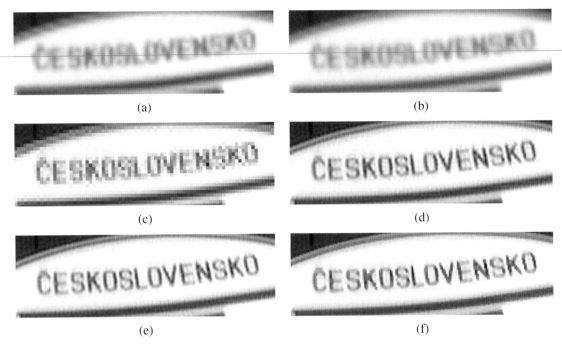

Figure 10.31 Super-resolution results using a variety of image priors (Capel 2001): (a) Low-res ROI (bicubic $3\times$ zoom); (b) average image; (c) MLE @ $1.25\times$ pixel-zoom; (d) simple $\|x\|^2$ prior ($\lambda = 0.004$); (e) GMRF ($\lambda = 0.003$); (f) HMRF ($\lambda = 0.01$, $\alpha = 0.04$). 10 images are used as input and a $3\times$ super-resolved image is produced in each case, except for the MLE result in (c).

As discussed in Section 3.7.2, when ρ_p is quadratic, this is a form of Tikhonov regularization (Section 3.7.1), and the overall problem is still linear least squares. The resulting prior image model is a Gaussian Markov random field (GMRF), which can be extended to other (e.g., diagonal) differences, as in (Capel 2004) (Figure 10.31).

Unfortunately, GMRFs tend to produce solutions with visible ripples, which can also be interpreted as increased noise sensitivity in middle frequencies (Exercise 3.17). A better image prior is a robust prior that encourages piecewise continuous solutions (Black and Rangarajan 1996), see Appendix B.3. Examples of such priors include the Huber potential (Schultz and Stevenson 1996; Capel and Zisserman 2003), which is a blend of a Gaussian with a longer-tailed Laplacian, and the even sparser (heavier-tailed) hyper-Laplacians used by Levin, Fergus, Durand *et al.* (2007) and Krishnan and Fergus (2009). It is also possible to learn the parameters for such priors using cross-validation (Capel 2004; Pickup 2007).

While sparse (robust) derivative priors can reduce rippling effects and increase edge sharpness, they cannot *hallucinate* higher-frequency texture or details. To do this, a training set of sample images can be used to find plausible mappings between low-frequency originals and the missing higher frequencies. Inspired by some of the example-based texture synthesis algorithms we discuss in Section 10.5, the *example-based super-resolution* algorithm developed by Freeman, Jones, and Pasztor (2002) uses training images to *learn* the mapping between local texture patches and missing higher-frequency details. To ensure that overlapping patches are similar in appearance, a Markov random field is used and optimized

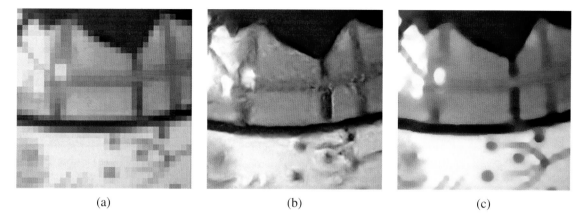

(a)   (b)   (c)

Figure 10.32 Example-based super-resolution: (a) original 32×32 low-resolution image; (b) example-based super-resolved 256×256 image (Freeman, Jones, and Pasztor 2002) © 2002 IEEE; (c) upsampling via imposed edge statistics (Fattal 2007) © 2007 ACM.

using either belief propagation (Freeman, Pasztor, and Carmichael 2000) or a raster-scan deterministic variant (Freeman, Jones, and Pasztor 2002). Figure 10.32 shows the results of hallucinating missing details using this approach and compares these results to a more recent algorithm by Fattal (2007). This latter algorithm learns to predict oriented gradient magnitudes in the finer resolution image based on a pixel's location relative to the nearest detected edge along with the corresponding edge statistics (magnitude and width). It is also possible to combine sparse (robust) derivative priors with example-based super-resolution, as shown by Tappen, Russell, and Freeman (2003).

An alternative (but closely related) form of hallucination is to *recognize* the parts of a training database of images to which a low-resolution pixel might correspond. In their work, Baker and Kanade (2002) use local derivative-of-Gaussian filter responses as features and then match *parent structure* vectors in a manner similar to De Bonet (1997).[19] The high-frequency gradient at each recognized training image location is then used as a constraint on the super-resolved image, along with the usual reconstruction (prediction) equation (10.27). Figure 10.33 shows the result of hallucinating higher-resolution faces from lower-resolution inputs; Baker and Kanade (2002) also show examples of super-resolving known-font text. Exercise 10.7 gives more details on how to implement and test one or more of these super-resolution techniques.

Under favorable conditions, super-resolution and related upsampling techniques can increase the resolution of a well-photographed image or image collection. When the input images are blurry to start with, the best one can often hope for is to reduce the amount of blur. This problem is closely related super-resolution, with the biggest differences being that the blur kernel b is usually much larger and the downsampling factor D is unity. A large literature on image deblurring exists; some of the more recent publications with nice literature reviews include those by Fergus, Singh, Hertzmann *et al.* (2006), Yuan, Sun, Quan *et al.* (2008), and Joshi, Zitnick, Szeliski *et al.* (2009). It is also possible to reduce blur by combining sharp (but noisy) images with blurrier (but cleaner) images (Yuan, Sun, Quan *et al.* 2007), take lots of

---

[19] For face super-resolution, where all the images are pre-aligned, only corresponding pixels in different images are examined.

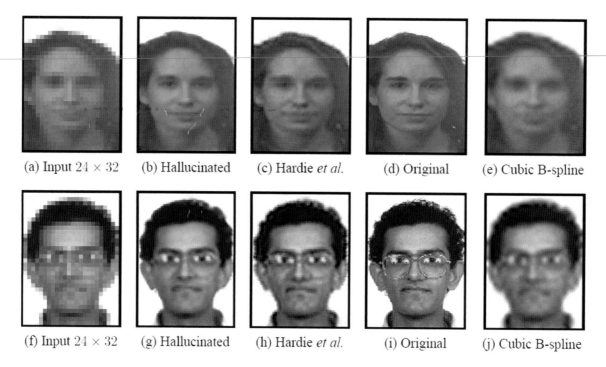

(a) Input 24×32 (b) Hallucinated   (c) Hardie *et al.*   (d) Original   (e) Cubic B-spline

(f) Input 24×32 (g) Hallucinated   (h) Hardie *et al.*   (i) Original   (j) Cubic B-spline

Figure 10.33 Recognition-based super-resolution (Baker and Kanade 2002) © 2002 IEEE. The *Hallucinated* column shows the results of the recognition-based algorithm compared to the regularization-based approach of Hardie, Barnard, and Armstrong (1997).

quick exposures[20] (Hasinoff and Kutulakos 2008; Hasinoff, Kutulakos, Durand *et al.* 2009; Hasinoff, Durand, and Freeman 2010), or use *coded aperture* techniques to simultaneously estimate depth and reduce blur (Levin, Fergus, Durand *et al.* 2007; Zhou, Lin, and Nayar 2009).

10.3.1 Color image demosaicing

A special case of super-resolution, which is used daily in most digital still cameras, is the process of *demosaicing* samples from a color filter array (CFA) into a full-color RGB image. Figure 10.34 shows the most commonly used CFA known as the *Bayer pattern*, which has twice as many green (G) sensors as red and blue sensors.

The process of going from the known CFA pixels values to the full RGB image is quite challenging. Unlike regular super-resolution, where small errors in guessing unknown values usually show up as blur or aliasing, demosaicing artifacts often produce spurious colors or high-frequency patterned *zippering*, which are quite visible to the eye (Figure 10.35b).

Over the years, a variety of techniques have been developed for image demosaicing (Kimmel 1999). Bennett, Uyttendaele, Zitnick *et al.* (2006) present a recently developed algorithm along with some good references, while Longere, Delahunt, Zhang *et al.* (2002) and Tappen, Russell, and Freeman (2003) compare some previously developed techniques using perceptually motivated metrics. To reduce the zippering effect, most techniques use the edge or

---

[20] The SONY DSC-WX1 takes multiple shots to produce better low-light photos.

G	R	G	R
B	G	B	G
G	R	G	R
B	G	B	G

(a)

rGb	Rgb	rGb	Rgb
rgB	rGb	rgB	rGb
rGb	Rgb	rGb	Rgb
rgB	rGb	rgB	rGb

(b)

Figure 10.34 Bayer RGB pattern: (a) color filter array layout; (b) interpolated pixel values, with unknown (guessed) values shown as lower case.

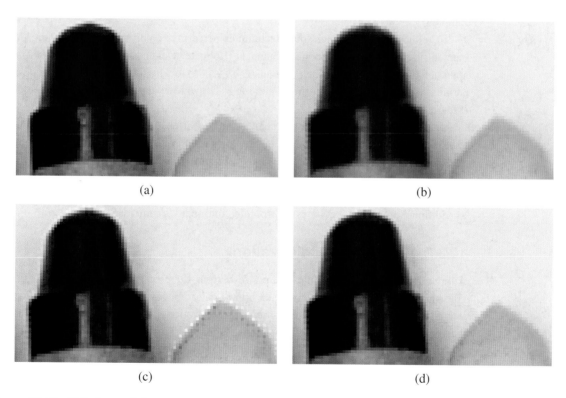

(a)   (b)

(c)   (d)

Figure 10.35 CFA demosaicing results (Bennett, Uyttendaele, Zitnick *et al.* 2006) © 2006 Springer: (a) original full-resolution image (a color subsampled version is used as the input to the algorithms); (b) bilinear interpolation results, showing color fringing near the tip of the blue crayon and zippering near its left (vertical) edge; (c) the high-quality linear interpolation results of Malvar, He, and Cutler (2004) (note the strong halo/checkerboard artifacts on the yellow crayon); (d) using the local two-color prior of Bennett, Uyttendaele, Zitnick *et al.* (2006).

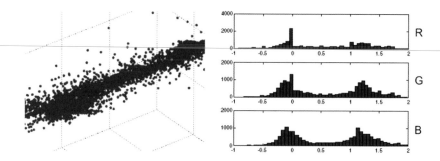

Figure 10.36 Two-color model computed from a collection of local 5×5 neighborhoods (Bennett, Uyttendaele, Zitnick *et al.* 2006) © 2006 Springer. After two-means clustering and reprojection along the line joining the two dominant colors (red dots), the majority of the pixels fall near the fitted line. The distribution along the line, projected along the RGB axes, is peaked at 0 and 1, the two dominant colors.

gradient information from the green channel, which is more reliable because it is sampled more densely, to infer plausible values for the red and blue channels, which are more sparsely sampled.

To reduce color fringing, some techniques perform a color space analysis, e.g., using median filtering on color opponent channels (Longere, Delahunt, Zhang *et al.* 2002). The approach of Bennett, Uyttendaele, Zitnick *et al.* (2006) locally forms a two-color model from an initial demosaicing result, using a moving 5×5 window to find the two dominant colors (Figure 10.36).[21]

Once the local color model has been estimated at each pixel, a Bayesian approach is then used to encourage pixel values to lie along each color line and to cluster around the dominant color values, which reduces halos (Figure 10.35d). The Bayesian approach also supports the simultaneous application of demosaicing and super-resolution, i.e., multiple CFA inputs can be merged into a higher-quality full-color image, which becomes more important as additional processing becomes incorporated into today's cameras.

10.3.2 *Application*: Colorization

Although not strictly an example of super-resolution, the process of *colorization*, i.e., manually adding colors to a "black and white" (grayscale) image, is another example of a sparse interpolation problem. In most applications of colorization, the user draws some scribbles indicating the desired colors in certain regions (Figure 10.37a) and the system interpolates the specified chrominance (u, v) values to the whole image, which are then re-combined with the input luminance channel to produce a final colorized image, as shown in Figure 10.37b. In the system developed by Levin, Lischinski, and Weiss (2004), the interpolation is performed using locally weighted regularization (3.100), where the local smoothness weights are inversely proportional to luminance gradients. This approach to locally weighted regularization has inspired later algorithms for high dynamic range tone mapping (Lischinski, Farbman, Uyttendaele *et al.* 2006a), see Section 10.2.1, as well as other applications of the weighted least

---

[21] Previous work on locally linear color models (Klinker, Shafer, and Kanade 1990; Omer and Werman 2004) focuses on color and illumination variation within a single material, whereas Bennett, Uyttendaele, Zitnick *et al.* (2006) use the two-color model to describe variations across color (material) edges.

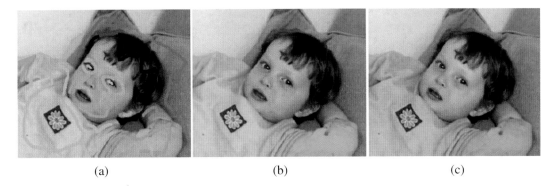

(a)   (b)   (c)

Figure 10.37 Colorization using optimization (Levin, Lischinski, and Weiss 2004) © 2004 ACM: (a) grayscale image some color scribbles overlaid; (b) resulting colorized image; (c) original color image from which the grayscale image and the chrominance values for the scribbles were derived. Original photograph by Rotem Weiss.

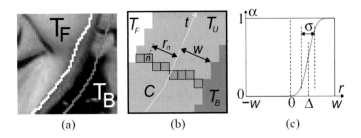

(a)   (b)   (c)

Figure 10.38 Softening a hard segmentation boundary (border matting) (Rother, Kolmogorov, and Blake 2004) © 2004 ACM: (a) the region surrounding a segmentation boundary where pixels of mixed foreground and background colors are visible; (b) pixel values along the boundary are used to compute a soft alpha matte; (c) at each point along the curve t, a displacement Δ and a width σ are estimated.

squares (WLS) formulation (Farbman, Fattal, Lischinski *et al.* 2008). An alternative approach to performing the sparse chrominance interpolation based on geodesic (edge-aware) distance functions has been developed by Yatziv and Sapiro (2006).

10.4 Image matting and compositing

Image matting and compositing is the process of cutting a foreground object out of one image and pasting it against a new background (Smith and Blinn 1996; Wang and Cohen 2007a). It is commonly used in television and film production to composite a live actor in front of computer-generated imagery such as weather maps or 3D virtual characters and scenery (Wright 2006; Brinkmann 2008).

We have already seen a number of tools for interactively segmenting objects in an image, including snakes (Section 5.1.1), scissors (Section 5.1.3), and GrabCut segmentation (Section 5.5). While these techniques can generate reasonable pixel-accurate segmentations, they fail to capture the subtle interplay of foreground and background colors at *mixed pixels* along the boundary (Szeliski and Golland 1999) (Figure 10.38a).

In order to successfully copy a foreground object from one image to another without

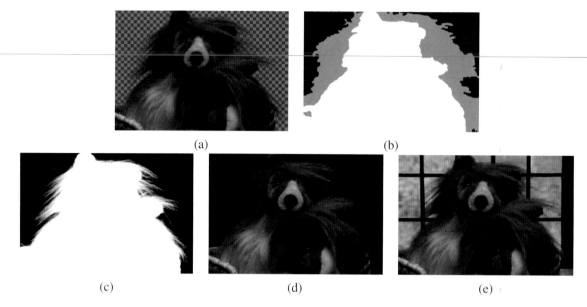

(a)   (b)

(c)   (d)   (e)

Figure 10.39 Natural image matting (Chuang, Curless, Salesin *et al.* 2001) © 2001 IEEE: (a) input image with a "natural" (non-constant) background; (b) hand-drawn trimap—gray indicates unknown regions; (c) extracted alpha map; (d) extracted (premultiplied) foreground colors; (e) composite over a new background.

visible discretization artifacts, we need to *pull a matte*, i.e., to estimate a soft opacity channel α and the uncontaminated foreground colors F from the input composite image C. Recall from Section 3.1.3 (Figure 3.4) that the compositing equation (3.8) can be written as

$$C = (1 - \alpha)B + \alpha F. \tag{10.30}$$

This operator attenuates the influence of the background image B by a factor $(1 - \alpha)$ and then adds in the (partial) color values corresponding to the foreground element F.

While the compositing operation is easy to implement, the reverse *matting* operation of estimating F, α, and B given an input image C is much more challenging (Figure 10.39). To see why, observe that while the composite pixel color C provides three measurements, the F, α, and B unknowns have a total of seven degrees of freedom. Devising techniques to estimate these unknowns despite the underconstrained nature of the problem is the essence of image matting.

In this section, we review a number of image matting techniques. We begin with *blue screen matting*, which assumes that the background is a constant known color, and discuss its variants, two-screen matting (when multiple backgrounds can be used) and difference matting (where the known background is arbitrary). We then discuss local variants of *natural image matting*, where both the foreground and background are unknown. In these applications, it is usual to first specify a *trimap*, i.e., a three-way labeling of the image into foreground, background, and unknown regions (Figure 10.39b). Next, we present some global optimization approaches to natural image matting. Finally, we discuss variants on the matting problem, including shadow matting, flash matting, and environment matting.

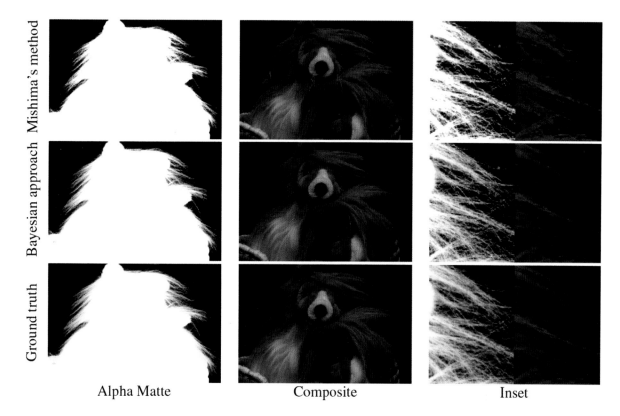

Figure 10.40 Blue-screen matting results (Chuang, Curless, Salesin *et al.* 2001) © 2001 IEEE. Mishima's method produces visible blue spill (color fringing in the hair), while Chuang's Bayesian matting approach produces accurate results.

10.4.1 Blue screen matting

Blue screen matting involves filming an actor (or object) in front of a constant colored background. While originally bright blue was the preferred color, bright green is now more commonly used (Wright 2006; Brinkmann 2008). Smith and Blinn (1996) discuss a number of techniques for blue screen matting, which are mostly described in patents rather than in the open research literature. Early techniques used linear combination of object color channels with user-tuned parameters to estimate the opacity α.

Chuang, Curless, Salesin *et al.* (2001) describe a newer technique called Mishima's algorithm, which involves fitting two polyhedral surfaces (centered at the mean background color), separating the foreground and background color distributions and then measuring the relative distance of a novel color to these surfaces to estimate α (Figure 10.41e). While this technique works well in many studio settings, it can still suffer from *blue spill*, where translucent pixels around the edges of an object acquire some of the background blue coloration (Figure 10.40).

Two-screen matting. In their paper, Smith and Blinn (1996) also introduce an algorithm called *triangulation matting* that uses more than one known background color to overconstrain the equations required to estimate the opacity α and foreground color F.

For example, consider in the compositing equation (10.30) setting the background color to black, i.e., $B = 0$. The resulting composite image C is therefore equal to αF. Replacing the background color with a different known non-zero value B now results in

$$C - \alpha F = (1 - \alpha)B, \qquad (10.31)$$

which is an overconstrained set of (color) equations for estimating α. In practice, B should be chosen so as not to saturate C and, for best accuracy, several values of B should be used. It is also important that colors be linearized before processing, which is the case for *all* image matting algorithms. Papers that generate ground truth alpha mattes for evaluation purposes normally use these techniques to obtain accurate matte estimates (Chuang, Curless, Salesin *et al.* 2001; Wang and Cohen 2007b; Levin, Acha, and Lischinski 2008; Rhemann, Rother, Rav-Acha *et al.* 2008; Rhemann, Rother, Wang *et al.* 2009).[22] Exercise 10.8 has you do this as well.

Difference matting. A related approach when the background is irregular but known is called *difference matting* (Wright 2006; Brinkmann 2008). It is most commonly used when the actor or object is filmed against a static background, e.g., for office videoconferencing, person tracking applications (Toyama, Krumm, Brumitt *et al.* 1999), or to produce silhouettes for volumetric 3D reconstruction techniques (Section 11.6.2) (Szeliski 1993; Seitz and Dyer 1997; Seitz, Curless, Diebel *et al.* 2006). It can also be used with a panning camera where the background is composited from frames where the foreground has been removed using a *garbage matte* (Section 10.4.5) (Chuang, Agarwala, Curless *et al.* 2002). Another recent application is the detection of visual continuity errors in films, i.e., differences in the background when a shot is re-taken at later time (Pickup and Zisserman 2009).

In the case where the foreground and background motions can both be specified with parametric transforms, high-quality mattes can be extracted using a generalization of triangulation matting (Wexler, Fitzgibbon, and Zisserman 2002). When frames need to be processed independently, however, the results are often of poor quality (Figure 10.42). In such cases, using a pair of stereo cameras as input can dramatically improve the quality of the results (Criminisi, Cross, Blake *et al.* 2006; Yin, Criminisi, Winn *et al.* 2007).

10.4.2 Natural image matting

The most general version of image matting is when nothing is known about the background except, perhaps, for a rough segmentation of the scene into foreground, background, and unknown regions, which is known as the *trimap* (Figure 10.39b). Some recent techniques, however, relax this requirement and allow the user to just draw a few strokes or scribbles in the image, see Figures 10.45 and 10.46 (Wang and Cohen 2005; Wang, Agrawala, and Cohen 2007; Levin, Lischinski, and Weiss 2008; Rhemann, Rother, Rav-Acha *et al.* 2008; Rhemann, Rother, and Gelautz 2008). Fully automated single image matting results have also been reported (Levin, Acha, and Lischinski 2008; Singaraju, Rother, and Rhemann 2009). The survey paper by Wang and Cohen (2007a) has detailed descriptions and comparisons of all of these techniques, a selection of which are described briefly below.

---

[22] See the alpha matting evaluation Web site at http://alphamatting.com/.

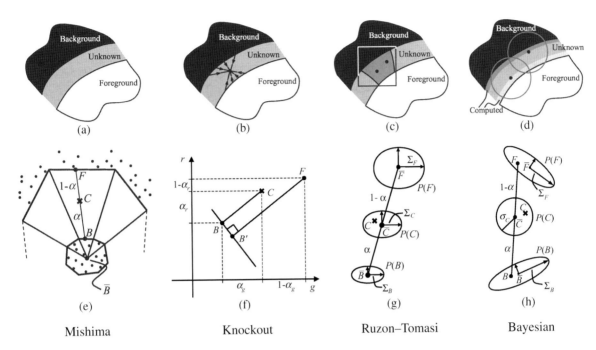

Mishima   Knockout   Ruzon–Tomasi   Bayesian

Figure 10.41 Image matting algorithms (Chuang, Curless, Salesin *et al.* 2001) © 2001 IEEE. Mishima's algorithm models global foreground and background color distribution as polyhedral surfaces centered around the mean background (blue) color. Knockout uses a local color estimate of foreground and background for each pixel and computes α along each color axis. Ruzon and Tomasi's algorithm locally models foreground and background colors and variances. Chuang *et al.*'s Bayesian matting approach computes a MAP estimate of (fractional) foreground color and opacity given the local foreground and background distributions.

A relatively simple algorithm for performing natural image matting is Knockout, as described by Chuang, Curless, Salesin *et al.* (2001) and illustrated in Figure 10.41f. In this algorithm, the nearest known foreground and background pixels (in image space) are determined and then blended with neighboring known pixels to produce a per-pixel foreground F and background B color estimate. The background color is then adjusted so that the measured color C lies on the line between F and B. Finally, opacity α is estimated on a per-channel basis, and the three estimates are combined based on per-channel color differences. (This is an approximation to the least squares solution for α.) Figure 10.42 shows that Knockout has problems when the background consists of more than one dominant local color.

More accurate matting results can be obtained if we treat the foreground and background colors as distributions sampled over some region (Figure 10.41g–h). Ruzon and Tomasi (2000) model local color distributions as mixtures of (uncorrelated) Gaussians and compute these models in strips. They then find the pairing of mixture components F and B that best describes the observed color C, compute the α as the relative distance between these means, and adjust the estimates of F and B so they are collinear with C.

Chuang, Curless, Salesin *et al.* (2001) and Hillman, Hannah, and Renshaw (2001) use full 3×3 color covariance matrices to model mixtures of correlated Gaussians, and compute estimates independently for each pixel. Matte extraction proceeds in strips starting from known color values growing into the unknown regions, so that recently computed F and B

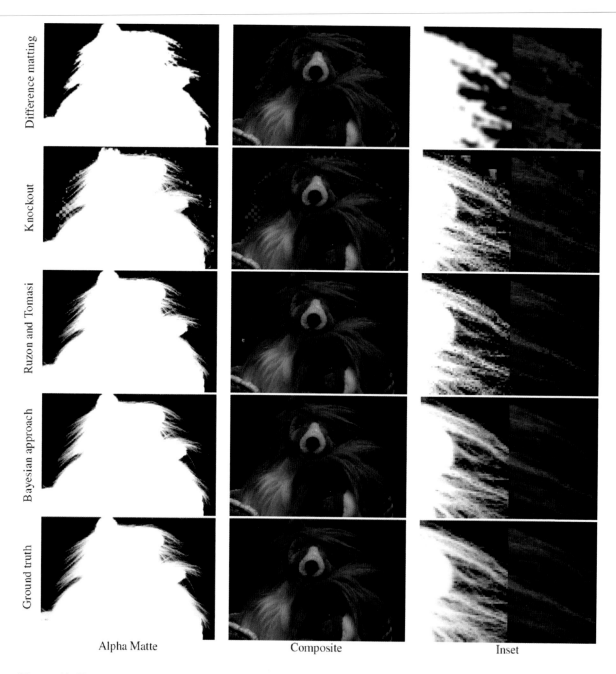

Figure 10.42   Natural image matting results (Chuang, Curless, Salesin *et al.* 2001) © 2001 IEEE. Difference matting and Knockout both perform poorly on this kind of background, while the more recent natural image matting techniques perform well. Chuang *et al.*'s results are slightly smoother and closer to the ground truth.

colors can be used in later stages.

To estimate the most likely value of an unknown pixel's opacity and (unmixed) foreground and background colors, Chuang *et al.* use a fully Bayesian formulation that maximizes

$$P(F, B, \alpha|C) = P(C|F, B, \alpha)P(F)P(B)P(\alpha)/P(C). \tag{10.32}$$

This is equivalent to minimizing the negative log likelihood

$$L(F, B, \alpha|C) = L(C|F, B, \alpha) + L(F) + L(B) + L(\alpha) \tag{10.33}$$

(dropping the $L(C)$ term since it is constant).

Let us examine each of these terms in turn. The first, $L(C|F, B, \alpha)$, is the likelihood that pixel color C was observed given values for the unknowns (F, B, α). If we assume Gaussian noise in our observation with variance σ_C^2, this negative log likelihood (data term) is

$$L(C) = {}^{1}\!/{}_{2}\|C - [\alpha F + (1 - \alpha)B]\|^2/\sigma_C^2, \tag{10.34}$$

as illustrated in Figure 10.41h.

The second term, $L(F)$, corresponds to the likelihood that a particular foreground color F comes from the mixture of Gaussians distribution. After partitioning the sample foreground colors into clusters, a weighted mean and covariance is computed, where the weights are proportional to a given foreground pixel's opacity and distance from the unknown pixel. The negative log likelihood for each cluster is thus given by

$$L(F) = (F - \overline{F})^T \Sigma_F^{-1} (F - \overline{F}). \tag{10.35}$$

A similar method is used to estimate unknown background color distributions. If the background is already known, i.e., for blue screen or difference matting applications, its measured color value and variance are used instead.

An alternative to modeling the foreground and background color distributions as mixtures of Gaussians is to keep around the original color samples and to compute the most likely pairings that explain the observed color C (Wang and Cohen 2005, 2007b). These techniques are described in more detail in (Wang and Cohen 2007a).

In their Bayesian matting paper, Chuang, Curless, Salesin *et al.* (2001) assume a constant (non-informative) distribution for $L(\alpha)$. More recent papers assume this distribution to be more peaked around 0 and 1, or sometimes use Markov random fields (MRFs) to define a global correlated prior on $P(\alpha)$ (Wang and Cohen 2007a).

To compute the most likely estimates for (F, B, α), the Bayesian matting algorithm alternates between computing (F, B) and α, since each of these problems is quadratic and hence can be solved as a small linear system. When several color clusters are estimated, the most likely pairing of foreground and background color clusters is used.

Bayesian image matting produces results that improve on the original natural image matting algorithm by Ruzon and Tomasi (2000), as can be seen in Figure 10.42. However, compared to more recent techniques (Wang and Cohen 2007a), its performance is not as good for complex background or inaccurate trimaps (Figure 10.44).

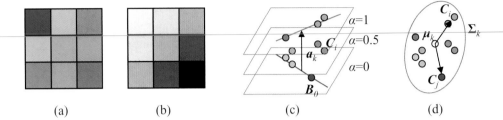

$$(a) \qquad\qquad (b) \qquad\qquad (c) \qquad\qquad (d)$$

Figure 10.43 Color line matting (Levin, Lischinski, and Weiss 2008): (a) local 3×3 patch of colors; (b) potential assignment of α values; (c) foreground and background color lines, the vector $\boldsymbol{a}_k$ joining their closest points of intersection, and the family of parallel planes of constant α values, $\alpha_i = \boldsymbol{a}_k \cdot (\boldsymbol{C}_i - \boldsymbol{B}_0)$; (d) a scatter plot of sample colors and the deviations from the mean μ_k for two sample colors $\boldsymbol{C}_i$ and $\boldsymbol{C}_j$.

10.4.3 Optimization-based matting

An alternative to estimating each pixel's opacity and foreground color independently is to use global optimization to compute a matte that takes into account correlations between neighboring α values. Two examples of this are border matting in the GrabCut interactive segmentation system (Rother, Kolmogorov, and Blake 2004) and Poisson Matting (Sun, Jia, Tang *et al.* 2004).

Border matting first dilates the region around the binary segmentation produced by Grab-Cut (Section 5.5) and then solves for a sub-pixel boundary location Δ and a blur width σ for every point along the boundary (Figure 10.38). Smoothness in these parameters along the boundary is enforced using regularization and the optimization is performed using dynamic programming. While this technique can obtain good results for smooth boundaries, such as a person's face, it has difficulty with fine details, such as hair.

Poisson matting (Sun, Jia, Tang *et al.* 2004) assumes a known foreground and background color for each pixel in the trimap (as with Bayesian matting). However, instead of independently estimating each α value, it assumes that the gradient of the alpha matte and the gradient of the color image are related by

$$\nabla\alpha = \frac{F - B}{\|F - B\|^2} \cdot \nabla C, \tag{10.36}$$

which can be derived by taking gradients of both sides of (10.30) and assuming that the foreground and background vary slowly. The per-pixel gradient estimates are then integrated into a continuous $\alpha(\boldsymbol{x})$ field using the regularization (least squares) technique first described in Section 3.7.1 (3.100) and subsequently used in Poisson blending (Section 9.3.4, 9.44) and gradient-based dynamic range compression mapping (Section 10.2.1, 10.19). This technique works well when good foreground and background color estimates are available and these colors vary slowly.

Instead of computing per-pixel foreground and background colors, Levin, Lischinski, and Weiss (2008) assume only that these color distribution can locally be well approximated as mixtures of two colors, which is known as the *color line model* (Figure 10.43a–c). Under this assumption, a closed-form estimate for α at each pixel i in a (say, 3×3) window W_k is given by

$$\alpha_i = \boldsymbol{a}_k \cdot (\boldsymbol{C}_i - \boldsymbol{B}_0) = \boldsymbol{a}_k \cdot \boldsymbol{C} + b_k, \tag{10.37}$$

where C_i is the pixel color treated as a three-vector, B_0 is any pixel along the background color line, and a_k is the vector joining the two closest points on the foreground and background color lines, as shown in Figure 10.43c. (Note that the geometric derivation shown in this figure is an alternative to the algebraic derivation presented by Levin, Lischinski, and Weiss (2008).) Minimizing the deviations of the alpha values α_i from their respective color line models (10.37) over all overlapping windows W_k in the image gives rise to the cost

$$E_\alpha = \sum_k \left(\sum_{i \in W_k} (\alpha_i - a_k \cdot C_i - b_k)^2 + \epsilon \|a_k\| \right), \tag{10.38}$$

where the ϵ term is used to regularize the value of a_k in the case where the two color distributions overlap (i.e., in constant α regions).

Because this formula is quadratic in the unknowns $\{(a_k, b_k)\}$, they can be eliminated inside each window W_k, leading to a final energy

$$E_\alpha = \alpha^T L \alpha, \tag{10.39}$$

where the entries in the L matrix are given by

$$L_{ij} = \sum_{k: i \in W_k \wedge j \in W_k} \left(\delta_{ij} - \frac{1}{M} \left(1 + (C_i - \mu_k)^T \hat{\Sigma}_k^{-1} (C_j - \mu_k) \right) \right), \tag{10.40}$$

where $M = |W_k|$ is the number of pixels in each (overlapping) window, μ_k is the mean color of the pixels in window W_k, and $\hat{\Sigma}_k$ is the 3×3 covariance of the pixel colors plus $\epsilon/_M I$.

Figure 10.43d shows the intuition behind the entries in this affinity matrix, which is called the *matting Laplacian*. Note how when two pixels C_i and C_j in W_k point in opposite directions away from the mean μ_k, their weighted dot product is close to -1, and so their affinity becomes close to 0. Pixels close to each other in color space (and hence with similar expected α values) will have affinities close to $-2/M$.

Minimizing the quadratic energy (10.39) constrained by the known values of $\alpha = \{0, 1\}$ at scribbles only requires the solution of a sparse set of linear equations, which is why the authors call their technique a *closed-form solution* to natural image matting. Once α has been computed, the foreground and background colors are estimated using a least squares minimization of the compositing equation (10.30) regularized with a spatially varying first-order smoothness,

$$E_{B,F} = \sum_i \|C_i - [\alpha + F_i + (1 - \alpha_i) B_i]\|^2 + \lambda |\nabla \alpha_i| (\|\nabla F_i\|^2 + \|\nabla B_i\|^2), \tag{10.41}$$

where the $|\nabla \alpha_i|$ weight is applied separately for the x and y components of the F and B derivatives (Levin, Lischinski, and Weiss 2008).

Laplacian (closed-form) matting is just one of many optimization-based techniques surveyed and compared by Wang and Cohen (2007a). Some of these techniques use alternative formulations for the affinities or smoothness terms on the α matte, alternative estimation techniques such as belief propagation, or alternative representations (e.g., local histograms) for modeling local foreground and background color distributions (Wang and Cohen 2005, 2007b,c). Some of these techniques also provide real-time results as the user draws a contour

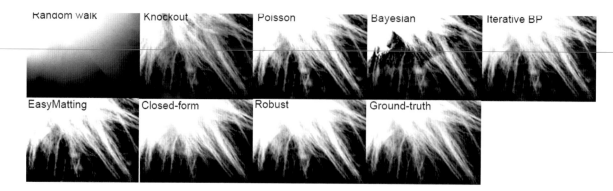

Figure 10.44 Comparative matting results for a medium accuracy trimap. Wang and Cohen (2007a) describe the individual techniques being compared.

line or sparse set of scribbles (Wang, Agrawala, and Cohen 2007; Rhemann, Rother, Rav-Acha *et al.* 2008) or even pre-segment the image into a small number of mattes that the user can select with simple clicks (Levin, Acha, and Lischinski 2008).

Figure 10.44 shows the results of running a number of the surveyed algorithms on a region of toy animal fur where a trimap has been specified, while Figure 10.45 shows results for techniques that can produce mattes with only a few scribbles as input. Figure 10.46 shows a result for an even more recent algorithm (Rhemann, Rother, Rav-Acha *et al.* 2008) that claims to outperform all of the techniques surveyed by Wang and Cohen (2007a).

Pasting. Once a matte has been pulled from an image, it is usually composited directly over the new background, unless the seams between the cutout and background regions are to be hidden, in which case Poisson blending (Pérez, Gangnet, and Blake 2003) can be used (Section 9.3.4).

In the latter case, it is helpful if the matte boundary passes through regions that either have little texture or look similar in the old and new images. Papers by Jia, Sun, Tang *et al.* (2006) and Wang and Cohen (2007c) explain how to do this.

10.4.4 Smoke, shadow, and flash matting

In addition to matting out solid objects with fractional boundaries, it is also possible to matte out translucent media such as smoke (Chuang, Agarwala, Curless *et al.* 2002). Starting with a video sequence, each pixel is modeled as a linear combination of its (unknown) background color and a constant foreground (smoke) color that is common to all pixels. Voting in color space is used to estimate this foreground color and the distance along each color line is used to estimate the per-pixel temporally varying alpha (Figure 10.47).

Extracting and re-inserting shadows is also possible using a related technique (Chuang, Goldman, Curless *et al.* 2003). Here, instead of assuming a constant foreground color, each pixel is assumed to vary between its fully lit and fully shadowed colors, which can be estimated by taking (robust) minimum and maximum values over time as a shadow passes over the scene (Exercise 10.9). The resulting fractional *shadow matte* can be used to re-project the shadow into a new scene. If the destination scene has a non-planar geometry, it can be

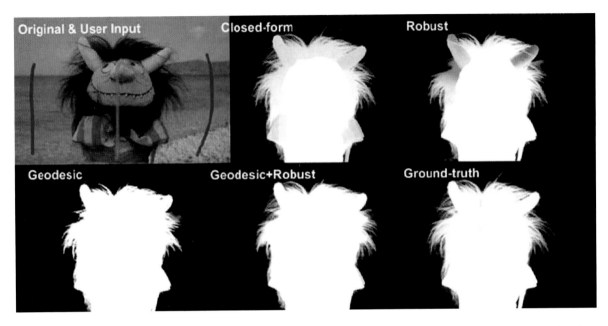

Figure 10.45 Comparative matting results with scribble-based inputs. Wang and Cohen (2007a) describe the individual techniques being compared.

Figure 10.46 Stroke-based segmentation result (Rhemann, Rother, Rav-Acha *et al.* 2008) © 2008 IEEE.

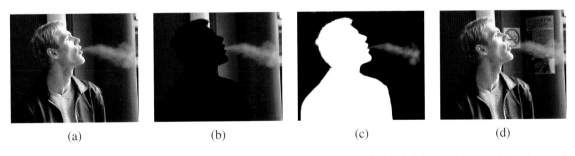

(a)   (b)   (c)   (d)

Figure 10.47 Smoke matting (Chuang, Agarwala, Curless *et al.* 2002) © 2002 ACM: (a) input video frame; (b) after removing the foreground object; (c) estimated alpha matte; (d) insertion of new objects into the background.

| (a) Foreground scene | (b) Background scene | (c) Blue screen composite | (d) Our method | (e) Reference photograph |

Figure 10.48 Shadow matting (Chuang, Goldman, Curless *et al.* 2003) © 2003 ACM. Instead of simply darkening the new scene with the shadow (c), shadow matting correctly dims the lit scene with the new shadow and drapes the shadow over 3D geometry (d).

scanned by waving a straight stick shadow across the scene. The new shadow matte can then be warped with the computed deformation field to have it drape correctly over the new scene (Figure 10.48).

The quality and reliability of matting algorithms can also be enhanced using more sophisticated acquisition systems. For example, taking a flash and non-flash image pair supports the reliable extraction of foreground mattes, which show up as regions of large illumination change between the two images (Sun, Li, Kang *et al.* 2006). Taking simultaneous video streams focused at different distances (McGuire, Matusik, Pfister *et al.* 2005) or using multi-camera arrays (Joshi, Matusik, and Avidan 2006) are also good approaches to producing high-quality mattes. These techniques are described in more detail in (Wang and Cohen 2007a).

Lastly, photographing a refractive object in front of a number of patterned backgrounds allows the object to be placed in novel 3D environments. These environment matting techniques (Zongker, Werner, Curless *et al.* 1999; Chuang, Zongker, Hindorff *et al.* 2000) are discussed in Section 13.4.

10.4.5 Video matting

While regular single-frame matting techniques such as blue or green screen matting (Smith and Blinn 1996; Wright 2006; Brinkmann 2008) can be applied to video sequences, the presence of moving objects can sometimes make the matting process easier, as portions of the background may get revealed in preceding or subsequent frames.

Chuang, Agarwala, Curless *et al.* (2002) describe a nice approach to this *video matting* problem, where foreground objects are first removed using a conservative *garbage matte* and the resulting *background plates* are aligned and composited to yield a high-quality background estimate. They also describe how trimaps drawn at sparse keyframes can be interpolated to in-between frames using bi-direction optic flow. Alternative approaches to video matting, such as rotoscoping, which involves drawing and tracking curves in video sequences (Agarwala, Hertzmann, Seitz *et al.* 2004), are discussed in the matting survey paper by Wang and Cohen (2007a).

radishes

lots more radishes

rocks

yogurt

(a) (b) (c)

Figure 10.49 Texture synthesis: (a) given a small patch of texture, the task is to synthesize (b) a similar-looking larger patch; (c) other semi-structured textures that are challenging to synthesize. (Images courtesy of Alyosha Efros.)

10.5 Texture analysis and synthesis

While texture analysis and synthesis may not at first seem like computational photography techniques, they are, in fact, widely used to repair defects, such as small holes, in images or to create non-photorealistic painterly renderings from regular photographs.

The problem of texture synthesis can be formulated as follows: given a small sample of a "texture" (Figure 10.49a), generate a larger similar-looking image (Figure 10.49b). As you can imagine, for certain sample textures, this problem can be quite challenging.

Traditional approaches to texture analysis and synthesis try to match the spectrum of the source image while generating shaped noise. Matching the frequency characteristics, which is equivalent to matching spatial correlations, is in itself not sufficient. The distributions of the responses at different frequencies must also match. Heeger and Bergen (1995) develop an algorithm that alternates between matching the histograms of multi-scale (steerable pyramid) responses and matching the final image histogram. Portilla and Simoncelli (2000) improve on this technique by also matching pairwise statistics across scale and orientations. De Bonet (1997) uses a coarse-to-fine strategy to find locations in the source texture with a similar *parent structure*, i.e., similar multi-scale oriented filter responses, and then randomly chooses one of these matching locations as the current sample value.

More recent texture synthesis algorithms sequentially generate texture pixels by looking for neighborhoods in the source texture that are similar to the currently synthesized image (Efros and Leung 1999). Consider the (as yet) unknown pixel p in the partially constructed texture on the left side of Figure 10.50. Since some of its neighboring pixels have been

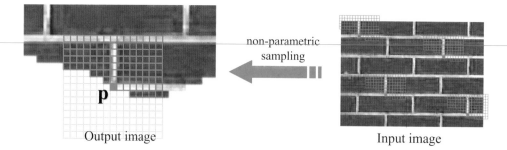

Figure 10.50 Texture synthesis using non-parametric sampling (Efros and Leung 1999). The value of the newest pixel p is randomly chosen from similar local (partial) patches in the source texture (input image). (Figure courtesy of Alyosha Efros.)

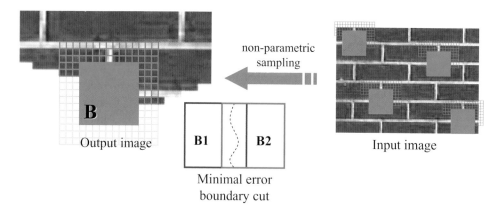

Figure 10.51 Texture synthesis by image quilting (Efros and Freeman 2001). Instead of generating a single pixel at a time, larger blocks are copied from the source texture. The transitions in the overlap regions between the selected blocks are then optimized using dynamic programming. (Figure courtesy of Alyosha Efros.)

already been synthesized, we can look for similar partial neighborhoods in the sample texture image on the right and randomly select one of these as the new value of p. This process can be repeated down the new image either in a raster fashion or by scanning around the periphery ("onion peeling") when filling holes, as discussed in (Section 10.5.1). In their actual implementation, Efros and Leung (1999) find the most similar neighborhood and then include all other neighborhoods within a $d = (1 + \epsilon)$ distance, with $\epsilon = 0.1$. They also optionally weight the random pixel selections by the similarity metric d.

To accelerate this process and improve its visual quality, Wei and Levoy (2000) extend this technique using a coarse-to-fine generation process, where coarser levels of the pyramid, which have already been synthesized, are also considered during the matching (De Bonet 1997). To accelerate the nearest neighbor finding, tree-structured vector quantization is used.

Efros and Freeman (2001) propose an alternative acceleration and visual quality improvement technique. Instead of synthesizing a single pixel at a time, overlapping square blocks are selected using similarity with previously synthesized regions (Figure 10.51). Once the appropriate blocks have been selected, the seam between newly overlapping blocks is determined using dynamic programming. (Full graph cut seam selection is not required, since only

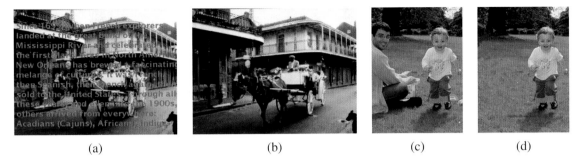

(a)   (b)   (c)   (d)

Figure 10.52 Image inpainting (hole filling): (a–b) propagation along isophote directions (Bertalmio, Sapiro, Caselles *et al.* 2000) © 2000 ACM; (c–d) exemplar-based inpainting with confidence-based filling order (Criminisi, Pérez, and Toyama 2004).

one seam location per row is needed for a vertical boundary.) Because this process involves selecting small patches and them stitching them together, Efros and Freeman (2001) call their system *image quilting*. Komodakis and Tziritas (2007b) present an MRF-based version of this block synthesis algorithm that uses a new, efficient version of loopy belief propagation they call "Priority-BP".

10.5.1 *Application*: Hole filling and inpainting

Filling holes left behind when objects or defects are excised from photographs, which is known as *inpainting*, is one of the most common applications of texture synthesis. Such techniques are used not only to remove unwanted people or interlopers from photographs (King 1997) but also to fix small defects in old photos and movies (*scratch removal*) or to remove wires holding props or actors in mid-air during filming (*wire removal*). Bertalmio, Sapiro, Caselles *et al.* (2000) solve the problem by propagating pixel values along isophote (constant-value) directions interleaved with some anisotropic diffusion steps (Figure 10.52a–b). Telea (2004) develops a faster technique that uses the fast marching method from level sets (Section 5.1.4). However, these techniques will not hallucinate texture in the missing regions. Bertalmio, Vese, Sapiro *et al.* (2003) augment their earlier technique by adding synthetic texture to the infilled regions.

The example-based (non-parametric) texture generation techniques discussed in the previous section can also be used by filling the holes from the outside in (the "onion-peel" ordering). However, this approach may fail to propagate strong oriented structures. Criminisi, Pérez, and Toyama (2004) use exemplar-based texture synthesis where the order of synthesis is determined by the strength of the gradient along the region boundary (Figures 10.1d and 10.52c–d). Sun, Yuan, Jia *et al.* (2004) present a related approach where the user draws interactive lines to indicate where structures should be preferentially propagated. Additional techniques related to these approaches include those developed by Drori, Cohen-Or, and Yeshurun (2003), Kwatra, Schödl, Essa *et al.* (2003), Kwatra, Essa, Bobick *et al.* (2005), Wilczkowiak, Brostow, Tordoff *et al.* (2005), Komodakis and Tziritas (2007b), and Wexler, Shechtman, and Irani (2007).

Most hole filling algorithms borrow small pieces of the original image to fill in the holes. When a large database of source images is available, e.g., when images are taken from a

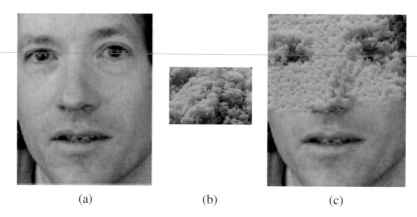

(a)   (b)   (c)

Figure 10.53 Texture transfer (Efros and Freeman 2001) © 2001 ACM: (a) reference (target) image; (b) source texture; (c) image (partially) rendered using the texture.

photo sharing site or the Internet, it is sometimes possible to copy a single contiguous image region to fill the hole. Hays and Efros (2007) present such a technique, which uses image context and boundary compatibility to select the source image, which is then blended with the original (holey) image using graph cuts and Poisson blending. This technique is discussed in more detail in Section 14.4.4 and Figure 14.46.

10.5.2 *Application*: Non-photorealistic rendering

Two more applications of the exemplar-based texture synthesis ideas are texture transfer (Efros and Freeman 2001) and image analogies (Hertzmann, Jacobs, Oliver *et al.* 2001), which are both examples of non-photorealistic rendering (Gooch and Gooch 2001).

In addition to using a source texture image, texture transfer also takes a reference (or target) image, and tries to match certain characteristics of the target image with the newly synthesized image. For example, the new image being rendered in Figure 10.53c not only tries to satisfy the usual similarity constraints with the source texture in Figure 10.53b, but it also tries to match the luminance characteristics of the reference image. Efros and Freeman (2001) mention that blurred image intensities or local image orientation angles are alternative quantities that could be matched.

Hertzmann, Jacobs, Oliver *et al.* (2001) formulate the following problem:

> Given a pair of images A and A' (the unfiltered and filtered source images, respectively), along with some additional unfiltered target image B, synthesize a new filtered target image B' such that

$$A : A' :: B : B'.$$

Instead of having the user program a certain non-photorealistic rendering effect, it is sufficient to supply the system with examples of before and after images, and let the system synthesize the novel image using exemplar-based synthesis, as shown in Figure 10.54.

The algorithm used to solve image analogies proceeds in a manner analogous to the texture synthesis algorithms of (Efros and Leung 1999; Wei and Levoy 2000). Once Gaussian pyramids have been computed for all of the source and reference images, the algorithm

A A' B B'

Figure 10.54 Image analogies (Hertzmann, Jacobs, Oliver *et al.* 2001) © 2001 ACM. Given an example pair of a source image A and its rendered (filtered) version A', generate the rendered version B' from another unfiltered source image B.

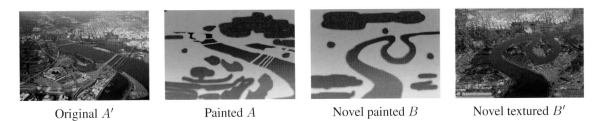

Original A' Painted A Novel painted B Novel textured B'

Figure 10.55 Texture-by-numbers (Hertzmann, Jacobs, Oliver *et al.* 2001) © 2001 ACM. Given a textured image A' and a hand-labeled (painted) version A, synthesize a new image B' given just the painted version B.

looks for neighborhoods in the source filtered pyramids generated from A' that are similar to the partially constructed neighborhood in B', while at the same time having similar multi-resolution appearances at corresponding locations in A and B. As with texture transfer, appearance characteristics can include not only (blurred) color or luminance values but also orientations.

This general framework allows image analogies to be applied to a variety of rendering tasks. In addition to exemplar-based non-photorealistic rendering, image analogies can be used for traditional texture synthesis, super-resolution, and texture transfer (using the same textured image for both A and A'). If only the filtered (rendered) image A' is available, as is the case with paintings, the missing reference image A can be hallucinated using a smart (edge preserving) blur operator. Finally, it is possible to train a system to perform *texture-by-numbers* by manually painting over a natural image with pseudocolors corresponding to pixels' semantic meanings, e.g., water, trees, and grass (Figure 10.55a–b). The resulting system can then convert a novel sketch into a fully rendered synthetic photograph (Figure 10.55c–d). In more recent work, Cheng, Vishwanathan, and Zhang (2008) add ideas from image quilting (Efros and Freeman 2001) and MRF inference (Komodakis, Tziritas, and Paragios 2008) to the basic image analogies algorithm, while Ramanarayanan and Bala (2007) recast this process as energy minimization, which means it can also be viewed as a conditional random field (Section 3.7.2), and devise an efficient algorithm to find a good minimum.

More traditional filtering and feature detection techniques can also be used for non-photorealistic rendering.[23] For example, pen-and-ink illustration (Winkenbach and Salesin

---

[23] For a good selection of papers, see the Symposia on Non-Photorealistic Animation and Rendering (NPAR) at http://www.npar.org/.

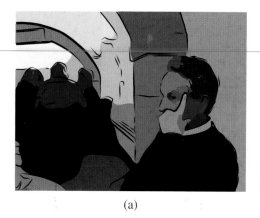 

(a)   (b)

Figure 10.56 Non-photorealistic abstraction of photographs: (a) DeCarlo and Santella (2002) © 2002 ACM and (b) Farbman, Fattal, Lischinski *et al.* (2008) © 2008 ACM.

1994) and painterly rendering techniques (Litwinowicz 1997) use local color, intensity, and orientation estimates as an input to their procedural rendering algorithms. Techniques for stylizing and simplifying photographs and video (DeCarlo and Santella 2002; Winnemöller, Olsen, and Gooch 2006; Farbman, Fattal, Lischinski *et al.* 2008), as in Figure 10.56, use combinations of edge-preserving blurring (Section 3.3.1) and edge detection and enhancement (Section 4.2.3).

10.6 Additional reading

A good overview of computational photography can be found in the book by Raskar and Tumblin (2010), survey articles by Nayar (2006), Cohen and Szeliski (2006), Levoy (2006), Debevec (2006), and Hayes (2008), as well as two special journal issues edited by Bimber (2006) and Durand and Szeliski (2007). Notes from the courses on computational photography mentioned at the beginning of this chapter are another great source of material and references.[24]

The sub-field of high dynamic range imaging has its own book discussing research in this area (Reinhard, Ward, Pattanaik *et al.* 2005), as well as some books describing related photographic techniques (Freeman 2008; Gulbins and Gulbins 2009). Algorithms for calibrating the radiometric response function of a camera can be found in articles by Mann and Picard (1995), Debevec and Malik (1997), and Mitsunaga and Nayar (1999).

The subject of tone mapping is treated extensively in (Reinhard, Ward, Pattanaik *et al.* 2005). Representative papers from the large volume of literature on this topic include those by Tumblin and Rushmeier (1993), Larson, Rushmeier, and Piatko (1997), Pattanaik, Ferwerda, Fairchild *et al.* (1998), Tumblin and Turk (1999), Durand and Dorsey (2002), Fattal, Lischinski, and Werman (2002), Reinhard, Stark, Shirley *et al.* (2002), Lischinski, Farbman, Uyttendaele *et al.* (2006b), and Farbman, Fattal, Lischinski *et al.* (2008).

---

[24] MIT 6.815/6.865, http://stellar.mit.edu/S/course/6/sp08/6.815/materials.html, CMU 15-463, http://graphics.cs.cmu.edu/courses/15-463/2008_fall/, Stanford CS 448A, http://graphics.stanford.edu/courses/cs448a-08-spring/, and SIGGRAPH courses, http://web.media.mit.edu/~raskar/photo/.

The literature on super-resolution is quite extensive (Chaudhuri 2001; Park, Park, and Kang 2003; Capel and Zisserman 2003; Capel 2004; van Ouwerkerk 2006). The term super-resolution usually describes techniques for aligning and merging multiple images to produce higher-resolution composites (Keren, Peleg, and Brada 1988; Irani and Peleg 1991; Cheeseman, Kanefsky, Hanson *et al.* 1993; Mann and Picard 1994; Chiang and Boult 1996; Bascle, Blake, and Zisserman 1996; Capel and Zisserman 1998; Smelyanskiy, Cheeseman, Maluf *et al.* 2000; Capel and Zisserman 2000; Pickup, Capel, Roberts *et al.* 2009; Gulbins and Gulbins 2009). However, single-image super-resolution techniques have also been developed (Freeman, Jones, and Pasztor 2002; Baker and Kanade 2002; Fattal 2007).

A good survey on image matting is given by Wang and Cohen (2007a). Representative papers, which include extensive comparisons with previous work, include those by Chuang, Curless, Salesin *et al.* (2001), Wang and Cohen (2007b), Levin, Acha, and Lischinski (2008), Rhemann, Rother, Rav-Acha *et al.* (2008), and Rhemann, Rother, Wang *et al.* (2009).

The literature on texture synthesis and hole filling includes traditional approaches to texture synthesis, which try to match image statistics between source and destination images (Heeger and Bergen 1995; De Bonet 1997; Portilla and Simoncelli 2000), as well as newer approaches, which search for matching neighborhoods or patches inside the source sample (Efros and Leung 1999; Wei and Levoy 2000; Efros and Freeman 2001). In a similar vein, traditional approaches to hole filling involve the solution of local variational (smooth continuation) problems (Bertalmio, Sapiro, Caselles *et al.* 2000; Bertalmio, Vese, Sapiro *et al.* 2003; Telea 2004). More recent techniques use data-driven texture synthesis approaches (Drori, Cohen-Or, and Yeshurun 2003; Kwatra, Schödl, Essa *et al.* 2003; Criminisi, Pérez, and Toyama 2004; Sun, Yuan, Jia *et al.* 2004; Kwatra, Essa, Bobick *et al.* 2005; Wilczkowiak, Brostow, Tordoff *et al.* 2005; Komodakis and Tziritas 2007b; Wexler, Shechtman, and Irani 2007).

10.7 Exercises

Ex 10.1: Radiometric calibration Implement one of the multi-exposure radiometric calibration algorithms described in Section 10.2 (Debevec and Malik 1997; Mitsunaga and Nayar 1999; Reinhard, Ward, Pattanaik *et al.* 2005). This calibration will be useful in a number of different applications, such as stitching images or stereo matching with different exposures and shape from shading.

1. Take a series of bracketed images with your camera on a tripod. If your camera has an automatic exposure bracketing (AEB) mode, taking three images may be sufficient to calibrate most of your camera's dynamic range, especially if your scene has a lot of bright and dark regions. (Shooting outdoors or through a window on a sunny day is best.)

2. If your images are not taken on a tripod, first perform a global alignment (similarity transform).

3. Estimate the radiometric response function using one of the techniques cited above.

4. Estimate the high dynamic range radiance image by selecting or blending pixels from

different exposures (Debevec and Malik 1997; Mitsunaga and Nayar 1999; Eden, Uyttendaele, and Szeliski 2006).

5. Repeat your calibration experiments under different conditions, e.g., indoors under incandescent light, to get a sense for the range of color balancing effects that your camera imposes.

6. If your camera supports RAW and JPEG mode, calibrate both sets of images simultaneously and to each other (the radiance at each pixel will correspond). See if you can come up with a model for what your camera does, e.g., whether it treats color balance as a diagonal or full 3×3 matrix multiply, whether it uses non-linearities in addition to gamma, whether it sharpens the image while "developing" the JPEG image, etc.

7. Develop an interactive viewer to change the exposure of an image based on the average exposure of a region around the mouse. (One variant is to show the adjusted image inside a window around the mouse. Another is to adjust the complete image based on the mouse position.)

8. Implement a tone mapping operator (Exercise 10.5) and use this to map your radiance image to a displayable gamut.

Ex 10.2: Noise level function Determine your camera's noise level function using either multiple shots or by analyzing smooth regions.

1. Set up your camera on a tripod looking at a calibration target or a static scene with a good variation in input levels and colors. (Check your camera's histogram to ensure that all values are being sampled.)

2. Take repeated images of the same scene (ideally with a remote shutter release) and average them to compute the variance at each pixel. Discarding pixels near high gradients (which are affected by camera motion), plot for each color channel the standard deviation at each pixel as a function of its output value.

3. Fit a lower envelope to these measurements and use this as your noise level function. How much variation do you see in the noise as a function of input level? How much of this is significant, i.e., away from flat regions in your camera response function where you do not want to be sampling anyway?

4. (Optional) Using the same images, develop a technique that segments the image into near-constant regions (Liu, Szeliski, Kang *et al.* 2008). (This is easier if you are photographing a calibration chart.) Compute the deviations for each region from a *single* image and use them to estimate the NLF. How does this compare to the multi-image technique, and how stable are your estimates from image to image?

Ex 10.3: Vignetting Estimate the amount of vignetting in some of your lenses using one of the following three techniques (or devise one of your choosing):

1. Take an image of a large uniform intensity region (well-illuminated wall or blue sky—but be careful of brightness gradients) and fit a radial polynomial curve to estimate the vignetting.

2. Construct a center-weighted panorama and compare these pixel values to the input image values to estimate the vignetting function. Weight pixels in slowly varying regions more highly, as small misalignments will give large errors at high gradients. Optionally estimate the radiometric response function as well (Litvinov and Schechner 2005; Goldman 2011).

3. Analyze the radial gradients (especially in low-gradient regions) and fit the robust means of these gradients to the derivative of the vignetting function, as described by Zheng, Yu, Kang *et al.* (2008).

For the parametric form of your vignetting function, you can either use a simple radial function, e.g.,

$$f(r) = 1 + \alpha_1 r + \alpha_2 r^2 + \cdots \tag{10.42}$$

or one of the specialized equations developed by Kang and Weiss (2000) and Zheng, Lin, and Kang (2006).

In all of these cases, be sure that you are using linearized intensity measurements, by using either RAW images or images linearized through a radiometric response function, or at least images where the gamma curve has been removed.

(Optional) What happens if you forget to undo the gamma before fitting a (multiplicative) vignetting function?

Ex 10.4: Optical blur (PSF) estimation Compute the optical PSF either using a known target (Figure 10.7) or by detecting and fitting step edges (Section 10.1.4) (Joshi, Szeliski, and Kriegman 2008).

1. Detect strong edges to sub-pixel precision.

2. Fit a local profile to each oriented edge and fill these pixels into an ideal target image, either at image resolution or at a higher resolution (Figure 10.9c–d).

3. Use least squares (10.1) at valid pixels to estimate the PSF kernel K, either globally or in locally overlapping sub-regions of the image.

4. Visualize the recovered PSFs and use them to remove chromatic aberration or de-blur the image.

Ex 10.5: Tone mapping Implement one of the tone mapping algorithms discussed in Section 10.2.1 (Durand and Dorsey 2002; Fattal, Lischinski, and Werman 2002; Reinhard, Stark, Shirley *et al.* 2002; Lischinski, Farbman, Uyttendaele *et al.* 2006b) or any of the numerous additional algorithms discussed by Reinhard, Ward, Pattanaik *et al.* (2005) and http://stellar.mit.edu/S/course/6/sp08/6.815/materials.html.

(Optional) Compare your algorithm to local histogram equalization (Section 3.1.4).

Ex 10.6: Flash enhancement Develop an algorithm to combine flash and non-flash photographs to best effect. You can use ideas from Eisemann and Durand (2004) and Petschnigg, Agrawala, Hoppe *et al.* (2004) or anything else you think might work well.

Ex 10.7: Super-resolution Implement one or more super-resolution algorithms and compare their performance.

1. Take a set of photographs of the same scene using a hand-held camera (to ensure that there is some jitter between the photographs).

2. Determine the PSF for the images you are trying to super-resolve using one of the techniques in Exercise 10.4.

3. Alternatively, simulate a collection of lower-resolution images by taking a high-quality photograph (avoid those with compression artifacts) and applying your own pre-filter kernel and downsampling.

4. Estimate the relative motion between the images using a parametric translation and rotation motion estimation algorithm (Sections 6.1.3 or 8.2).

5. Implement a basic least squares super-resolution algorithm by minimizing the difference between the observed and downsampled images (10.27–10.28).

6. Add in a gradient image prior, either as another least squares term or as a robust term that can be minimized using iteratively reweighted least squares (Appendix A.3).

7. (Optional) Implement one of the example-based super-resolution techniques, where matching against a set of exemplar images is used either to infer higher-frequency information to be added to the reconstruction (Freeman, Jones, and Pasztor 2002) or higher-frequency gradients to be matched in the super-resolved image (Baker and Kanade 2002).

8. (Optional) Use local edge statistic information to improve the quality of the super-resolved image (Fattal 2007).

Ex 10.8: Image matting Develop an algorithm for pulling a foreground matte from natural images, as described in Section 10.4.

1. Make sure that the images you are taking are linearized (Exercise 10.1 and Section 10.1) and that your camera exposure is fixed (full manual mode), at least when taking multiple shots of the same scene.

2. To acquire ground truth data, place your object in front of a computer monitor and display a variety of solid background colors as well as some natural imagery.

3. Remove your object and re-display the same images to acquire known background colors.

4. Use triangulation matting (Smith and Blinn 1996) to estimate the ground truth opacities α and pre-multiplied foreground colors αF for your objects.

5. Implement one or more of the natural image matting algorithms described in Section 10.4 and compare your results to the ground truth values you computed. Alternatively, use the matting test images published on http://alphamatting.com/.

6. (Optional) Run your algorithms on other images taken with the same calibrated camera (or other images you find interesting).

Ex 10.9: Smoke and shadow matting Extract smoke or shadow mattes from one scene and insert them into another (Chuang, Agarwala, Curless *et al.* 2002; Chuang, Goldman, Curless *et al.* 2003).

1. Take a still or video sequence of images with and without some intermittent smoke and shadows. (Remember to linearize your images before proceeding with any computations.)

2. For each pixel, fit a line to the observed color values.

3. If performing smoke matting, robustly compute the intersection of these lines to obtain the smoke color estimate. Then, estimate the background color as the other extremum (unless you already took a smoke-free background image).

    If performing shadow matting, compute robust shadow (minimum) and lit (maximum) values for each pixel.

4. Extract the smoke or shadow mattes from each frame as the fraction between these two values (background and smoke or shadowed and lit).

5. Scan a new (destination) scene or modify the original background with an image editor.

6. Re-insert the smoke or shadow matte, along with any other foreground objects you may have extracted.

7. (Optional) Using a series of cast stick shadows, estimate the deformation field for the destination scene in order to correctly warp (drape) the shadows across the new geometry. (This is related to the shadow scanning technique developed by Bouguet and Perona (1999) and implemented in Exercise 12.2.)

8. (Optional) Chuang, Goldman, Curless *et al.* (2003) only demonstrated their technique for planar source geometries. Can you extend their technique to capture shadows acquired from an irregular source geometry?

9. (Optional) Can you change the direction of the shadow, i.e., simulate the effect of changing the light source direction?

Ex 10.10: Texture synthesis Implement one of the texture synthesis or hole filling algorithms presented in Section 10.5. Here is one possible procedure:

1. Implement the basic Efros and Leung (1999) algorithm, i.e., starting from the outside (for hole filling) or in raster order (for texture synthesis), search for a similar neighborhood in the source texture image, and copy that pixel.

2. Add in the Wei and Levoy (2000) extension of generating the pixels in a coarse-to-fine fashion, i.e., generate a lower-resolution synthetic texture (or filled image), and use this as a guide for matching regions in the finer resolution version.

3. Add in the Criminisi, Pérez, and Toyama (2004) idea of prioritizing pixels to be filled by some function of the local structure (gradient or orientation strength).

4. Extend any of the above algorithms by selecting sub-blocks in the source texture and using optimization to determine the seam between the new block and the existing image that it overlaps (Efros and Freeman 2001).

5. (Optional) Implement one of the isophote (smooth continuation) inpainting algorithms (Bertalmio, Sapiro, Caselles *et al.* 2000; Telea 2004).

6. (Optional) Add the ability to supply a target (reference) image (Efros and Freeman 2001) or to provide sample filtered or unfiltered (reference and rendered) images (Hertzmann, Jacobs, Oliver *et al.* 2001), see Section 10.5.2.

Ex 10.11: Colorization   Implement the Levin, Lischinski, and Weiss (2004) colorization algorithm that is sketched out in Section 10.3.2 and Figure 10.37. Find some historic monochrome photographs and some modern color ones. Write an interactive tool that lets you "pick" colors from a modern photo and paint over the old one. Tune the algorithm parameters to give you good results. Are you pleased with the results? Can you think of ways to make them look more "antique", e.g., with softer (less saturated and edgy) colors?

Chapter 11

Stereo correspondence

R. Szeliski, *Computer Vision: Algorithms and Applications*, Texts in Computer Science,
DOI 10.1007/978-1-84882-935-0_11, © Springer-Verlag London Limited 2011

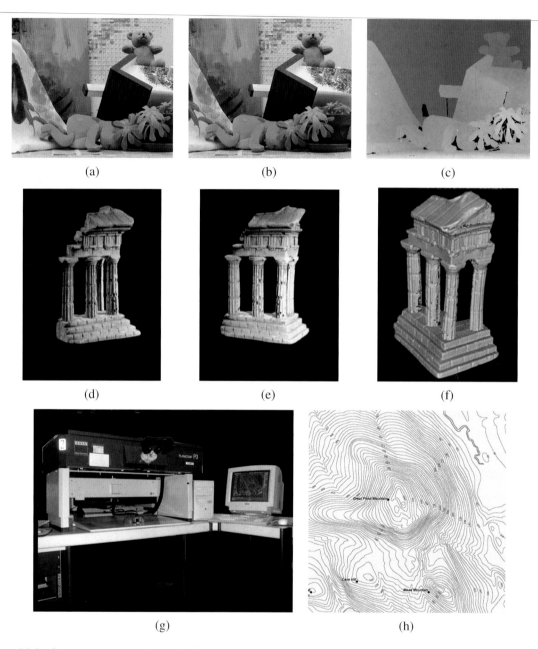

Figure 11.1 Stereo reconstruction techniques can convert (a–b) a pair of images into (c) a depth map (http://vision.middlebury.edu/stereo/data/scenes2003/) or (d–e) a sequence of images into (f) a 3D model (http://vision.middlebury.edu/mview/data/). (g) An analytical stereo plotter, courtesy of Kenney Aerial Mapping, Inc., can generate (h) contour plots.

Stereo matching is the process of taking two or more images and estimating a 3D model of the scene by finding matching pixels in the images and converting their 2D positions into 3D depths. In Chapters 6–7, we described techniques for recovering camera positions and building sparse 3D models of scenes or objects. In this chapter, we address the question of how to build a more complete 3D model, e.g., a sparse or dense *depth map* that assigns relative depths to pixels in the input images. We also look at the topic of *multi-view stereo* algorithms that produce complete 3D volumetric or surface-based object models.

Why are people interested in stereo matching? From the earliest inquiries into visual perception, it was known that we perceive depth based on the differences in appearance between the left and right eye.[1] As a simple experiment, hold your finger vertically in front of your eyes and close each eye alternately. You will notice that the finger jumps left and right relative to the background of the scene. The same phenomenon is visible in the image pair shown in Figure 11.1a–b, in which the foreground objects shift left and right relative to the background.

As we will shortly see, under simple imaging configurations (both eyes or cameras looking straight ahead), the amount of horizontal motion or *disparity* is inversely proportional to the distance from the observer. While the basic physics and geometry relating visual disparity to scene structure are well understood (Section 11.1), automatically measuring this disparity by establishing dense and accurate inter-image *correspondences* is a challenging task.

The earliest stereo matching algorithms were developed in the field of *photogrammetry* for automatically constructing topographic elevation maps from overlapping aerial images. Prior to this, operators would use photogrammetric stereo plotters, which displayed shifted versions of such images to each eye and allowed the operator to float a dot cursor around constant elevation contours (Figure 11.1g). The development of fully automated stereo matching algorithms was a major advance in this field, enabling much more rapid and less expensive processing of aerial imagery (Hannah 1974; Hsieh, McKeown, and Perlant 1992).

In computer vision, the topic of stereo matching has been one of the most widely studied and fundamental problems (Marr and Poggio 1976; Barnard and Fischler 1982; Dhond and Aggarwal 1989; Scharstein and Szeliski 2002; Brown, Burschka, and Hager 2003; Seitz, Curless, Diebel *et al.* 2006), and continues to be one of the most active research areas. While photogrammetric matching concentrated mainly on aerial imagery, computer vision applications include modeling the human visual system (Marr 1982), robotic navigation and manipulation (Moravec 1983; Konolige 1997; Thrun, Montemerlo, Dahlkamp *et al.* 2006), as well as view interpolation and image-based rendering (Figure 11.2a–d), 3D model building (Figure 11.2e–f and h–j), and mixing live action with computer-generated imagery (Figure 11.2g).

In this chapter, we describe the fundamental principles behind stereo matching, following the general taxonomy proposed by Scharstein and Szeliski (2002). We begin in Section 11.1 with a review of the *geometry* of stereo image matching, i.e., how to compute for a given pixel in one image the range of possible locations the pixel might appear at in the other image, i.e., its *epipolar line*. We describe how to pre-warp images so that corresponding epipolar lines are coincident (*rectification*). We also describe a general resampling algorithm called *plane sweep* that can be used to perform multi-image stereo matching with arbitrary camera configurations.

---

[1] The word *stereo* comes from the Greek for *solid*; stereo vision is how we perceive solid shape (Koenderink 1990).

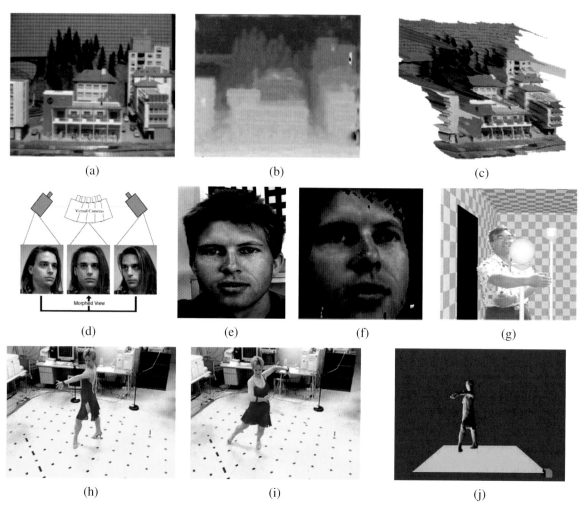

Figure 11.2 Applications of stereo vision: (a) input image, (b) computed depth map, and (c) new view generation from multi-view stereo (Matthies, Kanade, and Szeliski 1989) © 1989 Springer; (d) view morphing between two images (Seitz and Dyer 1996) © 1996 ACM; (e–f) 3D face modeling (images courtesy of Frédéric Devernay); (g) *z-keying* live and computer-generated imagery (Kanade, Yoshida, Oda *et al.* 1996) © 1996 IEEE; (h–j) building 3D surface models from multiple video streams in Virtualized Reality (Kanade, Rander, and Narayanan 1997).

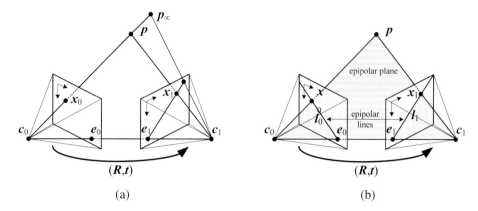

Figure 11.3 Epipolar geometry: (a) epipolar line segment corresponding to one ray; (b) corresponding set of epipolar lines and their epipolar plane.

Next, we briefly survey techniques for the *sparse* stereo matching of interest points and edge-like features (Section 11.2). We then turn to the main topic of this chapter, namely the estimation of a *dense* set of pixel-wise correspondences in the form of a *disparity map* (Figure 11.1c). This involves first selecting a pixel matching criterion (Section 11.3) and then using either local area-based aggregation (Section 11.4) or global optimization (Section 11.5) to help disambiguate potential matches. In Section 11.6, we discuss *multi-view stereo* methods that aim to reconstruct a complete 3D model instead of just a single disparity image (Figure 11.1d–f).

11.1 Epipolar geometry

Given a pixel in one image, how can we compute its correspondence in the other image? In Chapter 8, we saw that a variety of search techniques can be used to match pixels based on their local appearance as well as the motions of neighboring pixels. In the case of stereo matching, however, we have some additional information available, namely the positions and calibration data for the cameras that took the pictures of the same static scene (Section 7.2).

How can we exploit this information to reduce the number of potential correspondences, and hence both speed up the matching and increase its reliability? Figure 11.3a shows how a pixel in one image x_0 projects to an *epipolar line segment* in the other image. The segment is bounded at one end by the projection of the original viewing ray at infinity p_∞ and at the other end by the projection of the original camera center c_0 into the second camera, which is known as the *epipole* e_1. If we project the epipolar line in the second image back into the first, we get another line (segment), this time bounded by the other corresponding epipole e_0. Extending both line segments to infinity, we get a pair of corresponding *epipolar lines* (Figure 11.3b), which are the intersection of the two image planes with the *epipolar plane* that passes through both camera centers c_0 and c_1 as well as the point of interest p (Faugeras and Luong 2001; Hartley and Zisserman 2004).

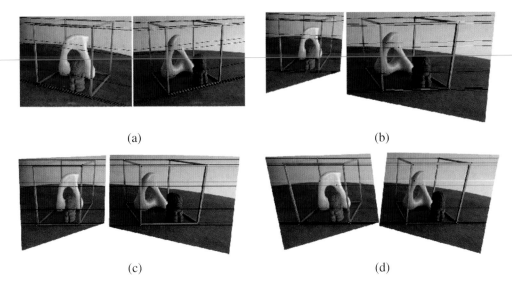

11.1.1 Rectification

As we saw in Section 7.2, the epipolar geometry for a pair of cameras is implicit in the
relative pose and calibrations of the cameras, and can easily be computed from seven or more
point matches using the fundamental matrix (or five or more points for the calibrated essential
matrix) (Zhang 1998a,b; Faugeras and Luong 2001; Hartley and Zisserman 2004). Once this
geometry has been computed, we can use the epipolar line corresponding to a pixel in one
image to constrain the search for corresponding pixels in the other image. One way to do this
is to use a general correspondence algorithm, such as optical flow (Section 8.4), but to only
consider locations along the epipolar line (or to project any flow vectors that fall off back onto
the line).

A more efficient algorithm can be obtained by first *rectifying* (i.e, warping) the input
images so that corresponding horizontal scanlines are epipolar lines (Loop and Zhang 1999;
Faugeras and Luong 2001; Hartley and Zisserman 2004).[2] Afterwards, it is possible to match
horizontal scanlines independently or to shift images horizontally while computing matching
scores (Figure 11.4).

A simple way to rectify the two images is to first rotate both cameras so that they are
looking perpendicular to the line joining the camera centers c_0 and c_1. Since there is a degree of freedom in the *tilt*, the smallest rotations that achieve this should be used. Next, to
determine the desired twist around the optical axes, make the *up vector* (the camera y axis)
perpendicular to the camera center line. This ensures that corresponding epipolar lines are

---

[2] This makes most sense if the cameras are next to each other, although by rotating the cameras, rectification can
be performed on any pair that is not *verged* too much or has too much of a scale change. In those latter cases, using
plane sweep (below) or hypothesizing small planar patch locations in 3D (Goesele, Snavely, Curless *et al.* 2007) may
be preferable.

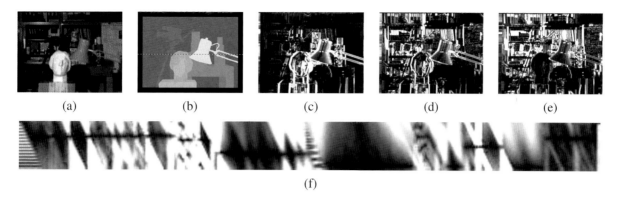

Figure 11.5 Slices through a typical disparity space image (DSI) (Scharstein and Szeliski 2002) © 2002 Springer: (a) original color image; (b) ground truth disparities; (c–e) three (x, y) slices for $d = 10, 16, 21$; (f) an (x, d) slice for $y = 151$ (the dashed line in (b)). Various dark (matching) regions are visible in (c–e), e.g., the bookshelves, table and cans, and head statue, and three disparity levels can be seen as horizontal lines in (f). The dark bands in the DSIs indicate regions that match at this disparity. (Smaller dark regions are often the result of textureless regions.) Additional examples of DSIs are discussed by Bobick and Intille (1999).

horizontal and that the disparity for points at infinity is 0. Finally, re-scale the images, if necessary, to account for different focal lengths, magnifying the smaller image to avoid aliasing. (The full details of this procedure can be found in Fusiello, Trucco, and Verri (2000) and Exercise 11.1.) Note that in general, it is not possible to rectify an arbitrary collection of images simultaneously unless their optical centers are collinear, although rotating the cameras so that they all point in the same direction reduces the inter-camera pixel movements to scalings and translations.

The resulting *standard rectified geometry* is employed in a lot of stereo camera setups and stereo algorithms, and leads to a very simple inverse relationship between 3D depths Z and disparities d,

$$d = f\frac{B}{Z}, \tag{11.1}$$

where f is the focal length (measured in pixels), B is the baseline, and

$$x' = x + d(x, y), \quad y' = y \tag{11.2}$$

describes the relationship between corresponding pixel coordinates in the left and right images (Bolles, Baker, and Marimont 1987; Okutomi and Kanade 1993; Scharstein and Szeliski 2002).[3] The task of extracting depth from a set of images then becomes one of estimating the *disparity map* $d(x, y)$.

After rectification, we can easily compare the similarity of pixels at corresponding locations (x, y) and $(x', y') = (x + d, y)$ and store them in a *disparity space image* (DSI) $C(x, y, d)$ for further processing (Figure 11.5). The concept of the disparity space (x, y, d) dates back to early work in stereo matching (Marr and Poggio 1976), while the concept of a disparity space image (volume) is generally associated with Yang, Yuille, and Lu (1993) and Intille and Bobick (1994).

---

[3] The term *disparity* was first introduced in the human vision literature to describe the difference in location of corresponding features seen by the left and right eyes (Marr 1982). Horizontal disparity is the most commonly studied phenomenon, but vertical disparity is possible if the eyes are verged.

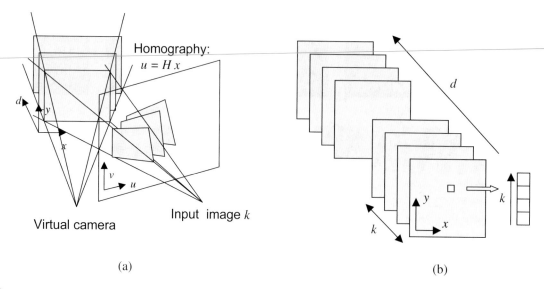

(a)   (b)

Figure 11.6 Sweeping a set of planes through a scene (Szeliski and Golland 1999) © 1999 Springer: (a) The set of planes seen from a virtual camera induces a set of homographies in any other source (input) camera image. (b) The warped images from all the other cameras can be stacked into a generalized disparity space volume $\tilde{I}(x, y, d, k)$ indexed by pixel location (x, y), disparity d, and camera k.

11.1.2 Plane sweep

An alternative to pre-rectifying the images before matching is to sweep a set of planes through the scene and to measure the *photoconsistency* of different images as they are re-projected onto these planes (Figure 11.6). This process is commonly known as the *plane sweep* algorithm (Collins 1996; Szeliski and Golland 1999; Saito and Kanade 1999).

As we saw in Section 2.1.5, where we introduced projective depth (also known as *plane plus parallax* (Kumar, Anandan, and Hanna 1994; Sawhney 1994; Szeliski and Coughlan 1997)), the last row of a full-rank 4×4 projection matrix $\tilde{P}$ can be set to an arbitrary plane equation $p_3 = s_3[\hat{n}_0 | c_0]$. The resulting four-dimensional projective transform (*collineation*) (2.68) maps 3D world points $p = (X, Y, Z, 1)$ into screen coordinates $x_s = (x_s, y_s, 1, d)$, where the *projective depth* (or *parallax*) d (2.66) is 0 on the reference plane (Figure 2.11).

Sweeping d through a series of disparity hypotheses, as shown in Figure 11.6a, corresponds to mapping each input image into the *virtual camera* $\tilde{P}$ defining the disparity space through a series of homographies (2.68–2.71),

$$\tilde{x}_k \sim \tilde{P}_k \tilde{P}^{-1} x_s = \tilde{H}_k \tilde{x} + t_k d = (\tilde{H}_k + t_k[0\ 0\ d])\tilde{x}, \qquad (11.3)$$

as shown in Figure 2.12b, where $\tilde{x}_k$ and $\tilde{x}$ are the homogeneous pixel coordinates in the source and virtual (reference) images (Szeliski and Golland 1999). The members of the family of homographies $\tilde{H}_k(d) = \tilde{H}_k + t_k[0\ 0\ d]$, which are parametererized by the addition of a rank-1 matrix, are related to each other through a *planar homology* (Hartley and Zisserman 2004, A5.2).

The choice of virtual camera and parameterization is application dependent and is what gives this framework a lot of its flexibility. In many applications, one of the input cameras (the *reference* camera) is used, thus computing a depth map that is registered with one of the input images and which can later be used for image-based rendering (Sections 13.1 and 13.2). In other applications, such as view interpolation for gaze correction in video-conferencing (Section 11.4.2) (Ott, Lewis, and Cox 1993; Criminisi, Shotton, Blake *et al.* 2003), a camera centrally located between the two input cameras is preferable, since it provides the needed per-pixel disparities to hallucinate the virtual middle image.

The choice of disparity sampling, i.e., the setting of the zero parallax plane and the scaling of integer disparities, is also application dependent, and is usually set to bracket the range of interest, i.e., the *working volume*, while scaling disparities to sample the image in pixel (or sub-pixel) shifts. For example, when using stereo vision for obstacle avoidance in robot navigation, it is most convenient to set up disparity to measure per-pixel elevation above the ground (Ivanchenko, Shen, and Coughlan 2009).

As each input image is warped onto the current planes parameterized by disparity d, it can be stacked into a *generalized disparity space image* $\tilde{I}(x, y, d, k)$ for further processing (Figure 11.6b) (Szeliski and Golland 1999). In most stereo algorithms, the photoconsistency (e.g., sum of squared or robust differences) with respect to the reference image I_r is calculated and stored in the DSI

$$C(x, y, d) = \sum_k \rho(\tilde{I}(x, y, d, k) - I_r(x, y)). \tag{11.4}$$

However, it is also possible to compute alternative statistics such as robust variance, focus, or entropy (Section 11.3.1) (Vaish, Szeliski, Zitnick *et al.* 2006) or to use this representation to reason about occlusions (Szeliski and Golland 1999; Kang and Szeliski 2004). The generalized DSI will come in particularly handy when we come back to the topic of multi-view stereo in Section 11.6.

Of course, planes are not the only surfaces that can be used to define a 3D sweep through the space of interest. Cylindrical surfaces, especially when coupled with panoramic photography (Chapter 9), are often used (Ishiguro, Yamamoto, and Tsuji 1992; Kang and Szeliski 1997; Shum and Szeliski 1999; Li, Shum, Tang *et al.* 2004; Zheng, Kang, Cohen *et al.* 2007). It is also possible to define other manifold topologies, e.g., ones where the camera rotates around a fixed axis (Seitz 2001).

Once the DSI has been computed, the next step in most stereo correspondence algorithms is to produce a univalued function in disparity space $d(x, y)$ that best describes the shape of the surfaces in the scene. This can be viewed as finding a surface embedded in the disparity space image that has some optimality property, such as lowest cost and best (piecewise) smoothness (Yang, Yuille, and Lu 1993). Figure 11.5 shows examples of slices through a typical DSI. More figures of this kind can be found in the paper by Bobick and Intille (1999).

11.2 Sparse correspondence

Early stereo matching algorithms were *feature-based*, i.e., they first extracted a set of potentially matchable image locations, using either interest operators or edge detectors, and then searched for corresponding locations in other images using a patch-based metric (Hannah 1974; Marr and Poggio 1979; Mayhew and Frisby 1980; Baker and Binford 1981; Arnold 1983; Grimson 1985; Ohta and Kanade 1985; Bolles, Baker, and Marimont 1987; Matthies, Kanade, and Szeliski 1989; Hsieh, McKeown, and Perlant 1992; Bolles, Baker, and Hannah

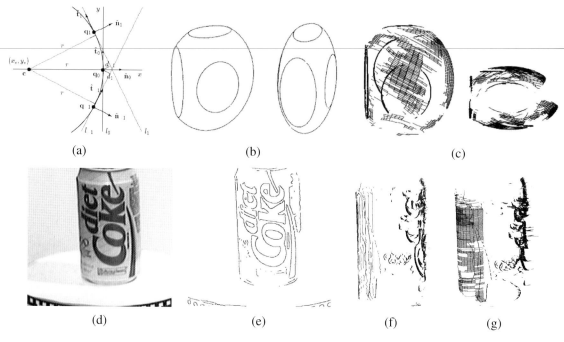

Figure 11.7 Surface reconstruction from occluding contours (Szeliski and Weiss 1998) © 2002 Springer: (a) circular arc fitting in the epipolar plane; (b) synthetic example of an ellipsoid with a truncated side and elliptic surface markings; (c) partially reconstructed surface mesh seen from an oblique and top-down view; (d) real-world image sequence of a soda can on a turntable; (e) extracted edges; (f) partially reconstructed profile curves; (g) partially reconstructed surface mesh. (Partial reconstructions are shown so as not to clutter the images.)

1993). This limitation to sparse correspondences was partially due to computational resource limitations, but was also driven by a desire to limit the answers produced by stereo algorithms to matches with high certainty. In some applications, there was also a desire to match scenes with potentially very different illuminations, where edges might be the only stable features (Collins 1996). Such sparse 3D reconstructions could later be interpolated using surface fitting algorithms such as those discussed in Sections 3.7.1 and 12.3.1.

More recent work in this area has focused on first extracting highly reliable features and then using these as *seeds* to grow additional matches (Zhang and Shan 2000; Lhuillier and Quan 2002). Similar approaches have also been extended to wide baseline multi-view stereo problems and combined with 3D surface reconstruction (Lhuillier and Quan 2005; Strecha, Tuytelaars, and Van Gool 2003; Goesele, Snavely, Curless *et al.* 2007) or free-space reasoning (Taylor 2003), as described in more detail in Section 11.6.

11.2.1 3D curves and profiles

Another example of sparse correspondence is the matching of *profile curves* (or *occluding contours*), which occur at the boundaries of objects (Figure 11.7) and at interior self occlusions, where the surface curves away from the camera viewpoint.

The difficulty in matching profile curves is that in general, the locations of profile curves vary as a function of camera viewpoint. Therefore, matching curves directly in two images and then triangulating these matches can lead to erroneous shape measurements. Fortunately, if three or more closely spaced frames are available, it is possible to fit a local circular arc to the locations of corresponding edgels (Figure 11.7a) and therefore obtain semi-dense curved surface meshes directly from the matches (Figures 11.7c and g). Another advantage of matching such curves is that they can be used to reconstruct surface shape for untextured surfaces, so long as there is a visible difference between foreground and background colors.

Over the years, a number of different techniques have been developed for reconstructing surface shape from profile curves (Giblin and Weiss 1987; Cipolla and Blake 1992; Vaillant and Faugeras 1992; Zheng 1994; Boyer and Berger 1997; Szeliski and Weiss 1998). Cipolla and Giblin (2000) describe many of these techniques, as well as related topics such as inferring camera motion from profile curve sequences. Below, we summarize the approach developed by Szeliski and Weiss (1998), which assumes a discrete set of images, rather than formulating the problem in a continuous differential framework.

Let us assume that the camera is moving smoothly enough that the local epipolar geometry varies slowly, i.e., the epipolar planes induced by the successive camera centers and an edgel under consideration are nearly co-planar. The first step in the processing pipeline is to extract and link edges in each of the input images (Figures 11.7b and e). Next, edgels in successive images are matched using pairwise epipolar geometry, proximity and (optionally) appearance. This provides a linked set of edges in the spatio-temporal volume, which is sometimes called the *weaving wall* (Baker 1989).

To reconstruct the 3D location of an individual edgel, along with its local in-plane normal and curvature, we project the viewing rays corresponding to its neighbors onto the instantaneous epipolar plane defined by the camera center, the viewing ray, and the camera velocity, as shown in Figure 11.7a. We then fit an *osculating circle* to the projected lines, parameterizing the circle by its centerpoint $c = (x_c, y_c)$ and radius r,

$$c_i x_c + s_i y_c + r = d_i, \tag{11.5}$$

where $c_i = \hat{t}_i \cdot \hat{t}_0$ and $s_i = -\hat{t}_i \cdot \hat{n}_0$ are the cosine and sine of the angle between viewing ray i and the central viewing ray 0, and $d_i = (q_i - q_0) \cdot \hat{n}_0$ is the perpendicular distance between viewing ray i and the local origin q_0, which is a point chosen on the central viewing ray close to the line intersections (Szeliski and Weiss 1998). The resulting set of linear equations can be solved using least squares, and the quality of the solution (residual error) can be used to check for erroneous correspondences.

The resulting set of 3D points, along with their spatial (in-image) and temporal (between-image) neighbors, form a 3D surface mesh with local normal and curvature estimates (Figures 11.7c and g). Note that whenever a curve is due to a surface marking or a sharp crease edge, rather than a smooth surface profile curve, this shows up as a 0 or small radius of curvature. Such curves result in isolated 3D space curves, rather than elements of smooth surface meshes, but can still be incorporated into the 3D surface model during a later stage of surface interpolation (Section 12.3.1).

11.3 Dense correspondence

While sparse matching algorithms are still occasionally used, most stereo matching algorithms today focus on dense correspondence, since this is required for applications such as image-based rendering or modeling. This problem is more challenging than sparse correspondence, since inferring depth values in textureless regions requires a certain amount of guesswork. (Think of a solid-colored background seen through a picket fence. What depth should it be?)

In this section, we review the taxonomy and categorization scheme for dense correspondence algorithms first proposed by Scharstein and Szeliski (2002). The taxonomy consists of a set of algorithmic "building blocks" from which a large set of algorithms can be constructed. It is based on the observation that stereo algorithms generally perform some subset of the following four steps:

1. matching cost computation;

2. cost (support) aggregation;

3. disparity computation and optimization; and

4. disparity refinement.

For example, *local* (window-based) algorithms (Section 11.4), where the disparity computation at a given point depends only on intensity values within a finite window, usually make implicit smoothness assumptions by aggregating support. Some of these algorithms can cleanly be broken down into steps 1, 2, 3. For example, the traditional sum-of-squared-differences (SSD) algorithm can be described as:

1. The matching cost is the squared difference of intensity values at a given disparity.

2. Aggregation is done by summing the matching cost over square windows with constant disparity.

3. Disparities are computed by selecting the minimal (winning) aggregated value at each pixel.

Some local algorithms, however, combine steps 1 and 2 and use a matching cost that is based on a support region, e.g. normalized cross-correlation (Hannah 1974; Bolles, Baker, and Hannah 1993) and the rank transform (Zabih and Woodfill 1994) and other ordinal measures (Bhat and Nayar 1998). (This can also be viewed as a preprocessing step; see (Section 11.3.1).)

Global algorithms, on the other hand, make explicit smoothness assumptions and then solve a a global optimization problem (Section 11.5). Such algorithms typically do not perform an aggregation step, but rather seek a disparity assignment (step 3) that minimizes a global cost function that consists of data (step 1) terms and smoothness terms. The main distinctions among these algorithms is the minimization procedure used, e.g., simulated annealing (Marroquin, Mitter, and Poggio 1987; Barnard 1989), probabilistic (mean-field) diffusion (Scharstein and Szeliski 1998), expectation maximization (EM) (Birchfield, Natarajan, and Tomasi 2007), graph cuts (Boykov, Veksler, and Zabih 2001), or loopy belief propagation (Sun, Zheng, and Shum 2003), to name just a few.

In between these two broad classes are certain iterative algorithms that do not explicitly specify a global function to be minimized, but whose behavior mimics closely that of iterative optimization algorithms (Marr and Poggio 1976; Zitnick and Kanade 2000). Hierarchical (coarse-to-fine) algorithms resemble such iterative algorithms, but typically operate on an image pyramid where results from coarser levels are used to constrain a more local search at finer levels (Witkin, Terzopoulos, and Kass 1987; Quam 1984; Bergen, Anandan, Hanna *et al.* 1992).

11.3.1 Similarity measures

The first component of any dense stereo matching algorithm is a similarity measure that compares pixel values in order to determine how likely they are to be in correspondence. In this section, we briefly review the similarity measures introduced in Section 8.1 and mention a few others that have been developed specifically for stereo matching (Scharstein and Szeliski 2002; Hirschmüller and Scharstein 2009).

The most common pixel-based matching costs include sums of *squared intensity differences* (SSD) (Hannah 1974) and *absolute intensity differences* (SAD) (Kanade 1994). In the video processing community, these matching criteria are referred to as the *mean-squared error* (MSE) and *mean absolute difference* (MAD) measures; the term *displaced frame difference* is also often used (Tekalp 1995).

More recently, robust measures (8.2), including truncated quadratics and contaminated Gaussians, have been proposed (Black and Anandan 1996; Black and Rangarajan 1996; Scharstein and Szeliski 1998). These measures are useful because they limit the influence of mismatches during aggregation. Vaish, Szeliski, Zitnick *et al.* (2006) compare a number of such robust measures, including a new one based on the entropy of the pixel values at a particular disparity hypothesis (Zitnick, Kang, Uyttendaele *et al.* 2004), which is particularly useful in multi-view stereo.

Other traditional matching costs include normalized cross-correlation (8.11) (Hannah 1974; Bolles, Baker, and Hannah 1993; Evangelidis and Psarakis 2008), which behaves similarly to sum-of-squared-differences (SSD), and binary matching costs (i.e., match or no match) (Marr and Poggio 1976), based on binary features such as edges (Baker and Binford 1981; Grimson 1985) or the sign of the Laplacian (Nishihara 1984). Because of their poor discriminability, simple binary matching costs are no longer used in dense stereo matching.

Some costs are insensitive to differences in camera gain or bias, for example gradient-based measures (Seitz 1989; Scharstein 1994), phase and filter-bank responses (Marr and Poggio 1979; Kass 1988; Jenkin, Jepson, and Tsotsos 1991; Jones and Malik 1992), filters that remove regular or robust (bilaterally filtered) means (Ansar, Castano, and Matthies 2004; Hirschmüller and Scharstein 2009), dense feature descriptor (Tola, Lepetit, and Fua 2010), and non-parametric measures such as rank and census transforms (Zabih and Woodfill 1994), ordinal measures (Bhat and Nayar 1998), or entropy (Zitnick, Kang, Uyttendaele *et al.* 2004; Zitnick and Kang 2007). The census transform, which converts each pixel inside a moving window into a bit vector representing which neighbors are above or below the central pixel, was found by Hirschmüller and Scharstein (2009) to be quite robust against large-scale, non-stationary exposure and illumination changes.

It is also possible to correct for differing global camera characteristics by performing a preprocessing or iterative refinement step that estimates inter-image bias–gain variations using global regression (Gennert 1988), histogram equalization (Cox, Roy, and Hingorani 1995), or mutual information (Kim, Kolmogorov, and Zabih 2003; Hirschmüller 2008). Local, smoothly varying compensation fields have also been proposed (Strecha, Tuytelaars, and Van Gool 2003; Zhang, McMillan, and Yu 2006).

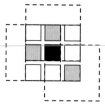

Figure 11.8 Shiftable window (Scharstein and Szeliski 2002) © 2002 Springer. The effect of trying all 3×3 shifted windows around the black pixel is the same as taking the minimum matching score across all *centered* (non-shifted) windows in the same neighborhood. (For clarity, only three of the neighboring shifted windows are shown here.)

In order to compensate for sampling issues, i.e., dramatically different pixel values in high-frequency areas, Birchfield and Tomasi (1998) proposed a matching cost that is less sensitive to shifts in image sampling. Rather than just comparing pixel values shifted by integral amounts (which may miss a valid match), they compare each pixel in the reference image against a linearly interpolated function of the other image. More detailed studies of these and additional matching costs are explored in (Szeliski and Scharstein 2004; Hirschmüller and Scharstein 2009). In particular, if you expect there to be significant exposure or appearance variation between images that you are matching, some of the more robust measures that performed well in the evaluation by Hirschmüller and Scharstein (2009), such as the census transform (Zabih and Woodfill 1994), ordinal measures (Bhat and Nayar 1998), bilateral subtraction (Ansar, Castano, and Matthies 2004), or hierarchical mutual information (Hirschmüller 2008), should be used.

11.4 Local methods

Local and window-based methods aggregate the matching cost by summing or averaging over a *support region* in the DSI $C(x, y, d)$.[4] A support region can be either two-dimensional at a fixed disparity (favoring fronto-parallel surfaces), or three-dimensional in x-y-d space (supporting slanted surfaces). Two-dimensional evidence aggregation has been implemented using square windows or Gaussian convolution (traditional), multiple windows anchored at different points, i.e., shiftable windows (Arnold 1983; Fusiello, Roberto, and Trucco 1997; Bobick and Intille 1999), windows with adaptive sizes (Okutomi and Kanade 1992; Kanade and Okutomi 1994; Kang, Szeliski, and Chai 2001; Veksler 2001, 2003), windows based on connected components of constant disparity (Boykov, Veksler, and Zabih 1998), or the results of color-based segmentation (Yoon and Kweon 2006; Tombari, Mattoccia, Di Stefano *et al.* 2008). Three-dimensional support functions that have been proposed include limited disparity difference (Grimson 1985), limited disparity gradient (Pollard, Mayhew, and Frisby 1985), Prazdny's coherence principle (Prazdny 1985), and the more recent work (which includes visibility and occlusion reasoning) by Zitnick and Kanade (2000).

---

[4] For two recent surveys and comparisons of such techniques, please see the work of Gong, Yang, Wang *et al.* (2007) and Tombari, Mattoccia, Di Stefano *et al.* (2008).

(a) (b) (c) (d)

Figure 11.9 Aggregation window sizes and weights adapted to image content (Tombari, Mattoccia, Di Stefano *et al.* 2008) © 2008 IEEE: (a) original image with selected evaluation points; (b) variable windows (Veksler 2003); (c) adaptive weights (Yoon and Kweon 2006); (d) segmentation-based (Tombari, Mattoccia, and Di Stefano 2007). Notice how the adaptive weights and segmentation-based techniques adapt their support to similarly colored pixels.

Aggregation with a fixed support region can be performed using 2D or 3D convolution,

$$C(x, y, d) = w(x, y, d) * C_0(x, y, d), \qquad (11.6)$$

or, in the case of rectangular windows, using efficient moving average box-filters (Section 3.2.2) (Kanade, Yoshida, Oda *et al.* 1996; Kimura, Shinbo, Yamaguchi *et al.* 1999). Shiftable windows can also be implemented efficiently using a separable sliding min-filter (Figure 11.8) (Scharstein and Szeliski 2002, Section 4.2). Selecting among windows of different shapes and sizes can be performed more efficiently by first computing a *summed area table* (Section 3.2.3, 3.30–3.32) (Veksler 2003). Selecting the right window is important, since windows must be large enough to contain sufficient texture and yet small enough so that they do not straddle depth discontinuities (Figure 11.9). An alternative method for aggregation is *iterative diffusion*, i.e., repeatedly adding to each pixel's cost the weighted values of its neighboring pixels' costs (Szeliski and Hinton 1985; Shah 1993; Scharstein and Szeliski 1998).

Of the local aggregation methods compared by Gong, Yang, Wang *et al.* (2007) and Tombari, Mattoccia, Di Stefano *et al.* (2008), the fast variable window approach of Veksler (2003) and the locally weighting approach developed by Yoon and Kweon (2006) consistently stood out as having the best tradeoff between performance and speed.[5] The local weighting technique, in particular, is interesting because, instead of using square windows with uniform weighting, each pixel within an aggregation window influences the final matching cost based on its color similarity and spatial distance, just as in bilinear filtering (Figure 11.9c). (In fact, their aggregation step is closely related to doing a joint bilateral filter on the color/disparity image, except that it is done symmetrically in both reference and target images.) The segmentation-based aggregation method of Tombari, Mattoccia, and Di Stefano (2007) did even better, although a fast implementation of this algorithm does not yet exist.

In local methods, the emphasis is on the matching cost computation and cost aggregation steps. Computing the final disparities is trivial: simply choose at each pixel the disparity associated with the minimum cost value. Thus, these methods perform a local "winner-take-all" (WTA) optimization at each pixel. A limitation of this approach (and many other

---

[5] More recent and extensive results from Tombari, Mattoccia, Di Stefano *et al.* (2008) can be found at http://www.vision.deis.unibo.it/spe/SPEHome.aspx.

correspondence algorithms) is that uniqueness of matches is only enforced for one image (the *reference image*), while points in the other image might match multiple points, unless cross-checking and subsequent hole filling is used (Fua 1993; Hirschmüller and Scharstein 2009).

11.4.1 Sub-pixel estimation and uncertainty

Most stereo correspondence algorithms compute a set of disparity estimates in some discretized space, e.g., for integer disparities (exceptions include continuous optimization techniques such as optical flow (Bergen, Anandan, Hanna *et al.* 1992) or splines (Szeliski and Coughlan 1997)). For applications such as robot navigation or people tracking, these may be perfectly adequate. However for image-based rendering, such quantized maps lead to very unappealing view synthesis results, i.e., the scene appears to be made up of many thin shearing layers. To remedy this situation, many algorithms apply a sub-pixel refinement stage after the initial discrete correspondence stage. (An alternative is to simply start with more discrete disparity levels (Szeliski and Scharstein 2004).)

Sub-pixel disparity estimates can be computed in a variety of ways, including iterative gradient descent and fitting a curve to the matching costs at discrete disparity levels (Ryan, Gray, and Hunt 1980; Lucas and Kanade 1981; Tian and Huhns 1986; Matthies, Kanade, and Szeliski 1989; Kanade and Okutomi 1994). This provides an easy way to increase the resolution of a stereo algorithm with little additional computation. However, to work well, the intensities being matched must vary smoothly, and the regions over which these estimates are computed must be on the same (correct) surface.

Recently, some questions have been raised about the advisability of fitting correlation curves to integer-sampled matching costs (Shimizu and Okutomi 2001). This situation may even be worse when sampling-insensitive dissimilarity measures are used (Birchfield and Tomasi 1998). These issues are explored in more depth by Szeliski and Scharstein (2004).

Besides sub-pixel computations, there are other ways of post-processing the computed disparities. Occluded areas can be detected using cross-checking, i.e., comparing left-to-right and right-to-left disparity maps (Fua 1993). A median filter can be applied to clean up spurious mismatches, and holes due to occlusion can be filled by surface fitting or by distributing neighboring disparity estimates (Birchfield and Tomasi 1999; Scharstein 1999; Hirschmüller and Scharstein 2009).

Another kind of post-processing, which can be useful in later processing stages, is to associate *confidences* with per-pixel depth estimates (Figure 11.10), which can be done by looking at the curvature of the correlation surface, i.e., how strong the minimum in the DSI image is at the winning disparity. Matthies, Kanade, and Szeliski (1989) show that under the assumption of small noise, photometrically calibrated images, and densely sampled disparities, the variance of a local depth estimate can be estimated as

$$Var(d) = \frac{\sigma_I^2}{a},\tag{11.7}$$

where a is the curvature of the DSI as a function of d, which can be measured using a local parabolic fit or by squaring all the horizontal gradients in the window, and σ_I^2 is the variance of the image noise, which can be estimated from the minimum SSD score. (See also Section 6.1.4, (8.44), and Appendix B.6.)

(a)   (b)   (c)

Figure 11.10 Uncertainty in stereo depth estimation (Szeliski 1991b): (a) input image; (b) estimated depth map (blue is closer); (c) estimated confidence(red is higher). As you can see, more textured areas have higher confidence.

11.4.2 *Application*: Stereo-based head tracking

A common application of real-time stereo algorithms is for tracking the position of a user interacting with a computer or game system. The use of stereo can dramatically improve the reliability of such a system compared to trying to use monocular color and intensity information (Darrell, Gordon, Harville *et al.* 2000). Once recovered, this information can be used in a variety of applications, including controlling a virtual environment or game, correcting the apparent gaze during video conferencing, and background replacement. We discuss the first two applications below and defer the discussion of background replacement to Section 11.5.3.

The use of head tracking to control a user's virtual viewpoint while viewing a 3D object or environment on a computer monitor is sometimes called *fish tank virtual reality*, since the user is observing a 3D world as if it were contained inside a fish tank (Ware, Arthur, and Booth 1993). Early versions of these systems used mechanical head tracking devices and stereo glasses. Today, such systems can be controlled using stereo-based head tracking and stereo glasses can be replaced with autostereoscopic displays. Head tracking can also be used to construct a "virtual mirror", where the user's head can be modified in real-time using a variety of visual effects (Darrell, Baker, Crow *et al.* 1997).

Another application of stereo head tracking and 3D reconstruction is in gaze correction (Ott, Lewis, and Cox 1993). When a user participates in a desktop video-conference or video chat, the camera is usually placed on top of the monitor. Since the person is gazing at a window somewhere on the screen, it appears as if they are looking down and away from the other participants, instead of straight at them. Replacing the single camera with two or more cameras enables a virtual view to be constructed right at the position where they are looking resulting in virtual eye contact. Real-time stereo matching is used to construct an accurate 3D head model and view interpolation (Section 13.1) is used to synthesize the novel in-between view (Criminisi, Shotton, Blake *et al.* 2003).

11.5 Global optimization

Global stereo matching methods perform some optimization or iteration steps after the disparity computation phase and often skip the aggregation step altogether, because the global smoothness constraints perform a similar function. Many global methods are formulated in an energy-minimization framework, where, as we saw in Sections 3.7 (3.100–3.102) and 8.4, the objective is to find a solution d that minimizes a global energy,

$$E(d) = E_d(d) + \lambda E_s(d). \tag{11.8}$$

The data term, $E_d(d)$, measures how well the disparity function d agrees with the input image pair. Using our previously defined disparity space image, we define this energy as

$$E_d(d) = \sum_{(x,y)} C(x, y, d(x, y)), \tag{11.9}$$

where C is the (initial or aggregated) matching cost DSI.

The smoothness term $E_s(d)$ encodes the smoothness assumptions made by the algorithm. To make the optimization computationally tractable, the smoothness term is often restricted to measuring only the differences between neighboring pixels' disparities,

$$E_s(d) = \sum_{(x,y)} \rho(d(x, y) - d(x + 1, y)) + \rho(d(x, y) - d(x, y + 1)), \tag{11.10}$$

where ρ is some monotonically increasing function of disparity difference. It is also possible to use larger neighborhoods, such as $\mathcal{N}_8$, which can lead to better boundaries (Boykov and Kolmogorov 2003), or to use second-order smoothness terms (Woodford, Reid, Torr *et al.* 2008), but such terms require more complex optimization techniques. An alternative to smoothness functionals is to use a lower-dimensional representation such as splines (Szeliski and Coughlan 1997).

In standard regularization (Section 3.7.1), ρ is a quadratic function, which makes d smooth everywhere and may lead to poor results at object boundaries. Energy functions that do not have this problem are called *discontinuity-preserving* and are based on robust ρ functions (Terzopoulos 1986b; Black and Rangarajan 1996). The seminal paper by Geman and Geman (1984) gave a Bayesian interpretation of these kinds of energy functions and proposed a discontinuity-preserving energy function based on Markov random fields (MRFs) and additional *line processes*, which are additional binary variables that control whether smoothness penalties are enforced or not. Black and Rangarajan (1996) show how independent line process variables can be replaced by robust pairwise disparity terms.

The terms in E_s can also be made to depend on the intensity differences, e.g.,

$$\rho_d(d(x, y) - d(x + 1, y)) \cdot \rho_I(\|I(x, y) - I(x + 1, y)\|), \tag{11.11}$$

where ρ_I is some monotonically decreasing function of intensity differences that lowers smoothness costs at high-intensity gradients. This idea (Gamble and Poggio 1987; Fua 1993; Bobick and Intille 1999; Boykov, Veksler, and Zabih 2001) encourages disparity discontinuities to coincide with intensity or color edges and appears to account for some of the good performance of global optimization approaches. While most researchers set these functions heuristically, Scharstein and Pal (2007) show how the free parameters in such *conditional random fields* (Section 3.7.2, (3.118)) can be learned from ground truth disparity maps.

Once the global energy has been defined, a variety of algorithms can be used to find a (local) minimum. Traditional approaches associated with regularization and Markov random fields include continuation (Blake and Zisserman 1987), simulated annealing (Geman and Geman 1984; Marroquin, Mitter, and Poggio 1987; Barnard 1989), highest confidence first (Chou and Brown 1990), and mean-field annealing (Geiger and Girosi 1991).

More recently, *max-flow* and *graph cut* methods have been proposed to solve a special class of global optimization problems (Roy and Cox 1998; Boykov, Veksler, and Zabih 2001; Ishikawa 2003). Such methods are more efficient than simulated annealing and have produced good results, as have techniques based on loopy belief propagation (Sun, Zheng, and Shum 2003; Tappen and Freeman 2003). Appendix B.5 and a recent survey paper on MRF inference (Szeliski, Zabih, Scharstein *et al.* 2008) discuss and compare such techniques in more detail.

While global optimization techniques currently produce the best stereo matching results, there are some alternative approaches worth studying.

Cooperative algorithms. Cooperative algorithms, inspired by computational models of human stereo vision, were among the earliest methods proposed for disparity computation (Dev 1974; Marr and Poggio 1976; Marroquin 1983; Szeliski and Hinton 1985; Zitnick and Kanade 2000). Such algorithms iteratively update disparity estimates using non-linear operations that result in an overall behavior similar to global optimization algorithms. In fact, for some of these algorithms, it is possible to explicitly state a global function that is being minimized (Scharstein and Szeliski 1998).

Coarse-to-fine and incremental warping. Most of today's best algorithms first enumerate all possible matches at all possible disparities and then select the best set of matches in some way. Faster approaches can sometimes be obtained using methods inspired by classic (infinitesimal) optical flow computation. Here, images are successively warped and disparity estimates incrementally updated until a satisfactory registration is achieved. These techniques are most often implemented within a coarse-to-fine hierarchical refinement framework (Quam 1984; Bergen, Anandan, Hanna *et al.* 1992; Barron, Fleet, and Beauchemin 1994; Szeliski and Coughlan 1997).

11.5.1 Dynamic programming

A different class of global optimization algorithm is based on *dynamic programming*. While the 2D optimization of Equation (11.8) can be shown to be NP-hard for common classes of smoothness functions (Veksler 1999), dynamic programming can find the global minimum for independent scanlines in polynomial time. Dynamic programming was first used for stereo vision in sparse, edge-based methods (Baker and Binford 1981; Ohta and Kanade 1985). More recent approaches have focused on the dense (intensity-based) scanline matching problem (Belhumeur 1996; Geiger, Ladendorf, and Yuille 1992; Cox, Hingorani, Rao *et al.* 1996; Bobick and Intille 1999; Birchfield and Tomasi 1999). These approaches work by computing the minimum-cost path through the matrix of all pairwise matching costs between two corresponding scanlines, i.e., through a horizontal slice of the DSI. Partial occlusion is

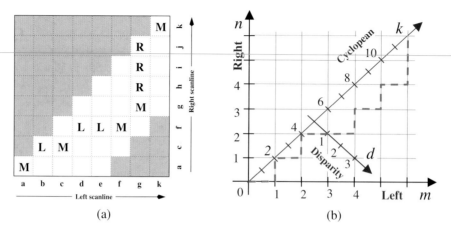

Figure 11.11 Stereo matching using dynamic programming, as illustrated by (a) Scharstein and Szeliski (2002) © 2002 Springer and (b) Kolmogorov, Criminisi, Blake *et al.* (2006). © 2006 IEEE. For each pair of corresponding scanlines, a minimizing path through the matrix of all pairwise matching costs (DSI) is selected. Lowercase letters (a–k) symbolize the intensities along each scanline. Uppercase letters represent the selected path through the matrix. Matches are indicated by M, while partially occluded points (which have a fixed cost) are indicated by L or R, corresponding to points only visible in the left or right images, respectively. Usually, only a limited disparity range is considered (0–4 in the figure, indicated by the non-shaded squares). The representation in (a) allows for diagonal moves while the representation in (b) does not. Note that these diagrams, which use the *Cyclopean* representation of depth, i.e., depth relative to a camera between the two input cameras, show an "unskewed" x-d slice through the DSI.

handled explicitly by assigning a group of pixels in one image to a single pixel in the other image. Figure 11.11 schematically shows how DP works, while Figure 11.5f shows a real DSI slice over which the DP is applied.

To implement dynamic programming for a scanline y, each entry (state) in a 2D cost matrix $D(m, n)$ is computed by combining its DSI value

$$C'(m, n) = C(m + n, m - n, y) \tag{11.12}$$

with one of its predecessor cost values. Using the representation shown in Figure 11.11a, which allows for "diagonal" moves, the aggregated match costs can be recursively computed as

$$
\begin{aligned}
D(m, n, M) &= \min(D(m-1, n-1, M), D(m-1, n, L), D(m-1, n-1, R)) \\
&\quad + C'(m, n) \\
D(m, n, L) &= \min(D(m-1, n-1, M), D(m-1, n, L)) + O \\
D(m, n, R) &= \min(D(m, n-1, M), D(m, n-1, R)) + O,
\end{aligned}
\tag{11.13}
$$

where O is a per-pixel occlusion cost. The aggregation rules corresponding to Figure 11.11b are given by Kolmogorov, Criminisi, Blake *et al.* (2006), who also use a two-state foreground–background model for bi-layer segmentation.

Problems with dynamic programming stereo include the selection of the right cost for occluded pixels and the difficulty of enforcing inter-scanline consistency, although several

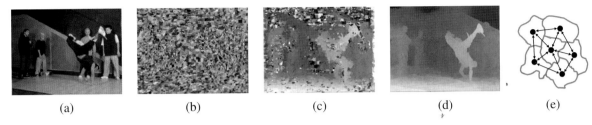

(a)   (b)   (c)   (d)   (e)

Figure 11.12 Segmentation-based stereo matching (Zitnick, Kang, Uyttendaele *et al.* 2004) © 2004 ACM: (a) input color image; (b) color-based segmentation; (c) initial disparity estimates; (d) final piecewise-smoothed disparities; (e) MRF neighborhood defined over the segments in the disparity space distribution (Zitnick and Kang 2007) © 2007 Springer.

methods propose ways of addressing the latter (Ohta and Kanade 1985; Belhumeur 1996; Cox, Hingorani, Rao *et al.* 1996; Bobick and Intille 1999; Birchfield and Tomasi 1999; Kolmogorov, Criminisi, Blake *et al.* 2006). Another problem is that the dynamic programming approach requires enforcing the *monotonicity* or *ordering constraint* (Yuille and Poggio 1984). This constraint requires that the relative ordering of pixels on a scanline remain the same between the two views, which may not be the case in scenes containing narrow foreground objects.

An alternative to traditional dynamic programming, introduced by Scharstein and Szeliski (2002), is to neglect the vertical smoothness constraints in (11.10) and simply optimize independent scanlines in the global energy function (11.8), which can easily be done using a recursive algorithm,

$$D(x, y, d) = C(x, y, d) + \min_{d'} \left\{ D(x - 1, y, d') + \rho_d(d - d') \right\}. \qquad (11.14)$$

The advantage of this *scanline optimization* algorithm is that it computes the same representation and minimizes a reduced version of the same energy function as the full 2D energy function (11.8). Unfortunately, it still suffers from the same streaking artifacts as dynamic programming.

A much better approach is to evaluate the cumulative cost function (11.14) from multiple directions, e.g, from the eight cardinal directions, N, E, W, S, NE, SE, SW, NW (Hirschmüller 2008). The resulting *semi-global* optimization performs quite well and is extremely efficient to implement.

Even though dynamic programming and scanline optimization algorithms do not generally produce *the* most accurate stereo reconstructions, when combined with sophisticated aggregation strategies, they can produce very fast and high-quality results.

11.5.2 Segmentation-based techniques

While most stereo matching algorithms perform their computations on a per-pixel basis, some of the more recent techniques first segment the images into regions and then try to label each region with a disparity.

For example, Tao, Sawhney, and Kumar (2001) segment the reference image, estimate per-pixel disparities using a local technique, and then do local plane fits inside each segment

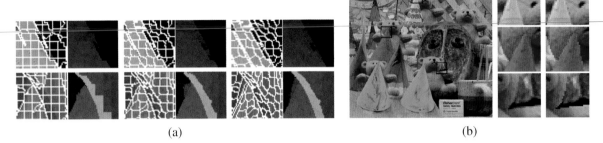

$\qquad$ (a) $\qquad\qquad\qquad\qquad\qquad\qquad\qquad$ (b)

Figure 11.13 Stereo matching with adaptive over-segmentation and matting (Taguchi, Wilburn, and Zitnick 2008) © 2008 IEEE: (a) segment boundaries are refined during the optimization, leading to more accurate results (e.g., the thin green leaf in the bottom row); (b) alpha mattes are extracted at segment boundaries, which leads to visually better compositing results (middle column).

before applying smoothness constraints between neighboring segments. Zitnick, Kang, Uyttendaele *et al.* (2004) and Zitnick and Kang (2007) use over-segmentation to mitigate initial bad segmentations. After a set of initial cost values for each segment has been stored into a *disparity space distribution* (DSD), iterative relaxation (or loopy belief propagation, in the more recent work of Zitnick and Kang (2007)) is used to adjust the disparity estimates for each segment, as shown in Figure 11.12. Taguchi, Wilburn, and Zitnick (2008) refine the segment shapes as part of the optimization process, which leads to much improved results, as shown in Figure 11.13.

Even more accurate results are obtained by Klaus, Sormann, and Karner (2006), who first segment the reference image using mean shift, run a small (3×3) SAD plus gradient SAD (weighted by cross-checking) to get initial disparity estimates, fit local planes, re-fit with global planes, and then run a final MRF on plane assignments with loopy belief propagation. When the algorithm was first introduced in 2006, it was the top ranked algorithm on the evaluation site at http://vision.middlebury.edu/stereo; in early 2010, it still had the top rank on the new evaluation datasets.

The highest ranked algorithm, by Wang and Zheng (2008), follows a similar approach of segmenting the image, doing local plane fits, and then performing cooperative optimization of neighboring plane fit parameters. Another highly ranked algorithm, by Yang, Wang, Yang *et al.* (2009), uses the color correlation approach of Yoon and Kweon (2006) and hierarchical belief propagation to obtain an initial set of disparity estimates. After left–right consistency checking to detect occluded pixels, the data terms for low-confidence and occluded pixels are recomputed using segmentation-based plane fits and one or more rounds of hierarchical belief propagation are used to obtain the final disparity estimates.

Another important ability of segmentation-based stereo algorithms, which they share with algorithms that use explicit layers (Baker, Szeliski, and Anandan 1998; Szeliski and Golland 1999) or boundary extraction (Hasinoff, Kang, and Szeliski 2006), is the ability to extract fractional pixel alpha mattes at depth discontinuities (Bleyer, Gelautz, Rother *et al.* 2009). This ability is crucial when attempting to create virtual view interpolation without clinging boundary or tearing artifacts (Zitnick, Kang, Uyttendaele *et al.* 2004) and also to seamlessly insert virtual objects (Taguchi, Wilburn, and Zitnick 2008), as shown in Figure 11.13b.

Figure 11.14 Background replacement using z-keying with a bi-layer segmentation algorithm (Kolmogorov, Criminisi, Blake *et al.* 2006) © 2006 IEEE.

Since new stereo matching algorithms continue to be introduced every year, it is a good idea to periodically check the Middlebury evaluation site at http://vision.middlebury.edu/stereo for a listing of the most recent algorithms to be evaluated.

11.5.3 *Application*: Z-keying and background replacement

Another application of real-time stereo matching is *z-keying*, which is the process of segmenting a foreground actor from the background using depth information, usually for the purpose of replacing the background with some computer-generated imagery, as shown in Figure 11.2g.

Originally, z-keying systems required expensive custom-built hardware to produce the desired depth maps in real time and were, therefore, restricted to broadcast studio applications (Kanade, Yoshida, Oda *et al.* 1996; Iddan and Yahav 2001). Off-line systems were also developed for estimating 3D multi-viewpoint geometry from video streams (Section 13.5.4) (Kanade, Rander, and Narayanan 1997; Carranza, Theobalt, Magnor *et al.* 2003; Zitnick, Kang, Uyttendaele *et al.* 2004; Vedula, Baker, and Kanade 2005). Recent advances in highly accurate real-time stereo matching, however, now make it possible to perform z-keying on regular PCs, enabling desktop videoconferencing applications such as those shown in Figure 11.14 (Kolmogorov, Criminisi, Blake *et al.* 2006).

11.6 Multi-view stereo

While matching pairs of images is a useful way of obtaining depth information, matching more images can lead to even better results. In this section, we review not only techniques for creating complete 3D object models, but also simpler techniques for improving the quality of depth maps using multiple source images.

As we saw in our discussion of plane sweep (Section 11.1.2), it is possible to resample all neighboring k images at each disparity hypothesis d into a generalized disparity space

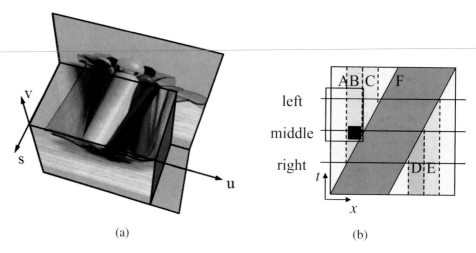

(a)   (b)

Figure 11.15 Epipolar plane image (EPI) (Gortler, Grzeszczuk, Szeliski *et al.* 1996) © 1996 ACM and a schematic EPI (Kang, Szeliski, and Chai 2001) © 2001 IEEE. (a) The Lumigraph (light field) (Section 13.3) is the 4D space of all light rays passing through a volume of space. Taking a 2D slice results in all of the light rays embedded in a plane and is equivalent to a scanline taken from a stacked EPI volume. Objects at different depths move sideways with velocities (slopes) proportional to their inverse depth. Occlusion (and translucency) effects can easily be seen in this representation. (b) The EPI corresponding to Figure 11.16 showing the three images (middle, left, and right) as slices through the EPI volume. The spatially and temporally shifted window around the black pixel is indicated by the rectangle, showing the right image is not being used in matching.

volume $\tilde{I}(x, y, d, k)$. The simplest way to take advantage of these additional images is to sum up their differences from the reference image I_r as in (11.4),

$$C(x, y, d) = \sum_k \rho(\tilde{I}(x, y, d, k) - I_r(x, y)).$$ (11.15)

This is the basis of the well-known sum of summed-squared-difference (SSSD) and SSAD approaches (Okutomi and Kanade 1993; Kang, Webb, Zitnick *et al.* 1995), which can be extended to reason about likely patterns of occlusion (Nakamura, Matsuura, Satoh *et al.* 1996). More recent work by Gallup, Frahm, Mordohai *et al.* (2008) show how to adapt the baselines used to the expected depth in order to get the best tradeoff between geometric accuracy (wide baseline) and robustness to occlusion (narrow baseline). Alternative multi-view cost metrics include measures such as synthetic focus sharpness and the entropy of the pixel color distribution (Vaish, Szeliski, Zitnick *et al.* 2006).

A useful way to visualize the multi-frame stereo estimation problem is to examine the *epipolar plane image* (EPI) formed by stacking corresponding scanlines from all the images, as shown in Figures 8.13c and 11.15 (Bolles, Baker, and Marimont 1987; Baker and Bolles 1989; Baker 1989). As you can see in Figure 11.15, as a camera translates horizontally (in a standard horizontally rectified geometry), objects at different depths move sideways at a rate inversely proportional to their depth (11.1).[6] Foreground objects occlude background objects,

---

[6] The four-dimensional generalization of the EPI is the *light field*, which we study in Section 13.3. In principle, there is enough information in a light field to recover both the shape and the BRDF of objects (Soatto, Yezzi, and Jin 2003), although relatively little progress has been made to date on this topic.

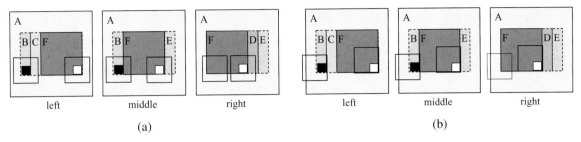

Figure 11.16 Spatio-temporally shiftable windows (Kang, Szeliski, and Chai 2001) © 2001 IEEE: A simple three-image sequence (the middle image is the reference image), which has a moving frontal gray square (marked F) and a stationary background. Regions B, C, D, and E are partially occluded. (a) A regular SSD algorithm will make mistakes when matching pixels in these regions (e.g. the window centered on the black pixel in region B) and in windows straddling depth discontinuities (the window centered on the white pixel in region F). (b) Shiftable windows help mitigate the problems in partially occluded regions and near depth discontinuities. The shifted window centered on the white pixel in region F matches correctly in all frames. The shifted window centered on the black pixel in region B matches correctly in the left image, but requires temporal selection to disable matching the right image. Figure 11.15b shows an EPI corresponding to this sequence and describes in more detail how temporal selection works.

which can be seen as *EPI-strips* (Criminisi, Kang, Swaminathan *et al.* 2005) occluding other strips in the EPI. If we are given a dense enough set of images, we can find such strips and reason about their relationships in order to both reconstruct the 3D scene and make inferences about translucent objects (Tsin, Kang, and Szeliski 2006) and specular reflections (Swaminathan, Kang, Szeliski *et al.* 2002; Criminisi, Kang, Swaminathan *et al.* 2005). Alternatively, we can treat the series of images as a set of sequential observations and merge them using Kalman filtering (Matthies, Kanade, and Szeliski 1989) or maximum likelihood inference (Cox 1994).

When fewer images are available, it becomes necessary to fall back on aggregation techniques such as sliding windows or global optimization. With additional input images, however, the likelihood of occlusions increases. It is therefore prudent to adjust not only the best window locations using a shiftable window approach, as shown in Figure 11.16a, but also to optionally select a subset of neighboring frames in order to discount those images where the region of interest is occluded, as shown in Figure 11.16b (Kang, Szeliski, and Chai 2001). Figure11.15b shows how such spatio-temporal selection or shifting of windows corresponds to selecting the most likely un-occluded volumetric region in the epipolar plane image volume.

The results of applying these techniques to the multi-frame *flower garden* image sequence are shown in Figure 11.17, which compares the results of using regular (non-shifted) SSSD with spatially shifted windows and full spatio-temporal window selection. (The task of applying stereo to a rigid scene filmed with a moving camera is sometimes called *motion stereo*). Similar improvements from using spatio-temporal selection are reported by (Kang and Szeliski 2004) and are evident even when local measurements are combined with global optimization.

While computing a depth map from multiple inputs outperforms pairwise stereo matching, even more dramatic improvements can be obtained by estimating multiple depth maps

(a) (b) (c) (d)

Figure 11.17 Local (5 × 5 window-based) matching results (Kang, Szeliski, and Chai 2001) © 2001 IEEE: (a) window that is not spatially perturbed (centered); (b) spatially perturbed window; (c) using the best five of 10 neighboring frames; (d) using the better half sequence. Notice how the results near the tree trunk are improved using temporal selection.

simultaneously (Szeliski 1999; Kang and Szeliski 2004). The existence of multiple depth maps enables more accurate reasoning about occlusions, as regions which are occluded in one image may be visible (and matchable) in others. The multi-view reconstruction problem can be formulated as the simultaneous estimation of depth maps at key frames (Figure 8.13c) while maximizing not only photoconsistency and piecewise disparity smoothness but also the consistency between disparity estimates at different frames. While Szeliski (1999) and Kang and Szeliski (2004) use soft (penalty-based) constraints to encourage multiple disparity maps to be consistent, Kolmogorov and Zabih (2002) show how such consistency measures can be encoded as hard constraints, which guarantee that the multiple depth maps are not only similar but actually identical in overlapping regions. Newer algorithms that simultaneously estimate multiple disparity maps include papers by Maitre, Shinagawa, and Do (2008) and Zhang, Jia, Wong *et al.* (2008).

A closely related topic to multi-frame stereo estimation is *scene flow*, in which multiple cameras are used to capture a dynamic scene. The task is then to simultaneously recover the 3D shape of the object at every instant in time and to estimate the full 3D motion of every surface point between frames. Representative papers in this area include those by Vedula, Baker, Rander *et al.* (2005), Zhang and Kambhamettu (2003), Pons, Keriven, and Faugeras (2007), Huguet and Devernay (2007), and Wedel, Rabe, Vaudrey *et al.* (2008). Figure 11.18a shows an image of the 3D scene flow for the tango dancer shown in Figure 11.2h–j, while Figure 11.18b shows 3D scene flows captured from a moving vehicle for the purpose of obstacle avoidance. In addition to supporting mensuration and safety applications, scene flow can be used to support both spatial and temporal view interpolation (Section 13.5.4), as demonstrated by Vedula, Baker, and Kanade (2005).

11.6.1 Volumetric and 3D surface reconstruction

According to Seitz, Curless, Diebel *et al.* (2006):

> The goal of multi-view stereo is to reconstruct a complete 3D object model from
> a collection of images taken from known camera viewpoints.

The most challenging but potentially most useful variant of multi-view stereo reconstruction is to create globally consistent 3D models. This topic has a long history in computer vision, starting with surface mesh reconstruction techniques such as the one developed by

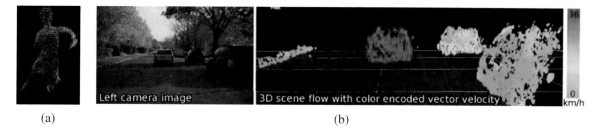

(a)   (b)

Figure 11.18 Three-dimensional scene flow: (a) computed from a multi-camera dome surrounding the dancer shown in Figure 11.2h–j (Vedula, Baker, Rander *et al.* 2005) © 2005 IEEE; (b) computed from stereo cameras mounted on a moving vehicle (Wedel, Rabe, Vaudrey *et al.* 2008) © 2008 Springer.

Fua and Leclerc (1995) (Figure 11.19a). A variety of approaches and representations have been used to solve this problem, including 3D voxel representations (Seitz and Dyer 1999; Szeliski and Golland 1999; De Bonet and Viola 1999; Kutulakos and Seitz 2000; Eisert, Steinbach, and Girod 2000; Slabaugh, Culbertson, Slabaugh *et al.* 2004; Sinha and Pollefeys 2005; Vogiatzis, Hernandez, Torr *et al.* 2007; Hiep, Keriven, Pons *et al.* 2009), level sets (Faugeras and Keriven 1998; Pons, Keriven, and Faugeras 2007), polygonal meshes (Fua and Leclerc 1995; Narayanan, Rander, and Kanade 1998; Hernandez and Schmitt 2004; Furukawa and Ponce 2009), and multiple depth maps (Kolmogorov and Zabih 2002). Figure 11.19 shows representative examples of 3D object models reconstructed using some of these techniques.

In order to organize and compare all these techniques, Seitz, Curless, Diebel *et al.* (2006) developed a six-point taxonomy that can help classify algorithms according to the *scene representation*, *photoconsistency measure*, *visibility model*, *shape priors*, *reconstruction algorithm*, and *initialization requirements* they use. Below, we summarize some of these choices and list a few representative papers. For more details, please consult the full survey paper (Seitz, Curless, Diebel *et al.* 2006) and the evaluation Web site, http://vision.middlebury.edu/mview/, which contains pointers to even more recent papers and results.

Scene representation. One of the more popular 3D representations is a uniform grid of 3D voxels,[7] which can be reconstructed using a variety of carving (Seitz and Dyer 1999; Kutulakos and Seitz 2000) or optimization (Sinha and Pollefeys 2005; Vogiatzis, Hernandez, Torr *et al.* 2007; Hiep, Keriven, Pons *et al.* 2009) techniques. Level set techniques (Section 5.1.4) also operate on a uniform grid but, instead of representing a binary occupancy map, they represent the signed distance to the surface (Faugeras and Keriven 1998; Pons, Keriven, and Faugeras 2007), which can encode a finer level of detail. Polygonal meshes are another popular representation (Fua and Leclerc 1995; Narayanan, Rander, and Kanade 1998; Isidoro and Sclaroff 2003; Hernandez and Schmitt 2004; Furukawa and Ponce 2009; Hiep, Keriven, Pons *et al.* 2009). Meshes are the standard representation used in computer graphics and also readily support the computation of visibility and occlusions. Finally, as we discussed in the previous section, multiple depth maps can also be used (Szeliski 1999; Kolmogorov and Zabih 2002; Kang and Szeliski 2004). Many algorithms also use more than a single representation, e.g., they may start by computing multiple depth maps and then merge

---

[7] For outdoor scenes that go to infinity, a non-uniform gridding of space may be preferable (Slabaugh, Culbertson, Slabaugh *et al.* 2004).

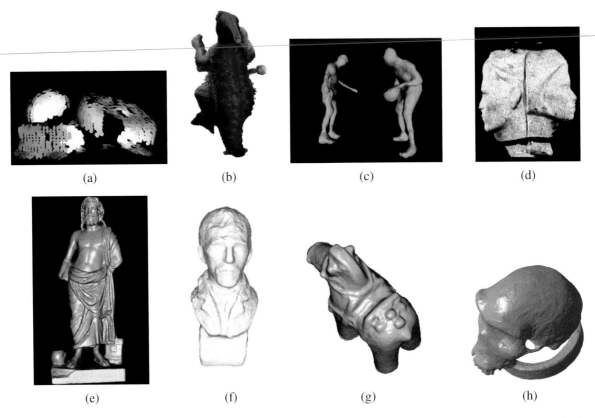

Figure 11.19 Multi-view stereo algorithms: (a) surface-based stereo (Fua and Leclerc 1995); (b) voxel coloring (Seitz and Dyer 1999) © 1999 Springer; (c) depth map merging (Narayanan, Rander, and Kanade 1998); (d) level set evolution (Faugeras and Keriven 1998) © 1998 IEEE; (e) silhouette and stereo fusion (Hernandez and Schmitt 2004) © 2004 Elsevier; (f) multi-view image matching (Pons, Keriven, and Faugeras 2005) © 2005 IEEE; (g) volumetric graph cut (Vogiatzis, Torr, and Cipolla 2005) © 2005 IEEE; (h) carved visual hulls (Furukawa and Ponce 2009) © 2009 Springer.

them into a 3D object model (Narayanan, Rander, and Kanade 1998; Furukawa and Ponce 2009; Goesele, Curless, and Seitz 2006; Goesele, Snavely, Curless *et al.* 2007; Furukawa, Curless, Seitz *et al.* 2010).

Photoconsistency measure. As we discussed in (Section 11.3.1), a variety of similarity measures can be used to compare pixel values in different images, including measures that try to discount illumination effects or be less sensitive to outliers. In multi-view stereo, algorithms have a choice of computing these measures directly on the surface of the model, i.e., in *scene space*, or projecting pixel values from one image (or from a textured model) back into another image, i.e., in *image space*. (The latter corresponds more closely to a Bayesian approach, since input images are noisy measurements of the colored 3D model.) The geometry of the object, i.e., its distance to each camera and its local surface normal, when available, can be used to adjust the matching windows used in the computation to account for foreshortening and scale change (Goesele, Snavely, Curless *et al.* 2007).

Visibility model. A big advantage that multi-view stereo algorithms have over single-depth-map approaches is their ability to reason in a principled manner about visibility and occlusions. Techniques that use the current state of the 3D model to predict which surface pixels are visible in each image (Kutulakos and Seitz 2000; Faugeras and Keriven 1998; Vogiatzis, Hernandez, Torr *et al.* 2007; Hiep, Keriven, Pons *et al.* 2009) are classified as using *geometric visibility models* in the taxonomy of Seitz, Curless, Diebel *et al.* (2006). Techniques that select a neighboring subset of image to match are called *quasi-geometric* (Narayanan, Rander, and Kanade 1998; Kang and Szeliski 2004; Hernandez and Schmitt 2004), while techniques that use traditional robust similarity measures are called *outlier-based*. While full geometric reasoning is the most principled and accurate approach, it can be very slow to evaluate and depends on the evolving quality of the current surface estimate to predict visibility, which can be a bit of a chicken-and-egg problem, unless conservative assumptions are used, as they are by Kutulakos and Seitz (2000).

Shape priors. Because stereo matching is often underconstrained, especially in texture-less regions, most matching algorithms adopt (either explicitly or implicitly) some form of prior model for the expected shape. Many of the techniques that rely on optimization use a 3D smoothness or area-based photoconsistency constraint, which, because of the natural tendency of smooth surfaces to shrink inwards, often results in a *minimal surface* prior (Faugeras and Keriven 1998; Sinha and Pollefeys 2005; Vogiatzis, Hernandez, Torr *et al.* 2007). Approaches that carve away the volume of space often stop once a photoconsistent solution is found (Seitz and Dyer 1999; Kutulakos and Seitz 2000), which corresponds to a *maximal surface* bias, i.e., these techniques tend to over-estimate the true shape. Finally, multiple depth map approaches often adopt traditional *image-based* smoothness (regularization) constraints.

Reconstruction algorithm. The details of how the actual reconstruction algorithm proceeds is where the largest variety—and greatest innovation—in multi-view stereo algorithms can be found.

Some approaches use global optimization defined over a three-dimensional photoconsistency volume to recover a complete surface. Approaches based on graph cuts use polynomial complexity binary segmentation algorithms to recover the object model defined on the voxel grid (Sinha and Pollefeys 2005; Vogiatzis, Hernandez, Torr *et al.* 2007; Hiep, Keriven, Pons *et al.* 2009). Level set approaches use a continuous surface evolution to find a good minimum in the configuration space of potential surfaces and therefore require a reasonably good initialization (Faugeras and Keriven 1998; Pons, Keriven, and Faugeras 2007). In order for the photoconsistency volume to be meaningful, matching costs need to be computed in some robust fashion, e.g., using sets of limited views or by aggregating multiple depth maps.

An alternative approach to global optimization is to sweep through the 3D volume while computing both photoconsistency and visibility simultaneously. The *voxel coloring* algorithm of Seitz and Dyer (1999) performs a front-to-back plane sweep. On every plane, any voxels that are sufficiently photoconsistent are labeled as part of the object. The corresponding pixels in the source images can then be "erased", since they are already accounted for, and therefore do not contribute to further photoconsistency computations. (A similar approach, albeit without the front-to-back sweep order, is used by Szeliski and Golland (1999).) The resulting 3D volume, under noise- and resampling-free conditions, is guaranteed to produce

Figure 11.20   The multi-view stereo data sets captured by Seitz, Curless, Diebel *et al.* (2006) © 2006 Springer. Only (a) and (b) are currently used for evaluation.

both a photoconsistent 3D model and to enclose whatever true 3D object model generated the images.

Unfortunately, voxel coloring is only guaranteed to work if all of the cameras lie on the same side of the sweep planes, which is not possible in general ring configurations of cameras. Kutulakos and Seitz (2000) generalize voxel coloring to *space carving*, where subsets of cameras that satisfy the voxel coloring constraint are iteratively selected and the 3D voxel grid is alternately carved away along different axes.

Another popular approach to multi-view stereo is to first independently compute multiple depth maps and then merge these partial maps into a complete 3D model. Approaches to depth map merging, which are discussed in more detail in Section 12.2.1, include signed distance functions (Curless and Levoy 1996), used by Goesele, Curless, and Seitz (2006), and Poisson surface reconstruction (Kazhdan, Bolitho, and Hoppe 2006), used by Goesele, Snavely, Curless *et al.* (2007). It is also possible to reconstruct sparser representations, such as 3D points and lines, and to interpolate them to full 3D surfaces (Section 12.3.1) (Taylor 2003).

Initialization requirements.   One final element discussed by Seitz, Curless, Diebel *et al.* (2006) is the varying degrees of initialization required by different algorithms. Because some algorithms refine or evolve a rough 3D model, they require a reasonably accurate (or overcomplete) initial model, which can often be obtained by reconstructing a volume from object silhouettes, as discussed in Section 11.6.2. However, if the algorithm performs a global optimization (Kolev, Klodt, Brox *et al.* 2009; Kolev and Cremers 2009), this dependence on initialization is not an issue.

Empirical evaluation.   In order to evaluate the large number of design alternatives in multi-view stereo, Seitz, Curless, Diebel *et al.* (2006) collected a dataset of calibrated images using a spherical gantry. A representative image from each of the six datasets is shown in Figure 11.20, although only the first two datasets have as yet been fully processed and used for evaluation. Figure 11.21 shows the results of running seven different algorithms on the *temple* dataset. As you can see, most of the techniques do an impressive job of capturing the fine details in the columns, although it is also clear that the techniques employ differing amounts of smoothing to achieve these results.

Since the publication of the survey by Seitz, Curless, Diebel *et al.* (2006), the field of

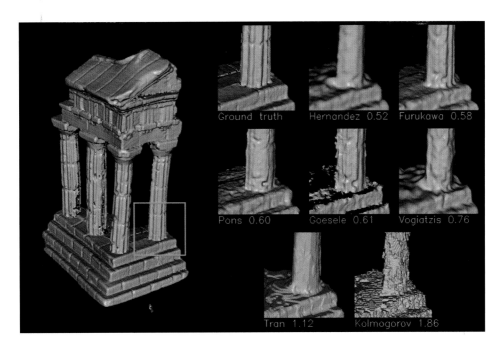

Figure 11.21 Reconstruction results (details) for seven algorithms (Hernandez and Schmitt 2004; Furukawa and Ponce 2009; Pons, Keriven, and Faugeras 2005; Goesele, Curless, and Seitz 2006; Vogiatzis, Torr, and Cipolla 2005; Tran and Davis 2002; Kolmogorov and Zabih 2002) evaluated by Seitz, Curless, Diebel *et al.* (2006) on the 47-image Temple Ring dataset. The numbers underneath each detail image are the accuracy of each of these techniques measured in millimeters.

multi-view stereo has continued to advance at a rapid pace (Strecha, Fransens, and Van Gool 2006; Hernandez, Vogiatzis, and Cipolla 2007; Habbecke and Kobbelt 2007; Furukawa and Ponce 2007; Vogiatzis, Hernandez, Torr *et al.* 2007; Goesele, Snavely, Curless *et al.* 2007; Sinha, Mordohai, and Pollefeys 2007; Gargallo, Prados, and Sturm 2007; Merrell, Akbarzadeh, Wang *et al.* 2007; Zach, Pock, and Bischof 2007b; Furukawa and Ponce 2008; Hornung, Zeng, and Kobbelt 2008; Bradley, Boubekeur, and Heidrich 2008; Zach 2008; Campbell, Vogiatzis, Hernández *et al.* 2008; Kolev, Klodt, Brox *et al.* 2009; Hiep, Keriven, Pons *et al.* 2009; Furukawa, Curless, Seitz *et al.* 2010). The multi-view stereo evaluation site, http://vision.middlebury.edu/mview/, provides quantitative results for these algorithms along with pointers to where to find these papers.

11.6.2 Shape from silhouettes

In many situations, performing a foreground–background segmentation of the object of interest is a good way to initialize or fit a 3D model (Grauman, Shakhnarovich, and Darrell 2003; Vlasic, Baran, Matusik *et al.* 2008) or to impose a convex set of constraints on multi-view stereo (Kolev and Cremers 2008). Over the years, a number of techniques have been developed to reconstruct a 3D volumetric model from the intersection of the binary silhouettes projected into 3D. The resulting model is called a *visual hull* (or sometimes a *line hull*), analogous with the convex hull of a set of points, since the volume is maximal with respect

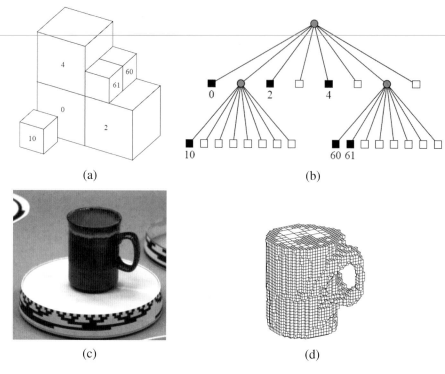

(a)   (b)

(c)   (d)

Figure 11.22   Volumetric octree reconstruction from binary silhouettes (Szeliski 1993) © 1993 Elsevier: (a) octree representation and its corresponding (b) tree structure; (c) input image of an object on a turntable; (d) computed 3D volumetric octree model.

to the visual silhouettes and surface elements are tangent to the viewing rays (lines) along the silhouette boundaries (Laurentini 1994). It is also possible to carve away a more accurate reconstruction using multi-view stereo (Sinha and Pollefeys 2005) or by analyzing cast shadows (Savarese, Andreetto, Rushmeier *et al.* 2007).

Some techniques first approximate each silhouette with a polygonal representation and then intersect the resulting faceted conical regions in three-space to produce polyhedral models (Baumgart 1974; Martin and Aggarwal 1983; Matusik, Buehler, and McMillan 2001), which can later be refined using triangular splines (Sullivan and Ponce 1998). Other approaches use voxel-based representations, usually encoded as octrees (Samet 1989), because of the resulting space–time efficiency. Figures 11.22a–b show an example of a 3D octree model and its associated colored tree, where black nodes are interior to the model, white nodes are exterior, and gray nodes are of mixed occupancy. Examples of octree-based reconstruction approaches include those by Potmesil (1987), Noborio, Fukada, and Arimoto (1988), Srivasan, Liang, and Hackwood (1990), and Szeliski (1993).

The approach of Szeliski (1993) first converts each binary silhouette into a one-sided variant of a distance map, where each pixel in the map indicates the largest square that is completely inside (or outside) the silhouette. This makes it fast to project an octree cell into the silhouette to confirm whether it is completely inside or outside the object, so that it can be colored black, white, or left as gray (mixed) for further refinement on a smaller grid. The octree construction algorithm proceeds in a coarse-to-fine manner, first building an octree at a relatively coarse resolution, and then refining it by revisiting and subdividing all the input images for the gray (mixed) cells whose occupancy has not yet been determined. Figure 11.22d shows the resulting octree model computed from a coffee cup rotating on a turntable.

More recent work on visual hull computation borrows ideas from image-based rendering, and is hence called an *image-based visual hull* (Matusik, Buehler, Raskar *et al.* 2000). Instead of precomputing a global 3D model, an image-based visual hull is recomputed for each new viewpoint, by successively intersecting viewing ray segments with the binary silhouettes in each image. This not only leads to a fast computation algorithm but also enables fast texturing of the recovered model with color values from the input images. This approach can also be combined with high-quality deformable templates to capture and re-animate whole body motion (Vlasic, Baran, Matusik *et al.* 2008).

11.7 Additional reading

The field of stereo correspondence and depth estimation is one of the oldest and most widely studied topics in computer vision. A number of good surveys have been written over the years (Marr and Poggio 1976; Barnard and Fischler 1982; Dhond and Aggarwal 1989; Scharstein and Szeliski 2002; Brown, Burschka, and Hager 2003; Seitz, Curless, Diebel *et al.* 2006) and they can serve as good guides to this extensive literature.

Because of computational limitations and the desire to find appearance-invariant correspondences, early algorithms often focused on finding *sparse correspondences* (Hannah 1974; Marr and Poggio 1979; Mayhew and Frisby 1980; Baker and Binford 1981; Arnold 1983; Grimson 1985; Ohta and Kanade 1985; Bolles, Baker, and Marimont 1987; Matthies, Kanade, and Szeliski 1989; Hsieh, McKeown, and Perlant 1992; Bolles, Baker, and Hannah 1993).

The topic of computing epipolar geometry and pre-rectifying images is covered in Sections 7.2 and 11.1 and is also treated in textbooks on multi-view geometry (Faugeras and Luong 2001; Hartley and Zisserman 2004) and articles specifically on this topic (Torr and Murray 1997; Zhang 1998a,b). The concepts of the *disparity space* and *disparity space image* are often associated with the seminal work by Marr (1982) and the papers of Yang, Yuille, and Lu (1993) and Intille and Bobick (1994). The plane sweep algorithm was first popularized by Collins (1996) and then generalized to a full arbitrary projective setting by Szeliski and Golland (1999) and Saito and Kanade (1999). Plane sweeps can also be formulated using cylindrical surfaces (Ishiguro, Yamamoto, and Tsuji 1992; Kang and Szeliski 1997; Shum and Szeliski 1999; Li, Shum, Tang *et al.* 2004; Zheng, Kang, Cohen *et al.* 2007) or even more general topologies (Seitz 2001).

Once the topology for the cost volume or DSI has been set up, we need to compute the actual photoconsistency measures for each pixel and potential depth. A wide range of such measures have been proposed, as discussed in Section 11.3.1. Some of these are compared in recent surveys and evaluations of matching costs (Scharstein and Szeliski 2002; Hirschmüller and Scharstein 2009).

To compute an actual depth map from these costs, some form of optimization or selection criterion must be used. The simplest of these are sliding windows of various kinds, which are discussed in Section 11.4 and surveyed by Gong, Yang, Wang *et al.* (2007) and Tombari,

Mattoccia, Di Stefano *et al.* (2008). More commonly, global optimization frameworks are used to compute the best disparity field, as described in Section 11.5. These techniques include dynamic programming and truly global optimization algorithms, such as graph cuts and loopy belief propagation. Because the literature on this is so extensive, it is described in more detail in Section 11.5. A good place to find pointers to the latest results in this field is the Middlebury Stereo Vision Page at http://vision.middlebury.edu/stereo.

Algorithms for multi-view stereo typically fall into two categories. The first include algorithms that compute traditional depth maps using several images for computing photoconsistency measures (Okutomi and Kanade 1993; Kang, Webb, Zitnick *et al.* 1995; Nakamura, Matsuura, Satoh *et al.* 1996; Szeliski and Golland 1999; Kang, Szeliski, and Chai 2001; Vaish, Szeliski, Zitnick *et al.* 2006; Gallup, Frahm, Mordohai *et al.* 2008). Optionally, some of these techniques compute multiple depth maps and use additional constraints to encourage the different depth maps to be consistent (Szeliski 1999; Kolmogorov and Zabih 2002; Kang and Szeliski 2004; Maitre, Shinagawa, and Do 2008; Zhang, Jia, Wong *et al.* 2008).

The second category consists of papers that compute true 3D volumetric or surface-based object models. Again, because of the large number of papers published on this topic, rather than citing them here, we refer you to the material in Section 11.6.1, the survey by Seitz, Curless, Diebel *et al.* (2006), and the on-line evaluation Web site at http://vision.middlebury.edu/mview/.

11.8 Exercises

Ex 11.1: Stereo pair rectification   Implement the following simple algorithm (Section 11.1.1):

1. Rotate both cameras so that they are looking perpendicular to the line joining the two camera centers c_0 and c_1. The smallest rotation can be computed from the cross product between the original and desired optical axes.

2. Twist the optical axes so that the horizontal axis of each camera looks in the direction of the other camera. (Again, the cross product between the current x-axis after the first rotation and the line joining the cameras gives the rotation.)

3. If needed, scale up the smaller (less detailed) image so that it has the same resolution (and hence line-to-line correspondence) as the other image.

Now compare your results to the algorithm proposed by Loop and Zhang (1999). Can you think of situations where their approach may be preferable?

Ex 11.2: Rigid direct alignment   Modify your spline-based or optical flow motion estimator from Exercise 8.4 to use epipolar geometry, i.e. to only estimate disparity.

(Optional) Extend your algorithm to simultaneously estimate the epipolar geometry (without first using point correspondences) by estimating a base homography corresponding to a reference plane for the dominant motion and then an epipole for the residual parallax (motion).

Ex 11.3: Shape from profiles   Reconstruct a surface model from a series of edge images (Section 11.2.1).

1. Extract edges and link them (Exercises 4.7–4.8).

2. Based on previously computed epipolar geometry, match up edges in triplets (or longer sets) of images.

3. Reconstruct the 3D locations of the curves using osculating circles (11.5).

4. Render the resulting 3D surface model as a sparse mesh, i.e., drawing the reconstructed 3D profile curves and links between 3D points in neighboring images with similar osculating circles.

Ex 11.4: Plane sweep   Implement a plane sweep algorithm (Section 11.1.2).

If the images are already pre-rectified, this consists simply of shifting images relative to each other and comparing pixels. If the images are not pre-rectified, compute the homography that resamples the target image into the reference image's coordinate system for each plane.

Evaluate a subset of the following similarity measures (Section 11.3.1) and compare their performance by visualizing the disparity space image (DSI), which should be dark for pixels at correct depths:

- squared difference (SD);

- absolute difference (AD);

- truncated or robust measures;

- gradient differences;

- rank or census transform (the latter usually performs better);

- mutual information from a pre-computed joint density function.

Consider using the Birchfield and Tomasi (1998) technique of comparing ranges between neighboring pixels (different shifted or warped images). Also, try pre-compensating images for bias or gain variations using one or more of the techniques discussed in Section 11.3.1.

Ex 11.5: Aggregation and window-based stereo   Implement one or more of the matching cost aggregation strategies described in Section 11.4:

- convolution with a box or Gaussian kernel;

- shifting window locations by applying a min filter (Scharstein and Szeliski 2002);

- picking a window that maximizes some match-reliability metric (Veksler 2001, 2003);

- weighting pixels by their similarity to the central pixel (Yoon and Kweon 2006).

Once you have aggregated the costs in the DSI, pick the winner at each pixel (winner-take-all), and then optionally perform one or more of the following post-processing steps:

1. compute matches both ways and pick only the reliable matches (draw the others in another color);

2. tag matches that are unsure (whose confidence is too low);

3. fill in the matches that are unsure from neighboring values;

4. refine your matches to sub-pixel disparity by either fitting a parabola to the DSI values around the winner or by using an iteration of Lukas–Kanade.

Ex 11.6: Optimization-based stereo   Compute the disparity space image (DSI) volume using one of the techniques you implemented in Exercise 11.4 and then implement one (or more) of the global optimization techniques described in Section 11.5 to compute the depth map. Potential choices include:

- dynamic programming or scanline optimization (relatively easy);

- semi-global optimization (Hirschmüller 2008), which is a simple extension of scanline optimization and performs well;

- graph cuts using alpha expansions (Boykov, Veksler, and Zabih 2001), for which you will need to find a max-flow or min-cut algorithm (http://vision.middlebury.edu/stereo);

- loopy belief propagation (Appendix B.5.3).

Evaluate your algorithm by running it on the Middlebury stereo data sets.

How well does your algorithm do against local aggregation (Yoon and Kweon 2006)? Can you think of some extensions or modifications to make it even better?

Ex 11.7: View interpolation, revisited   Compute a dense depth map using one of the techniques you developed above and use it (or, better yet, a depth map for each source image) to generate smooth in-between views from a stereo data set.

Compare your results against using the ground truth depth data (if available).

What kinds of artifacts do you see? Can you think of ways to reduce them?

More details on implementing such algorithms can be found in Section 13.1 and Exercises 13.1–13.4.

Ex 11.8: Multi-frame stereo   Extend one of your previous techniques to use multiple input frames (Section 11.6) and try to improve the results you obtained with just two views.

If helpful, try using temporal selection (Kang and Szeliski 2004) to deal with the increased number of occlusions in multi-frame data sets.

You can also try to simultaneously estimate multiple depth maps and make them consistent (Kolmogorov and Zabih 2002; Kang and Szeliski 2004).

Test your algorithms out on some standard multi-view data sets.

Ex 11.9: Volumetric stereo   Implement voxel coloring (Seitz and Dyer 1999) as a simple extension to the plane sweep algorithm you implemented in Exercise 11.4.

1. Instead of computing the complete DSI all at once, evaluate each plane one at a time from front to back.

2. Tag every voxel whose photoconsistency is below a certain threshold as being part of the object and remember its average (or robust) color (Seitz and Dyer 1999; Eisert, Steinbach, and Girod 2000; Kutulakos 2000; Slabaugh, Culbertson, Slabaugh *et al.* 2004).

3. Erase the input pixels corresponding to tagged voxels in the input images, e.g., by setting their alpha value to 0 (or to some reduced number, depending on occupancy).

4. As you evaluate the next plane, use the source image alpha values to modify your photoconsistency score, e.g., only consider pixels that have full alpha or weight pixels by their alpha values.

5. If the cameras are not all on the same side of your plane sweeps, use space carving (Kutulakos and Seitz 2000) to cycle through different subsets of source images while carving away the volume from different directions.

Ex 11.10: Depth map merging   Use the technique you developed for multi-frame stereo in Exercise 11.8 or a different technique, such as the one described by Goesele, Snavely, Curless *et al.* (2007), to compute a depth map for every input image.

Merge these depth maps into a coherent 3D model, e.g., using Poisson surface reconstruction (Kazhdan, Bolitho, and Hoppe 2006).

Ex 11.11: Shape from silhouettes   Build a silhouette-based volume reconstruction algorithm (Section 11.6.2). Use an octree or some other representation of your choosing.

Chapter 12

3D reconstruction

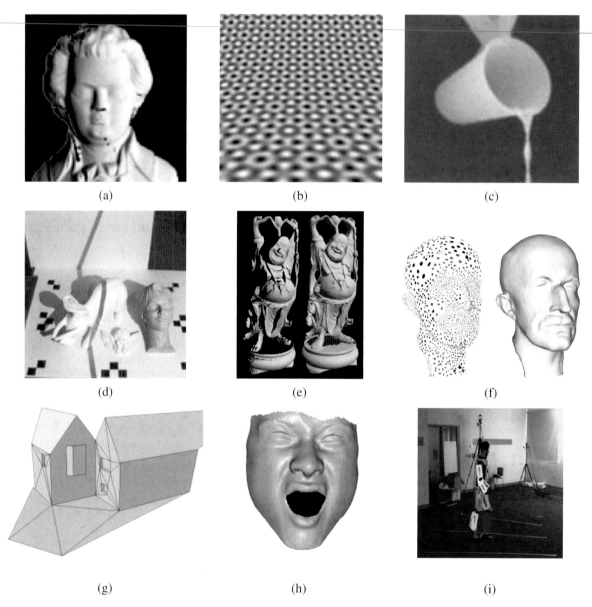

(a)   (b)   (c)

(d)   (e)   (f)

(g)   (h)   (i)

Figure 12.1   3D shape acquisition and modeling techniques: (a) shaded image (Zhang, Tsai, Cryer *et al.* 1999) © 1999 IEEE; (b) texture gradient (Garding 1992) © 1992 Springer; (c) real-time depth from focus (Nayar, Watanabe, and Noguchi 1996) © 1996 IEEE; (d) scanning a scene with a stick shadow (Bouguet and Perona 1999) © 1999 Springer; (e) merging range maps into a 3D model (Curless and Levoy 1996) © 1996 ACM; (f) point-based surface modeling (Pauly, Keiser, Kobbelt *et al.* 2003) © 2003 ACM; (g) automated modeling of a 3D building using lines and planes (Werner and Zisserman 2002) © 2002 Springer; (h) 3D face model from spacetime stereo (Zhang, Snavely, Curless *et al.* 2004) © 2004 ACM; (i) person tracking (Sigal, Bhatia, Roth *et al.* 2004) © 2004 IEEE.

As we saw in the previous chapter, a variety of stereo matching techniques have been developed to reconstruct high quality 3D models from two or more images. However, stereo is just one of the many potential cues that can be used to infer shape from images. In this chapter, we investigate a number of such techniques, which include not only visual cues such as shading and focus, but also techniques for merging multiple range or depth images into 3D models, as well as techniques for reconstructing specialized models, such as heads, bodies, or architecture.

Among the various cues that can be used to infer shape, the shading on a surface (Figure 12.1a) can provide a lot of information about local surface orientations and hence overall surface shape (Section 12.1.1). This approach becomes even more powerful when lights shining from different directions can be turned on and off separately (*photometric stereo*). Texture gradients (Figure 12.1b), i.e., the foreshortening of regular patterns as the surface slants or bends away from the camera, can provide similar cues on local surface orientation (Section 12.1.2). Focus is another powerful cue to scene depth, especially when two or more images with different focus settings are used (Section 12.1.3).

3D shape can also be estimated using active illumination techniques such as light stripes (Figure 12.1d) or time of flight range finders (Section 12.2). The partial surface models obtained using such techniques (or passive image-based stereo) can then be merged into more coherent 3D surface models (Figure 12.1e), as discussed in Section 12.2.1. Such techniques have been used to construct highly detailed and accurate models of cultural heritage such as historic sites (Section 12.2.2). The resulting surface models can then be simplified to support viewing at different resolutions and streaming across the Web (Section 12.3.2). An alternative to working with continuous surfaces is to represent 3D surfaces as dense collections of 3D oriented points (Section 12.4) or as volumetric primitives (Section 12.5).

3D modeling can be more efficient and effective if we know something about the objects we are trying to reconstruct. In Section 12.6, we look at three specialized but commonly occurring examples, namely architecture (Figure 12.1g), heads and faces (Figure 12.1h), and whole bodies (Figure 12.1i). In addition to modeling people, we also discuss techniques for tracking them.

The last stage of shape and appearance modeling is to extract some textures to paint onto our 3D models (Section 12.7). Some techniques go beyond this and actually estimate full BRDFs (Section 12.7.1).

Because there exists such a large variety of techniques to perform 3D modeling, this chapter does not go into detail on any one of these. Readers are encouraged to find more information in the cited references or more specialized publications and conferences devoted to these topics, e.g., the International Symposium on 3D Data Processing, Visualization, and Transmission (3DPVT), the International Conference on 3D Digital Imaging and Modeling (3DIM), the International Conference on Automatic Face and Gesture Recognition (FG), the IEEE Workshop on Analysis and Modeling of Faces and Gestures, and the International Workshop on Tracking Humans for the Evaluation of their Motion in Image Sequences (THEMIS).

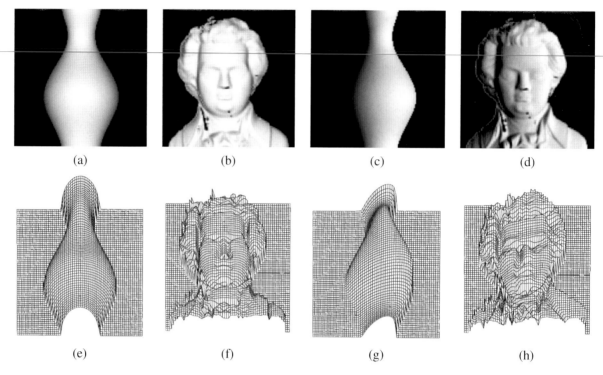

(a)   (b)   (c)   (d)

(e)   (f)   (g)   (h)

Figure 12.2 Synthetic shape from shading (Zhang, Tsai, Cryer *et al.* 1999) © 1999 IEEE: shaded images, (a–b) with light from in front $(0, 0, 1)$ and (c–d) with light the front right $(1, 0, 1)$; (e–f) corresponding shape from shading reconstructions using the technique of Tsai and Shah (1994).

12.1 Shape from X

In addition to binocular disparity, shading, texture, and focus all play a role in how we perceive shape. The study of how shape can be inferred from such cues is sometimes called *shape from X*, since the individual instances are called *shape from shading*, *shape from texture*, and *shape from focus*.[1] In this section, we look at these three cues and how they can be used to reconstruct 3D geometry. A good overview of all these topics can be found in the collection of papers on physics-based shape inference edited by Wolff, Shafer, and Healey (1992b).

12.1.1 Shape from shading and photometric stereo

When you look at images of smooth shaded objects, such as the ones shown in Figure 12.2, you can clearly see the shape of the object from just the shading variation. How is this possible? The answer is that as the surface normal changes across the object, the apparent brightness changes as a function of the angle between the local surface orientation and the incident illumination, as shown in Figure 2.15 (Section 2.2.2).

The problem of recovering the shape of a surface from this intensity variation is known as

---

[1] We have already seen examples of shape from stereo, shape from profiles, and shape from silhouettes in Chapter 11.

shape from shading and is one of the classic problems in computer vision (Horn 1975). The collection of papers edited by Horn and Brooks (1989) is a great source of information on this topic, especially the chapter on variational approaches. The survey by Zhang, Tsai, Cryer *et al.* (1999) not only reviews more recent techniques, but also provides some comparative results.

Most shape from shading algorithms assume that the surface under consideration is of a uniform albedo and reflectance, and that the light source directions are either known or can be calibrated by the use of a reference object. Under the assumptions of distant light sources and observer, the variation in intensity (*irradiance equation*) become purely a function of the local surface orientation,

$$I(x, y) = R(p(x, y), q(x, y)), \tag{12.1}$$

where $(p, q) = (z_x, z_y)$ are the depth map derivatives and $R(p, q)$ is called the *reflectance map*. For example, a diffuse (Lambertian) surface has a reflectance map that is the (non-negative) dot product (2.88) between the surface normal $\hat{n} = (p, q, 1)/\sqrt{1 + p^2 + q^2}$ and the light source direction $v = (v_x, v_y, v_z)$,

$$R(p, q) = \max\left(0, \rho \frac{p v_x + q v_y + v_z}{\sqrt{1 + p^2 + q^2}}\right), \tag{12.2}$$

where ρ is the surface reflectance factor (albedo).

In principle, Equations (12.1–12.2) can be used to estimate (p, q) using non-linear least squares or some other method. Unfortunately, unless additional constraints are imposed, there are more unknowns per pixel (p, q) than there are measurements (I). One commonly used constraint is the smoothness constraint,

$$\mathcal{E}_s = \int p_x^2 + p_y^2 + q_x^2 + q_y^2 \, dx \, dy = \int \|\nabla p\|^2 + \|\nabla q\|^2 \, dx \, dy, \tag{12.3}$$

which we already saw in Section 3.7.1 (3.94). The other is the *integrability constraint*,

$$\mathcal{E}_i = \int (p_y - q_x)^2 \, dx \, dy, \tag{12.4}$$

which arises naturally, since for a valid depth map $z(x, y)$ with $(p, q) = (z_x, z_y)$, we have $p_y = z_{xy} = z_{yx} = q_x$.

Instead of first recovering the orientation fields (p, q) and integrating them to obtain a surface, it is also possible to directly minimize the discrepancy in the image formation equation (12.1) while finding the optimal depth map $z(x, y)$ (Horn 1990). Unfortunately, shape from shading is susceptible to local minima in the search space and, like other variational problems that involve the simultaneous estimation of many variables, can also suffer from slow convergence. Using multi-resolution techniques (Szeliski 1991a) can help accelerate the convergence, while using more sophisticated optimization techniques (Dupuis and Oliensis 1994) can help avoid local minima.

In practice, surfaces other than plaster casts are rarely of a single uniform albedo. Shape from shading therefore needs to be combined with some other technique or extended in some way to make it useful. One way to do this is to combine it with stereo matching (Fua and Leclerc 1995) or known texture (surface patterns) (White and Forsyth 2006). The stereo and texture components provide information in textured regions, while shape from shading helps fill in the information across uniformly colored regions and also provides finer information about surface shape.

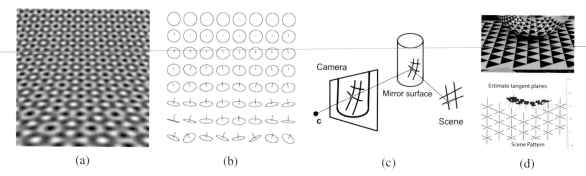

(a)   (b)   (c)   (d)

Figure 12.3 Synthetic shape from texture (Garding 1992) © 1992 Springer: (a) regular texture wrapped onto a curved surface and (b) the corresponding surface normal estimates. Shape from mirror reflections (Savarese, Chen, and Perona 2005) © 2005 Springer: (c) a regular pattern reflecting off a curved mirror gives rise to (d) curved lines, from which 3D point locations and normals can be inferred.

Photometric stereo. Another way to make shape from shading more reliable is to use multiple light sources that can be selectively turned on and off. This technique is called *photometric stereo*, since the light sources play a role analogous to the cameras located at different locations in traditional stereo (Woodham 1981).[2] For each light source, we have a different reflectance map, $R_1(p,q)$, $R_2(p,q)$, etc. Given the corresponding intensities I_1, I_2, etc. at a pixel, we can in principle recover both an unknown albedo ρ and a surface orientation estimate (p,q).

For diffuse surfaces (12.2), if we parameterize the local orientation by $\hat{n}$, we get (for non-shadowed pixels) a set of linear equations of the form

$$I_k = \rho\hat{n} \cdot v_k, \tag{12.5}$$

from which we can recover $\rho\hat{n}$ using linear least squares. These equations are well conditioned as long as the (three or more) vectors v_k are linearly independent, i.e., they are not along the same azimuth (direction away from the viewer).

Once the surface normals or gradients have been recovered at each pixel, they can be integrated into a depth map using a variant of regularized surface fitting (3.100). (Nehab, Rusinkiewicz, Davis *et al.* (2005) and Harker and O'Leary (2008) have produced some recent work in this area.)

When surfaces are specular, more than three light directions may be required. In fact, the irradiance equation given in (12.1) not only requires that the light sources and camera be distant from the surface, it also neglects inter-reflections, which can be a significant source of the shading observed on object surfaces, e.g., the darkening seen inside concave structures such as grooves and crevasses (Nayar, Ikeuchi, and Kanade 1991).

12.1.2 Shape from texture

The variation in foreshortening observed in regular textures can also provide useful information about local surface orientation. Figure 12.3 shows an example of such a pattern, along

---

[2] An alternative to turning lights on-and-off is to use three colored lights (Woodham 1994; Hernandez, Vogiatzis, Brostow *et al.* 2007; Hernandez and Vogiatzis 2010).

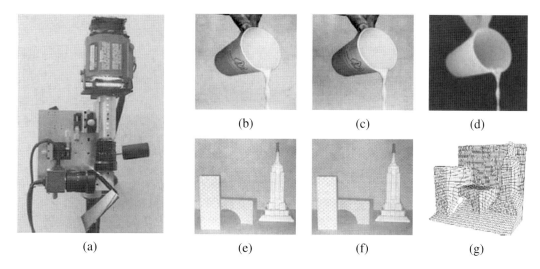

Figure 12.4 Real time depth from defocus (Nayar, Watanabe, and Noguchi 1996) © 1996 IEEE: (a) the real-time focus range sensor, which includes a half-silvered mirror between the two telecentric lenses (lower right), a prism that splits the image into two CCD sensors (lower left), and an edged checkerboard pattern illuminated by a Xenon lamp (top); (b–c) input video frames from the two cameras along with (d) the corresponding depth map; (e–f) two frames (you can see the texture if you zoom in) and (g) the corresponding 3D mesh model.

with the estimated local surface orientations. Shape from texture algorithms require a number of processing steps, including the extraction of repeated patterns or the measurement of local frequencies in order to compute local affine deformations, and a subsequent stage to infer local surface orientation. Details on these various stages can be found in the research literature (Witkin 1981; Ikeuchi 1981; Blostein and Ahuja 1987; Garding 1992; Malik and Rosenholtz 1997; Lobay and Forsyth 2006).

When the original pattern is regular, it is possible to fit a regular but slightly deformed grid to the image and use this grid for a variety of image replacement or analysis tasks (Liu, Collins, and Tsin 2004; Liu, Lin, and Hays 2004; Hays, Leordeanu, Efros *et al.* 2006; Lin, Hays, Wu *et al.* 2006; Park, Brocklehurst, Collins *et al.* 2009). This process becomes even easier if specially printed textured cloth patterns are used (White and Forsyth 2006; White, Crane, and Forsyth 2007).

The deformations induced in a regular pattern when it is viewed in the reflection of a curved mirror, as shown in Figure 12.3c–d, can be used to recover the shape of the surface (Savarese, Chen, and Perona 2005; Rozenfeld, Shimshoni, and Lindenbaum 2007). It is is also possible to infer local shape information from *specular flow*, i.e., the motion of specularities when viewed from a moving camera (Oren and Nayar 1997; Zisserman, Giblin, and Blake 1989; Swaminathan, Kang, Szeliski *et al.* 2002).

12.1.3 Shape from focus

A strong cue for object depth is the amount of blur, which increases as the object's surface moves away from the camera's focusing distance. As shown in Figure 2.19, moving the object surface away from the focus plane increases the circle of confusion, according to a formula that is easy to establish using similar triangles (Exercise 2.4).

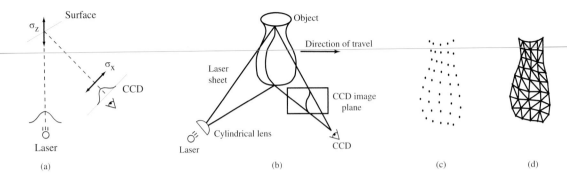

Figure 12.5 Range data scanning (Curless and Levoy 1996) © 1996 ACM: (a) a laser dot on a surface is imaged by a CCD sensor; (b) a laser stripe (sheet) is imaged by the sensor (the deformation of the stripe encodes the distance to the object); (c) the resulting set of 3D points are turned into (d) a triangulated mesh.

A number of techniques have been developed to estimate depth from the amount of defocus (*depth from defocus*) (Pentland 1987; Nayar and Nakagawa 1994; Nayar, Watanabe, and Noguchi 1996; Watanabe and Nayar 1998; Chaudhuri and Rajagopalan 1999; Favaro and Soatto 2006). In order to make such a technique practical, a number issues need to be addressed:

- The amount of blur increase in *both* directions as you move away from the focus plane. Therefore, it is necessary to use two or more images captured with different focus distance settings (Pentland 1987; Nayar, Watanabe, and Noguchi 1996) or to translate the object in depth and look for the point of maximum sharpness (Nayar and Nakagawa 1994).

- The magnification of the object can vary as the focus distance is changed or the object is moved. This can be modeled either explicitly (making correspondence more difficult) or using *telecentric optics*, which approximate an orthographic camera and require an aperture in front of the lens (Nayar, Watanabe, and Noguchi 1996).

- The amount of defocus must be reliably estimated. A simple approach is to average the squared gradient in a region but this suffers from several problems, including the image magnification problem mentioned above. A better solution is to use carefully designed *rational filters* (Watanabe and Nayar 1998).

Figure 12.4 shows an example of a real-time depth from defocus sensor, which employs two imaging chips at slightly different depths sharing a common optical path, as well as an active illumination system that projects a checkerboard pattern from the same direction. As you can see in Figure 12.4b–g, the system produces high-accuracy real-time depth maps for both static and dynamic scenes.

12.2 Active rangefinding

As we have seen in the previous section, actively lighting a scene, whether for the purpose of estimating normals using photometric stereo or for adding artificial texture for shape from

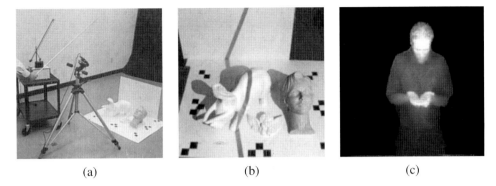

(a)   (b)   (c)

Figure 12.6 Shape scanning using cast shadows (Bouguet and Perona 1999) © 1999 Springer: (a) camera setup with a point light source (a desk lamp without its reflector), a hand-held stick casting a shadow, and (b) the objects being scanned in front of two planar backgrounds. (c) Real-time depth map using a pulsed illumination system (Iddan and Yahav 2001) © 2001 SPIE.

defocus, can greatly improve the performance of vision systems. This kind of *active illu-mination* has been used from the earliest days of machine vision to construct highly reliable sensors for estimating 3D depth images using a variety of *rangefinding* (or *range sensing*) techniques (Besl 1989; Curless 1999; Hebert 2000).

One of the most popular active illumination sensors is a laser or light stripe sensor, which sweeps a plane of light across the scene or object while observing it from an offset viewpoint, as shown in Figure 12.5b (Rioux and Bird 1993; Curless and Levoy 1995). As the stripe falls across the object, it deforms its shape according to the shape of the surface it is illuminating. It is then a simple matter of using *optical triangulation* to estimate the 3D locations of all the points seen in a particular stripe. In more detail, knowledge of the 3D plane equation of the light stripe allows us to infer the 3D location corresponding to each illuminated pixel, as pre-viously discussed in (2.70–2.71). The accuracy of light striping techniques can be improved by finding the exact temporal peak in illumination for each pixel (Curless and Levoy 1995). The final accuracy of a scanner can be determined using slant edge modulation techniques, i.e., by imaging sharp creases in a calibration object (Goesele, Fuchs, and Seidel 2003).

An interesting variant on light stripe rangefinding is presented by Bouguet and Perona (1999). Instead of projecting a light stripe, they simply wave a stick casting a shadow over a scene or object illuminated by a point light source such as a lamp or the sun (Figure 12.6a). As the shadow falls across two background planes whose orientation relative to the cam-era is known (or inferred during pre-calibration), the plane equation for each stripe can be inferred from the two projected lines, whose 3D equations are known (Figure 12.6b). The deformation of the shadow as it crosses the object being scanned then reveals its 3D shape, as with regular light stripe rangefinding (Exercise 12.2). This technique can also be used to estimate the 3D geometry of a background scene and how its appearance varies as it moves into shadow, in order to cast new shadows onto the scene (Chuang, Goldman, Curless *et al.* 2003) (Section 10.4.3).

The time it takes to scan an object using a light stripe technique is proportional to the number of depth planes used, which is usually comparable to the number of pixels across an image. A much faster scanner can be constructed by turning different projector pixels on

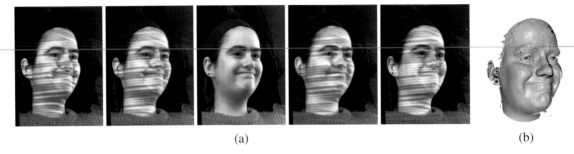

(a)   (b)

Figure 12.7   Real-time dense 3D face capture using spacetime stereo (Zhang, Snavely, Curless *et al.* 2004) ©
2004 ACM: (a) set of five consecutive video frames from one of two stereo cameras (every fifth frame is free of
stripe patterns, in order to extract texture); (b) resulting high-quality 3D surface model (depth map visualized as a
shaded rendering).

and off in a structured manner, e.g., using a binary or Gray code (Besl 1989). For example,
let us assume that the LCD projector we are using has 1024 columns of pixels. Taking the
10-bit binary code corresponding to each column's address ($0 \ldots 1023$), we project the first
bit, then the second, etc. After 10 projections (e.g., a third of a second for a synchronized
30Hz camera-projector system), each pixel in the camera knows which of the 1024 columns
of projector light it is seeing. A similar approach can also be used to estimate the refractive
properties of an object by placing a monitor behind the object (Zongker, Werner, Curless *et al.*
1999; Chuang, Zongker, Hindorff *et al.* 2000) (Section 13.4). Very fast scanners can also be
constructed with a single laser beam, i.e., a real-time *flying spot* optical triangulation scanner
(Rioux, Bechthold, Taylor *et al.* 1987).

   If even faster, i.e., frame-rate, scanning is required, we can project a single textured pattern into the scene. Proesmans, Van Gool, and Defoort (1998) describe a system where a
checkerboard grid is projected onto an object (e.g., a person's face) and the deformation of
the grid is used to infer 3D shape. Unfortunately, such a technique only works if the surface
is continuous enough to link all of the grid points.

   A much better system can be constructed using high-speed custom illumination and sensing hardware. Iddan and Yahav (2001) describe the construction of their 3DV Zcam video-
rate depth sensing camera, which projects a pulsed plane of light onto the scene and then
integrates the returning light for a short interval, essentially obtaining time-of-flight measurement for the distance to individual pixels in the scene. A good description of earlier
time-of-flight systems, including amplitude and frequency modulation schemes for LIDAR,
can be found in (Besl 1989).

   Instead of using a single camera, it is also possible to construct an active illumination
range sensor using stereo imaging setups. The simplest way to do this is to just project random stripe patterns onto the scene to create synthetic texture, which helps match textureless
surfaces (Kang, Webb, Zitnick *et al.* 1995). Projecting a known series of stripes, just as in
coded pattern single-camera rangefinding, makes the correspondence between pixels unam-
biguous and allows for the recovery of depth estimates at pixels only seen in a single camera
(Scharstein and Szeliski 2003). This technique has been used to produce large numbers of
highly accurate registered multi-image stereo pairs and depth maps for the purpose of evaluating stereo correspondence algorithms (Scharstein and Szeliski 2002; Hirschmüller and

Scharstein 2009) and learning depth map priors and parameters (Scharstein and Pal 2007).

While projecting multiple patterns usually requires the scene or object to remain still, additional processing can enable the production of real-time depth maps for dynamic scenes. The basic idea (Davis, Ramamoorthi, and Rusinkiewicz 2003; Zhang, Curless, and Seitz 2003) is to assume that depth is nearly constant within a 3D space–time window around each pixel and to use the 3D window for matching and reconstruction. Depending on the surface shape and motion, this assumption may be error-prone, as shown in (Davis, Nahab, Ramamoorthi *et al.* 2005). To model shapes more accurately, Zhang, Curless, and Seitz (2003) model the linear disparity variation within the space–time window and show that better results can be obtained by globally optimizing disparity and disparity gradient estimates over video volumes (Zhang, Snavely, Curless *et al.* 2004). Figure 12.7 shows the results of applying this system to a person's face; the frame-rate 3D surface model can then be used for further model-based fitting and computer graphics manipulation (Section 12.6.2).

12.2.1 Range data merging

While individual range images can be useful for applications such as real-time z-keying or facial motion capture, they are often used as building blocks for more complete 3D object modeling. In such applications, the next two steps in processing are the registration (alignment) of partial 3D surface models and their integration into coherent 3D surfaces (Curless 1999). If desired, this can be followed by a model fitting stage using either parametric representations such as generalized cylinders (Agin and Binford 1976; Nevatia and Binford 1977; Marr and Nishihara 1978; Brooks 1981), superquadrics (Pentland 1986; Solina and Bajcsy 1990; Terzopoulos and Metaxas 1991), or non-parametric models such as triangular meshes (Boissonat 1984) or physically-based models (Terzopoulos, Witkin, and Kass 1988; Delingette, Hebert, and Ikeuichi 1992; Terzopoulos and Metaxas 1991; McInerney and Terzopoulos 1993; Terzopoulos 1999). A number of techniques have also been developed for segmenting range images into simpler constituent surfaces (Hoover, Jean-Baptiste, Jiang *et al.* 1996).

The most widely used 3D registration technique is the *iterated closest point* (ICP) algorithm, which alternates between finding the closest point matches between the two surfaces being aligned and then solving a 3D *absolute orientation* problem (Section 6.1.5, (6.31–6.32) (Besl and McKay 1992; Chen and Medioni 1992; Zhang 1994; Szeliski and Lavallée 1996; Gold, Rangarajan, Lu *et al.* 1998; David, DeMenthon, Duraiswami *et al.* 2004; Li and Hartley 2007; Enqvist, Josephson, and Kahl 2009).[3] Since the two surfaces being aligned usually only have partial overlap and may also have outliers, robust matching criteria (Section 6.1.4 and Appendix B.3) are typically used. In order to speed up the determination of the closest point, and also to make the distance-to-surface computation more accurate, one of the two point sets (e.g., the current merged model) can be converted into a *signed distance function*, optionally represented using an *octree spline* for compactness (Lavallée and Szeliski 1995). Variants on the basic ICP algorithm can be used to register 3D point sets under non-rigid deformations, e.g., for medical applications (Feldmar and Ayache 1996; Szeliski and Lavallée 1996). Color values associated with the points or range measurements can also be used as part of the registration process to improve robustness (Johnson and Kang 1997; Pulli 1999).

---

[3] Some techniques, such as the one developed by Chen and Medioni (1992), use local surface tangent planes to make this computation more accurate and to accelerate convergence.

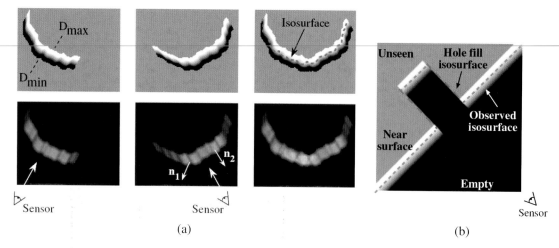

Figure 12.8   Range data merging (Curless and Levoy 1996) © 1996 ACM: (a) two signed distance functions (top left) are merged with their (weights) bottom left to produce a combined set of functions (right column) from which an isosurface can be extracted (green dashed line); (b) the signed distance functions are combined with empty and unseen space labels to fill holes in the isosurface.

Unfortunately, the ICP algorithm and its variants can only find a locally optimal alignment between 3D surfaces. If this is not known *a priori*, more global correspondence or search techniques, based on local descriptors invariant to 3D rigid transformations, need to be used. An example of such a descriptor is the *spin image*, which is a local circular projection of a 3D surface patch around the local normal axis (Johnson and Hebert 1999). Another (earlier) example is the *splash* representation introduced by Stein and Medioni (1992).

Once two or more 3D surfaces have been aligned, they can be merged into a single model. One approach is to represent each surface using a triangulated mesh and combine these meshes using a process that is sometimes called *zippering* (Soucy and Laurendeau 1992; Turk and Levoy 1994). Another, now more widely used, approach is to compute a signed distance function that fits all of the 3D data points (Hoppe, DeRose, Duchamp *et al.* 1992; Curless and Levoy 1996; Hilton, Stoddart, Illingworth *et al.* 1996; Wheeler, Sato, and Ikeuchi 1998).

Figure 12.8 shows one such approach, the *volumetric range image processing* (VRIP) technique developed by Curless and Levoy (1996), which first computes a weighted signed distance function from each range image and then merges them using a weighted averaging process. To make the representation more compact, run-length coding is used to encode the empty, seen, and varying (signed distance) voxels, and only the signed distance values near each surface are stored.[4] Once the merged signed distance function has been computed, a zero-crossing surface extraction algorithm, such as *marching cubes* (Lorensen and Cline 1987), can be used to recover a meshed surface model. Figure 12.9 shows an example of the complete range data merging and isosurface extraction pipeline.

Volumetric range data merging techniques based on signed distance or characteristic (inside–outside) functions are also widely used to extract smooth well-behaved surfaces from oriented or unoriented sets of points (Hoppe, DeRose, Duchamp *et al.* 1992; Ohtake, Belyaev,

---

[4] An alternative, even more compact, representation could be to use octrees (Lavallée and Szeliski 1995).

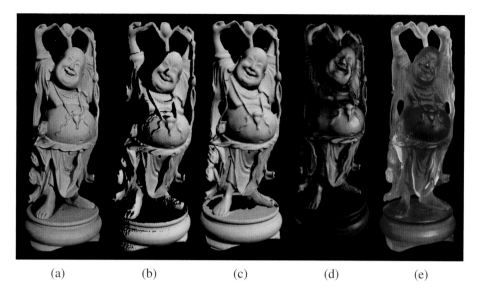

(a)   (b)   (c)   (d)   (e)

Figure 12.9 Reconstruction and hardcopy of the "Happy Buddha" statuette (Curless and Levoy 1996) © 1996 ACM: (a) photograph of the original statue after spray painting with matte gray; (b) partial range scan; (c) merged range scans; (d) colored rendering of the reconstructed model; (e) hardcopy of the model constructed using stereolithography.

Alexa *et al.* 2003; Kazhdan, Bolitho, and Hoppe 2006; Lempitsky and Boykov 2007; Zach, Pock, and Bischof 2007b; Zach 2008), as discussed in more detail in Section 12.5.1.

12.2.2 *Application*: Digital heritage

Active rangefinding technologies, combined with surface modeling and appearance modeling techniques (Section 12.7), are widely used in the fields of archeological and historical preservation, which often also goes under the name *digital heritage* (MacDonald 2006). In such applications, detailed 3D models of cultural objects are acquired and later used for applications such as analysis, preservation, restoration, and the production of duplicate artwork (Rioux and Bird 1993).

A more recent example of such an endeavor is the Digital Michelangelo project of Levoy, Pulli, Curless *et al.* (2000), which used Cyberware laser stripe scanners and high-quality digital SLR cameras mounted on a large gantry to obtain detailed scans of Michelangelo's David and other sculptures in Florence. The project also took scans of the *Forma Urbis Romae*, an ancient stone map of Rome that had shattered into pieces, for which new matches were obtained using digital techniques. The whole process, from initial planning, to software development, acquisition, and post-processing, took several years (and many volunteers), and produced a wealth of 3D shape and appearance modeling techniques as a result.

Even larger-scale projects are now being attempted, for example, the scanning of complete temple sites such as Angkor-Thom (Ikeuchi and Sato 2001; Ikeuchi and Miyazaki 2007; Banno, Masuda, Oishi *et al.* 2008). Figure 12.10 shows details from this project, including a sample photograph, a detailed 3D (sculptural) head model scanned from ground level, and an aerial overview of the final merged 3D site model, which was acquired using a balloon.

(a)   (b)   (c)

Figure 12.10   Laser range modeling of the Bayon temple at Angkor-Thom (Banno, Masuda, Oishi *et al.* 2008) © 2008 Springer: (a) sample photograph from the site; (b) a detailed head model scanned from the ground; (c) final merged 3D model of the temple scanned using a laser range sensor mounted on a balloon.

12.3 Surface representations

In previous sections, we have seen different representations being used to integrate 3D range scans. We now look at several of these representations in more detail. Explicit surface representations, such as triangle meshes, splines (Farin 1992, 1996), and subdivision surfaces (Stollnitz, DeRose, and Salesin 1996; Zorin, Schröder, and Sweldens 1996; Warren and Weimer 2001; Peters and Reif 2008), enable not only the creation of highly detailed models but also processing operations, such as interpolation (Section 12.3.1), fairing or smoothing, and decimation and simplification (Section 12.3.2). We also examine discrete point-based representations (Section 12.4) and volumetric representations (Section 12.5).

12.3.1 Surface interpolation

One of the most common operations on surfaces is their reconstruction from a set of sparse data constraints, i.e. *scattered data interpolation*. When formulating such problems, surfaces may be parameterized as height fields $f(x)$, as 3D parametric surfaces $f(x)$, or as non-parametric models such as collections of triangles.

In the section on image processing, we saw how two-dimensional function interpolation and approximation problems $\{d_i\} \rightarrow f(x)$ could be cast as energy minimization problems using regularization (Section 3.7.1 (3.94–3.98).[5] Such problems can also specify the locations of discontinuities in the surface as well as local orientation constraints (Terzopoulos 1986b; Zhang, Dugas-Phocion, Samson *et al.* 2002).

One approach to solving such problems is to discretize both the surface and the energy on a discrete grid or mesh using finite element analysis (3.100–3.102) (Terzopoulos 1986b). Such problems can then be solved using sparse system solving techniques, such as multigrid (Briggs, Henson, and McCormick 2000) or hierarchically preconditioned conjugate gradient (Szeliski 2006b). The surface can also be represented using a hierarchical combination of multilevel B-splines (Lee, Wolberg, and Shin 1996).

---

[5] The difference between interpolation and approximation is that the former requires the surface or function to pass through the data while the latter allows the function to pass near the data, and can therefore be used for surface smoothing as well.

An alternative approach is to use *radial basis* (or *kernel*) functions (Boult and Kender 1986; Nielson 1993). To interpolate a field $f(x)$ through (or near) a number of data values d_i located at x_i, the *radial basis function* approach uses

$$f(x) = \frac{\sum_i w_i(x) d_i}{\sum_i w_i(x)}, \tag{12.6}$$

where the weights,

$$w_i(x) = K(\|x - x_i\|), \tag{12.7}$$

are computed using a *radial basis* (spherically symmetrical) function $K(r)$.

If we want the function $f(x)$ to exactly interpolate the data points, the kernel functions must either be singular at the origin, $\lim_{r \to 0} K(r) \to \infty$ (Nielson 1993), or a dense linear system must be solved to determine the magnitude associated with each basis function (Boult and Kender 1986). It turns out that, for certain regularized problems, e.g., (3.94–3.96), there exist radial basis functions (kernels) that give the same results as a full analytical solution (Boult and Kender 1986). Unfortunately, because the dense system solving is cubic in the number of data points, basis function approaches can only be used for small problems such as feature-based image morphing (Beier and Neely 1992).

When a three-dimensional *parametric surface* is being modeled, the vector-valued function f in (12.6) or (3.94–3.102) encodes 3D coordinates (x, y, z) on the surface and the domain $x = (s, t)$ encodes the surface parameterization. One example of such surfaces are symmetry-seeking parametric models, which are elastically deformable versions of *generalized cylinders*[6] (Terzopoulos, Witkin, and Kass 1987). In these models, s is the parameter *along* the spine of the deformable tube and t is the parameter *around* the tube. A variety of smoothness and radial symmetry forces are used to constrain the model while it is fitted to image-based silhouette curves.

It is also possible to define *non-parametric* surface models such as general triangulated meshes and to equip such meshes (using finite element analysis) with both internal smoothness metrics and external data fitting metrics (Sander and Zucker 1990; Fua and Sander 1992; Delingette, Hebert, and Ikeuichi 1992; McInerney and Terzopoulos 1993). While most of these approaches assume a standard *elastic* deformation model, which uses quadratic internal smoothness terms, it is also possible to use sub-linear energy models in order to better preserve surface creases (Diebel, Thrun, and Brünig 2006). Triangle meshes can also be augmented with either spline elements (Sullivan and Ponce 1998) or subdivision surfaces (Stollnitz, DeRose, and Salesin 1996; Zorin, Schröder, and Sweldens 1996; Warren and Weimer 2001; Peters and Reif 2008) to produce surfaces with better smoothness control.

Both parametric and non-parametric surface models assume that the topology of the surface is known and fixed ahead of time. For more flexible surface modeling, we can either represent the surface as a collection of oriented points (Section 12.4) or use 3D implicit functions (Section 12.5.1), which can also be combined with elastic 3D surface models (McInerney and Terzopoulos 1993).

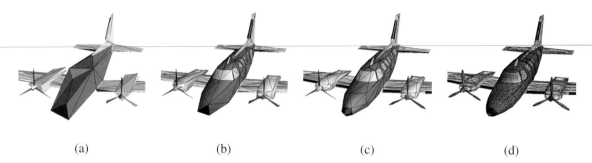

(a)   (b)   (c)   (d)

Figure 12.11 Progressive mesh representation of an airplane model (Hoppe 1996) © 1996 ACM: (a) base mesh M^0 (150 faces); (b) mesh M^{175} (500 faces); (c) mesh M^{425} (1000 faces); (d) original mesh $M = M^n$ (13,546 faces).

12.3.2 Surface simplification

Once a triangle mesh has been created from 3D data, it is often desirable to create a hierarchy of mesh models, for example, to control the displayed *level of detail* (LOD) in a computer graphics application. (In essence, this is a 3D analog to image pyramids (Section 3.5).) One approach to doing this is to approximate a given mesh with one that has *subdivision connectivity*, over which a set of triangular wavelet coefficients can then be computed (Eck, DeRose, Duchamp *et al.* 1995). A more continuous approach is to use sequential *edge collapse* operations to go from the original fine-resolution mesh to a coarse base-level mesh (Hoppe 1996). The resulting *progressive mesh* (PM) representation can be used to render the 3D model at arbitrary levels of detail, as shown in Figure 12.11.

12.3.3 Geometry images

While multi-resolution surface representations such as (Eck, DeRose, Duchamp *et al.* 1995; Hoppe 1996) support level of detail operations, they still consist of an irregular collection of triangles, which makes them more difficult to compress and store in a cache-efficient manner.[7]

To make the triangulation completely regular (uniform and gridded), Gu, Gortler, and Hoppe (2002) describe how to create *geometry images* by cutting surface meshes along well-chosen lines and "flattening" the resulting representation into a square. Figure 12.12a shows the resulting (x, y, z) values of the surface mesh mapped over the unit square, while Figure 12.12b shows the associated (n_x, n_y, n_z) *normal map*, i.e., the surface normals associated with each mesh vertex, which can be used to compensate for loss in visual fidelity if the original geometry image is heavily compressed.

---

[6] A generalized cylinder (Brooks 1981) is a *solid of revolution*, i.e., the result of rotating a (usually smooth) curve around an axis. It can also be generated by sweeping a slowly varying circular cross-section along the axis. (These two interpretations are equivalent.)

[7] Subdivision triangulations, such as those in (Eck, DeRose, Duchamp *et al.* 1995), are *semi-regular*, i.e., regular (ordered and nested) within each subdivided base triangle.

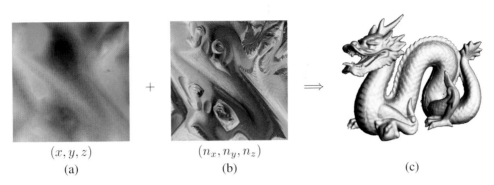

(x, y, z) (n_x, n_y, n_z)
(a) (b) (c)

Figure 12.12 Geometry images (Gu, Gortler, and Hoppe 2002) © 2002 ACM: (a) the 257×257 geometry image defines a mesh over the surface; (b) the 512×512 normal map defines vertex normals; (c) final lit 3D model.

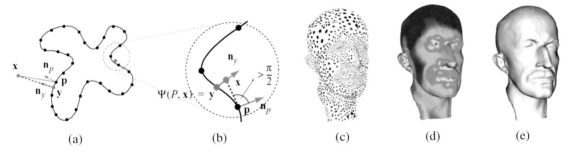

(a) (b) (c) (d) (e)

Figure 12.13 Point-based surface modeling with moving least squares (MLS) (Pauly, Keiser, Kobbelt *et al.* 2003) © 2003 ACM: (a) a set of points (black dots) is turned into an implicit inside–outside function (black curve); (b) the signed distance to the nearest oriented point can serve as an approximation to the inside–outside distance; (c) a set of oriented points with variable sampling density representing a 3D surface (head model); (d) local estimate of sampling density, which is used in the moving least squares; (e) reconstructed continuous 3D surface.

12.4 Point-based representations

As we mentioned previously, triangle-based surface models assume that the topology (and often the rough shape) of the 3D model is known ahead of time. While it is possible to re-mesh a model as it is being deformed or fitted, a simpler solution is to dispense with an explicit triangle mesh altogether and to have triangle vertices behave as *oriented points*, or particles, or *surface elements* (surfels) (Szeliski and Tonnesen 1992).

In order to endow the resulting particle system with internal smoothness constraints, pairwise interaction potentials can be defined that approximate the equivalent elastic bending energies that would be obtained using local finite-element analysis.[8] Instead of defining the finite element neighborhood for each particle (vertex) ahead of time, a soft influence function is used to couple nearby particles. The resulting 3D model can change both topology and particle density as it evolves and can therefore be used to interpolate partial 3D data with holes (Szeliski, Tonnesen, and Terzopoulos 1993b). Discontinuities in both the surface orientation and crease curves can also be modeled (Szeliski, Tonnesen, and Terzopoulos 1993a).

---

[8] As mentioned before, an alternative is to use *sub-linear* interaction potentials, which encourage the preservation of surface creases (Diebel, Thrun, and Brünig 2006).

To render the particle system as a continuous surface, local dynamic triangulation heuristics (Szeliski and Tonnesen 1992) or direct surface element *splatting* (Pfister, Zwicker, van Baar *et al.* 2000) can be used. Another alternative is to first convert the point cloud into an implicit signed distance or inside–outside function, using either minimum signed distances to the oriented points (Hoppe, DeRose, Duchamp *et al.* 1992) or by interpolating a characteristic (inside–outside) function using radial basis functions (Turk and O'Brien 2002; Dinh, Turk, and Slabaugh 2002). Even greater precision over the implicit function fitting, including the ability to handle irregular point densities, can be obtained by computing a *moving least squares* (MLS) estimate of the signed distance function (Alexa, Behr, Cohen-Or *et al.* 2003; Pauly, Keiser, Kobbelt *et al.* 2003), as shown in Figure 12.13. Further improvements can be obtained using local sphere fitting (Guennebaud and Gross 2007), faster and more accurate re-sampling (Guennebaud, Germann, and Gross 2008), and kernel regression to better tolerate outliers (Oztireli, Guennebaud, and Gross 2008).

12.5 Volumetric representations

A third alternative for modeling 3D surfaces is to construct 3D volumetric inside–outside functions. We already saw examples of this in Section 11.6.1, where we looked at voxel coloring (Seitz and Dyer 1999), space carving (Kutulakos and Seitz 2000), and level set (Faugeras and Keriven 1998; Pons, Keriven, and Faugeras 2007) techniques for stereo matching, and Section 11.6.2, where we discussed using binary silhouette images to reconstruct volumes.

In this section, we look at continuous *implicit* (inside–outside) functions to represent 3D shape.

12.5.1 Implicit surfaces and level sets

While polyhedral and voxel-based representations can represent three-dimensional shapes to an arbitrary precision, they lack some of the intrinsic smoothness properties available with continuous implicit surfaces, which use an *indicator function* (*characteristic function*) $F(x, y, z)$ to indicate which 3D points are inside $F(x, y, z) < 0$ or outside $F(x, y, z) > 0$ the object.

An early example of using implicit functions to model 3D objects in computer vision are superquadrics, which are a generalization of quadric (e.g., ellipsoidal) parametric volumetric models,

$$F(x, y, z) = \left(\left(\frac{x}{a_1} \right)^{2/\epsilon_2} + \left(\frac{y}{a_2} \right)^{2/\epsilon_2} \right)^{\epsilon_2/\epsilon_1} + \left(\frac{x}{a_1} \right)^{2/\epsilon_1} - 1 = 0 \qquad (12.8)$$

(Pentland 1986; Solina and Bajcsy 1990; Waithe and Ferrie 1991; Leonardis, Jaklič, and Solina 1997). The values of (a_1, a_2, a_3) control the extent of model along each (x, y, z) axis, while the values of (ϵ_1, ϵ_2) control how "square" it is. To model a wider variety of shapes, superquadrics are usually combined with either rigid or non-rigid deformations (Terzopoulos and Metaxas 1991; Metaxas and Terzopoulos 2002). Superquadric models can either be fit to range data or used directly for stereo matching.

A different kind of implicit shape model can be constructed by defining a *signed distance function* over a regular three-dimensional grid, optionally using an octree spline to represent this function more coarsely away from its surface (zero-set) (Lavallée and Szeliski 1995; Szeliski and Lavallée 1996; Frisken, Perry, Rockwood *et al.* 2000; Ohtake, Belyaev, Alexa *et al.* 2003). We have already seen examples of signed distance functions being used to represent distance transforms (Section 3.3.3), level sets for 2D contour fitting and tracking (Section 5.1.4), volumetric stereo (Section 11.6.1), range data merging (Section 12.2.1), and point-based modeling (Section 12.4). The advantage of representing such functions directly on a grid is that it is quick and easy to look up distance function values for any (x, y, z) location and also easy to extract the isosurface using the marching cubes algorithm (Lorensen and Cline 1987). The work of Ohtake, Belyaev, Alexa *et al.* (2003) is particularly notable since it allows for several distance functions to be used simultaneously and then combined locally to produce sharp features such as creases.

Poisson surface reconstruction (Kazhdan, Bolitho, and Hoppe 2006) uses a closely related volumetric function, namely a smoothed 0/1 inside–outside (characteristic) function, which can be thought of as a clipped signed distance function. The gradients for this function are set to lie along oriented surface normals near known surface points and 0 elsewhere. The function itself is represented using a quadratic tensor-product B-spline over an octree, which provides a compact representation with larger cells away from the surface or in regions of lower point density, and also admits the efficient solution of the related Poisson equations (3.100–3.102), see Section 9.3.4 (Pérez, Gangnet, and Blake 2003).

It is also possible to replace the quadratic penalties used in the Poisson equations with L_1 (total variation) constraints and still obtain a convex optimization problem, which can be solved using either continuous (Zach, Pock, and Bischof 2007b; Zach 2008) or discrete graph cut (Lempitsky and Boykov 2007) techniques.

Signed distance functions also play an integral role in level-set evolution equations ((Sections 5.1.4 and 11.6.1), where the values of distance transforms on the mesh are updated as the surface evolves to fit multi-view stereo photoconsistency measures (Faugeras and Keriven 1998).

12.6 Model-based reconstruction

When we know something ahead of time about the objects we are trying to model, we can construct more detailed and reliable 3D models using specialized techniques and representations. For example, architecture is usually made up of large planar regions and other parametric forms (such as surfaces of revolution), usually oriented perpendicular to gravity and to each other (Section 12.6.1). Heads and faces can be represented using low-dimensional, non-rigid shape models, since the variability in shape and appearance of human faces, while extremely large, is still bounded (Section 12.6.2). Human bodies or parts, such as hands, form highly articulated structures, which can be represented using kinematic chains of piecewise rigid skeletal elements linked by joints (Section 12.6.4).

In this section, we highlight some of the main ideas, representations, and modeling algorithms used for these three cases. Additional details and references can be found in specialized conferences and workshops devoted to these topics, e.g., the International Symposium on 3D Data Processing, Visualization, and Transmission (3DPVT), the International Conference on 3D Digital Imaging and Modeling (3DIM), the International Conference on Automatic Face and Gesture Recognition (FG), the IEEE Workshop on Analysis and Modeling of Faces

Figure 12.14 Interactive architectural modeling using the Façade system (Debevec, Taylor, and Malik 1996) ©️ 1996 ACM: (a) input image with user-drawn edges shown in green; (b) shaded 3D solid model; (c) geometric primitives overlaid onto the input image; (d) final view-dependent, texture-mapped 3D model.

and Gestures, and the International Workshop on Tracking Humans for the Evaluation of their Motion in Image Sequences (THEMIS).

12.6.1 Architecture

Architectural modeling, especially from aerial photography, has been one of the longest studied problems in both photogrammetry and computer vision (Walker and Herman 1988). Recently, the development of reliable image-based modeling techniques, as well as the prevalence of digital cameras and 3D computer games, has spurred renewed interest in this area.

The work by Debevec, Taylor, and Malik (1996) was one of the earliest hybrid geometry- and image-based modeling and rendering systems. Their Façade system combines an interactive image-guided geometric modeling tool with model-based (local plane plus parallax) stereo matching and view-dependent texture mapping. During the interactive photogrammetric modeling phase, the user selects block elements and aligns their edges with visible edges in the input images (Figure 12.14a). The system then automatically computes the dimensions and locations of the blocks along with the camera positions using constrained optimization (Figure 12.14b–c). This approach is intrinsically more reliable than general feature-based structure from motion, because it exploits the strong geometry available in the block primitives. Related work by Becker and Bove (1995), Horry, Anjyo, and Arai (1997), and Criminisi, Reid, and Zisserman (2000) exploits similar information available from vanishing points. In the interactive, image-based modeling system of Sinha, Steedly, Szeliski *et al.* (2008), vanishing point directions are used to guide the user drawing of polygons, which are then automatically fitted to sparse 3D points recovered using structure from motion.

Once the rough geometry has been estimated, more detailed offset maps can be computed for each planar face using a local plane sweep, which Debevec, Taylor, and Malik (1996) call *model-based stereo*. Finally, during rendering, images from different viewpoints are warped and blended together as the camera moves around the scene, using a process (related to light field and Lumigraph rendering, see Section 13.3) called *view-dependent texture mapping* (Figure 12.14d).

For interior modeling, instead of working with single pictures, it is more useful to work

 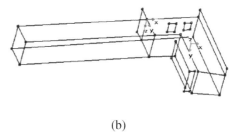

(a)   (b)

Figure 12.15 Interactive 3D modeling from panoramas (Shum, Han, and Szeliski 1998) © 1998 IEEE: (a) wide-angle view of a panorama with user-drawn vertical and horizontal (axis-aligned) lines; (b) single-view reconstruction of the corridors.

with panoramas, since you can see larger extents of walls and other structures. The 3D modeling system developed by Shum, Han, and Szeliski (1998) first constructs calibrated panoramas from multiple images (Section 7.4) and then has the user draw vertical and horizontal lines in the image to demarcate the boundaries of planar regions. The lines are initially used to establish an absolute rotation for each panorama and are later used (along with the inferred vertices and planes) to optimize the 3D structure, which can be recovered up to scale from one or more images (Figure 12.15). 360° high dynamic range panoramas can also be used for outdoor modeling, since they provide highly reliable estimates of relative camera orientations as well as vanishing point directions (Antone and Teller 2002; Teller, Antone, Bodnar *et al.* 2003).

While earlier image-based modeling systems required some user authoring, Werner and Zisserman (2002) present a fully automated line-based reconstruction system. As described in Section 7.5.1, they first detect lines and vanishing points and use them to calibrate the camera; then they establish line correspondences using both appearance matching and trifocal tensors, which enables them to reconstruct families of 3D line segments, as shown in Figure 12.16a. They then generate plane hypotheses, using both co-planar 3D lines and a plane sweep (Section 11.1.2) based on cross-correlation scores evaluated at interest points. Intersections of planes are used to determine the extent of each plane, i.e., an initial coarse geometry, which is then refined with the addition of rectangular or wedge-shaped indentations and extrusions (Figure 12.16c). Note that when top-down maps of the buildings being modeled are available, these can be used to further constrain the 3D modeling process (Robertson and Cipolla 2002, 2009). The idea of using matched 3D lines for estimating vanishing point directions and dominant planes continues to be used in a number of recent fully automated image-based architectural modeling systems (Zebedin, Bauer, Karner *et al.* 2008; Mičušík and Košecká 2009; Furukawa, Curless, Seitz *et al.* 2009b; Sinha, Steedly, and Szeliski 2009).

Another common characteristic of architecture is the repeated use of primitives such as windows, doors, and colonnades. Architectural modeling systems can be designed to search for such repeated elements and to use them as part of the structure inference process (Dick, Torr, and Cipolla 2004; Mueller, Zeng, Wonka *et al.* 2007; Schindler, Krishnamurthy, Lublinerman *et al.* 2008; Sinha, Steedly, Szeliski *et al.* 2008).

The combination of all these techniques now makes it possible to reconstruct the structure of large 3D scenes (Zhu and Kanade 2008). For example, the *Urbanscan* system of Polle-

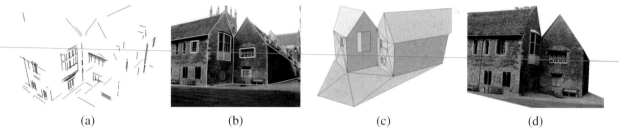

(a)   (b)   (c)   (d)

Figure 12.16   Automated architectural reconstruction using 3D lines and planes (Werner and Zisserman 2002) © 2002 Springer: (a) reconstructed 3D lines, color coded by their vanishing directions; (b) wire-frame model superimposed onto an input image; (c) triangulated piecewise-planar model with windows; (d) final texture-mapped model.

feys, Nistér, Frahm *et al.* (2008) reconstructs texture-mapped 3D models of city streets from videos acquired with a GPS-equipped vehicle. To obtain real-time performance, they use both optimized on-line structure-from-motion algorithms, as well as GPU implementations of plane-sweep stereo aligned to dominant planes and depth map fusion. Cornelis, Leibe, Cornelis *et al.* (2008) present a related system that also uses plane-sweep stereo (aligned to vertical building façades) combined with object recognition and segmentation for vehicles. Mičušík and Košecká (2009) build on these results using omni-directional images and super-pixel-based stereo matching along dominant plane orientations. Reconstruction directly from active range scanning data combined with color imagery that has been compensated for exposure and lighting variations is also possible (Chen and Chen 2008; Stamos, Liu, Chen *et al.* 2008; Troccoli and Allen 2008).

12.6.2 Heads and faces

Another area in which specialized shape and appearance models are extremely helpful is in the modeling of heads and faces. Even though the appearance of people seems at first glance to be infinitely variable, the actual shape of a person's head and face can be described reasonably well using a few dozen parameters (Pighin, Hecker, Lischinski *et al.* 1998; Guenter, Grimm, Wood *et al.* 1998; DeCarlo, Metaxas, and Stone 1998; Blanz and Vetter 1999; Shan, Liu, and Zhang 2001).

Figure 12.17 shows an example of an image-based modeling system, where user-specified keypoints in several images are used to fit a generic head model to a person's face. As you can see in Figure 12.17c, after specifying just over 100 keypoints, the shape of the face has become quite adapted and recognizable. Extracting a texture map from the original images and then applying it to the head model results in an animatable model with striking visual fidelity (Figure 12.18a).

A more powerful system can be built by applying *principal component analysis* (PCA) to a collection of 3D scanned faces, which is a topic we discuss in Section 12.6.3. As you can see in Figure 12.19, it is then possible to fit morphable 3D models to single images and to use such models for a variety of animation and visual effects (Blanz and Vetter 1999). It is also possible to design stereo matching algorithms that optimize directly for the head model parameters (Shan, Liu, and Zhang 2001; Kang and Jones 2002) or to use the output of real-

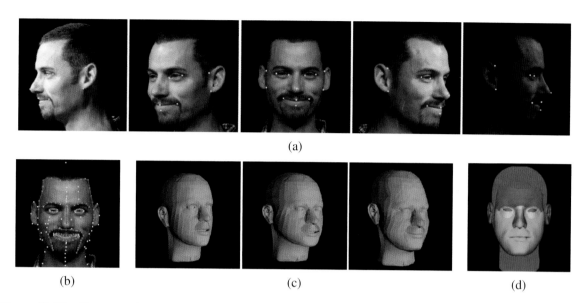

(a)

(b)   (c)   (d)

Figure 12.17 3D model fitting to a collection of images: (Pighin, Hecker, Lischinski *et al.* 1998) © 1998 ACM: (a) set of five input images along with user-selected keypoints; (b) the complete set of keypoints and curves; (c) three meshes—the original, adapted after 13 keypoints, and after an additional 99 keypoints; (d) the partition of the image into separately animatable regions.

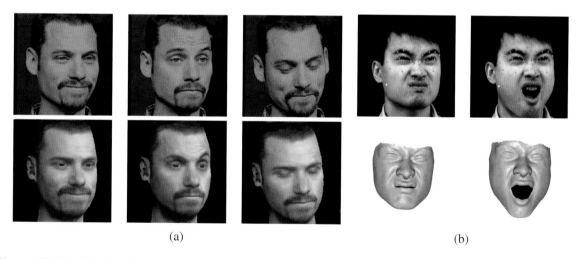

(a)   (b)

Figure 12.18 Head and expression tracking and re-animation using deformable 3D models. (a) Models fit directly to five input video streams (Pighin, Szeliski, and Salesin 2002) © 2002 Springer: The bottom row shows the results of re-animating a synthetic texture-mapped 3D model with pose and expression parameters fitted to the input images in the top row. (b) Models fit to frame-rate spacetime stereo surface models (Zhang, Snavely, Curless *et al.* 2004) © 2004 ACM: The top row shows the input images with synthetic green markers overlaid, while the bottom row shows the fitted 3D surface model.

time stereo with active illumination (Zhang, Snavely, Curless *et al.* 2004) (Figures 12.7 and 12.18b).

As the sophistication of 3D facial capture systems evolves, so does the detail and realism in the reconstructed models. Newer systems can capture (in real-time) not only surface details such as wrinkles and creases, but also accurate models of skin reflection, translucency, and sub-surface scattering (Weyrich, Matusik, Pfister *et al.* 2006; Golovinskiy, Matusik, ster *et al.* 2006; Bickel, Botsch, Angst *et al.* 2007; Igarashi, Nishino, and Nayar 2007).

Once a 3D head model has been constructed, it can be used in a variety of applications, such as head tracking (Toyama 1998; Lepetit, Pilet, and Fua 2004; Matthews, Xiao, and Baker 2007), as shown in Figures 4.29 and 14.24, and face transfer, i.e., replacing one person's face with another in a video (Bregler, Covell, and Slaney 1997; Vlasic, Brand, Pfister *et al.* 2005). Additional applications include face beautification by warping face images toward a more attractive "standard" (Leyvand, Cohen-Or, Dror *et al.* 2008), face de-identification for privacy protection (Gross, Sweeney, De la Torre *et al.* 2008), and face swapping (Bitouk, Kumar, Dhillon *et al.* 2008).

12.6.3 *Application*: Facial animation

Perhaps the most widely used application of 3D head modeling is facial animation. Once a parameterized 3D model of shape and appearance (surface texture) has been constructed, it can be used directly to track a person's facial motions (Figure 12.18a) and to animate a different character with these same motions and expressions (Pighin, Szeliski, and Salesin 2002).

An improved version of such a system can be constructed by first applying principal component analysis (PCA) to the space of possible head shapes and facial appearances. Blanz and Vetter (1999) describe a system where they first capture a set of 200 colored range scans of faces (Figure 12.19a), which can be represented as a large collection of (X, Y, Z, R, G, B) samples (vertices).[9] In order for 3D morphing to be meaningful, corresponding vertices in different people's scans must first be put into correspondence (Pighin, Hecker, Lischinski *et al.* 1998). Once this is done, PCA can be applied to more naturally parameterize the 3D morphable model. The flexibility of this model can be increased by performing separate analyses in different subregions, such as the eyes, nose, and mouth, just as in modular eigenspaces (Moghaddam and Pentland 1997).

After computing a subspace representation, different directions in this space can be associated with different characteristics such as gender, facial expressions, or facial features (Figure 12.19a). As in the work of Rowland and Perrett (1995), faces can be turned into caricatures by exaggerating their displacement from the mean image.

3D morphable models can be fitted to a single image using gradient descent on the error between the input image and the re-synthesized model image, after an initial manual placement of the model in an approximately correct pose, scale, and location (Figures 12.19b–c). The efficiency of this fitting process can be increased using inverse compositional image alignment (8.64–8.65), as described by Romdhani and Vetter (2003).

The resulting texture-mapped 3D model can then be modified to produce a variety of vi-

---

[9] A cylindrical coordinate system provides a natural two-dimensional embedding for this collection, but such an embedding is not necessary to perform PCA.

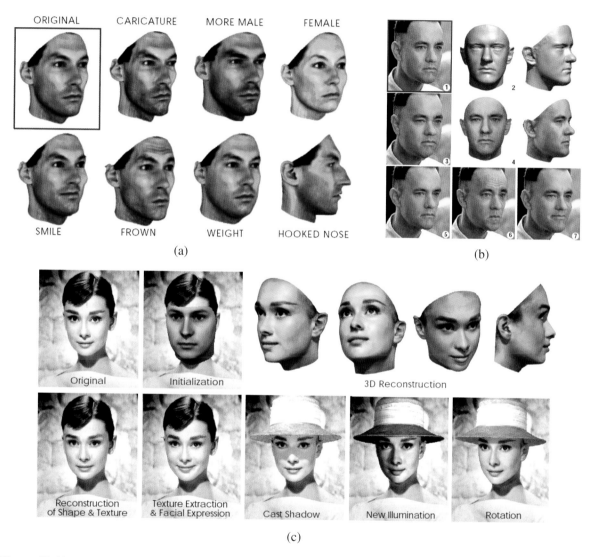

Figure 12.19 3D morphable face model (Blanz and Vetter 1999) © 1999 ACM: (a) original 3D face model with the addition of shape and texture variations in specific directions: deviation from the mean (caricature), gender, expression, weight, and nose shape; (b) a 3D morphable model is fit to a single image, after which its weight or expression can be manipulated; (c) another example of a 3D reconstruction along with a different set of 3D manipulations such as lighting and pose change.

sual effects, including changing a person's weight or expression, or three-dimensional effects such as re-lighting or 3D video-based animation (Section 13.5.1). Such models can also be used for video compression, e.g., by only transmitting a small number of facial expression and pose parameters to drive a synthetic avatar (Eisert, Wiegand, and Girod 2000; Gao, Chen, Wang *et al.* 2003).

3D facial animation is often matched to the performance of an actor, in what is known as *performance-driven animation* (Section 4.1.5) (Williams 1990). Traditional performance-driven animation systems use marker-based motion capture (Ma, Jones, Chiang *et al.* 2008), while some newer systems use video footage to control the animation (Buck, Finkelstein, Jacobs *et al.* 2000; Pighin, Szeliski, and Salesin 2002; Zhang, Snavely, Curless *et al.* 2004; Vlasic, Brand, Pfister *et al.* 2005).

An example of the latter approach is the system developed for the film *Benjamin Button*, in which Digital Domain used the CONTOUR system from Mova[10] to capture actor Brad Pitt's facial motions and expressions (Roble and Zafar 2009). CONTOUR uses a combination of phosphorescent paint and multiple high-resolution video cameras to capture real-time 3D range scans of the actor. These 3D models were then translated into Facial Action Coding System (FACS) shape and expression parameters (Ekman and Friesen 1978) to drive a different (older) synthetically animated computer-generated imagery (CGI) character.

12.6.4 Whole body modeling and tracking

The topics of tracking humans, modeling their shape and appearance, and recognizing their activities, are some of the most actively studied areas of computer vision. Annual conferences[11] and special journal issues (Hilton, Fua, and Ronfard 2006) are devoted to this subject, and two recent surveys (Forsyth, Arikan, Ikemoto *et al.* 2006; Moeslund, Hilton, and Krüger 2006) each list over 400 papers devoted to these topics.[12] The HumanEva database of articulated human motions[13] contains multi-view video sequences of human actions along with corresponding motion capture data, evaluation code, and a reference 3D tracker based on particle filtering. The companion paper by Sigal, Balan, and Black (2010) not only describes the database and evaluation but also has a nice survey of important work in this field.

Given the breadth of this area, it is difficult to categorize all of this research, especially since different techniques usually build on each other. Moeslund, Hilton, and Krüger (2006) divide their survey into initialization, tracking (which includes background modeling and segmentation), pose estimation, and action (activity) recognition. Forsyth, Arikan, Ikemoto *et al.* (2006) divide their survey into sections on tracking (background subtraction, deformable templates, flow, and probabilistic models), recovering 3D pose from 2D observations, and data association and body parts. They also include a section on motion synthesis, which is more widely studied in computer graphics (Arikan and Forsyth 2002; Kovar, Gleicher, and Pighin 2002; Lee, Chai, Reitsma *et al.* 2002; Li, Wang, and Shum 2002; Pullen and Bregler

---

[10] http://www.mova.com.

[11] International Conference on Automatic Face and Gesture Recognition (FG), IEEE Workshop on Analysis and Modeling of Faces and Gestures, and International Workshop on Tracking Humans for the Evaluation of their Motion in Image Sequences (THEMIS).

[12] Older surveys include those by Gavrila (1999) and Moeslund and Granum (2001). Some surveys on gesture recognition, which we do not cover in this book, include those by Pavlović, Sharma, and Huang (1997) and Yang, Ahuja, and Tabb (2002).

[13] http://vision.cs.brown.edu/humaneva/.

2002), see Section 13.5.2. Another potential taxonomy for work in this field would be along the lines of whether 2D or 3D (or multi-view) images are used as input and whether 2D or 3D kinematic models are used.

In this section, we briefly review some of the more seminal and widely cited papers in the areas of background subtraction, initialization and detection, tracking with flow, 3D kinematic models, probabilistic models, adaptive shape modeling, and activity recognition. We refer the reader to the previously mentioned surveys for other topics and more details.

Background subtraction. One of the first steps in many (but certainly not all) human tracking systems is to model the background in order to extract the moving foreground objects (silhouettes) corresponding to people. Toyama, Krumm, Brumitt *et al.* (1999) review several *difference matting* and *background maintenance* (modeling) techniques and provide a good introduction to this topic. Stauffer and Grimson (1999) describe some techniques based on mixture models, while Sidenbladh and Black (2003) develop a more comprehensive treatment, which models not only the background image statistics but also the appearance of the foreground objects, e.g., their edge and motion (frame difference) statistics.

Once silhouettes have been extracted from one or more cameras, they can then be modeled using deformable templates or other contour models (Baumberg and Hogg 1996; Wren, Azarbayejani, Darrell *et al.* 1997). Tracking such silhouettes over time supports the analysis of multiple people moving around a scene, including building shape and appearance models and detecting if they are carrying objects (Haritaoglu, Harwood, and Davis 2000; Mittal and Davis 2003; Dimitrijevic, Lepetit, and Fua 2006).

Initialization and detection. In order to track people in a fully automated manner, it is necessary to first detect (or re-acquire) their presence in individual video frames. This topic is closely related to *pedestrian detection*, which is often considered as a kind of object recognition (Mori, Ren, Efros *et al.* 2004; Felzenszwalb and Huttenlocher 2005; Felzenszwalb, McAllester, and Ramanan 2008), and is therefore treated in more depth in Section 14.1.2. Additional techniques for initializing 3D trackers based on 2D images include those described by Howe, Leventon, and Freeman (2000), Rosales and Sclaroff (2000), Shakhnarovich, Viola, and Darrell (2003), Sminchisescu, Kanaujia, Li *et al.* (2005), Agarwal and Triggs (2006), Lee and Cohen (2006), Sigal and Black (2006), and Stenger, Thayananthan, Torr *et al.* (2006).

Single-frame human detection and pose estimation algorithms can sometimes be used by themselves to perform tracking (Ramanan, Forsyth, and Zisserman 2005; Rogez, Rihan, Ramalingam *et al.* 2008; Bourdev and Malik 2009), as described in Section 4.1.4. More often, however, they are combined with frame-to-frame tracking techniques to provide better reliability (Fossati, Dimitrijevic, Lepetit *et al.* 2007; Andriluka, Roth, and Schiele 2008; Ferrari, Marin-Jimenez, and Zisserman 2008).

Tracking with flow. The tracking of people and their pose from frame to frame can be enhanced by computing optic flow or matching the appearance of their limbs from one frame to another. For example, the *cardboard people* model of Ju, Black, and Yacoob (1996) models the appearance of each leg portion (upper and lower) as a moving rectangle, and uses optic flow to estimate their location in each subsequent frame. Cham and Rehg (1999) and Sidenbladh, Black, and Fleet (2000) track limbs using optical flow and templates, along with

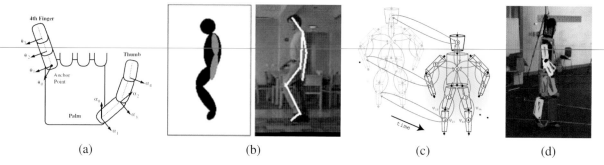

(a)   (b)   (c)   (d)

Figure 12.20 Tracking 3D human motion: (a) kinematic chain model for a human hand (Rehg, Morris, and Kanade 2003) © 2003, reprinted by permission of SAGE; (b) tracking a kinematic chain blob model in a video sequence (Bregler, Malik, and Pullen 2004) © 2004 Springer; (c–d) probabilistic loose-limbed collection of body parts (Sigal, Bhatia, Roth *et al.* 2004)

techniques for dealing with multiple hypotheses and uncertainty. Bregler, Malik, and Pullen (2004) use a full 3D model of limb and body motion, as described below. It is also possible to match the estimated motion field itself to some prototypes in order to identify the particular phase of a running motion or to match two low-resolution video portions in order to perform video replacement (Efros, Berg, Mori *et al.* 2003).

3D kinematic models. The effectiveness of human modeling and tracking can be greatly enhanced using a more accurate 3D model of a person's shape and motion. Underlying such representations, which are ubiquitous in 3D computer animation in games and special effects, is a *kinematic model* or *kinematic chain*, which specifies the length of each limb in a skeleton as well as the 2D or 3D rotation angles between the limbs or segments (Figure 12.20a–b). Inferring the values of the joint angles from the locations of the visible surface points is called *inverse kinematics* (IK) and is widely studied in computer graphics.

Figure 12.20a shows the kinematic model for a human hand used by Rehg, Morris, and Kanade (2003) to track hand motion in a video. As you can see, the attachment points between the fingers and the thumb have two degrees of freedom, while the finger joints themselves have only one. Using this kind of model can greatly enhance the ability of an edge-based tracker to cope with rapid motion, ambiguities in 3D pose, and partial occlusions.

Kinematic chain models are even more widely used for whole body modeling and tracking (O'Rourke and Badler 1980; Hogg 1983; Rohr 1994). One popular approach is to associate an ellipsoid or superquadric with each rigid limb in the kinematic model, as shown in Figure 12.20b. This model can then be fitted to each frame in one or more video streams either by matching silhouettes extracted from known backgrounds or by matching and tracking the locations of occluding edges (Gavrila and Davis 1996; Kakadiaris and Metaxas 2000; Bregler, Malik, and Pullen 2004; Kehl and Van Gool 2006). Note that some techniques use 2D models coupled to 2D measurements, some use 3D measurements (range data or multi-view video) with 3D models, and some use monocular video to infer and track 3D models directly.

It is also possible to use temporal models to improve the tracking of periodic motions, such as walking, by analyzing the joint angles as functions of time (Polana and Nelson 1997; Seitz and Dyer 1997; Cutler and Davis 2000). The generality and applicability of such tech-

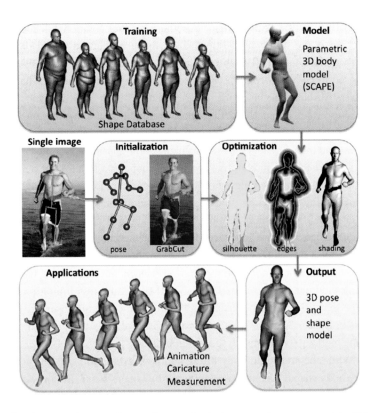

Figure 12.21 Estimating human shape and pose from a single image using a parametric 3D model (Guan, Weiss, Bălan *et al.* 2009) © 2009 IEEE.

niques can be improved by learning typical motion patterns using principal component analysis (Sidenbladh, Black, and Fleet 2000; Urtasun, Fleet, and Fua 2006).

Probabilistic models. Because tracking can be such a difficult task, sophisticated probabilistic inference techniques are often used to estimate the likely states of the person being tracked. One popular approach, called *particle filtering* (Isard and Blake 1998), was originally developed for tracking the outlines of people and hands, as described in Section 5.1.2 (Figures 5.6–5.8). It was subsequently applied to whole-body tracking (Deutscher, Blake, and Reid 2000; Sidenbladh, Black, and Fleet 2000; Deutscher and Reid 2005) and continues to be used in modern trackers (Ong, Micilotta, Bowden *et al.* 2006). Alternative approaches to handling the uncertainty inherent in tracking include multiple hypothesis tracking (Cham and Rehg 1999) and inflated covariances (Sminchisescu and Triggs 2001).

Figure 12.20c–d shows an example of a sophisticated spatio-temporal probabilistic graphical model called *loose-limbed people*, which models not only the geometric relationship between various limbs, but also their likely temporal dynamics (Sigal, Bhatia, Roth *et al.* 2004). The conditional probabilities relating various limbs and time instances are learned from training data, and particle filtering is used to perform the final pose inference.

Adaptive shape modeling. Another essential component of whole body modeling and tracking is the fitting of parameterized shape models to visual data. As we saw in Section 12.6.3 (Figure 12.19), the availability of large numbers of registered 3D range scans can be used to create *morphable models* of shape and appearance (Allen, Curless, and Popović 2003). Building on this work, Anguelov, Srinivasan, Koller *et al.* (2005) develop a sophisticated system called SCAPE (Shape Completion and Animation for PEople), which first acquires a large number of range scans of different people and of one person in different poses, and then registers these scans using semi-automated marker placement. The registered datasets are used to model the variation in shape as a function of personal characteristics and skeletal pose, e.g., the bulging of muscles as certain joints are flexed (Figure 12.21, top row). The resulting system can then be used for *shape completion*, i.e., the recovery of a full 3D mesh model from a small number of captured markers, by finding the best model parameters in both shape and pose space that fit the measured data.

Because it is constructed completely from scans of people in close-fitting clothing and uses a parametric shape model, the SCAPE system cannot cope with people wearing loose-fitting clothing. Bălan and Black (2008) overcome this limitation by estimating the body shape that fits within the visual hull of the same person observed in multiple poses, while Vlasic, Baran, Matusik *et al.* (2008) adapt an initial surface mesh fitted with a parametric shape model to better match the visual hull.

While the preceding body fitting and pose estimation systems use multiple views to estimate body shape, even more recent work by Guan, Weiss, Bălan *et al.* (2009) can fit a human shape and pose model to a single image of a person on a natural background. Manual initialization is used to estimate a rough pose (skeleton) and height model, and this is then used to segment the person's outline using the Grab Cut segmentation algorithm (Section 5.5). The shape and pose estimate are then refined using a combination of silhouette edge cues and shading information (Figure 12.21). The resulting 3D model can be used to create novel animations.

Activity recognition. The final widely studied topic in human modeling is motion, activity, and action recognition (Bobick 1997; Hu, Tan, Wang *et al.* 2004; Hilton, Fua, and Ronfard 2006). Examples of actions that are commonly recognized include walking and running, jumping, dancing, picking up objects, sitting down and standing up, and waving. Recent representative papers on these topics have been written by Robertson and Reid (2006), Sminchisescu, Kanaujia, and Metaxas (2006), Weinland, Ronfard, and Boyer (2006), Yilmaz and Shah (2006), and Gorelick, Blank, Shechtman *et al.* (2007).

12.7 Recovering texture maps and albedos

After a 3D model of an object or person has been acquired, the final step in modeling is usually to recover a *texture map* to describe the object's surface appearance. This first requires establishing a parameterization for the (u, v) texture coordinates as a function of 3D surface position. One simple way to do this is to associate a separate texture map with each triangle (or pair of triangles). More space-efficient techniques involve unwrapping the surface onto one or more maps, e.g., using a subdivision mesh (Section 12.3.2) (Eck, DeRose, Duchamp *et al.* 1995) or a geometry image (Section 12.3.3) (Gu, Gortler, and Hoppe 2002).

(a)   (b)   (c)

Figure 12.22 Estimating the diffuse albedo and reflectance parameters for a scanned 3D model (Sato, Wheeler, and Ikeuchi 1997) © 1997 ACM: (a) set of input images projected onto the model; (b) the complete diffuse reflection (albedo) model; (c) rendering from the reflectance model including the specular component.

Once the (u, v) coordinates for each triangle have been fixed, the perspective projection equations mapping from texture (u, v) to an image j's pixel (u_j, v_j) coordinates can be obtained by concatenating the affine $(u, v) \rightarrow (X, Y, Z)$ mapping with the perspective homography $(X, Y, Z) \rightarrow (u_j, v_j)$ (Szeliski and Shum 1997). The color values for the (u, v) texture map can then be re-sampled and stored, or the original image can itself be used as the texture source using projective texture mapping (OpenGL-ARB 1997).

The situation becomes more involved when more than one source image is available for appearance recovery, which is the usual case. One possibility is to use a *view-dependent texture map* (Section 13.1.1), in which a different source image (or combination of source images) is used for each polygonal face based on the angles between the virtual camera, the surface normals, and the source images (Debevec, Taylor, and Malik 1996; Pighin, Hecker, Lischinski *et al.* 1998). An alternative approach is to estimate a complete Surface Light Field for each surface point (Wood, Azuma, Aldinger *et al.* 2000), as described in Section 13.3.2.

In some situations, e.g., when using models in traditional 3D games, it is preferable to merge all of the source images into a single coherent texture map during pre-processing. Ideally, each surface triangle should select the source image where it is seen most directly (perpendicular to its normal) and at the resolution best matching the texture map resolution.[14] This can be posed as a graph cut optimization problem, where the smoothness term encourages adjacent triangles to use similar source images, followed by blending to compensate for exposure differences (Lempitsky and Ivanov 2007; Sinha, Steedly, Szeliski *et al.* 2008). Even better results can be obtained by explicitly modeling geometric and photometric misalignments between the source images (Shum and Szeliski 2000; Gal, Wexler, Ofek *et al.* 2010).

These kinds of approaches produce good results when the lighting stays fixed with respect to the object, i.e., when the camera moves around the object or space. When the lighting is strongly directional, however, and the object is being moved relative to this lighting, strong shading effects or specularities may be present, which will interfere with the reliable recovery of a texture (albedo) map. In this case, it is preferable to explicitly undo the shading effects (Section 12.1) by modeling the light source directions and estimating the surface reflectance properties while recovering the texture map (Sato and Ikeuchi 1996; Sato, Wheeler, and Ikeuchi 1997; Yu and Malik 1998; Yu, Debevec, Malik *et al.* 1999). Figure 12.22 shows

---

[14] When surfaces are seen at oblique viewing angles, it may be necessary to blend different images together to obtain the best resolution (Wang, Kang, Szeliski *et al.* 2001).

the results of one such approach, where the specularities are first removed while estimating the matte reflectance component (albedo) and then later re-introduced by estimating the specular component k_s in a Torrance–Sparrow reflection model (2.91).

12.7.1 Estimating BRDFs

A more ambitious approach to the problem of view-dependent appearance modeling is to estimate a general bidirectional reflectance distribution function (BRDF) for each point on an object's surface. Dana, van Ginneken, Nayar *et al.* (1999), Jensen, Marschner, Levoy *et al.* (2001), and Lensch, Kautz, Goesele *et al.* (2003) present different techniques for estimating such functions, while Dorsey, Rushmeier, and Sillion (2007) and Weyrich, Lawrence, Lensch *et al.* (2008) present more recent surveys of the topics of BRDF modeling, recovery, and rendering.

As we saw in Section 2.2.2 (2.81), the BRDF can be written as

$$f_r(\theta_i, \phi_i, \theta_r, \phi_r; \lambda), \tag{12.9}$$

where (θ_i, ϕ_i) and (θ_r, ϕ_r) are the angles the incident $\hat{v}_i$ and reflected $\hat{v}_r$ light ray directions make with the local surface coordinate frame $(\hat{d}_x, \hat{d}_y, \hat{n})$ shown in Figure 2.15. When modeling the appearance of an object, as opposed to the appearance of a patch of material, we need to estimate this function at every point (x, y) on the object's surface, which gives us the *spatially varying* BRDF, or SVBRDF (Weyrich, Lawrence, Lensch *et al.* 2008),

$$f_v(x, y, \theta_i, \phi_i, \theta_r, \phi_r; \lambda). \tag{12.10}$$

If sub-surface scattering effects are being modeled, such as the long-range transmission of light through materials such as alabaster, the eight-dimensional bidirectional scattering-surface reflectance-distribution function (BSSRDF) is used instead,

$$f_e(x_i, y_i, \theta_i, \phi_i, x_e, y_e, \theta_e, \phi_e; \lambda), \tag{12.11}$$

where the e subscript now represents the *emitted* rather than the *reflected* light directions.

Weyrich, Lawrence, Lensch *et al.* (2008) provide a nice survey of these and related topics, including basic photometry, BRDF models, traditional BRDF acquisition using *gonio reflectometry* (the precise measurement of visual angles and reflectances), multiplexed illumination (Schechner, Nayar, and Belhumeur 2009), skin modeling (Debevec, Hawkins, Tchou *et al.* 2000; Weyrich, Matusik, Pfister *et al.* 2006), and image-based acquisition techniques, which simultaneously recover an object's 3D shape and reflectometry from multiple photographs.

A nice example of this latter approach is the system developed by Lensch, Kautz, Goesele *et al.* (2003), who estimate locally varying BRDFs and refine their shape models using local estimates of surface normals. To build up their models, they first associate a *lumitexels*, which contains a 3D position, a surface normal, and a set of sparse radiance samples, with each surface point. Next, they cluster such lumitexels into materials that share common properties, using a Lafortune reflectance model (Lafortune, Foo, Torrance *et al.* 1997) and a divisive clustering approach (Figure 12.23a). Finally, in order to model detailed spatially varying appearance, each lumitexel (surface point) is projected onto the basis of clustered appearance models (Figure 12.23b).

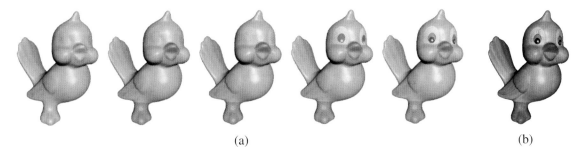

Figure 12.23 Image-based reconstruction of appearance and detailed geometry (Lensch, Kautz, Goesele *et al.* 2003) © 2003 ACM. (a) Appearance models (BRDFs) are re-estimated using divisive clustering. (b) In order to model detailed spatially varying appearance, each lumitexel is projected onto the basis formed by the clustered materials.

While most of the techniques discussed in this section require large numbers of views to estimate surface properties, a challenging future direction will be to take these techniques out of the lab and into the real world, and to combine them with regular and Internet photo image-based modeling approaches.

12.7.2 *Application*: 3D photography

The techniques described in this chapter for building complete 3D models from multiple images and then recovering their surface appearance have opened up a whole new range of applications that often go under the name *3D photography*. Pollefeys and Van Gool (2002) provide a nice introduction to this field, including the processing steps of feature matching, structure from motion recovery,[15] dense depth map estimation, 3D model building, and texture map recovery. A complete Web-based system for automatically performing all of these tasks, called ARC3D, is described by Vergauwen and Van Gool (2006) and Moons, Van Gool, and Vergauwen (2010). The latter paper provides not only an in-depth survey of this whole field but also a detailed description of their complete end-to-end system.

An alternative to such fully automated systems is to put the user in the loop in what is sometimes called *interactive computer vision*. van den Hengel, Dick, Thormhlen *et al.* (2007) describe their VideoTrace system, which performs automated point tracking and 3D structure recovery from video and then lets the user draw triangles and surfaces on top of the resulting point cloud, as well as interactively adjusting the locations of model vertices. Sinha, Steedly, Szeliski *et al.* (2008) describe a related system that uses matched vanishing points in multiple images (Figure 4.45) to infer 3D line orientations and plane normals. These are then used to guide the user drawing axis-aligned planes, which are automatically fitted to the recovered 3D point cloud. Fully automated variants on these ideas are described by Zebedin, Bauer, Karner *et al.* (2008), Furukawa, Curless, Seitz *et al.* (2009a), Furukawa, Curless, Seitz *et al.* (2009b), Mičušík and Košecká (2009), and Sinha, Steedly, and Szeliski (2009).

As the sophistication and reliability of these techniques continues to improve, we can expect to see even more user-friendly applications for photorealistic 3D modeling from images (Exercise 12.8).

---

[15] These earlier steps are also discussed in Section 7.4.4.

12.8 Additional reading

Shape from shading is one of the classic problems in computer vision (Horn 1975). Some representative papers in this area include those by Horn (1977), Ikeuchi and Horn (1981), Pentland (1984), Horn and Brooks (1986), Horn (1990), Szeliski (1991a), Mancini and Wolff (1992), Dupuis and Oliensis (1994), and Fua and Leclerc (1995). The collection of papers edited by Horn and Brooks (1989) is a great source of information on this topic, especially the chapter on variational approaches. The survey by Zhang, Tsai, Cryer *et al.* (1999) not only reviews more recent techniques but also provides some comparative results.

Woodham (1981) wrote the seminal paper of photometric stereo. Shape from texture techniques include those by Witkin (1981), Ikeuchi (1981), Blostein and Ahuja (1987), Garding (1992), Malik and Rosenholtz (1997), Liu, Collins, and Tsin (2004), Liu, Lin, and Hays (2004), Hays, Leordeanu, Efros *et al.* (2006), Lin, Hays, Wu *et al.* (2006), Lobay and Forsyth (2006), White and Forsyth (2006), White, Crane, and Forsyth (2007), and Park, Brocklehurst, Collins *et al.* (2009). Good papers and books on depth from defocus have been written by Pentland (1987), Nayar and Nakagawa (1994), Nayar, Watanabe, and Noguchi (1996), Watanabe and Nayar (1998), Chaudhuri and Rajagopalan (1999), and Favaro and Soatto (2006). Additional techniques for recovering shape from various kinds of illumination effects, including inter-reflections (Nayar, Ikeuchi, and Kanade 1991), are discussed in the book on shape recovery edited by Wolff, Shafer, and Healey (1992b).

Active rangefinding systems, which use laser or natural light illumination projected into the scene, have been described by Besl (1989), Rioux and Bird (1993), Kang, Webb, Zitnick *et al.* (1995), Curless and Levoy (1995), Curless and Levoy (1996), Proesmans, Van Gool, and Defoort (1998), Bouguet and Perona (1999), Curless (1999), Hebert (2000), Iddan and Yahav (2001), Goesele, Fuchs, and Seidel (2003), Scharstein and Szeliski (2003), Davis, Ramamoorthi, and Rusinkiewicz (2003), Zhang, Curless, and Seitz (2003), Zhang, Snavely, Curless *et al.* (2004), and Moons, Van Gool, and Vergauwen (2010). Individual range scans can be aligned using 3D correspondence and distance optimization techniques such as *iterated closest points* and its variants (Besl and McKay 1992; Zhang 1994; Szeliski and Lavallée 1996; Johnson and Kang 1997; Gold, Rangarajan, Lu *et al.* 1998; Johnson and Hebert 1999; Pulli 1999; David, DeMenthon, Duraiswami *et al.* 2004; Li and Hartley 2007; Enqvist, Josephson, and Kahl 2009). Once they have been aligned, range scans can be merged using techniques that model the signed distance of surfaces to volumetric sample points (Hoppe, DeRose, Duchamp *et al.* 1992; Curless and Levoy 1996; Hilton, Stoddart, Illingworth *et al.* 1996; Wheeler, Sato, and Ikeuchi 1998; Kazhdan, Bolitho, and Hoppe 2006; Lempitsky and Boykov 2007; Zach, Pock, and Bischof 2007b; Zach 2008).

Once constructed, 3D surfaces can be modeled and manipulated using a variety of three-dimensional representations, which include triangle meshes (Eck, DeRose, Duchamp *et al.* 1995; Hoppe 1996), splines (Farin 1992, 1996; Lee, Wolberg, and Shin 1996), subdivision surfaces (Stollnitz, DeRose, and Salesin 1996; Zorin, Schröder, and Sweldens 1996; Warren and Weimer 2001; Peters and Reif 2008), and geometry images (Gu, Gortler, and Hoppe 2002). Alternatively, they can be represented as collections of point samples with local orientation estimates (Hoppe, DeRose, Duchamp *et al.* 1992; Szeliski and Tonnesen 1992; Turk and O'Brien 2002; Pfister, Zwicker, van Baar *et al.* 2000; Alexa, Behr, Cohen-Or *et al.* 2003; Pauly, Keiser, Kobbelt *et al.* 2003; Diebel, Thrun, and Brünig 2006; Guennebaud and Gross

2007; Guennebaud, Germann, and Gross 2008; Oztireli, Guennebaud, and Gross 2008). They can also be modeled using implicit inside–outside characteristic or signed distance functions sampled on regular or irregular (octree) volumetric grids (Lavallée and Szeliski 1995; Szeliski and Lavallée 1996; Frisken, Perry, Rockwood *et al.* 2000; Dinh, Turk, and Slabaugh 2002; Kazhdan, Bolitho, and Hoppe 2006; Lempitsky and Boykov 2007; Zach, Pock, and Bischof 2007b; Zach 2008).

The literature on model-based 3D reconstruction is extensive. For modeling architecture and urban scenes, both interactive and fully automated systems have been developed. A special journal issue devoted to the reconstruction of large-scale 3D scenes (Zhu and Kanade 2008) is a good source of references and Robertson and Cipolla (2009) give a nice description of a complete system. Lots of additional references can be found in Section 12.6.1.

Face and whole body modeling and tracking is a very active sub-field of computer vision, with its own conferences and workshops, e.g., the International Conference on Automatic Face and Gesture Recognition (FG), the IEEE Workshop on Analysis and Modeling of Faces and Gestures, and the International Workshop on Tracking Humans for the Evaluation of their Motion in Image Sequences (THEMIS). Recent survey articles on the topic of whole body modeling and tracking include those by Forsyth, Arikan, Ikemoto *et al.* (2006), Moeslund, Hilton, and Krüger (2006), and Sigal, Balan, and Black (2010).

12.9 Exercises

Ex 12.1: Shape from focus   Grab a series of focused images with a digital SLR set to manual focus (or get one that allows for programmatic focus control) and recover the depth of an object.

1. Take some calibration images, e.g., of a checkerboard, so you can compute a mapping between the amount of defocus and the focus setting.

2. Try both a fronto-parallel planar target and one which is slanted so that it covers the working range of the sensor. Which one works better?

3. Now put a real object in the scene and perform a similar focus sweep.

4. For each pixel, compute the local sharpness and fit a parabolic curve over focus settings to find the most in-focus setting.

5. Map these focus settings to depth and compare your result to ground truth. If you are using a known simple object, such as sphere or cylinder (a ball or a soda can), it's easy to measure its true shape.

6. (Optional) See if you can recover the depth map from just two or three focus settings.

7. (Optional) Use an LCD projector to project artificial texture onto the scene. Use a pair of cameras to compare the accuracy of your shape from focus and shape from stereo techniques.

8. (Optional) Create an all-in-focus image using the technique of Agarwala, Dontcheva, Agrawala *et al.* (2004).

Ex 12.2: Shadow striping   Implement the handheld shadow striping system of Bouguet and Perona (1999). The basic steps include the following.

1. Set up two background planes behind the object of interest and calculate their orientation relative to the viewer, e.g., with fiducial marks.

2. Cast a moving shadow with a stick across the scene; record the video or capture the data with a webcam.

3. Estimate each light plane equation from the projections of the cast shadow against the two backgrounds.

4. Triangulate to the remaining points on each curve to get a 3D stripe and display the stripes using a 3D graphics engine.

5. (Optional) remove the requirement for a known second (vertical) plane and infer its location (or that of the light source) using the techniques described by Bouguet and Perona (1999). The techniques from Exercise 10.9 may also be helpful here.

Ex 12.3: Range data registration   Register two or more 3D datasets using either iterated closest points (ICP) (Besl and McKay 1992; Zhang 1994; Gold, Rangarajan, Lu *et al.* 1998) or octree signed distance fields (Szeliski and Lavallée 1996) (Section 12.2.1).

Apply your technique to narrow-baseline stereo pairs, e.g., obtained by moving a camera around an object, using structure from motion to recover the camera poses, and using a standard stereo matching algorithm.

Ex 12.4: Range data merging   Merge the datasets that you registered in the previous exercise using signed distance fields (Curless and Levoy 1996; Hilton, Stoddart, Illingworth *et al.* 1996). You can optionally use an octree to represent and compress this field if you already implemented it in the previous registration step.

Extract a meshed surface model from the signed distance field using marching cubes and display the resulting model.

Ex 12.5: Surface simplification   Use progressive meshes (Hoppe 1996) or some other technique from Section 12.3.2 to create a hierarchical simplification of your surface model.

Ex 12.6: Architectural modeler   Build a 3D interior or exterior model of some architectural structure, such as your house, from a series of handheld wide-angle photographs.

1. Extract lines and vanishing points (Exercises 4.11–4.15) to estimate the dominant directions in each image.

2. Use structure from motion to recover all of the camera poses and match up the vanishing points.

3. Let the user sketch the locations of the walls by drawing lines corresponding to wall bottoms, tops, and horizontal extents onto the images (Sinha, Steedly, Szeliski *et al.* 2008)—see also Exercise 6.9. Do something similar for openings (doors and windows) and simple furniture (tables and countertops).

4. Convert the resulting polygonal meshes into a 3D model (e.g., VRML) and optionally texture-map these surfaces from the images.

Ex 12.7: Body tracker   Download the video sequences from the HumanEva Web site.[16] Either implement a human motion tracker from scratch or extend the code on that Web site (Sigal, Balan, and Black 2010) in some interesting way.

Ex 12.8: 3D photography   Combine all of your previously developed techniques to produce a system that takes a series of photographs or a video and constructs a photorealistic texture-mapped 3D model.

---

[16] http://vision.cs.brown.edu/humaneva/.

Chapter 13

Image-based rendering

R. Szeliski, *Computer Vision: Algorithms and Applications*, Texts in Computer Science,
DOI 10.1007/978-1-84882-935-0_13, © Springer-Verlag London Limited 2011

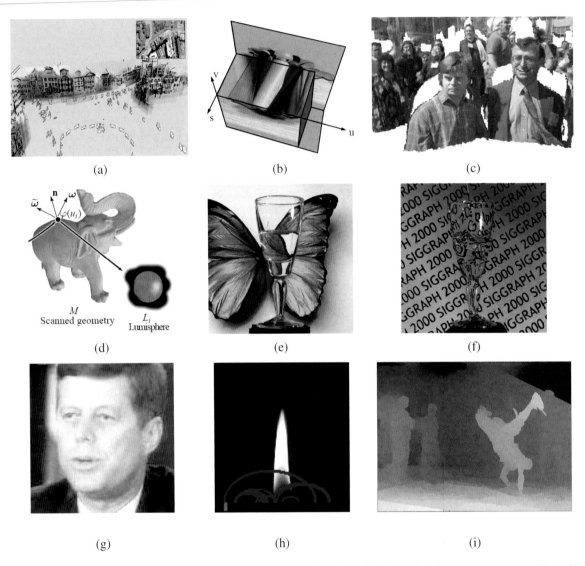

Figure 13.1 Image-based and video-based rendering: (a) a 3D view of a Photo Tourism reconstruction (Snavely, Seitz, and Szeliski 2006) © 2006 ACM; (b) a slice through a 4D light field (Gortler, Grzeszczuk, Szeliski *et al.* 1996) © 1996 ACM; (c) sprites with depth (Shade, Gortler, He *et al.* 1998) © 1998 ACM; (d) surface light field (Wood, Azuma, Aldinger *et al.* 2000) © 2000 ACM; (e) environment matte in front of a novel background (Zongker, Werner, Curless *et al.* 1999) © 1999 ACM; (f) real-time video environment matte (Chuang, Zongker, Hindorff *et al.* 2000) © 2000 ACM; (g) Video Rewrite used to re-animate old video (Bregler, Covell, and Slaney 1997) © 1997 ACM; (h) video texture of a candle flame (Schödl, Szeliski, Salesin *et al.* 2000) © 2000 ACM; (i) video view interpolation (Zitnick, Kang, Uyttendaele *et al.* 2004) © 2004 ACM.

Over the last two decades, image-based rendering has emerged as one of the most exciting applications of computer vision (Kang, Li, Tong *et al.* 2006; Shum, Chan, and Kang 2007). In image-based rendering, 3D reconstruction techniques from computer vision are combined with computer graphics rendering techniques that use multiple views of a scene to create interactive photo-realistic experiences, such as the Photo Tourism system shown in Figure 13.1a. Commercial versions of such systems include immersive street-level navigation in on-line mapping systems[1] and the creation of 3D Photosynths[2] from large collections of casually acquired photographs.

In this chapter, we explore a variety of image-based rendering techniques, such as those illustrated in Figure 13.1. We begin with *view interpolation* (Section 13.1), which creates a seamless transition between a pair of reference images using one or more pre-computed depth maps. Closely related to this idea are *view-dependent texture maps* (Section 13.1.1), which blend multiple texture maps on a 3D model's surface. The representations used for both the color imagery and the 3D geometry in view interpolation include a number of clever variants such as *layered depth images* (Section 13.2) and *sprites with depth* (Section 13.2.1).

We continue our exploration of image-based rendering with the *light field* and *Lumigraph* four-dimensional representations of a scene's appearance (Section 13.3), which can be used to render the scene from any arbitrary viewpoint. Variants on these representations include the *unstructured Lumigraph* (Section 13.3.1), *surface light fields* (Section 13.3.2), *concentric mosaics* (Section 13.3.3), and *environment mattes* (Section 13.4).

The last part of this chapter explores the topic of *video-based rendering*, which uses one or more videos in order to create novel video-based experiences (Section 13.5). The topics we cover include video-based facial animation (Section 13.5.1), as well as *video textures* (Section 13.5.2), in which short video clips can be seamlessly looped to create dynamic real-time video-based renderings of a scene. We close with a discussion of *3D videos* created from multiple video streams (Section 13.5.4), as well as *video-based walkthroughs* of environments (Section 13.5.5), which have found widespread application in immersive outdoor mapping and driving direction systems.

13.1 View interpolation

While the term *image-based rendering* first appeared in the papers by Chen (1995) and McMillan and Bishop (1995), the work on *view interpolation* by Chen and Williams (1993) is considered as the seminal paper in the field. In view interpolation, pairs of rendered color images are combined with their pre-computed depth maps to generate interpolated views that mimic what a virtual camera would see in between the two reference views.

View interpolation combines two ideas that were previously used in computer vision and computer graphics. The first is the idea of pairing a recovered depth map with the reference image used in its computation and then using the resulting texture-mapped 3D model to generate novel views (Figure 11.1). The second is the idea of *morphing* (Section 3.6.3) (Figure 3.53), where correspondences between pairs of images are used to warp each reference image to an in-between location while simultaneously cross-dissolving between the two warped images.

---

[1] http://maps.bing.com and http://maps.google.com.
[2] http://photosynth.net.

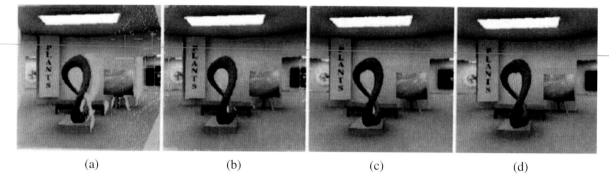

| (a) | (b) | (c) | (d) |

Figure 13.2 View interpolation (Chen and Williams 1993) © 1993 ACM: (a) holes from one source image (shown in blue); (b) holes after combining two widely spaced images; (c) holes after combining two closely spaced images; (d) after interpolation (hole filling).

Figure 13.2 illustrates this process in more detail. First, both source images are warped to the novel view, using both the knowledge of the reference and virtual 3D camera pose along with each image's depth map (2.68–2.70). In the paper by Chen and Williams (1993), a *forward warping* algorithm (Algorithm 3.1 and Figure 3.46) is used. The depth maps are represented as quadtrees for both space and rendering time efficiency (Samet 1989).

During the forward warping process, multiple pixels (which occlude one another) may land on the same destination pixel. To resolve this conflict, either a *z-buffer* depth value can be associated with each destination pixel or the images can be warped in back-to-front order, which can be computed based on the knowledge of epipolar geometry (Chen and Williams 1993; Laveau and Faugeras 1994; McMillan and Bishop 1995).

Once the two reference images have been warped to the novel view (Figure 13.2a–b), they can be merged to create a coherent composite (Figure 13.2c). Whenever one of the images has a *hole* (illustrated as a cyan pixel), the other image is used as the final value. When both images have pixels to contribute, these can be blended as in usual morphing, i.e., according to the relative distances between the virtual and source cameras. Note that if the two images have very different exposures, which can happen when performing view interpolation on real images, the hole-filled regions and the blended regions will have different exposures, leading to subtle artifacts.

The final step in view interpolation (Figure 13.2d) is to fill any remaining holes or cracks due to the forward warping process or lack of source data (scene visibility). This can be done by copying pixels from the *further* pixels adjacent to the hole. (Otherwise, foreground objects are subject to a "fattening effect".)

The above process works well for rigid scenes, although its visual quality (lack of aliasing) can be improved using a two-pass, forward–backward algorithm (Section 13.2.1) (Shade, Gortler, He *et al.* 1998) or full 3D rendering (Zitnick, Kang, Uyttendaele *et al.* 2004). In the case where the two reference images are views of a non-rigid scene, e.g., a person smiling in one image and frowning in the other, *view morphing*, which combines ideas from view interpolation with regular morphing, can be used (Seitz and Dyer 1996).

While the original view interpolation paper describes how to generate novel views based on similar pre-computed (linear perspective) images, the *plenoptic modeling* paper of McMillan and Bishop (1995) argues that cylindrical images should be used to store the pre-computed

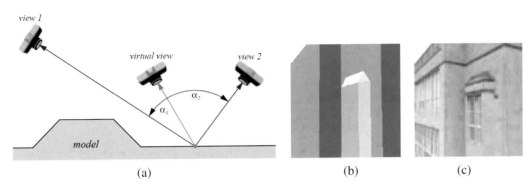

Figure 13.3 View-dependent texture mapping (Debevec, Taylor, and Malik 1996) © 1996 ACM. (a) The weighting given to each input view depends on the relative angles between the novel (virtual) view and the original views; (b) simplified 3D model geometry; (c) with view-dependent texture mapping, the geometry appears to have more detail (recessed windows).

rendering or real-world images. (Chen 1995) also propose using environment maps (cylindrical, cubic, or spherical) as source images for view interpolation.

13.1.1 View-dependent texture maps

View-dependent texture maps (Debevec, Taylor, and Malik 1996) are closely related to view interpolation. Instead of associating a separate depth map with each input image, a single 3D model is created for the scene, but different images are used as texture map sources depending on the virtual camera's current position (Figure 13.3a).[3]

In more detail, given a new virtual camera position, the similarity of this camera's view of each polygon (or pixel) is compared to that of potential source images. The images are then blended using a weighting that is inversely proportional to the angles α_i between the virtual view and the source views (Figure 13.3a). Even though the geometric model can be fairly coarse (Figure 13.3b), blending between different views gives a strong sense of more detailed geometry because of the parallax (visual motion) between corresponding pixels. While the original paper performs the weighted blend computation separately at each pixel or coarsened polygon face, follow-on work by Debevec, Yu, and Borshukov (1998) presents a more efficient implementation based on precomputing contributions for various portions of viewing space and then using projective texture mapping (OpenGL-ARB 1997).

The idea of view-dependent texture mapping has been used in a large number of subsequent image-based rendering systems, including facial modeling and animation (Pighin, Hecker, Lischinski *et al.* 1998) and 3D scanning and visualization (Pulli, Abi-Rached, Duchamp *et al.* 1998). Closely related to view-dependent texture mapping is the idea of blending between light rays in 4D space, which forms the basis of the Lumigraph and unstructured Lumigraph systems (Section 13.3) (Gortler, Grzeszczuk, Szeliski *et al.* 1996; Buehler, Bosse, McMillan *et al.* 2001).

---

[3] The term *image-based modeling*, which is now commonly used to describe the creation of texture-mapped 3D models from multiple images, appears to have first been used by Debevec, Taylor, and Malik (1996), who also used the term *photogrammetric modeling* to describe the same process.

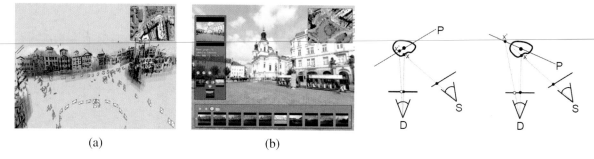

(a)   (b)

Figure 13.4 Photo Tourism (Snavely, Seitz, and Szeliski 2006): © 2006 ACM: (a) a 3D overview of the scene, with translucent washes and lines painted onto the planar impostors; (b) once the user has selected a region of interest, a set of related thumbnails is displayed along the bottom; (c) planar proxy selection for optimal stabilization (Snavely, Garg, Seitz *et al.* 2008) © 2008 ACM.

In order to provide even more realism in their Façade system, Debevec, Taylor, and Malik (1996) also include a *model-based stereo* component, which optionally computes an offset (parallax) map for each coarse planar facet of their 3D model. They call the resulting analysis and rendering system a *hybrid geometry- and image-based* approach, since it uses traditional 3D geometric modeling to create the global 3D model, but then uses local depth offsets, along with view interpolation, to add visual realism.

13.1.2 *Application*: Photo Tourism

While view interpolation was originally developed to accelerate the rendering of 3D scenes on low-powered processors and systems without graphics acceleration, it turns out that it can be applied directly to large collections of casually acquired photographs. The *Photo Tourism* system developed by Snavely, Seitz, and Szeliski (2006) uses structure from motion to compute the 3D locations and poses of all the cameras taking the images, along with a sparse 3D point-cloud model of the scene (Section 7.4.4, Figure 7.11).

To perform an image-based exploration of the resulting *sea of images* (Aliaga, Funkhouser, Yanovsky *et al.* 2003), Photo Tourism first associates a 3D proxy with each image. While a triangulated mesh obtained from the point cloud can sometimes form a suitable proxy, e.g., for outdoor terrain models, a simple dominant plane fit to the 3D points visible in each image often performs better, because it does not contain any erroneous segments or connections that pop out as artifacts. As automated 3D modeling techniques continue to improve, however, the pendulum may swing back to more detailed 3D geometry (Goesele, Snavely, Curless *et al.* 2007; Sinha, Steedly, and Szeliski 2009).

The resulting image-based navigation system lets users move from photo to photo, either by selecting cameras from a top-down view of the scene (Figure 13.4a) or by selecting regions of interest in an image, navigating to nearby views, or selecting related thumbnails (Figure 13.4b). To create a background for the 3D scene, e.g., when being viewed from above, non-photorealistic techniques (Section 10.5.2), such as translucent color washes or highlighted 3D line segments, can be used (Figure 13.4a). The system can also be used to annotate regions of images and to automatically propagate such annotations to other photographs.

The 3D planar proxies used in Photo Tourism and the related Photosynth system from Microsoft result in non-photorealistic transitions reminiscent of visual effects such as "page flips". Selecting a stable 3D axis for all the planes can reduce the amount of swimming and enhance the perception of 3D (Figure 13.4c) (Snavely, Garg, Seitz *et al.* 2008). It is also possible to automatically detect objects in the scene that are seen from multiple views and create "orbits" of viewpoints around such objects. Furthermore, nearby images in both 3D position and viewing direction can be linked to create "virtual paths", which can then be used to navigate between arbitrary pairs of images, such as those you might take yourself while walking around a popular tourist site (Snavely, Garg, Seitz *et al.* 2008).

The spatial matching of image features and regions performed by Photo Tourism can also be used to infer more information from large image collections. For example, Simon, Snavely, and Seitz (2007) show how the match graph between images of popular tourist sites can be used to find the most *iconic* (commonly photographed) objects in the collection, along with their related tags. In follow-on work, Simon and Seitz (2008) show how such tags can be propagated to sub-regions of each image, using an analysis of which 3D points appear in the central portions of photographs. Extensions of these techniques to *all* of the world's images, including the use of GPS tags where available, have been investigated as well (Li, Wu, Zach *et al.* 2008; Quack, Leibe, and Van Gool 2008; Crandall, Backstrom, Huttenlocher *et al.* 2009; Li, Crandall, and Huttenlocher 2009; Zheng, Zhao, Song *et al.* 2009).

13.2 Layered depth images

Traditional view interpolation techniques associate a single depth map with each source or reference image. Unfortunately, when such a depth map is warped to a novel view, holes and cracks inevitably appear behind the foreground objects. One way to alleviate this problem is to keep several depth and color values (*depth pixels*) at every pixel in a reference image (or, at least for pixels near foreground–background transitions) (Figure 13.5). The resulting data structure, which is called a *layered depth image* (LDI), can be used to render new views using a back-to-front forward warping (splatting) algorithm (Shade, Gortler, He *et al.* 1998).

13.2.1 Impostors, sprites, and layers

An alternative to keeping lists of color-depth values at each pixel, as is done in the LDI, is to organize objects into different *layers* or *sprites*. The term sprite originates in the computer game industry, where it is used to designate flat animated characters in games such as Pac-Man or Mario Bros. When put into a 3D setting, such objects are often called *impostors*, because they use a piece of flat, alpha-matted geometry to represent simplified versions of 3D objects that are far away from the camera (Shade, Lischinski, Salesin *et al.* 1996; Lengyel and Snyder 1997; Torborg and Kajiya 1996). In computer vision, such representations are usually called *layers* (Wang and Adelson 1994; Baker, Szeliski, and Anandan 1998; Torr, Szeliski, and Anandan 1999; Birchfield, Natarajan, and Tomasi 2007). Section 8.5.2 discusses the topics of transparent layers and reflections, which occur on specular and transparent surfaces such as glass.

While flat layers can often serve as an adequate representation of geometry and appearance for far-away objects, better geometric fidelity can be achieved by also modeling the

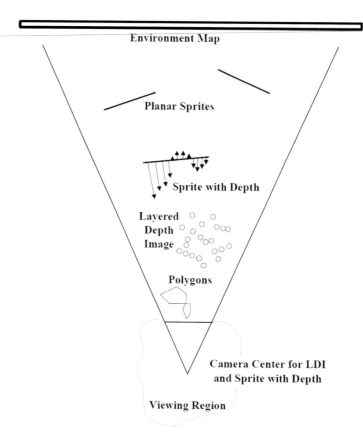

Figure 13.5 A variety of image-based rendering primitives, which can be used depending on the distance between the camera and the object of interest (Shade, Gortler, He *et al.* 1998) ©️ 1998 ACM. Closer objects may require more detailed polygonal representations, while mid-level objects can use a layered depth image (LDI), and far-away objects can use sprites (potentially with depth) and environment maps.

    (a)   (b)   (c)   (d)

Figure 13.6 Sprites with depth (Shade, Gortler, He *et al.* 1998) ©️ 1998 ACM: (a) alpha-matted color sprite; (b) corresponding relative depth or parallax; (c) rendering without relative depth; (d) rendering with depth (note the curved object boundaries).

per-pixel offsets relative to a base plane, as shown in Figures 13.5 and 13.6a–b. Such representations are called *plane plus parallax* in the computer vision literature (Kumar, Anandan, and Hanna 1994; Sawhney 1994; Szeliski and Coughlan 1997; Baker, Szeliski, and Anandan 1998), as discussed in Section 8.5 (Figure 8.16). In addition to fully automated stereo techniques, it is also possible to paint in depth layers (Kang 1998; Oh, Chen, Dorsey *et al.* 2001; Shum, Sun, Yamazaki *et al.* 2004) or to infer their 3D structure from monocular image cues (Section 14.4.4) (Hoiem, Efros, and Hebert 2005b; Saxena, Sun, and Ng 2009).

How can we render a sprite with depth from a novel viewpoint? One possibility, as with a regular depth map, is to just forward warp each pixel to its new location, which can cause aliasing and cracks. A better way, which we already mentioned in Section 3.6.2, is to first warp the depth (or (u, v) displacement) map to the novel view, fill in the cracks, and then use higher-quality inverse warping to resample the color image (Shade, Gortler, He *et al.* 1998). Figure 13.6d shows the results of applying such a two-pass rendering algorithm. From this still image, you can appreciate that the foreground sprites look more rounded; however, to fully appreciate the improvement in realism, you would have to look at the actual animated sequence.

Sprites with depth can also be rendered using conventional graphics hardware, as described in (Zitnick, Kang, Uyttendaele *et al.* 2004). Rogmans, Lu, Bekaert *et al.* (2009) describe GPU implementations of both real-time stereo matching and real-time forward and inverse rendering algorithms.

13.3 Light fields and Lumigraphs

While image-based rendering approaches can synthesize scene renderings from novel viewpoints, they raise the following more general question:

> *Is is possible to capture and render the appearance of a scene from all possible viewpoints and, if so, what is the complexity of the resulting structure?*

Let us assume that we are looking at a static scene, i.e., one where the objects and illuminants are fixed, and only the observer is moving around. Under these conditions, we can describe each image by the location and orientation of the virtual camera (6 dof) as well as its intrinsics (e.g., its focal length). However, if we capture a two-dimensional *spherical* image around each possible camera location, we can re-render any view from this information.[4] Thus, taking the cross-product of the three-dimensional space of camera positions with the 2D space of spherical images, we obtain the 5D *plenoptic function* of Adelson and Bergen (1991), which forms the basis of the image-based rendering system of McMillan and Bishop (1995).

Notice, however, that when there is no light dispersion in the scene, i.e., no smoke or fog, all the coincident rays along a portion of free space (between solid or refractive objects) have the same color value. Under these conditions, we can reduce the 5D plenoptic function to the 4D *light field* of all possible rays (Gortler, Grzeszczuk, Szeliski *et al.* 1996; Levoy and Hanrahan 1996; Levoy 2006).[5]

---

[4] Since we are counting dimensions, we ignore for now any sampling or resolution issues.
[5] Levoy and Hanrahan (1996) borrowed the term *light field* from a paper by Gershun (1939). Another name for this representation is the *photic field* (Moon and Spencer 1981).

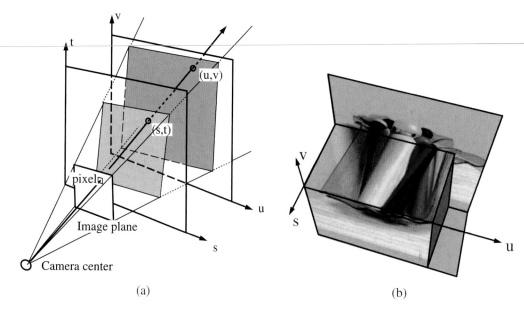

(a)   (b)

Figure 13.7 The Lumigraph (Gortler, Grzeszczuk, Szeliski *et al.* 1996) © 1996 ACM: (a) a ray is represented by its 4D two-plane parameters (s, t) and (u, v); (b) a slice through the 3D light field subset (u, v, s).

To make the parameterization of this 4D function simpler, let us put two planes in the 3D scene roughly bounding the area of interest, as shown in Figure 13.7a. Any light ray terminating at a camera that lives in front of the st plane (assuming that this space is empty) passes through the two planes at (s, t) and (u, v) and can be described by its 4D coordinate (s, t, u, v). This diagram (and parameterization) can be interpreted as describing a family of cameras living on the st plane with their image planes being the uv plane. The uv plane can be placed at infinity, which corresponds to all the virtual cameras looking in the same direction.

In practice, if the planes are of finite extent, the finite *light slab* $L(s, t, u, v)$ can be used to generate any synthetic view that a camera would see through a (finite) *viewport* in the st plane with a view frustum that wholly intersects the far uv plane. To enable the camera to move all the way around an object, the 3D space surrounding the object can be split into multiple domains, each with its own light slab parameterization. Conversely, if the camera is moving inside a bounded volume of free space looking outward, multiple cube faces surrounding the camera can be used as (s, t) planes.

Thinking about 4D spaces is difficult, so let us drop our visualization by one dimension. If we fix the row value t and constrain our camera to move along the s axis while looking at the uv plane, we can stack all of the stabilized images the camera sees to get the (u, v, s) *epipolar volume*, which we discussed in Section 11.6. A "horizontal" cross-section through this volume is the well-known *epipolar plane image* (Bolles, Baker, and Marimont 1987), which is the us slice shown in Figure 13.7b.

As you can see in this slice, each color pixel moves along a linear track whose slope is related to its depth (parallax) from the uv plane. (Pixels exactly on the uv plane appear "vertical", i.e., they do not move as the camera moves along s.) Furthermore, pixel tracks

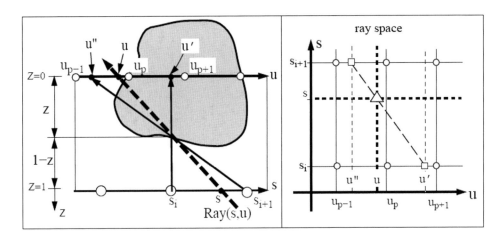

Figure 13.8 Depth compensation in the Lumigraph (Gortler, Grzeszczuk, Szeliski *et al.* 1996) © 1996 ACM. To resample the (s, u) dashed light ray, the u parameter corresponding to each discrete s_i camera location is modified according to the out-of-plane depth z to yield new coordinates u and u'; in (u, s) ray space, the original sample ($\triangle$) is resampled from the (s_i, u') and (s_{i+1}, u'') samples, which are themselves linear blends of their adjacent (○) samples.

occlude one another as their corresponding 3D surface elements occlude. Translucent pixels, however, composite *over* background pixels (Section 3.1.3, (3.8)) rather than occluding them. Thus, we can think of adjacent pixels sharing a similar planar geometry as *EPI strips* or *EPI tubes* (Criminisi, Kang, Swaminathan *et al.* 2005).

The equations mapping from pixels (x, y) in a virtual camera and the corresponding (s, t, u, v) coordinates are relatively straightforward to derive and are sketched out in Exercise 13.7. It is also possible to show that the set of pixels corresponding to a regular orthographic or perspective camera, i.e., one that has a linear projective relationship between 3D points and (x, y) pixels (2.63), lie along a two-dimensional hyperplane in the (s, t, u, v) light field (Exercise 13.7).

While a light field can be used to render a complex 3D scene from novel viewpoints, a much better rendering (with less ghosting) can be obtained if something is known about its 3D geometry. The Lumigraph system of Gortler, Grzeszczuk, Szeliski *et al.* (1996) extends the basic light field rendering approach by taking into account the 3D location of surface points corresponding to each 3D ray.

Consider the ray (s, u) corresponding to the dashed line in Figure 13.8, which intersects the object's surface at a distance z from the uv plane. When we look up the pixel's color in camera s_i (assuming that the light field is discretely sampled on a regular 4D (s, t, u, v) grid), the actual pixel coordinate is u', instead of the original u value specified by the (s, u) ray. Similarly, for camera s_{i+1} (where $s_i \le s \le s_{i+1}$), pixel address u'' is used. Thus, instead of using quadri-linear interpolation of the nearest sampled (s, t, u, v) values around a given ray to determine its color, the (u, v) values are modified for each discrete (s_i, t_i) camera.

Figure 13.8 also shows the same reasoning in *ray space*. Here, the original continuous-valued (s, u) ray is represented by a triangle and the nearby sampled discrete values are shown as circles. Instead of just blending the four nearest samples, as would be indicated by the vertical and horizontal dashed lines, the modified (s_i, u') and (s_{i+1}, u'') values are sampled instead and their values are then blended.

The resulting rendering system produces images of much better quality than a proxy-free light field and is the method of choice whenever 3D geometry can be inferred. In subsequent work, Isaksen, McMillan, and Gortler (2000) show how a planar proxy for the scene, which is a simpler 3D model, can be used to simplify the resampling equations. They also describe how to create synthetic aperture photos, which mimic what might be seen by a wide-aperture lens, by blending more nearby samples (Levoy and Hanrahan 1996). A similar approach can be used to re-focus images taken with a plenoptic (microlens array) camera (Ng, Levoy, Bréedif *et al.* 2005; Ng 2005) or a light field microscope (Levoy, Ng, Adams *et al.* 2006). It can also be used to see through obstacles, using extremely large synthetic apertures focused on a background that can blur out foreground objects and make them appear translucent (Wilburn, Joshi, Vaish *et al.* 2005; Vaish, Szeliski, Zitnick *et al.* 2006).

Now that we understand how to render new images from a light field, how do we go about capturing such data sets? One answer is to move a calibrated camera with a motion control rig or *gantry*.[6] Another approach is to take handheld photographs and to determine the pose and intrinsic calibration of each image using either a calibrated stage or structure from motion. In this case, the images need to be *rebinned* into a regular 4D (s, t, u, v) space before they can be used for rendering (Gortler, Grzeszczuk, Szeliski *et al.* 1996). Alternatively, the original images can be used directly using a process called the *unstructured Lumigraph*, which we describe below.

Because of the large number of images involved, light fields and Lumigraphs can be quite voluminous to store and transmit. Fortunately, as you can tell from Figure 13.7b, there is a tremendous amount of redundancy (coherence) in a light field, which can be made even more explicit by first computing a 3D model, as in the Lumigraph. A number of techniques have been developed to compress and progressively transmit such representations (Gortler, Grzeszczuk, Szeliski *et al.* 1996; Levoy and Hanrahan 1996; Rademacher and Bishop 1998; Magnor and Girod 2000; Wood, Azuma, Aldinger *et al.* 2000; Shum, Kang, and Chan 2003; Magnor, Ramanathan, and Girod 2003; Shum, Chan, and Kang 2007).

13.3.1 Unstructured Lumigraph

When the images in a Lumigraph are acquired in an unstructured (irregular) manner, it can be counterproductive to resample the resulting light rays into a regularly binned (s, t, u, v) data structure. This is both because resampling always introduces a certain amount of aliasing and because the resulting gridded light field can be populated very sparsely or irregularly.

The alternative is to render directly from the acquired images, by finding for each light ray in a virtual camera the closest pixels in the original images. The *unstructured Lumigraph* rendering (ULR) system of Buehler, Bosse, McMillan *et al.* (2001) describes how to select such pixels by combining a number of fidelity criteria, including *epipole consistency* (distance of rays to a source camera's center), *angular deviation* (similar incidence direction on the surface), *resolution* (similar sampling density along the surface), *continuity* (to nearby pixels), and *consistency* (along the ray). These criteria can all be combined to determine a weighting

---

[6] See http://lightfield.stanford.edu/acq.html for a description of some of the gantries and camera arrays built at the Stanford Computer Graphics Laboratory. This Web site also provides a number of light field data sets that are a great source of research and project material.

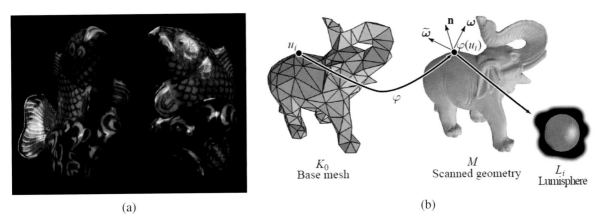

Figure 13.9 Surface light fields (Wood, Azuma, Aldinger *et al.* 2000) © 2000 ACM: (a) example of a highly specular object with strong inter-reflections; (b) the surface light field stores the light emanating from each surface point in all visible directions as a "Lumisphere".

function between each virtual camera's pixel and a number of candidate input cameras from which it can draw colors. To make the algorithm more efficient, the computations are performed by discretizing the virtual camera's image plane using a regular grid overlaid with the polyhedral object mesh model and the input camera centers of projection and interpolating the weighting functions between vertices.

The unstructured Lumigraph generalizes previous work in both image-based rendering and light field rendering. When the input cameras are gridded, the ULR behaves the same way as regular Lumigraph rendering. When fewer cameras are available but the geometry is accurate, the algorithm behaves similarly to view-dependent texture mapping (Section 13.1.1).

13.3.2 Surface light fields

Of course, using a two-plane parameterization for a light field is not the only possible choice. (It is the one usually presented first since the projection equations and visualizations are the easiest to draw and understand.) As we mentioned on the topic of light field compression, if we know the 3D shape of the object or scene whose light field is being modeled, we can effectively compress the field because nearby rays emanating from nearby surface elements have similar color values.

In fact, if the object is totally diffuse, ignoring occlusions, which can be handled using 3D graphics algorithms or z-buffering, all rays passing through a given surface point will have the same color value. Hence, the light field "collapses" to the usual 2D texture-map defined over an object's surface. Conversely, if the surface is totally specular (e.g., mirrored), each surface point reflects a miniature copy of the environment surrounding that point. In the absence of inter-reflections (e.g., a convex object in a large open space), each surface point simply reflects the far-field *environment map* (Section 2.2.1), which again is two-dimensional. Therefore, is seems that re-parameterizing the 4D light field to lie on the object's surface can be extremely beneficial.

These observations underlie the *surface light field* representation introduced by Wood, Azuma, Aldinger *et al.* (2000). In their system, an accurate 3D model is built of the object being represented. Then the *Lumisphere* of all rays emanating from each surface point is estimated or captured (Figure 13.9). Nearby Lumispheres will be highly correlated and hence amenable to both compression and manipulation.

To estimate the diffuse component of each Lumisphere, a median filtering over all visible exiting directions is first performed for each channel. Once this has been subtracted from the Lumisphere, the remaining values, which should consist mostly of the specular components, are *reflected* around the local surface normal (2.89), which turns each Lumisphere into a copy of the local environment around that point. Nearby Lumispheres can then be compressed using predictive coding, vector quantization, or principal component analysis.

The decomposition into a diffuse and specular component can also be used to perform editing or manipulation operations, such as re-painting the surface, changing the specular component of the reflection (e.g., by blurring or sharpening the specular Lumispheres), or even geometrically deforming the object while preserving detailed surface appearance.

13.3.3 *Application*: Concentric mosaics

A useful and simple version of light field rendering is a panoramic image with parallax, i.e., a video or series of photographs taken from a camera swinging in front of some rotation point. Such panoramas can be captured by placing a camera on a boom on a tripod, or even more simply, by holding a camera at arm's length while rotating your body around a fixed axis.

The resulting set of images can be thought of as a *concentric mosaic* (Shum and He 1999; Shum, Wang, Chai *et al.* 2002) or a *layered depth panorama* (Zheng, Kang, Cohen *et al.* 2007). The term "concentric mosaic" comes from a particular structure that can be used to re-bin all of the sampled rays, essentially associating each column of pixels with the "radius" of the concentric circle to which it is tangent (Shum and He 1999; Peleg, Ben-Ezra, and Pritch 2001).

Rendering from such data structures is fast and straightforward. If we assume that the scene is far enough away, for any virtual camera location, we can associate each column of pixels in the virtual camera with the nearest column of pixels in the input image set. (For a regularly captured set of images, this computation can be performed analytically.) If we have some rough knowledge of the depth of such pixels, columns can be stretched vertically to compensate for the change in depth between the two cameras. If we have an even more detailed depth map (Peleg, Ben-Ezra, and Pritch 2001; Li, Shum, Tang *et al.* 2004; Zheng, Kang, Cohen *et al.* 2007), we can perform pixel-by-pixel depth corrections.

While the virtual camera's motion is constrained to lie in the plane of the original cameras and within the radius of the original capture ring, the resulting experience can exhibit complex rendering phenomena, such as reflections and translucencies, which cannot be captured using a texture-mapped 3D model of the world. Exercise 13.10 has you construct a concentric mosaic rendering system from a series of hand-held photos or video.

13.4 Environment mattes

So far in this chapter, we have dealt with view interpolation and light fields, which are techniques for modeling and rendering complex static scenes seen from different viewpoints.

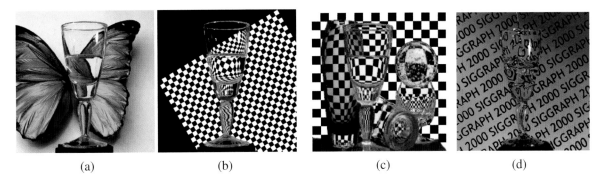

Figure 13.10 Environment mattes: (a–b) a refractive object can be placed in front of a series of backgrounds and their light patterns will be correctly refracted (Zongker, Werner, Curless *et al.* 1999) (c) multiple refractions can be handled using a mixture of Gaussians model and (d) real-time mattes can be pulled using a single graded colored background (Chuang, Zongker, Hindorff *et al.* 2000) © 2000 ACM.

What if instead of moving around a virtual camera, we take a complex, refractive object, such as the water goblet shown in Figure 13.10, and place it in front of a new background? Instead of modeling the 4D space of rays emanating from a scene, we now need to model how each pixel in our view of this object refracts incident light coming from its environment.

What is the intrinsic dimensionality of such a representation and how do we go about capturing it? Let us assume that if we trace a light ray from the camera at pixel (x, y) toward the object, it is reflected or refracted back out toward its environment at an angle (ϕ, θ). If we assume that other objects and illuminants are sufficiently distant (the same assumption we made for surface light fields in Section 13.3.2), this 4D mapping $(x, y) \rightarrow (\phi, \theta)$ captures all the information between a refractive object and its environment. Zongker, Werner, Curless *et al.* (1999) call such a representation an *environment matte*, since it generalizes the process of object matting (Section 10.4) to not only cut and paste an object from one image into another but also take into account the subtle refractive or reflective interplay between the object and its environment.

Recall from Equations (3.8) and (10.30) that a foreground object can be represented by its premultiplied colors and opacities $(\alpha F, \alpha)$. Such a matte can then be composited onto a new background B using

$$C_i = \alpha_i F_i + (1 - \alpha_i) B_i, \qquad (13.1)$$

where i is the pixel under consideration. In environment matting, we augment this equation with a reflective or refractive term to model indirect light paths between the environment and the camera. In the original work of Zongker, Werner, Curless *et al.* (1999), this indirect component I_i is modeled as

$$I_i = R_i \int A_i(\boldsymbol{x}) B(\boldsymbol{x}) d\boldsymbol{x}, \qquad (13.2)$$

where A_i is the rectangular *area of support* for that pixel, R_i is the colored reflectance or transmittance (for colored glossy surfaces or glass), and $B(\boldsymbol{x})$ is the background (environment) image, which is integrated over the area $A_i(\boldsymbol{x})$. In follow-on work, Chuang, Zongker,

Hindorff *et al.* (2000) use a superposition of oriented Gaussians,

$$I_i = \sum_j R_{ij} \int G_{ij}(\boldsymbol{x}) B(\boldsymbol{x}) d\boldsymbol{x}, \tag{13.3}$$

where each 2D Gaussian

$$G_{ij}(\boldsymbol{x}) = G_{2D}(\boldsymbol{x}; \boldsymbol{c}_{ij}, \boldsymbol{\sigma}_{ij}, \theta_{ij}) \tag{13.4}$$

is modeled by its center $\boldsymbol{c}_{ij}$, unrotated widths $\boldsymbol{\sigma}_{ij} = (\sigma_{ij}^x, \sigma_{ij}^y)$, and orientation θ_{ij}.

Given a representation for an environment matte, how can we go about estimating it for a particular object? The trick is to place the object in front of a monitor (or surrounded by a set of monitors), where we can change the illumination patterns $B(\boldsymbol{x})$ and observe the value of each composite pixel C_i.[7]

As with traditional two-screen matting (Section 10.4.1), we can use a variety of solid colored backgrounds to estimate each pixel's foreground color $\alpha_i F_i$ and partial coverage (opacity) α_i. To estimate the area of support A_i in (13.2), Zongker, Werner, Curless *et al.* (1999) use a series of periodic horizontal and vertical solid stripes at different frequencies and phases, which is reminiscent of the structured light patterns used in active rangefinding (Section 12.2). For the more sophisticated mixture of Gaussian model (13.3), Chuang, Zongker, Hindorff *et al.* (2000) sweep a series of narrow Gaussian stripes at four different orientations (horizontal, vertical, and two diagonals), which enables them to estimate multiple oriented Gaussian responses at each pixel.

Once an environment matte has been "pulled", it is then a simple matter to replace the background with a new image $B(\boldsymbol{x})$ to obtain a novel composite of the object placed in a different environment (Figure 13.10a–c). The use of multiple backgrounds during the matting process, however, precludes the use of this technique with dynamic scenes, e.g., water pouring into a glass (Figure 13.10d). In this case, a single graded color background can be used to estimate a single 2D monochromatic displacement for each pixel (Chuang, Zongker, Hindorff *et al.* 2000).

13.4.1 Higher-dimensional light fields

As you can tell from the preceding discussion, an environment matte in principle maps every pixel (x, y) into a 4D distribution over light rays and is, hence, a six-dimensional representation. (In practice, each 2D pixel's response is parameterized using a dozen or so parameters, e.g., $\{F, \alpha, B, R, A\}$, instead of a full mapping.) What if we want to model an object's refractive properties from every potential point of view? In this case, we need a mapping from every incoming 4D light ray to every potential exiting 4D light ray, which is an 8D representation. If we use the same trick as with surface light fields, we can parameterize each surface point by its 4D BRDF to reduce this mapping back down to 6D but this loses the ability to handle multiple refractive paths.

If we want to handle dynamic light fields, we need to add another temporal dimension. (Wenger, Gardner, Tchou *et al.* (2005) gives a nice example of a dynamic appearance and illumination acquisition system.) Similarly, if we want a continuous distribution over wavelengths, this becomes another dimension.

---

[7] If we relax the assumption that the environment is distant, the monitor can be placed at several depths to estimate a depth-dependent mapping function (Zongker, Werner, Curless *et al.* 1999).

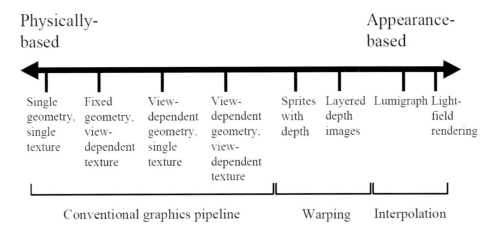

Figure 13.11 The geometry-image continuum in image-based rendering (Kang, Szeliski, and Anandan 2000) ©
2000 IEEE. Representations at the left of the spectrum use more detailed geometry and simpler image representations, while representations and algorithms on the right use more images and less geometry.

These examples illustrate how modeling the full complexity of a visual scene through
sampling can be extremely expensive. Fortunately, constructing specialized models, which
exploit knowledge about the physics of light transport along with the natural coherence of
real-world objects, can make these problems more tractable.

13.4.2 The modeling to rendering continuum

The image-based rendering representations and algorithms we have studied in this chapter
span a continuum ranging from classic 3D texture-mapped models all the way to pure sampled
ray-based representations such as light fields (Figure 13.11). Representations such as view-
dependent texture maps and Lumigraphs still use a single global geometric model, but select
the colors to map onto these surfaces from nearby images. View-dependent geometry, e.g.,
multiple depth maps, sidestep the need for coherent 3D geometry, and can sometimes better
model local non-rigid effects such as specular motion (Swaminathan, Kang, Szeliski *et al.*
2002; Criminisi, Kang, Swaminathan *et al.* 2005). Sprites with depth and layered depth
images use image-based representations of both color and geometry and can be efficiently
rendered using warping operations rather than 3D geometric rasterization.

The best choice of representation and rendering algorithm depends on both the quantity
and quality of the input imagery as well as the intended application. When nearby views are
being rendered, image-based representations capture more of the visual fidelity of the real
world because they directly sample its appearance. On the other hand, if only a few input
images are available or the image-based models need to be manipulated, e.g., to change their
shape or appearance, more abstract 3D representations such as geometric and local reflection
models are a better fit. As we continue to capture and manipulate increasingly larger quantities of visual data, research into these aspects of image-based modeling and rendering will
continue to evolve.

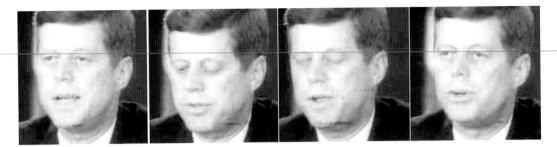

Figure 13.12 Video Rewrite (Bregler, Covell, and Slaney 1997) © 1997 ACM: the video frames are composed from bits and pieces of old video footage matched to a new audio track.

13.5 Video-based rendering

Since multiple images can be used to render new images or interactive experiences, can something similar be done with video? In fact, a fair amount of work has been done in the area of *video-based rendering* and *video-based animation*, two terms first introduced by Schödl, Szeliski, Salesin *et al.* (2000) to denote the process of generating new video sequences from captured video footage. An early example of such work is Video Rewrite (Bregler, Covell, and Slaney 1997), in which archival video footage is "re-animated" by having actors say new utterances (Figure 13.12). More recently, the term video-based rendering has been used by some researchers to denote the creation of virtual camera moves from a set of synchronized video cameras placed in a studio (Magnor 2005). (The terms *free-viewpoint video* and *3D video* are also sometimes used, see Section 13.5.4.)

In this section, we present a number of video-based rendering systems and applications. We start with *video-based animation* (Section 13.5.1), in which video footage is re-arranged or modified, e.g., in the capture and re-rendering of facial expressions. A special case of this are *video textures* (Section 13.5.2), in which source video is automatically cut into segments and re-looped to create infinitely long video animations. It is also possible to create such animations from still pictures or paintings, by segmenting the image into separately moving regions and animating them using stochastic motion fields (Section 13.5.3).

Next, we turn our attention to *3D video* (Section 13.5.4), in which multiple synchronized video cameras are used to film a scene from different directions. The source video frames can then be re-combined using image-based rendering techniques, such as view interpolation, to create virtual camera paths between the source cameras as part of a real-time viewing experience. Finally, we discuss capturing environments by driving or walking through them with panoramic video cameras in order to create interactive video-based walkthrough experiences (Section 13.5.5).

13.5.1 Video-based animation

As we mentioned above, an early example of video-based animation is Video Rewrite, in which frames from original video footage are rearranged in order to match them to novel spoken utterances, e.g., for movie dubbing (Figure 13.12). This is similar in spirit to the way that *concatenative speech synthesis* systems work (Taylor 2009).

In their system, Bregler, Covell, and Slaney (1997) first use speech recognition to extract phonemes from both the source video material and the novel audio stream. Phonemes are grouped into *triphones* (triplets of phonemes), since these better model the *coarticulation* effect present when people speak. Matching triphones are then found in the source footage and audio track. The mouth images corresponding to the selected video frames are then cut and pasted into the desired video footage being re-animated or dubbed, with appropriate geometric transformations to account for head motion. During the analysis phase, features corresponding to the lips, chin, and head are tracked using computer vision techniques. During synthesis, image morphing techniques are used to blend and stitch adjacent mouth shapes into a more coherent whole. In more recent work, Ezzat, Geiger, and Poggio (2002) describe how to use a *multidimensional morphable model* (Section 12.6.2) combined with regularized trajectory synthesis to improve these results.

A more sophisticated version of this system, called *face transfer*, uses a novel source video, instead of just an audio track, to drive the animation of a previously captured video, i.e., to re-render a video of a talking head with the appropriate visual speech, expression, and head pose elements (Vlasic, Brand, Pfister *et al.* 2005). This work is one of many *performance-driven animation* systems (Section 4.1.5), which are often used to animate 3D facial models (Figures 12.18–12.19). While traditional performance-driven animation systems use marker-based motion capture (Williams 1990; Litwinowicz and Williams 1994; Ma, Jones, Chiang *et al.* 2008), video footage can now often be used directly to control the animation (Buck, Finkelstein, Jacobs *et al.* 2000; Pighin, Szeliski, and Salesin 2002; Zhang, Snavely, Curless *et al.* 2004; Vlasic, Brand, Pfister *et al.* 2005; Roble and Zafar 2009).

In addition to its most common application to facial animation, video-based animation can also be applied to whole body motion (Section 12.6.4), e.g., by matching the flow fields between two different source videos and using one to drive the other (Efros, Berg, Mori *et al.* 2003). Another approach to video-based rendering is to use flow or 3D modeling to *unwrap* surface textures into stabilized images, which can then be manipulated and re-rendered onto the original video (Pighin, Szeliski, and Salesin 2002; Rav-Acha, Kohli, Fitzgibbon *et al.* 2008).

13.5.2 Video textures

Video-based animation is a powerful means of creating photo-realistic videos by re-purposing existing video footage to match some other desired activity or script. What if instead of constructing a special animation or narrative, we simply want the video to continue playing in a plausible manner? For example, many Web sites use images or videos to highlight their destinations, e.g., to portray attractive beaches with surf and palm trees waving in the wind. Instead of using a static image or a video clip that has a discontinuity when it loops, can we transform the video clip into an infinite-length animation that plays forever?

This idea is the basis of *video textures*, in which a short video clip can be arbitrarily extended by re-arranging video frames while preserving visual continuity (Schödl, Szeliski, Salesin *et al.* 2000). The basic problem in creating video textures is how to perform this re-arrangement without introducing visual artifacts. Can you think of how you might do this?

The simplest approach is to match frames by visual similarity (e.g., L_2 distance) and to jump between frames that appear similar. Unfortunately, if the motions in the two frames are different, a dramatic visual artifact will occur (the video will appear to "stutter"). For

(a)   (b)   (c)

(d)   (e)   (f)

(g)   (h)   (i)

Figure 13.13   Video textures (Schödl, Szeliski, Salesin *et al.* 2000) © 2000 ACM: (a) a clock pendulum, with correctly matched direction of motion; (b) a candle flame, showing temporal transition arcs; (c) the flag is generated using morphing at jumps; (d) a bonfire uses longer cross-dissolves; (e) a waterfall cross-dissolves several sequences at once; (f) a smiling animated face; (g) two swinging children are animated separately; (h) the balloons are automatically segmented into separate moving regions; (i) a synthetic fish tank consisting of bubbles, plants, and fish. Videos corresponding to these images can be found at http://www.cc.gatech.edu/gvu/perception/projects/videotexture/.

example, if we fail to match the motions of the clock pendulum in Figure 13.13a, it can suddenly change direction in mid-swing.

How can we extend our basic frame matching to also match motion? In principle, we could compute optic flow at each frame and match this. However, flow estimates are often unreliable (especially in textureless regions) and it is not clear how to weight the visual and motion similarities relative to each other. As an alternative, Schödl, Szeliski, Salesin *et al.* (2000) suggest matching *triplets* or larger neighborhoods of adjacent video frames, much in the same way as Video Rewrite matches triphones. Once we have constructed an $n \times n$ similarity matrix between all video frames (where n is the number of frames), a simple finite impulse response (FIR) filtering of each match sequence can be used to emphasize subsequences that match well.

The results of this match computation gives us a *jump table* or, equivalently, a transition probability between any two frames in the original video. This is shown schematically as red arcs in Figure 13.13b, where the red bar indicates which video frame is currently being displayed, and arcs light up as a forward or backward transition is taken. We can view these transition probabilities as encoding the *hidden Markov model* (HMM) that underlies a stochastic video generation process.

Sometimes, it is not possible to find exactly matching subsequences in the original video. In this case, morphing, i.e., warping and blending frames during transitions (Section 3.6.3) can be used to hide the visual differences (Figure 13.13c). If the motion is chaotic enough, as in a bonfire or a waterfall (Figures 13.13d–e), simple blending (extended cross-dissolves) may be sufficient. Improved transitions can also be obtained by performing 3D graph cuts on the spatio-temporal volume around a transition (Kwatra, Schödl, Essa *et al.* 2003).

Video textures need not be restricted to chaotic random phenomena such as fire, wind, and water. Pleasing video textures can be created of people, e.g., a smiling face (as in Figure 13.13f) or someone running on a treadmill (Schödl, Szeliski, Salesin *et al.* 2000). When multiple people or objects are moving independently, as in Figures 13.13g–h, we must first segment the video into independently moving regions and animate each region separately. It is also possible to create large panoramic video textures from a slowly panning camera (Agarwala, Zheng, Pal *et al.* 2005).

Instead of just playing back the original frames in a stochastic (random) manner, video textures can also be used to create scripted or interactive animations. If we extract individual elements, such as fish in a fishtank (Figure 13.13i) into separate *video sprites*, we can animate them along pre-specified paths (by matching the path direction with the original sprite motion) to make our video elements move in a desired fashion (Schödl and Essa 2002). In fact, work on video textures inspired research on systems that re-synthesize new motion sequences from motion capture data, which some people refer to as "mocap soup" (Arikan and Forsyth 2002; Kovar, Gleicher, and Pighin 2002; Lee, Chai, Reitsma *et al.* 2002; Li, Wang, and Shum 2002; Pullen and Bregler 2002).

While video textures primarily analyze the video as a sequence of frames (or regions) that can be re-arranged in time, *temporal textures* (Szummer and Picard 1996; Bar-Joseph, El-Yaniv, Lischinski *et al.* 2001) and *dynamic textures* (Doretto, Chiuso, Wu *et al.* 2003; Yuan, Wen, Liu *et al.* 2004; Doretto and Soatto 2006) treat the video as a 3D spatio-temporal volume with textural properties, which can be described using auto-regressive temporal models.

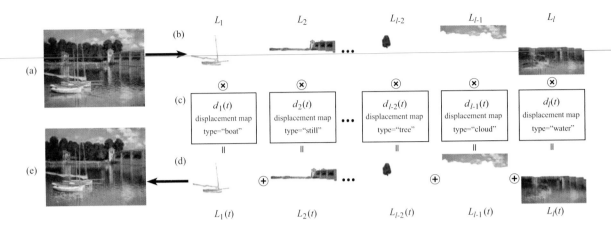

Figure 13.14 Animating still pictures (Chuang, Goldman, Zheng *et al.* 2005) © 2005 ACM. (a) The input still image is manually segmented into (b) several layers. (c) Each layer is then animated with a different stochastic motion texture (d) The animated layers are then composited to produce (e) the final animation

13.5.3 *Application*: Animating pictures

While video textures can turn a short video clip into an infinitely long video, can the same thing be done with a single still image? The answer is yes, if you are willing to first segment the image into different layers and then animate each layer separately.

Chuang, Goldman, Zheng *et al.* (2005) describe how an image can be decomposed into separate layers using interactive matting techniques. Each layer is then animated using a class-specific synthetic motion. As shown in Figure 13.14, boats rock back and forth, trees sway in the wind, clouds move horizontally, and water ripples, using a shaped noise displacement map. All of these effects can be tied to some global control parameters, such as the velocity and direction of a virtual wind. After being individually animated, the layers can be composited to create a final dynamic rendering.

13.5.4 3D Video

In recent years, the popularity of 3D movies has grown dramatically, with recent releases ranging from *Hannah Montana*, through U2's 3D concert movie, to James Cameron's *Avatar*. Currently, such releases are filmed using stereoscopic camera rigs and displayed in theaters (or at home) to viewers wearing polarized glasses.[8] In the future, however, home audiences may wish to view such movies with multi-zone auto-stereoscopic displays, where each person gets his or her own customized stereo stream and can move around a scene to see it from different perspectives.[9]

The stereo matching techniques developed in the computer vision community along with image-based rendering (view interpolation) techniques from graphics are both essential components in such scenarios, which are sometimes called *free-viewpoint video* (Carranza, Theobalt, Magnor *et al.* 2003) or *virtual viewpoint video* (Zitnick, Kang, Uyttendaele *et al.* 2004). In

---

[8] http://www.3d-summit.com/.
[9] http://www.siggraph.org/s2008/attendees/caf/3d/.

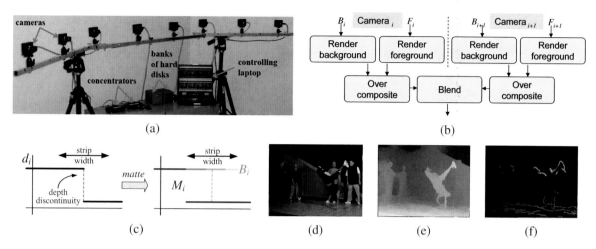

Figure 13.15 Video view interpolation (Zitnick, Kang, Uyttendaele *et al.* 2004) © 2004 ACM: (a) the capture hardware consists of eight synchronized cameras; (b) the background and foreground images from each camera are rendered and composited before blending; (c) the two-layer representation, before and after boundary matting; (d) background color estimates; (e) background depth estimates; (f) foreground color estimates.

addition to solving a series of per-frame reconstruction and view interpolation problems, the depth maps or proxies produced by the analysis phase must be temporally consistent in order to avoid flickering artifacts.

Shum, Chan, and Kang (2007) and Magnor (2005) present nice overviews of various video view interpolation techniques and systems. These include the Virtualized Reality system of Kanade, Rander, and Narayanan (1997) and Vedula, Baker, and Kanade (2005), Immersive Video (Moezzi, Katkere, Kuramura *et al.* 1996), Image-Based Visual Hulls (Matusik, Buehler, Raskar *et al.* 2000; Matusik, Buehler, and McMillan 2001), and Free-Viewpoint Video (Carranza, Theobalt, Magnor *et al.* 2003), which all use global 3D geometric models (surface-based (Section 12.3) or volumetric (Section 12.5)) as their proxies for rendering. The work of Vedula, Baker, and Kanade (2005) also computes *scene flow*, i.e., the 3D motion between corresponding surface elements, which can then be used to perform spatio-temporal interpolation of the multi-view video stream.

The Virtual Viewpoint Video system of Zitnick, Kang, Uyttendaele *et al.* (2004), on the other hand, associates a two-layer depth map with each input image, which allows them to accurately model occlusion effects such as the mixed pixels that occur at object boundaries. Their system, which consists of eight synchronized video cameras connected to a disk array (Figure 13.15a), first uses segmentation-based stereo to extract a depth map for each input image (Figure 13.15e). Near object boundaries (depth discontinuities), the background layer is extended along a strip behind the foreground object (Figure 13.15c) and its color is estimated from the neighboring images where it is not occluded (Figure 13.15d). Automated matting techniques (Section 10.4) are then used to estimate the fractional opacity and color of boundary pixels in the foreground layer (Figure 13.15f).

At render time, given a new virtual camera that lies between two of the original cameras, the layers in the neighboring cameras are rendered as texture-mapped triangles and the foreground layer (which may have fractional opacities) is then composited over the background layer (Figure 13.15b). The resulting two images are merged and blended by comparing their respective z-buffer values. (Whenever the two z-values are sufficiently close, a linear blend of the two colors is computed.) The interactive rendering system runs in real time using regular graphics hardware. It can therefore be used to change the observer's viewpoint while playing the video or to freeze the scene and explore it in 3D. More recently, Rogmans, Lu, Bekaert *et al.* (2009) have developed GPU implementations of both real-time stereo matching and real-time rendering algorithms, which enable them to explore algorithmic alternatives in a real-time setting.

At present, the depth maps computed from the eight stereo cameras using off-line stereo matching have produced the highest quality depth maps associated with live video.[10] They are therefore often used in studies of 3D video compression, which is an active area of research (Smolic and Kauff 2005; Gotchev and Rosenhahn 2009). Active video-rate depth sensing cameras, such as the 3DV Zcam (Iddan and Yahav 2001), which we discussed in Section 12.2.1, are another potential source of such data.

When large numbers of closely spaced cameras are available, as in the Stanford Light Field Camera (Wilburn, Joshi, Vaish *et al.* 2005), it may not always be necessary to compute explicit depth maps to create video-based rendering effects, although the results are usually of higher quality if you do (Vaish, Szeliski, Zitnick *et al.* 2006).

13.5.5 *Application*: Video-based walkthroughs

Video camera arrays enable the simultaneous capture of 3D dynamic scenes from multiple viewpoints, which can then enable the viewer to explore the scene from viewpoints near the original capture locations. What if instead we wish to capture an extended area, such as a home, a movie set, or even an entire city?

In this case, it makes more sense to move the camera through the environment and play back the video as an interactive video-based walkthrough. In order to allow the viewer to look around in all directions, it is preferable to use a panoramic video camera (Uyttendaele, Criminisi, Kang *et al.* 2004).[11]

One way to structure the acquisition process is to capture these images in a 2D horizontal plane, e.g., over a grid superimposed inside a room. The resulting *sea of images* (Aliaga, Funkhouser, Yanovsky *et al.* 2003) can be used to enable continuous motion between the captured locations.[12] However, extending this idea to larger settings, e.g., beyond a single room, can become tedious and data-intensive.

Instead, a natural way to explore a space is often to just walk through it along some pre-specified paths, just as museums or home tours guide users along a particular path, say down the middle of each room.[13] Similarly, city-level exploration can be achieved by driving down the middle of each street and allowing the user to branch at each intersection. This idea dates back to the Aspen MovieMap project (Lippman 1980), which recorded analog video taken from moving cars onto videodiscs for later interactive playback.

---

[10] http://research.microsoft.com/en-us/um/redmond/groups/ivm/vvv/.

[11] See http://www.cis.upenn.edu/~kostas/omni.html for descriptions of panoramic (omnidirectional) vision systems and associated workshops.

[12] (The Photo Tourism system of Snavely, Seitz, and Szeliski (2006) applies this idea to less structured collections.

[13] In computer games, restricting a player to forward and backward motion along predetermined paths is called *rail-based gaming*.

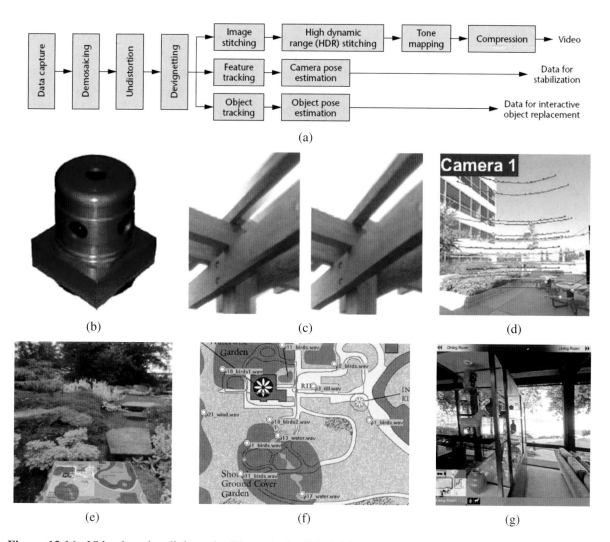

Figure 13.16 Video-based walkthroughs (Uyttendaele, Criminisi, Kang *et al.* 2004) © 2004 IEEE: (a) system diagram of video pre-processing; (b) the Point Grey Ladybug camera; (c) ghost removal using multi-perspective plane sweep; (d) point tracking, used both for calibration and stabilization; (e) interactive garden walkthrough with map below; (f) overhead map authoring and sound placement; (g) interactive home walkthrough with navigation bar (top) and icons of interest (bottom).

Recent improvements in video technology now enable the capture of panoramic (spherical) video using a small co-located array of cameras, such as the Point Grey Ladybug camera[14] (Figure 13.16b) developed by Uyttendaele, Criminisi, Kang *et al.* (2004) for their interactive video-based walkthrough project. In their system, the synchronized video streams from the six cameras (Figure 13.16a) are stitched together into 360° panoramas using a variety of techniques developed specifically for this project.

Because the cameras do not share the same center of projection, parallax between the cameras can lead to ghosting in the overlapping fields of view (Figure 13.16c). To remove this, a multi-perspective plane sweep stereo algorithm is used to estimate per-pixel depths at each column in the overlap area. To calibrate the cameras relative to each other, the camera is spun in place and a constrained structure from motion algorithm (Figure 7.8) is used to estimate the relative camera poses and intrinsics. Feature tracking is then run on the walkthrough video in order to stabilize the video sequence—Liu, Gleicher, Jin *et al.* (2009) have carried out more recent work along these lines.

Indoor environments with windows, as well as sunny outdoor environments with strong shadows, often have a dynamic range that exceeds the capabilities of video sensors. For this reason, the Ladybug camera has a programmable exposure capability that enables the bracketing of exposures at subsequent video frames. In order to merge the resulting video frames into high dynamic range (HDR) video, pixels from adjacent frames need to be motion-compensated before being merged (Kang, Uyttendaele, Winder *et al.* 2003).

The interactive walk-through experience becomes much richer and more navigable if an overview map is available as part of the experience. In Figure 13.16f, the map has annotations, which can show up during the tour, and localized sound sources, which play (with different volumes) when the viewer is nearby. The process of aligning the video sequence with the map can be automated using a process called *map correlation* (Levin and Szeliski 2004).

All of these elements combine to provide the user with a rich, interactive, and immersive experience. Figure 13.16e shows a walk through the Bellevue Botanical Gardens, with an overview map in perspective below the live video window. Arrows on the ground are used to indicate potential directions of travel. The viewer simply orients his view towards one of the arrows (the experience can be driven using a game controller) and "walks" forward along the desired path.

Figure 13.16g shows an indoor home tour experience. In addition to a schematic map in the lower left corner and adjacent room names along the top navigation bar, icons appear along the bottom whenever items of interest, such as a homeowner's art pieces, are visible in the main window. These icons can then be clicked to provide more information and 3D views.

The development of interactive video tours spurred a renewed interest in 360° video-based virtual travel and mapping experiences, as evidenced by commercial sites such as Google's Street View and Bing Maps. The same videos can also be used to generate turn-by-turn driving directions, taking advantage of both expanded fields of view and image-based rendering to enhance the experience (Chen, Neubert, Ofek *et al.* 2009).

As we continue to capture more and more of our real world with large amounts of high-quality imagery and video, the interactive modeling, exploration, and rendering techniques described in this chapter will play an even bigger role in bringing virtual experiences based

[14] http://www.ptgrey.com/.

on remote areas of the world closer to everyone.

13.6 Additional reading

Two good recent surveys of image-based rendering are by Kang, Li, Tong *et al.* (2006) and Shum, Chan, and Kang (2007), with earlier surveys available from Kang (1999), McMillan and Gortler (1999), and Debevec (1999). The term *image-based rendering* was introduced by McMillan and Bishop (1995), although the seminal paper in the field is the view interpolation paper by Chen and Williams (1993). Debevec, Taylor, and Malik (1996) describe their Façade system, which not only created a variety of image-based modeling tools but also introduced the widely used technique of *view-dependent texture mapping*.

Early work on planar impostors and layers was carried out by Shade, Lischinski, Salesin *et al.* (1996), Lengyel and Snyder (1997), and Torborg and Kajiya (1996), while newer work based on *sprites with depth* is described by Shade, Gortler, He *et al.* (1998).

The two foundational papers in image-based rendering are *Light field rendering* by Levoy and Hanrahan (1996) and *The Lumigraph* by Gortler, Grzeszczuk, Szeliski *et al.* (1996). Buehler, Bosse, McMillan *et al.* (2001) generalize the Lumigraph approach to irregularly spaced collections of images, while Levoy (2006) provides a survey and more gentle introduction to the topic of light field and image-based rendering.

Surface light fields (Wood, Azuma, Aldinger *et al.* 2000) provide an alternative parameterization for light fields with accurately known surface geometry and support both better compression and the possibility of editing surface properties. Concentric mosaics (Shum and He 1999; Shum, Wang, Chai *et al.* 2002) and panoramas with depth (Peleg, Ben-Ezra, and Pritch 2001; Li, Shum, Tang *et al.* 2004; Zheng, Kang, Cohen *et al.* 2007), provide useful parameterizations for light fields captured with panning cameras. Multi-perspective images (Rademacher and Bishop 1998) and manifold projections (Peleg and Herman 1997), although not true light fields, are also closely related to these ideas.

Among the possible extensions of light fields to higher-dimensional structures, environment mattes (Zongker, Werner, Curless *et al.* 1999; Chuang, Zongker, Hindorff *et al.* 2000) are the most useful, especially for placing captured objects into new scenes.

Video-based rendering, i.e., the re-use of video to create new animations or virtual experiences, started with the seminal work of Szummer and Picard (1996), Bregler, Covell, and Slaney (1997), and Schödl, Szeliski, Salesin *et al.* (2000). Important follow-on work to these basic re-targeting approaches was carried out by Schödl and Essa (2002), Kwatra, Schödl, Essa *et al.* (2003), Doretto, Chiuso, Wu *et al.* (2003), Wang and Zhu (2003), Zhong and Sclaroff (2003), Yuan, Wen, Liu *et al.* (2004), Doretto and Soatto (2006), Zhao and Pietikäinen (2007), and Chan and Vasconcelos (2009).

Systems that allow users to change their 3D viewpoint based on multiple synchronized video streams include those by Moezzi, Katkere, Kuramura *et al.* (1996), Kanade, Rander, and Narayanan (1997), Matusik, Buehler, Raskar *et al.* (2000), Matusik, Buehler, and McMillan (2001), Carranza, Theobalt, Magnor *et al.* (2003), Zitnick, Kang, Uyttendaele *et al.* (2004), Magnor (2005), and Vedula, Baker, and Kanade (2005). 3D (multiview) video coding and compression is also an active area of research (Smolic and Kauff 2005; Gotchev and Rosenhahn 2009), with 3D Blu-Ray discs, encoded using the multiview video coding (MVC) extension to H.264/MPEG-4 AVC, expected by the end of 2010.

13.7 Exercises

Ex 13.1: Depth image rendering   Develop a "view extrapolation" algorithm to re-render a previously computed stereo depth map coupled with its corresponding reference color image.

1. Use a 3D graphics mesh rendering system such as OpenGL or Direct3D, with two triangles per pixel quad and perspective (projective) texture mapping (Debevec, Yu, and Borshukov 1998).

2. Alternatively, use the one- or two-pass forward warper you constructed in Exercise 3.24, extended using (2.68–2.70) to convert from disparities or depths into displacements.

3. (Optional) Kinks in straight lines introduced during view interpolation or extrapolation are visually noticeable, which is one reason why image morphing systems let you specify line correspondences (Beier and Neely 1992). Modify your depth estimation algorithm to match and estimate the geometry of straight lines and incorporate it into your image-based rendering algorithm.

Ex 13.2: View interpolation   Extend the system you created in the previous exercise to render two reference views and then blend the images using a combination of z-buffering, hole filing, and blending (morphing) to create the final image (Section 13.1).

1. (Optional) If the two source images have very different exposures, the hole-filled regions and the blended regions will have different exposures. Can you extend your algorithm to mitigate this?

2. (Optional) Extend your algorithm to perform three-way (trilinear) interpolation between neighboring views. You can triangulate the reference camera poses and use barycentric coordinates for the virtual camera in order to determine the blending weights.

Ex 13.3: View morphing   Modify your view interpolation algorithm to perform morphs between views of a non-rigid object, such as a person changing expressions.

1. Instead of using a pure stereo algorithm, use a general flow algorithm to compute displacements, but separate them into a rigid displacement due to camera motion and a non-rigid deformation.

2. At render time, use the rigid geometry to determine the new pixel location but then add a fraction of the non-rigid displacement as well.

3. Alternatively, compute a stereo depth map but let the user specify additional correspondences or use a feature-based matching algorithm to provide them automatically.

4. (Optional) Take a single image, such as the Mona Lisa or a friend's picture, and create an animated 3D view morph (Seitz and Dyer 1996).

   (a) Find the vertical axis of symmetry in the image and reflect your reference image to provide a virtual pair (assuming the person's hairstyle is somewhat symmetric).

   (b) Use structure from motion to determine the relative camera pose of the pair.

(c) Use dense stereo matching to estimate the 3D shape.

(d) Use view morphing to create a 3D animation.

Ex 13.4: View dependent texture mapping Use a 3D model you created along with the original images to implement a view-dependent texture mapping system.

1. Use one of the 3D reconstruction techniques you developed in Exercises 7.3, 11.9, 11.10, or 12.8 to build a triangulated 3D image-based model from multiple photographs.

2. Extract textures for each model face from your photographs, either by performing the appropriate resampling or by figuring out how to use the texture mapping software to directly access the source images.

3. At run time, for each new camera view, select the best source image for each visible model face.

4. Extend this to blend between the top two or three textures. This is trickier, since it involves the use of texture blending or pixel shading (Debevec, Taylor, and Malik 1996; Debevec, Yu, and Borshukov 1998; Pighin, Hecker, Lischinski *et al.* 1998).

Ex 13.5: Layered depth images Extend your view interpolation algorithm (Exercise 13.2) to store more than one depth or color value per pixel (Shade, Gortler, He *et al.* 1998), i.e., a layered depth image (LDI). Modify your rendering algorithm accordingly. For your data, you can use synthetic ray tracing, a layered reconstructed model, or a volumetric reconstruction.

Ex 13.6: Rendering from sprites or layers Extend your view interpolation algorithm to handle multiple planes or sprites (Section 13.2.1) (Shade, Gortler, He *et al.* 1998).

1. Extract your layers using the technique you developed in Exercise 8.9.

2. Alternatively, use an interactive painting and 3D placement system to extract your layers (Kang 1998; Oh, Chen, Dorsey *et al.* 2001; Shum, Sun, Yamazaki *et al.* 2004).

3. Determine a back-to-front order based on expected visibility or add a z-buffer to your rendering algorithm to handle occlusions.

4. Render and composite all of the resulting layers, with optional alpha matting to handle the edges of layers and sprites.

Ex 13.7: Light field transformations Derive the equations relating regular images to 4D light field coordinates.

1. Determine the mapping between the far plane (u, v) coordinates and a virtual camera's (x, y) coordinates.

   (a) Start by parameterizing a 3D point on the uv plane in terms of its (u, v) coordinates.

   (b) Project the resulting 3D point to the camera pixels $(x, y, 1)$ using the usual 3×4 camera matrix $\boldsymbol{P}$ (2.63).

   (c) Derive the 2D homography relating (u, v) and (x, y) coordinates.

2. Write down a similar transformation for (s, t) to (x, y) coordinates.

3. Prove that if the virtual camera is actually on the (s, t) plane, the (s, t) value depends only on the camera's optical center and is independent of (x, y).

4. Prove that an image taken by a regular orthographic or perspective camera, i.e., one that has a linear projective relationship between 3D points and (x, y) pixels (2.63), samples the (s, t, u, v) light field along a two-dimensional hyperplane.

Ex 13.8: Light field and Lumigraph rendering   Implement a light field or Lumigraph rendering system:

1. Download one of the light field data sets from http://lightfield.stanford.edu/.

2. Write an algorithm to synthesize a new view from this light field, using quadri-linear interpolation of (s, t, u, v) ray samples.

3. Try varying the focal plane corresponding to your desired view (Isaksen, McMillan, and Gortler 2000) and see if the resulting image looks sharper.

4. Determine a 3D proxy for the objects in your scene. You can do this by running multi-view stereo over one of your light fields to obtain a depth map per image.

5. Implement the Lumigraph rendering algorithm, which modifies the sampling of rays according to the 3D location of each surface element.

6. Collect a set of images yourself and determine their pose using structure from motion.

7. Implement the unstructured Lumigraph rendering algorithm from Buehler, Bosse, McMillan *et al.* (2001).

Ex 13.9: Surface light fields   Construct a surface light field (Wood, Azuma, Aldinger *et al.* 2000) and see how well you can compress it.

1. Acquire an interesting light field of a specular scene or object, or download one from http://lightfield.stanford.edu/.

2. Build a 3D model of the object using a multi-view stereo algorithm that is robust to outliers due to specularities.

3. Estimate the Lumisphere for each surface point on the object.

4. Estimate its diffuse components. Is the median the best way to do this? Why not use the minimum color value? What happens if there is Lambertian shading on the diffuse component?

5. Model and compress the remaining portion of the Lumisphere using one of the techniques suggested by Wood, Azuma, Aldinger *et al.* (2000) or invent one of your own.

6. Study how well your compression algorithm works and what artifacts it produces.

7. (Optional) Develop a system to edit and manipulate your surface light field.

Ex 13.10: Handheld concentric mosaics   Develop a system to navigate a handheld concentric mosaic.

1. Stand in the middle of a room with a camcorder held at arm's length in front of you and spin in a circle.

2. Use a structure from motion system to determine the camera pose and sparse 3D structure for each input frame.

3. (Optional) Re-bin your image pixels into a more regular concentric mosaic structure.

4. At view time, determine from the new camera's view (which should be near the plane of your original capture) which source pixels to display. You can simplify your computations to determine a source column (and scaling) for each output column.

5. (Optional) Use your sparse 3D structure, interpolated to a dense depth map, to improve your rendering (Zheng, Kang, Cohen *et al.* 2007).

Ex 13.11: Video textures   Capture some videos of natural phenomena, such as a water fountain, fire, or smiling face, and loop the video seamlessly into an infinite length video (Schödl, Szeliski, Salesin *et al.* 2000).

1. Compare all the frames in the original clip using an L_2 (sum of square difference) metric. (This assumes the videos were shot on a tripod or have already been stabilized.)

2. Filter the comparison table temporally to accentuate temporal sub-sequences that match well together.

3. Convert your similarity table into a jump probability table through some exponential distribution. Be sure to modify transitions near the end so you do not get "stuck" in the last frame.

4. Starting with the first frame, use your transition table to decide whether to jump forward, backward, or continue to the next frame.

5. (Optional) Add any of the other extensions to the original video textures idea, such as multiple moving regions, interactive control, or graph cut spatio-temporal texture seaming.

Chapter 14

Recognition

R. Szeliski, *Computer Vision: Algorithms and Applications*, Texts in Computer Science,
DOI 10.1007/978-1-84882-935-0_14, © Springer-Verlag London Limited 2011

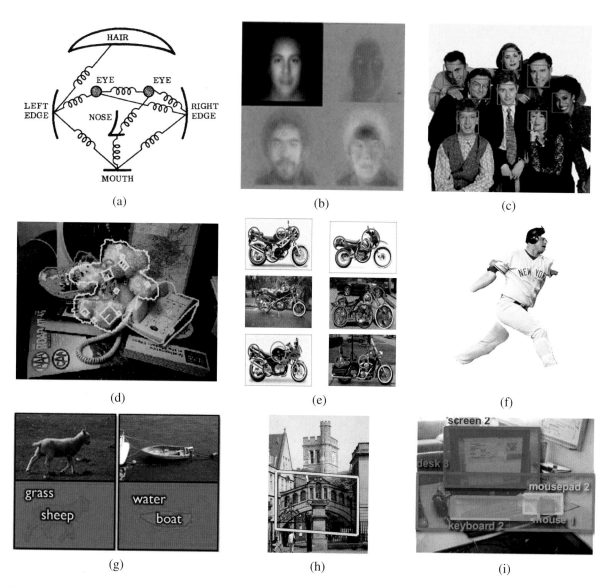

Figure 14.1 Recognition: face recognition with (a) pictorial structures (Fischler and Elschlager 1973) © 1973 IEEE and (b) eigenfaces (Turk and Pentland 1991b); (c) real-time face detection (Viola and Jones 2004) © 2004 Springer; (d) instance (known object) recognition (Lowe 1999) © 1999 IEEE; (e) feature-based recognition (Fergus, Perona, and Zisserman 2007); (f) region-based recognition (Mori, Ren, Efros *et al.* 2004) © 2004 IEEE; (g) simultaneous recognition and segmentation (Shotton, Winn, Rother *et al.* 2009) © 2009 Springer; (h) location recognition (Philbin, Chum, Isard *et al.* 2007) © 2007 IEEE; (i) using context (Russell, Torralba, Liu *et al.* 2007).

Of all the visual tasks we might ask a computer to perform, analyzing a scene and recognizing all of the constituent objects remains the most challenging. While computers excel at accurately reconstructing the 3D shape of a scene from images taken from different views, they cannot name all the objects and animals present in a picture, even at the level of a two-year-old child. There is not even any consensus among researchers on when this level of performance might be achieved.

Why is recognition so hard? The real world is made of a jumble of objects, which all occlude one another and appear in different poses. Furthermore, the variability intrinsic within a class (e.g., dogs), due to complex non-rigid articulation and extreme variations in shape and appearance (e.g., between different breeds), makes it unlikely that we can simply perform exhaustive matching against a database of exemplars.[1]

The recognition problem can be broken down along several axes. For example, if we know what we are looking for, the problem is one of *object detection* (Section 14.1), which involves quickly scanning an image to determine where a match may occur (Figure 14.1c). If we have a specific rigid object we are trying to recognize (*instance recognition*, Section 14.3), we can search for characteristic feature points (Section 4.1) and verify that they align in a geometrically plausible way (Section 14.3.1) (Figure 14.1d).

The most challenging version of recognition is general *category* (or *class*) recognition (Section 14.4), which may involve recognizing instances of extremely varied classes such as animals or furniture. Some techniques rely purely on the presence of features (known as a "bag of words" model—see Section 14.4.1), their relative positions (*part-based models* (Section 14.4.2)), Figure 14.1e, while others involve segmenting the image into semantically meaningful regions (Section 14.4.3) (Figure 14.1f). In many instances, recognition depends heavily on the *context* of surrounding objects and scene elements (Section 14.5). Woven into all of these techniques is the topic of *learning* (Section 14.5.1), since hand-crafting specific object recognizers seems like a futile approach given the complexity of the problem.

Given the extremely rich and complex nature of this topic, this chapter is structured to build from simpler concepts to more complex ones. We begin with a discussion of face and object detection (Section 14.1), where we introduce a number of machine-learning techniques such as boosting, neural networks, and support vector machines. Next, we study face recognition (Section 14.2), which is one of the more widely known applications of recognition. This topic serves as an introduction to subspace (PCA) models and Bayesian approaches to recognition and classification. We then present techniques for instance recognition (Section 14.3), building upon earlier topics in this book, such as feature detection, matching, and geometric alignment (Section 14.3.1). We introduce topics from the information and document retrieval communities, such as frequency vectors, feature quantization, and inverted indices (Section 14.3.2). We also present applications of location recognition (Section 14.3.3).

In the second half of the chapter, we address the most challenging variant of recognition, namely the problem of category recognition (Section 14.4). This includes approaches that use bags of features (Section 14.4.1), parts (Section 14.4.2), and segmentation (Section 14.4.3). We show how such techniques can be used to automate photo editing tasks, such as 3D modeling, scene completion, and creating collages (Section 14.4.4). Next, we discuss the role that context can play in both individual object recognition and more holistic scene under-

---

[1] However, some recent research suggests that direct image matching may be feasible for large enough databases (Russell, Torralba, Liu *et al.* 2007; Malisiewicz and Efros 2008; Torralba, Freeman, and Fergus 2008).

standing (Section 14.5). We close this chapter with a discussion of databases and test sets for constructing and evaluating recognition systems (Section 14.6).

While there is no comprehensive reference on object recognition, an excellent set of notes can be found in the ICCV 2009 short course (Fei-Fei, Fergus, and Torralba 2009), Antonio Torralba's more comprehensive MIT course (Torralba 2008), and two recent collections of papers (Ponce, Hebert, Schmid *et al.* 2006; Dickinson, Leonardis, Schiele *et al.* 2007) and a survey on object categorization (Pinz 2005). An evaluation of some of the best performing recognition algorithms can be found on the PASCAL Visual Object Classes (VOC) Challenge Web site at http://pascallin.ecs.soton.ac.uk/challenges/VOC/.

14.1 Object detection

If we are given an image to analyze, such as the group portrait in Figure 14.2, we could try to apply a recognition algorithm to every possible sub-window in this image. Such algorithms are likely to be both slow and error-prone. Instead, it is more effective to construct special-purpose *detectors*, whose job it is to rapidly find likely regions where particular objects might occur.

We begin this section with face detectors, which are some of the more successful examples of recognition. For example, such algorithms are built into most of today's digital cameras to enhance auto-focus and into video conferencing systems to control pan-tilt heads. We then look at pedestrian detectors, as an example of more general methods for object detection. Such detectors can be used in automotive safety applications, e.g., detecting pedestrians and other cars from moving vehicles (Leibe, Cornelis, Cornelis *et al.* 2007).

14.1.1 Face detection

Before face recognition can be applied to a general image, the locations and sizes of any faces must first be found (Figures 14.1c and 14.2). In principle, we could apply a face recognition algorithm at every pixel and scale (Moghaddam and Pentland 1997) but such a process would be too slow in practice.

Over the years, a wide variety of fast face detection algorithms have been developed. Yang, Kriegman, and Ahuja (2002) provide a comprehensive survey of earlier work in this field; Yang's ICPR 2004 tutorial[2] and the Torralba (2007) short course provide more recent reviews.[3]

According to the taxonomy of Yang, Kriegman, and Ahuja (2002), face detection techniques can be classified as feature-based, template-based, or appearance-based. Feature-based techniques attempt to find the locations of distinctive image features such as the eyes, nose, and mouth, and then verify whether these features are in a plausible geometrical arrangement. These techniques include some of the early approaches to face recognition (Fischler and Elschlager 1973; Kanade 1977; Yuille 1991), as well as more recent approaches based on modular eigenspaces (Moghaddam and Pentland 1997), local filter jets (Leung, Burl, and Perona 1995; Penev and Atick 1996; Wiskott, Fellous, Krüger *et al.* 1997), support

---
[2] http://vision.ai.uiuc.edu/mhyang/face-detection-survey.html.
[3] An alternative approach to detecting faces is to look for regions of skin color in the image (Forsyth and Fleck 1999; Jones and Rehg 2001). See Exercise 2.8 for some additional discussion and references.

Figure 14.2 Face detection results produced by Rowley, Baluja, and Kanade (1998a) © 1998 IEEE. Can you find the one false positive (a box around a non-face) among the 57 true positive results?

vector machines (Heisele, Ho, Wu *et al.* 2003; Heisele, Serre, and Poggio 2007), and boosting (Schneiderman and Kanade 2004).

Template-based approaches, such as active appearance models (AAMs) (Section 14.2.2), can deal with a wide range of pose and expression variability. Typically, they require good initialization near a real face and are therefore not suitable as fast face detectors.

Appearance-based approaches scan over small overlapping rectangular patches of the image searching for likely face candidates, which can then be refined using a *cascade* of more expensive but selective detection algorithms (Sung and Poggio 1998; Rowley, Baluja, and Kanade 1998a; Romdhani, Torr, Schölkopf *et al.* 2001; Fleuret and Geman 2001; Viola and Jones 2004). In order to deal with scale variation, the image is usually converted into a sub-octave pyramid and a separate scan is performed on each level. Most appearance-based approaches today rely heavily on training classifiers using sets of labeled face and non-face patches.

Sung and Poggio (1998) and Rowley, Baluja, and Kanade (1998a) present two of the earliest appearance-based face detectors and introduce a number of innovations that are widely used in later work by others.

To start with, both systems collect a set of labeled face patches (Figure 14.2) as well as a set of patches taken from images that are known not to contain faces, such as aerial images or vegetation (Figure 14.3b). The collected face images are augmented by artificially mirroring, rotating, scaling, and translating the images by small amounts to make the face detectors less sensitive to such effects (Figure 14.3a).

After an initial set of training images has been collected, some optional pre-processing can be performed, such as subtracting an average gradient (linear function) from the image to compensate for global shading effects and using histogram equalization to compensate for

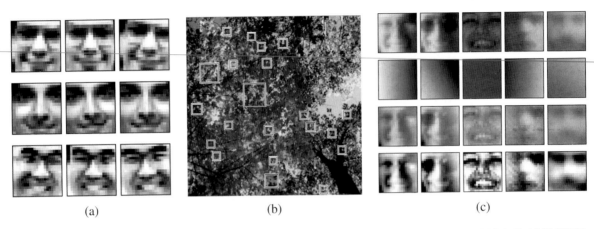

Figure 14.3 Pre-processing stages for face detector training (Rowley, Baluja, and Kanade 1998a) © 1998 IEEE: (a) artificially mirroring, rotating, scaling, and translating training images for greater variability; (b) using images without faces (looking up at a tree) to generate non-face examples; (c) pre-processing the patches by subtracting a best fit linear function (constant gradient) and histogram equalizing.

varying camera contrast (Figure 14.3c).

Clustering and PCA. Once the face and non-face patterns have been pre-processed, Sung and Poggio (1998) cluster each of these datasets into six separate clusters using k-means and then fit PCA subspaces to each of the resulting 12 clusters (Figure 14.4). At detection time, the DIFS and DFFS metrics first developed by Moghaddam and Pentland (1997) (see Figure 14.14 and (14.14)) are used to produce 24 Mahalanobis distance measurements (two per cluster). The resulting 24 measurements are input to a multi-layer perceptron (MLP), which is a neural network with alternating layers of weighted summations and sigmoidal non-linearities trained using the "backpropagation" algorithm (Rumelhart, Hinton, and Williams 1986).

Neural networks. Instead of first clustering the data and computing Mahalanobis distances to the cluster centers, Rowley, Baluja, and Kanade (1998a) apply a neural network (MLP) directly to the 20×20 pixel patches of gray-level intensities, using a variety of differently sized hand-crafted "receptive fields" to capture both large-scale and smaller scale structure (Figure 14.5). The resulting neural network directly outputs the likelihood of a face at the center of every overlapping patch in a multi-resolution pyramid. Since several overlapping patches (in both space and resolution) may fire near a face, an additional merging network is used to merge overlapping detections. The authors also experiment with training several networks and merging their outputs. Figure 14.2 shows a sample result from their face detector.

To make the detector run faster, a separate network operating on 30×30 patches is trained to detect both faces and faces shifted by ± 5 pixels. This network is evaluated at every 10th pixel in the image (horizontally and vertically) and the results of this "coarse" or "sloppy" detector are used to select regions on which to run the slower single-pixel overlap technique. To deal with in-plane rotations of faces, Rowley, Baluja, and Kanade (1998b) train a *router*

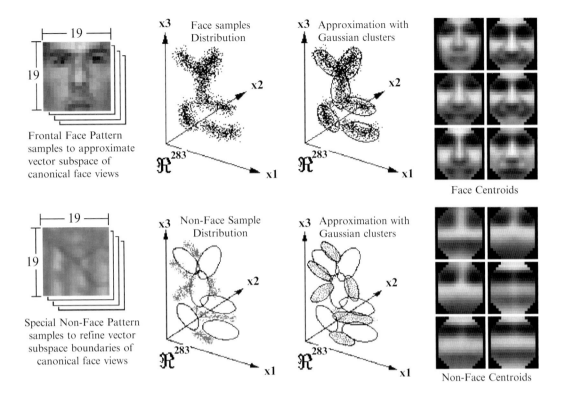

Figure 14.4 Learning a mixture of Gaussians model for face detection (Sung and Poggio 1998) © 1998 IEEE. The face and non-face images (19^2-long vectors) are first clustered into six separate clusters (each) using k-means and then analyzed using PCA. The cluster centers are shown in the right-hand columns.

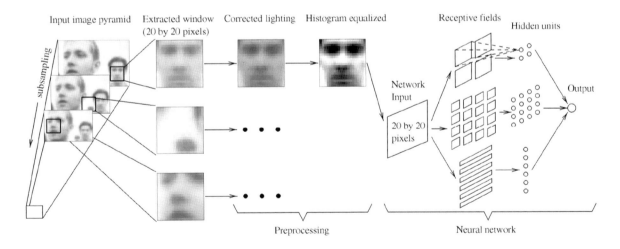

Figure 14.5 A neural network for face detection (Rowley, Baluja, and Kanade 1998a) © 1998 IEEE. Overlapping patches are extracted from different levels of a pyramid and then pre-processed as shown in Figure 14.3b. A three-layer neural network is then used to detect likely face locations.

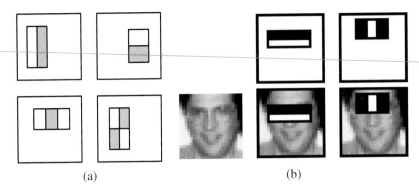

Figure 14.6 Simple features used in boosting-based face detector (Viola and Jones 2004) © 2004 Springer: (a) difference of rectangle feature composed of 2–4 different rectangles (pixels inside the white rectangles are subtracted from the gray ones); (b) the first and second features selected by AdaBoost. The first feature measures the differences in intensity between the eyes and the cheeks, the second one between the eyes and the bridge of the nose.

network to estimate likely rotation angles from input patches and then apply the estimated rotation to each patch before running the result through their upright face detector.

Support vector machines. Instead of using a neural network to classify patches, Osuna, Freund, and Girosi (1997) use a *support vector machine* (SVM) (Hastie, Tibshirani, and Friedman 2001; Schölkopf and Smola 2002; Bishop 2006; Lampert 2008) to classify the same preprocessed patches as Sung and Poggio (1998). An SVM searches for a series of *maximum margin* separating planes in feature space between different classes (in this case, face and non-face patches). In those cases where linear classification boundaries are insufficient, the feature space can be lifted into higher-dimensional features using *kernels* (Hastie, Tibshirani, and Friedman 2001; Schölkopf and Smola 2002; Bishop 2006). SVMs have been used by other researchers for both face detection and face recognition (Heisele, Ho, Wu *et al.* 2003; Heisele, Serre, and Poggio 2007) and are a widely used tool in object recognition in general.

Boosting. Of all the face detectors currently in use, the one introduced by Viola and Jones (2004) is probably the best known and most widely used. Their technique was the first to introduce the concept of *boosting* to the computer vision community, which involves training a series of increasingly discriminating simple classifiers and then blending their outputs (Hastie, Tibshirani, and Friedman 2001; Bishop 2006).

In more detail, boosting involves constructing a *classifier* $h(\boldsymbol{x})$ as a sum of simple *weak learners*,

$$h(\boldsymbol{x}) = \text{sign} \left[\sum_{j=0}^{m-1} \alpha_j h_j(\boldsymbol{x}) \right], \tag{14.1}$$

where each of the weak learners $h_j(\boldsymbol{x})$ is an extremely simple function of the input, and hence is not expected to contribute much (in isolation) to the classification performance.

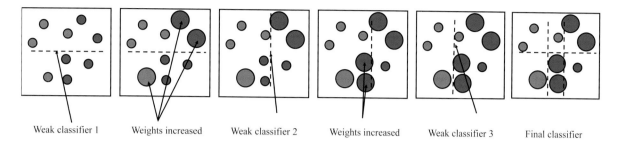

Weak classifier 1   Weights increased   Weak classifier 2   Weights increased   Weak classifier 3   Final classifier

Figure 14.7 Schematic illustration of boosting, courtesy of Svetlana Lazebnik, after original illustrations from Paul Viola and David Lowe. After each weak classifier (decision stump or hyperplane) is selected, data points that are erroneously classified have their weights increased. The final classifier is a linear combination of the simple weak classifiers.

In most variants of boosting, the weak learners are threshold functions,

$$h_j(\boldsymbol{x}) = a_j[f_j < \theta_j] + b_j[f_j \ge \theta_j] = \begin{cases} a_j & \text{if } f_j < \theta_j \\ b_j & \text{otherwise,} \end{cases} \qquad (14.2)$$

which are also known as *decision stumps* (basically, the simplest possible version of *decision trees*). In most cases, it is also traditional (and simpler) to set a_j and b_j to ± 1, i.e., $a_j = -s_j$, $b_j = +s_j$, so that only the feature f_j, the threshold value θ_j, and the polarity of the threshold $s_j \in \pm 1$ need to be selected.[4]

In many applications of boosting, the features are simply coordinate axes x_k, i.e., the boosting algorithm selects one of the input vector components as the best one to threshold. In Viola and Jones' face detector, the features are differences of rectangular regions in the input patch, as shown in Figure 14.6. The advantage of using these features is that, while they are more discriminating than single pixels, they are extremely fast to compute once a summed area table has been pre-computed, as described in Section 3.2.3 (3.31–3.32). Essentially, for the cost of an $O(N)$ pre-computation phase (where N is the number of pixels in the image), subsequent differences of rectangles can be computed in $4r$ additions or subtractions, where $r \in \{2, 3, 4\}$ is the number of rectangles in the feature.

The key to the success of boosting is the method for incrementally selecting the weak learners and for re-weighting the training examples after each stage (Figure 14.7). The AdaBoost (Adaptive Boosting) algorithm (Hastie, Tibshirani, and Friedman 2001; Bishop 2006) does this by re-weighting each sample as a function of whether it is correctly classified at each stage, and using the stage-wise average classification error to determine the final weightings α_j among the weak classifiers, as described in Algorithm 14.1. While the resulting classifier is extremely fast in practice, the training time can be quite slow (in the order of weeks), because of the large number of feature (difference of rectangle) hypotheses that need to be examined at each stage.

To further increase the speed of the detector, it is possible to create a *cascade* of classifiers, where each classifier uses a small number of tests (say, a two-term AdaBoost classifier) to reject a large fraction of non-faces while trying to pass through all potential face candidates

---

[4]Some variants, such as that of Viola and Jones (2004), use $(a_j, b_j) \in [0, 1]$ and adjust the learning algorithm accordingly.

1. Input the positive and negative training examples along with their labels $\{(\boldsymbol{x}_i, y_i)\}$, where $y_i = 1$ for positive (face) examples and $y_i = -1$ for negative examples.

2. Initialize all the weights to $w_{i,1} \leftarrow \frac{1}{N}$, where N is the number of training examples. (Viola and Jones (2004) use a separate N_1 and N_2 for positive and negative examples.)

3. For each training stage $j = 1 \ldots M$:

   (a) Renormalize the weights so that they sum up to 1 (divide them by their sum).

   (b) Select the best classifier $h_j(\boldsymbol{x}; f_j, \theta_j, s_j)$ by finding the one that minimizes the weighted classification error

   $$e_j = \sum_{i=0}^{N-1} w_{i,j} e_{i,j}, \qquad (14.3)$$

   $$e_{i,j} = 1 - \delta(y_i, h_j(\boldsymbol{x}_i; f_j, \theta_j, s_j)). \qquad (14.4)$$

   For any given f_j function, the optimal values of (θ_j, s_j) can be found in linear time using a variant of weighted median computation (Exercise 14.2).

   (c) Compute the modified error rate β_j and classifier weight α_j,

   $$\beta_j = \frac{e_j}{1 - e_j} \quad \text{and} \quad \alpha_j = -\log \beta_j. \qquad (14.5)$$

   (d) Update the weights according to the classification errors $e_{i,j}$

   $$w_{i,j+1} \leftarrow w_{i,j} \beta_j^{1 - e_{i,j}}, \qquad (14.6)$$

   i.e., downweight the training samples that were correctly classified in proportion to the overall classification error.

4. Set the final classifier to

   $$h(\boldsymbol{x}) = \text{sign} \left[\sum_{j=0}^{m-1} \alpha_j h_j(\boldsymbol{x}) \right]. \qquad (14.7)$$

Algorithm 14.1 The AdaBoost training algorithm, adapted from Hastie, Tibshirani, and Friedman (2001), Viola and Jones (2004), and Bishop (2006).

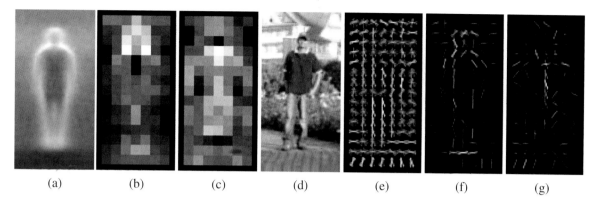

(a)	(b)	(c)	(d)	(e)	(f)	(g)

Figure 14.8 Pedestrian detection using histograms of oriented gradients (Dalal and Triggs 2005) © 2005 IEEE: (a) the average gradient image over the training examples; (b) each "pixel" shows the maximum positive SVM weight in the block centered on the pixel; (c) likewise, for the negative SVM weights; (d) a test image; (e) the computed R-HOG (rectangular histogram of gradients) descriptor; (f) the R-HOG descriptor weighted by the positive SVM weights; (g) the R-HOG descriptor weighted by the negative SVM weights.

(Fleuret and Geman 2001; Viola and Jones 2004). An even faster algorithm for performing cascade learning has recently been developed by Brubaker, Wu, Sun *et al.* (2008).

14.1.2 Pedestrian detection

While a lot of the research on object detection has focused on faces, the detection of other objects, such as pedestrians and cars, has also received widespread attention (Gavrila and Philomin 1999; Gavrila 1999; Papageorgiou and Poggio 2000; Mohan, Papageorgiou, and Poggio 2001; Schneiderman and Kanade 2004). Some of these techniques maintain the same focus as face detection on speed and efficiency. Others, however, focus instead on accuracy, viewing detection as a more challenging variant of generic class recognition (Section 14.4) in which the locations and extents of objects are to be determined as accurately as possible. (See, for example, the PASCAL VOC detection challenge, http://pascallin.ecs.soton.ac.uk/challenges/VOC/.)

An example of a well-known pedestrian detector is the algorithm developed by Dalal and Triggs (2005), who use a set of overlapping *histogram of oriented gradients* (HOG) descriptors fed into a support vector machine (Figure 14.8). Each HOG has cells to accumulate magnitude-weighted votes for gradients at particular orientations, just as in the scale invariant feature transform (SIFT) developed by Lowe (2004), which we discussed in Section 4.1.2 and Figure 4.18. Unlike SIFT, however, which is only evaluated at interest point locations, HOGs are evaluated on a regular overlapping grid and their descriptor magnitudes are normalized using an even coarser grid; they are only computed at a single scale and a fixed orientation. In order to capture the subtle variations in orientation around a person's outline, a large number of orientation bins is used and no smoothing is performed in the central difference gradient computation—see the work of Dalal and Triggs (2005) for more implementation details. Figure 14.8d shows a sample input image, while Figure 14.8e shows the associated HOG descriptors.

Once the descriptors have been computed, a support vector machine (SVM) is trained

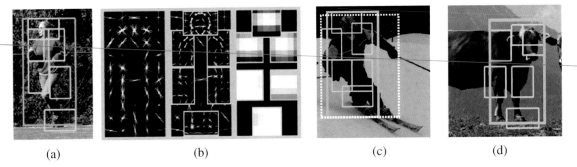

(a)　　　　　　　　　(b)　　　　　　　　　(c)　　　　　　　(d)

Figure 14.9 Part-based object detection (Felzenszwalb, McAllester, and Ramanan 2008) © 2008 IEEE: (a) An input photograph and its associated person (blue) and part (yellow) detection results. (b) The detection model is defined by a coarse template, several higher resolution part templates, and a spatial model for the location of each part. (c) True positive detection of a skier and (d) false positive detection of a cow (labeled as a person).

on the resulting high-dimensional continuous descriptor vectors. Figures 14.8b–c show a diagram of the (most) positive and negative SVM weights in each block, while Figures 14.8f–g show the corresponding weighted HOG responses for the central input image. As you can see, there are a fair number of positive responses around the head, torso, and feet of the person, and relatively few negative responses (mainly around the middle and the neck of the sweater).

The fields of pedestrian and general object detection have continued to evolve rapidly over the last decade (Belongie, Malik, and Puzicha 2002; Mikolajczyk, Schmid, and Zisserman 2004; Leibe, Seemann, and Schiele 2005; Opelt, Pinz, and Zisserman 2006; Torralba 2007; Andriluka, Roth, and Schiele 2009, 2010; Dollàr, Belongie, and Perona 2010). Munder and Gavrila (2006) compare a number of pedestrian detectors and conclude that those based on local receptive fields and SVMs perform the best, with a boosting-based approach coming close. Maji, Berg, and Malik (2008) improve on the best of these results using non-overlapping multi-resolution HOG descriptors and a histogram intersection kernel SVM based on a spatial pyramid match kernel from Lazebnik, Schmid, and Ponce (2006).

When detectors for several different classes are being constructed simultaneously, Torralba, Murphy, and Freeman (2007) show that sharing features and weak learners between detectors yields better performance, both in terms of faster computation times and fewer training examples. To find the features and decision stumps that work best in a shared manner, they introduce a novel *joint boosting* algorithm that optimizes, at each stage, a summed expected exponential loss function using the "gentleboost" algorithm of Friedman, Hastie, and Tibshirani (2000).

In more recent work, Felzenszwalb, McAllester, and Ramanan (2008) extend the histogram of oriented gradients person detector to incorporate flexible parts models (Section 14.4.2). Each part is trained and detected on HOGs evaluated at two pyramid levels below the overall object model and the locations of the parts relative to the parent node (the overall bounding box) are also learned and used during recognition (Figure 14.9b). To compensate for inaccuracies or inconsistencies in the training example bounding boxes (dashed white lines in Figure 14.9c), the "true" location of the parent (blue) bounding box is considered a latent (hidden) variable and is inferred during both training and recognition. Since the locations

Figure 14.10 Part-based object detection results for people, bicycles, and horses (Felzenszwalb, McAllester, and Ramanan 2008) © 2008 IEEE. The first three columns show correct detections, while the rightmost column shows false positives.

of the parts are also latent, the system can be trained in a semi-supervised fashion, without needing part labels in the training data. An extension to this system (Felzenszwalb, Girshick, McAllester *et al.* 2010), which includes among its improvements a simple contextual model, was among the two best object detection systems in the 2008 Visual Object Classes detection challenge. Other recent improvements to part-based person detection and pose estimation include the work by Andriluka, Roth, and Schiele (2009) and Kumar, Zisserman, and H.S.Torr (2009).

An even more accurate estimate of a person's pose and location is presented by Rogez, Rihan, Ramalingam *et al.* (2008), who compute both the phase of a person in a walk cycle and the locations of individual joints, using random forests built on top of HOGs (Figure 14.11). Since their system produces full 3D pose information, it is closer in its application domain to 3D person trackers (Sidenbladh, Black, and Fleet 2000; Andriluka, Roth, and Schiele 2010), which we discussed in Section 12.6.4.

One final note on person and object detection. When video sequences are available, the additional information present in the optic flow and motion discontinuities can greatly aid in the detection task, as discussed by Efros, Berg, Mori *et al.* (2003), Viola, Jones, and Snow (2003), and Dalal, Triggs, and Schmid (2006).

Figure 14.11 Pose detection using random forests (Rogez, Rihan, Ramalingam *et al.* 2008) © 2008 IEEE. The estimated pose (state of the kinematic model) is drawn over each input frame.

Figure 14.12 Humans can recognize low-resolution faces of familiar people (Sinha, Balas, Ostrovsky *et al.* 2006) © 2006 IEEE.

14.2 Face recognition

Among the various recognition tasks that computers might be asked to perform, face recognition is the one where they have arguably had the most success.[5] While computers cannot pick out suspects from thousands of people streaming in front of video cameras (even people cannot readily distinguish between similar people with whom they are not familiar (O'Toole, Jiang, Roark *et al.* 2006; O'Toole, Phillips, Jiang *et al.* 2009)), their ability to distinguish among a small number of family members and friends has found its way into consumer-level photo applications, such as Picasa and iPhoto. Face recognition can also be used in a variety of additional applications, including human–computer interaction (HCI), identity verification (Kirovski, Jojic, and Jancke 2004), desktop login, parental controls, and patient monitoring (Zhao, Chellappa, Phillips *et al.* 2003).

Today's face recognizers work best when they are given full frontal images of faces under relatively uniform illumination conditions, although databases that include large amounts of pose and lighting variation have been collected (Phillips, Moon, Rizvi *et al.* 2000; Sim,

---

[5]Instance recognition, i.e., the re-recognition of known objects such as locations or planar objects, is the other most successful application of general image recognition. In the general domain of *biometrics*, i.e., identity recognition, specialized images such as irises and fingerprints perform even better (Jain, Bolle, and Pankanti 1999; Pankanti, Bolle, and Jain 2000; Daugman 2004).

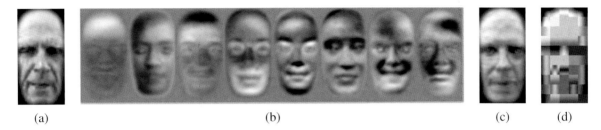

    (a)   (b)   (c)   (d)

Figure 14.13 Face modeling and compression using eigenfaces (Moghaddam and Pentland 1997) © 1997 IEEE: (a) input image; (b) the first eight eigenfaces; (c) image reconstructed by projecting onto this basis and compressing the image to 85 bytes; (d) image reconstructed using JPEG (530 bytes).

Baker, and Bsat 2003; Gross, Shi, and Cohn 2005; Huang, Ramesh, Berg *et al.* 2007; Phillips, Scruggs, O'Toole *et al.* 2010). (See Table 14.1 in Section 14.6 for more details.)

Some of the earliest approaches to face recognition involved finding the locations of distinctive image features, such as the eyes, nose, and mouth, and measuring the distances between these feature locations (Fischler and Elschlager 1973; Kanade 1977; Yuille 1991). More recent approaches rely on comparing gray-level images projected onto lower dimensional subspaces called *eigenfaces* (Section 14.2.1) and jointly modeling shape and appearance variations (while discounting pose variations) using *active appearance models* (Section 14.2.2).

Descriptions of additional face recognition techniques can be found in a number of surveys and books on this topic (Chellappa, Wilson, and Sirohey 1995; Zhao, Chellappa, Phillips *et al.* 2003; Li and Jain 2005) as well as the Face Recognition Web site.[6] The survey on face recognition by humans by Sinha, Balas, Ostrovsky *et al.* (2006) is also well worth reading; it includes a number of surprising results, such as humans' ability to recognize low-resolution images of familiar faces (Figure 14.12) and the importance of eyebrows in recognition.

14.2.1 Eigenfaces

Eigenfaces rely on the observation first made by Kirby and Sirovich (1990) that an arbitrary face image x can be compressed and reconstructed by starting with a mean image m (Figure 14.1b) and adding a small number of scaled signed images u_i,[7]

$$\tilde{x} = m + \sum_{i=0}^{M-1} a_i u_i, \tag{14.8}$$

where the signed basis images (Figure 14.13b) can be derived from an ensemble of training images using *principal component analysis* (also known as *eigenvalue analysis* or the *Karhunen–Loève transform*). Turk and Pentland (1991a) recognized that the coefficients a_i in the eigenface expansion could themselves be used to construct a fast image matching algorithm.

---

[6] http://www.face-rec.org/.

[7] In previous chapters, we used I to indicate images; in this chapter, we use the more abstract quantities x and u to indicate collections of pixels in an image turned into a vector.

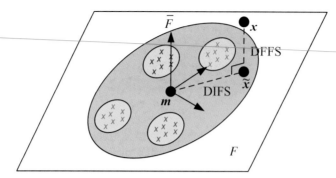

Figure 14.14 Projection onto the linear subspace spanned by the eigenface images (Moghaddam and Pentland 1997) © 1997 IEEE. The distance from face space (DFFS) is the orthogonal distance to the plane, while the distance in face space (DIFS) is the distance along the plane from the mean image. Both distances can be turned into Mahalanobis distances and given probabilistic interpretations.

In more detail, let us start with a collection of *training images* $\{x_j\}$, from which we can compute the mean image m and a *scatter* or *covariance* matrix

$$C = \frac{1}{N} \sum_{j=0}^{N-1} (x_j - m)(x_j - m)^T. \tag{14.9}$$

We can apply the eigenvalue decomposition (A.6) to represent this matrix as

$$C = U \Lambda U^T = \sum_{i=0}^{N-1} \lambda_i u_i u_i^T, \tag{14.10}$$

where the λ_i are the eigenvalues of C and the u_i are the *eigenvectors*. For general images, Kirby and Sirovich (1990) call these vectors *eigenpictures*; for faces, Turk and Pentland (1991a) call them *eigenfaces* (Figure 14.13b).[8]

Two important properties of the eigenvalue decomposition are that the optimal (best approximation) coefficients a_i for any new image x can be computed as

$$a_i = (x - m) \cdot u_i, \tag{14.11}$$

and that, assuming the eigenvalues $\{\lambda_i\}$ are sorted in decreasing order, truncating the approximation given in (14.8) at any point M gives the best possible approximation (least error) between $\tilde{x}$ and x. Figure 14.13c shows the resulting approximation corresponding to Figure 14.13a and shows how much better it is at compressing a face image than JPEG.

Truncating the eigenface decomposition of a face image (14.8) after M components is equivalent to projecting the image onto a linear subspace F, which we can call the *face space* (Figure 14.14). Because the eigenvectors (eigenfaces) are orthogonal and of unit norm, the

---

[8] In actual practice, the full $P \times P$ scatter matrix (14.9) is never computed. Instead, a smaller $N \times N$ matrix consisting of the inner products between all the signed deviations $(x_i - m)$ is accumulated instead. See Appendix A.1.2 (A.13–A.14) for details.

distance of a projected face $\tilde{x}$ to the mean face m can be written as

$$\text{DIFS} = \|\tilde{x} - m\| = \sqrt{\sum_{i=0}^{M-1} a_i^2}, \tag{14.12}$$

where DIFS stands for *distance in face space* (Moghaddam and Pentland 1997). The remaining distance between the original image x and its projection onto face space $\tilde{x}$, i.e., the *distance from face space* (DFFS), can be computed directly in pixel space and represents the "faceness" of a particular image.[9] It is also possible to measure the distance between two different faces in face space as

$$\text{DIFS}(x, y) = \|\tilde{x} - \tilde{y}\| = \sqrt{\sum_{i=0}^{M-1} (a_i - b_i)^2}, \tag{14.13}$$

where the $b_i = (y - m) \cdot u_i$ are the eigenface coefficients corresponding to y.

Computing such distances in Euclidean vector space, however, does not exploit the additional information that the eigenvalue decomposition of our covariance matrix (14.10) provides. If we interpret the covariance matrix C as the covariance of a multi-variate Gaussian (Appendix B.1.1),[10] we can turn the DIFS into a log likelihood by computing the *Mahalanobis distance*

$$\text{DIFS}' = \|\tilde{x} - m\|_{C^{-1}} = \sqrt{\sum_{i=0}^{M-1} a_i^2 / \lambda_i^2}. \tag{14.14}$$

Instead of measuring the squared distance along each principal component in face space F, the Mahalanobis distance measures the *ratio* between the squared distance and the corresponding *variance* $\sigma_i^2 = \lambda_i$ and then sums these squared ratios (per-component log-likelihoods). An alternative way to implement this is to pre-scale each eigenvector by the inverse square root of its corresponding eigenvalue,

$$\hat{U} = U \Lambda^{-1/2}. \tag{14.15}$$

This *whitening* transformation then means that Euclidean distances in feature (face) space now correspond directly to log likelihoods (Moghaddam, Jebara, and Pentland 2000). (This same whitening approach can also be used in feature-based matching algorithms, as discussed in Section 4.1.3.)

If the distribution in eigenface space is very elongated, the Mahalanobis distance properly scales the components to come up with a sensible (probabilistic) distance from the mean. A similar analysis can be performed for computing a sensible difference from face space (DFFS) (Moghaddam and Pentland 1997) and the two terms can be combined to produce an estimate of the likelihood of being a true face, which can be useful in doing face detection (Section 14.1.1). More detailed explanations of probabilistic and Bayesian PCA can be found in textbooks on statistical learning (Hastie, Tibshirani, and Friedman 2001; Bishop 2006), which also discuss techniques for selecting the optimum number of components M to use in modeling a distribution.

---

[9] This can be used to form a simple face detector, as mentioned in Section 14.1.1.

[10] The ellipse shown in Figure 14.14 denotes an equi-probability contour of this multi-variate Gaussian.

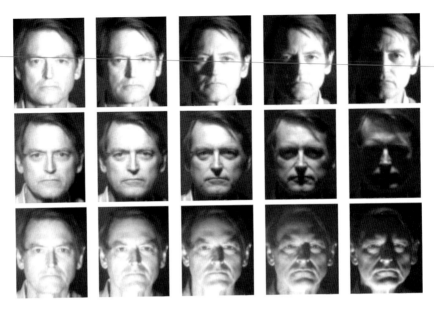

Figure 14.15 Images from the Harvard database used by Belhumeur, Hespanha, and Kriegman (1997) © 1997 IEEE. Note the wide range of illumination variation, which can be more dramatic than inter-personal variations.

One of the biggest advantages of using eigenfaces is that they reduce the comparison of a new face image x to a prototype (training) face image x_k (one of the colored xs in Figure 14.14) from a P-dimensional difference in pixel space to an M-dimensional difference in face space,

$$\|x - x_k\| = \|a - a_k\|, \tag{14.16}$$

where $a = U^T(x - m)$ (14.11) involves computing a dot product between the signed difference-from-mean image $(x - m)$ and each of the eigenfaces u_i. Once again, however, this Euclidean distance ignores the fact that we have more information about face likelihoods available in the distribution of training images.

Consider the set of images of one person taken under a wide range of illuminations shown in Figure 14.15. As you can see, the *intrapersonal* variability within these images is much greater than the typical *extrapersonal* variability between any two people taken under the same illumination. Regular PCA analysis fails to distinguish between these two sources of variability and may, in fact, devote most of its principal components to modeling the intrapersonal variability.

If we are going to approximate faces by a linear subspace, it is more useful to have a space that *discriminates* between different classes (people) and is less sensitive to within-class variations (Belhumeur, Hespanha, and Kriegman 1997). Consider the three classes shown as different colors in Figure 14.16. As you can see, the distributions within a class (indicated by the tilted colored axes) are elongated and tilted with respect to the main face space PCA, which is aligned with the black x and y axes. We can compute the total *within-class* scatter matrix as

$$S_{\mathrm{W}} = \sum_{k=0}^{K-1} S_k = \sum_{k=0}^{K-1} \sum_{i \in C_k} (x_i - m_k)(x_i - m_k)^T, \tag{14.17}$$

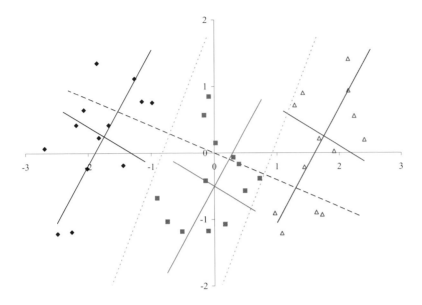

Figure 14.16 Simple example of Fisher linear discriminant analysis. The samples come from three different classes, shown in different colors along with their principal axes, which are scaled to $2\sigma_i$. (The intersections of the tilted axes are the class means $\boldsymbol{m}_k$.) The dashed line is the (dominant) Fisher linear discriminant direction and the dotted lines are the linear discriminants between the classes. Note how the discriminant direction is a blend between the principal directions of the between-class and within-class scatter matrices.

where $\boldsymbol{m}_k$ is the mean of class k and $\boldsymbol{S}_k$ is its within-class scatter matrix.[11] Similarly, we can compute the *between-class* scatter as

$$\boldsymbol{S}_{\mathrm{B}} = \sum_{k=0}^{K-1} N_k (\boldsymbol{m}_k - \boldsymbol{m})(\boldsymbol{m}_k - \boldsymbol{m})^T, \qquad (14.18)$$

where N_k are the number of exemplars in each class and $\boldsymbol{m}$ is the overall mean. For the three distributions shown in Figure 14.16, we have

$$\boldsymbol{S}_{\mathrm{W}} = 3N \begin{bmatrix} 0.246 & 0.183 \\ 0.183 & 0.457 \end{bmatrix} \quad \text{and} \quad \boldsymbol{S}_{\mathrm{B}} = N \begin{bmatrix} 6.125 & 0 \\ 0 & 0.375 \end{bmatrix}, \qquad (14.19)$$

where $N = N_k = 13$ is the number of samples in each class.

To compute the most discriminating direction, *Fisher's linear discriminant* (FLD) (Belhumeur, Hespanha, and Kriegman 1997; Hastie, Tibshirani, and Friedman 2001; Bishop 2006), which is also known as *linear discriminant analysis* (LDA), selects the direction $\boldsymbol{u}$ that results in the largest ratio between the projected between-class and within-class variations

$$\boldsymbol{u}^* = \arg\max_{\boldsymbol{u}} \frac{\boldsymbol{u}^T \boldsymbol{S}_{\mathrm{B}} \boldsymbol{u}}{\boldsymbol{u}^T \boldsymbol{S}_{\mathrm{W}} \boldsymbol{u}}, \qquad (14.20)$$

---

[11] To be consistent with Belhumeur, Hespanha, and Kriegman (1997), we use $\boldsymbol{S}_{\mathrm{W}}$ and $\boldsymbol{S}_{\mathrm{B}}$ to denote the scatter matrices, even though we use $\boldsymbol{C}$ elsewhere (14.9).

which is equivalent to finding the eigenvector corresponding to the largest eigenvalue of the generalized eigenvalue problem

$$S_{\mathrm{B}} u = \lambda S_{\mathrm{W}} u \quad \text{or} \quad \lambda u = S_{\mathrm{W}}^{-1} S_{\mathrm{B}} u. \tag{14.21}$$

For the problem shown in Figure 14.16,

$$S_{\mathrm{W}}^{-1} S_{\mathrm{B}} = \begin{bmatrix} 11.796 & -0.289 \\ -4.715 & 0.3889 \end{bmatrix} \quad \text{and} \quad u = \begin{bmatrix} 0.926 \\ -0.379 \end{bmatrix} \tag{14.22}$$

As you can see, using this direction results in a better separation between the classes than using the dominant PCA direction, which is the horizontal axis. In their paper, Belhumeur, Hespanha, and Kriegman (1997) show that Fisherfaces significantly outperform the original eigenfaces algorithm, especially when faces have large amounts of illumination variation, as in Figure 14.15.

An alternative for modeling within-class (intrapersonal) and between-class (extrapersonal) variations is to model each distribution separately and then use Bayesian techniques to find the closest exemplar (Moghaddam, Jebara, and Pentland 2000). Instead of computing the mean for each class and then the within-class and between-class distributions, consider evaluating the difference images

$$\boldsymbol{\Delta}_{ij} = \boldsymbol{x}_i - \boldsymbol{x}_j \tag{14.23}$$

between all pairs of training images $(\boldsymbol{x}_i, \boldsymbol{x}_j)$. The differences between pairs that are in the same class (the same person) are used to estimate the intrapersonal covariance matrix $\boldsymbol{\Sigma}_I$, while differences between different people are used to estimate the extrapersonal covariance $\boldsymbol{\Sigma}_E$.[12] The principal components (eigenfaces) corresponding to these two classes are shown in Figure 14.17.

At recognition time, we can compute the distance $\boldsymbol{\Delta}_i$ between a new face $\boldsymbol{x}$ and a stored training image $\boldsymbol{x}_i$ and evaluate its intrapersonal likelihood as

$$p_I(\boldsymbol{\Delta}_i) = p_{\mathcal{N}}(\boldsymbol{\Delta}_i; \boldsymbol{\Sigma}_I) = \frac{1}{|2\pi \boldsymbol{\Sigma}_I|^{1/2}} \exp -\|\boldsymbol{\Delta}_i\|_{\boldsymbol{\Sigma}_I^{-1}}^2, \tag{14.24}$$

where $p_{\mathcal{N}}$ is a normal (Gaussian) distribution with covariance $\boldsymbol{\Sigma}_I$ and

$$|2\pi \boldsymbol{\Sigma}_I|^{1/2} = (2\pi)^{M/2} \prod_{j=1}^{M} \lambda_j^{1/2} \tag{14.25}$$

is its volume. The Mahalanobis distance

$$\|\boldsymbol{\Delta}_i\|_{\boldsymbol{\Sigma}_I^{-1}}^2 = \boldsymbol{\Delta}_i^T \boldsymbol{\Sigma}_I^{-1} \boldsymbol{\Delta}_i = \|\boldsymbol{a}^I - \boldsymbol{a}_i^I\|^2 \tag{14.26}$$

can be computed more efficiently by first projecting the new image $\boldsymbol{x}$ into the whitened intrapersonal face space (14.15)

$$\boldsymbol{a}^I = \hat{\boldsymbol{U}}^I \boldsymbol{x} \tag{14.27}$$

and then computing a Euclidean distance to the training image vector $\boldsymbol{a}_i^I$, which can be precomputed offline. The extrapersonal likelihood $p_E(\boldsymbol{\Delta}_i)$ can be computed in a similar fashion.

---

[12] Note that the difference distributions are zero mean because for every $\boldsymbol{\Delta}_{ij}$ there corresponds a negative $\boldsymbol{\Delta}_{ji}$.

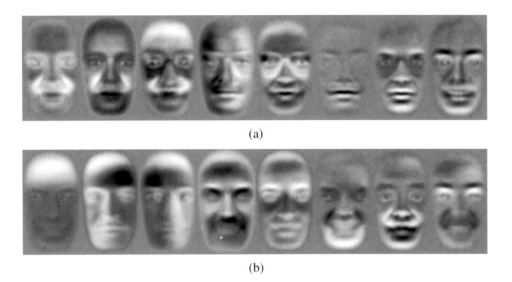

(a)

(b)

Figure 14.17 "Dual" eigenfaces (Moghaddam, Jebara, and Pentland 2000) © 2000 Elsevier: (a) intrapersonal and (b) extrapersonal.

Once the intrapersonal and extrapersonal likelihoods have been computed, we can compute the Bayesian likelihood of a new image x matching a training image x_i as

$$p(\mathbf{\Delta}_i) = \frac{p_I(\mathbf{\Delta}_i)l_I}{p_I(\mathbf{\Delta}_i)l_I + p_E(\mathbf{\Delta}_i)l_E}, \tag{14.28}$$

where l_I and l_E are the prior probabilities of two images being in the same or in different classes (Moghaddam, Jebara, and Pentland 2000). A simpler approach, which does not require the evaluation of extrapersonal probabilities, is to simply choose the training image with the highest likelihood $p_I(\mathbf{\Delta}_i)$. In this case, nearest neighbor search techniques in the space spanned by the precomputed $\{a_i^I\}$ vectors could be used to speed up finding the best match.[13]

Another way to improve the performance of eigenface-based approaches is to break up the image into separate regions such as the eyes, nose, and mouth (Figure 14.18) and to match each of these *modular eigenspaces* independently (Moghaddam and Pentland 1997; Heisele, Ho, Wu *et al.* 2003; Heisele, Serre, and Poggio 2007). The advantage of such a modular approach is that it can tolerate a wider range of viewpoints, because each part can move relative to the others. It also supports a larger variety of combinations, e.g., we can model one person as having a narrow nose and bushy eyebrows, without requiring the eigenfaces to span all possible combinations of nose, mouth, and eyebrows. (If you remember the cardboard children's books where you can select different top and bottom faces, or Mr. Potato Head, you get the idea.)

Another approach to dealing with large variability in appearance is to create *view-based* (view-specific) eigenspaces, as shown in Figure 14.19 (Moghaddam and Pentland 1997). We can think of these view-based eigenspaces as local descriptors that select different axes depending on which part of the face space you are in. Note that such approaches, however,

---

[13] Note that while the covariance matrices $\mathbf{\Sigma}_I$ and $\mathbf{\Sigma}_E$ are computed by looking at differences between *all* pairs of images, the run-time evaluation selects the *nearest* image to determine the facial identity. Whether this is statistically correct is explored in Exercise 14.4.

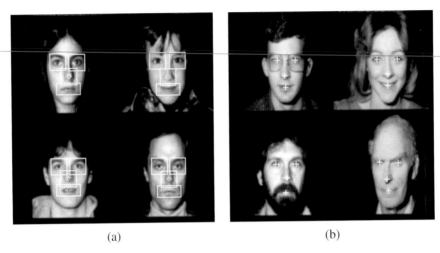

(a)   (b)

Figure 14.18 Modular eigenspace for face recognition (Moghaddam and Pentland 1997) © 1997 IEEE. (a) By detecting separate features in the faces (eyes, nose, mouth), separate eigenspaces can be estimated for each one. (b) The relative positions of each feature can be detected at recognition time, thus allowing for more flexibility in viewpoint and expression.

potentially require large amounts of training data, i.e., pictures of every person in every possible pose or expression. This is in contrast to the shape and appearance models we study in Section 14.2.2, which can learn deformations across all individuals.

It is also possible to generalize the bilinear factorization implicit in PCA and SVD approaches to multilinear (tensor) formulations that can model several interacting factors simultaneously (Vasilescu and Terzopoulos 2007). These ideas are related to currently active topics in machine learning such as *subspace learning* (Cai, He, Hu *et al.* 2007), *local distance functions* (Frome, Singer, Sha *et al.* 2007), and *metric learning* (Ramanan and Baker 2009). Learning approaches play an increasingly important role in face recognition, e.g., in the work of Sivic, Everingham, and Zisserman (2009) and Guillaumin, Verbeek, and Schmid (2009).

14.2.2 Active appearance and 3D shape models

The need to use modular or view-based eigenspaces for face recognition is symptomatic of a more general observation, i.e., that facial appearance and identifiability depend as much on *shape* as they do on color or texture (which is what eigenfaces capture). Furthermore, when dealing with 3D head rotations, the *pose* of a person's head should be discounted when performing recognition.

In fact, the earliest face recognition systems, such as those by Fischler and Elschlager (1973), Kanade (1977), and Yuille (1991), found distinctive feature points on facial images and performed recognition on the basis of their relative positions or distances. Newer techniques such as *local feature analysis* (Penev and Atick 1996) and *elastic bunch graph matching* (Wiskott, Fellous, Krüger *et al.* 1997) combine local filter responses (jets) at distinctive feature locations together with shape models to perform recognition.

A visually compelling example of why both shape and texture are important is the work of Rowland and Perrett (1995), who manually traced the contours of facial features and then

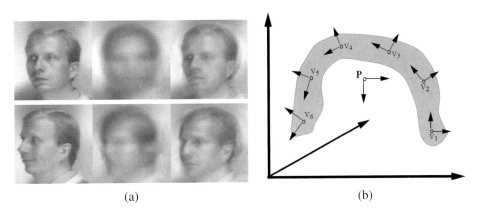

(a)   (b)

Figure 14.19 View-based eigenspace (Moghaddam and Pentland 1997) © 1997 IEEE. (a) Comparison between a regular (parametric) eigenspace reconstruction (middle column) and a view-based eigenspace reconstruction (right column) corresponding to the input image (left column). The top row is from a training image, the bottom row is from the test set. (b) A schematic representation of the two approaches, showing how each view computes its own local basis representation.

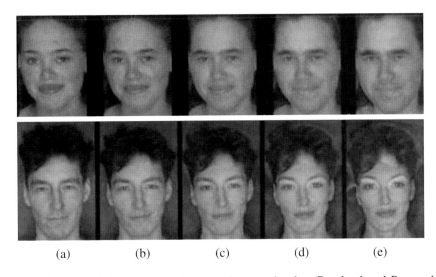

(a)   (b)   (c)   (d)   (e)

Figure 14.20 Manipulating facial appearance through shape and color (Rowland and Perrett 1995) © 1995 IEEE. By adding or subtracting gender-specific shape and color characteristics to (b) an input image, different amounts of gender variation can be induced. The amounts added (from the mean) are: (a) +50% (gender enhancement), (c) -50% (near "androgyny"), (d) -100% (gender switched), and (e) -150% (opposite gender attributes enhanced).

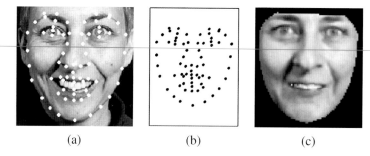

(a)   (b)   (c)

Figure 14.21 Active Appearance Models (Cootes, Edwards, and Taylor 2001) © 2001 IEEE: (a) input image with registered feature points; (b) the feature points (shape vector s); (c) the shape-free appearance image (texture vector t).

used these contours to normalize (warp) each image to a canonical shape. After analyzing both the shape and color images for deviations from the mean, they were able to associate certain shape and color deformations with personal characteristics such as age and gender (Figure 14.20). Their work demonstrates that both shape and color have an important influence on the perception of such characteristics.

Around the same time, researchers in computer vision were beginning to use simultaneous shape deformations and texture interpolation to model the variability in facial appearance caused by identity or expression (Beymer 1996; Vetter and Poggio 1997), developing techniques such as Active Shape Models (Lanitis, Taylor, and Cootes 1997), 3D Morphable Models (Blanz and Vetter 1999), and Elastic Bunch Graph Matching (Wiskott, Fellous, Krüger *et al.* 1997).[14]

Of all these techniques, the *active appearance models* (AAMs) of Cootes, Edwards, and Taylor (2001) are among the most widely used for face recognition and tracking. Like other shape and texture models, an AAM models both the variation in the shape of an image s, which is normally encoded by the location of key feature points on the image (Figure 14.21b), as well as the variation in texture t, which is normalized to a canonical shape before being analyzed (Figure 14.21c).[15]

Both shape and texture are represented as deviations from a mean shape $\bar{s}$ and texture $\bar{t}$,

$$s = \bar{s} + U_s a \tag{14.29}$$

$$t = \bar{t} + U_t a, \tag{14.30}$$

where the eigenvectors in U_s and U_t have been pre-scaled (whitened) so that unit vectors in a represent one standard deviation of variation observed in the training data. In addition to these principal deformations, the shape parameters are transformed by a global similarity to match the location, size, and orientation of a given face. Similarly, the texture image contains a scale and offset to best match novel illumination conditions.

As you can see, the same appearance parameters a in (14.29–14.30) simultaneously control both the shape and texture deformations from the mean, which makes sense if we believe

---

[14] We have already seen the application of PCA to 3D head and face modeling and animation in Section 12.6.3.

[15] When only the shape variation is being captured, such models are called *active shape models* (ASMs) (Cootes, Cooper, Taylor *et al.* 1995; Davies, Twining, and Taylor 2008). These were already discussed in Section 5.1.1 (5.13–5.17).

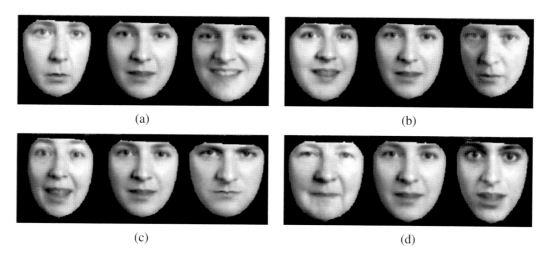

(a)   (b)

(c)   (d)

Figure 14.22 Principal modes of variation in active appearance models (Cootes, Edwards, and Taylor 2001) © 2001 IEEE. The four images show the effects of simultaneously changing the first four modes of variation in both shape and texture by $\pm\sigma$ from the mean. You can clearly see how the shape of the face and the shading are simultaneously affected.

them to be correlated. Figure 14.22 shows how moving three standard deviations along each of the first four principal directions ends up changing several correlated factors in a person's appearance, including expression, gender, age, and identity.

In order to fit an active appearance model to a novel image, Cootes, Edwards, and Taylor (2001) pre-compute a set of "difference decomposition" images, using an approach related to other fast techniques for incremental tracking, such as those we discussed in Sections 4.1.4, 8.1.3, and 8.2 (Gleicher 1997; Hager and Belhumeur 1998), which often *learn* a discriminative mapping between matching errors and incremental displacements (Avidan 2001; Jurie and Dhome 2002; Liu, Chen, and Kumar 2003; Sclaroff and Isidoro 2003; Romdhani and Vetter 2003; Williams, Blake, and Cipolla 2003).

In more detail, Cootes, Edwards, and Taylor (2001) compute the derivatives of a set of training images with respect to each of the parameters in a using finite differences and then compute a set of *displacement weight* images

$$W = \left[\frac{\partial x^T}{\partial a} \frac{\partial x}{\partial a}\right]^{-1} \frac{\partial x^T}{\partial a}, \tag{14.31}$$

which can be multiplied by the current error residual to produce an update step in the parameters, $\delta a = -W r$. Matthews and Baker (2004) use their *inverse compositional method*, which they first developed for parametric optical flow (8.64–8.65), to further speed up active appearance model fitting and tracking. Examples of AAMs being fitted to two input images are shown in Figure 14.23.

Although active appearance models are primarily designed to accurately capture the variability in appearance and deformation that are characteristic of faces, they can be adapted to face recognition by computing an identity subspace that separates variation in identity from other sources of variability such as lighting, pose, and expression (Costen, Cootes, Edwards *et al.* 1999). The basic idea, which is modeled after similar work in eigenfaces (Belhumeur,

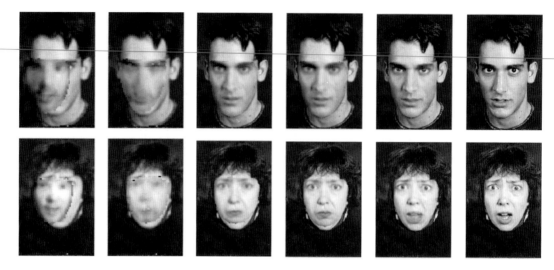

Figure 14.23 Multiresolution model fitting (search) in active appearance models (Cootes, Edwards, and Taylor 2001) © 2001 IEEE. The columns show the initial model, the results after 3, 8, and 11 iterations, and the final convergence. The rightmost column shows the input image.

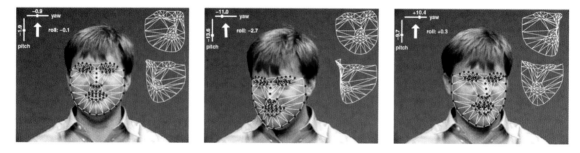

Figure 14.24 Head tracking with 3D AAMs (Matthews, Xiao, and Baker 2007) © 2007 Springer. Each image shows a video frame along with the estimate yaw, pitch, and roll parameters and the fitted 3D deformable mesh.

Hespanha, and Kriegman 1997; Moghaddam, Jebara, and Pentland 2000), is to compute separate statistics for intrapersonal and extrapersonal variation and then find discriminating directions in these subspaces. While AAMs have sometimes been used directly for recognition (Blanz and Vetter 2003), their main use in the context of recognition is to align faces into a canonical pose (Liang, Xiao, Wen *et al.* 2008) so that more traditional methods of face recognition (Penev and Atick 1996; Wiskott, Fellous, Krüger *et al.* 1997; Ahonen, Hadid, and Pietikäinen 2006; Zhao and Pietikäinen 2007; Cao, Yin, Tang *et al.* 2010) can be used. AAMs (or, actually, their simpler version, Active Shape Models (ASMs)) can also be used to align face images to perform automated morphing (Zanella and Fuentes 2004).

Active appearance models continue to be an active research area, with enhancements to deal with illumination and viewpoint variation (Gross, Baker, Matthews *et al.* 2005) as well as occlusions (Gross, Matthews, and Baker 2006). One of the most significant extensions is to construct 3D models of shape (Matthews, Xiao, and Baker 2007), which are much better at capturing and explaining the full variability of facial appearance across wide changes in pose.

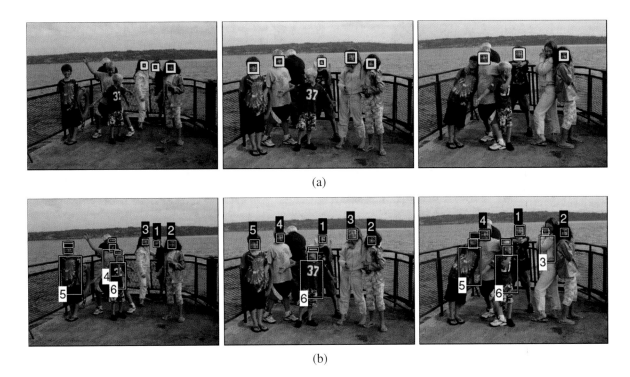

Figure 14.25 Person detection and re-recognition using a combined face, hair, and torso model (Sivic, Zitnick, and Szeliski 2006) © 2006 Springer. (a) Using face detection alone, several of the heads are missed. (b) The combined face and clothing model successfully re-finds all the people.

Such models can be constructed either from monocular video sequences (Matthews, Xiao, and Baker 2007), as shown in Figure 14.24, or from multi-view video sequences (Ramnath, Koterba, Xiao *et al.* 2008), which provide even greater reliability and accuracy in reconstruction and tracking. (For a recent review of progress in head pose estimation, please see the survey paper by Murphy-Chutorian and Trivedi (2009).)

14.2.3 *Application*: Personal photo collections

In addition to digital cameras automatically finding faces to aid in auto-focusing and video cameras finding faces in video conferencing to center on the speaker (either mechanically or digitally), face detection has found its way into most consumer-level photo organization packages, such as iPhoto, Picasa, and Windows Live Photo Gallery. Finding faces and allowing users to tag them makes it easier to find photos of selected people at a later date or to automatically share them with friends. In fact, the ability to tag friends in photos is one of the more popular features on Facebook.

Sometimes, however, faces can be hard to find and recognize, especially if they are small, turned away from the camera, or otherwise occluded. In such cases, combining face recognition with person detection and clothes recognition can be very effective, as illustrated in Figure 14.25 (Sivic, Zitnick, and Szeliski 2006). Combining person recognition with other kinds of context, such as location recognition (Section 14.3.3) or activity or event recognition, can also help boost performance (Lin, Kapoor, Hua *et al.* 2010).

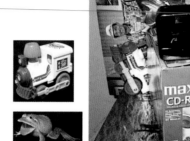 

Figure 14.26 Recognizing objects in a cluttered scene (Lowe 2004) © 2004 Springer. Two of the training images in the database are shown on the left. They are matched to the cluttered scene in the middle using SIFT features, shown as small squares in the right image. The affine warp of each recognized database image onto the scene is shown as a larger parallelogram in the right image.

14.3 Instance recognition

General object recognition falls into two broad categories, namely *instance recognition* and *class recognition*. The former involves re-recognizing a known 2D or 3D rigid object, potentially being viewed from a novel viewpoint, against a cluttered background, and with partial occlusions. The latter, which is also known as *category-level* or *generic* object recognition (Ponce, Hebert, Schmid *et al.* 2006), is the much more challenging problem of recognizing any instance of a particular general class such as "cat", "car", or "bicycle".

Over the years, many different algorithms have been developed for instance recognition. Mundy (2006) surveys earlier approaches, which focused on extracting lines, contours, or 3D surfaces from images and matching them to known 3D object models. Another popular approach was to acquire images from a large set of viewpoints and illuminations and to represent them using an eigenspace decomposition (Murase and Nayar 1995). More recent approaches (Lowe 2004; Rothganger, Lazebnik, Schmid *et al.* 2006; Ferrari, Tuytelaars, and Van Gool 2006b; Gordon and Lowe 2006; Obdržálek and Matas 2006; Sivic and Zisserman 2009) tend to use viewpoint-invariant 2D features, such as those we saw in Section 4.1.2. After extracting informative sparse 2D features from both the new image and the images in the database, image features are matched against the object database, using one of the sparse feature matching strategies described in Section 4.1.3. Whenever a sufficient number of matches have been found, they are verified by finding a geometric transformation that aligns the two sets of features (Figure 14.26).

Below, we describe some of the techniques that have been proposed for representing the geometric relationships between such features (Section 14.3.1). We also discuss how to make the feature matching process more efficient using ideas from text and information retrieval (Section 14.3.2).

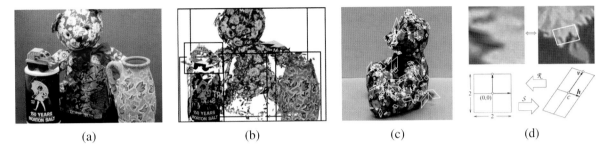

(a)   (b)   (c)   (d)

Figure 14.27 3D object recognition with affine regions (Rothganger, Lazebnik, Schmid *et al.* 2006) © 2006 Springer: (a) sample input image; (b) five of the recognized (reprojected) objects along with their bounding boxes; (c) a few of the local affine regions; (d) local affine region (patch) reprojected into a canonical (square) frame, along with its geometric affine transformations.

14.3.1 Geometric alignment

To recognize one or more instances of some known objects, such as those shown in the left column of Figure 14.26, the recognition system first extracts a set of interest points in each database image and stores the associated descriptors (and original positions) in an indexing structure such as a search tree (Section 4.1.3). At recognition time, features are extracted from the new image and compared against the stored object features. Whenever a sufficient number of matching features (say, three or more) are found for a given object, the system then invokes a *match verification* stage, whose job is to determine whether the spatial arrangement of matching features is consistent with those in the database image.

Because images can be highly cluttered and similar features may belong to several objects, the original set of feature matches can have a large number of outliers. For this reason, Lowe (2004) suggests using a Hough transform (Section 4.3.2) to accumulate votes for likely geometric transformations. In his system, he uses an affine transformation between the database object and the collection of scene features, which works well for objects that are mostly planar, or where at least several corresponding features share a quasi-planar geometry.[16]

Since SIFT features carry with them their own location, scale, and orientation, Lowe uses a four-dimensional similarity transformation as the original Hough binning structure, i.e., each bin denotes a particular location for the object center, scale, and in-plane rotation. Each matching feature votes for the nearest 2^4 bins and peaks in the transform are then selected for a more careful affine motion fit. Figure 14.26 (right image) shows three instances of the two objects on the left that were recognized by the system. Obdržálek and Matas (2006) generalize Lowe's approach to use feature descriptors with full local affine frames and evaluate their approach on a number of object recognition databases.

Another system that uses local affine frames is the one developed by Rothganger, Lazebnik, Schmid *et al.* (2006). In their system, the affine region detector of Mikolajczyk and Schmid (2004) is used to rectify local image patches (Figure 14.27d), from which both a SIFT descriptor and a 10×10 UV color histogram are computed and used for matching and recognition. Corresponding patches in different views of the same object, along with

---

[16] When a larger number of features is available, a full fundamental matrix can be used (Brown and Lowe 2002; Gordon and Lowe 2006). When image stitching is being performed (Brown and Lowe 2007), the motion models discussed in Section 9.1 can be used instead.

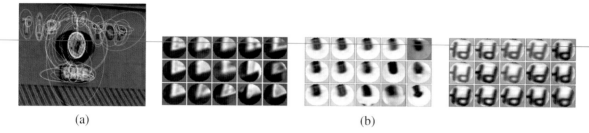

(a)   (b)

Figure 14.28 Visual words obtained from elliptical normalized affine regions (Sivic and Zisserman 2009) ©
2009 IEEE. (a) Affine covariant regions are extracted from each frame and clustered into visual words using k-
means clustering on SIFT descriptors with a learned Mahalanobis distance. (b) The central patch in each grid
shows the query and the surrounding patches show the nearest neighbors.

their local affine deformations, are used to compute a 3D affine model for the object using
an extension of the factorization algorithm of Section 7.3, which can then be upgraded to a
Euclidean reconstruction (Tomasi and Kanade 1992).

At recognition time, local Euclidean neighborhood constraints are used to filter potential
matches, in a manner analogous to the affine geometric constraints used by Lowe (2004) and
Obdržálek and Matas (2006). Figure 14.27 shows the results of recognizing five objects in a
cluttered scene using this approach.

While feature-based approaches are normally used to detect and localize known objects in
scenes, it is also possible to get pixel-level segmentations of the scene based on such matches.
Ferrari, Tuytelaars, and Van Gool (2006b) describe such a system for simultaneously recognizing objects and segmenting scenes, while Kannala, Rahtu, Brandt *et al.* (2008) extend this
approach to non-rigid deformations. Section 14.4.3 re-visits this topic of joint recognition
and segmentation in the context of generic class (category) recognition.

14.3.2 Large databases

As the number of objects in the database starts to grow large (say, millions of objects or video
frames being searched), the time it takes to match a new image against each database image
can become prohibitive. Instead of comparing the images one at a time, techniques are needed
to quickly narrow down the search to a few likely images, which can then be compared using
a more detailed and conservative verification stage.

The problem of quickly finding partial matches between documents is one of the central problems in *information retrieval* (IR) (Baeza-Yates and Ribeiro-Neto 1999; Manning,
Raghavan, and Schütze 2008). The basic approach in fast document retrieval algorithms is to
pre-compute an *inverted index* between individual words and the documents (or Web pages
or news stories) where they occur. More precisely, the *frequency* of occurrence of particular
words in a document is used to quickly find documents that match a particular query.

Sivic and Zisserman (2009) were the first to adapt IR techniques to visual search. In their
Video Google system, affine invariant features are first detected in all the video frames they
are indexing using both *shape adapted* regions around Harris feature points (Schaffalitzky
and Zisserman 2002; Mikolajczyk and Schmid 2004) and maximally stable extremal regions
(Matas, Chum, Urban *et al.* 2004), (Section 4.1.1), as shown in Figure 14.28a. Next, 128-

(a)   (b)

Figure 14.29 Matching based on visual words (Sivic and Zisserman 2009) © 2009 IEEE. (a) Features in the query region on the left are matched to corresponding features in a highly ranked video frame. (b) Results after removing the stop words and filtering the results using spatial consistency.

dimensional SIFT descriptors are computed from each normalized region (i.e., the patches shown in Figure 14.28b). Then, an average covariance matrix for these descriptors is estimated by accumulating statistics for features tracked from frame to frame. The feature descriptor covariance Σ is then used to define a Mahalanobis distance between feature descriptors,

$$d(\boldsymbol{x}_0, \boldsymbol{x}_1) = \|\boldsymbol{x}_0 - \boldsymbol{x}_1\|_{\Sigma^{-1}} = \sqrt{(\boldsymbol{x}_0 - \boldsymbol{x}_1)^T \Sigma^{-1}(\boldsymbol{x}_0 - \boldsymbol{x}_1)}. \qquad (14.32)$$

In practice, feature descriptors are *whitened* by pre-multiplying them by $\Sigma^{-1/2}$ so that Euclidean distances can be used.[17]

In order to apply fast information retrieval techniques to images, the high-dimensional feature descriptors that occur in each image must first be mapped into discrete *visual words*. Sivic and Zisserman (2003) perform this mapping using k-means clustering, while some of newer methods discussed below (Nistér and Stewénius 2006; Philbin, Chum, Isard *et al.* 2007) use alternative techniques, such as vocabulary trees or randomized forests. To keep the clustering time manageable, only a few hundred video frames are used to learn the cluster centers, which still involves estimating several thousand clusters from about 300,000 descriptors. At visual query time, each feature in a new query region (e.g., Figure 14.28a, which is a cropped region from a larger video frame) is mapped to its corresponding visual word. To keep very common patterns from contaminating the results, a *stop list* of the most common visual words is created and such words are dropped from further consideration.

Once a query image or region has been mapped into its constituent visual words, likely matching images or video frames must then be retrieved from the database. Information retrieval systems do this by matching word distributions (*term frequencies*) n_{id}/n_d between the query and target documents, where n_{id} is how many times word i occurs in document d, and n_d is the total number of words in document d. In order to downweight words that occur frequently and to focus the search on rarer (and hence, more informative) terms, an *inverse document frequency* weighting $\log N/N_i$ is applied, where N_i is the number of documents containing word i, and N is the total number of documents in the database. The combination of these two factors results in the *term frequency-inverse document frequency (tf-idf)* measure,

$$t_i = \frac{n_{id}}{n_d} \log \frac{N}{N_i}. \qquad (14.33)$$

---

[17] Note that the computation of feature covariances from matched feature points is much more sensible than simply performing a PCA on the descriptor space (Winder and Brown 2007). This corresponds roughly to the *within-class scatter matrix* (14.17) we studied in Section 14.2.1.

1. **Vocabulary construction (off-line)**

   (a) Extract affine covariant regions from each database image.

   (b) Compute descriptors and optionally whiten them to make Euclidean distances meaningful (Sivic and Zisserman 2009).

   (c) Cluster the descriptors into visual words, either using k-means (Sivic and Zisserman 2009), hierarchical clustering (Nistér and Stewénius 2006), or randomized k-d trees (Philbin, Chum, Isard *et al.* 2007).

   (d) Decide which words are too common and put them in the stop list.

2. **Database construction (off-line)**

   (a) Compute term frequencies for the visual word in each image, document frequencies for each word, and normalized *tf-idf* vectors for each document.

   (b) Compute inverted indices from visual words to images (with word counts).

3. **Image retrieval (on-line)**

   (a) Extract regions, descriptors, and visual words, and compute a *tf-idf* vector for the query image or region.

   (b) Retrieve the top image candidates, either by exhaustively comparing sparse *tf-idf* vectors (Sivic and Zisserman 2009) or by using inverted indices to examine only a subset of the images (Nistér and Stewénius 2006).

   (c) Optionally re-rank or verify all the candidate matches, using either spatial consistency (Sivic and Zisserman 2009) or an affine (or simpler) transformation model (Philbin, Chum, Isard *et al.* 2007).

   (d) Optionally expand the answer set by re-submitting highly ranked matches as new queries (Chum, Philbin, Sivic *et al.* 2007).

Algorithm 14.2 Image retrieval using visual words (Sivic and Zisserman 2009; Nistér and Stewénius 2006; Philbin, Chum, Isard *et al.* 2007; Chum, Philbin, Sivic *et al.* 2007; Philbin, Chum, Sivic *et al.* 2008).

At match time, each document (or query region) is represented by its *tf-idf* vector,

$$\boldsymbol{t} = (t_1, \ldots, t_i, \ldots t_m). \tag{14.34}$$

The similarity between two documents is measured by the dot product between their corresponding normalized vectors $\hat{\boldsymbol{t}} = \boldsymbol{t}/\|\boldsymbol{t}\|$, which means that their dissimilarity is proportional to their Euclidean distance. In their journal paper, Sivic and Zisserman (2009) compare this simple metric to a dozen other metrics and conclude that it performs just about as well as more complicated metrics. Because the number of non-zero t_i terms in a typical query or document is small ($M \approx 200$) compared to the number of visual words ($V \approx 20,000$), the distance between pairs of (sparse) *tf-idf* vectors can be computed quite quickly.

After retrieving the top $N_s = 500$ documents based on word frequencies, Sivic and Zisserman (2009) re-rank these results using spatial consistency. This step involves taking every matching feature and counting the number of $k = 15$ nearest adjacent features that also match between the two documents. (This latter process is accelerated using inverted files, which we discuss in more detail below.) As shown in Figure 14.29, this step helps remove spurious false positive matches and produces a better estimate of which frames and regions in the video are actually true matches. Algorithm 14.2 summarizes the processing steps involved in image retrieval using visual words.

While this approach works well for tens of thousand of visual words and thousands of keyframes, as the size of the database continues to increase, both the time to quantize each feature and to find potential matching frames or images can become prohibitive. Nistér and Stewénius (2006) address this problem by constructing a hierarchical *vocabulary tree*, where feature vectors are hierarchically clustered into a k-way tree of prototypes. (This technique is also known as *tree-structured vector quantization* (Gersho and Gray 1991).) At both database construction time and query time, each descriptor vector is compared to several prototypes at a given level in the vocabulary tree and the branch with the closest prototype is selected for further refinement (Figure 14.30). In this way, vocabularies with millions (10^6) of words can be supported, which enables individual words to be far more discriminative, while only requiring $10 \cdot 6$ comparisons for quantizing each descriptor.

At query time, each node in the vocabulary tree keeps its own inverted file index, so that features that match a particular node in the tree can be rapidly mapped to potential matching images. (Interior leaf nodes just use the inverted indices of their corresponding leaf-node descendants.) To score a particular query *tf-idf* vector $\boldsymbol{t}_q$ against all document vectors $\{\boldsymbol{t}_j\}$ using an L_p metric,[18] the non-zero t_{iq} entries in $\boldsymbol{t}_q$ are used to fetch corresponding non-zero t_{ij} entries, and the L_p norm is efficiently computed as

$$\|\boldsymbol{t}_q - \boldsymbol{t}_j\|_p^p = 2 + \sum_{i|t_{iq}>0 \wedge t_{ij}>0} \left(|t_{iq} - t_{ij}|^p - |t_{iq}|^p - |t_{ij}|^p \right). \tag{14.35}$$

In order to mitigate quantization errors due to noise in the descriptor vectors, Nistér and Stewénius (2006) not only score leaf nodes in the vocabulary tree (corresponding to visual words), but also score interior nodes in the tree, which correspond to clusters of similar visual words.

Because of the high efficiency in both quantizing and scoring features, their vocabulary-tree-based recognition system is able to process incoming images in real time against a

---

[18] In their actual implementation, Nistér and Stewénius (2006) use an L_1 metric.

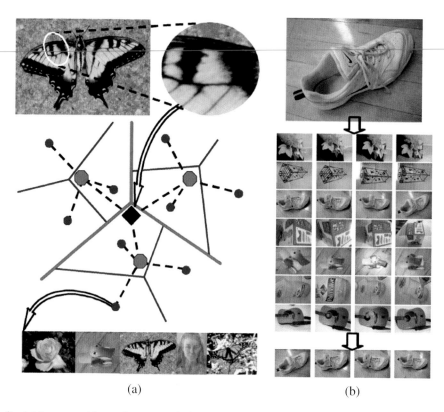

(a)   (b)

Figure 14.30 Scalable recognition using a vocabulary tree (Nistér and Stewénius 2006) © 2006 IEEE. (a) Each MSER elliptical region is converted into a SIFT descriptor, which is then quantized by comparing it hierarchically to some prototype descriptors in a vocabulary tree. Each leaf node stores its own inverted index (sparse list of non-zero *tf-idf* counts) into images that contain that feature. (b) A recognition result, showing a query image (top row) being indexed into a database of 6000 test images and correctly finding the corresponding four images.

database of 40,000 CD covers and at 1Hz when matching a database of one million frames taken from six feature-length movies. Figure 14.30b shows some typical images from the database of objects taken under varying viewpoints and illumination that was used to train and test the vocabulary tree recognition system.

The state of the art in instance recognition continues to improve rapidly. Philbin, Chum, Isard *et al.* (2007) have shown that randomized forest of k-d trees perform better than vocabulary trees on a large location recognition task (Figure 14.31). They also compare the effects of using different 2D motion models (Section 2.1.2) in the verification stage. In follow-on work, Chum, Philbin, Sivic *et al.* (2007) apply another idea from information retrieval, namely *query expansion*, which involves re-submitting top-ranked images from the initial query as additional queries to generate additional candidate results, to further improve recognition rates for difficult (occluded or oblique) examples. Philbin, Chum, Sivic *et al.* (2008) show how to mitigate quantization problems in visual words selection using *soft assignment*, where each feature descriptor is mapped to a number of visual words based on its distance from the cluster prototypes. The soft weights derived from these distances are used, in turn, to weight the counts used in the *tf-idf* vectors and to retrieve additional images for later verification.

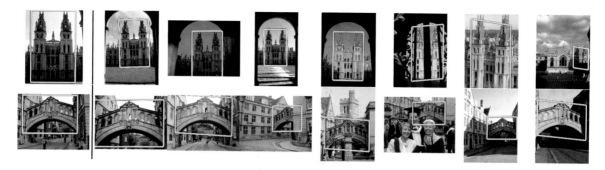

Figure 14.31 Location or building recognition using randomized trees (Philbin, Chum, Isard *et al.* 2007) © 2007 IEEE. The left image is the query, the other images are the highest-ranked results.

Taken together, these recent advances hold the promise of extending current instance recognition algorithms to performing Web-scale retrieval and matching tasks (Agarwal, Snavely, Simon *et al.* 2009; Agarwal, Furukawa, Snavely *et al.* 2010; Snavely, Simon, Goesele *et al.* 2010).

14.3.3 *Application*: Location recognition

One of the most exciting applications of instance recognition today is in the area of location recognition, which can be used both in desktop applications (where did I take this holiday snap?) and in mobile (cell-phone) applications. The latter case includes not only finding out your current location based on a cell-phone image but also providing you with navigation directions or annotating your images with useful information, such as building names and restaurant reviews (i.e., a portable form of *augmented reality*).

Some approaches to location recognition assume that the photos consist of architectural scenes for which vanishing directions can be used to pre-rectify the images for easier matching (Robertson and Cipolla 2004). Other approaches use general affine covariant interest points to perform *wide baseline matching* (Schaffalitzky and Zisserman 2002). The Photo Tourism system of Snavely, Seitz, and Szeliski (2006) (Section 13.1.2) was the first to apply these kinds of ideas to large-scale image matching and (implicit) location recognition from Internet photo collections taken under a wide variety of viewing conditions.

The main difficulty in location recognition is in dealing with the extremely large community (user-generated) photo collections on Web sites such as Flickr (Philbin, Chum, Isard *et al.* 2007; Chum, Philbin, Sivic *et al.* 2007; Philbin, Chum, Sivic *et al.* 2008; Turcot and Lowe 2009) or commercially captured databases (Schindler, Brown, and Szeliski 2007). The prevalence of commonly appearing elements such as foliage, signs, and common architectural elements further complicates the task. Figure 14.31 shows some results on location recognition from community photo collections, while Figure 14.32 shows sample results from denser commercially acquired datasets. In the latter case, the overlap between adjacent database images can be used to verify and prune potential matches using "temporal" filtering, i.e., requiring the query image to match nearby overlapping database images before accepting the match.

Another variant on location recognition is the automatic discovery of *landmarks*, i.e.,

(a)   (b)   (c)

Figure 14.32 Feature-based location recognition (Schindler, Brown, and Szeliski 2007) © 2007 IEEE: (a) three typical series of overlapping street photos; (b) handheld camera shots and (c) their corresponding database photos.

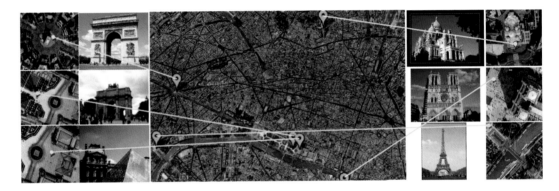

Figure 14.33 Automatic mining, annotation, and localization of community photo collections (Quack, Leibe, and Van Gool 2008) © 2008 ACM. This figure does not show the textual annotations or corresponding Wikipedia entries, which are also discovered.

frequently photographed objects and locations. Simon, Snavely, and Seitz (2007) show how these kinds of objects can be discovered simply by analyzing the matching graph constructed as part of the 3D modeling process in Photo Tourism. More recent work has extended this approach to larger data sets using efficient clustering techniques (Philbin and Zisserman 2008; Li, Wu, Zach *et al.* 2008; Chum, Philbin, and Zisserman 2008; Chum and Matas 2010) as well as combining meta-data such as GPS and textual tags with visual search (Quack, Leibe, and Van Gool 2008; Crandall, Backstrom, Huttenlocher *et al.* 2009), as shown in Figure 14.33. It is now even possible to automatically associate object tags with images based on their co-occurrence in multiple loosely tagged images (Simon and Seitz 2008; Gammeter, Bossard, Quack *et al.* 2009).

The concept of organizing the world's photo collections by location has even been recently extended to organizing all of the universe's (astronomical) photos in an application called *astrometry*, http://astrometry.net/. The technique used to match any two star fields is

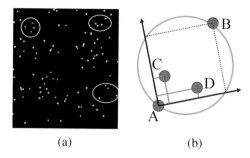

(a)   (b)

Figure 14.34 Locating star fields using astrometry, http://astrometry.net/. (a) Input star field and some selected star quads. (b) The 2D coordinates of stars C and D are encoded relative to the unit square defined by A and B.

to take quadruplets of nearby stars (a pair of stars and another pair inside their diameter) to form a 30-bit *geometric hash* by encoding the relative positions of the second pair of points using the inscribed square as the reference frame, as shown in Figure 14.34. Traditional information retrieval techniques (k-d trees built for different parts of a sky atlas) are then used to find matching quads as potential star field location hypotheses, which can then be verified using a similarity transform.

14.4 Category recognition

While instance recognition techniques are relatively mature and are used in commercial applications, such as Photosynth (Section 13.1.2), generic category (class) recognition is still a largely unsolved problem. Consider for example the set of photographs in Figure 14.35, which shows objects taken from 10 different visual categories. (I'll leave it up to you to name each of the categories.) How would you go about writing a program to categorize each of these images into the appropriate class, especially if you were also given the choice "none of the above"?

As you can tell from this example, visual category recognition is an *extremely* challenging problem; no one has yet constructed a system that approaches the performance level of a two-year-old child. However, the progress in the field has been quite dramatic, if judged by how much better today's algorithms are compared to those of a decade ago.

Figure 14.54 shows a sample image from each of the 20 categories used in the 2008 PASCAL Visual Object Classes Challenge. The yellow boxes represent the extent of each of the objects found in a given image. On such *closed world* collections where the task is to decide among 20 categories, today's classification algorithms can do remarkably well.

In this section, we look at a number of approaches to solving category recognition. While historically, *part-based* representations and recognition algorithms (Section 14.4.2) were the preferred approach (Fischler and Elschlager 1973; Felzenszwalb and Huttenlocher 2005; Fergus, Perona, and Zisserman 2007), we begin by describing simpler *bag-of-features* approaches (Section 14.4.1) that represent objects and images as unordered collections of feature descriptors. We then look at the problem of simultaneously segmenting images while recognizing objects (Section 14.4.3) and also present some applications of such techniques to photo manipulation (Section 14.4.4). In Section 14.5, we look at how context and scene un-

Figure 14.35 Sample images from the Xerox 10 class dataset (Csurka, Dance, Perronnin *et al.* 2006) © 2007 Springer. Imagine trying to write a program to distinguish such images from other photographs.

derstanding, as well as machine learning, can improve overall recognition results. Additional details on the techniques presented in this section can be found in (Pinz 2005; Ponce, Hebert, Schmid *et al.* 2006; Dickinson, Leonardis, Schiele *et al.* 2007; Fei-Fei, Fergus, and Torralba 2009).

14.4.1 Bag of words

One of the simplest algorithms for category recognition is the *bag of words* (also known as *bag of features* or *bag of keypoints*) approach (Csurka, Dance, Fan *et al.* 2004; Lazebnik, Schmid, and Ponce 2006; Csurka, Dance, Perronnin *et al.* 2006; Zhang, Marszalek, Lazebnik *et al.* 2007). As shown in Figure 14.36, this algorithm simply computes the distribution (histogram) of visual words found in the query image and compares this distribution to those found in the training images. We have already seen elements of this approach in Section 14.3.2, Equations (14.33–14.35) and Algorithm 14.2. The biggest difference from instance recognition is the absence of a geometric verification stage (Section 14.3.1), since individual instances of generic visual categories, such as those shown in Figure 14.35, have relatively little spatial coherence to their features (but see the work by Lazebnik, Schmid, and Ponce (2006)).

Csurka, Dance, Fan *et al.* (2004) were the first to use the term *bag of keypoints* to describe such approaches and among the first to demonstrate the utility of frequency-based techniques for category recognition. Their original system used affine covariant regions and SIFT de-

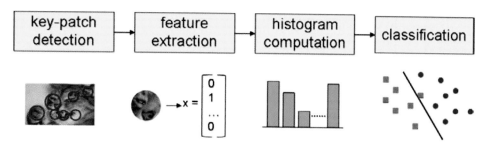

Figure 14.36 A typical processing pipeline for a bag-of-words category recognition system (Csurka, Dance, Perronnin *et al.* 2006) © 2007 Springer. Features are first extracted at keypoints and then quantized to get a distribution (histogram) over the learned *visual words* (feature cluster centers). The feature distribution histogram is used to learn a decision surface using a classification algorithm, such as a support vector machine.

scriptors, k-means visual vocabulary construction, and both a naïve Bayesian classifier and support vector machines for classification. (The latter was found to perform better.) Their newer system (Csurka, Dance, Perronnin *et al.* 2006) uses regular (non-affine) SIFT patches, boosting instead of SVMs, and incorporates a small amount of geometric consistency information.

Zhang, Marszalek, Lazebnik *et al.* (2007) perform a more detailed study of such bag of features systems. They compare a number of feature detectors (Harris–Laplace (Mikolajczyk and Schmid 2004) and Laplacian (Lindeberg 1998b)), descriptors (SIFT, RIFT, and SPIN (Lazebnik, Schmid, and Ponce 2005)), and SVM kernel functions. To estimate distances for the kernel function, they form an *image signature*

$$S = ((t_1, \boldsymbol{m}_1), \ldots, (t_m, \boldsymbol{m}_m)), \tag{14.36}$$

analogous to the *tf-idf* vector $\boldsymbol{t}$ in (14.34), where the cluster centers $\boldsymbol{m}_i$ are made explicit. They then investigate two different kernels for comparing such image signatures. The first is the *earth mover's distance* (EMD) (Rubner, Tomasi, and Guibas 2000),

$$EMD(S, S') = \frac{\sum_i \sum_j f_{ij} d(\boldsymbol{m}_i, \boldsymbol{m}'_j)}{\sum_i \sum_j f_{ij}}, \tag{14.37}$$

where f_{ij} is a *flow* value that can be computed using a linear program and $d(\boldsymbol{m}_i, \boldsymbol{m}'_j)$ is the *ground distance* (Euclidean distance) between $\boldsymbol{m}_i$ and $\boldsymbol{m}'_j$. Note that the EMD can be used to compare two signatures of different lengths, where the entries do not need to correspond. The second is a χ^2 distance

$$\chi^2(S, S') = \frac{1}{2} \sum_i \frac{(t_i - t'_i)^2}{t_i + t'_i}, \tag{14.38}$$

which measures the likelihood that the two signatures were generated from consistent random processes. These distance metrics are then converted into SVM kernels using a generalized Gaussian kernel

$$K(S, S') = \exp\left(-\frac{1}{A} D(S, S')\right), \tag{14.39}$$

where A is a scaling parameter set to the mean distance between training images. In their experiments, they find that the EMD works best for visual category recognition and the χ^2 measure is best for texture recognition.

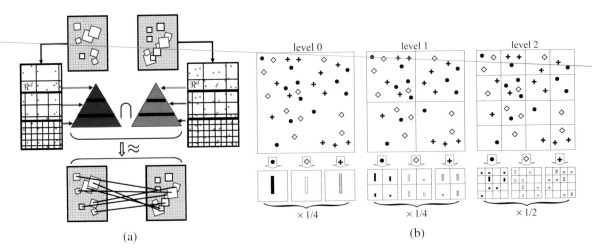

level 0   level 1   level 2

×1/4   ×1/4   ×1/2

(a)   (b)

Figure 14.37 Comparing collections of feature vectors using pyramid matching. (a) The feature-space pyramid match kernel (Grauman and Darrell 2007b) constructs a pyramid in high-dimensional feature space and uses it to compute distances (and implicit correspondences) between sets of feature vectors. (b) Spatial pyramid matching (Lazebnik, Schmid, and Ponce 2006) © 2006 IEEE divides the image into a pyramid of pooling regions and computes separate visual word histograms (distributions) inside each spatial bin.

Instead of quantizing feature vectors to visual words, Grauman and Darrell (2007b) develop a technique for directly computing an approximate distance between two variably sized collections of feature vectors. Their approach is to bin the feature vectors into a multi-resolution pyramid defined in feature space (Figure 14.37a) and count the number of features that land in corresponding bins B_{il} and B'_{il} (Figure 14.38a–c). The distance between the two sets of feature vectors (which can be thought of as points in a high-dimensional space) is computed using histogram intersection between corresponding bins

$$C_l = \sum_i \min(B_{il}, B'_{il}) \tag{14.40}$$

(Figure 14.38d). These per-level counts are then summed up in a weighted fashion

$$D_\Delta = \sum_l w_l N_l \quad \text{with} \quad N_l = C_l - C_{l-1} \quad \text{and} \quad w_l = \frac{1}{d2^l} \tag{14.41}$$

(Figure 14.38e), which discounts matches already found at finer levels while weighting finer matches more heavily. (d is the dimension of the embedding space, i.e., the length of the feature vectors.) In follow-on work, Grauman and Darrell (2007a) show how an explicit construction of the pyramid can be avoided using hashing techniques.

Inspired by this work, Lazebnik, Schmid, and Ponce (2006) show how a similar idea can be employed to augment bags of keypoints with loose notions of 2D spatial location analogous to the pooling performed by SIFT (Lowe 2004) and "gist" (Torralba, Murphy, Freeman et al. 2003). In their work, they extract affine region descriptors (Lazebnik, Schmid, and Ponce 2005) and quantize them into visual words. (Based on previous results by Fei-Fei and Perona (2005), the feature descriptors are extracted densely (on a regular grid) over the image, which can be helpful in describing textureless regions such as the sky.) They then form

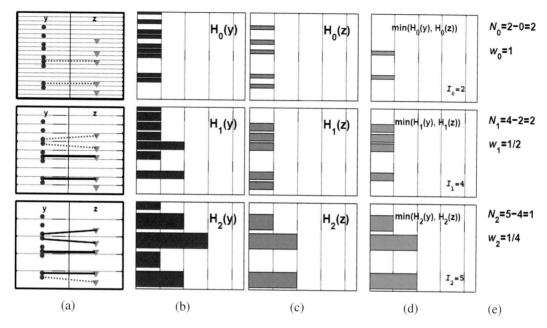

Figure 14.38 A one-dimensional illustration of comparing collections of feature vectors using the pyramid match kernel (Grauman and Darrell 2007b): (a) distribution of feature vectors (point sets) into the pyramidal bins; (b–c) histogram of point counts in bins B_{il} and B'_{il} for the two images; (d) histogram intersections (minimum values); (e) per-level similarity scores, which are weighted and summed to form the final distance/similarity metric.

a spatial pyramid of bins containing word counts (histograms), as shown in Figure 14.37b, and use a similar pyramid match kernel to combine histogram intersection counts in a hierarchical fashion.

The debate about whether to use quantized feature descriptors or continuous descriptors and also whether to use sparse or dense features continues to this day. Boiman, Shechtman, and Irani (2008) show that if query images are compared to *all* the features representing a given class, rather than just each class image individually, nearest-neighbor matching followed by a naïve Bayes classifier outperforms quantized visual words (Figure 14.39). Instead of using generic feature detectors and descriptors, some authors have been investigating *learning* class-specific features (Ferencz, Learned-Miller, and Malik 2008), often using randomized forests (Philbin, Chum, Isard *et al.* 2007; Moosmann, Nowak, and Jurie 2008; Shotton, Johnson, and Cipolla 2008) or combining the feature generation and image classification stages (Yang, Jin, Sukthankar *et al.* 2008). Others, such as Serre, Wolf, and Poggio (2005) and Mutch and Lowe (2008) use hierarchies of dense feature transforms inspired by biological (visual cortical) processing combined with SVMs for final classification.

14.4.2 Part-based models

Recognizing an object by finding its constituent parts and measuring their geometric relationships is one of the oldest approaches to object recognition (Fischler and Elschlager 1973; Kanade 1977; Yuille 1991). We have already seen examples of part-based approaches being used for face recognition (Figure 14.18) (Moghaddam and Pentland 1997; Heisele, Ho, Wu

Figure 14.39 "Image-to-Image" vs. "Image-to-Class" distance comparison (Boiman, Shechtman, and Irani 2008) © 2008 IEEE. The query image on the upper left may not match the feature distribution of any of the database images in the bottom row. However, if each feature in the query is matched to its closest analog in *all* the class images, a good match can be found.

et al. 2003; Heisele, Serre, and Poggio 2007) and pedestrian detection (Figure 14.9) (Felzenszwalb, McAllester, and Ramanan 2008).

In this section, we look more closely at some of the central issues in part-based recognition, namely, the representation of geometric relationships, the representation of individual parts, and algorithms for learning such descriptions and recognizing them at run time. More details on part-based models for recognition can be found in the course notes of Fergus (2007b, 2009).

The earliest approaches to representing geometric relationships were dubbed *pictorial structures* by Fischler and Elschlager (1973) and consisted of spring-like connections between different feature locations (Figure 14.1a). To fit a pictorial structure to an image, an energy function of the form

$$E = \sum_i V_i(\boldsymbol{l}_i) + \sum_{ij \in E} V_{ij}(\boldsymbol{l}_i, \boldsymbol{l}_j) \qquad (14.42)$$

is minimized over all potential part locations or poses $\{\boldsymbol{l}_i\}$ and pairs of parts (i, j) for which an edge (geometric relationship) exists in E. Note how this energy is closely related to that used with Markov random fields (3.108–3.109), which can be used to embed pictorial structures in a probabilistic framework that makes parameter learning easier (Felzenszwalb and Huttenlocher 2005).

Part-based models can have different topologies for the geometric connections between the parts (Figure 14.41). For example, Felzenszwalb and Huttenlocher (2005) restrict the connections to a tree (Figure 14.41d), which makes learning and inference more tractable. A tree topology enables the use of a recursive Viterbi (dynamic programming) algorithm (Pearl 1988; Bishop 2006), in which leaf nodes are first optimized as a function of their parents, and the resulting values are then plugged in and eliminated from the energy function—see Appendix B.5.2. The Viterbi algorithm computes an optimal match in $O(N^2|E| + NP)$ time,

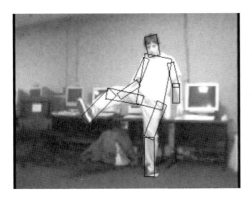

Figure 14.40 Using pictorial structures to locate and track a person (Felzenszwalb and Huttenlocher 2005) © 2005 Springer. The structure consists of articulated rectangular body parts (torso, head, and limbs) connected in a tree topology that encodes relative part positions and orientations. To fit a pictorial structure model, a binary silhouette image is first computed using background subtraction.

where N is the number of potential locations or poses for each part, $|E|$ is the number of edges (pairwise constraints), and $P = |V|$ is the number of parts (vertices in the graphical model, which is equal to $|E| + 1$ in a tree). To further increase the efficiency of the inference algorithm, Felzenszwalb and Huttenlocher (2005) restrict the pairwise energy functions $V_{ij}(l_i, l_j)$ to be Mahalanobis distances on functions of location variables and then use fast distance transform algorithms to minimize each pairwise interaction in time that is closer to linear in N.

Figure 14.40 shows the results of using their pictorial structures algorithm to fit an articulated body model to a binary image obtained by background segmentation. In this application of pictorial structures, parts are parameterized by the locations, sizes, and orientations of their approximating rectangles. Unary matching potentials $V_i(l_i)$ are determined by counting the percentage of foreground and background pixels inside and just outside the tilted rectangle representing each part.

Over the last decade, a large number of different graphical models have been proposed for part-based recognition, as shown in Figure 14.41. Carneiro and Lowe (2006) discuss a number of these models and propose one of their own, which they call a *sparse flexible model*; it involves ordering the parts and having each part's location depend on at most k of its ancestor locations.

The simplest models, which we saw in Section 14.4.1, are bags of words, where there are no geometric relationships between different parts or features. While such models can be very efficient, they have a very limited capacity to express the spatial arrangement of parts. Trees and stars (a special case of trees where all leaf nodes are directly connected to a common root) are the most efficient in terms of inference and hence also learning (Felzenszwalb and Huttenlocher 2005; Fergus, Perona, and Zisserman 2005; Felzenszwalb, McAllester, and Ramanan 2008). Directed acyclic graphs (Figure 14.41f–g) come next in terms of complexity and can still support efficient inference, although at the cost of imposing a causal structure on the part model (Bouchard and Triggs 2005; Carneiro and Lowe 2006). k-fans, in which a clique of size k forms the root of a star-shaped model (Figure 14.41c) have inference complexity $O(N^{k+1})$, although with distance transforms and Gaussian priors, this can be lowered to

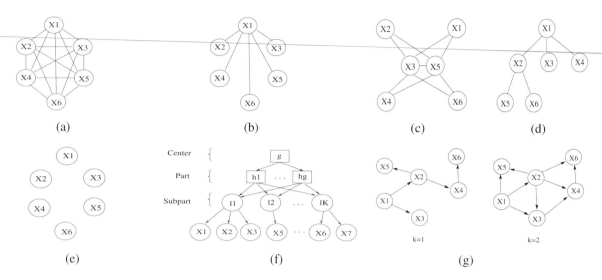

Figure 14.41 Graphical models for geometric spatial priors (Carneiro and Lowe 2006) © 2006 Springer: (a) constellation (Fergus, Perona, and Zisserman 2007); (b) star (Crandall, Felzenszwalb, and Huttenlocher 2005; Fergus, Perona, and Zisserman 2005); (c) k-fan ($k = 2$) (Crandall, Felzenszwalb, and Huttenlocher 2005); (d) tree (Felzenszwalb and Huttenlocher 2005); (e) bag of features (Csurka, Dance, Fan *et al.* 2004); (f) hierarchy (Bouchard and Triggs 2005); (g) sparse flexible model (Carneiro and Lowe 2006).

$O(N^k)$ (Crandall, Felzenszwalb, and Huttenlocher 2005; Crandall and Huttenlocher 2006). Finally, fully connected *constellation* models (Figure 14.41a) are the most general, but the assignment of features to parts becomes intractable for moderate numbers of parts P, since the complexity of such an assignment is $O(N^P)$ (Fergus, Perona, and Zisserman 2007).

The original constellation model was developed by Burl, Weber, and Perona (1998) and consists of a number of parts whose relative positions are encoded by their mean locations and a full covariance matrix, which is used to denote not only positional uncertainty but also potential correlations (covariance) between different parts (Figure 14.42a). Weber, Welling, and Perona (2000) extended this technique to a weakly supervised setting, where both the appearance of each part and its locations are automatically learned given only whole image labels. Fergus, Perona, and Zisserman (2007) further extend this approach to simultaneous learning of appearance and shape models from scale-invariant keypoint detections.

Figure 14.42a shows the shape model learned for the motorcycle class. The top figure shows the mean relative locations for each part along with their position covariances (inter-part covariances are not shown) and likelihood of occurrence. The bottom curve shows the Gaussian PDFs for the relative log-scale of each part with respect to the "landmark" feature. Figure 14.42b shows the appearance model learned for each part, visualized as the patches around detected features in the training database that best match the appearance model. Figure 14.42c shows the features detected in the test database (pink dots) along with the corresponding parts that they were assigned to (colored circles). As you can see, the system has successfully learned and then used a fairly complex model of motorcycle appearance.

The part-based approach to recognition has also been extended to learning new categories from small numbers of examples, building on recognition components developed for other classes (Fei-Fei, Fergus, and Perona 2006). More complex hierarchical part-based models can

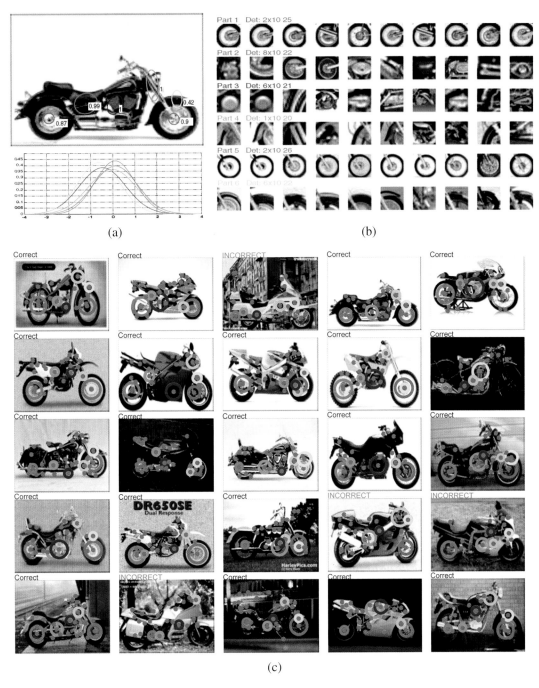

Figure 14.42 Part-based recognition (Fergus, Perona, and Zisserman 2007) © 2007 Springer: (a) locations and covariance ellipses for each part, along with their occurrence probabilities (top) and relative log-scale densities (bottom); (b) part examples drawn from the training images that best match the average appearance; (c) recognition results for the motorcycle class, showing detected features (pink dots) and parts (colored circles).

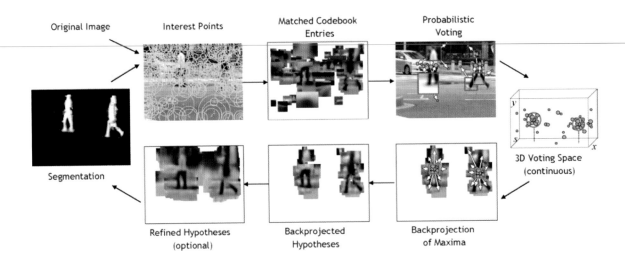

Figure 14.43 Interleaved recognition and segmentation (Leibe, Leonardis, and Schiele 2008) © 2008 Springer. The process starts by re-recognizing visual words (codebook entries) in a new image (scene) and having each part vote for likely locations and size in a 3D (x, y, s) voting space (top row). Once a maximum has been found, the parts (features) corresponding to this instance are determined by *backprojecting* the contributing votes. The foreground–background segmentation for each object can be found by backprojecting probabilistic masks associated with each codebook entry. The whole recognition and segmentation process can then be repeated.

be developed using the concept of grammars (Bouchard and Triggs 2005; Zhu and Mumford 2006). A simpler way to use parts is to have keypoints that are recognized as being part of a class vote for the estimated part locations, as shown in the top row of Figure 14.43 (Leibe, Leonardis, and Schiele 2008). (Implicitly, this corresponds to having a star-shaped geometric model.)

14.4.3 Recognition with segmentation

The most challenging version of generic object recognition is to simultaneously perform recognition with accurate boundary segmentation (Fergus 2007a). For instance recognition (Section 14.3.1), this can sometimes be achieved by backprojecting the object model into the scene (Lowe 2004), as shown in Figure 14.1d, or matching portions of the new scene to pre-learned (segmented) object models (Ferrari, Tuytelaars, and Van Gool 2006b; Kannala, Rahtu, Brandt *et al.* 2008).

For more complex (flexible) object models, such as those for humans Figure 14.1f, a different approach is to pre-segment the image into larger or smaller pieces (Chapter 5) and then match such pieces to portions of the model (Mori, Ren, Efros *et al.* 2004; Mori 2005; He, Zemel, and Ray 2006; Gu, Lim, Arbelaez *et al.* 2009).

An alternative approach by Leibe, Leonardis, and Schiele (2008), which we introduced in the previous section, votes for potential object locations and scales based on the detection of features corresponding to pre-clustered visual codebook entries (Figure 14.43). To support segmentation, each codebook entry has an associated foreground–background mask, which is learned as part of the codebook clustering process from pre-labeled object segmentation masks. During recognition, once a maximum in the voting space is found, the masks associated with the entries that voted for this instance are combined to obtain an object segmentation, as shown on the left side of Figure 14.43.

A more holistic approach to recognition and segmentation is to formulate the problem as one of labeling every pixel in an image with its class membership, and to solve this problem using energy minimization or Bayesian inference techniques, i.e., conditional random fields (Section 3.7.2, (3.118)) (Kumar and Hebert 2006; He, Zemel, and Carreira-Perpiñán 2004). The TextonBoost system of Shotton, Winn, Rother *et al.* (2009) uses unary (pixelwise) potentials based on image-specific color distributions (Section 5.5) (Boykov and Jolly 2001; Rother, Kolmogorov, and Blake 2004), location information (e.g., foreground objects are more likely to be in the middle of the image, sky is likely to be higher, and road is likely to be lower), and novel texture-layout classifiers trained using shared boosting. It also uses traditional pairwise potentials that look at image color gradients (Veksler 2001; Boykov and Jolly 2001; Rother, Kolmogorov, and Blake 2004). The texton-layout features first filter the image with a series of 17 oriented filter banks and then cluster the responses to classify each pixel into 30 different texton classes (Malik, Belongie, Leung *et al.* 2001). The responses are then filtered using offset rectangular regions trained with joint boosting (Viola and Jones 2004) to produce the texton-layout features used as unary potentials.

Figure 14.44a shows some examples of images successfully labeled and segmented using TextonBoost, while Figure 14.44b shows examples where it does not do as well. As you can see, this kind of semantic labeling can be extremely challenging.

The TextonBoost conditional random field framework has been extended to LayoutCRFs by Winn and Shotton (2006), who incorporate additional constraints to recognize multiple object instances and deal with occlusions (Figure 14.45), and even more recently by Hoiem, Rother, and Winn (2007) to incorporate full 3D models.

Conditional random fields continue to be widely used and extended for simultaneous recognition and segmentation applications (Kumar and Hebert 2006; He, Zemel, and Ray 2006; Levin and Weiss 2006; Verbeek and Triggs 2007; Yang, Meer, and Foran 2007; Rabinovich, Vedaldi, Galleguillos *et al.* 2007; Batra, Sukthankar, and Chen 2008; Larlus and Jurie 2008; He and Zemel 2008; Kumar, Torr, and Zisserman 2010), producing some of the best results on the difficult PASCAL VOC segmentation challenge (Shotton, Johnson, and Cipolla 2008; Kohli, Ladický, and Torr 2009). Approaches that first segment the image into unique or multiple segmentations (Borenstein and Ullman 2008; He, Zemel, and Ray 2006; Russell, Efros, Sivic *et al.* 2006) (potentially combined with CRF models) also do quite well: Csurka and Perronnin (2008) have one of the top algorithms in the VOC segmentation challenge. Hierarchical (multi-scale) and grammar (parsing) models are also sometimes used (Tu, Chen, Yuille *et al.* 2005; Zhu, Chen, Lin *et al.* 2008).

14.4.4 *Application*: Intelligent photo editing

Recent advances in object recognition and scene understanding have greatly increased the power of intelligent (semi-automated) photo editing applications. One example is the Photo Clip Art system of Lalonde, Hoiem, Efros *et al.* (2007), which recognizes and segments objects of interest, such as pedestrians, in Internet photo collections and then allows users to paste them into their own photos. Another is the scene completion system of Hays and Efros (2007), which tackles the same *inpainting* problem we studied in Section 10.5. Given an image in which we wish to erase and fill in a large section (Figure 14.46a–b), where do you

(a)

(b)

Figure 14.44 Simultaneous recognition and segmentation using TextonBoost (Shotton, Winn, Rother *et al.* 2009) © 2009 Springer: (a) successful recognition results; (b) less successful results.

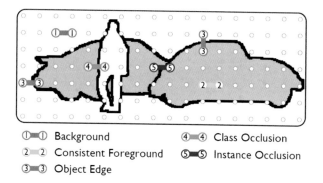

①■① Background	④■④ Class Occlusion
②■② Consistent Foreground	⑤■⑤ Instance Occlusion
③■③ Object Edge	

Figure 14.45 Layout consistent random field (Winn and Shotton 2006) © 2006 IEEE. The numbers indicate the kind of neighborhood relations that can exist between pixels assigned to the same or different classes. Each pairwise relationship carries its own likelihood (energy penalty).

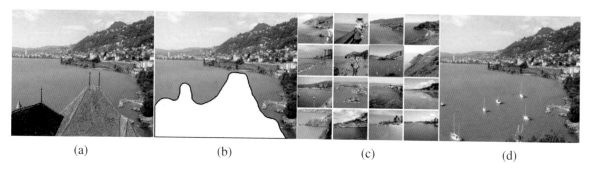

(a)   (b)   (c)   (d)

Figure 14.46 Scene completion using millions of photographs (Hays and Efros 2007) © 2007 ACM: (a) original image; (b) after unwanted foreground removal; (c) plausible scene matches, with the one the user selected highlighted in red; (d) output image after replacement and blending.

get the pixels to fill in the gaps in the edited image? Traditional approaches either use smooth continuation (Bertalmio, Sapiro, Caselles *et al.* 2000) or borrowing pixels from other parts of the image (Efros and Leung 1999; Criminisi, Pérez, and Toyama 2004; Efros and Freeman 2001). With the advent of huge repositories of images on the Web (a topic we return to in Section 14.5.1), it often makes more sense to find a *different* image to serve as the source of the missing pixels.

In their system, Hays and Efros (2007) compute the *gist* of each image (Oliva and Torralba 2001; Torralba, Murphy, Freeman *et al.* 2003) to find images with similar colors and composition. They then run a graph cut algorithm that minimizes image gradient differences and composite the new replacement piece into the original image using Poisson image blending (Section 9.3.4) (Pérez, Gangnet, and Blake 2003). Figure 14.46d shows the resulting image with the erased foreground rooftops region replaced with sailboats.

A different application of image recognition and segmentation is to infer 3D structure from a single photo by recognizing certain scene structures. For example, Criminisi, Reid, and Zisserman (2000) detect vanishing points and have the user draw basic structures, such as walls, in order infer the 3D geometry (Section 6.3.3). Hoiem, Efros, and Hebert (2005a) on the other hand, work with more "organic" scenes such as the one shown in Figure 14.47.

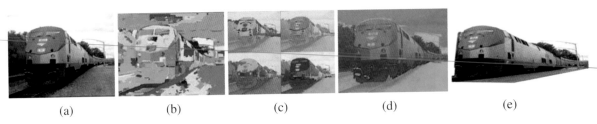

(a)   (b)   (c)   (d)   (e)

Figure 14.47   Automatic photo pop-up (Hoiem, Efros, and Hebert 2005a) © 2005 ACM: (a) input image; (b) superpixels are grouped into (c) multiple regions; (d) labelings indicating ground (green), vertical (red), and sky (blue); (e) novel view of resulting piecewise-planar 3D model.

Their system uses a variety of classifiers and statistics learned from labeled images to classify each pixel as either ground, vertical, or sky (Figure 14.47d). To do this, they begin by computing superpixels (Figure 14.47b) and then group them into plausible regions that are likely to share similar geometric labels (Figure 14.47c). After all the pixels have been labeled, the boundaries between the vertical and ground pixels can be used to infer 3D lines along which the image can be folded into a "pop-up" (after removing the sky pixels), as shown in Figure 14.47e. In related work, Saxena, Sun, and Ng (2009) develop a system that directly infers the depth and orientation of each pixel instead of using just three geometric class labels.

Face detection and localization can also be used in a variety of photo editing applications (in addition to being used in-camera to provide better focus, exposure, and flash settings). Zanella and Fuentes (2004) use active shape models (Section 14.2.2) to register facial features for creating automated morphs. Rother, Bordeaux, Hamadi *et al.* (2006) use face and sky detection to determine regions of interest in order to decide which pieces from a collection of images to stitch into a collage. Bitouk, Kumar, Dhillon *et al.* (2008) describe a system that matches a given face image to a large collection of Internet face images, which can then be used (with careful relighting algorithms) to replace the face in the original image. Applications they describe include de-identification and getting the best possible smile from everyone in a "burst mode" group shot. Leyvand, Cohen-Or, Dror *et al.* (2008) show how accurately locating facial features using an active shape model (Cootes, Edwards, and Taylor 2001; Zhou, Gu, and Zhang 2003) can be used to warp such features (and hence the image) towards configurations resembling those found in images whose facial attractiveness was highly rated, thereby "beautifying" the image without completely losing a person's identity.

Most of these techniques rely either on a set of labeled training images, which is an essential component of all learning techniques, or the even more recent explosion in images available on the Internet. The assumption in some of this work (and in recognition systems based on such very large databases (Section 14.5.1)) is that as the collection of accessible (and potentially partially labeled) images gets larger, finding a close match gets easier. As Hays and Efros (2007) state in their abstract "Our chief insight is that while the space of images is effectively infinite, the space of semantically differentiable scenes is actually not that large." In an interesting commentary on their paper, Levoy (2008) disputes this assertion, claiming that "features in natural scenes form a heavy-tailed distribution, meaning that while some features in photographs are more common than others, the relative occurrence of less common features drops slowly. In other words, there are many unusual photographs in the world." He does, however agree that in computational photography, as in many other applications such

(a)   (b)   (c)   (d)   (e)

Figure 14.48 The importance of context (images courtesy of Antonio Torralba). Can you name all of the objects in images (a–b), especially those that are circled in (c–d). Look carefully at the circled objects. Did you notice that they all have the same shape (after being rotated), as shown in column (e)?

as speech recognition, synthesis, and translation, "simple machine learning algorithms often outperform more sophisticated ones if trained on large enough databases." He also goes on to point out both the potential advantages of such systems, such as better automatic color balancing, and potential issues and pitfalls with the kind of image fakery that these new approaches enable.

For additional examples of photo editing and computational photography applications enabled by Internet computer vision, please see recent workshops on this topic,[19] as well as the special journal issue (Avidan, Baker, and Shan 2010), and the course on Internet Vision by Tamara Berg (2008).

14.5 Context and scene understanding

Thus far, we have mostly considered the task of recognizing and localizing objects in isolation from that of understanding the scene (context) in which the object occur. This is a severe limitation, as context plays a very important role in human object recognition (Oliva and Torralba 2007). As we will see in this section, it can greatly improve the performance of object recognition algorithms (Divvala, Hoiem, Hays *et al.* 2009), as well as providing useful semantic clues for general scene understanding (Torralba 2008).

Consider the two photographs in Figure 14.48a–b. Can you name all of the objects, especially those circled in images (c–d)? Now have a closer look at the circled objects. Do see any similarity in their shapes? In fact, if you rotate them by $90°$, they are all the same as the "blob" shown in Figure 14.48e. So much for our ability to recognize object by their shape! Another (perhaps more artificial) example of recognition in context is shown in Figure 14.49. Try to name all of the letters and numbers, and then see if you guessed right.

Even though we have not addressed context explicitly earlier in this chapter, we have already seen several instances of this general idea being used. A simple way to incorporate spatial information into a recognition algorithm is to compute feature statistics over different regions, as in the spatial pyramid system of Lazebnik, Schmid, and Ponce (2006). Part-based models (Section 14.4.2, Figures 14.40–14.43), use a kind of local context, where various parts need to be arranged in a proper geometric relationship to constitute an object.

---

[19] http://www.internetvisioner.org/.

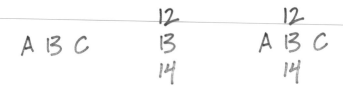

Figure 14.49 More examples of context: read the letters in the first group, the numbers in the second, and the letters and numbers in the third. (Images courtesy of Antonio Torralba.)

The biggest difference between part-based and context models is that the latter combine objects into scenes and the number of constituent objects from each class is not known in advance. In fact, it is possible to combine part-based and context models into the same recognition architecture (Murphy, Torralba, and Freeman 2003; Sudderth, Torralba, Freeman *et al.* 2008; Crandall and Huttenlocher 2007).

Consider the street and office scenes shown in Figure 14.50a–b. If we have enough training images with labeled regions, such as buildings, cars, and roads or monitors, keyboards, and mice, we can develop a geometric model for describing their relative positions. Sudderth, Torralba, Freeman *et al.* (2008) develop such a model, which can be thought of as a two-level constellation model. At the top level, the distributions of objects relative to each other (say, buildings with respect to cars) is modeled as a Gaussian (Figure 14.50c, upper right corners). At the bottom level, the distribution of parts (affine covariant features) with respect to the object center is modeled using a mixture of Gaussians (Figure 14.50c, lower two rows). However, since the number of objects in the scene and parts in each object is unknown, a *latent Dirichlet process* (LDP) is used to model object and part creation in a generative framework. The distributions for all of the objects and parts are learned from a large labeled database and then later used during inference (recognition) to label the elements of a scene.

Another example of context is in simultaneous segmentation and recognition (Section 14.4.3) (Figures 14.44–14.45), where the arrangements of various objects in a scene are used as part of the labeling process. Torralba, Murphy, and Freeman (2004) describe a conditional random field where the estimated locations of building and roads influence the detection of cars, and where boosting is used to learn the structure of the CRF. Rabinovich, Vedaldi, Galleguillos *et al.* (2007) use context to improve the results of CRF segmentation by noting that certain adjacencies (relationships) are more likely than others, e.g., a person is more likely to be on a horse than on a dog.

Context also plays an important role in 3D inference from single images (Figure 14.47), using computer vision techniques for labeling pixels as belonging to the ground, vertical surfaces, or sky (Hoiem, Efros, and Hebert 2005a,b). This line of work has been extended to a more holistic approach that simultaneously reasons about object identity, location, surface orientations, occlusions, and camera viewing parameters (Hoiem, Efros, and Hebert 2008a,b).

A number of approaches use the *gist* of a scene (Torralba 2003; Torralba, Murphy, Freeman *et al.* 2003) to determine where instances of particular objects are likely to occur. For example, Murphy, Torralba, and Freeman (2003) train a regressor to predict the vertical loca-

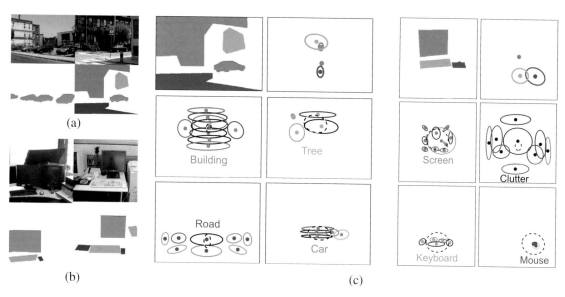

Figure 14.50 Contextual scene models for object recognition (Sudderth, Torralba, Freeman *et al.* 2008) © 2008 Springer: (a) some street scenes and their corresponding labels (magenta = buildings, red = cars, green = trees, blue = road); (b) some office scenes (red = computer screen, green = keyboard, blue = mouse); (c) learned contextual models built from these labeled scenes. The top row shows a sample label image and the distribution of the objects relative to the center red (car or screen) object. The bottom rows show the distributions of parts that make up each object.

tions of objects such as pedestrians, cars, and buildings (or screens and keyboard for indoor office scenes) based on the gist of an image. These location distributions are then used with classic object detectors to improve the performance of the detectors. Gists can also be used to directly match complete images, as we saw in the scene completion work of Hays and Efros (2007).

Finally, some of the most recent work in scene understanding exploits the existence of large numbers of labeled (or even unlabeled) images to perform matching directly against whole images, where the images themselves implicitly encode the expected relationships between objects (Figure 14.51) (Russell, Torralba, Liu *et al.* 2007; Malisiewicz and Efros 2008). We discuss such techniques in the next section, where we look at the influence that large image databases have had on object recognition and scene understanding.

14.5.1 Learning and large image collections

Given how learning techniques are widely used in recognition algorithms, you may wonder whether the topic of learning deserves its own section (or even chapter), or whether it is just part of the basic fabric of all recognition tasks. In fact, trying to build a recognition system without lots of training data for anything other than a basic pattern such as a UPC code has proven to be a dismal failure.

In this chapter, we have already seen lots of techniques borrowed from the machine learning, statistics, and pattern recognition communities. These include principal component, subspace, and discriminant analysis (Section 14.2.1) and more sophisticated discriminative clas-

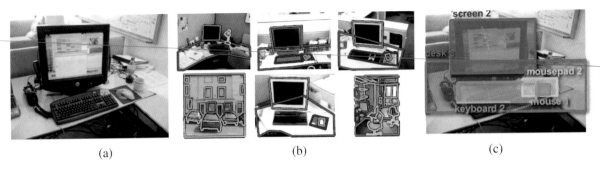

(a)   (b)   (c)

Figure 14.51 Recognition by scene alignment (Russell, Torralba, Liu *et al.* 2007): (a) input image; (b) matched images with similar scene configurations; (c) final labeling of the input image.

sification algorithms such as neural networks, support vector machines, and boosting (Section 14.1.1). Some of the best-performing techniques on challenging recognition benchmarks (Varma and Ray 2007; Felzenszwalb, McAllester, and Ramanan 2008; Fritz and Schiele 2008; Vedaldi, Gulshan, Varma *et al.* 2009) rely heavily on the latest machine learning techniques, whose development is often being driven by challenging vision problems (Freeman, Perona, and Schölkopf 2008).

A distinction sometimes made in the recognition community is between problems where most of the variables of interest (say, parts) are already (partially) labeled and systems that learn more of the problem structure with less supervision (Fergus, Perona, and Zisserman 2007; Fei-Fei, Fergus, and Perona 2006). In fact, recent work by Sivic, Russell, Zisserman *et al.* (2008) has demonstrated the ability to learn visual hierarchies (hierarchies of object parts with related visual appearance) and scene segmentations in a totally unsupervised framework.

Perhaps the most dramatic change in the recognition community has been the appearance of very large databases of training images.[20] Early learning-based algorithms, such as those for face and pedestrian detection (Section 14.1), used relatively few (in the hundreds) labeled examples to train recognition algorithm parameters (say, the thresholds used in boosting). Today, some recognition algorithms use databases such as LabelMe (Russell, Torralba, Murphy *et al.* 2008), which contain tens of thousands of labeled examples.

The existence of such large databases opens up the possibility of matching directly against the training images rather than using them to learn the parameters of recognition algorithms. Russell, Torralba, Liu *et al.* (2007) describe a system where a new image is matched against each of the training images, from which a consensus labeling for the unknown objects in the scene can be inferred, as shown in Figure 14.51. Malisiewicz and Efros (2008) start by over-segmenting each image and then use the LabelMe database to search for similar images and configurations in order to obtain per-pixel category labelings. It is also possible to combine feature-based correspondence algorithms with large labeled databases to perform simultaneous recognition and segmentation (Liu, Yuen, and Torralba 2009).

When the database of images becomes large enough, it is even possible to directly match complete images with the expectation of finding a good match. Torralba, Freeman, and Fergus (2008) start with a database of 80 million tiny (32×32) images and compensate for the poor accuracy in their image labels, which are collected automatically from the Internet, by using

---

[20] We have already seen some computational photography applications of such databases in Section 14.4.4.

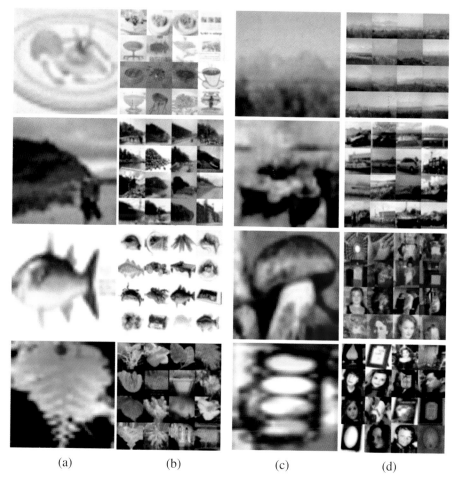

(a)   (b)   (c)   (d)

Figure 14.52 Recognition using tiny images (Torralba, Freeman, and Fergus 2008) © 2008 IEEE: columns (a) and (c) show sample input images and columns (b) and (d) show the corresponding 16 nearest neighbors in the database of 80 million tiny images.

a semantic taxonomy (Wordnet) to infer the most likely labels for a new image. Somewhere in the 80 million images, there are enough examples to associate some set of images with each of the 75,000 non-abstract nouns in Wordnet that they use in their system. Some sample recognition results are shown in Figure 14.52.

Another example of a large labeled database of images is ImageNet (Deng, Dong, Socher *et al.* 2009), which is collecting images for the 80,000 nouns (synonym sets) in WordNet (Fellbaum 1998). As of April 2010, about 500–1000 carefully vetted examples for 14841 synsets have been collected (Figure 14.53). The paper by Deng, Dong, Socher *et al.* (2009) also has a nice review of related databases.

As we mentioned in Section 14.4.3, the existence of large databases of partially labeled Internet imagery has given rise to a new sub-field of Internet computer vision, with its own workshops[21] and a special journal issue (Avidan, Baker, and Shan 2010).

---

[21] http://www.internetvisioner.org/.

Figure 14.53 ImageNet (Deng, Dong, Socher *et al.* 2009) © 2009 IEEE. This database contains over 500 carefully vetted images for each of 14,841 (as of April, 2010) nouns from the WordNet hierarchy.

14.5.2 *Application*: Image search

Even though visual recognition algorithms are by some measures still in their infancy, they are already starting to have some impact on image search, i.e., the retrieval of images from the Web using combinations of keywords and visual similarity. Today, most image search engines rely mostly on textual keywords found in captions, nearby text, and filenames, augmented by user click-through data (Craswell and Szummer 2007). As recognition algorithms continue to improve, however, visual features and visual similarity will start being used to recognize images with missing or erroneous keywords.

The topic of searching by visual similarity has a long history and goes by a variety of names, including content-based image retrieval (CBIR) (Smeulders, Worring, Santini *et al.* 2000; Lew, Sebe, Djeraba *et al.* 2006; Vasconcelos 2007; Datta, Joshi, Li *et al.* 2008) and query by image content (QBIC) (Flickner, Sawhney, Niblack *et al.* 1995). Original publications in these fields were based primarily on simple whole-image similarity metrics, such as color and texture (Swain and Ballard 1991; Jacobs, Finkelstein, and Salesin 1995; Manjunathi and Ma 1996).

In more recent work, Fergus, Perona, and Zisserman (2004) use a feature-based learning and recognition algorithm to re-rank the outputs from a traditional keyword-based image search engine. In follow-on work, Fergus, Fei-Fei, Perona *et al.* (2005) cluster the results returned by image search using an extension of probabilistic latest semantic analysis (PLSA) (Hofmann 1999) and then select the clusters associated with the highest ranked results as the representative images for that category.

Even more recent work relies on carefully annotated image databases such as LabelMe (Russell, Torralba, Murphy *et al.* 2008). For example, Malisiewicz and Efros (2008) describe a system that, given a query image, can find similar LabelMe images, whereas Liu, Yuen, and Torralba (2009) combine feature-based correspondence algorithms with the labeled database to perform simultaneous recognition and segmentation.

14.6 Recognition databases and test sets

In addition to rapid advances in machine learning and statistical modeling techniques, one of the key ingredients in the continued improvement of recognition algorithms has been the increased availability and quality of image recognition databases.

Tables 14.1 and 14.2, which are based on similar tables in Fei-Fei, Fergus, and Torralba (2009), updated with more recent entries and URLs, show some of the mostly widely used recognition databases. Some of these databases, such as the ones for face recognition and localization, date back over a decade. The most recent ones, such as the PASCAL database, are refreshed annually with ever more challenging problems. Table 14.1 shows examples of databases used primarily for (whole image) recognition while Table 14.2 shows databases where more accurate localization or segmentation information is available and expected.

Ponce, Berg, Everingham *et al.* (2006) discuss some of the problems with earlier datasets and describe how the latest PASCAL Visual Object Classes Challenge aims to overcome these. Some examples of the 20 visual classes in the 2008 challenge are shown in Figure 14.54. The slides from the VOC workshops,[22] are a great source for pointers to the best recognition techniques currently available.

Two of the most recent trends in recognition databases are the emergence of Web-based annotation and data collection tools, and the use of search and recognition algorithms to build up databases (Ponce, Berg, Everingham *et al.* 2006). Some of the most interesting work in human annotation of images comes from a series of interactive multi-person games such as ESP (von Ahn and Dabbish 2004) and Peekaboom (von Ahn, Liu, and Blum 2006). In these games, people help each other guess the identity of a hidden image by giving textual clues as to its contents, which implicitly labels either the whole image or just regions. A more "serious" volunteer effort is the LabelMe database, in which vision researchers contribute manual polygonal region annotations in return for gaining access to the database (Russell, Torralba, Murphy *et al.* 2008).

The use of computer vision algorithms for collecting recognition databases dates back to the work of Fergus, Fei-Fei, Perona *et al.* (2005), who cluster the results returned by Google image search using an extension of PLSA and then select the clusters associated with the highest ranked results. More recent examples of related techniques include the work of Berg and Forsyth (2006) and Li and Fei-Fei (2010).

Whatever methods are used to collect and validate recognition databases, they will continue to grow in size, utility, and difficulty from year to year. They will also continue to be an essential component of research into the recognition and scene understanding problems, which remain, as always, the grand challenges of computer vision.

14.7 Additional reading

Although there are currently no specialized textbooks on image recognition and scene understanding, some surveys (Pinz 2005) and collections of papers (Ponce, Hebert, Schmid *et al.* 2006; Dickinson, Leonardis, Schiele *et al.* 2007) can be found that describe the latest approaches. Other good sources of recent research are courses on this topic, such as the ICCV

---

[22] http://pascallin.ecs.soton.ac.uk/challenges/VOC/.

Name / URL	Extents	Contents / Reference
Face and person recognition		
Yale face database	Centered face images	Frontal faces
http://www1.cs.columbia.edu/~belhumeur/		Belhumeur, Hespanha, and Kriegman (1997)
Resources for face detection	Various databases	Faces in various poses
http://vision.ai.uiuc.edu/mhyang/face-detection-survey.html		Yang, Kriegman, and Ahuja (2002)
FERET	Centered face images	Frontal faces
http://www.frvt.org/FERET		Phillips, Moon, Rizvi *et al.* (2000)
FRVT	Centered face images	Faces in various poses
http://www.frvt.org/		Phillips, Scruggs, O'Toole *et al.* (2010)
CMU PIE database	Centered face image	Faces in various poses
http://www.ri.cmu.edu/projects/project_418.html		Sim, Baker, and Bsat (2003)
CMU Multi-PIE database	Centered face image	Faces in various poses
http://multipie.org		Gross, Matthews, Cohn *et al.* (2010)
Faces in the Wild	Internet images	Faces in various poses
http://vis-www.cs.umass.edu/lfw/		Huang, Ramesh, Berg *et al.* (2007)
Consumer image person DB	Complete images	People
http://chenlab.ece.cornell.edu/people/Andy/GallagherDataset.html		Gallagher and Chen (2008)
Object recognition		
Caltech 101	Segmentation masks	101 categories
http://www.vision.caltech.edu/Image_Datasets/Caltech101/		Fei-Fei, Fergus, and Perona (2006)
Caltech 256	Centered objects	256 categories and clutter
http://www.vision.caltech.edu/Image_Datasets/Caltech256/		Griffin, Holub, and Perona (2007)
COIL-100	Centered objects	100 instances
http://www1.cs.columbia.edu/CAVE/software/softlib/coil-100.php		Nene, Nayar, and Murase (1996)
ETH-80	Centered objects	8 instances, 10 views
http://www.mis.tu-darmstadt.de/datasets		Leibe and Schiele (2003)
Instance recognition benchmark	Objects in various poses	2550 objects
http://vis.uky.edu/~stewe/ukbench/		Nistér and Stewénius (2006)
Oxford buildings dataset	Pictures of buildings	5062 images
http://www.robots.ox.ac.uk/~vgg/data/oxbuildings/		Philbin, Chum, Isard *et al.* (2007)
NORB	Bounding box	50 toys
http://www.cs.nyu.edu/~ylclab/data/norb-v1.0/		LeCun, Huang, and Bottou (2004)
Tiny images	Complete images	75,000 (Wordnet) things
http://people.csail.mit.edu/torralba/tinyimages/		Torralba, Freeman, and Fergus (2008)
ImageNet	Complete images	14,000 (Wordnet) things
http://www.image-net.org/		Deng, Dong, Socher *et al.* (2009)

Table 14.1 Image databases for recognition, adapted and expanded from Fei-Fei, Fergus, and Torralba (2009).

Name / URL	Extents	Contents / Reference
Object detection / localization		
CMU frontal faces	Patches	Frontal faces
http://vasc.ri.cmu.edu/idb/html/face/frontal_images		Rowley, Baluja, and Kanade (1998a)
MIT frontal faces	Patches	Frontal faces
http://cbcl.mit.edu/software-datasets/FaceData2.html		Sung and Poggio (1998)
CMU face detection databases	Multiple faces	Faces in various poses
http://www.ri.cmu.edu/research_project_detail.html?project_id=419		Schneiderman and Kanade (2004)
UIUC Image DB	Bounding boxes	Cars
http://l2r.cs.uiuc.edu/~cogcomp/Data/Car/		Agarwal and Roth (2002)
Caltech Pedestrian Dataset	Bounding boxes	Pedestrians
http://www.vision.caltech.edu/Image_Datasets/CaltechPedestrians/		Dollàr, Wojek, Schiele *et al.* (2009)
Graz-02 Database	Segmentation masks	Bikes, cars, people
http://www.emt.tugraz.at/~pinz/data/GRAZ_02/		Opelt, Pinz, Fussenegger *et al.* (2006)
ETHZ Toys	Cluttered images	Toys, boxes, magazines
http://www.vision.ee.ethz.ch/~calvin/datasets.html		Ferrari, Tuytelaars, and Van Gool (2006b)
TU Darmstadt DB	Segmentation masks	Motorbikes, cars, cows
http://www.vision.ee.ethz.ch/~bleibe/data/datasets.html		Leibe, Leonardis, and Schiele (2008)
MSR Cambridge	Segmentation masks	23 classes
http://research.microsoft.com/en-us/projects/objectclassrecognition/		Shotton, Winn, Rother *et al.* (2009)
LabelMe dataset	Polygonal boundary	>500 categories
http://labelme.csail.mit.edu/		Russell, Torralba, Murphy *et al.* (2008)
Lotus Hill	Segmentation masks	Scenes and hierarchies
http://www.imageparsing.com/		Yao, Yang, Lin *et al.* (2010)
On-line annotation tools		
ESP game	Image descriptions	Web images
http://www.gwap.com/gwap/		von Ahn and Dabbish (2004)
Peekaboom	Labeled regions	Web images
http://www.gwap.com/gwap/		von Ahn, Liu, and Blum (2006)
LabelMe	Polygonal boundary	High-resolution images
http://labelme.csail.mit.edu/		Russell, Torralba, Murphy *et al.* (2008)
Collections of challenges		
PASCAL	Segmentation, boxes	Various
http://pascallin.ecs.soton.ac.uk/challenges/VOC/		Everingham, Van Gool, Williams *et al.* (2010)

Table 14.2 Image databases for detection and localization, adapted and expanded from Fei-Fei, Fergus, and Torralba (2009).

airplane   bicycle   bird   boat   bottle

bus   car   cat   chair   cow

diningtable   dog   horse   motorbike   person

pottedplant   sheep   sofa   train   tvmonitor

Figure 14.54 Sample images from the PASCAL Visual Object Classes Challenge 2008 (VOC2008) database (Everingham, Van Gool, Williams *et al.* 2008). The original images were obtained from flickr (http://www.flickr.com/) and the database rights are explained on http://pascallin.ecs.soton.ac.uk/challenges/VOC/voc2008/.

2009 short course (Fei-Fei, Fergus, and Torralba 2009) and Antonio Torralba's more comprehensive MIT course (Torralba 2008). The PASCAL VOC Challenge Web site contains workshop slides that summarize today's best performing algorithms.

The literature on face, pedestrian, car, and other object detection is quite extensive. Seminal papers in face detection include those by Osuna, Freund, and Girosi (1997), Sung and Poggio (1998), Rowley, Baluja, and Kanade (1998a), and Viola and Jones (2004), with Yang, Kriegman, and Ahuja (2002) providing a comprehensive survey of early work in this field. More recent examples include (Heisele, Ho, Wu *et al.* 2003; Heisele, Serre, and Poggio 2007).

Early work in pedestrian and car detection was carried out by Gavrila and Philomin (1999), Gavrila (1999), Papageorgiou and Poggio (2000), Mohan, Papageorgiou, and Poggio (2001), and Schneiderman and Kanade (2004). More recent examples include the work of Belongie, Malik, and Puzicha (2002), Mikolajczyk, Schmid, and Zisserman (2004), Dalal and Triggs (2005), Leibe, Seemann, and Schiele (2005), Dalal, Triggs, and Schmid (2006), Opelt, Pinz, and Zisserman (2006), Torralba (2007), Andriluka, Roth, and Schiele (2008), Felzenszwalb, McAllester, and Ramanan (2008), Rogez, Rihan, Ramalingam *et al.* (2008), Andriluka, Roth, and Schiele (2009), Kumar, Zisserman, and H.S.Torr (2009), Dollàr, Belongie, and Perona (2010). and Felzenszwalb, Girshick, McAllester *et al.* (2010).

While some of the earliest approaches to face recognition involved finding the distinctive image features and measuring the distances between them (Fischler and Elschlager 1973; Kanade 1977; Yuille 1991), more recent approaches rely on comparing gray-level images, often projected onto lower dimensional subspaces (Turk and Pentland 1991a; Belhumeur, Hespanha, and Kriegman 1997; Moghaddam and Pentland 1997; Moghaddam, Jebara, and Pentland 2000; Heisele, Ho, Wu *et al.* 2003; Heisele, Serre, and Poggio 2007). Additional details on principal component analysis (PCA) and its Bayesian counterparts can be found in Appendix B.1.1 and books and articles on this topic (Hastie, Tibshirani, and Friedman 2001; Bishop 2006; Roweis 1998; Tipping and Bishop 1999; Leonardis and Bischof 2000; Vidal, Ma, and Sastry 2010). The topics of subspace learning, local distance functions, and metric learning are covered by Cai, He, Hu *et al.* (2007), Frome, Singer, Sha *et al.* (2007), Guillaumin, Verbeek, and Schmid (2009), Ramanan and Baker (2009), and Sivic, Everingham, and Zisserman (2009). An alternative to directly matching gray-level images or patches is to use non-linear local transforms such as local binary patterns (Ahonen, Hadid, and Pietikäinen 2006; Zhao and Pietikäinen 2007; Cao, Yin, Tang *et al.* 2010).

In order to boost the performance of what are essentially 2D appearance-based models, a variety of shape and pose deformation models have been developed (Beymer 1996; Vetter and Poggio 1997), including Active Shape Models (Lanitis, Taylor, and Cootes 1997; Cootes, Cooper, Taylor *et al.* 1995; Davies, Twining, and Taylor 2008), Elastic Bunch Graph Matching (Wiskott, Fellous, Krüger *et al.* 1997), 3D Morphable Models (Blanz and Vetter 1999), and Active Appearance Models (Costen, Cootes, Edwards *et al.* 1999; Cootes, Edwards, and Taylor 2001; Gross, Baker, Matthews *et al.* 2005; Gross, Matthews, and Baker 2006; Matthews, Xiao, and Baker 2007; Liang, Xiao, Wen *et al.* 2008; Ramnath, Koterba, Xiao *et al.* 2008). The topic of head pose estimation, in particular, is covered in a recent survey by Murphy-Chutorian and Trivedi (2009).

Additional information about face recognition can be found in a number of surveys and books on this topic (Chellappa, Wilson, and Sirohey 1995; Zhao, Chellappa, Phillips *et al.* 2003; Li and Jain 2005) as well as on the Face Recognition Web site.[23] Databases for face recognition are discussed by Phillips, Moon, Rizvi *et al.* (2000), Sim, Baker, and Bsat (2003), Gross, Shi, and Cohn (2005), Huang, Ramesh, Berg *et al.* (2007), and Phillips, Scruggs, O'Toole *et al.* (2010).

Algorithms for instance recognition, i.e., the detection of static man-made objects that only vary slightly in appearance but may vary in 3D pose, are mostly based on detecting 2D points of interest and describing them using viewpoint-invariant descriptors (Lowe 2004; Rothganger, Lazebnik, Schmid *et al.* 2006; Ferrari, Tuytelaars, and Van Gool 2006b; Gordon and Lowe 2006; Obdržálek and Matas 2006; Kannala, Rahtu, Brandt *et al.* 2008; Sivic and Zisserman 2009).

As the size of the database being matched increases, it becomes more efficient to quantize the visual descriptors into words (Sivic and Zisserman 2003; Schindler, Brown, and Szeliski 2007; Sivic and Zisserman 2009; Turcot and Lowe 2009), and to then use information-retrieval techniques, such as inverted indices (Nistér and Stewénius 2006; Philbin, Chum, Isard *et al.* 2007; Philbin, Chum, Sivic *et al.* 2008), query expansion (Chum, Philbin, Sivic *et al.* 2007; Agarwal, Snavely, Simon *et al.* 2009), and min hashing (Philbin and Zisserman 2008; Li, Wu, Zach *et al.* 2008; Chum, Philbin, and Zisserman 2008; Chum and Matas 2010) to perform efficient retrieval and clustering.

---

[23] http://www.face-rec.org/.

A number of surveys, collections of papers, and course notes have been written on the topic of category recognition (Pinz 2005; Ponce, Hebert, Schmid *et al.* 2006; Dickinson, Leonardis, Schiele *et al.* 2007; Fei-Fei, Fergus, and Torralba 2009). Some of the seminal papers on the bag of words (bag of keypoints) approach to whole-image category recognition have been written by Csurka, Dance, Fan *et al.* (2004), Lazebnik, Schmid, and Ponce (2006), Csurka, Dance, Perronnin *et al.* (2006), Grauman and Darrell (2007b), and Zhang, Marszalek, Lazebnik *et al.* (2007). Additional and more recent papers in this area include Sivic, Russell, Efros *et al.* (2005), Serre, Wolf, and Poggio (2005), Opelt, Pinz, Fussenegger *et al.* (2006), Grauman and Darrell (2007a), Torralba, Murphy, and Freeman (2007), Boiman, Shechtman, and Irani (2008), Ferencz, Learned-Miller, and Malik (2008), and Mutch and Lowe (2008). It is also possible to recognize objects based on their contours, e.g., using shape contexts (Belongie, Malik, and Puzicha 2002) or other techniques (Jurie and Schmid 2004; Shotton, Blake, and Cipolla 2005; Opelt, Pinz, and Zisserman 2006; Ferrari, Tuytelaars, and Van Gool 2006a).

Many object recognition algorithms use part-based decompositions to provide greater invariance to articulation and pose. Early algorithms focused on the relative positions of the parts (Fischler and Elschlager 1973; Kanade 1977; Yuille 1991) while newer algorithms use more sophisticated models of appearance (Felzenszwalb and Huttenlocher 2005; Fergus, Perona, and Zisserman 2007; Felzenszwalb, McAllester, and Ramanan 2008). Good overviews on part-based models for recognition can be found in the course notes of Fergus 2007b; 2009.

Carneiro and Lowe (2006) discuss a number of graphical models used for part-based recognition, which include trees and stars (Felzenszwalb and Huttenlocher 2005; Fergus, Perona, and Zisserman 2005; Felzenszwalb, McAllester, and Ramanan 2008), k-fans (Crandall, Felzenszwalb, and Huttenlocher 2005; Crandall and Huttenlocher 2006), and constellations (Burl, Weber, and Perona 1998; Weber, Welling, and Perona 2000; Fergus, Perona, and Zisserman 2007). Other techniques that use part-based recognition include those developed by Dorkó and Schmid (2003) and Bar-Hillel, Hertz, and Weinshall (2005).

Combining object recognition with scene segmentation can yield strong benefits. One approach is to pre-segment the image into pieces and then match the pieces to portions of the model (Mori, Ren, Efros *et al.* 2004; Mori 2005; He, Zemel, and Ray 2006; Russell, Efros, Sivic *et al.* 2006; Borenstein and Ullman 2008; Csurka and Perronnin 2008; Gu, Lim, Arbelaez *et al.* 2009). Another is to vote for potential object locations and scales based on object detection (Leibe, Leonardis, and Schiele 2008). One of the currently most popular approaches is to use conditional random fields (Kumar and Hebert 2006; He, Zemel, and Carreira-Perpiñán 2004; He, Zemel, and Ray 2006; Levin and Weiss 2006; Winn and Shotton 2006; Hoiem, Rother, and Winn 2007; Rabinovich, Vedaldi, Galleguillos *et al.* 2007; Verbeek and Triggs 2007; Yang, Meer, and Foran 2007; Batra, Sukthankar, and Chen 2008; Larlus and Jurie 2008; He and Zemel 2008; Shotton, Winn, Rother *et al.* 2009; Kumar, Torr, and Zisserman 2010), which produce some of the best results on the difficult PASCAL VOC segmentation challenge (Shotton, Johnson, and Cipolla 2008; Kohli, Ladický, and Torr 2009).

More and more recognition algorithms are starting to use scene context as part of their recognition strategy. Representative papers in this area include those by Torralba (2003), Torralba, Murphy, Freeman *et al.* (2003), Murphy, Torralba, and Freeman (2003), Torralba, Murphy, and Freeman (2004), Crandall and Huttenlocher (2007), Rabinovich, Vedaldi, Galleguillos *et al.* (2007), Russell, Torralba, Liu *et al.* (2007), Hoiem, Efros, and Hebert (2008a),

Hoiem, Efros, and Hebert (2008b), Sudderth, Torralba, Freeman *et al.* (2008), and Divvala, Hoiem, Hays *et al.* (2009).

Sophisticated machine learning techniques are also becoming a key component of successful object detection and recognition algorithms (Varma and Ray 2007; Felzenszwalb, McAllester, and Ramanan 2008; Fritz and Schiele 2008; Sivic, Russell, Zisserman *et al.* 2008; Vedaldi, Gulshan, Varma *et al.* 2009), as is exploiting large human-labeled databases (Russell, Torralba, Liu *et al.* 2007; Malisiewicz and Efros 2008; Torralba, Freeman, and Fergus 2008; Liu, Yuen, and Torralba 2009). Rough three-dimensional models are also making a comeback for recognition, as evidenced in some recent papers (Savarese and Fei-Fei 2007, 2008; Sun, Su, Savarese *et al.* 2009; Su, Sun, Fei-Fei *et al.* 2009). As always, the latest conferences on computer vision are your best reference for the newest algorithms in this rapidly evolving field.

14.8 Exercises

Ex 14.1: Face detection Build and test one of the face detectors presented in Section 14.1.1.

1. Download one or more of the labeled face detection databases in Table 14.2.

2. Generate your own negative examples by finding photographs that do not contain any people.

3. Implement one of the following face detectors (or devise one of your own):

   - boosting (Algorithm 14.1) based on simple area features, with an optional cascade of detectors (Viola and Jones 2004);

   - PCA face subspace (Moghaddam and Pentland 1997);

   - distances to clustered face and non-face prototypes, followed by a neural network (Sung and Poggio 1998) or SVM (Osuna, Freund, and Girosi 1997) classifier;

   - a multi-resolution neural network trained directly on normalized gray-level patches (Rowley, Baluja, and Kanade 1998a).

4. Test the performance of your detector on the database by evaluating the detector at every location in a sub-octave pyramid. Optionally retrain your detector on false positive examples you get on non-face images.

Ex 14.2: Determining the threshold for AdaBoost Given a set of function evaluations on the training examples x_i, $f_i = f(x_i) \in \pm 1$, training labels $y_i \in \pm 1$, and weights $w_i \in (0, 1)$, as explained in Algorithm 14.1, devise an efficient algorithm to find values of θ and $s = \pm 1$ that maximize

$$\sum_i w_i y_i h(s f_i, \theta), \tag{14.43}$$

where $h(x, \theta) = \text{sign}(x - \theta)$.

Ex 14.3: Face recognition using eigenfaces Collect a set of facial photographs and then build a recognition system to re-recognize the same people.

1. Take several photos of each of your classmates and store them.

2. Align the images by automatically or manually detecting the corners of the eyes and using a similarity transform to stretch and rotate each image to a canonical position.

3. Compute the average image and a PCA subspace for the face images

4. Take a new set of photographs a week later and use them as your test set.

5. Compare each new image to each database image and select the nearest one as the recognized identity. Verify that the distance in PCA space is close to the distance computed with a full SSD (sum of squared difference) measure.

6. (Optional) Compute different principal components for identity and expression, and use them to improve your recognition results.

Ex 14.4: Bayesian face recognition Moghaddam, Jebara, and Pentland (2000) compute separate covariance matrices Σ_I and Σ_E by looking at differences between *all* pairs of images. At run time, they select the *nearest* image to determine the facial identity. Does it make sense to estimate statistics for all pairs of images and use them for testing the distance to the nearest exemplar? Discuss whether this is statistically correct.

How is the all-pair intrapersonal covariance matrix Σ_I related to the within-class scatter matrix S_W? Does a similar relationship hold between Σ_E and S_B?

Ex 14.5: Modular eigenfaces Extend your face recognition system to separately match the eye, nose, and mouth regions, as shown in Figure 14.18.

1. After normalizing face images to a canonical scale and location, manually segment out some of the eye, nose, and face regions.

2. Build separate detectors for these three (or four) kinds of region, either using a subspace (PCA) approach or one of the techniques presented in Section 14.1.1.

3. For each new image to be recognized, first detect the locations of the facial features.

4. Then, match the individual features against your database and note the locations of these features.

5. Train and test a classifier that uses the individual feature matching IDs as well as (optionally) the feature locations to perform face recognition.

Ex 14.6: Recognition-based color balancing Build a system that recognizes the most important color areas in common photographs (sky, grass, skin) and color balances the image accordingly. Some references and ideas for skin detection are given in Exercise 2.8 and by Forsyth and Fleck (1999), Jones and Rehg (2001), Vezhnevets, Sazonov, and Andreeva (2003), and Kakumanu, Makrogiannis, and Bourbakis (2007). These may give you ideas for how to detect other regions or you can try more sophisticated MRF-based approaches (Shotton, Winn, Rother *et al.* 2009).

Ex 14.7: Pedestrian detection Build and test one of the pedestrian detectors presented in Section 14.1.2.

Ex 14.8: Simple instance recognition   Use the feature detection, matching, and alignment algorithms you developed in Exercises 4.1–4.4 and 9.2 to find matching images given a query image or region (Figure 14.26).

Evaluate several feature detectors, descriptors, and robust geometric verification strategies, either on your own or by comparing your results with those of classmates.

Ex 14.9: Large databases and location recognition   Extend the previous exercise to larger databases using quantized visual words and information retrieval techniques, as described in Algorithm 14.2.

Test your algorithm on a large database, such as the one used by Nistér and Stewénius (2006) or Philbin, Chum, Sivic *et al.* (2008), which are listed in Table 14.1. Alternatively, use keyword search on the Web or in a photo sharing site (e.g., for a city) to create your own database.

Ex 14.10: Bag of words   Adapt the feature extraction and matching pipeline developed in Exercise 14.8 to category (class) recognition, using some of the techniques described in Section 14.4.1.

1. Download the training and test images from one or more of the databases listed in Tables 14.1 and 14.2, e.g., Caltech 101, Caltech 256, or PASCAL VOC.

2. Extract features from each of the training images, quantize them, and compute the *tf-idf* vectors (bag of words histograms).

3. As an option, consider not quantizing the features and using pyramid matching (14.40–14.41) (Grauman and Darrell 2007b) or using a spatial pyramid for greater selectivity (Lazebnik, Schmid, and Ponce 2006).

4. Choose a classification algorithm (e.g., nearest neighbor classification or support vector machine) and "train" your recognizer, i.e., build up the appropriate data structures (e.g., k-d trees) or set the appropriate classifier parameters.

5. Test your algorithm on the test data set using the same pipeline you developed in steps 2–4 and compare your results to the best reported results.

6. Explain why your results differ from the previously reported ones and give some ideas for how you could improve your system.

You can find a good synopsis of the best-performing classification algorithms and their approaches in the report of the PASCAL Visual Object Classes Challenge found on their Web site (http://pascallin.ecs.soton.ac.uk/challenges/VOC/).

Ex 14.11: Object detection and localization   Extend the classification algorithm developed in the previous exercise to localize the objects in an image by reporting a bounding box around each detected object. The easiest way to do this is to use a sliding window approach. Some pointers to recent techniques in this area can be found in the workshop associated with the PASCAL VOC 2008 Challenge.

Ex 14.12: Part-based recognition   Choose one or more of the techniques described in Section 14.4.2 and implement a part-based recognition system. Since these techniques are fairly involved, you will need to read several of the research papers in this area, select which general approach you want to follow, and then implement your algorithm. A good starting point could be the paper by Felzenszwalb, McAllester, and Ramanan (2008), since it performed well in the PASCAL VOC 2008 detection challenge.

Ex 14.13: Recognition and segmentation   Choose one or more of the techniques described in Section 14.4.3 and implement a simultaneous recognition and segmentation system. Since these techniques are fairly involved, you will need to read several of the research papers in this area, select which general approach you want to follow, and then implement your algorithm. Test your algorithm on one or more of the segmentation databases in Table 14.2.

Ex 14.14: Context   Implement one or more of the context and scene understanding systems described in Section 14.5 and report on your experience. Does context or whole scene understanding perform better at naming objects than stand-alone systems?

Ex 14.15: Tiny images   Download the tiny images database from http://people.csail.mit.edu/torralba/tinyimages/ and build a classifier based on comparing your test images directly against all of the labeled training images. Does this seem like a promising approach?

Chapter 15

Conclusion

In this book, we have covered a broad range of computer vision topics. Starting with image formation, we have seen how images can be pre-processed to remove noise or blur, segmented into regions, or converted into feature descriptors. Multiple images can be matched and registered, with the results used to estimate motion, track people, reconstruct 3D models, or merge images into more attractive and interesting composites and renderings. Images can also be analyzed to produce semantic descriptions of their content. However, the gap between computer and human performance in this area is still large and is likely to remain so for many years.

Our study has also exposed us to a wide range of mathematical techniques. These include continuous mathematics, such as signal processing, variational approaches, three-dimensional and projective geometry, linear algebra, and least squares. We have also studied topics in discrete mathematics and computer science, such as graph algorithms, combinatorial optimization, and even database techniques for information retrieval. Since many problems in computer vision are inverse problems that involve estimating unknown quantities from noisy input data, we have also looked at Bayesian statistical inference techniques, as well as machine learning techniques to learn probabilistic models from large amounts of training data. As the availability of partially labeled visual imagery on the Internet continues to increase exponentially, this latter approach will continue to have a major impact on our field.

You may ask: why is our field so broad and aren't there any unifying principles that can be used to simplify our study? Part of the answer lies in the expansive definition of computer vision, which is the analysis of images and video, as well as the incredible complexity inherent in the formation of visual imagery. In some ways, our field is as complex as the study of automotive engineering, which requires an understanding of internal combustion, mechanics, aerodynamics, ergonomics, electrical circuitry, and control systems, among other topics. Computer vision similarly draws on a wide variety of sub-disciplines, which makes it challenging to cover in a one-semester course, let alone to achieve mastery during a course of graduate studies. Conversely, the incredible breadth and technical complexity of computer vision problems is what draws many people to this research field.

Because of this richness and the difficulty in making and measuring progress, I have attempted to instill in my students and in readers of this book a discipline founded on principles from engineering, science, and statistics.

R. Szeliski, *Computer Vision: Algorithms and Applications*, Texts in Computer Science, DOI 10.1007/978-1-84882-935-0_15, © Springer-Verlag London Limited 2011

The engineering approach to problem solving is to first carefully define the overall problem being tackled and to question the basic assumptions and goals inherent in this process. Once this has been done, a number of alternative solutions or approaches are implemented and carefully tested, paying attention to issues such as reliability and computational cost. Finally, one or more solutions are deployed and evaluated in real-world settings. For this reason, this book contains many different alternatives for solving vision problems, many of which are sketched out in the exercises for students to implement and test on their own.

The scientific approach builds upon a basic understanding of physical principles. In the case of computer vision, this includes the physics of man-made and natural structures, image formation, including lighting and atmospheric effects, optics, and noisy sensors. The task is to then invert this formation using stable and efficient algorithms to obtain reliable descriptions of the scene and other quantities of interest. The scientific approach also encourages us to formulate and test hypotheses, which is similar to the extensive testing and evaluation inherent in engineering disciplines.

Lastly, because so much about the image formation process is inherently uncertain and ambiguous, a statistical approach that models both uncertainty in the world (e.g., the number and types of animals in a picture) and noise in the image formation process, is often essential. Bayesian inference techniques can then be used to combine prior and measurement models to estimate the unknowns and to model their uncertainty. Machine learning techniques can be used to create the probabilistic models in the first place. Efficient learning and inference algorithms, such as dynamic programming, graph cuts, and belief propagation, often play a crucial role in this process.

Given the breadth of material we have covered in this book, what new developments are we likely to see in the future? As I have mentioned before, one of the recent trends in computer vision is using the massive amounts of partially labeled visual data on the Internet as sources for learning visual models of scenes and objects. We have already seen data-driven approaches succeed in related fields such as speech recognition, machine translation, speech and music synthesis, and even computer graphics (both in image-based rendering and animation from motion capture). A similar process has been occurring in computer vision, with some of the most exciting new work occurring at the intersection of the object recognition and machine learning fields.

More traditional quantitative techniques in computer vision such as motion estimation, stereo correspondence, and image enhancement, all benefit from better prior models for images, motions, and disparities, as well as efficient statistical inference techniques such as those for inhomogeneous and higher-order Markov random fields. Some techniques, such as feature matching and structure from motion, have matured to where they can be applied to almost arbitrary collections of images of static scenes. This has resulted in an explosion of work in 3D modeling from Internet datasets, which again is related to visual recognition from massive amounts of data.

While these are all encouraging developments, the gap between human and machine performance in semantic scene understanding remains large. It may be many years before computers can name and outline all of the objects in a photograph with the same skill as a two-year-old child. However, we have to remember that human performance is often the result of many years of training and familiarity and often works best in special ecologically important situations. For example, while humans appear to be experts at face recognition, our actual performance when shown people we do not know well is not that good. Combining vision algorithms with general inference techniques that reason about the real world will likely lead to more breakthroughs, although some of the problems may turn out to be "AI-complete", in the sense that a full emulation of human experience and intelligence may be necessary.

Whatever the outcome of these research endeavors, computer vision is already having a tremendous impact in many areas, including digital photography, visual effects, medical imaging, safety and surveillance, and Web-based search. The breadth of the problems and techniques inherent in this field, combined with the richness of the mathematics and the utility of the resulting algorithms, will ensure that this remains an exciting area of study for years to come.

Linear algebra and numerical techniques

In this appendix, we introduce some elements of linear algebra and numerical techniques that are used elsewhere in the book. We start with some basic decompositions in matrix algebra, including the singular value decomposition (SVD), eigenvalue decompositions, and other matrix decompositions (factorizations). Next, we look at the problem of linear least squares, which can be solved using either the QR decomposition or normal equations. This is followed by non-linear least squares, which arise when the measurement equations are not linear in the unknowns or when robust error functions are used. Such problems require iteration to find a solution. Next, we look at direct solution (factorization) techniques for sparse problems, where the ordering of the variables can have a large influence on the computation and memory requirements. Finally, we discuss iterative techniques for solving large linear (or linearized) least squares problems. Good general references for much of this material include the work by Björck (1996), Golub and Van Loan (1996), Trefethen and Bau (1997), Meyer (2000), Nocedal and Wright (2006), and Björck and Dahlquist (2010).

A note on vector and matrix indexing.   To be consistent with the rest of the book and with the general usage in the computer science and computer vision communities, I adopt a 0-based indexing scheme for vector and matrix element indexing. Please note that most mathematical textbooks and papers use 1-based indexing, so you need to be aware of the differences when you read this book.

Software implementations.   Highly optimized and tested libraries corresponding to the algorithms described in this appendix are readily available and are listed in Appendix C.2.

A.1 Matrix decompositions

In order to better understand the structure of matrices and more stably perform operations such as inversion and system solving, a number of decompositions (or factorizations) can be used. In this section, we review singular value decomposition (SVD), eigenvalue decomposition, QR factorization, and Cholesky factorization.

A.1.1 Singular value decomposition

One of the most useful decompositions in matrix algebra is the *singular value decomposition* (SVD), which states that any real-valued $M \times N$ matrix A can be written as

$$A_{M \times N} = U_{M \times P} \Sigma_{P \times P} V_{P \times N}^T \tag{A.1}$$

$$= \left[\begin{array}{c|c|c} & & \\ u_0 & \cdots & u_{p-1} \\ & & \end{array} \right] \left[\begin{array}{ccc} \sigma_0 & & \\ & \ddots & \\ & & \sigma_{p-1} \end{array} \right] \left[\begin{array}{c} v_0^T \\ \hline \cdots \\ \hline v_{p-1}^T \end{array} \right],$$

where $P = \min(M, N)$. The matrices U and V are orthonormal, i.e., $U^T U = I$ and $V^T V = I$, and so are their column vectors,

$$u_i \cdot u_j = v_i \cdot v_j = \delta_{ij}. \tag{A.2}$$

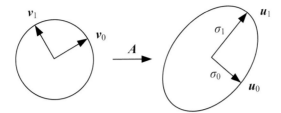

Figure A.1 The action of a matrix A can be visualized by thinking of the domain as being spanned by a set of orthonormal vectors v_j, each of which is transformed to a new orthogonal vector u_j with a length σ_j. When A is interpreted as a covariance matrix and its eigenvalue decomposition is performed, each of the u_j axes denote a principal direction (component) and each σ_j denotes one standard deviation along that direction.

The singular values are all non-negative and can be ordered in decreasing order

$$\sigma_0 \geq \sigma_1 \geq \cdots \geq \sigma_{p-1} \geq 0. \tag{A.3}$$

A geometric intuition for the SVD of a matrix A can be obtained by re-writing $A = U\Sigma V^T$ in (A.2) as

$$AV = U\Sigma \quad \text{or} \quad Av_j = \sigma_j u_j. \tag{A.4}$$

This formula says that the matrix A takes any basis vector v_j and maps it to a direction u_j with length σ_j, as shown in Figure A.1

If only the first r singular values are positive, the matrix A is of *rank* r and the index p in the SVD decomposition (A.2) can be replaced by r. (In other words, we can drop the last $p - r$ columns of U and V.)

An important property of the singular value decomposition of a matrix (also true for the eigenvalue decomposition of a real symmetric non-negative definite matrix) is that if we truncate the expansion

$$A = \sum_{j=0}^{t} \sigma_j u_j v_j^T, \tag{A.5}$$

we obtain the best possible least squares approximation to the original matrix A. This is used both in eigenface-based face recognition systems (Section 14.2.1) and in the separable approximation of convolution kernels (3.21).

A.1.2 Eigenvalue decomposition

If the matrix C is symmetric $(m = n)$,[1] it can be written as an eigenvalue decomposition,

$$
C = U\Lambda U^T = \begin{bmatrix} u_0 & \cdots & u_{n-1} \end{bmatrix} \begin{bmatrix} \lambda_0 & & \\ & \ddots & \\ & & \lambda_{n-1} \end{bmatrix} \begin{bmatrix} u_0^T \\ \cdots \\ u_{n-1}^T \end{bmatrix}
$$

$$
= \sum_{i=0}^{n-1} \lambda_i u_i u_i^T. \tag{A.6}
$$

---

[1] In this appendix, we denote symmetric matrices using C and general rectangular matrices using A.

(The eigenvector matrix U is sometimes written as $\mathbf{\Phi}$ and the eigenvectors u as ϕ.) In this case, the eigenvalues

$$\lambda_0 \geq \lambda_1 \geq \cdots \geq \lambda_{n-1} \tag{A.7}$$

can be both positive and negative.[2]

A special case of the symmetric matrix C occurs when it is constructed as the sum of a number of outer products

$$C = \sum_i a_i a_i^T = AA^T, \tag{A.8}$$

which often occurs when solving least squares problems (Appendix A.2), where the matrix A consists of all the a_i column vectors stacked side-by-side. In this case, we are guaranteed that all of the eigenvalues λ_i are non-negative. The associated matrix C is *positive semi-definite*

$$x^T C x \geq 0, \quad \forall x. \tag{A.9}$$

If the matrix C is of full rank, the eigenvalues are all positive and the matrix is called *symmetric positive definite* (SPD).

Symmetric positive semi-definite matrices also arise in the statistical analysis of data, since they represent the *covariance* of a set of $\{x_i\}$ points around their mean $\bar{x}$,

$$C = \frac{1}{n} \sum_i (x_i - \bar{x})(x_i - \bar{x})^T. \tag{A.10}$$

In this case, performing the eigenvalue decomposition is known as *principal component analysis* (PCA), since it models the principal directions (and magnitudes) of variation of the point distribution around their mean, as shown in Section 5.1.1 (5.13–5.15), Section 14.2.1 (14.9), and Appendix B.1.1 (B.10). Figure A.1 shows how the principal components of the covariance matrix C denote the principal axes u_j of the uncertainty ellipsoid corresponding to this point distribution and how the $\sigma_j = \sqrt{\lambda_j}$ denote the standard deviations along each axis.

The eigenvalues and eigenvectors of C and the singular values and singular vectors of A are closely related. Given

$$A = U\Sigma V^T, \tag{A.11}$$

we get

$$C = AA^T = U\Sigma V^T V \Sigma U^T = U\Lambda U^T. \tag{A.12}$$

From this, we see that $\lambda_i = \sigma_i^2$ and that the left singular vectors of A are the eigenvectors of C.

This relationship gives us an efficient method for computing the eigenvalue decomposition of large matrices that are rank deficient, such as the scatter matrices observed in computing eigenfaces (Section 14.2.1). Observe that the covariance matrix C in (14.9) is exactly the same as C in (A.8). Note also that the individual difference-from-mean images $a_i = x_i - \bar{x}$ are long vectors of length P (the number of pixels in the image), while the total number of exemplars N (the number of faces in the training database) is much smaller. Instead of forming $C = AA^T$, which is $P \times P$, we form the matrix

$$\hat{C} = A^T A, \tag{A.13}$$

---

[2] Eigenvalue decompositions can be computed for non-symmetric matrices but the eigenvalues and eigenvectors can have complex entries in that case.

which is $N \times N$. (This involves taking the dot product between every pair of difference images a_i and a_j.) The eigenvalues of $\hat{C}$ are the squared singular values of A, namely Σ^2, and are hence also the eigenvalues of C. The eigenvectors of $\hat{C}$ are the right singular vectors V of A, from which the desired eigenfaces U, which are the left singular vectors of A, can be computed as

$$U = AV\Sigma^{-1}. \tag{A.14}$$

This final step is essentially computing the eigenfaces as linear combinations of the difference images (Turk and Pentland 1991a). If you have access to a high-quality linear algebra package such as LAPACK, routines for efficiently computing a small number of the left singular vectors and singular values of rectangular matrices such as A are usually provided (Appendix C.2). However, if storing all of the images in memory is prohibitive, the construction of $\hat{C}$ in (A.13) can be used instead.

How can eigenvalue and singular value decompositions actually be computed? Notice that an eigenvector is defined by the equation

$$\lambda_i u_i = C u_i \quad \text{or} \quad (\lambda_i I - C) u_i = 0. \tag{A.15}$$

(This can be derived from (A.6) by post-multiplying both sides by u_i.) Since the latter equation is *homogeneous*, i.e., it has a zero right-hand-side, it can only have a non-zero (non-trivial) solution for u_i if the system is rank deficient, i.e.,

$$|(\lambda I - C)| = 0. \tag{A.16}$$

Evaluating this determinant yields a *characteristic* polynomial equation in λ, which can be solved for small problems, e.g., 2×2 or 3×3 matrices, in closed form.

For larger matrices, iterative algorithms that first reduce the matrix C to a real symmetric tridiagonal form using orthogonal transforms and then perform QR iterations are normally used (Golub and Van Loan 1996; Trefethen and Bau 1997; Björck and Dahlquist 2010). Since these techniques are rather involved, it is best to use a linear algebra package such as LAPACK (Anderson, Bai, Bischof *et al.* 1999)—see Appendix C.2.

Factorization with missing data requires different kinds of iterative algorithms, which often involve either hallucinating the missing terms or minimizing some weighted reconstruction metric, which is intrinsically much more challenging than regular factorization. This area has been widely studied in computer vision (Shum, Ikeuchi, and Reddy 1995; De la Torre and Black 2003; Huynh, Hartley, and Heyden 2003; Buchanan and Fitzgibbon 2005; Gross, Matthews, and Baker 2006; Torresani, Hertzmann, and Bregler 2008) and is sometimes called *generalized PCA*. However, this term is also sometimes used to denote algebraic subspace clustering techniques, which is the subject of a forthcoming monograph by Vidal, Ma, and Sastry (2010).

A.1.3 QR factorization

A widely used technique for stably solving poorly conditioned least squares problems (Björck 1996) and as the basis of more complex algorithms, such as computing the SVD and eigenvalue decompositions, is the QR factorization,

$$A = QR, \tag{A.17}$$

procedure *Cholesky*($\boldsymbol{C}, \boldsymbol{R}$):

$\quad \boldsymbol{R} = \boldsymbol{C}$

$\quad$ **for** $i = 0 \ldots n - 1$

$\quad\quad$ **for** $j = i + 1 \ldots n - 1$

$\quad\quad\quad \boldsymbol{R}_{j,j:n-1} = \boldsymbol{R}_{j,j:n-1} - r_{ij} r_{ii}^{-1} \boldsymbol{R}_{i,j:n-1}$

$\quad\quad \boldsymbol{R}_{i,i:n-1} = r_{ii}^{-1/2} \boldsymbol{R}_{i,i:n-1}$

Algorithm A.1 Cholesky decomposition of the matrix $\boldsymbol{C}$ into its upper triangular form $\boldsymbol{R}$.

where $\boldsymbol{Q}$ is an *orthonormal* (or *unitary*) matrix $\boldsymbol{Q}\boldsymbol{Q}^T = \boldsymbol{I}$ and $\boldsymbol{R}$ is upper triangular.[3] In computer vision, QR can be used to convert a camera matrix into a rotation matrix and an upper-triangular calibration matrix (6.35) and also in various self-calibration algorithms (Section 7.2.2). The most common algorithms for computing QR decompositions, modified Gram–Schmidt, Householder transformations, and Givens rotations, are described by Golub and Van Loan (1996), Trefethen and Bau (1997), and Björck and Dahlquist (2010) and are also found in LAPACK. Unlike the SVD and eigenvalue decompositions, QR factorization does not require iteration and can be computed exactly in $O(MN^2 + N^3)$ operations, where M is the number of rows and N is the number of columns (for a tall matrix).

A.1.4 Cholesky factorization

Cholesky factorization can be applied to any symmetric positive definite matrix $\boldsymbol{C}$ to convert it into a product of symmetric lower and upper triangular matrices,

$$\boldsymbol{C} = \boldsymbol{L}\boldsymbol{L}^T = \boldsymbol{R}^T\boldsymbol{R}, \qquad\qquad (A.18)$$

where $\boldsymbol{L}$ is a lower-triangular matrix and $\boldsymbol{R}$ is an upper-triangular matrix. Unlike Gaussian elimination, which may require pivoting (row and column reordering) or may become unstable (sensitive to roundoff errors or reordering), Cholesky factorization remains stable for positive definite matrices, such as those that arise from normal equations in least squares problems (Appendix A.2). Because of the form of (A.18), the matrices $\boldsymbol{L}$ and $\boldsymbol{R}$ are sometimes called *matrix square roots*.[4]

The algorithm to compute an upper triangular Cholesky decomposition of $\boldsymbol{C}$ is a straightforward symmetric generalization of Gaussian elimination and is based on the decomposition (Björck 1996; Golub and Van Loan 1996)

$$\boldsymbol{C} = \begin{bmatrix} \gamma & \boldsymbol{c}^T \\ \boldsymbol{c} & \boldsymbol{C}_{11} \end{bmatrix} \qquad\qquad (A.19)$$

---

[3] The term "R" comes from the German name for the lower–upper (LU) decomposition, which is LR for "links" and "rechts" (left and right of the diagonal).

[4] In fact, there exists a whole family of matrix square roots. Any matrix of the form $\boldsymbol{L}\boldsymbol{Q}$ or $\boldsymbol{Q}\boldsymbol{R}$, where $\boldsymbol{Q}$ is a unitary matrix, is a square root of $\boldsymbol{C}$.

$$
=
\begin{bmatrix}
\gamma^{1/2} & \mathbf{0}^T \\
\mathbf{c}\gamma^{-1/2} & \mathbf{I}
\end{bmatrix}
\begin{bmatrix}
1 & \mathbf{0}^T \\
\mathbf{0} & \mathbf{C}_{11} - \mathbf{c}\gamma^{-1}\mathbf{c}^T
\end{bmatrix}
\begin{bmatrix}
\gamma^{1/2} & \gamma^{-1/2}\mathbf{c}^T \\
\mathbf{0} & \mathbf{I}
\end{bmatrix}
\tag{A.20}
$$

$$
= \mathbf{R}_0^T \mathbf{C}_1 \mathbf{R}_0, \tag{A.21}
$$

which, through recursion, can be turned into

$$
\mathbf{C} = \mathbf{R}_0^T \ldots \mathbf{R}_{n-1}^T \mathbf{R}_{n-1} \ldots \mathbf{R}_0 = \mathbf{R}^T \mathbf{R}. \tag{A.22}
$$

Algorithm A.1 provides a more procedural definition, which can store the upper-triangular matrix $\mathbf{R}$ in the same space as $\mathbf{C}$, if desired. The total operation count for Cholesky factorization is $O(N^3)$ for a dense matrix but can be significantly lower for sparse matrices with low fill-in (Appendix A.4).

Note that Cholesky decomposition can also be applied to block-structured matrices, where the term γ in (A.19) is now a square block sub-matrix and $\mathbf{c}$ is a rectangular matrix (Golub and Van Loan 1996). The computation of square roots can be avoided by leaving the γ on the diagonal of the middle factor in (A.20), which results in the $\mathbf{C} = \mathbf{LDL}^T$ factorization, where $\mathbf{D}$ is a diagonal matrix. However, since square roots are relatively fast on modern computers, this is not worth the bother and Cholesky factorization is usually preferred.

A.2 Linear least squares

Least squares fitting problems are pervasive in computer vision. For example, the alignment of images based on matching feature points involves the minimization of a squared distance objective function (6.2),

$$
E_{\mathrm{LS}} = \sum_i \|\mathbf{r}_i\|^2 = \sum_i \|\mathbf{f}(\mathbf{x}_i; \mathbf{p}) - \mathbf{x}_i'\|^2, \tag{A.23}
$$

where

$$
\mathbf{r}_i = \mathbf{f}(\mathbf{x}_i; \mathbf{p}) - \mathbf{x}_i' = \hat{\mathbf{x}}_i' - \tilde{\mathbf{x}}_i' \tag{A.24}
$$

is the *residual* between the measured location $\hat{\mathbf{x}}_i'$ and its corresponding current *predicted* location $\tilde{\mathbf{x}}_i' = \mathbf{f}(\mathbf{x}_i; \mathbf{p})$. More complex versions of least squares problems, such as large-scale structure from motion (Section 7.4), may involve the minimization of functions of thousands of variables. Even problems such as image filtering (Section 3.4.3) and regularization (Section 3.7.1) may involve the minimization of sums of squared errors.

Figure A.2a shows an example of a simple least squares line fitting problem, where the quantities being estimated are the line equation parameters (m, b). When the sampled vertical values y_i are assumed to be noisy versions of points on the line $y = mx + b$, the optimal estimates for (m, b) can be found by minimizing the squared vertical residuals

$$
E_{\mathrm{VLS}} = \sum_i |y_i - (mx_i + b)|^2. \tag{A.25}
$$

Note that the function being fitted need not itself be linear to use linear least squares. All that is required is that the function be linear in the unknown parameters. For example, polynomial fitting can be written as

$$
E_{\mathrm{PLS}} = \sum_i |y_i - (\sum_{j=0}^{p} a_j x_i^j)|^2, \tag{A.26}
$$

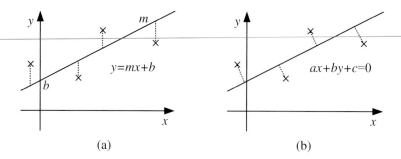

Figure A.2 Least squares regression. (a) The line $y = mx + b$ is fit to the four noisy data points, $\{(x_i, y_i)\}$, denoted by $\times$ by minimizing the squared vertical residuals between the data points and the line, $\sum_i \|y_i - (mx_i + b)\|^2$. (b) When the measurements $\{(x_i, y_i)\}$ are assumed to have noise in all directions, the sum of orthogonal squared distances to the line $\sum_i \|ax_i + by_i + c\|^2$ is minimized using total least squares.

while sinusoid fitting with unknown amplitude A and phase ϕ (but known frequency f) can be written as

$$E_{\mathrm{SLS}} = \sum_i |y_i - A\sin(2\pi f x_i + \phi)|^2 = \sum_i |y_i - (B\sin 2\pi f x_i + C\cos 2\pi f x_i)|^2, \quad (A.27)$$

which is linear in (B, C).

In general, it is more common to denote the unknown parameters using $\boldsymbol{x}$ and to write the general form of linear least squares as[5]

$$E_{\mathrm{LLS}} = \sum_i |\boldsymbol{a}_i \boldsymbol{x} - b_i|^2 = \|\boldsymbol{A}\boldsymbol{x} - \boldsymbol{b}\|^2. \quad (A.28)$$

Expanding the above equation gives us

$$E_{\mathrm{LLS}} = \boldsymbol{x}^T(\boldsymbol{A}^T\boldsymbol{A})\boldsymbol{x} - 2\boldsymbol{x}^T(\boldsymbol{A}^T\boldsymbol{b}) + \|\boldsymbol{b}\|^2, \quad (A.29)$$

whose minimum value for $\boldsymbol{x}$ can be found by solving the associated *normal equations* (Björck 1996; Golub and Van Loan 1996)

$$(\boldsymbol{A}^T\boldsymbol{A})\boldsymbol{x} = \boldsymbol{A}^T\boldsymbol{b}. \quad (A.30)$$

The preferred way to solve the normal equations is to use Cholesky factorization. Let

$$\boldsymbol{C} = \boldsymbol{A}^T\boldsymbol{A} = \boldsymbol{R}^T\boldsymbol{R}, \quad (A.31)$$

where $\boldsymbol{R}$ is the upper-triangular Cholesky factor of the Hessian $\boldsymbol{C}$, and

$$\boldsymbol{d} = \boldsymbol{A}^T\boldsymbol{b}. \quad (A.32)$$

After factorization, the solution for $\boldsymbol{x}$ can be obtained as

$$\boldsymbol{R}^T\boldsymbol{z} = \boldsymbol{d}, \quad \boldsymbol{R}\boldsymbol{x} = \boldsymbol{z}, \quad (A.33)$$

---

[5] Be extra careful in interpreting the variable names here. In the 2D line-fitting example, x is used to denote the horizontal axis, but in the general least squares problem, $\boldsymbol{x} = (m, b)$ denotes the unknown parameter vector.

which involves the solution of two triangular systems, i.e., forward and backward substitution (Björck 1996).

In cases where the least squares problem is numerically poorly conditioned (which should generally be avoided by adding sufficient regularization or prior knowledge about the parameters, (Appendix A.3)), it is possible to use QR factorization or SVD directly on the matrix A (Björck 1996; Golub and Van Loan 1996; Trefethen and Bau 1997; Nocedal and Wright 2006; Björck and Dahlquist 2010), e.g.,

$$Ax = QRx = b \quad \longrightarrow \quad Rx = Q^T b. \tag{A.34}$$

Note that the upper triangular matrices R produced by the Cholesky factorization of $C = A^T A$ and the QR factorization of A are the same, but that solving (A.34) is generally more stable (less sensitive to roundoff error) but slower (by a constant factor).

A.2.1 Total least squares

In some problems, e.g., when performing geometric line fitting in 2D images or 3D plane fitting to point cloud data, instead of having measurement error along one particular axis, the measured points have uncertainty in all directions, which is known as the *errors-in-variables* model (Van Huffel and Lemmerling 2002; Matei and Meer 2006). In this case, it makes more sense to minimize a set of homogeneous squared errors of the form

$$E_{\mathrm{TLS}} = \sum_i (a_i x)^2 = \|Ax\|^2, \tag{A.35}$$

which is known as *total least squares* (TLS) (Van Huffel and Vandewalle 1991; Björck 1996; Golub and Van Loan 1996; Van Huffel and Lemmerling 2002).

The above error metric has a trivial minimum solution at $x = 0$ and is, in fact, homogeneous in x. For this reason, we augment this minimization problem with the requirement that $\|x\|^2 = 1$. which results in the eigenvalue problem

$$x = \arg\min_x x^T (A^T A) x \quad \text{such that} \quad \|x\|^2 = 1. \tag{A.36}$$

The value of x that minimizes this constrained problem is the eigenvector associated with the smallest eigenvalue of $A^T A$. This is the same as the last right singular vector of A, since

$$A = U\Sigma V, \tag{A.37}$$
$$A^T A = V\Sigma^2 V, \tag{A.38}$$
$$A^T A v_k = \sigma_k^2, \tag{A.39}$$

which is minimized by selecting the smallest σ_k value.

Figure A.2b shows a line fitting problem where, in this case, the measurement errors are assumed to be isotropic in (x, y). The solution for the best line equation $ax + by + c = 0$ is found by minimizing

$$E_{\mathrm{TLS-2D}} = \sum_i (ax_i + by_i + c)^2, \tag{A.40}$$

i.e., finding the eigenvector associated with the smallest eigenvalue of[6]

$$C = A^T A = \sum_i \begin{bmatrix} x_i \\ y_i \\ 1 \end{bmatrix} \begin{bmatrix} x_i & y_i & 1 \end{bmatrix}. \tag{A.41}$$

Notice, however, that minimizing $\sum_i (a_i x)^2$ in (A.35) is only statistically optimal (Appendix B.1.1) if all of the measured terms in the a_i, e.g., the $(x_i, y_i, 1)$ measurements, have equal noise. This is definitely not the case in the line-fitting example of Figure A.2b (A.40), since the 1 values are noise-free. To mitigate this, we first subtract the mean x and y values from all the measured points

$$\hat{x}_i = x_i - \bar{x} \tag{A.42}$$
$$\hat{y}_i = y_i - \bar{y} \tag{A.43}$$

and then fit the 2D line equation $a(x - \bar{x}) + b(y - \bar{y}) = 0$ by minimizing

$$E_{\text{TLS}-2\text{Dm}} = \sum_i (a\hat{x}_i + b\hat{y}_i)^2. \tag{A.44}$$

The more general case where each individual measurement component can have different noise level, as is the case in estimating essential and fundamental matrices (Section 7.2), is called the *heteroscedastic* errors-in-variable (HEIV) model and is discussed by Matei and Meer (2006).

A.3 Non-linear least squares

In many vision problems, such as structure from motion, the least squares problem formulated in (A.23) involves functions $f(x_i; p)$ that are *not* linear in the unknown parameters p. This problem is known as *non-linear least squares* or *non-linear regression* (Björck 1996; Madsen, Nielsen, and Tingleff 2004; Nocedal and Wright 2006). It is usually solved by iteratively re-linearizing (A.23) around the current estimate of p using the gradient derivative (Jacobian) $J = \partial f / \partial p$ and computing an incremental improvement Δp.

As shown in Equations (6.13–6.17), this results in

$$E_{\text{NLS}}(\Delta p) = \sum_i \| f(x_i; p + \Delta p) - x_i' \|^2 \tag{A.45}$$

$$\approx \sum_i \| J(x_i; p) \Delta p - r_i \|^2, \tag{A.46}$$

where the Jacobians $J(x_i; p)$ and residual vectors r_i play the same role in forming the normal equations as a_i and b_i in (A.28).

Because the above approximation only holds near a local minimum or for small values of Δp, the update $p \leftarrow p + \Delta p$ may not always decrease the summed square residual error (A.45). One way to mitigate this problem is to take a smaller step,

$$p \leftarrow p + \alpha \Delta p, \quad 0 < \alpha \le 1. \tag{A.47}$$

---

[6] Again, be careful with the variable names here. The measurement equation is $a_i = (x_i, y_i, 1)$ and the unknown parameters are $x = (a, b, c)$.

A simple way to determine a reasonable value of α is to start with 1 and successively halve the value, which is a simple form of *line search* (Al-Baali and Fletcher. 1986; Björck 1996; Nocedal and Wright 2006).

Another approach to ensuring a downhill step in error is to add a diagonal damping term to the approximate Hessian

$$C = \sum_i J^T(x_i) J(x_i), \tag{A.48}$$

i.e., to solve

$$[C + \lambda \operatorname{diag}(C)]\Delta p = d, \tag{A.49}$$

where

$$d = \sum_i J^T(x_i) r_i, \tag{A.50}$$

which is called a *damped Gauss–Newton* method. The damping parameter λ is increased if the squared residual is not decreasing as fast as expected, i.e., as predicted by (A.46), and is decreased if the expected decrease is obtained (Madsen, Nielsen, and Tingleff 2004). The combination of the Newton (first-order Taylor series) approximation (A.46) and the adaptive damping parameter λ is commonly known as the Levenberg–Marquardt algorithm (Levenberg 1944; Marquardt 1963) and is an example of more general *trust region methods*, which are discussed in more detail in (Björck 1996; Conn, Gould, and Toint 2000; Madsen, Nielsen, and Tingleff 2004; Nocedal and Wright 2006).

When the initial solution is far away from its quadratic region of convergence around a local minimum, *large residual methods*, e.g., *Newton-type methods*, which add a second-order term to the Taylor series expansion in (A.46), may converge faster. Quasi-Newton methods such as BFGS, which require only gradient evaluations, can also be useful if memory size is an issue. Such techniques are discussed in textbooks and papers on numerical optimization (Toint 1987; Björck 1996; Conn, Gould, and Toint 2000; Nocedal and Wright 2006).

A.4 Direct sparse matrix techniques

Many optimization problems in computer vision, such as bundle adjustment (Szeliski and Kang 1994; Triggs, McLauchlan, Hartley *et al.* 1999; Hartley and Zisserman 2004; Snavely, Seitz, and Szeliski 2008b; Agarwal, Snavely, Simon *et al.* 2009) have Jacobian and (approximate) Hessian matrices that are extremely sparse (Section 7.4.1). For example, Figure 7.9a shows the *bipartite* model typical of structure from motion problems, in which most points are only observed by a subset of the cameras, which results in the sparsity patterns for the Jacobian and Hessian shown in Figure 7.9b–c.

Whenever the Hessian matrix is sparse enough, it is more efficient to use sparse Cholesky factorization instead of regular Cholesky factorization. In such sparse direct techniques, the Hessian matrix C and its associated Cholesky factor R are stored in *compressed form*, in which the amount of storage is proportional to the number of (potentially) non-zero entries (Björck 1996; Davis 2006).[7] Algorithms for computing the non-zero elements in C and R

---

[7] For example, you can store a list of (i, j, c_{ij}) triples. One example of such a scheme is *compressed sparse row (CSR)* storage. An alternative storage method called *skyline*, which stores adjacent vertical spans of non-zero elements (Bathe 2007), is sometimes used in finite element analysis. Banded systems such as snakes (5.3) can store just the non-zero band elements (Björck 1996, Section 6.2) and can be solved in $O(nb^2)$, where n is the number of

from the sparsity pattern of the Jacobian matrix J are given by Björck (1996, Section 6.4), and algorithms for computing the numerical Cholesky and QR decompositions (once the sparsity pattern has been computed and storage allocated) are discussed by Björck (1996, Section 6.5).

A.4.1 Variable reordering

The key to efficiently solving sparse problems using direct (non-iterative) techniques is to determine an efficient *ordering* for the variables, which reduces the amount of *fill-in*, i.e., the number of non-zero entries in R that were zero in the original C matrix. We already saw in Section 7.4.1 how storing the more numerous 3D point parameters before the camera parameters and using the Schur complement (7.56) results in a more efficient algorithm. Similarly, sorting parameters by time in video-based reconstruction problems usually results in lower fill-in. Furthermore, any problem whose adjacency graph (the graph corresponding to the sparsity pattern) is a tree can be solved in linear time with an appropriate reordering of the variables (putting all the children before their parents). All of these are examples of good reordering techniques.

In the general case of unstructured data, there are many heuristics available to find good reorderings (Björck 1996; Davis 2006).[8] For general adjacency (sparsity) graphs, *minimum degree orderings* generally produce good results. For planar graphs, which often arise on image or spline grids (Section 8.3), *nested dissection*, which recursively splits the graph into two equal halves along a *frontier* (or boundary) of small size, generally works well. Such *domain decomposition* (or *multi-frontal*) techniques also enable the use of parallel processing, since independent sub-graphs can be processed in parallel on separate processors (Davis 2008).

The overall set of steps used to perform the direct solution of sparse least squares problems are summarized in Algorithm A.2, which is a modified version of Algorithm 6.6.1 by Björck (1996, Section 6.6)). If a series of related least squares problems is being solved, as is the case in iterative non-linear least squares (Appendix A.3), steps 1–3 can be performed ahead of time and reused for each new invocation with different C and d values. When the problem is block-structured, as is the case in structure from motion where point (structure) variables have dense 3×3 sub-entries in C and cameras have 6×6 (or larger) entries, the cost of performing the reordering computation is small compared to the actual numerical factorization, which can benefit from block-structured matrix operations (Golub and Van Loan 1996). It is also possible to apply sparse reordering and multifrontal techniques to QR factorization (Davis 2008), which may be preferable when the least squares problems are poorly conditioned.

A.5 Iterative techniques

When problems become large, the amount of memory required to store the Hessian matrix C and its factor R, and the amount of time it takes to compute the factorization, can become prohibitively large, especially when there are large amounts of fill-in. This is often the case with image processing problems defined on pixel grids, since, even with the optimal reordering (nested dissection) the amount of fill can still be large.

---

variables and b is the bandwidth.

[8]Finding the optimal reordering with minimal fill-in is provably NP-hard.

---

procedure *SparseCholeskySolve*(C, d):

1. Determine symbolically the structure of C, i.e., the adjacency graph.

2. (Optional) Compute a reordering for the variables, taking into account any block structure inherent in the problem.

3. Determine the fill-in pattern for R and allocate the compressed storage for R as well as storage for the permuted right hand side $\hat{d}$.

4. Copy the elements of C and d into R and $\hat{d}$, permuting the values according to the computed ordering.

5. Perform the numerical factorization of R using Algorithm A.1.

6. Solve the factored system (A.33), i.e.,

$$R^T z = \hat{d}, \quad Rx = z.$$

7. Return the solution x, after undoing the permutation.

Algorithm A.2 Sparse least squares using a sparse Cholesky decomposition of the matrix C.

A preferable approach to solving such linear systems is to use iterative techniques, which compute a series of estimates that converge to the final solution, e.g., by taking a series of downhill steps in an energy function such as (A.29).

A large number of iterative techniques have been developed over the years, including such well-known algorithms as successive overrelaxation and multi-grid. These are described in specialized textbooks on iterative solution techniques (Axelsson 1996; Saad 2003) as well as in more general books on numerical linear algebra and least squares techniques (Björck 1996; Golub and Van Loan 1996; Trefethen and Bau 1997; Nocedal and Wright 2006; Björck and Dahlquist 2010).

A.5.1 Conjugate gradient

The iterative solution technique that often performs best is conjugate gradient descent, which takes a series of downhill steps that are *conjugate* to each other with respect to the C matrix, i.e., if the u and v descent directions satisfy $u^T C v = 0$. In practice, conjugate gradient descent outperforms other kinds of gradient descent algorithm because its convergence rate is proportional to the square root of the *condition number* of C instead of the condition number itself.[9] Shewchuk (1994) provides a nice introduction to this topic, with clear intuitive explanations of the reasoning behind the conjugate gradient algorithm and its performance.

Algorithm A.3 describes the conjugate gradient algorithm and its related least squares counterpart, which can be used when the original set of least squares linear equations are

---

[9] The condition number $\kappa(C)$ is the ratio of the largest and smallest eigenvalues of C. The actual convergence rate depends on the clustering of the eigenvalues, as discussed in the references cited in this section.

$ConjugateGradient(\boldsymbol{C}, \boldsymbol{d}, \boldsymbol{x}_0)$	$ConjugateGradientLS(\boldsymbol{A}, \boldsymbol{b}, \boldsymbol{x}_0)$
1. $\boldsymbol{r}_0 = \boldsymbol{d} - \boldsymbol{C}\boldsymbol{x}_0$	1. $\boldsymbol{q}_0 = \boldsymbol{b} - \boldsymbol{A}\boldsymbol{x}_0, \quad \boldsymbol{r}_0 = \boldsymbol{A}^T\boldsymbol{q}_0$
2. $\boldsymbol{p}_0 = \boldsymbol{r}_0$	2. $\boldsymbol{p}_0 = \boldsymbol{r}_0$
3. for $k = 0 \ldots$	3. for $k = 0 \ldots$
4. $\quad \boldsymbol{w}_k = \boldsymbol{C}\boldsymbol{p}_k$	4. $\quad \boldsymbol{v}_k = \boldsymbol{A}\boldsymbol{p}_k$
5. $\quad \alpha_k = \|\boldsymbol{r}_k\|^2 / (\boldsymbol{p}_k \cdot \boldsymbol{w}_k)$	5. $\quad \alpha_k = \|\boldsymbol{r}_k\|^2 / \|\boldsymbol{v}_k\|^2$
6. $\quad \boldsymbol{x}_{k+1} = \boldsymbol{x}_k + \alpha_k\boldsymbol{p}_k$	6. $\quad \boldsymbol{x}_{k+1} = \boldsymbol{x}_k + \alpha_k\boldsymbol{p}_k$
7. $\quad \boldsymbol{r}_{k+1} = \boldsymbol{r}_k - \alpha_k\boldsymbol{w}_k$	7. $\quad \boldsymbol{q}_{k+1} = \boldsymbol{q}_k - \alpha_k\boldsymbol{v}_k$
8.	8. $\quad \boldsymbol{r}_{k+1} = \boldsymbol{A}^T\boldsymbol{q}_{k+1}$
9. $\quad \beta_{k+1} = \|\boldsymbol{r}_{k+1}\|^2 / \|\boldsymbol{r}_k\|^2$	9. $\quad \beta_{k+1} = \|\boldsymbol{r}_{k+1}\|^2 / \|\boldsymbol{r}_k\|^2$
10. $\quad \boldsymbol{p}_{k+1} = \boldsymbol{r}_{k+1} + \beta_k\boldsymbol{p}_k$	10. $\quad \boldsymbol{p}_{k+1} = \boldsymbol{r}_{k+1} + \beta_k\boldsymbol{p}_k$

Algorithm A.3 Conjugate gradient and conjugate gradient least squares algorithms. The algorithm is described in more detail in the text, but in brief, they choose descent directions $\boldsymbol{p}_k$ that are conjugate to each other with respect to $\boldsymbol{C}$ by computing a factor β by which to discount the previous search direction $\boldsymbol{p}_{k-1}$. They then find the optimal step size α and take a downhill step by an amount $\alpha_k\boldsymbol{p}_k$.

available in the form of $\boldsymbol{A}\boldsymbol{x} = \boldsymbol{b}$ (A.28). While it is easy to convince yourself that the two forms are mathematically equivalent, the least squares form is preferable if rounding errors start to affect the results because of poor conditioning. It may also be preferable if, due to the sparsity structure of $\boldsymbol{A}$, multiplies with the original $\boldsymbol{A}$ matrix are faster or more space efficient than multiplies with $\boldsymbol{C}$.

The conjugate gradient algorithm starts by computing the current residual $\boldsymbol{r}_0 = \boldsymbol{d} - \boldsymbol{C}\boldsymbol{x}_0$, which is the direction of steepest descent of the energy function (A.28). It sets the original descent direction $\boldsymbol{p}_0 = \boldsymbol{r}_0$. Next, it multiplies the descent direction by the quadratic form (Hessian) matrix $\boldsymbol{C}$ and combines this with the residual to estimate the optimal step size α_k. The solution vector $\boldsymbol{x}_k$ and the residual vector $\boldsymbol{r}_k$ are then updated using this step size. (Notice how the least squares variant of the conjugate gradient algorithm splits the multiplication by the $\boldsymbol{C} = \boldsymbol{A}^T\boldsymbol{A}$ matrix across steps 4 and 8.) Finally, a new search direction is calculated by first computing a factor β as the ratio of current to previous residual magnitudes. The new search direction $\boldsymbol{p}_{k+1}$ is then set to the residual plus β times the old search direction $\boldsymbol{p}_k$, which keeps the directions conjugate with respect to $\boldsymbol{C}$.

It turns out that conjugate gradient descent can also be directly applied to non-quadratic energy functions, e.g., those arising from non-linear least squares (Appendix A.3). Instead of explicitly forming a local quadratic approximation $\boldsymbol{C}$ and then computing residuals $\boldsymbol{r}_k$, non-linear conjugate gradient descent computes the gradient of the energy function E (A.45) directly inside each iteration and uses it to set the search direction (Nocedal and Wright 2006). Since the quadratic approximation to the energy function may not exist or may be inaccurate, line search is often used to determine the step size α_k. Furthermore, to compensate for errors in finding the true function minimum, alternative formulas for β_{k+1} such as Polak–Ribière,

$$\beta_{k+1} = \frac{\nabla E(\boldsymbol{x}_{k+1})[\nabla E(\boldsymbol{x}_{k+1}) - \nabla E(\boldsymbol{x}_k)]}{\|\nabla E(\boldsymbol{x}_k)\|^2} \tag{A.51}$$

are often used (Nocedal and Wright 2006).

A.5.2 Preconditioning

As we mentioned previously, the rate of convergence of the conjugate gradient algorithm is governed in large part by the condition number $\kappa(\boldsymbol{C})$. Its effectiveness can therefore be increased dramatically by reducing this number, e.g., by rescaling elements in $\boldsymbol{x}$, which corresponds to rescaling rows and columns in $\boldsymbol{C}$.

In general, preconditioning is usually thought of as a change of basis from the vector $\boldsymbol{x}$ to a new vector

$$\hat{x} = \boldsymbol{S}\boldsymbol{x}. \tag{A.52}$$

The corresponding linear system being solved then becomes

$$\boldsymbol{A}\boldsymbol{S}^{-1}\hat{x} = \boldsymbol{S}^{-1}\boldsymbol{b} \quad \text{or} \quad \hat{\boldsymbol{A}}\hat{x} = \hat{\boldsymbol{b}}, \tag{A.53}$$

with a corresponding least squares energy (A.29) of the form

$$E_{\mathrm{PLS}} = \hat{x}^T(\boldsymbol{S}^{-T}\boldsymbol{C}\boldsymbol{S}^{-1})\hat{x} - 2\hat{x}^T(\boldsymbol{S}^{-T}\boldsymbol{d}) + \|\hat{\boldsymbol{b}}\|^2. \tag{A.54}$$

The actual preconditioned matrix $\hat{\boldsymbol{C}} = \boldsymbol{S}^{-T}\boldsymbol{C}\boldsymbol{S}^{-1}$ is usually not explicitly computed. Instead, Algorithm A.3 is extended to insert $\boldsymbol{S}^{-T}$ and $\boldsymbol{S}^T$ operations at the appropriate places (Björck 1996; Golub and Van Loan 1996; Trefethen and Bau 1997; Saad 2003; Nocedal and Wright 2006).

A good preconditioner $\boldsymbol{S}$ is easy and cheap to compute, but is also a decent approximation to a square root of $\boldsymbol{C}$, so that $\kappa(\boldsymbol{S}^{-T}\boldsymbol{C}\boldsymbol{S}^{-1})$ is closer to 1. The simplest such choice is the square root of the diagonal matrix $\boldsymbol{S} = \boldsymbol{D}^{1/2}$, with $\boldsymbol{D} = \mathrm{diag}(\boldsymbol{C})$. This has the advantage that any scalar change in variables (e.g., using radians instead of degrees for angular measurements) has no effect on the range of convergence of the iterative technique. For problems that are naturally block-structured, e.g., for structure from motion, where 3D point positions or 6D camera poses are being estimated, a block diagonal preconditioner is often a good choice.

A wide variety of more sophisticated preconditioners have been developed over the years (Björck 1996; Golub and Van Loan 1996; Trefethen and Bau 1997; Saad 2003; Nocedal and Wright 2006), many of which can be directly applied to problems in computer vision (Byröd and øAström 2009; Jeong, Nistér, Steedly *et al.* 2010; Agarwal, Snavely, Seitz *et al.* 2010). Some of these are based on an *incomplete Cholesky* factorization of $\boldsymbol{C}$, i.e., one in which the amount of fill-in in $\boldsymbol{R}$ is strictly limited, e.g., to just the original non-zero elements in $\boldsymbol{C}$.[10] Other preconditioners are based on a sparsified, e.g., tree-based or clustered, approximation to $\boldsymbol{C}$ (Koutis 2007; Koutis and Miller 2008; Grady 2008; Koutis, Miller, and Tolliver 2009), since these are known to have efficient inversion properties.

---

[10] If a complete Cholesky factorization $\boldsymbol{C} = \boldsymbol{R}^T\boldsymbol{R}$ is used, we get $\hat{\boldsymbol{C}} = \boldsymbol{R}^{-T}\boldsymbol{C}\boldsymbol{R}^{-1} = \boldsymbol{I}$ and all iterative algorithms converge in a single step, thereby obviating the need to use them, but the complete factorization is often too expensive. Note that incomplete factorization can also benefit from reordering.

For grid-based image-processing applications, *parallel* or *hierarchical* preconditioners often perform extremely well (Yserentant 1986; Szeliski 1990b; Pentland 1994; Saad 2003; Szeliski 2006b). These approaches use a change of basis transformation S that resembles the pyramidal or wavelet representations discussed in Section 3.5, and are hence amenable to parallel and GPU-based implementations. Coarser elements in the new representation quickly converge to the low-frequency components in the solution, while finer-level elements encode the higher-frequency components. Some of the relationships between hierarchical preconditioners, incomplete Cholesky factorization, and multigrid techniques are explored by Saad (2003) and Szeliski (2006b).

A.5.3 Multigrid

One other class of iterative techniques widely used in computer vision is *multigrid* techniques (Briggs, Henson, and McCormick 2000; Trottenberg, Oosterlee, and Schuller 2000), which have been applied to problems such as surface interpolation (Terzopoulos 1986a), optical flow (Terzopoulos 1986a; Bruhn, Weickert, Kohlberger *et al.* 2006), high dynamic range tone mapping (Fattal, Lischinski, and Werman 2002), colorization (Levin, Lischinski, and Weiss 2004), natural image matting (Levin, Lischinski, and Weiss 2008), and segmentation (Grady 2008).

The main idea behind multigrid is to form coarser (lower-resolution) versions of the problems and use them to compute the low-frequency components of the solution. However, unlike simple coarse-to-fine techniques, which use the coarse solutions to initialize the fine solution, multigrid techniques only *correct* the low-frequency component of the current solution and use multiple rounds of coarsening and refinement (in what are often called "V" and "W" patterns of motion across the pyramid) to obtain rapid convergence.

On certain simple homogeneous problems (such as solving Poisson equations), multigrid techniques can achieve optimal performance, i.e., computation times linear in the number of variables. However, for more inhomogeneous problems or problems on irregular grids, variants on these techniques, such as *algebraic multigrid* (AMG) approaches, which look at the structure of C to derive coarse level problems, may be preferable. Saad (2003) has a nice discussion of the relationship between multigrid and parallel preconditioners and on the relative merits of using multigrid or conjugate gradient approaches.

Appendix B

Bayesian modeling and inference

The following problem commonly recurs in this book: Given a number of measurements (images, feature positions, etc.), estimate the values of some unknown structure or parameter (camera positions, object shape, etc.). These kinds of problems are in general called *inverse* problems because they involve estimating unknown model parameters instead of simulating the forward formation equations.[1] Computer graphics is a classic forward modeling problem (given some objects, cameras, and lighting, simulate the images that would result), while computer vision problems are usually of the inverse kind (given one or more images, recover the scene that gave rise to these images).

Given an instance of an inverse problem, there are, in general, several ways to proceed. For instance, through clever (or sometimes straightforward) algebraic manipulation, a closed form solution for the unknowns can sometimes be derived. Consider, for example, the *camera matrix calibration* problem (Section 6.2.1): given an image of a calibration pattern consisting of known 3D point positions, compute the 3×4 camera matrix P that maps these points onto the image plane.

In more detail, we can write this problem as (6.33–6.34)

$$x_i = \frac{p_{00}X_i + p_{01}Y_i + p_{02}Z_i + p_{03}}{p_{20}X_i + p_{21}Y_i + p_{22}Z_i + p_{23}} \tag{B.1}$$

$$y_i = \frac{p_{10}X_i + p_{11}Y_i + p_{12}Z_i + p_{13}}{p_{20}X_i + p_{21}Y_i + p_{22}Z_i + p_{23}}, \tag{B.2}$$

where (x_i, y_i) is the feature position of the ith point measured in the image plane, (X_i, Y_i, Z_i) is the corresponding 3D point position, and the p_{ij} are the unknown entries of the camera matrix P. Moving the denominator over to the left hand side, we end up with a set of simultaneous linear equations,

$$x_i(p_{20}X_i + p_{21}Y_i + p_{22}Z_i + p_{23}) = p_{00}X_i + p_{01}Y_i + p_{02}Z_i + p_{03}, \tag{B.3}$$

$$y_i(p_{20}X_i + p_{21}Y_i + p_{22}Z_i + p_{23}) = p_{10}X_i + p_{11}Y_i + p_{12}Z_i + p_{13}, \tag{B.4}$$

which we can solve using linear least squares (Appendix A.2) to obtain an estimate of P.

The question then arises: is this set of equations the right ones to be solving? If the measurements are totally noise-free or we do not care about getting the best possible answer, then the answer is yes. However, in general, we cannot be sure that we have a reasonable algorithm unless we make a model of the likely sources of error and devise an algorithm that performs as well as possible given these potential errors.

B.1 Estimation theory

The study of such inference problems from noisy data is often called *estimation theory* (Gelb 1974), and its extension to problems where we explicitly choose a loss function is called *statistical decision theory* (Berger 1993; Hastie, Tibshirani, and Friedman 2001; Bishop 2006; Robert 2007). We first start by writing down the forward process that leads from our unknowns (and knowns) to a set of noise-corrupted measurements. We then devise an algorithm that will give us an estimate (or set of estimates) that are both insensitive to the noise (as best they can be) and also quantify the reliability of these estimates.

---

[1] In machine learning, these problems are called *regression problems*, because we are trying to estimate a *continuous* quantity from noisy inputs, as opposed to a discrete *classification* task (Bishop 2006).

The specific equations above (B.1) are just a particular instance of a more general set of *measurement equations*,

$$\boldsymbol{y}_i = \boldsymbol{f}_i(\boldsymbol{x}) + \boldsymbol{n}_i. \tag{B.5}$$

Here, the $\boldsymbol{y}_i$ are the noise-corrupted *measurements*, e.g., (x_i, y_i) in Equation (B.1), and $\boldsymbol{x}$ is the unknown *state vector*.[2]

Each measurement comes with its associated *measurement model* $\boldsymbol{f}_i(\boldsymbol{x})$, which maps the unknown into that particular measurement. An alternative formulation would be to have one general function $\boldsymbol{f}(\boldsymbol{x}, \boldsymbol{p}_i)$ and to use a per-measurement parameter vector $\boldsymbol{p}_i$ to distinguish between different measurements, e.g., (X_i, Y_i, Z_i) in Equation (B.1). Note that the use of the $\boldsymbol{f}_i(\boldsymbol{x})$ form makes it straightforward to have measurements of different dimensions, which becomes useful when we start adding in prior information (Appendix B.4).

Each measurement is also contaminated with some noise $\boldsymbol{n}_i$. In Equation (B.5), we have indicated that $\boldsymbol{n}_i$ is a zero-mean normal (Gaussian) random variable with a covariance matrix $\boldsymbol{\Sigma}_i$. In general, the noise need not be Gaussian and, in fact, it is usually prudent to assume that some measurements may be outliers. However, we defer this discussion to Appendix B.3, after we have explored the simpler Gaussian noise case more fully. We also assume that the noise vectors $\boldsymbol{n}_i$ are independent. In the case where they are not (e.g., when some constant gain or offset contaminates all of the pixels in a given image), we can add this effect as a *nuisance parameter* to our state vector $\boldsymbol{x}$ and later estimate its value (and discard it, if so desired).

B.1.1 Likelihood for multivariate Gaussian noise

Given all of the noisy measurements $\boldsymbol{y} = \{\boldsymbol{y}_i\}$, we would like to infer a probability distribution on the unknown $\boldsymbol{x}$ vector. We can write the *likelihood* of having observed the $\{\boldsymbol{y}_i\}$ given a particular value of $\boldsymbol{x}$ as

$$L = p(\boldsymbol{y}|\boldsymbol{x}) = \prod_i p(\boldsymbol{y}_i|\boldsymbol{x}) = \prod_i p(\boldsymbol{y}_i|\boldsymbol{f}_i(\boldsymbol{x})) = \prod_i p(\boldsymbol{n}_i). \tag{B.6}$$

When each noise vector $\boldsymbol{n}_i$ is a multivariate Gaussian with covariance $\boldsymbol{\Sigma}_i$,

$$\boldsymbol{n}_i \sim \mathcal{N}(0, \boldsymbol{\Sigma}_i), \tag{B.7}$$

we can write this likelihood as

$$
\begin{aligned}
L &= \prod_i |2\pi\boldsymbol{\Sigma}_i|^{-1/2} \exp\left(-\frac{1}{2}(\boldsymbol{y}_i - \boldsymbol{f}_i(\boldsymbol{x}))^T \boldsymbol{\Sigma}_i^{-1}(\boldsymbol{y}_i - \boldsymbol{f}_i(\boldsymbol{x}))\right) \\
&= \prod_i |2\pi\boldsymbol{\Sigma}_i|^{-1/2} \exp\left(-\frac{1}{2}\|\boldsymbol{y}_i - \boldsymbol{f}_i(\boldsymbol{x})\|^2_{\boldsymbol{\Sigma}_i^{-1}}\right),
\end{aligned}
\tag{B.8}
$$

where the matrix norm $\|\boldsymbol{x}\|^2_{\boldsymbol{A}}$ is a shorthand notation for $\boldsymbol{x}^T \boldsymbol{A} \boldsymbol{x}$.

The norm $\|\boldsymbol{y}_i - \overline{\boldsymbol{y}}_i\|_{\boldsymbol{\Sigma}_i^{-1}}$ is often called the *Mahalanobis distance* (5.26 and 14.14) and is used to measure the distance between a measurement and the mean of a multivariate Gaussian distribution. Contours of equal Mahalanobis distance are equi-probability contours. Note

---

[2] In the Kalman filtering literature (Gelb 1974), it is more common to use $\boldsymbol{z}$ instead of $\boldsymbol{y}$ to denote measurements.

that when the measurement covariance is isotropic (the same in all directions), i.e., when $\mathbf{\Sigma}_i = \sigma_i^2 \mathbf{I}$, the likelihood can be written as

$$L = \prod_i (2\pi\sigma_i^2)^{-N_i/2} \exp\left(-\frac{1}{2\sigma_i^2}\|\mathbf{y}_i - \mathbf{f}_i(\mathbf{x})\|^2\right), \tag{B.9}$$

where N_i is the length of the ith measurement vector $\mathbf{y}_i$.

We can more easily visualize the structure of the covariance matrix and the corresponding Mahalanobis distance if we first perform an *eigenvalue* or *principal component* analysis (PCA) of the covariance matrix (A.6),

$$\mathbf{\Sigma} = \mathbf{\Phi} \, \text{diag}(\lambda_0 \dots \lambda_{N-1}) \, \mathbf{\Phi}^T. \tag{B.10}$$

Equal-probability contours of the corresponding multi-variate Gaussian, which are also equidistance contours in the Mahalanobis distance (Figure 14.14), are multi-dimensional ellipsoids whose axis directions are given by the columns of $\mathbf{\Phi}$ (the *eigenvectors*) and whose lengths are given by the $\sigma_j = \sqrt{\lambda_j}$ (Figure A.1).

It is usually more convenient to work with the negative log likelihood, which we can think of as a *cost* or *energy*

$$E = -\log L = \frac{1}{2}\sum_i (\mathbf{y}_i - \mathbf{f}_i(\mathbf{x}))^T \mathbf{\Sigma}_i^{-1}(\mathbf{y}_i - \mathbf{f}_i(\mathbf{x})) + k \tag{B.11}$$

$$= \frac{1}{2}\sum_i \|\mathbf{y}_i - \mathbf{f}_i(\mathbf{x})\|^2_{\mathbf{\Sigma}_i^{-1}} + k, \tag{B.12}$$

where $k = \sum_i \log|2\pi\mathbf{\Sigma}_i|$ is a constant that depends on the measurement variances, but is independent of $\mathbf{x}$.

Notice that the inverse covariance $\mathbf{C}_i = \mathbf{\Sigma}_i^{-1}$ plays the role of a *weight* on each of the measurement error *residuals*, i.e., the difference between the contaminated measurement $\mathbf{y}_i$ and its uncontaminated (predicted) value $\mathbf{f}_i(\mathbf{x})$. In fact, the inverse covariance is often called the (Fisher) *information matrix* (Bishop 2006), since it tells us how much information is contained in a given measurement, i.e., how well it constrains the final estimate. We can also think of this matrix as denoting the amount of *confidence* to associate with each measurement (hence the letter $\mathbf{C}$).

In this formulation, it is quite acceptable for some information matrices to be singular (of degenerate rank) or even zero (if the measurement is missing altogether). Rank-deficient measurements often occur, for example, when using a line feature or edge to measure a 3D edge-like feature, since its exact position along the edge is unknown (of infinite or extremely large variance) §8.1.3.

In order to make the distinction between the noise contaminated measurement and its expected value for a particular setting of $\mathbf{x}$ more explicit, we adopt the notation $\tilde{\mathbf{y}}$ for the former (think of the tilde as the approximate or noisy value) and $\hat{\mathbf{y}} = \mathbf{f}_i(\mathbf{x})$ for the latter (think of the hat as the predicted or expected value). We can then write the negative log likelihood as

$$E = -\log L = \sum_i \|\tilde{\mathbf{y}}_i - \hat{\mathbf{y}}_i\|_{\mathbf{\Sigma}_i^{-1}} + k. \tag{B.13}$$

B.2 Maximum likelihood estimation and least squares

Now that we have presented the likelihood and log likelihood functions, how can we find the optimal value for our state estimate x? One plausible choice might be to select the value of x that maximizes $L = p(y|x)$. In fact, in the absence of any prior model for x (Appendix B.4), we have

$$L = p(y|x) = p(y, x) = p(x|y).$$

Therefore, choosing the value of x that maximizes the likelihood is equivalent to choosing the maximum of our probability density estimate for x.

When might this be a good idea? If the data (measurements) constrain the possible values of x so that they all cluster tightly around one value (e.g., if the distribution $p(x|y)$ is a unimodal Gaussian), the maximum likelihood estimate is the optimal one in that it is both unbiased and has the least possible variance. In many other cases, e.g., if a single estimate is all that is required, it is still often the best estimate.[3] However, if the probability is multimodal, i.e., it has several local minima in the log likelihood (Figure 5.7), much more care may be required. In particular, it might be necessary to defer certain decisions (such as the ultimate position of an object being tracked) until more measurements have been taken. The CONDENSATION algorithm presented in Section 5.1.2 is one possible method for modeling and updating such multi-modal distributions but is just one example of more general *particle filtering* and *Markov Chain Monte Carlo* (MCMC) techniques (Andrieu, de Freitas, Doucet *et al.* 2003; Bishop 2006; Koller and Friedman 2009).

Another possible way to choose the best estimate is to maximize the *expected utility* (or, conversely, to minimize the expected risk or loss) associated with obtaining the correct estimate, i.e., by minimizing

$$E_{\text{loss}}(x, y) = \int l(x - z)p(z|y)dz. \tag{B.14}$$

For example, if a robot wants to avoid hitting a wall at all costs, the loss function will be high whenever the estimate underestimates the true distance to the wall. When $l(x - y) = \delta(x - y)$, we obtain the maximum likelihood estimate, whereas when $l(x - y) = \|x - y\|^2$, we obtain the *mean square error* (MSE) or *expected value* estimate. The explicit modeling of a utility or loss function is what characterizes *statistical decision theory* (Berger 1993; Hastie, Tibshirani, and Friedman 2001; Bishop 2006; Robert 2007).

How do we find the maximum likelihood estimate? If the measurement noise is Gaussian, we can minimize the quadratic objective function (B.13). This becomes even simpler if the measurement equations are linear, i.e.,

$$f_i(x) = H_i x, \tag{B.15}$$

where H is the *measurement matrix* relating unknown state variables x to measurements $\tilde{y}$. In this case, (B.13) becomes

$$E = \sum_i \|\tilde{y}_i - H_i x\|_{\Sigma_i^{-1}} = \sum_i (\tilde{y}_i - H_i x)^T C_i(\tilde{y}_i - H_i x), \tag{B.16}$$

---

[3] According to the Gauss-Markov theorem, least squares produces the best linear unbiased estimator (BLUE) for a linear measurement model regardless of the actual noise distribution, assuming that the noise is zero mean and uncorrelated.

which is a simple quadratic form in x, which can be solved using linear least squares (Appendix A.2). When the measurements are non-linear, the system must be solved iteratively using non-linear least squares (Appendix A.3).

B.3 Robust statistics

In Appendix B.1.1, we assumed that the noise being added to each measurement (B.5) was multivariate Gaussian (B.7). This is an appropriate model if the noise is the result of lots of tiny errors being added together, e.g., from thermal noise in a silicon imager. In most cases, however, measurements can be contaminated with larger *outliers*, i.e., gross failures in the measurement process. Examples of such outliers include bad feature matches (Section 6.1.4), occlusions in stereo matching (Chapter 11), and discontinuities in an otherwise smooth image, depth map, or label image (Sections 3.7.1 and 3.7.2).

In such cases, it makes more sense to model the measurement noise with a long-tailed *contaminated* noise model such as a Laplacian. The negative log likelihood in this case, rather than being quadratic in the measurement residuals (B.12–B.16), has a slower growth in the penalty function to account for the increased likelihood of large errors.

This formulation of the inference problem is called an *M-estimator* in the robust statistics literature (Huber 1981; Hampel, Ronchetti, Rousseeuw *et al.* 1986; Black and Rangarajan 1996; Stewart 1999) and involves applying a robust penalty function $\rho(r)$ to the residuals

$$E_{\mathrm{RLS}}(\Delta \boldsymbol{p}) = \sum_i \rho(\|\boldsymbol{r}_i\|) \qquad (\mathrm{B}.17)$$

instead of squaring them.

As we mentioned in Section 6.1.4, we can take the derivative of this function with respect to $\boldsymbol{p}$ and set it to 0,

$$\sum_i \psi(\|\boldsymbol{r}_i\|) \frac{\partial \|\boldsymbol{r}_i\|}{\partial \boldsymbol{p}} = \sum_i \frac{\psi(\|\boldsymbol{r}_i\|)}{\|\boldsymbol{r}_i\|} \boldsymbol{r}_i^T \frac{\partial \boldsymbol{r}_i}{\partial \boldsymbol{p}} = 0, \qquad (\mathrm{B}.18)$$

where $\psi(r) = \rho'(r)$ is the derivative of ρ and is called the *influence function*. If we introduce a *weight function*, $w(r) = \Psi(r)/r$, we observe that finding the stationary point of (B.17) using (B.18) is equivalent to minimizing the *iteratively re-weighted least squares* (IRLS) problem

$$E_{\mathrm{IRLS}} = \sum_i w(\|\boldsymbol{r}_i\|) \|\boldsymbol{r}_i\|^2, \qquad (\mathrm{B}.19)$$

where the $w(\|\boldsymbol{r}_i\|)$ play the same local weighting role as $C_i = \Sigma_i^{-1}$ in (B.12). Black and Anandan (1996) describe a variety of robust penalty functions and their corresponding influence and weighting function.

The IRLS algorithm alternates between computing the influence functions $w(\|\boldsymbol{r}_i\|)$ and solving the resulting weighted least squares problem (with fixed w values). Alternative incremental robust least squares algorithms can be found in the work of Sawhney and Ayer (1996); Black and Anandan (1996); Black and Rangarajan (1996); Baker, Gross, Ishikawa *et al.* (2003) and textbooks and tutorials on robust statistics (Huber 1981; Hampel, Ronchetti, Rousseeuw *et al.* 1986; Rousseeuw and Leroy 1987; Stewart 1999). It is also possible to apply general optimization techniques (Appendix A.3) directly to the non-linear cost function given in Equation (B.19), which may sometimes have better convergence properties.

Most robust penalty functions involve a scale parameter, which should typically be set to the variance (or standard deviation, depending on the formulation) of the non-contaminated (inlier) noise. Estimating such noise levels directly from the measurements or their residuals, however, can be problematic, as such estimates themselves become contaminated by outliers. The robust statistics literature contains a variety of techniques to estimate such parameters. One of the simplest and most effective is the *median absolute deviation* (MAD),

$$MAD = \text{med}_i \|\boldsymbol{r}_i\|, \tag{B.20}$$

which, when multiplied by 1.4, provides a robust estimate of the standard deviation of the inlier noise process.

As mentioned in Section 6.1.4, it is often better to start iterative non-linear minimization techniques, such as IRLS, in the vicinity of a good solution by first randomly selecting small subsets of measurements until a good set of inliers is found. The best known of these techniques is RANdom SAmple Consensus (RANSAC) (Fischler and Bolles 1981), although even better variants such as Preemptive RANSAC (Nistér 2003) and PROgressive SAmple Consensus (PROSAC) (Chum and Matas 2005) have since been developed.

B.4 Prior models and Bayesian inference

While maximum likelihood estimation can often lead to good solutions, in some cases the range of possible solutions consistent with the measurements is too large to be useful. For example, consider the problem of image denoising (Sections 3.4.4 and 3.7.3). If we estimate each pixel separately based on just its noisy version, we cannot make any progress, as there are a large number of values that could lead to each noisy measurement.[4] Instead, we need to rely on typical properties of images, e.g., that they tend to be piecewise smooth (Section 3.7.1).

The propensity of images to be piecewise smooth can be encoded in a *prior distribution* $p(\boldsymbol{x})$, which measures the likelihood of an image being a natural image. For example, to encode piecewise smoothness, we can use a *Markov random field* model (3.109 and B.24) whose negative log likelihood is proportional to a robustified measure of image smoothness (gradient magnitudes).

Prior models need not be restricted to image processing applications. For example, we may have some external knowledge about the rough dimensions of an object being scanned, the focal length of a lens being calibrated, or the likelihood that a particular object might appear in an image. All of these are examples of prior distributions or probabilities and they can be used to produce more reliable estimates.

As we have already seen in (3.68) and (3.106), Bayes' Rule states that a *posterior* distribution $p(\boldsymbol{x}|\boldsymbol{y})$ over the unknowns $\boldsymbol{x}$ given the measurements $\boldsymbol{y}$ can be obtained by multiplying the measurement likelihood $p(\boldsymbol{y}|\boldsymbol{x})$ by the prior distribution $p(\boldsymbol{x})$,

$$p(\boldsymbol{x}|\boldsymbol{y}) = \frac{p(\boldsymbol{y}|\boldsymbol{x})p(\boldsymbol{x})}{p(\boldsymbol{y})}, \tag{B.21}$$

where $p(\boldsymbol{y}) = \int_{\boldsymbol{x}} p(\boldsymbol{y}|\boldsymbol{x})p(\boldsymbol{x})$ is a normalizing constant used to make the $p(\boldsymbol{x}|\boldsymbol{y})$ distribution *proper* (integrate to 1). Taking the negative logarithm of both sides of Equation (B.21), we

---

[4] In fact, the maximum likelihood estimate is just the noisy image itself.

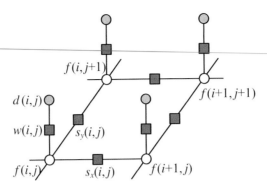

Figure B.1   Graphical model for an $\mathcal{N}_4$ neighborhood Markov random field. The white circles are the unknowns $f(i,j)$, while the dark circles are the input data $d(i,j)$. The $s_x(i,j)$ and $s_y(i,j)$ black boxes denote arbitrary *interaction potentials* between adjacent nodes in the random field, and the $w(i,j)$ denote the *data penalty* functions. They are all examples of the general potentials $V_{i,j,k,l}(f(i,j),f(k,l))$ used in Equation (B.24).

get

$$- \log p(\boldsymbol{x}|\boldsymbol{y}) = - \log p(\boldsymbol{y}|\boldsymbol{x}) - \log p(\boldsymbol{x}) + \log p(\boldsymbol{y}), \qquad \text{(B.22)}$$

which is the *negative posterior log likelihood*. It is common to drop the constant $\log p(\boldsymbol{y})$ because its value does not matter during energy minimization. However, if the prior distribution $p(\boldsymbol{x})$ depends on some unknown parameters, we may wish to keep $\log p(\boldsymbol{y})$ in order to compute the most likely value of these parameters using *Occam's razor*, i.e., by maximizing the likelihood of the observations, or to select the correct number of free parameters using *model selection* (Hastie, Tibshirani, and Friedman 2001; Torr 2002; Bishop 2006; Robert 2007).

To find the most likely (*maximum a posteriori* or MAP) solution $\boldsymbol{x}$ given some measurements $\boldsymbol{y}$, we simply minimize this negative log likelihood, which can also be thought of as an *energy*,

$$E(\boldsymbol{x},\boldsymbol{y}) = E_d(\boldsymbol{x},\boldsymbol{y}) + E_p(\boldsymbol{x}). \qquad \text{(B.23)}$$

The first term $E_d(\boldsymbol{x},\boldsymbol{y})$ is the *data energy* or *data penalty* and measures the negative log likelihood that the measurements $\boldsymbol{y}$ were observed given the unknown state $\boldsymbol{x}$. The second term $E_p(\boldsymbol{x})$ is the *prior energy* and it plays a role analogous to the smoothness energy in regularization. Note that the MAP estimate may not always be desirable, since it selects the "peak" in the posterior distribution rather than some more stable statistic such as MSE—see the discussion in Appendix B.2 about loss functions and decision theory.

B.5 Markov random fields

Markov random fields (Blake, Kohli, and Rother 2010) are the most popular types of prior model for gridded image-like data,[5] which include not only regular natural images (Section 3.7.2) but also two-dimensional fields such as optic flow (Chapter 8) or depth maps (Chapter 11), as well as binary fields, such as segmentations (Section 5.5).

---

[5] Alternative formulations include power spectra (Section 3.4.3) and non-local means (Buades, Coll, and Morel 2008).

As we discussed in Section 3.7.2, the prior probability $p(\boldsymbol{x})$ for a Markov random field is a *Gibbs* or *Boltzmann distribution*, whose negative log likelihood (according to the Hammersley–Clifford Theorem) can be written as a sum of pairwise *interaction potentials*,

$$E_p(\boldsymbol{x}) = \sum_{\{(i,j),(k,l)\}\in\mathcal{N}} V_{i,j,k,l}(f(i,j), f(k,l)), \tag{B.24}$$

where $\mathcal{N}(i,j)$ denotes the *neighbors* of pixel (i,j). In the more general case, MRFs can also contain unary potentials, as well as *higher-order potentials* defined over larger cardinality *cliques* (Kindermann and Snell 1980; Geman and Geman 1984; Bishop 2006; Potetz and Lee 2008; Kohli, Kumar, and Torr 2009; Kohli, Ladický, and Torr 2009; Rother, Kohli, Feng *et al.* 2009; Alahari, Kohli, and Torr 2011). They can also contain *line processes*, i.e., additional binary variables that mediate discontinuities between adjacent elements (Geman and Geman 1984). Black and Rangarajan (1996) show how independent line process variables can be eliminated and incorporated into regular MRFs using robust pairwise penalty functions.

The most commonly used neighborhood in Markov random field modeling is the $\mathcal{N}_4$ neighborhood, where each pixel in the field $f(i,j)$ interacts only with its immediate neighbors— Figure B.1 shows such an $\mathcal{N}_4$ MRF. The $s_x(i,j)$ and $s_y(i,j)$ black boxes denote arbitrary interaction potentials between adjacent nodes in the random field and the $w(i,j)$ denote the elemental data penalty terms in E_d (B.23). These square nodes can also be interpreted as *factors* in a *factor graph* version of the undirected graphical model (Bishop 2006; Wainwright and Jordan 2008; Koller and Friedman 2009), which is another name for interaction potentials. (Strictly speaking, the factors are improper probability functions whose product is the un-normalized posterior distribution.)

More complex and higher-dimensional interaction models and neighborhoods are also possible. For example, 2D grids can be enhanced with the addition of diagonal connections (an $\mathcal{N}_8$ neighborhood) or even larger numbers of pairwise terms (Boykov and Kolmogorov 2003; Rother, Kolmogorov, Lempitsky *et al.* 2007). 3D grids can be used to compute globally optimal segmentations in 3D volumetric medical images (Boykov and Funka-Lea 2006) (Section 5.5.1). Higher-order cliques can also be used to develop more sophisticated models (Potetz and Lee 2008; Kohli, Ladický, and Torr 2009; Kohli, Kumar, and Torr 2009).

One of the biggest challenges in using MRF models is to develop efficient *inference algorithms* that will find low-energy solutions (Veksler 1999; Boykov, Veksler, and Zabih 2001; Kohli 2007; Kumar 2008). Over the years, a large variety of such algorithms have been developed, including simulated annealing, graph cuts, and loopy belief propagation. The choice of inference technique can greatly affect the overall performance of a vision system. For example, most of the top-performing algorithms on the Middlebury Stereo Evaluation page either use belief propagation or graph cuts.

In the next few subsections, we review some of the more widely used MRF inference techniques. More in-depth descriptions of most of these algorithms can be found in a recently published book on advances in MRF techniques (Blake, Kohli, and Rother 2010). Experimental comparisons, along with test datasets and reference software, are provided by Szeliski, Zabih, Scharstein *et al.* (2008).[6]

---

[6] http://vision.middlebury.edu/MRF/.

B.5.1 Gradient descent and simulated annealing

The simplest optimization technique is gradient descent, which minimizes the energy by changing independent subsets of nodes to take on lower-energy configurations. Such techniques go under a variety of names, including *contextual classification* (Kittler and Föglein 1984) and *iterated conditional modes* (ICM) (Besag 1986).[7] Variables can either be updated sequentially, e.g., in raster scan, or in parallel, e.g., using red–black coloring on a checkerboard. Chou and Brown (1990) suggests using highest confidence first (HCF), i.e., choosing variables based on how large a difference they make in reducing the energy.

The problem with gradient descent is that it is prone to getting stuck in local minima, which is almost always the case with MRF problems. One way around this is to use *stochastic gradient descent* or *Markov chain Monte Carlo* (MCMC) (Metropolis, Rosenbluth, Rosenbluth *et al.* 1953), i.e., to randomly take occasional uphill steps in order to get out of such minima. One popular update rule is the *Gibbs sampler* (Geman and Geman 1984); rather than choosing the lowest energy state for a variable being updated, it chooses the state with probability

$$p(\boldsymbol{x}) \propto e^{-E(\boldsymbol{x})/T}, \qquad\qquad\qquad (B.25)$$

where T is called the *temperature* and controls how likely the system is to choose a more random update. Stochastic gradient descent is usually combined with *simulated annealing* (Kirkpatrick, Gelatt, and Vecchi 1983), which starts at a relatively high temperature, thereby randomly exploring a large part of the state space, and gradually cools (anneals) the temperature to find a good local minimum. During the late 1980s, simulated annealing was the method of choice for solving MRF inference problems (Szeliski 1986; Marroquin, Mitter, and Poggio 1985; Barnard 1989).

Another variant on simulated annealing is the Swendsen–Wang algorithm (Swendsen and Wang 1987; Barbu and Zhu 2003, 2005). Here, instead of "flipping" (changing) single variables, a connected subset of variables, chosen using a random walk based on MRF connectively strengths, is selected as the basic update unit. This can sometimes help make larger state changes, and hence find better-quality solutions in less time.

While simulated annealing has largely been superseded by the newer graph cuts and loopy belief propagation techniques, it still occasionally finds use, especially in highly connected and highly non-submodular graphs (Rother, Kolmogorov, Lempitsky *et al.* 2007).

B.5.2 Dynamic programming

Dynamic programming (DP) is an efficient inference procedure that works for any tree-structured graphical model, i.e., one that does not have any cycles. Given such a tree, pick any node as the root r and figuratively pick up the tree by its root. The depth or distance of all the other nodes from this root induces a partial ordering over the vertices, from which a total ordering can be obtained by arbitrarily breaking ties. Let us now lay out this graph as a tree with the root on the right and indices increasing from left to right, as shown in Figure B.2a.

Before describing the DP algorithm, let us re-write the potential function of Equation (B.24)

---

[7] The name comes from iteratively setting variables to the mode (most likely, i.e., lowest energy) state conditioned on its currently fixed neighbors.

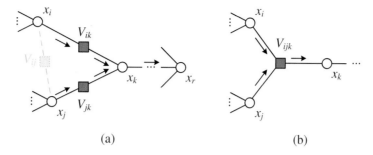

(a)   (b)

Figure B.2 Dynamic programming over a tree drawn as a factor graph. (a) To compute the lowest energy solution $\hat{E}_k(x_k)$ at node x_k conditioned on the best solutions to the left of this node, we enumerate all possible values of $\hat{E}_i(x_i) + V_{ik}(x_i, x_k)$ and pick the smallest one (and similarly for j). (b) For higher-order cliques, we need to try all combinations of (x_i, x_j) in order to select the best possible configuration. The arrows show the basic flow of the computation. The lightly shaded factor V_{ij} in (a) shows an additional connection that turns the tree into a cyclic graph, for which exact inference cannot be efficiently computed.

in a more general but succinct form,

$$E(\boldsymbol{x}) = \sum_{(i,j)\in\mathcal{N}} V_{i,j}(x_i, x_j) + \sum_i V_i(x_i), \qquad (\text{B.26})$$

where instead of using pixel indices (i, j) and (k, l), we just use scalar index variables i and j. We also replace the function value $f(i, j)$ with the more succinct notation x_i, with the $\{x_i\}$ variables making up the state vector $\boldsymbol{x}$. We can simplify this function even further by adding dummy nodes (vertices) i^- for every node that has a non-zero $V_i(x_i)$ and setting $V_{i,i^-}(x_i, x_{i^-}) = V_i(x_i)$, which lets us drop the V_i terms from (B.26).

Dynamic programming proceeds by computing partial sums in a left-to-right fashion, i.e., in order of increasing variable index. Let $\mathcal{C}_k$ be the children of k, i.e., $i < k, (i, k) \in \mathcal{N}$. Then, define

$$\tilde{E}_k(\boldsymbol{x}) = \sum_{i<k,\, j\leq k} V_{i,j}(x_i, x_j) = \sum_{i\in\mathcal{C}_k} \left[V_{i,k}(x_i, x_k) + \tilde{E}_i(\boldsymbol{x}) \right], \qquad (\text{B.27})$$

as a partial sum of (B.26) over all variables up to and including k, i.e., over all parts of the graph shown in Figure B.2a to the left of x_k. This sum depends on the state of all the unknown variables in $\boldsymbol{x}$ with $i \leq k$.

Now suppose we wish to find the setting for all variables $i < k$ that minimizes this sum. It turns out that we can use a simple recursive formula

$$\hat{E}_k(x_k) = \min_{\{x_i,\, i<k\}} \tilde{E}_k(\boldsymbol{x}) = \sum_{i\in\mathcal{C}_k} \min_{x_i} \left[V_{i,k}(x_i, x_k) + \hat{E}_i(x_i) \right] \qquad (\text{B.28})$$

to find this minimum. Visually, this is easy to understand. Looking at Figure B.2a, associate an energy $\hat{E}_k(x_k)$ with each node k and each possible setting of its value x_k that is based on the *best* possible setting of variables to the left of that node. It is easy to convince yourself that in this figure, you only need to know $\hat{E}_i(x_i)$ and $\hat{E}_j(x_j)$ in order to compute this value.

Once the flow of information in the tree has been processed from left to right, the minimum value of $\hat{E}_r(x_r)$ at the root gives the MAP (lowest-energy) solution for $E(\boldsymbol{x})$. The root node is set to the choice of x_r that minimizes this function, and other nodes are set in a *backward chaining* pass by selecting the values of child nodes $i \in \mathcal{C}_k$ that were minimal in the original recursion (B.28).

Dynamic programming is not restricted to trees with pairwise potentials. Figure B.2b shows an example of a three-way potential $V_{ijk}(x_i, x_j, x_k)$ inside a tree. To compute the optimum value of $\hat{E}_k(x_k)$, the recursion formula in (B.28) now has to evaluate the minimum over all combinations of possible state values leading into a factor node (gray box). For this reason, dynamic programming is normally exponential in complexity in the order of the clique size, i.e., a clique of size n with l labels at each node requires the evaluation of l^{n-1} possible states (Potetz and Lee 2008; Kohli, Kumar, and Torr 2009). However, for certain kinds of potential functions $V_{i,k}(x_i, x_k)$, including the Potts model (delta function), absolute values (total variation), and quadratic (Gaussian MRF), Felzenszwalb and Huttenlocher (2006) show how to reduce the complexity of the min-finding step (B.28) from $O(l^2)$ to $O(l)$. In Appendix B.5.3, we also discuss how Potetz and Lee (2008) reduce the complexity for special kinds of higher-order clique, i.e., linear summations followed by non-linearities.

Figure B.2a also shows what happens if we add an extra factor between nodes i and j. In this case, the graph is no longer a tree, i.e., it contains a cycle. It is no longer possible to use the recursion formula (B.28), since $\hat{E}_i(x_i)$ now appears in two different terms inside the summation, i.e., as a child of both nodes j and k, and the same setting for x_i may not minimize both. In other words, when loops exist, there is no ordering of the variables that allows the recursion (elimination) in (B.28) to be well-founded.

It is, however, possible to convert small loops into higher-order factors and to solve these as shown in Figure B.2b. However, graphs with long loops or meshes result in extremely large clique sizes and hence an amount of computation potentially exponential in the size of the graph.

B.5.3 Belief propagation

Belief propagation is an inference technique originally developed for trees (Pearl 1988) but more recently extended to "loopy" (cyclic) graphs such as MRFs (Frey and MacKay 1997; Freeman, Pasztor, and Carmichael 2000; Yedidia, Freeman, and Weiss 2001; Weiss and Freeman 2001a,b; Yuille 2002; Sun, Zheng, and Shum 2003; Felzenszwalb and Huttenlocher 2006). It is closely related to dynamic programming, in that both techniques pass messages forward and backward over a tree or graph. In fact, one of the two variants of belief propagation, the *max-product rule*, performs the exact same computation (inference) as dynamic programming, albeit using probabilities instead of energies.

Recall that the energy we are minimizing in MAP estimation (B.26) is the negative log likelihood (B.12, B.13, and B.22) of a factored Gibbs posterior distribution,

$$p(\boldsymbol{x}) = \prod_{(i,j)\in\mathcal{N}} \phi_{i,j}(x_i, x_j), \tag{B.29}$$

where

$$\phi_{i,j}(x_i, x_j) = e^{-V_{i,j}(x_i, x_j)} \tag{B.30}$$

are the pairwise *interaction potentials*. We can rewrite (B.27) as

$$\tilde{p}_k(\boldsymbol{x}) = \prod_{i<k,\ j\leq k} \phi_{i,j}(x_i, x_j) = \prod_{i\in\mathcal{C}_k} \tilde{p}_{i,k}(\boldsymbol{x}), \tag{B.31}$$

where

$$\tilde{p}_{i,k}(\boldsymbol{x}) = \phi_{i,k}(x_i, x_k)\tilde{p}_i(\boldsymbol{x}). \tag{B.32}$$

We can therefore rewrite (B.28) as

$$\hat{p}_k(x_k) = \max_{\{x_i,\ i<k\}} \tilde{p}_k(\boldsymbol{x}) = \prod_{i\in\mathcal{C}_k} \hat{p}_{i,k}(\boldsymbol{x}), \tag{B.33}$$

with

$$\hat{p}_{i,k}(\boldsymbol{x}) = \max_{x_i} \phi_{i,k}(x_i, x_k)\hat{p}_i(\boldsymbol{x}). \tag{B.34}$$

Equation (B.34) is the *max* update rule evaluated at all square box factors in Figure B.2a, while (B.33) is the *product* rule evaluated at the nodes. The probability distribution $\hat{p}_{i,k}(\boldsymbol{x})$ is often interpreted as a *message* passing information about child i to parent k and is hence written as $m_{i,k}(x_k)$ (Yedidia, Freeman, and Weiss 2001) or $\mu_{i\to k}(x_k)$ (Bishop 2006).

The max-product rule can be used to compute the MAP estimate in a tree using the same kind of forward and backward sweep as in dynamic programming (which is sometimes called the *max-sum* algorithm (Bishop 2006)). An alternative rule, known as the *sum–product*, sums over all possible values in (B.34) rather than taking the maximum, in essence computing the *expected* distribution rather than the *maximum likelihood* distribution. This produces a set of probability estimates that can be used to compute the *marginal* distributions $b_i(x_i) = \sum_{\boldsymbol{x}\backslash x_i} p(\boldsymbol{x})$ (Pearl 1988; Yedidia, Freeman, and Weiss 2001; Bishop 2006).

Belief propagation may not produce optimal estimates for cyclic graphs for the same reason that dynamic programming fails to work, i.e., because a node with multiple parents may take on different optimal values for each of the parents, i.e., there is no unique elimination ordering. Early algorithms for extending belief propagation to graphs with cycles, dubbed *loopy belief propagation*, performed the updates in parallel over the graph, i.e., using *synchronous updates* (Frey and MacKay 1997; Freeman, Pasztor, and Carmichael 2000; Yedidia, Freeman, and Weiss 2001; Weiss and Freeman 2001a,b; Yuille 2002; Sun, Zheng, and Shum 2003; Felzenszwalb and Huttenlocher 2006).

For example, Felzenszwalb and Huttenlocher (2006) split an $\mathcal{N}_4$ graph into its red and black (checkerboard) components and alternate between sending messages from the red nodes to the black and vice versa. They also use multi-grid (coarser level) updates to speed up the convergence. As discussed previously, to reduce the complexity of the basic max-product update rule (B.28) from $O(l^2)$ to $O(l)$, they develop specialized update algorithms for several cost functions $V_{i,k}(x_i, x_k)$, including the Potts model (delta function), absolute values (total variation), and quadratic (Gaussian MRF). A related algorithm, *mean field diffusion* (Scharstein and Szeliski 1998), also uses synchronous updates between nodes to compute marginal distributions. Yuille (2010) discusses the relationships between mean field theory and loopy belief propagation.

More recent loopy belief propagation algorithms and their variants use sequential scans through the graph (Szeliski, Zabih, Scharstein *et al.* 2008). For example, Tappen and Freeman (2003) pass messages from left to right along each row and then reverse the direction once they reach the end. This is similar to treating each row as an independent tree (chain), except that messages from nodes above and below the row are also incorporated. They then perform similar computations along columns. These sequential updates allow the information to propagate much more quickly across the image than synchronous updates.

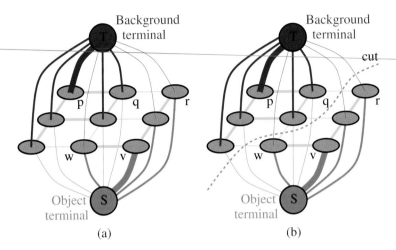

Figure B.3 Graph cuts for minimizing binary sub-modular MRF energies (Boykov and Jolly 2001) © 2001 IEEE: (a) energy function encoded as a max flow problem; (b) the minimum cut determines the region boundary.

The other belief propagation variant tested by Szeliski, Zabih, Scharstein *et al.* (2008), which they call BP-S or TRW-S, is based on Kolmogorov's (2006) sequential extension of the *tree-reweighted message passing* of Wainwright, Jaakkola, and Willsky (2005). TRW first selects a set of trees from the neighborhood graph and computes a set of probability distributions over each tree. These are then used to reweight the messages being passed during loopy belief propagation. The sequential version of TRW, called TRW-S, processed nodes in scan-line order, with a forward and backward pass. In the forward pass, each node sends messages to its right and bottom neighbors. In the backward pass, messages are sent to the left and upper neighbors. TRW-S also computes a lower bound on the energy, which is used by Szeliski, Zabih, Scharstein *et al.* (2008) to estimate how close to the best possible solution all of the MRF inference algorithms being evaluated get.

As with dynamic programming, belief propagation techniques also become less efficient as the order of each factor clique increases. Potetz and Lee (2008) shows how this complexity can be reduced back to linear in the clique order for continuous-valued problems where the factors involve linear summations followed by a non-linearity, which is typical of more sophisticated MRF models such as fields of experts (Roth and Black 2009) and steerable random fields (Roth and Black 2007b). Kohli, Kumar, and Torr (2009) and Alahari, Kohli, and Torr (2011) develop alternative ways for dealing with higher-order cliques in the context of graph cut algorithms.

B.5.4 Graph cuts

The computer vision community has adopted "graph cuts" as an informal name to describe a large family of MRF inference algorithms based on solving one or more min-cut or max-flow problems (Boykov, Veksler, and Zabih 2001; Boykov and Kolmogorov 2010; Boykov, Veksler, and Zabih 2010; Ishikawa and Veksler 2010).

The simplest example of an MRF graph cut is the polynomial-time algorithm for performing exact minimization of a binary MRF originally developed by Greig, Porteous, and Seheult

(1989) and brought to the attention of the computer vision community by Boykov, Veksler, and Zabih (2001) and Boykov and Jolly (2001). The basic construction of the min-cut graph from an MRF energy function is shown in Figure B.3 and described in Sections 3.7.2 and 5.5. In brief, the nodes in an MRF are connected to special source and sink nodes, and the minimum cut between these two nodes, whose cost is exactly that of the MRF energy under a binary assignment of labels, is computed using a polynomial-time max flow algorithm (Goldberg and Tarjan 1988; Boykov and Kolmogorov 2004).

As discussed in Section 5.5, important extensions of this basic algorithm have been made for the case of directed edges (Kolmogorov and Boykov 2005), larger neighborhoods (Boykov and Kolmogorov 2003; Kolmogorov and Boykov 2005), connectivity priors (Vicente, Kolmogorov, and Rother 2008), and shape priors (Lempitsky and Boykov 2007; Lempitsky, Blake, and Rother 2008). Kolmogorov and Zabih (2004) formally characterize the class of binary energy potentials (*regularity conditions*) for which these algorithms find the global minimum. Komodakis, Tziritas, and Paragios (2008) and Rother, Kolmogorov, Lempitsky *et al.* (2007) provide good algorithms for the cases when they do not.

Binary MRF problems can also be approximately solved by turning them into continuous $[0, 1]$ problems, solving them either as linear systems (Grady 2006; Sinop and Grady 2007; Grady and Alvino 2008; Grady 2008; Grady and Ali 2008; Singaraju, Grady, and Vidal 2008; Couprie, Grady, Najman *et al.* 2009) (the *random walker model*) or by computing geodesic distances (Bai and Sapiro 2009; Criminisi, Sharp, and Blake 2008) and then thresholding the results. More details on these techniques are provided in Section 5.5 and a nice review can be found in the work of Singaraju, Grady, Sinop *et al.* (2010). A different connection to continuous segmentation techniques, this time to the literature on level sets (Section 5.1.4), is made by Boykov, Kolmogorov, Cremers *et al.* (2006), who develop an approach to solving surface propagation PDEs based on combinatorial graph cut algorithms—Boykov and Funka-Lea (2006) discuss this and related techniques.

Multi-valued MRF inference problems usually require solving a series of related binary MRF problems (Boykov, Veksler, and Zabih 2001), although for special cases, such as some convex functions, a single graph cut may suffice (Ishikawa 2003; Schlesinger and Flach 2006). The seminal work in this area is that of Boykov, Veksler, and Zabih (2001), who introduced two algorithms, called the *swap move* and the *expansion move*, which are sketched in Figure B.4. The α–β-swap move selects two labels (usually by cycling through all possible pairings) and then formulates a binary MRF problem that allows any pixels currently labeled as either α or β to optionally switch their values to the other label. The α-expansion move allows any pixel in the MRF to take on the α label or to keep its current identity. It is easy to see by inspection that both of these moves result in binary MRFs with well-defined energy functions.

Because these algorithms use a binary MRF optimization inside their inner loop, they are subject to the constraints on the energy functions that occur in the binary labeling case (Kolmogorov and Zabih 2004). However, more recent algorithms such as those developed by Komodakis, Tziritas, and Paragios (2008) and Rother, Kolmogorov, Lempitsky *et al.* (2007) can be used to provide approximate solutions for more general energy functions. Efficient algorithms for re-using previous solutions (*flow-* and *cut-recycling*) have been developed for on-line applications such as *dynamic MRFs* (Kohli and Torr 2005; Juan and Boykov 2006; Alahari, Kohli, and Torr 2011) and coarse-to-fine banded graph cuts (Agarwala, Zheng, Pal *et*

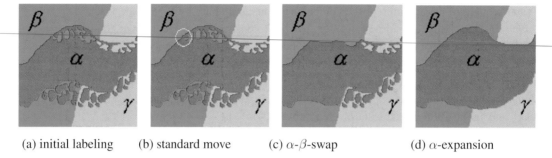

(a) initial labeling   (b) standard move   (c) α-β-swap   (d) α-expansion

Figure B.4 Multi-level graph optimization from (Boykov, Veksler, and Zabih 2001) © 2001 IEEE: (a) initial problem configuration; (b) the standard move changes only one pixel; (c) the α–β-swap optimally exchanges all α- and β-labeled pixels; (d) the α-expansion move optimally selects among current pixel values and the α label.

al. 2005; Lombaert, Sun, Grady *et al.* 2005; Juan and Boykov 2006). It is also now possible to minimize the number of labels used as part of the alpha-expansion process (Delong, Osokin, Isack *et al.* 2010).

In experimental comparisons, α-expansions usually converge faster to a good solution than α–β-swaps (Szeliski, Zabih, Scharstein *et al.* 2008), especially for problems that involve large regions of identical labels, such as the labeling of source imagery in image stitching (Figure 3.60). For truncated convex energy functions defined over ordinal values, more accurate algorithms that consider complete ranges of labels inside each min-cut and often produce lower energies have been developed (Veksler 2007; Kumar and Torr 2008; Kumar, Veksler, and Torr 2010). The whole field of efficient MRF inference algorithms is rapidly developing, as witnessed by a recent special journal issue (Kohli and Torr 2008; Komodakis, Tziritas, and Paragios 2008; Olsson, Eriksson, and Kahl 2008; Potetz and Lee 2008), articles (Alahari, Kohli, and Torr 2011), and a forthcoming book (Blake, Kohli, and Rother 2010).

B.5.5 Linear programming

[8] Many successful algorithms for MRF optimization are based on the *linear programming* (LP) relaxation of the energy function (Weiss, Yanover, and Meltzer 2010). For some practical MRF problems, LP-based techniques can produce globally minimal solutions (Meltzer, Yanover, and Weiss 2005), even though MRF inference is in general NP-hard. In order to describe this relaxation, let us first rewrite the energy function (B.26) as

$$E(\boldsymbol{x}) \;=\; \sum_{(i,j)\in\mathcal{N}} V_{i,j}(x_i, x_j) + \sum_i V_i(x_i) \tag{B.35}$$

$$=\; \sum_{i,j,\alpha,\beta} V_{i,j}(\alpha,\beta) x_{i,j;\alpha,\beta} + \sum_{i,\alpha} V_i(\alpha) x_{i;\alpha} \tag{B.36}$$

$$\text{subject to} \quad x_{i;\alpha} \;=\; \sum_{\beta} x_{i,j;\alpha,\beta} \quad \forall (i,j) \in \mathcal{N}, \alpha, \tag{B.37}$$

$$x_{j;\beta} \;=\; \sum_{\alpha} x_{i,j;\alpha,\beta} \quad \forall (i,j) \in \mathcal{N}, \beta, \quad \text{and} \tag{B.38}$$

$$x_{i,\alpha}, \; x_{i,j;\alpha,\beta} \;\in\; \{0,1\}. \tag{B.39}$$

---

[8] This section was contributed by Vladimir Kolmogorov. Thanks!

Here, α and β range over label values and $x_{i;\alpha} = \delta(x_i - \alpha)$ and $x_{ij;\alpha\beta} = \delta(x_i - \alpha)\delta(x_j - \beta)$ are indicator variables of assignments $x_i = \alpha$ and $(x_i, x_j) = (\alpha, \beta)$, respectively. The LP relaxation is obtained by replacing the discreteness constraints (B.39) with linear constraints $x_{ij;\alpha\beta} \in [0, 1]$. It is easy to show that the optimal value of (B.36) is a lower bound on (B.26).

This relaxation has been extensively studied in the literature, starting with the work of Schlesinger (1976). An important question is how to solve this LP efficiently. Unfortunately, general-purpose LP solvers cannot handle large problems in vision (Yanover, Meltzer, and Weiss 2006). A large number of customized iterative techniques have been proposed. Most of these solve the dual problem, i.e., they formulate a lower bound on (B.36) and then try to maximize this bound. The bound is often formulated using a convex combination of trees, as proposed in (Wainwright, Jaakkola, and Willsky 2005).

The LP lower bound can be maximized via a number of techniques, such as *max-sum diffusion* (Werner 2007), *tree-reweighted message passing* (TRW) (Wainwright, Jaakkola, and Willsky 2005; Kolmogorov 2006), subgradient methods (Schlesinger and Giginyak 2007a,b; Komodakis, Paragios, and Tziritas 2007), and Bregman projections (Ravikumar, Agarwal, and Wainwright 2008). Note that the max-sum diffusion and TRW algorithms are not guaranteed to converge to a global maximum of LP—they may get stuck at a suboptimal point (Kolmogorov 2006; Werner 2007). However, in practice, this does not appear to be a problem (Kolmogorov 2006).

For some vision applications, algorithms based on relaxation (B.36) produce excellent results. However, this is not guaranteed in all cases—after all, the problem is NP-hard. Recently, researchers have investigated alternative linear programming relaxations (Sontag and Jaakkola 2007; Sontag, Meltzer, Globerson *et al.* 2008; Komodakis and Paragios 2008; Schraudolph 2010). These algorithms are capable of producing tighter bounds compared to (B.36) at the expense of additional computational cost.

LP relaxation and alpha expansion. Solving a linear program produces primal and dual solutions that satisfy *complementary slackness conditions*. In general, the primal solution of (B.36) does not have to be integer-valued so, in practice, we may have to round it to obtain a valid labeling $\boldsymbol{x}$. An alternative proposed by Komodakis and Tziritas (2007a); Komodakis, Tziritas, and Paragios (2007) is to search for primal and dual solutions such that they satisfy *approximate* complementary slackness conditions and the primal solution is already integer-valued. Several max-flow-based algorithms are proposed by (Komodakis and Tziritas 2007a; Komodakis, Tziritas, and Paragios 2007) for this purpose and the *Fast-PD* method (Komodakis, Tziritas, and Paragios 2007) is shown to perform best. In the case of metric interactions, the default version of Fast-PD produces the same primal solution as the alpha-expansion algorithm (Boykov, Veksler, and Zabih 2001). This provides an interesting interpretation of the alpha expansion algorithm as trying to approximately solve relaxation (B.36).

Unlike the standard alpha expansion algorithm, Fast-PD also maintains a dual solution and thus runs faster in practice. Fast-PD can be extended to the case of semi-metric interactions (Komodakis, Tziritas, and Paragios 2007). The primal version of such extension was also given by Rother, Kumar, Kolmogorov *et al.* (2005).

B.6 Uncertainty estimation (error analysis)

In addition to computing the most likely estimate, many applications require an estimate for the *uncertainty* in this estimate.[9] The most general way to do this is to compute a complete probability distribution over all of the unknowns but this is generally intractable. The one special case where it is easy to obtain a simple description for this distribution is linear estimation problems with Gaussian noise, where the joint energy function (negative log likelihood of the posterior estimate) is a quadratic. In this case, the posterior distribution is a multi-variate Gaussian and the covariance can be computed directly from the inverse of the problem Hessian. (Another name for the inverse covariance matrix, which is equal to the Hessian in such simple cases, is the *information matrix*.)

Even here, however, the full covariance matrix may be too large to compute and store. For example, in large structure from motion problems, a large sparse Hessian normally results in a full dense covariance matrix. In such cases, it is often considered acceptable to report only the variance in the estimated quantities or simple covariance estimates on individual parameters, such as 3D point positions or camera pose estimates (Szeliski 1990a). More insight into the problem, e.g., the dominant *modes* of uncertainty, can be obtained using eigenvalue analysis (Szeliski and Kang 1997).

For problems where the posterior energy is non-quadratic, e.g., in non-linear or robustified least squares, it is still often possible to obtain an estimate of the Hessian in the vicinity of the optimal solution. In this case, the *Cramer–Rao lower bound* on the uncertainty (covariance) can be computed as the inverse of the Hessian. Another way of saying this is that while the local Hessian can underestimate how "wide" the energy function can be, the covariance can never be smaller than the estimate based on this local quadratic approximation. It is also possible to estimate a different kind of uncertainty (min-marginal energies) in general MRFs where the MAP inference is performed using graph cuts (Kohli and Torr 2008).

While many computer vision applications ignore uncertainty modeling, it is often useful to compute these estimates just to get an intuitive feeling for the reliability of the estimates. Certain applications, such as Kalman filtering, require the computation of this uncertainty (either explicitly as posterior covariances or implicitly as inverse covariances) in order to optimally integrate new measurements with previously computed estimates.

---

[9] This is particularly true of classic photogrammetry applications, where the reporting of precision is almost always considered mandatory (Förstner 2005).

Appendix C

Supplementary material

In this final appendix, I summarize some of the supplementary materials that may be useful to students, instructors, and researchers. The book's Web site at http://szeliski.org/Book contains updated lists of datasets and software, so please check there as well.

C.1 Data sets

One of the keys to developing reliable vision algorithms is to test your procedures on challenging and representative data sets. When ground truth or other people's results are available, such test can be even more informative (and quantitative).

Over the years, a large number of datasets have been developed for testing and evaluating computer vision algorithms. A number of these datasets (and software) are indexed on the Computer Vision Homepage.[1] Some newer Web sites, such as CVonline (http://homepages. inf.ed.ac.uk/rbf/CVonline/), VisionBib.Com (http://datasets.visionbib.com/), and Computer Vision online (http://computervisiononline.com/), have more recent pointers.

Below, I list some of the more popular data sets, grouped by the book chapters to which they most closely correspond:

Chapter 2: Image formation

CUReT: Columbia-Utrecht Reflectance and Texture Database, http://www1.cs.columbia. edu/CAVE/software/curet/ (Dana, van Ginneken, Nayar *et al.* 1999).

Middlebury Color Datasets: registered color images taken by different cameras to study how they transform gamuts and colors, http://vision.middlebury.edu/color/data/ (Chakrabarti, Scharstein, and Zickler 2009).

Chapter 3: Image processing

Middlebury test datasets for evaluating MRF minimization/inference algorithms, http: //vision.middlebury.edu/MRF/results/ (Szeliski, Zabih, Scharstein *et al.* 2008).

Chapter 4: Feature detection and matching

Affine Covariant Features database for evaluating feature detector and descriptor matching quality and repeatability, http://www.robots.ox.ac.uk/~vgg/research/affine/ (Mikolajczyk and Schmid 2005; Mikolajczyk, Tuytelaars, Schmid *et al.* 2005).

Database of matched image patches for learning and feature descriptor evaluation, http://cvlab.epfl.ch/~brown/patchdata/patchdata.html (Winder and Brown 2007; Hua, Brown, and Winder 2007).

Chapter 5: Segmentation

Berkeley Segmentation Dataset and Benchmark of 1000 images labeled by 30 humans, along with an evaluation, http://www.eecs.berkeley.edu/Research/Projects/CS/vision/ grouping/segbench/ (Martin, Fowlkes, Tal *et al.* 2001).

[1] http://www.cs.cmu.edu/~cil/vision.html, although it has not been maintained since 2004.

Weizmann segmentation evaluation database of 100 grayscale images with ground truth segmentations, http://www.wisdom.weizmann.ac.il/~vision/Seg_Evaluation_DB/index.html (Alpert, Galun, Basri *et al.* 2007).

Chapter 8: Dense motion estimation

The Middlebury optic flow evaluation Web site, http://vision.middlebury.edu/flow/data (Baker, Scharstein, Lewis *et al.* 2009).

The Human-Assisted Motion Annotation database, http://people.csail.mit.edu/celiu/motionAnnotation/ (Liu, Freeman, Adelson *et al.* 2008)

Chapter 10: Computational photography

High Dynamic Range radiance maps, http://www.debevec.org/Research/HDR/ (Debevec and Malik 1997).

Alpha matting evaluation Web site, http://alphamatting.com/ (Rhemann, Rother, Wang *et al.* 2009).

Chapter 11: Stereo correspondence

Middlebury Stereo Datasets and Evaluation, http://vision.middlebury.edu/stereo/ (Scharstein and Szeliski 2002).

Stereo Classification and Performance Evaluation of different aggregation costs for stereo matching, http://www.vision.deis.unibo.it/spe/SPEHome.aspx (Tombari, Mattoccia, Di Stefano *et al.* 2008).

Middlebury Multi-View Stereo Datasets, http://vision.middlebury.edu/mview/data/ (Seitz, Curless, Diebel *et al.* 2006).

Multi-view and Oxford Colleges building reconstructions, http://www.robots.ox.ac.uk/~vgg/data/data-mview.html.

Multi-View Stereo Datasets, http://cvlab.epfl.ch/data/strechamvs/ (Strecha, Fransens, and Van Gool 2006).

Multi-View Evaluation, http://cvlab.epfl.ch/~strecha/multiview/ (Strecha, von Hansen, Van Gool *et al.* 2008).

Chapter 12: 3D reconstruction

HumanEva: synchronized video and motion capture dataset for evaluation of articulated human motion, http://vision.cs.brown.edu/humaneva/ (Sigal, Balan, and Black 2010).

Chapter 13: Image-based rendering

The (New) Stanford Light Field Archive, http://lightfield.stanford.edu/ (Wilburn, Joshi, Vaish *et al.* 2005).

Virtual Viewpoint Video: multi-viewpoint video with per-frame depth maps, http: //research.microsoft.com/en-us/um/redmond/groups/ivm/vvv/ (Zitnick, Kang, Uytten- daele *et al.* 2004).

Chapter 14: Recognition

For a list of visual recognition datasets, see Tables 14.1–14.2. In addition to those, there are also:

Buffy pose classes, http://www.robots.ox.ac.uk/~vgg/data/buffy_pose_classes/ and Buffy stickmen V2.1, http://www.robots.ox.ac.uk/~vgg/data/stickmen/index.html (Ferrari, Marin-Jimenez, and Zisserman 2009; Eichner and Ferrari 2009).

H3D database of pose/joint annotated photographs of humans, http://www.eecs.berkeley. edu/~lbourdev/h3d/ (Bourdev and Malik 2009).

Action Recognition Datasets, http://www.cs.berkeley.edu/projects/vision/action, has point- ers to several datasets for action and activity recognition, as well as some papers. The human action database at http://www.nada.kth.se/cvap/actions/ contains more action sequences.

C.2 Software

One of the best sources for computer vision algorithms is the Open Source Computer Vision (OpenCV) library (http://opencv.willowgarage.com/wiki/), which was developed by Gary Bradski and his colleagues at Intel and is now being maintained and extended at Willow Garage (Bradsky and Kaehler 2008). A partial list of the available functions, taken from http://opencv.willowgarage.com/documentation/cpp/ includes:

- image processing and transforms (filtering, morphology, pyramids);
- geometric image transformations (rotations, resizing);
- miscellaneous image transformations (Fourier transforms, distance transforms);
- histograms;
- segmentation (watershed, mean shift);
- feature detection (Canny, Harris, Hough, MSER, SURF);
- motion analysis and object tracking (Lucas–Kanade, mean shift);
- camera calibration and 3D reconstruction;
- machine learning (k nearest neighbors, support vector machines, decision trees, boost- ing, random trees, expectation-maximization, and neural networks).

The Intel Performance Primitives (IPP) library, http://software.intel.com/en-us/intel-ipp/, contains highly optimized code for a variety of image processing tasks. Many of the routines in OpenCV take advantage of this library, if it is installed, to run even faster. In terms of functionality, it has many of the same operators as those found in OpenCV, plus additional libraries for image and video compression, signal and speech processing, and matrix algebra.

The MATLAB Image Processing Toolbox, http://www.mathworks.com/products/image/, contains routines for spatial transformations (rotations, resizing), normalized cross-correlation, image analysis and statistics (edges, Hough transform), image enhancement (adaptive histogram equalization, median filtering) and restoration (deblurring), linear filtering (convolution), image transforms (Fourier and DCT), and morphological operations (connected components and distance transforms).

Two older libraries, which no longer appear to be under active development but contain many useful routines, are VXL (C++ Libraries for Computer Vision Research and Implementation, http://vxl.sourceforge.net/) and LTI-Lib 2 (http://www.ie.itcr.ac.cr/palvarado/ltilib-2/homepage/).

Photo editing and viewing packages, such as Windows Live Photo Gallery, iPhoto, Picasa, GIMP, and IrfanView, can be useful for performing common processing tasks, converting formats, and viewing your results. They can also serve as interesting reference implementations for image processing algorithms (such as tone correction or denoising) that you are trying to develop from scratch.

There are also software packages and infrastructure that can be helpful for building real-time video processing demos. Vision on Tap (http://www.visionontap.com/) provides a Web service that will process your webcam video in real time (Chiu and Raskar 2009). Video-Man (VideoManager, http://videomanlib.sourceforge.net/) can be useful for getting real-time video-based demos and applications running. You can also use `imread` in MATLAB to read directly from any URL, such as a webcam.

Below, I list some additional software that can be found on the Web, grouped by the book chapters to which they most correspond:

Chapter 3: Image processing

matlabPyrTools—MATLAB source code for Laplacian pyramids, QMF/Wavelets, and steerable pyramids, http://www.cns.nyu.edu/~lcv/software.php (Simoncelli and Adelson 1990a; Simoncelli, Freeman, Adelson *et al.* 1992).

BLS-GSM image denoising, http://decsai.ugr.es/~javier/denoise/ (Portilla, Strela, Wainwright *et al.* 2003).

Fast bilateral filtering code, http://people.csail.mit.edu/jiawen/#code (Chen, Paris, and Durand 2007).

C++ implementation of the fast distance transform algorithm, http://people.cs.uchicago.edu/~pff/dt/ (Felzenszwalb and Huttenlocher 2004a).

GREYC's Magic Image Converter, including image restoration software using regularization and anisotropic diffusion, http://gmic.sourceforge.net/gimp.shtml (Tschumperlé and Deriche 2005).

Chapter 4: Feature detection and matching

VLFeat, an open and portable library of computer vision algorithms, http://vlfeat.org/ (Vedaldi and Fulkerson 2008).

SiftGPU: A GPU Implementation of Scale Invariant Feature Transform (SIFT), http://www.cs.unc.edu/~ccwu/siftgpu/ (Wu 2010).

SURF: Speeded Up Robust Features, http://www.vision.ee.ethz.ch/~surf/ (Bay, Tuytelaars, and Van Gool 2006).

FAST corner detection, http://mi.eng.cam.ac.uk/~er258/work/fast.html (Rosten and Drummond 2005, 2006).

Linux binaries for affine region detectors and descriptors, as well as MATLAB files to compute repeatability and matching scores, http://www.robots.ox.ac.uk/~vgg/research/affine/.

Kanade–Lucas–Tomasi feature trackers: KLT, http://www.ces.clemson.edu/~stb/klt/ (Shi and Tomasi 1994); GPU-KLT, http://cs.unc.edu/~cmzach/opensource.html (Zach, Gallup, and Frahm 2008); and Lucas–Kanade 20 Years On, http://www.ri.cmu.edu/projects/project_515.html (Baker and Matthews 2004).

Chapter 5: Segmentation

Efficient graph-based image segmentation, http://people.cs.uchicago.edu/~pff/segment/ (Felzenszwalb and Huttenlocher 2004b).

EDISON, edge detection and image segmentation, http://coewww.rutgers.edu/riul/research/code/EDISON/ (Meer and Georgescu 2001; Comaniciu and Meer 2002).

Normalized cuts segmentation including intervening contours, http://www.cis.upenn.edu/~jshi/software/ (Shi and Malik 2000; Malik, Belongie, Leung et al. 2001).

Segmentation by weighted aggregation (SWA), http://www.cs.weizmann.ac.il/~vision/SWA/ (Alpert, Galun, Basri et al. 2007).

Chapter 6: Feature-based alignment and calibration

Non-iterative PnP algorithm, http://cvlab.epfl.ch/software/EPnP/ (Moreno-Noguer, Lepetit, and Fua 2007).

Tsai Camera Calibration Software, http://www-2.cs.cmu.edu/~rgw/TsaiCode.html (Tsai 1987).

Easy Camera Calibration Toolkit, http://research.microsoft.com/en-us/um/people/zhang/Calib/ (Zhang 2000).

Camera Calibration Toolbox for MATLAB, http://www.vision.caltech.edu/bouguetj/calib_doc/; a C version is included in OpenCV.

MATLAB functions for multiple view geometry, http://www.robots.ox.ac.uk/~vgg/hzbook/code/ (Hartley and Zisserman 2004).

Chapter 7: Structure from motion

SBA: A generic sparse bundle adjustment C/C++ package based on the Levenberg–Marquardt algorithm, http://www.ics.forth.gr/~lourakis/sba/ (Lourakis and Argyros 2009).

Simple sparse bundle adjustment (SSBA), http://cs.unc.edu/~cmzach/opensource.html.

Bundler, structure from motion for unordered image collections, http://phototour.cs. washington.edu/bundler/ (Snavely, Seitz, and Szeliski 2006).

Chapter 8: Dense motion estimation

Optical flow software, http://www.cs.brown.edu/~black/code.html (Black and Anandan 1996).

Optical flow using total variation and conjugate gradient descent, http://people.csail. mit.edu/celiu/OpticalFlow/ (Liu 2009).

TV-L1 optical flow on the GPU, http://cs.unc.edu/~cmzach/opensource.html (Zach, Pock, and Bischof 2007a).

elastix: a toolbox for rigid and nonrigid registration of images, http://elastix.isi.uu.nl/ (Klein, Staring, and Pluim 2007).

Deformable image registration using discrete optimization, http://www.mrf-registration. net/deformable/index.html (Glocker, Komodakis, Tziritas *et al.* 2008).

Chapter 9: Image stitching

Microsoft Research Image Compositing Editor for stitching images, http://research. microsoft.com/en-us/um/redmond/groups/ivm/ice/.

Chapter 10: Computational photography

HDRShop software for combining bracketed exposures into high-dynamic range radiance images, http://projects.ict.usc.edu/graphics/HDRShop/.

Super-resolution code, http://www.robots.ox.ac.uk/~vgg/software/SR/ (Pickup 2007; Pickup, Capel, Roberts *et al.* 2007, 2009).

Chapter 11: Stereo correspondence

StereoMatcher, standalone C++ stereo matching code, http://vision.middlebury.edu/ stereo/code/ (Scharstein and Szeliski 2002).

Patch-based multi-view stereo software (PMVS Version 2), http://grail.cs.washington. edu/software/pmvs/ (Furukawa and Ponce 2011).

Chapter 12: 3D reconstruction

Scanalyze: a system for aligning and merging range data, http://graphics.stanford.edu/ software/scanalyze/ (Curless and Levoy 1996).

MeshLab: software for processing, editing, and visualizing unstructured 3D triangular meshes, http://meshlab.sourceforge.net/.

VRML viewers (various) are also a good way to visualize texture-mapped 3D models.

Section 12.6.4: Whole body modeling and tracking

Bayesian 3D person tracking, http://www.cs.brown.edu/~black/code.html (Sidenbladh, Black, and Fleet 2000; Sidenbladh and Black 2003).

HumanEva: baseline code for the tracking of articulated human motion, http://vision. cs.brown.edu/humaneva/ (Sigal, Balan, and Black 2010).

Section 14.1.1: Face detection

Sample face detection code and evaluation tools, http://vision.ai.uiuc.edu/mhyang/face-detection-survey.html.

Section 14.1.2: Pedestrian detection

A simple object detector with boosting, http://people.csail.mit.edu/torralba/shortCourseRLOC/ boosting/boosting.html (Hastie, Tibshirani, and Friedman 2001; Torralba, Murphy, and Freeman 2007).

Discriminatively trained deformable part models, http://people.cs.uchicago.edu/~pff/ latent/ (Felzenszwalb, Girshick, McAllester *et al.* 2010).

Upper-body detector, http://www.robots.ox.ac.uk/~vgg/software/UpperBody/ (Ferrari, Marin-Jimenez, and Zisserman 2008).

2D articulated human pose estimation software, http://www.vision.ee.ethz.ch/~calvin/ articulated_human_pose_estimation_code/ (Eichner and Ferrari 2009).

Section 14.2.2: Active appearance and 3D shape models

AAMtools: An active appearance modeling toolbox, http://cvsp.cs.ntua.gr/software/ AAMtools/ (Papandreou and Maragos 2008).

Section 14.3: Instance recognition

FASTANN and FASTCLUSTER for approximate k-means (AKM), http://www.robots. ox.ac.uk/~vgg/software/ (Philbin, Chum, Isard *et al.* 2007).

Feature matching using fast approximate nearest neighbors, http://people.cs.ubc.ca/ ~mariusm/index.php/FLANN/FLANN (Muja and Lowe 2009).

Section 14.4.1: Bag of words

Two bag of words classifiers, http://people.csail.mit.edu/fergus/iccv2005/bagwords.html (Fei-Fei and Perona 2005; Sivic, Russell, Efros *et al.* 2005).

Bag of features and hierarchical k-means, http://www.vlfeat.org/ (Nistér and Stewénius 2006; Nowak, Jurie, and Triggs 2006).

Section 14.4.2: Part-based models

A simple parts and structure object detector, http://people.csail.mit.edu/fergus/iccv2005/ partsstructure.html (Fischler and Elschlager 1973; Felzenszwalb and Huttenlocher 2005).

Section 14.5.1: Machine learning software

Support vector machines (SVM) software (http://www.support-vector-machines.org/ SVM_soft.html) has pointers to lots of SVM libraries, including SVM^{light}, http:// svmlight.joachims.org/; LIBSVM, http://www.csie.ntu.edu.tw/~cjlin/libsvm/ (Fan, Chen, and Lin 2005); and LIBLINEAR, http://www.csie.ntu.edu.tw/~cjlin/liblinear/ (Fan, Chang, Hsieh *et al.* 2008).

Kernel Machines: links to SVM, Gaussian processes, boosting, and other machine learning algorithms, http://www.kernel-machines.org/software.

Multiple kernels for image classification, http://www.robots.ox.ac.uk/~vgg/software/ MKL/ (Varma and Ray 2007; Vedaldi, Gulshan, Varma *et al.* 2009).

Appendix A.1–A.2: Matrix decompositions and linear least squares[2]

BLAS (Basic Linear Algebra Subprograms), http://www.netlib.org/blas/ (Blackford, Demmel, Dongarra *et al.* 2002).

LAPACK (Linear Algebra PACKage), http://www.netlib.org/lapack/ (Anderson, Bai, Bischof *et al.* 1999).

GotoBLAS, http://www.tacc.utexas.edu/tacc-projects/.

ATLAS (Automatically Tuned Linear Algebra Software), http://math-atlas.sourceforge. net/ (Demmel, Dongarra, Eijkhout *et al.* 2005).

Intel Math Kernel Library (MKL), http://software.intel.com/en-us/intel-mkl/.

AMD Core Math Library (ACML), http://developer.amd.com/cpu/Libraries/acml/Pages/ default.aspx.

Robust PCA code, http://www.salle.url.edu/~ftorre/papers/rpca2.html (De la Torre and Black 2003).

Appendix A.3: Non-linear least squares

MINPACK, http://www.netlib.org/minpack/.

levmar: Levenberg–Marquardt nonlinear least squares algorithms, http://www.ics.forth. gr/~lourakis/levmar/ (Madsen, Nielsen, and Tingleff 2004).

Appendix A.4–A.5: Direct and iterative sparse matrix solvers

SuiteSparse (various reordering algorithms, CHOLMOD) and SuiteSparse QR, http: //www.cise.ufl.edu/research/sparse/SuiteSparse/ (Davis 2006, 2008).

PARDISO (iterative and sparse direct solution), http://www.pardiso-project.org/.

TAUCS (sparse direct, iterative, out of core, preconditioners), http://www.tau.ac.il/ ~stoledo/taucs/.

HSL Mathematical Software Library, http://www.hsl.rl.ac.uk/index.html.

---

[2] Thanks to Sameer Agarwal for suggesting and describing most of these sites.

Templates for the solution of linear systems, http://www.netlib.org/linalg/html_templates/ Templates.html (Barrett, Berry, Chan *et al.* 1994). Download the PDF for instructions on how to get the software.

ITSOL, MIQR, and other sparse solvers, http://www-users.cs.umn.edu/~saad/software/ (Saad 2003).

ILUPACK, http://www-public.tu-bs.de/~bolle/ilupack/.

Appendix B: Bayesian modeling and inference

Middlebury source code for MRF minimization, http://vision.middlebury.edu/MRF/ code/ (Szeliski, Zabih, Scharstein *et al.* 2008).

C++ code for efficient belief propagation for early vision, http://people.cs.uchicago. edu/~pff/bp/ (Felzenszwalb and Huttenlocher 2006).

FastPD MRF optimization code, http://www.csd.uoc.gr/~komod/FastPD (Komodakis and Tziritas 2007a; Komodakis, Tziritas, and Paragios 2008)

Gaussian noise generation. A lot of basic software packages come with a uniform random noise generator (e.g., the `rand()` routine in Unix), but not all have a Gaussian random noise generator. To compute a normally distributed random variable, you can use the Box–Muller transform (Box and Muller 1958), whose C code is given in Algorithm C.1— note that this routine returns pairs of random variables. Alternative methods for generating Gaussian random numbers are given by Thomas, Luk, Leong *et al.* (2007).

Pseudocolor generation. In many applications, it is convenient to be able to visualize the set of labels assigned to an image (or to image features such as lines). One of the easiest ways to do this is to assign a unique color to each integer label. In my work, I have found it convenient to distribute these labels in a quasi-uniform fashion around the RGB color cube using the following idea.

For each (non-negative) label value, consider the bits as being split among the three color channels, e.g., for a nine-bit value, the bits could be labeled RGBRGBRGB. After collecting each of the three color values, *reverse* the bits so that the low-order bits vary the most quickly. In practice, for eight-bit color channels, this bit reverse can be stored in a table or a complete table mapping from labels to pseudocolors (say with 4092 entries) can be pre-computed. Figure 8.16 shows an example of such a pseudo-color mapping.

GPU implementation

The advent of programmable GPUs with capabilities such as pixel shaders and compute shaders has led to the development of fast computer vision algorithms for real-time applications such as segmentation, tracking, stereo, and motion estimation (Pock, Unger, Cremers *et al.* 2008; Vineet and Narayanan 2008; Zach, Gallup, and Frahm 2008). A good source for learning about such algorithms is the CVPR 2008 workshop on Visual Computer Vision on GPUs (CVGPU), http://www.cs.unc.edu/~jmf/Workshop_on_Computer_Vision_on_GPU. html, whose papers can be found on the CVPR 2008 proceedings DVD. Additional sources

```
double urand()
{
  return ((double) rand()) / ((double) RAND_MAX);
}
void grand(double& g1, double& g2)
{
#ifndef M_PI
#define M_PI 3.14159265358979323846
#endif // M_PI

  double n1 = urand();
  double n2 = urand();
  double x1 = n1 + (n1 == 0); /* guard against log(0) */
  double sqlogn1 = sqrt(-2.0 * log (x1));
  double ang1 = (2.0 * M_PI) * n2;
  g1 = sqlogn1 * cos(ang1);
  g2 = sqlogn1 * sin(ang1);
}
```

Algorithm C.1 C algorithm for Gaussian random noise generation, using the Box–Muller transform.

for GPU algorithms include the GPGPU Web site and workshops, http://gpgpu.org/, and the OpenVIDIA Web site, http://openvidia.sourceforge.net/index.php/OpenVIDIA.

C.3 Slides and lectures

As I mentioned in the preface, I hope to post slides corresponding to the material in the book. Until these are ready, your best bet is to look at the slides from the courses I have co-taught at the University of Washington, as well as related courses that have used a similar syllabus. Here is a partial list of such courses:

UW 455: Undergraduate Computer Vision, http://www.cs.washington.edu/education/courses/455/.

UW 576: Graduate Computer Vision, http://www.cs.washington.edu/education/courses/576/.

Stanford CS233B: Introduction to Computer Vision, http://vision.stanford.edu/teaching/cs223b/.

MIT 6.869: Advances in Computer Vision, http://people.csail.mit.edu/torralba/courses/6.869/6.869.computervision.htm.

Berkeley CS 280: Computer Vision, http://www.eecs.berkeley.edu/~trevor/CS280.html.

UNC COMP 776: Computer Vision, http://www.cs.unc.edu/~lazebnik/spring10/.

Middlebury CS 453: Computer Vision, http://www.cs.middlebury.edu/~schar/courses/cs453-s10/.

Related courses have also been taught on the topic of Computational Photography, e.g.,

CMU 15-463: Computational Photography, http://graphics.cs.cmu.edu/courses/15-463/.

MIT 6.815/6.865: Advanced Computational Photography, http://stellar.mit.edu/S/course/6/sp09/6.815/.

Stanford CS 448A: Computational photography on cell phones, http://graphics.stanford.edu/courses/cs448a-10/.

SIGGRAPH courses on Computational Photography, http://web.media.mit.edu/~raskar/photo/.

There is also an excellent set of on-line lectures available on a range of computer vision topics, such as belief propagation and graph cuts, at the UW-MSR Course of Vision Algorithms http://www.cs.washington.edu/education/courses/577/04sp/.

C.4 Bibliography

While a bibliography (BibTex .bib file) for all of the references cited in this book is available on the book's Web site, a much more comprehensive partially annotated bibliography of nearly *all* computer vision publications is maintained by Keith Price at http://iris.usc.edu/Vision-Notes/bibliography/contents.html. There is also a searchable computer graphics bibliography at http://www.siggraph.org/publications/bibliography/. Additional good sources for technical papers are Google Scholar and CiteSeer[X].

References

Abdel-Hakim, A. E. and Farag, A. A. (2006). CSIFT: A SIFT descriptor with color invariant characterstics. In *IEEE Computer Society Conference on Computer Vision and Pattern Recognition (CVPR'2006)*, pp. 1978–1983, New York City, NY.

Adelson, E. H. and Bergen, J. (1991). The plenoptic function and the elements of early vision. In *Computational Models of Visual Processing*, pp. 3–20.

Adelson, E. H., Simoncelli, E., and Hingorani, R. (1987). Orthogonal pyramid transforms for image coding. In *SPIE Vol. 845, Visual Communications and Image Processing II*, pp. 50–58, Cambridge, Massachusetts.

Adiv, G. (1989). Inherent ambiguities in recovering 3-D motion and structure from a noisy flow field. *IEEE Transactions on Pattern Analysis and Machine Intelligence*, 11(5):477–490.

Agarwal, A. and Triggs, B. (2006). Recovering 3D human pose from monocular images. *IEEE Transactions on Pattern Analysis and Machine Intelligence*, 28(1):44–58.

Agarwal, S. and Roth, D. (2002). Learning a sparse representation for object detection. In *Seventh European Conference on Computer Vision (ECCV 2002)*, pp. 113–127, Copenhagen.

Agarwal, S., Snavely, N., Seitz, S. M., and Szeliski, R. (2010). Bundle adjustment in the large. In *Eleventh European Conference on Computer Vision (ECCV 2010)*, Heraklion, Crete.

Agarwal, S., Snavely, N., Simon, I., Seitz, S. M., and Szeliski, R. (2009). Building Rome in a day. In *Twelfth IEEE International Conference on Computer Vision (ICCV 2009)*, Kyoto, Japan.

Agarwal, S., Furukawa, Y., Snavely, N., Curless, B., Seitz, S. M., and Szeliski, R. (2010). Reconstructing Rome. *Computer*, 43(6):40–47.

Agarwala, A. (2007). Efficient gradient-domain compositing using quadtrees. *ACM Transactions on Graphics*, 26(3).

Agarwala, A., Hertzmann, A., Seitz, S., and Salesin, D. (2004). Keyframe-based tracking for rotoscoping and animation. *ACM Transactions on Graphics (Proc. SIGGRAPH 2004)*, 23(3):584–591.

Agarwala, A., Agrawala, M., Cohen, M., Salesin, D., and Szeliski, R. (2006). Photographing long scenes with multi-viewpoint panoramas. *ACM Transactions on Graphics (Proc. SIGGRAPH 2006)*, 25(3):853–861.

Agarwala, A., Dontcheva, M., Agrawala, M., Drucker, S., Colburn, A., Curless, B., Salesin, D. H., and Cohen, M. F. (2004). Interactive digital photomontage. *ACM Transactions on Graphics (Proc. SIGGRAPH 2004)*, 23(3):292–300.

Agarwala, A., Zheng, K. C., Pal, C., Agrawala, M., Cohen, M., Curless, B., Salesin, D., and Szeliski, R. (2005). Panoramic video textures. *ACM Transactions on Graphics (Proc. SIGGRAPH 2005)*, 24(3):821–827.

Aggarwal, J. K. and Nandhakumar, N. (1988). On the computation of motion from sequences of images—a review. *Proceedings of the IEEE*, 76(8):917–935.

Agin, G. J. and Binford, T. O. (1976). Computer description of curved objects. *IEEE Transactions on Computers*, C-25(4):439–449.

Ahonen, T., Hadid, A., and Pietikäinen, M. (2006). Face description with local binary patterns: Application to face recognition. *IEEE Transactions on Pattern Analysis and Machine Intelligence*, 28(12):2037–2041.

Akenine-Möller, T. and Haines, E. (2002). *Real-Time Rendering*. A K Peters, Wellesley, Massachusetts, second edition.

Al-Baali, M. and Fletcher., R. (1986). An efficient line search for nonlinear least squares. *Journal Journal of Optimization Theory and Applications*, 48(3):359–377.

Alahari, K., Kohli, P., and Torr, P. (2011). Dynamic hybrid algorithms for discrete MAP MRF inference. *IEEE Transactions on Pattern Analysis and Machine Intelligence*.

Alexa, M., Behr, J., Cohen-Or, D., Fleishman, S., Levin, D., and Silva, C. T. (2003). Computing and rendering point set surfaces. *IEEE Transactions on Visualization and Computer Graphics*, 9(1):3–15.

Aliaga, D. G., Funkhouser, T., Yanovsky, D., and Carlbom, I. (2003). Sea of images. *IEEE Computer Graphics and Applications*, 23(6):22–30.

Allen, B., Curless, B., and Popović, Z. (2003). The space of human body shapes: reconstruction and parameterization from range scans. *ACM Transactions on Graphics (Proc. SIGGRAPH 2003)*, 22(3):587–594.

Allgower, E. L. and Georg, K. (2003). *Introduction to Numerical Continuation Methods*. Society for Industrial and Applied Mathematics.

Aloimonos, J. (1990). Perspective approximations. *Image and Vision Computing*, 8:177–192.

Alpert, S., Galun, M., Basri, R., and Brandt, A. (2007). Image segmentation by probabilistic bottom-up aggregation and cue integration. In *IEEE Computer Society Conference on Computer Vision and Pattern Recognition (CVPR 2007)*, Minneapolis, MN.

Amini, A. A., Weymouth, T. E., and Jain, R. C. (1990). Using dynamic programming for solving variational problems in vision. *IEEE Transactions on Pattern Analysis and Machine Intelligence*, 12(9):855–867.

Anandan, P. (1984). Computing dense displacement fields with confidence measures in scenes containing occlusion. In *Image Understanding Workshop*, pp. 236–246, New Orleans.

Anandan, P. (1989). A computational framework and an algorithm for the measurement of visual motion. *International Journal of Computer Vision*, 2(3):283–310.

Anandan, P. and Irani, M. (2002). Factorization with uncertainty. *International Journal of Computer Vision*, 49(2-3):101–116.

Anderson, E., Bai, Z., Bischof, C., Blackford, S., Demmel, J. W. *et al.* (1999). *LAPACK Users' Guide*. Society for Industrial and Applied Mathematics, 3rd edition.

Andrieu, C., de Freitas, N., Doucet, A., and Jordan, M. I. (2003). An introduction to MCMC for machine learning. *Machine Learning*, 50(1-2):5–43.

Andriluka, M., Roth, S., and Schiele, B. (2008). People-tracking-by-detection and people-detection-by-tracking. In *IEEE Computer Society Conference on Computer Vision and Pattern Recognition (CVPR 2008)*, Anchorage, AK.

Andriluka, M., Roth, S., and Schiele, B. (2009). Pictorial structures revisited: People detection and articulated pose estimation. In *IEEE Computer Society Conference on Computer Vision and Pattern Recognition (CVPR 2009)*, Miami Beach, FL.

Andriluka, M., Roth, S., and Schiele, B. (2010). Monocular 3d pose estimation and tracking by detection. In *IEEE Computer Society Conference on Computer Vision and Pattern Recognition (CVPR 2010)*, San Francisco, CA.

Anguelov, D., Srinivasan, P., Koller, D., Thrun, S., Rodgers, J., and Davis, J. (2005). SCAPE: Shape completion and animation of people. *ACM Transactions on Graphics (Proc. SIGGRAPH 2005)*, 24(3):408–416.

Ansar, A., Castano, A., and Matthies, L. (2004). Enhanced real-time stereo using bilateral filtering. In *International Symposium on 3D Data Processing, Visualization, and Transmission (3DPVT)*.

Antone, M. and Teller, S. (2002). Scalable extrinsic calibration of omni-directional image networks. *International Journal of Computer Vision*, 49(2-3):143–174.

Arbeláez, P., Maire, M., Fowlkes, C., and Malik, J. (2010). *Contour Detection and Hierarchical Image Segmentation*. Technical Report UCB/EECS-2010-17, EECS Department, University of California, Berkeley. Submitted to PAMI.

Argyriou, V. and Vlachos, T. (2003). Estimation of sub-pixel motion using gradient cross-correlation. *Electronic Letters*, 39(13):980–982.

Arikan, O. and Forsyth, D. A. (2002). Interactive motion generation from examples. *ACM Transactions on Graphics*, 21(3):483–490.

Arnold, R. D. (1983). *Automated Stereo Perception*. Technical Report AIM-351, Artificial Intelligence Laboratory, Stanford University.

Arya, S., Mount, D. M., Netanyahu, N. S., Silverman, R., and Wu, A. Y. (1998). An optimal algorithm for approximate nearest neighbor searching in fixed dimensions. *Journal of the ACM*, 45(6):891–923.

Ashdown, I. (1993). Near-field photometry: A new approach. *Journal of the Illuminating Engineering Society*, 22(1):163–180.

Atkinson, K. B. (1996). *Close Range Photogrammetry and Machine Vision*. Whittles Publishing, Scotland, UK.

Aurich, V. and Weule, J. (1995). Non-linear Gaussian filters performing edge preserving diffusion. In *17th DAGM-Symposium*, pp. 538–545, Bielefeld.

Avidan, S. (2001). Support vector tracking. In *IEEE Computer Society Conference on Computer Vision and Pattern Recognition (CVPR'2001)*, pp. 283–290, Kauai, Hawaii.

Avidan, S., Baker, S., and Shan, Y. (2010). Special issue on Internet Vision. *Proceedings of the IEEE*, 98(8):1367–1369.

Axelsson, O. (1996). *Iterative Solution Methods*. Cambridge University Press, Cambridge.

Ayache, N. (1989). *Vision Stéréoscopique et Perception Multisensorielle*. InterEditions, Paris.

Azarbayejani, A. and Pentland, A. P. (1995). Recursive estimation of motion, structure, and focal length. *IEEE Transactions on Pattern Analysis and Machine Intelligence*, 17(6):562–575.

Azuma, R. T., Baillot, Y., Behringer, R., Feiner, S. K., Julier, S., and MacIntyre, B. (2001). Recent advances in augmented reality. *IEEE Computer Graphics and Applications*, 21(6):34–47.

Bab-Hadiashar, A. and Suter, D. (1998a). Robust optic flow computation. *International Journal of Computer Vision*, 29(1):59–77.

Bab-Hadiashar, A. and Suter, D. (1998b). Robust total least squares based optic flow computation. In *Asian Conference on Computer Vision (ACCV'98)*, pp. 566–573, Hong Kong.

Badra, F., Qumsieh, A., and Dudek, G. (1998). Rotation and zooming in image mosaicing. In *IEEE Workshop on Applications of Computer Vision (WACV'98)*, pp. 50–55, Princeton.

Bae, S., Paris, S., and Durand, F. (2006). Two-scale tone management for photographic look. *ACM Transactions on Graphics*, 25(3):637–645.

Baeza-Yates, R. and Ribeiro-Neto, B. (1999). *Modern Information Retrieval*. Addison Wesley.

Bai, X. and Sapiro, G. (2009). Geodesic matting: A framework for fast interactive image and video segmentation and matting. *International Journal of Computer Vision*, 82(2):113–132.

Bajcsy, R. and Kovacic, S. (1989). Multiresolution elastic matching. *Computer Vision, Graphics, and Image Processing*, 46(1):1–21.

Baker, H. H. (1977). Three-dimensional modeling. In *Fifth International Joint Conference on Artificial Intelligence (IJCAI-77)*, pp. 649–655.

Baker, H. H. (1982). *Depth from Edge and Intensity Based Stereo*. Technical Report AIM-347, Artificial Intelligence Laboratory, Stanford University.

Baker, H. H. (1989). Building surfaces of evolution: The weaving wall. *International Journal of Computer Vision*, 3(1):50–71.

Baker, H. H. and Binford, T. O. (1981). Depth from edge and intensity based stereo. In *IJCAI81*, pp. 631–636.

Baker, H. H. and Bolles, R. C. (1989). Generalizing epipolar-plane image analysis on the spatiotemporal surface. *International Journal of Computer Vision*, 3(1):33–49.

Baker, S. and Kanade, T. (2002). Limits on super-resolution and how to break them. *IEEE Transactions on Pattern Analysis and Machine Intelligence*, 24(9):1167–1183.

Baker, S. and Matthews, I. (2004). Lucas-Kanade 20 years on: A unifying framework: Part 1: The quantity approximated, the warp update rule, and the gradient descent approximation. *International Journal of Computer Vision*, 56(3):221–255.

Baker, S. and Nayar, S. (1999). A theory of single-viewpoint catadioptric image formation. *International Journal of Computer Vision*, 5(2):175–196.

Baker, S. and Nayar, S. K. (2001). Single viewpoint catadioptric cameras. In Benosman, R. and Kang, S. B. (eds), *Panoramic Vision: Sensors, Theory, and Applications*, pp. 39–71, Springer, New York.

Baker, S., Gross, R., and Matthews, I. (2003). *Lucas-Kanade 20 Years On: A Unifying Framework: Part 3*. Technical Report CMU-RI-TR-03-35, The Robotics Institute, Carnegie Mellon University.

Baker, S., Gross, R., and Matthews, I. (2004). *Lucas-Kanade 20 Years On: A Unifying Framework: Part 4*. Technical Report CMU-RI-TR-04-14, The Robotics Institute, Carnegie Mellon University.

Baker, S., Szeliski, R., and Anandan, P. (1998). A layered approach to stereo reconstruction. In *IEEE Computer Society Conference on Computer Vision and Pattern Recognition (CVPR'98)*, pp. 434–441, Santa Barbara.

Baker, S., Gross, R., Ishikawa, T., and Matthews, I. (2003). *Lucas-Kanade 20 Years On: A Unifying Framework: Part 2*. Technical Report CMU-RI-TR-03-01, The Robotics Institute, Carnegie Mellon University.

Baker, S., Black, M., Lewis, J. P., Roth, S., Scharstein, D., and Szeliski, R. (2007). A database and evaluation methodology for optical flow. In *Eleventh International Conference on Computer Vision (ICCV 2007)*, Rio de Janeiro, Brazil.

Baker, S., Scharstein, D., Lewis, J., Roth, S., Black, M. J., and Szeliski, R. (2009). *A Database and Evaluation Methodology for Optical Flow*. Technical Report MSR-TR-2009-179, Microsoft Research.

Ballard, D. H. (1981). Generalizing the Hough transform to detect arbitrary patterns. *Pattern Recognition*, 13(2):111–122.

Ballard, D. H. and Brown, C. M. (1982). *Computer Vision*. Prentice-Hall, Englewood Cliffs, New Jersey.

Banno, A., Masuda, T., Oishi, T., and Ikeuchi, K. (2008). Flying laser range sensor for large-scale site-modeling and its applications in Bayon digital archival project. *International Journal of Computer Vision*, 78(2-3):207–222.

Bar-Hillel, A., Hertz, T., and Weinshall, D. (2005). Object class recognition by boosting a part based model. In *IEEE Computer Society Conference on Computer Vision and Pattern Recognition (CVPR'2005)*, pp. 701–708, San Diego, CA.

Bar-Joseph, Z., El-Yaniv, R., Lischinski, D., and Werman, M. (2001). Texture mixing and texture movie synthesis using statistical learning. *IEEE Transactions on Visualization and Computer Graphics*, 7(2):120–135.

Bar-Shalom, Y. and Fortmann, T. E. (1988). *Tracking and data association*. Academic Press, Boston.

Barash, D. (2002). A fundamental relationship between bilateral filtering, adaptive smoothing, and the nonlinear diffusion equation. *IEEE Transactions on Pattern Analysis and Machine Intelligence*, 24(6):844–847.

Barash, D. and Comaniciu, D. (2004). A common framework for nonlinear diffusion, adaptive smoothing, bilateral filtering and mean shift. *Image and Vision Computing*, 22(1):73–81.

Barbu, A. and Zhu, S.-C. (2003). Graph partition by Swendsen–Wang cuts. In *Ninth International Conference on Computer Vision (ICCV 2003)*, pp. 320–327, Nice, France.

Barbu, A. and Zhu, S.-C. (2005). Generalizing Swendsen–Wang to sampling arbitrary posterior probabilities. *IEEE Transactions on Pattern Analysis and Machine Intelligence*, 27(9):1239–1253.

Barkans, A. C. (1997). High quality rendering using the Talisman architecture. In *Proceedings of the Eurographics Workshop on Graphics Hardware*.

Barnard, S. T. (1989). Stochastic stereo matching over scale. *International Journal of Computer Vision*, 3(1):17–32.

Barnard, S. T. and Fischler, M. A. (1982). Computational stereo. *Computing Surveys*, 14(4):553–572.

Barnes, C., Jacobs, D. E., Sanders, J., Goldman, D. B., Rusinkiewicz, S., Finkelstein, A., and Agrawala, M. (2008). Video puppetry: A performative interface for cutout animation. *ACM Transactions on Graphics*, 27(5).

Barreto, J. P. and Daniilidis, K. (2005). Fundamental matrix for cameras with radial distortion. In *Tenth International Conference on Computer Vision (ICCV 2005)*, pp. 625–632, Beijing, China.

Barrett, R., Berry, M., Chan, T. F., Demmel, J., Donato, J. *et al.* (1994). *Templates for the Solution of Linear Systems: Building Blocks for Iterative Methods, 2nd Edition*. SIAM, Philadelphia, PA.

Barron, J. L., Fleet, D. J., and Beauchemin, S. S. (1994). Performance of optical flow techniques. *International Journal of Computer Vision*, 12(1):43–77.

Barrow, H. G. and Tenenbaum, J. M. (1981). Computational vision. *Proceedings of the IEEE*, 69(5):572–595.

Bartels, R. H., Beatty, J. C., and Barsky, B. A. (1987). *An Introduction to Splines for use in Computer Graphics and Geeometric Modeling*. Morgan Kaufmann Publishers, Los Altos.

Bartoli, A. (2003). Towards gauge invariant bundle adjustment: A solution based on gauge dependent damping. In *Ninth International Conference on Computer Vision (ICCV 2003)*, pp. 760–765, Nice, France.

Bartoli, A. and Sturm, P. (2003). Multiple-view structure and motion from line correspondences. In *Ninth International Conference on Computer Vision (ICCV 2003)*, pp. 207–212, Nice, France.

Bartoli, A., Coquerelle, M., and Sturm, P. (2004). A framework for pencil-of-points structure-from-motion. In *Eighth European Conference on Computer Vision (ECCV 2004)*, pp. 28–40, Prague.

Bascle, B., Blake, A., and Zisserman, A. (1996). Motion deblurring and super-resolution from an image sequence. In *Fourth European Conference on Computer Vision (ECCV'96)*, pp. 573–582, Cambridge, England.

Bathe, K.-J. (2007). *Finite Element Procedures*. Prentice-Hall, Inc., Englewood Cliffs, New Jersey.

Batra, D., Sukthankar, R., and Chen, T. (2008). Learning class-specific affinities for image labelling. In *IEEE Computer Society Conference on Computer Vision and Pattern Recognition (CVPR 2008)*, Anchorage, AK.

Baudisch, P., Tan, D., Steedly, D., Rudolph, E., Uyttendaele, M., Pal, C., and Szeliski, R. (2006). An exploration of user interface designs for real-time panoramic photography. *Australian Journal of Information Systems*, 13(2).

Baumberg, A. (2000). Reliable feature matching across widely separated views. In *IEEE Computer Society Conference on Computer Vision and Pattern Recognition (CVPR'2000)*, pp. 774–781, Hilton Head Island.

Baumberg, A. M. and Hogg, D. C. (1996). Generating spatiotemporal models from examples. *Image and Vision Computing*, 14(8):525–532.

Baumgart, B. G. (1974). *Geometric Modeling for Computer Vision*. Technical Report AIM-249, Artificial Intelligence Laboratory, Stanford University.

Bay, H., Ferrari, V., and Van Gool, L. (2005). Wide-baseline stereo matching with line segments. In *IEEE Computer Society Conference on Computer Vision and Pattern Recognition (CVPR'2005)*, pp. 329–336, San Diego, CA.

Bay, H., Tuytelaars, T., and Van Gool, L. (2006). SURF: Speeded up robust features. In *Ninth European Conference on Computer Vision (ECCV 2006)*, pp. 404–417.

Bayer, B. E. (1976). Color imaging array. US Patent No. 3,971,065.

Beardsley, P., Torr, P., and Zisserman, A. (1996). 3D model acquisition from extended image sequences. In *Fourth European Conference on Computer Vision (ECCV'96)*, pp. 683–695, Cambridge, England.

Beare, R. (2006). A locally constrained watershed transform. *IEEE Transactions on Pattern Analysis and Machine Intelligence*, 28(7):1063–1074.

Becker, S. and Bove, V. M. (1995). Semiautomatic 3-D model extraction from uncalibrated 2-D camera views. In *SPIE Vol. 2410, Visual Data Exploration and Analysis II*, pp. 447–461, San Jose.

Beier, T. and Neely, S. (1992). Feature-based image metamorphosis. *Computer Graphics (SIGGRAPH '92)*, 26(2):35–42.

Beis, J. S. and Lowe, D. G. (1999). Indexing without invariants in 3D object recognition. *IEEE Transactions on Pattern Analysis and Machine Intelligence*, 21(10):1000–1015.

Belhumeur, P. N. (1996). A Bayesian approach to binocular stereopsis. *International Journal of Computer Vision*, 19(3):237–260.

Belhumeur, P. N., Hespanha, J. P., and Kriegman, D. J. (1997). Eigenfaces vs. Fisherfaces: Recognition using class specific linear projection. *IEEE Transactions on Pattern Analysis and Machine Intelligence*, 19(7):711–720.

Belongie, S. and Malik, J. (1998). Finding boundaries in natural images: a new method using point descriptors and area completion. In *Fifth European Conference on Computer Vision (ECCV'98)*, pp. 751–766, Freiburg, Germany.

Belongie, S., Malik, J., and Puzicha, J. (2002). Shape matching and object recognition using shape contexts. *IEEE Transactions on Pattern Analysis and Machine Intelligence*, 24(4):509–522.

Belongie, S., Fowlkes, C., Chung, F., and Malik, J. (2002). Spectral partitioning with indefinite kernels using the Nyström extension. In *Seventh European Conference on Computer Vision (ECCV 2002)*, pp. 531–543, Copenhagen.

Bennett, E., Uyttendaele, M., Zitnick, L., Szeliski, R., and Kang, S. B. (2006). Video and image Bayesian demosaicing with a two color image prior. In *Ninth European Conference on Computer Vision (ECCV 2006)*, pp. 508–521, Graz.

Benosman, R. and Kang, S. B. (eds). (2001). *Panoramic Vision: Sensors, Theory, and Applications*, Springer, New York.

Berg, T. (2008). Internet vision. SUNY Stony Brook Course CSE 690, http://www.tamaraberg.com/teaching/Fall_08/.

Berg, T. and Forsyth, D. (2006). Animals on the web. In *IEEE Computer Society Conference on Computer Vision and Pattern Recognition (CVPR'2006)*, pp. 1463–1470, New York City, NY.

Bergen, J. R., Anandan, P., Hanna, K. J., and Hingorani, R. (1992). Hierarchical model-based motion estimation. In *Second European Conference on Computer Vision (ECCV'92)*, pp. 237–252, Santa Margherita Liguere, Italy.

Bergen, J. R., Burt, P. J., Hingorani, R., and Peleg, S. (1992). A three-frame algorithm for estimating two-component image motion. *IEEE Transactions on Pattern Analysis and Machine Intelligence*, 14(9):886–896.

Berger, J. O. (1993). *Statistical Decision Theory and Bayesian Analysis*. Springer, New York, second edition.

Bertalmio, M., Sapiro, G., Caselles, V., and Ballester, C. (2000). Image inpainting. In *ACM SIGGRAPH 2000 Conference Proceedings*, pp. 417–424.

Bertalmio, M., Vese, L., Sapiro, G., and Osher, S. (2003). Simultaneous structure and texture image inpainting. *IEEE Transactions on Image Processing*, 12(8):882–889.

Bertero, M., Poggio, T. A., and Torre, V. (1988). Ill-posed problems in early vision. *Proceedings of the IEEE*, 76(8):869–889.

Besag, J. (1986). On the statistical analysis of dirty pictures. *Journal of the Royal Statistical Society B*, 48(3):259–302.

Besl, P. (1989). Active optical range imaging sensors. In Sanz, J. L. (ed.), *Advances in Machine Vision*, chapter 1, pp. 1–63, Springer-Verlag.

Besl, P. J. and Jain, R. C. (1985). Three-dimensional object recognition. *Computing Surveys*, 17(1):75–145.

Besl, P. J. and McKay, N. D. (1992). A method for registration of 3-D shapes. *IEEE Transactions on Pattern Analysis and Machine Intelligence*, 14(2):239–256.

Betrisey, C., Blinn, J. F., Dresevic, B., Hill, B., Hitchcock, G. *et al.* (2000). Displaced filtering for patterned displays. In *Society for Information Display Symposium,*, pp. 296–299.

Beymer, D. (1996). Feature correspondence by interleaving shape and texture computations. In *IEEE Computer Society Conference on Computer Vision and Pattern Recognition (CVPR'96)*, pp. 921–928, San Francisco.

Bhat, D. N. and Nayar, S. K. (1998). Ordinal measures for image correspondence. *IEEE Transactions on Pattern Analysis and Machine Intelligence*, 20(4):415–423.

Bickel, B., Botsch, M., Angst, R., Matusik, W., Otaduy, M., Pfister, H., and Gross, M. (2007). Multi-scale capture of facial geometry and motion. *ACM Transactions on Graphics*, 26(3).

Billinghurst, M., Kato, H., and Poupyrev, I. (2001). The MagicBook: a transitional AR interface. *Computers & Graphics*, 25:745–753.

Bimber, O. (2006). Computational photography—the next big step. *Computer*, 39(8):28–29.

Birchfield, S. and Tomasi, C. (1998). A pixel dissimilarity measure that is insensitive to image sampling. *IEEE Transactions on Pattern Analysis and Machine Intelligence*, 20(4):401–406.

Birchfield, S. and Tomasi, C. (1999). Depth discontinuities by pixel-to-pixel stereo. *International Journal of Computer Vision*, 35(3):269–293.

Birchfield, S. T., Natarajan, B., and Tomasi, C. (2007). Correspondence as energy-based segmentation. *Image and Vision Computing*, 25(8):1329–1340.

Bishop, C. M. (2006). *Pattern Recognition and Machine Learning*. Springer, New York, NY.

Bitouk, D., Kumar, N., Dhillon, S., Belhumeur, P., and Nayar, S. K. (2008). Face swapping: Automatically replacing faces in photographs. *ACM Transactions on Graphics*, 27(3).

Björck, A. (1996). *Numerical Methods for Least Squares Problems*. Society for Industrial and Applied Mathematics.

Björck, A. and Dahlquist, G. (2010). *Numerical Methods in Scientific Computing*. Volume II, Society for Industrial and Applied Mathematics.

Black, M., Yacoob, Y., Jepson, A. D., and Fleet, D. J. (1997). Learning parameterized models of image motion. In *IEEE Computer Society Conference on Computer Vision and Pattern Recognition (CVPR'97)*, pp. 561–567, San Juan, Puerto Rico.

Black, M. J. and Anandan, P. (1996). The robust estimation of multiple motions: Parametric and piecewise-smooth flow fields. *Computer Vision and Image Understanding*, 63(1):75–104.

Black, M. J. and Jepson, A. D. (1996). Estimating optical flow in segmented images using variable-order parametric models with local deformations. *IEEE Transactions on Pattern Analysis and Machine Intelligence*, 18(10):972–986.

Black, M. J. and Jepson, A. D. (1998). EigenTracking: robust matching and tracking of articulated objects using a view-based representation. *International Journal of Computer Vision*, 26(1):63–84.

Black, M. J. and Rangarajan, A. (1996). On the unification of line processes, outlier rejection, and robust statistics with applications in early vision. *International Journal of Computer Vision*, 19(1):57–91.

Black, M. J., Sapiro, G., Marimont, D. H., and Heeger, D. (1998). Robust anisotropic diffusion. *IEEE Transactions on Image Processing*, 7(3):421–432.

Blackford, L. S., Demmel, J., Dongarra, J., Duff, I., Hammarling, S. *et al.* (2002). An updated set of basic linear algebra subprograms (BLAS). *ACM Transactions on Mathematical Software*, 28(2):135–151.

Blake, A. and Isard, M. (1998). *Active Contours: The Application of Techniques from Graphics, Vision, Control Theory and Statistics to Visual Tracking of Shapes in Motion*. Springer Verlag, London.

Blake, A. and Zisserman, A. (1987). *Visual Reconstruction*. MIT Press, Cambridge, Massachusetts.

Blake, A., Curwen, R., and Zisserman, A. (1993). A framework for spatio-temporal control in the tracking of visual contour. *International Journal of Computer Vision*, 11(2):127–145.

Blake, A., Kohli, P., and Rother, C. (eds). (2010). *Advances in Markov Random Fields*, MIT Press.

Blake, A., Zimmerman, A., and Knowles, G. (1985). Surface descriptions from stereo and shading. *Image and Vision Computing*, 3(4):183–191.

Blake, A., Rother, C., Brown, M., Perez, P., and Torr, P. (2004). Interactive image segmentation using an adaptive GMMRF model. In *Eighth European Conference on Computer Vision (ECCV 2004)*, pp. 428–441, Prague.

Blanz, V. and Vetter, T. (1999). A morphable model for the synthesis of 3D faces. In *ACM SIGGRAPH 1999 Conference Proceedings*, pp. 187–194.

Blanz, V. and Vetter, T. (2003). Face recognition based on fitting a 3D morphable model. *IEEE Transactions on Pattern Analysis and Machine Intelligence*, 25():1063–1074.

Bleyer, M., Gelautz, M., Rother, C., and Rhemann, C. (2009). A stereo approach that handles the matting problem via image warping. In *IEEE Computer Society Conference on Computer Vision and Pattern Recognition (CVPR 2009)*, Miami Beach, FL.

Blinn, J. (1998). *Dirty Pixels*. Morgan Kaufmann Publishers, San Francisco.

Blinn, J. F. (1994a). Jim Blinn's corner: Compositing, part 1: Theory. *IEEE Computer Graphics and Applications*, 14(5):83–87.

Blinn, J. F. (1994b). Jim Blinn's corner: Compositing, part 2: Practice. *IEEE Computer Graphics and Applications*, 14(6):78–82.

Blinn, J. F. and Newell, M. E. (1976). Texture and reflection in computer generated images. *Communications of the ACM*, 19(10):542–547.

Blostein, D. and Ahuja, N. (1987). Shape from texture: Integrating texture-element extraction and surface estimation. *IEEE Transactions on Pattern Analysis and Machine Intelligence*, 11(12):1233–1251.

Bobick, A. F. (1997). Movement, activity and action: the role of knowledge in the perception of motion. *Proceedings of the Royal Society of London*, B 352:1257–1265.

Bobick, A. F. and Intille, S. S. (1999). Large occlusion stereo. *International Journal of Computer Vision*, 33(3):181–200.

Boden, M. A. (2006). *Mind As Machine: A History of Cognitive Science*. Oxford University Press, Oxford, England.

Bogart, R. G. (1991). View correlation. In Arvo, J. (ed.), *Graphics Gems II*, pp. 181–190, Academic Press, Boston.

Boiman, O., Shechtman, E., and Irani, M. (2008). In defense of nearest-neighbor based image classification. In *IEEE Computer Society Conference on Computer Vision and Pattern Recognition (CVPR 2008)*, Anchorage, AK.

Boissonat, J.-D. (1984). Representing 2D and 3D shapes with the Delaunay triangulation. In *Seventh International Conference on Pattern Recognition (ICPR'84)*, pp. 745–748, Montreal, Canada.

Bolles, R. C., Baker, H. H., and Hannah, M. J. (1993). The JISCT stereo evaluation. In *Image Understanding Workshop*, pp. 263–274.

Bolles, R. C., Baker, H. H., and Marimont, D. H. (1987). Epipolar-plane image analysis: An approach to determining structure from motion. *International Journal of Computer Vision*, 1:7–55.

Bookstein, F. L. (1989). Principal warps: Thin-plate splines and the decomposition of deformations. *IEEE Transactions on Pattern Analysis and Machine Intelligence*, 11(6):567–585.

Borenstein, E. and Ullman, S. (2008). Combined top-down/bottom-up segmentation. *IEEE Transactions on Pattern Analysis and Machine Intelligence*, 30(12):2109–2125.

Borgefors, G. (1986). Distance transformations in digital images. *Computer Vision, Graphics and Image Processing*, 34(3):227–248.

Bouchard, G. and Triggs, B. (2005). Hierarchical part-based visual object categorization. In *IEEE Computer Society Conference on Computer Vision and Pattern Recognition (CVPR'2005)*, pp. 709–714, San Diego, CA.

Bougnoux, S. (1998). From projective to Euclidean space under any practical situation, a criticism of self-calibration. In *Sixth International Conference on Computer Vision (ICCV'98)*, pp. 790–798, Bombay.

Bouguet, J.-Y. and Perona, P. (1999). 3D photography using shadows in dual-space geometry. *International Journal of Computer Vision*, 35(2):129–149.

Boult, T. E. and Kender, J. R. (1986). Visual surface reconstruction using sparse depth data. In *IEEE Computer Society Conference on Computer Vision and Pattern Recognition (CVPR'86)*, pp. 68–76, Miami Beach.

Bourdev, L. and Malik, J. (2009). Poselets: Body part detectors trained using 3D human pose annotations. In *Twelfth International Conference on Computer Vision (ICCV 2009)*, Kyoto, Japan.

Bovik, A. (ed.). (2000). *Handbook of Image and Video Processing*, Academic Press, San Diego.

Bowyer, K. W., Kranenburg, C., and Dougherty, S. (2001). Edge detector evaluation using empirical ROC curves. *Computer Vision and Image Understanding*, 84(1):77–103.

Box, G. E. P. and Muller, M. E. (1958). A note on the generation of random normal deviates. *Annals of Mathematical Statistics*, 29(2).

Boyer, E. and Berger, M. O. (1997). 3D surface reconstruction using occluding contours. *International Journal of Computer Vision*, 22(3):219–233.

Boykov, Y. and Funka-Lea, G. (2006). Graph cuts and efficient N-D image segmentation. *International Journal of Computer Vision*, 70(2):109–131.

Boykov, Y. and Jolly, M.-P. (2001). Interactive graph cuts for optimal boundary and region segmentation of objects in N-D images. In *Eighth International Conference on Computer Vision (ICCV 2001)*, pp. 105–112, Vancouver, Canada.

Boykov, Y. and Kolmogorov, V. (2003). Computing geodesics and minimal surfaces via graph cuts. In *Ninth International Conference on Computer Vision (ICCV 2003)*, pp. 26–33, Nice, France.

Boykov, Y. and Kolmogorov, V. (2004). An experimental comparison of min-cut/max-flow algorithms for energy minimization in vision. *IEEE Transactions on Pattern Analysis and Machine Intelligence*, 26(9):1124–1137.

Boykov, Y. and Kolmogorov, V. (2010). Basic graph cut algorithms. In Blake, A., Kohli, P., and Rother, C. (eds), *Advances in Markov Random Fields*, MIT Press.

Boykov, Y., Veksler, O., and Zabih, R. (1998). A variable window approach to early vision. *IEEE Transactions on Pattern Analysis and Machine Intelligence*, 20(12):1283–1294.

Boykov, Y., Veksler, O., and Zabih, R. (2001). Fast approximate energy minimization via graph cuts. *IEEE Transactions on Pattern Analysis and Machine Intelligence*, 23(11):1222–1239.

Boykov, Y., Veksler, O., and Zabih, R. (2010). Optimizing multi-label MRFs by move making algorithms. In Blake, A., Kohli, P., and Rother, C. (eds), *Advances in Markov Random Fields*, MIT Press.

Boykov, Y., Kolmogorov, V., Cremers, D., and Delong, A. (2006). An integral solution to surface evolution PDEs via Geo-cuts. In *Ninth European Conference on Computer Vision (ECCV 2006)*, pp. 409–422.

Bracewell, R. N. (1986). *The Fourier Transform and its Applications*. McGraw-Hill, New York, 2nd edition.

Bradley, D., Boubekeur, T., and Heidrich, W. (2008). Accurate multi-view reconstruction using robust binocular stereo and surface meshing. In *IEEE Computer Society Conference on Computer Vision and Pattern Recognition (CVPR 2008)*, Anchorage, AK.

Bradsky, G. and Kaehler, A. (2008). *Learning OpenCV: Computer Vision with the OpenCV Library*. O'Reilly, Sebastopol, CA.

Brandt, A. (1986). Algebraic multigrid theory: The symmetric case. *Applied Mathematics and Computation*, 19(1-4):23–56.

Bregler, C. and Malik, J. (1998). Tracking people with twists and exponential maps. In *IEEE Computer Society Conference on Computer Vision and Pattern Recognition (CVPR'98)*, pp. 8–15, Santa Barbara.

Bregler, C., Covell, M., and Slaney, M. (1997). Video rewrite: Driving visual speech with audio. In *ACM SIGGRAPH 1997 Conference Proceedings*, pp. 353–360.

Bregler, C., Malik, J., and Pullen, K. (2004). Twist based acquisition and tracking of animal and human kinematics. *International Journal of Computer Vision*, 56(3):179–194.

Breu, H., Gil, J., Kirkpatrick, D., and Werman, M. (1995). Linear time Euclidean distance transform algorithms. *IEEE Transactions on Pattern Analysis and Machine Intelligence*, 17(5):529–533.

Brice, C. R. and Fennema, C. L. (1970). Scene analysis using regions. *Artificial Intelligence*, 1(3-4):205–226.

Briggs, W. L., Henson, V. E., and McCormick, S. F. (2000). *A Multigrid Tutorial*. Society for Industrial and Applied Mathematics, Philadelphia, second edition.

Brillaut-O'Mahoney, B. (1991). New method for vanishing point detection. *Computer Vision, Graphics, and Image Processing*, 54(2):289–300.

Brinkmann, R. (2008). *The Art and Science of Digital Compositing*. Morgan Kaufmann Publishers, San Francisco, 2nd edition.

Brooks, R. A. (1981). Symbolic reasoning among 3-D models and 2-D images. *Artificial Intelligence*, 17:285–348.

Brown, D. C. (1971). Close-range camera calibration. *Photogrammetric Engineering*, 37(8):855–866.

Brown, L. G. (1992). A survey of image registration techniques. *Computing Surveys*, 24(4):325–376.

Brown, M. and Lowe, D. (2002). Invariant features from interest point groups. In *British Machine Vision Conference*, pp. 656–665, Cardiff, Wales.

Brown, M. and Lowe, D. (2003). Unsupervised 3D object recognition and reconstruction in unordered datasets. In *International Conference on 3D Imaging and Modelling*, pp. 1218–1225, Nice, France.

Brown, M. and Lowe, D. (2007). Automatic panoramic image stitching using invariant features. *International Journal of Computer Vision*, 74(1):59–73.

Brown, M., Hartley, R., and Nistér, D. (2007). Minimal solutions for panoramic stitching. In *IEEE Computer Society Conference on Computer Vision and Pattern Recognition (CVPR 2007)*, Minneapolis, MN.

Brown, M., Szeliski, R., and Winder, S. (2004). *Multi-Image Matching Using Multi-Scale Oriented Patches*. Technical Report MSR-TR-2004-133, Microsoft Research.

Brown, M., Szeliski, R., and Winder, S. (2005). Multi-image matching using multi-scale oriented patches. In *IEEE Computer Society Conference on Computer Vision and Pattern Recognition (CVPR'2005)*, pp. 510–517, San Diego, CA.

Brown, M. Z., Burschka, D., and Hager, G. D. (2003). Advances in computational stereo. *IEEE Transactions on Pattern Analysis and Machine Intelligence*, 25(8):993–1008.

Brox, T., Bregler, C., and Malik, J. (2009). Large displacement optical flow. In *IEEE Computer Society Conference on Computer Vision and Pattern Recognition (CVPR 2009)*, Miami Beach, FL.

Brox, T., Bruhn, A., Papenberg, N., and Weickert, J. (2004). High accuracy optical flow estimation based on a theory for warping. In *Eighth European Conference on Computer Vision (ECCV 2004)*, pp. 25–36, Prague.

Brubaker, S. C., Wu, J., Sun, J., Mullin, M. D., and Rehg, J. M. (2008). On the design of cascades of boosted ensembles for face detection. *International Journal of Computer Vision*, 77(1-3):65–86.

Bruhn, A., Weickert, J., and Schnörr, C. (2005). Lucas/Kanade meets Horn/Schunck: Combining local and global optic flow methods. *International Journal of Computer Vision*, 61(3):211–231.

Bruhn, A., Weickert, J., Kohlberger, T., and Schnörr, C. (2006). A multigrid platform for real-time motion computation with discontinuity-preserving variational methods. *International Journal of Computer Vision*, 70(3):257–277.

Buades, A., Coll, B., and Morel, J.-M. (2008). Nonlocal image and movie denoising. *International Journal of Computer Vision*, 76(2):123–139.

Bălan, A. O. and Black, M. J. (2008). The naked truth: Estimating body shape under clothing. In *Tenth European Conference on Computer Vision (ECCV 2008)*, pp. 15–29, Marseilles.

Buchanan, A. and Fitzgibbon, A. (2005). Damped Newton algorithms for matrix factorization with missing data. In *IEEE Computer Society Conference on Computer Vision and Pattern Recognition (CVPR'2005)*, pp. 316–322, San Diego, CA.

Buck, I., Finkelstein, A., Jacobs, C., Klein, A., Salesin, D. H., Seims, J., Szeliski, R., and Toyama, K. (2000). Performance-driven hand-drawn animation. In *Symposium on Non Photorealistic Animation and Rendering*, pp. 101–108, Annecy.

Buehler, C., Bosse, M., McMillan, L., Gortler, S. J., and Cohen, M. F. (2001). Unstructured Lumigraph rendering. In *ACM SIGGRAPH 2001 Conference Proceedings*, pp. 425–432.

Bugayevskiy, L. M. and Snyder, J. P. (1995). *Map Projections: A Reference Manual*. CRC Press.

Burger, W. and Burge, M. J. (2008). *Digital Image Processing: An Algorithmic Introduction Using Java*. Springer, New York, NY.

Burl, M. C., Weber, M., and Perona, P. (1998). A probabilistic approach to object recognition using local photometry and global geometry. In *Fifth European Conference on Computer Vision (ECCV'98)*, pp. 628–641, Freiburg, Germany.

Burns, J. B., Hanson, A. R., and Riseman, E. M. (1986). Extracting straight lines. *IEEE Transactions on Pattern Analysis and Machine Intelligence*, PAMI-8(4):425–455.

Burns, P. D. and Williams, D. (1999). Using slanted edge analysis for color registration measurement. In *IS&T PICS Conference*, pp. 51–53.

Burt, P. J. and Adelson, E. H. (1983a). The Laplacian pyramid as a compact image code. *IEEE Transactions on Communications*, COM-31(4):532–540.

Burt, P. J. and Adelson, E. H. (1983b). A multiresolution spline with applications to image mosaics. *ACM Transactions on Graphics*, 2(4):217–236.

Burt, P. J. and Kolczynski, R. J. (1993). Enhanced image capture through fusion. In *Fourth International Conference on Computer Vision (ICCV'93)*, pp. 173–182, Berlin, Germany.

Byröd, M. and øAström, K. (2009). Bundle adjustment using conjugate gradients with multiscale preconditioning. In *British Machine Vision Conference (BMVC 2009)*.

Cai, D., He, X., Hu, Y., Han, J., and Huang, T. (2007). Learning a spatially smooth subspace for face recognition. In *IEEE Computer Society Conference on Computer Vision and Pattern Recognition (CVPR 2007)*, Minneapolis, MN.

Campbell, N. D. F., Vogiatzis, G., Hernández, C., and Cipolla, R. (2008). Using multiple hypotheses to improve depth-maps for multi-view stereo. In *Tenth European Conference on Computer Vision (ECCV 2008)*, pp. 766–779, Marseilles.

Can, A., Stewart, C., Roysam, B., and Tanenbaum, H. (2002). A feature-based, robust, hierarchical algorithm for registering pairs of images of the curved human retina. *IEEE Transactions on Pattern Analysis and Machine Intelligence*, 24(3):347–364.

Canny, J. (1986). A computational approach to edge detection. *IEEE Transactions on Pattern Analysis and Machine Intelligence*, PAMI-8(6):679–698.

Cao, Z., Yin, Q., Tang, X., and Sun, J. (2010). Face recognition with learning-based descriptor. In *IEEE Computer Society Conference on Computer Vision and Pattern Recognition (CVPR 2010)*, San Francisco, CA.

Capel, D. (2004). *Image Mosaicing and Super-resolution. Distinguished Dissertation Series, British Computer Society*, Springer-Verlag.

Capel, D. and Zisserman, A. (1998). Automated mosaicing with super-resolution zoom. In *IEEE Computer Society Conference on Computer Vision and Pattern Recognition (CVPR'98)*, pp. 885–891, Santa Barbara.

Capel, D. and Zisserman, A. (2000). Super-resolution enhancement of text image sequences. In *Fifteenth International Conference on Pattern Recognition (ICPR'2000)*, pp. 600–605, Barcelona, Spain.

Capel, D. and Zisserman, A. (2003). Computer vision applied to super resolution. *IEEE Signal Processing Magazine*, 20(3):75–86.

Capel, D. P. (2001). *Super-resolution and Image Mosaicing*. Ph.D. thesis, University of Oxford.

Caprile, B. and Torre, V. (1990). Using vanishing points for camera calibration. *International Journal of Computer Vision*, 4(2):127–139.

Carneiro, G. and Jepson, A. (2005). The distinctiveness, detectability, and robustness of local image features. In *IEEE Computer Society Conference on Computer Vision and Pattern Recognition (CVPR'2005)*, pp. 296–301, San Diego, CA.

Carneiro, G. and Lowe, D. (2006). Sparse flexible models of local features. In *Ninth European Conference on Computer Vision (ECCV 2006)*, pp. 29–43.

Carnevali, P., Coletti, L., and Patarnello, S. (1985). Image processing by simulated annealing. *IBM Journal of Research and Development*, 29(6):569–579.

Carranza, J., Theobalt, C., Magnor, M. A., and Seidel, H.-P. (2003). Free-viewpoint video of human actors. *ACM Transactions on Graphics (Proc. SIGGRAPH 2003)*, 22(3):569–577.

Carroll, R., Agrawala, M., and Agarwala, A. (2009). Optimizing content-preserving projections for wide-angle images. *ACM Transactions on Graphics*, 28(3).

Caselles, V., Kimmel, R., and Sapiro, G. (1997). Geodesic active contours. *International Journal of Computer Vision*, 21(1):61–79.

Catmull, E. and Smith, A. R. (1980). 3-D transformations of images in scanline order. *Computer Graphics (SIGGRAPH '80)*, 14(3):279–285.

Celniker, G. and Gossard, D. (1991). Deformable curve and surface finite-elements for free-form shape design. *Computer Graphics (SIGGRAPH '91)*, 25(4):257–266.

Chakrabarti, A., Scharstein, D., and Zickler, T. (2009). An empirical camera model for internet color vision. In *British Machine Vision Conference (BMVC 2009)*, London, UK.

Cham, T. J. and Cipolla, R. (1998). A statistical framework for long-range feature matching in uncalibrated image mosaicing. In *IEEE Computer Society Conference on Computer Vision and Pattern Recognition (CVPR'98)*, pp. 442–447, Santa Barbara.

Cham, T.-J. and Rehg, J. M. (1999). A multiple hypothesis approach to figure tracking. In *IEEE Computer Society Conference on Computer Vision and Pattern Recognition (CVPR'99)*, pp. 239–245, Fort Collins.

Champleboux, G., Lavallée, S., Sautot, P., and Cinquin, P. (1992). Accurate calibration of cameras and range imaging sensors, the NPBS method. In *IEEE International Conference on Robotics and Automation*, pp. 1552–1558, Nice, France.

Champleboux, G., Lavallée, S., Szeliski, R., and Brunie, L. (1992). From accurate range imaging sensor calibration to accurate model-based 3-D object localization. In *IEEE Computer Society Conference on Computer Vision and Pattern Recognition (CVPR'92)*, pp. 83–89, Champaign, Illinois.

Chan, A. B. and Vasconcelos, N. (2009). Layered dynamic textures. *IEEE Transactions on Pattern Analysis and Machine Intelligence*, 31(10):1862–1879.

Chan, T. F. and Vese, L. A. (1992). Active contours without edges. *IEEE Transactions on Image Processing*, 10(2):266–277.

Chan, T. F., Osher, S., and Shen, J. (2001). The digital TV filter and nonlinear denoising. *IEEE Transactions on Image Processing*, 10(2):231–241.

Chang, M. M., Tekalp, A. M., and Sezan, M. I. (1997). Simultaneous motion estimation and segmentation. *IEEE Transactions on Image Processing*, 6(9):1326–1333.

Chaudhuri, S. (2001). *Super-Resolution Imaging*. Springer.

Chaudhuri, S. and Rajagopalan, A. N. (1999). *Depth from Defocus: A Real Aperture Imaging Approach*. Springer.

Cheeseman, P., Kanefsky, B., Hanson, R., and Stutz, J. (1993). *Super-Resolved Surface Reconstruction From Multiple Images*. Technical Report FIA-93-02, NASA Ames Research Center, Artificial Intelligence Branch.

Chellappa, R., Wilson, C., and Sirohey, S. (1995). Human and machine recognition of faces: A survey. *Proceedings of the IEEE*, 83(5):705–740.

Chen, B., Neubert, B., Ofek, E., Deussen, O., and Cohen, M. F. (2009). Integrated videos and maps for driving directions. In *UIST '09: Proceedings of the 22nd annual ACM symposium on User interface software and technology*, pp. 223–232, Victoria, BC, Canada, New York, NY, USA.

Chen, C.-Y. and Klette, R. (1999). Image stitching - comparisons and new techniques. In *Computer Analysis of Images and Patterns (CAIP'99)*, pp. 615–622, Ljubljana.

Chen, J. and Chen, B. (2008). Architectural modeling from sparsely scanned range data. *International Journal of Computer Vision*, 78(2-3):223–236.

Chen, J., Paris, S., and Durand, F. (2007). Real-time edge-aware image processing with the bilateral grid. *ACM Transactions on Graphics*, 26(3).

Chen, S. and Williams, L. (1993). View interpolation for image synthesis. In *ACM SIGGRAPH 1993 Conference Proceedings*, pp. 279–288.

Chen, S. E. (1995). QuickTime VR – an image-based approach to virtual environment navigation. In *ACM SIGGRAPH 1995 Conference Proceedings*, pp. 29–38, Los Angeles.

Chen, Y. and Medioni, G. (1992). Object modeling by registration of multiple range images. *Image and Vision Computing*, 10(3):145–155.

Cheng, L., Vishwanathan, S. V. N., and Zhang, X. (2008). Consistent image analogies using semi-supervised learning. In *IEEE Computer Society Conference on Computer Vision and Pattern Recognition (CVPR 2008)*, Anchorage, AK.

Cheng, Y. (1995). Mean shift, mode seeking, and clustering. *IEEE Transactions on Pattern Analysis and Machine Intelligence*, 17(8):790–799.

Chiang, M.-C. and Boult, T. E. (1996). Efficient image warping and super-resolution. In *IEEE Workshop on Applications of Computer Vision (WACV'96)*, pp. 56–61, Sarasota.

Chiu, K. and Raskar, R. (2009). Computer vision on tap. In *Second IEEE Workshop on Internet Vision*, Miami Beach, Florida.

Chou, P. B. and Brown, C. M. (1990). The theory and practice of Bayesian image labeling. *International Journal of Computer Vision*, 4(3):185–210.

Christensen, G., Joshi, S., and Miller, M. (1997). Volumetric transformation of brain anatomy. *IEEE Transactions on Medical Imaging*, 16(6):864–877.

Christy, S. and Horaud, R. (1996). Euclidean shape and motion from multiple perspective views by affine iterations. *IEEE Transactions on Pattern Analysis and Machine Intelligence*, 18(11):1098–1104.

Chuang, Y.-Y., Curless, B., Salesin, D. H., and Szeliski, R. (2001). A Bayesian approach to digital matting. In *IEEE Computer Society Conference on Computer Vision and Pattern Recognition (CVPR'2001)*, pp. 264–271, Kauai, Hawaii.

Chuang, Y.-Y., Agarwala, A., Curless, B., Salesin, D. H., and Szeliski, R. (2002). Video matting of complex scenes. *ACM Transactions on Graphics (Proc. SIGGRAPH 2002)*, 21(3):243–248.

Chuang, Y.-Y., Goldman, D. B., Curless, B., Salesin, D. H., and Szeliski, R. (2003). Shadow matting. *ACM Transactions on Graphics (Proc. SIGGRAPH 2003)*, 22(3):494–500.

Chuang, Y.-Y., Goldman, D. B., Zheng, K. C., Curless, B., Salesin, D. H., and Szeliski, R. (2005). Animating pictures with stochastic motion textures. *ACM Transactions on Graphics (Proc. SIGGRAPH 2005)*, 24(3):853–860.

Chuang, Y.-Y., Zongker, D., Hindorff, J., Curless, B., Salesin, D. H., and Szeliski, R. (2000). Environment matting extensions: Towards higher accuracy and real-time capture. In *ACM SIGGRAPH 2000 Conference Proceedings*, pp. 121–130, New Orleans.

Chui, C. K. (1992). *Wavelet Analysis and Its Applications*. Academic Press, New York.

Chum, O. and Matas, J. (2005). Matching with PROSAC—progressive sample consensus. In *IEEE Computer Society Conference on Computer Vision and Pattern Recognition (CVPR'2005)*, pp. 220–226, San Diego, CA.

Chum, O. and Matas, J. (2010). Large-scale discovery of spatially related images. *IEEE Transactions on Pattern Analysis and Machine Intelligence*, 32(2):371–377.

Chum, O., Philbin, J., and Zisserman, A. (2008). Near duplicate image detection: min-hash and tf-idf weighting. In *British Machine Vision Conference (BMVC 2008)*, Leeds, England.

Chum, O., Philbin, J., Sivic, J., Isard, M., and Zisserman, A. (2007). Total recall: Automatic query expansion with a generative feature model for object retrieval. In *Eleventh International Conference on Computer Vision (ICCV 2007)*, Rio de Janeiro, Brazil.

Cipolla, R. and Blake, A. (1990). The dynamic analysis of apparent contours. In *Third International Conference on Computer Vision (ICCV'90)*, pp. 616–623, Osaka, Japan.

Cipolla, R. and Blake, A. (1992). Surface shape from the deformation of apparent contours. *International Journal of Computer Vision*, 9(2):83–112.

Cipolla, R. and Giblin, P. (2000). *Visual Motion of Curves and Surfaces*. Cambridge University Press, Cambridge.

Cipolla, R., Drummond, T., and Robertson, D. P. (1999). Camera calibration from vanishing points in images of architectural scenes. In *British Machine Vision Conference (BMVC99)*.

Claus, D. and Fitzgibbon, A. (2005). A rational function lens distortion model for general cameras. In *IEEE Computer Society Conference on Computer Vision and Pattern Recognition (CVPR'2005)*, pp. 213–219, San Diego, CA.

Clowes, M. B. (1971). On seeing things. *Artificial Intelligence*, 2:79–116.

Cohen, L. D. and Cohen, I. (1993). Finite-element methods for active contour models and balloons for 2-D and 3-D images. *IEEE Transactions on Pattern Analysis and Machine Intelligence*, 15(11):1131–1147.

Cohen, M. and Wallace, J. (1993). *Radiosity and Realistic Image Synthesis*. Morgan Kaufmann.

Cohen, M. F. and Szeliski, R. (2006). The Moment Camera. *Computer*, 39(8):40–45.

Collins, R. T. (1996). A space-sweep approach to true multi-image matching. In *IEEE Computer Society Conference on Computer Vision and Pattern Recognition (CVPR'96)*, pp. 358–363, San Francisco.

Collins, R. T. and Liu, Y. (2003). On-line selection of discriminative tracking features. In *Ninth International Conference on Computer Vision (ICCV 2003)*, pp. 346–352, Nice, France.

Collins, R. T. and Weiss, R. S. (1990). Vanishing point calculation as a statistical inference on the unit sphere. In *Third International Conference on Computer Vision (ICCV'90)*, pp. 400–403, Osaka, Japan.

Comaniciu, D. and Meer, P. (2002). Mean shift: A robust approach toward feature space analysis. *IEEE Transactions on Pattern Analysis and Machine Intelligence*, 24(5):603–619.

Comaniciu, D. and Meer, P. (2003). An algorithm for data-driven bandwidth selection. *IEEE Transactions on Pattern Analysis and Machine Intelligence*, 25(2):281–288.

Conn, A. R., Gould, N. I. M., and Toint, P. L. (2000). *Trust-Region Methods*. Society for Industrial and Applied Mathematics, Philadephia.

Cook, R. L. and Torrance, K. E. (1982). A reflectance model for computer graphics. *ACM Transactions on Graphics*, 1(1):7–24.

Coorg, S. and Teller, S. (2000). Spherical mosaics with quaternions and dense correlation. *International Journal of Computer Vision*, 37(3):259–273.

Cootes, T., Edwards, G. J., and Taylor, C. J. (2001). Active appearance models. *IEEE Transactions on Pattern Analysis and Machine Intelligence*, 23(6):681–685.

Cootes, T., Cooper, D., Taylor, C., and Graham, J. (1995). Active shape models—their training and application. *Computer Vision and Image Understanding*, 61(1):38–59.

Cootes, T., Taylor, C., Lanitis, A., Cooper, D., and Graham, J. (1993). Building and using flexible models incorporating grey-level information. In *Fourth International Conference on Computer Vision (ICCV'93)*, pp. 242–246, Berlin, Germany.

Cootes, T. F. and Taylor, C. J. (2001). Statistical models of appearance for medical image analysis and computer vision. In *Medical Imaging*.

Coquillart, S. (1990). Extended free-form deformations: A sculpturing tool for 3D geometric modeling. *Computer Graphics (SIGGRAPH '90)*, 24(4):187–196.

Cormen, T. H. (2001). *Introduction to Algorithms*. MIT Press, Cambridge, Massachusetts.

Cornelis, N., Leibe, B., Cornelis, K., and Van Gool, L. (2008). 3D urban scene modeling integrating recognition and reconstruction. *International Journal of Computer Vision*, 78(2-3):121–141.

Corso, J. and Hager, G. (2005). Coherent regions for concise and stable image description. In *IEEE Computer Society Conference on Computer Vision and Pattern Recognition (CVPR'2005)*, pp. 184–190, San Diego, CA.

Costeira, J. and Kanade, T. (1995). A multi-body factorization method for motion analysis. In *Fifth International Conference on Computer Vision (ICCV'95)*, pp. 1071–1076, Cambridge, Massachusetts.

Costen, N., Cootes, T. F., Edwards, G. J., and Taylor, C. J. (1999). Simultaneous extraction of functional face subspaces. In *IEEE Computer Society Conference on Computer Vision and Pattern Recognition (CVPR'99)*, pp. 492–497, Fort Collins.

Couprie, C., Grady, L., Najman, L., and Talbot, H. (2009). Power watersheds: A new image segmentation framework extending graph cuts, random walker and optimal spanning forest. In *Twelfth International Conference on Computer Vision (ICCV 2009)*, Kyoto, Japan.

Cour, T., Bénézit, F., and Shi, J. (2005). Spectral segmentation with multiscale graph decomposition. In *IEEE Computer Society Conference on Computer Vision and Pattern Recognition (CVPR'2005)*, pp. 1123–1130, San Diego, CA.

Cox, D., Little, J., and O'Shea, D. (2007). *Ideals, Varieties, and Algorithms: An Introduction to Computational Algebraic Geometry and Commutative Algebra*. Springer.

Cox, I. J. (1994). A maximum likelihood N-camera stereo algorithm. In *IEEE Computer Society Conference on Computer Vision and Pattern Recognition (CVPR'94)*, pp. 733–739, Seattle.

Cox, I. J., Roy, S., and Hingorani, S. L. (1995). Dynamic histogram warping of image pairs for constant image brightness. In *IEEE International Conference on Image Processing (ICIP'95)*, pp. 366–369.

Cox, I. J., Hingorani, S. L., Rao, S. B., and Maggs, B. M. (1996). A maximum likelihood stereo algorithm. *Computer Vision and Image Understanding*, 63(3):542–567.

Crandall, D. and Huttenlocher, D. (2007). Composite models of objects and scenes for category recognition. In *IEEE Computer Society Conference on Computer Vision and Pattern Recognition (CVPR 2007)*, Minneapolis, MN.

Crandall, D., Felzenszwalb, P., and Huttenlocher, D. (2005). Spatial priors for part-based recognition using statistical models. In *IEEE Computer Society Conference on Computer Vision and Pattern Recognition (CVPR'2005)*, pp. 10–17, San Diego, CA.

Crandall, D., Backstrom, L., Huttenlocher, D., and Kleinberg, J. (2009). Mapping the world's photos. In *18th Int. World Wide Web Conference*, pp. 761–770, Madrid.

Crandall, D. J. and Huttenlocher, D. P. (2006). Weakly supervised learning of part-based spatial models for visual object recognition. In *Ninth European Conference on Computer Vision (ECCV 2006)*, pp. 16–29.

Crane, R. (1997). *A Simplified Approach to Image Processing*. Prentice Hall, Upper Saddle River, NJ.

Craswell, N. and Szummer, M. (2007). Random walks on the click graph. In *ACM SIGIR Conference on Research and Development in Informaion Retrieval*, pp. 239–246, New York, NY.

Cremers, D. and Soatto, S. (2005). Motion competition: A variational framework for piecewise parametric motion segmentation. *International Journal of Computer Vision*, 62(3):249–265.

Cremers, D., Rousson, M., and Deriche, R. (2007). A review of statistical approaches to level set segmentation: integrating color, texture, motion and shape. *International Journal of Computer Vision*, 72(2):195–215.

Crevier, D. (1993). *AI: The Tumultuous Search for Artificial Intelligence*. BasicBooks, New York, NY.

Criminisi, A., Pérez, P., and Toyama, K. (2004). Region filling and object removal by exemplar-based inpainting. *IEEE Transactions on Image Processing*, 13(9):1200–1212.

Criminisi, A., Reid, I., and Zisserman, A. (2000). Single view metrology. *International Journal of Computer Vision*, 40(2):123–148.

Criminisi, A., Sharp, T., and Blake, A. (2008). Geos: Geodesic image segmentation. In *Tenth European Conference on Computer Vision (ECCV 2008)*, pp. 99–112, Marseilles.

Criminisi, A., Cross, G., Blake, A., and Kolmogorov, V. (2006). Bilayer segmentation of live video. In *IEEE Computer Society Conference on Computer Vision and Pattern Recognition (CVPR'2006)*, pp. 53–60, New York City, NY.

Criminisi, A., Shotton, J., Blake, A., and Torr, P. (2003). Gaze manipulation for one-to-one teleconferencing. In *Ninth International Conference on Computer Vision (ICCV 2003)*, pp. 191–198, Nice, France.

Criminisi, A., Kang, S. B., Swaminathan, R., Szeliski, R., and Anandan, P. (2005). Extracting layers and analyzing their specular properties using epipolar-plane-image analysis. *Computer Vision and Image Understanding*, 97(1):51–85.

Criminisi, A., Shotton, J., Blake, A., Rother, C., and Torr, P. H. S. (2007). Efficient dense stereo with occlusion by four-state dynamic programming. *International Journal of Computer Vision*, 71(1):89–110.

Crow, F. C. (1984). Summed-area table for texture mapping. *Computer Graphics (SIGGRAPH '84)*, 18(3):207–212.

Crowley, J. L. and Stern, R. M. (1984). Fast computation of the difference of low-pass transform. *IEEE Transactions on Pattern Analysis and Machine Intelligence*, 6(2):212–222.

Csurka, G. and Perronnin, F. (2008). A simple high performance approach to semantic segmentation. In *British Machine Vision Conference (BMVC 2008)*, Leeds.

Csurka, G., Dance, C. R., Perronnin, F., and Willamowski, J. (2006). Generic visual categorization using weak geometry. In Ponce, J., Hebert, M., Schmid, C., and Zisserman, A. (eds), *Toward Category-Level Object Recognition*, pp. 207–224, Springer, New York.

Csurka, G., Dance, C. R., Fan, L., Willamowski, J., and Bray, C. (2004). Visual categorization with bags of keypoints. In *ECCV International Workshop on Statistical Learning in Computer Vision*, Prague.

Cui, J., Yang, Q., Wen, F., Wu, Q., Zhang, C., Van Gool, L., and Tang, X. (2008). Transductive object cutout. In *IEEE Computer Society Conference on Computer Vision and Pattern Recognition (CVPR 2008)*, Anchorage, AK.

Curless, B. (1999). From range scans to 3D models. *Computer Graphics*, 33(4):38–41.

Curless, B. and Levoy, M. (1995). Better optical triangulation through spacetime analysis. In *Fifth International Conference on Computer Vision (ICCV'95)*, pp. 987–994, Cambridge, Massachusetts.

Curless, B. and Levoy, M. (1996). A volumetric method for building complex models from range images. In *ACM SIGGRAPH 1996 Conference Proceedings*, pp. 303–312, New Orleans.

Cutler, R. and Davis, L. S. (2000). Robust real-time periodic motion detection, analysis, and applications. *IEEE Transactions on Pattern Analysis and Machine Intelligence*, 22(8):781–796.

Cutler, R. and Turk, M. (1998). View-based interpretation of real-time optical flow for gesture recognition. In *IEEE International Conference on Automatic Face and Gesture Recognition*, pp. 416–421, Nara, Japan.

Dai, S., Baker, S., and Kang, S. B. (2009). An MRF-based deinterlacing algorithm with exemplar-based refinement. *IEEE Transactions on Image Processing*, 18(5):956–968.

Dalal, N. and Triggs, B. (2005). Histograms of oriented gradients for human detection. In *IEEE Computer Society Conference on Computer Vision and Pattern Recognition (CVPR'2005)*, pp. 886–893, San Diego, CA.

Dalal, N., Triggs, B., and Schmid, C. (2006). Human detection using oriented histograms of flow and appearance. In *Ninth European Conference on Computer Vision (ECCV 2006)*, pp. 428–441.

Dana, K. J., van Ginneken, B., Nayar, S. K., and Koenderink, J. J. (1999). Reflectance and texture of real world surfaces. *ACM Transactions on Graphics*, 18(1):1–34.

Danielsson, P. E. (1980). Euclidean distance mapping. *Computer Graphics and Image Processing*, 14(3):227–248.

Darrell, T. and Pentland, A. (1991). Robust estimation of a multi-layered motion representation. In *IEEE Workshop on Visual Motion*, pp. 173–178, Princeton, New Jersey.

Darrell, T. and Pentland, A. (1995). Cooperative robust estimation using layers of support. *IEEE Transactions on Pattern Analysis and Machine Intelligence*, 17(5):474–487.

Darrell, T. and Simoncelli, E. (1993). "Nulling" filters and the separation of transparent motion. In *IEEE Computer Society Conference on Computer Vision and Pattern Recognition (CVPR'93)*, pp. 738–739, New York.

Darrell, T., Gordon, G., Harville, M., and Woodfill, J. (2000). Integrated person tracking using stereo, color, and pattern detection. *International Journal of Computer Vision*, 37(2):175–185.

Darrell, T., Baker, H., Crow, F., Gordon, G., and Woodfill, J. (1997). Magic morphin mirror: face-sensitive distortion and exaggeration. In *ACM SIGGRAPH 1997 Visual Proceedings*, Los Angeles.

Datta, R., Joshi, D., Li, J., and Wang, J. Z. (2008). Image retrieval: Ideas, influences, and trends of the new age. *ACM Computing Surveys*, 40(2).

Daugman, J. (2004). How iris recognition works. *IEEE Transactions on Circuits and Systems for Video Technology*, 14(1):21–30.

David, P., DeMenthon, D., Duraiswami, R., and Samet, H. (2004). SoftPOSIT: Simultaneous pose and correspondence determination. *International Journal of Computer Vision*, 59(3):259–284.

Davies, R., Twining, C., and Taylor, C. (2008). *Statistical Models of Shape*. Springer-Verlag, London.

Davis, J. (1998). Mosaics of scenes with moving objects. In *IEEE Computer Society Conference on Computer Vision and Pattern Recognition (CVPR'98)*, pp. 354–360, Santa Barbara.

Davis, J., Ramamoorthi, R., and Rusinkiewicz, S. (2003). Spacetime stereo: A unifying framework for depth from triangulation. In *IEEE Computer Society Conference on Computer Vision and Pattern Recognition (CVPR'2003)*, pp. 359–366, Madison, WI.

Davis, J., Nahab, D., Ramamoorthi, R., and Rusinkiewicz, S. (2005). Spacetime stereo: A unifying framework for depth from triangulation. *IEEE Transactions on Pattern Analysis and Machine Intelligence*, 27(2):296–302.

Davis, L. (1975). A survey of edge detection techniques. *Computer Graphics and Image Processing*, 4(3):248–270.

Davis, T. A. (2006). *Direct Methods for Sparse Linear Systems*. SIAM.

Davis, T. A. (2008). Multifrontal multithreaded rank-revealing sparse QR factorization. *ACM Trans. on Mathematical Software*, (submitted).

Davison, A., Reid, I., Molton, N. D., and Stasse, O. (2007). MonoSLAM: Real-time single camera SLAM. *IEEE Transactions on Pattern Analysis and Machine Intelligence*, 29(6):1052–1067.

de Agapito, L., Hayman, E., and Reid, I. (2001). Self-calibration of rotating and zooming cameras. *International Journal of Computer Vision*, 45(2):107–127.

de Berg, M., Cheong, O., van Kreveld, M., and Overmars, M. (2006). *Computational Geometry: Algorithms and Applications*. Springer, New York, NY, third edition.

De Bonet, J. (1997). Multiresolution sampling procedure for analysis and synthesis of texture images. In *ACM SIGGRAPH 1997 Conference Proceedings*, pp. 361–368, Los Angeles.

De Bonet, J. S. and Viola, P. (1999). Poxels: Probabilistic voxelized volume reconstruction. In *Seventh International Conference on Computer Vision (ICCV'99)*, pp. 418–425, Kerkyra, Greece.

De Castro, E. and Morandi, C. (1987). Registration of translated and rotated images using finite Fourier transforms. *IEEE Transactions on Pattern Analysis and Machine Intelligence*, PAMI-9(5):700–703.

de Haan, G. and Bellers, E. B. (1998). Deinterlacing—an overview. *Proceedings of the IEEE*, 86:1839–1857.

De la Torre, F. and Black, M. J. (2003). A framework for robust subspace learning. *International Journal of Computer Vision*, 54(1/2/3):117–142.

Debevec, P. (1998). Rendering synthetic objects into real scenes: Bridging traditional and image-based graphics with global illumination and high dynamic range photography. In *ACM SIGGRAPH 1998 Conference Proceedings*, pp. 189–198.

Debevec, P. (2006). Virtual cinematography: Relighting through computation. *Computer*, 39(8):57–65.

Debevec, P., Hawkins, T., Tchou, C., Duiker, H.-P., Sarokin, W., and Sagar, M. (2000). Acquiring the reflectance field of a human face. In *ACM SIGGRAPH 2000 Conference Proceedings*, pp. 145–156.

Debevec, P., Wenger, A., Tchou, C., Gardner, A., Waese, J., and Hawkins, T. (2002). A lighting reproduction approach to live-action compositing. *ACM Transactions on Graphics (Proc. SIGGRAPH 2002)*, 21(3):547–556.

Debevec, P. E. (1999). Image-based modeling and lighting. *Computer Graphics*, 33(4):46–50.

Debevec, P. E. and Malik, J. (1997). Recovering high dynamic range radiance maps from photographs. In *ACM SIGGRAPH 1997 Conference Proceedings*, pp. 369–378.

Debevec, P. E., Taylor, C. J., and Malik, J. (1996). Modeling and rendering architecture from photographs: A hybrid geometry- and image-based approach. In *ACM SIGGRAPH 1996 Conference Proceedings*, pp. 11–20, New Orleans.

Debevec, P. E., Yu, Y., and Borshukov, G. D. (1998). Efficient view-dependent image-based rendering with projective texture-mapping. In *Eurographics Rendering Workshop 1998*, pp. 105–116.

DeCarlo, D. and Santella, A. (2002). Stylization and abstraction of photographs. *ACM Transactions on Graphics (Proc. SIGGRAPH 2002)*, 21(3):769–776.

DeCarlo, D., Metaxas, D., and Stone, M. (1998). An anthropometric face model using variational techniques. In *ACM SIGGRAPH 1998 Conference Proceedings*, pp. 67–74.

Delingette, H., Hebert, M., and Ikeuichi, K. (1992). Shape representation and image segmentation using deformable surfaces. *Image and Vision Computing*, 10(3):132–144.

Dellaert, F. and Collins, R. (1999). Fast image-based tracking by selective pixel integration. In *ICCV Workshop on Frame-Rate Vision*, pp. 1–22.

Delong, A., Osokin, A., Isack, H. N., and Boykov, Y. (2010). Fast approximate energy minimization with label costs. In *IEEE Computer Society Conference on Computer Vision and Pattern Recognition (CVPR 2010)*, San Francisco, CA.

DeMenthon, D. I. and Davis, L. S. (1995). Model-based object pose in 25 lines of code. *International Journal of Computer Vision*, 15(1-2):123–141.

Demmel, J., Dongarra, J., Eijkhout, V., Fuentes, E., Petitet, A. *et al.* (2005). Self-adapting linear algebra algorithms and software. *Proceedings of the IEEE*, 93(2):293–312.

Dempster, A., Laird, N. M., and Rubin, D. B. (1977). Maximum likelihood from incomplete data via the EM algorithm. *Journal of the Royal Statistical Society B*, 39(1):1–38.

Deng, J., Dong, W., Socher, R., Li, L.-J., Li, K., and Fei-Fei, L. (2009). ImageNet: A large-scale hierarchical image database. In *IEEE Computer Society Conference on Computer Vision and Pattern Recognition (CVPR 2009)*, Miami Beach, FL.

Deriche, R. (1987). Using Canny's criteria to derive a recursively implemented optimal edge detector. *International Journal of Computer Vision*, 1(2):167–187.

Deriche, R. (1990). Fast algorithms for low-level vision. *IEEE Transactions on Pattern Analysis and Machine Intelligence*, 12(1):78–87.

Deutscher, J. and Reid, I. (2005). Articulated body motion capture by stochastic search. *International Journal of Computer Vision*, 61(2):185–205.

Deutscher, J., Blake, A., and Reid, I. (2000). Articulated body motion capture by annealed particle filtering. In *IEEE Computer Society Conference on Computer Vision and Pattern Recognition (CVPR'2000)*, pp. 126–133, Hilton Head Island.

Dev, P. (1974). *Segmentation Processes in Visual Perception: A Cooperative Neural Model*. COINS Technical Report 74C-5, University of Massachusetts at Amherst.

Dhond, U. R. and Aggarwal, J. K. (1989). Structure from stereo—a review. *IEEE Transactions on Systems, Man, and Cybernetics*, 19(6):1489–1510.

Dick, A., Torr, P. H. S., and Cipolla, R. (2004). Modelling and interpretation of architecture from several images. *International Journal of Computer Vision*, 60(2):111–134.

Dickinson, S., Leonardis, A., Schiele, B., and Tarr, M. J. (eds). (2007). *Object Categorization: Computer and Human Vision Perspectives*, Cambridge University Press, New York.

Dickmanns, E. D. and Graefe, V. (1988). Dynamic monocular machine vision. *Machine Vision and Applications*, 1:223–240.

Diebel, J. (2006). *Representing Attitude: Euler Angles, Quaternions, and Rotation Vectors*. Technical Report, Stanford University. http://ai.stanford.edu/~diebel/attitude.html.

Diebel, J. R., Thrun, S., and Brünig, M. (2006). A Bayesian method for probable surface reconstruction and decimation. *ACM Transactions on Graphics*, 25(1).

Dimitrijevic, M., Lepetit, V., and Fua, P. (2006). Human body pose detection using Bayesian spatio-temporal templates. *Computer Vision and Image Understanding*, 104(2-3):127–139.

Dinh, H. Q., Turk, G., and Slabaugh, G. (2002). Reconstructing surfaces by volumetric regularization using radial basis functions. *IEEE Transactions on Pattern Analysis and Machine Intelligence*, 24(10):1358–1371.

Divvala, S., Hoiem, D., Hays, J., Efros, A. A., and Hebert, M. (2009). An empirical study of context in object detection. In *IEEE Computer Society Conference on Computer Vision and Pattern Recognition (CVPR 2009)*, Miami, FL.

Dodgson, N. A. (1992). *Image Resampling*. Technical Report TR261, Wolfson College and Computer Laboratory, University of Cambridge.

Dollàr, P., Belongie, S., and Perona, P. (2010). The fastest pedestrian detector in the west. In *British Machine Vision Conference (BMVC 2010)*, Aberystwyth, Wales, UK.

Dollàr, P., Wojek, C., Schiele, B., and Perona, P. (2009). Pedestrian detection: A benchmark. In *IEEE Computer Society Conference on Computer Vision and Pattern Recognition (CVPR 2009)*, Miami Beach, FL.

Doretto, G. and Soatto, S. (2006). Dynamic shape and appearance models. *IEEE Transactions on Pattern Analysis and Machine Intelligence*, 28(12):2006–2019.

Doretto, G., Chiuso, A., Wu, Y. N., and Soatto, S. (2003). Dynamic textures. *International Journal of Computer Vision*, 51(2):91–109.

Dorkó, G. and Schmid, C. (2003). Selection of scale-invariant parts for object class recognition. In *Ninth International Conference on Computer Vision (ICCV 2003)*, pp. 634–640, Nice, France.

Dorsey, J., Rushmeier, H., and Sillion, F. (2007). *Digital Modeling of Material Appearance*. Morgan Kaufmann, San Francisco.

Douglas, D. H. and Peucker, T. K. (1973). Algorithms for the reduction of the number of points required to represent a digitized line or its caricature. *The Canadian Cartographer*, 10(2):112–122.

Drori, I., Cohen-Or, D., and Yeshurun, H. (2003). Fragment-based image completion. *ACM Transactions on Graphics (Proc. SIGGRAPH 2003)*, 22(3):303–312.

Duda, R. O. and Hart, P. E. (1972). Use of the Hough transform to detect lines and curves in pictures. *Communications of the ACM*, 15(1):11–15.

Duda, R. O., Hart, P. E., and Stork, D. G. (2001). *Pattern Classification*. John Wiley & Sons, New York, 2nd edition.

Dupuis, P. and Oliensis, J. (1994). An optimal control formulation and related numerical methods for a problem in shape reconstruction. *Annals of Applied Probability*, 4(2):287–346.

Durand, F. and Dorsey, J. (2002). Fast bilateral filtering for the display of high-dynamic-range images. *ACM Transactions on Graphics (Proc. SIGGRAPH 2002)*, 21(3):257–266.

Durand, F. and Szeliski, R. (2007). Computational photography. *IEEE Computer Graphics and Applications*, 27(2):21–22. Guest Editors' Introduction to Special Issue.

Durbin, R. and Willshaw, D. (1987). An analogue approach to the traveling salesman problem using an elastic net method. *Nature*, 326:689–691.

Durbin, R., Szeliski, R., and Yuille, A. (1989). An analysis of the elastic net approach to the travelling salesman problem. *Neural Computation*, 1(3):348–358.

Eck, M., DeRose, T., Duchamp, T., Hoppe, H., Lounsbery, M., and Stuetzle, W. (1995). Multiresolution analysis of arbitrary meshes. In *ACM SIGGRAPH 1995 Conference Proceedings*, pp. 173–182, Los Angeles.

Eden, A., Uyttendaele, M., and Szeliski, R. (2006). Seamless image stitching of scenes with large motions and exposure differences. In *IEEE Computer Society Conference on Computer Vision and Pattern Recognition (CVPR'2006)*, pp. 2498–2505, New York, NY.

Efros, A. A. and Freeman, W. T. (2001). Image quilting for texture synthesis and transfer. In *ACM SIGGRAPH 2001 Conference Proceedings*, pp. 341–346.

Efros, A. A. and Leung, T. K. (1999). Texture synthesis by non-parametric sampling. In *Seventh International Conference on Computer Vision (ICCV'99)*, pp. 1033–1038, Kerkyra, Greece.

Efros, A. A., Berg, A. C., Mori, G., and Malik, J. (2003). Recognizing action at a distance. In *Ninth International Conference on Computer Vision (ICCV 2003)*, pp. 726–733, Nice, France.

Eichner, M. and Ferrari, V. (2009). Better appearance models for pictorial structures. In *British Machine Vision Conference (BMVC 2009)*.

Eisemann, E. and Durand, F. (2004). Flash photography enhancement via intrinsic relighting. *ACM Transactions on Graphics*, 23(3):673–678.

Eisert, P., Steinbach, E., and Girod, B. (2000). Automatic reconstruction of stationary 3-D objects from multiple uncalibrated camera views. *IEEE Transactions on Circuits and Systems for Video Technology*, 10(2):261–277.

Eisert, P., Wiegand, T., and Girod, B. (2000). Model-aided coding: a new approach to incorporate facial animation into motion-compensated video coding. *IEEE Transactions on Circuits and Systems for Video Technology*, 10(3):344–358.

Ekman, P. and Friesen, W. V. (1978). *Facial Action Coding System: A Technique for the Measurement of Facial Movement*. Consulting Psychologists press, Palo Alto, CA.

El-Melegy, M. and Farag, A. (2003). Nonmetric lens distortion calibration: Closed-form solutions, robust estimation and model selection. In *Ninth International Conference on Computer Vision (ICCV 2003)*, pp. 554–559, Nice, France.

Elder, J. H. (1999). Are edges incomplete? *International Journal of Computer Vision*, 34(2/3):97–122.

Elder, J. H. and Goldberg, R. M. (2001). Image editing in the contour domain. *IEEE Transactions on Pattern Analysis and Machine Intelligence*, 23(3):291–296.

Elder, J. H. and Zucker, S. W. (1998). Local scale control for edge detection and blur estimation. *IEEE Transactions on Pattern Analysis and Machine Intelligence*, 20(7):699–716.

Engels, C., Stewénius, H., and Nistér, D. (2006). Bundle adjustment rules. In *Photogrammetric Computer Vision (PCV'06)*, Bonn, Germany.

Engl, H. W., Hanke, M., and Neubauer, A. (1996). *Regularization of Inverse Problems*. Kluwer Academic Publishers, Dordrecht.

Enqvist, O., Josephson, K., and Kahl, F. (2009). Optimal correspondences from pairwise constraints. In *Twelfth International Conference on Computer Vision (ICCV 2009)*, Kyoto, Japan.

Estrada, F. J. and Jepson, A. D. (2009). Benchmarking image segmentation algorithms. *International Journal of Computer Vision*, 85(2):167–181.

Estrada, F. J., Jepson, A. D., and Chennubhotla, C. (2004). Spectral embedding and min-cut for image segmentation. In *British Machine Vision Conference (BMVC 2004)*, pp. 317–326, London.

Evangelidis, G. D. and Psarakis, E. Z. (2008). Parametric image alignment using enhanced correlation coefficient maximization. *IEEE Transactions on Pattern Analysis and Machine Intelligence*, 30(10):1858–1865.

Everingham, M., Van Gool, L., Williams, C. K. I., Winn, J., and Zisserman, A. (2008). The PASCAL Visual Object Classes Challenge 2008 (VOC2008) Results. http://www.pascal-network.org/challenges/VOC/voc2008/workshop/index.html.

Everingham, M., Van Gool, L., Williams, C. K. I., Winn, J., and Zisserman, A. (2010). The PASCAL visual object classes (VOC) challenge. *International Journal of Computer Vision*, 88(2):147–168.

Ezzat, T., Geiger, G., and Poggio, T. (2002). Trainable videorealistic speech animation. *ACM Transactions on Graphics (Proc. SIGGRAPH 2002)*, 21(3):388–398.

Fabbri, R., Costa, L. D. F., Torelli, J. C., and Bruno, O. M. (2008). 2D Euclidean distance transform algorithms: A comparative survey. *ACM Computing Surveys*, 40(1).

Fairchild, M. D. (2005). *Color Appearance Models*. Wiley, 2nd edition.

Fan, R.-E., Chen, P.-H., and Lin, C.-J. (2005). Working set selection using second order information for training support vector machines. *Journal of Machine Learning Research*, 6:1889–1918.

Fan, R.-E., Chang, K.-W., Hsieh, C.-J., Wang, X.-R., and Lin, C.-J. (2008). LIBLINEAR: A library for large linear classification. *Journal of Machine Learning Research*, 9:1871–1874.

Farbman, Z., Fattal, R., Lischinski, D., and Szeliski, R. (2008). Edge-preserving decompositions for multi-scale tone and detail manipulation. *ACM Transactions on Graphics (Proc. SIGGRAPH 2008)*, 27(3).

Farenzena, M., Fusiello, A., and Gherardi, R. (2009). Structure-and-motion pipeline on a hierarchical cluster tree. In *IEEE International Workshop on 3D Digital Imaging and Modeling (3DIM 2009)*, Kyoto, Japan.

Farin, G. (1992). From conics to NURBS: A tutorial and survey. *IEEE Computer Graphics and Applications*, 12(5):78–86.

Farin, G. E. (1996). *Curves and Surfaces for Computer Aided Geometric Design: A Practical Guide.* Academic Press, Boston, Massachusetts, 4th edition.

Fattal, R. (2007). Image upsampling via imposed edge statistics. *ACM Transactions on Graphics*, 26(3).

Fattal, R. (2009). Edge-avoiding wavelets and their applications. *ACM Transactions on Graphics*, 28(3).

Fattal, R., Lischinski, D., and Werman, M. (2002). Gradient domain high dynamic range compression. *ACM Transactions on Graphics (Proc. SIGGRAPH 2002)*, 21(3):249–256.

Faugeras, O. (1993). *Three-dimensional computer vision: A geometric viewpoint.* MIT Press, Cambridge, Massachusetts.

Faugeras, O. and Keriven, R. (1998). Variational principles, surface evolution, PDEs, level set methods, and the stereo problem. *IEEE Transactions on Image Processing*, 7(3):336–344.

Faugeras, O. and Luong, Q.-T. (2001). *The Geometry of Multiple Images.* MIT Press, Cambridge, MA.

Faugeras, O. D. (1992). What can be seen in three dimensions with an uncalibrated stereo rig? In *Second European Conference on Computer Vision (ECCV'92)*, pp. 563–578, Santa Margherita Liguere, Italy.

Faugeras, O. D. and Hebert, M. (1987). The representation, recognition and positioning of 3-D shapes from range data. In Kanade, T. (ed.), *Three-Dimensional Machine Vision*, pp. 301–353, Kluwer Academic Publishers, Boston.

Faugeras, O. D., Luong, Q.-T., and Maybank, S. J. (1992). Camera self-calibration: Theory and experiments. In *Second European Conference on Computer Vision (ECCV'92)*, pp. 321–334, Santa Margherita Liguere, Italy.

Favaro, P. and Soatto, S. (2006). *3-D Shape Estimation and Image Restoration: Exploiting Defocus and Motion-Blur.* Springer.

Fawcett, T. (2006). An introduction to ROC analysis. *Pattern Recognition Letters*, 27(8):861–874.

Fei-Fei, L. and Perona, P. (2005). A Bayesian hierarchical model for learning natural scene categories. In *IEEE Computer Society Conference on Computer Vision and Pattern Recognition (CVPR'2005)*, pp. 524–531, San Diego, CA.

Fei-Fei, L., Fergus, R., and Perona, P. (2006). One-shot learning of object categories. *IEEE Transactions on Pattern Analysis and Machine Intelligence*, 28(4):594–611.

Fei-Fei, L., Fergus, R., and Torralba, A. (2009). ICCV 2009 short course on recognizing and learning object categories. In *Twelfth International Conference on Computer Vision (ICCV 2009)*, Kyoto, Japan. http://people.csail.mit.edu/torralba/shortCourseRLOC/.

Feilner, M., Van De Ville, D., and Unser, M. (2005). An orthogonal family of quincunx wavelets with continuously adjustable order. *IEEE Transactions on Image Processing*, 14(4):499–520.

Feldmar, J. and Ayache, N. (1996). Rigid, affine, and locally affine registration of free-form surfaces. *International Journal of Computer Vision*, 18(2):99–119.

Fellbaum, C. (ed.). (1998). *WordNet: An Electronic Lexical Database*, Bradford Books.

Felzenszwalb, P., McAllester, D., and Ramanan, D. (2008). A discriminatively trained, multiscale, deformable part model. In *IEEE Computer Society Conference on Computer Vision and Pattern Recognition (CVPR 2008)*, Anchorage, AK.

Felzenszwalb, P. F. and Huttenlocher, D. P. (2004a). *Distance Transforms of Sampled Functions.* Technical Report TR2004-1963, Cornell University Computing and Information Science.

Felzenszwalb, P. F. and Huttenlocher, D. P. (2004b). Efficient graph-based image segmentation. *International Journal of Computer Vision*, 59(2):167–181.

Felzenszwalb, P. F. and Huttenlocher, D. P. (2005). Pictorial structures for object recognition. *International Journal of Computer Vision*, 61(1):55–79.

Felzenszwalb, P. F. and Huttenlocher, D. P. (2006). Efficient belief propagation for early vision. *International Journal of Computer Vision*, 70(1):41–54.

Felzenszwalb, P. F., Girshick, R. B., McAllester, D., and Ramanan, D. (2010). Object detection with discriminatively trained part-based models. *IEEE Transactions on Pattern Analysis and Machine Intelligence*, 32(9):1627–1645.

Ferencz, A., Learned-Miller, E. G., and Malik, J. (2008). Learning to locate informative features for visual identification. *International Journal of Computer Vision*, 77(1-3):3–24.

Fergus, R. (2007a). Combined segmentation and recognition. In *CVPR 2007 Short Course on Recognizing and Learning Object Categories*. http://people.csail.mit.edu/torralba/shortCourseRLOC/.

Fergus, R. (2007b). Part-based models. In *CVPR 2007 Short Course on Recognizing and Learning Object Categories*. http://people.csail.mit.edu/torralba/shortCourseRLOC/.

Fergus, R. (2009). Classical methods for object recognition. In *ICCV 2009 Short Course on Recognizing and Learning Object Categories*, Kyoto, Japan. http://people.csail.mit.edu/torralba/shortCourseRLOC/.

Fergus, R., Perona, P., and Zisserman, A. (2004). A visual category filter for Google images. In *Eighth European Conference on Computer Vision (ECCV 2004)*, pp. 242–256, Prague.

Fergus, R., Perona, P., and Zisserman, A. (2005). A sparse object category model for efficient learning and exhaustive recognition. In *IEEE Computer Society Conference on Computer Vision and Pattern Recognition (CVPR'2005)*, pp. 380–387, San Diego, CA.

Fergus, R., Perona, P., and Zisserman, A. (2007). Weakly supervised scale-invariant learning of models for visual recognition. *International Journal of Computer Vision*, 71(3):273–303.

Fergus, R., Fei-Fei, L., Perona, P., and Zisserman, A. (2005). Learning object categories from Google's image search. In *Tenth International Conference on Computer Vision (ICCV 2005)*, pp. 1816–1823, Beijing, China.

Fergus, R., Singh, B., Hertzmann, A., Roweis, S. T., and Freeman, W. T. (2006). Removing camera shake from a single photograph. *ACM Transactions on Graphics*, 25(3):787–794.

Ferrari, V., Marin-Jimenez, M., and Zisserman, A. (2009). Pose search: retrieving people using their pose. In *IEEE Computer Society Conference on Computer Vision and Pattern Recognition (CVPR 2009)*, Miami Beach, FL.

Ferrari, V., Marin-Jimenez, M. J., and Zisserman, A. (2008). Progressive search space reduction for human pose estimation. In *IEEE Computer Society Conference on Computer Vision and Pattern Recognition (CVPR 2008)*, Anchorage, AK.

Ferrari, V., Tuytelaars, T., and Van Gool, L. (2006a). Object detection by contour segment networks. In *Ninth European Conference on Computer Vision (ECCV 2006)*, pp. 14–28.

Ferrari, V., Tuytelaars, T., and Van Gool, L. (2006b). Simultaneous object recognition and segmentation from single or multiple model views. *International Journal of Computer Vision*, 67(2):159–188.

Field, D. J. (1987). Relations between the statistics of natural images and the response properties of cortical cells. *Journal of the Optical Society of America A*, 4(12):2379–2394.

Finkelstein, A. and Salesin, D. H. (1994). Multiresolution curves. In *ACM SIGGRAPH 1994 Conference Proceedings*, pp. 261–268.

Fischler, M. A. and Bolles, R. C. (1981). Random sample consensus: A paradigm for model fitting with applications to image analysis and automated cartography. *Communications of the ACM*, 24(6):381–395.

Fischler, M. A. and Elschlager, R. A. (1973). The representation and matching of pictorial structures. *IEEE Transactions on Computers*, 22(1):67–92.

Fischler, M. A. and Firschein, O. (1987). *Readings in Computer Vision*. Morgan Kaufmann Publishers, Inc., Los Altos.

Fischler, M. A., Firschein, O., Barnard, S. T., Fua, P. V., and Leclerc, Y. (1989). *The Vision Problem: Exploiting Parallel Computation*. Technical Note 458, SRI International, Menlo Park.

Fitzgibbon, A. W. and Zisserman, A. (1998). Automatic camera recovery for closed and open image sequences. In *Fifth European Conference on Computer Vision (ECCV'98)*, pp. 311–326, Freiburg, Germany.

Fitzgibbon, A. W., Cross, G., and Zisserman, A. (1998). Automatic 3D model construction for turn-table sequences. In *European Workshop on 3D Structure from Multiple Images of Large-Scale Environments (SMILE)*, pp. 155–170, Freiburg.

Fleet, D. and Jepson, A. (1990). Computation of component image velocity from local phase information. *International Journal of Computer Vision*, 5(1):77–104.

Fleuret, F. and Geman, D. (2001). Coarse-to-fine face detection. *International Journal of Computer Vision*, 41(1/2):85–107.

Flickner, M., Sawhney, H., Niblack, W., Ashley, J., Huang, Q. *et al.* (1995). Query by image and video content: The QBIC system. *Computer*, 28(9):23–32.

Foley, J. D., van Dam, A., Feiner, S. K., and Hughes, J. F. (1995). *Computer Graphics: Principles and Practice*. Addison-Wesley, Reading, MA, 2 edition.

Förstner, W. (1986). A feature-based correspondence algorithm for image matching. *Intl. Arch. Photogrammetry & Remote Sensing*, 26(3):150–166.

Förstner, W. (2005). Uncertainty and projective geometry. In Bayro-Corrochano, E. (ed.), *Handbook of Geometric Computing*, pp. 493–534, Springer, New York.

Forsyth, D. and Ponce, J. (2003). *Computer Vision: A Modern Approach*. Prentice Hall, Upper Saddle River, NJ.

Forsyth, D. A. and Fleck, M. M. (1999). Automatic detection of human nudes. *International Journal of Computer Vision*, 32(1):63–77.

Forsyth, D. A., Arikan, O., Ikemoto, L., O'Brien, J., and Ramanan, D. (2006). Computational studies of human motion: Part 1, tracking and motion synthesis. *Foundations and Trends in Computer Graphics and Computer Vision*, 1(2/3):77–254.

Fossati, A., Dimitrijevic, M., Lepetit, V., and Fua, P. (2007). Bridging the gap between detection and tracking for 3D monocular video-based motion capture. In *IEEE Computer Society Conference on Computer Vision and Pattern Recognition (CVPR 2007)*, Minneapolis, MN.

Frahm, J.-M. and Koch, R. (2003). Camera calibration with known rotation. In *Ninth International Conference on Computer Vision (ICCV 2003)*, pp. 1418–1425, Nice, France.

Freeman, M. (2008). *Mastering HDR Photography*. Amphoto Books, New York.

Freeman, W., Perona, P., and Schölkopf, B. (2008). Guest editorial: Special issue on machine learning for vision. *International Journal of Computer Vision*, 77(1-3):1.

Freeman, W. T. (1992). *Steerable Filters and Local Analysis of Image Structure*. Ph.D. thesis, Massachusetts Institute of Technology.

Freeman, W. T. and Adelson, E. H. (1991). The design and use of steerable filters. *IEEE Transactions on Pattern Analysis and Machine Intelligence*, 13(9):891–906.

Freeman, W. T., Jones, T. R., and Pasztor, E. C. (2002). Example-based super-resolution. *IEEE Computer Graphics and Applications*, 22(2):56–65.

Freeman, W. T., Pasztor, E. C., and Carmichael, O. T. (2000). Learning low-level vision. *International Journal of Computer Vision*, 40(1):25–47.

Frey, B. J. and MacKay, D. J. C. (1997). A revolution: Belief propagation in graphs with cycles. In *Advances in Neural Information Processing Systems*.

Friedman, J., Hastie, T., and Tibshirani, R. (2000). Additive logistic regression: a statistical view of boosting. *Annals of Statistics*, 38(2):337–374.

Frisken, S. F., Perry, R. N., Rockwood, A. P., and Jones, T. R. (2000). Adaptively sampled distance fields: A general representation of shape for computer graphics. In *ACM SIGGRAPH 2000 Conference Proceedings*, pp. 249–254.

Fritz, M. and Schiele, B. (2008). Decomposition, discovery and detection of visual categories using topic models. In *IEEE Computer Society Conference on Computer Vision and Pattern Recognition (CVPR 2008)*, Anchorage, AK.

Frome, A., Singer, Y., Sha, F., and Malik, J. (2007). Learning globally-consistent local distance functions for shape-based image retrieval and classification. In *Eleventh International Conference on Computer Vision (ICCV 2007)*, Rio de Janeiro, Brazil.

Fua, P. (1993). A parallel stereo algorithm that produces dense depth maps and preserves image features. *Machine Vision and Applications*, 6(1):35–49.

Fua, P. and Leclerc, Y. G. (1995). Object-centered surface reconstruction: Combining multi-image stereo and shading. *International Journal of Computer Vision*, 16(1):35–56.

Fua, P. and Sander, P. (1992). Segmenting unstructured 3D points into surfaces. In *Second European Conference on Computer Vision (ECCV'92)*, pp. 676–680, Santa Margherita Liguere, Italy.

Fuh, C.-S. and Maragos, P. (1991). Motion displacement estimation using an affine model for image matching. *Optical Engineering*, 30(7):881–887.

Fukunaga, K. and Hostetler, L. D. (1975). The estimation of the gradient of a density function, with applications in pattern recognition. *IEEE Transactions on Information Theory*, 21:32–40.

Furukawa, Y. and Ponce, J. (2007). Accurate, dense, and robust multi-view stereopsis. In *IEEE Computer Society Conference on Computer Vision and Pattern Recognition (CVPR 2007)*, Minneapolis, MN.

Furukawa, Y. and Ponce, J. (2008). Accurate calibration from multi-view stereo and bundle adjustment. In *IEEE Computer Society Conference on Computer Vision and Pattern Recognition (CVPR 2008)*, Anchorage, AK.

Furukawa, Y. and Ponce, J. (2009). Carved visual hulls for image-based modeling. *International Journal of Computer Vision*, 81(1):53–67.

Furukawa, Y. and Ponce, J. (2011). Accurate, dense, and robust multi-view stereopsis. *IEEE Transactions on Pattern Analysis and Machine Intelligence*.

Furukawa, Y., Curless, B., Seitz, S. M., and Szeliski, R. (2009a). Manhattan-world stereo. In *IEEE Computer Society Conference on Computer Vision and Pattern Recognition (CVPR 2009)*, Miami, FL.

Furukawa, Y., Curless, B., Seitz, S. M., and Szeliski, R. (2009b). Reconstructing building interiors from images. In *Twelfth IEEE International Conference on Computer Vision (ICCV 2009)*, Kyoto, Japan.

Furukawa, Y., Curless, B., Seitz, S. M., and Szeliski, R. (2010). Towards internet-scale multi-view stereo. In *IEEE Computer Society Conference on Computer Vision and Pattern Recognition (CVPR 2010)*, San Francisco, CA.

Fusiello, A., Roberto, V., and Trucco, E. (1997). Efficient stereo with multiple windowing. In *IEEE Computer Society Conference on Computer Vision and Pattern Recognition (CVPR'97)*, pp. 858–863, San Juan, Puerto Rico.

Fusiello, A., Trucco, E., and Verri, A. (2000). A compact algorithm for rectification of stereo pairs. *Machine Vision and Applications*, 12(1):16–22.

Gai, J. and Kang, S. B. (2009). Matte-based restoration of vintage video. *IEEE Transactions on Image Processing*, 18:2185–2197.

Gal, R., Wexler, Y., Ofek, E., Hoppe, H., and Cohen-Or, D. (2010). Seamless montage for texturing models. In *Proceedings of Eurographics 2010*.

Gallagher, A. C. and Chen, T. (2008). Multi-image graph cut clothing segmentation for recognizing people. In *IEEE Computer Society Conference on Computer Vision and Pattern Recognition (CVPR 2008)*, Anchorage, AK.

Gallup, D., Frahm, J.-M., Mordohai, P., and Pollefeys, M. (2008). Variable baseline/resolution stereo. In *IEEE Computer Society Conference on Computer Vision and Pattern Recognition (CVPR 2008)*, Anchorage, AK.

Gamble, E. and Poggio, T. (1987). *Visual integration and detection of discontinuities: the key role of intensity edges*. A. I. Memo 970, Artificial Intelligence Laboratory, Massachusetts Institute of Technology.

Gammeter, S., Bossard, L., Quack, T., and Van Gool, L. (2009). I know what you did last summer: Object-level auto-annotation of holiday snaps. In *Twelfth International Conference on Computer Vision (ICCV 2009)*, Kyoto, Japan.

Gao, W., Chen, Y., Wang, R., Shan, S., and Jiang, D. (2003). Learning and synthesizing MPEG-4 compatible 3-D face animation from video sequence. *IEEE Transactions on Circuits and Systems for Video Technology*, 13(11):1119–1128.

Garding, J. (1992). Shape from texture for smooth curved surfaces in perspective projection. *Journal of Mathematical Imaging and Vision*, 2:329–352.

Gargallo, P., Prados, E., and Sturm, P. (2007). Minimizing the reprojection error in surface reconstruction from images. In *Eleventh International Conference on Computer Vision (ICCV 2007)*, Rio de Janeiro, Brazil.

Gavrila, D. M. (1999). The visual analysis of human movement: A survey. *Computer Vision and Image Understanding*, 73(1):82–98.

Gavrila, D. M. and Davis, L. S. (1996). 3D model-based tracking of humans in action: A multi-view approach. In *IEEE Computer Society Conference on Computer Vision and Pattern Recognition (CVPR'96)*, pp. 73–80, San Francisco.

Gavrila, D. M. and Philomin, V. (1999). Real-time object detection for smart vehicles. In *Seventh International Conference on Computer Vision (ICCV'99)*, pp. 87–93, Kerkyra, Greece.

Geiger, D. and Girosi, F. (1991). Parallel and deterministic algorithms for MRFs: Surface reconstruction. *IEEE Transactions on Pattern Analysis and Machine Intelligence*, 13(5):401–412.

Geiger, D., Ladendorf, B., and Yuille, A. (1992). Occlusions and binocular stereo. In *Second European Conference on Computer Vision (ECCV'92)*, pp. 425–433, Santa Margherita Liguere, Italy.

Gelb, A. (ed.). (1974). *Applied Optimal Estimation*. MIT Press, Cambridge, Massachusetts.

Geller, T. (2008). Overcoming the uncanny valley. *IEEE Computer Graphics and Applications*, 28(4):11–17.

Geman, S. and Geman, D. (1984). Stochastic relaxation, Gibbs distribution, and the Bayesian restoration of images. *IEEE Transactions on Pattern Analysis and Machine Intelligence*, PAMI-6(6):721–741.

Gennert, M. A. (1988). Brightness-based stereo matching. In *Second International Conference on Computer Vision (ICCV'88)*, pp. 139–143, Tampa.

Gersho, A. and Gray, R. M. (1991). *Vector Quantization and Signal Compression*. Springer.

Gershun, A. (1939). The light field. *Journal of Mathematics and Physics*, XVIII:51–151.

Gevers, T., van de Weijer, J., and Stokman, H. (2006). Color feature detection. In Lukac, R. and Plataniotis, K. N. (eds), *Color Image Processing: Methods and Applications*, CRC Press.

Giblin, P. and Weiss, R. (1987). Reconstruction of surfaces from profiles. In *First International Conference on Computer Vision (ICCV'87)*, pp. 136–144, London, England.

Gionis, A., Indyk, P., and Motwani, R. (1999). Similarity search in high dimensions via hashing. In *25th International Conference on Very Large Data Bases (VLDB'99)*, pp. 518–529.

Girod, B., Greiner, G., and Niemann, H. (eds). (2000). *Principles of 3D Image Analysis and Synthesis*, Kluwer, Boston.

Glassner, A. S. (1995). *Principles of Digital Image Synthesis*. Morgan Kaufmann Publishers, San Francisco.

Gleicher, M. (1995). Image snapping. In *ACM SIGGRAPH 1995 Conference Proceedings*, pp. 183–190.

Gleicher, M. (1997). Projective registration with difference decomposition. In *IEEE Computer Society Conference on Computer Vision and Pattern Recognition (CVPR'97)*, pp. 331–337, San Juan, Puerto Rico.

Gleicher, M. and Witkin, A. (1992). Through-the-lens camera control. *Computer Graphics (SIGGRAPH '92)*, 26(2):331–340.

Glocker, B., Komodakis, N., Tziritas, G., Navab, N., and Paragios, N. (2008). Dense image registration through MRFs and efficient linear programming. *Medical Image Analysis*, 12(6):731–741.

Glocker, B., Paragios, N., Komodakis, N., Tziritas, G., and Navab, N. (2008). Optical flow estimation with uncertainties through dynamic MRFs. In *IEEE Computer Society Conference on Computer Vision and Pattern Recognition (CVPR 2008)*, Anchorage, AK.

Gluckman, J. (2006a). Higher order image pyramids. In *Ninth European Conference on Computer Vision (ECCV 2006)*, pp. 308–320.

Gluckman, J. (2006b). Scale variant image pyramids. In *IEEE Computer Society Conference on Computer Vision and Pattern Recognition (CVPR'2006)*, pp. 1069–1075, New York City, NY.

Goesele, M., Curless, B., and Seitz, S. (2006). Multi-view stereo revisited. In *IEEE Computer Society Conference on Computer Vision and Pattern Recognition (CVPR'2006)*, pp. 2402–2409, New York City, NY.

Goesele, M., Fuchs, C., and Seidel, H.-P. (2003). Accuracy of 3D range scanners by measurement of the slanted edge modulation transfer function. In *Fourth International Conference on 3-D Digital Imaging and Modeling*, Banff.

Goesele, M., Snavely, N., Curless, B., Hoppe, H., and Seitz, S. M. (2007). Multi-view stereo for community photo collections. In *Eleventh International Conference on Computer Vision (ICCV 2007)*, Rio de Janeiro, Brazil.

Gold, S., Rangarajan, A., Lu, C., Pappu, S., and Mjolsness, E. (1998). New algorithms for 2D and 3D point matching: Pose estimation and correspondence. *Pattern Recognition*, 31(8):1019–1031.

Goldberg, A. V. and Tarjan, R. E. (1988). A new approach to the maximum-flow problem. *Journal of the ACM*, 35(4):921–940.

Goldluecke, B. and Cremers, D. (2009). Superresolution texture maps for multiview reconstruction. In *Twelfth International Conference on Computer Vision (ICCV 2009)*, Kyoto, Japan.

Goldman, D. B. (2011). Vignette and exposure calibration and compensation. *IEEE Transactions on Pattern Analysis and Machine Intelligence*.

Golovinskiy, A., Matusik, W., ster, H. P., Rusinkiewicz, S., and Funkhouser, T. (2006). A statistical model for synthesis of detailed facial geometry. *ACM Transactions on Graphics*, 25(3):1025–1034.

Golub, G. and Van Loan, C. F. (1996). *Matrix Computation, third edition*. The John Hopkins University Press, Baltimore and London.

Gomes, J. and Velho, L. (1997). *Image Processing for Computer Graphics*. Springer-Verlag, New York.

Gomes, J., Darsa, L., Costa, B., and Velho, L. (1999). *Warping and Morphing of Graphical Objects*. Morgan Kaufmann Publishers, San Francisco.

Gong, M., Yang, R., Wang, L., and Gong, M. (2007). A performance study on different cost aggregation approaches used in realtime stereo matching. *International Journal of Computer Vision*, 75(2):283–296.

Gonzales, R. C. and Woods, R. E. (2008). *Digital Image Processing*. Prentice-Hall, Upper Saddle River, NJ, 3rd edition.

Gooch, B. and Gooch, A. (2001). *Non-Photorealistic Rendering*. A K Peters, Ltd, Natick, Massachusetts.

Gordon, I. and Lowe, D. G. (2006). What and where: 3D object recognition with accurate pose. In Ponce, J., Hebert, M., Schmid, C., and Zisserman, A. (eds), *Toward Category-Level Object Recognition*, pp. 67–82, Springer, New York.

Gorelick, L., Blank, M., Shechtman, E., Irani, M., and Basri, R. (2007). Actions as space-time shapes. *IEEE Transactions on Pattern Analysis and Machine Intelligence*, 29(12):2247–2253.

Gortler, S. J. and Cohen, M. F. (1995). Hierarchical and variational geometric modeling with wavelets. In *Symposium on Interactive 3D Graphics*, pp. 35–43, Monterey, CA.

Gortler, S. J., Grzeszczuk, R., Szeliski, R., and Cohen, M. F. (1996). The Lumigraph. In *ACM SIGGRAPH 1996 Conference Proceedings*, pp. 43–54, New Orleans.

Goshtasby, A. (1989). Correction of image deformation from lens distortion using Bézier patches. *Computer Vision, Graphics, and Image Processing*, 47(4):385–394.

Goshtasby, A. (2005). *2-D and 3-D Image Registration*. Wiley, New York.

Gotchev, A. and Rosenhahn, B. (eds). (2009). *Proceedings of the 3DTV Conference: The True Vision—Capture, Transmission and Display of 3D Video*, IEEE Computer Society Press.

Govindu, V. M. (2006). Revisiting the brightness constraint: Probabilistic formulation and algorithms. In *Ninth European Conference on Computer Vision (ECCV 2006)*, pp. 177–188.

Grady, L. (2006). Random walks for image segmentation. *IEEE Transactions on Pattern Analysis and Machine Intelligence*, 28(11):1768–1783.

Grady, L. (2008). A lattice-preserving multigrid method for solving the inhomogeneous Poisson equations used in image analysis. In *Tenth European Conference on Computer Vision (ECCV 2008)*, pp. 252–264, Marseilles.

Grady, L. and Ali, S. (2008). Fast approximate random walker segmentation using eigenvector precomputation. In *IEEE Computer Society Conference on Computer Vision and Pattern Recognition (CVPR 2008)*, Anchorage, AK.

Grady, L. and Alvino, C. (2008). Reformulating and optimizing the Mumford–Shah functional on a graph — a faster, lower energy solution. In *Tenth European Conference on Computer Vision (ECCV 2008)*, pp. 248–261, Marseilles.

Grauman, K. and Darrell, T. (2005). Efficient image matching with distributions of local invariant features. In *IEEE Computer Society Conference on Computer Vision and Pattern Recognition (CVPR'2005)*, pp. 627–634, San Diego, CA.

Grauman, K. and Darrell, T. (2007a). Pyramid match hashing: Sub-linear time indexing over partial correspondences. In *IEEE Computer Society Conference on Computer Vision and Pattern Recognition (CVPR 2007)*, Minneapolis, MN.

Grauman, K. and Darrell, T. (2007b). The pyramid match kernel: Efficient learning with sets of features. *Journal of Machine Learning Research*, 8:725–760.

Grauman, K., Shakhnarovich, G., and Darrell, T. (2003). Inferring 3D structure with a statistical image-based shape model. In *Ninth International Conference on Computer Vision (ICCV 2003)*, pp. 641–648, Nice, France.

Greene, N. (1986). Environment mapping and other applications of world projections. *IEEE Computer Graphics and Applications*, 6(11):21–29.

Greene, N. and Heckbert, P. (1986). Creating raster Omnimax images from multiple perspective views using the elliptical weighted average filter. *IEEE Computer Graphics and Applications*, 6(6):21–27.

Greig, D., Porteous, B., and Seheult, A. (1989). Exact maximum a posteriori estimation for binary images. *Journal of the Royal Statistical Society, Series B*, 51(2):271–279.

Gremban, K. D., Thorpe, C. E., and Kanade, T. (1988). Geometric camera calibration using systems of linear equations. In *IEEE International Conference on Robotics and Automation*, pp. 562–567, Philadelphia.

Griffin, G., Holub, A., and Perona, P. (2007). *Caltech-256 Object Category Dataset*. Technical Report 7694, California Institute of Technology.

Grimson, W. E. L. (1983). An implementation of a computational theory of visual surface interpolation. *Computer Vision, Graphics, and Image Processing*, 22:39–69.

Grimson, W. E. L. (1985). Computational experiments with a feature based stereo algorithm. *IEEE Transactions on Pattern Analysis and Machine Intelligence*, PAMI-7(1):17–34.

Gross, R., Matthews, I., and Baker, S. (2006). Active appearance models with occlusion. *Image and Vision Computing*, 24(6):593–604.

Gross, R., Shi, J., and Cohn, J. F. (2005). Quo vadis face recognition? In *IEEE Workshop on Empirical Evaluation Methods in Computer Vision*, San Diego.

Gross, R., Baker, S., Matthews, I., and Kanade, T. (2005). Face recognition across pose and illumination. In Li, S. Z. and Jain, A. K. (eds), *Handbook of Face Recognition*, Springer.

Gross, R., Sweeney, L., De la Torre, F., and Baker, S. (2008). Semi-supervised learning of multi-factor models for face de-identification. In *IEEE Computer Society Conference on Computer Vision and Pattern Recognition (CVPR 2008)*, Anchorage, AK.

Gross, R., Matthews, I., Cohn, J., Kanade, T., and Baker, S. (2010). Multi-PIE. *Image and Vision Computing*, 28(5):807–813.

Grossberg, M. D. and Nayar, S. K. (2001). A general imaging model and a method for finding its parameters. In *Eighth International Conference on Computer Vision (ICCV 2001)*, pp. 108–115, Vancouver, Canada.

Grossberg, M. D. and Nayar, S. K. (2004). Modeling the space of camera response functions. *IEEE Transactions on Pattern Analysis and Machine Intelligence*, 26(10):1272–1282.

Gu, C., Lim, J., Arbelaez, P., and Malik, J. (2009). Recognition using regions. In *IEEE Computer Society Conference on Computer Vision and Pattern Recognition (CVPR 2009)*, Miami Beach, FL.

Gu, X., Gortler, S. J., and Hoppe, H. (2002). Geometry images. *ACM Transactions on Graphics*, 21(3):355–361.

Guan, P., Weiss, A., Bălan, A. O., and Black, M. J. (2009). Estimating human shape and pose from a single image. In *Twelfth International Conference on Computer Vision (ICCV 2009)*, Kyoto, Japan.

Guennebaud, G. and Gross, M. (2007). Algebraic point set surfaces. *ACM Transactions on Graphics*, 26(3).

Guennebaud, G., Germann, M., and Gross, M. (2008). Dynamic sampling and rendering of algebraic point set surfaces. *Computer Graphics Forum*, 27(2):653–662.

Guenter, B., Grimm, C., Wood, D., Malvar, H., and Pighin, F. (1998). Making faces. In *ACM SIGGRAPH 1998 Conference Proceedings*, pp. 55–66.

Guillaumin, M., Verbeek, J., and Schmid, C. (2009). Is that you? Metric learning approaches for face identification. In *Twelfth International Conference on Computer Vision (ICCV 2009)*, Kyoto, Japan.

Gulbins, J. and Gulbins, R. (2009). *Photographic Multishot Techniques: High Dynamic Range, Super-Resolution, Extended Depth of Field, Stitching*. Rocky Nook.

Habbecke, M. and Kobbelt, L. (2007). A surface-growing approach to multi-view stereo reconstruction. In *IEEE Computer Society Conference on Computer Vision and Pattern Recognition (CVPR 2007)*, Minneapolis, MN.

Hager, G. D. and Belhumeur, P. N. (1998). Efficient region tracking with parametric models of geometry and illumination. *IEEE Transactions on Pattern Analysis and Machine Intelligence*, 20(10):1025–1039.

Hall, R. (1989). *Illumination and Color in Computer Generated Imagery*. Springer-Verlag, New York.

Haller, M., Billinghurst, M., and Thomas, B. (2007). *Emerging Technologies of Augmented Reality: Interfaces and Design*. IGI Publishing.

Hampel, F. R., Ronchetti, E. M., Rousseeuw, P. J., and Stahel, W. A. (1986). *Robust Statistics : The Approach Based on Influence Functions*. Wiley, New York.

Han, F. and Zhu, S.-C. (2005). Bottom-up/top-down image parsing by attribute graph grammar. In *Tenth International Conference on Computer Vision (ICCV 2005)*, pp. 1778–1785, Beijing, China.

Hanna, K. J. (1991). Direct multi-resolution estimation of ego-motion and structure from motion. In *IEEE Workshop on Visual Motion*, pp. 156–162, Princeton, New Jersey.

Hannah, M. J. (1974). *Computer Matching of Areas in Stereo Images*. Ph.D. thesis, Stanford University.

Hannah, M. J. (1988). Test results from SRI's stereo system. In *Image Understanding Workshop*, pp. 740–744, Cambridge, Massachusetts.

Hansen, M., Anandan, P., Dana, K., van der Wal, G., and Burt, P. (1994). Real-time scene stabilization and mosaic construction. In *IEEE Workshop on Applications of Computer Vision (WACV'94)*, pp. 54–62, Sarasota.

Hanson, A. R. and Riseman, E. M. (eds). (1978). *Computer Vision Systems*, Academic Press, New York.

Haralick, R. M. and Shapiro, L. G. (1985). Image segmentation techniques. *Computer Vision, Graphics, and Image Processing*, 29(1):100–132.

Haralick, R. M. and Shapiro, L. G. (1992). *Computer and Robot Vision*. Addison-Wesley, Reading, MA.

Haralick, R. M., Lee, C.-N., Ottenberg, K., and Nölle, M. (1994). Review and analysis of solutions of the three point perspective pose estimation problem. *International Journal of Computer Vision*, 13(3):331–356.

Hardie, R. C., Barnard, K. J., and Armstrong, E. E. (1997). Joint MAP registration and high-resolution image estimation using a sequence of undersampled images. *IEEE Transactions on Image Processing*, 6(12):1621–1633.

Haritaoglu, I., Harwood, D., and Davis, L. S. (2000). W^4: Real-time surveillance of people and their activities. *IEEE Transactions on Pattern Analysis and Machine Intelligence*, 22(8):809–830.

Harker, M. and O'Leary, P. (2008). Least squares surface reconstruction from measured gradient fields. In *IEEE Computer Society Conference on Computer Vision and Pattern Recognition (CVPR 2008)*, Anchorage, AK.

Harris, C. and Stephens, M. J. (1988). A combined corner and edge detector. In *Alvey Vision Conference*, pp. 147–152.

Hartley, R. and Kang, S. B. (2007). Parameter-free radial distortion correction with center of distortion estimation. *IEEE Transactions on Pattern Analysis and Machine Intelligence*, 31(8):1309–1321.

Hartley, R., Gupta, R., and Chang, T. (1992). Estimation of relative camera positions for uncalibrated cameras. In *Second European Conference on Computer Vision (ECCV'92)*, pp. 579–587, Santa Margherita Liguere, Italy.

Hartley, R. I. (1994a). Projective reconstruction and invariants from multiple images. *IEEE Transactions on Pattern Analysis and Machine Intelligence*, 16(10):1036–1041.

Hartley, R. I. (1994b). Self-calibration from multiple views of a rotating camera. In *Third European Conference on Computer Vision (ECCV'94)*, pp. 471–478, Stockholm, Sweden.

Hartley, R. I. (1997a). In defense of the 8-point algorithm. *IEEE Transactions on Pattern Analysis and Machine Intelligence*, 19(6):580–593.

Hartley, R. I. (1997b). Self-calibration of stationary cameras. *International Journal of Computer Vision*, 22(1):5–23.

Hartley, R. I. (1998). Chirality. *International Journal of Computer Vision*, 26(1):41–61.

Hartley, R. I. and Kang, S. B. (2005). Parameter-free radial distortion correction with centre of distortion estimation. In *Tenth International Conference on Computer Vision (ICCV 2005)*, pp. 1834–1841, Beijing, China.

Hartley, R. I. and Sturm, P. (1997). Triangulation. *Computer Vision and Image Understanding*, 68(2):146–157.

Hartley, R. I. and Zisserman, A. (2004). *Multiple View Geometry*. Cambridge University Press, Cambridge, UK.

Hartley, R. I., Hayman, E., de Agapito, L., and Reid, I. (2000). Camera calibration and the search for infinity. In *IEEE Computer Society Conference on Computer Vision and Pattern Recognition (CVPR'2000)*, pp. 510–517, Hilton Head Island.

Hasinoff, S. W. and Kutulakos, K. N. (2008). Light-efficient photography. In *Tenth European Conference on Computer Vision (ECCV 2008)*, pp. 45–59, Marseilles.

Hasinoff, S. W., Durand, F., and Freeman, W. T. (2010). Noise-optimal capture for high dynamic range photography. In *IEEE Computer Society Conference on Computer Vision and Pattern Recognition (CVPR 2010)*, San Francisco, CA.

Hasinoff, S. W., Kang, S. B., and Szeliski, R. (2006). Boundary matting for view synthesis. *Computer Vision and Image Understanding*, 103(1):22–32.

Hasinoff, S. W., Kutulakos, K. N., Durand, F., and Freeman, W. T. (2009). Time-constrained photography. In *Twelfth International Conference on Computer Vision (ICCV 2009)*, Kyoto, Japan.

Hastie, T., Tibshirani, R., and Friedman, J. (2001). *The Elements of Statistical Learning: Data Mining, Inference, and Prediction*. Springer-Verlag, New York.

Hayes, B. (2008). Computational photography. *American Scientist*, 96:94–99.

Hays, J. and Efros, A. A. (2007). Scene completion using millions of photographs. *ACM Transactions on Graphics*, 26(3).

Hays, J., Leordeanu, M., Efros, A. A., and Liu, Y. (2006). Discovering texture regularity as a higher-order correspondence problem. In *Ninth European Conference on Computer Vision (ECCV 2006)*, pp. 522–535.

He, L.-W. and Zhang, Z. (2005). Real-time whiteboard capture and processing using a video camera for teleconferencing. In *IEEE International Conference on Acoustics, Speech, and Signal Processing (ICASSP 2005)*, pp. 1113–1116, Philadelphia.

He, X. and Zemel, R. S. (2008). Learning hybrid models for image annotation with partially labeled data. In *Advances in Neural Information Processing Systems*.

He, X., Zemel, R. S., and Carreira-Perpiñán, M. A. (2004). Multiscale conditional random fields for image labeling. In *IEEE Computer Society Conference on Computer Vision and Pattern Recognition (CVPR'2004)*, pp. 695–702, Washington, DC.

He, X., Zemel, R. S., and Ray, D. (2006). Learning and incorporating top-down cues in image segmentation. In *Ninth European Conference on Computer Vision (ECCV 2006)*, pp. 338–351.

Healey, G. E. and Kondepudy, R. (1994). Radiometric CCD camera calibration and noise estimation. *IEEE Transactions on Pattern Analysis and Machine Intelligence*, 16(3):267–276.

Healey, G. E. and Shafer, S. A. (1992). *Color. Physics-Based Vision: Principles and Practice*, Jones & Bartlett, Cambridge, MA.

Heath, M. D., Sarkar, S., Sanocki, T., and Bowyer, K. W. (1998). Comparison of edge detectors. *Computer Vision and Image Understanding*, 69(1):38–54.

Hebert, M. (2000). Active and passive range sensing for robotics. In *IEEE International Conference on Robotics and Automation*, pp. 102–110, San Francisco.

Hecht, E. (2001). *Optics*. Pearson Addison Wesley, Reading, MA, 4th edition.

Heckbert, P. (1986). Survey of texture mapping. *IEEE Computer Graphics and Applications*, 6(11):56–67.

Heckbert, P. (1989). *Fundamentals of Texture Mapping and Image Warping*. Master's thesis, The University of California at Berkeley.

Heeger, D. J. (1988). Optical flow using spatiotemporal filters. *International Journal of Computer Vision*, 1(1):279–302.

Heeger, D. J. and Bergen, J. R. (1995). Pyramid-based texture analysis/synthesis. In *ACM SIGGRAPH 1995 Conference Proceedings*, pp. 229–238.

Heisele, B., Serre, T., and Poggio, T. (2007). A component-based framework for face detection and identification. *International Journal of Computer Vision*, 74(2):167–181.

Heisele, B., Ho, P., Wu, J., and Poggio, T. (2003). Face recognition: component-based versus global approaches. *Computer Vision and Image Understanding*, 91(1-2):6–21.

Herley, C. (2005). Automatic occlusion removal from minimum number of images. In *International Conference on Image Processing (ICIP 2005)*, pp. 1046–1049–16, Genova.

Hernandez, C. and Schmitt, F. (2004). Silhouette and stereo fusion for 3D object modeling. *Computer Vision and Image Understanding*, 96(3):367–392.

Hernandez, C. and Vogiatzis, G. (2010). Self-calibrating a real-time monocular 3d facial capture system. In *Fifth International Symposium on 3D Data Processing, Visualization and Transmission (3DPVT'10)*, Paris.

Hernandez, C., Vogiatzis, G., and Cipolla, R. (2007). Probabilistic visibility for multi-view stereo. In *IEEE Computer Society Conference on Computer Vision and Pattern Recognition (CVPR 2007)*, Minneapolis, MN.

Hernandez, C., Vogiatzis, G., Brostow, G. J., Stenger, B., and Cipolla, R. (2007). Non-rigid photometric stereo with colored lights. In *Eleventh International Conference on Computer Vision (ICCV 2007)*, Rio de Janeiro, Brazil.

Hershberger, J. and Snoeyink, J. (1992). *Speeding Up the Douglas-Peucker Line-Simplification Algorithm*. Technical Report TR-92-07, Computer Science Department, The University of British Columbia.

Hertzmann, A., Jacobs, C. E., Oliver, N., Curless, B., and Salesin, D. H. (2001). Image analogies. In *ACM SIGGRAPH 2001 Conference Proceedings*, pp. 327–340.

Hiep, V. H., Keriven, R., Pons, J.-P., and Labatut, P. (2009). Towards high-resolution large-scale multi-view stereo. In *IEEE Computer Society Conference on Computer Vision and Pattern Recognition (CVPR 2009)*, Miami Beach, FL.

Hillman, P., Hannah, J., and Renshaw, D. (2001). Alpha channel estimation in high resolution images and image sequences. In *IEEE Computer Society Conference on Computer Vision and Pattern Recognition (CVPR'2001)*, pp. 1063–1068, Kauai, Hawaii.

Hilton, A., Fua, P., and Ronfard, R. (2006). Modeling people: Vision-based understanding of a person's shape, appearance, movement, and behaviour. *Computer Vision and Image Understanding*, 104(2-3):87–89.

Hilton, A., Stoddart, A. J., Illingworth, J., and Windeatt, T. (1996). Reliable surface reconstruction from multiple range images. In *Fourth European Conference on Computer Vision (ECCV'96)*, pp. 117–126, Cambridge, England.

Hinckley, K., Sinclair, M., Hanson, E., Szeliski, R., and Conway, M. (1999). The VideoMouse: a camera-based multi-degree-of-freedom input device. In *12th annual ACM symposium on User interface software and technology*, pp. 103–112.

Hinterstoisser, S., Benhimane, S., Navab, N., Fua, P., and Lepetit, V. (2008). Online learning of patch perspective rectification for efficient object detection. In *IEEE Computer Society Conference on Computer Vision and Pattern Recognition (CVPR 2008)*, Anchorage, AK.

Hinton, G. E. (1977). *Relaxation and its Role in Vision*. Ph.D. thesis, University of Edinburgh.

Hirschmüller, H. (2008). Stereo processing by semiglobal matching and mutual information. *IEEE Transactions on Pattern Analysis and Machine Intelligence*, 30(2):328–341.

Hirschmüller, H. and Scharstein, D. (2009). Evaluation of stereo matching costs on images with radiometric differences. *IEEE Transactions on Pattern Analysis and Machine Intelligence*, 31(9):1582–1599.

Hjaltason, G. R. and Samet, H. (2003). Index-driven similarity search in metric spaces. *ACM Transactions on Database Systems*, 28(4):517–580.

Hofmann, T. (1999). Probabilistic latent semantic indexing. In *ACM SIGIR Conference on Research and Development in Informaion Retrieval*, pp. 50–57, Berkeley, CA.

Hogg, D. (1983). Model-based vision: A program to see a walking person. *Image and Vision Computing*, 1(1):5–20.

Hoiem, D., Efros, A. A., and Hebert, M. (2005a). Automatic photo pop-up. *ACM Transactions on Graphics (Proc. SIGGRAPH 2005)*, 24(3):577–584.

Hoiem, D., Efros, A. A., and Hebert, M. (2005b). Geometric context from a single image. In *Tenth International Conference on Computer Vision (ICCV 2005)*, pp. 654–661, Beijing, China.

Hoiem, D., Efros, A. A., and Hebert, M. (2008a). Closing the loop in scene interpretation. In *IEEE Computer Society Conference on Computer Vision and Pattern Recognition (CVPR 2008)*, Anchorage, AK.

Hoiem, D., Efros, A. A., and Hebert, M. (2008b). Putting objects in perspective. *International Journal of Computer Vision*, 80(1):3–15.

Hoiem, D., Rother, C., and Winn, J. (2007). 3D LayoutCRF for multi-view object class recognition and segmentation. In *IEEE Computer Society Conference on Computer Vision and Pattern Recognition (CVPR 2007)*, Minneapolis, MN.

Hoover, A., Jean-Baptiste, G., Jiang, X., Flynn, P. J., Bunke, H. *et al.* (1996). An experimental comparison of range image segmentation algorithms. *IEEE Transactions on Pattern Analysis and Machine Intelligence*, 18(7):673–689.

Hoppe, H. (1996). Progressive meshes. In *ACM SIGGRAPH 1996 Conference Proceedings*, pp. 99–108, New Orleans.

Hoppe, H., DeRose, T., Duchamp, T., McDonald, J., and Stuetzle, W. (1992). Surface reconstruction from unorganized points. *Computer Graphics (SIGGRAPH '92)*, 26(2):71–78.

Horn, B. K. P. (1974). Determining lightness from an image. *Computer Graphics and Image Processing*, 3(1):277–299.

Horn, B. K. P. (1975). Obtaining shape from shading information. In Winston, P. H. (ed.), *The Psychology of Computer Vision*, pp. 115–155, McGraw-Hill, New York.

Horn, B. K. P. (1977). Understanding image intensities. *Artificial Intelligence*, 8(2):201–231.

Horn, B. K. P. (1986). *Robot Vision*. MIT Press, Cambridge, Massachusetts.

Horn, B. K. P. (1987). Closed-form solution of absolute orientation using unit quaternions. *Journal of the Optical Society of America A*, 4(4):629–642.

Horn, B. K. P. (1990). Height and gradient from shading. *International Journal of Computer Vision*, 5(1):37–75.

Horn, B. K. P. and Brooks, M. J. (1986). The variational approach to shape from shading. *Computer Vision, Graphics, and Image Processing*, 33:174–208.

Horn, B. K. P. and Brooks, M. J. (eds). (1989). *Shape from Shading*, MIT Press, Cambridge, Massachusetts.

Horn, B. K. P. and Schunck, B. G. (1981). Determining optical flow. *Artificial Intelligence*, 17:185–203.

Horn, B. K. P. and Weldon Jr., E. J. (1988). Direct methods for recovering motion. *International Journal of Computer Vision*, 2(1):51–76.

Hornung, A., Zeng, B., and Kobbelt, L. (2008). Image selection for improved multi-view stereo. In *IEEE Computer Society Conference on Computer Vision and Pattern Recognition (CVPR 2008)*, Anchorage, AK.

Horowitz, S. L. and Pavlidis, T. (1976). Picture segmentation by a tree traversal algorithm. *Journal of the ACM*, 23(2):368–388.

Horry, Y., Anjyo, K.-I., and Arai, K. (1997). Tour into the picture: Using a spidery mesh interface to make animation from a single image. In *ACM SIGGRAPH 1997 Conference Proceedings*, pp. 225–232.

Hough, P. V. C. (1962). Method and means for recognizing complex patterns. *U. S. Patent*, 3,069,654.

Houhou, N., Thiran, J.-P., and Bresson, X. (2008). Fast texture segmentation using the shape operator and active contour. In *IEEE Computer Society Conference on Computer Vision and Pattern Recognition (CVPR 2008)*, Anchorage, AK.

Howe, N. R., Leventon, M. E., and Freeman, W. T. (2000). Bayesian reconstruction of 3D human motion from single-camera video. In *Advances in Neural Information Processing Systems*.

Hsieh, Y. C., McKeown, D., and Perlant, F. P. (1992). Performance evaluation of scene registration and stereo matching for cartographic feature extraction. *IEEE Transactions on Pattern Analysis and Machine Intelligence*, 14(2):214–238.

Hu, W., Tan, T., Wang, L., and Maybank, S. (2004). A survey on visual surveillance of object motion and behaviors. *IEEE Transactions on Systems, Man, and Cybernetics, Part C: Applications and Reviews*, 34(3):334–352.

Hua, G., Brown, M., and Winder, S. (2007). Discriminant embedding for local image descriptors. In *Eleventh International Conference on Computer Vision (ICCV 2007)*, Rio de Janeiro, Brazil.

Huang, G. B., Ramesh, M., Berg, T., and Learned-Miller, E. (2007). *Labeled Faces in the Wild: A Database for Studying Face Recognition in Unconstrained Environments*. Technical Report 07-49, University of Massachusetts, Amherst.

Huang, T. S. (1981). *Image Sequence Analysis*. Springer-Verlag, Berlin, Heidelberg.

Huber, P. J. (1981). *Robust Statistics*. John Wiley & Sons, New York.

Huffman, D. A. (1971). Impossible objects and nonsense sentences. *Machine Intelligence*, 8:295–323.

Huguet, F. and Devernay, F. (2007). A variational method for scene flow estimation from stereo sequences. In *Eleventh International Conference on Computer Vision (ICCV 2007)*, Rio de Janeiro, Brazil.

Huttenlocher, D. P., Klanderman, G., and Rucklidge, W. (1993). Comparing images using the Hausdorff distance. *IEEE Transactions on Pattern Analysis and Machine Intelligence*, 15(9):850–863.

Huynh, D. Q., Hartley, R., and Heyden, A. (2003). Outlier correcton in image sequences for the affine camera. In *Ninth International Conference on Computer Vision (ICCV 2003)*, pp. 585–590, Nice, France.

Iddan, G. J. and Yahav, G. (2001). 3D imaging in the studio (and elsewhere...). In *Three-Dimensional Image Capture and Applications IV*, pp. 48–55.

Igarashi, T., Nishino, K., and Nayar, S. (2007). The appearance of human skin: A survey. *Foundations and Trends in Computer Graphics and Computer Vision*, 3(1):1–95.

Ikeuchi, K. (1981). Shape from regular patterns. *Artificial Intelligence*, 22(1):49–75.

Ikeuchi, K. and Horn, B. K. P. (1981). Numerical shape from shading and occluding boundaries. *Artificial Intelligence*, 17:141–184.

Ikeuchi, K. and Miyazaki, D. (eds). (2007). *Digitally Archiving Cultural Objects*, Springer, Boston, MA.

Ikeuchi, K. and Sato, Y. (eds). (2001). *Modeling From Reality*, Kluwer Academic Publishers, Boston.

Illingworth, J. and Kittler, J. (1988). A survey of the Hough transform. *Computer Vision, Graphics, and Image Processing*, 44:87–116.

Intille, S. S. and Bobick, A. F. (1994). Disparity-space images and large occlusion stereo. In *Third European Conference on Computer Vision (ECCV'94)*, Stockholm, Sweden.

Irani, M. and Anandan, P. (1998). Video indexing based on mosaic representations. *Proceedings of the IEEE*, 86(5):905–921.

Irani, M. and Peleg, S. (1991). Improving resolution by image registration. *Graphical Models and Image Processing*, 53(3):231–239.

Irani, M., Hsu, S., and Anandan, P. (1995). Video compression using mosaic representations. *Signal Processing: Image Communication*, 7:529–552.

Irani, M., Rousso, B., and Peleg, S. (1994). Computing occluding and transparent motions. *International Journal of Computer Vision*, 12(1):5–16.

Irani, M., Rousso, B., and Peleg, S. (1997). Recovery of ego-motion using image stabilization. *IEEE Transactions on Pattern Analysis and Machine Intelligence*, 19(3):268–272.

Isaksen, A., McMillan, L., and Gortler, S. J. (2000). Dynamically reparameterized light fields. In *ACM SIGGRAPH 2000 Conference Proceedings*, pp. 297–306.

Isard, M. and Blake, A. (1998). CONDENSATION—conditional density propagation for visual tracking. *International Journal of Computer Vision*, 29(1):5–28.

Ishiguro, H., Yamamoto, M., and Tsuji, S. (1992). Omni-directional stereo. *IEEE Transactions on Pattern Analysis and Machine Intelligence*, 14(2):257–262.

Ishikawa, H. (2003). Exact optimization for Markov random fields with convex priors. *IEEE Transactions on Pattern Analysis and Machine Intelligence*, 25(10):1333–1336.

Ishikawa, H. and Veksler, O. (2010). Convex and truncated convex priors for multi-label MRFs. In Blake, A., Kohli, P., and Rother, C. (eds), *Advances in Markov Random Fields*, MIT Press.

Isidoro, J. and Sclaroff, S. (2003). Stochastic refinement of the visual hull to satisfy photometric and silhouette consistency constraints. In *Ninth International Conference on Computer Vision (ICCV 2003)*, pp. 1335–1342, Nice, France.

Ivanchenko, V., Shen, H., and Coughlan, J. (2009). Elevation-based stereo implemented in real-time on a GPU. In *IEEE Workshop on Applications of Computer Vision (WACV 2009)*, Snowbird, Utah.

Jacobs, C. E., Finkelstein, A., and Salesin, D. H. (1995). Fast multiresolution image querying. In *ACM SIGGRAPH 1995 Conference Proceedings*, pp. 277–286.

Jähne, B. (1997). *Digital Image Processing*. Springer-Verlag, Berlin.

Jain, A. K. and Dubes, R. C. (1988). *Algorithms for Clustering Data*. Prentice Hall, Englewood Cliffs, New Jersey.

Jain, A. K., Bolle, R. M., and Pankanti, S. (eds). (1999). *Biometrics: Personal Identification in Networked Society*, Kluwer.

Jain, A. K., Duin, R. P. W., and Mao, J. (2000). Statistical pattern recognition: A review. *IEEE Transactions on Pattern Analysis and Machine Intelligence*, 22(1):4–37.

Jain, A. K., Topchy, A., Law, M. H. C., and Buhmann, J. M. (2004). Landscape of clustering algorithms. In *International Conference on Pattern Recognition (ICPR 2004)*, pp. 260–263.

Jenkin, M. R. M., Jepson, A. D., and Tsotsos, J. K. (1991). Techniques for disparity measurement. *CVGIP: Image Understanding*, 53(1):14–30.

Jensen, H. W., Marschner, S. R., Levoy, M., and Hanrahan, P. (2001). A practical model for subsurface light transport. In *ACM SIGGRAPH 2001 Conference Proceedings*, pp. 511–518.

Jeong, Y., Nistér, D., Steedly, D., Szeliski, R., and Kweon, I.-S. (2010). Pushing the envelope of modern methods for bundle adjustment. In *IEEE Computer Society Conference on Computer Vision and Pattern Recognition (CVPR 2010)*, San Francisco, CA.

Jia, J. and Tang, C.-K. (2003). Image registration with global and local luminance alignment. In *Ninth International Conference on Computer Vision (ICCV 2003)*, pp. 156–163, Nice, France.

Jia, J., Sun, J., Tang, C.-K., and Shum, H.-Y. (2006). Drag-and-drop pasting. *ACM Transactions on Graphics*, 25(3):631–636.

Jiang, Z., Wong, T.-T., and Bao, H. (2003). Practical super-resolution from dynamic video sequences. In *IEEE Computer Society Conference on Computer Vision and Pattern Recognition (CVPR'2003)*, pp. 549–554, Madison, WI.

Johnson, A. E. and Hebert, M. (1999). Using spin images for efficient object recognition in cluttered 3D scenes. *IEEE Transactions on Pattern Analysis and Machine Intelligence*, 21(5):433–448.

Johnson, A. E. and Kang, S. B. (1997). Registration and integration of textured 3-D data. In *International Conference on Recent Advances in 3-D Digital Imaging and Modeling*, pp. 234–241, Ottawa.

Jojic, N. and Frey, B. J. (2001). Learning flexible sprites in video layers. In *IEEE Computer Society Conference on Computer Vision and Pattern Recognition (CVPR'2001)*, pp. 199–206, Kauai, Hawaii.

Jones, D. G. and Malik, J. (1992). A computational framework for determining stereo correspondence from a set of linear spatial filters. In *Second European Conference on Computer Vision (ECCV'92)*, pp. 397–410, Santa Margherita Liguere, Italy.

Jones, M. J. and Rehg, J. M. (2001). Statistical color models with application to skin detection. *International Journal of Computer Vision*, 46(1):81–96.

Joshi, N., Matusik, W., and Avidan, S. (2006). Natural video matting using camera arrays. *ACM Transactions on Graphics*, 25(3):779–786.

Joshi, N., Szeliski, R., and Kriegman, D. J. (2008). PSF estimation using sharp edge prediction. In *IEEE Computer Society Conference on Computer Vision and Pattern Recognition (CVPR 2008)*, Anchorage, AK.

Joshi, N., Zitnick, C. L., Szeliski, R., and Kriegman, D. J. (2009). Image deblurring and denoising using color priors. In *IEEE Computer Society Conference on Computer Vision and Pattern Recognition (CVPR 2009)*, Miami, FL.

Ju, S. X., Black, M. J., and Jepson, A. D. (1996). Skin and bones: Multi-layer, locally affine, optical flow and regularization with transparency. In *IEEE Computer Society Conference on Computer Vision and Pattern Recognition (CVPR'96)*, pp. 307–314, San Francisco.

Ju, S. X., Black, M. J., and Yacoob, Y. (1996). Cardboard people: a parameterized model of articulated image motion. In *2nd International Conference on Automatic Face and Gesture Recognition*, pp. 38–44, Killington, VT.

Juan, O. and Boykov, Y. (2006). Active graph cuts. In *IEEE Computer Society Conference on Computer Vision and Pattern Recognition (CVPR'2006)*, pp. 1023–1029, New York City, NY.

Jurie, F. and Dhome, M. (2002). Hyperplane approximation for template matching. *IEEE Transactions on Pattern Analysis and Machine Intelligence*, 24(7):996–1000.

Jurie, F. and Schmid, C. (2004). Scale-invariant shape features for recognition of object categories. In *IEEE Computer Society Conference on Computer Vision and Pattern Recognition (CVPR'2004)*, pp. 90–96, Washington, DC.

Kadir, T., Zisserman, A., and Brady, M. (2004). An affine invariant salient region detector. In *Eighth European Conference on Computer Vision (ECCV 2004)*, pp. 228–241, Prague.

Kaftory, R., Schechner, Y., and Zeevi, Y. (2007). Variational distance-dependent image restoration. In *IEEE Computer Society Conference on Computer Vision and Pattern Recognition (CVPR 2007)*, Minneapolis, MN.

Kahl, F. and Hartley, R. (2008). Multiple-view geometry under the l_∞-norm. *IEEE Transactions on Pattern Analysis and Machine Intelligence*, 30(11):1603–1617.

Kakadiaris, I. and Metaxas, D. (2000). Model-based estimation of 3D human motion. *IEEE Transactions on Pattern Analysis and Machine Intelligence*, 22(12):1453–1459.

Kakumanu, P., Makrogiannis, S., and Bourbakis, N. (2007). A survey of skin-color modeling and detection methods. *Pattern Recognition*, 40(3):1106–1122.

Kamvar, S. D., Klein, D., and Manning, C. D. (2002). Interpreting and extending classical agglomerative clustering algorithms using a model-based approach. In *International Conference on Machine Learning*, pp. 283–290.

Kanade, T. (1977). *Computer Recognition of Human Faces*. Birkhauser, Basel.

Kanade, T. (1980). A theory of the origami world. *Artificial Intelligence*, 13:279–311.

Kanade, T. (ed.). (1987). *Three-Dimensional Machine Vision*, Kluwer Academic Publishers, Boston.

Kanade, T. (1994). Development of a video-rate stereo machine. In *Image Understanding Workshop*, pp. 549–557, Monterey.

Kanade, T. and Okutomi, M. (1994). A stereo matching algorithm with an adaptive window: Theory and experiment. *IEEE Transactions on Pattern Analysis and Machine Intelligence*, 16(9):920–932.

Kanade, T., Rander, P. W., and Narayanan, P. J. (1997). Virtualized reality: constructing virtual worlds from real scenes. *IEEE MultiMedia Magazine*, 4(1):34–47.

Kanade, T., Yoshida, A., Oda, K., Kano, H., and Tanaka, M. (1996). A stereo machine for video-rate dense depth mapping and its new applications. In *IEEE Computer Society Conference on Computer Vision and Pattern Recognition (CVPR'96)*, pp. 196–202, San Francisco.

Kanatani, K. and Morris, D. D. (2001). Gauges and gauge transformations for uncertainty description of geometric structure with indeterminacy. *IEEE Transactions on Information Theory*, 47(5):2017–2028.

Kang, S. B. (1998). *Depth Painting for Image-based Rendering Applications*. Technical Report, Compaq Computer Corporation, Cambridge Research Lab.

Kang, S. B. (1999). A survey of image-based rendering techniques. In *Videometrics VI*, pp. 2–16, San Jose.

Kang, S. B. (2001). Radial distortion snakes. *IEICE Trans. Inf. & Syst.*, E84-D(12):1603–1611.

Kang, S. B. and Jones, M. (2002). Appearance-based structure from motion using linear classes of 3-D models. *International Journal of Computer Vision*, 49(1):5–22.

Kang, S. B. and Szeliski, R. (1997). 3-D scene data recovery using omnidirectional multibaseline stereo. *International Journal of Computer Vision*, 25(2):167–183.

Kang, S. B. and Szeliski, R. (2004). Extracting view-dependent depth maps from a collection of images. *International Journal of Computer Vision*, 58(2):139–163.

Kang, S. B. and Weiss, R. (1997). Characterization of errors in compositing panoramic images. In *IEEE Computer Society Conference on Computer Vision and Pattern Recognition (CVPR'97)*, pp. 103–109, San Juan, Puerto Rico.

Kang, S. B. and Weiss, R. (1999). Characterization of errors in compositing panoramic images. *Computer Vision and Image Understanding*, 73(2):269–280.

Kang, S. B. and Weiss, R. (2000). Can we calibrate a camera using an image of a flat, textureless Lambertian surface? In *Sixth European Conference on Computer Vision (ECCV 2000)*, pp. 640–653, Dublin, Ireland.

Kang, S. B., Szeliski, R., and Anandan, P. (2000). The geometry-image representation tradeoff for rendering. In *International Conference on Image Processing (ICIP-2000)*, pp. 13–16, Vancouver.

Kang, S. B., Szeliski, R., and Chai, J. (2001). Handling occlusions in dense multi-view stereo. In *IEEE Computer Society Conference on Computer Vision and Pattern Recognition (CVPR'2001)*, pp. 103–110, Kauai, Hawaii.

Kang, S. B., Szeliski, R., and Shum, H.-Y. (1997). A parallel feature tracker for extended image sequences. *Computer Vision and Image Understanding*, 67(3):296–310.

Kang, S. B., Szeliski, R., and Uyttendaele, M. (2004). *Seamless Stitching using Multi-Perspective Plane Sweep*. Technical Report MSR-TR-2004-48, Microsoft Research.

Kang, S. B., Li, Y., Tong, X., and Shum, H.-Y. (2006). Image-based rendering. *Foundations and Trends in Computer Graphics and Computer Vision*, 2(3):173–258.

Kang, S. B., Uyttendaele, M., Winder, S., and Szeliski, R. (2003). High dynamic range video. *ACM Transactions on Graphics (Proc. SIGGRAPH 2003)*, 22(3):319–325.

Kang, S. B., Webb, J., Zitnick, L., and Kanade, T. (1995). A multibaseline stereo system with active illumination and real-time image acquisition. In *Fifth International Conference on Computer Vision (ICCV'95)*, pp. 88–93, Cambridge, Massachusetts.

Kannala, J., Rahtu, E., Brandt, S. S., and Heikkila, J. (2008). Object recognition and segmentation by non-rigid quasi-dense matching. In *IEEE Computer Society Conference on Computer Vision and Pattern Recognition (CVPR 2008)*, Anchorage, AK.

Kass, M. (1988). Linear image features in stereopsis. *International Journal of Computer Vision*, 1(4):357–368.

Kass, M., Witkin, A., and Terzopoulos, D. (1988). Snakes: Active contour models. *International Journal of Computer Vision*, 1(4):321–331.

Kato, H., Billinghurst, M., Poupyrev, I., Imamoto, K., and Tachibana, K. (2000). Virtual object manipulation on a table-top AR environment. In *International Symposium on Augmented Reality (ISAR 2000)*.

Kaufman, L. and Rousseeuw, P. J. (1990). *Finding Groups in Data: An Introduction to Cluster Analysis*. John Wiley & Sons, Hoboken.

Kazhdan, M., Bolitho, M., and Hoppe, H. (2006). Poisson surface reconstruction. In *Eurographics Symposium on Geometry Processing*, pp. 61–70.

Ke, Y. and Sukthankar, R. (2004). PCA-SIFT: a more distinctive representation for local image descriptors. In *IEEE Computer Society Conference on Computer Vision and Pattern Recognition (CVPR'2004)*, pp. 506–513, Washington, DC.

Kehl, R. and Van Gool, L. (2006). Markerless tracking of complex human motions from multiple views. *Computer Vision and Image Understanding*, 104(2-3):190–209.

Kenney, C., Zuliani, M., and Manjunath, B. (2005). An axiomatic approach to corner detection. In *IEEE Computer Society Conference on Computer Vision and Pattern Recognition (CVPR'2005)*, pp. 191–197, San Diego, CA.

Keren, D., Peleg, S., and Brada, R. (1988). Image sequence enhancement using sub-pixel displacements. In *IEEE Computer Society Conference on Computer Vision and Pattern Recognition (CVPR'88)*, pp. 742–746, Ann Arbor, Michigan.

Kim, J., Kolmogorov, V., and Zabih, R. (2003). Visual correspondence using energy minimization and mutual information. In *Ninth International Conference on Computer Vision (ICCV 2003)*, pp. 1033–1040, Nice, France.

Kimmel, R. (1999). Demosaicing: image reconstruction from color CCD samples. *IEEE Transactions on Image Processing*, 8(9):1221–1228.

Kimura, S., Shinbo, T., Yamaguchi, H., Kawamura, E., and Nakano, K. (1999). A convolver-based real-time stereo machine (SAZAN). In *IEEE Computer Society Conference on Computer Vision and Pattern Recognition (CVPR'99)*, pp. 457–463, Fort Collins.

Kindermann, R. and Snell, J. L. (1980). *Markov Random Fields and Their Applications*. American Mathematical Society.

King, D. (1997). *The Commissar Vanishes*. Henry Holt and Company.

Kirby, M. and Sirovich, L. (1990). Application of the Karhunen–Lòeve procedure for the characterization of human faces. *IEEE Transactions on Pattern Analysis and Machine Intelligence*, 12(1):103–108.

Kirkpatrick, S., Gelatt, C. D. J., and Vecchi, M. P. (1983). Optimization by simulated annealing. *Science*, 220:671–680.

Kirovski, D., Jojic, N., and Jancke, G. (2004). Tamper-resistant biometric IDs. In *ISSE 2004 - Securing Electronic Business Processes: Highlights of the Information Security Solutions Europe 2004 Conference*, pp. 160–175.

Kittler, J. and Föglein, J. (1984). Contextual classification of multispectral pixel data. *Image and Vision Computing*, 2(1):13–29.

Klaus, A., Sormann, M., and Karner, K. (2006). Segment-based stereo matching using belief propagation and a self-adapting dissimilarity measure. In *International Conference on Pattern Recognition (ICPR 2006)*, pp. 15–18.

Klein, G. and Murray, D. (2007). Parallel tracking and mapping for small AR workspaces. In *International Symposium on Mixed and Augmented Reality (ISMAR 2007)*, Nara.

Klein, G. and Murray, D. (2008). Improving the agility of keyframe-based slam. In *Tenth European Conference on Computer Vision (ECCV 2008)*, pp. 802–815, Marseilles.

Klein, S., Staring, M., and Pluim, J. P. W. (2007). Evaluation of optimization methods for nonrigid medical image registration using mutual information and B-splines. *IEEE Transactions on Image Processing*, 16(12):2879–2890.

Klinker, G. J. (1993). *A Physical Approach to Color Image Understanding*. A K Peters, Wellesley, Massachusetts.

Klinker, G. J., Shafer, S. A., and Kanade, T. (1990). A physical approach to color image understanding. *International Journal of Computer Vision*, 4(1):7–38.

Koch, R., Pollefeys, M., and Van Gool, L. J. (2000). Realistic surface reconstruction of 3D scenes from uncalibrated image sequences. *Journal Visualization and Computer Animation*, 11:115–127.

Koenderink, J. J. (1990). *Solid Shape*. MIT Press, Cambridge, Massachusetts.

Koethe, U. (2003). Integrated edge and junction detection with the boundary tensor. In *Ninth International Conference on Computer Vision (ICCV 2003)*, pp. 424–431, Nice, France.

Kohli, P. (2007). *Minimizing Dynamic and Higher Order Energy Functions using Graph Cuts*. Ph.D. thesis, Oxford Brookes University.

Kohli, P. and Torr, P. H. S. (2005). Effciently solving dynamic Markov random fields using graph cuts. In *Tenth International Conference on Computer Vision (ICCV 2005)*, pp. 922–929, Beijing, China.

Kohli, P. and Torr, P. H. S. (2007). Dynamic graph cuts for efficient inference in markov random fields. *IEEE Transactions on Pattern Analysis and Machine Intelligence*, 29(12):2079–2088.

Kohli, P. and Torr, P. H. S. (2008). Measuring uncertainty in graph cut solutions. *Computer Vision and Image Understanding*, 112(1):30–38.

Kohli, P., Kumar, M. P., and Torr, P. H. S. (2009). $\mathcal{P}^3$ & beyond: Move making algorithms for solving higher order functions. *IEEE Transactions on Pattern Analysis and Machine Intelligence*, 31(9):1645–1656.

Kohli, P., Ladický, L., and Torr, P. H. S. (2009). Robust higher order potentials for enforcing label consistency. *International Journal of Computer Vision*, 82(3):302–324.

Kokaram, A. (2004). On missing data treatment for degraded video and film archives: a survey and a new Bayesian approach. *IEEE Transactions on Image Processing*, 13(3):397–415.

Kolev, K. and Cremers, D. (2008). Integration of multiview stereo and silhouettes via convex functionals on convex domains. In *Tenth European Conference on Computer Vision (ECCV 2008)*, pp. 752–765, Marseilles.

Kolev, K. and Cremers, D. (2009). Continuous ratio optimization via convex relaxation with applications to multiview 3D reconstruction. In *IEEE Computer Society Conference on Computer Vision and Pattern Recognition (CVPR 2009)*, Miami Beach, FL.

Kolev, K., Klodt, M., Brox, T., and Cremers, D. (2009). Continuous global optimization in multiview 3D reconstruction. *International Journal of Computer Vision*, 84(1):80–96.

Koller, D. and Friedman, N. (2009). *Probabilistic Graphical Models: Principles and Techniques*. MIT Press, Cambridge, Massachusetts.

Kolmogorov, V. (2006). Convergent tree-reweighted message passing for energy minimization. *IEEE Transactions on Pattern Analysis and Machine Intelligence*, 28(10):1568–1583.

Kolmogorov, V. and Boykov, Y. (2005). What metrics can be approximated by geo-cuts, or global optimization of length/area and flux. In *Tenth International Conference on Computer Vision (ICCV 2005)*, pp. 564–571, Beijing, China.

Kolmogorov, V. and Zabih, R. (2002). Multi-camera scene reconstruction via graph cuts. In *Seventh European Conference on Computer Vision (ECCV 2002)*, pp. 82–96, Copenhagen.

Kolmogorov, V. and Zabih, R. (2004). What energy functions can be minimized via graph cuts? *IEEE Transactions on Pattern Analysis and Machine Intelligence*, 26(2):147–159.

Kolmogorov, V., Criminisi, A., Blake, A., Cross, G., and Rother, C. (2006). Probabilistic fusion of stereo with color and contrast for bi-layer segmentation. *IEEE Transactions on Pattern Analysis and Machine Intelligence*, 28(9):1480–1492.

Komodakis, N. and Paragios, N. (2008). Beyond loose LP-relaxations: Optimizing MRFs by repairing cycles. In *Tenth European Conference on Computer Vision (ECCV 2008)*, pp. 806–820, Marseilles.

Komodakis, N. and Tziritas, G. (2007a). Approximate labeling via graph cuts based on linear programming. *IEEE Transactions on Pattern Analysis and Machine Intelligence*, 29(8):1436–1453.

Komodakis, N. and Tziritas, G. (2007b). Image completion using efficient belief propagation via priority scheduling and dynamic pruning. *IEEE Transactions on Image Processing*, 29(11):2649–2661.

Komodakis, N., Paragios, N., and Tziritas, G. (2007). MRF optimization via dual decomposition: Message-passing revisited. In *Eleventh International Conference on Computer Vision (ICCV 2007)*, Rio de Janeiro, Brazil.

Komodakis, N., Tziritas, G., and Paragios, N. (2007). Fast, approximately optimal solutions for single and dynamic MRFs. In *IEEE Computer Society Conference on Computer Vision and Pattern Recognition (CVPR 2007)*, Minneapolis, MN.

Komodakis, N., Tziritas, G., and Paragios, N. (2008). Performance vs computational efficiency for optimizing single and dynamic MRFs: Setting the state of the art with primal dual strategies. *Computer Vision and Image Understanding*, 112(1):14–29.

Konolige, K. (1997). Small vision systems: Hardware and implementation. In *Eighth International Symposium on Robotics Research*, pp. 203–212, Hayama, Japan.

Kopf, J., Cohen, M. F., Lischinski, D., and Uyttendaele, M. (2007). Joint bilateral upsampling. *ACM Transactions on Graphics*, 26(3).

Kopf, J., Uyttendaele, M., Deussen, O., and Cohen, M. F. (2007). Capturing and viewing gigapixel images. *ACM Transactions on Graphics*, 26(3).

Kopf, J., Lischinski, D., Deussen, O., Cohen-Or, D., and Cohen, M. (2009). Locally adapted projections to reduce panorama distortions. *Computer Graphics Forum (Proceedings of EGSR 2009)*, 28(4).

Koutis, I. (2007). *Combinatorial and algebraic tools for optimal multilevel algorithms*. Ph.D. thesis, Carnegie Mellon University. Technical Report CMU-CS-07-131.

Koutis, I. and Miller, G. L. (2008). Graph partitioning into isolated, high conductance clusters: theory, computation and applications to preconditioning. In *Symposium on Parallel Algorithms and Architectures*, pp. 137–145, Munich.

Koutis, I., Miller, G. L., and Tolliver, D. (2009). Combinatorial preconditioners and multilevel solvers for problems in computer vision and image processing. In *5th International Symposium on Visual Computing (ISVC09)*, Las Vegas.

Kovar, L., Gleicher, M., and Pighin, F. (2002). Motion graphs. *ACM Transactions on Graphics*, 21(3):473–482.

Košecká, J. and Zhang, W. (2005). Extraction, matching and pose recovery based on dominant rectangular structures. *Computer Vision and Image Understanding*, 100(3):174–293.

Kraus, K. (1997). *Photogrammetry*. Dümmler, Bonn.

Krishnan, D. and Fergus, R. (2009). Fast image deconvolution using hyper-Laplacian priors. In *Advances in Neural Information Processing Systems*.

Kuglin, C. D. and Hines, D. C. (1975). The phase correlation image alignment method. In *IEEE 1975 Conference on Cybernetics and Society*, pp. 163–165, New York.

Kulis, B. and Grauman, K. (2009). Kernelized locality-sensitive hashing for scalable image search. In *Twelfth International Conference on Computer Vision (ICCV 2009)*, Kyoto, Japan.

Kumar, M. P. (2008). *Combinatorial and Convex Optimization for Probabilistic Models in Computer Vision*. Ph.D. thesis, Oxford Brookes University.

Kumar, M. P. and Torr, P. H. S. (2006). Fast memory-efficient generalized belief propagation. In *Ninth European Conference on Computer Vision (ECCV 2006)*, pp. 451–463.

Kumar, M. P. and Torr, P. H. S. (2008). Improved moves for truncated convex models. In *Advances in Neural Information Processing Systems*.

Kumar, M. P., Torr, P. H. S., and Zisserman, A. (2008). Learning layered motion segmentations of video. *International Journal of Computer Vision*, 76(3):301–319.

Kumar, M. P., Torr, P. H. S., and Zisserman, A. (2010). OBJCUT: Efficient segmentation using top-down and bottom-up cues. *IEEE Transactions on Pattern Analysis and Machine Intelligence*, 32(3).

Kumar, M. P., Veksler, O., and Torr, P. H. S. (2010). Improved moves for truncated convex models. *Journal of Machine Learning Research*, (sumbitted).

Kumar, M. P., Zisserman, A., and H.S.Torr, P. (2009). Efficient discriminative learning of parts-based models. In *Twelfth International Conference on Computer Vision (ICCV 2009)*, Kyoto, Japan.

Kumar, R., Anandan, P., and Hanna, K. (1994). Direct recovery of shape from multiple views: A parallax based approach. In *Twelfth International Conference on Pattern Recognition (ICPR'94)*, pp. 685–688, Jerusalem, Israel.

Kumar, R., Anandan, P., Irani, M., Bergen, J., and Hanna, K. (1995). Representation of scenes from collections of images. In *IEEE Workshop on Representations of Visual Scenes*, pp. 10–17, Cambridge, Massachusetts.

Kumar, S. and Hebert, M. (2003). Discriminative random fields: A discriminative framework for contextual interaction in classification. In *Ninth International Conference on Computer Vision (ICCV 2003)*, pp. 1150–1157, Nice, France.

Kumar, S. and Hebert, M. (2006). Discriminative random fields. *International Journal of Computer Vision*, 68(2):179–202.

Kundur, D. and Hatzinakos, D. (1996). Blind image deconvolution. *IEEE Signal Processing Magazine*, 13(3):43–64.

Kutulakos, K. N. (2000). Approximate N-view stereo. In *Sixth European Conference on Computer Vision (ECCV 2000)*, pp. 67–83, Dublin, Ireland.

Kutulakos, K. N. and Seitz, S. M. (2000). A theory of shape by space carving. *International Journal of Computer Vision*, 38(3):199–218.

Kwatra, V., Essa, I., Bobick, A., and Kwatra, N. (2005). Graphcut textures: Image and video synthesis using graph cuts. *ACM Transactions on Graphics (Proc. SIGGRAPH 2005)*, 24(5):795–802.

Kwatra, V., Schödl, A., Essa, I., Turk, G., and Bobick, A. (2003). Graphcut textures: Image and video synthesis using graph cuts. *ACM Transactions on Graphics (Proc. SIGGRAPH 2003)*, 22(3):277–286.

Kybic, J. and Unser, M. (2003). Fast parametric elastic image registration. *IEEE Transactions on Image Processing*, 12(11):1427–1442.

Lafferty, J., McCallum, A., and Pereira, F. (2001). Conditional random fields: Probabilistic models for segmenting and labeling sequence data. In *International Conference on Machine Learning*.

Lafortune, E. P. F., Foo, S.-C., Torrance, K. E., and Greenberg, D. P. (1997). Non-linear approximation of reflectance functions. In *ACM SIGGRAPH 1997 Conference Proceedings*, pp. 117–126, Los Angeles.

Lai, S.-H. and Vemuri, B. C. (1997). Physically based adaptive preconditioning for early vision. *IEEE Transactions on Pattern Analysis and Machine Intelligence*, 19(6):594–607.

Lalonde, J.-F., Hoiem, D., Efros, A. A., Rother, C., Winn, J., and Criminisi, A. (2007). Photo clip art. *ACM Transactions on Graphics*, 26(3).

Lampert, C. H. (2008). Kernel methods in computer vision. *Foundations and Trends in Computer Graphics and Computer Vision*, 4(3):193–285.

Langer, M. S. and Zucker, S. W. (1994). Shape from shading on a cloudy day. *Journal Optical Society America, A*, 11(2):467–478.

Lanitis, A., Taylor, C. J., and Cootes, T. F. (1997). Automatic interpretation and coding of face images using flexible models. *IEEE Transactions on Pattern Analysis and Machine Intelligence*, 19(7):742–756.

Larlus, D. and Jurie, F. (2008). Combining appearance models and Markov random fields for category level object segmentation. In *IEEE Computer Society Conference on Computer Vision and Pattern Recognition (CVPR 2008)*, Anchorage, AK.

Larson, G. W. (1998). LogLuv encoding for full-gamut, high-dynamic range images. *Journal of Graphics Tools*, 3(1):15–31.

Larson, G. W., Rushmeier, H., and Piatko, C. (1997). A visibility matching tone reproduction operator for high dynamic range scenes. *IEEE Transactions on Visualization and Computer Graphics*, 3(4):291–306.

Laurentini, A. (1994). The visual hull concept for silhouette-based image understanding. *IEEE Transactions on Pattern Analysis and Machine Intelligence*, 16(2):150–162.

Lavallée, S. and Szeliski, R. (1995). Recovering the position and orientation of free-form objects from image contours using 3-D distance maps. *IEEE Transactions on Pattern Analysis and Machine Intelligence*, 17(4):378–390.

Laveau, S. and Faugeras, O. D. (1994). 3-D scene representation as a collection of images. In *Twelfth International Conference on Pattern Recognition (ICPR'94)*, pp. 689–691, Jerusalem, Israel.

Lazebnik, S., Schmid, C., and Ponce, J. (2005). A sparse texture representation using local affine regions. *IEEE Transactions on Pattern Analysis and Machine Intelligence*, 27(8):1265–1278.

Lazebnik, S., Schmid, C., and Ponce, J. (2006). Beyond bags of features: Spatial pyramid matching for recognizing natural scene categories. In *IEEE Computer Society Conference on Computer Vision and Pattern Recognition (CVPR'2006)*, pp. 2169–2176, New York City, NY.

Le Gall, D. (1991). MPEG: A video compression standard for multimedia applications. *Communications of the ACM*, 34(4):46–58.

Leclerc, Y. G. (1989). Constructing simple stable descriptions for image partitioning. *International Journal of Computer Vision*, 3(1):73–102.

LeCun, Y., Huang, F. J., and Bottou, L. (2004). Learning methods for generic object recognition with invariance to pose and lighting. In *IEEE Computer Society Conference on Computer Vision and Pattern Recognition (CVPR'2004)*, pp. 97–104, Washington, DC.

Lee, J., Chai, J., Reitsma, P. S. A., Hodgins, J. K., and Pollard, N. S. (2002). Interactive control of avatars animated with human motion data. *ACM Transactions on Graphics*, 21(3):491–500.

Lee, M.-C., ge Chen, W., lung Bruce Lin, C., Gu, C., Markoc, T., Zabinsky, S. I., and Szeliski, R. (1997). A layered video object coding system using sprite and affine motion model. *IEEE Transactions on Circuits and Systems for Video Technology*, 7(1):130–145.

Lee, M. E. and Redner, R. A. (1990). A note on the use of nonlinear filtering in computer graphics. *IEEE Computer Graphics and Applications*, 10(3):23–29.

Lee, M. W. and Cohen, I. (2006). A model-based approach for estimating human 3D poses in static images. *IEEE Transactions on Pattern Analysis and Machine Intelligence*, 28(6):905–916.

Lee, S., Wolberg, G., and Shin, S. Y. (1996). Data interpolation using multilevel b-splines. *IEEE Transactions on Visualization and Computer Graphics*, 3(3):228–244.

Lee, S., Wolberg, G., Chwa, K.-Y., and Shin, S. Y. (1996). Image metamorphosis with scattered feature constraints. *IEEE Transactions on Visualization and Computer Graphics*, 2(4):337–354.

Lee, Y. D., Terzopoulos, D., and Waters, K. (1995). Realistic facial modeling for animation. In *ACM SIGGRAPH 1995 Conference Proceedings*, pp. 55–62.

Lei, C. and Yang, Y.-H. (2009). Optical flow estimation on coarse-to-fine region-trees using discrete optimization. In *Twelfth International Conference on Computer Vision (ICCV 2009)*, Kyoto, Japan.

Leibe, B. and Schiele, B. (2003). Analyzing appearance and contour based methods for object categorization. In *IEEE Computer Society Conference on Computer Vision and Pattern Recognition (CVPR'2003)*, pp. 409–415, Madison, WI.

Leibe, B., Leonardis, A., and Schiele, B. (2008). Robust object detection with interleaved categorization and segmentation. *International Journal of Computer Vision*, 77(1-3):259–289.

Leibe, B., Seemann, E., and Schiele, B. (2005). Pedestrian detection in crowded scenes. In *IEEE Computer Society Conference on Computer Vision and Pattern Recognition (CVPR'2005)*, pp. 878–885, San Diego, CA.

Leibe, B., Cornelis, N., Cornelis, K., and Van Gool, L. (2007). Dynamic 3D scene analysis from a moving vehicle. In *IEEE Computer Society Conference on Computer Vision and Pattern Recognition (CVPR 2007)*, Minneapolis, MN.

Leibowitz, D. (2001). *Camera Calibration and Reconstruction of Geometry from Images*. Ph.D. thesis, University of Oxford.

Lempitsky, V. and Boykov, Y. (2007). Global optimization for shape fitting. In *IEEE Computer Society Conference on Computer Vision and Pattern Recognition (CVPR 2007)*, Minneapolis, MN.

Lempitsky, V. and Ivanov, D. (2007). Seamless mosaicing of image-based texture maps. In *IEEE Computer Society Conference on Computer Vision and Pattern Recognition (CVPR 2007)*, Minneapolis, MN.

Lempitsky, V., Blake, A., and Rother, C. (2008). Image segmentation by branch-and-mincut. In *Tenth European Conference on Computer Vision (ECCV 2008)*, pp. 15–29, Marseilles.

Lempitsky, V., Roth, S., and Rother., C. (2008). FlowFusion: Discrete-continuous optimization for optical flow estimation. In *IEEE Computer Society Conference on Computer Vision and Pattern Recognition (CVPR 2008)*, Anchorage, AK.

Lempitsky, V., Rother, C., and Blake, A. (2007). Logcut - efficient graph cut optimization for Markov random fields. In *Eleventh International Conference on Computer Vision (ICCV 2007)*, Rio de Janeiro, Brazil.

Lengyel, J. and Snyder, J. (1997). Rendering with coherent layers. In *ACM SIGGRAPH 1997 Conference Proceedings*, pp. 233–242, Los Angeles.

Lensch, H. P. A., Kautz, J., Goesele, M., Heidrich, W., and Seidel, H.-P. (2003). Image-based reconstruction of spatial appearance and geometric detail. *ACM Transactions on Graphics*, 22(2):234–257.

Leonardis, A. and Bischof, H. (2000). Robust recognition using eigenimages. *Computer Vision and Image Understanding*, 78(1):99–118.

Leonardis, A., Jaklič, A., and Solina, F. (1997). Superquadrics for segmenting and modeling range data. *IEEE Transactions on Pattern Analysis and Machine Intelligence*, 19(11):1289–1295.

Lepetit, V. and Fua, P. (2005). Monocular model-based 3D tracking of rigid objects. *Foundations and Trends in Computer Graphics and Computer Vision*, 1(1).

Lepetit, V., Pilet, J., and Fua, P. (2004). Point matching as a classification problem for fast and robust object pose estimation. In *IEEE Computer Society Conference on Computer Vision and Pattern Recognition (CVPR'2004)*, pp. 244–250, Washington, DC.

Lepetit, V., Pilet, J., and Fua, P. (2006). Keypoint recognition using randomized trees. *IEEE Transactions on Pattern Analysis and Machine Intelligence*, 28(9):1465–1479.

Leung, T. K., Burl, M. C., and Perona, P. (1995). Finding faces in cluttered scenes using random labeled graph matching. In *Fifth International Conference on Computer Vision (ICCV'95)*, pp. 637–644, Cambridge, Massachusetts.

Levenberg, K. (1944). A method for the solution of certain problems in least squares. *Quarterly of Applied Mathematics*, 2:164–168.

Levin, A. (2006). Blind motion deblurring using image statistics. In *Advances in Neural Information Processing Systems*.

Levin, A. and Szeliski, R. (2004). Visual odometry and map correlation. In *IEEE Computer Society Conference on Computer Vision and Pattern Recognition (CVPR'2004)*, pp. 611–618, Washington, DC.

Levin, A. and Szeliski, R. (2006). *Motion Uncertainty and Field of View*. Technical Report MSR-TR-2006-37, Microsoft Research.

Levin, A. and Weiss, Y. (2006). Learning to combine bottom-up and top-down segmentation. In *Ninth European Conference on Computer Vision (ECCV 2006)*, pp. 581–594.

Levin, A. and Weiss, Y. (2007). User assisted separation of reflections from a single image using a sparsity prior. *IEEE Transactions on Pattern Analysis and Machine Intelligence*, 29(9):1647–1654.

Levin, A., Acha, A. R., and Lischinski, D. (2008). Spectral matting. *IEEE Transactions on Pattern Analysis and Machine Intelligence*, 30(10):1699–1712.

Levin, A., Lischinski, D., and Weiss, Y. (2004). Colorization using optimization. *ACM Transactions on Graphics*, 23(3):689–694.

Levin, A., Lischinski, D., and Weiss, Y. (2008). A closed form solution to natural image matting. *IEEE Transactions on Pattern Analysis and Machine Intelligence*, 30(2):228–242.

Levin, A., Zomet, A., and Weiss, Y. (2004). Separating reflections from a single image using local features. In *IEEE Computer Society Conference on Computer Vision and Pattern Recognition (CVPR'2004)*, pp. 306–313, Washington, DC.

Levin, A., Fergus, R., Durand, F., and Freeman, W. T. (2007). Image and depth from a conventional camera with a coded aperture. *ACM Transactions on Graphics*, 26(3).

Levin, A., Weiss, Y., Durand, F., and Freeman, B. (2009). Understanding and evaluating blind deconvolution algorithms. In *IEEE Computer Society Conference on Computer Vision and Pattern Recognition (CVPR 2009)*, Miami Beach, FL.

Levin, A., Zomet, A., Peleg, S., and Weiss, Y. (2004). Seamless image stitching in the gradient domain. In *Eighth European Conference on Computer Vision (ECCV 2004)*, pp. 377–389, Prague.

Levoy, M. (1988). Display of surfaces from volume data. *IEEE Computer Graphics and Applications*, 8(3):29–37.

Levoy, M. (2006). Light fields and computational imaging. *Computer*, 39(8):46–55.

Levoy, M. (2008). Technical perspective: Computational photography on large collections of images. *Communications of the ACM*, 51(10):86.

Levoy, M. and Hanrahan, P. (1996). Light field rendering. In *ACM SIGGRAPH 1996 Conference Proceedings*, pp. 31–42, New Orleans.

Levoy, M. and Whitted, T. (1985). *The Use of Points as a Display Primitive*. Technical Report 85-022, University of North Carolina at Chapel Hill.

Levoy, M., Ng, R., Adams, A., Footer, M., and Horowitz, M. (2006). Light field microscopy. *ACM Transactions on Graphics*, 25(3):924–934.

Levoy, M., Pulli, K., Curless, B., Rusinkiewicz, S., Koller, D. *et al.* (2000). The digital Michelangelo project: 3D scanning of large statues. In *ACM SIGGRAPH 2000 Conference Proceedings*, pp. 131–144.

Lew, M. S., Sebe, N., Djeraba, C., and Jain, R. (2006). Content-based multimedia information retrieval: State of the art and challenges. *ACM Transactions on Multimedia Computing, Communications and Applications*, 2(1):1–19.

Leyvand, T., Cohen-Or, D., Dror, G., and Lischinski, D. (2008). Data-driven enhancement of facial attractiveness. *ACM Transactions on Graphics*, 27(3).

Lhuillier, M. and Quan, L. (2002). Match propagation for image-based modeling and rendering. *IEEE Transactions on Pattern Analysis and Machine Intelligence*, 24(8):1140–1146.

Lhuillier, M. and Quan, L. (2005). A quasi-dense approach to surface reconstruction from uncalibrated images. *IEEE Transactions on Pattern Analysis and Machine Intelligence*, 27(3):418–433.

Li, H. and Hartley, R. (2007). The 3D–3D registration problem revisited. In *Eleventh International Conference on Computer Vision (ICCV 2007)*, Rio de Janeiro, Brazil.

Li, L.-J. and Fei-Fei, L. (2010). Optimol: Automatic object picture collection via incremental model learning. *International Journal of Computer Vision*, 88(2):147–168.

Li, S. (1995). *Markov Random Field Modeling in Computer Vision*. Springer-Verlag.

Li, S. Z. and Jain, A. K. (eds). (2005). *Handbook of Face Recognition*, Springer.

Li, X., Wu, C., Zach, C., Lazebnik, S., and Frahm, J.-M. (2008). Modeling and recognition of landmark image collections using iconic scene graphs. In *Tenth European Conference on Computer Vision (ECCV 2008)*, pp. 427–440, Marseilles.

Li, Y. and Huttenlocher, D. P. (2008). Learning for optical flow using stochastic optimization. In *Tenth European Conference on Computer Vision (ECCV 2008)*, pp. 379–391, Marseilles.

Li, Y., Crandall, D. J., and Huttenlocher, D. P. (2009). Landmark classification in large-scale image collections. In *Twelfth International Conference on Computer Vision (ICCV 2009)*, Kyoto, Japan.

Li, Y., Wang, T., and Shum, H.-Y. (2002). Motion texture: a two-level statistical model for character motion synthesis. *ACM Transactions on Graphics*, 21(3):465–472.

Li, Y., Shum, H.-Y., Tang, C.-K., and Szeliski, R. (2004). Stereo reconstruction from multiperspective panoramas. *IEEE Transactions on Pattern Analysis and Machine Intelligence*, 26(1):44–62.

Li, Y., Sun, J., Tang, C.-K., and Shum, H.-Y. (2004). Lazy snapping. *ACM Transactions on Graphics (Proc. SIGGRAPH 2004)*, 23(3):303–308.

Liang, L., Xiao, R., Wen, F., and Sun, J. (2008). Face alignment via component-based discriminative search. In *Tenth European Conference on Computer Vision (ECCV 2008)*, pp. 72–85, Marseilles.

Liang, L., Liu, C., Xu, Y.-Q., Guo, B., and Shum, H.-Y. (2001). Real-time texture synthesis by patch-based sampling. *ACM Transactions on Graphics*, 20(3):127–150.

Liebowitz, D. and Zisserman, A. (1998). Metric rectification for perspective images of planes. In *IEEE Computer Society Conference on Computer Vision and Pattern Recognition (CVPR'98)*, pp. 482–488, Santa Barbara.

Lim, J. (1990). *Two-Dimensional Signal and Image Processing*. Prentice-Hall, Englewood, NJ.

Lim, J. J., Arbeláez, P., Gu, C., and Malik, J. (2009). Context by region ancestry. In *Twelfth International Conference on Computer Vision (ICCV 2009)*, Kyoto, Japan.

Lin, D., Kapoor, A., Hua, G., and Baker, S. (2010). Joint people, event, and location recognition in personal photo collections using cross-domain context. In *Eleventh European Conference on Computer Vision (ECCV 2010)*, Heraklion, Crete.

Lin, W.-C., Hays, J., Wu, C., Kwatra, V., and Liu, Y. (2006). Quantitative evaluation of near regular texture synthesis algorithms. In *IEEE Computer Society Conference on Computer Vision and Pattern Recognition (CVPR'2006)*, pp. 427–434, New York City, NY.

Lindeberg, T. (1990). Scale-space for discrete signals. *IEEE Transactions on Pattern Analysis and Machine Intelligence*, 12(3):234–254.

Lindeberg, T. (1993). Detecting salient blob-like image structures and their scales with a scale-space primal sketch: a method for focus-of-attention. *International Journal of Computer Vision*, 11(3):283–318.

Lindeberg, T. (1994). Scale-space theory: A basic tool for analysing structures at different scales. *Journal of Applied Statistics*, 21(2):224–270.

Lindeberg, T. (1998a). Edge detection and ridge detection with automatic scale selection. *International Journal of Computer Vision*, 30(2):116–154.

Lindeberg, T. (1998b). Feature detection with automatic scale selection. *International Journal of Computer Vision*, 30(2):79–116.

Lindeberg, T. and Garding, J. (1997). Shape-adapted smoothing in estimation of 3-D shape cues from affine deformations of local 2-D brightness structure. *Image and Vision Computing*, 15(6):415–434.

Lippman, A. (1980). Movie maps: An application of the optical videodisc to computer graphics. *Computer Graphics (SIGGRAPH '80)*, 14(3):32–43.

Lischinski, D., Farbman, Z., Uyttendaele, M., and Szeliski, R. (2006a). Interactive local adjustment of tonal values. *ACM Transactions on Graphics (Proc. SIGGRAPH 2006)*, 25(3):646–653.

Lischinski, D., Farbman, Z., Uyttendaele, M., and Szeliski, R. (2006b). Interactive local adjustment of tonal values. *ACM Transactions on Graphics*, 25(3):646–653.

Litvinov, A. and Schechner, Y. Y. (2005). Radiometric framework for image mosaicking. *Journal of the Optical Society of America A*, 22(5):839–848.

Litwinowicz, P. (1997). Processing images and video for an impressionist effect. In *ACM SIGGRAPH 1997 Conference Proceedings*, pp. 407–414.

Litwinowicz, P. and Williams, L. (1994). Animating images with drawings. In *ACM SIGGRAPH 1994 Conference Proceedings*, pp. 409–412.

Liu, C. (2009). *Beyond Pixels: Exploring New Representations and Applications for Motion Analysis*. Ph.D. thesis, Massachusetts Institute of Technology.

Liu, C., Yuen, J., and Torralba, A. (2009). Nonparametric scene parsing: Label transfer via dense scene alignment. In *IEEE Computer Society Conference on Computer Vision and Pattern Recognition (CVPR 2009)*, Miami Beach, FL.

Liu, C., Freeman, W. T., Adelson, E., and Weiss, Y. (2008). Human-assisted motion annotation. In *IEEE Computer Society Conference on Computer Vision and Pattern Recognition (CVPR 2008)*, Anchorage, AK.

Liu, C., Szeliski, R., Kang, S. B., Zitnick, C. L., and Freeman, W. T. (2008). Automatic estimation and removal of noise from a single image. *IEEE Transactions on Pattern Analysis and Machine Intelligence*, 30(2):299–314.

Liu, F., Gleicher, M., Jin, H., and Agarwala, A. (2009). Content-preserving warps for 3d video stabilization. *ACM Transactions on Graphics*, 28(3).

Liu, X., Chen, T., and Kumar, B. V. (2003). Face authentication for multiple subjects using eigenflow. *Pattern Recognition*, 36(2):313–328.

Liu, Y., Collins, R. T., and Tsin, Y. (2004). A computational model for periodic pattern perception based on frieze and wallpaper groups. *IEEE Transactions on Pattern Analysis and Machine Intelligence*, 26(3):354–371.

Liu, Y., Lin, W.-C., and Hays, J. (2004). Near-regular texture analysis and manipulation. *ACM Transactions on Graphics*, 23(3):368–376.

Livingstone, M. (2008). *Vision and Art: The Biology of Seeing*. Abrams, New York.

Lobay, A. and Forsyth, D. A. (2006). Shape from texture without boundaries. *International Journal of Computer Vision*, 67(1):71–91.

Lombaert, H., Sun, Y., Grady, L., and Xu, C. (2005). A multilevel banded graph cuts method for fast image segmentation. In *Tenth International Conference on Computer Vision (ICCV 2005)*, pp. 259–265, Beijing, China.

Longere, P., Delahunt, P. B., Zhang, X., and Brainard, D. H. (2002). Perceptual assessment of demosaicing algorithm performance. *Proceedings of the IEEE*, 90(1):123–132.

Longuet-Higgins, H. C. (1981). A computer algorithm for reconstructing a scene from two projections. *Nature*, 293:133–135.

Loop, C. and Zhang, Z. (1999). Computing rectifying homographies for stereo vision. In *IEEE Computer Society Conference on Computer Vision and Pattern Recognition (CVPR'99)*, pp. 125–131, Fort Collins.

Lorensen, W. E. and Cline, H. E. (1987). Marching cubes: A high resolution 3D surface construction algorithm. *Computer Graphics (SIGGRAPH '87)*, 21(4):163–169.

Lorusso, A., Eggert, D., and Fisher, R. B. (1995). A comparison of four algorithms for estimating 3-D rigid transformations. In *British Machine Vision Conference (BMVC95)*, pp. 237–246, Birmingham, England.

Lourakis, M. I. A. and Argyros, A. A. (2009). SBA: A software package for generic sparse bundle adjustment. *ACM Transactions on Mathematical Software*, 36(1).

Lowe, D. G. (1988). Organization of smooth image curves at multiple scales. In *Second International Conference on Computer Vision (ICCV'88)*, pp. 558–567, Tampa.

Lowe, D. G. (1989). Organization of smooth image curves at multiple scales. *International Journal of Computer Vision*, 3(2):119–130.

Lowe, D. G. (1999). Object recognition from local scale-invariant features. In *Seventh International Conference on Computer Vision (ICCV'99)*, pp. 1150–1157, Kerkyra, Greece.

Lowe, D. G. (2004). Distinctive image features from scale-invariant keypoints. *International Journal of Computer Vision*, 60(2):91–110.

Lucas, B. D. and Kanade, T. (1981). An iterative image registration technique with an application in stereo vision. In *Seventh International Joint Conference on Artificial Intelligence (IJCAI-81)*, pp. 674–679, Vancouver.

Luong, Q.-T. and Faugeras, O. D. (1996). The fundamental matrix: Theory, algorithms, and stability analysis. *International Journal of Computer Vision*, 17(1):43–75.

Luong, Q.-T. and Viéville, T. (1996). Canonical representations for the geometries of multiple projective views. *Computer Vision and Image Understanding*, 64(2):193–229.

Lyu, S. and Simoncelli, E. (2008). Nonlinear image representation using divisive normalization. In *IEEE Computer Society Conference on Computer Vision and Pattern Recognition (CVPR 2008)*, Anchorage, AK.

Lyu, S. and Simoncelli, E. (2009). Modeling multiscale subbands of photographic images with fields of Gaussian scale mixtures. *IEEE Transactions on Pattern Analysis and Machine Intelligence*, 31(4):693–706.

Ma, W.-C., Jones, A., Chiang, J.-Y., Hawkins, T., Frederiksen, S., Peers, P., Vukovic, M., Ouhyoung, M., and Debevec, P. (2008). Facial performance synthesis using deformation-driven polynomial displacement maps. *ACM Transactions on Graphics*, 27(5).

Ma, Y., Derksen, H., Hong, W., and Wright, J. (2007). Segmentation of multivariate mixed data via lossy data coding and compression. *IEEE Transactions on Pattern Analysis and Machine Intelligence*, 29(9):1546–1562.

MacDonald, L. (ed.). (2006). *Digital Heritage: Applying Digital Imaging to Cultural Heritage*, Butterworth-Heinemann.

Madsen, K., Nielsen, H. B., and Tingleff, O. (2004). Methods for non-linear least squares problems. Informatics and Mathematical Modelling, Technical University of Denmark (DTU).

Maes, F., Collignon, A., Vandermeulen, D., Marchal, G., and Suetens, P. (1997). Multimodality image registration by maximization of mutual information. *IEEE Transactions on Medical Imaging*, 16(2):187–198.

Magnor, M. (2005). *Video-Based Rendering*. A. K. Peters, Wellesley, MA.

Magnor, M. and Girod, B. (2000). Data compression for light-field rendering. *IEEE Transactions on Circuits and Systems for Video Technology*, 10(3):338–343.

Magnor, M., Ramanathan, P., and Girod, B. (2003). Multi-view coding for image-based rendering using 3-D scene geometry. *IEEE Transactions on Circuits and Systems for Video Technology*, 13(11):1092–1106.

Mahajan, D., Huang, F.-C., Matusik, W., Ramamoorthi, R., and Belhumeur, P. (2009). Moving gradients: A path-based method for plausible image interpolation. *ACM Transactions on Graphics*, 28(3).

Maimone, M., Cheng, Y., and Matthies, L. (2007). Two years of visual odometry on the Mars exploration rovers. *Journal of Field Robotics*, 24(3).

Maire, M., Arbelaez, P., Fowlkes, C., and Malik, J. (2008). Using contours to detect and localize junctions in natural images. In *IEEE Computer Society Conference on Computer Vision and Pattern Recognition (CVPR 2008)*, Anchorage, AK.

Maitin-Shepard, J., Cusumano-Towner, M., Lei, J., and Abbeel, P. (2010). Cloth grasp point detection based on multiple-view geometric cues with application to robotic towel folding. In *IEEE International Conference on Robotics and Automation*, Anchorage, AK.

Maitre, M., Shinagawa, Y., and Do, M. N. (2008). Symmetric multi-view stereo reconstruction from planar camera arrays. In *IEEE Computer Society Conference on Computer Vision and Pattern Recognition (CVPR 2008)*, Anchorage, AK.

Maji, S., Berg, A., and Malik, J. (2008). Classification using intersection kernel support vector machines is efficient. In *IEEE Computer Society Conference on Computer Vision and Pattern Recognition (CVPR 2008)*, Anchorage, AK.

Malik, J. and Rosenholtz, R. (1997). Computing local surface orientation and shape from texture for curved surfaces. *International Journal of Computer Vision*, 23(2):149–168.

Malik, J., Belongie, S., Leung, T., and Shi, J. (2001). Contour and texture analysis for image segmentation. *International Journal of Computer Vision*, 43(1):7–27.

Malisiewicz, T. and Efros, A. A. (2008). Recognition by association via learning per-exemplar distances. In *IEEE Computer Society Conference on Computer Vision and Pattern Recognition (CVPR 2008)*, Anchorage, AK.

Malladi, R., Sethian, J. A., and Vemuri, B. C. (1995). Shape modeling with front propagation. *IEEE Transactions on Pattern Analysis and Machine Intelligence*, 17(2):158–176.

Mallat, S. G. (1989). A theory for multiresolution signal decomposition: the wavelet representation. *IEEE Transactions on Pattern Analysis and Machine Intelligence*, PAMI-11(7):674–693.

Malvar, H. S. (1990). Lapped transforms for efficient transform/subband coding. *IEEE Transactions on Acoustics, Speech, and Signal Processing*, 38(6):969–978.

Malvar, H. S. (1998). Biorthogonal and nonuniform lapped transforms for transform coding with reduced blocking and ringing artifacts. *IEEE Transactions on Signal Processing*, 46(4):1043–1053.

Malvar, H. S. (2000). Fast progressive image coding without wavelets. In *IEEE Data Compressions Conference*, pp. 243–252, Snowbird, UT.

Malvar, H. S., He, L.-W., and Cutler, R. (2004). High-quality linear interpolation for demosaicing of Bayer-patterned color images. In *IEEE International Conference on Acoustics, Speech, and Signal Processing (ICASSP'04)*, pp. 485–488, Montreal.

Mancini, T. A. and Wolff, L. B. (1992). 3D shape and light source location from depth and reflectance. In *IEEE Computer Society Conference on Computer Vision and Pattern Recognition (CVPR'92)*, pp. 707–709, Champaign, Illinois.

Manjunathi, B. S. and Ma, W. Y. (1996). Texture features for browsing and retrieval of image data. *IEEE Transactions on Pattern Analysis and Machine Intelligence*, 18(8):837–842.

Mann, S. and Picard, R. W. (1994). Virtual bellows: Constructing high-quality images from video. In *First IEEE International Conference on Image Processing (ICIP-94)*, pp. 363–367, Austin.

Mann, S. and Picard, R. W. (1995). On being 'undigital' with digital cameras: Extending dynamic range by combining differently exposed pictures. In *IS&T's 48th Annual Conference*, pp. 422–428, Washington, D. C.

Manning, C. D., Raghavan, P., and Schütze, H. (2008). *Introduction to Information Retrieval*. Cambridge University Press.

Marquardt, D. W. (1963). An algorithm for least-squares estimation of nonlinear parameters. *Journal of the Society for Industrial and Applied Mathematics*, 11(2):431–441.

Marr, D. (1982). *Vision: A Computational Investigation into the Human Representation and Processing of Visual Information*. W. H. Freeman, San Francisco.

Marr, D. and Hildreth, E. (1980). Theory of edge detection. *Proceedings of the Royal Society of London*, B 207:187–217.

Marr, D. and Nishihara, H. K. (1978). Representation and recognition of the spatial organization of three-dimensional shapes. *Proc. Roy. Soc. London, B*, 200:269–294.

Marr, D. and Poggio, T. (1976). Cooperative computation of stereo disparity. *Science*, 194:283–287.

Marr, D. C. and Poggio, T. (1979). A computational theory of human stereo vision. *Proceedings of the Royal Society of London*, B 204:301–328.

Marroquin, J., Mitter, S., and Poggio, T. (1985). Probabilistic solution of ill-posed problems in computational vision. In *Image Understanding Workshop*, pp. 293–309, Miami Beach.

Marroquin, J., Mitter, S., and Poggio, T. (1987). Probabilistic solution of ill-posed problems in computational vision. *Journal of the American Statistical Association*, 82(397):76–89.

Marroquin, J. L. (1983). *Design of Cooperative Networks*. Working Paper 253, Artificial Intelligence Laboratory, Massachusetts Institute of Technology.

Martin, D., Fowlkes, C., and Malik, J. (2004). Learning to detect natural image boundaries using local brightness, color, and texture cues. *IEEE Transactions on Pattern Analysis and Machine Intelligence*, 26(5):530–549.

Martin, D., Fowlkes, C., Tal, D., and Malik, J. (2001). A database of human segmented natural images and its application to evaluating segmentation algorithms and measuring ecological statistics. In *Eighth International Conference on Computer Vision (ICCV 2001)*, pp. 416–423, Vancouver, Canada.

Martin, W. N. and Aggarwal, J. K. (1983). Volumetric description of objects from multiple views. *IEEE Transactions on Pattern Analysis and Machine Intelligence*, PAMI-5(2):150–158.

Martinec, D. and Pajdla, T. (2007). Robust rotation and translation estimation in multiview reconstruction. In *IEEE Computer Society Conference on Computer Vision and Pattern Recognition (CVPR 2007)*, Minneapolis, MN.

Massey, M. and Bender, W. (1996). Salient stills: Process and practice. *IBM Systems Journal*, 35(3&4):557–573.

Matas, J., Chum, O., Urban, M., and Pajdla, T. (2004). Robust wide baseline stereo from maximally stable extremal regions. *Image and Vision Computing*, 22(10):761–767.

Matei, B. C. and Meer, P. (2006). Estimation of nonlinear errors-in-variables models for computer vision applications. *IEEE Transactions on Pattern Analysis and Machine Intelligence*, 28(10):1537–1552.

Matsushita, Y. and Lin, S. (2007). Radiometric calibration from noise distributions. In *IEEE Computer Society Conference on Computer Vision and Pattern Recognition (CVPR 2007)*, Minneapolis, MN.

Matsushita, Y., Ofek, E., Ge, W., Tang, X., and Shum, H.-Y. (2006). Full-frame video stabilization with motion inpainting. *IEEE Transactions on Pattern Analysis and Machine Intelligence*, 28(7):1150–1163.

Matthews, I. and Baker, S. (2004). Active appearance models revisited. *International Journal of Computer Vision*, 60(2):135–164.

Matthews, I., Xiao, J., and Baker, S. (2007). 2D vs. 3D deformable face models: Representational power, construction, and real-time fitting. *International Journal of Computer Vision*, 75(1):93–113.

Matthies, L., Kanade, T., and Szeliski, R. (1989). Kalman filter-based algorithms for estimating depth from image sequences. *International Journal of Computer Vision*, 3(3):209–236.

Matusik, W., Buehler, C., and McMillan, L. (2001). Polyhedral visual hulls for real-time rendering. In *12th Eurographics Workshop on Rendering Techniques*, pp. 115–126, London.

Matusik, W., Buehler, C., Raskar, R., Gortler, S. J., and McMillan, L. (2000). Image-based visual hulls. In *ACM SIGGRAPH 2000 Conference Proceedings*, pp. 369–374.

Mayhew, J. E. W. and Frisby, J. P. (1980). The computation of binocular edges. *Perception*, 9:69–87.

Mayhew, J. E. W. and Frisby, J. P. (1981). Psychophysical and computational studies towards a theory of human stereopsis. *Artificial Intelligence*, 17(1-3):349–408.

McCamy, C. S., Marcus, H., and Davidson, J. G. (1976). A color-rendition chart. *Journal of Applied Photogrammetric Engineering*, 2(3):95–99.

McCane, B., Novins, K., Crannitch, D., and Galvin, B. (2001). On benchmarking optical flow. *Computer Vision and Image Understanding*, 84(1):126–143.

McGuire, M., Matusik, W., Pfister, H., Hughes, J. F., and Durand, F. (2005). Defocus video matting. *ACM Transactions on Graphics (Proc. SIGGRAPH 2005)*, 24(3):567–576.

McInerney, T. and Terzopoulos, D. (1993). A finite element model for 3D shape reconstruction and nonrigid motion tracking. In *Fourth International Conference on Computer Vision (ICCV'93)*, pp. 518–523, Berlin, Germany.

McInerney, T. and Terzopoulos, D. (1996). Deformable models in medical image analysis: A survey. *Medical Image Analysis*, 1(2):91–108.

McInerney, T. and Terzopoulos, D. (1999). Topology adaptive deformable surfaces for medical image volume segmentation. *IEEE Transactions on Medical Imaging*, 18(10):840–850.

McInerney, T. and Terzopoulos, D. (2000). T-snakes: Topology adaptive snakes. *Medical Image Analysis*, 4:73–91.

McLauchlan, P. F. (2000). A batch/recursive algorithm for 3D scene reconstruction. In *IEEE Computer Society Conference on Computer Vision and Pattern Recognition (CVPR'2000)*, pp. 738–743, Hilton Head Island.

McLauchlan, P. F. and Jaenicke, A. (2002). Image mosaicing using sequential bundle adjustment. *Image and Vision Computing*, 20(9-10):751–759.

McLean, G. F. and Kotturi, D. (1995). Vanishing point detection by line clustering. *IEEE Transactions on Pattern Analysis and Machine Intelligence*, 17(11):1090–1095.

McMillan, L. and Bishop, G. (1995). Plenoptic modeling: An image-based rendering system. In *ACM SIGGRAPH 1995 Conference Proceedings*, pp. 39–46.

McMillan, L. and Gortler, S. (1999). Image-based rendering: A new interface between computer vision and computer graphics. *Computer Graphics*, 33(4):61–64.

Meehan, J. (1990). *Panoramic Photography*. Watson-Guptill.

Meer, P. and Georgescu, B. (2001). Edge detection with embedded confidence. *IEEE Transactions on Pattern Analysis and Machine Intelligence*, 23(12):1351–1365.

Meilă, M. and Shi, J. (2000). Learning segmentation by random walks. In *Advances in Neural Information Processing Systems*.

Meilă, M. and Shi, J. (2001). A random walks view of spectral segmentation. In *Workshop on Artificial Intelligence and Statistics*, pp. 177–182, Key West, FL.

Meltzer, J. and Soatto, S. (2008). Edge descriptors for robust wide-baseline correspondence. In *IEEE Computer Society Conference on Computer Vision and Pattern Recognition (CVPR 2008)*, Anchorage, AK.

Meltzer, T., Yanover, C., and Weiss, Y. (2005). Globally optimal solutions for energy minimization in stereo vision using reweighted belief propagation. In *Tenth International Conference on Computer Vision (ICCV 2005)*, pp. 428–435, Beijing, China.

Mémin, E. and Pérez, P. (2002). Hierarchical estimation and segmentation of dense motion fields. *International Journal of Computer Vision*, 44(2):129–155.

Menet, S., Saint-Marc, P., and Medioni, G. (1990a). Active contour models: overview, implementation and applications. In *IEEE International Conference on Systems, Man and Cybernetics*, pp. 194–199, Los Angeles.

Menet, S., Saint-Marc, P., and Medioni, G. (1990b). B-snakes: implementation and applications to stereo. In *Image Understanding Workshop*, pp. 720–726, Pittsburgh.

Merrell, P., Akbarzadeh, A., Wang, L., Mordohai, P., Frahm, J.-M., Yang, R., Nister, D., and Pollefeys, M. (2007). Real-time visibility-based fusion of depth maps. In *Eleventh International Conference on Computer Vision (ICCV 2007)*, Rio de Janeiro, Brazil.

Mertens, T., Kautz, J., and Reeth, F. V. (2007). Exposure fusion. In *Proceedings of Pacific Graphics 2007*, pp. 382–390.

Metaxas, D. and Terzopoulos, D. (2002). Dynamic deformation of solid primitives with constraints. *ACM Transactions on Graphics (Proc. SIGGRAPH 2002)*, 21(3):309–312.

Metropolis, N., Rosenbluth, A. W., Rosenbluth, M. N., Teller, A. H., and Teller, E. (1953). Equations of state calculations by fast computing machines. *Journal of Chemical Physics*, 21:1087–1091.

Meyer, C. D. (2000). *Matrix Analysis and Applied Linear Algebra*. Society for Industrial and Applied Mathematics, Philadephia.

Meyer, Y. (1993). *Wavelets: Algorithms and Applications*. Society for Industrial and Applied Mathematics, Philadephia.

Mikolajczyk, K. and Schmid, C. (2004). Scale & affine invariant interest point detectors. *International Journal of Computer Vision*, 60(1):63–86.

Mikolajczyk, K. and Schmid, C. (2005). A performance evaluation of local descriptors. *IEEE Transactions on Pattern Analysis and Machine Intelligence*, 27(10):1615–1630.

Mikolajczyk, K., Schmid, C., and Zisserman, A. (2004). Human detection based on a probabilistic assembly of robust part detectors. In *Eighth European Conference on Computer Vision (ECCV 2004)*, pp. 69–82, Prague.

Mikolajczyk, K., Tuytelaars, T., Schmid, C., Zisserman, A., Matas, J., Schaffalitzky, F., Kadir, T., and Van Gool, L. J. (2005). A comparison of affine region detectors. *International Journal of Computer Vision*, 65(1-2):43–72.

Milgram, D. L. (1975). Computer methods for creating photomosaics. *IEEE Transactions on Computers*, C-24(11):1113–1119.

Milgram, D. L. (1977). Adaptive techniques for photomosaicking. *IEEE Transactions on Computers*, C-26(11):1175–1180.

Miller, I., Campbell, M., Huttenlocher, D., Kline, F.-R., Nathan, A. *et al.* (2008). Team Cornell's Skynet: Robust perception and planning in an urban environment. *Journal of Field Robotics*, 25(8):493–527.

Mitiche, A. and Bouthemy, P. (1996). Computation and analysis of image motion: A synopsis of current problems and methods. *International Journal of Computer Vision*, 19(1):29–55.

Mitsunaga, T. and Nayar, S. K. (1999). Radiometric self calibration. In *IEEE Computer Society Conference on Computer Vision and Pattern Recognition (CVPR'99)*, pp. 374–380, Fort Collins.

Mittal, A. and Davis, L. S. (2003). M_2 tracker: A multi-view approach to segmenting and tracking people in a cluttered scene. *International Journal of Computer Vision*, 51(3):189–203.

Mičušík, B. and Košecká, J. (2009). Piecewise planar city 3D modeling from street view panoramic sequences. In *IEEE Computer Society Conference on Computer Vision and Pattern Recognition (CVPR 2009)*, Miami Beach, FL.

Mičušik, B., Wildenauer, H., and Košecká, J. (2008). Detection and matching of rectilinear structures. In *IEEE Computer Society Conference on Computer Vision and Pattern Recognition (CVPR 2008)*, Anchorage, AK.

Moeslund, T. B. and Granum, E. (2001). A survey of computer vision-based human motion capture. *Computer Vision and Image Understanding*, 81(3):231–268.

Moeslund, T. B., Hilton, A., and Krüger, V. (2006). A survey of advances in vision-based human motion capture and analysis. *Computer Vision and Image Understanding*, 104(2-3):90–126.

Moezzi, S., Katkere, A., Kuramura, D., and Jain, R. (1996). Reality modeling and visualization from multiple video sequences. *IEEE Computer Graphics and Applications*, 16(6):58–63.

Moghaddam, B. and Pentland, A. (1997). Probabilistic visual learning for object representation. *IEEE Transactions on Pattern Analysis and Machine Intelligence*, 19(7):696–710.

Moghaddam, B., Jebara, T., and Pentland, A. (2000). Bayesian face recognition. *Pattern Recognition*, 33(11):1771–1782.

Mohan, A., Papageorgiou, C., and Poggio, T. (2001). Example-based object detection in images by components. *IEEE Transactions on Pattern Analysis and Machine Intelligence*, 23(4):349–361.

Möller, K. D. (1988). *Optics*. University Science Books, Mill Valley, CA.

Montemerlo, M., Becker, J., Bhat, S., Dahlkamp, H., Dolgov, D. *et al.* (2008). Junior: The Stanford entry in the Urban Challenge. *Journal of Field Robotics*, 25(9):569–597.

Moon, P. and Spencer, D. E. (1981). *The Photic Field*. MIT Press, Cambridge, Massachusetts.

Moons, T., Van Gool, L., and Vergauwen, M. (2010). 3D reconstruction from multiple images. *Foundations and Trends in Computer Graphics and Computer Vision*, 4(4).

Moosmann, F., Nowak, E., and Jurie, F. (2008). Randomized clustering forests for image classification. *IEEE Transactions on Pattern Analysis and Machine Intelligence*, 30(9):1632–1646.

Moravec, H. (1977). Towards automatic visual obstacle avoidance. In *Fifth International Joint Conference on Artificial Intelligence (IJCAI'77)*, p. 584, Cambridge, Massachusetts.

Moravec, H. (1983). The Stanford cart and the CMU rover. *Proceedings of the IEEE*, 71(7):872–884.

Moreno-Noguer, F., Lepetit, V., and Fua, P. (2007). Accurate non-iterative $O(n)$ solution to the PnP problem. In *Eleventh International Conference on Computer Vision (ICCV 2007)*, Rio de Janeiro, Brazil.

Mori, G. (2005). Guiding model search using segmentation. In *Tenth International Conference on Computer Vision (ICCV 2005)*, pp. 1417–1423, Beijing, China.

Mori, G., Ren, X., Efros, A., and Malik, J. (2004). Recovering human body configurations: Combining segmentation and recognition. In *IEEE Computer Society Conference on Computer Vision and Pattern Recognition (CVPR'2004)*, pp. 326–333, Washington, DC.

Mori, M. (1970). The uncanny valley. *Energy*, 7(4):33–35. http://www.androidscience.com/theuncannyvalley/proceedings2005/uncannyvalley.html.

Morimoto, C. and Chellappa, R. (1997). Fast 3D stabilization and mosaic construction. In *IEEE Computer Society Conference on Computer Vision and Pattern Recognition (CVPR'97)*, pp. 660–665, San Juan, Puerto Rico.

Morita, T. and Kanade, T. (1997). A sequential factorization method for recovering shape and motion from image streams. *IEEE Transactions on Pattern Analysis and Machine Intelligence*, 19(8):858–867.

Morris, D. D. and Kanade, T. (1998). A unified factorization algorithm for points, line segments and planes with uncertainty models. In *Sixth International Conference on Computer Vision (ICCV'98)*, pp. 696–702, Bombay.

Morrone, M. and Burr, D. (1988). Feature detection in human vision: A phase dependent energy model. *Proceedings of the Royal Society of London B*, 235:221–245.

Mortensen, E. N. (1999). Vision-assisted image editing. *Computer Graphics*, 33(4):55–57.

Mortensen, E. N. and Barrett, W. A. (1995). Intelligent scissors for image composition. In *ACM SIGGRAPH 1995 Conference Proceedings*, pp. 191–198.

Mortensen, E. N. and Barrett, W. A. (1998). Interactive segmentation with intelligent scissors. *Graphical Models and Image Processing*, 60(5):349–384.

Mortensen, E. N. and Barrett, W. A. (1999). Toboggan-based intelligent scissors with a four parameter edge model. In *IEEE Computer Society Conference on Computer Vision and Pattern Recognition (CVPR'99)*, pp. 452–458, Fort Collins.

Mueller, P., Zeng, G., Wonka, P., and Van Gool, L. (2007). Image-based procedural modeling of facades. *ACM Transactions on Graphics*, 26(3).

Mühlich, M. and Mester, R. (1998). The role of total least squares in motion analysis. In *Fifth European Conference on Computer Vision (ECCV'98)*, pp. 305–321, Freiburg, Germany.

Muja, M. and Lowe, D. G. (2009). Fast approximate nearest neighbors with automatic algorithm configuration. In *International Conference on Computer Vision Theory and Applications (VISAPP)*, Lisbon, Portugal.

Mumford, D. and Shah, J. (1989). Optimal approximations by piecewise smooth functions and variational problems. *Comm. Pure Appl. Math.*, XLII(5):577–685.

Munder, S. and Gavrila, D. M. (2006). An experimental study on pedestrian classification. *IEEE Transactions on Pattern Analysis and Machine Intelligence*, 28(11):1863–1868.

Mundy, J. L. (2006). Object recognition in the geometric era: A retrospective. In Ponce, J., Hebert, M., Schmid, C., and Zisserman, A. (eds), *Toward Category-Level Object Recognition*, pp. 3–28, Springer, New York.

Mundy, J. L. and Zisserman, A. (eds). (1992). *Geometric Invariance in Computer Vision*. MIT Press, Cambridge, Massachusetts.

Murase, H. and Nayar, S. K. (1995). Visual learning and recognition of 3-D objects from appearance. *International Journal of Computer Vision*, 14(1):5–24.

Murphy, E. P. (2005). *A Testing Procedure to Characterize Color and Spatial Quality of Digital Cameras Used to Image Cultural Heritage*. Master's thesis, Rochester Institute of Technology.

Murphy, K., Torralba, A., and Freeman, W. T. (2003). Using the forest to see the trees: A graphical model relating features, objects, and scenes. In *Advances in Neural Information Processing Systems*.

Murphy-Chutorian, E. and Trivedi, M. M. (2009). Head pose estimation in computer vision: A survey. *IEEE Transactions on Pattern Analysis and Machine Intelligence*, 31(4):607–626.

Murray, R. M., Li, Z. X., and Sastry, S. S. (1994). *A Mathematical Introduction to Robotic Manipulation*. CRC Press.

Mutch, J. and Lowe, D. G. (2008). Object class recognition and localization using sparse features with limited receptive fields. *International Journal of Computer Vision*, 80(1):45–57.

Nagel, H. H. (1986). Image sequences—ten (octal) years—from phenomenology towards a theoretical foundation. In *Eighth International Conference on Pattern Recognition (ICPR'86)*, pp. 1174–1185, Paris.

Nagel, H.-H. and Enkelmann, W. (1986). An investigation of smoothness constraints for the estimation of displacement vector fields from image sequences. *IEEE Transactions on Pattern Analysis and Machine Intelligence*, PAMI-8(5):565–593.

Nakamura, Y., Matsuura, T., Satoh, K., and Ohta, Y. (1996). Occlusion detectable stereo—occlusion patterns in camera matrix. In *IEEE Computer Society Conference on Computer Vision and Pattern Recognition (CVPR'96)*, pp. 371–378, San Francisco.

Nakao, T., Kashitani, A., and Kaneyoshi, A. (1998). Scanning a document with a small camera attached to a mouse. In *IEEE Workshop on Applications of Computer Vision (WACV'98)*, pp. 63–68, Princeton.

Nalwa, V. S. (1987). Edge-detector resolution improvement by image interpolation. *IEEE Transactions on Pattern Analysis and Machine Intelligence*, PAMI-9(3):446–451.

Nalwa, V. S. (1993). *A Guided Tour of Computer Vision*. Addison-Wesley, Reading, MA.

Nalwa, V. S. and Binford, T. O. (1986). On detecting edges. *IEEE Transactions on Pattern Analysis and Machine Intelligence*, PAMI-8(6):699–714.

Narasimhan, S. G. and Nayar, S. K. (2005). Enhancing resolution along multiple imaging dimensions using assorted pixels. *IEEE Transactions on Pattern Analysis and Machine Intelligence*, 27(4):518–530.

Narayanan, P., Rander, P., and Kanade, T. (1998). Constructing virtual worlds using dense stereo. In *Sixth International Conference on Computer Vision (ICCV'98)*, pp. 3–10, Bombay.

Nayar, S., Watanabe, M., and Noguchi, M. (1995). Real-time focus range sensor. In *Fifth International Conference on Computer Vision (ICCV'95)*, pp. 995–1001, Cambridge, Massachusetts.

Nayar, S. K. (2006). Computational cameras: Redefining the image. *Computer*, 39(8):30–38.

Nayar, S. K. and Branzoi, V. (2003). Adaptive dynamic range imaging: Optical control of pixel exposures over space and time. In *Ninth International Conference on Computer Vision (ICCV 2003)*, pp. 1168–1175, Nice, France.

Nayar, S. K. and Mitsunaga, T. (2000). High dynamic range imaging: Spatially varying pixel exposures. In *IEEE Computer Society Conference on Computer Vision and Pattern Recognition (CVPR'2000)*, pp. 472–479, Hilton Head Island.

Nayar, S. K. and Nakagawa, Y. (1994). Shape from focus. *IEEE Transactions on Pattern Analysis and Machine Intelligence*, 16(8):824–831.

Nayar, S. K., Ikeuchi, K., and Kanade, T. (1991). Shape from interreflections. *International Journal of Computer Vision*, 6(3):173–195.

Nayar, S. K., Watanabe, M., and Noguchi, M. (1996). Real-time focus range sensor. *IEEE Transactions on Pattern Analysis and Machine Intelligence*, 18(12):1186–1198.

Negahdaripour, S. (1998). Revised definition of optical flow: Integration of radiometric and geometric cues for dynamic scene analysis. *IEEE Transactions on Pattern Analysis and Machine Intelligence*, 20(9):961–979.

Nehab, D., Rusinkiewicz, S., Davis, J., and Ramamoorthi, R. (2005). Efficiently combining positions and normals for precise 3d geometry. *ACM Transactions on Graphics (Proc. SIGGRAPH 2005)*, 24(3):536–543.

Nene, S. and Nayar, S. K. (1997). A simple algorithm for nearest neighbor search in high dimensions. *IEEE Transactions on Pattern Analysis and Machine Intelligence*, 19(9):989–1003.

Nene, S. A., Nayar, S. K., and Murase, H. (1996). *Columbia Object Image Library (COIL-100)*. Technical Report CUCS-006-96, Department of Computer Science, Columbia University.

Netravali, A. and Robbins, J. (1979). Motion-compensated television coding: Part 1. *Bell System Tech.*, 58(3):631–670.

Nevatia, R. (1977). A color edge detector and its use in scene segmentation. *IEEE Transactions on Systems, Man, and Cybernetics*, SMC-7(11):820–826.

Nevatia, R. and Binford, T. (1977). Description and recognition of curved objects. *Artificial Intelligence*, 8:77–98.

Ng, A. Y., Jordan, M. I., and Weiss, Y. (2001). On spectral clustering: Analysis and an algorithm. In *Advances in Neural Information Processing Systems*, pp. 849–854.

Ng, R. (2005). Fourier slice photography. *ACM Transactions on Graphics (Proc. SIGGRAPH 2005)*, 24(3):735–744.

Ng, R., Levoy, M., Bréedif, M., Duval, G., Horowitz, M., and Hanrahan, P. (2005). *Light Field Photography with a Hand-held Plenoptic Camera*. Technical Report CSTR 2005-02, Stanford University.

Nielsen, M., Florack, L. M. J., and Deriche, R. (1997). Regularization, scale-space, and edge-detection filters. *Journal of Mathematical Imaging and Vision*, 7(4):291–307.

Nielson, G. M. (1993). Scattered data modeling. *IEEE Computer Graphics and Applications*, 13(1):60–70.

Nir, T., Bruckstein, A. M., and Kimmel, R. (2008). Over-parameterized variational optical flow. *International Journal of Computer Vision*, 76(2):205–216.

Nishihara, H. K. (1984). Practical real-time imaging stereo matcher. *OptEng*, 23(5):536–545.

Nistér, D. (2003). Preemptive RANSAC for live structure and motion estimation. In *Ninth International Conference on Computer Vision (ICCV 2003)*, pp. 199–206, Nice, France.

Nistér, D. (2004). An efficient solution to the five-point relative pose problem. *IEEE Transactions on Pattern Analysis and Machine Intelligence*, 26(6):756–777.

Nistér, D. and Stewénius, H. (2006). Scalable recognition with a vocabulary tree. In *IEEE Computer Society Conference on Computer Vision and Pattern Recognition (CVPR'2006)*, pp. 2161–2168, New York City, NY.

Nistér, D. and Stewénius, H. (2008). Linear time maximally stable extremal regions. In *Tenth European Conference on Computer Vision (ECCV 2008)*, pp. 183–196, Marseilles.

Nistér, D., Naroditsky, O., and Bergen, J. (2006). Visual odometry for ground vehicle applications. *Journal of Field Robotics*, 23(1):3–20.

Noborio, H., Fukada, S., and Arimoto, S. (1988). Construction of the octree approximating three-dimensional objects by using multiple views. *IEEE Transactions on Pattern Analysis and Machine Intelligence*, PAMI-10(6):769–782.

Nocedal, J. and Wright, S. J. (2006). *Numerical Optimization*. Springer, New York, second edition.

Nomura, Y., Zhang, L., and Nayar, S. K. (2007). Scene collages and flexible camera arrays. In *Eurographics Symposium on Rendering*.

Nordström, N. (1990). Biased anisotropic diffusion: A unified regularization and diffusion approach to edge detection. *Image and Vision Computing*, 8(4):318–327.

Nowak, E., Jurie, F., and Triggs, B. (2006). Sampling strategies for bag-of-features image classification. In *Ninth European Conference on Computer Vision (ECCV 2006)*, pp. 490–503.

Obdržálek, S. and Matas, J. (2006). Object recognition using local affine frames on maximally stable extremal regions. In Ponce, J., Hebert, M., Schmid, C., and Zisserman, A. (eds), *Toward Category-Level Object Recognition*, pp. 83–104, Springer, New York.

Oh, B. M., Chen, M., Dorsey, J., and Durand, F. (2001). Image-based modeling and photo editing. In *ACM SIGGRAPH 2001 Conference Proceedings*, pp. 433–442.

Ohlander, R., Price, K., and Reddy, D. R. (1978). Picture segmentation using a recursive region splitting method. *Computer Graphics and Image Processing*, 8(3):313–333.

Ohta, Y. and Kanade, T. (1985). Stereo by intra- and inter-scanline search using dynamic programming. *IEEE Transactions on Pattern Analysis and Machine Intelligence*, PAMI-7(2):139–154.

Ohtake, Y., Belyaev, A., Alexa, M., Turk, G., and Seidel, H.-P. (2003). Multi-level partition of unity implicits. *ACM Transactions on Graphics (Proc. SIGGRAPH 2003)*, 22(3):463–470.

Okutomi, M. and Kanade, T. (1992). A locally adaptive window for signal matching. *International Journal of Computer Vision*, 7(2):143–162.

Okutomi, M. and Kanade, T. (1993). A multiple baseline stereo. *IEEE Transactions on Pattern Analysis and Machine Intelligence*, 15(4):353–363.

Okutomi, M. and Kanade, T. (1994). A stereo matching algorithm with an adaptive window: Theory and experiment. *IEEE Transactions on Pattern Analysis and Machine Intelligence*, 16(9):920–932.

Oliensis, J. (2005). The least-squares error for structure from infinitesimal motion. *International Journal of Computer Vision*, 61(3):259–299.

Oliensis, J. and Hartley, R. (2007). Iterative extensions of the Sturm/Triggs algorithm: Convergence and nonconvergence. *IEEE Transactions on Pattern Analysis and Machine Intelligence*, 29(12):2217–2233.

Oliva, A. and Torralba, A. (2001). Modeling the shape of the scene: a holistic representation of the spatial envelope. *International Journal of Computer Vision*, 42(3):145–175.

Oliva, A. and Torralba, A. (2007). The role of context in object recognition. *Trends in Cognitive Sciences*, 11(12):520–527.

Olsson, C., Eriksson, A. P., and Kahl, F. (2008). Improved spectral relaxation methods for binary quadratic optimization problems. *Computer Vision and Image Understanding*, 112(1):3–13.

Omer, I. and Werman, M. (2004). Color lines: Image specific color representation. In *IEEE Computer Society Conference on Computer Vision and Pattern Recognition (CVPR'2004)*, pp. 946–953, Washington, DC.

Ong, E.-J., Micilotta, A. S., Bowden, R., and Hilton, A. (2006). Viewpoint invariant exemplar-based 3D human tracking. *Computer Vision and Image Understanding*, 104(2-3):178–189.

Opelt, A., Pinz, A., and Zisserman, A. (2006). A boundary-fragment-model for object detection. In *Ninth European Conference on Computer Vision (ECCV 2006)*, pp. 575–588.

Opelt, A., Pinz, A., Fussenegger, M., and Auer, P. (2006). Generic object recognition with boosting. *IEEE Transactions on Pattern Analysis and Machine Intelligence*, 28(3):614–641.

OpenGL-ARB. (1997). *OpenGL Reference Manual: The Official Reference Document to OpenGL, Version 1.1*. Addison-Wesley, Reading, MA, 2nd edition.

Oppenheim, A. V. and Schafer, A. S. (1996). *Signals and Systems*. Prentice Hall, Englewood Cliffs, New Jersey, 2nd edition.

Oppenheim, A. V., Schafer, R. W., and Buck, J. R. (1999). *Discrete-Time Signal Processing*. Prentice Hall, Englewood Cliffs, New Jersey, 2nd edition.

Oren, M. and Nayar, S. (1997). A theory of specular surface geometry. *International Journal of Computer Vision*, 24(2):105–124.

O'Rourke, J. and Badler, N. I. (1980). Model-based image analysis of human motion using constraint propagation. *IEEE Transactions on Pattern Analysis and Machine Intelligence*, 2(6):522–536.

Osher, S. and Paragios, N. (eds). (2003). *Geometric Level Set Methods in Imaging, Vision, and Graphics*, Springer.

Osuna, E., Freund, R., and Girosi, F. (1997). Training support vector machines: An application to face detection. In *IEEE Computer Society Conference on Computer Vision and Pattern Recognition (CVPR'97)*, pp. 130–136, San Juan, Puerto Rico.

O'Toole, A. J., Jiang, F., Roark, D., and Abdi, H. (2006). Predicting human face recognition. In Zhao, W.-Y. and Chellappa, R. (eds), *Face Processing: Advanced Methods and Models*, Elsevier.

O'Toole, A. J., Phillips, P. J., Jiang, F., Ayyad, J., Pénard, N., and Abdi, H. (2009). Face recognition algorithms surpass humans matching faces over changes in illumination. *IEEE Transactions on Pattern Analysis and Machine Intelligence*, 29(9):1642–1646.

Ott, M., Lewis, J. P., and Cox, I. J. (1993). Teleconferencing eye contact using a virtual camera. In *INTERACT'93 and CHI'93 conference companion on Human factors in computing systems*, pp. 109–110, Amsterdam.

Otte, M. and Nagel, H.-H. (1994). Optical flow estimation: advances and comparisons. In *Third European Conference on Computer Vision (ECCV'94)*, pp. 51–60, Stockholm, Sweden.

Oztireli, C., Guennebaud, G., and Gross, M. (2008). Feature preserving point set surfaces. *Computer Graphics Forum*, 28(2):493–501.

Özuysal, M., Calonder, M., Lepetit, V., and Fua, P. (2010). Fast keypoint recognition using random ferns. *IEEE Transactions on Pattern Analysis and Machine Intelligence*, 32(3).

Paglieroni, D. W. (1992). Distance transforms: Properties and machine vision applications. *Graphical Models and Image Processing*, 54(1):56–74.

Pal, C., Szeliski, R., Uyttendaele, M., and Jojic, N. (2004). Probability models for high dynamic range imaging. In *IEEE Computer Society Conference on Computer Vision and Pattern Recognition (CVPR'2004)*, pp. 173–180, Washington, DC.

Palmer, S. E. (1999). *Vision Science: Photons to Phenomenology*. The MIT Press, Cambridge, Massachusetts.

Pankanti, S., Bolle, R. M., and Jain, A. K. (2000). Biometrics: The future of identification. *Computer*, 21(2):46–49.

Papageorgiou, C. and Poggio, T. (2000). A trainable system for object detection. *International Journal of Computer Vision*, 38(1):15–33.

Papandreou, G. and Maragos, P. (2008). Adaptive and constrained algorithms for inverse compositional active appearance model fitting. In *IEEE Computer Society Conference on Computer Vision and Pattern Recognition (CVPR 2008)*, Anchorage, AK.

Papenberg, N., Bruhn, A., Brox, T., Didas, S., and Weickert, J. (2006). Highly accurate optic flow computation with theoretically justified warping. *International Journal of Computer Vision*, 67(2):141–158.

Papert, S. (1966). *The Summer Vision Project*. Technical Report AIM-100, Artificial Intelligence Group, Massachusetts Institute of Technology. http://hdl.handle.net/1721.1/6125.

Paragios, N. and Deriche, R. (2000). Geodesic active contours and level sets for the detection and tracking of moving objects. *IEEE Transactions on Pattern Analysis and Machine Intelligence*, 22(3):266–280.

Paragios, N. and Sgallari, F. (2009). Special issue on scale space and variational methods in computer vision. *International Journal of Computer Vision*, 84(2).

Paragios, N., Faugeras, O. D., Chan, T., and Schnörr, C. (eds). (2005). *Third International Workshop on Variational, Geometric, and Level Set Methods in Computer Vision (VLSM 2005)*, Springer.

Paris, S. and Durand, F. (2006). A fast approximation of the bilateral filter using a signal processing approach. In *Ninth European Conference on Computer Vision (ECCV 2006)*, pp. 568–580.

Paris, S. and Durand, F. (2007). A topological approach to hierarchical segmentation using mean shift. In *IEEE Computer Society Conference on Computer Vision and Pattern Recognition (CVPR 2007)*, Minneapolis, MN.

Paris, S., Kornprobst, P., Tumblin, J., and Durand, F. (2008). Bilateral filtering: Theory and applications. *Foundations and Trends in Computer Graphics and Computer Vision*, 4(1):1–73.

Park, M., Brocklehurst, K., Collins, R. T., and Liu, Y. (2009). Deformed lattice detection in real-world images using mean-shift belief propagation. *IEEE Transactions on Pattern Analysis and Machine Intelligence*, 31(10):1804–1816.

Park, S. C., Park, M. K., and Kang, M. G. (2003). Super-resolution image reconstruction: A technical overview. *IEEE Signal Processing Magazine*, 20:21–36.

Parke, F. I. and Waters, K. (1996). *Computer Facial Animation*. A K Peters, Wellesley, Massachusetts.

Parker, J. A., Kenyon, R. V., and Troxel, D. E. (1983). Comparison of interpolating methods for image resampling. *IEEE Transactions on Medical Imaging*, MI-2(1):31–39.

Pattanaik, S. N., Ferwerda, J. A., Fairchild, M. D., and Greenberg, D. P. (1998). A multiscale model of adaptation and spatial vision for realistic image display. In *ACM SIGGRAPH 1998 Conference Proceedings*, pp. 287–298, Orlando.

Pauly, M., Keiser, R., Kobbelt, L. P., and Gross, M. (2003). Shape modeling with point-sampled geometry. *ACM Transactions on Graphics (Proc. SIGGRAPH 2003)*, 21(3):641–650.

Pavlidis, T. (1977). *Structural Pattern Recognition*. Springer-Verlag, Berlin; New York.

Pavlidis, T. and Liow, Y.-T. (1990). Integrating region growing and edge detection. *IEEE Transactions on Pattern Analysis and Machine Intelligence*, 12(3):225–233.

Pavlović, V., Sharma, R., and Huang, T. S. (1997). Visual interpretation of hand gestures for human-computer interaction: A review. *IEEE Transactions on Pattern Analysis and Machine Intelligence*, 19(7):677–695.

Pearl, J. (1988). *Probabilistic reasoning in intelligent systems: networks of plausible inference*. Morgan Kaufmann Publishers, Los Altos.

Peleg, R., Ben-Ezra, M., and Pritch, Y. (2001). Omnistereo: Panoramic stereo imaging. *IEEE Transactions on Pattern Analysis and Machine Intelligence*, 23(3):279–290.

Peleg, S. (1981). Elimination of seams from photomosaics. *Computer Vision, Graphics, and Image Processing*, 16(1):1206–1210.

Peleg, S. and Herman, J. (1997). Panoramic mosaics by manifold projection. In *IEEE Computer Society Conference on Computer Vision and Pattern Recognition (CVPR'97)*, pp. 338–343, San Juan, Puerto Rico.

Peleg, S. and Rav-Acha, A. (2006). Lucas-Kanade without iterative warping. In *International Conference on Image Processing (ICIP-2006)*, pp. 1097–1100, Atlanta.

Peleg, S., Rousso, B., Rav-Acha, A., and Zomet, A. (2000). Mosaicing on adaptive manifolds. *IEEE Transactions on Pattern Analysis and Machine Intelligence*, 22(10):1144–1154.

Penev, P. and Atick, J. (1996). Local feature analysis: A general statistical theory for object representation. *Network Computation and Neural Systems*, 7:477–500.

Pentland, A. P. (1984). Local shading analysis. *IEEE Transactions on Pattern Analysis and Machine Intelligence*, PAMI-6(2):170–179.

Pentland, A. P. (1986). Perceptual organization and the representation of natural form. *Artificial Intelligence*, 28(3):293–331.

Pentland, A. P. (1987). A new sense for depth of field. *IEEE Transactions on Pattern Analysis and Machine Intelligence*, PAMI-9(4):523–531.

Pentland, A. P. (1994). Interpolation using wavelet bases. *IEEE Transactions on Pattern Analysis and Machine Intelligence*, 16(4):410–414.

Pérez, P., Blake, A., and Gangnet, M. (2001). JetStream: Probabilistic contour extraction with particles. In *Eighth International Conference on Computer Vision (ICCV 2001)*, pp. 524–531, Vancouver, Canada.

Pérez, P., Gangnet, M., and Blake, A. (2003). Poisson image editing. *ACM Transactions on Graphics (Proc. SIGGRAPH 2003)*, 22(3):313–318.

Perona, P. (1995). Deformable kernels for early vision. *IEEE Transactions on Pattern Analysis and Machine Intelligence*, 17(5):488–499.

Perona, P. and Malik, J. (1990a). Detecting and localizing edges composed of steps, peaks and roofs. In *Third International Conference on Computer Vision (ICCV'90)*, pp. 52–57, Osaka, Japan.

Perona, P. and Malik, J. (1990b). Scale space and edge detection using anisotropic diffusion. *IEEE Transactions on Pattern Analysis and Machine Intelligence*, 12(7):629–639.

Peters, J. and Reif, U. (2008). *Subdivision Surfaces*. Springer.

Petschnigg, G., Agrawala, M., Hoppe, H., Szeliski, R., Cohen, M., and Toyama, K. (2004). Digital photography with flash and no-flash image pairs. *ACM Transactions on Graphics (Proc. SIGGRAPH 2004)*, 23(3):664–672.

Pfister, H., Zwicker, M., van Baar, J., and Gross, M. (2000). Surfels: Surface elements as rendering primitives. In *ACM SIGGRAPH 2000 Conference Proceedings*, pp. 335–342.

Pflugfelder, R. (2008). *Self-calibrating Cameras in Video Surveillance*. Ph.D. thesis, Graz University of Technology.

Philbin, J. and Zisserman, A. (2008). Object mining using a matching graph on very large image collections. In *Indian Conference on Computer Vision, Graphics and Image Processing*, Bhubaneswar, India.

Philbin, J., Chum, O., Isard, M., Sivic, J., and Zisserman, A. (2007). Object retrieval with large vocabularies and fast spatial matching. In *IEEE Computer Society Conference on Computer Vision and Pattern Recognition (CVPR 2007)*, Minneapolis, MN.

Philbin, J., Chum, O., Sivic, J., Isard, M., and Zisserman, A. (2008). Lost in quantization: Improving particular object retrieval in large scale image databases. In *IEEE Computer Society Conference on Computer Vision and Pattern Recognition (CVPR 2008)*, Anchorage, AK.

Phillips, P. J., Moon, H., Rizvi, S. A., and Rauss, P. J. (2000). The FERET evaluation methodology for face recognition algorithms. *IEEE Transactions on Pattern Analysis and Machine Intelligence*, 22(10):1090–1104.

Phillips, P. J., Scruggs, W. T., O'Toole, A. J., Flynn, P. J., Bowyer, K. W. *et al.* (2010). FRVT 2006 and ICE 2006 large-scale experimental results. *IEEE Transactions on Pattern Analysis and Machine Intelligence*, 32(5):831–846.

Phong, B. T. (1975). Illumination for computer generated pictures. *Communications of the ACM*, 18(6):311–317.

Pickup, L. C. (2007). *Machine Learning in Multi-frame Image Super-resolution*. Ph.D. thesis, University of Oxford.

Pickup, L. C. and Zisserman, A. (2009). Automatic retrieval of visual continuity errors in movies. In *ACM International Conference on Image and Video Retrieval*, Santorini, Greece.

Pickup, L. C., Capel, D. P., Roberts, S. J., and Zisserman, A. (2007). Overcoming registration uncertainty in image super-resolution: Maximize or marginalize? *EURASIP Journal on Advances in Signal Processing*, 2010(Article ID 23565).

Pickup, L. C., Capel, D. P., Roberts, S. J., and Zisserman, A. (2009). Bayesian methods for image super-resolution. *The Computer Journal*, 52.

Pighin, F., Szeliski, R., and Salesin, D. H. (2002). Modeling and animating realistic faces from images. *International Journal of Computer Vision*, 50(2):143–169.

Pighin, F., Hecker, J., Lischinski, D., Salesin, D. H., and Szeliski, R. (1998). Synthesizing realistic facial expressions from photographs. In *ACM SIGGRAPH 1998 Conference Proceedings*, pp. 75–84, Orlando.

Pilet, J., Lepetit, V., and Fua, P. (2008). Fast non-rigid surface detection, registration, and realistic augmentation. *International Journal of Computer Vision*, 76(2).

Pinz, A. (2005). Object categorization. *Foundations and Trends in Computer Graphics and Computer Vision*, 1(4):255–353.

Pizer, S. M., Amburn, E. P., Austin, J. D., Cromartie, R., Geselowitz, A. *et al.* (1987). Adaptive histogram equalization and its variations. *Computer Vision, Graphics, and Image Processing*, 39(3):355–368.

Platel, B., Balmachnova, E., Florack, L., and ter Haar Romeny, B. (2006). Top-points as interest points for image matching. In *Ninth European Conference on Computer Vision (ECCV 2006)*, pp. 418–429.

Platt, J. C. (2000). Optimal filtering for patterned displays. *IEEE Signal Processing Letters*, 7(7):179–180.

Pock, T., Unger, M., Cremers, D., and Bischof, H. (2008). Fast and exact solution of total variation models on the GPU. In *CVPR 2008 Workshop on Visual Computer Vision on GPUs (CVGPU)*, Anchorage, AK.

Poelman, C. J. and Kanade, T. (1997). A paraperspective factorization method for shape and motion recovery. *IEEE Transactions on Pattern Analysis and Machine Intelligence*, 19(3):206–218.

Poggio, T. and Koch, C. (1985). Ill-posed problems in early vision: from computational theory to analogue networks. *Proceedings of the Royal Society of London*, B 226:303–323.

Poggio, T., Gamble, E., and Little, J. (1988). Parallel integration of vision modules. *Science*, 242(4877):436–440.

Poggio, T., Torre, V., and Koch, C. (1985). Computational vision and regularization theory. *Nature*, 317(6035):314–319.

Poggio, T., Little, J., Gamble, E., Gillet, W., Geiger, D. *et al.* (1988). The MIT vision machine. In *Image Understanding Workshop*, pp. 177–198, Boston.

Polana, R. and Nelson, R. C. (1997). Detection and recognition of periodic, nonrigid motion. *International Journal of Computer Vision*, 23(3):261–282.

Pollard, S. B., Mayhew, J. E. W., and Frisby, J. P. (1985). PMF: A stereo correspondence algorithm using a disparity gradient limit. *Perception*, 14:449–470.

Pollefeys, M. and Van Gool, L. (2002). From images to 3D models. *Communications of the ACM*, 45(7):50–55.

Pollefeys, M., Nistér, D., Frahm, J.-M., Akbarzadeh, A., Mordohai, P. *et al.* (2008). Detailed real-time urban 3D reconstruction from video. *International Journal of Computer Vision*, 78(2-3):143–167.

Ponce, J., Hebert, M., Schmid, C., and Zisserman, A. (eds). (2006). *Toward Category-Level Object Recognition*, Springer, New York.

Ponce, J., Berg, T., Everingham, M., Forsyth, D., Hebert, M. *et al.* (2006). Dataset issues in object recognition. In Ponce, J., Hebert, M., Schmid, C., and Zisserman, A. (eds), *Toward Category-Level Object Recognition*, pp. 29–48, Springer, New York.

Pons, J.-P., Keriven, R., and Faugeras, O. (2005). Modelling dynamic scenes by registering multi-view image sequences. In *IEEE Computer Society Conference on Computer Vision and Pattern Recognition (CVPR'2005)*, pp. 822–827, San Diego, CA.

Pons, J.-P., Keriven, R., and Faugeras, O. (2007). Multi-view stereo reconstruction and scene flow estimation with a global image-based matching score. *International Journal of Computer Vision*, 72(2):179–193.

Porter, T. and Duff, T. (1984). Compositing digital images. *Computer Graphics (SIGGRAPH '84)*, 18(3):253–259.

Portilla, J. and Simoncelli, E. P. (2000). A parametric texture model based on joint statistics of complex wavelet coefficients. *International Journal of Computer Vision*, 40(1):49–71.

Portilla, J., Strela, V., Wainwright, M., and Simoncelli, E. P. (2003). Image denoising using scale mixtures of Gaussians in the wavelet domain. *IEEE Transactions on Image Processing*, 12(11):1338–1351.

Potetz, B. and Lee, T. S. (2008). Efficient belief propagation for higher-order cliques using linear constraint nodes. *Computer Vision and Image Understanding*, 112(1):39–54.

Potmesil, M. (1987). Generating octree models of 3D objects from their silhouettes in a sequence of images. *Computer Vision, Graphics, and Image Processing*, 40:1–29.

Pratt, W. K. (2007). *Digital Image Processing*. Wiley-Interscience, Hoboken, NJ, 4th edition.

Prazdny, K. (1985). Detection of binocular disparities. *Biological Cybernetics*, 52:93–99.

Pritchett, P. and Zisserman, A. (1998). Wide baseline stereo matching. In *Sixth International Conference on Computer Vision (ICCV'98)*, pp. 754–760, Bombay.

Proesmans, M., Van Gool, L., and Defoort, F. (1998). Reading between the lines – a method for extracting dynamic 3D with texture. In *Sixth International Conference on Computer Vision (ICCV'98)*, pp. 1081–1086, Bombay.

Protter, M. and Elad, M. (2009). Super resolution with probabilistic motion estimation. *IEEE Transactions on Image Processing*, 18(8):1899–1904.

Pullen, K. and Bregler, C. (2002). Motion capture assisted animation: texturing and synthesis. *ACM Transactions on Graphics*, 21(3):501–508.

Pulli, K. (1999). Multiview registration for large data sets. In *Second International Conference on 3D Digital Imaging and Modeling (3DIM'99)*, pp. 160–168, Ottawa, Canada.

Pulli, K., Abi-Rached, H., Duchamp, T., Shapiro, L., and Stuetzle, W. (1998). Acquisition and visualization of colored 3D objects. In *International Conference on Pattern Recognition (ICPR'98)*, pp. 11–15.

Quack, T., Leibe, B., and Van Gool, L. (2008). World-scale mining of objects and events from community photo collections. In *Conference on Image and Video Retrieval*, pp. 47–56, Niagara Falls.

Quam, L. H. (1984). Hierarchical warp stereo. In *Image Understanding Workshop*, pp. 149–155, New Orleans.

Quan, L. and Lan, Z. (1999). Linear N-point camera pose determination. *IEEE Transactions on Pattern Analysis and Machine Intelligence*, 21(8):774–780.

Quan, L. and Mohr, R. (1989). Determining perspective structures using hierarchical Hough transform. *Pattern Recognition Letters*, 9(4):279–286.

Rabinovich, A., Vedaldi, A., Galleguillos, C., Wiewiora, E., and Belongie, S. (2007). Objects in context. In *Eleventh International Conference on Computer Vision (ICCV 2007)*, Rio de Janeiro, Brazil.

Rademacher, P. and Bishop, G. (1998). Multiple-center-of-projection images. In *ACM SIGGRAPH 1998 Conference Proceedings*, pp. 199–206, Orlando.

Raginsky, M. and Lazebnik, S. (2009). Locality-sensitive binary codes from shift-invariant kernels. In *Advances in Neural Information Processing Systems*.

Raman, S. and Chaudhuri, S. (2007). A matte-less, variational approach to automatic scene compositing. In *Eleventh International Conference on Computer Vision (ICCV 2007)*, Rio de Janeiro, Brazil.

Raman, S. and Chaudhuri, S. (2009). Bilateral filter based compositing for variable exposure photography. In *Proceedings of Eurographics 2009*.

Ramanan, D. and Baker, S. (2009). Local distance functions: A taxonomy, new algorithms, and an evaluation. In *Twelfth International Conference on Computer Vision (ICCV 2009)*, Kyoto, Japan.

Ramanan, D., Forsyth, D., and Zisserman, A. (2005). Strike a pose: Tracking people by finding stylized poses. In *IEEE Computer Society Conference on Computer Vision and Pattern Recognition (CVPR'2005)*, pp. 271–278, San Diego, CA.

Ramanarayanan, G. and Bala, K. (2007). Constrained texture synthesis via energy minimization. *IEEE Transactions on Visualization and Computer Graphics*, 13(1):167–178.

Ramer, U. (1972). An iterative procedure for the polygonal approximation of plane curves. *Computer Graphics and Image Processing*, 1(3):244–256.

Ramnath, K., Koterba, S., Xiao, J., Hu, C., Matthews, I., Baker, S., Cohn, J., and Kanade, T. (2008). Multi-view AAM fitting and construction. *International Journal of Computer Vision*, 76(2):183–204.

Raskar, R. and Tumblin, J. (2010). *Computational Photography: Mastering New Techniques for Lenses, Lighting, and Sensors*. A K Peters, Wellesley, Massachusetts.

Raskar, R., Tan, K.-H., Feris, R., Yu, J., and Turk, M. (2004). Non-photorealistic camera: Depth edge detection and stylized rendering using multi-flash imaging. *ACM Transactions on Graphics*, 23(3):679–688.

Rav-Acha, A., Kohli, P., Fitzgibbon, A., and Rother, C. (2008). Unwrap mosaics: A new representation for video editing. *ACM Transactions on Graphics*, 27(3).

Rav-Acha, A., Pritch, Y., Lischinski, D., and Peleg, S. (2005). Dynamosaics: Video mosaics with non-chronological time. In *IEEE Computer Society Conference on Computer Vision and Pattern Recognition (CVPR'2005)*, pp. 58–65, San Diego, CA.

Ravikumar, P., Agarwal, A., and Wainwright, M. J. (2008). Message-passing for graph-structured linear programs: Proximal projections, convergence and rounding schemes. In *International Conference on Machine Learning*, pp. 800–807.

Ray, S. F. (2002). *Applied Photographic Optics*. Focal Press, Oxford, 3rd edition.

Rehg, J. and Kanade, T. (1994). Visual tracking of high DOF articulated structures: an application to human hand tracking. In *Third European Conference on Computer Vision (ECCV'94)*, pp. 35–46, Stockholm, Sweden.

Rehg, J. and Witkin, A. (1991). Visual tracking with deformation models. In *IEEE International Conference on Robotics and Automation*, pp. 844–850, Sacramento.

Rehg, J., Morris, D. D., and Kanade, T. (2003). Ambiguities in visual tracking of articulated objects using two- and three-dimensional models. *International Journal of Robotics Research*, 22(6):393–418.

Reichenbach, S. E., Park, S. K., and Narayanswamy, R. (1991). Characterizing digital image acquisition devices. *Optical Engineering*, 30(2):170–177.

Reinhard, E., Stark, M., Shirley, P., and Ferwerda, J. (2002). Photographic tone reproduction for digital images. *ACM Transactions on Graphics (Proc. SIGGRAPH 2002)*, 21(3):267–276.

Reinhard, E., Ward, G., Pattanaik, S., and Debevec, P. (2005). *High Dynamic Range Imaging: Acquisition, Display, and Image-Based Lighting*. Morgan Kaufmann.

Rhemann, C., Rother, C., and Gelautz, M. (2008). Improving color modeling for alpha matting. In *British Machine Vision Conference (BMVC 2008)*, Leeds.

Rhemann, C., Rother, C., Rav-Acha, A., and Sharp, T. (2008). High resolution matting via interactive trimap segmentation. In *IEEE Computer Society Conference on Computer Vision and Pattern Recognition (CVPR 2008)*, Anchorage, AK.

Rhemann, C., Rother, C., Wang, J., Gelautz, M., Kohli, P., and Rott, P. (2009). A perceptually motivated online benchmark for image matting. In *IEEE Computer Society Conference on Computer Vision and Pattern Recognition (CVPR 2009)*, Miami Beach, FL.

Richardson, I. E. G. (2003). *H.264 and MPEG-4 Video Compression: Video Coding for Next Generation Multimedia*. Wiley.

Rioul, O. and Vetterli, M. (1991). Wavelets and signal processing. *IEEE Signal Processing Magazine*, 8(4):14–38.

Rioux, M. and Bird, T. (1993). White laser, synced scan. *IEEE Computer Graphics and Applications*, 13(3):15–17.

Rioux, M., Bechthold, G., Taylor, D., and Duggan, M. (1987). Design of a large depth of view three-dimensional camera for robot vision. *Optical Engineering*, 26(12):1245–1250.

Riseman, E. M. and Arbib, M. A. (1977). Computational techniques in the visual segmentation of static scenes. *Computer Graphics and Image Processing*, 6(3):221–276.

Ritter, G. X. and Wilson, J. N. (2000). *Handbook of Computer Vision Algorithms in Image Algebra*. CRC Press, Boca Raton, 2nd edition.

Robert, C. P. (2007). *The Bayesian Choice: From Decision-Theoretic Foundations to Computational Implementation*. Springer-Verlag, New York.

Roberts, L. G. (1965). Machine perception of three-dimensional solids. In Tippett, J. T., Borkowitz, D. A., Clapp, L. C., Koester, C. J., and Vanderburgh Jr., A. (eds), *Optical and Electro-Optical Information Processing*, pp. 159–197, MIT Press, Cambridge, Massachusetts.

Robertson, D. and Cipolla, R. (2004). An image-based system for urban navigation. In *British Machine Vision Conference*, pp. 656–665, Kingston.

Robertson, D. P. and Cipolla, R. (2002). Building architectural models from many views using map constraints. In *Seventh European Conference on Computer Vision (ECCV 2002)*, pp. 155–169, Copenhagen.

Robertson, D. P. and Cipolla, R. (2009). Architectural modelling. In Varga, M. (ed.), *Practical Image Processing and Computer Vision*, John Wiley.

Robertson, N. and Reid, I. (2006). A general method for human activity recognition in video. *Computer Vision and Image Understanding*, 104(2-3):232–248.

Roble, D. (1999). Vision in film and special effects. *Computer Graphics*, 33(4):58–60.

Roble, D. and Zafar, N. B. (2009). Don't trust your eyes: cutting-edge visual effects. *Computer*, 42(7):35–41.

Rogez, G., Rihan, J., Ramalingam, S., Orrite, C., and Torr, P. H. S. (2008). Randomized trees for human pose detection. In *IEEE Computer Society Conference on Computer Vision and Pattern Recognition (CVPR 2008)*, Anchorage, AK.

Rogmans, S., Lu, J., Bekaert, P., and Lafruit, G. (2009). Real-time stereo-based views synthesis algorithms: A unified framework and evaluation on commodity GPUs. *Signal Processing: Image Communication*, 24:49–64.

Rohr, K. (1994). Towards model-based recognition of human movements in image sequences. *Computer Vision, Graphics, and Image Processing*, 59(1):94–115.

Román, A. and Lensch, H. P. A. (2006). Automatic multiperspective images. In *Eurographics Symposium on Rendering*, pp. 83–92.

Román, A., Garg, G., and Levoy, M. (2004). Interactive design of multi-perspective images for visualizing urban landscapes. In *IEEE Visualization 2004*, pp. 537–544, Minneapolis.

Romdhani, S. and Vetter, T. (2003). Efficient, robust and accurate fitting of a 3D morphable model. In *Ninth International Conference on Computer Vision (ICCV 2003)*, pp. 59–66, Nice, France.

Romdhani, S., Torr, P. H. S., Schölkopf, B., and Blake, A. (2001). Computationally efficient face detection. In *Eighth International Conference on Computer Vision (ICCV 2001)*, pp. 695–700, Vancouver, Canada.

Rosales, R. and Sclaroff, S. (2000). Inferring body pose without tracking body parts. In *IEEE Computer Society Conference on Computer Vision and Pattern Recognition (CVPR'2000)*, pp. 721–727, Hilton Head Island.

Rosenfeld, A. (1980). Quadtrees and pyramids for pattern recognition and image processing. In *Fifth International Conference on Pattern Recognition (ICPR'80)*, pp. 802–809, Miami Beach.

Rosenfeld, A. (ed.). (1984). *Multiresolution Image Processing and Analysis*, Springer-Verlag, New York.

Rosenfeld, A. and Davis, L. S. (1979). Image segmentation and image models. *Proceedings of the IEEE*, 67(5):764–772.

Rosenfeld, A. and Kak, A. C. (1976). *Digital Picture Processing*. Academic Press, New York.

Rosenfeld, A. and Pfaltz, J. L. (1966). Sequential operations in digital picture processing. *Journal of the ACM*, 13(4):471–494.

Rosenfeld, A., Hummel, R. A., and Zucker, S. W. (1976). Scene labeling by relaxation operations. *IEEE Transactions on Systems, Man, and Cybernetics*, SMC-6:420–433.

Rosten, E. and Drummond, T. (2005). Fusing points and lines for high performance tracking. In *Tenth International Conference on Computer Vision (ICCV 2005)*, pp. 1508–1515, Beijing, China.

Rosten, E. and Drummond, T. (2006). Machine learning for high-speed corner detection. In *Ninth European Conference on Computer Vision (ECCV 2006)*, pp. 430–443.

Roth, S. and Black, M. J. (2007a). On the spatial statistics of optical flow. *International Journal of Computer Vision*, 74(1):33–50.

Roth, S. and Black, M. J. (2007b). Steerable random fields. In *Eleventh International Conference on Computer Vision (ICCV 2007)*, Rio de Janeiro, Brazil.

Roth, S. and Black, M. J. (2009). Fields of experts. *International Journal of Computer Vision*, 82(2):205–229.

Rother, C. (2002). A new approach for vanishing point detection in architectural environments. *Image and Vision Computing*, 20(9-10):647–656.

Rother, C. (2003). Linear multi-view reconstruction of points, lines, planes and cameras using a reference plane. In *Ninth International Conference on Computer Vision (ICCV 2003)*, pp. 1210–1217, Nice, France.

Rother, C. and Carlsson, S. (2002). Linear multi view reconstruction and camera recovery using a reference plane. *International Journal of Computer Vision*, 49(2/3):117–141.

Rother, C., Kolmogorov, V., and Blake, A. (2004). "GrabCut"—interactive foreground extraction using iterated graph cuts. *ACM Transactions on Graphics (Proc. SIGGRAPH 2004)*, 23(3):309–314.

Rother, C., Bordeaux, L., Hamadi, Y., and Blake, A. (2006). Autocollage. *ACM Transactions on Graphics*, 25(3):847–852.

Rother, C., Kohli, P., Feng, W., and Jia, J. (2009). Minimizing sparse higher order energy functions of discrete variables. In *IEEE Computer Society Conference on Computer Vision and Pattern Recognition (CVPR 2009)*, Miami Beach, FL.

Rother, C., Kolmogorov, V., Lempitsky, V., and Szummer, M. (2007). Optimizing binary MRFs via extended roof duality. In *IEEE Computer Society Conference on Computer Vision and Pattern Recognition (CVPR 2007)*, Minneapolis, MN.

Rother, C., Kumar, S., Kolmogorov, V., and Blake, A. (2005). Digital tapestry. In *IEEE Computer Society Conference on Computer Vision and Pattern Recognition (CVPR'2005)*, pp. 589–596, San Diego, CA.

Rothganger, F., Lazebnik, S., Schmid, C., and Ponce, J. (2006). 3D object modeling and recognition using local affine-invariant image descriptors and multi-view spatial constraints. *International Journal of Computer Vision*, 66(3):231–259.

Rousseeuw, P. J. (1984). Least median of squares regresssion. *Journal of the American Statistical Association*, 79:871–880.

Rousseeuw, P. J. and Leroy, A. M. (1987). *Robust Regression and Outlier Detection*. Wiley, New York.

Rousson, M. and Paragios, N. (2008). Prior knowledge, level set representations, and visual grouping. *International Journal of Computer Vision*, 76(3):231–243.

Roweis, S. (1998). EM algorithms for PCA and SPCA. In *Advances in Neural Information Processing Systems*, pp. 626–632.

Rowland, D. A. and Perrett, D. I. (1995). Manipulating facial appearance through shape and color. *IEEE Computer Graphics and Applications*, 15(5):70–76.

Rowley, H. A., Baluja, S., and Kanade, T. (1998a). Neural network-based face detection. *IEEE Transactions on Pattern Analysis and Machine Intelligence*, 20(1):23–38.

Rowley, H. A., Baluja, S., and Kanade, T. (1998b). Rotation invariant neural network-based face detection. In *IEEE Computer Society Conference on Computer Vision and Pattern Recognition (CVPR'98)*, pp. 38–44, Santa Barbara.

Roy, S. and Cox, I. J. (1998). A maximum-flow formulation of the N-camera stereo correspondence problem. In *Sixth International Conference on Computer Vision (ICCV'98)*, pp. 492–499, Bombay.

Rozenfeld, S., Shimshoni, I., and Lindenbaum, M. (2007). Dense mirroring surface recovery from 1d homographies and sparse correspondences. In *IEEE Computer Society Conference on Computer Vision and Pattern Recognition (CVPR 2007)*, Minneapolis, MN.

Rubner, Y., Tomasi, C., and Guibas, L. J. (2000). The earth mover's distance as a metric for image retrieval. *International Journal of Computer Vision*, 40(2):99–121.

Rumelhart, D. E., Hinton, G. E., and Williams, R. J. (1986). Learning internal representations by error propagation. In Rumelhart, D. E., McClelland, J. L., and the PDP research group (eds), *Parallel distributed processing: Explorations in the microstructure of cognition*, pp. 318–362, Bradford Books, Cambridge, Massachusetts.

Rusinkiewicz, S. and Levoy, M. (2000). Qsplat: A multiresolution point rendering system for large meshes. In *ACM SIGGRAPH 2000 Conference Proceedings*, pp. 343–352.

Russ, J. C. (2007). *The Image Processing Handbook*. CRC Press, Boca Raton, 5th edition.

Russell, B., Efros, A., Sivic, J., Freeman, W., and Zisserman, A. (2006). Using multiple segmentations to discover objects and their extent in image collections. In *IEEE Computer Society Conference on Computer Vision and Pattern Recognition (CVPR'2006)*, pp. 1605–1612, New York City, NY.

Russell, B. C., Torralba, A., Murphy, K. P., and Freeman, W. T. (2008). LabelMe: A database and web-based tool for image annotation. *International Journal of Computer Vision*, 77(1-3):157–173.

Russell, B. C., Torralba, A., Liu, C., Fergus, R., and Freeman, W. T. (2007). Object recognition by scene alignment. In *Advances in Neural Information Processing Systems*.

Ruzon, M. A. and Tomasi, C. (2000). Alpha estimation in natural images. In *IEEE Computer Society Conference on Computer Vision and Pattern Recognition (CVPR'2000)*, pp. 18–25, Hilton Head Island.

Ruzon, M. A. and Tomasi, C. (2001). Edge, junction, and corner detection using color distributions. *IEEE Transactions on Pattern Analysis and Machine Intelligence*, 23(11):1281–1295.

Ryan, T. W., Gray, R. T., and Hunt, B. R. (1980). Prediction of correlation errors in stereo-pair images. *Optical Engineering*, 19(3):312–322.

Saad, Y. (2003). *Iterative Methods for Sparse Linear Systems*. Society for Industrial and Applied Mathematics, second edition.

Saint-Marc, P., Chen, J. S., and Medioni, G. (1991). Adaptive smoothing: A general tool for early vision. *IEEE Transactions on Pattern Analysis and Machine Intelligence*, 13(6):514–529.

Saito, H. and Kanade, T. (1999). Shape reconstruction in projective grid space from large number of images. In *IEEE Computer Society Conference on Computer Vision and Pattern Recognition (CVPR'99)*, pp. 49–54, Fort Collins.

Samet, H. (1989). *The Design and Analysis of Spatial Data Structures*. Addison-Wesley, Reading, Massachusetts.

Sander, P. T. and Zucker, S. W. (1990). Inferring surface trace and differential structure from 3-D images. *IEEE Transactions on Pattern Analysis and Machine Intelligence*, 12(9):833–854.

Sapiro, G. (2001). *Geometric Partial Differential Equations and Image Analysis*. Cambridge University Press.

Sato, Y. and Ikeuchi, K. (1996). Reflectance analysis for 3D computer graphics model generation. *Graphical Models and Image Processing*, 58(5):437–451.

Sato, Y., Wheeler, M., and Ikeuchi, K. (1997). Object shape and reflectance modeling from observation. In *ACM SIGGRAPH 1997 Conference Proceedings*, pp. 379–387, Los Angeles.

Savarese, S. and Fei-Fei, L. (2007). 3D generic object categorization, localization and pose estimation. In *Eleventh International Conference on Computer Vision (ICCV 2007)*, Rio de Janeiro, Brazil.

Savarese, S. and Fei-Fei, L. (2008). View synthesis for recognizing unseen poses of object classes. In *Tenth European Conference on Computer Vision (ECCV 2008)*, pp. 602–615, Marseilles.

Savarese, S., Chen, M., and Perona, P. (2005). Local shape from mirror reflections. *International Journal of Computer Vision*, 64(1):31–67.

Savarese, S., Andreetto, M., Rushmeier, H. E., Bernardini, F., and Perona, P. (2007). 3D reconstruction by shadow carving: Theory and practical evaluation. *International Journal of Computer Vision*, 71(3):305–336.

Sawhney, H. S. (1994). Simplifying motion and structure analysis using planar parallax and image warping. In *Twelfth International Conference on Pattern Recognition (ICPR'94)*, pp. 403–408, Jerusalem, Israel.

Sawhney, H. S. and Ayer, S. (1996). Compact representation of videos through dominant multiple motion estimation. *IEEE Transactions on Pattern Analysis and Machine Intelligence*, 18(8):814–830.

Sawhney, H. S. and Hanson, A. R. (1991). Identification and 3D description of 'shallow' environmental structure over a sequence of images. In *IEEE Computer Society Conference on Computer Vision and Pattern Recognition (CVPR'91)*, pp. 179–185, Maui, Hawaii.

Sawhney, H. S. and Kumar, R. (1999). True multi-image alignment and its application to mosaicing and lens distortion correction. *IEEE Transactions on Pattern Analysis and Machine Intelligence*, 21(3):235–243.

Sawhney, H. S., Kumar, R., Gendel, G., Bergen, J., Dixon, D., and Paragano, V. (1998). VideoBrush: Experiences with consumer video mosaicing. In *IEEE Workshop on Applications of Computer Vision (WACV'98)*, pp. 56–62, Princeton.

Sawhney, H. S., Arpa, A., Kumar, R., Samarasekera, S., Aggarwal, M., Hsu, S., Nister, D., and Hanna, K. (2002). Video flashlights: real time rendering of multiple videos for immersive model visualization. In *Proceedings of the 13th Eurographics Workshop on Rendering*, pp. 157–168, Pisa, Italy.

Saxena, A., Sun, M., and Ng, A. Y. (2009). Make3D: Learning 3D scene structure from a single still image. *IEEE Transactions on Pattern Analysis and Machine Intelligence*, 31(5):824–840.

Schaffalitzky, F. and Zisserman, A. (2000). Planar grouping for automatic detection of vanishing lines and points. *Image and Vision Computing*, 18:647–658.

Schaffalitzky, F. and Zisserman, A. (2002). Multi-view matching for unordered image sets, or "How do I organize my holiday snaps?". In *Seventh European Conference on Computer Vision (ECCV 2002)*, pp. 414–431, Copenhagen.

Scharr, H., Black, M. J., and Haussecker, H. W. (2003). Image statistics and anisotropic diffusion. In *Ninth International Conference on Computer Vision (ICCV 2003)*, pp. 840–847, Nice, France.

Scharstein, D. (1994). Matching images by comparing their gradient fields. In *Twelfth International Conference on Pattern Recognition (ICPR'94)*, pp. 572–575, Jerusalem, Israel.

Scharstein, D. (1999). *View Synthesis Using Stereo Vision*. Volume 1583, Springer-Verlag.

Scharstein, D. and Pal, C. (2007). Learning conditional random fields for stereo. In *IEEE Computer Society Conference on Computer Vision and Pattern Recognition (CVPR 2007)*, Minneapolis, MN.

Scharstein, D. and Szeliski, R. (1998). Stereo matching with nonlinear diffusion. *International Journal of Computer Vision*, 28(2):155–174.

Scharstein, D. and Szeliski, R. (2002). A taxonomy and evaluation of dense two-frame stereo correspondence algorithms. *International Journal of Computer Vision*, 47(1):7–42.

Scharstein, D. and Szeliski, R. (2003). High-accuracy stereo depth maps using structured light. In *IEEE Computer Society Conference on Computer Vision and Pattern Recognition (CVPR'2003)*, pp. 195–202, Madison, WI.

Schechner, Y. Y., Nayar, S. K., and Belhumeur, P. N. (2009). Multiplexing for optimal lighting. *IEEE Transactions on Pattern Analysis and Machine Intelligence*, 29(8):1339–1354.

Schindler, G., Brown, M., and Szeliski, R. (2007). City-scale location recognition. In *IEEE Computer Society Conference on Computer Vision and Pattern Recognition (CVPR 2007)*, Minneapolis, MN.

Schindler, G., Krishnamurthy, P., Lublinerman, R., Liu, Y., and Dellaert, F. (2008). Detecting and matching repeated patterns for automatic geo-tagging in urban environments. In *IEEE Computer Society Conference on Computer Vision and Pattern Recognition (CVPR 2008)*, Anchorage, AK.

Schlesinger, D. and Flach, B. (2006). *Transforming an arbitrary minsum problem into a binary one*. Technical Report TUD-FI06-01, Dresden University of Technology.

Schlesinger, M. I. (1976). Syntactic analysis of two-dimensional visual signals in noisy conditions. *Kibernetika*, 4:113–130.

Schlesinger, M. I. and Giginyak, V. V. (2007a). Solution to structural recognition (max,+)-problems by their equivalent transformations – part 1. *Control Systems and Computers*, 2007(1):3–15.

Schlesinger, M. I. and Giginyak, V. V. (2007b). Solution to structural recognition (max,+)-problems by their equivalent transformations – part 2. *Control Systems and Computers*, 2007(2):3–18.

Schmid, C. and Mohr, R. (1997). Local grayvalue invariants for image retrieval. *IEEE Transactions on Pattern Analysis and Machine Intelligence*, 19(5):530–534.

Schmid, C. and Zisserman, A. (1997). Automatic line matching across views. In *IEEE Computer Society Conference on Computer Vision and Pattern Recognition (CVPR'97)*, pp. 666–671, San Juan, Puerto Rico.

Schmid, C., Mohr, R., and Bauckhage, C. (2000). Evaluation of interest point detectors. *International Journal of Computer Vision*, 37(2):151–172.

Schneiderman, H. and Kanade, T. (2004). Object detection using the statistics of parts. *International Journal of Computer Vision*, 56(3):151–177.

Schödl, A. and Essa, I. (2002). Controlled animation of video sprites. In *ACM Symposium on Computater Animation*, San Antonio.

Schödl, A., Szeliski, R., Salesin, D. H., and Essa, I. (2000). Video textures. In *ACM SIGGRAPH 2000 Conference Proceedings*, pp. 489–498, New Orleans.

Schoenemann, T. and Cremers, D. (2008). High resolution motion layer decomposition using dual-space graph cuts. In *IEEE Computer Society Conference on Computer Vision and Pattern Recognition (CVPR 2008)*, Anchorage, AK.

Schölkopf, B. and Smola, A. (eds). (2002). *Learning with Kernels: Support Vector Machines, Regularization, Optimization and Beyond*. MIT Press, Cambridge, Massachusetts.

Schraudolph, N. N. (2010). Polynomial-time exact inference in NP-hard binary MRFs via reweighted perfect matching. In *13th International Conference on Artificial Intelligence and Statistics (AISTATS)*, pp. 717–724.

Schröder, P. and Sweldens, W. (1995). Spherical wavelets: Efficiently representing functions on the sphere. In *ACM SIGGRAPH 1995 Conference Proceedings*, pp. 161–172.

Schultz, R. R. and Stevenson, R. L. (1996). Extraction of high-resolution frames from video sequences. *IEEE Transactions on Image Processing*, 5(6):996–1011.

Sclaroff, S. and Isidoro, J. (2003). Active blobs: region-based, deformable appearance models. *Computer Vision and Image Understanding*, 89(2-3):197–225.

Scott, G. L. and Longuet-Higgins, H. C. (1990). Feature grouping by relocalization of eigenvectors of the proximity matrix. In *British Machine Vision Conference*, pp. 103–108.

Sebastian, T. B. and Kimia, B. B. (2005). Curves vs. skeletons in object recognition. *Signal Processing*, 85(2):246–263.

Sederberg, T. W. and Parry, S. R. (1986). Free-form deformations of solid geometric models. *Computer Graphics (SIGGRAPH '86)*, 20(4):151–160.

Sederberg, T. W., Gao, P., Wang, G., and Mu, H. (1993). 2D shape blending: An intrinsic solution to the vertex path problem. In *ACM SIGGRAPH 1993 Conference Proceedings*, pp. 15–18.

Seitz, P. (1989). Using local orientation information as image primitive for robust object recognition. In *SPIE Vol. 1199, Visual Communications and Image Processing IV*, pp. 1630–1639.

Seitz, S. (2001). The space of all stereo images. In *Eighth International Conference on Computer Vision (ICCV 2001)*, pp. 26–33, Vancouver, Canada.

Seitz, S. and Szeliski, R. (1999). Applications of computer vision to computer graphics. *Computer Graphics*, 33(4):35–37. Guest Editors' introduction to the Special Issue.

Seitz, S., Curless, B., Diebel, J., Scharstein, D., and Szeliski, R. (2006). A comparison and evaluation of multi-view stereo reconstruction algorithms. In *IEEE Computer Society Conference on Computer Vision and Pattern Recognition (CVPR'2006)*, pp. 519–526, New York, NY.

Seitz, S. M. and Baker, S. (2009). Filter flow. In *Twelfth International Conference on Computer Vision (ICCV 2009)*, Kyoto, Japan.

Seitz, S. M. and Dyer, C. M. (1996). View morphing. In *ACM SIGGRAPH 1996 Conference Proceedings*, pp. 21–30, New Orleans.

Seitz, S. M. and Dyer, C. M. (1997). Photorealistic scene reconstruction by voxel coloring. In *IEEE Computer Society Conference on Computer Vision and Pattern Recognition (CVPR'97)*, pp. 1067–1073, San Juan, Puerto Rico.

Seitz, S. M. and Dyer, C. M. (1999). Photorealistic scene reconstruction by voxel coloring. *International Journal of Computer Vision*, 35(2):151–173.

Seitz, S. M. and Dyer, C. R. (1997). View invariant analysis of cyclic motion. *International Journal of Computer Vision*, 25(3):231–251.

Serra, J. (1982). *Image Analysis and Mathematical Morphology*. Academic Press, New York.

Serra, J. and Vincent, L. (1992). An overview of morphological filtering. *Circuits, Systems and Signal Processing*, 11(1):47–108.

Serre, T., Wolf, L., and Poggio, T. (2005). Object recognition with features inspired by visual cortex. In *IEEE Computer Society Conference on Computer Vision and Pattern Recognition (CVPR'2005)*, pp. 994–1000, San Diego, CA.

Sethian, J. (1999). *Level Set Methods and Fast Marching Methods*. Cambridge University Press, Cambridge, 2nd edition.

Shade, J., Gortler, S., He, L., and Szeliski, R. (1998). Layered depth images. In *ACM SIGGRAPH 1998 Conference Proceedings*, pp. 231–242, Orlando.

Shade, J., Lischinski, D., Salesin, D., DeRose, T., and Snyder, J. (1996). Hierarchical images caching for accelerated walkthroughs of complex environments. In *ACM SIGGRAPH 1996 Conference Proceedings*, pp. 75–82, New Orleans.

Shafer, S. A. (1985). Using color to separate reflection components. *COLOR Research and Applications*, 10(4):210–218.

Shafer, S. A., Healey, G., and Wolff, L. (1992). *Physics-Based Vision: Principles and Practice*. Jones & Bartlett, Cambridge, MA.

Shafique, K. and Shah, M. (2005). A noniterative greedy algorithm for multiframe point correspondence. *IEEE Transactions on Pattern Analysis and Machine Intelligence*, 27(1):51–65.

Shah, J. (1993). A nonlinear diffusion model for discontinuous disparity and half-occlusion in stereo. In *IEEE Computer Society Conference on Computer Vision and Pattern Recognition (CVPR'93)*, pp. 34–40, New York.

Shakhnarovich, G., Darrell, T., and Indyk, P. (eds). (2006). *Nearest-Neighbor Methods in Learning and Vision: Theory and Practice*, MIT Press.

Shakhnarovich, G., Viola, P., and Darrell, T. (2003). Fast pose estimation with parameter-sensitive hashing. In *Ninth International Conference on Computer Vision (ICCV 2003)*, pp. 750–757, Nice, France.

Shan, Y., Liu, Z., and Zhang, Z. (2001). Model-based bundle adjustment with application to face modeling. In *Eighth International Conference on Computer Vision (ICCV 2001)*, pp. 644–641, Vancouver, Canada.

Sharon, E., Galun, M., Sharon, D., Basri, R., and Brandt, A. (2006). Hierarchy and adaptivity in segmenting visual scenes. *Nature*, 442(7104):810–813.

Shashua, A. and Toelg, S. (1997). The quadric reference surface: Theory and applications. *International Journal of Computer Vision*, 23(2):185–198.

Shashua, A. and Wexler, Y. (2001). Q-warping: Direct computation of quadratic reference surfaces. *IEEE Transactions on Pattern Analysis and Machine Intelligence*, 23(8):920–925.

Shaw, D. and Barnes, N. (2006). Perspective rectangle detection. In *Workshop on Applications of Computer Vision at ECCV'2006*.

Shewchuk, J. R. (1994). An introduction to the conjugate gradient method without the agonizing pain. Unpublished manuscript, available on author's homepage (http://www.cs.berkeley.edu/~jrs/). An earlier version appeared as a Carnegie Mellon University Technical Report, CMU-CS-94-125.

Shi, J. and Malik, J. (2000). Normalized cuts and image segmentation. *IEEE Transactions on Pattern Analysis and Machine Intelligence*, 8(22):888–905.

Shi, J. and Tomasi, C. (1994). Good features to track. In *IEEE Computer Society Conference on Computer Vision and Pattern Recognition (CVPR'94)*, pp. 593–600, Seattle.

Shimizu, M. and Okutomi, M. (2001). Precise sub-pixel estimation on area-based matching. In *Eighth International Conference on Computer Vision (ICCV 2001)*, pp. 90–97, Vancouver, Canada.

Shirley, P. (2005). *Fundamentals of Computer Graphics*. A K Peters, Wellesley, Massachusetts, second edition.

Shizawa, M. and Mase, K. (1991). A unified computational theory of motion transparency and motion boundaries based on eigenenergy analysis. In *IEEE Computer Society Conference on Computer Vision and Pattern Recognition (CVPR'91)*, pp. 289–295, Maui, Hawaii.

Shoemake, K. (1985). Animating rotation with quaternion curves. *Computer Graphics (SIGGRAPH '85)*, 19(3):245–254.

Shotton, J., Blake, A., and Cipolla, R. (2005). Contour-based learning for object detection. In *Tenth International Conference on Computer Vision (ICCV 2005)*, pp. 503–510, Beijing, China.

Shotton, J., Johnson, M., and Cipolla, R. (2008). Semantic texton forests for image categorization and segmentation. In *IEEE Computer Society Conference on Computer Vision and Pattern Recognition (CVPR 2008)*, Anchorage, AK.

Shotton, J., Winn, J., Rother, C., and Criminisi, A. (2009). Textonboost for image understanding: Multiclass object recognition and segmentation by jointly modeling appearance, shape and context. *International Journal of Computer Vision*, 81(1):2–23.

Shufelt, J. (1999). Performance evaluation and analysis of vanishing point detection techniques. *IEEE Transactions on Pattern Analysis and Machine Intelligence*, 21(3):282–288.

Shum, H.-Y. and He, L.-W. (1999). Rendering with concentric mosaics. In *ACM SIGGRAPH 1999 Conference Proceedings*, pp. 299–306, Los Angeles.

Shum, H.-Y. and Szeliski, R. (1999). Stereo reconstruction from multiperspective panoramas. In *Seventh International Conference on Computer Vision (ICCV'99)*, pp. 14–21, Kerkyra, Greece.

Shum, H.-Y. and Szeliski, R. (2000). Construction of panoramic mosaics with global and local alignment. *International Journal of Computer Vision*, 36(2):101–130. Erratum published July 2002, 48(2):151–152.

Shum, H.-Y., Chan, S.-C., and Kang, S. B. (2007). *Image-Based Rendering*. Springer, New York, NY.

Shum, H.-Y., Han, M., and Szeliski, R. (1998). Interactive construction of 3D models from panoramic mosaics. In *IEEE Computer Society Conference on Computer Vision and Pattern Recognition (CVPR'98)*, pp. 427–433, Santa Barbara.

Shum, H.-Y., Ikeuchi, K., and Reddy, R. (1995). Principal component analysis with missing data and its application to polyhedral modeling. *IEEE Transactions on Pattern Analysis and Machine Intelligence*, 17(9):854–867.

Shum, H.-Y., Kang, S. B., and Chan, S.-C. (2003). Survey of image-based representations and compression techniques. *IEEE Transactions on Circuits and Systems for Video Technology*, 13(11):1020–1037.

Shum, H.-Y., Wang, L., Chai, J.-X., and Tong, X. (2002). Rendering by manifold hopping. *International Journal of Computer Vision*, 50(2):185–201.

Shum, H.-Y., Sun, J., Yamazaki, S., Li, Y., and Tang, C.-K. (2004). Pop-up light field: An interactive image-based modeling and rendering system. *ACM Transactions on Graphics*, 23(2):143–162.

Sidenbladh, H. and Black, M. J. (2003). Learning the statistics of people in images and video. *International Journal of Computer Vision*, 54(1):189–209.

Sidenbladh, H., Black, M. J., and Fleet, D. J. (2000). Stochastic tracking of 3D human figures using 2D image motion. In *Sixth European Conference on Computer Vision (ECCV 2000)*, pp. 702–718, Dublin, Ireland.

Sigal, L. and Black, M. J. (2006). Predicting 3D people from 2D pictures. In *AMDO 2006 - IV Conference on Articulated Motion and Deformable Objects*, pp. 185–195, Mallorca, Spain.

Sigal, L., Balan, A., and Black, M. J. (2010). Humaneva: Synchronized video and motion capture dataset and baseline algorithm for evaluation of articulated human motion. *International Journal of Computer Vision*, 87(1-2):4–27.

Sigal, L., Bhatia, S., Roth, S., Black, M. J., and Isard, M. (2004). Tracking loose-limbed people. In *IEEE Computer Society Conference on Computer Vision and Pattern Recognition (CVPR'2004)*, pp. 421–428, Washington, DC.

Sillion, F. and Puech, C. (1994). *Radiosity and Global Illumination*. Morgan Kaufmann.

Sim, T., Baker, S., and Bsat, M. (2003). The CMU pose, illumination, and expression database. *IEEE Transactions on Pattern Analysis and Machine Intelligence*, 25(12):1615–1618.

Simard, P. Y., Bottou, L., Haffner, P., and Cun, Y. L. (1998). Boxlets: a fast convolution algorithm for signal processing and neural networks. In *Advances in Neural Information Processing Systems 13*, pp. 571–577.

Simon, I. and Seitz, S. M. (2008). Scene segmentation using the wisdom of crowds. In *Tenth European Conference on Computer Vision (ECCV 2008)*, pp. 541–553, Marseilles.

Simon, I., Snavely, N., and Seitz, S. M. (2007). Scene summarization for online image collections. In *Eleventh International Conference on Computer Vision (ICCV 2007)*, Rio de Janeiro, Brazil.

Simoncelli, E. P. (1999). Bayesian denoising of visual images in the wavelet domain. In Müller, P. and Vidakovic, B. (eds), *Bayesian Inference in Wavelet Based Models*, pp. 291–308, Springer-Verlag, New York.

Simoncelli, E. P. and Adelson, E. H. (1990a). Non-separable extensions of quadrature mirror filters to multiple dimensions. *Proceedings of the IEEE*, 78(4):652–664.

Simoncelli, E. P. and Adelson, E. H. (1990b). Subband transforms. In Woods, J. (ed.), *Subband Coding*, pp. 143–191, Kluwer Academic Press, Norwell, MA.

Simoncelli, E. P., Adelson, E. H., and Heeger, D. J. (1991). Probability distributions of optic flow. In *IEEE Computer Society Conference on Computer Vision and Pattern Recognition (CVPR'91)*, pp. 310–315, Maui, Hawaii.

Simoncelli, E. P., Freeman, W. T., Adelson, E. H., and Heeger, D. J. (1992). Shiftable multiscale transforms. *IEEE Transactions on Information Theory*, 38(3):587–607.

Singaraju, D., Grady, L., and Vidal, R. (2008). Interactive image segmentation via minimization of quadratic energies on directed graphs. In *IEEE Computer Society Conference on Computer Vision and Pattern Recognition (CVPR 2008)*, Anchorage, AK.

Singaraju, D., Rother, C., and Rhemann, C. (2009). New appearance models for natural image matting. In *IEEE Computer Society Conference on Computer Vision and Pattern Recognition (CVPR 2009)*, Miami Beach, FL.

Singaraju, D., Grady, L., Sinop, A. K., and Vidal, R. (2010). A continuous valued MRF for image segmentation. In Blake, A., Kohli, P., and Rother, C. (eds), *Advances in Markov Random Fields*, MIT Press.

Sinha, P., Balas, B., Ostrovsky, Y., and Russell, R. (2006). Face recognition by humans: Nineteen results all computer vision researchers should know about. *Proceedings of the IEEE*, 94(11):1948–1962.

Sinha, S., Mordohai, P., and Pollefeys, M. (2007). Multi-view stereo via graph cuts on the dual of an adaptive tetrahedral mesh. In *Eleventh International Conference on Computer Vision (ICCV 2007)*, Rio de Janeiro, Brazil.

Sinha, S. N. and Pollefeys, M. (2005). Multi-view reconstruction using photo-consistency and exact silhouette constraints: A maximum-flow formulation. In *Tenth International Conference on Computer Vision (ICCV 2005)*, pp. 349–356, Beijing, China.

Sinha, S. N., Steedly, D., and Szeliski, R. (2009). Piecewise planar stereo for image-based rendering. In *Twelfth IEEE International Conference on Computer Vision (ICCV 2009)*, Kyoto, Japan.

Sinha, S. N., Steedly, D., Szeliski, R., Agrawala, M., and Pollefeys, M. (2008). Interactive 3D architectural modeling from unordered photo collections. *ACM Transactions on Graphics (Proc. SIGGRAPH Asia 2008)*, 27(5).

Sinop, A. K. and Grady, L. (2007). A seeded image segmentation framework unifying graph cuts and random walker which yields a new algorithm. In *Eleventh International Conference on Computer Vision (ICCV 2007)*, Rio de Janeiro, Brazil.

Sivic, J. and Zisserman, A. (2003). Video Google: A text retrieval approach to object matching in videos. In *Ninth International Conference on Computer Vision (ICCV 2003)*, pp. 1470–1477, Nice, France.

Sivic, J. and Zisserman, A. (2009). Efficient visual search of videos cast as text retrieval. *IEEE Transactions on Pattern Analysis and Machine Intelligence*, 31(4):591–606.

Sivic, J., Everingham, M., and Zisserman, A. (2009). "Who are you?"—Learning person specific classifiers from video. In *IEEE Computer Society Conference on Computer Vision and Pattern Recognition (CVPR 2009)*, Miami Beach, FL.

Sivic, J., Zitnick, C. L., and Szeliski, R. (2006). Finding people in repeated shots of the same scene. In *British Machine Vision Conference (BMVC 2006)*, pp. 909–918, Edinburgh.

Sivic, J., Russell, B., Zisserman, A., Freeman, W. T., and Efros, A. A. (2008). Unsupervised discovery of visual object class hierarchies. In *IEEE Computer Society Conference on Computer Vision and Pattern Recognition (CVPR 2008)*, Anchorage, AK.

Sivic, J., Russell, B. C., Efros, A. A., Zisserman, A., and Freeman, W. T. (2005). Discovering objects and their localization in images. In *Tenth International Conference on Computer Vision (ICCV 2005)*, pp. 370–377, Beijing, China.

Slabaugh, G. G., Culbertson, W. B., Slabaugh, T. G., Culbertson, B., Malzbender, T., and Stevens, M. (2004). Methods for volumetric reconstruction of visual scenes. *International Journal of Computer Vision*, 57(3):179–199.

Slama, C. C. (ed.). (1980). *Manual of Photogrammetry*. American Society of Photogrammetry, Falls Church, Virginia, fourth edition.

Smelyanskiy, V. N., Cheeseman, P., Maluf, D. A., and Morris, R. D. (2000). Bayesian super-resolved surface reconstruction from images. In *IEEE Computer Society Conference on Computer Vision and Pattern Recognition (CVPR'2000)*, pp. 375–382, Hilton Head Island.

Smeulders, A. W. M., Worring, M., Santini, S., Gupta, A., and Jain, R. C. (2000). Content-based image retrieval at the end of the early years. *IEEE Transactions on Pattern Analysis and Machine Intelligence*, 22(12):477–490.

Sminchisescu, C. and Triggs, B. (2001). Covariance scaled sampling for monocular 3D body tracking. In *IEEE Computer Society Conference on Computer Vision and Pattern Recognition (CVPR'2001)*, pp. 447–454, Kauai, Hawaii.

Sminchisescu, C., Kanaujia, A., and Metaxas, D. (2006). Conditional models for contextual human motion recognition. *Computer Vision and Image Understanding*, 104(2-3):210–220.

Sminchisescu, C., Kanaujia, A., Li, Z., and Metaxas, D. (2005). Discriminative density propagation for 3D human motion estimation. In *IEEE Computer Society Conference on Computer Vision and Pattern Recognition (CVPR'2005)*, pp. 390–397, San Diego, CA.

Smith, A. R. and Blinn, J. F. (1996). Blue screen matting. In *ACM SIGGRAPH 1996 Conference Proceedings*, pp. 259–268, New Orleans.

Smith, B. M., Zhang, L., Jin, H., and Agarwala, A. (2009). Light field video stabilization. In *Twelfth International Conference on Computer Vision (ICCV 2009)*, Kyoto, Japan.

Smith, S. M. and Brady, J. M. (1997). SUSAN—a new approach to low level image processing. *International Journal of Computer Vision*, 23(1):45–78.

Smolic, A. and Kauff, P. (2005). Interactive 3-D video representation and coding technologies. *Proceedings of the IEEE*, 93(1):98–110.

Snavely, N., Seitz, S. M., and Szeliski, R. (2006). Photo tourism: Exploring photo collections in 3D. *ACM Transactions on Graphics (Proc. SIGGRAPH 2006)*, 25(3):835–846.

Snavely, N., Seitz, S. M., and Szeliski, R. (2008a). Modeling the world from Internet photo collections. *International Journal of Computer Vision*, 80(2):189–210.

Snavely, N., Seitz, S. M., and Szeliski, R. (2008b). Skeletal graphs for efficient structure from motion. In *IEEE Computer Society Conference on Computer Vision and Pattern Recognition (CVPR 2008)*, Anchorage, AK.

Snavely, N., Garg, R., Seitz, S. M., and Szeliski, R. (2008). Finding paths through the world's photos. *ACM Transactions on Graphics (Proc. SIGGRAPH 2008)*, 27(3).

Snavely, N., Simon, I., Goesele, M., Szeliski, R., and Seitz, S. M. (2010). Scene reconstruction and visualization from community photo collections. *Proceedings of the IEEE*, 98(8):1370–1390.

Soatto, S., Yezzi, A. J., and Jin, H. (2003). Tales of shape and radiance in multiview stereo. In *Ninth International Conference on Computer Vision (ICCV 2003)*, pp. 974–981, Nice, France.

Soille, P. (2006). Morphological image compositing. *IEEE Transactions on Pattern Analysis and Machine Intelligence*, 28(5):673–683.

Solina, F. and Bajcsy, R. (1990). Recovery of parametric models from range images: The case for superquadrics with global deformations. *IEEE Transactions on Pattern Analysis and Machine Intelligence*, 12(2):131–147.

Sontag, D. and Jaakkola, T. (2007). New outer bounds on the marginal polytope. In *Advances in Neural Information Processing Systems*.

Sontag, D., Meltzer, T., Globerson, A., Jaakkola, T., and Weiss, Y. (2008). Tightening LP relaxations for MAP using message passing. In *Uncertainty in Artificial Intelligence (UAI)*.

Soucy, M. and Laurendeau, D. (1992). Multi-resolution surface modeling from multiple range views. In *IEEE Computer Society Conference on Computer Vision and Pattern Recognition (CVPR'92)*, pp. 348–353, Champaign, Illinois.

Srinivasan, S., Chellappa, R., Veeraraghavan, A., and Aggarwal, G. (2005). Electronic image stabilization and mosaicking algorithms. In Bovik, A. (ed.), *Handbook of Image and Video Processing*, Academic Press.

Srivasan, P., Liang, P., and Hackwood, S. (1990). Computational geometric methods in volumetric intersections for 3D reconstruction. *Pattern Recognition*, 23(8):843–857.

Stamos, I., Liu, L., Chen, C., Wolberg, G., Yu, G., and Zokai, S. (2008). Integrating automated range registration with multiview geometry for the photorealistic modeling of large-scale scenes. *International Journal of Computer Vision*, 78(2-3):237–260.

Stark, J. A. (2000). Adaptive image contrast enhancement using generalizations of histogram equalization. *IEEE Transactions on Image Processing*, 9(5):889–896.

Stauffer, C. and Grimson, W. (1999). Adaptive background mixture models for real-time tracking. In *IEEE Computer Society Conference on Computer Vision and Pattern Recognition (CVPR'99)*, pp. 246–252, Fort Collins.

Steedly, D. and Essa, I. (2001). Propagation of innovative information in non-linear least-squares structure from motion. In *Eighth International Conference on Computer Vision (ICCV 2001)*, pp. 223–229, Vancouver, Canada.

Steedly, D., Essa, I., and Dellaert, F. (2003). Spectral partitioning for structure from motion. In *Ninth International Conference on Computer Vision (ICCV 2003)*, pp. 996–1003, Nice, France.

Steedly, D., Pal, C., and Szeliski, R. (2005). Efficiently registering video into panoramic mosaics. In *Tenth International Conference on Computer Vision (ICCV 2005)*, pp. 1300–1307, Beijing, China.

Steele, R. and Jaynes, C. (2005). Feature uncertainty arising from covariant image noise. In *IEEE Computer Society Conference on Computer Vision and Pattern Recognition (CVPR'2005)*, pp. 1063–1070, San Diego, CA.

Steele, R. M. and Jaynes, C. (2006). Overconstrained linear estimation of radial distortion and multi-view geometry. In *Ninth European Conference on Computer Vision (ECCV 2006)*, pp. 253–264.

Stein, A., Hoiem, D., and Hebert, M. (2007). Learning to extract object boundaries using motion cues. In *Eleventh International Conference on Computer Vision (ICCV 2007)*, Rio de Janeiro, Brazil.

Stein, F. and Medioni, G. (1992). Structural indexing: Efficient 3-D object recognition. *IEEE Transactions on Pattern Analysis and Machine Intelligence*, 14(2):125–145.

Stein, G. (1995). Accurate internal camera calibration using rotation, with analysis of sources of error. In *Fifth International Conference on Computer Vision (ICCV'95)*, pp. 230–236, Cambridge, Massachusetts.

Stein, G. (1997). Lens distortion calibration using point correspondences. In *IEEE Computer Society Conference on Computer Vision and Pattern Recognition (CVPR'97)*, pp. 602–608, San Juan, Puerto Rico.

Stenger, B., Thayananthan, A., Torr, P. H. S., and Cipolla, R. (2006). Model-based hand tracking using a hierarchical bayesian filter. *IEEE Transactions on Pattern Analysis and Machine Intelligence*, 28(9):1372–1384.

Stewart, C. V. (1999). Robust parameter estimation in computer vision. *SIAM Reviews*, 41(3):513–537.

Stiller, C. and Konrad, J. (1999). Estimating motion in image sequences: A tutorial on modeling and computation of 2D motion. *IEEE Signal Processing Magazine*, 16(4):70–91.

Stollnitz, E. J., DeRose, T. D., and Salesin, D. H. (1996). *Wavelets for Computer Graphics: Theory and Applications*. Morgan Kaufmann, San Francisco.

Strang, G. (1988). *Linear Algebra and its Applications*. Harcourt, Brace, Jovanovich, Publishers, San Diego, 3rd edition.

Strang, G. (1989). Wavelets and dilation equations: A brief introduction. *SIAM Reviews*, 31(4):614–627.

Strecha, C., Fransens, R., and Van Gool, L. (2006). Combined depth and outlier estimation in multi-view stereo. In *IEEE Computer Society Conference on Computer Vision and Pattern Recognition (CVPR'2006)*, pp. 2394–2401, New York City, NY.

Strecha, C., Tuytelaars, T., and Van Gool, L. (2003). Dense matching of multiple wide-baseline views. In *Ninth International Conference on Computer Vision (ICCV 2003)*, pp. 1194–1201, Nice, France.

Strecha, C., von Hansen, W., Van Gool, L., Fua, P., and Thoennessen, U. (2008). On benchmarking camera calibration and multi-view stereo. In *IEEE Computer Society Conference on Computer Vision and Pattern Recognition (CVPR 2008)*, Anchorage, AK.

Sturm, P. (2005). Multi-view geometry for general camera models. In *IEEE Computer Society Conference on Computer Vision and Pattern Recognition (CVPR'2005)*, pp. 206–212, San Diego, CA.

Sturm, P. and Ramalingam, S. (2004). A generic concept for camera calibration. In *Eighth European Conference on Computer Vision (ECCV 2004)*, pp. 1–13, Prague.

Sturm, P. and Triggs, W. (1996). A factorization based algorithm for multi-image projective structure and motion. In *Fourth European Conference on Computer Vision (ECCV'96)*, pp. 709–720, Cambridge, England.

Su, H., Sun, M., Fei-Fei, L., and Savarese, S. (2009). Learning a dense multi-view representation for detection, viewpoint classification and synthesis of object categories. In *Twelfth International Conference on Computer Vision (ICCV 2009)*, Kyoto, Japan.

Sudderth, E. B., Torralba, A., Freeman, W. T., and Willsky, A. S. (2008). Describing visual scenes using transformed objects and parts. *International Journal of Computer Vision*, 77(1-3):291–330.

Sullivan, S. and Ponce, J. (1998). Automatic model construction and pose estimation from photographs using triangular splines. *IEEE Transactions on Pattern Analysis and Machine Intelligence*, 20(10):1091–1096.

Sun, D., Roth, S., Lewis, J. P., and Black, M. J. (2008). Learning optical flow. In *Tenth European Conference on Computer Vision (ECCV 2008)*, pp. 83–97, Marseilles.

Sun, J., Zheng, N., and Shum, H. (2003). Stereo matching using belief propagation. *IEEE Transactions on Pattern Analysis and Machine Intelligence*, 25(7):787–800.

Sun, J., Jia, J., Tang, C.-K., and Shum, H.-Y. (2004). Poisson matting. *ACM Transactions on Graphics (Proc. SIGGRAPH 2004)*, 23(3):315–321.

Sun, J., Li, Y., Kang, S. B., and Shum, H.-Y. (2006). Flash matting. *ACM Transactions on Graphics*, 25(3):772–778.

Sun, J., Yuan, L., Jia, J., and Shum, H.-Y. (2004). Image completion with structure propagation. *ACM Transactions on Graphics (Proc. SIGGRAPH 2004)*, 24(3):861–868.

Sun, M., Su, H., Savarese, S., and Fei-Fei, L. (2009). A multi-view probabilistic model for 3D object classes. In *IEEE Computer Society Conference on Computer Vision and Pattern Recognition (CVPR 2009)*, Miami Beach, FL.

Sung, K.-K. and Poggio, T. (1998). Example-based learning for view-based human face detection. *IEEE Transactions on Pattern Analysis and Machine Intelligence*, 20(1):39–51.

Sutherland, I. E. (1974). Three-dimensional data input by tablet. *Proceedings of the IEEE*, 62(4):453–461.

Swain, M. J. and Ballard, D. H. (1991). Color indexing. *International Journal of Computer Vision*, 7(1):11–32.

Swaminathan, R., Kang, S. B., Szeliski, R., Criminisi, A., and Nayar, S. K. (2002). On the motion and appearance of specularities in image sequences. In *Seventh European Conference on Computer Vision (ECCV 2002)*, pp. 508–523, Copenhagen.

Sweldens, W. (1996). Wavelets and the lifting scheme: A 5 minute tour. *Z. Angew. Math. Mech.*, 76 (Suppl. 2):41–44.

Sweldens, W. (1997). The lifting scheme: A construction of second generation wavelets. *SIAM J. Math. Anal.*, 29(2):511–546.

Swendsen, R. H. and Wang, J.-S. (1987). Nonuniversal critical dynamics in Monte Carlo simulations. *Physical Review Letters*, 58(2):86–88.

Szeliski, R. (1986). *Cooperative Algorithms for Solving Random-Dot Stereograms*. Technical Report CMU-CS-86-133, Computer Science Department, Carnegie Mellon University.

Szeliski, R. (1989). *Bayesian Modeling of Uncertainty in Low-Level Vision*. Kluwer Academic Publishers, Boston.

Szeliski, R. (1990a). Bayesian modeling of uncertainty in low-level vision. *International Journal of Computer Vision*, 5(3):271–301.

Szeliski, R. (1990b). Fast surface interpolation using hierarchical basis functions. *IEEE Transactions on Pattern Analysis and Machine Intelligence*, 12(6):513–528.

Szeliski, R. (1991a). Fast shape from shading. *CVGIP: Image Understanding*, 53(2):129–153.

Szeliski, R. (1991b). Shape from rotation. In *IEEE Computer Society Conference on Computer Vision and Pattern Recognition (CVPR'91)*, pp. 625–630, Maui, Hawaii.

Szeliski, R. (1993). Rapid octree construction from image sequences. *CVGIP: Image Understanding*, 58(1):23–32.

Szeliski, R. (1994). Image mosaicing for tele-reality applications. In *IEEE Workshop on Applications of Computer Vision (WACV'94)*, pp. 44–53, Sarasota.

Szeliski, R. (1996). Video mosaics for virtual environments. *IEEE Computer Graphics and Applications*, 16(2):22–30.

Szeliski, R. (1999). A multi-view approach to motion and stereo. In *IEEE Computer Society Conference on Computer Vision and Pattern Recognition (CVPR'99)*, pp. 157–163, Fort Collins.

Szeliski, R. (2006a). Image alignment and stitching: A tutorial. *Foundations and Trends in Computer Graphics and Computer Vision*, 2(1):1–104.

Szeliski, R. (2006b). Locally adapted hierarchical basis preconditioning. *ACM Transactions on Graphics (Proc. SIGGRAPH 2006)*, 25(3):1135–1143.

Szeliski, R. and Coughlan, J. (1997). Spline-based image registration. *International Journal of Computer Vision*, 22(3):199–218.

Szeliski, R. and Golland, P. (1999). Stereo matching with transparency and matting. *International Journal of Computer Vision*, 32(1):45–61. Special Issue for Marr Prize papers.

Szeliski, R. and Hinton, G. (1985). Solving random-dot stereograms using the heat equation. In *IEEE Computer Society Conference on Computer Vision and Pattern Recognition (CVPR'85)*, pp. 284–288, San Francisco.

Szeliski, R. and Ito, M. R. (1986). New Hermite cubic interpolator for two-dimensional curve generation. *IEE Proceedings E*, 133(6):341–347.

Szeliski, R. and Kang, S. B. (1994). Recovering 3D shape and motion from image streams using nonlinear least squares. *Journal of Visual Communication and Image Representation*, 5(1):10–28.

Szeliski, R. and Kang, S. B. (1995). Direct methods for visual scene reconstruction. In *IEEE Workshop on Representations of Visual Scenes*, pp. 26–33, Cambridge, Massachusetts.

Szeliski, R. and Kang, S. B. (1997). Shape ambiguities in structure from motion. *IEEE Transactions on Pattern Analysis and Machine Intelligence*, 19(5):506–512.

Szeliski, R. and Lavallée, S. (1996). Matching 3-D anatomical surfaces with non-rigid deformations using octree-splines. *International Journal of Computer Vision*, 18(2):171–186.

Szeliski, R. and Scharstein, D. (2004). Sampling the disparity space image. *IEEE Transactions on Pattern Analysis and Machine Intelligence*, 26(3):419–425.

Szeliski, R. and Shum, H.-Y. (1996). Motion estimation with quadtree splines. *IEEE Transactions on Pattern Analysis and Machine Intelligence*, 18(12):1199–1210.

Szeliski, R. and Shum, H.-Y. (1997). Creating full view panoramic image mosaics and texture-mapped models. In *ACM SIGGRAPH 1997 Conference Proceedings*, pp. 251–258, Los Angeles.

Szeliski, R. and Tonnesen, D. (1992). Surface modeling with oriented particle systems. *Computer Graphics (SIGGRAPH '92)*, 26(2):185–194.

Szeliski, R. and Torr, P. (1998). Geometrically constrained structure from motion: Points on planes. In *European Workshop on 3D Structure from Multiple Images of Large-Scale Environments (SMILE)*, pp. 171–186, Freiburg, Germany.

Szeliski, R. and Weiss, R. (1998). Robust shape recovery from occluding contours using a linear smoother. *International Journal of Computer Vision*, 28(1):27–44.

Szeliski, R., Avidan, S., and Anandan, P. (2000). Layer extraction from multiple images containing reflections and transparency. In *IEEE Computer Society Conference on Computer Vision and Pattern Recognition (CVPR'2000)*, pp. 246–253, Hilton Head Island.

Szeliski, R., Tonnesen, D., and Terzopoulos, D. (1993a). Curvature and continuity control in particle-based surface models. In *SPIE Vol. 2031, Geometric Methods in Computer Vision II*, pp. 172–181, San Diego.

Szeliski, R., Tonnesen, D., and Terzopoulos, D. (1993b). Modeling surfaces of arbitrary topology with dynamic particles. In *IEEE Computer Society Conference on Computer Vision and Pattern Recognition (CVPR'93)*, pp. 82–87, New York.

Szeliski, R., Uyttendaele, M., and Steedly, D. (2008). *Fast Poisson Blending using Multi-Splines*. Technical Report MSR-TR-2008-58, Microsoft Research.

Szeliski, R., Winder, S., and Uyttendaele, M. (2010). *High-quality multi-pass image resampling*. Technical Report MSR-TR-2010-10, Microsoft Research.

Szeliski, R., Zabih, R., Scharstein, D., Veksler, O., Kolmogorov, V., Agarwala, A., Tappen, M., and Rother, C. (2008). A comparative study of energy minimization methods for Markov random fields with smoothness-based priors. *IEEE Transactions on Pattern Analysis and Machine Intelligence*, 30(6):1068–1080.

Szummer, M. and Picard, R. W. (1996). Temporal texture modeling. In *IEEE International Conference on Image Processing (ICIP-96)*, pp. 823–826, Lausanne.

Tabb, M. and Ahuja, N. (1997). Multiscale image segmentation by integrated edge and region detection. *IEEE Transactions on Image Processing*, 6(5):642–655.

Taguchi, Y., Wilburn, B., and Zitnick, C. L. (2008). Stereo reconstruction with mixed pixels using adaptive over-segmentation. In *IEEE Computer Society Conference on Computer Vision and Pattern Recognition (CVPR 2008)*, Anchorage, AK.

Tanaka, M. and Okutomi, M. (2008). Locally adaptive learning for translation-variant MRF image priors. In *IEEE Computer Society Conference on Computer Vision and Pattern Recognition (CVPR 2008)*, Anchorage, AK.

Tao, H., Sawhney, H. S., and Kumar, R. (2001). A global matching framework for stereo computation. In *Eighth International Conference on Computer Vision (ICCV 2001)*, pp. 532–539, Vancouver, Canada.

Tappen, M. F. (2007). Utilizing variational optimization to learn Markov random fields. In *IEEE Computer Society Conference on Computer Vision and Pattern Recognition (CVPR 2007)*, Minneapolis, MN.

Tappen, M. F. and Freeman, W. T. (2003). Comparison of graph cuts with belief propagation for stereo, using identical MRF parameters. In *Ninth International Conference on Computer Vision (ICCV 2003)*, pp. 900–907, Nice, France.

Tappen, M. F., Freeman, W. T., and Adelson, E. H. (2005). Recovering intrinsic images from a single image. *IEEE Transactions on Pattern Analysis and Machine Intelligence*, 27(9):1459–1472.

Tappen, M. F., Russell, B. C., and Freeman, W. T. (2003). Exploiting the sparse derivative prior for super-resolution and image demosaicing. In *Third International Workshop on Statistical and Computational Theories of Vision*, Nice, France.

Tappen, M. F., Liu, C., Freeman, W., and Adelson, E. (2007). Learning Gaussian conditional random fields for low-level vision. In *IEEE Computer Society Conference on Computer Vision and Pattern Recognition (CVPR 2007)*, Minneapolis, MN.

Tardif, J.-P. (2009). Non-iterative approach for fast and accurate vanishing point detection. In *Twelfth International Conference on Computer Vision (ICCV 2009)*, Kyoto, Japan.

Tardif, J.-P., Sturm, P., and Roy, S. (2007). Plane-based self-calibration of radial distortion. In *Eleventh International Conference on Computer Vision (ICCV 2007)*, Rio de Janeiro, Brazil.

Tardif, J.-P., Sturm, P., Trudeau, M., and Roy, S. (2009). Calibration of cameras with radially symmetric distortion. *IEEE Transactions on Pattern Analysis and Machine Intelligence*, 31(9):1552–1566.

Taubin, G. (1995). Curve and surface smoothing without shrinkage. In *Fifth International Conference on Computer Vision (ICCV'95)*, pp. 852–857, Cambridge, Massachusetts.

Taubman, D. S. and Marcellin, M. W. (2002). Jpeg2000: standard for interactive imaging. *Proceedings of the IEEE*, 90(8):1336–1357.

Taylor, C. J. (2003). Surface reconstruction from feature based stereo. In *Ninth International Conference on Computer Vision (ICCV 2003)*, pp. 184–190, Nice, France.

Taylor, C. J., Debevec, P. E., and Malik, J. (1996). Reconstructing polyhedral models of architectural scenes from photographs. In *Fourth European Conference on Computer Vision (ECCV'96)*, pp. 659–668, Cambridge, England.

Taylor, C. J., Kriegman, D. J., and Anandan, P. (1991). Structure and motion in two dimensions from multiple images: A least squares approach. In *IEEE Workshop on Visual Motion*, pp. 242–248, Princeton, New Jersey.

Taylor, P. (2009). *Text-to-Speech Synthesis*. Cambridge University Press, Cambridge.

Tek, K. and Kimia, B. B. (2003). Symmetry maps of free-form curve segments via wave propagation. *International Journal of Computer Vision*, 54(1-3):35–81.

Tekalp, M. (1995). *Digital Video Processing*. Prentice Hall, Upper Saddle River, NJ.

Telea, A. (2004). An image inpainting technique based on fast marching method. *Journal of Graphics Tools*, 9(1):23–34.

Teller, S., Antone, M., Bodnar, Z., Bosse, M., Coorg, S., Jethwa, M., and Master, N. (2003). Calibrated, registered images of an extended urban area. *International Journal of Computer Vision*, 53(1):93–107.

Teodosio, L. and Bender, W. (1993). Salient video stills: Content and context preserved. In *ACM Multimedia 93*, pp. 39–46, Anaheim, California.

Terzopoulos, D. (1983). Multilevel computational processes for visual surface reconstruction. *Computer Vision, Graphics, and Image Processing*, 24:52–96.

Terzopoulos, D. (1986a). Image analysis using multigrid relaxation methods. *IEEE Transactions on Pattern Analysis and Machine Intelligence*, PAMI-8(2):129–139.

Terzopoulos, D. (1986b). Regularization of inverse visual problems involving discontinuities. *IEEE Transactions on Pattern Analysis and Machine Intelligence*, PAMI-8(4):413–424.

Terzopoulos, D. (1988). The computation of visible-surface representations. *IEEE Transactions on Pattern Analysis and Machine Intelligence*, PAMI-10(4):417–438.

Terzopoulos, D. (1999). Visual modeling for computer animation: Graphics with a vision. *Computer Graphics*, 33(4):42–45.

Terzopoulos, D. and Fleischer, K. (1988). Deformable models. *The Visual Computer*, 4(6):306–331.

Terzopoulos, D. and Metaxas, D. (1991). Dynamic 3D models with local and global deformations: Deformable superquadrics. *IEEE Transactions on Pattern Analysis and Machine Intelligence*, 13(7):703–714.

Terzopoulos, D. and Szeliski, R. (1992). Tracking with Kalman snakes. In Blake, A. and Yuille, A. L. (eds), *Active Vision*, pp. 3–20, MIT Press, Cambridge, Massachusetts.

Terzopoulos, D. and Waters, K. (1990). Analysis of facial images using physical and anatomical models. In *Third International Conference on Computer Vision (ICCV'90)*, pp. 727–732, Osaka, Japan.

Terzopoulos, D. and Witkin, A. (1988). Physically-based models with rigid and deformable components. *IEEE Computer Graphics and Applications*, 8(6):41–51.

Terzopoulos, D., Witkin, A., and Kass, M. (1987). Symmetry-seeking models and 3D object reconstruction. *International Journal of Computer Vision*, 1(3):211–221.

Terzopoulos, D., Witkin, A., and Kass, M. (1988). Constraints on deformable models: Recovering 3D shape and nonrigid motion. *Artificial Intelligence*, 36(1):91–123.

Thayananthan, A., Iwasaki, M., and Cipolla, R. (2008). Principled fusion of high-level model and low-level cues for motion segmentation. In *IEEE Computer Society Conference on Computer Vision and Pattern Recognition (CVPR 2008)*, Anchorage, AK.

Thirthala, S. and Pollefeys, M. (2005). The radial trifocal tensor: A tool for calibrating the radial distortion of wide-angle cameras. In *IEEE Computer Society Conference on Computer Vision and Pattern Recognition (CVPR'2005)*, pp. 321–328, San Diego, CA.

Thomas, D. B., Luk, W., Leong, P. H., and Villasenor, J. D. (2007). Gaussian random number generators. *ACM Computing Surveys*, 39(4).

Thrun, S., Burgard, W., and Fox, D. (2005). *Probabilistic Robotics*. The MIT Press, Cambridge, Massachusetts.

Thrun, S., Montemerlo, M., Dahlkamp, H., Stavens, D., Aron, A. *et al.* (2006). Stanley, the robot that won the DARPA Grand Challenge. *Journal of Field Robotics*, 23(9):661–692.

Tian, Q. and Huhns, M. N. (1986). Algorithms for subpixel registration. *Computer Vision, Graphics, and Image Processing*, 35:220–233.

Tikhonov, A. N. and Arsenin, V. Y. (1977). *Solutions of Ill-Posed Problems*. V. H. Winston, Washington, D. C.

Tipping, M. E. and Bishop, C. M. (1999). Probabilistic principal components analysis. *Journal of the Royal Statistical Society, Series B*, 61(3):611–622.

Toint, P. L. (1987). On large scale nonlinear least squares calculations. *SIAM J. Sci. Stat. Comput.*, 8(3):416–435.

Tola, E., Lepetit, V., and Fua, P. (2010). DAISY: An efficient dense descriptor applied to wide-baseline stereo. *IEEE Transactions on Pattern Analysis and Machine Intelligence*, 32(5):815–830.

Tolliver, D. and Miller, G. (2006). Graph partitioning by spectral rounding: Applications in image segmentation and clustering. In *IEEE Computer Society Conference on Computer Vision and Pattern Recognition (CVPR'2006)*, pp. 1053–1060, New York City, NY.

Tomasi, C. and Kanade, T. (1992). Shape and motion from image streams under orthography: A factorization method. *International Journal of Computer Vision*, 9(2):137–154.

Tomasi, C. and Manduchi, R. (1998). Bilateral filtering for gray and color images. In *Sixth International Conference on Computer Vision (ICCV'98)*, pp. 839–846, Bombay.

Tombari, F., Mattoccia, S., and Di Stefano, L. (2007). Segmentation-based adaptive support for accurate stereo correspondence. In *Pacific-Rim Symposium on Image and Video Technology*.

Tombari, F., Mattoccia, S., Di Stefano, L., and Addimanda, E. (2008). Classification and evaluation of cost aggregation methods for stereo correspondence. In *IEEE Computer Society Conference on Computer Vision and Pattern Recognition (CVPR 2008)*, Anchorage, AK.

Tommasini, T., Fusiello, A., Trucco, E., and Roberto, V. (1998). Making good features track better. In *IEEE Computer Society Conference on Computer Vision and Pattern Recognition (CVPR'98)*, pp. 178–183, Santa Barbara.

Torborg, J. and Kajiya, J. T. (1996). Talisman: Commodity realtime 3D graphics for the PC. In *ACM SIGGRAPH 1996 Conference Proceedings*, pp. 353–363, New Orleans.

Torr, P. H. S. (2002). Bayesian model estimation and selection for epipolar geometry and generic manifold fitting. *International Journal of Computer Vision*, 50(1):35–61.

Torr, P. H. S. and Fitzgibbon, A. W. (2004). Invariant fitting of two view geometry. *IEEE Transactions on Pattern Analysis and Machine Intelligence*, 26(5):648–650.

Torr, P. H. S. and Murray, D. (1997). The development and comparison of robust methods for estimating the fundamental matrix. *International Journal of Computer Vision*, 24(3):271–300.

Torr, P. H. S., Szeliski, R., and Anandan, P. (1999). An integrated Bayesian approach to layer extraction from image sequences. In *Seventh International Conference on Computer Vision (ICCV'99)*, pp. 983–990, Kerkyra, Greece.

Torr, P. H. S., Szeliski, R., and Anandan, P. (2001). An integrated Bayesian approach to layer extraction from image sequences. *IEEE Transactions on Pattern Analysis and Machine Intelligence*, 23(3):297–303.

Torralba, A. (2003). Contextual priming for object detection. *International Journal of Computer Vision*, 53(2):169–191.

Torralba, A. (2007). Classifier-based methods. In *CVPR 2007 Short Course on Recognizing and Learning Object Categories*. http://people.csail.mit.edu/torralba/shortCourseRLOC/.

Torralba, A. (2008). Object recognition and scene understanding. MIT Course 6.870, http://people.csail.mit.edu/torralba/courses/6.870/6.870.recognition.htm.

Torralba, A., Freeman, W. T., and Fergus, R. (2008). 80 million tiny images: a large dataset for non-parametric object and scene recognition. *IEEE Transactions on Pattern Analysis and Machine Intelligence*, 30(11):1958–1970.

Torralba, A., Murphy, K. P., and Freeman, W. T. (2004). Contextual models for object detection using boosted random fields. In *Advances in Neural Information Processing Systems*.

Torralba, A., Murphy, K. P., and Freeman, W. T. (2007). Sharing visual features for multiclass and multiview object detection. *IEEE Transactions on Pattern Analysis and Machine Intelligence*, 29(5):854–869.

Torralba, A., Weiss, Y., and Fergus, R. (2008). Small codes and large databases of images for object recognition. In *IEEE Computer Society Conference on Computer Vision and Pattern Recognition (CVPR 2008)*, Anchorage, AK.

Torralba, A., Murphy, K. P., Freeman, W. T., and Rubin, M. A. (2003). Context-based vision system for place and object recognition. In *Ninth International Conference on Computer Vision (ICCV 2003)*, pp. 273–280, Nice, France.

Torrance, K. E. and Sparrow, E. M. (1967). Theory for off-specular reflection from roughened surfaces. *Journal of the Optical Society of America A*, 57(9):1105–1114.

Torresani, L., Hertzmann, A., and Bregler, C. (2008). Non-rigid structure-from-motion: Estimating shape and motion with hierarchical priors. *IEEE Transactions on Pattern Analysis and Machine Intelligence*, 30(5):878–892.

Toyama, K. (1998). *Prolegomena for Robust Face Tracking*. Technical Report MSR-TR-98-65, Microsoft Research.

Toyama, K., Krumm, J., Brumitt, B., and Meyers, B. (1999). Wallflower: Principles and practice of background maintenance. In *Seventh International Conference on Computer Vision (ICCV'99)*, pp. 255–261, Kerkyra, Greece.

Tran, S. and Davis, L. (2002). 3D surface reconstruction using graph cuts with surface constraints. In *Seventh European Conference on Computer Vision (ECCV 2002)*, pp. 219–231, Copenhagen.

Trefethen, L. N. and Bau, D. (1997). *Numerical Linear Algebra*. SIAM.

Treisman, A. (1985). Preattentive processing in vision. *Computer Vision, Graphics, and Image Processing*, 31(2):156–177.

Triggs, B. (1996). Factorization methods for projective structure and motion. In *IEEE Computer Society Conference on Computer Vision and Pattern Recognition (CVPR'96)*, pp. 845–851, San Francisco.

Triggs, B. (2004). Detecting keypoints with stable position, orientation, and scale under illumination changes. In *Eighth European Conference on Computer Vision (ECCV 2004)*, pp. 100–113, Prague.

Triggs, B., McLauchlan, P. F., Hartley, R. I., and Fitzgibbon, A. W. (1999). Bundle adjustment — a modern synthesis. In *International Workshop on Vision Algorithms*, pp. 298–372, Kerkyra, Greece.

Trobin, W., Pock, T., Cremers, D., and Bischof, H. (2008). Continuous energy minimization via repeated binary fusion. In *Tenth European Conference on Computer Vision (ECCV 2008)*, pp. 677–690, Marseilles.

Troccoli, A. and Allen, P. (2008). Building illumination coherent 3D models of large-scale outdoor scenes. *International Journal of Computer Vision*, 78(2-3):261–280.

Trottenberg, U., Oosterlee, C. W., and Schuller, A. (2000). *Multigrid*. Academic Press.

Trucco, E. and Verri, A. (1998). *Introductory Techniques for 3-D Computer Vision*. Prentice Hall, Upper Saddle River, NJ.

Tsai, P. S. and Shah, M. (1994). Shape from shading using linear approximation. *Image and Vision Computing*, 12:487–498.

Tsai, R. Y. (1987). A versatile camera calibration technique for high-accuracy 3D machine vision metrology using off-the-shelf TV cameras and lenses. *IEEE Journal of Robotics and Automation*, RA-3(4):323–344.

Tschumperlé, D. (2006). Curvature-preserving regularization of multi-valued images using PDEs. In *Ninth European Conference on Computer Vision (ECCV 2006)*, pp. 295–307.

Tschumperlé, D. and Deriche, R. (2005). Vector-valued image regularization with PDEs: A common framework for different applications. *IEEE Transactions on Pattern Analysis and Machine Intelligence*, 27:506–517.

Tsin, Y., Kang, S. B., and Szeliski, R. (2006). Stereo matching with linear superposition of layers. *IEEE Transactions on Pattern Analysis and Machine Intelligence*, 28(2):290–301.

Tsin, Y., Ramesh, V., and Kanade, T. (2001). Statistical calibration of CCD imaging process. In *Eighth International Conference on Computer Vision (ICCV 2001)*, pp. 480–487, Vancouver, Canada.

Tu, Z., Chen, X., Yuille, A. L., and Zhu, S.-C. (2005). Image parsing: Unifying segmentation, detection, and recognition. *International Journal of Computer Vision*, 63(2):113–140.

Tumblin, J. and Rushmeier, H. E. (1993). Tone reproduction for realistic images. *IEEE Computer Graphics and Applications*, 13(6):42–48.

Tumblin, J. and Turk, G. (1999). LCIS: A boundary hierarchy for detail-preserving contrast reduction. In *ACM SIGGRAPH 1999 Conference Proceedings*, pp. 83–90, Los Angeles.

Tumblin, J., Agrawal, A., and Raskar, R. (2005). Why I want a gradient camera. In *IEEE Computer Society Conference on Computer Vision and Pattern Recognition (CVPR'2005)*, pp. 103–110, San Diego, CA.

Turcot, P. and Lowe, D. G. (2009). Better matching with fewer features: The selection of useful features in large database recognition problems. In *ICCV Workshop on Emergent Issues in Large Amounts of Visual Data (WS-LAVD)*, Kyoto, Japan.

Turk, G. and Levoy, M. (1994). Zippered polygonal meshes from range images. In *ACM SIGGRAPH 1994 Conference Proceedings*, pp. 311–318.

Turk, G. and O'Brien, J. (2002). Modelling with implicit surfaces that interpolate. *ACM Transactions on Graphics*, 21(4):855–873.

Turk, M. and Pentland, A. (1991a). Eigenfaces for recognition. *Journal of Cognitive Neuroscience*, 3(1):71–86.

Turk, M. and Pentland, A. (1991b). Face recognition using eigenfaces. In *IEEE Computer Society Conference on Computer Vision and Pattern Recognition (CVPR'91)*, pp. 586–591, Maui, Hawaii.

Tuytelaars, T. and Mikolajczyk, K. (2007). Local invariant feature detectors. *Foundations and Trends in Computer Graphics and Computer Vision*, 3(1).

Tuytelaars, T. and Van Gool, L. (2004). Matching widely separated views based on affine invariant regions. *International Journal of Computer Vision*, 59(1):61–85.

Tuytelaars, T., Van Gool, L., and Proesmans, M. (1997). The cascaded Hough transform. In *International Conference on Image Processing (ICIP'97)*, pp. 736–739.

Ullman, S. (1979). The interpretation of structure from motion. *Proceedings of the Royal Society of London*, B-203:405–426.

Unnikrishnan, R., Pantofaru, C., and Hebert, M. (2007). Toward objective evaluation of image segmentation algorithms. *IEEE Transactions on Pattern Analysis and Machine Intelligence*, 29(6):828–944.

Unser, M. (1999). Splines: A perfect fit for signal and image processing. *IEEE Signal Processing Magazine*, 16(6):22–38.

Urmson, C., Anhalt, J., Bagnell, D., Baker, C., Bittner, R. *et al.* (2008). Autonomous driving in urban environments: Boss and the urban challenge. *Journal of Field Robotics*, 25(8):425–466.

Urtasun, R., Fleet, D. J., and Fua, P. (2006). Temporal motion models for monocular and multiview 3D human body tracking. *Computer Vision and Image Understanding*, 104(2-3):157–177.

Uyttendaele, M., Eden, A., and Szeliski, R. (2001). Eliminating ghosting and exposure artifacts in image mosaics. In *IEEE Computer Society Conference on Computer Vision and Pattern Recognition (CVPR'2001)*, pp. 509–516, Kauai, Hawaii.

Uyttendaele, M., Criminisi, A., Kang, S. B., Winder, S., Hartley, R., and Szeliski, R. (2004). Image-based interactive exploration of real-world environments. *IEEE Computer Graphics and Applications*, 24(3):52–63.

Vaillant, R. and Faugeras, O. D. (1992). Using extremal boundaries for 3-D object modeling. *IEEE Transactions on Pattern Analysis and Machine Intelligence*, 14(2):157–173.

Vaish, V., Szeliski, R., Zitnick, C. L., Kang, S. B., and Levoy, M. (2006). Reconstructing occluded surfaces using synthetic apertures: Shape from focus vs. shape from stereo. In *IEEE Computer Society Conference on Computer Vision and Pattern Recognition (CVPR'2006)*, pp. 2331–2338, New York, NY.

van de Weijer, J. and Schmid, C. (2006). Coloring local feature extraction. In *Ninth European Conference on Computer Vision (ECCV 2006)*, pp. 334–348.

van den Hengel, A., Dick, A., Thormhlen, T., Ward, B., and Torr, P. H. S. (2007). Videotrace: Rapid interactive scene modeling from video. *ACM Transactions on Graphics*, 26(3).

Van Huffel, S. and Lemmerling, P. (eds). (2002). *Total Least Squares and Errors-in-Variables Modeling*, Springer.

Van Huffel, S. and Vandewalle, J. (1991). *The Total Least Squares Problem: Computational Aspects and Analysis*. Society for Industrial and Applied Mathematics, Philadephia.

van Ouwerkerk, J. D. (2006). Image super-resolution survey. *Image and Vision Computing*, 24(10):1039–1052.

Varma, M. and Ray, D. (2007). Learning the discriminative power-invariance trade-off. In *Eleventh International Conference on Computer Vision (ICCV 2007)*, Rio de Janeiro, Brazil.

Vasconcelos, N. (2007). From pixels to semantic spaces: Advances in content-based image retrieval. *Computer*, 40(7):20–26.

Vasilescu, M. A. O. and Terzopoulos, D. (2007). Multilinear (tensor) image synthesis, analysis, and recognition. *IEEE Signal Processing Magazine*, 24(6):118–123.

Vedaldi, A. and Fulkerson, B. (2008). VLFeat: An open and portable library of computer vision algorithms. http://www.vlfeat.org/.

Vedaldi, A., Gulshan, V., Varma, M., and Zisserman, A. (2009). Multiple kernels for object detection. In *Twelfth International Conference on Computer Vision (ICCV 2009)*, Kyoto, Japan.

Vedula, S., Baker, S., and Kanade, T. (2005). Image-based spatio-temporal modeling and view interpolation of dynamic events. *ACM Transactions on Graphics*, 24(2):240–261.

Vedula, S., Baker, S., Rander, P., Collins, R., and Kanade, T. (2005). Three-dimensional scene flow. *IEEE Transactions on Pattern Analysis and Machine Intelligence*, 27(3):475–480.

Veeraraghavan, A., Raskar, R., Agrawal, A., Mohan, A., and Tumblin, J. (2007). Dappled photography: Mask enhanced cameras for heterodyned light fields and coded aperture refocusing. *ACM Transactions on Graphics*, 26(3).

Veksler, O. (1999). *Efficient Graph-based Energy Minimization Methods in Computer Vision*. Ph.D. thesis, Cornell University.

Veksler, O. (2001). Stereo matching by compact windows via minimum ratio cycle. In *Eighth International Conference on Computer Vision (ICCV 2001)*, pp. 540–547, Vancouver, Canada.

Veksler, O. (2003). Fast variable window for stereo correspondence using integral images. In *IEEE Computer Society Conference on Computer Vision and Pattern Recognition (CVPR'2003)*, pp. 556–561, Madison, WI.

Veksler, O. (2007). Graph cut based optimization for MRFs with truncated convex priors. In *IEEE Computer Society Conference on Computer Vision and Pattern Recognition (CVPR 2007)*, Minneapolis, MN.

Verbeek, J. and Triggs, B. (2007). Region classification with Markov field aspect models. In *IEEE Computer Society Conference on Computer Vision and Pattern Recognition (CVPR 2007)*, Minneapolis, MN.

Vergauwen, M. and Van Gool, L. (2006). Web-based 3D reconstruction service. *Machine Vision and Applications*, 17(2):321–329.

Vetter, T. and Poggio, T. (1997). Linear object classes and image synthesis from a single example image. *IEEE Transactions on Pattern Analysis and Machine Intelligence*, 19(7):733–742.

Vezhnevets, V., Sazonov, V., and Andreeva, A. (2003). A survey on pixel-based skin color detection techniques. In *GRAPHICON03*, pp. 85–92.

Vicente, S., Kolmogorov, V., and Rother, C. (2008). Graph cut based image segmentation with connectivity priors. In *IEEE Computer Society Conference on Computer Vision and Pattern Recognition (CVPR 2008)*, Anchorage, AK.

Vidal, R., Ma, Y., and Sastry, S. S. (2010). *Generalized Principal Component Analysis*. Springer.

Viéville, T. and Faugeras, O. D. (1990). Feedforward recovery of motion and structure from a sequence of 2D-lines matches. In *Third International Conference on Computer Vision (ICCV'90)*, pp. 517–520, Osaka, Japan.

Vincent, L. and Soille, P. (1991). Watersheds in digital spaces: An efficient algorithm based on immersion simulations. *IEEE Transactions on Pattern Analysis and Machine Intelligence*, 13(6):583–596.

Vineet, V. and Narayanan, P. J. (2008). CUDA cuts: Fast graph cuts on the GPU. In *CVPR 2008 Workshop on Visual Computer Vision on GPUs (CVGPU)*, Anchorage, AK.

Viola, P. and Wells III, W. (1997). Alignment by maximization of mutual information. *International Journal of Computer Vision*, 24(2):137–154.

Viola, P., Jones, M. J., and Snow, D. (2003). Detecting pedestrians using patterns of motion and appearance. In *Ninth International Conference on Computer Vision (ICCV 2003)*, pp. 734–741, Nice, France.

Viola, P. A. and Jones, M. J. (2004). Robust real-time face detection. *International Journal of Computer Vision*, 57(2):137–154.

Vlasic, D., Baran, I., Matusik, W., and Popović, J. (2008). Articulated mesh animation from multi-view silhouettes. *ACM Transactions on Graphics*, 27(3).

Vlasic, D., Brand, M., Pfister, H., and Popović, J. (2005). Face transfer with multilinear models. *ACM Transactions on Graphics (Proc. SIGGRAPH 2005)*, 24(3):426–433.

Vogiatzis, G., Torr, P., and Cipolla, R. (2005). Multi-view stereo via volumetric graph-cuts. In *IEEE Computer Society Conference on Computer Vision and Pattern Recognition (CVPR'2005)*, pp. 391–398, San Diego, CA.

Vogiatzis, G., Hernandez, C., Torr, P., and Cipolla, R. (2007). Multi-view stereo via volumetric graph-cuts and occlusion robust photo-consistency. *IEEE Transactions on Pattern Analysis and Machine Intelligence*, 29(12):2241–2246.

von Ahn, L. and Dabbish, L. (2004). Labeling images with a computer game. In *CHI'04: SIGCHI Conference on Human Factors in Computing Systems*, pp. 319–326, Vienna, Austria.

von Ahn, L., Liu, R., and Blum, M. (2006). Peekaboom: A game for locating objects in images. In *CHI'06: SIGCHI Conference on Human Factors in Computing Systems*, pp. 55–64, Montréal, Québec, Canada.

Wainwright, M. J. and Jordan, M. I. (2008). Graphical models, exponential families, and variational inference. *Foundations and Trends in Machine Learning*, 1(1-2):1–305.

Wainwright, M. J., Jaakkola, T. S., and Willsky, A. S. (2005). MAP estimation via agreement on trees: message-passing and linear programming. *IEEE Transactions on Information Theory*, 51(11):3697–3717.

Waithe, P. and Ferrie, F. (1991). From uncertainty to visual exploration. *IEEE Transactions on Pattern Analysis and Machine Intelligence*, 13(10):1038–1049.

Walker, E. L. and Herman, M. (1988). Geometric reasoning for constructing 3D scene descriptions from images. *Artificial Intelligence*, 37:275–290.

Wallace, G. K. (1991). The JPEG still picture compression standard. *Communications of the ACM*, 34(4):30–44.

Wallace, J. R., Cohen, M. F., and Greenberg, D. P. (1987). A two-pass solution to the rendering equation: A synthesis of ray tracing and radiosity methods. *Computer Graphics (SIGGRAPH '87)*, 21(4):311–320.

Waltz, D. L. (1975). Understanding line drawings of scenes with shadows. In Winston, P. H. (ed.), *The Psychology of Computer Vision*, McGraw-Hill, New York.

Wang, H. and Oliensis, J. (2010). Shape matching by segmentation averaging. *IEEE Transactions on Pattern Analysis and Machine Intelligence*, 32(4):619–635.

Wang, J. and Cohen, M. F. (2005). An iterative optimization approach for unified image segmentation and matting. In *Tenth International Conference on Computer Vision (ICCV 2005)*, Beijing, China.

Wang, J. and Cohen, M. F. (2007a). Image and video matting: A survey. *Foundations and Trends in Computer Graphics and Computer Vision*, 3(2).

Wang, J. and Cohen, M. F. (2007b). Optimized color sampling for robust matting. In *IEEE Computer Society Conference on Computer Vision and Pattern Recognition (CVPR 2007)*, Minneapolis, MN.

Wang, J. and Cohen, M. F. (2007c). Simultaneous matting and compositing. In *IEEE Computer Society Conference on Computer Vision and Pattern Recognition (CVPR 2007)*, Minneapolis, MN.

Wang, J., Agrawala, M., and Cohen, M. F. (2007). Soft scissors: An interactive tool for realtime high quality matting. *ACM Transactions on Graphics*, 26(3).

Wang, J., Thiesson, B., Xu, Y., and Cohen, M. (2004). Image and video segmentation by anisotropic kernel mean shift. In *Eighth European Conference on Computer Vision (ECCV 2004)*, pp. 238–249, Prague.

Wang, J., Bhat, P., Colburn, R. A., Agrawala, M., and Cohen, M. F. (2005). Video cutout. *ACM Transactions on Graphics (Proc. SIGGRAPH 2005)*, 24(3):585–594.

Wang, J. Y. A. and Adelson, E. H. (1994). Representing moving images with layers. *IEEE Transactions on Image Processing*, 3(5):625–638.

Wang, L., Kang, S. B., Szeliski, R., and Shum, H.-Y. (2001). Optimal texture map reconstruction from multiple views. In *IEEE Computer Society Conference on Computer Vision and Pattern Recognition (CVPR'2001)*, pp. 347–354, Kauai, Hawaii.

Wang, Y. and Zhu, S.-C. (2003). Modeling textured motion: Particle, wave and sketch. In *Ninth International Conference on Computer Vision (ICCV 2003)*, pp. 213–220, Nice, France.

Wang, Z., Bovik, A. C., and Simoncelli, E. P. (2005). Structural approaches to image quality assessment. In Bovik, A. C. (ed.), *Handbook of Image and Video Processing*, pp. 961–974, Elsevier Academic Press.

Wang, Z., Bovik, A. C., Sheikh, H. R., and Simoncelli, E. P. (2004). Image quality assessment: From error visibility to structural similarity. *IEEE Transactions on Image Processing*, 13(4):600–612.

Wang, Z.-F. and Zheng, Z.-G. (2008). A region based stereo matching algorithm using cooperative optimization. In *IEEE Computer Society Conference on Computer Vision and Pattern Recognition (CVPR 2008)*, Anchorage, AK.

Ward, G. (1992). Measuring and modeling anisotropic reflection. *Computer Graphics (SIGGRAPH '92)*, 26(4):265–272.

Ward, G. (1994). The radiance lighting simulation and rendering system. In *ACM SIGGRAPH 1994 Conference Proceedings*, pp. 459–472.

Ward, G. (2003). Fast, robust image registration for compositing high dynamic range photographs from hand-held exposures. *Journal of Graphics Tools*, 8(2):17–30.

Ward, G. (2004). High dynamic range image encodings. http://www.anyhere.com/gward/hdrenc/hdr_encodings.html.

Ware, C., Arthur, K., and Booth, K. S. (1993). Fish tank virtual reality. In *INTERCHI'03*, pp. 37–42, Amsterdam.

Warren, J. and Weimer, H. (2001). *Subdivision Methods for Geometric Design: A Constructive Approach*. Morgan Kaufmann.

Watanabe, M. and Nayar, S. K. (1998). Rational filters for passive depth from defocus. *International Journal of Computer Vision*, 27(3):203–225.

Watt, A. (1995). *3D Computer Graphics*. Addison-Wesley, Harlow, England, third edition.

Weber, J. and Malik, J. (1995). Robust computation of optical flow in a multi-scale differential framework. *International Journal of Computer Vision*, 14(1):67–81.

Weber, M., Welling, M., and Perona, P. (2000). Unsupervised learning of models for recognition. In *Sixth European Conference on Computer Vision (ECCV 2000)*, pp. 18–32, Dublin, Ireland.

Wedel, A., Cremers, D., Pock, T., and Bischof, H. (2009). Structure- and motion-adaptive regularization for high accuracy optic flow. In *Twelfth International Conference on Computer Vision (ICCV 2009)*, Kyoto, Japan.

Wedel, A., Rabe, C., Vaudrey, T., Brox, T., Franke, U., and Cremers, D. (2008). Efficient dense scene flow from sparse or dense stereo data. In *Tenth European Conference on Computer Vision (ECCV 2008)*, pp. 739–751, Marseilles.

Wei, C. Y. and Quan, L. (2004). Region-based progressive stereo matching. In *IEEE Computer Society Conference on Computer Vision and Pattern Recognition (CVPR'2005)*, pp. 106–113, Washington, D. C.

Wei, L.-Y. and Levoy, M. (2000). Fast texture synthesis using tree-structured vector quantization. In *ACM SIGGRAPH 2000 Conference Proceedings*, pp. 479–488.

Weickert, J. (1998). *Anisotropic Diffusion in Image Processing*. Tuebner, Stuttgart.

Weickert, J., ter Haar Romeny, B. M., and Viergever, M. A. (1998). Efficient and reliable schemes for nonlinear diffusion filtering. *IEEE Transactions on Image Processing*, 7(3):398–410.

Weinland, D., Ronfard, R., and Boyer, E. (2006). Free viewpoint action recognition using motion history volumes. *Computer Vision and Image Understanding*, 104(2-3):249–257.

Weiss, Y. (1997). Smoothness in layers: Motion segmentation using nonparametric mixture estimation. In *IEEE Computer Society Conference on Computer Vision and Pattern Recognition (CVPR'97)*, pp. 520–526, San Juan, Puerto Rico.

Weiss, Y. (1999). Segmentation using eigenvectors: A unifying view. In *Seventh International Conference on Computer Vision (ICCV'99)*, pp. 975–982, Kerkyra, Greece.

Weiss, Y. (2001). Deriving intrinsic images from image sequences. In *Eighth International Conference on Computer Vision (ICCV 2001)*, pp. 7–14, Vancouver, Canada.

Weiss, Y. and Adelson, E. H. (1996). A unified mixture framework for motion segmentation: Incorporating spatial coherence and estimating the number of models. In *IEEE Computer Society Conference on Computer Vision and Pattern Recognition (CVPR'96)*, pp. 321–326, San Francisco.

Weiss, Y. and Freeman, B. (2007). What makes a good model of natural images? In *IEEE Computer Society Conference on Computer Vision and Pattern Recognition (CVPR 2007)*, Minneapolis, MN.

Weiss, Y. and Freeman, W. T. (2001a). Correctness of belief propagation in Gaussian graphical models of arbitrary topology. *Neural Computation*, 13(10):2173–2200.

Weiss, Y. and Freeman, W. T. (2001b). On the optimality of solutions of the max-product belief propagation algorithm in arbitrary graphs. *IEEE Transactions on Information Theory*, 47(2):736–744.

Weiss, Y., Torralba, A., and Fergus, R. (2008). Spectral hashing. In *Advances in Neural Information Processing Systems*.

Weiss, Y., Yanover, C., and Meltzer, T. (2010). Linear programming and variants of belief propagation. In Blake, A., Kohli, P., and Rother, C. (eds), *Advances in Markov Random Fields*, MIT Press.

Wells, III, W. M. (1986). Efficient synthesis of Gaussian filters by cascaded uniform filters. *IEEE Transactions on Pattern Analysis and Machine Intelligence*, 8(2):234–239.

Weng, J., Ahuja, N., and Huang, T. S. (1993). Optimal motion and structure estimation. *IEEE Transactions on Pattern Analysis and Machine Intelligence*, 15(9):864–884.

Wenger, A., Gardner, A., Tchou, C., Unger, J., Hawkins, T., and Debevec, P. (2005). Performance relighting and reflectance transformation with time-multiplexed illumination. *ACM Transactions on Graphics (Proc. SIGGRAPH 2005)*, 24(3):756–764.

Werlberger, M., Trobin, W., Pock, T., Bischof, H., Wedel, A., and Cremers, D. (2009). Anisotropic Huber-L1 optical flow. In *British Machine Vision Conference (BMVC 2009)*, London.

Werner, T. (2007). A linear programming approach to max-sum problem: A review. *IEEE Transactions on Pattern Analysis and Machine Intelligence*, 29(7):1165–1179.

Werner, T. and Zisserman, A. (2002). New techniques for automated architectural reconstruction from photographs. In *Seventh European Conference on Computer Vision (ECCV 2002)*, pp. 541–555, Copenhagen.

Westin, S. H., Arvo, J. R., and Torrance, K. E. (1992). Predicting reflectance functions from complex surfaces. *Computer Graphics (SIGGRAPH '92)*, 26(4):255–264.

Westover, L. (1989). Interactive volume rendering. In *Workshop on Volume Visualization*, pp. 9–16, Chapel Hill.

Wexler, Y., Fitzgibbon, A., and Zisserman, A. (2002). Bayesian estimation of layers from multiple images. In *Seventh European Conference on Computer Vision (ECCV 2002)*, pp. 487–501, Copenhagen.

Wexler, Y., Shechtman, E., and Irani, M. (2007). Space-time completion of video. *IEEE Transactions on Pattern Analysis and Machine Intelligence*, 29(3):463–476.

Weyrich, T., Lawrence, J., Lensch, H. P. A., Rusinkiewicz, S., and Zickler, T. (2008). Principles of appearance acquisition and representation. *Foundations and Trends in Computer Graphics and Computer Vision*, 4(2):75–191.

Weyrich, T., Matusik, W., Pfister, H., Bickel, B., Donner, C. *et al.* (2006). Analysis of human faces using a measurement-based skin reflectance model. *ACM Transactions on Graphics*, 25(3):1013–1024.

Wheeler, M. D., Sato, Y., and Ikeuchi, K. (1998). Consensus surfaces for modeling 3D objects from multiple range images. In *Sixth International Conference on Computer Vision (ICCV'98)*, pp. 917–924, Bombay.

White, R. and Forsyth, D. (2006). Combining cues: Shape from shading and texture. In *IEEE Computer Society Conference on Computer Vision and Pattern Recognition (CVPR'2006)*, pp. 1809–1816, New York City, NY.

White, R., Crane, K., and Forsyth, D. A. (2007). Capturing and animating occluded cloth. *ACM Transactions on Graphics*, 26(3).

Wiejak, J. S., Buxton, H., and Buxton, B. F. (1985). Convolution with separable masks for early image processing. *Computer Vision, Graphics, and Image Processing*, 32(3):279–290.

Wilburn, B., Joshi, N., Vaish, V., Talvala, E.-V., Antunez, E. *et al.* (2005). High performance imaging using large camera arrays. *ACM Transactions on Graphics (Proc. SIGGRAPH 2005)*, 24(3):765–776.

Wilczkowiak, M., Brostow, G. J., Tordoff, B., and Cipolla, R. (2005). Hole filling through photomontage. In *British Machine Vision Conference (BMVC 2005)*, pp. 492–501, Oxford Brookes.

Williams, D. and Burns, P. D. (2001). Diagnostics for digital capture using MTF. In *IS&T PICS Conference*, pp. 227–232.

Williams, D. J. and Shah, M. (1992). A fast algorithm for active contours and curvature estimation. *Computer Vision, Graphics, and Image Processing*, 55(1):14–26.

Williams, L. (1983). Pyramidal parametrics. *Computer Graphics (SIGGRAPH '83)*, 17(3):1–11.

Williams, L. (1990). Performace driven facial animation. *Computer Graphics (SIGGRAPH '90)*, 24(4):235–242.

Williams, O., Blake, A., and Cipolla, R. (2003). A sparse probabilistic learning algorithm for real-time tracking. In *Ninth International Conference on Computer Vision (ICCV 2003)*, pp. 353–360, Nice, France.

Williams, T. L. (1999). *The Optical Transfer Function of Imaging Systems*. Institute of Physics Publishing, London.

Winder, S. and Brown, M. (2007). Learning local image descriptors. In *IEEE Computer Society Conference on Computer Vision and Pattern Recognition (CVPR 2007)*, Minneapolis, MN.

Winkenbach, G. and Salesin, D. H. (1994). Computer-generated pen-and-ink illustration. In *ACM SIGGRAPH 1994 Conference Proceedings*, pp. 91–100, Orlando, Florida.

Winn, J. and Shotton, J. (2006). The layout consistent random field for recognizing and segmenting partially occluded objects. In *IEEE Computer Society Conference on Computer Vision and Pattern Recognition (CVPR'2006)*, pp. 37–44, New York City, NY.

Winnemöller, H., Olsen, S. C., and Gooch, B. (2006). Real-time video abstraction. *ACM Transactions on Graphics*, 25(3):1221–1226.

Winston, P. H. (ed.). (1975). *The Psychology of Computer Vision*, McGraw-Hill, New York.

Wiskott, L., Fellous, J.-M., Krüger, N., and von der Malsburg, C. (1997). Face recognition by elastic bunch graph matching. *IEEE Transactions on Pattern Analysis and Machine Intelligence*, 19(7):775–779.

Witkin, A. (1981). Recovering surface shape and orientation from texture. *Artificial Intelligence*, 17(1-3):17–45.

Witkin, A. (1983). Scale-space filtering. In *Eighth International Joint Conference on Artificial Intelligence (IJCAI-83)*, pp. 1019–1022.

Witkin, A., Terzopoulos, D., and Kass, M. (1986). Signal matching through scale space. In *Fifth National Conference on Artificial Intelligence (AAAI-86)*, pp. 714–719, Philadelphia.

Witkin, A., Terzopoulos, D., and Kass, M. (1987). Signal matching through scale space. *International Journal of Computer Vision*, 1:133–144.

Wolberg, G. (1990). *Digital Image Warping*. IEEE Computer Society Press, Los Alamitos.

Wolberg, G. and Pavlidis, T. (1985). Restoration of binary images using stochastic relaxation with annealing. *Pattern Recognition Letters*, 3:375–388.

Wolff, L. B., Shafer, S. A., and Healey, G. E. (eds). (1992a). *Radiometry. Physics-Based Vision: Principles and Practice*, Jones & Bartlett, Cambridge, MA.

Wolff, L. B., Shafer, S. A., and Healey, G. E. (eds). (1992b). *Shape Recovery. Physics-Based Vision: Principles and Practice*, Jones & Bartlett, Cambridge, MA.

Wood, D. N., Finkelstein, A., Hughes, J. F., Thayer, C. E., and Salesin, D. H. (1997). Multiperspective panoramas for cel animation. In *ACM SIGGRAPH 1997 Conference Proceedings*, pp. 243–250, Los Angeles.

Wood, D. N., Azuma, D. I., Aldinger, K., Curless, B., Duchamp, T., Salesin, D. H., and Stuetzle, W. (2000). Surface light fields for 3D photography. In *ACM SIGGRAPH 2000 Conference Proceedings*, pp. 287–296.

Woodford, O., Reid, I., Torr, P. H., and Fitzgibbon, A. (2008). Global stereo reconstruction under second order smoothness priors. In *IEEE Computer Society Conference on Computer Vision and Pattern Recognition (CVPR 2008)*, Anchorage, AK.

Woodham, R. J. (1981). Analysing images of curved surfaces. *Artificial Intelligence*, 17:117–140.

Woodham, R. J. (1994). Gradient and curvature from photometric stereo including local confidence estimation. *Journal of the Optical Society of America, A*, 11:3050–3068.

Wren, C. R., Azarbayejani, A., Darrell, T., and Pentland, A. P. (1997). Pfinder: Real-time tracking of the human body. *IEEE Transactions on Pattern Analysis and Machine Intelligence*, 19(7):780–785.

Wright, S. (2006). *Digital Compositing for Film and Video*. Focal Press, 2nd edition.

Wu, C. (2010). SiftGPU: A GPU implementation of scale invariant feature transform (SIFT). http://www.cs. unc.edu/~ccwu/siftgpu/.

Wyszecki, G. and Stiles, W. S. (2000). *Color Science: Concepts and Methods, Quantitative Data and Formulae.* John Wiley & Sons, New York, 2nd edition.

Xiao, J. and Shah, M. (2003). Two-frame wide baseline matching. In *Ninth International Conference on Computer Vision (ICCV 2003)*, pp. 603–609, Nice, France.

Xiao, J. and Shah, M. (2005). Motion layer extraction in the presence of occlusion using graph cuts. *IEEE Transactions on Pattern Analysis and Machine Intelligence*, 27(10):1644–1659.

Xiong, Y. and Turkowski, K. (1997). Creating image-based VR using a self-calibrating fisheye lens. In *IEEE Computer Society Conference on Computer Vision and Pattern Recognition (CVPR'97)*, pp. 237–243, San Juan, Puerto Rico.

Xiong, Y. and Turkowski, K. (1998). Registration, calibration and blending in creating high quality panoramas. In *IEEE Workshop on Applications of Computer Vision (WACV'98)*, pp. 69–74, Princeton.

Xu, L., Chen, J., and Jia, J. (2008). A segmentation based variational model for accurate optical flow estimation. In *Tenth European Conference on Computer Vision (ECCV 2008)*, pp. 671–684, Marseilles.

Yang, D., El Gamal, A., Fowler, B., and Tian, H. (1999). A 640x512 CMOS image sensor with ultra-wide dynamic range floating-point pixel level ADC. *IEEE Journal of Solid State Circuits*, 34(12):1821–1834.

Yang, L. and Albregtsen, F. (1996). Fast and exact computation of Cartesian geometric moments using discrete Green's theorem. *Pattern Recognition*, 29(7):1061–1073.

Yang, L., Meer, P., and Foran, D. (2007). Multiple class segmentation using a unified framework over mean-shift patches. In *IEEE Computer Society Conference on Computer Vision and Pattern Recognition (CVPR 2007)*, Minneapolis, MN.

Yang, L., Jin, R., Sukthankar, R., and Jurie, F. (2008). Unifying discriminative visual codebook generation with classifier training for object category recognition. In *IEEE Computer Society Conference on Computer Vision and Pattern Recognition (CVPR 2008)*, Anchorage, AK.

Yang, M.-H., Ahuja, N., and Tabb, M. (2002). Extraction of 2D motion trajectories and its application to hand gesture recognition. *IEEE Transactions on Pattern Analysis and Machine Intelligence*, 24(8):1061–1074.

Yang, M.-H., Kriegman, D. J., and Ahuja, N. (2002). Detecting faces in images: A survey. *IEEE Transactions on Pattern Analysis and Machine Intelligence*, 24(1):34–58.

Yang, Q., Wang, L., Yang, R., Stewénius, H., and Nistér, D. (2009). Stereo matching with color-weighted correlation, hierarchical belief propagation and occlusion handling. *IEEE Transactions on Pattern Analysis and Machine Intelligence*, 31(3):492–504.

Yang, Y., Yuille, A., and Lu, J. (1993). Local, global, and multilevel stereo matching. In *IEEE Computer Society Conference on Computer Vision and Pattern Recognition (CVPR'93)*, pp. 274–279, New York.

Yanover, C., Meltzer, T., and Weiss, Y. (2006). Linear programming relaxations and belief propagation — an empirical study. *Journal of Machine Learning Research*, 7:1887–1907.

Yao, B. Z., Yang, X., Lin, L., Lee, M. W., and Zhu, S.-C. (2010). I2T: Image parsing to text description. *Proceedings of the IEEE*, 98(8):1485–1508.

Yaou, M.-H. and Chang, W.-T. (1994). Fast surface interpolation using multiresolution wavelets. *IEEE Transactions on Pattern Analysis and Machine Intelligence*, 16(7):673–689.

Yatziv, L. and Sapiro, G. (2006). Fast image and video colorization using chrominance blending. *IEEE Transactions on Image Processing*, 15(5):1120–1129.

Yedidia, J. S., Freeman, W. T., and Weiss, Y. (2001). Understanding belief propagation and its generalization. In *International Joint Conference on Artificial Intelligence (IJCAI 2001)*.

Yezzi, Jr., A. J., Kichenassamy, S., Kumar, A., Olver, P., and Tannenbaum, A. (1997). A geometric snake model for segmentation of medical imagery. *IEEE Transactions on Medical Imaging*, 16(2):199–209.

Yilmaz, A. and Shah, M. (2006). Matching actions in presence of camera motion. *Computer Vision and Image Understanding*, 104(2-3):221–231.

Yilmaz, A., Javed, O., and Shah, M. (2006). Object tracking: A survey. *ACM Computing Surveys*, 38(4).

Yin, P., Criminisi, A., Winn, J., and Essa, I. (2007). Tree-based classifiers for bilayer video segmentation. In *IEEE Computer Society Conference on Computer Vision and Pattern Recognition (CVPR 2007)*, Minneapolis, MN.

Yoon, K.-J. and Kweon, I.-S. (2006). Adaptive support-weight approach for correspondence search. *IEEE Transactions on Pattern Analysis and Machine Intelligence*, 28(4):650–656.

Yserentant, H. (1986). On the multi-level splitting of finite element spaces. *Numerische Mathematik*, 49:379–412.

Yu, S. X. and Shi, J. (2003). Multiclass spectral clustering. In *Ninth International Conference on Computer Vision (ICCV 2003)*, pp. 313–319, Nice, France.

Yu, Y. and Malik, J. (1998). Recovering photometric properties of architectural scenes from photographs. In *ACM SIGGRAPH 1996 Conference Proceedings*, pp. 207–218, Orlando.

Yu, Y., Debevec, P., Malik, J., and Hawkins, T. (1999). Inverse global illumination: Recovering reflectance models of real scenes from photographs. In *ACM SIGGRAPH 1999 Conference Proceedings*, pp. 215–224.

Yuan, L., Sun, J., Quan, L., and Shum, H.-Y. (2007). Image deblurring with blurred/noisy image pairs. *ACM Transactions on Graphics*, 26(3).

Yuan, L., Sun, J., Quan, L., and Shum, H.-Y. (2008). Progressive inter-scale and intra-scale non-blind image deconvolution. *ACM Transactions on Graphics*, 27(3).

Yuan, L., Wen, F., Liu, C., and Shum, H.-Y. (2004). Synthesizing dynamic texture with closed-loop linear dynamic system. In *Eighth European Conference on Computer Vision (ECCV 2004)*, pp. 603–616, Prague.

Yuille, A. (1991). Deformable templates for face recognition. *Journal of Cognitive Neuroscience*, 3(1):59–70.

Yuille, A. (2002). CCCP algorithms to minimize the Bethe and Kikuchi free energies: Convergent alternatives to belief propagation. *Neural Computation*, 14(7):1691–1722.

Yuille, A. (2010). Loopy belief propagation, mean-field and Bethe approximations. In Blake, A., Kohli, P., and Rother, C. (eds), *Advances in Markov Random Fields*, MIT Press.

Yuille, A. and Poggio, T. (1984). *A Generalized Ordering Constraint for Stereo Correspondence*. A. I. Memo 777, Artificial Intelligence Laboratory, Massachusetts Institute of Technology.

Yuille, A., Vincent, L., and Geiger, D. (1992). Statistical morphology and Bayesian reconstruction. *Journal of Mathematical Imaging and Vision*, 1(3):223–238.

Zabih, R. and Woodfill, J. (1994). Non-parametric local transforms for computing visual correspondence. In *Third European Conference on Computer Vision (ECCV'94)*, pp. 151–158, Stockholm, Sweden.

Zach, C. (2008). Fast and high quality fusion of depth maps. In *Fourth International Symposium on 3D Data Processing, Visualization and Transmission (3DPVT'08)*, Atlanta.

Zach, C., Gallup, D., and Frahm, J.-M. (2008). Fast gain-adaptive KLT tracking on the GPU. In *CVPR 2008 Workshop on Visual Computer Vision on GPUs (CVGPU)*, Anchorage, AK.

Zach, C., Klopschitz, M., and Pollefeys, M. (2010). Disambiguating visual relations using loop constraints. In *IEEE Computer Society Conference on Computer Vision and Pattern Recognition (CVPR 2010)*, San Francisco, CA.

Zach, C., Pock, T., and Bischof, H. (2007a). A duality based approach for realtime TV-L1 optical flow. In *Pattern Recognition (DAGM 2007)*.

Zach, C., Pock, T., and Bischof, H. (2007b). A globally optimal algorithm for robust TV-L^1 range image integration. In *Eleventh International Conference on Computer Vision (ICCV 2007)*, Rio de Janeiro, Brazil.

Zanella, V. and Fuentes, O. (2004). An approach to automatic morphing of face images in frontal view. In *Mexican International Conference on Artificial Intelligence (MICAI 2004)*, pp. 679–687, Mexico City.

Zebedin, L., Bauer, J., Karner, K., and Bischof, H. (2008). Fusion of feature- and area-based information for urban buildings modeling from aerial imagery. In *Tenth European Conference on Computer Vision (ECCV 2008)*, pp. 873–886, Marseilles.

Zelnik-Manor, L. and Perona, P. (2007). Automating joiners. In *Symposium on Non Photorealistic Animation and Rendering*, Annecy.

Zhang, G., Jia, J., Wong, T.-T., and Bao, H. (2008). Recovering consistent video depth maps via bundle optimization. In *IEEE Computer Society Conference on Computer Vision and Pattern Recognition (CVPR 2008)*, Anchorage, AK.

Zhang, J., McMillan, L., and Yu, J. (2006). Robust tracking and stereo matching under variable illumination. In *IEEE Computer Society Conference on Computer Vision and Pattern Recognition (CVPR'2006)*, pp. 871–878, New York City, NY.

Zhang, J., Marszalek, M., Lazebnik, S., and Schmid, C. (2007). Local features and kernels for classification of texture and object categories: a comprehensive study. *International Journal of Computer Vision*, 73(2):213–238.

Zhang, L., Curless, B., and Seitz, S. (2003). Spacetime stereo: Shape recovery for dynamic scenes. In *IEEE Computer Society Conference on Computer Vision and Pattern Recognition (CVPR'2003)*, pp. 367–374, Madison, WI.

Zhang, L., Dugas-Phocion, G., Samson, J.-S., and Seitz, S. M. (2002). Single view modeling of free-form scenes. *Journal of Visualization and Computer Animation*, 13(4):225–235.

Zhang, L., Snavely, N., Curless, B., and Seitz, S. M. (2004). Spacetime faces: High resolution capture for modeling and animation. *ACM Transactions on Graphics*, 23(3):548–558.

Zhang, R., Tsai, P.-S., Cryer, J. E., and Shah, M. (1999). Shape from shading: A survey. *IEEE Transactions on Pattern Analysis and Machine Intelligence*, 21(8):690–706.

Zhang, Y. and Kambhamettu, C. (2003). On 3D scene flow and structure recovery from multiview image sequences. *IEEE Transactions on Systems, Man, and Cybernetics*, 33(4):592–606.

Zhang, Z. (1994). Iterative point matching for registration of free-form curves and surfaces. *International Journal of Computer Vision*, 13(2):119–152.

Zhang, Z. (1998a). Determining the epipolar geometry and its uncertainty: A review. *International Journal of Computer Vision*, 27(2):161–195.

Zhang, Z. (1998b). On the optimization criteria used in two-view motion analysis. *IEEE Transactions on Pattern Analysis and Machine Intelligence*, 20(7):717–729.

Zhang, Z. (2000). A flexible new technique for camera calibration. *IEEE Transactions on Pattern Analysis and Machine Intelligence*, 22(11):1330–1334.

Zhang, Z. and He, L.-W. (2007). Whiteboard scanning and image enhancement. *Digital Signal Processing*, 17(2):414–432.

Zhang, Z. and Shan, Y. (2000). A progressive scheme for stereo matching. In *Second European Workshop on 3D Structure from Multiple Images of Large-Scale Environments (SMILE 2000)*, pp. 68–85, Dublin, Ireland.

Zhang, Z., Deriche, R., Faugeras, O., and Luong, Q. (1995). A robust technique for matching two uncalibrated images through the recovery of the unknown epipolar geometry. *Artificial Intelligence*, 78:87–119.

Zhao, G. and Pietikäinen, M. (2007). Dynamic texture recognition using local binary patterns with an application to facial expressions. *IEEE Transactions on Pattern Analysis and Machine Intelligence*, 29(6):915–928.

Zhao, W., Chellappa, R., Phillips, P. J., and Rosenfeld, A. (2003). Face recognition: A literature survey. *ACM Computing Surveys*, 35(4):399–358.

Zheng, J. Y. (1994). Acquiring 3-D models from sequences of contours. *IEEE Transactions on Pattern Analysis and Machine Intelligence*, 16(2):163–178.

Zheng, K. C., Kang, S. B., Cohen, M., and Szeliski, R. (2007). Layered depth panoramas. In *IEEE Computer Society Conference on Computer Vision and Pattern Recognition (CVPR 2007)*, Minneapolis, MN.

Zheng, Y., Lin, S., and Kang, S. B. (2006). Single-image vignetting correction. In *IEEE Computer Society Conference on Computer Vision and Pattern Recognition (CVPR'2006)*, pp. 461–468, New York City, NY.

Zheng, Y., Yu, J., Kang, S.-B., Lin, S., and Kambhamettu, C. (2008). Single-image vignetting correction using radial gradient symmetry. In *IEEE Computer Society Conference on Computer Vision and Pattern Recognition (CVPR 2008)*, Anchorage, AK.

Zheng, Y., Zhou, X. S., Georgescu, B., Zhou, S. K., and Comaniciu, D. (2006). Example based non-rigid shape detection. In *Ninth European Conference on Computer Vision (ECCV 2006)*, pp. 423–436.

Zheng, Y.-T., Zhao, M., Song, Y., Adam, H., Buddemeier, U., Bissacco, A., Brucher, F., Chua, T.-S., and Neven, H. (2009). Tour the world: building a web-scale landmark recognition engine. In *IEEE Computer Society Conference on Computer Vision and Pattern Recognition (CVPR 2009)*, Miami Beach, FL.

Zhong, J. and Sclaroff, S. (2003). Segmenting foreground objects from a dynamic, textured background via a robust Kalman filter. In *Ninth International Conference on Computer Vision (ICCV 2003)*, pp. 44–50, Nice, France.

Zhou, C., Lin, S., and Nayar, S. (2009). Coded aperture pairs for depth from defocus. In *Twelfth International Conference on Computer Vision (ICCV 2009)*, Kyoto, Japan.

Zhou, Y., Gu, L., and Zhang, H.-J. (2003). Bayesian tangent shape model: Estimating shape and pose parameters via Bayesian inference. In *IEEE Computer Society Conference on Computer Vision and Pattern Recognition (CVPR'2003)*, pp. 109–116, Madison, WI.

Zhu, L., Chen, Y., Lin, Y., Lin, C., and Yuille, A. (2008). Recursive segmentation and recognition templates for 2D parsing. In *Advances in Neural Information Processing Systems*.

Zhu, S.-C. and Mumford, D. (2006). A stochastic grammar of images. *Foundations and Trends in Computer Graphics and Computer Vision*, 2(4).

Zhu, S. C. and Yuille, A. L. (1996). Region competition: Unifying snakes, region growing, and Bayes/MDL for multiband image segmentation. *IEEE Transactions on Pattern Analysis and Machine Intelligence*, 18(9):884–900.

Zhu, Z. and Kanade, T. (2008). Modeling and representations of large-scale 3D scenes. *International Journal of Computer Vision*, 78(2-3):119–120.

Zisserman, A., Giblin, P. J., and Blake, A. (1989). The information available to a moving observer from specularities. *Image and Vision Computing*, 7(1):38–42.

Zitnick, C. L. and Kanade, T. (2000). A cooperative algorithm for stereo matching and occlusion detection. *IEEE Transactions on Pattern Analysis and Machine Intelligence*, 22(7):675–684.

Zitnick, C. L. and Kang, S. B. (2007). Stereo for image-based rendering using image over-segmentation. *International Journal of Computer Vision*, 75(1):49–65.

Zitnick, C. L., Jojic, N., and Kang, S. B. (2005). Consistent segmentation for optical flow estimation. In *Tenth International Conference on Computer Vision (ICCV 2005)*, pp. 1308–1315, Beijing, China.

Zitnick, C. L., Kang, S. B., Uyttendaele, M., Winder, S., and Szeliski, R. (2004). High-quality video view interpolation using a layered representation. *ACM Transactions on Graphics (Proc. SIGGRAPH 2004)*, 23(3):600–608.

Zitov'aa, B. and Flusser, J. (2003). Image registration methods: A survey. *Image and Vision Computing*, 21:997–1000.

Zoghlami, I., Faugeras, O., and Deriche, R. (1997). Using geometric corners to build a 2D mosaic from a set of images. In *IEEE Computer Society Conference on Computer Vision and Pattern Recognition (CVPR'97)*, pp. 420–425, San Juan, Puerto Rico.

Zongker, D. E., Werner, D. M., Curless, B., and Salesin, D. H. (1999). Environment matting and compositing. In *ACM SIGGRAPH 1999 Conference Proceedings*, pp. 205–214.

Zorin, D., Schröder, P., and Sweldens, W. (1996). Interpolating subdivision for meshes with arbitrary topology. In *ACM SIGGRAPH 1997 Conference Proceedings*, pp. 189–192, New Orleans.

Index